T0214890

# Lecture Notes in Computer Science    13535

More information about this series at https://link.springer.com/bookseries/558

Shiqi Yu · Zhaoxiang Zhang · Pong C. Yuen ·
Junwei Han · Tieniu Tan · Yike Guo ·
Jianhuang Lai · Jianguo Zhang (Eds.)

# Pattern Recognition and Computer Vision

5th Chinese Conference, PRCV 2022
Shenzhen, China, November 4–7, 2022
Proceedings, Part II

Springer

*Editors*
Shiqi Yu
Southern University of Science
and Technology
Shenzhen, China

Pong C. Yuen
Hong Kong Baptist University
Hong Kong, China

Tieniu Tan
Institute of Automation
Chinese Academy of Sciences
Beijing, China

Jianhuang Lai
Sun Yat-sen University
Guangzhou, China

Zhaoxiang Zhang
Institute of Automation
Chinese Academy of Sciences
Beijing, China

Junwei Han
Northwestern Polytechnical University
Xi'an, China

Yike Guo
Hong Kong Baptist University
Hong Kong, China

Jianguo Zhang
Southern University of Science
and Technology
Shenzhen, China

ISSN 0302-9743          ISSN 1611-3349 (electronic)
Lecture Notes in Computer Science
ISBN 978-3-031-18909-8          ISBN 978-3-031-18910-4 (eBook)
https://doi.org/10.1007/978-3-031-18910-4

This Springer imprint is published by the registered company Springer Nature Switzerland AG
The registered company address is: Gewerbestrasse 11, 6330 Cham, Switzerland

# Preface

Welcome to the proceedings of the 5th Chinese Conference on Pattern Recognition and Computer Vision (PRCV 2022) held in Shenzhen, China!

PRCV was established to further boost the impact of the Chinese community in pattern recognition and computer vision, which are two core areas of artificial intelligence, and further improve the quality of academic communication. Accordingly, PRCV is co-sponsored by four major academic societies of China: the China Society of Image and Graphics (CSIG), the Chinese Association for Artificial Intelligence (CAAI), the China Computer Federation (CCF), and the Chinese Association of Automation (CAA).

PRCV aims at providing an interactive communication platform for researchers from academia and from industry. It promotes not only academic exchange but also communication between academia and industry. In order to keep track of the frontier of academic trends and share the latest research achievements, innovative ideas, and scientific methods, international and local leading experts and professors are invited to deliver keynote speeches, introducing the latest advances in theories and methods in the fields of pattern recognition and computer vision.

PRCV 2022 was hosted by the Southern University of Science and Technology and Shenzhen Polytechnic. We received 564 full submissions. Each submission was reviewed by at least three reviewers selected from the Program Committee and other qualified researchers. Based on the reviewers' reports, 233 papers were finally accepted for presentation at the conference, comprising 40 oral presentations and 193 posters. The acceptance rate was 41%. The conference took place during November 4–7, 2022, and the proceedings are published in this volume in Springer's Lecture Notes in Computer Science (LNCS) series.

We are grateful to the keynote speakers, Alan Yuille from Johns Hopkins University, USA, Kyoung Mu Lee from the Korea National Open University, South Korea, Zhengyou Zhang from the Tencent AI Lab, China, Yaonan Wang from Hunan University, China, Wen Gao from the Pengcheng Laboratory and Peking University, China, Hong Qiao from the Institute of Automation, Chinese Academy of Sciences, China, and Muming Poo from the Institute of Neuroscience, Chinese Academy of Sciences, China.

We give sincere thanks to the authors of all submitted papers, the Program Committee members and the reviewers, and the Organizing Committee. Without their contributions, this conference would not have been possible. Special thanks also go to all of the sponsors.

October 2022

Tieniu Tan
Yike Guo
Jianhuang Lai
Jianguo Zhang
Shiqi Yu
Zhaoxiang Zhang
Pong C. Yuen
Junwei Han

# Organization

## Steering Committee Chair

Tieniu Tan — Institute of Automation, Chinese Academy of Sciences, China

## Steering Committee

| | |
|---|---|
| Xilin Chen | Institute of Computing Technology, Chinese Academy of Sciences, China |
| Chenglin Liu | Institute of Automation, Chinese Academy of Sciences, China |
| Yong Rui | Lenovo, China |
| Hongbing Zha | Peking University, China |
| Nanning Zheng | Xi'an Jiaotong University, China |
| Jie Zhou | Tsinghua University, China |

## Steering Committee Secretariat

Liang Wang — Institute of Automation, Chinese Academy of Sciences, China

## General Chairs

| | |
|---|---|
| Tieniu Tan | Institute of Automation, Chinese Academy of Sciences, China |
| Yike Guo | Hong Kong Baptist University, Hong Kong, China |
| Jianhuang Lai | Sun Yat-sen University, China |
| Jianguo Zhang | Southern University of Science and Technology, China |

## Program Chairs

| | |
|---|---|
| Shiqi Yu | Southern University of Science and Technology, China |
| Zhaoxiang Zhang | Institute of Automation, Chinese Academy of Sciences, China |
| Pong C. Yuen | Hong Kong Baptist University, Hong Kong, China |
| Junwei Han | Northwest Polytechnic University, China |

## Organizing Committee Chairs

| | |
|---|---|
| Jinfeng Yang | Shenzhen Polytechnic, China |
| Guangming Lu | Harbin Institute of Technology, Shenzhen, China |
| Baoyuan Wu | The Chinese University of Hong Kong, Shenzhen, China |
| Feng Zheng | Northwest Polytechnic University, China |

## Sponsorship Chairs

| | |
|---|---|
| Liqiang Nie | Harbin Institute of Technology, Shenzhen, China |
| Yu Qiao | Shenzhen Institute of Advanced Technology, Chinese Academy of Sciences, China |
| Zhenan Sun | Institute of Automation, Chinese Academy of Sciences, China |
| Xiaochun Cao | Sun Yat-sen University, China |

## Publicity Chairs

| | |
|---|---|
| Weishi Zheng | Sun Yat-sen University, China |
| Wei Jia | Hefei University of Technology, China |
| Lifang Wu | Beijing University of Technology, China |
| Junping Zhang | Fudan University, China |

## Local Arrangement Chairs

| | |
|---|---|
| Yujiu Yang | Tsinghua Shenzhen International Graduate School, China |
| Yanjie Wei | Shenzhen Institute of Advanced Technology, Chinese Academy of Sciences, China |

## International Liaison Chairs

| | |
|---|---|
| Jingyi Yu | ShanghaiTech University, China |
| Qifeng Liu | Shenzhen Polytechnic, China |
| Song Guo | Hong Kong Polytechnic University, Hong Kong, China |

## Competition Chairs

| | |
|---|---|
| Wangmeng Zuo | Harbin Institute of Technology, China |
| Di Huang | Beihang University, China |
| Bin Fan | University of Science and Technology Beijing, China |

## Tutorial Chairs

Jiwen Lu      Tsinghua University, China
Ran He      Institute of Automation, Chinese Academy of
Sciences, China
Xi Li      Zhejiang University, China
Jiaying Liu      Peking University, China

## Special Session Chairs

Jing Dong      Institute of Automation, Chinese Academy of
Sciences, China
Zhouchen Lin      Peking University, China
Xin Geng      Southeast University, China
Yong Xia      Northwest Polytechnic University, China

## Doctoral Forum Chairs

Tianzhu Zhang      University of Science and Technology of China,
China
Shanshan Zhang      Nanjing University of Science and Technology,
China
Changdong Wang      Sun Yat-sen University, China

## Publication Chairs

Kui Jia      South China University of Technology, China
Yang Cong      Institute of Automation, Chinese Academy of
Sciences, China
Cewu Lu      Shanghai Jiao Tong University, China

## Registration Chairs

Weihong Deng      Beijing University of Posts and
Telecommunications, China
Wenxiong Kang      South China University of Technology, China
Xiaohu Yan      Shenzhen Polytechnic, China

## Exhibition Chairs

Hongmin Liu      University of Science and Technology Beijing,
China
Rui Huang      The Chinese University of Hong Kong, Shenzhen,
China

Kai Lei                          Peking University Shenzhen Graduate School,
                                     China
Zechao Li                        Nanjing University of Science and Technology,
                                     China

## Finance Chairs

Xu Wang                          Shenzhen Polytechnic, China
Li Liu                           Southern University of Science and Technology,
                                     China

## Website Chairs

Zhaofeng He                      Beijing University of Posts and
                                     Telecommunications, China
Mengyuan Liu                     Sun Yat-sen University, China
Hanyang Peng                     Pengcheng Laboratory, China

## Program Committee

Yuntao Chen                      TuSimple, China
Gong Cheng                       Northwest Polytechnic University, China
Runmin Cong                      Beijing Jiaotong University, China
Bin Fan                          University of Science and Technology Beijing,
                                     China
Chen Gong                        Nanjing University of Science and Technology,
                                     China
Fuyuan Hu                        Suzhou University of Science and Technology,
                                     China
Huaibo Huang                     Institute of Automation, Chinese Academy of
                                     Sciences, China
Sheng Huang                      Chongqing University, China
Du Huynh                         University of Western Australia, Australia
Sen Jia                          Shenzhen University, China
Baiying Lei                      Shenzhen University, China
Changsheng Li                    Beijing Institute of Technology, China
Haibo Liu                        Harbin Engineering University, China
Chao Ma                          Shanghai Jiao Tong University, China
Vishal M. Patel                  Johns Hopkins University, USA
Hanyang Peng                     Pengcheng Laboratory, China
Manivannan Siyamalan             University of Jaffna, Sri Lanka
Anwaar Ulhaq                     Charles Sturt University, Australia
Changdong Wang                   Sun Yat-sen University, China

# Contents – Part II

## Pattern Classification and Clustering

# Biomedical Image Processing
# and Analysis

# ED-AnoNet: Elastic Distortion-Based Unsupervised Network for OCT Image Anomaly Detection

Yajing Li, Junhua Li, Hailan Shen(✉) ⓘ, and Zailiang Chen

School of Computer Science and Engineering, Central South University, Hunan 410083, China
hn_shl@126.com

**Abstract.** The use of anomaly detection methods based on the deep convolutional neural network has shown its success on optical coherence tomography (OCT) images. However, these methods only train normal samples from healthy subjects, which are insensitive to abnormalities caused by small lesions, and are prone to missed diagnoses. To alleviate this shortcoming, this paper proposes an unsupervised anomaly detection network called ED-AnoNet, which is based on elastic distortion (ED), to improve OCT images anomaly detection. Different distortion fields are generated by adjusting the parameters of ED to simulate the damage of the hierarchical structure of the retina by the lesions. Subsequently, the normal OCT images are used to resample the distortion field to generate the pseudo abnormal OCT (Pseudo-abnorOCT) images and use them to train ED-AnoNet. On the spatial feature map, the spatial similarity retention loss function is used to increase the similarity between normal OCT and reconstructed images. Meanwhile, the spatial difference retention loss function is used to reduce the similarity between normal OCT and Pseudo-abnorOCT images. ED-AnoNet is promoted to extract more expressive feature maps, in which the anomaly detection performance can be improved. Results on public datasets show that the proposed method outperforms current state-of-the-art methods in terms of the area under the curve significantly.

**Keywords:** Anomaly detection · Unsupervised · Retinal OCT image · Elastic distortion · ED-AnoNet

## 1 Introduction

The incidence of various retinal diseases is increasing annually, which is one of the serious threats to people's health [1]. Medical imaging allows the easy observation of markers associated with the disease status. Optical coherence tomography (OCT) is a noninvasive imaging method that can provide the volume scanning of the micrometer resolution of the retina [2]. Various ocular diseases, such as age-related macular degeneration (AMD) [3], can be diagnosed through OCT images. Given the rise of deep learning in computer vision [4], the adoption of deep learning-based methods in medical imaging analysis has increased dramatically [5–7]. In retinal OCT imaging, supervised

© The Author(s), under exclusive license to Springer Nature Switzerland AG 2022
S. Yu et al. (Eds.): PRCV 2022, LNCS 13535, pp. 3–15, 2022.
https://doi.org/10.1007/978-3-031-18910-4_1

methods have been used extensively. References [8, 9] applied convolutional classification networks to achieve the retinal OCT image screening, and references [10] proposed the detection of AMD lesions in retinal OCT images. However, these methods require increased effort to annotate many OCT images, thus limiting the application of deep learning in medical image analysis.

By contrast, unsupervised methods are relatively easy by using normal OCT images. Anomaly detection can be achieved by training only normal OCT images, thus reducing the cost of labeling. [11]. Inspired by the generative adversarial network (GAN) [12], Schlegl et al. [13] proposed AnoGAN to identify abnormal OCT images. This method requires a lot of computational costs, and the experimental results are easily affected by noise when reconstruction error is used. Later, Schlegl et al. [14] further proposed f-AnoGAN with higher computational efficiency than AnoGAN. However, these networks are not trained end-to-end, which may cause them to fall into a local optimal state. Zhou et al. [15] proposed the Sparse-GAN framework, which regularized the sparsity of latent features, to realize the image-to-image GAN medical images anomaly detection. Later, Luo et al. [16] proposed P-Net to segment the hierarchical structure of the retina to determine whether the OCT images are abnormal. Seeböck et al. [17] used weak labels to train the Bayesian U-Net network to obtain the segmentation probability map of the retinal hierarchical structure. However, these approaches tend to be insensitive to OCT image abnormalities caused by small lesions, in which images lie relatively close to the distribution of normal OCT images.

To alleviate this problem, we propose a novel anomaly detection architecture called ED-AnoNet, which is based on the elastic distortion algorithm (EDA) [18]. We simulate the damage of the retina by lesions and use EDA to generate pseudo abnormal OCT (Pseudo-abnorOCT) images. The normal OCT and Pseudo-abnorOCT images are paired into training ED-AnoNet. Considering that the spatial distribution of the normal OCT and the pseudo-anor OCT images are inconsistent, we use the loss function to retain the difference between the two in the spatial feature map. Promoting the encoder abstracts more discriminative feature maps, which can improve the accuracy of discrimination and reduce the effect of noise.

In summary, the main contributions of this paper are presented as follows.

1. We develop a novel ED-based method, using Pseudo-abnorOCT images. To the best of our knowledge, this work is the first to use Pseudo-abnorOCT images for anomaly detection by introducing ED.
2. The ED-AnoNet is an end-to-end learning approach that is driven entirely by normal OCT images without using any heuristics or handcrafting of features.
3. The ED-AnoNet achieves state-of-the-art performance on a large public OCT dataset [9].

## 2   Method

The proposed ED-AnoNet architecture consists of three major parts, as shown in Fig. 1. ED-AnoNet learns feature representations for anomaly detection from the retinal OCT images in an end-to-end manner, which avoids several handcrafted works [19, 20]. The normal representation network (NoR-Net) is mainly used to encode and decode the normal OCT images and extract the spatial feature maps of the normal OCT images. The elastic distortion module (EDM) is used to generate Pseudo-abnorOCT images. The abnormal representation network (AbR-Net) is mainly used to encode and decode Pseudo-abnorOCT images and extract the spatial feature maps of Pseudo-abnorOCT images.

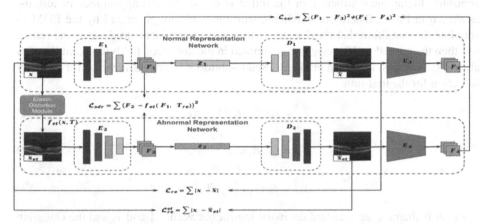

**Fig. 1.** Overview architecture of the proposed ED-AnoNet. The normal and abnormal representation network extracts feature maps of normal and abnormal images, respectively. EDM is applied to obtain Pseudo-abnorOCT images.

## 2.1 Normal Representation Network

Different from the unsupervised OCT image anomaly detection networks, such as AnoGAN [13], f-AnoGAN [14], and Sparse-GAN [15], our proposed ED-AnoNet adopts a two-way encoding and decoding architecture. NoR-Net is used to process normal OCT images. To reduce the amount of calculation, the encoder $E_1$ and the encode $E_3$ share parameters during training. Inspired by [21], we use ResNet34 [22] as the feature extractor of $E_1$ and $E_3$, which retain the first four feature-extracting blocks without the average pooling layer and the fully connected layers. ResNet34 adds the shortcut mechanism to avoid gradient vanishing and accelerate the network convergence, which is crucial for ED-AnoNet. After the input image $x$ is encoded by $E_1$, the spatial feature map $F_1$ is mapped to the spatial feature vector $z_1$ using continuous Convolution-BatchNorm-ReLu operations, and the reconstructed image is obtained through the decoder $D_1$. For the decoder $D_1$, the feature decoder module of the CENet [21] is modified for decoding $z_1$ to obtain a reconstruction image $\hat{x}$. We have exploited the encoder $E_3$ to transform $\hat{x}$ into the feature map space to obtain the feature map $F_3$ and reduce the influence of speckle noise on the experimental results.

## 2.2  Elastic Distortion Module

This very challenging task guarantees the difference in input and the consistency of output between the abnormal and the normal representation networks while promoting the encoders to abstract a discriminative feature map. The EDA [18], which is used for data enhancement [23], is suitable for handling this challenge. We propose an elastic distortion module (EDM) based on EDA. Compared with normal OCT images, the abnormal hierarchical structure of the retina is caused by the appearance of lesions, as shown in Fig. 2. Therefore, random distortion fields are generated by the EDM to simulate the condition that the disease destroys the hierarchical structure of the retina, and then the normal OCT images are resampled in the distortion fields to obtain Pseudo-abnorOCT images, as shown in Fig. 3. Pseudo-abnorOCT images are used for anomaly detection for the first time.

$$T_x = f_{gf}(R, \alpha, \sigma) + d_x \tag{1}$$

$$T_y = f_{gf}(R, \alpha, \sigma) + d_y \tag{2}$$

$$x_{et} = f_{et}(x, T[T_x, T_y]) \tag{3}$$

where $R$ is the random standard deviation matrix between $-1$ and $1$, and the Gaussian filter $f_{gf}$ is used to filter the $R$ of each dimension. Parameter factors $\alpha$ and $\sigma$ are used to control the deviation range. $T_x$ and $T_y$, $d_x$ and $d_y$ are two-dimensional grid coordinates, and cascade operations $T_x$ and $T_y$ obtain the distortion field matrix $T$. Finally, the normal OCT images can be resampled on the distortion field matrix $T$ to obtain Pseudo-abnorOCT images $x_{et}$. Generally, a small $\alpha$ and a large $\sigma$ will lead to smaller deviations, thereby making the pseudo-abnorOCT image more similar to the original image, as shown in Fig. 3.

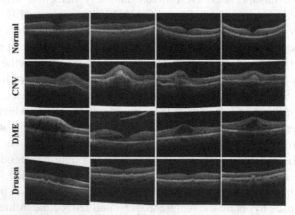

**Fig. 2.** The comparisons of normal OCT images with abnormal OCT images. The lesion will change the structure of the retina in a different direction.

## 2.3 Abnormal Representation Network

AbR-Net has the same network architecture as NoR-Net, which is used to process Pseudo-abnorOCT images. To reduce the amount of calculation during training, AbR-Net and NoR-Net share parameters. In the training process, the normal OCT and the Pseudo-abnorOCT images are input into the network in pairs and decoded into the same normal OCT images. Compared with the previous methods, considering that $D_2$ can decode the Pseudo-abnorOCT images into the original normal OCT images, the robustness is better. Therefore, the problem of network robustness to abnormal OCT images is alleviated.

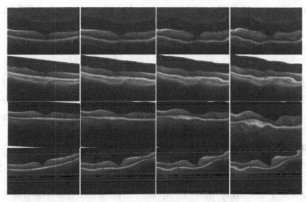

**Fig. 3.** A schematic diagram of a pseudo-abnorOCT image. The first column is an input normal OCT image, and the second, third, and fourth columns are Pseudo-abnorOCT images obtained by resampling under different parameter distortion fields.

## 2.4 Network Losses

When training a deep learning network, selecting an appropriate loss function can not only make the network converge quickly, but also improve the performance of the network. When training ED-AnoNet, three types of loss functions, namely, reconstruction error (RE), spatial similarity retention (SSR), and spatial difference retention (SDR), are introduced to train the network jointly.

**Reconstruction Error Loss**
We encoded and decoded the Pseudo-abnorOCT images to obtain the normal OCT images and solve the problem of network robustness to abnormal OCT images.

$$\mathcal{L}_{re} = \sum |x - \hat{x}| \tag{4}$$

$$\mathcal{L}_{re}^{et} = \sum |x - \hat{x}_{et}| \tag{5}$$

In the spirit of [24], we defined the reconstruction error loss function that measures the visual dissimilarity between decoded images $\hat{x}$ and $\hat{x}_{et}$ and the input image $x$ in the image space.

**Spatial Similarity Retention Loss**
When directly detecting whether a test OCT image is abnormal by using the reconstruction error loss, the noise of the test OCT image influences the results of the experiment. The reconstruction error loss is only zero in an ideal situation, that is, the detection results of normal and abnormal OCT images will be affected. Moreover, the abnormality to be detected by this task only appears in the retinal area, and the abnormality only occupies a small part of the entire image. Thus, detecting abnormalities caused by small lesions is difficult. To alleviate this problem, under the influence of Schlegl et al. [13] and Salimans et al. [25], the SSR loss function is defined.

$$\mathcal{L}_{ssr} = \sum (F_1 - F_3)^2 + (F_1 - F_4)^2 \tag{6}$$

where the outputs of the intermediate layer of the encoders $E_1$, $E_3$, and $E_4$ are used to specify the similarity statistics between the input images and the decoded images for anomaly detection to reduce the influence of noise on experimental results.

**Spatial Difference Retention Loss**
We propose $\mathcal{L}_{sdr}$ loss to keep the difference between the normal and the abnormal OCT images on the spatial feature maps, which improves the performance of anomaly detection. In the OCT anomaly detection, we have tried this for the first time, and subsequent experiments also prove that the attempt is effective. We scale the distortion field matrix $T$ in Eq. (3) to a size that matches the spatial feature map $F_1$ and use the spatial feature map $F_2$ of the Pseudo-abnorOCT image minus the resampling of the normal OCT image spatial feature map on $T_{re}$. Therefore, a small spatial difference retention loss results in a large difference between the normal and the abnormal OCT images on the spatial feature map and increased the advantage of distinction. The $\mathcal{L}_{sdr}$ loss can be written as

$$T_{re} = resize(T) \tag{7}$$

$$\mathcal{L}_{sdr} = \sum (F_2 - f_{et}(F_1, T_{re}))^2 \tag{8}$$

Our full objective is

$$\mathcal{L} = \lambda \cdot \mathcal{L}_{re} + \lambda \cdot \mathcal{L}_{er}^{et} + \mu \cdot \mathcal{L}_{ssr} + v \cdot \mathcal{L}_{sdr} \tag{9}$$

$\mathcal{L}$ is utilized to optimize the proposed ED-AnoNet, where $\lambda$, $\mu$, and $v$ are balance hyperparameters.

## 3 Experiments and Results

We have implemented our proposed ED-AnoNet based on the Pytorch, which is a public and common deep learning library. We have adopted the Adam algorithm to optimize the network, and the learning rate is 0.0001. The input size of the network is 448 × 448. Four GeForce RTX 2080TI GPUs are utilized to train the networks. Empirically, we have obtained the best experimental results when we debug $\lambda = 80$, $\mu = 120$, and $\nu = 60$ during training.

### 3.1 Dataset and Metrics

We have evaluated our method on two publicly available datasets to validate the effectiveness of the proposed ED-AnoNet. ZhangLabData (ZD), the first experimental data set is published by Kermany et al. [9]. This dataset contains four types of data, which can be divided into normal OCT images, and the other three types of abnormal OCT images of drusen, diabetic Macular edema (DME), and choroidal neo-vasplasmin (CNV) of different lesions.

Through the research of the ZD dataset, the image size of this dataset is non-uniform in size. And these images have irregular blank areas, some of which occupy more than half of the entire image. For the image itself, these areas are noise. Therefore, the ZD dataset is preprocessed, and the blank area is removed from the images without affecting the content, and then the size of the image is unified. To distinguish, the dataset is named ZD_clear after removing the blank area, and the original dataset is named ZD_unclear.

The second experimental dataset OCTA500 is published by Li et al. [26]. For normal OCT images, a total of 36400 OCT images come from 91 volumes data were reported. For abnormal OCT images, a total of 8837 OCT images, which come from 43 AMD, 14 CSC, 35 diabetic retinopathy and 10 central retinal vein occlusion volumes data, according to the volume data labels given by the author. To reduce the over-fitting phenomenon that may occur during ED-AnoNet network training, the training images are expanded by horizontal flipping.

The OCT image anomaly detection can be regarded as a classical binary classification task, where the commonly used metrics in this task mainly include accuracy, sensitivity, precision, specificity, and area under curve (AUC). In this paper, we adopt these metrics to evaluate our and other comparative methods.

### 3.2 Comparison with State-of-the-Art Methods

We have compared ED-AnoNet with state-of-the-art networks, including Auto-Encoder, AnoGAN [13], f-AnoGAN [14], and sparse-GAN [15] on the same dataset to demonstrate the advantage of our proposed method. Experimental results are shown in Table 1. Where #1 and #2 represent the experimental results of ED-AnoNet on the ZD_unclear and ZD_clear datasets, respectively.

Table 1 shows that among the five evaluation indexes, the proposed method ED-AnoNet obtained the four best results. Another evaluation index also obtained the second-best result, and the difference from the best result is very small. Comparing the evaluation index AUC, the performance of ED-AnoNet on the ZD_unclear dataset is significantly better than Auto-Encoder, AnoGAN [13], and f-AnoGAN [14] methods and can be compared with Sparse-GAN [15]. However, ED-AnoNet directly increases the AUC from 0.925 to 0.960 on the ZD_clear dataset, which is far better than Sparse-GAN. This finding verifies the previous conjecture that the blank area will affect the result of

**Table 1.** Comparison with state-of-the-art methods on test dataset.

| Method | Acc | Pre | Sen | Spe | AUC |
|---|---|---|---|---|---|
| Auto-Encoder | 0.751 | 0.834 | 0.834 | 0.502 | 0.783 |
| AnoGAN [13] | 0.789 | 0.828 | 0.917 | 0.405 | 0.846 |
| f-AnoGAN [14] | 0.808 | 0.818 | 0.871 | 0.619 | 0.882 |
| Sparse-GAN [15] | 0.841 | 0.854 | **0.951** | 0.512 | 0.925 |
| ED-AnoNet #1 | 0.867 | 0.910 | 0.912 | 0.732 | 0.925 |
| ED-AnoNet #2 | **0.910** | **0.933** | 0.948 | **0.796** | **0.960** |

anomaly detection as noise in the OCT images. By comparing other evaluation indexes on ZD_unclear dataset, ED-AnoNet is better than Sparse-GAN. In the index Acc that reflects the overall detection performance, ED-AnoNet is significantly better than the Sparse-GAN method, which directly increases from 0.841 to 0.867. For the evaluation index Pre, it also directly increases from 0.854 to 0.910, which is close to six percentage points. Evaluation indexes Sen and Spe reflect the ability to recognize abnormal and normal OCT images, respectively. Although ED-AnoNet is weaker than Sparse-GAN in terms of the recognition of abnormal OCT images, it is far superior to Sparse-GAN for the recognition of normal OCT images. It directly increases Spe from 0.512 to 0.732, which is more than 20%. This is very important for abnormal detection of OCT images. Because the number of normal OCT images in a real scene is much greater than the number of abnormal OCT images, it is necessary to ensure the recognition accuracy of normal OCT images while ensuring the recognition accuracy of abnormal OCT images. If the recognition accuracy of normal OCT images is very low, a lot of misdiagnosis in the clinical scene will be given, which is undesirable for doctors. Therefore, the feature representation ability extracted by ED-AnoNet is relatively strong and has good distinguishability.

## 4   Discussion

### 4.1   Ablation Study Analysis

In this section, we have analyzed the effect of $\mathcal{L}_{ssr}$ and $\mathcal{L}_{sdr}$ on the experimental results and used the same ED coefficient to make a comparative test on the ZD_clear dataset. $\mathcal{L}_{ssr}$ and $\mathcal{L}_{sdr}$ are removed and recorded as ED-AnoNet ($\mathcal{L}_{ssr}$) and ED-AnoNet ($\mathcal{L}_{sdr}$), respectively. In addition, NoR-Net and ED-AnoNet are directly compared to verify the effectiveness of ED for OCT image anomaly detection. Table 2 shows the results.

In theory, our proposed method uses $\mathcal{L}_{sdr}$ to preserve the difference between normal and Pseudo-abnorOCT images on the spatial feature maps, and $\mathcal{L}_{ssr}$ is used to retain the similarity between normal and reconstructed OCT images on the spatial feature maps. In accordance with the experimental results in Table 2, when $\mathcal{L}_{ssr}$ is removed, the Spe dropped drastically from 0.796 to 0.212. This result proves that $\mathcal{L}_{ssr}$ can retain the similarity in the spatial feature map between the normal and reconstructed OCT images, thereby increasing the distinguishability of the normal OCT images. At the same time, Sen also improved after removing $\mathcal{L}_{ssr}$. The reason for this phenomenon is that the ability of ED-AnoNet to optimize $\mathcal{L}_{sdr}$, which can retain the difference between normal and abnormal OCT images is strengthened, thereby making it easier to distinguish between abnormal OCT images. When $\mathcal{L}_{sdr}$ is removed, Sen does not decrease because ED-AnoNet originally retains the difference information between normal and abnormal images on the spatial feature maps. In general, under the combined effect of $\mathcal{L}_{ssr}$ and $\mathcal{L}_{sdr}$, ED-AnoNet can extract feature maps with strong representation ability, thus increasing the distinction between normal and abnormal OCT images.

**Table 2.** Comparison with state-of-the-art methods and quantitative results for ablation studies on test dataset.

| Method | $\mathcal{L}_{re}$ | $\mathcal{L}_{er}^{et}$ | $\mathcal{L}_{ssr}$ | $\mathcal{L}_{sdr}$ | Acc | Pre | Sen | Spe | AUC |
|---|---|---|---|---|---|---|---|---|---|
| ED-AnoNet | surd | surd | surd | surd | **0.910** | **0.933** | 0.948 | **0.796** | **0.960** |
| ED-AnoNet ($\mathcal{L}_{ssr}$) | surd | surd | surd | surd | 0.778 | 0.786 | **0.967** | 0.212 | 0.869 |
| ED-AnoNet ($\mathcal{L}_{sdr}$) | surd | surd | | | 0.858 | 0.867 | 0.955 | 0.568 | 0.924 |
| NoR-Net | | | | | 0.855 | 0.876 | 0.938 | 0.604 | 0.923 |

To more intuitively reflect that the loss functions $\mathcal{L}_{ssr}$ and $\mathcal{L}_{sdr}$ can help ED-AnoNet extract more expressive feature maps, Class Activation Map (CAM) of abnormal OCT images on the ZD_clear dataset is calculated. However, anomaly detection is different from supervised classification. The calculation of CAM is not suitable for direct application to ED-AnoNet. Therefore, we modify the calculation of anomaly activation map (AAM) [15] to calculate the CAM of abnormal OCT images. The experimental

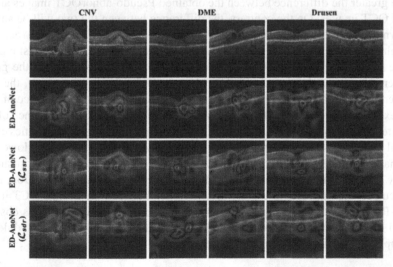

**Fig. 4.** The CAM comparison of abnormal images obtained in the ablation experiment on the ZD_clear dataset. ED-AnoNet with all loss, ED-AnoNet ($\mathcal{L}_{ssr}$) without $\mathcal{L}_{ssr}$, , and ED-AnoNet ($\mathcal{L}_{sdr}$) without $\mathcal{L}_{sdr}$.

results obtained are shown in Fig. 3, and the darker color means stronger representation ability of the feature maps. Comparison shows that when $\mathcal{L}_{ssr}$ and $\mathcal{L}_{sdr}$ loss function is removed, the representation ability of the model ED-AnoNet ($\mathcal{L}_{ssr}$) and ED-AnoNet ($\mathcal{L}_{sdr}$) to extract feature maps is reduced. Therefore, the entire lesion area is difficult to locate in CAM, even if it is located in a small part of the lesion area, as shown CNV and DME OCT images in Fig. 4.

On the contrary, ED-AnoNet uses $\mathcal{L}_{ssr}$ and $\mathcal{L}_{sdr}$ loss functions to extract feature maps with very strong representation ability. CAM cannot only locate abnormal areas of large lesions well, but also locate abnormal OCT images of small lesions, such as Drusen. However, ED-AnoNet ($\mathcal{L}_{ssr}$) and ED-AnoNet ($\mathcal{L}_{sdr}$) have almost no effect on Drusen abnormal OCT images. By calculating the CAM of abnormal OCT images, the effectiveness of $\mathcal{L}_{ssr}$ and $\mathcal{L}_{sdr}$ loss functions for ED-AnoNet's feature map extraction and anomaly detection is further verified. Besides, by comparing the experimental results of NoR-Net and ED-AnoNet on the ZD_clear dataset, the effect of ED on ED-AnoNet anomaly detection is very obvious. The Pseudo-abnorOCT images generated by the EDM can help ED-AnoNet extract more distinguishable feature maps and improve the performance of OCT image anomaly detection.

### 4.2 Elastic Distortion Coefficient Analysis

We have performed elastic distortion coefficient studies to show the influence of different coefficients on experimental results. Five sets of comparative experiments with different elastic distortion coefficients are designed on the ZD_clear dataset. According to the principle of the controlled variable method, the value of $\sigma$ keeps a constant during the experiment, and the value of $\alpha$ is 2, 3, 4, 5, and 6 for comparison, corresponding to Model1, Model2, Model3, Model4. And Model5, respectively. The greater the value of $\alpha$, the greater the difference between the obtained Pseudo-abnorOCT images and the original OCT images. On the contrary, the difference between the two will be smaller, as shown in Fig. 3. Experimental results are shown in Table 3. It can be seen from the results in Table 3 that it is not that the greater the difference of the elastic distortion, the better the performance of anomaly detection. The reason is that the greater the difference causes the greater the difficulty of ED-AnoNet optimization, the noise contained in the reconstructed image obtained will increase, and the influence of noise on the experimental results will also increase. In addition, due to the existence of $\mathcal{L}_{sdr}$, the greater the difference will also cause ED-AnoNet to ignore the abnormalities caused by small lesions, and cause the performance of ED-AnoNet to decrease. However, it is not that the smaller the difference of elastic distortion, the better the performance of anomaly detection. Because the smaller the difference of the elastic distortion, it will be difficult for ED-AnoNet to capture the difference between the normal OCT images and the Pseudo-abnorOCT images. Moreover, when $\alpha = \sigma$, no difference is observed between the input images and the output images of the elastic distortion module, and the complexity of ED-AnoNet is also increased.

**Table 3.** The performance of anomaly detection under different elastic distortion parameters.

| Model | $\alpha : \sigma$ | Acc | Pre | Sen | Spe | AUC |
|---|---|---|---|---|---|---|
| Model-1 | 2: 0.066 | **0.910** | **0.933** | 0.948 | **0.796** | **0.960** |
| Model-2 | 3: 0.066 | 0.891 | 0.925 | 0.931 | 0.772 | 0.952 |
| Model-3 | 4: 0.066 | 0.879 | 0.895 | 0.951 | 0.664 | 0.943 |
| Model-4 | 5: 0.066 | 0.876 | 0.894 | 0.947 | 0.664 | 0.942 |
| Model-5 | 6: 0.066 | 0.873 | 0.864 | **0.985** | 0.536 | 0.956 |

### 4.3 Generalization Ability Assessment

Finally, the ED-AnoNet generalization ability is tested on an OCTA500 dataset. For the training of ED-AnoNet, the settings in Table 3 are still used, and the experimental results are shown in Table 4. By comparison, Ed-Anonet has strong generalization ability to the OCTA500 dataset. Moreover, the influence of the elastic deformation parameter $\alpha : \sigma$ on the experimental results is still obvious.

**Table 4.** Comparison of ED-AnoNet and fully supervised two classification models on the OCTA500 dataset.

| Model | $\alpha : \sigma$ | Acc | Pre | Sen | Spe | AUC |
|---|---|---|---|---|---|---|
| Model-1 | 2:0.066 | 0.881 | 0.812 | 0.974 | 0.788 | 0.972 |
| Model-2 | 3:0.066 | 0.944 | 0.918 | 0.974 | 0.914 | 0.988 |
| Model-3 | 4:0.066 | 0.954 | 0.935 | 0.976 | 0.932 | 0.987 |
| Model-4 | 5:0.066 | 0.929 | 0.984 | 0.872 | 0.986 | 0.993 |
| Model-5 | 6:0.066 | 0.963 | 0.985 | 0.940 | 0.986 | 0.996 |

## 5 Conclusion

In this work, we have proposed a novel OCT image anomaly detection network called ED-AnoNet. We have obtained Pseudo-abnorOCT images through the elastic distortion of normal OCT images, which can promote the ED-AnoNet to learn discriminant feature maps during the training process. The results on two public datasets show that our method can effectively detect different known anomalies, such as CNV, Drusen, and DME, which have never been seen during training. In contrast to prior work, this study shows that the utilization of the Pseudo-abnorOCT images can yield improved results, thereby validating that the use of Pseudo-abnorOCT images in promoting ED-AnoNet learning with discrimination feature maps is effective.

**Acknowledgments.** This work was supported by the National Natural Science Foundation of China (No. 61972419, 61672542 and 61702558), Natural Science Foundation of Hunan Province of China (No. 2020JJ4120).

# References

1. Yanagihara, R.T., Lee, C.S., Ting, D., Lee, A.Y.: Methodological challenges of deep learning in optical coherence tomography for retinal diseases: a review. Transl. Vis. Sci. Technol. **9**(2), 11 (2020)
2. Huang, D., Swanson, E.A., Lin, C.P., et al.: Optical coherence tomography. Science **254**(5035), 1178–1181 (1991). https://doi.org/10.1126/science.1957169
3. Sadda, S.V.R., Abdelfattah, N.S., Lei, J., et al.: Spectral-domain OCT analysis of risk factors for macular atrophy development in the harbor study for neovascular age-related macular degeneration. Ophthalmology **127**(10), 1360–1370 (2020)
4. Krizhevsky, A., Sutskever, I., Hinton, G.E.: Imagenet classification with deep convolutional neural networks. Adv. Neural. Inf. Process. Syst. **60**(6), 84–90 (2012). https://doi.org/10.1145/3065386
5. Chen, Z., Peng, P., Shen, H., et al.: Region-segmentation strategy for Bruch's membrane opening detection in spectral domain optical coherence tomography images. Biomed. Opt. Express **10**(2), 526–538 (2019)
6. Pekala, M., Joshi, N., Liu, T.Y.A., et al.: Deep learning based retinal OCT segmentation. Comput. Biol. Med. **114**, 103445 (2019)
7. Wei, H., Shen, H., Li, J., et al.: AneNet: A lightweight network for the real-time anemia screening from retinal vessel optical coherence tomography images. Opt. Laser Technol. **136**, 106773 (2020)
8. De, F.J., Ledsam, J.R., Romera-Paredes, B., et al.: Clinically applicable deep learning for diagnosis and referral in retinal disease. Nat. Med. **24**(9), 1342–1350 (2018)
9. Kermany, D.S., Goldbaum, M., Cai, W., et al.: Identifying medical diagnoses and treatable diseases by image-based deep learning. Cell **172**(5), 1122–1131 (2018)
10. Lee, C.S., Baughman, D.M., Lee, A.Y.: Deep learning is effective for classifying normal versus age-related macular degeneration OCT images. Ophthalmol. Retina **1**(4), 322–327 (2017)
11. Pimentel, M.A.F., Clifton, D.A., Clifton, L., et al.: A review of novelty detection. Signal Process. **99**, 215–249 (2014)
12. Goodfellow, I., Pouget-Abadie, J., Mirza, M., et al.: Generative adversarial nets. Adv. Neural. Inf. Process. Syst. **63**(11), 139–144 (2014)
13. Schlegl, T., Seeböck, P., Waldstein, S.M., Schmidt-Erfurth, U., Langs, G.: Unsupervised anomaly detection with generative adversarial networks to guide marker discovery. In: Niethammer, M., et al. (eds.) IPMI 2017. LNCS, vol. 10265, pp. 146–157. Springer, Cham (2017). https://doi.org/10.1007/978-3-319-59050-9_12
14. Schlegl, T., Seeböck, P., Waldstein, S.M., et al.: f-AnoGAN: fast unsupervised anomaly detection with generative adversarial networks. Med. Image Anal. **54**, 30–44 (2019)
15. Zhou, K., Gao, S., Cheng, J., et al.: Sparse-GAN: sparsity-constrained generative adversarial network for anomaly detection in retinal OCT image. In: 2020 IEEE 17th International Symposium on Biomedical Imaging (ISBI), pp. 1227–1231.IEEE (2020)
16. Zhou, K., et al.: Encoding structure-texture relation with P-Net for anomaly detection in retinal images. In: Vedaldi, A., Bischof, H., Brox, T., Frahm, J.-M. (eds.) ECCV 2020. LNCS, vol. 12365, pp. 360–377. Springer, Cham (2020). https://doi.org/10.1007/978-3-030-58565-5_22

17. Seeböck, P., Orlando, J.I., Schlegl, T., et al.: Exploiting epistemic uncertainty of anatomy segmentation for anomaly detection in retinal OCT. IEEE Trans. Med. Imaging **39**(1), 87–98 (2019)

18. Simard, P.Y., Steinkraus, D., Platt, J.C.: Best practices for convolutional neural networks applied to visual document analysis. In: Seventh International Conference on Document Analysis and Recognition, p. 958. IEEE (2003)

19. Chen, Z., Mo, Y., Ouyang, P., Shen, H., Li, D., Zhao, R.: Retinal vessel optical coherence tomography images for anemia screening. Med. Biol. Eng. Comput. **57**(4), 953–966 (2018). https://doi.org/10.1007/s11517-018-1927-8

20. Chen, Z., Wei, H., Shen, H., et al.: Intraretinal layer segmentation and parameter measurement in optic nerve head region through energy function of spatial-gradient continuity constraint. J. Cent. South Univ. **25**(8), 1938–1947 (2018)

21. Gu, Z., Cheng, J., Fu, H., et al.: CE-Net: context encoder network for 2D medical image segmentation. IEEE Trans. Med. Imaging **38**(10), 2281–2292 (2019)

22. He, K., Zhang, X., Ren, S., et al.: Deep residual learning for image recognition. In: 2016 IEEE Conference on Computer Vision and Pattern Recognition (CVPR), pp. 770–778. IEEE (2016)

23. Namozov, A., Im, C.Y.: An improvement for medical image analysis using data enhancement techniques in deep learning. In: 2018 International Conference on Information and Communication Technology Robotics (ICT-ROBOT), pp. 1–3. IEEE (2018)

24. Yeh, R.A., Chen, C., Yian, L. T., et al.: Semantic image inpainting with deep generative models. In: 2017 IEEE Conference on Computer Vision and Pattern Recognition (CVPR), pp. 6882–6890. IEEE (2017)

25. Salimans, T., Goodfellow, I., Zaremba, W., et al.: Improved techniques for training gans. arXiv preprint arXiv:1606.03498 (2016)

26. Li, M., Chen, Y., Ji, Z., et al.: Image projection network: 3D to 2D image segmentation in OCTA images. IEEE Trans. Med. Imaging **39**(11), 3343–3354 (2020)

# BiDFNet: Bi-decoder and Feedback Network for Automatic Polyp Segmentation with Vision Transformers

Shu Tang[✉], Junlin Qiu, Xianzhong Xie, Haiheng Ran, and Guoli Zhang

Chongqing University of Posts and Telecommunications, Chongqing, China
tangshu@stu.cqupt.edu.cn

**Abstract.** Accurate polyp segmentation is becoming increasingly important in the early diagnosis of rectal cancer. In recent years, polyp segmentation methods represented by deep learning neural network have achieved great success, especially for the U-Net, however, accurate poly segmentation is still an extremely challenging task due to the low contrast and indistinct boundary between the foreground poly and the background, and diverse in the shape, size, color and texture at different stages of rectal cancer. To address these challenges and achieve more accurate polyp segmentation from the colonoscopy images, we propose a novel network called bi-Decoder network with feedback (BiDFNet) to further improve the accuracy of polyp segmentation, especially for the small ones. It is well known that different scales information and different level features play important roles in accurate target segmentation, therefore, in the proposed BiDFNet, we first propose a bi-decoder with feedback architecture which works in both "coarse-to-fine" and "fine-to-coarse" manners for achieving better information flow exploitation across different scales. Then, at each scale, we construct a residual connection mode (RCM) to dynamically fuse shallow-level features and deep-level features for distilling more effective information. Extensive experiments on five popular polyp segmentation benchmarks (Kvasir, CVC-ClinicDB, ETIS, CVC-ColonDB and Endoscene) shows that our approach has stronger generalization and robustness. The results outperform the state-of-the-art methods by a large margin both on the objective evaluation metric and the subjective visual effect.

**Keywords:** Polyp segmentation · Dual decoder · From coarse to fine · From fine to coarse · Adaptive fusion

## 1 Introduction

Colorectal cancer (CRC) has become one of the most serious cancers that threaten human health, and colorectal cancer ranks third in terms of incidence, and second in terms of mortality. The cells, growing in the lining of the colon or rectum, called polyp are the main reason of colorectal cancer. As time goes on,

© The Author(s), under exclusive license to Springer Nature Switzerland AG 2022
S. Yu et al. (Eds.): PRCV 2022, LNCS 13535, pp. 16–27, 2022.
https://doi.org/10.1007/978-3-031-18910-4_2

some polyps will turn to colorectal cancer. Therefore, early detection and remove polyps are crucial before they turn to colorectal cancer. Colonoscopy is the most popular procedure for examining polyps. However, due to various reasons, the results of colonoscopy have high miss rate. Therefore, an accurate and effective computer-aided automatic polyp segmentation method can greatly help doctors to improve the accuracy of diagnosis.

With the development of deep learning, convolutional neural networks (CNNs) have become the mainstream in polyp segmentation. Especially the encoder-decoder based network Unet [16], which has shown excellent segmentation performance. Many polyp segmentation networks [3, 5, 8, 10, 11, 11, 13, 14, 22, 26] have adopted the U-shaped architecture.

However, in the various U-shaped structures, there still remain two big challenges in polyp segmentation. Firstly, deep features lack spatial information, which cannot locate the location of the polyps accurately. Many exist methods such as [4, 5, 7, 11, 22] only use deep features to predict the final prediction which cannot split the small polyps. Secondly, the decoder leverages multi-level features to generate the final high-resolution prediction. However, if the flow of information in the model is not effectively controlled and fused, some redundant features, will enter the information flow of the model, and may lead to the performance degradation, such as obscure boundaries.

In order to better solve the above challenges. We propose a novel U-shape network named BiDFNet. Firstly, to solve the disappearance of spatial information, we use both deep and shadow features, and design an architecture which contains two decoders with a feedback path. From bottom to top, we propose an adaptive fusion module (AFM) to fuse adjacent multi-scale features. The AFM implements the attention mechanism to aggregate semantic features. From top to bottom, aggregated features are feedback into different scales for further corresponding features refinement. Secondly, at each scale, to remove the background noise and redundant features, we propose a RCM. RCM is designed for further fusion and enhance interactions of contextual cues. These two module types can be integrated into our framework to build an efficient semantic segmentation mode and boost the performance of the polyp segmentation.

In summary, our contribution can be summarized as follows:

1. We propose a novel network structure which consists of an encoder and two decoders. We use pyramid vision transformer as the encoder, which will extract richer and more powerful features. Two parallel decoders with a feedback path structure enables the model to get more accurate segmentation results.

2. We propose an adaptive fusion module (AFM) and a residual connection module (RCM). The AFM is an attention block which is proposed to fuse features of different scales and suppress background noise. And the RCM is proposed for further distillation more effective information from different levels.

3. Extensive experiments conducted on five typical polyp segmentation datasets show that our methods outperforms the previous state-of-the-art methods

by a large margin, and our method has better performance for small polyp segmentation.

## 2  Related Work

Earlier polyp segmentation methods depend on hand-crafted features such as color, textures, shape and appearance [2,18] but the effectiveness of these methods is generally limited due to the low representation capability of hand-crafted features.

In recent years, methods based on deep learning have achieved excellent performance in polyp segmentation. Fully convolutional networks (FCN) [12] realized end-to-end semantic segmentation for the first time. The encoder-decoder based network Unet [16] is widely used in polyp segmentation, which has become the baseline of most state-of-the-art segmentation methods.

Base on the U-Net, many novel architectures for polyp segmentation were introduced. Such as Unet++ [26], ResUnet++ [10], DoubleUnet [8] which have achieve expressive performance. ResUnet++ uses many advanced modules such as squeeze and excitation, atrous spatial pyramidal pooling (ASPP), and residual blocks. DoubleUnet skillfully combines two Unets with an encoder using VGG-16. Different from the U-shaped structure, SFA [5] adds another area-boundary branch for polyp segmentation, PraNet [4] forces on the boundary of polyp and uses the high-level feature aggregation, parallel partial decoder and reverse attention to improve the result. MSEG [7] improve the PraNet architecture and get better result than PraNet. More recent works, MSNet [25] designs a subtraction unit to produce the difference features. SANet [22] proposes a shallow attention module which has better performance on small polyps.

Recently, the novel architecture transformer [19] has caused great attention on computer vision. Vision transformer (ViT), splits the image into patches and models the correlation between these patches as sequences with transformer, and achieves comparable performance with other state-of-the-art (SOTA) CNN-based methods. For polyp segmentation with transformer, TransFuse [24], proposes a method to fuse the features extracted by transformer and CNNs. Moreover, pyramid vision transformer (PVT) [21], use a hierarchical transformer with four stages, has achieve great performance on polyp segmentation tasks, such as Polyp-PVT [3]. Due to the excellent ability of long-range dependencies modeling, PVT inherits the strengths of CNN and transformer, we would adopt PVT as our backbone.

## 3  Proposed Method

### 3.1  Overall Network Architecture

Figure 1 describes the overall structure of the proposed BiDFNet. The network is a U-shaped architecture which consists of one encoder and two decoders. The encoder network consists of 4 encoder-blocks ($E_i, i \in \{1, 2, 3, 4\}$), whereas each decoder network also consists of 4 decoder blocks ($D - Block_i, i \in \{1, 2, 3, 4, 5, 6, 7, 8\}$). Besides, the model also contains two types of modules: the adaptive fusion module (AFM) and the residual Connection Module (RCM). For encoder, We first use pyramid vision transformer(PVT) as the backbone of the network to extract features of four scales with different resolutions, respectively. Then, at each scale, we separately use a $1 \times 1$ convolution to reduce the number of feature channels to 32 ($X_i, i \in \{1, 2, 3, 4\}$) which helps to save the computation. For decoder, we use two decoders $Decoder_1$ and $Decoder_2$ to predict the result. Firstly, features ($X_i, i \in \{1, 2, 3, 4\}$) from encoder are feed to $Decoder_1$, get output $out_1$ and the input ($X_i', i \in \{1, 2, 3, 4\}$) of $Decoder_2$. Secondly, each $X_i'$ is feed to $Decoder_2$ and get the output of the $Decoder_2$, $out_2$. Finally, we feed $out_1$ and $out_2$ to two convolution modules respectively and get the mask predictions $predicition_1$ and $predicition_2$. We use the sum of the $predicition_1$ and the $predicition_2$ as the final prediction result. We will describe our approach in details in the following sections.

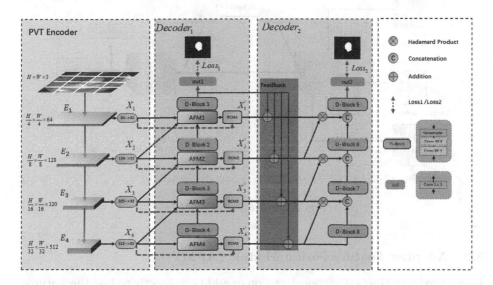

**Fig. 1.** Overall architecture of the proposed BiDFNet.

## 3.2 Bi-decoder

**Bi-decoder.** As show in Fig. 1, we propose two parallel decoders ($Decoder_1$ and $Decoder_2$) in our network which work in both "coarse-to-fine" and "fine-to-coarse" manners for achieving effective fusion of different scales information. $Decoder_1$ consists of four $D - Blocks$, AFM and RCM modules, and each output of the encoder is fed to the corresponding scale of $Decoder_1$, and each scale output of $Decoder_1$ is feed to the corresponding scale of the $Decoder_2$. Each $D - Block$ in the decoder performs a bi-linear up-sampling on the feature resolution space, and reduces the channel to 32. $Decoder_2$ contains four $D - Blocks$ and a feedback path. To explore the correlations between the features from adjacent layers, each input of the $D - Block$ is multiplied element-wisely by the input of the previous layer.

**Feedback Path.** We consider that the output of the $D - Block_1$ of the $Decoder_1$ contains different scales information. Therefore we propose a top-down feedback path, in which the output of $Decoder_1$ is downsampled and added to corresponding scale features exported by RCM for further refining them. These refined features will be sent to the $Decoder_2$ to generate the second output $out_2$. The two parallel decoders are linked, and the features are refined, so our network has the potential to capture more complex and concealed features and achieve more accuracy polyp segmentation.

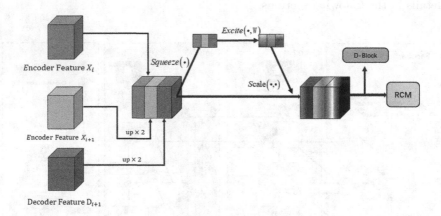

**Fig. 2.** Illustration of AFM

## 3.3   Adaptive Feature Fusion Module (AFM)

In most existing Unets, the concatenation or addition directly to fuse the features of different scales, which ignore the differences between these different features, resulting in redundant features and weakening useful features. We believe that an effective features fusion approach for different scales can capture both fine-grained and coarse-grained information well, which is beneficial to accurate polyp segmentation. So that we propose an AFM, as shown in Fig. 2, which is used to effectively aggregate features from different scales. In $(AFM_i, i \in \{1, 2, 3, 4\})$, $AFM_i$ receives the feature from encoder of the same scale feature $X_i$, coarse scale feature $X_{i+1}$, the output of the $D - Block_{i+1}$ from the coarse scale. After the concatenation of the features from adjacent scales, we apply a channel attention mechanism (Squeeze-and-Excite block [6]) on the concatenated features to re-weight each channel for robust representation. The result is used as the inputs of $RCM_i$ and $D - Block_{i-1}$, respectively.

## 3.4  Residual Connection Module (RCM)

The residual connection module(RCM), as shown in Fig. 3, is a small but useful module. The input of $(CFM_i, i \in \{1,2,3,4\})$ contains the output of encoder $(X_i, i \in \{1,2,3,4\})$ and the output of the $(AFM_i, i \in 1,2,3,4)$. We first use a $1 \times 1$ convolution to reduce the channel of the output feature of the $AFM_i$ to 32, the compressed features are added into $X_i$, and then the result is feed to a $3 \times 3$ convolution to generate $X_i'$, which is the input of the $Decoder_2$.

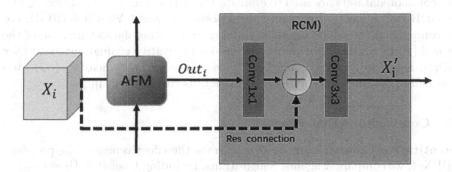

**Fig. 3.** Illustration of RCM

## 3.5  Loss Function

The total training loss for our method can be written as:

$$\mathcal{L}_{total} = \mathcal{L}_{decoder1} + \mathcal{L}_{decoder2}$$

where $\mathcal{L}_{decoder1}$ represents the loss of the $Decoder_1$, and $\mathcal{L}_{decoder2}$ represents the loss of $Decoder_2$.

$\mathcal{L}_{decoder1}$ is the loss between $predicition_1$ and ground truth $G$:

$$\mathcal{L}_{decoder1} = \mathcal{L}_{IoU}^{\omega} + \mathcal{L}_{BCE}^{\omega}$$

$\mathcal{L}_{decoder2}$ is the loss between $predicition_2$ and ground truth $G$:

$$\mathcal{L}_{decoder2} = \mathcal{L}_{IoU}^{\omega} + \mathcal{L}_{BCE}^{\omega}$$

$\mathcal{L}_{IoU}^{\omega}$ represents the weighted IoU loss, while $\mathcal{L}_{BCE}^{\omega}$ represents the binary cross entropy (BCE) loss which have been widely used in segmentation tasks [3,4,7,25] and their effectiveness has been validated in these works.

# 4  Experiments

## 4.1  Implementation Details

All the experiments are performed on a 2080Ti GPU using the PyTorch 1.7 framework. We train our model for 100 epochs with mini-batch size 8. Besides, we train our model with AdamW [24] optimizer, the momentum, weight decay and learning rate are set as 0.9, 1e−4 and 1e−4, respectively. All the images are resized to $352 \times 352$ in the training phase, and in the test phase, we adjust the test images to $352 \times 352$ without any post-processing steps. For dataset augmentation, multi-scale training strategy (as the PraNet [4]) is used in all experiments.

## 4.2   Datasets and Evaluation Metrics

Five common datasets are used to evaluate the performance of our model: CVC-ColonDB [18], ETIS [17], Kvasir [9], Endoscene [20] and CVC-ClinicDB [1]. For fair comparison, we adopt the same training and testing dataset division of the method [4]. In addition, six metrics are used quantitative evaluation: mean Dice (mDic), mean IoU (mIoU), weighted F- measure ($F_\beta^\omega$), S-measure ($S_\alpha$), and E-measure ($E_\xi$), mean absolute error (MAE), as the PraNet [4].

## 4.3   Comparisons Experiments

**Quantitative Comparison.** To demonstrate the effectiveness of the proposed BiDFNet, we compare it against 8 algorithms, including Unet [16], Unet++ [26], MSEG [7], PraNet [4], ACSNet [23], EU-Net [15], SANet [22], MSNet [25]. For fair comparison, the results of these competitors are directly acquired from their respective papers or computed by their released codes. As shown in Table 1, compared with other counterparts, our approach achieves the best scores on all the five datasets with respect to seven metrics(best scores on mDic, mIoU, $F_\beta^\omega$ and $S_\alpha$, while the second-best scores on mDic, $mE_\xi$, $maxE_\xi$ for Endoscene).

Specifically, for the first two datasets, compared to the second-best model MSNet, our model increases the mDic and mIoU by 1.3% and 1.7% on the Kvasir-SEG and 1.9% and 2.1% on the ClinicDB, respectively. For the last three datasets, which are unseen and used to validate the generalization ability of our model. On ColonDB, our model achieves a mDic of 0.813 and a mIoU of 0.729, which has 6.2% improvement on mDic and 5.8 % improvement on mIoU over the second-best model MSNet.

**Visual Comparison.** We visualize some segmentation results produced by our model and other approaches in Fig. 4. It can be observed that our proposed method not only highlights the polyp regions clearly, but also well suppresses the background noises. It excels in dealing with various challenging size and shape, including very small polyps (row1, row3, row5), multiple polyps (row2) and large size polyps (row4, row6). Besides, compared with other counterparts, our results also has clearer edges. In short, out method outperforms state-of-the-art methods on the both metrics and visual appearances, which demonstrates the superior capability of our method.

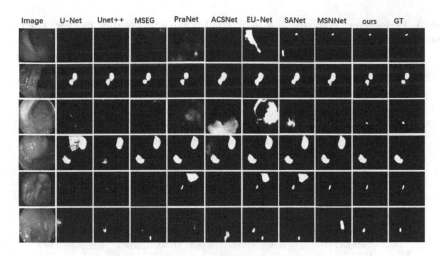

**Fig. 4.** Visual comparison of different methods.

## 4.4 Ablation Study

In order to evaluate the effectiveness of each component in our proposed method, we further conduct ablation studies on four variants of our BiDFNet. The datasets we select and the training setting are the same with the mentioned in the Sects. 3.2 and 3.3. In No.1 (Backbone) experiment, we remove all component except the encoder, then use the last layer of encoder to predict the result. In No.2 (Without F) experiment, we remove the feedback path. In No.3 (Without-AFM), we removed all the AFM modules, and replace it with a convolution layer. In No.4 (Without-RCM), we remove the residual connection path of RCM. The results are shown in Table 2.

**Effectiveness of Feedback Paths.** We investigate the importance of the feedback paths. From Table 2, we observe that No.2 (Backbone without F) outperforms No.1 (Backbone), in particular, the mDic drops from 0.799 to 0.774, clearly showing that the feedback paths is necessary for improving performance.

**Effectiveness of AFM.** To analyze the effectiveness of the AFM, we utilize a convolution layer instead of the AFM. As shown in Table 2, it can be observed that BiDFNet outperforms No.3 on five datasets in terms of two evaluation metrics. Specifically, removing the AFM causes the mDic to drop from 0.813 to 0.800 on CVC-ColonDB.

**Effectiveness of RCM.** We further investigate the contribution of the RCM, we observe that without RCM, the mDic decreases by 0.9% on Kvasir and 4.2% on EITS. Although the mDic of ColonDB increases, the accuracy only increases by 0.4%. And without RCM, the average mDic of five datasets decreases by 1.5%. So, Table 2 demonstrates the effectiveness of the RCM.

**Table 1.** Performance comparison with different polyp segmentation models. The highest scores are highlight in red.

| Dataset | Model | mDic | mIoU | $F_\beta^\omega$ | $S_\alpha$ | $mE_\xi$ | $maxE_\xi$ | MAE |
|---|---|---|---|---|---|---|---|---|
| Kvasir | Unet [16] | 0.818 | 0.746 | 0.794 | 0.858 | 0.881 | 0.893 | 0.055 |
| | Unet++ [26] | 0.821 | 0.743 | 0.808 | 0.862 | 0.886 | 0.909 | 0.048 |
| | MSEG [7] | 0.897 | 0.839 | 0.885 | 0.912 | 0.942 | 0.948 | 0.028 |
| | PraNet [4] | 0.898 | 0.840 | 0.885 | 0.915 | 0.944 | 0.948 | 0.030 |
| | ACSNet [23] | 0.898 | 0.838 | 0.882 | 0.920 | 0.941 | 0.952 | 0.032 |
| | EU-Net [15] | 0.908 | 0.854 | 0.893 | 0.917 | 0.951 | 0.954 | 0.028 |
| | SANet [22] | 0.904 | 0.847 | 0.892 | 0.915 | 0.949 | 0.953 | 0.028 |
| | MSNNet [25] | 0.905 | 0.849 | 0.892 | 0.923 | 0.947 | 0.954 | 0.028 |
| | BiDFNet (ours) | 0.918 | 0.866 | 0.906 | 0.925 | 0.959 | 0.962 | 0.023 |
| ClinicDB | Unet [16] | 0.823 | 0.755 | 0.811 | 0.889 | 0.913 | 0.954 | 0.019 |
| | Unet++ [26] | 0.794 | 0.729 | 0.785 | 0.873 | 0.891 | 0.931 | 0.022 |
| | MSEG [7] | 0.909 | 0.864 | 0.907 | 0.938 | 0.961 | 0.969 | 0.007 |
| | PraNet [4] | 0.899 | 0.849 | 0.896 | 0.936 | 0.959 | 0.979 | 0.009 |
| | ACSNet [23] | 0.882 | 0.826 | 0.873 | 0.927 | 0.947 | 0.959 | 0.011 |
| | EU-Net [15] | 0.902 | 0.846 | 0.891 | 0.939 | 0.959 | 0.965 | 0.011 |
| | SANet [22] | 0.904 | 0.847 | 0.892 | 0.915 | 0.949 | 0.953 | 0.028 |
| | MSNNet [25] | 0.918 | 0.869 | 0.913 | 0.946 | 0.973 | 0.979 | 0.008 |
| | BiDFNet (ours) | 0.937 | 0.890 | 0.935 | 0.950 | 0.985 | 0.989 | 0.006 |
| ColonDB | Unet [16] | 0.512 | 0.444 | 0.498 | 0.712 | 0.696 | 0.776 | 0.061 |
| | Unet++ [26] | 0.483 | 0.410 | 0.467 | 0.691 | 0.680 | 0.760 | 0.064 |
| | MSEG [7] | 0.735 | 0.666 | 0.724 | 0.834 | 0.859 | 0.875 | 0.038 |
| | PraNet [4] | 0.712 | 0.640 | 0.699 | 0.820 | 0.847 | 0.872 | 0.043 |
| | ACSNet [23] | 0.716 | 0.649 | 0.697 | 0.829 | 0.839 | 0.851 | 0.039 |
| | EU-Net [15] | 0.756 | 0.681 | 0.730 | 0.831 | 0.863 | 0.872 | 0.045 |
| | SANet [22] | 0.753 | 0.670 | 0.726 | 0.837 | 0.869 | 0.878 | 0.043 |
| | MSNNet [25] | 0.751 | 0.671 | 0.736 | 0.838 | 0.872 | 0.883 | 0.041 |
| | BiDFNet (ours) | 0.813 | 0.729 | 0.795 | 0.869 | 0.918 | 0.924 | 0.029 |
| EITS | Unet [16] | 0.398 | 0.335 | 0.366 | 0.684 | 0.643 | 0.740 | 0.036 |
| | Unet++ [26] | 0.401 | 0.344 | 0.390 | 0.683 | 0.629 | 0.776 | 0.035 |
| | MSEG [7] | 0.700 | 0.630 | 0.671 | 0.828 | 0.854 | 0.890 | 0.015 |
| | PraNet [4] | 0.628 | 0.567 | 0.600 | 0.794 | 0.808 | 0.841 | 0.031 |
| | ACSNet [23] | 0.578 | 0.509 | 0.530 | 0.754 | 0.737 | 0.764 | 0.059 |
| | EU-Net [15] | 0.687 | 0.609 | 0.636 | 0.793 | 0.807 | 0.841 | 0.067 |
| | SANet [22] | 0.750 | 0.654 | 0.685 | 0.849 | 0.881 | 0.897 | 0.015 |
| | MSNNet [25] | 0.723 | 0.652 | 0.677 | 0.845 | 0.876 | 0.890 | 0.020 |
| | BiDFNet (ours) | 0.799 | 0.722 | 0.765 | 0.883 | 0.906 | 0.923 | 0.016 |
| Endoscene | Unet [16] | 0.710 | 0.627 | 0.684 | 0.843 | 0.847 | 0.875 | 0.022 |
| | Unet++ [26] | 0.707 | 0.624 | 0.687 | 0.839 | 0.834 | 0.898 | 0.018 |
| | MSEG [7] | 0.874 | 0.804 | 0.852 | 0.924 | 0.948 | 0.957 | 0.009 |
| | PraNet [4] | 0.871 | 0.797 | 0.843 | 0.925 | 0.950 | 0.972 | 0.010 |
| | ACSNet [23] | 0.573 | 0.519 | 0.547 | 0.703 | 0.698 | 0.941 | 0.941 |
| | EU-Net [15] | 0.837 | 0.765 | 0.805 | 0.904 | 0.919 | 0.933 | 0.015 |
| | SANet [22] | 0.888 | 0.815 | 0.859 | 0.928 | 0.962 | 0.972 | 0.008 |
| | MSNNet [25] | 0.865 | 0.799 | 0.848 | 0.926 | 0.945 | 0.953 | 0.010 |
| | BiDFNet (ours) | 0.885 | 0.815 | 0.865 | 0.931 | 0.956 | 0.967 | 0.010 |

**Table 2.** Ablation study for BiDFNet with different datasets. The highest scores are highlight in red.

| No | dataset | Kvasir-SEG | | ClinicDB | | ColonDB | | EITS | | Endoscene | |
|----|---------|------|------|------|------|------|------|------|------|------|------|
| | Metrics | mDic | mIoU | mDic | mIoU | mDic | mIoU | mDic | mIoU | mDic | mIoU |
| 1 | Backbone | 0.895 | 0.833 | 0.911 | 0.849 | 0.766 | 0.675 | 0.739 | 0.649 | 0.857 | 0.780 |
| 2 | Without -F | 0.911 | 0.858 | 0.920 | 0.872 | 0.810 | 0.728 | 0.774 | 0.699 | 0.879 | 0.811 |
| 3 | Without- AFM | 0.904 | 0.849 | 0.923 | 0.876 | 0.800 | 0.715 | 0.783 | 0.705 | 0.883 | 0.813 |
| 4 | Without- RCM | 0.909 | 0.875 | 0.918 | 0.807 | 0.817 | 0.731 | 0.765 | 0.684 | 0.875 | 0.870 |
| 5 | BiDFNet | 0.918 | 0.866 | 0.937 | 0.890 | 0.813 | 0.729 | 0.799 | 0.722 | 0.886 | 0.815 |

### 4.5   Computing Complexity

In terms of speed on a RTX 2080Ti GPU(showing in Table 3), Our method achieves a speed about ~17 FPS. Because of one transformer encoder and double decoders, our method gets lower speed. However, our method achieves the best performance in the most of cases. In the future, we will try to speed up our method.

**Table 3.** The average speed of different methods.

| Methods | Unet | Unet++ | MSEG | ParNet | SANNet | MSNNet | BiDFNet (ours) |
|---------|------|--------|------|--------|--------|--------|----------------|
| Average speed | ~8 fps | ~7 fps | ~86 fps | ~50 fps | ~72 fps | ~70 fps | ~17 fps |

## 5   Conclusion

In this paper, we present a novel bi-decoder and feedback Network (BiDFNet) for accurate polyp segmentation. We design a novel structure which contains one transformer encoder and two parallel decoders. We propose a top-down path, which feeds fused information from adjacent scales back to each scale of the $Decoder_2$. To further improve feature fusion and enhance interactions of contextual cues, we propose an AFM and a RCM. The proposed feedback architecture, AFM and RCM together achieve effective information fusion from different scales and different levels, which can further improve the accuracy of polyp segmentation, especially for the small polyps. Extensive experimental results demonstrate that the proposed BiDFNet outperforms the state-of-the-art methods on both qualitative evaluation and quantitative metrics. In the future, we plan to further improve the performance of the bi-decoder architecture and extend the proposed BiDFNet to other medical-related tasks such as instance segmentation and disease classification.

# References

1. Bernal, J., Sánchez, F.J., Fernández-Esparrach, G., Gil, D., Rodríguez, C., Vilariño, F.: WM-DOVA maps for accurate polyp highlighting in colonoscopy: validation vs. saliency maps from physicians. Computer. Med. Imaging Graph. **43**, 99–111 (2015)
2. Bernal, J., Sánchez, J., Vilarino, F.: Towards automatic polyp detection with a polyp appearance model. Pattern Recogn. **45**(9), 3166–3182 (2012)
3. Dong, B., Wang, W., Fan, D.P., Li, J., Fu, H., Shao, L.: Polyp-PVT: polyp segmentation with pyramid vision transformers. arXiv preprint arXiv:2108.06932 (2021)
4. Fan, D.-P., et al.: PraNet: parallel reverse attention network for polyp segmentation. In: Martel, A.L., et al. (eds.) MICCAI 2020. LNCS, vol. 12266, pp. 263–273. Springer, Cham (2020). https://doi.org/10.1007/978-3-030-59725-2_26
5. Fang, Y., Chen, C., Yuan, Y., Tong, K.: Selective feature aggregation network with area-boundary constraints for polyp segmentation. In: Shen, D., et al. (eds.) MICCAI 2019. LNCS, vol. 11764, pp. 302–310. Springer, Cham (2019). https://doi.org/10.1007/978-3-030-32239-7_34
6. Hu, J., Shen, L., Sun, G.: Squeeze-and-excitation networks. In: Proceedings of the IEEE Conference on Computer Vision and Pattern Recognition, pp. 7132–7141 (2018)
7. Huang, C.H., Wu, H.Y., Lin, Y.L.: HardNet-MSEG: a simple encoder-decoder polyp segmentation neural network that achieves over 0.9 mean dice and 86 fps. arXiv preprint arXiv:2101.07172 (2021)
8. Jha, D., Riegler, M.A., Johansen, D., Halvorsen, P., Johansen, H.D.: Doubleu-Net: a deep convolutional neural network for medical image segmentation. In: 2020 IEEE 33rd International Symposium on Computer-Based Medical Systems (CBMS), pp. 558–564. IEEE (2020)
9. Jha, D., et al.: Kvasir-SEG: a segmented polyp dataset. In: Ro, Y.M., et al. (eds.) MMM 2020. LNCS, vol. 11962, pp. 451–462. Springer, Cham (2020). https://doi.org/10.1007/978-3-030-37734-2_37
10. Jha, D., et al.: ResuNet++: an advanced architecture for medical image segmentation. In: 2019 IEEE International Symposium on Multimedia (ISM), pp. 225–2255. IEEE (2019)
11. Kim, T., Lee, H., Kim, D.: Uacanet: uncertainty augmented context attention for polyp segmentation. In: Proceedings of the 29th ACM International Conference on Multimedia, pp. 2167–2175 (2021)
12. Long, J., Shelhamer, E., Darrell, T.: Fully convolutional networks for semantic segmentation. In: Proceedings of the IEEE Conference on Computer Vision and Pattern Recognition, pp. 3431–3440 (2015)
13. Lou, A., Guan, S., Loew, M.: CaraNet: context axial reverse attention network for segmentation of small medical objects. arXiv preprint arXiv:2108.07368 (2021)
14. Murugesan, B., Sarveswaran, K., Shankaranarayana, S.M., Ram, K., Joseph, J., Sivaprakasam, M.: Psi-Net: Shape and boundary aware joint multi-task deep network for medical image segmentation. In: 2019 41st Annual International Conference of the IEEE Engineering in Medicine and Biology Society (EMBC), pp. 7223–7226. IEEE (2019)
15. Patel, K., Bur, A.M., Wang, G.: Enhanced u-net: a feature enhancement network for polyp segmentation. In: 2021 18th Conference on Robots and Vision (CRV), pp. 181–188. IEEE (2021)

16. Ronneberger, O., Fischer, P., Brox, T.: U-net: convolutional networks for biomedical image segmentation. In: Navab, N., Hornegger, J., Wells, W.M., Frangi, A.F. (eds.) MICCAI 2015. LNCS, vol. 9351, pp. 234–241. Springer, Cham (2015). https://doi.org/10.1007/978-3-319-24574-4_28

17. Silva, J., Histace, A., Romain, O., Dray, X., Granado, B.: Toward embedded detection of polyps in WCE images for early diagnosis of colorectal cancer. Int. J. Comput. Assist. Radiol. Surg. **9**(2), 283–293 (2014)

18. Tajbakhsh, N., Gurudu, S.R., Liang, J.: Automated polyp detection in colonoscopy videos using shape and context information. IEEE Trans. Med. Imaging **35**(2), 630–644 (2015)

19. Vaswani, A., et al.: Attention is all you need. Adv. Neural Inf. Process. Syst. **30** (2017)

20. Vázquez, D., et al.: A benchmark for endoluminal scene segmentation of colonoscopy images. J. Healthc. Eng. **2017** (2017)

21. Wang, W., et al.: Pvt v2: improved baselines with pyramid vision transformer. Comput. Vis. Media, 1–10 (2022)

22. Wei, J., Hu, Y., Zhang, R., Li, Z., Zhou, S.K., Cui, S.: Shallow attention network for polyp segmentation. In: de Bruijne, M., et al. (eds.) MICCAI 2021. LNCS, vol. 12901, pp. 699–708. Springer, Cham (2021). https://doi.org/10.1007/978-3-030-87193-2_66

23. Zhang, R., Li, G., Li, Z., Cui, S., Qian, D., Yu, Y.: Adaptive context selection for polyp segmentation. In: Martel, A.L., et al. (eds.) MICCAI 2020. LNCS, vol. 12266, pp. 253–262. Springer, Cham (2020). https://doi.org/10.1007/978-3-030-59725-2_25

24. Zhang, Y., Liu, H., Hu, Q.T.: Fusing transformers and CNNs for medical image segmentation. arxiv. arXiv preprint arXiv:2102.08005 (2021)

25. Zhao, X., Zhang, L., Lu, H.: Automatic polyp segmentation via multi-scale subtraction network. In: de Bruijne, M., et al. (eds.) MICCAI 2021. LNCS, vol. 12901, pp. 120–130. Springer, Cham (2021). https://doi.org/10.1007/978-3-030-87193-2_12

26. Zhou, Z., Rahman Siddiquee, M.M., Tajbakhsh, N., Liang, J.: UNet++: a nested U-net architecture for medical image segmentation. In: Stoyanov, D., et al. (eds.) DLMIA/ML-CDS -2018. LNCS, vol. 11045, pp. 3–11. Springer, Cham (2018). https://doi.org/10.1007/978-3-030-00889-5_1

# FundusGAN: A One-Stage Single Input GAN for Fundus Synthesis

Chao Cai, Xue Xia$^{(\boxtimes)}$, and Yuming Fang

Jiangxi University of Finance and Economics, Nanchang 330013, China
yeziandkuma@qq.com

**Abstract.** Annotating medical images, especially fundus images that contain complex structures, needs expertise and time. To this end, fundus image synthesis methods were proposed to obtain specific categories of samples by combining vessel components and basic fundus images, during which well-segmented vessels from real fundus images were always required. Being different from these methods, We present a one-stage fundus image generating network to obtain healthy fundus images from scratch. First, we propose a basic attention Generator to present both global and local features. Second, we guide the Generator to focus on multi-scale fundus texture and structure features for better synthesis. Third, we design a self-motivated strategy to construct a vessel assisting module for vessel refining. By integrating the three proposed submodules, our fundus synthesis network, termed as FundusGAN, is built to provide one-stage fundus image generation without extra references. As a result, the synthetic fundus images are anatomically consistent with real images and demonstrate both diversity and reasonable visual quality.

**Keywords:** Medical image processing · Retinal fundus · Generative adversarial networks · Synthesis

## 1 Introduction

More than 2.2 billion people (about 29% of the global population) suffer from varying degrees of visual impairment, among which 80% of blinding diseases can be avoided through early screening, diagnosis, and treatment. Analyzing fundus images provide diagnosis for ophthalmology diseases such as age-related macular degeneration (AMD), diabetic retinopathy (DR), glaucoma, and cardiovascular conditions [1]. In recent years, researchers have paid attention to machine learning-aided auto-ophthalmic diseases diagnosis, especially on lesion segmentation and disease grading. However, these works need a large amount of annotated data, which relies on professional ophthalmologists. Moreover, due to different image obtaining devices, varying image capturing environments and different photographer behavior, the captured image quality varies a lot. Consequently, it costs a lot to get high-quality and well-annotated fundus images for auto-diagnosis algorithms.

© The Author(s), under exclusive license to Springer Nature Switzerland AG 2022
S. Yu et al. (Eds.): PRCV 2022, LNCS 13535, pp. 28–40, 2022.
https://doi.org/10.1007/978-3-031-18910-4_3

Image synthesis has been supposed to be a solution to annotation scarcity. In [2], the authors generate background and fovea, optic disc, and vessels using three modules. Generative Adversarial Network(GAN) [3] dramatically simplifies the synthesis process and boosts performance. Existing fundus synthesis methods always follow a two-stage strategy that generates the basic fundus images (non-vascular regions) and vessels separately [2,4,5]. The former mainly consists of fundus background, fovea, and optic disc, while the latter generally contains the vessel component. The reason may be two folds: 1) high-quality data is insufficient for the Generator to learn critical features, 2) lack of proper guidance for Generator to focus on vessels.

**Landmark GANs for Natural Images:** GANs [3] benefit image generation tasks. However, the gradient fluctuations or instability in GAN training bothers. To this end, Kurach et al. [6] and Roth et al. [7] proposed regularizations to support training. Salimans and Goodfellow et al. [8] presented multi techniques such as feature matching and one-sided label smoothing to improve GAN training. Denton et al. [9] used a cascade of CNN within a Laplacian pyramid to generate high-quality samples of natural images.

Arjovsky et al. [10] introduced Wasserstein distance to estimate the similarity between two non-overlapped distributions (WGAN), which greatly improves training stability. Jiang et al. [12] firstly build a Transformer-module based GAN without convolutions, termed as TransGAN. This proves the effectiveness of involving global attention modules. However, generating a $256 \times 256$ image using Transformer encoders costs huge GPU memory due to the matrix products among intermediate feature map pixels.

**GANs for Retinal Fundus Images:** Existing GAN-based fundus image synthesis methods can be mainly divided into two categories. **One** relies on real fundus images. Kamran et al. [13] proposed a GAN for Fluroscein Angiograms synthesis, in which two generators are used for fine and coarse features, and a vision transformer is adopted as the Discriminator. The GAN proposed by Yu et al. [14] takes vessel, optic cup, and optic disc components as inputs for generation. Other works require extra inputs. Liu et al. [15] involved style transferring in fundus image synthesizing. Healthy fundus images were used for style transferring, while those with diseases were for image generating. Results demonstrate that this method works like a data augmentor rather than a new content Generator. **The other** category needs extra vessel components. Zhao et al. [16] proposed tubGAN to obtain synthetic images from random noise together with tubular structures. To acquire diversity, a feature network for style-supervision was adopted. Costa et al. [4] generated fundus images from vessel binary maps and trained the Discriminator to distinguish vessel and fundus pairs rather than single images. Costa et al. [5] proposed a two-stage GAN, in which an autoencoder was trained to learn the mapping from random noise to binary vessel trees, and a standard GAN was used to generate fundus images from the generated binary vessel trees. These two works obtain fundus from segmented or generated vessels, and inspired many other researches. Sengupta et al. [17] adopted similar thinking, the main differences lie in a de-noise module and a super-resolution module for quality enhancement.

Except for the two-stage GAN in [5], all works involved either real fundus images or vessels as references. The latter was either used for new vessel component generation or direct fundus fusion. Some works even involved more than one Generator to synthesize different fundus regions.

This paper proposes a one-stage end-to-end generative adversarial network to synthesize retinal fundus images. Thus the proposed net is termed as Fundus-GAN. Our FundusGAN outputs fundus images with reasonable visual quality by accepting a random noise. The contributions of our network can be summarized as follows.

- We propose a one-stage GAN to generate fundus by making the best use of features and supervised learning. Especially, a stackable attention module aggregating global and local features is proposed as the Generator.
- We guide the Generator to focus on texture and structure features in a simple yet efficient way. Thus the vessel components generation performance is boosted.
- Moreover, a vessel assisting module is proposed to re-supervise the vessel components generation through a learning-free segmentation net for detail compensation.

## 2    Proposed Method

In this work, we present a one-stage GAN that only accepts a random noise to synthesize retinal fundus images (FundusGAN). The overall network architecture is illustrated in Fig. 1. Our GAN contains a proposed attention-based Generator and a basic Discriminator, and we propose a multi-scale structure and texture guidance and a vessel assisting module for the Generator. By feeding a random noise $z$, the FundusGAN directly generates a color retinal fundus image.

### 2.1    Network Architecture

For the sake of training stability, we adopt a modified Wasserstein Generative Adversarial Net(WGAN) as the backbone of our network.

**Attention Generator:** We embedded Transformer encoders into a basic Generator for attention acquisition, shown in Fig. 2. Generating a whole image from a noise vector requires global sights, while conventional upsampling modules, either interpolation or deconvolution, consider the information in a relatively local neighborhood. Therefore, we design an attention Generator in which two *Transformer Encoder Blocks* [12] are leveraged as a global feature extractor to work with the basic Generator modules. One *Transformer Block* consists of self-attention computation, normalization, and feed-forward MLP.

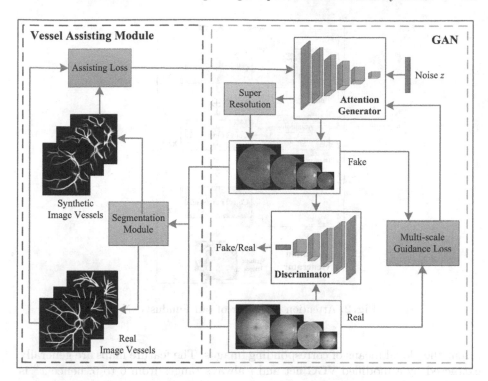

**Fig. 1.** The overall architecture of our FundusGAN. The GAN is embedded with attention modules and a texture and structure guidance module (in orange dotted box), and is equipped with a self-motivated vessel assisting modules (in violet dotted box). (Color figure online)

**Multi-scale Texture and Structure Guidance:** Even with attention mechanism involved, it's still challenging to learn vessel components due to its complex structure and abundant details. Many works synthesize vessels using an extra net. As a simplification, we endeavor to find an assessment metric DISTS (Deep Image Structure and Texture Similarity) [18] that perceptually evaluates texture properties and structure details. We concated multi-scale DISTS metrics for acquiring local and global features to guide the Generator. Under this guide, the Generator will focus on how to synthesize retinal fundus textures and structures rather than simply re-create pixels. Here we adopt multi-scale DISTS as a loss function for the Generator.

Since DISTS holds similarity of structure and texture between a pair of images, the texture similarity is computed through (1):

$$l(r_j^i, syn_j^i) = \frac{2\mu_{r_j}^i \mu_{syn_j}^i + C_1}{(\mu_{r_j}^i)^2 + (\mu_{syn_j}^i)^2 + C_1} \tag{1}$$

where $r_j^i$ and $syn_j^i$ denote the $j$-th feature map of the $i$-th convolution layer from a real image and a synthetic image, respectively. While $\mu_{r_j}^i$ and $\mu_{syn_j}^i$ rep-

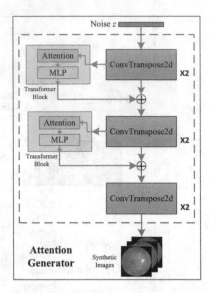

**Fig. 2.** Attention generator of our FundusGAN

resent the global means of corresponding images. The feature maps are generally extracted by a modified VGG net and $i$ always ranges from 0 to 5, hence $x^0$ is actually the input $x$. Similarly, the structure similarity between $r$ and $syn$ can be calculated by (2):

$$s(r_j^i, syn_j^i) = \frac{2\sigma_{r_j syn_j}^i + C_2}{(\sigma_{r_j}^i)^2 + (\sigma_{syn_j}^i)^2 + C_2} \tag{2}$$

where $\sigma_{r_j}^i$ and $\sigma_{syn_j}^i$ are the global variances of $r_j^i$ and $syn_j^i$, respectively. While $\sigma_{r_j syn_j}^i$ represents the global covariance between the pair of $r_j{}^i$ and $syn_j{}^i$. $C_1$ and $C_2$ are constants that avoid dividing by zero.

By unifying $l(r, syn)$ and $s(r, syn)$, the texture and structure similarity is obtained by (3). Based on this, the cost function of our guidance module is shown in (4):

$$sim(r, syn; \theta_1, \theta_2) = \sum_i \sum_j (\theta_1^{ij} l(r_j{}^i, syn_j{}^i)$$

$$+ \theta_2^{ij} s(r_j{}^i, syn_j{}^i)) \tag{3}$$

$$s.t. \sum_i \sum_j (\theta_1^{ij} + \theta_2^{ij}) = 1$$

$$\mathcal{L}_{guid} = 1 - sim(r, syn; \theta_1, \theta_2) \tag{4}$$

where $\theta_1^{ij}$ and $\theta_2^{ij}$ are two positive learnable weights, and the goal of the guidance module is to maximize the similarity. Hence, $\mathcal{L}_{guid}$ is the DISTS metric. To better guide the synthesis in different generating stages, multi-scale outputs from different Generator layers rather than single output from the last layer are employed. Therefore, the multi-scale guidance loss, termed as $L_{ms\_guid}$, is calculated through (5).

$$\mathcal{L}_{ms\_guid} = \mathcal{L}_{guid1} + \mathcal{L}_{guid2} + \mathcal{L}_{guid3} + \mathcal{L}_{guid4} \tag{5}$$

where $\mathcal{L}_{guid1}$, $\mathcal{L}_{guid2}$, $\mathcal{L}_{guid3}$ and $\mathcal{L}_{guid4}$ denote the loss of the image in size $32 \times 32$, $64 \times 64$, $128 \times 128$, and $256 \times 256$.

**Vessel Assisting Module:** The aforementioned works fail to generate the whole fundus without either existing or synthesizing vessel trees. The reason may be the lack of vessel-related information or supervision. Therefore, to further assist our attention Generator in acquiring better vessel-related information, we propose a self-motivated strategy relying on existing vessel segmentation methods. As illustrated in Fig. 1, a generated fundus image is sent into a well-trained segmentation network for getting its corresponding vessel component map. The assisting network can be either a sophisticated semantic segmentation network or a network designed for medical image, whose weights are not updated.

We hope the vessel map segmented from a synthetic image to be similar to, rather than exactly the same as, the one segmented from a real fundus image. Hence, the Structural Similarity index (SSIM) [19] is adopted as the criterion to help the synthetic image contain vision-satisfied vessels. The criterion is shown as follows:

$$\mathcal{L}_{assist} = 1 - SSIM(r, syn) \tag{6}$$

$$SSIM(r, syn) = \frac{(2\mu_r\mu_{syn} + \alpha_1)(2\sigma_{r,syn} + \alpha_2)}{(\mu_r^2 + \mu_{syn}^2 + \alpha_1)(\sigma_r^2 + \sigma_{syn}^2 + \alpha_2)} \tag{7}$$

where $\mathcal{L}_{assist}$ stands for the loss function in vessel domain. $SSIM(r, syn)$ is the mean value of window-based SSIM between a real image $r$ and a synthetic one $syn$. $\alpha_1$ and $\alpha_2$ are constants that avoid dividing by zero.

**Fundus Super Resolution:** Since global attention acquired by multi-head self-attention and MLP inevitably increases computation consumption, we simply added a pre-trained super resolution module after our attention Generator to obtain fundus images in size of $256 \times 256$.

## 2.2   Adversarial Cost Functions

The objective function of our Discriminator is described in (8). $p_r$ and $p_{syn}$ are the distribution of real images and synthetic ones, respectively. $D^*$ is the optimal solution.

$$D^* = \underset{D}{argmax}[\mathbb{E}_{x \sim p_r}[D(x)] - \mathbb{E}_{x \sim p_{syn}}[D(x)]] \tag{8}$$

The $x \sim p_{syn}$ is actually $x \sim p(x|z, w_g)$ being obtained by $G(z, w_g)$. $z$ is a random noise and $w_g$ indicates the weights of the Generator.

Since our Generator consists of a basic attention Generator, a texture and structure guidance, and a vessel assistance, the final Generator loss function is described as (9):

$$\mathcal{L}_G = \eta_1 \mathcal{L}_{att\_g} + \eta_2 \mathcal{L}_1 + \eta_3 \mathcal{L}_{assist} + \eta_4 \mathcal{L}_{ms\_guid} \tag{9}$$

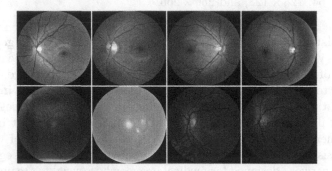

**Fig. 3.** Healthy samples from DDR, Messidor, and ODIR-5K datasets. First row: High quality fundus images, Second row: Low quality fundus images.

where $\mathcal{L}_{att\_g}$ is the basic Generator loss function in (10). For $x \sim p_r$, $x \sim p_{(x|z,w_g)}$ and $z \sim p(z)$, hence $D^*(x) = D^*(G(z, w_g))$.

$$\mathcal{L}_{att\_g} = -\mathbb{E}_{x \sim p_{syn}}[D^*(x)] \tag{10}$$

$\mathcal{L}_1$ is the Mean Absolute Error(MAE) between real images $r$ and synthetic ones $syn$ being illustrated in (11).

$$\mathcal{L}_1 = \frac{1}{N} \sum_{i=1}^{N} |r_i - syn_i| \tag{11}$$

## 3   Experiments

### 3.1   Experimental Settings

**Datasets:** Due to differences in varying fundus cameras, capture environments, and photographing operations, fundus images are diverse in appearance and qualities. As shown in Fig. 3, healthy fundus image qualities are vary in DDR [20], Messidor [21], and ODIR-5K[1] which may lead to training failure. Hence we manually selected 2000 normal fundus images from the three public datasets, where 998 images from DDR, 470 images from Messidor and 532 images from ODIR-5K,

---

[1] The dataset is available at https://odir2019.grand-challenge.org/dataset.

to compose a new mix dataset termed as MIX. Besides, we also collected 3600 high-quality real healthy fundus images from the ophthalmic hospital, termed as OUR. We will make the dataset OUR public once being permitted.

**Implementation Details:** As mentioned above, a trained segmentator is adopted for self-motivated information obtaining in our vessel assisting module. Since it's learning-free, any trained vessel segmentation network is available. We used the UNet [22]-based LadderNet[2] for vessel segmentation and pretrained SRGAN [23] for fundus super resolution.

All experiments are run in PyTorch. We adopt a fixed learning rate $2 \times 10^{-5}$ for Generator and $5 \times 10^{-5}$ for Discriminator with RMSprop optimizer. The batch size is set to 8 and the max epoch is 500. We empirically set $\eta_1 = 0.5$, $\eta_2 = 1$, $\eta_3 = 0.5$, and $\eta_4 = 0.5$ for the final loss function $\mathcal{L}_G$. We conduct our experiments on an NVIDIA RTX3090 and an NVIDIA GTX1080Ti.

**Metric:** Two common metrics for evaluating generative models are Inception Score (IS) [8] and Fréchet Inception Distance (FID) [24]. The former is a class-related metric that reflects diversity. Since we only focus on a single class, *i.e.*, healthy fundus, we only report FID, which calculates the distance between the synthetic image features and the real ones. The feature is the output of the FC layer in Inception Net-V3. FID score is computed through:

$$FID(r, syn) = ||\mu_r - \mu_{syn}||_2^2$$
$$+ Tr(\Sigma_r + \Sigma_{syn} - 2(\Sigma_r \Sigma_{syn})^{\frac{1}{2}}) \tag{12}$$

where $\mu_r$ and $\mu_{syn}$ refer to the feature-wise means of the real and generated images, $\Sigma r$ and $\Sigma syn$ are the covariance matrices of the real and generated image feature vectors, respectively. $Tr(A)$ is the trace of matrix $A$. This reflects the difference between the two distributions. Thus a lower value indicates a better GAN model.

**Preprocessing:** We involved three preprocessing methods,

- Background removing through a mask that filters out extra black area and makes the color fundus region in the center of an image.
- All images are resized to a fixed size before being fed into the network. In our experiments, $128 \times 128$ and $256 \times 256$ images are generated.
- All left eye fundus images are horizontally flipped, thus all inputs can be regarded as right eye fundus for simplification.

---

[2] The code is available at https://github.com/juntang-zhuang/LadderNet.

**Table 1.** FID of comparison methods on two datasets (128 × 128 images generated)

| Methods | MIX | OUR |
|---|---|---|
| DCGAN [25] | 120.35 | 85.58 |
| WGAN [10] | 78.63 | 51.91 |
| WGAN-GP [11] | 56.42 | 39.0 |
| TransGAN [12] | 109.08 | 108.38 |
| StyleGAN-V2 [26] | 41.90 | 41.95 |
| **FundusGAN** | **38.54** | **37.41** |

## 3.2   Comparisons

To evaluate the performance of our FundusGAN, we involve five representative GANs, which are DCGAN [25], WGAN, WGAN-GP [11], StyleGAN-V2 [26], and TransGAN. The performance generating images in size of 128 × 128 and 256 × 256 are illustrated in Table 1 and Table 2, respectively. The visualize of synthetic images with all comparison methods is shown in Fig. 4. Although DCGAN, WGAN, and WGAN-GP generate fundus images with macula and optic disc, they fail in synthesizing vessel features. The main reason is that these basic GANs are designed for low-resolution digit number generation. Thus they achieve bad performance when generating higher resolution color fundus images. TransGAN suffers from a gridding effect due to the patches in Transformer. While StyleGAN v2 and FundusGAN are well-designed to capture the real data distribution, hence fundus images generated by the two methods are anatomically consistent with real fundus and demonstrate both diversity and reasonable visual quality. In addition, all synthetic images on OUR have higher visual quality than those on MIX, indicating that the image quality of OUR dataset is better than MIX.

Overall, there are three findings. 1) Our method achieves the lowest FID scores in generating 128 × 128 fundus images on both datasets. 2) For some light GANs, such as WGAN and DCGAN, the FID scores on MIX are overall higher than those on OUR, which indicates that our dataset is more consistency in colors and illuminance, and this devotes to fundus generation. However, the Generator of TransGAN, StyleGAN-V2 and FundusGAN are well-designed to extract important features, thus high-quality data may devote less to the FID metric in more complicated networks.

**Table 2.** FID of comparison methods on two datasets (256 × 256 images generated)

| Methods | MIX | OUR |
|---|---|---|
| DCGAN [25] | 117.66 | 74.83 |
| WGAN [10] | 160.2 | 114.8 |
| WGAN-GP [11] | 161.86 | 66.83 |
| SAGAN [27] | 132.17 | 176.71 |
| TransGAN [12] | 166.99 | 199.43 |
| **FundusGAN** | **47.01** | **55.19** |

3) In order to obtain large size fundus images based on the existing proposed network, a pretrained SR is added to upsample the 128 × 128 fundus to 256 × 256 ones. It's obvious that the FID scores of 128 × 128 fundus are much lower. Especially, our method outperforms others a lot. Potential reason is that the comparison methods are designed for low-resolution image synthesis. To obtain 256 × 256, we modified them by stacking deconvolution modules, which is inferior to the well-designed FundusGAN.

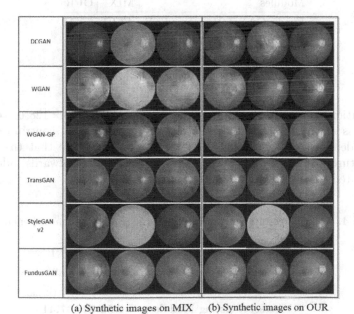

(a) Synthetic images on MIX    (b) Synthetic images on OUR

**Fig. 4.** Visualization of comparison results on MIX (a) and OUR (b). The six rows represent the synthetic images of DCGAN, WGAN, WGAN-GP, TransGAN, StyleGAN-V2, and our FundusGAN from top to bottom.

To find out whether SR module works, ablation of the SR module are conducted. We conduct two interpolation experiments Bilinear and Bicubic compared with super resolution module, as illustrate in Table 4, pretrained super resolution module achieved the best performance with the lowest FID score.

## 3.3   Ablation Results

To verify the effectiveness of SR, comparison of SR module and commonly used interpolations are presented in Table 3. The FID scores on both datasets demonstrate that SR brings a better upsampling performance than conventional interpolations. Then the reason why FID scores on $256 \times 256$ images are higher than those on $128 \times 128$ ones may be that our network (as well as WGAN and TransGAN) fails in synthesizing abundant and correct details for larger images while DCGAN does. Consequently, our future work may focus on how to take better use of convolutions for larger size of images, since DCGAN depends on convolutional modules.

**Table 3.** Ablation of SR module on two datasets ($256 \, times \, 256$ images generated)

| Modules | MIX | OUR |
|---|---|---|
| FundusGAN + Pretrained SR | **47.01** | **55.19** |
| FundusGAN + Bilinear | 72.80 | 83.08 |
| FundusGAN + Bicubic | 65.91 | 72.60 |

In addition, we conduct ablation experiments of size $128 \times 128$ to verify the effectiveness of the claimed three sub-modules that mainly contribute to our work. As demonstrated in Table 4, the FID scores indicate that the Texture and Structure Guidance does boost the performance. Afterwards, adding the self-motivated Vessel Assisting Module refines the results.

**Table 4.** Ablation results on two datasets ($128 \, times \, 128$ images generated)

| Modules | MIX | OUR |
|---|---|---|
| Basic Attention Generator | 98.33 | 69.9 |
| +Texture and Structure Guidance | 40.12 | 40.79 |
| +Vessel Assisting Module | **38.54** | **37.41** |

# 4   Conclusions

We propose a one-stage GAN, termed as FundusGAN, for retinal fundus image synthesis. Our FundusGAN is different from existing works in: 1) We combine global attention with the conventional features by adding, thus the global information can be regarded as a residual path to convolutional layers. 2) We model vessel generating as a texture and structure similarity estimation problem, and successfully generate vessels in spatial domain by a proper metric. 3) We design a self-motivated assisting module for vessel refinement in vessel domain. Experimental results show that the FundusGAN successfully obtains fundus images with neither references nor extra training-required generators. Furthermore, the synthetic fundus images are of reasonable visual quality yet need improving. Our future works may focus on involving multi-scale information for vessel inner-consistency optimization and on generating fundus with diseases to deal with scarce annotation problem.

# References

1. Abràmoff, M.D., Garvin, M.K., Sonka, M.: Retinal imaging and image analysis. IEEE Rev. Biomed. Eng. **3**, 169–208 (2010)
2. Fiorini, S., et al.: Automatic generation of synthetic retinal fundus images: vascular network. In: 20th Conference on Medical Image Understanding and Analysis (MIUA), pp. 54–60. Springer, Leicestershire (2016). https://doi.org/10.1016/j.procs.2016.07.010
3. Goodfellow, I., et al.: Generative adversarial nets. In: NIPS, pp. 2678–2680. MIT, Montreal (2014)
4. Costa, P., Galdran, A., Meyer, M.I., Abramoff, M.D., Niemeijer, M., Mendonça, A., Campilho, A.: Towards adversarial retinal image synthesis. arXiv preprint arXiv:1701.08974 (2017)
5. Costa, P., Galdran, A., Meyer, M.I., Niemeijer, M., Abràmoff, M., Mendonça, A.M., Campilho, A.: End-to-end adversarial retinal image synthesis. IEEE Trans. Med. Imaging **37**(3), 781–791 (2018)
6. Kurach, K., Lučić, M., Zhai, X., Michalski, M., Gelly, S.: A large-scale study on regularization and normalization in GANs. In: ICML (2019)
7. Roth, K., Lucchi, A., Nowozin, S., Hofmann, T.: Stabilizing training of generative adversarial networks through regularization. In: NIPS, pp. 2015–2025. MIT, California (2017)
8. Salimans, T., Goodfellow, I., Zaremba, W., Cheung, V., Radford, A., Chen, X.: Improved techniques for training GANs. In: NIPS, pp. 2234–2242. MIT, Barcelona (2016)
9. Denton, E., Chintala, S., Szlam, A., Fergus, R.: Deep generative image models using a Laplacian pyramid of adversarial networks. In: NIPS, pp. 1486–1494. MIT, Barcelona (2016)
10. Arjovsky, M., Chintala, S., Bottou, L.: Wasserstein generative adversarial networks. In: ICML (2017)
11. Gulrajani, I., Ahmed, F., Arjovsky, M., Dumoulin, V., Courville, A.: Improved training of Wasserstein GANs. In: NIPS, pp. 5769–5779. MIT, California (2017)

12. Jiang, Y., Chang, S., Wang, Z.: TransGAN: two pure transformers can make one strong GAN, and that can scale up. In: NIPS, pp. 14745–14758. Curran Associates Inc, New Orleans (2021)

13. Kamran, S.A., Hossain, K.F., Tavakkoli, A., Zuckerbrod, S.L., Baker, S.A.: VTGAN: semi-supervised retinal image synthesis and disease prediction using vision Transformers. In: ICCV (2021)

14. Yu, Z., Xiang, Q., Meng, J., Kou, C., Ren, Q., Lu, Y.: Retinal image synthesis from multiple-landmarks input with generative adversarial networks. Biomed. Eng. Online **10**(1), 1–15 (2019)

15. Liu, Y.-C., et al.: Synthesizing new retinal symptom images by multiple generative models. In: Carneiro, G., You, S. (eds.) ACCV 2018. LNCS, vol. 11367, pp. 235–250. Springer, Cham (2019). https://doi.org/10.1007/978-3-030-21074-8_19

16. He, Z., Huiqi, L., Sebastian, M., Li, C.: Synthesizing retinal and neuronal images with generative adversarial nets. Med. Image Anal. **49**, 14–26 (2018)

17. Sengupta, S., Athwale, A., Gulati, T., Zelek, J., Lakshminarayanan, V.: FunSyn-Net: enhanced residual variational auto-encoder and image-to-image translation network for fundus image synthesis. In: Medical Imaging 2020: Image Processing, vol. 11313, pp. 15–10 (2020)

18. Ding, K., Ma, K., Wang, S., Simoncelli, E.P.: Image quality assessment: unifying structure and texture similarity. IEEE Trans. Pattern Anal. Mach. Intell. **445**(5), 2567–2581 (2022)

19. Wang, Z., Bovik, A.C., Sheikh, H.R., Simoncelli, E.P.: Image quality assessment: from error visibility to structural similarity. IEEE Trans. Image Process. **13**(4), 600–612 (2004)

20. Li, T., Gao, Y., Wang, K., Guo, S., Liu, H., Kang, H.: Diagnostic assessment of deep learning algorithms for diabetic retinopathy screening. Inf. Sci. **501**, 511–522 (2019)

21. Decencière, E., et al.: Feedback on a publicly distributed database: the Messidor database. Image Anal. Stereol. **33**, 231–234 (2014)

22. Li, K., Qi, X., Luo, Y., Yao, Z., Zhou, X., Sun, M.: Accurate retinal vessel segmentation in color fundus images via fully attention-based networks. IEEE J. Biomed. Health Inform. **25**, 2071–2081 (2021)

23. Christian L., et al.: Photo-realistic single image super-resolution using a generative adversarial network. In: CVPR, pp. 105–114 (2017)

24. Heusel, M., Ramsauer, H., Unterthiner, T., Nessler, B., Hochreiter, S.: GANs trained by a two time-Scale update rule converge to a local Nash equilibrium. In: NIPS, pp. 6629–6640. Curran Associates Inc., California (2017)

25. Radford, A., Metz, L., Chintala, S.: Unsupervised representation learning with deep convolutional generative adversarial networks. arXiv preprint arXiv:1511.06434 (2015)

26. Karras, T., Laine, S., Aittala, M., Hellsten, J., Lehtinen, J., Aila, T.: Analyzing, improving the image quality of StyleGAN. In: CVPR, pp. 8110–8119 (2020)

27. Zhang, H., Goodfellow, I., Metaxas, D., Odena, A.: Self-attention generative adversarial networks. In: ICML (2019)

# DIT-NET: Joint Deformable Network and Intra-class Transfer GAN for Cross-domain 3D Neonatal Brain MRI Segmentation

Bo Li[1]([✉]), Xinge You[1,3], Qinmu Peng[1,3], Jing Wang[2], and Chuanwu Yang[1]

[1] School of Electronic Information and Communication,
Huazhong University of Science and Technology, Wuhan 430074, China
`lb_whu@hust.edu.cn`
[2] Department of Radiology, Union Hospital, Tongji Medical College,
Huazhong University of Science and Technology, Wuhan, China
[3] Shenzhen Research Institute, Huazhong University of Science and Technology,
Shenzhen 518000, China

**Abstract.** In neonatal brain Magnetic Resonance Image (MRI) segmentation, the model we trained on dataset from medical institutions fails to adapt to the clinical data. Because the clinical data (target domain) is largely different from the training dataset (source domain) in terms of scale, shape and intensity distribution. Current GAN-based unsupervised domain adaptation (UDA) models mainly focus on transferring the global intensity distribution, but cannot transform the shape and cover the intra-class similarity. And current deformable network can only transform the shape from the source domain to the target domain, while the intensity cannot be transferred. Thus, the whole cross-domain segmentation can not be trained end-to-end and require complex deformable registration preprocessing. Meanwhile, the deformable preprocessing and UDA method are adversely affected by cross-domain differences in intensity distribution and shape respectively. In this case, we propose a joint framework with Deformable network and Intra-class Transfer GAN (DIT-NET), both of which are trained to perform intra-class intensity and shape transformation for 3D cross-domain segmentation. The Intra-class Transfer GAN is designed not only to intra-classly transfer the intensity for reducing the cross-domain intensity difference, but also to make the deformable network better align the multi-class regions. Our experiments show that the proposed DIT-NET can make the segmentation network better adapt to the target domain end-to-end and it also achieves state-of-the-art results in the comparison with the current UDA models for the 3D neonatal brain MRI segmentation.

**Keywords:** Neonatal brain MRI · Unsupervised Domain Adaptation · 3D segmentation · Deformable network

© The Author(s), under exclusive license to Springer Nature Switzerland AG 2022
S. Yu et al. (Eds.): PRCV 2022, LNCS 13535, pp. 41–53, 2022.
https://doi.org/10.1007/978-3-031-18910-4_4

# 1  Introduction

The analysis of the neonatal brain morphological structure is crucial for assessing the brain development [1]. Most of the brain disorders and diseases are reflected by the abnormalities of the morphological structure [2]. An accurate and automatic segmentation of brain MRI images can help physicians better assess the neonatal brain and make therapeutic interventions. Among the current segmentation methods, the 3D convolutional neural network(CNN) achieves the best results [3,4].

However, 3D CNNs trained on specific database from medical institutions perform poorly in clinical practice. It is caused by the large cross-domain gap. This gap results mainly from the following three reasons: (1) The rapid development of the brain during the perinatal period leads to large shape difference between domains [1]. (2) Different scanners, image acquisition protocols, and scanned subjects between the two domains result in the difference of intensity distribution [5]. (3) In the task of multi-class segmentation, the considerable cross-domain misalignments make the 3D segmentation worse. In addition, labeling all the tissues in the clinic practice is time-consuming. Therefore, we need to make cross-domain neonatal brain MRI segmentation with the Unsupervised Domain Adaptation issue.

Recently, many UDA methods have been used to make the cross-domain segmentation in some fields, such as Self-training, Adversarial Learning, and Generative-based Approach. Due to the large gap between the domains, most of the methods fail to apply to our case. For example, Self-training approach would produce the considerable misclassified pseudo-label which have negative effects on segmentation, even if with a suitable confidence threshold [6]. Adversarial-learning approach is weak in the case of the insufficient dataset because of its strategy of common feature refinement [11]. While, the dataset provided for training is always insufficient in brain MRI segmentation. Generative-based approach is more suitable to our case and it, in fact, has been widely used in current UDA tasks for medical image segmentation [5,7].

CycleGAN is the most widespread one in the generative-based methods. Huo et al. [8] implement CycleGAN to synthesize CT images from labeled MRI for spleen segmentation, in which an additional segmentation network is trained on the synthesized images for a better generalization. Chen et al. [9] combine the CycleGAN and segmentation network into a common encoder, in which it can receive the information from another modal(MRI) for cardiac CT segmentation. But, due to the large gap between domains, the cycle consistency of CycleGAN cannot completely preserve the semantic information of source images, which would lead to shape distortion [11]. Many works apply semantic constraint of segmentation network to force the generator of GAN to maintain the semantic information. For example, CyCADA [12] introduces FCN8s as a segmenter for providing semantic constraint for CycleGANs in cityscapes semantic segmentation. Zhang et al. [11] apply Unet [10] with a semantic consistency loss to CycleGAN for preserving semantic information of source domain.

However, the current generative-based approaches mentioned above cannot work well in the UDA task of neonatal brain segmentation. Firstly, the large shape differences between domains cannot be directly bridged by the UDA approaches. Therefore, they can not work end-to-end in cross-domain segmentation and the source-domain images have to be registered before UDA, which is time-consuming [18]. In fact, many current UDA works regard the deformable registration as a preprocessing to overcome the shape difference between domains [13,18]. Secondly, the preprocessing deformable network is always influenced by different intensity distribution between domains. Because the registration loss tends to align the voxels with similar intensity distribution to the same place regardless of their classes. Thirdly, current UDA models tend to achieve the global intensity similarity to the target with a strong semantic constraint which makes it difficult for them to align intra-class features in the transferring. Intra-class features are extracted from the same semantic content of images in the different domains. Fourthly, the GPU memory consumption of current GAN-based models is too high, especially those 3D ones. Thus, they have to be trained independently apart from segmentation network which set barriers to clinical practice.

To address these issues, we propose a 3D joint Deformable network and Intra-class Transfer GAN (DIT-NET) for the end-to-end cross-domain brain MRI segmentation. Deformable network (D-NET) is to make the synthesized images closer to the target domain in shape, while the designed intra-class transfer GAN (IT-GAN) is to achieve the intra-class intensity distribution of the target domain with a semantic supervision. They can promote each other. More similar intra-class intensity can make D-NET better align to target-domain image, and better alignment can enable the IT-GAN to obtain the synthesized images more similar to the target domain. As shown in the experimental result, the proposed method achieves the state-of-the-art results in the compared UDA models for the 3D segmentation task.

Our main contributions can be summarized as follows: (a) We designed a novel DIT-NET for end-to-end cross-domain neonatal brain MRI segmentation, which can transfer both the intensity and the shape simultaneously to make the segmentation model more adaptive in the target domain. (b) We introduce deformative network for the first time into UDA model in brain MRI segmentation. (c) The proposed IT-GAN can achieve the intra-class similarity to the target domain and reduce the class misalignments for D-NET. (d) The DIT-NET only contains 1/4 parameters of the segmentation model, thus the whole training of cross-domain segmentation(UDA and Segmentation) only needs to be performed once end-to-end which is beneficial to clinical practice.

The rest of this paper is organized as follows. Firstly, we introduce the related work in Sect. 2 and our proposed work is presented in Sect. 3. Secondly, experiment details and segmentation result are presented in Sects. 4. Thirdly, we summarize this paper in Sect. 5.

## 2   Related Work

Traditional registration methods align voxels between domains with enforced constraints by solving a pairwise optimization problem. This pairwise registration strategy requires intensive calculations, therefore its algorithms on CPU require hours to register only one pair of 3D images [14]. But in most of the cases, deep learning networks for segmentation often require a large amount of training data, especially unlabeled target-domain data.

Recent registration methods apply the deep network on GPU to solve this issue. VoxelMorph [14] firstly propose a learning architecture, which uses a deep network to obtain the deformation field by training the network. Compared to the pair-wised registration, VoxelMorph is much time-saving. Marek Wodzinski et al. [15] suggest a modified U-NET to make nonrigid image registration for real-time breast tumor bed localization, which is helpful to improve real-time radiation therapy after the tumor resection. Beljaards et al. [16] proposed a so-called cross-stitch unit to exchange the information between a joint segmentation and registration network for better performance of both in Adaptive Radiotherapy. Mahapatra et al. [17] propose a GAN-based(generative adversarial networks) framework to ensure that the features extracted by the encoders are invariant to the input image type. Thus, their model trained on one dataset can give better registration performance for other datasets. Qin et al. [23] suggest a unsupervised multi-modal deformable image registration method (UMDIR) to align multi-modal images without deformable field by decomposing images into a shape representation and a appearance code. Compared to conventional registration approaches, this image-to-image translation based on MUNIT [20] make significant improvements in terms of both accuracy and speed. The current registration networks focus on designing different model to transform moving image for a shape similarity to the fixed image and maintain its appearance.

However, we wish to transfer both the shape and appearance for making the segmentation network better adapt to the target domain in the case of large cross-domain difference. Meanwhile, the current UDA models is too costly to make an end-to-end cross-domain segmentation for the 3D neonatal brain MRI. Finally, due to the semantic constraints from the source domain, current UDA models for segmentation tend to transfer incorrect feature for the target domain.

## 3   Method

The proposed DIT-NET is composed of deformable network (D-NET), intra-class transfer GAN (IT-GAN) and segmentation network (S-NET). The data preprocessing for all experiments is the same N4 correction [24] and Sigmoid normalization. Experiments are conducted on the whole brain MR images without the Brain extraction (BET) [19].

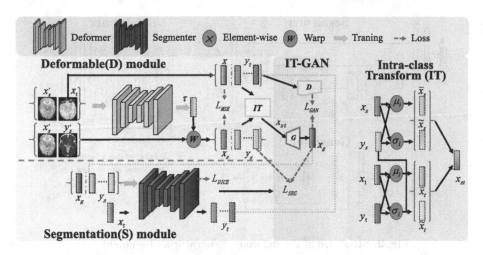

**Fig. 1.** The overview of the proposed DIT-NET.

## 3.1 Framework of Proposed DIT-NET

As shown in Fig. 1, D-NET, IT-GAN and S-NET are all 3D U-NET structure. They are trained as follows: (i) The D-NET without Intra-class Transform Layer (ITL) is pre-trained by the source images $x'_s$ and target images $x_t$. (ii) The trained D-NET transforms $x'_s$ and $y'_s$ to $x_s$ and $y_s$. Then S-NET can be trained by the deformed $x_s$ and their corresponding label $y_s$. (iii) The D-NET and IT-GAN are initialized and retrained by $x'_s$ and $x_t$. Here, the S-NET trained in step (ii) can provide the pseudo-labels $y_t$ of $x_t$ for ITL calculation in IT-GAN. (iv) The trained D-NET and IT-GAN transforms the $x'_s$ and $y'_s$ into the transformed image $x_{st}$ and $y_{st}$. Finally, S-NET can be retrained by the UDA result $x_{st}$ and $y_{st}$.

## 3.2 Deformable Network

The proposed Deformable Network(D-NET) and IT-GAN aim to transform $x'_s$ of size $L \times W \times H$ into synthesized image $x_{st}$ with the shape and intensity distribution similar to $x_t$, and keep the semantic content of the source-domain label $y_s$. Among them, D-NET is mainly used for shape transfer. In step (i), instead of training IT-GAN, we train the D-NET separately. Because S-NET has not been pre-trained at this time to provide pseudo-label $y_t$ for IT-GAN. In the training of D-NET, the volumetric input is a pair of $x'_s$ and $x_t$ and the output is the deformation field $\tau$ which is used to transform $x'_s$ and $y'_s$ into $x_s$ and $y_s$. Its MSE loss can be expressed as follows:

$$\mathcal{L}_{MSE} = \frac{\sum_{n=1}^{N}(x_t(n) - \tau(x'_s(n)))^2}{N} \tag{1}$$

where $N = L \times W \times H$ is the voxel number of image, $\tau(x'_s(n)) = x_s$ is the transformed image.

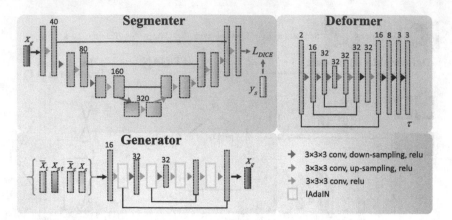

**Fig. 2.** Structure of the deformer, generator and segmenter.

In step (i), D-NET can provide a coarse registration result for the training of S-NET in step (ii). Due to the large difference of intra-class intensity between the domains, the trained D-NET would lead to considerable misalignments. Its loss function tends to align the voxels with similar intensity regardless of their classes. However, compared with directly training on $x'_s$, the S-NET trained on $x_s$ can provide better pseudo-labels $y_t$ for $x_t$ which can be used for ITL calculation in step (iii). Although the provided $y_t$ are too inaccurate to be a criterion for segmentation, it is sufficient to calculate the intra-class mean and variance in IT-GAN. In D-NET we design an Intra-class Transform Layer(ITL) for the intra-class intensity transfer of IT-GAN in step (iii), which will be introduced in the next subsection.

### 3.3 Intra-class Transfer GAN

Intra-class Transfer GAN (IT-GAN) is used for the transfer of the intensity distribution for the target domain. In step (iii), we introduce the ITL and IT-GAN to D-NET and initialize their parameter for retraining. To obtain the intra-class intensity similarity to the target domain, as shown in Fig. 1, ITL calculation is proposed as follow:

$$ITL(x_s, y_s, x_t, y_t) = \widetilde{x}_t \left( \frac{x_s - \overline{x}_s}{\widetilde{x}_s} \right) + \overline{x}_t \tag{2}$$

where $x_s$ is the registered source-domain image by D-NET, $\overline{x}_s$ and $\widetilde{x}_s$ are respectively the intra-class mean and variance images of $x_s$, $\overline{x}_t$ and $\widetilde{x}_t$ are respectively the intra-class mean and variance images of $x_t$. They have the same size $L \times W \times H$. As shown on the right of Fig. 1, they can be obtained as follows:

$$\overline{x}_s = \sum_{i=1}^{C} m_s^i \cdot y_s^i, \quad \widetilde{x}_s = \sum_{i=1}^{C} v_s^i \cdot y_s^i, \quad \overline{x}_t = \sum_{i=1}^{C} m_t^i \cdot y_s^i, \quad \widetilde{x}_t = \sum_{i=1}^{C} v_t^i \cdot y_s^i \tag{3}$$

where $y_s^i$ is the i-th class one-hot label image of $y_s$ with size $L \times W \times H$. $m_s^i$ is the i-th class mean value of $x_s$ and can be calculate as $m_s^i = \frac{\sum_{n=1}^{N} x_s(n) \cdot y_s^i}{\sum_{n=1}^{N} y_s^i}$. $v_s^i$ is the i-th class variance value of $x_s$ and can be calculate as $v_s^i = \sqrt{\frac{\sum_{n=1}^{N} (x_s(n) - \overline{x}_s(n))^2 \cdot y_s^i(n)}{\sum_{n=1}^{N} y_s^i(n)}}$.

Similarly, for $x_t$ and $y_t$, intra-class mean value can be calculated as $m_t^i = \frac{\sum_{n=1}^{N} x_t(n) \cdot y_t^i}{\sum_{n=1}^{N} y_t^i}$ and intra-class variance value can be calculated as $v_t^i = \sqrt{\frac{\sum_{n=1}^{N} (x_t(n) - \overline{x}_t(n))^2 \cdot y_t^i(n)}{\sum_{n=1}^{N} y_t^i(n)}}$. And thus, for training step(iii) the MSE loss is as follow:

$$\mathcal{L}_{MSE} = \frac{\sum_{n=1}^{N} (x_t(n) - ITL(\tau(x_s'(n))))^2}{N} \tag{4}$$

where $ITL()$ is the ITL calculation.

In addition, to obtain better transfer results, we introduce the Local Adaptive Instance Normalization (LAdaIN) algorithm from the work [18]. As shown in Fig. 2, A generator with a completely different structure from this work [18] is designed, in which LAdaIN is implemented in each layer of the generator. Its calculation is as follows:

$$\text{LAdaIN}(F_l^h) = \gamma_t^h \left( \frac{F_l^h(x_s) - F_l^h(\overline{x}_s)}{\sigma_s^i} \right) + F_l^h(\overline{x}_{st}) \tag{5}$$

where $F_l^h$ denotes the LAdaIN feature map of the h-th channel at the l-th layer. $\overline{x}_s$, $\sigma_s$, $\overline{x}_{st}$ and $\gamma_t$ are the intra-class mean and variance of each class $c$. For specific calculations, please refer to the work [18].

### 3.4 Segmentation Network

As mentioned above, we apply a 3D U-NET for segmentation. In step (iii), The S-NET is inactive and acts as a segmenter to provide pseudo-labels for D-NET. In stage (ii) and (iv), it is trained as a segmenter on the output of the D-NET. Dice loss is implemented in both steps as follow:

$$\mathcal{L}_{DICE} = \frac{1}{C} \cdot \sum_{i=1}^{C} (1 - \frac{2f_{seg}^i(x_{st}) \cdot y_s^i + \gamma}{f_{seg}^i(x_{st})^2 + (y_s^i)^2 + \gamma}) \tag{6}$$

where $C$ denote the class number, $f_{seg}^i$ is the prediction of the segmenter for the i-th class, $y_s^i$ is the registered one-hot label.

The network of the Deformer of D-NET, Segmenter (S-NET) and Generator of IT-GAN is shown in Fig. 2. To guarantee a better segmentation result, we design a deeper segmenter and reduce the number of filters of the Deformer and Generator. Their encoders consist of 3D convolutions with a kernel size of 3 and stride of 2 and decoder is composed of 3D convolutions, the upsampling and the skip connections. After each 3D convolutions, a ReLU layer is followed. The output of Deformer, Segmenter and Generator are the deformable matrix $\tau$, prediction $y_t$ and fake image $x_{st}$ respectively.

## 4   Experiments

The datasets selected for the two different domains in our experiment are Neo-brainS12 [21] and dHCP [22], which exist large difference in the shape and intensity distribution between them. NeobrainS12 dataset selects 40 weeks infants for MRI scan on Philips SENSE head 3T scanner. There are 7 T2-weighted axial MR images in NeobrainS12, in which resolution = $0.35 \times 0.35 \times 2$ mm$^3$, TR/TE = 6293/120 ms, image size = $512 \times 512 \times 50$. dHCP dataset selects 37–44 weeks infants for MRI scan on Philips Achieva 3T scanner. 40 T2-weighted MR images are provided, resolution = $0.8 \times 0.8 \times 0.8$ mm$^3$, TR/TE = 12000/156 ms, image size = $290 \times 290 \times 155$. For a easily labeling, we down-sample the dHCP images to $290 \times 290 \times 50$. Then a expert physician make manual segmentations slice by slice for a week on a ROI Editor software. Finally, the images of the both datasets are cropped to the same size $272 \times 208 \times 48$. NeobrinS12 is selected as the source domain and the dHCP as the target domain in our experiment.

The experimental detail is as follow. In step (i) and (iii), the learning rate for training register is initially used as $1 \times 10^{-5}$ and is then decreased to $1 \times 10^{-6}$ in 200 epochs. In step (ii) and (iv), the learning rate for training segmentation starts with $1 \times 10^{-3}$ and decayed to $1 \times 10^{-5}$ in 300 epochs. Both networks are using TensorFlow and Adam optimization and Momentum is 0.5 with a batch size of 1. We implement a standard workstation with an Intel Xeon (E5-2682) CPU and a NVIDIA TITAN X GPU 12G. For the proposed method, each step of training takes about 2 to 4 h, and the entire training process can be completed in half a day.

### 4.1   Adaptive Transfer Result

The synthesized MR images by all compared methods and the corresponding input images of the two domains are shown in Fig. 3. For a fair comparison of transferring, all the compared UDA methods use Voxelmorph as a preprocessing of registration. While the proposed method is to make end-to-end synthesis and segmentation. 'Voxelmorph Label' and 'Proposed Label' in Fig. 3 refer to the transformed label image by Voxelmorph and the proposed method respectively. For better display, we enlarge a part of the synthesized images.

As shown in Fig. 3, there are considerable shape and intensity difference between NeobrainS12 and dHCP. Thus GAN-based UDA model without a preprocessing of registration can not work in this case. As shown in the enlarged images of Fig. 3, the images synthesized by the proposed method are more similar to the target domain than the compared methods. In addition, the synthesized images by proposed DIT-NET shows the best appearance similarity to 'dHCP (target)' and maintains a good semantic consistency with 'Proposed Label'. Although the images synthesized by CYCADA well preserves the semantic content of the source domain, the appearance transfer is relatively poor. Unfortunately, due to the missing of supervision 'CycleGAN' and 'MUNIT' cannot maintain the semantic consistency with 'Voxelmorph Label'. Many shape distortions can be found in their synthesized images.

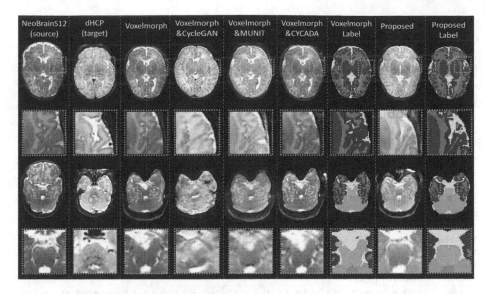

**Fig. 3.** Visual results of the synthesized T2 MR images by the compared methods. The images in the 1st and 3rd rows are from different subjects and the images in the same row are from the slice at the same position.

As shown in Table 1, we introduce Mean Squared Error (MSE) and Structural Similarity (SSIM) to quantitatively evaluate the effect of transferring to the target domain. We calculate the MSE distance and SSIM between all the synthesized images and their corresponding target-domain images. The average MSE value of each voxel and the average SSIM value of each sample are listed in Table 1. Table 1 shows that the images synthesized by the proposed method has the shortest MSE distance and the best structural similarity to the target domain. Finally, image SNR(Signal Noise Ratio) is used to measure the quality of the synthesized images. Since the SNR of the entire source-domain image is low, the SNR value of images registered by 'Voxelmorph' is much lower than other compared methods.

**Table 1.** The adaptive transfer result.

| Indicator | Voxelmorph | CycleGAN | CYCADA | MUNIT | Proposed |
|---|---|---|---|---|---|
| MSE (target) | 0.0154 ± 0.0005 | 0.0152 ± 0.0004 | 0.0245 ± 0.0006 | 0.0144 ± 0.0003 | **0.0133 ± 0.0004** |
| SSIM (target) | 0.6039 ± 0.0088 | 0.5812 ± 0.0125 | 0.5534 ± 0.0113 | 0.5877 ± 0.0088 | **0.6163 ± 0.0079** |
| SNR | 0.6812 ± 0.0032 | **0.7315 ± 0.0045** | 0.7063 ± 0.0078 | 0.7176 ± 0.0057 | 0.7218 ± 0.0038 |

### 4.2 Segmentation Result

We compare our proposed 3D model with the state-of-art UDA methods: MUNIT [20] and CYCADA [12]. Both of them are trained on 2D slices of the registered

NeoBrainS12 (source) and dHCP (target). The 2D slices synthesized by them are composed of 3D images and then are trained on a same 3D Unet as the proposed method for segmentation test. Human brain is segmented into seven different classes: cortical gray matter (CGM), basal ganglia and thalami (BGT), white matter (WM), brain stem (BS), cerebellum (CB), ventricles (VENT), and cerebrospinal fluid (CSF).

**Table 2.** Segmentation result.

| | CGM | WM | BGT | BS | CB | VENT | CSF | AVG |
|---|---|---|---|---|---|---|---|---|
| Method | Dice score (%) | | | | | | | |
| Baseline | 76.5 ± 1.8 | 54.5 ± 4.1 | 82.9 ± 2.2 | 18.3 ± 3.1 | 65.9 ± 2.5 | 53.6 ± 1.7 | 69.5 ± 1.5 | 60.2 ± 1.8 |
| Scaling | 78.9 ± 1.2 | 60.4 ± 5.2 | 85.6 ± 1.8 | 20.3 ± 2.4 | 72.9 ± 2.2 | 52.5 ± 3.1 | 72.7 ± 1.4 | 63.4 ± 2.2 |
| VM | 87.7 ± 1.4 | 74.1 ± 2.8 | 90.5 ± 1.5 | 74.2 ± 1.9 | 85.6 ± 1.5 | 65.3 ± 2.5 | 82.5 ± 1.6 | 79.7 ± 1.1 |
| VM&Munit | 84.2 ± 1.5 | 61.6 ± 3.8 | 86.2 ± 1.4 | 75.6 ± 1.4 | 75.4 ± 1.6 | 60.1 ± 2.8 | 78.3 ± 1.3 | 74.5 ± 0.7 |
| VM&Cycada | 88.2 ± 1.2 | 73.2 ± 2.5 | 90.5 ± 1.2 | 74.9 ± 2.6 | 86.8 ± 1.4 | 63.3 ± 1.8 | 83.7 ± 1.3 | 80.1 ± 0.9 |
| Proposed | **89.4 ± 1.1** | **81.1 ± 1.7** | **92.1 ± 0.9** | **82.2 ± 1.8** | **89.6 ± 1.2** | **71.1 ± 2.1** | **86.5 ± 1.5** | **84.6 ± 0.8** |
| Method | Sensitivity (%) | | | | | | | |
| Baseline | 73.8 ± 2.1 | 48.7 ± 5.8 | 90.3 ± 1.9 | 15.6 ± 2.7 | 58.1 ± 2.4 | 56.6 ± 2.2 | 85.3 ± 1.4 | 61.2 ± 1.9 |
| Scaling | 78.5 ± 1.5 | 47.9 ± 4.7 | 90.6 ± 1.6 | 17.5 ± 2.8 | 68.8 ± 2.7 | 54.3 ± 3.5 | 78.1 ± 1.2 | 62.2 ± 1.8 |
| VM | 89.8 ± 1.2 | 67.7 ± 3.2 | 90.4 ± 1.8 | 64.2 ± 2.1 | 78.5 ± 1.6 | 73.4 ± 2.4 | 86.2 ± 1.8 | 78.6 ± 1.7 |
| VM&Munit | 85.3 ± 1.6 | 53.9 ± 3.5 | 88.5 ± 1.6 | 81.9 ± 1.5 | 73.4 ± 1.9 | 65.1 ± 2.1 | 84.3 ± 1.3 | 76.1 ± 1.1 |
| VM&Cycada | **90.4 ± 0.9** | 63.5 ± 3.2 | 91.1 ± 1.5 | 71.7 ± 2.3 | 86.6 ± 1.6 | 75.6 ± 1.6 | 85.3 ± 1.5 | 80.6 ± 1.2 |
| Proposed | 89.2 ± 1.3 | **75.4 ± 2.0** | **93.5 ± 0.5** | **82.0 ± 1.6** | **86.7 ± 1.4** | **81.9 ± 2.3** | **88.7 ± 1.3** | **85.3 ± 0.9** |

The segmentation results are shown in Table 2, in which the 'Baseline' directly use original source-domain images and 'Scaling' is a common scaling (scaling factor = 0.9) on them. We display the average Dice Score and Sensitivity over three experiments. It can be seen that without registration the 3D segmentation network trained on the 'Baseline' images completely fails in the target domain. Meanwhile, MUNIT reduces the Dice score of the segmentation network, which is due to the inconsistency between the synthesized images and its labels. And CYCADA has limited improvements to the segmentation network. This demonstrate that although the semantic constraints in CYCADA can maintain semantic consistency, it also limits the transfer effect to the target domain. The proposed DIT-NET increases the average dice score by 5%, which shows that it greatly improves the generalization of the segmentation network in the target domain. As shown in Fig. 4, the proposed method significantly outperforms the compared ones 'BS', 'CB' and 'VENT' regions. The synthesized images are shown in Fig. 3.

In fact, the shape difference between domains has greater impact on 3D segmentation network than 2D ones. Compared to the same-domain segmentation, cross-domain task exists considerable misclassifications between WM and CB, VENT, BS regions which have large gap in shape. These misclassifications are more serious in the 3D model. It is why the accuracy of WM is lower than that of CGM in our experiment. Meanwhile, since the slice number of one sample is 48, the training samples of the 3D network are 48 times less than those of the

2D network. Thus, the shape diversity of 3D samples is largely limited. Compared to the 2D UDA work [18], although the 3D DIT-NET achieves better segmentation results in CGM and CSF regions which have small shape difference between domains, the segmentation results of other regions are even worse than that of the 2D network. We hope that the additional training samples for 3D cross-domain segmentation in the future can alleviate this issue.

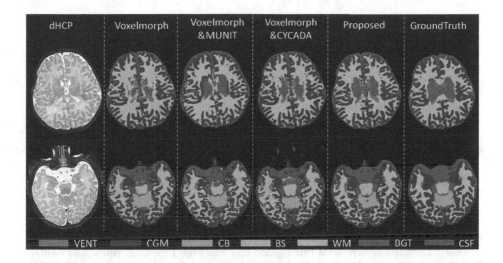

**Fig. 4.** The display of segmentation results on two different slices from different subjects.

## 5 Discussion and Conclusion

In this work, a joint Deformable network and Intra-class Transfer GAN(DIT-NET) is proposed to make the segmentation model (S-NET) be adaptive to the target domain. They can be trained together and realize an end-to-end system for cross-domain segmentation of 3D brain MR images. The proposed IT-GAN and D-NET can effectively transform both the shape and intra-class appearance across domains to make a better UDA for S-NET in the target domain. Experiments show that the MR images synthesized by the proposed DIT-NET are more similar to the target-domain images than existing UDA methods in shape and intra-class intensity distribution and thus our method achieves the state-of-the-art segmentation result, which outperforms all compared UDA models.

**Acknowledgments.** This work was supported in part by the National Natural Science Foundation of China under Grant 11671161, Grant 61571205, and Grant 61772220, in part by the Key Program for International S&T Cooperation Projects of China under Grant 2016YFE0121200, in part by the Special Projects for Technology Innovation of Hubei Province under Grant 2018ACA135, in part by the Key Science and

Technology Innovation Program of Hubei Province under Grant 2017AAA017, in part by the Natural Science Foundation of Hubei Province under Grant 2018CFB691, and in part by the Science, Technology and Innovation Commission of Shenzhen Municipality under Grant JCYJ20180305180637611, Grant JCYJ20180305180804836, and Grant JSGG20180507182030600.

# References

1. Makropoulos, A., Counsell, S.J., Rueckert, D.: A review on automatic fetal and neonatal brain MRI segmentation. NeuroImage **170**, 231–248 (2018)
2. Illavarason, P., Arokia, J.R., Mohan, P.K.: A study on the quality of life of CP children requiring early rehabilitation interventions. In: IEEE International Conference on Image Processing, pp. 91–97 (2018)
3. Xu, Y., Geraud, T., Bloch, I.: From neonatal to adult brain MR image segmentation in a few seconds using 3D-like fully convolutional network and transfer learning. In: International Conference on Science Technology Engineering and Mathematics, pp. 4417–4421 (2017)
4. Nie, D., Wang, L., Gao, Y.: Fully convolutional networks for multi-modality isointense infant brain image segmentation. In: International Symposium on Biomedical Imaging, pp. 1342–1345 (2016)
5. Tajbakhsh, N., Jeyaseelan, L., Li, Q., Chiang, J.N., et al.: Embracing imperfect datasets: a review of deep learning solutions for medical image segmentation. Med. Image Anal. **63**, 101693 (2020)
6. Zhu, X., Goldberg, A.B., et al.: Introduction to semi-supervised learning. In: Synthesis Lectures on Artificial Intelligence and Machine Learning, pp. 1–130 (2009)
7. Oliver, A., Odena, A., et al.: Realistic evaluation of deep semi-supervised learning algorithms. arXiv preprint arXiv:1804.09170 (2018)
8. Huo, Y., Xu, Z., et al.: SynSeg-Net: synthetic segmentation without target modality ground truth. IEEE Trans. Med. Imag. **38**, 1016–1025 (2009)
9. Chen, C., Dou, Q., et al.: Synergistic image and feature adaptation: Towards cross-modality domain adaptation for medical image segmentation. Association for the Advancement of Artificial Intelligence (2019)
10. Ronneberger, O., Fischer, P., Brox, T.: U-Net: convolutional networks for biomedical image segmentation. In: Navab, N., Hornegger, J., Wells, W.M., Frangi, A.F. (eds.) MICCAI 2015. LNCS, vol. 9351, pp. 234–241. Springer, Cham (2015). https://doi.org/10.1007/978-3-319-24574-4_28
11. Zhang, Z., Yang, L., et al.: Translating and segmenting multimodal medical volumes with cycle- and shape-consistency generative adversarial network. In: IEEE Conference on Computer Vision and Pattern Recognition, pp. 9242–9251 (2018)
12. Hoffman, J., Tzeng, E., et al.: CyCADA: cycle-consistent adversarial domain adaptation. In: International Conference on Machine Learning, pp. 1994–2003 (2018)
13. Ackaouy, A., Courty, N., et al.: Unsupervised domain adaptation with optimal transport in multi-site segmentation of multiple sclerosis lesions from MRI data. Front. Comput. Neurosci. **14**, 19 (2020)
14. Balakrishnan, G., Zhao, A., et al.: VoxelMorph: a learning framework for deformable medical image registration. IEEE Trans. Med. Imag. **38**, 1788–1800 (2019)
15. Wodzinski, M., Ciepiela, I., et al.: Semi-supervised deep learning-based image registration method with volume penalty for real-time breast tumor bed localization. Sensors(Basel, Switzerland) **21**(12), 4085 (2021)

16. Beljaards, L., Elmahdy, M., Verbeek, F., Staring, M.: A cross-stitch architecture for joint registration and segmentation in adaptive radiotherapy. In: Medical Imaging with Deep Learning (2020)

17. Mahapatra, D., Ge, Z.: Training data independent image registration using generative adversarial networks and domain adaptation. Pattern Recogn. **100**, 107109 (2020)

18. Li, B., You, X., Peng, Q., et al.: IAS-NET: joint intraclassly adaptive GAN and segmentation network for unsupervised cross-domain in neonatal brain MRI segmentation. Med. Phys. **48**(11), 6962–6975 (2021)

19. Stephen, M.S.: Fast robust automated brain extraction. Hum. Brain Mapp. **17**(3), 143–155 (2002)

20. Huang, X., Liu, M., et al.: Multimodal unsupervised image-to-image translation. In: IEEE European Conference on Computer Vision, pp. 172–189 (2018)

21. Isgum, I., Benders, M., et al.: Evaluation of automatic neonatal brain segmentation algorithms: the NeoBrainS12 challenge. Med. Image Anal. **20**, 135–151 (2015)

22. Makropoulos, A., Robinson, E.C., et al.: The developing human connectome project: a minimal processing pipeline for neonatal cortical surface reconstruction. NeuroImage **173**, 88–112 (2018)

23. Qin, C., Shi, B., Liao, R., Mansi, T., Rueckert, D., Kamen, A.: Unsupervised deformable registration for multi-modal images via disentangled representations. In: Chung, A.C.S., Gee, J.C., Yushkevich, P.A., Bao, S. (eds.) IPMI 2019. LNCS, vol. 11492, pp. 249–261. Springer, Cham (2019). https://doi.org/10.1007/978-3-030-20351-1_19

24. Tustison, N.J., et al.: N4ITK: improved N3 bias correction. IEEE Trans. Med. Imag. **29**(6), 1310–1320 (2010)

# Classification of sMRI Images for Alzheimer's Disease by Using Neural Networks

Ying Xing[1], Yu Guan[1(✉)], Bin Yang[2], and Jingze Liu[3]

[1] School of Artificial Intelligence, Beijing University of Posts
and Telecommunications, Beijing, China
guanyu@bupt.edu.cn
[2] China Unicom Research Institute, Beijing, China
[3] College of Life Science, Hebei Normal University, Shijiazhuang, China

**Abstract.** Alzheimer's disease is a kind of chronic disease, and its early detection have a positive impact on the outcome of subsequent treatment. However, relying entirely on manual diagnosis is time-consuming and requires high expertise. Therefore, computer-aided diagnosis becomes very urgent. Considering the wide application of deep learning in computer-aided diagnosis, a method based on deep learning to assist in the diagnosis of Alzheimer's disease was proposed in this paper. Specifically, this method started with brain extraction on the original sMRI images, and selected some sMRI images slices from the extracted images. Then it used ResNet and Attention network to extract features from the selected sMRI images slices. Finally, the extracted features were fed into the fully connected network for classification. We designed two ablation experiments and one comparative experiment. The results of the ablation experiments showed the effects of sMRI images slice numbers and Attention neural network on our method. Comparative experiment result showed that the Accuracy and Specificity of the proposed method reach 95.33%, 97.38% respectively, which were better than state-of-the-art methods.

**Keywords:** Alzheimer's disease · Brain extraction · sMRI images slice · Attention nerual network

## 1 Introduction

Alzheimer's disease (AD) is one of the top ten leading causes of death in the world [1]. Patients with AD can exhibit symptoms of atrophy in the hippocampus, parietal lobes and other areas. Structural magnetic resonance imaging (sMRI) can measure the morphology of the brain, capture neuronal loss and gray matter atrophy at the microscopic level, which plays an important role in AD diagnosis [2]. However, the analysis of sMRI images is now often performed manually, which requires specific knowledge and consuming [3]. Machine learning, due to

© The Author(s), under exclusive license to Springer Nature Switzerland AG 2022
S. Yu et al. (Eds.): PRCV 2022, LNCS 13535, pp. 54–66, 2022.
https://doi.org/10.1007/978-3-031-18910-4_5

its superior performance, has been widely used in various fields, including applications to assist in AD diagnosis [4,5]. However, the application of sMRI images to machine learning for the classification of AD requires consideration of an issue: the original sMRI images contains a lot of useless noise, which not only reduce the accuracy of AD classification, but also increases the computational cost. Changes in brain structure are one of the main manifestations of AD [6], so brain extraction on the original sMRI images is very useful for the diagnosis of AD. Considering that in information theory, entropy is often used to reflect the complexity of information systems. sMRI images slices can also be viewed as a kind of image information, therefore, we attempted to combine both information theory and sMRI slices for the classification of AD.

In this paper, we proposed a method to classify AD and Normal using the annotated sMRI images from the Alzheimer's Disease Neuroimaging Initiative (ADNI) database. The method firstly performed brain extraction on the original sMRI images, and used information entropy to select a certain number of sMRI images slices that contain more brain information. Then, ResNet and fully-connected network (FCN) were adopted for feature extraction and AD classification, respectively. Furthermore, channel attention network and spatial attention network were used in our model to improve the performance. All the codes of our method are available at https://github.com/guanyu1998/ADNI--Alzheimer-s-Disease. In summary, our contributions include:

1. Slice entropy and brain extraction were combined to select quality sMRI images slices.
2. ResNet, channel attention network, spatial attention network and FCN were used for AD classification.
3. The effectiveness of our proposed method was verified through ablation experiments and comparative experiments, which were performed by 20-fold cross-validation.

## 2   Related Work

From the perspective of relevant methods, AD diagnosis belongs to the problem of image classification. From the perspective of application, AD diagnosis belongs to AD classification. In this section, we discuss image classification and the Alzheimer's disease classification in detail.

### 2.1   Image Classification

The classification problem has been one of the top three problems in computer vision [8]. LeCun et al. [9] proposed the convolutional-pooling-fully connected neural network structure-LeNet, for recognizing handwritten character images in 1998. Alex Krizhevskyet et al. [10] inherited LeCun's ideas and proposed the AlexNet network in 2012, which significantly reduced the classification error rate in the ImageNet challenge that year. Karen Simonyan et al. [11] proposed VGGNet in 2014, which further improved the classification accuracy. Christian

Szegedy *et al.* [12] proposed GoogLeNet, which made more efficient use of computational resources by using the idea of $1 \times 1$ convolution and reaggregation of convolution on multiple dimensions to extract more features with the same amount of computation, thus improving the training results. However, AlexNet, VGGNet and other structures increase the depth (number of layers) of the network to obtain better training results, causing the model degradation problem. He *et al.* [13] proposed the ResNet network, which can solve the model degradation problem by using residual blocks.

Experiments show that due to the bottleneck of information processing, only part of all visible information is noticed by human beings [14]. So, only using CNN typically ignores channel and spatial information, which often hinders further improvement of network performance. For this question, Zhong *et al.* [15] applied pixel-group attention to the traditional convolution to enhance the extraction of features, and achieved better performance. Chen *et al.* [16] embedded channel attention network and spatial attention network into his model, which greatly improved the feature extraction performance.

## 2.2   AD Classification

Among diseases, Alzheimer's disease has gradually attracted the attention of scholars due to its inherent high prevalence, incurability, and time-consuming diagnosis. Pan *et al.* [17] constructed an algorithm based on brain sMRI scans to diagnose AD using sparse autoencoders and 3D convolutional neural networks, and validated the algorithm on the ADNI dataset. Liu *et al.* [18] proposed an hierarchical network based on 3D texture features of brain images, combining edge features and node features for AD classification through a multi-core combination framework. Wang *et al.* [19] performed the diagnosis of AD by introducing dense connections to maximize information flow and connecting each layer directly to all subsequent layers. Feng *et al.* [20] performed downsampling and reconstruction step for sMRI images, then weighted the edges between any two nodes using the connection strength (CS), finally concatenated node features and edge features at different scales for AD classification. Ju *et al.* [21] used sMRI to construct a targeted automatic coding network and combined it with clinical textual information, such as age and gender for the diagnosis of AD. Jha *et al.* [22] used double tree complex wavelet transform (DTCWT), principal component analysis, linear discriminant analysis, and extreme value learning machine (ELM) to distinguish AD patients from healthy controls. Zhang *et al.* [23] proposed PM-method, which used two different networks to predict AD by using PET and sMRI images separately. In summary, the work of the aforementioned scholars did not consider further processing of the sMRI data. The original sMRI images contain a large amount of information irrelevant to AD diagnosis, which usually hinders further improvement of model performance. To solve this problem, some scholars avoided the use of irrelevant information by selecting partial sMRI images slices. Khan *et al.* [24] selected some sMRI images slices while fine-tuning the VGGNet to perform AD classification. Bumshik *et al.* [25] selected different slices to constitute the training data for multidimensional channels after outlier processing of the slices and used AlexNet network for the classification of AD. Kang *et al.* [25] employed an integrated approach with multiple models and multiple slices for the classification of AD. Other scholars used methods that avoid the use of irrelevant information by extracting parts of the brain. Li *et al.* [26] extracted the hippocampus in sMRI images and fed them into two convolutional neural networks for feature extraction and finally weighted the extracted features for AD classification. Zhang *et al.* [27] performed brain imaging for skull stripping and spatial normalization, then selected an axial slice and extracted texture features using smooth wavelet entropy (SWE), finally used a single hidden layer neural network for AD classification.

## 3   Methodology

To avoid useless information in sMRI images and achieve better performance, our method mainly included: (i) Brain extraction; (ii) Slice selection; (iii) Model building using ResNet and Attention network. Specifically, Brain extraction and Slice selection were used to reduce the use of irrelevant information; model building using ResNet and Attention network was used to extract features and avoid the impact of a small sample size on model performance. Figure 1 shows the overview of our proposed method.

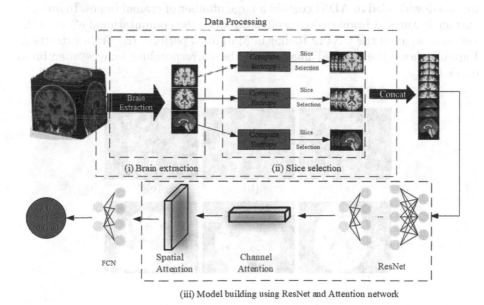

**Fig. 1.** Overview of the proposed framework

### 3.1   Data Processing

In this section, we discuss brain extraction and slice selection.

**Brain Extraction:** sMRI slices at different locations contain different information. In order to show the differences clearly, we selected a few extreme slices as sample presentations, as shown in Fig. 2. It is clear that sMRI images slices located at the edges contain less or no brain information, while sMRI images slices located in the middle contained more brain structures.

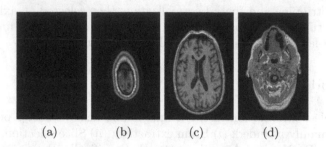

(a)          (b)          (c)          (d)

**Fig. 2.** sMRI images slice at different locations. a, b, c, d represents respectively slice = 0, slice = 27, slice = 90, slice = 190

The main lesion area of Alzheimer's patients is the brain. The original MRI images downloaded in ADNI contain a large number of cranial bones. In order to extract features of brain regions well and reduce the computational effort of the network, we used the CAT12 toolkit in Matlab to perform the brain extraction. Figure 3 shows the original images and the corresponding images after brain extraction.

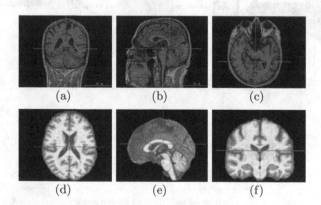

(a)                    (b)                    (c)

(d)                    (e)                    (f)

**Fig. 3.** Original images and the corresponding images after brain extraction. a, b, c are the original images; d, e, f are the corresponding images after brain extraction.

**Entropy-based Slice Selection:** In information theory, entropy is considered to be a measure characterizing the degree of order in the state of motion of an object, so the magnitude of the entropy value reflects the degree of disorder. In image processing, the entropy $H$ of an image can be defined based on the orderliness of the grayscale distribution of individual pixel points of the image, which reflects the degree of information richness of the image. When the image is a pure color map (i.e., white or black), there is only one gray value, the entropy is minimum; when each pixel of the image has a different gray value, the entropy is maximum.

To reduce noise interference in sMRI images and select high-quality sMRI images slices, the information entropy of sMRI images slices are calculated by Formula 1, and a certain number of sMRI images slices are selected in the order from the largest to the smallest.

$$H_k = - \sum_{i=1}^{M} p_i \times log p_i \tag{1}$$

where $H_k$ is the slice entropy of the $k - th$ image, $p_i$ is the probability that the $i - th$ pixel appears in the $k - th$ image, and $M$ is the number of pixel types.

## 3.2 Model Building Using ResNet and Attention Network

Residual network solves the problem of model degradation by adding inputs and outputs, as shown in Fig. 4. The output features after going through multiple convolution layers will be added to the input features. ResNet can stack more convolutional layers to obtain deeper features by using this structure. ResNet is often used as a backbone in traditional image classification, and sMRI images classification can be considered as a slice class of images to some extent, so it can also be the backbone of our method.

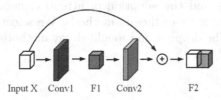

Fig. 4. The structure of residual network. Conv represents convolution layer, F1, F2 represent feature, and Input X represents input.

Attention network is widely used in natural language processing and computer vision. By imitating the human attention mechanism, the Attention network quickly scans the global image to obtain the target area, while suppressing other useless information. Similarly, when processing the features extracted from the backbone network, we need to avoid the focus on useless features while improving the learning of useful features, so the attention network can largely satisfy our needs.

Based on the above discussion, we have made a combination of different networks and adopt a fine-tuning strategy for feature extraction. Then, the extracted feature was fed into the channel attention network (shown in Fig. 5) and spatial attention network (shown in Fig. 6) successively. Finally, FCN and SoftMax were used for AD classification.

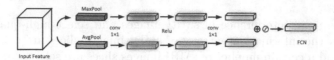

**Fig. 5.** The structure of channel attention network. The features are summed after MaxPool, Conv1 × 1, Relu, Conv1 × 1 and AvgPool, Conv1 × 1, Relu, Conv1 × 1, respectively, then they are fed into FCN.

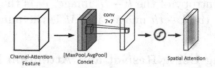

**Fig. 6.** The structure of spatial attention network. MaxPool, AvgPool and Concat operation are used for the Channel-Attention feature, finally the feature is fed into Spatial Attention after passing through the Conv7 × 7.

## 4    Expermients and Results

In this section, we performed ablation experiments in terms of different numbers of sMRI images slices and the adoption of attention network, and compared our method with other state-of-the-art methods. We select 1146 images as the experiment dataset. The dropout and weight decay methods are used to prevent overfitting, respectively.

### 4.1    Dataset

The Alzheimer's Disease Neuroimaging Initiative (ADNI) [29] is the most commonly used open dataset for AD classification, and the ADNI is a longitudinal multicenter study to develop clinical, imaging, genetic, and biochemical biomarkers for the early detection and follow-up of Alzheimer's disease. In this paper, we select a total of 1146 samples of sMRI subjects with the field strength of 1.5T, weighting of T1 in ADNI-1. The samples are all over 60 years old, including 565 samples of male gender and 581 samples of female gender; the number of sMRI samples labeled AD is 372 and the number of sMRI samples labeled Normal is 774. All sMRI images are acquired by Magnetization-Prepared Rapid Gradient Echo (MP-RAGE) and proposed by GradWarp, B1 Correction, N3, Scaled. Relevant samples can be obtained from https://adni.loni.usc.edu.

## 4.2   Analysis of Different sMRI Images Slice Numbers

As described in Sect. 3, slices at different locations contain different information, and the information entropy can be used to measure the information complexity of each slice. In our selected dataset, the sMRI image of each patient contains 225 slices. To be able to avoid the use of useless information, we need to select from 225 slices. Model performance based on different numbers of sMRI images slices could effectively reflect the extent of our invalid information rejection. In this ablation experiment, the only variable was the number of the sMRI images slices, and the rest of the conditions were guaranteed to be consistent. In terms of number of sMRI images slices, we selected the numbers of 8, 16, 32, 64, according to the computer uses a power of 2 for storage. The experimental results are shown in Fig. 7, and the detailed information is shown in Table 1. For reasons of the python library itself, the upper and lower edges of boxplot indicate the maximum and minimum observed values respectively, the SD in Table 1 means Standard Deviation.

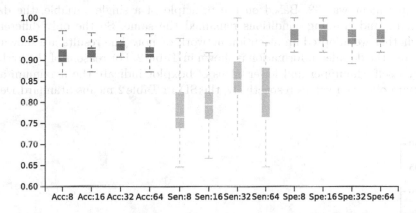

**Fig. 7.** Experimental results of different slice numbers. Red boxplot represents Accuracy, green boxplot represents Sensitivity, and blue boxplot represents Specificity. Acc, Sen and Spe indicated Accuracy, Sensitivity and Specificity, respectively. The number in the horizontal coordinate represents the number of slices. (Color figure online)

**Table 1.** Experimental results of different slice numbers.

| Slice number | Average accuracy | SD | Average sensitivity | SD | Average specificity | SD |
|---|---|---|---|---|---|---|
| 8 | 91.25% | 0.0316 | 77.12% | 0.0977 | 94.46% | **0.0223** |
| 16 | 93.03% | 0.0291 | 79.20% | 0.0921 | **97.09%** | 0.0241 |
| 32 | **94.34%** | **0.0192** | **84.91%** | 0.0772 | 95.35% | 0.0317 |
| 64 | 91.93% | 0.0278 | 83.05% | **0.0754** | 94.89% | 0.0238 |

From the experimental results, it can be found that the model performance was affected by the number of sMRI images slices. On the whole, when the number of slices was 8 or 16, the model could not give full play to its performance, because the selected slices could not contain enough brain information; as the number of slices increased, the performance of the model gradually becomed better; when the number of selected slices was 64, the selected slices contained much useless information, which would affect the model performance. When the number was 32, our model performed best overall, ranking first in both Accuracy and Sensitivity metrics with 94.34% and 84.91%, respectively, and ranking second in Specificity metric with a result of 95.35%. In addition, the standard deviation of all the results is less than 0.1. those results indicates that the dispersion of all the results in the cross-validation is small and the experimental results are relatively reliable.

## 4.3   Adoption of Attention Network

To verify the effect of the Attention network, an ablation experiment was conducted. Based on the results of Sect. 4.2, the number of sMRI images slice in this expermient was 32. Based on the principle of a single variable, the data processing and training conditions remained the same. So the only difference was whether we adopted an attention network or not. The results are shown in Fig. 8 and the detailed information is shown in Table 2. For reasons of the python library itself, the upper and lower edges of boxplot indicate the maximum and minimum observed values respectively, the SD in Table 2 means Standard Deviation.

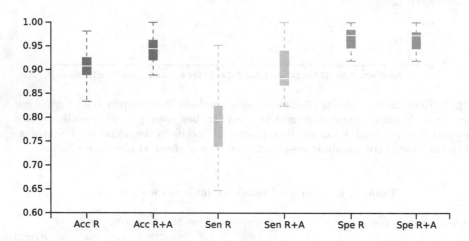

**Fig. 8.** Experimental results on Attention networks. Red boxplot represents Accuracy, green boxplot represents Sensitivity, and blue boxplot represents Specificity. In the horizontal coordinate, R is ResNet, R+A is ResNet+Attention, Acc, Sen and Spe indicated Accuracy, Sensitivity and Specificity, respectively. (Color figure online)

**Table 2.** Experimental results on attention networks.

|                  | Average accuracy | SD     | Average sensitivity | SD     | Average specificity | SD     |
| ---------------- | ---------------- | ------ | ------------------- | ------ | ------------------- | ------ |
| ResNet+Attention | **95.33**%       | **0.0301** | **88.99**%       | **0.0588** | **97.38**%       | 0.0288 |
| ResNet           | 94.34%           | 0.0351 | 84.91%              | 0.0978 | 95.35%              | **0.0241** |

From the experimental results, It was clear that the performance of the model in terms of Accuracy, Sensitivity and Specificity were significantly improved with adopted the Attention network, and the performance of model improved by 0.99%, 4.08% and 2.03% in the three given metrics, respectively. Attention mechanisms could be able to extract further features. As mentioned above, the attention mechanism could pay more attention to the target area and suppress other useless information, thus improving the performance of the model. Based on the experiments, our model performed the best when adopting the attention mechanism. In addition, the standard deviation of all the results is less than 0.1. those results indicates that the dispersion of all the results in the cross-validation is small and the experimental results are relatively reliable.

## 4.4   Comparison with Other Methods

Deep learning can automatically capture features and perform more complex nonlinear fits [28], so it has advantages over traditional machine learning. To further validate the feasibility of our method, we compared our proposed method with other eight deep learning methods [18,20–23,25–27]. All methods used the ADNI-1 dataset. In terms of evaluation metrics, we adopted three medically commonly used metrics, namely, Accuracy, Sensitivity and Specificity. The results are shown in Table 3.

**Table 3.** Results for different methods.

| Method         | Average accuracy | Average sensitivity | Average specificity |
| -------------- | ---------------- | ------------------- | ------------------- |
| NCSIN [16]     | 94.21%           | **96.58**%          | 92.44%              |
| IHN-F [14]     | 93.95%           | 91.07%              | 95.66%              |
| RSB-F [17]     | 92.92%           | 94.00%              | 89.85%              |
| SWE-F [24]     | 92.70%           | 93.67%              | 91.77%              |
| Hipp-F [23]    | 87.51%           | 87.60%              | 87.42%              |
| CDTWS-F [18]   | 90.16%           | 90.22%              | 90.15%              |
| PM-method [19] | 94.97%           | 84.31%              | 88.20%              |
| EL [22]        | 90.36%           | 93.94%              | 83.78%              |
| Our Method     | **95.33**%       | 88.99%              | **97.38**%          |

Table 3 gives the results of different models for AD and Normal classification. It could be observed from Table 3 that our proposed method scored 95.33% and 97.38% for Accuracy and Specificity, respectively, which were the highest scores. Among the compared models, the PM-method and Hipp-F had the highest score of 94.97% and the lowest score of 87.51% for Accuracy, which were 0.36% and 7.82% lower than our proposed method, respectively; the IHN-F and EL had the highest score of 95.66% and 83.78% for Specificity, which were 1.72% and 13.60% lower than our model. However, the relatively low score of our model on Sensitivity may be caused by the small number of sMRI images of AD subjects in the dataset itself. In future experiments, it is necessary to select the appropriate number of samples as much as possible, and try to ensure that the ratio of our positive to negative sample size is 1:1.

## 5    Conclusion

In this paper, we presented a method for AD diagnosis, this method contained data processing part and model building part. In the data processing part, our method first performed brain extraction on the original sMRI images to remove the irrelevant parts for AD diagnosis. Then, slice entropy was used to select sMRI images slices. In model building part, ResNet and Attention network were used for feature extraction, fully-connected network was used for AD classification. Finally, we conducted two ablation experiments and a comparative experiment to analyze our method, the experimental results proved the effectiveness of the proposed method in AD diagnosis. In the future, we plan to use more advanced models or use datasets with more data to optimize our model.

**Declaration of Competing Interest.** The authors declare that they have no known competing financial interests or personal relationships that could have appeared to influence the work reported in this paper.

## References

1. Jagust, W.: Vulnerable neural systems and the borderland of brain aging and neurodegeneration. Neuron **77**(2), 219–234 (2013)
2. Vasilakos, A.V., Tang, Y., Yao, Y.: Neural networks for computer-aided diagnosis in medicine: a review. Neurocomputing **216**, 700–708 (2016)
3. Odusami, M., Maskeliūnas, R., Damaševičius, R., et al.: Analysis of features of Alzheimer's disease: detection of early stage from functional brain changes in magnetic resonance images using a finetuned ResNet18 network. Diagnostics **11**(6), 1071 (2021)
4. Yang, X., Goh, A., Chen, S.H.A., et al.: Evolution of hippocampal shapes across the human lifespan. Hum. Brain Mapping **34**(11), 3075–3085 (2013)
5. Cui, Y., Liu, B., Luo, S., et al.: Identification of conversion from mild cognitive impairment to Alzheimer's disease using multivariate predictors. PloS One **6**(7), e21896 (2011)

6. Jagust, W.: Imaging the evolution and pathophysiology of Alzheimer disease. Nat. Rev. Neurosci. **19**(11), 687–700 (2018)
7. Oizumi, M., Albantakis, L., Tononi, G.: From the phenomenology to the mechanisms of consciousness: integrated information theory 3.0. PLoS Computat. Biol. **10**(5), e1003588 (2014)
8. Sultana, F., Sufian, A., Dutta, P.: Advancements in image classification using convolutional neural network. In: 2018 Fourth International Conference on Research in Computational Intelligence and Communication Networks (ICRCICN), pp. 122–129. IEEE (2018)
9. LeCun, Y., Bottou, L., Bengio, Y., et al.: Gradient-based learning applied to document recognition. Proc. IEEE **86**(11), 2278–2324 (1998)
10. Krizhevsky, A., Sutskever, I., Hinton, G.E.: ImageNet classification with deep convolutional neural networks. Adv. Neural Inf. Process. Syst. **25**, 1097–1105 (2012)
11. Simonyan, K., Zisserman, A.: Very deep convolutional networks for large-scale image recognition. arXiv preprint arXiv:1409.1556 (2014)
12. Szegedy, C., Liu, W., Jia, Y., et al.: Going deeper with convolutions. In: Proceedings of the IEEE Conference on Computer Vision and Pattern Recognition, pp. 1–9 (2015)
13. He, K., Zhang, X., Ren, S., et al.: Deep residual learning for image recognition. In: Proceedings of the IEEE Conference on Computer Vision and Pattern Recognition, pp. 770–778 (2016)
14. Yang, X.: An overview of the attention mechanisms in computer vision. J. Phys. Conf. Series **1693**(1), 012173 (2020)
15. Zhong, Z., Lin, Z.Q., Bidart, R., et al.: Squeeze-and-attention networks for semantic segmentation. In: Proceedings of the IEEE/CVF Conference on Computer Vision and Pattern Recognition, pp. 13065–13074 (2020)
16. Chen, L., Tian, X., Chai, G., et al.: A new CBAM-P-Net model for few-shot forest species classification using airborne hyperspectral images. Remote Sens. **13**(7), 1269 (2021)
17. Payan, A., Montana, G.: Predicting Alzheimer's disease: a neuroimaging study with 3D convolutional neural networks. arXiv preprint arXiv:1502.02506 (2015)
18. Liu, J., Wang, J., Hu, B., et al.: Alzheimer's disease classification based on individual hierarchical networks constructed with 3-D texture features. IEEE Trans. Banobiosci. **16**(6), 428–437 (2017)
19. Wang, H., Shen, Y., Wang, S., et al.: Ensemble of 3D densely connected convolutional network for diagnosis of mild cognitive impairment and Alzheimer's disease. Neurocomputing **333**, 145–156 (2019)
20. Feng, J., Zhang, S.W., Chen, L., et al.: Alzheimer's disease classification using features extracted from nonsubsampled contourlet subband-based individual networks. Neurocomputing **421**, 260–272 (2021)
21. Ju, R., Hu, C., Li, Q.: Early diagnosis of Alzheimer's disease based on resting-state brain networks and deep learning. IEEE/ACM Trans. Comput. Biol. Bioinf. **16**(1), 244–257 (2017)
22. Jha, D., Alam, S., Pyun, J.Y., et al.: Alzheimer's disease detection using extreme learning machine, complex dual tree wavelet principal coefficients and linear discriminant analysis. J. Med. Imaging Health Inf. **8**(5), 881–890 (2018)
23. Zhang, F., Li, Z., Zhang, B., et al.: Multi-modal deep learning model for auxiliary diagnosis of Alzheimer's disease. Neurocomputing **361**, 185–195 (2019)
24. Khan, N.M., Abraham, N., Hon, M.: Transfer learning with intelligent training data selection for prediction of Alzheimer's disease. IEEE Access **7**, 72726–72735 (2019)

25. Lee, B., Ellahi, W., Choi, J.Y.: Using deep CNN with data permutation scheme for classification of Alzheimer's disease in structural magnetic resonance imaging (sMRI). IEICE Trans. Inform. Syst. **102**(7), 1384–1395 (2019)
26. Li, H., Habes, M., Wolk, D.A., et al.: A deep learning model for early prediction of Alzheimer's disease dementia based on hippocampal magnetic resonance imaging data. Alzheimer's Dementia **15**(8), 1059–1070 (2019)
27. Zhang, Y., Wang, S., Sui, Y., et al.: Multivariate approach for Alzheimer's disease detection using stationary wavelet entropy and predator-prey particle swarm optimization. J. Alzheimer's Dis. **65**(3), 855–869 (2018)
28. Singha, A., Thakur, R.S., Patel, T.: Deep learning applications in medical image analysis. Biomedical Data Mining for Information Retrieval: Methodologies, Techniques and Applications, pp. 293–350 (2021)
29. Jack, C.R., Jr., Bernstein, M.A., Fox, N.C., et al.: The Alzheimer's disease neuroimaging initiative (ADNI): MRI methods. J. Magn. Reson. Imaging Official J. Int. Soc. Magn. Reson. Med. **27**(4), 685–691 (2008)

# Semi-supervised Distillation Learning Based on Swin Transformer for MRI Reconstruction

Yuanyuan Tan and Jun Lyu[✉]

School of Computer and Control Engineering, Yantai University, Yantai 264205, China
ljdream0710@pku.edu.cn

**Abstract.** Deep learning-based magnetic resonance imaging (MRI) reconstruction obtains extremely high reconstruction performance by training with large amounts of data. However, the acquisition of fully sampled MRI data is expensive and time-consuming, making it difficult to obtain large amounts of fully sampled data. This not only poses a challenge for models that require more fully sampled data for training but also limits the generalization ability of network models. To address the above problems, we propose a semi-supervised MRI reconstruction algorithm based on migration learning by analyzing the characteristics of undersampled MRI reconstruction. To address the lack of data scarcity and generalization in the reconstruction process. The model fuses shallow features extracted from the convolutional layer and deep features obtained from the Swin Transformer Block (STB) to greatly improve the reconstruction capability of the network. However, the process of distillation cannot predict the goodness of the knowledge transferred, which hinders the performance of the semi-supervised algorithm. We further propose the use of privilege loss as a way to improve the distillation of useful knowledge. Experimental results show that student networks trained by this algorithm are able to rival supervised teacher networks and outperform unsupervised network models in brain data reconstruction.

**Keywords:** Magnetic resonance imaging · Swin transformer · Knowledge distillation · Privileged information

## 1 Introduction

Magnetic resonance imaging (MRI) is an important medical imaging technique with many advantages, such as high contrast and no radiation, and is widely used in clinical practice. Deep learning makes an important contribution at every stage of MRI, but the need for additional storage space for models in real-world applications presents a huge challenge for computing devices.

Therefore, it is important to develop a lightweight network model. An effective way to obtain compact models that are easy to deploy is a knowledge distillation (KD) [1]. The method uses a large teacher network to assist a small student network for joint training, while the student network incorporates the probability distribution of the teacher network output for learning [2]. This probability distribution can provide richer supervision information than ground truth images.

S. Yu et al. (Eds.): PRCV 2022, LNCS 13535, pp. 67–76, 2022.
https://doi.org/10.1007/978-3-031-18910-4_6

MRI reconstruction is performed in the frequency domain (k-space) or image domain. Specifically, the imaging method based on k-space data in the k-space domain is mainly performed by interpolating the under-sampled k-space data by ANN (Artificial Neural Network) before imaging. Hao et al. [3] used the under-sampled data as input to interpolate the k-space data through a convoluted network to accomplish MRI reconstruction. While in the image domain, Wang et al. [4] designed a Convolutional Neural Networks (CNN) to reduce the random artifacts generated by sampling. Lee et al. [5] introduced residual learning to MR fast imaging. The amount of data on training and the generalization ability of the neural network being trained determine the success of these algorithms.

MRI is limited by its own imaging mechanism and follows Nyquist's sampling theorem making acquisition times long. Prolonged scanning can cause discomfort to the collector and may also introduce motion artefacts [6]. This poses a huge difficulty in training the model. There is therefore an urgent need to enhance the generalization capabilities of small sample-based networks. The amount of fully - sampled images greatly affect the final performance of the model, and how to reduce or not use fully-sampled data at all is a pressing issue. The above problem has been studied by some scholars in terms of unsupervised [7] and semi-supervised [8]. In unsupervised learning, the model clusters unlabeled data by means of shallow features to complete the entire learning process [9]. In semi-supervised learning, the model is trained by establishing associations between unlabeled data and the learning task [10]. Affected by data labels with strong supervision signals, the performance gap between unsupervised learning and semi-supervised learning and supervised learning is large. Compared with shallow features in unsupervised learning, deep features are more robust [11]. The generalization ability of the trained neural network is affected by the training data set. One effective method to solve this problem is distillation learning. In knowledge distillation, the neural network obtains rich reconstructed knowledge by training in the source data domain.

Based on the above problems and needs, we designed a novel SEMI-KD network for MRI reconstruction, which is a Swin Transformer based semi-supervised distillation learning method for MR image reconstruction. The method allows the student network to fit the deep features of the teacher's network output as a supervised signal, and this method has advantages over general supervised and semi-supervised learning: 1) The need for a fully sampled dataset for supervised learning can be avoided, and full use can be made of unlabeled data; 2) It is also possible to avoid the association model that needs to be built in semi-supervised learning during the training phase, ensuring robustness. Second, we add Swin Transformer residual blocks to the network, which has the advantage of solving the edge pixel problem in the patch by sliding the window [12]. It also further improves the reconstruction performance of the network by reducing the interference of irrelevant knowledge through privileged imitation loss. The method further compresses the student network parameters and improves its performance to achieve the goal of using richer data and compressing smaller models.

We conducted extensive experiments with $2\times$, $4\times$ and $6\times$ under-sampled data. We experimentally demonstrate that our method not only has lower verification errors, but also improves the efficiency of feature knowledge transfer between networks compared to common distillation and unsupervised methods.

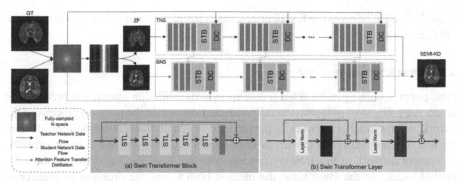

**Fig. 1.** The overall structure of the SEMI-KD network. ZF: zero-filled image. GT: ground truth. TNS: Teacher network structure (with 5 cascaded layers, each with 5 convolutional layers, a STB and a DC layer) SNS: Student network structure (with 5 cascaded layers, each with 3 convolutional layers, a STB and a DC layer) (a)STB: Swin Transformer Block; (b)STL: Swin Transformer Layer; Training process: step1, train the teacher network first; step2, use the attention shift loss ($L_{AT}$) to train the student network; step3, load the parameters in step2 to retrain the student network.

## 2 Method

### 2.1 MRI Reconstruction

In the Compressed Sensing MRI (CS-MRI), the reconstruction process is to reconstruct x from the partially sampled data y expressed by the equation:

$$y = F_\Phi x + m \tag{1}$$

where $F_\Phi$ is the under-sampled Fourier encoding matrix, x is the MR image to be reconstructed. m is the effect on measurements of noise and scanner imprecisions. The optimal solution x is reconstructed using the classical method in the under-sampling mode:

$$\arg\min_x \|F_\Phi x - y\|_2^2 + R(x) \tag{2}$$

where the first term is the data fidelity term and the second term is the regularization term. The Half-quadratic splitting [13] optimizes Eq. (2) by introducing an auxiliary variable $q$:

$$q^{(i)} = \arg\min_q \|x^{(i-1)} - q\|_2^2 + R(q) \tag{3a}$$

$$x^{i+1} = \arg\min_x \|F_\Phi x - y\|_2^2 + \lambda\|x - q^{(i)}\|_2^2 \tag{3b}$$

where $\lambda \geq 0$ is hyper-parameter, $q^{(i)}$ is the intermediate variable Eq. (3b) has a fixed solution at the sampling location n in k-space. This can be used as a data consistency layer (DC) in the network [14] with the following procedure:

$$\hat{x}^{i+1}[n] = \begin{cases} \frac{y[n] + \lambda\hat{q}^{(i)}[n]}{1+\lambda}, & n \in \Phi \\ \hat{q}^{(i)}[n], & n \notin \Phi \end{cases} \tag{4}$$

where $\hat{x}^{i+1}$ and $\hat{q}^{(i)}$ denote the fast Fourier transforms of $x^{i+1}$ and $q^{(i)}$. $\lambda \geq 0$ is the noise level (i.e., $\lambda \to \infty$).

## 2.2  Network Structure

In this paper, a training method for semi-supervised distillation learning is proposed to address the problem of reducing the fully sampled dataset. In the training process of the network, a large teacher network is first trained to obtain the reconstruction information, and this information is trained as semi-supervised labels by the student network. The student network in this training process does not need the assistance of the fully sampled image. At the same time, the method both solves the problem of inaccurate pseudo-label generation in general semi-supervised learning and reduces the need for many fully sampled datasets for training. During the training of the student model, the supervised signals provided by the teacher network are used directly for learning as a way to complete the whole training process.

The proposed SEMI-KD network was established under a semi-supervised framework (Fig. 1). We used a DC-CNN network containing Swin Transformer residual blocks to accomplish the distillation of MRI reconstruction and demonstrated the effectiveness of this method. This choice takes into account the simple design of fully convolutional layers and the scalability of CNN-based MRI reconstruction architectures [4, 15]. Each cascade block in the network consists of a convolutional layer CNN [14] and a data consistency (DC) layer as well as a Swin Transformer residual block. Each convolutional layer has a kernel size of $3 \times 3$ and a step size of 1. To maintain the image size, the padding value is set to 1.

The initial convolutional layer accepts a single channel as input (an under-sampled image) and produces 32 feature maps; the final convolutional layer accepts 32 feature maps as input and produces a single channel as the output. Other convolutional layers have 32 input and output feature maps. To introduce non-linearity between convolution layers, a Leaky ReLU is used. To provide consistency in the Fourier domain, the DC layer fills the anticipated k-space with known values. The cascade is equipped with a long skip connection (LSC) that connects the cascade's output to its input, allowing the network to concentrate on learning high frequency information.

## 2.3  Swin Transformer Block

In Fig. 1(a), the Swin Transformer block (STB) has multiple Swin Transformer layers (STL) and one convolutional layer. STL completes local attention and cross-window interaction, convolution enhances features, and residual join completes feature aggregation. Given the input features $F_0$ of STB, the intermediate features $F_f$ are extracted and expressed by the Swin Transformer layer as:

$$F_f = H_{STL}(F_0) \tag{5}$$

where $H_{STL}(\cdot)$ is the Swin Transformer layer in STB. STB uses the residual learning method to ensure the stability of feature extraction. The output of the STB is given by:

$$F_{out} = F_{CON}(F_f) + F_0 \tag{6}$$

where $F_{CON}(\cdot)$ is the convolutional layer. Transformer can be considered as a concrete instance of spatially varying convolution [16, 17]. Moreover, residual connections aggregate features at different levels.

The Swin Transformer Layer (STL) [12] is based on the original Transformer Layer's basic multi-headed self-attentiveness. The primary distinctions are the mechanisms governing local attention and window shifting. STL is composed of two components, as illustrated in Fig. 1(b): Multiheaded Self-Attention (MSA) and Multilayer Perceptron (MLP). Swin Transformer will divide the given input into non-overlapping local windows and compute the standard self-attention for each window separately.

In practice, we apply the attention function in parallel h times and then concatenate the results for MSA in accordance with [18]. The MLP has two fully connected layers with GELU nonlinearity between them for further feature transformation. Both MSA and MLP have layer norm (LN) layers, and both modules use residual connections. Swin Transformer extracts more deep features for reconstruction.

## 2.4 Attention Based Feature Distillation

Inspired by attentional mechanisms, Komodakis [19] et al. introduced such mechanisms to knowledge distillation and treated attentional feature maps as knowledge to be learned by student networks. Students can improve their similarity to the teacher's network by learning the attentional profile map in the teacher's network. This approach has been shown to be scientifically valid and the attention migration algorithm outperforms most distillation algorithms. The teacher network provides the most direct form of supervision for the student network. The goal of attention-based feature distillation is to enhance the reconstruction of student networks by allowing them to learn the attention map of the teacher's network.

Our feature attention map in this experiment is given by $F_{sum}(A) = \sum_{i=1}^{C} |A_i|^2$, where $A$ is the feature map after activation and $C$ is the number of channels. The following attentional transfer losses were used to achieve effective information distillation:

$$L_{AT} = \sum_{j \in J} \left\| \frac{V_S^j}{\left\| V_S^j \right\|_2} - \frac{V_T^j}{\left\| V_T^j \right\|_2} \right\|_2 \tag{7}$$

where $V_S^j$ and $V_T^j$ are the vectorized forms of the $j$-th pair of student-teacher attention graphs. $J$ denotes the teacher-student convolutional layer selected for attentional transfer.

## 2.5 Loss Functions

We follow the Hinton [1] knowledge distillation strategy to encourage the student network to learn more of the softened class distribution in the teacher network. However, teachers' projections may provide non-helpful information as there may be redundant information or incorrect projections. In the detailed and fuzzy areas of the tumors, students need more help from the teacher, but they also need to avoid the wrong predictions made by the teacher. Therefore, pixel-level regularization of knowledge transfer (*i.e.*, privileged information) is recommended to guide students to focus on simulating softened distributions from teacher predictions that are accurate.

Specifically, a regularization factor mapping was constructed to moderate the contribution of soft labels. Let $l_s$, $l_T$ denote the PSNR of the teacher-student model at location $p$, with $\Delta p = l_s - l_T$ denote the difference between their values. The value of $\Delta p$ can represent the teacher's and students' relative prediction performance for each position. With an active $\Delta p$, the teacher will make more accurate predictions and encourage students to actively imitate them. The larger the positive $\Delta p$ value, the more knowledge the student has gained. Whereas negative $\Delta p$ may be associated with the transfer of potentially irrelevant information, teachers should avoid transferring knowledge to students.

In addition, we require that knowledge transfer is only allowed if the teacher makes a correct prediction at a different location. We had designed a regularized factor mapping with each element $\partial$ defined as follows:

$$\partial = \begin{cases} \Delta p & \text{if } \Delta p > 0 \\ 0 \end{cases} \tag{8}$$

$\Delta p$ has greater value for ill-defined tumour/organ regions, and regularization factors constructed based on Eq. (3b) can highlight distillation of important tumor/organ regions. Following that, the regularized knowledge distillation loss was obtained by pixel-level multiplication of the cross-entropy loss of teachers and students by the regularization factor $\partial$:

$$L_{rkd} = \partial \|\sigma(rec_T), \sigma(rec_S)\| \tag{9}$$

where $\|\cdot\|$ denotes the loss of cross-entropy, $rec_T$ and $rec_S$ denote the teacher's and student's outputs at the $p$-th position, and $\sigma$ denotes the Tanh function. The regularization factor $\partial$ is a constant in the calculation of the loss gradient.

Saputra [20] proposed adding imitation loss to the student loss constraint and demonstrated better performance of the student network. This loss was included in our approach since it is a regularized version of the student reconstruction loss. The total reconstruction losses for students were:

$$L_s = L_{rkd} + L_{soft} \tag{10}$$

## 3  Experiments

### 3.1  Experimental Parameters

Our proposed semi-supervised training method is deployed in PyTorch. The training and testing make is a graphics processing unit (GPU) is NVIDIA Tesla V100 GPU (4 $\times$ 16 GB). We set the learning rate and epoch to $1e^{-4}$, 130. For training and testing, respectively, and used an optimizer with ADAM [21].

## 3.2 Experimental Data

The experiments in this paper used the multimodal Brain Tumour Segmentation Challenge 2018 (BraTs2018) dataset [22]. This dataset exposes MRI samples from 285 patients. In this study, T2 image data were used with the imaging orientation in the axial direction. The size of each image was 240 × 240. In addition, we randomly divided the 285 subjects into 80% for training and 20% for testing. For network training, the k-space data were under-sampling using Cartesian under-sampling with various acceleration factors (R = 2×, 4× and 6×) along the phase encoding direction.

## 3.3 Experimental Assessment Methods

The image metrics used are peak signal to noise ratio (PSNR) and structural similarity (SSIM). The larger the value of PSNR, the higher the overall accuracy of the reconstructed image, and the closer the value of SSIM to 1, the clearer the image. The performance of the model reconstruction is assessed by the PSNR and SSIM metrics.

## 3.4 Results

In order to verify the effectiveness of the proposed algorithm, the Cartesian under-sampling model, which is commonly used in fast MRI studies, was used. Cartesian sampling trajectories are widely used in modern commercial MRI instruments due to their simple hardware design and ease of implementation. Three under-sampling factors are used in this paper 2×, 4× and 6×.

The proposed method SEMI-KD is compared with Teacher, SUP-KD [23] and Cycle-GAN [7]. The teacher is the teacher network that guides SEMI-KD. SUP-KD is a supervised knowledge distillation reconstruction method and CycleGAN is an unsupervised depth reconstruction method using cyclic consistency loss.

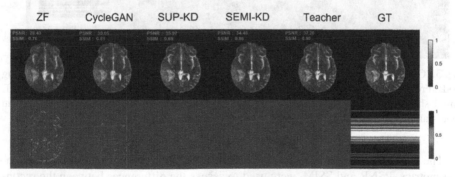

**Fig. 2.** Comparison of brain data reconstruction results of different methods in 4 × under-sampling mode. From left to right are the images of ZF, CycleGAN, SUP-KD, SEMI-KD, Teacher and GT. Row 1 shows the reconstruction results, row 2 is the error map and the corresponding Cartesian under-sampling mask.

Figure 2 provides a qualitative comparison of the above methods. It is clear from the figure that the reconstruction obtained using SEMI-KD is closer to SUP-KD, and Cycle-GAN reconstructs an image that still suffers from loss of detail in certain regions and a less satisfactory reconstruction. The CycleGAN sampling mode was able to recover some detail, but not enough. The performance exhibited by SEMI-KD is due to a combination of attention shifting and privilege loss, which helps to reconstruct the structure. Imitation loss is expected to act as a regularized for student reconstruction loss, while attention transfer helps students learn the intermediate representation of the teacher. In contrast to SUP-KD, the student network still has strong reconstruction capabilities without access to a fully sampled dataset. The reconstruction capability of the network is still comparable to that of traditional supervised methods.

To better demonstrate the reconstruction capability of our algorithm, a comparison is made with other algorithms in 6× under-sampling mode. As shown in Fig. 3, it is observed that the reconstruction obtained using SEMI-KD is closer to SUP-KD, reducing reconstruction artifacts and providing relatively smooth edges. The sampling k-space learning range of CycleGAN (unsupervised model) is small because of high under-sampling. Although the obvious aliasing artifacts in CycleGAN results are reduced, the reconstructed images are still blurred and the details are seriously lost. Compared to CycleGAN, SEMI-KD can provide more and sharper edge detail. As the student model is supported by a strong teacher network, the results can be better reconstructed without using real data in the training and the image quality is significantly improved.

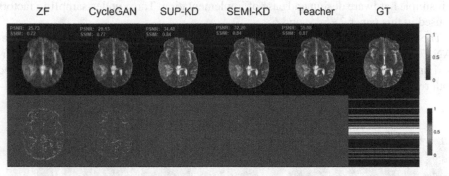

**Fig. 3.** Comparison of brain reconstruction results of different methods in 6× under-sampling mode. From left to right are the images of ZF, CycleGAN, SUP-KD, SEMI-KD, Teacher and GT. Row 1 shows the reconstruction results, row 2 is the error map and the corresponding Cartesian under-sampling mask.

The average quantitative results are shown in Table 1. Two general image evaluation metrics, PSNR and SSIM, were used to assess the differences between the reconstruction results of different methods. As the table indicates, our technique consistently outperforms CycleGAN and achieves better metric scores despite the high magnification under-sampling. With increasing under-sampling multipliers, our method is still comparable to SUP-KD.

**Table 1.** Reconstruction accuracy (mean and standard deviation of PSNR, SSIM) of different reconstruction methods in the brain dataset.

| | 2× | | 4× | | 6× | |
|---|---|---|---|---|---|---|
| | PSNR | SSIM | PSNR | SSIM | PSNR | SSIM |
| ZF | 34.10 ± 1.35 | 0.90 ± 0.02 | 28.23 ± 1.34 | 0.77 ± 0.02 | 25.63 ± 1.35 | 0.71 ± 0.02 |
| CycleGAN | 36.71 ± 2.96 | 0.91 ± 0.01 | 30.01 ± 2.35 | 0.80 ± 0.02 | 28.91 ± 2.12 | 0.76 ± 0.03 |
| SUP-KD | 37.67 ± 1.73 | 0.93 ± 0.01 | 35.58 ± 1.70 | 0.88 ± 0.01 | 33.98 ± 1.71 | 0.84 ± 0.01 |
| SEMI-KD | 37.53 ± 1.89 | 0.92 ± 0.01 | 34.19 ± 1.83 | 0.85 ± 0.01 | 32.09 ± 1.79 | 0.83 ± 0.02 |
| Teacher | 38.89 ± 1.57 | 0.93 ± 0.00 | 36.87 ± 1.28 | 0.89 ± 0.01 | 35.12 ± 1.38 | 0.87 ± 0.01 |

## 4 Discussion and Conclusion

Based on the traditional knowledge distillation framework, we propose a medical image reconstruction method based on Swin Transformer. The algorithm uses a convolutional layer with Swin Transformer residual blocks and a DC layer to construct residual groups and adds feature distillation and privileged distillation losses between the teacher and student networks to fully capture the feature information about the teacher images. This method enables small models to better simulate the performance of large models, while effectively utilizing unlabeled data to avoid the difficulty of obtaining fully sampled MRI data. In the absence of fully sampled images, the images reconstructed by SEMI-KD are rich in details and clear in texture. In future research, we will explore more deeply the knowledge distillation aspect of label-free MRI reconstruction and extend the study of semi-supervised training based on knowledge distillation to other fields.

## References

1. Hinton, G., et al.: Distilling the knowledge in a neural network. Comput. Sci. **14**(7), 38–39 (2015)
2. Yim, J., et al.: A gift from knowledge distillation: fast optimization, network minimization and transfer learning. In: 2017 IEEE Conference on Computer Vision and Pattern Recognition (CVPR), pp. 4133–4141 (2017)
3. Hao, X., et al.: Deep learning. Int. J. Semant. Comput. **10**(03), 417–439 (2016)
4. Wang, S., et al.: Accelerating magnetic resonance imaging via deep learning. In: 2016 13th International Symposium on Biomedical Imaging (ISBI), pp. 514–517. IEEE (2016)
5. Lee, D., et al.: Deep residual learning for accelerated MRI using magnitude and phase networks. IEEE Trans. Biomed. Eng. **65**(9), 1985–1995 (2018)
6. Lustig, M., et al.: Compressed sensing MRI. IEEE Signal Process. Mag. **25**(2), 72–82 (2008)
7. Zhu, J. Y., et al.: Unpaired image-to-image translation using cycle-consistent adversarial networks. In: Proceedings of the IEEE International Conference on Computer Vision (ICCV), pp. 2223–2232 (2017)
8. Yurt, M., et al.: Semi-supervised learning of mutually accelerated MRI synthesis without fully-sampled ground truths. arXiv preprint, arXiv:2011.14347 (2020)
9. Huang, C., et al.: Unsupervised learning of discriminative attributes and visual representations. In: Proceedings of the IEEE conference on Computer Vision & Pattern Recognition, pp. 5175–5184 (2016)

10. Xie, Q., et al.: Self-training with noisy student improves IMAGENET classification. In: Proceedings of the IEEE/CVF Conference on Computer Vision and Pattern Recognition, pp. 10687–10698 (2020)

11. Masi, I., et al.: Deep face recognition: a survey. In: 2018 31st SIBGRAPI Conference on Graphics, Patterns and Images (SIBGRAPI), pp. 471–478. IEEE (2018)

12. Liu, Z., et al.: Swin transformer: hierarchical vision transformer using shifted windows. In: Proceedings of the IEEE/CVF International Conference on Computer Vision, pp. 10012–10022 (2021)

13. Geman, D., et al.: Nonlinear image recovery with half-quadratic regularization. IEEE Trans. Image Process. Publ. IEEE Signal Process. Soc. 4(7), 932–946 (1995)

14. Schlemper, J., Caballero, J., Hajnal, J.V., Price, A., Rueckert, D.: A deep cascade of convolutional neural networks for MR image reconstruction. In: Niethammer, M., et al. (eds.) IPMI 2017. LNCS, vol. 10265, pp. 647–658. Springer, Cham (2017). https://doi.org/10.1007/978-3-319-59050-9_51

15. Souza, R., et al.: A hybrid, dual domain, cascade of convolutional neural networks for magnetic resonance image reconstruction. In: International Conference on Medical Imaging with Deep Learning, pp. 437–446 (2019)

16. Elsayed, G.F., et al.: Revisiting spatial invariance with low-rank local connectivity. In: International Conference on Machine Learning, pp. 2868–2879 (2020)

17. Vaswani, A., et al.: Scaling local self-attention for parameter efficient visual backbones. In: Proceedings of the IEEE/CVF Conference on Computer Vision and Pattern Recognition (CVPR), pp. 12894–12904 (2021)

18. Vaswani, A., et al.: Attention is all you need. In: Advances in Neural Information Processing Systems, 30 (2017)

19. Zagoruyko, S., et al.: Paying more attention to attention: improving the performance of convolutional neural networks via attention transfer. arXiv preprint, arXiv:1612.03928 (2016)

20. Saputra, M., et al.: Distilling knowledge from a deep pose regressor network. In: IEEE/CVF International Conference on Computer Vision (ICCV), pp. 263–272 (2019)

21. Kingma, D., et al.: Adam: a method for stochastic optimization. arXiv preprint, arXiv:1412.6980 (2014)

22. Menze, B., et al.: The multimodal brain tumor image segmentation benchmark (BRATS). IEEE Trans. Med. Imaging 34(10),1993–2024 (2014)

23. Murugesan, B., et al.: KD-MRI: a knowledge distillation framework for image reconstruction and image restoration in MRI workflow. In: Medical Imaging with Deep Learning, pp. 515–526 (2020)

# Multi-scale Multi-target Domain Adaptation for Angle Closure Classification

Zhen Qiu[1,5], Yifan Zhang[2], Fei Li[3], Xiulan Zhang[3], Yanwu Xu[4],
and Mingkui Tan[1,6(✉)]

[1] South China University of Technology, Guangzhou, China
mingkuitan@scut.edu.cn
[2] National University of Singapore, Singapore, Singapore
[3] Sun Yat-sen University, Guangzhou, China
[4] Baidu Inc., Beijing, China
[5] Pazhou Laboratory, Guangzhou, China
[6] Key Laboratory of Big Data and Intelligent Robot,
Ministry of Education, Beijing, China

**Abstract.** Deep learning (DL) has made significant progress in angle closure classification with anterior segment optical coherence tomography (AS-OCT) images. These AS-OCT images are often acquired by different imaging devices/conditions, which results in a vast change of underlying data distributions (called "data domains"). Moreover, due to practical labeling difficulties, some domains (*e.g.,* devices) may not have any data labels. As a result, deep models trained on one specific domain (*e.g.,* a specific device) are difficult to adapt to and thus may perform poorly on other domains (*e.g.,* other devices). To address this issue, we present a multi-target domain adaptation paradigm to transfer a model trained on one labeled source domain to multiple unlabeled target domains. Specifically, we propose a novel Multi-scale Multi-target Domain Adversarial Network (M2DAN) for angle closure classification. M2DAN conducts multi-domain adversarial learning for extracting domain-invariant features and develops a multi-scale module for capturing local and global information of AS-OCT images. Based on these domain-invariant features at different scales, the deep model trained on the source domain is able to classify angle closure on multiple target domains even without any annotations in these domains. Extensive experiments on a real-world AS-OCT dataset demonstrate the effectiveness of the proposed method.

**Keywords:** Angle closure classification · Unsupervised multi-target domain adaptation · Anterior segment optical coherence tomography

## 1 Introduction

Glaucoma is the foremost cause of irreversible blindness [28,31]. Since the vision loss is irreversible, early detection and precise diagnosis for glaucoma are essential to vision preservation. A common type of glaucoma is angle closure, where

© The Author(s), under exclusive license to Springer Nature Switzerland AG 2022
S. Yu et al. (Eds.): PRCV 2022, LNCS 13535, pp. 77–88, 2022.
https://doi.org/10.1007/978-3-031-18910-4_7

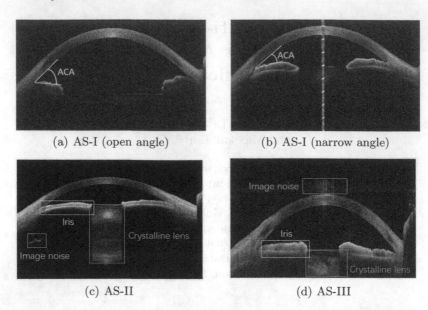

(a) AS-I (open angle)          (b) AS-I (narrow angle)

(c) AS-II                      (d) AS-III

**Fig. 1.** Illustration of different types of anterior chamber angle (ACA) and different data domains. Specifically, ACA consists of two categories: open angle (a) and narrow angle (b). In addition, different imaging devices/techniques may result in different data domains of anterior segment (AS) images, *e.g.,* AS-I (a-b), AS-II (c) and AS-III (d), which differ in terms of the crystalline lens [4], image noises [1], and image resolutions.

the anterior chamber angle (ACA) is narrow as shown in Fig. 1(b). Such an issue leads to blockage of drainage channels that results in pressure on the optic nerve [7]. To identify this, anterior segment optical coherence tomography (AS-OCT) has been shown an effective approach for the evaluation of the ACA structure [15] and is thus widely used for angle closure classification [12,13].

Despite the success of deep learning in computer-aided diagnosis, it hinges on massive annotated images for training [18]. Thanks to AS-OCT devices and hence a growing number of labeled AS-OCT data for deep model training, remarkable performance has been achieved on angle closure classification [5,23]. However, different imaging devices/conditions intrinsically lead to a vast change of underlying data distributions [38], which means that the AS-OCT images may come from different "domains". As a result, deep models trained on one domain (*e.g.,* a specific device) can hardly generalize to other domains [22] (*e.g.,* other devices). More critically, it is impractical to customize deep models for each domain, since annotation costs for such specific-customized images are inevitably expensive. Note that due to labeling difficulties, we may not have any labeled data for some domains.

To solve this issue, one may explore unsupervised domain adaptation [2, 10,19,27,32–34,41], which leverages the labeled data on a source domain to improve the performance on an unlabeled target domain. Most existing methods [3,16,29,38,40] focus on pair-wise adaptation from one source domain to one target domain. However, in angle closure classification tasks, AS-OCT images are often acquired via diverse imaging devices (*e.g.,* CASIA-I or CASIA-II), imaging conditions (*e.g.,* light or dark environment) and preprocessing techniques. In other words, doctors need to classify AS-OCT images from different domains. Therefore, it is more practical to study multi-target domain adaptation [11, 26, 36] for angle closure classification. To be specific, multi-target domain adaptation aims to leverage the annotations on one source domain to improve the performance of multiple unlabeled target domains. Despite the importance, it remains largely unexplored for medical images analysis, especially in angle closure classification.

Multi-target domain adaptation with AS-OCT image poses two challenges. The first challenge is the domain discrepancies among multiple domains, which results from different imaging devices, imaging conditions, and preprocessing techniques. As shown in Fig. 1, the AS-OCT images from different domains may differ in terms of the crystalline lens [4], image noises [1] and image resolutions. As a result, directly applying the model trained on the source domain tends to perform poorly on the multi-target domains. The second challenge is how to capture both local and global information of AS-OCT images for angle closure classification. In practice, ophthalmologists classify angle closure based on both local information (*e.g.,* anterior chamber angle (ACA) and iris curvature) and global information (*e.g.,* anterior chamber width and cornea structure) [6]. However, most deep neural networks (DNNs) tend to learn global features without paying attention to fine-grained information of the images, *e.g.,* ACA in AS-OCT images. Since the measurement of small regions (*e.g.,* trabecular iris angle and angle opening distance [6]) in ACA is highly important for this task, it is difficult for existing DNN models to effectively classify angle closure. As a result, most existing DNN-based unsupervised domain adaptation methods may fail to handle such a challenging task.

To handle the two challenges, we explore multi-domain adversarial learning and multi-scale feature extraction for angle closure classification. Specifically, to alleviate the domain discrepancies, we resort to domain adversarial learning, which is one of the mainstream paradigms for pair-wise unsupervised domain adaptation [38, 40]. Meanwhile, since there exists low contrast and vast noise in local regions of AS-OCT images (*e.g.,* trabecular iris angle and angle opening distance [6]), capturing fine-grained information with a fixed scale of neural filter is intractable. Therefore, we propose to explore multi-scale convolutional filters for promoting fine-grained representation extraction [7, 37]. Following these ideas, we present a novel Multi-scale Multi-target Domain Adversarial Network (M2DAN). In M2DAN, a new multi-scale module is developed to capture global and local information of AS-OCT images. Such a module consists of three convolutional branches with different filter sizes, which are used to extract multi-scale features. Meanwhile, M2DAN conducts multi-domain adversarial learning for each convolutional branch separately, so that it can learn domain-invariant features at different scales. Based on the extracted multi-scale domain-invariant features, the classifier trained on the source domain is able to conduct angle closure classification effectively on the multiple target domains.

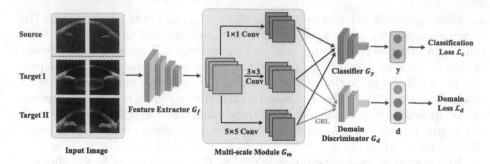

**Fig. 2.** The scheme of Multi-scale Multi-target Domain Adversarial Network. Specifically, the multi-scale module consists of three convolutional branches with different filter sizes. Then, we use a shared domain discriminator to distinguish features from each branch separately for scale-aware domain adaptation, while we concatenate all features for classification. We implement domain adversarial training through Gradient Reverse Layer (GRL) [8].

We summarize the main contributions of this paper as follows:

- We propose a novel Multi-scale Multi-target Domain Adversarial Network for angle closure classification. By exploring a new multi-scale scheme and multi-domain adversarial learning, the proposed method is able to learn multi-scale domain-invariant features and effectively classify the angle closure.
- To the best of our knowledge, our work is the first to study multi-target domain adaptation for angle closure classification, which enhances the applications of deep learning in early detection and precise diagnosis for angle closure glaucoma.
- Extensive experiments demonstrate the effectiveness and superiority of the proposed method on a real-world anterior segment optical coherence tomography dataset with three domains.

## 2   Method

### 2.1   Problem Definition

We consider two practical challenges in AS-OCT based angle closure classification task: 1) the distribution changes of different domains (*e.g.*, devices); 2) the lack of labeled data for multiple domains. We tackle them by adapting a model learned on a source domain to $B$ target domains. In total we consider $(B+1)$ domains. For convenience, we introduce a domain label vector $\mathbf{d}_i \in \{0,1\}^{B+1}$ to indicate the domain labels of each sample. Then, let $\mathcal{D}_s = \{\mathbf{x}_i, \mathbf{y}_i, \mathbf{d}_i\}_{i=1}^{n_s}$ be the source domain data and $\mathcal{D}_t = \{\mathbf{x}_j, \mathbf{d}_j\}_{j=1}^{n_t}$ be the unlabeled data collected from $B$ target domains, where $\mathbf{y}_i$ denotes the class label of source domain data, and $n_s$ and $n_t$ denote the numbers of samples in $\mathcal{D}_s$ and $\mathcal{D}_t$, respectively.

Note that given a specific task, all domains share the same label space, but only the source domain data are labeled. The primary goal of this paper is to learn a well-performed deep neural network for multiple target domains, using both labeled source samples and unlabeled target samples. Unfortunately, since we have no labeled target data, how to conduct effective domain adaptation to multiple target domains is very challenging.

## 2.2 Multi-scale Multi-target Domain Adversarial Network

To enforce effective domain adaptation from the source domain $\mathcal{D}_s$ to the multiple target domain $\mathcal{D}_t$, we address the challenges from two aspects: (1) we seek to alleviate the domain discrepancies among multiple domains with domain adversarial learning; (2) Note that beyond the distribution changes, the $B + 1$ domains also share some intrinsic properties as they are dealing with the same task, *e.g.*, angle closure classification. We thus exploit both local and global information of AS-OCT images for angle closure classification with a multi-scale scheme. Given the above motivations, we propose a multi-scale multi-target domain adversarial network (M2DAN). As shown in Fig. 2, M2DAN consists of four components: a feature extractor $G_f$ and a multi-scale module $G_m$, a classifier $G_y$ for task prediction, and a domain discriminator $G_d$ to discriminate multi-scale features of images from different domains. To be specific, the multi-scale module $G_m$ is developed to extract features with multi-scale information.

In the angle closure classification, both local information ( *e.g.*, iris curvature and angle opening distance ) and global information ( *e.g.*, cornea structure [7]) plays important roles. The local information can be used to obtain several major clinical measurements for clinical diagnosis [24], while the global cornea structure offers various cues associated with risk factors for angle-closure glaucoma [7]. To capture them, the multi-scale module consists of three parallel convolutional branches with different filter sizes ( *i.e.*, $1 \times 1$, $3 \times 3$ and $5 \times 5$) to extract features from different scales. Here, all feature maps have the same spatial size through padding. We then send the feature maps at different scales into the domain discriminator separately for multiple domain adaptation, while we concatenate all these features for classification. In this way, we are able to extract domain-invariant features with multi-scale information, which helps the classifier to make more accurate predictions on the target domains.

To train M2DAN, we employ the following two strategies. First, inspired by most domain adaptation methods [3, 26, 38], we adopt domain adversarial learning to enforce the multi-scale feature extractor $G_m \circ G_f$ to capture multi-scale domain-invariant features, so that the discrepancy among multiple domains is minimized. To be specific, a shared domain discriminator $G_d$ is trained to adequately distinguish features of images from different domains by minimizing a domain loss $\mathcal{L}_d$. Meanwhile, $G_m \circ G_f$ is trained to confuse the domain discriminator by maximizing $\mathcal{L}_d$. Note that, domain adversarial learning is applied to each branch of the multi-scale module separately for learning multi-scale domain-invariant features. Second, we train the backbone network $(G_f, G_m, G_y)$ via a classification loss $\mathcal{L}_c$ to make it imbalance-aware and discriminative. The overall training of M2DAN is to solve the following problem:

$$\min_{\theta_f, \theta_m, \theta_y} \max_{\theta_d} \underbrace{-\alpha \mathcal{L}_d(\theta_f, \theta_m, \theta_d)}_{\text{domain loss}} + \underbrace{\lambda \mathcal{L}_c(\theta_f, \theta_m, \theta_y)}_{\text{classification loss}} \qquad (1)$$

where $\theta_f, \theta_m, \theta_y, \theta_d$ indicate the parameters of $G_f$, $G_m$, $G_y$ and $G_d$, respectively. Moreover, $\alpha$ and $\lambda$ denote the trade-off parameters for different losses. In next sections, we will detail the domain loss $\mathcal{L}_d$ and the classification loss $\mathcal{L}_c$.

## 2.3  Domain Loss for Multi-target Domain Adaptation

Diverse imaging devices and techniques intrinsically result in discrepancies among image domains. In practice, doctors often need to classify angle closure based on AS-OCT images from multiple target domains. However, existing unsupervised domain adaptation for medical images mainly focuses on two domains and cannot handle this practical problem.

To solve this, inspired by multi-class classification via cross-entropy, we conduct multi-target domain adaptation via a multi-domain loss as follows:

$$\mathcal{L}_d(\theta_f, \theta_m, \theta_d) = -\frac{1}{n} \sum_{i=1}^{n} \mathbf{d}_i^\top \log(\hat{\mathbf{d}}_i), \qquad (2)$$

where $\hat{\mathbf{d}}_i = G_d(G_m(G_f(\mathbf{x}_i)))$ denotes the prediction of the domain discriminator $w.r.t.$ $\mathbf{x}_i$, and $n$ denotes the overall number of data. Moreover, since different branches in the multi-scale module share the same domain discriminator, we use the same domain loss for them without explicitly mentioning branches. In this way, M2DAN is able to capture domain-invariant features at different scales.

## 2.4  Classification Loss for Angle Closure Classification

For the task of angle closure classification, we can adopt any classification losses to train the network, $e.g.$, cross-entropy. Nevertheless, since the class-imbalanced issue commonly exist in this task, we use the focal loss [17] as follows:

$$\mathcal{L}_{fo}(\theta_f, \theta_m, \theta_y) = -\frac{1}{n_s} \sum_{i=1}^{n_s} \mathbf{y}_i^\top \left((1 - \hat{\mathbf{y}}_i)^\gamma \odot \log(\hat{\mathbf{y}}_i)\right), \qquad (3)$$

where $\hat{\mathbf{y}}_i = G_y(G_m(G_f(\mathbf{x}_i))$ denotes the prediction of the classifier $w.r.t.$ $\mathbf{x}_i$, and $n_s$ denotes the number of **labeled source samples**. Moreover, $\odot$ denotes the element-wise product and $\gamma$ is hyperparameter in focal loss. Note that, the focal loss is a widely-used loss for class imbalance issue [38,39]. To further improve the classification performance, we encourage high-density compactness of intra-class samples and low-density separation of inter-class samples for all domains via entropy minimization [21]:

$$\mathcal{L}_{en}(\theta_f, \theta_m, \theta_y) = -\frac{1}{n_t + n_s} \sum_{i=1}^{n_t + n_s} \hat{\mathbf{y}}_i^\top \log(\hat{\mathbf{y}}_i). \qquad (4)$$

**Table 1.** Statistics of the AS-OCT dataset.

| Domain | Data | Country | Device | Training set | | | Test set | | |
|--------|------|---------|--------|--------|-------|--------|---------|-------|--------|
| | | | | #Narrow | #Open | #Total | #Narrow | #Open | #Total |
| Source | AS-I | China | CASIA-I | 3,006 | 6,024 | 9,030 | 790 | 1412 | 2,202 |
| Target I | AS-II | China | CASIA-II | 62 | 464 | 526 | 64 | 464 | 526 |
| Target II | AS-III | Singapore | CASIA-I | 416 | 1,406 | 1,822 | 418 | 1,406 | 1,824 |

Based on the above, we summarize the overall classification loss $\mathcal{L}_c$ as follows:

$$\mathcal{L}_c(\theta_f, \theta_m, \theta_y) = \mathcal{L}_{fo}(\theta_f, \theta_m, \theta_y) + \eta \mathcal{L}_{en}(\theta_f, \theta_m, \theta_y), \tag{5}$$

where $\eta$ is a hyperparameter to trade-off between the two losses.

## 3  Experiments

**Dataset.** In this paper, we conduct our experiments on one anterior segment optical coherence tomography (AS-OCT) dataset, provided by Zhongshan Ophthalmic Center. Such a dataset consists of a well-labeled source domain (**AS-I**) and two unlabeled target domains (**AS-II** and **AS-III**). The data from different domains are acquired from different OCT devices and/or different countries. The statistics of the dataset are shown in Table 1.

**Compared Methods.** We compare our proposed M2DAN with one baseline (**Source-only**), several state-of-the-art unsupervised domain adaptation methods (**DSN** [3], **DANN** [8], **DMAN** [38] and **ToAlign** [35]), and one advanced multi-target domain adaptation methods for natural images (**MTDA** [11]). The baseline Source-only is trained only on the labeled source domain.

**Implementation Details.** We implement our proposed method based on PyTorch [25]. For a fair comparison, we use res2net [9] as the feature extractor in all considered methods. (one can also use other DNN models, *e.g.*, ResNet [14] and MobileNetV2 [30]). For all compared methods, we keep the same hyperparameters as the original paper. Note that we conduct pair-wise domain adaptation for each target domain separately when implementing unsupervised domain adaptation methods. For M2DAN, both classifier and domain discriminator consist of three fully connected layers. In the training process, we use an SGD optimizer with a learning rate of 0.001 to train the network. For the trade-off parameters, we set $\lambda = 1.0$, $\eta = 0.1$ and $\alpha = 0.03$ through cross-validation. Following [17], we set $\gamma = 2.0$ for the focal loss. Following [6], we cut the images in half as the input of the network.

### 3.1  Comparisons with State-of-the-Art Methods

We compare our M2DAN with several state-of-the-art methods in terms of two metrics, *i.e.*, accuracy and AUC [20]. From Table 2, all domain adaptation methods perform better than Source-only, which verifies the contribution of unsupervised domain adaptation. Moreover, our proposed M2DAN outperforms all

**Table 2.** Comparisons of six methods in accuracy and AUC on two target domains.

| Method | AS-II | | AS-III | | Mean acc. | Mean AUC |
|---|---|---|---|---|---|---|
| | Acc. | AUC | Acc. | AUC | | |
| Source-only | 0.638 | 0.834 | 0.737 | 0.911 | 0.688 | 0.872 |
| DANN [8] | 0.723 | 0.866 | 0.836 | 0.912 | 0.780 | 0.889 |
| DSN [3] | 0.762 | 0.888 | 0.848 | 0.915 | 0.805 | 0.901 |
| DMAN [38] | 0.786 | 0.906 | 0.834 | 0.922 | 0.810 | 0.914 |
| DANN+ToAlign [35] | 0.842 | 0.685 | 0.688 | 0.607 | 0.765 | 0.646 |
| MTDA [11] | 0.667 | 0.791 | 0.735 | 0.806 | 0.701 | 0.799 |
| M2DAN (ours) | **0.856** | **0.914** | **0.869** | **0.928** | **0.862** | **0.921** |

**Table 3.** Effect of the filter size in the multi-scale module. The variant M2DAN-S$k$ represents the convolutional layers in all three branches of the multi-scale module use the same filter size $k$, where $k = 1, 3, 5$.

| Method | AS II | | AS III | | Mean acc. | Mean AUC |
|---|---|---|---|---|---|---|
| | Acc. | AUC | Acc. | AUC | | |
| M2DAN-S1 | 0.737 | 0.847 | 0.807 | 0.909 | 0.772 | 0.878 |
| M2DAN-S3 | 0.756 | 0.913 | 0.748 | 0.916 | 0.752 | 0.914 |
| M2DAN-S5 | 0.757 | 0.902 | 0.792 | 0.921 | 0.775 | 0.914 |
| M2DAN | **0.856** | **0.914** | **0.869** | **0.928** | **0.862** | **0.921** |

pair-wise unsupervised domain adaptation methods (*i.e.,* DSN, DANN, DMAN and DANN+ToAlign). The result indicates that those pair-wise domain adaptation methods may fail to alleviate the discrepancies among multiple domains since they focus on pair-wise adaptation and cannot capture correlation among domains effectively. In addition, M2DAN also outperforms MTDA in terms of both metrics, which demonstrates the superiority of our proposed method in handling multi-target domain adaptation for angle closure classification. In M2DAN, the multi-scale scheme helps to extract multi-scale domain-invariant features of AS-OCT images for angle closure classification. Note that the performance of MTDA is worse than pair-wise domain adaptation methods. Such poor performance of MTDA results from the poor reconstruction which includes a lot of noise for fine-grained anterior chamber angle in AS-OCT images.

## 3.2    Ablation Studies

**The Effectiveness of Multi-scale Module.** To verify the effectiveness of the proposed multi-scale module, we compare our method with three variants, namely **M2DAN-S1**, **M2DAN-S3** and **M2DAN-S5**. The variant **M2DAN-S$k$** uses the same filter size $k$ in all three branches of convolutional layers in the multi-scale module. In this case, the feature maps in each variant are extracted at the same scale. From Table 3, M2DAN achieves better performance than all three

**Table 4.** Ablation study for the losses (*i.e.*, $\mathcal{L}_{fo}$, $\mathcal{L}_d$ and $\mathcal{L}_{en}$). Note that $\mathcal{L}_{ce}$ denotes the cross-entropy loss for angle closure classification.

| Backbone | $\mathcal{L}_{ce}$ | $\mathcal{L}_{fo}$ | $\mathcal{L}_d$ | $\mathcal{L}_{en}$ | AS II | | AS III | | Mean acc. | Mean AUC |
|---|---|---|---|---|---|---|---|---|---|---|
| | | | | | Acc. | AUC | Acc. | AUC | | |
| ✓ | ✓ | | | | 0.784 | 0.826 | 0.780 | 0.903 | 0.782 | 0.865 |
| ✓ | | ✓ | | | 0.828 | 0.843 | 0.814 | 0.894 | 0.821 | 0.868 |
| ✓ | | ✓ | ✓ | | 0.856 | 0.876 | 0.841 | 0.916 | 0.848 | 0.896 |
| ✓ | | ✓ | ✓ | ✓ | **0.856** | **0.914** | **0.869** | **0.928** | **0.862** | **0.921** |

**Table 5.** Influence of the trade-off parameter $\alpha$ on AUC performance of our method. The value of $\alpha$ is selected among $[0.0003, 0.003, 0.03, 0.3]$, while fixing other parameters.

| $\alpha$ | AS-II | AS-III | Mean AUC |
|---|---|---|---|
| $3e-04$ | 0.828 | 0.910 | 0.869 |
| $3e-03$ | 0.909 | 0.892 | 0.901 |
| $3e-02$ | **0.914** | **0.928** | **0.921** |
| $3e-01$ | 0.813 | 0.843 | 0.828 |

**Table 6.** Influence of the trade-off parameter $\eta$ on AUC performance of our method. The value of $\eta$ is selected among $[0.001, 0.01, 0.1, 1]$, while fixing other parameters.

| $\eta$ | AS-II | AS-III | Mean AUC |
|---|---|---|---|
| $1e-03$ | 0.791 | 0.871 | 0.831 |
| $1e-02$ | 0.825 | 0.876 | 0.851 |
| $1e-01$ | **0.914** | **0.928** | **0.921** |
| $1$ | 0.884 | 0.922 | 0.903 |

variants in terms of two target domains. The results demonstrate the superiority of the proposed multi-scale module.

**Ablation Studies on Difference Losses.** To investigate the effect of all losses ($\mathcal{L}_{fo}$, $\mathcal{L}_d$ and $\mathcal{L}_{en}$), we evaluate the model optimized by different losses. From Table 4, our method with $\mathcal{L}_{fo}$ performs better than that with $\mathcal{L}_{ce}$, verifying that the focal loss helps to handle the class-imbalanced issue. When introducing $\mathcal{L}_d$, the performance improves a lot, which indicates that such a loss succeeds in alleviating domain discrepancies among domains. By combining all the losses, we obtain the best result. Such a result demonstrates that encouraging high-density compactness of intra-class samples and low-density separation of inter-class samples further facilitates the classification of angle closure.

### 3.3 Influence of Hyper-parameter

In this section, we investigate the impact of the hyper-parameters $\alpha$, $\eta$ and $\lambda$. We evaluate one parameter a time while fixing other parameters. As shown

**Table 7.** Influence of the trade-off parameter $\lambda$ on AUC performance of our method. The value of $\lambda$ is selected among [0.001, 0.01, 0.1, 1], while fixing other parameters.

| $\lambda$ | AS-II | AS-III | Mean AUC |
|---|---|---|---|
| $1e-03$ | 0.663 | 0.671 | 0.667 |
| $1e-02$ | 0.709 | 0.647 | 0.678 |
| $1e-01$ | 0.659 | 0.815 | 0.737 |
| 1 | **0.914** | **0.928** | **0.921** |

in Tables 5, 6 and 7, our method achieves the best performance when setting $\alpha = 0.03$, $\eta = 0.1$ and $\lambda = 1$. To some extent, our method is non-sensitive to hyper-parameters. Moreover, it is crucial to set a reasonable classification loss weight which helps to classify angle closure effectively.

## 4   Conclusion

In this paper, we have proposed a novel Multi-scale Multi-target Domain Adversarial Network (M2DAN) for angle closure classification. M2DAN aims to transfer a deep model learned on one labeled source domain to multiple unlabeled target domains. To be specific, we devise a multi-scale module to extract features regarding both local and global information. By performing multi-domain adversarial learning at different scales, M2DAN is able to extract domain-invariant features and effectively classify angle closure in multiple target domains. Extensive experiments demonstrate the effectiveness of our proposed method.

**Acknowledgments.** This work was partially supported by Key-Area Research and Development Program Guangdong Province 2019B010155001, Key Realm R&D Program of Guangzhou (202007030007), National Natural Science Foundation of China (NS-FC) 62072190 and Program for Guangdong Introducing Innovative and Enterpreneurial Teams 2017ZT07X183.

## References

1. Azzeh, J., Zahran, B., Alqadi, Z.: Salt and pepper noise: effects and removal. JOIV: Int. J. Inform. Vis. **2**(4), 252–256 (2018)
2. Benaim, S., Wolf, L.: One-sided unsupervised domain mapping. In: Advances in Neural Information Processing Systems, pp. 752–762 (2017)
3. Bousmalis, K., Trigeorgis, G., et al.: Domain separation networks. In: Advances in Neural Information Processing Systems, pp. 343–351 (2016)
4. Dubbelman, M., Van der Heijde, G., et al.: Change in shape of the aging human crystalline lens with accommodation. Vision. Res. **45**(1), 117–132 (2005)
5. Fu, H., Li, F., Sun, X., et al.: Age challenge: angle closure glaucoma evaluation in anterior segment optical coherence tomography. Med. Image Anal. **66**, 101798 (2020)

6. Fu, H., Xu, Y., Lin, S., et al.: Segmentation and quantification for angle-closure glaucoma assessment in anterior segment oct. IEEE Trans. Med. Imaging **36**(9), 1930–1938 (2017)
7. Fu, H., et al.: Multi-context deep network for angle-closure glaucoma screening in anterior segment OCT. In: Frangi, A.F., Schnabel, J.A., Davatzikos, C., Alberola-López, C., Fichtinger, G. (eds.) MICCAI 2018. LNCS, vol. 11071, pp. 356–363. Springer, Cham (2018). https://doi.org/10.1007/978-3-030-00934-2_40
8. Ganin, Y., Lempitsky, V.: Unsupervised domain adaptation by backpropagation. arXiv preprint arXiv:1409.7495 (2014)
9. Gao, S., Cheng, M.M., Zhao, K., et al.: Res2net: a new multi-scale backbone architecture. IEEE Trans. Pattern Anal. Mach. Intell. **43**, 652–662 (2019)
10. Ghafoorian, M., et al.: Transfer learning for domain adaptation in MRI: application in brain lesion segmentation. In: Descoteaux, M., Maier-Hein, L., Franz, A., Jannin, P., Collins, D.L., Duchesne, S. (eds.) MICCAI 2017. LNCS, vol. 10435, pp. 516–524. Springer, Cham (2017). https://doi.org/10.1007/978-3-319-66179-7_59
11. Gholami, B., Sahu, P., Rudovic, O., et al.: Unsupervised multi-target domain adaptation: an information theoretic approach. IEEE Trans. Image Process. **29**, 3993–4002 (2020)
12. Hao, H., Zhao, Y., Yan, Q., et al.: Angle-closure assessment in anterior segment oct images via deep learning. Med. Image Anal. **69**, 101956 (2021)
13. Hao, J., Li, F., Hao, H., et al.: Hybrid variation-aware network for angle-closure assessment in as-OCT. IEEE Trans. Med. Imaging **41**, 254–265 (2021)
14. He, K., Zhang, X., Ren, S., Sun, J.: Deep residual learning for image recognition. In: Proceedings of the IEEE Conference on Computer Vision and Pattern Recognition, pp. 770–778 (2016)
15. Leung, C.K., Weinreb, R.: Anterior chamber angle imaging with optical coherence tomography. Eye **25**(3), 261–267 (2011)
16. Lin, H., Zhang, Y., Qiu, Z., et al.: Prototype-guided continual adaptation for class-incremental unsupervised domain adaptation. In: European Conference on Computer Vision (2022)
17. Lin, T.Y., Goyal, P., Girshick, R., et al.: Focal loss for dense object detection. In: Proceedings of the IEEE International Conference on Computer Vision, pp. 2980–2988 (2017)
18. Litjens, G., Kooi, T., Bejnordi, B.E., et al.: A survey on deep learning in medical image analysis. Med. Image Anal. **42**, 60–88 (2017)
19. Liu, Y., Du, X.: DUDA: deep unsupervised domain adaptation learning for multi-sequence cardiac MR image segmentation. In: Peng, Y., et al. (eds.) PRCV 2020. LNCS, vol. 12305, pp. 503–515. Springer, Cham (2020). https://doi.org/10.1007/978-3-030-60633-6_42
20. Lobo, J.M., Jiménez-Valverde, A., Real, R.: AUC: a misleading measure of the performance of predictive distribution models. Glob. Ecol. Biogeogr. **17**(2), 145–151 (2008)
21. Mangin, J.F.: Entropy minimization for automatic correction of intensity nonuniformity. In: Proceedings IEEE Workshop on Mathematical Methods in Biomedical Image Analysis. MMBIA-2000 (Cat. No. PR00737), pp. 162–169. IEEE (2000)
22. Niu, S., Wu, J., Zhang, Y., et al.: Efficient test-time model adaptation without forgetting. In: International Conference on Machine Learning (2022)
23. Niwas, S.I., Lin, W., Bai, X., et al.: Automated anterior segment oct image analysis for angle closure glaucoma mechanisms classification. Comput. Methods Programs Biomed. **130**, 65–75 (2016)

24. Nongpiur, M.E., Haaland, B.A., Friedman, D.S., et al.: Classification algorithms based on anterior segment optical coherence tomography measurements for detection of angle closure. Ophthalmology **120**(1), 48–54 (2013)
25. Paszke, A., Gross, S., Massa, F., et al.: PyTorch: an imperative style, high-performance deep learning library. In: Advances in Neural Information Processing Systems, pp. 8024–8035 (2019)
26. Peng, X., Huang, Z., Sun, X., Saenko, K.: Domain agnostic learning with disentangled representations. arXiv preprint arXiv:1904.12347 (2019)
27. Qiu, Z., Zhang, Y., Lin, H., et al.: Source-free domain adaptation via avatar prototype generation and adaptation. In: International Joint Conference on Artificial Intelligence (2021)
28. Quigley, H.A., Broman, A.T.: The number of people with glaucoma worldwide in 2010 and 2020. Br. J. Ophthalmol. **90**(3), 262–267 (2006)
29. Ren, J., Hacihaliloglu, I., Singer, E.A., Foran, D.J., Qi, X.: Adversarial domain adaptation for classification of prostate histopathology whole-slide images. In: Frangi, A.F., Schnabel, J.A., Davatzikos, C., Alberola-López, C., Fichtinger, G. (eds.) MICCAI 2018. LNCS, vol. 11071, pp. 201–209. Springer, Cham (2018). https://doi.org/10.1007/978-3-030-00934-2_23
30. Sandler, M., Howard, A., Zhu, M., et al.: MobileNetV 2: inverted residuals and linear bottlenecks. In: Proceedings of the IEEE Conference on Computer Vision and Pattern Recognition, pp. 4510–4520 (2018)
31. Thylefors, B., Negrel, A., Pararajasegaram, R., Dadzie, K.: Global data on blindness. Bull. World Health Organ. **73**(1), 115 (1995)
32. Tzeng, E., Hoffman, J., Saenko, K., Darrell, T.: Adversarial discriminative domain adaptation. In: Proceedings of the IEEE Conference on Computer Vision and Pattern Recognition, pp. 7167–7176 (2017)
33. Tzeng, E., Hoffman, J., Zhang, N., et al.: Deep domain confusion: maximizing for domain invariance. arXiv preprint arXiv:1412.3474 (2014)
34. Wang, S., Zhang, L.: LSTN: latent subspace transfer network for unsupervised domain adaptation. In: Lai, J.-H., et al. (eds.) PRCV 2018. LNCS, vol. 11257, pp. 273–284. Springer, Cham (2018). https://doi.org/10.1007/978-3-030-03335-4_24
35. Wei, G., Lan, C., Zeng, W., Chen, Z.: ToAlign: task-oriented alignment for unsupervised domain adaptation. In: NeurIPS (2021)
36. Yang, J., Dvornek, N.C., Zhang, F., et al.: Domain-agnostic learning with anatomy-consistent embedding for cross-modality liver segmentation. In: Proceedings of the IEEE International Conference on Computer Vision Workshops (2019)
37. Zhang, X., Luo, H., Fan, X., et al.: AlignedReID: surpassing human-level performance in person re-identification. arXiv preprint arXiv:1711.08184 (2017)
38. Zhang, Y., et al.: From whole slide imaging to microscopy: deep microscopy adaptation network for histopathology cancer image classification. In: Shen, D., et al. (eds.) MICCAI 2019. LNCS, vol. 11764, pp. 360–368. Springer, Cham (2019). https://doi.org/10.1007/978-3-030-32239-7_40
39. Zhang, Y., Kang, B., Hooi, B., et al.: Deep long-tailed learning: a survey. arXiv preprint arXiv:2110.04596 (2021)
40. Zhang, Y., Wei, Y., Wu, Q., et al.: Collaborative unsupervised domain adaptation for medical image diagnosis. IEEE Trans. Image Process. **29**, 7834–7844 (2020)
41. Zhou, J., Wu, F., Sun, Y., Wu, S., Yang, M., Jing, X.-Y.: Adversarial domain alignment feature similarity enhancement learning for unsupervised domain adaptation. In: Lin, Z., et al. (eds.) PRCV 2019. LNCS, vol. 11859, pp. 259–271. Springer, Cham (2019). https://doi.org/10.1007/978-3-030-31726-3_22

# Automatic Glottis Segmentation Method Based on Lightweight U-net

Xiangyu Huang[1], Junjie Deng[1], Xi Wang[2], Peiyun Zhuang[3], Lianfen Huang[1], and Caidan Zhao[1]([⊠])

[1] School of Informatics, Xiamen University, Xiamen, China
zcd@xmu.edu.cn
[2] School of Medicine, Xiamen University, Xiamen, China
[3] Department of Voice, Zhongshan Hospital, Xiamen, China

**Abstract.** U-net is one of the common segmentation frameworks in the field of medical semantic segmentation. By utilizing skip-connection and multi-scale feature fusion tricks, U-net shows excellent segmentation performance. However, traditional U-net architectures have a large number of parameters, which may make image processing slow. In this paper, a fast and effective glottis segmentation method based on a lightweight U-net is designed to solve the problem of throat glottis segmentation, which ensures the accuracy of the segmentation while taking into account the processing speed. We simplify the model structure and introduce a self-attention module to improve segmentation performance. Besides, we also propose a hybrid loss for glottis region segmentation. Compared with the mainstream segmentation networks such as U-net, PSPNET, Segnet, and NestedU-net, the total number of model parameters we design is less, and the proposed method can achieve higher dice score, mIoU, FWIoU, and mPA.

**Keywords:** Semantic segmentation · Convolutional neural network · Glottis segmentation

## 1 Introduction

The change of the glottis area is one of the crucial references for the diagnosis of throat-related diseases. With the help of high-speed photography equipment, doctors can observe the changes in the glottis area of the patient's throat in detail and then make predictions of related diseases according to the characteristics of the glottis area. For example, irregular changes in the glottis area may be caused by dysfunction of the patient's throat cartilage. When the curve of the glottis

This work was supported in part by the National Natural Science Foundation of China under Grant No. 61971368, in part by the Natural Science Foundation of Fujian Province of China No. 2019J01003, in part by the National Natural Science Foundation of China under Grant No. U20A20162, in part by the National Natural Science Foundation of China (grant number 61731012).

area is not zero, there is a certain probability that the patient's glottis is not entirely closed. At the current stage, doctors mostly make judgments based on the videos taken, which requires doctors to watch a lot of videos to give accurate results. It is time-consuming and labor-intensive. Therefore, this paper proposes a simple automatic segmentation convolutional neural network to efficiently and quickly segment out the glottis area so as to obtain the change characteristics of the throat glottis area more easily and quickly and realize the diagnosis task of assisting doctors.

In the early days, Chen [1] proposed a glottal region segmentation scheme combining thresholds, morphological operations, and region growing. Through image processing techniques such as global threshold processing, morphological binary calculation, and region generation, continuous segmentation results of the throat glottis region under high-speed video are achieved. Their experimental results show that it is feasible to segment the throat glottis and obtain the corresponding pathology of the patient according to the change in the glottis area. Amaia [2] designed an automatic glottis segmentation algorithm based on the Gabor filter. They calculated the gradient of the preprocess picture after gray equalization and then used prior medical knowledge to do threshold segmentation on the preprocess images. Compared with the region growing algorithm, which needs to calibrate the generated area manually, Amaia's algorithm is efficient and straightforward, indirectly showing that the automatic segmentation of the glottis is feasible. Arriola [3] also compared the proposed watershed automatic glottal segmentation algorithm with the other methods and further verified the application possibility of an automatic segmentation algorithm in the glottis. Badri [4] considers the inaccuracy of segmentation region positioning, uses a geodesic active contour model to locate the glottis region, and controls the evolution of the active contour according to the statistical distribution of the glottis region of the image to reduce the probability of wrong segmentation. Gloger [5] introduces Bayesian probability maps into the field of glottis segmentation and uses the special shape of the glottis region to construct an a priori model to improve the segmentation accuracy and speed.

Although traditional image processing algorithms, such as Gabor transform, region growing, watershed algorithm, etc., can achieve the segmentation task of the glottis, they are limited by the scene, and the segmentation accuracy fluctuates wildly. In recent years, due to the excellent image processing capabilities of deep learning algorithms, researchers have constructed a variety of segmentation networks to complete specific image segmentation tasks. FCN (Fully Convolutional Networks for Semantic Segmentation) proposed by Evan [6] is a milestone model of segmentation network. They designed a fully convolutional structure to extract the object information of the input picture. By building down-sampling and up-sampling modules, FCN achieves pixel-level object segmentation performance. However, down-sampling operations may cause the loss of detailed image information, and the U-net [7] network is proposed to solve this problem. U-net uses skip connections to alleviate the problem of information loss. And the skip connections have proved effective in recovering fine-grained details of the target objects. Segnet [8] is improved on the model structure of FCN. The maximum pooling operation of the encoder part records the position (index) of the maximum value and then realizes nonlinear upsampling through the corresponding pooling index so that there is no need to fit parameters in the upsampling stage. After upsampling, a sparse feature map is obtained, and then a dense feature map is obtained through convolution operation. The advantage of Segnet is that instead of saving the feature map of the entire encoder part, only the pooled index needs to be saved. Zhou [9] finds that U-Net directly concatenates coarse-grained feature maps from the decoder sub-network with semantic features and low-level fine-grained feature maps from the encoder sub-network, which creates a semantic gap. Therefore, they use the dense skip pathway technique to design the NestedU-net to segment the input picture from multiple feature scales, alleviating the semantic gap. Attention U-net [10] is a network based on the gate attention mechanism. Compared with the gate attention based on the global feature vector, the proposed attention gate can be easily integrated into the standard CNN (convolutional neural networks) architecture, such as the U-Net model, which has a small computational overhead, while improving the model sensitivity and prediction accuracy. PSPNet [11] adopts the pyramid pooling module to aggregate the context information of different regions, thereby improving the ability to obtain global information.

**Fig. 1.** Glottis pictures and ground truth of corresponding glottic segmentation area

Figure 1 shows part of the video pictures captured by high-speed photography video. The size of the area to be segmented varies widely, and it is difficult to train a neural network suitable for the segmentation of objects of different scales using traditional segmentation loss. Moreover, many segmentation models have a slow calculation speed and massive parameters, which cannot meet the task of fast throat image processing. Based on the above problems, this paper proposes a hybrid loss for glottis region segmentation, simplifies the traditional

U-net network, and introduces the self-attention mechanism module to improve segmentation performance and speed. Compared with the mainstream semantic segmentation algorithm, the proposed method has a faster processing speed and higher segmentation accuracy.

The contributions of this paper can be summarized as follows:

- We simplify the traditional U-net and introduce the self-attention mechanism module to design a framework for the glottis segmentation.
- We propose a hybrid loss for the glottis region segmentation with changeable scales to improve the segmentation model's performance.
- We propose a new dataset for fast glottis segmentation. And we demonstrate the effectiveness of the proposed glottis segmentation method, and experimental results show that our method achieves better performance on the proposed dataset compared with the mainstream segmentation algorithm.

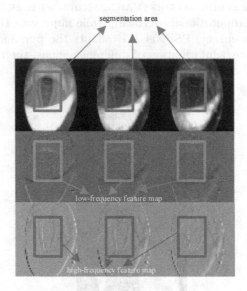

**Fig. 2.** Partial features of wavelet decomposition of throat glottis

## 2   Proposed Method

Before training the segmentation neural network, we usually need to manually label the segmentation data so that the constructed model can calculate the corresponding segmentation loss according to the labeled segmentation area and then update the network parameters through the backpropagation algorithm. The calculation formula of the entire segmentation model can be expressed as $f_{cnn}(x) = y$, where $x$ is the image to be segmented, $y$ is the output image after segmentation, and $f_{cnn}$ is the constructed semantic segmentation model. It is known that any picture contains high-frequency and low-frequency information, so we can think of the picture as being composed of the addition of a high-frequency feature map and a low-frequency feature map, from which we can get the following expression:

$$x = \sum_{i=1}^{N} x_i \tag{1}$$

In the above formula, $x$ is the input picture; $x_i$ is the feature map; $N$ is the total number of feature maps; A picture can be decomposed into the addition of different feature maps, and as can be seen from Fig. 2, the contribution of different feature maps to the region segmentation is different. For example, features with too much low-frequency information cannot be distinguished by obvious edge structures, which is not conducive to the final determination of the segmentation, and the feature maps rich in high-frequency information can clearly see the contour of the area to be segmented, making the algorithm network better determine the edge of the object. More generally in convolutional neural works, each convolution operation can get hundreds of feature maps and each feature map has a different importance for the final segmentation results, so we introduce the SENet [12] module. The module can be expressed by the following expression:

$$\begin{aligned} x_{\text{new}} &= \sum_{i=1}^{N} \alpha_i x_i \\ \text{s.t. } x &= \sum_{i=1}^{N} x_i \end{aligned} \tag{2}$$

By introducing a new learnable weight $\alpha_i$, the model can automatically learn the importance of different channel features so that the constructed CNN model achieves a better semantic segmentation result.

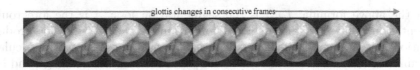

**Fig. 3.** Continuous frame glottis under high-speed photography video

In the throat high-speed photography video, the throat glottis is in the cycle of opening and closing, and the area of the throat glottis varies significantly with the movement state of the glottis. Figure 3 also shows the process of continuous movement of the glottis, and the area of the glottis to be divided presents a periodic change process. When using the pixel-level cross-entropy loss to calculate the segmentation area, the expression can be written as:

$$\begin{aligned} L_{CE} &= -\frac{1}{row*col} \sum_{i=0}^{row} \sum_{j=0}^{col} \sum_{c=0}^{1} g_{ijc} \log g_{ijc} \\ \text{s.t } \sum_{c=0}^{1} g_{ijc} &= 1, 0 \leq i \leq row, 0 \leq j \leq col \end{aligned} \tag{3}$$

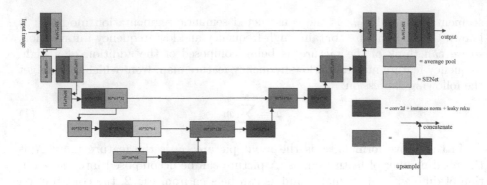

**Fig. 4.** Lightweight U-net

In the above formula, $L_{CE}$ is the segmentation loss, and *row* and *col* are the length and width of the segmented image; $g_{ijc}$ is the probability that the pixel in the i-th row and j-column belongs to the c-th category, and a pixel belongs to only one category; we define the background category as 0, and the foreground (glottis) category is 1. The glottis region accounts for a relatively small number of pixels in some frames, which makes the model still have a very low loss when dividing the entire input picture into the background, which is not conducive to the training of the model, causing the model to fall into an under-fitting situation. As shown in Fig. 3, the throat glottis area is less than the background area, and it is not feasible to use the cross-entropy loss for training. Therefore, some researchers have proposed to use dice loss to deal with the problem of small object segmentation. And the dice loss expressions can be written as:

$$L_{\text{dice}} = \frac{2 A \cap B|}{(|A| + |B|)} \tag{4}$$

In the above formula, $L_{dice}$ is the segmentation loss; $A$ is the foreground segmentation area; $B$ is the predicted foreground area; $\cap$ is the dot product operation; $\|$ is the sum of the matrix values; When dice loss is used to calculate the semantic segmentation loss, it does not pay attention to the background but pays too much attention to the foreground area, which increases the possibility of incorrect segmentation. Therefore, this paper combines the features of the throat region to propose a hybrid semantic segmentation loss. Its expression is as follows:

$$L_{hybrid} = \lambda_{\text{CE-focal}} * L_{\text{CE-focal}}\left(y_{\text{fore}}, x_{\text{fore}}\right) + L_{\text{CE-focal}}\left(y_{\text{back}}, x_{\text{back}}\right) \\ + L_{\text{dice}}\left(y_{\text{fore}}, x_{\text{fore}}\right) \tag{5}$$

where $\lambda_{\text{CE-focal}} = e^{\frac{|y_{\text{fore}}|+|y_{\text{back}}|}{3*|y_{\text{fore}}|}}$.

In the above formula, $x_{fore}$ is the output foreground area; $y_{fore}$ is the corresponding manually labeled foreground area; $x_{back}$ is the output background area;

$y_{back}$ is the corresponding manually labeled background area; $L_{hybrid}$ is the proposed hybrid loss; $L_{CE-focal}$ is the combination of cross-entropy loss and focal loss [13], which is used to solve the pixels that are difficult to segment and reduce the loss of pixels that are easy to segment. And $\lambda_{CE-focal}$ is a weighted weight we designed based on the ratio of background to foreground to highlight the foreground area to prevent the problem of being unable to effectively update the model caused by too few foreground pixels when calculating the loss. Besides, we also use dice loss to guide the small object segmentation.

## 3 Network Architecture, Training Setup and Datasets

### 3.1 Network Architecture and Training Setup

U-net is a convolutional neural network that shows great performance on biomedical image segmentation. But traditional U-net works with low efficiency, and it is not suitable for our task. To avoid it, we modify the architecture and decrease the number of convolutional layers. The details are illustrated in Fig. 4. The average pooling layer is used as the down-sample module, and its receptive field is 2 * 2; each convolution block is composed of a convolutional layer, instance normalization layer, and activation layer; the receptive field of each convolutional kernel is 3 * 3; In the down-sampling stage, the feature map is downsampled or skip-connected after passing through the SENet module; In the upsampling stage, the method of combining bilinear sampling and a convolutional layer is used to replace the deconvolutional layer to avoid checkboard artifacts. And we remove the activation layer in the final convolutional block to avoid the vanishing gradient problem during training. The optimization function is set as Adam with an initial learning rate of 1e–4. During the training process, the training set is randomly divided into some mini-batches with a batch size of 8.

### 3.2 Datasets

The high-speed glottis videos for training and testing were provided by the Department of the throat, Xiamen University Zhongshan Hospital. The frame rate of capture video is 4000, and the video resolution is 320 * 256. When the frame rate is too high, the difference between the pictures of adjacent frames is tiny. Therefore, we take one of the collected patient videos every 100 frames and obtain a total of 9700 high-speed photography pictures of 47 patients, of which 1700 are used for testing. Another 8000 images are used for training. As shown in Fig. 5, we acquired the glottis data in the glottis acquisition room of Xiamen Zhongshan Hospital and then used the MIT labelme software to label the data.

## 4 Experimental Performance Analysis

We use the same training set to train U-net [7], AttentionU-net [10], NestedU-net [9], Segnet [8], PSPNet [11] and FCN [6] semantic segmentation networks.

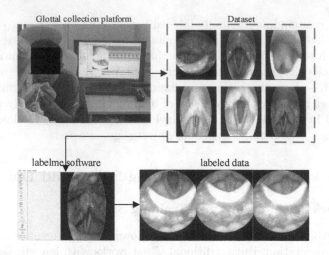

**Fig. 5.** Glottal data collection and label process

Then, we give a detailed performance analysis of different neural networks on the glottis segmentation test datasets and compare the complexity of different segmentation models.

### 4.1 Metrics

In order to evaluate the segmentation performance of the model, we use CPA (Class Pixel Accuray), mPA (mean Pixel Accuracy), mIoU (mean Intersection over Union), dice score, and FWIoU (Frequency Weighted Intersection over Union).

- $PA_1 = \text{background PA} = \frac{TP}{TP+FP}$
- $PA_2 = \text{foreground PA} = \frac{TN}{TN+FN}$
- $mPA = \frac{PA_1+PA_2}{2}$
- $mIoU = \frac{\left(\frac{TP}{TP+FP+FN} + \frac{TN}{TN+FN+FP}\right)}{2}$
- $FWIoU = \left[\frac{(TP+FN)}{(TP+FP+TN+FN)}\right] * \left[\frac{TP}{TP+FP+FN}\right]$
- $\text{dice score} = \frac{2|A \cap B|}{(|A|+|B|)}$

### 4.2 Comparison of Different Methods

Table 1 shows the performance comparison of different models in the segmentation task of throat glottis. "lightweight U-net + SENet + hybrid loss" denotes the segmentation algorithm proposed in this paper. We have achieved the best score in four of the five evaluation metrics. NestedU-net with the highest background PA scores has the lowest mPA, mIoU, FWIoU, and dice scores, which indirectly

**Table 1.** Comparison of proposed method and other methods. The best results are highlighted in bold.

| Algorithm | FWIoU | mPA | background PA | foreground PA | mIoU | dice score |
|---|---|---|---|---|---|---|
| lightweight U-net + SENet + hybrid loss | **0.9971** | **0.9421** | 0.9993 | **0.9063** | **0.9028** | **0.8813** |
| U-net [7] | 0.9952 | 0.8882 | 0.9996 | 0.7768 | 0.8693 | 0.8204 |
| Attention U-net [10] | 0.9971 | 0.9225 | 0.9994 | 0.7768 | 0.8924 | 0.8606 |
| NestedU-net [9] | 0.9742 | 0.7310 | **0.9999** | 0.4621 | 0.7310 | 0.5245 |
| Segnet [8] | 0.9960 | 0.8638 | 0.9998 | 0.7278 | 0.8508 | 0.7926 |
| FCN [6] | 0.9938 | 0.8263 | 0.9998 | 0.6529 | 0.8171 | 0.7345 |
| PSPNet [11] | 0.9964 | 0.8789 | 0.9997 | 0.7582 | 0.8629 | 0.8120 |

**Table 2.** Ablation experiments: using different losses and training block. The best results are highlighted in bold.

| Algorithm | FWIoU | mPA | background PA | foreground PA | mIoU | dice score |
|---|---|---|---|---|---|---|
| lightweight U-net + SENet + hybrid loss | **0.9971** | **0.9421** | 0.9993 | **0.9063** | **0.9028** | **0.8813** |
| lightweight U-net + SENet + ce | 0.9918 | 0.8148 | 0.9997 | 0.6299 | 0.8011 | 0.6994 |
| lightweight U-net + SENet + dice | 0.9961 | 0.9306 | 0.9993 | 0.8620 | 0.8843 | 0.8535 |
| lightweight U-net + hybrid loss | 0.9960 | 0.9360 | 0.9993 | 0.8727 | 0.8854 | 0.8561 |
| lightweight U-net + ce | 0.9876 | 0.7288 | **0.9999** | 0.4576 | 0.7231 | 0.5468 |
| lightweight U-net + dice | 0.9950 | 0.9030 | 0.9993 | 0.8066 | 0.8704 | 0.8322 |

shows that in small object segmentation, excessive attention to the background area may make the segmentation results worse. Figure 6 shows some visual segmentation results. The proposed algorithm has good segmentation results no matter whether the glottal area is large or small. For example, in the first row of test results in Fig. 6, the glottis area of the input picture is very small, and the existing methods can only effectively segment the upper half of the glottis. However, the smaller glottis area located in the lower half is erroneously determined as the background.

**Table 3.** Comparison of the complexity of different neural networks.

| Algorithm | params | FLOPs | MAdd | memory |
|---|---|---|---|---|
| lightweight U-net + SENet | 0.292M | 896.98M | 1.78G | 35.69 MB |
| lightweight U-net | 0.290M | 896.97M | 1.78G | 35.69 MB |
| U-net [7] | 31.527M | 59.59G | 120.45G | 489.62 MB |
| Attention U-net [10] | 34.878M | 81.89G | 166.36G | 749.68 MB |
| NestedU-net [9] | 36.629 | 83.20G | 344.94G | 847.19 MB |
| Segnet [8] | 18.818M | 36.51G | 72.92G | 384.38 MB |
| FCN [6] | 18.643M | 25.13G | 53.57G | 227.66 MB |
| PSPNet [11] | 27.566M | 49.82G | 99.59G | 257.70 MB |

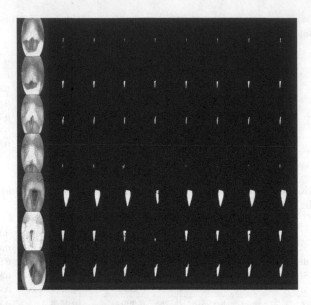

**Fig. 6.** Comparison of visualization results of glottis segmentation. From left to right are input image, ground truth, Attention U-net, FCN, NestedU-Net, PSPNet, Segnet, U-net, lightweight U-net+SENet+hybrid loss

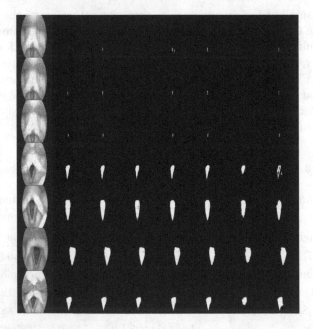

**Fig. 7.** Visualization results of ablation experiments. From left to right are input image, ground truth, lightweight U-net+SENet+hybrid loss, lightweight U-net+SENet+ce, lightweight U-net+SENet+ce, lightweight U-net+hybrid loss, lightweight U-net+ce, lightweight U-net+dice

As shown in Table 3, we also test detailed parameters about different models based on the Pytorch. "params" denotes the total number of parameters; "MAdd" indicates the theoretical amount of multiply-adds; "FLOPs" is the theoretical amount of floating point arithmetics; "memory" denotes memory usage; "lightweight U-net" represents the lightweight U-net designed in this paper, and "lightweight U-net+SENet" is a lightweight network that incorporates a self-attention module. The proposed algorithm reduces the depth of the convolutional feature map and at the same time uses a simple SENet to implement the self-attention mechanism without increasing too many parameters while improving performance. The traditional U-net not only requires a large amount of calculation but also performs poorly in segmentation performance.

## 4.3 Ablation Study

Figure 7 and Table 2 show the ablation experiment results using different segmentation losses on the proposed model. We fixed other training parameters and only changed the SENet module and training loss. For convenience, "ce" and "dice" denotes cross-entropy loss and dice loss, respectively, to train the proposed model. In the small object segmentation scenario, the performance of the model trained with cross-entropy loss is poor, and the target object cannot be segmented at all. After using the dice loss training model, although the segmentation effect has improved, compared with the proposed hybrid loss, it is still not good enough. Furthermore, after using the SENet module, whether the cross-entropy loss or the proposed hybrid is used, the segmentation performance of the throat glottis region has been further improved, which also shows the effectiveness of the SENet module.

## 5 Conclusion

In this paper, we simplify the traditional U-net network for the fast glottis segmentation task and add a self-attention mechanism module to improve the model segmentation performance without adding too many parameters. Furthermore, we propose a hybrid segmentation loss for segmentation of the glottis to further improve the model segmentation accuracy. According to the analysis of experimental results, the proposed algorithm performs better in model complexity and segmentation results. In future work, we will continue to study the segmentation network and segmentation loss for the throat glottis region segmentation task, improve model segmentation performance, and design more lightweight models.

## References

1. Chen, X., Bless, D., Yan, Y.: A segmentation scheme based on Rayleigh distribution model for extracting glottal waveform from high-speed laryngeal images. In: 2005 IEEE Engineering in Medicine and Biology 27th Annual Conference, pp. 6269–6272. IEEE (2005)

2. Mendez, A., Garcia, B., Ruiz, I., Iturricha, I.: Glottal area segmentation without initialization using Gabor filters. In: 2008 IEEE International Symposium on Signal Processing and Information Technology, pp. 18–22. IEEE (2008)

3. Gutiérrez-Arriola, J.M., Osma-Ruiz, V., Sáenz-Lechón, N., Godino-Llorente, J.I., Fraile, R., Arias-Londoño, J.D.: Objective measurements to evaluate glottal space segmentation from laryngeal images. In: 2012 Annual International Conference of the IEEE Engineering in Medicine and Biology Society, pp. 5396–5399. IEEE (2012)

4. Ammar-Badri, H., Benazza-Benyahia, A.: Statistical glottal segmentation of videoendoscopic images using geodesic active contours. In: 2014 1st International Conference on Advanced Technologies for Signal and Image Processing (ATSIP), pp. 198–203. IEEE (2014)

5. Gloger, O., Lehnert, B., Schrade, A., Völzke, H.: Fully automated glottis segmentation in endoscopic videos using local color and shape features of glottal regions. IEEE Trans. Biomed. Eng. **62**(3), 795–806 (2014)

6. Long, J., Shelhamer, E., Darrell, T.: Fully convolutional networks for semantic segmentation. In: Proceedings of the IEEE Conference on Computer Vision and Pattern Recognition, pp. 3431–3440. IEEE (2015)

7. Ronneberger, O., Fischer, P., Brox, T.: U-Net: convolutional networks for biomedical image segmentation. In: Navab, N., Hornegger, J., Wells, W.M., Frangi, A.F. (eds.) MICCAI 2015. LNCS, vol. 9351, pp. 234–241. Springer, Cham (2015). https://doi.org/10.1007/978-3-319-24574-4_28

8. Badrinarayanan, V., Kendall, A., Cipolla, R.: SegNet: a deep convolutional encoder-decoder architecture for image segmentation. IEEE Trans. Pattern Anal. Mach. Intell. **39**(12), 2481–2495 (2017)

9. Zhou, Z., Rahman Siddiquee, M.M., Tajbakhsh, N., Liang, J.: UNet++: a nested U-Net architecture for medical image segmentation. In: Stoyanov, D., et al. (eds.) DLMIA/ML-CDS -2018. LNCS, vol. 11045, pp. 3–11. Springer, Cham (2018). https://doi.org/10.1007/978-3-030-00889-5_1

10. Oktay, O., et al.: Attention U-Net: Learning where to look for the pancreas. arXiv preprint arXiv:1804.03999 (2018)

11. Zhao, H., Shi, J., Qi, X., Wang, X., Jia, J.: Pyramid scene parsing network. In: Proceedings of the IEEE Conference on Computer Vision and Pattern Recognition, pp. 2881–2890 (2017)

12. Hu, J., Shen, L., Sun, G.: Squeeze-and-excitation networks. In: Proceedings of the IEEE Conference on Computer Vision and Pattern Recognition, pp. 7132–7141 (2018)

13. Lin, T.Y., Goyal, P., Girshick, R., He, K., Dollár, P.: Focal loss for dense object detection. In: Proceedings of the IEEE International Conference on Computer Vision, pp. 2980–2988. IEEE (2017)

# Decouple U-Net: A Method for the Segmentation and Counting of Macrophages in Whole Slide Imaging

Zining Chen[1] ⓘ, Huifang Yang[2], Mengqi Gao[1], Xiao Hu[1], Yunpeng Li[1], and Lin Wang[3](✉) ⓘ

[1] Peking University School and Hospital of Stomatology, Beijing 100081, People's Republic of China
[2] Center of Digital Dentistry, Peking University School and Hospital of Stomatology, Beijing 100081, People's Republic of China
[3] Department of Oral and Maxillofacial Surgery, Peking University School and Hospital of Stomatology, Beijing 100081, People's Republic of China
linwang@bjmu.edu.cn

**Abstract.** At present, tumor-associated macrophages (TAMs) are receiving substantial attention owing to their potential as new therapeutic targets. However, the recognition and counting of TAMs remains an open problem. The results of existing algorithms and procedures are unsatisfactory and exhibit multiple defects such as blurred edges or a long inference time. In this work, we first propose an algorithm based on simple linear iterative clustering for the automatic selection of TAMs-dense hot spots in huge whole slide imaging. Subsequently, we present an end-to-end method based on U-Net for the segmentation and counting of pleomorphic TAMs. Edge detection is incorporated into the network architecture and nuclei information is used for verification. The experimental results demonstrate that our method achieved the highest F1-score and relatively good edge segmentation accuracy with an acceptable parameter size on a constructed dataset. The average counting results of our method also exhibited a comparatively small deviation, thereby demonstrating the possibility for clinical application.

The code and dataset are available at https://github.com/Meteorsc9/Decouple-U-Net.

**Keywords:** Computational pathology · Medical image segmentation · Whole slide imaging · Tumor-associated macrophages

## 1 Introduction

Tumor-associated macrophages (TAMs), which account for the largest fraction of infiltrating immune cells in tumor microenvironments, play vital roles in tumorigenesis, progression, angiogenesis, and metastasis [1, 2]. Numerous studies and clinical trials have

---

Z. Chen and H. Yang—These authors have contributed equally to this work.

© The Author(s), under exclusive license to Springer Nature Switzerland AG 2022
S. Yu et al. (Eds.): PRCV 2022, LNCS 13535, pp. 101–112, 2022.
https://doi.org/10.1007/978-3-031-18910-4_9

focused on TAMs owing to their significant value as a therapeutic target [2, 3]. Nevertheless, several issues remain, one of which is the improved recognition and counting of TAMs.

Pathological slides are considered as the gold standard for disease diagnosis. Immunohistochemistry (IHC) staining slides with specific antibodies (such as CD163) for identifying cell types are commonly used for the recognition of TAMs [4, 5]. However, to date, the counting of macrophages remains challenging owing to their pleomorphic and variable nature [6]. In clinical practice, well-trained pathologists select several high-magnification hot spots for recognition and counting [7]. On the one hand, the accurate selection of these fields of view is strongly dependent on the working experience of the pathologists, and on the other hand, the counting results are inevitably affected by subjective bias.

In recent years, digital pathology has been expanding with the increasing demands on precision medicine. Whole slide imaging (WSI), which is achieved by microscope scanning, has become popular in numerous fields owing to its high resolution and ease of retrospection [8]. However, it is very difficult to count all TAMs manually owing to the huge size of WSIs.

Based on WSIs, integration of algorithms that are derived from artificial intelligence enables researchers to explore additional information and reduce subjective bias [9]. Perfect segmentation is necessary for precise counting. Nevertheless, pleomorphic, cell-to-cell overlaps and adhesions are very common in the WSIs of TAMs. At present, no methods are available specifically for staining the nuclei of TAMs that can be applied on a large scale, which means that substantial difficulties remain in the segmentation and counting of TAMs.

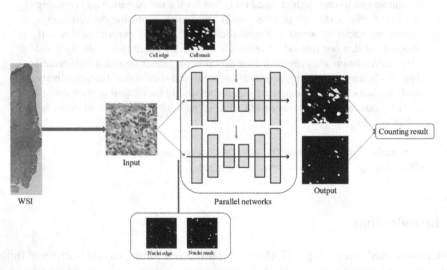

**Fig. 1.** Macrophage counting flowchart. Our method is a combination of direct segmentation and edge detection, which uses nuclei information for verification when cells overlap.

The main contributions of this study are as follows:

1. An algorithm based on simple linear iterative clustering (SLIC) [10] is proposed, which can automatically select TAMs-dense hot spots, or regions of interest (ROI) in huge WSIs. The algorithm is used for dataset construction and the subsequent clinical applications.
2. An improved convolutional neural network (CNN) architecture based on U-Net [11] is presented to achieve the precise semantic segmentation of TAMs in WSIs.
3. Accurate counting of TAMs is achieved using two parallel improved CNNs by explicitly incorporating the nuclei information into the training process of the neural network.

The overall pipeline is depicted in Fig. 1.

## 2  Related Works

Superpixel algorithms, the motivation for which is to use a single cluster center to represent a pre-existing complex region, involves dividing an image into different regions by considering similarity measures that are defined by color, spatial or other features. Therefore, superpixel algorithms are generally employed as a preprocessing procedure or for rough segmentation to reduce the computational complexity.

A fixed rectangular grid does not conform to the shape characteristics of ROIs. Thus, an algorithm such as the region proposal network (RPN) in Faster R-CNN [12] is required to obtain multiple candidate regions with a relatively acceptable inference time. Several methods have been developed to generate superpixels, such as the mean shift [13] and normalized cuts [14]. We selected SLIC, which meets all of the above requirements. In SLIC, RGB images are first converted into CIELab color space, and every pixel is represented by a 5-dimensional vector $(l, a, b, x, y)$, where $x$ and $y$ are the pixel coordinates. Subsequently, K-means clustering is applied to all vectors.

Semantic segmentation, the goal of which is to train a classifier that can classify every pixel in an input image, is a fundamental task in computer vision. A series of classic algorithms have been proposed in this field, including Otsu [15], Canny [16], Grab Cut [17], and SNAKE [18]. However, with the rise of the CNN, various CNN-based network architectures, such as FCN [19], ResNet [20], and Deeplab [21], have been proven to exhibit superior comprehensive performance. Among these models, U-Net has a simple structure with robust performance, and it is suitable for small sample problems. With various advantages, it has become the most commonly used baseline in medical image processing, and several variants such as U-Net++ [22] and Attention U-Net [23] have been proposed. However, the multiple max pooling operations in the U-Net structure make it insufficient for retaining adequate edge information. Although the skip connection partially alleviates this problem, the performance of U-Net is not satisfactory when highly overlapping TAMs are segmented. The edges of the cells in the segmentation results are blurred (Fig. 2), which makes it difficult to count the TAMs in the post-processing procedure.

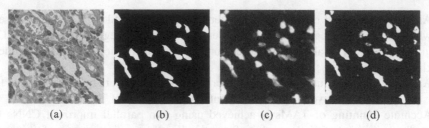

(a)                    (b)                    (c)                    (d)

**Fig. 2.** (a) Original images, (b) manually annotated masks, (c) U-Net segmentation result with blurred edges, and (d) Decouple U-Net segmentation result.

A common method for solving this problem is the use of atrous convolution [21] to achieve expansion of the receptive field without downsampling, such as DeeplabV3+ [24]; Another method is the explicitly integration of the edge information into the network structure. Related methods in this area include GSCNN [25], RPCNet [26], and DecoupleSegNet [27]. In our proposed Decouple U-Net, both types of methods are applied simultaneously.

In recent decades, there have been some works on the counting of macrophages. [28] uses transferred U-Net and [6] is based on Rudin-Osher-Fatemi (ROF) filter. However, macrophages in [28] are from mouses and cultured in vitro, while datasets in [6] mainly consist of fluorescent immunostained tissue sections. IHC slides, which are in color and can provide more comprehensive information, are routinely used for the diagnosis and grading of carcinoma patients. Therefore, effective counting method of TAMs in IHC slides is needed.

## 3 Methodology

### 3.1 Pre-processing

CD163 protein was selected as the M2 type TAMs in this study. Furthermore, IHC was routinely completed using the CD163 antibody from Abcam in the pathological slides of head and neck squamous cell carcinoma patients. Thereafter, we used microscopes produced by Hamamatsu to scan the pathological slides. And different magnifications could be selected with the generated NDPI files. In this work, we used 5× and 40×.

Owing to hardware limitations, we performed a sparse non-negative matrix factorization (SNMF)-based algorithm [29] for unsupervised structure-preserving stain separation on the 5× -sized WSI to exclude interference from other cells in the background. Subsequently, we applied SLIC to the Diaminobenzidine (DAB) channel images, which performed rough segmentation to generate the ROIs. We used the minimum circumscribed rectangle as the bounding box for ROIs with irregular shapes. Moreover, we converted the color image of the DAB channel into a grayscale image, and performed binarization. As the cytoplasm of TAMs are stained brown, they appeared predominantly black in the binarized images. Thereafter, we traversed all candidate ROIs, sorted them according to the proportion of black pixels, selected a certain number of ROIs with more black pixels, obtained their coordinates from the thumbnail, and cropped the corresponding region in the original 40× -sized image. The process is illustrated in Fig. 3.

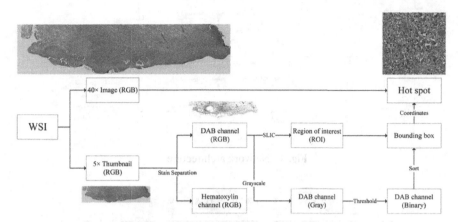

**Fig. 3.** Pre-processing procedure

During the dataset construction process, the generated ROIs were first cropped to the specified size, 512 × 512, and color normalization [29] was performed using the same algorithm based on SNMF to reduce the impact of staining differences on the training. Thereafter, the images were manually annotated by experienced pathologists to obtain ground-truth (GT) semantic labels, and the Canny algorithm was used to process the GT semantic labels to obtain GT binary edge masks.

Before the images were sent to the CNN, they were cropped to generate 256 × 256 patches with a 50% overlap between each patch, which enabled a larger batch size to be used. Data augmentation including rotation and mirroring was also applied.

## 3.2 Network Architecture

The proposed Decouple U-Net retains the U-shaped symmetrical structure of U-Net (Fig. 4), which consists of three sections: the residual block, body generation module and segmentation module. The residual block continuously processed the input images to achieve feature extraction. The body generation module [27] separated the edge and body of the images. The segmentation module integrated the features maps at different levels to obtain the final segmentation result.

Every residual block (Fig. 5) consisted of two cascade conv-batch normalization-ReLU structures, and shortcut connections from ResNet and the channel attention module from SENet [30] were added for more effective and robust feature extraction. Max pooling was performed between two residual blocks expect for block 4 and 5. And the 3 × 3 conv in block 4 and 5 was replaced with atrous convolution to reduce downsampling times.

The skip connections in the original U-Net are not designed to separate the various body and edge features effectively. Therefore, we incorporated the body generation

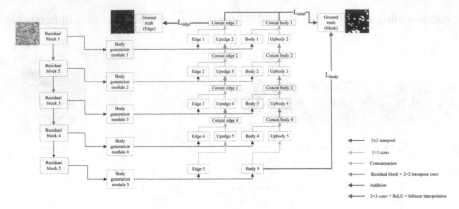

**Fig. 4.** Network architecture

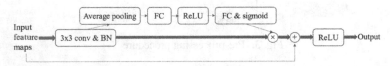

**Fig. 5.** Every residual block consisted of two cascade structures.

module from DecoupleSegNet into the existing skip-layer connections. We selected this method for two reasons. This module achieves results that are comparable to or better than those of other methods with less increased parameters, and the module can easily be plugged into U-Net without many adaptions. In the image, the edge part with high frequency is processed separately from the body part with low frequency, which is beneficial to the segmentation of cells with severe adhesion.

In the segmentation module, we integrated feature maps at the bottom of the network which contain more semantic information, with upper feature maps including more edge information layer by layer, and finally re-merged the edge and body parts simply in an additive manner to obtain the segmentation result.

### 3.3  Loss Function

Let $\hat{s}$ represent the GT semantic labels, $\hat{e}$ represent the GT binary edge masks, $s$ represent the final semantic labels, $e$ represent the edge segmentation result, and $b$ represent the body segmentation result. Our loss function can be defined as:

$$L = \lambda_1 L_{total}(s, \hat{s}) + \lambda_2 L_{edge1}(e, \hat{e}) + \lambda_3 L_{edge2}(e, \hat{e}) + \lambda_4 L_{body}(b, \hat{s}) \quad (1)$$

where $\lambda_1$, $\lambda_2$, $\lambda_3$, and $\lambda_4$ are four hyper parameters. In this study, $\lambda_1$, $\lambda_2$, and $\lambda_4$ were set to 1 and $\lambda_3$ was set to 0.01.

We used the focal loss [31] as the total loss, which can be defined as:

$$L_{focal} = -|\alpha(1 - s)^\gamma \hat{s} log(s) + (1 - \alpha)s^\gamma(1 - \hat{s})log(1 - s)| \quad (2)$$

where $\alpha$ is the percentage of non-zero pixels in the GT semantic labels and $\gamma$ was set to 2. In the edge loss, we used the focal loss as above for $L_{edge1}$ and the dice loss for $L_{edge2}$ to obtain a combined loss function. For the body loss, because $b$ was downsampled multiple times and contained few edge information, the boundaries relaxation loss [32] was used to alleviate over-fitting during training.

### 3.4 Parallel Networks

Although edge factors were considered in the network architecture and loss function, several overlapping cells still could not be separated correctly (Fig. 6), which had a negative impact on the counting results. Therefore, we decided to train a Decouple U-Net with TAMs as the segmentation object, and subsequently used it as a pre-trained model to train an additional Decouple U-Net to identify the nuclei of the TAMs.

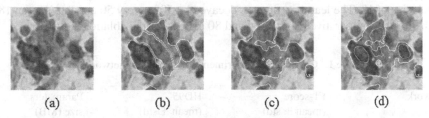

    (a)            (b)            (c)            (d)

**Fig. 6.** (a) Original image, (b) manually annotated masks, (c) incorrect cell segmentation result without parallel networks, and (d) cell segmentation result (white) and nuclei segmentation result (green). The nuclei segmentation network corrected the original results.

We recorded the size of all TAMs in the GT semantic labels. Only the "large" cells with a quantile of 90% or above in the first network segmentation results were subdivided to reduce the calculation amount. The number of inner nuclei was used to distinguish multiple overlapping cells from truly large cells, and the connected domain with an area of less than 250 pixels was removed to exclude noise. Finally, the connected domain analysis method was used to obtain the count result.

## 4    Experiments

### 4.1    Metrics

In this study, we used the F1-score and 95% Hausdorff distance (HD95) as evaluation metrics. The F1-score is defined as follows:

$$F1 = \frac{2TP}{2TP + FP + FN} \tag{3}$$

where TP means true positive, FP means false positive, and FN means false negative. The F1-score could measure the similarity between the GT labels and segmentation result.

Let $\hat{e}$ represent the GT binary edge masks, and $e_s$ denote for the edge segmentation that is calculated from the final semantic labels $s$. The HD95 can be defined as follows:

$$HD95 = P_{95}\left[h(\hat{e}, e_s), h(e_s, \hat{e})\right] \tag{4}$$

$$h(\hat{e}, e_s) = \max_{a \in \hat{e}}\{\min_{b \in e_s}\|a - b\|\} \tag{5}$$

where $\|\cdot\|$ is a type of distance measure, for which we selected the Euclidean distance. Therefore, the HD95 could measure the edge segmentation accuracy [33].

## 4.2  Comparative Experiment

Experiments were carried out on the dataset that we constructed, which consisted of 32 images for training and 8 images for testing. All networks were trained using same settings. We used Adam [34] as the optimizer with an initial learning rate of 1e−4 and a batch size of 12. The learning rate was decayed by 50% every 50 epochs. We ran 180 epochs for the comparative experiment and 80 epochs for the ablation experiment.

**Table 1.** Comparative experiment among several networks

| Network | F1-score (mean ± std) | HD95 (mean ± std) | Parameters size (MB) |
|---|---|---|---|
| U-Net | 0.8014 ± 0.0097 | 38.41 ± 0.8800 | 118.42 |
| U-Net++ | 0.8010 ± 0.0025 | 33.75 ± 1.7322 | 123.75 |
| Attention U-Net | 0.7987 ± 0.0023 | 40.22 ± 2.2249 | 137.99 |
| DeeplabV3+ (ResNet-101) | 0.7756 ± 0.0048 | 41.06 ± 1.9732 | 227.66 |
| GSCNN (ResNet-101) | 0.7917 ± 0.0018 | 29.42 ± 1.8319 | 226.81 |
| DecoupleSegNet (ResNet-101) | 0.7821 ± 0.0048 | 32.60 ± 1.8171 | 231.69 |
| Our method | **0.8136 ± 0.0020** | **33.30 ± 0.9792** | **172.51** |

The experimental results are displayed in Table 1. It can be observed that our method achieved the highest F1-score and a relatively low HD95 with acceptable size of parameters, which means that a balanced situation existed among the three metrics. U-Net and its variants such as U-Net++ and Attention U-Net achieved a higher F1-score but rough contours, whereas the performance of the edge-based networks was exactly the opposite. Our Decouple U-Net could successfully combine the advantages of both.

## 4.3  Ablation Experiment

The results of the ablation experiment are presented in Table 2. It can be observed that the application of shortcut connections from ResNet improved the F1-score at the expense of

**Table 2.** Ablation experiment

| U-Net | Shortcut connections | Channel attention | Atrous conv | Body generation module | Our loss function | F1-score | HD95 |
|-------|---------------------|-------------------|-------------|------------------------|-------------------|----------|------|
| + | | | | | | 0.7946 | 36.18 |
| + | + | | | | | 0.7998 | 44.85 |
| + | + | + | | | | 0.7993 | 43.37 |
| + | + | + | + | | | 0.7987 | 42.87 |
| + | + | + | + | + | | 0.7992 | 32.70 |
| + | + | + | + | + | + | **0.8062** | **35.47** |

**Table 3.** Counting result

| Image number | 1 | 2 | 3 | 4 | 5 | 6 | 7 | 8 | Mean |
|--------------|---|---|---|---|---|---|---|---|------|
| Manual counting | 21 | 18 | 20 | 16 | 24 | 18 | 17 | 20 | 19.25 |
| ImageJ | 32 | 16 | 26 | 28 | 23 | 27 | 27 | 18 | 24.625 |
| Our method | 22 | 17 | 29 | 13 | 22 | 19 | 18 | 22 | 20.25 |

a reduced quality of the edge segmentation. The channel attention and atrous convolution had similar effects in the opposite direction. However, with the body generation module, HD95 decreased significantly, whereas the F1-score remained at the same level. We also find that changing loss functions cannot improve F1-score and reduce HD95 at the same time. Therefore, our loss function aims to make Higher F1-score while ensuring better quality of edge segmentation than U-Net.

### 4.4 Counting Results

The p-value of paired Student's t-test between manual counting and our method is 0.465, which indicates that the average counting result of our method were not significantly different from the true value. Among available software, ImageJ with Weka segmentation plugin was selected as the comparison, and the p-value is 0.041, hence showing the performance improvement of our method. Therefore, our method may be quite practical when applied in clinic (Table 3).

## 5  Conclusions

We have proposed a complete process consisting of the extraction of hot spots, semantic segmentation and counting of TAMs. The SLIC-based algorithm makes it possible to select TAM-dense hot spots automatically within a relatively short time. The network architecture was refined using the body generation module and combined loss function, thereby achieving superior performance over existing methods. The two parallel networks, namely one for the whole cell and one for its nucleus, work together to obtain more precise counting results. We believe that this work contributes to the development of the automatic segmentation and counting of TAMs, so that pathologists will be able to gradually move away from this meaningless and repetitive work and focus on other more challenging tasks.

**Acknowledgements.** This work is supported by Clinical Medicine Plus X - Young Scholars Project, Peking University, the Fundamental Research Funds for the Central Universities PKU2022LCXQ19 and Innovative Experiment Project for Undergraduates of Peking University Health Science Center 2021-SSDC-14. We would like to thank Yan Gao and Jianyun Zhang for their work on annotating images.

# References

1. Cheng, N., Bai, X., Shu, Y., Ahmad, O., Shen, P.: Targeting tumor-associated macrophages as an antitumor strategy. Biochem. Pharmacol. **183**, 114354 (2021)
2. Petty, A.J., Owen, D.H., Yang, Y., Huang, X.: Targeting tumor-associated macrophages in cancer immunotherapy. Cancers **13**, 5318 (2021)
3. Pan, Y., Yu, Y., Wang, X., Zhang, T.: Tumor-associated macrophages in tumor immunity. Front. Immunol., 3151 (2020)
4. Duraiyan, J., Govindarajan, R., Kaliyappan, K., Palanisamy, M.: Applications of immuno-histochemistry. J. Pharm. Bioallied Sci. **4**, S307 (2012)
5. Yoshida, C., et al.: Tumor-associated CD163+ macrophage as a predictor of tumor spread through air spaces and with CD25+ lymphocyte as a prognostic factor in resected stage I lung adenocarcinoma. Lung Cancer **167**, 34–40 (2022)
6. Wagner, M., et al.: Automated macrophage counting in DLBCL tissue samples: a ROF filter based approach. Biol. Proced. Online **21**, 1–18 (2019)
7. Cassetta, L., et al.: Human tumor-associated macrophage and monocyte transcriptional landscapes reveal cancer-specific reprogramming, biomarkers, and therapeutic targets. Cancer Cell **35**, 588–602, e510 (2019)
8. Kumar, N., Gupta, R., Gupta, S.: Whole slide imaging (WSI) in pathology: current perspectives and future directions. J. Digit. Imaging **33**, 1034–1040 (2020)
9. Baxi, V., Edwards, R., Montalto, M., Saha, S.: Digital pathology and artificial intelligence in translational medicine and clinical practice. Mod. Pathol., 1–10 (2021)
10. Achanta, R., Shaji, A., Smith, K., Lucchi, A., Fua, P., Süsstrunk, S.: SLIC superpixels compared to state-of-the-art superpixel methods. IEEE Trans. Pattern Anal. Mach. Intell. **34**, 2274–2282 (2012)
11. Ronneberger, O., Fischer, P., Brox, T.: U-Net: convolutional networks for biomedical image segmentation. In: Navab, N., Hornegger, J., Wells, W., Frangi, A. (eds.) MICCAI 2015. LNCS, vol. 9351, pp. 234–241. Springer, Cham (2015). https://doi.org/10.1007/978-3-319-24574-4_28
12. Ren, S., He, K., Girshick, R., Sun, J.: Faster R-CNN: towards real-time object detection with region proposal networks. In: Advances in Neural Information Processing Systems 28 (2015)
13. Comaniciu, D., Meer, P.: Mean shift: a robust approach toward feature space analysis. IEEE Trans. Pattern Anal. Mach. Intell. **24**, 603–619 (2002)
14. Shi, J., Malik, J.: Normalized cuts and image segmentation. IEEE Trans. Pattern Anal. Mach. Intell. **22**, 888–905 (2000)

15. Otsu, N.: A threshold selection method from gray-level histograms. IEEE Trans. Syst. Man Cybern. **9**, 62–66 (1979)
16. Canny, J.: A computational approach to edge detection. IEEE Trans. Pattern Anal. Mach. Intell. **6**, 679–698 (1986)
17. Rother, C., Kolmogorov, V., Blake, A.: "GrabCut" interactive foreground extraction using iterated graph cuts. ACM Trans. Graph. (TOG) **23**, 309–314 (2004)
18. Kass, M., Witkin, A., Terzopoulos, D.: Snakes: active contour models. Int. J. Comput. Vis. **1**, 321–331 (1988)
19. Long, J., Shelhamer, E., Darrell, T.: Fully convolutional networks for semantic segmentation. In: Proceedings of the IEEE Conference on Computer Vision and Pattern Recognition, pp. 3431–3440 (2015)
20. He, K., Zhang, X., Ren, S., Sun, J.: Deep residual learning for image recognition. In: Proceedings of the IEEE Conference on Computer Vision and Pattern Recognition, pp. 770–778 (2016)
21. Chen, L.-C., Papandreou, G., Kokkinos, I., Murphy, K., Yuille, A.L.: DEEPLAB: semantic image segmentation with deep convolutional nets, atrous convolution, and fully connected CRFs. IEEE Trans. Pattern Anal. Mach. Intell. **40**, 834–848 (2017)
22. Zhou, Z., Rahman Siddiquee, M.M., Tajbakhsh, N., Liang, J.: UNet++: a nested U-Net architecture for medical image segmentation. In: Stoyanov, D., et al. (eds.) DLMIA ML-CDS 2018 2018. LNCS, vol. 11045, pp. 3–11. Springer, Cham (2018). https://doi.org/10.1007/978-3-030-00889-5_1
23. Oktay, O., et al.: Attention U-Net: learning where to look for the pancreas. arXiv preprint arXiv:1804.03999 (2018)
24. Chen, L.-C., Zhu, Y., Papandreou, G., Schroff, F., Adam, H.: Encoder-decoder with atrous separable convolution for semantic image segmentation. In: Ferrari, V., Hebert, M., Sminchisescu, C., Weiss, Y. (eds.) ECCV 2018. LNCS, vol. 11211, pp. 833–851. Springer, Cham (2018). https://doi.org/10.1007/978-3-030-01234-2_49
25. Takikawa, T., Acuna, D., Jampani, V., Fidler, S.: Gated-SCNN: gated shape CNNs for semantic segmentation. In: Proceedings of the IEEE/CVF International Conference on Computer Vision, pp. 5229–5238 (2019)
26. Zhen, M., et al.: Joint semantic segmentation and boundary detection using iterative pyramid contexts. In: Proceedings of the IEEE/CVF Conference on Computer Vision and Pattern Recognition, pp. 13666–13675 (2020)
27. Li, X., et al.: Improving semantic segmentation via decoupled body and edge supervision. In: Vedaldi, A., Bischof, H., Brox, T., Frahm, JM. (eds.) ECCV 2020. LNCS, vol. 12362, pp. 435–452. Springer, Cham (2020). https://doi.org/10.1007/978-3-030-58520-4_26
28. Zhan, G., Wang, W., Sun, H., Hou, Y., Feng, L.: Auto-CSC: a transfer learning based automatic cell segmentation and count framework. Cyborg Bionic Syst. **2022** (2022)
29. Vahadane, A., et al.: Structure-preserving color normalization and sparse stain separation for histological images. IEEE Trans. Med. Imaging **35**, 1962–1971 (2016)
30. Hu, J., Shen, L., Sun, G.: Squeeze-and-excitation networks. In: Proceedings of the IEEE Conference on Computer Vision and Pattern Recognition, pp. 7132–7141 (2018)
31. Lin, T.-Y., Goyal, P., Girshick, R., He, K., Dollár, P.: Focal loss for dense object detection. In: Proceedings of the IEEE International Conference on Computer Vision, pp. 2980–2988 (2017)
32. Zhu, Y., et al.: Improving semantic segmentation via video propagation and label relaxation. In: Proceedings of the IEEE/CVF Conference on Computer Vision and Pattern Recognition, pp. 8856–8865 (2019)
33. Crum, W.R., Camara, O., Hill, D.L.: Generalized overlap measures for evaluation and validation in medical image analysis. IEEE Trans. Med. Imaging **25**, 1451–1461 (2006)

34. Kingma, D.P., Ba, J.: Adam: A method for stochastic optimization. arXiv preprint arXiv:
    1412.6980 (2014)

# A Zero-Training Method for RSVP-Based Brain Computer Interface

Xujin Li[1,2], Shuang Qiu[1,2], Wei Wei[1], and Huiguang He[1,2,3(✉)]

[1] Research Center for Brain-Inspired Intelligence, National Laboratory of Pattern Recognition, Institute of Automation, Chinese Academy of Sciences, Beijing, China
{lixujin2021,shuang.qiu,weiwei2018,huiguang.he}@ia.ac.cn
[2] University of Chinese Academy of Sciences, Beijing, China
[3] Center for Excellence in Brain Science and Intelligence Technology, Chinese Academy of Sciences, Beijing, China

**Abstract.** Brain-Computer Interface (BCI) is a communication system that transmits information between the brain and the outside world which does not rely on peripheral nerves and muscles. Rapid Serial Visual Presentation (RSVP)-based BCI system is an efficient and robust information retrieval method based on human vision. However, the current RSVP-BCI system requires a time-consuming calibration procedure for one new subject, which greatly restricts the use of the BCI system. In this study, we propose a zero-training method based on convolutional neural network and graph attention network with adaptive graph learning. Firstly, a single-layer convolutional neural network is used to extract EEG features. Then, the extracted features from similar samples were adaptively connected to construct the graph. Graph attention network was employed to classify the target sample through decoding the connection relationship of adjacent samples in one graph. Our proposed method achieves 86.76% mean balanced-accuracy (BA) in one self-collected dataset containing 31 subjects, which performs better than the comparison methods. This indicates our method can realize zero-calibration for an RSVP-based BCI system.

**Keywords:** Brain-Computer Interface (BCI) · Adaptive graph learning · Graph attention network · Zero-training · RSVP

## 1 Introduction

Brain-computer interface (BCI) system collects and decodes brain neural activity information to build a direct information interaction pathway between the brain and the external machine, which can be used to replace, repair, enhance, supplement or improve the normal output of central nerves system [1]. Electroencephalogram (EEG)-based BCI has attracted much attention because of its non-invasive technology, easy to measure brain signals and low equipment cost. Rapid Serial Visual Presentation (RSVP) is a visual evoked paradigm which displays images in sequence at the same position with high display rates. The

S. Yu et al. (Eds.): PRCV 2022, LNCS 13535, pp. 113–125, 2022.
https://doi.org/10.1007/978-3-031-18910-4_10

RSVP-based BCI system can be used to recognize sonar images to detect some objects [2] and implement speller [3,4], image retrieval system [5], image classification system [6,7] and abnormal pattern recognition system [3].

RSVP paradigm uses a high rate presented picture sequence containing a small number of target pictures to induce specific event-related potential (ERP) components. Many researchers have proposed many efficient methods to improve EEG decoding performance in RSVP tasks. In 2006, Gerson, A.D. et al. proposed a method called Hierarchical Discriminant Component Analysis (HDCA), which introduced linear discrimination to reveal target images' differences [6]. Information geometry has also been tried to help improve performance [8]. Barachan et al. [9] proposed the Minimum Distance to Riemannian Mean (MDRM) method to transform the original EEG data to covariance matrices and then classify them according to the minimum distance to mean. In recent years, convolutional neural networks (CNN) have been proven to be useful in decoding EEG signals [10] such as MCNN [11] in RSVP tasks and One Convolutional Layer Neural Network (OCLNN) [12] in P300 speller. Lawhern V.J. et al. (2018) proposed EEGNet [13] which is a multi-layer convolutional neural network. Its second layer is a depthwise separable convolution [14] which can simplify the network structure and reduce the number of parameters. Although these methods can improve the decoding accuracy to a certain extent, these methods which are named as within-subject methods require new subjects data to calibrate classifiers for one new subject [15]. This process is one of the factors that have limited the use of BCI systems in the real world. To overcome this shortcoming, researchers came up with an idea that uses a large amount of data from other subjects to train the machine learning classifier of BCI for one new subject. Thus, subjects can directly use the BCI device without calibration. We call this kind of training method without calibration the zero-training method.

Research on zero-training methods in RSVP tasks can improve the efficiency of target retrieval, and help the entire BCI research field progress. Some attempts have been made to eliminate the calibration process [16]. Recently, Lee et al. proposed an EEGNet-based model which increased the number of feature maps in the first convolution layer and the number of groups of the second depthwise separable convolution layer in EEGNet for P300 detection [15], which achieved reasonable performance and showed no statistical difference when compared to the traditional approach in the same offline data. But few work on zero-training methods has been done for decoding EEG signals in RSVP tasks. Therefore, it is necessary to design a noval zero-training method for the RSVP-based BCI system.

Previous studies showed that convolutional neural networks have become an effective method for EEG signals classification in RSVP tasks. These methods use each single sample for training and testing rather than mining information between similar samples. Considering that RSVP task is a fast visual presentation process, there are a large number of relevant samples in the training and testing stages. Thus, we proposed a novel zero-training framework based on convolutional neural network and graph attention network with adaptive graph learning to decoding EEG signals in RSVP tasks. The convoluational neural network was used to extract features, and extracted features from different samples were adaptively constructed the graph. Graph attention network (GAT) is a kind of spatial based graph convolutional network, which uses attention mechanism to implicitly specify different weights to different nodes in a neighborhood to determine the importance of each neighbor node to the central node, without requiring any kind of costly matrix operation (such as inversion) or depending on knowing the graph structure in advance [17]. In this study, we applied GAT to aggregate features of neighbor samples to improve the classification performance of the test sample.

We collected EEG data from 31 subjects and constructed an RSVP dataset. Then we proposed a zero-training method which is composed of a single-layer convolutional neural network and a graph attention layer with adaptive graph learning, and conducted experiments to verify the effectiveness of our proposed method.

## 2    Materials

### 2.1    Subjects

The experiment included 31 participants (19 males and 12 females; aged 24.9 ± 2.8, 28 right-handed). All participants had corrected-to-normal or normal vision, and were naive in respect RSVP-based BCI experiments. All participants were voluntary, fully informed, and have written consent. This study was ethically approved by the Institutional Review Board of the Institute of Automation, Chinese Academy of Sciences. All subjects gave their written informed consent before testing.

### 2.2    RSVP Paradigm

The visual stimuli for our experiment included 1,400 images (500 × 500 pixels) from the scene and object database [18] published by MIT CSAIL. These images were divided into target images with pedestrians and non-target images without pedestrians (See Fig. 1(a), (b)). Images were randomly presented at a frequency 10 Hz, in which the probability of the target image appearance was 4%. The experiment required subjects to sit 1 m from a monitor with 1920 × 1080 resolution. The subjects need to press the space bar on the keyboard as fast as possible when they found the target images.

The experimental session had 10 blocks, and each block contained 1,400 images, divided into 14 sequences (See Fig. 1.(c)). Each sequence contained 100 images, and the interval between two sequences was controlled by subjects, around 4–6 s. Each block took about five minutes to complete with 2–3 min between two adjacent blocks.

## 2.3   Data Acquisition and Preprocessing

The EEG data were recorded by the SynAmp2 system (NeuroScan, Australia) using 64-channel Ag/AgCl electrodes placed according to the international 10/20 system, with a sampling rate of 1000 Hz Hz. All the electrodes with the impedance 10 k$\Omega$ or lower were referenced to the vertex and grounded to the forehead.

In the preprocessing stage, the EEG data were downsampled 250 Hz. After that, a linear phase 3-order ButterWorth filter with a bandpass between 0.5 15 Hz is used to filter the signal to remove slow drift and high-frequency noise and prevent delay distortions. Then the preprocessed data of each block was segmented into EEG trials. Each trial contained 1 s EEG data starting from the stimulation onset to 1000 milliseconds (0 s to 1 s) after the stimulation onset. For each trial, data were normalized to zero mean and variance one. The subsequent analysis and classification of EEG were based on these segmented EEG trials (samples). According to our experimental paradigm, each subject had 10 (blocks) ×1400 (trials) EEG samples, in which 560 are target samples and the rest are non-target samples.

## 3   Method

In this section, we present our proposed zero-training method based on adaptive GAT (See Fig. 2.). Firstly, we use a single-layer convolutional neural network to extract features. Secondly, We define the graph learning method (See Fig. 2.(b)) to calculate adjacency matrix. Finally, we feed the extracted features into the graph attention layer followed by a linear layer and a softmax operation for the classification. Experience shows that the performance is better when the graph attention layer is stacked shallowly [17], so we use one graph attention layer for classification.

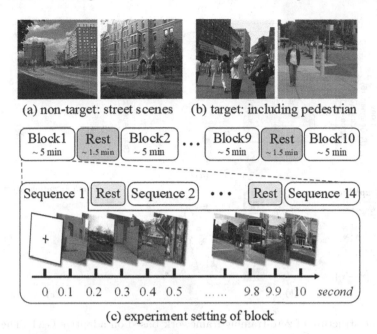

(a) non-target: street scenes     (b) target: including pedestrian

(c) experiment setting of block

**Fig. 1.** (a) non-target image examples (b) target image examples (c) experiments settings about division of blocks and sequences.

## 3.1 EEG Feature Extraction

We use $X \in \mathbb{R}^{N \times 1 \times C \times T}$ to denote the input data in a graph, where $N$ is the number of nodes in a graph, $C$ is the number of EEG channels and $T$ denotes the number of sampling points.

Inspired by OCLNN which used one simple convolution layer and achieved high generalization performance. We use a two-dimension convolution layer with $F1 \times (C, kernLength)$ convolution kernel, where $F1$ is the number of unbiased feature maps with padding $(0, 3)$ and stride $(1, kernLength)$. Then we use BatchNormalization and the activation function is the ReLU activation function. Finally, each feature is stretched to a one-dimension feature.

## 3.2 Adaptive Graph Learning

The input of the graph attention layer are the feature matrix ($H \in \mathbb{R}^{N \times F}$) and the adjacency matrix ($Adj$), where $F$ represents the feature dimension of each node. We feed the output of the feature extractor to the graph attention layer as the feature matrix. In this part, we will introduce how to calculate the adjacency matrix adaptively using the feature similarity between sample nodes. The dimension of the adjacency matrix is $(N, N)$, whose elements are 0 or 1. The element $Adj(i, j) = 1$ indicates $i \rightarrow j$ is related. The adjacency matrix is symmetric since the input graph is undirected.

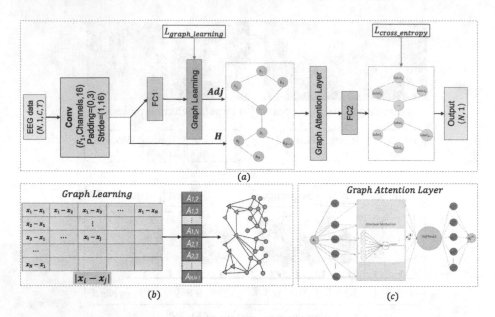

**Fig. 2.** The structure of zero-training framework based on adaptive GAT. The model is made up of a convolution layer, a graph learning block, and a graph attention layer. $\boldsymbol{x}_i$ denotes $softmax(\boldsymbol{W}_a\boldsymbol{h}_i)$, $N$ denotes the number of nodes in a graph, $\boldsymbol{Adj}$ and $\boldsymbol{H}$ denotes the adjacency matrix and feature matrix respectively. The structure of attention mechanism is a single-layer fully connected neural network: the bottom layer has $2F'$ neurons, and each neuron has a value of the element of $[\boldsymbol{x}||\boldsymbol{y}]$ with the element of $\boldsymbol{a}^T$ as the parameter. The activation function is LeakyReLU.

We define a non-negative function $A_{mn} = f(\boldsymbol{h}_m, \boldsymbol{h}_n)(m, n \in \{1, 2, \cdots, N\})$ to represent the connection relationship between the m-th node and the n-th node based on the input feature matrix $\boldsymbol{H} = \left(\boldsymbol{h}_1, \boldsymbol{h}_2, \cdots, \boldsymbol{h}_N\right)^T$. $f(\boldsymbol{h}_m, \boldsymbol{h}_n)$ is implemented through a single-layer fully-connected network, which has the learnable weight matrix $\boldsymbol{W}_a \in \mathbb{R}^{2 \times F}$. The learned graph structure matrix $\boldsymbol{A}$ is defined as:

$$A_{mn} = f(\boldsymbol{h}_m, \boldsymbol{h}_n) = ReLU(\theta_a - |softmax(\boldsymbol{W}_a\boldsymbol{h}_m) - softmax(\boldsymbol{W}_a\boldsymbol{h}_n)|) \quad (1)$$

$$Adj_{mn} = \begin{cases} 0 & A_{mn} = 0 \\ 1 & A_{mn} > 0 \end{cases} \quad (2)$$

where rectified linear unit (ReLU) is an activation function to guarantee that $A_{mn}$ is non-negative. $\theta_a$ is a hyperparameter that selects similar nodes. The weight matrix $\boldsymbol{W}_a$ is updated by minimizing the following loss function:

$$L_{graph\_learning} = L_{middle} + \lambda \|\boldsymbol{A}\|_{L_1} \quad (3)$$

$$L_{middle} = -\frac{1}{N} \sum_{n=1}^{N} \sum_{r=1}^{R} y_{n,r} \log \hat{y}_{n,r}^{middle} \tag{4}$$

where $\lambda > 0$ is a regularization parameter and we set $\lambda = \frac{1}{N}$. The $L_1$ norm of $A$ is used to prevent excessive aggregation of node information and lack of differentiation due to dense connections. $L_{middle}$ uses the cross entropy loss which can use label information directly to optimize the parameters of graph learning and $R$ denotes the number of classes. $y$ is the true label and $\hat{y}^{middle}$ is the value predicted from $softmax(W_a h_n)$.

## 3.3   Graph Attention Layer

In the graph attention module, we use one graph attention layer (See Fig. 2.(c)), which is used to aggregate information of neighbor nodes. In order to determine the importance of each neighbor node to the central node, when the features are aggregated. We define the attention mechanism in the graph attention layer to compute weights as follows:

$$\alpha_{ij} = \frac{exp\left(LeakyReLU\left(a^T[W h_i \| W h_j]\right)\right)}{\sum_{k \in M_i} exp\left(LeakyReLU\left(a^T[W h_i \| W h_k]\right)\right)} \tag{5}$$

The set of neighbor nodes of the $i$-th node is represented by $M_i$. $a^T \subset \mathbb{R}^{2F'}$ is a parameter vector and $[x \| y]$ represents concatenating $x$ and $y$ to a new vector. $W \in \mathbb{R}^{F' \times F}$ is defined as the parameter matrix, which acts on the feature matrix to transform input features into higher-level output features, where $F'$ is the hidden feature dimension of this attention mechanism.

Above, we have defined an attention mechanism in the graph attention layer. In order to make the graph attention layer more stable, multiple attention mechanisms [19] are adopted in our graph attention layer. There are $K(K > 1)$ attention mechanisms in the attention layer, and the method of output features calculation in each attention mechanism is the same as above. It concatenates output features of all attention mechanisms as the output feature.

$$h_i' = \|_{k=1}^{K} \sigma \left( \sum_{j \in M_i} \alpha_{ij}^k W^k h_j \right) \tag{6}$$

The difference between the attention mechanisms is due to the difference between $\alpha_{ij}^k$ and $W^k$, i.e. the parameters $a^k$ and $W^k$. The output feature dimension of the graph attention layer with $K$ attention mechanisms is $KF'$, and the size of the output feature matrix $H'$ is $(N, KF')$.

In the graph attention layer, the input feature dimension is the output feature dimension of the feature extraction network. There are $K = 10$ attention mechanisms in this layer, and the output dimension of each attention mechanism is $F' = 16$. The activation function ($\sigma$) is ELU activation function using dropout technique ($Dropoutrate = 0.5$).

### 3.4   Loss Function

The output size of the graph attention layer is $(N, KF')$. We use a fully-connected layer with softmax activation function to map features into 2 dimensions at the end. The loss function uses cross entropy loss and graph learning loss defined in SectionIII.B.:

$$L_{loss} = L_{cross\_entropy} + L_{graph\_learning} \tag{7}$$

$$L_{cross\_entropy} = -\frac{1}{N} \sum_{n=1}^{N} \sum_{r=1}^{R} y_{n,r} \log \hat{y}_{n,r} \tag{8}$$

$y$ indicates the real label and $\hat{y}$ is the value predicted by the model.

## 4   Experiment

### 4.1   Dataset Setup and Parameters

We conducted zero-training experiment in a Leave-One-Subject-Out (LOSO) way. Each subject will be as the test set alone and the rest as the training set. To overcome the influence made by the extreme imbalance of two classes, we adopt resampling. Downsampling the non-target class to the same number as the target class. This operation is limited to the training set.

We set the length of convolution kernel ($kernLength$) of the single-layer neural network as 16, and the number of feature maps ($F_1$) as 16. The threshold ($\theta_a$) for selecting similar samples in graph learning block is set to $5 \times 10^{-4}$. We set the number of nodes in a graph ($N$) as 1120 for training and 700 for testing. The impact of $N$ will be discussed in Section V.D. and the other hyperparameters selection is based on the experience.

We use PyTorch framework. The overall network is trained by minimizing the loss function ($L_{loss}$) defined in SectionIII.D. Adam optimizer [20] is adopted for model optimization and the learning rate is 0.0002. And the weight decay coefficient is 0.01. Set the maximum training epochs to 200.

### 4.2   Compared Methods

We compare our proposed network with the following methods:

- HDCA [6]: a linear discrimination method that learns weights on the channel and time window of EEG. We set time window to 25 sampling points.
- MDRM [8]: a Riemannian geometry classifier, classify samples according to the geodesic distance to the center of the category. The method is re-implemented based on the Python package pyriemann.
- OCLNN: a single-layer CNN, we re-implemented the network under the description in [12].
- MCNN: a three-layer CNN proposed by Manor, we re-implemented the network under the description in [11].

- EEGNet [13]: a four-layer CNN with depthwise separable convolution layer. https://github.com/vlawhern/arl-eegmodels.
- Lee [15]: a zero-training method based on EEGNet.

Down-sampling operation is also used in the training dataset of the above comparative method. Lee belongs to zero-training methods. HDCA, MDRM, OCLNN, MCNN, and EEGNet belong to within-subject method and the training setting is as follows: for each subject who has 10 blocks data, the data of $b$ blocks are selected as the training set, and the data of the remaining $10 - b$ blocks are used as the test set ($b = 1, 2, 3$). Moreover, we also use these methods to carry out zero-training experiments to compare with our proposed model.

### 4.3   Evaluation Metrics

This RSVP image retrieval task is a binary classification task. Because the test set is not down-sampled, there is still an extreme imbalance of categories in the test set. In order to reduce the impact of unbalanced classes on model performance evaluation, balanced-accuracy (BA) is used to evaluate model performance. The results are expressed as average BA ± standard deviation for all test subjects. The calculation formula is as follows:

$$\begin{cases} BA = \left( \frac{TP}{TP+FN} + \frac{TN}{TN+FP} \right) /2 \\ TPR = \frac{TP}{TP+FN} \\ FPR = \frac{FP}{TN+FP} \end{cases} \tag{9}$$

True Positive Rate (TPR) represents the classification accuracy of positive samples. False Positive Rate (FPR) represents the classification error rate of negative samples. TP represents the number of correctly classified positive samples, and FN represents the number of incorrectly classified positive samples. TN represents the number of correctly classified negative samples, and FP represents the number of incorrectly classified negative samples.

## 5   Result and Discussion

### 5.1   Comparison Results

The comparative experiment was conducted according to our dataset, and the BA of classification is presented in Table 1.

Among all the compared methods, Lee (85.03%) has the highest BA value in zero-training experiments. Because Lee uses depthwise separable convolution with a large number of feature maps, which improves the generalization performance of the model without greatly increasing the number of parameters. The T-test revealed that the mean BA of our proposed model (86.76%) is significantly higher than that of the Lee and other methods ($all : p < 0.02$) in zero-training experiments. Moreover, the classification accuracy of our method for positive samples (TPR) (83.79%) is also significantly higher than other comparison methods $(all : p < 0.02)$ on the condition that the misclassification rate of negative samples (FPR) does not increase, which shows that our methods are the best under zero-training. This may be due to adaptive graph learning and graph attention layer can improve the generalization performance by taking advantage of other similar samples.

In within-subject experiments, HDCA (82.14%, 84.26%, 86.43%) has the highest performance compared with other comparative methods with one, two and three blocks. And the mean BA of our model is significantly higher than that of HDCA (82.14%, 84.26%) $(all : p < 0.02)$ with one and two blocks and higher than that of HDCA (86.43%) with three blocks calibration. Therefore, we reduce the calibration time of at least three blocks. Which shows the use of big data training in advance compensates for the use of subjects' own data for calibration. Therefore, our zero-training model is effective.

## 5.2  Ablation Experiments

To evaluate the effectiveness of our feature extractor and an adaptive GAT module, we conduct ablation experiments. The results are listed in Table 2. After adding adaptive graph attention layer to the feature extractor, the performance (86.76%) is significantly improved $(p < 0.05)$ and the TPR and TNR are also significantly improved $(all : p < 0.05)$, which indicates that the adaptive GAT is effective.

**Table 1.** Comparison of classification performance of different methods

| Methods | Zero-training | | | Within-subject | | |
|---|---|---|---|---|---|---|
| | | | | 1 block | 2 blocks | 3 blocks |
| | BA (%) | TPR (%) | FPR (%) | BA (%) | BA (%) | BA (%) |
| HDCA | 82.59 ±4.48 | 80.48 ± 9.14 | 15.3 ± 2.93 | **82.14 ± 5.35** | **84.26 ± 4.10** | **86.43 ± 3.86** |
| MDRM | 82.69 ± 6.84 | 78.63 ± 8.86 | 13.25 ± 3.72 | 81.41 ± 6.43 | 82.38 ± 5.44 | 82.98 ± 5.85 |
| OCLNN | 84.61 ± 4.05 | **81.93 ± 8.06** | 12.70 ± 0.97 | 80.24 ± 5.82 | 83.92 ± 4.62 | 85.99 ± 3.49 |
| MCNN | 83.05 ± 4.95 | 79.16 ± 8.30 | 13.05 ± 2.63 | 72.75 ± 8.07 | 76.14 ± 7.93 | 80.57 ± 5.52 |
| EEGNet | 79.99 ± 3.97 | 78.88 ± 6.00 | 18.89 ± 1.27 | 75.95 ± 3.77 | 81.85 ± 3.54 | 84.44 ± 3.12 |
| Lee | **85.03 ± 4.70** | 80.60 ± 9.90 | **10.54 ± 3.23** | | | |
| Ours | **86.76 ± 3.93** | **83.79 ± 7.44** | **10.26 ± 2.35** | | | |

**Table 2.** Results of ablation experiments

| Model | BA (%) | TPR (%) | FPR (%) |
|---|---|---|---|
| Feature extractor | 85.45 ± 4.05 | 82.36 ± 8.37 | 11.46 ± 1.68 |
| Ours | **86.76 ± 3.93** | **83.79 ± 7.44** | **10.26 ± 2.35** |

The experimental set of feature extractor is the same as that of contrast methods in Table 1, which is comparable. It can be seen that the performance of the feature extractor (85.45%) is better than that of the Lee (85.03%) in zero-training, indicating that the feature extractor can extract features and separate different classes of features effectively.

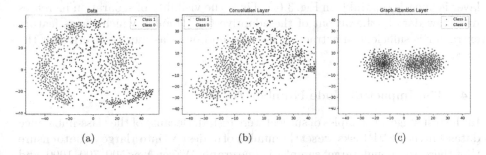

(a)                         (b)                         (c)

**Fig. 3.** The t-SNE visualization results of different spaces in the network: (a) raw data, (b) the output of convolution layer, (c) the output of graph attention layer. The red dots indicate target samples, and the blue dots indicate non-target samples.

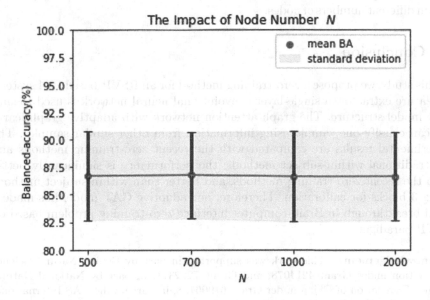

**Fig. 4.** Results of our method under different numbers of nodes ($N$).

## 5.3  Visualization

In order to explore how our proposed method works for classification, we applied t-distributed Stochastic Neighbor Embedding (t-SNE) to project the output of each layer into 2 dimensions. We took one subject as an example and sampled balanced non-target data to project and draw scatter plots.

As revealed in Fig. 3.(a), we can see the maximum overlap in t-SNE visualization for raw data. After extracting features by convolution layer, the samples of each class clustered into multiple block obviously but still cannot be linearly separated, which can be seen in Fig. 3.(b). The output of the graph attention layer is linearly separable in Fig. 3.(c). Thus, the visibility of separation increases from raw data to the output of the adaptive GAT model, which shows feature extractor is sufficient in extracting features and our classifier is effective for the classification task.

### 5.4   The Impact of Node Number $N$

In the test stage, all samples of subject were tested. Because of the class-imbalance dataset in the RSVP tasks, we set the number of nodes ($N$) into a large value to ensure that there are enough target samples in one graph. We set $N$ as 500, 700, 1000, and 2000 to conduct experiments in order to explore the impact of the number of nodes on classification performance. The results can be seen in Fig. 4. The mean BA are 86.69%, 86.76%, 86.63%, 86.65% respectively, which shows no statistical difference between each pair of comparisons ($all : p > 0.1$). Therefore, our method can perform well in different numbers of nodes.

## 6   Conclusion

In this study, we propose a zero-training method for an RSVP-based BCI system. In feature extractor, a single-layer convolutional neural network is used to simplify model structure. The graph attention network with adaptive graph learning can classify one sample using information from other similar samples. The experimental results are compared with the recent zero-training methods and the traditional within-subject methods: the performance is significantly better than the recent zero-training methods, and better than within-subject methods using 3 blocks for calibration. Therefore, our adaptive GAT model has made a good breakthrough in Brain-computer interface zero-training problem based on RSVP paradigm.

**Acknowledgements.** This work was supported in part by Beijing Natural Science Foundation under Grant 4214078, and Grant 7222311; in part by National Natural Science Foundation of China under Grant 61906188; in part by the CAS International Collaboration Key Project under Grant 173211KYSB20190024; and in part by the Strategic Priority Research Program of CAS under Grant XDB32040200.

## References

1. Wolpaw, J.R., et al.: Brain-computer interfaces for communication and control. Clin. Neurophysiol. **113**(6), pp. 767–791 (2002)

2.  Barngrover, C., et al.: A brain-computer interface (BCI) for the detection of mine-like objects in sidescan sonar imagery. IEEE J. Ocean. Eng. **41**(1), 123–138 (2015)
3.  Acqualagna, L., Blankertz, B.: Gaze-independent BCI-spelling using rapid serial visual presentation (RSVP). Clin. Neurophysiol. **124**(5), 901–908 (2013)
4.  Lin, Z., et al.: A novel P300 BCI speller based on the triple RSVP paradigm. Sci. Rep. **8**(1), 1–9 (2018)
5.  Pohlmeyer, E.A., et al.: Closing the loop in cortically-coupled computer vision: a brain-computer interface for searching image databases. J. Neural Eng. **8**(3), 036025 (2011)
6.  Gerson, A.D., et al.: Cortically coupled computer vision for rapid image search. IEEE Trans. Neural Syst. Rehabil. Eng. **14**(2), 174–179 (2006)
7.  Marathe, A.R., et al.: Improved neural signal classification in a rapid serial visual presentation task using active learning. IEEE Trans. Neural Syst. Rehabil. Eng. **24**(3), 333–343 (2015)
8.  Barachant, A., Congedo, M.: A plug play P300 BCI using information geometry, August 2014. arXiv:1409.0107
9.  Zanini, P., Congedo, M., Jutten, C., Said, S., Berthoumieu, Y.: Transfer learning: a Riemannian geometry framework with applications to brain-computer interfaces. IEEE Trans. Biomed. Eng. **65**(5), 1107–1116 (2018). https://doi.org/10.1109/TBME.2017.2742541
10. Cecotti, H., Graser, A.: Convolutional neural networks for P300 detection with application to brain-computer interfaces. IEEE Trans. Pattern Anal. Mach. Intell. **33**(3), 433–445 (2011). https://doi.org/10.1109/TPAMI.2010.125
11. Manor, R., Geva, A.B.: Convolutional neural network for multi-category rapid serial visual presentation BCI. Front. Comput. Neurosci. **9**, 146 (2015)
12. Shan, H., Liu, Y., Stefanov, T.P.: A simple convolutional neural network for accurate P300 detection and character spelling in brain computer interface. In: IJCAI, pp. 1604–1610, July 2018
13. Lawhern, V.J., et al.: EEGNet: a compact convolutional neural network for EEG-based brain-computer interfaces. J. Neural Eng. **15**(5), 056013 (2018)
14. Chollet, F.: Xception: deep learning with depthwise separable convolutions. CoRR, vol. abs/1610.02357 (2016). http://arxiv.org/abs/1610.02357
15. Lee, J., et al.: CNN with large data achieves true zero-training in online P300 brain-computer interface. IEEE Access **8**, 74385–74400 (2020)
16. Naz, S., Bawane, N.: Recent trends in BCI based speller system: a survey report. Int. J. Eng. Sci. **6**(7) (2016)
17. Velickovic, P., Cucurull, G., Casanova, A., Romero, A., Lio, P., Bengio, Y.: Graph attention networks. In: Proceedings of ICLR (2018)
18. Torralba, A ., et al.: The MIT-CSAIL Database of Objects and Scenes. http://web.mit.edu/torralba/www/database.html
19. Vaswani, A., et al.: Attention is all you need. arXiv preprint arXiv:1706.03762 (2017)
20. Kingma, D.P., Ba, J.: Adam: a method for stochastic optimization. arXiv preprint, arXiv:1412.6980, December 2014

# An Improved Tensor Network for Image Classification in Histopathology

Yongxian Fan[(⊠)] [iD] and Hao Gong[iD]

Guilin University of Electronic Technology, Guilin 541004, China
yongxian.fan@gmail.com

**Abstract.** As some machine learning tools such as neural networks are adopted in several fields, some interesting connections and comparisons of concepts between these fields are beginning to emerge. Tensor networks have been an enabling tool for the analysis of quantum many-body systems in physics in the past and now are applied to medical image analysis tasks. Through inter-domain concept migration, we propose an Unordered Stacked Tensor Network model (UnSTNet). We extend the matrix product state to adapt to the medical image analysis task, and embed the classical image domain concept, local disorder of images, to preserve the global structure of images. In addition, we stack unordered blocks within tensor blocks to integrate global information, and stack the outputs of multiple tensor blocks to fuse image features in different states for global evaluation. We evaluate on three publicly available histopathology image datasets and demonstrate that the proposed method obtains improved performance compared to related tensor learning methods. The results also show that, compared with the advanced deep learning method, our model can perform well with fewer computing resources and hyperparameters.

**Keywords:** Histopathology image · Pattern recognition and classification · Tensor network

## 1 Introduction

In recent years, automated histopathological image analysis has become an important research topic in the field of medical imaging. Although different imaging techniques such as diagnostic radiographs, magnetic resonance imaging and ultrasonography exist to detect and diagnose tumors, histopathological analysis of diseased tissue by pathologists is the only way to diagnose tumors with confidence. Histopathological analysis is a very time-consuming professional task, depending on the skills and experience of the pathologist, and the diagnosis is, after all, subjective and could be impacted by a variety of factors, such as fatigue and distraction. In addition, there is often a lack of consensus among experts on diagnosis. The continuous accumulation of clinical cases has led to an increased demand for histopathological image analysis. Based on these facts, there is an urgent requirement for computer-aided diagnostic systems that can automatically detect and classify to reduce the workload of professionals while increasing efficiency [1].

© The Author(s), under exclusive license to Springer Nature Switzerland AG 2022
S. Yu et al. (Eds.): PRCV 2022, LNCS 13535, pp. 126–137, 2022.
https://doi.org/10.1007/978-3-031-18910-4_11

Support vector machine (SVM), a very popular classification algorithm for traditional machine learning, is a general type of feed-forward network. It is based on the same theory [2–4] as other kernel methods, where complex problems in low dimensions become easier when boosted to higher levels. The same idea is shared by the tensor network approach. The key lies in how to treat the large-scale data mapped into the high-dimensional feature space to prevent the curse of dimensionality. The solution given by tensor networks is to decompose the high-order tensor space into a compressed sequence of low-dimensional tensors and perform an approximation of the high-order space using a series of efficient algorithms [5, 6].

In machine learning, tensor network can be used to solve non-convex optimization tasks [7, 8] and has made progress in many other important problems [9–11], such as learning features for images [11] and compressing neural networks with weight layers [9]. Phan et al. [10] decomposed multiplexed data based on the orthogonal tensor and embedded higher-order discriminant analysis to extract essential factors and salient features from the core tensor for classification. Chen et al. [12] implemented binary image classification feature representation utilizing techniques such as constrained rank tensor approximation, QR decomposition and multilevel tensor decomposition. Moreover, researchers have put considerable effort and made many contributions in tensor networks applied to the image domain. For example, Stoudenmire et al. [13] converted 2D input images into 1D vectors before encoding them into high-dimensional space and used tensor networks for approximate conversion. They used flattening to preprocess images and focused on preserving the relevance of pixels as much as possible using an improved flattening strategy. For small resolution images, such as MNIST or Fashion MNIST datasets, tensor networks can exploit the residual correlation in flattened images [14]. However, in medical image tasks, where such low-resolution images are largely absent, the global structure of the image can be lost by the flattening operation which may result in the missing of vital information. Selvan et al. [15] proposed a locally disordered tensor network (LoTeNet), which, according to the classical theory of locally disordered images [16], can ignore the local order of pixels while still capturing the global structure by operating at different scales to obtain statistical information about the minor neighborhoods of an image. The proposed LoTeNet model is designed for linear classification in high-dimensional space and end-to-end optimization by propagating error signals backward through the tensor network. Nevertheless, the constant simplification of features during training can result in the loss of some information. A single transfer of features between layers may also widen the error and thus lose contact with the original data.

In response to the above challenges, an unordered stacked tensor network model is proposed in this paper. The model utilizes disorder theory to divide the image into multiple disordered blocks, increasing the dimension of features while retaining the global structure. We also use stacking operations to integrate unordered blocks to achieve a multi-layer network. At the same time, we stack the network layers to mitigate the transmission of errors and improve the accuracy of the diagnosis to a greater extent. The mapping mechanism is a key part of the projection of raw data into the feature space, which directly affects the quality of data compression and assembly [15, 17]. Thus, we extend the mapping function to add features at different scales [17]. Magnifying the mapping can reveal the data state in different dimensions and extract information hidden in the features for classification. We conduct experiments on three publicly available medical image datasets: the BreaKHis dataset [18], the IDC dataset [19, 20] and the PCAM dataset [21]. The results show that, compared with the related tensor learning methods, the proposed model has higher performance. Meanwhile, we can achieve effects comparable to the advanced deep learning method with a much smaller resource footprint and hyperparameters.

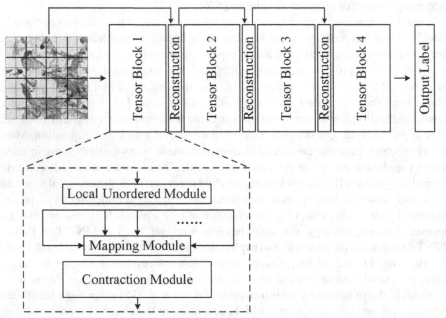

**Fig. 1.** The overall structure of the proposed UnSTNet model. The model consists of four continuous tensor blocks and reconstruction modules interspersed with them. Each tensor block is composed of local unordered module, mapping module and contraction module in sequence.

In conclusion, the main contributions of this paper are as follows:

1) A new unordered stacked tensor network model is proposed to enhance the communication between the network layers and improve the robustness of the network.
2) The scale of the feature representation is extended to reveal more detail.
3) The proposed method is implemented in the histopathology image classification task with good results.

The rest of the paper is organized as follows: Sect. 2 describes the proposed network; Sect. 3 gives experiments and results; Sect. 3.4 provides a detailed discussion of the system.

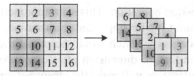

**Fig. 2.** The 4 × 4 image is converted into 4 local unordered sub-blocks using the compression operation of k = 2.

## 2 Method

The proposed unordered stacked tensor network consists of four contiguous tensor blocks and reconstruction modules interspersed among them. Each tensor block is composed of local unordered module, mapping module and contraction module in sequence. The local unordered module is designed to increase the dimension of features and retain global structure using unordered partitions; Mapping module is used to extend the data scale for extracting refined features; The contraction module employs efficient algorithms to simplify the calculation of high-dimensional spaces, further reducing the number of parameters and resource consumption; The reconstruction module is applied to shape multi-scale features and utilizes the idea of stacking to superimpose tensor block feature maps to slow down the propagation of errors. The diagram of our model is shown in Fig. 1. We now delve into the details of this model.

### 2.1 Local Unordered Partition

Mapping the data to high-dimensional space, the 2D image needs to be smoothed to a 1D associated tensor, and feature space complexity increases exponentially with the number of data points, which has a relatively strict requirement on the image resolution size. In order to adapt to the medical image data size, a local disordered image region is proposed based on the theory of local disordered images [12, 16]. This divides the whole image into multiple local unordered subblocks before representing it as the tensor network, so that it will not violate the image size requirement of tensor networks and can also adapt to the medical image analysis task.

The local disorder of the sub-blocks means that they are not divided along one dimension of the image, but utilize multiple scales both to obtain appropriately sized sub-blocks and preserve the structural layout of the image, as shown in Fig. 2.

Sampling operations of size $k$ are carried out along each dimension of the image, which has three dimensions (channels: $C$, height: $H$, width: $W$). For a single-channel image $X \in R^{H \times W}$, the sub-block obtained after compression is $x \in R^{(W/k) \times (H/k)}$, and a total of $k^2$ sub-blocks are achieved. For the multi-channel transformation, the channel superposition needs to be considered as follows:

$$\varphi(X; k) : \left\{ X \in R^{C \times H \times W} \right\} \rightarrow \left\{ x \in R^{C \times \frac{H}{k} \times \frac{W}{k}}, N = k^2 \right\} \tag{1}$$

where $N$ denotes the number of sub-blocks. The step size of the kernel $k$ determines the spatial dimension and the corresponding feature dimension of the image compression. The larger $k$ is, the smaller the spatial dimension and the larger the feature dimension of the image after the compression operation. This sampling method preserves the global structure of the image without losing important information. In addition, the feature dimension after compression is $k^2$, which would be one if the original image is used directly. In comparison, the feature dimension after compression is larger and these increased feature spatial dimensions will make the tensor network more expressive [22].

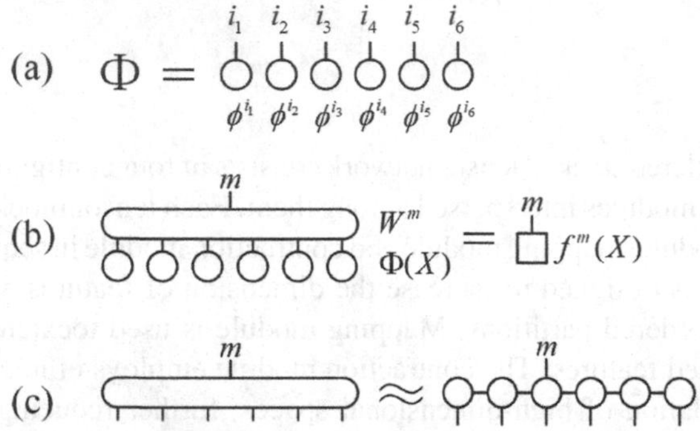

**Fig. 3.** The diagram of (a) joint feature map, (b) decision function and (c) tensor contraction.

## 2.2  Mapping to High-Dimensional Space

Classifiers in high-dimensional space are very powerful [23], and support vector machines are implemented by mapping data into high-dimensional spaces using kernel functions [2]. In this section, we describe the specific implementation of encoding image data into high-dimensional feature spaces.

For the 2D image with $N$ pixels, we achieve an $N$ dimensional vector $X$ by smoothing operations. Before mapping to the higher dimensional space, we need to scale each pixel in it. Most previous work has used two-dimensional mapping to scale pixels into feature space [12, 17]. In our work, we implement feature mapping using three-dimensional vectors to complete the preparation before input to the tensor network:

$$\phi^i(x) = \left[\cos^2\left(\frac{\pi}{2}x\right), \sqrt{2}\cos\left(\frac{\pi}{2}x\right)\sin\left(\frac{\pi}{2}x\right), \sin^2\left(\frac{\pi}{2}x\right)\right] \tag{2}$$

where $x$ indicates the pixel point of the image, $i$ denotes the dimension of the pixel expansion and $\phi^i(\cdot)$ represents the pixel-wise feature map.

Compared to a two-dimensional tensor, a three-dimensional mapping maps $X$ to a higher-dimensional Hilbert space, from which more accurate features for discrimination can be extracted. All pixel-wise features are mapped into the tensor network via the tensor product, forming a joint feature mapping (Fig. 3(a)).

$$\Phi^{i_1,i_2\cdots i_N}(X) = \phi^{i_1}(x_1) \otimes \phi^{i_2}(x_2) \otimes \cdots \phi^{i_N}(x_N) \tag{3}$$

where $\otimes$ represents the tensor product, $\Phi^{i_1,i_2\cdots i_N}(\cdot)$ represents the joint feature map through tensor network feature mapping, and $i_1, i_2 \cdots i_N$ denotes each dimension of the joint feature mapping. The global joint feature representation contains $N$ local features with dimension $d = 3$, which constitutes the scale of each component in the high-dimensional feature space.

Given the high-dimensional feature mapping, for the input data $X$, the multi-classification decision function can be expressed as follows:

$$f^m(X) = \left( W_m^{i_1,i_2\cdots i_N}(X) \right) \cdot \left( \Phi^{i_1,i_2\cdots i_N}(X) \right) \tag{4}$$

where $W(\cdot)$ represents the image-wise features and $m$ denotes an $M$ dimensional label prediction vector, where $M$ is the total number of categories. As shown above, $W(\cdot)$ is an $N + 1$ dimensional tensor, in which the previous $N$ dimensions correspond to the $N$ dimensional joint feature map $\Phi(\cdot)$ and the rest represents the output dimension, corresponding to the predicted probability of each category (Fig. 3(b)).

## 2.3  Contraction Sequences for Low-Order Tensors

Considering that high dimensional spaces containing a large number of parameters necessarily increase the complexity of the calculation, we apply an efficient algorithm for optimization. We utilize matrix product state [24] to represent the high-dimensional tensor, which is approximate to a contraction sequence of low-order tensors, as shown in the Fig. 3(c). In this way, the amount of calculation is greatly reduced while decreasing the number of parameters. Specifically, it can be calculated as

$$W_m^{i_1,i_2\cdots i_N}(X) = \sum_{\alpha_1,\alpha_2\cdots\alpha_N} A_{\alpha_1}^{i_1} A_{\alpha_1\alpha_2}^{i_2} A_{\alpha_2\alpha_3}^{i_3} \cdots A_{m;\alpha_j\alpha_{j+1}}^{i_j} \cdots A_{\alpha_N}^{i_N} \tag{5}$$

where $A$ denotes the parameter of the matrix product state approximation and virtual dimensions $\alpha_1, \alpha_2 \cdots \alpha_N$ appear as subscripts in its index. The virtual dimension is the bridge to the contraction sequence, also known as the key dimension. It is the hyper-parameter that controls the quality of the low-order tensor sequences. Certainly, this pattern is not fixed, and it can be optimized and adapted for different tasks [13].

## 2.4  Reconstruction Feature

As shown in the Fig. 1, the original image is divided into multiple unordered blocks by the local unordered module. These unordered blocks are then dispatched into the mapping module to raise the scale and obtain hidden information. As the mapping functions are unified, they share a common mapping mechanism. Afterwards, the contraction module receives a number of high-dimensional tensors and approximates them as contraction sequences of low-order tensors. It is worth noting that each high-dimensional space is transformed using a separate matrix product state. Finally, the feature maps generated by the training of multiple unordered blocks are fed into the reconstruction module.

The reconstruction module reshapes these feature maps into high-resolution multi-scale feature maps according to the global structure. Furthermore, the features of multiple tensor blocks are stacked to slow down the feedforward network error transmission and improve the accuracy of the diagnosis to a certain extent.

**Table 1.** Performance achieved by the proposed method and other tensor network methods

| Models | BreaKHis | | IDC | | PCam | |
|---|---|---|---|---|---|---|
| | ACC | AUC | ACC | AUC | ACC | AUC |
| TensorNet-5 | 83.6 | 91.6 | 82.0 | 89.4 | 73.0 | 79.7 |
| TensorNet-10 | 84.8 | 92.7 | 82.5 | 90.2 | 72.4 | 78.7 |
| LoTeNet | 86.5 | 95.3 | 85.7 | 93.0 | 78.4 | 87.0 |
| UnSTNet (ours) | 90.1 | 97.2 | 86.6 | 93.8 | 81.3 | 89.0 |

Previous models could only train on the output of a single layer, which would prevent the features extracted in the shallow layers from being used more. Since the features extracted by the network layer depend on the quality of the features in the previous layer, many intermediate parameters have little impact on the decision, or even lose their role and take up computational resources for nothing. Moreover, the errors in the network will continue to grow as the layers deepen, even losing their correlation with the input. The usage of stacking strategies will avoid the classifier relying directly on the most complex features of the last layer in the network to make the final decision. This allows us to make comprehensive use of features of lower complexity at shallow levels, making it easier to obtain smooth decision functions with better generalization performance and avoiding overfitting as much as possible. The proposed model is an adaptive network where we only need to set the size of the virtual dimension, which is the only hyperparameter that needs to be adjusted in the model.

## 3 Data and Experiments

### 3.1 Data

We conduct experiments on three publicly available histopathology image datasets with the task of image binary classification.

**BreaKHis Dataset:** In order to further enhance the integration of computer technology with breast cancer diagnosis, a Breast Cancer Histopathological Database (BreakHis) was proposed for research [18]. This dataset comprises of 9109 microscopic images of breast tumor tissue collected from 82 patients. It contains 2480 benign samples and 5429 malignant samples, all of which are 3-channel RGB images with a size of 700 × 460 pixel. To keep the class balance of the dataset, we performed a random extraction operation on the images and then divided them into training, validation and test sets according to 60:20:20 for the experiments.

**IDC Dataset:** Invasive ductal carcinoma (IDC) is the most common subtype of all breast cancers. In order to assign an aggressiveness grade to the entire sample, pathologists usually focus on the area containing the IDC. Therefore, one of the common preprocessing steps for automated aggressiveness grading is to depict the exact region of IDC within the entire mounting slide. The original dataset [19, 20] consisted of 162 full slide images of breast cancer (BCa) specimens scanned at 40x, from which 277,524 50 × 50-sized patches containing 198,738 IDC negatives and 78,786 IDC positives were extracted. We extract the dataset further, keeping the balance of positive and negative classes of the data 50–50. Similarly, we divide the dataset according to 60:20:20 to complete the training, validation and testing process in the experiment, respectively.

**Table 2.** Performance obtained by the proposed method and advanced deep learning method

| Models | BreaKHis | | IDC | | PCam | |
|---|---|---|---|---|---|---|
| | ACC | AUC | ACC | AUC | ACC | AUC |
| DenseNet | 89.7 | 97.3 | 87.0 | 94.1 | 77.8 | 85.6 |
| UnSTNet (ours) | 90.1 | 97.2 | 86.6 | 93.8 | 81.3 | 89.0 |

**Table 3.** GPU resources used in the training process for all methods in the experiment (GB)

| Datasets | TensorNet-5 | TensorNet-10 | LoTeNet | UnSTNet | DenseNet |
|---|---|---|---|---|---|
| BreaKHis | 7.6 | 11.1 | 1.5 | 2.6 | 10.2 |
| IDC | 2.2 | 7.1 | 1.0 | 1.1 | 4.5 |
| PCam | 4.6 | 7.9 | 1.2 | 1.8 | 8.7 |

**PCam Dataset:** The PatchCamelyon (PCam) dataset is a new challenging image classification dataset proposed by Veeling and Linmans et al. [21]. It contains image patches of 96 × 96 pixel extracted from histopathological scans of lymph nodes sections. Each image is annotated with a binary label indicating presence of metastatic tissue. A positive label indicates the presence of at least one pixel of tumor tissue in the 32 × 32 region at the center of the image, otherwise negative label. The dataset contains a total of 327680 image patches with a balance of 50–50 between positive and negative classes. It is split into training set, validation set and test set according to 80: 10: 10 respectively.

The mean and standard deviation of all images in the experimental dataset are normalized to 0.5. We employ random rotation, random horizontal and vertical flips to enhance the training data. To make the experimental data fit the model more closely, we reshaped the BreaKHis and IDC images to 128 × 128 pixel and 64 × 64 pixel sizes before feeding them into the network.

### 3.2  Experimental Settings

The only hyperparameter of the whole model, the virtual dimension, is set to 5 [15]. We used an Adam optimizer with a learning rate of 0.0005 and a batch size of 512 to train the data, and set a maximum number of 100 epochs for training. Depending on the dataset, the learning rate also needs to be dynamically adjusted to achieve the best performance. During the training process, the validation set is utilized to evaluate the model at each iteration. The test set is used to generate the classification evaluation metrics whenever optimal values are reached. The training will be terminated without performance improvement for 10 consecutive epochs and the best model will be saved.

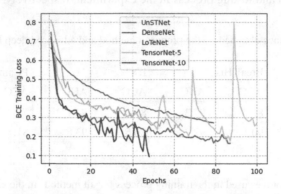

**Fig. 4.** Losses during training on the BreaKHis dataset for all methods used in our experiments.

In our experiments, we mainly use three metrics to evaluate proposed method as well as other comparison methods. Two of them register the accuracy and area under the curve of the model evaluated on the test set, which directly express the quality of the model. The detailed data can be seen in Table 1 and Table 2. The remaining captures the GPU resources absorbed by the model during training, which indirectly evaluates the model, as illustrated in Table 3

### 3.3  Results

We search for relevant tensor networks and advanced deep learning methods for comparison experiments, namely the tensor network methods TensorNet and LoTeNet, together with the DenseNet neural network method, where the TensorNet method employs two virtual dimensions 5 and 10 for experiments.

In our work, the DenseNet method adopts a four-layer network architecture with a growth rate of 12 [25]. TensorNet is actually a single-layer tensor network architecture. LoTeNet is also implemented based on the multi-layer tensor network with layers $L = 3$[15].

As shown from the data in Table 1, our method achieves 90.1% and 97.2% performance in terms of accuracy and area under the curve, respectively, for the BreaKHis dataset. Compared to the other tensor networks TensorNet-5, TensorNet-10 and LoTeNet, our method outperforms them by 3%–6% in terms of ACC, and 2%–6% in AUC. This conclusion also applies to the other two datasets. Compared to the second ranked tensor network, our method obtains 0.9% and 0.8% increases in ACC and AUC on IDC, as well as 2.9% and 2.0% on PCam. All the above data and analysis show that our method has better capability than other tensor network methods.

Table 2 shows that the DenseNet method achieves 89.7% and 97.3%, 87.0% and 94.1% as well as 77.8% and 85.6% performance on ACC and AUC in turn, and the proposed method produces 90.1% and 97.2%, 86.6% and 93.8% as well as 81.3% and 89.0%. From the data analysis, the proposed method can obtain comparable performance to the DenseNet network. Table 3 records the GPU resources consumed by the various methods during the experiments, focusing on the resource consumption of the proposed method and the deep learning method. The data shows that our method consumes 2.6 GB, 1.1 GB and 1.8 GB of GPU resources on the three datasets in turn, while the deep learning method consumes 10.2 GB, 4.5 GB and 8.7 GB of resources. In contrast, the deep learning method consumes several times more resources than we do. In conclusion, the advantage of the proposed method is that it takes fewer work resources to achieve the same diagnostic effect.

### 3.4 Discussion and Conclusions

The method proposed in this paper employs high-order space to deal with low-dimensional problems. Capturing the state of the data in Hilbert space using tensor networks and decomposing the high-dimensional data into low-order tensor chains is to achieve compressed higher-order pattern data, which can capture local correlations between adjacent subsystems [26] and reduce training parameters while improving the robustness of the training algorithm. The tensor network form of the feature parameters also allows extracting information hidden in the training model and speed up the training by utilizing techniques such as parallel optimization of different internal tensors. We adopt the matrix product state as the built-in tensor network and reproduce the approximate output of the higher-order tensor by shrinking the core tensor. The compressed sequence of high-dimensional arrays reshaped into low-order tensors are computationally more efficient, plus such low-order objects usually take fewer storage resources [27]. Utilizing local disorder image theory, we divide the whole image into multiple sub-blocks, which neglect the local pixel order but retain the important information of global structure, and the overall image still behaves as a global association. By preserving the spatial relationship inside the image structure, the feature minimizes the intra-class invariance of the tensor and improves the prediction accuracy. The idea of stacking makes network initialization more robust. The single tensor transmission network will produce a large number of matrix product operations, which can easily lead to the explosion or disappearance of gradients. The same problems often lead to the failure of traditional deep neural network training. The usage of stacking allows for the fusion of predictions from multiple layers, enhancing the fault tolerance of the network.

The proposed network is an adaptive image classification method that greatly reduces the dependence on hyperparameters. The model has only one unique hyperparameter, the virtual dimension, which needs to be determined before use, and it is even possible to default this parameter without any changes. Applying our model to different datasets essentially yields similar performance as expected, since we do not need to configure a complex architecture to cope with a specific dataset. The deep learning method needs to configure various parameters such as convolution layers, activation layers, pooling layers and full connection layers. In comparison, our method appears to be simpler. Our model has better generality and robustness than approaches with good performance for specific data, as shown in the Fig. 4.

Compared to deep learning methods, our approach has a significantly lower footprint on the GPU, mainly owing to the fact that deep learning relies on the delivery of deep intermediate feature maps to automatically filter available features when building complex models, but intermediate feature maps take up a large amount of GPU memory [28]. In contrast, the proposed model is based on compressing the input data of the entire pipeline into a much smaller tensor, so it does not increase memory consumption as the layers go deeper, nor does it need to maintain a large number of intermediate feature maps. This greatly reduces the GPU usage of the model, which means that larger images and larger batches can be processed.

In this paper, we propose an unordered stacked tensor network model. The model contains local unordered module, mapping module, contraction module and reconstruction module. Each module plays an integral role. We evaluate the proposed method on three publicly available histopathological image datasets. The results show that the model proposed in this paper has higher performance in comparison with existing tensor network methods and is able to achieve comparable effects to the deep learning method with fewer resources. We demonstrate the effectiveness of the proposed method for the diagnosis of histopathological images.

# References

1. Gurcan, M.N., Boucheron, L.E., et al.: Histopathological image analysis: a review. IEEE Rev. Biomed. Eng. **2**, 147–171 (2009)
2. Hofmann, T., Scholkopf, B., Smola, A.J.: Kernel methods in machine learning. Ann. Stat. **36**(3), 1171–1220 (2008)
3. Cortes, C., Vapnik, V.: Support-vector networks. Mach. Learn. **20**(3), 273–297 (1995)
4. Boser, B.E., Guyon, I.M., Vapnik, V.N.: A training algorithm for optimal margin classifiers. In: Proceedings of the Fifth Annual Workshop on Computational Learning Theory, Pittsburgh, Pennsylvania, USA, pp. 144–152. Association for Computing Machinery (1992)
5. Oseledets, I.V.: Tensor-train decomposition. SIAM J. Sci. Comput. **33**(5), 2295–2317 (2011)
6. Bridgeman, J.C., Chubb, C.T.: Hand-waving and interpretive dance: an introductory course on tensor networks. J. Phys. Math. Theor. **50**(22), 61 (2017)
7. Anandkumar, A., Ge, R., et al.: Tensor decompositions for learning latent variable models. J. Mach. Learn. Res. **15**, 2773–2832 (2014)
8. Anandkumar, A., Ge, R., et al.: A tensor approach to learning mixed membership community models. J. Mach. Learn. Res. **15**, 2239–2312 (2014)
9. Novikov, A., Podoprikhin, D., et al.: Tensorizing neural networks. In: Proceedings of the 28th International Conference on Neural Information Processing Systems - Volume 1, Montreal, Canada, pp. 442–450. MIT Press (2015)
10. Phan, A.H., Cichocki, A.: Tensor decompositions for feature extraction and classification of high dimensional datasets. Nonlinear Theory Appl. IEICE **1**(1), 37–68 (2010)
11. Bengua, J.A., Phien, H.N., Tuan, H.D.: Optimal feature extraction and classification of tensors via matrix product state decomposition. In: 2015 IEEE International Congress on Big Data (2015)
12. Chen, G., Chen, Q., et al.: Tensor network for image classification. In: 2020 8th International Conference on Digital Home (ICDH). IEEE (2020)
13. Stoudenmire, E.M., Schwab, D.J.: Supervised learning with tensor networks. In: 30th Conference on Neural Information Processing Systems (NIPS). Neural Information Processing Systems (Nips), Barcelona, Spain (2016)

14. Baharudin, B., Lee, L.H., Khan, K.: A review of machine learning algorithms for text-documents classification. J. Adv. Inf. Technol. **1**, 4–20 (2010)
15. Selvan, R., Dam, E.B.: Tensor networks for medical image classification. In: Tal, A., Ismail Ben, A., et al. (eds.) Proceedings of the Third Conference on Medical Imaging with Deep Learning, pp. 721–732. PMLR: Proceedings of Machine Learning Research (2020)
16. Koenderink, J.J., Van Doorn, A.J.: The structure of locally orderless images. Int. J. Comput. Vis. **31**(2–3), 159–168 (1999)
17. Sun, Z.Z., Peng, C., et al.: Generative tensor network classification model for supervised machine learning. Phys. Rev. B **101**(7), 6 (2020)
18. Spanhol, F.A., Oliveira, L.S., et al.: A dataset for breast cancer histopathological image classification. IEEE Trans. Biomed. Eng. **63**(7), 1455–1462 (2016)
19. Janowczyk, A., Madabhushi, A.: Deep learning for digital pathology image analysis: a comprehensive tutorial with selected use cases. J. Pathol. Inform. **7**, 29 (2016)
20. Cruz-Roa, A., Basavanhally, A., et al.: Automatic detection of invasive ductal carcinoma in whole slide images with convolutional neural networks. In: 2nd Conference on Medical Imaging - Digital Pathology, San Diego, CA. Spie-Int Soc Optical Engineering (2014)
21. Veeling, B.S., Linmans, J., Winkens, J., Cohen, T., Welling, M.: Rotation equivariant CNNs for digital pathology. In: Frangi, A.F., Schnabel, J.A., Davatzikos, C., Alberola-López, C., Fichtinger, G. (eds.) MICCAI 2018. LNCS, vol. 11071, pp. 210–218. Springer, Cham (2018). https://doi.org/10.1007/978-3-030-00934-2_24
22. Shi, Y.Y., Duan, L.M., Vidal, G.: Classical simulation of quantum many-body systems with a tree tensor network. Phys. Rev. A **74**(2), 4 (2006)
23. Novikov, A., Trofimov, M., Oseledets, I.: Exponential machines. Bull. Polish Acad. Sci. Techn. Sci. **66**(6) (2018)
24. Perez-Garcia, D., Verstraete, F., et al.: Matrix product state representations. Quantum Inf. Comput. **7**(5–6), 401–430 (2007)
25. Huang, G., Liu, Z., et al.: Densely connected convolutional networks. In: 30th IEEE/CVF Conference on Computer Vision and Pattern Recognition (CVPR), Honolulu, HI (2017). IEEE
26. Chen, Y.W., Guo, K., et al.: Robust supervised learning based on tensor network method. In: 33rd Youth Academic Annual Conference of Chinese Association of Automation (YAC), Nanjing. Peoples R China (2018)
27. Zdunek, R., Fonal, K.: Nonnegatively constrained tensor network for classification problems. In: 11th International Conference on Ubiquitous and Future Networks (ICUFN), Zagreb, Croatia. IEEE (2019)
28. Rhu, M., Gimelshein, N., et al.: vDNN: virtualized deep neural networks for scalable, memory-efficient neural network design. In: 49th Annual IEEE/ACM International Symposium on Microarchitecture (MICRO), Taipei, Taiwan (2016)

# Gradient-Rebalanced Uncertainty Minimization for Cross-Site Adaptation of Medical Image Segmentation

Jiaming Li[1], Chaowei Fang[2](✉), and Guanbin Li[1]

[1] School of Data and Computer Science, Sun Yet-Sen University,
Guangzhou 510006, China
`lijm48@mail2.sysu.edu.cn`, `liguanbin@mail.sysu.edu.cn`
[2] School of Artificial Intelligence, Xidian University, Xi'an 710071, China
`chaoweifang@outlook.com`

**Abstract.** Automatically adapting image segmentation across data sites benefits to reduce the data annotation burden in medical image analysis. Due to variations in image collection procedures, there usually exists moderate domain gap between medical image datasets from different sites. Increasing the prediction certainty is beneficial for gradually reducing the category-wise domain shift. However, uncertainty minimization naturally leads to bias towards major classes since the target object usually occupies a small portion of pixels in the input image. In this paper, we propose a gradient-rebalanced uncertainty minimization scheme which is capable of eliminating the learning bias. First, the foreground pixels and background pixels are reweighted according to the total gradient amplitude of every class. Furthermore, we devise a feature-level adaptation scheme to reduce the overall domain gap between source and target datasets, based on feature norm regularization and adversarial learning. Experiments on CT pancreas segmentation and MRI prostate segmentation validate that, our method outperforms existing cross-site adaptation algorithms by around 3% on the DICE similarity coefficient.

**Keywords:** Medical image segmentation · Domain alignment · Uncertainty minimization · Adversarial learning

## 1 Introduction

Recently, deep convolutional neural networks achieve encouraging progress in medical image segmentation [2]. However, segmentation models trained on the source dataset hardly generalize to the target dataset collected from other sites, considering that the target dataset usually has moderate domain shift compared

**Supplementary Information** The online version contains supplementary material available at https://doi.org/10.1007/978-3-031-18910-4_12.

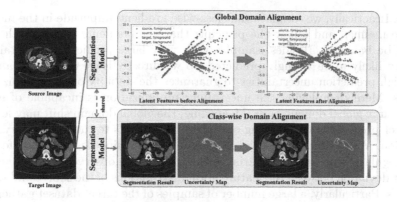

**Fig. 1.** An example of pancreas segmentation for illustrating the performance of our devised global and class-wise domain alignment strategies. The global domain alignment based on joint feature norm regularization and adversarial learning can effectively reduce the overall domain gap and increase the inter-class separability in the latent feature space. Meanwhile, the gradient-based uncertainty minimization helps to further reduce the class-wise domain gap and improve the segmentation result.

to the source dataset because of differences in imaging protocols, devices, etc. Re-annotating every target dataset is uneconomical and labor-intensive. Thus, we focus on implementing the cross-site adaptation of medical image segmentation without data re-annotation in this paper.

Unsupervised domain adaptation (UDA) is an effective solution to the cross-site adaptation problem. A large number of UDA algorithms are devised based on domain alignment in the input space [5,24,32,33] or the intermediate feature space [7,9,14,26] via adversarial learning [11]. However, it is challenging for adversarial learning to achieve the alignment of distribution details (e.g. the inter-class decision boundary) between source and target domains. The class-wise distribution alignment can be refined via minimizing the uncertainty estimated by entropy loss [1,27,28] or maximum squares loss [3]. Such uncertainty minimization helps to implement the class-wise distribution alignment, since it is able to increase the intra-class compactness while preserving the inter-class separability. In some scenarios of medical image segmentation, such as segmenting the pancreas or prostate organ, pixels of different classes are severely imbalanced. Pure uncertainty minimization schemes based on entropy or maximum squares losses induce to severe learning bias. To alleviate the above issue, the class-wise frequencies can be used to re-weight the estimated uncertainty map [3] or constrain the class distribution of the network predictions [1]. However, the frequency values can not reflect the practical influence degrees on the network optimization, thus limiting the capacity in data re-balancing for these methods.

In this paper, we propose a gradient-rebalanced uncertainty minimization mechanism. The uncertainty regularization losses of samples are re-weighted with the accumulated gradient amplitudes of classes. This is helpful for maintaining the equilibrium among the optimization influences caused by different classes. Practically, we estimate the class-wise gradient amplitude in the moving average manner, and follow the principle that the gradients toward each class should be balanced. Besides, samples with very large prediction uncertainties are very likely to be wrongly predicted, so we directly leave out those samples with high prediction uncertainties to guarantee the stability of the optimization process. Merely employing the uncertainty minimization is incapable of eliminating large global domain shift. Meanwhile, the global domain shift may lead to incorrect predictions which bring optimization artifacts to the uncertainty minimization. We devise a global domain alignment pipeline based on the feature norm regularization and adversarial learning. First, we observe that there exists evident deviation between the feature norm distributions of the source and target datasets. Particularly, a large number of samples of the target dataset gather in a compact and small feature space, which harms the inter-class separability. Hence, we constrain latent features of images from both source and target datasets to approach a fixed norm value like in [29]. This benefits the feature distribution alignment across datasets and improve the inter-class separability of samples by making them scatter in a relatively larger feature space. Furthermore, a gradient reversal layer is employed to take advantage of adversarial learning for generating domain-indiscriminative feature representation. Actually, the training process of our method is composed of three stages: 1) We first pre-train the segmentation network on the source dataset; 2) Then, the feature norm regularization and adversarial learning are applied for eliminating the global domain shift; 3) Finally, we implement fine-grained class-wise domain alignment with the help of the gradient-rebalanced uncertainty minimization. An example of pancreas segmentation is provided in Fig. 1 to illustrate the efficacy of our method. Extensive experiments on the pancreas and prostate segmentation tasks indicate our proposed method outperforms existing cross-site adaptation methods by large margins.

Main contributions of this paper are as follows:

1) A gradient-rebalanced uncertainty minimization strategy is proposed for simultaneously reducing class-wise domain shift and relieving the class imbalance issue in the unsupervised cross-site adaptation of medical image segmentation.
2) To ensure the effectiveness of uncertainty minimization, we propose to reduce the global domain shift between source and target datasets based on feature norm regularization and domain-adversarial learning.
3) Extensive experiments on the pancreas and prostate segmentation tasks indicate that our proposed method achieves significantly better performance than state-of-the-art unsupervised cross-site adaptation algorithms.

## 2   Related Work

The main challenge in unsupervised cross-site adaptation is to eliminate the domain shift between the source and target datasets. The majority of existing

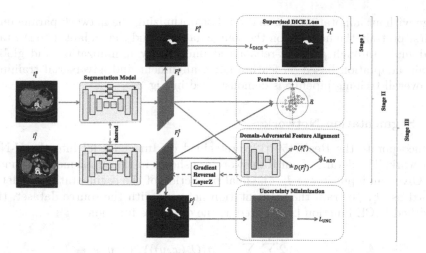

**Fig. 2.** The training pipeline of our method. The training procedure is constituted by three stages: 1) The segmentation network is pre-trained on source images; 2) The norm regularization and adversarial learning are utilized to alleviate the global domain gap; 3) The adaptation is further refined via applying the uncertainty minimization on unlabeled target images.

methods for solving the unsupervised domain adaptation of image segmentation models attempt to mitigate the domain shift on input images [4,5,13,18,24,31] or certain latent space [7,14,15,22,26,27,34]. Inspired from [29], we introduce the feature norm regularization to bridge the global domain gap between source and target datasets, via constraining the average of feature norms to an fixed constant with the $L_2$-distance metric. Furthermore, the adversarial learning is incorporated to align feature distributions of source and target domains with the gradient reversal layer.

Self-training algorithms, such as pseudo labeling [35] and uncertainty minimization based on the entropy loss [1,27] or the maximum squares loss [3], are proved to be effective in unsupervised domain adaption. In this paper, we propose to mitigate the imbalance problem more thoroughly through estimating the re-balancing coefficients with respect to the accumulated gradient amplitude of different classes.

## 3 Method

This paper aims at leveraging a source medical image dataset with pixel-wise annotations to train a segmentation model for the target dataset without annotations. Suppose the source dataset is composed of $N^s$ images $\{(I_i^s, Y_i^s) \mid i = 1, \cdots, N^s\}$, and the target dataset contains $N^t$ unlabeled images $\{I_i^t | i = 1, \cdots, N^t\}$. $I_i^s \in \mathbb{R}^{h \times w \times c}$ and $Y_i^s \in \{0,1\}^{h \times w}$ represent a source image and its pixel-wise annotation respectively. $h$, $w$ and $c$ denotes the height, width and channel size of the input image, respectively. $I^t$ denotes a target domain image without annotation information. For optimizing the network parameters, we first pretrain the network on the source dataset, and then adapt it to the target domain through gradient-rebalanced uncertainty minimization and global domain adaptation based on feature norm alignment and adversarial training. The overall training pipeline is demonstrated in Fig. 2.

## 3.1   Segmentation Network

We incorporate the ResNet50 [12] pretrained on Imagenet [8] into the U-Net framework. The details of our framework are shown in the supplementary material. Given an input image $I_i^s$, the final prediction of the segmentation model is defined as $O_i^s$. To train the segmentation network with the source dataset, the smoothed DICE function [20] is used as the objective function,

$$L_{\text{DICE}} = 1 - \frac{2\sum_{i=1}^{N^s}\sum_{x=1}^{h}\sum_{y=1}^{w}\sigma(O_i^s(x,y))Y_i^s(x,y) + \epsilon}{\sum_{i=1}^{N^s}\sum_{x=1}^{h}\sum_{y=1}^{w}[\sigma(O_i^s(x,y))^2 + Y_i^s(x,y)^2] + \epsilon}, \tag{1}$$

where $\epsilon$ is a constant for smoothing, and $\sigma(\cdot)$ is the Sigmoid function. $O_i^s(x,y)$ and $Y_i^s(x,y)$ indicates the value at position $(x,y)$ of $O_i^s$ and $Y_i^s$, respectively.

## 3.2   Eliminating Global Domain Shift

Inspired from [29], we devise a feature norm regularization constraint to eliminate the global domain shift, via constraining the average norms of features from source or target domain into a predefined value. This also helps to prevent features from gathering in a small space, which harms the inter-class separability.

Given an input source or target domain image $I_i^s/I_i^t$, we denote the feature maps produced by the penultimate layer of the segmentation network be $F_i^s/F_i^t$ with shape of $h' \times w' \times d$. The feature norm regularization term is formulated as follows,

$$L_{\text{FNA}} = (\frac{\sum_{i=1}^{N^s}\sum_{x=1}^{h'}\sum_{y=1}^{w'}||F_i^s(x,y)||_2^2}{N^s h' w'} - \kappa)^2$$
$$+ (\frac{\sum_{i=1}^{N^t}\sum_{x=1}^{h'}\sum_{y=1}^{w'}||F_i^t(x,y)||_2^2}{N^t h' w'} - \kappa)^2, \tag{2}$$

where $\kappa$ is a constant. The above regularization penalizes the feature norm deviation between the source and target domains, via pushing the averaged feature norms of source and target domains to a constant. In contrast to directly minimize the Euclidean distance between the two averaged feature norms, the utilization of an intermediate value avoids trivial solutions in which all feature values vanish to zero. Instead of regarding $\kappa$ as a hyper-parameter in [29], we choose $\kappa$ through averaging the feature norms of all source images with the model pretrained on the source dataset.

The feature norm regularization can not guarantee to explicitly reduce the feature distribution difference between two domains. Thus, we further adopt the adversarial learning to construct a feature space in which the source and target domains are indivisible. The discriminator model in [26] is utilized to identify whether the input feature maps $F_i^s$-s and $F_i^t$-s are from the source or target domain. The adversarial learning algorithm based on the least squares loss function [19] is adopted for network optimization. Denote the discriminator network as $D$. The loss function for optimizing the discriminator and the segmentation model is as follows,

$$L_{\text{ADV}} = \frac{1}{N^s hw} ||D(F_i^s) - 1||_2^2 + \frac{1}{N^t hw} ||D(F_i^t)||_2^2, \tag{3}$$

$D(F)$ denotes the domain indication map predicted by the discriminator on the input feature map $F$. The discriminator and feature extraction module are learned via solving the minimax problem under the supervision of the above loss function. The parameters of the discriminator are updated through minimizing (3), while those of the feature extraction module are updated through maximizing (3). Like in [10], we employ the gradient reversal layer to jointly implement two goals by minimizing (3). During the forward propagation pass, the gradient reversal layer plays the role of identity mapping function. During the backward propagation pass, it multiplies the gradients with $-1$.

### 3.3 Refining Class-wise Domain Alignment via Gradient-Rebalanced Uncertainty Minimization

On the basis of globally aligned features, we further employ the uncertainty minimization to achieve fine-grained class-wise domain alignment. In this paper, we use the maximum squares loss proposed in [3], to calculate the uncertainty map, $\mathcal{R}(v) = -\sigma(v)^2 - (1 - \sigma(v))^2$.

Pixels with large prediction uncertainty values are very likely to be incorrect. Thus, we directly disregard these pixels during the uncertainty minimization with a low threshold $\delta_l$ and a high threshold $\delta_h$. In medical image segmentation, there usually exists severe data imbalance. For example, when segmenting the pancreas or prostate organ, the target object only occupies a small part of pixels in input images. Under such circumstance, the uncertainty minimization is dominated by the majority class, which causes severe learning bias. To re-balance the training data, we propose to re-weight the estimated uncertainty values. The uncertainty minimization objective can be formulated as follows,

$$L_{\text{UNC}} = \frac{1}{N^t hw} \sum_{j=1}^{N^t} \sum_{x=1}^{h} \sum_{y=1}^{w} [\alpha \mathcal{R}(O_j^t(x,y))(\sigma(O_j^t(x,y)) > \delta_h)$$
$$+ (1 - \alpha)\mathcal{R}(O_j^t(x,y))(\sigma(O_j^t(x,y)) < \delta_l)]. \tag{4}$$

$\alpha$ is the weight coefficient and $\delta$ is the threshold to distinguish foreground and background pixel. Existing methods [1,3] depend on class frequency for data rebalancing. However, this can not reflect the actual influence of class imbalance on the optimization of network parameters. Compared to foreground predictions, the background predictions are always more confident in medical segmentation. The uncertainty of background predictions are relatively small so that the mean gradient of background predictions is much smaller. Thus, the gradient of model will bias toward foreground classes with class-frequency based re-balancing. To settle the class imbalance issue more thoroughly, we propose to estimate the weight coefficient following the principle that the accumulated gradient magnitude of foreground pixels (those pixels belong to the target object) should be equivalent to that of background pixels. The derivative of $L_{\text{UNC}}$ with respect to $O_j^t(x, y)$ is formulated as below,

$$\frac{\partial L_{\text{UNC}}}{\partial O_j^t(x,y)} = \begin{cases} \frac{\alpha}{N^t h w} \frac{\partial \mathcal{R}(v)}{\partial v}|_{v=O_j^t(x,y)}, & \text{if } \sigma(O_j^t(x,y)) > \delta_h; \\ \frac{1-\alpha}{N^t h w} \frac{\partial \mathcal{R}(v)}{\partial v}|_{v=O_j^t(x,y)}, & \text{if } \sigma(O_j^t(x,y)) < \delta_l. \end{cases} \quad (5)$$

We assume $\{(x, y)|\sigma(O_j^t(x, y)) > \delta_h\}$ and $\{(x, y)|\sigma(O_j^t(x, y)) < \delta_l\}$ be the foreground and background set respectively. For rebalancing the importance of foreground and background in network optimization, $\alpha$ is calculated as follows,

$$\tilde{\alpha} = \frac{\sum\limits_{j=1}^{N^t} \sum\limits_{x=1}^{h} \sum\limits_{y=1}^{w} (\sigma(O_j^t(x,y)) < \delta_l) |\frac{d\mathcal{R}(v)}{dv}|_{v=O_j^t(x,y)}|}{\sum\limits_{j=1}^{N^t} \sum\limits_{x=1}^{h} \sum\limits_{y=1}^{w} (\sigma(O_j^t(x,y)) < \delta_l \text{ or } \sigma(O_j^t(x,y)) > \delta_h) |\frac{d\mathcal{R}(v)}{dv}|_{v=O_j^t(x,y)}|}. \quad (6)$$

To increase the anti-noise capacity, the moving average strategy is employed to temporally smooth $\alpha$: $\tilde{\alpha}^k = \eta\tilde{\alpha}^{k-1} + (1 - \eta)\alpha$, where $\tilde{\alpha}^k$ denotes the weight in the $k$-th optimization iteration.

### 3.4   Training Process

The training procedure is composed of three phases. In the first phase, we pretrain the segmentation model on the source dataset with the DICE loss function (1): $L = L_{\text{DICE}}$. Then, the feature norm regularization (2) and domain-adversarial learning (3) are employed for eliminating the global domain shift with the objective function: $L = L_{\text{DICE}} + \lambda_{\text{FNA}} L_{\text{FNA}} + \lambda_{\text{ADV}} L_{\text{ADV}}$. $\lambda_{\text{ADV}}$ and $\lambda_{\text{FNA}}$ are the weights for $L_{\text{ADV}}$ and $L_{\text{FNA}}$ respectively.

Afterwards, we involve in the gradient-rebalanced uncertainty minimization (4) for further reducing class-wise domain shift with the following loss function,

$$L = L_{\text{DICE}} + \lambda_{\text{FNA}} L_{\text{FNA}} + \lambda_{\text{ADV}} L_{\text{ADV}} + \lambda_{\text{UNC}} L_{\text{UNC}}. \quad (7)$$

$\lambda_{\text{UNC}}$ is the weight for $L_{\text{UNC}}$.

## 4   Experiments

### 4.1   Datasets

**Pancreas Segmentation.** Two CT datasets collected by different institutes are used to validate UDA algorithms. 1) The NIHC dataset [23] which includes

**Table 1.** Comparison with unsupervised domain adaptation and semi-supervised learning methods on the pancreas segmentation task. 'w/o adapt.' indicates the baseline segmentation model trained with only source images. ↑ indicates the higher value is better, while ↓ indicates the lower value is better.

| Method | Metric | | |
|---|---|---|---|
| | DSC ↑ | IoU ↑ | ASSD ↓ |
| w/o adapt | 0.6438 | 0.4820 | 2.0163 |
| Mean Teacher [6] | 0.7009 | 0.5456 | 2.5534 |
| TUNA-Net [24] | 0.7164 | 0.5641 | 1.1858 |
| SRDA [1] | 0.7236 | 0.5724 | 1.1191 |
| Synth [5] | 0.7317 | 0.5815 | 1.6768 |
| MPA [30] | 0.7403 | 0.5895 | 1.0232 |
| Ours | **0.7714** | **0.6319** | **0.5471** |

**Table 2.** Comparison with unsupervised domain adaptation and semi-supervised learning methods on the prostate segmentation task under DSC. 'mean' indicates metric values averaged from five folds.

| Method | I2CVB | | | | | |
|---|---|---|---|---|---|---|
| | fold 1 | fold 2 | fold 3 | fold 4 | fold 5 | mean |
| w/ adapt. | 0.5959 | 0.5892 | 0.6314 | 0.4797 | 0.5184 | 0.5629 |
| Mean teacher [6] | 0.7439 | 0.7968 | 0.7861 | 0.8010 | 0.8413 | 0.7938 |
| TUNA-Net [24] | 0.7499 | 0.7832 | 0.8083 | 0.7541 | 0.7699 | 0.7731 |
| SRDA [1] | 0.7972 | 0.7599 | 0.7742 | 0.7687 | 0.8208 | 0.7842 |
| Synth [5] | 0.7809 | 0.7801 | 0.7735 | 0.7862 | 0.7951 | 0.7832 |
| MPA [30] | 0.8025 | 0.8132 | 0.7998 | 0.7893 | 0.8240 | 0.8058 |
| Ours | 0.8290 | 0.8250 | 0.8220 | 0.8053 | 0.8381 | 0.8239 |

82 contrast-enhanced abdominal CT volumes with pixel-wise annotations is regarded as the source dataset. 2) The MALC (short for Multi-atlas Labeling Challenge) [16] provides 50 abdomen CT-s as the target dataset. We randomly select 35 CT-s for training and 15 CT-s for testing.

**Prostate Segmentation.** Two MRI datasets are collected to validate the effectiveness of our method in prostate segmentation. The source dataset is from the NCI-ISBI 2013 challenge [21] which is composed of 80 volumes. The I2CVB (Initiative for Collaborative Computer Vision Benchmarking) [17], including 40 MRI-s, is selected as the target dataset. 5-fold cross-validation is conducted for comparing different cross-site adaptation methods. In each fold, 32 and 8 MRI-s are chosen for training and testing respectively.

The mean DICE similarity coefficient (DSC), intersection over union (IoU), and average symmetric surface distance (ASSD) are used for measuring the performance of segmentation algorithms.

## 4.2  Implementation Details

During training, random cropping, rotation and elastic deformation are applied for data augmentation. In the first stage, we train the source model using a batch size of 16 and a learning rate of $10^{-4}$ for 1,600 epochs. Then, the learning rate is reduced to $1 \times 10^{-5}$. The second and third stage cost 400 epochs and 200 epochs respectively. The smoothness coefficient $\epsilon$ in the DICE loss function (1) is set to 1. The thresholds for trimming the uncertainty map in (4) are set as: $\delta_l = 0.3$ and $\delta_h = 0.7$. The weighting factors $\lambda_{\text{FNA}}$, $\lambda_{\text{ADV}}$ and $\lambda_{\text{UNC}}$, are set to 0.1, 1 and 50 respectively. The parameter $\eta$ is set to 0.95.

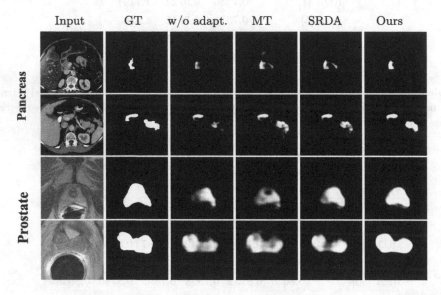

**Fig. 3.** Qualitative comparisons of different methods on the pancreas segmentation and prostate segmentation task. Our method achieves better segmentation results than the baseline model without adaptation, the mean teacher algorithm(MT) [6], and SRDA [1].

## 4.3  Experimental Results

**Comparisons with Other Methods.** As presented in Table 1 and 2, we compare our approach against four existing unsupervised domain adaptation methods, including TUNA-Net [24], SRDA [1], Synth [5], and MPA [30], and one semi-supervised learning method [6] which is devised based on the mean teacher model [25]. The experimental results on the pancreas segmentation task are presented in Table 1. As can be observed, our proposed method outperforms other methods significantly. Particularly, it surpasses the second best UDA method MPA by 3.11% in DSC, 4.24% in IoU, and 0.4761 in ASSD, respectively. Our method obtains a drastic gain of 12.76% under the DSC metric, compared to the baseline model without adaptation.

**Table 3.** Comparisons between different domain alignment strategies. 'FNR', 'DAFA', and 'GRUM' denotes feature norm regularization, domain-adversarial feature alignment, and gradient-rebalanced uncertainty minimization respectively. The evaluation metric is DSC.

| No. | FNR | DAFA | GRUM | Pancreas | Prostate |
|-----|-----|------|------|----------|----------|
| 1   |     |      |      | 0.6438   | 0.5629   |
| 2   | √   |      |      | 0.7129   | 0.7696   |
| 3   |     | √    |      | 0.7141   | 0.7586   |
| 4   |     |      | √    | 0.7588   | 0.7428   |
| 5   | √   | √    |      | 0.7229   | 0.8099   |
| 6   | √   |      | √    | 0.7671   | 0.8128   |
| 7   |     | √    | √    | 0.7650   | 0.7899   |
| 8   | √   | √    | √    | 0.7714   | 0.8239   |

**Table 4.** Comparisons between different rebalancing strategies under DSC. 'None' denotes the variant without data rebalancing. 'Class ratio' or 'Gradient' means that the weighting coefficient is estimated by class ratios or class-wise gradient amplitudes.

| Rebalancing strategy | Pancreas | Prostate |
|----------------------|----------|----------|
| None                 | 0.7229   | 0.8099   |
| Class ratio          | 0.7274   | 0.8107   |
| Gradient             | 0.7714   | 0.8239   |

On the prostate segmentation task, we conduct the 5-fold cross-validation to compare our method against different methods. The experimental results are reported in Table 2. Our method achieves better performance than other algorithms under most metrics of five testing folds. In particular, it surpasses the second best method (MPA in [30]) by 1.79% under DSC. Compared to the baseline model merely trained with the source dataset ('w/o adapt.'), our method produces segmentation results with 26.10% higher DSC score. Qualitative comparisons on the pancreas and prostate segmentation tasks are visualized in Fig. 3.

**Ablation Study.** We attempt to apply different domain alignment strategies for bridging the distribution gap between the source and target datasets. The experimental results on pancreas and prostate segmentation are presented in Table 3. The baseline model which is trained on the source dataset only is denoted by No. 1. Using the feature norm regularization (FNR, No. 2), domain adversarial feature alignment (DAFA, No. 3), or gradient-rebalanced uncertainty minimization (GRUM, No. 4) alone can bring significant performance improvement. For example, FNR, DAFA and GRUM causes 10.73%, 10.92% and 17.86% DSC gain respectively, on the pancreas segmentation task. For global domain alignment,

FNR and DAFA are complementary to each other FNR aims at eliminating the deviation of feature norms and preventing the features from gathering in a small space while DAFA is targeted at producing domain-indistinguishable feature representation. Hence, the utilization of both FNR and DAFA as indicated by No. 5 outperforms pure FNR (No. 2) or DAFA (No. 3). On the other hand, The class-wise alignment implemented via our devised uncertainty minimization can significantly promote the segmentation performance. In contrast to No. 2, 3 and 5, the involvement of GRUM leads to DSC gain of 7.60%, 7.13% and 6.71% in No. 6, 7 and 8 respectively. This indicates the necessity of applying the finer-grained class-wise domain alignment on the basis of global domain alignment.

*Performance of Using Different Rebalancing Strategies in Uncertainty Minimization.* As control experiments, two variants of our method are implemented: 1) $\alpha$ is fixed as 0.5, which means that no rebalancing strategy is adopted; 2) $\alpha$ is estimated based on the class ratios as in Eq. 5. The experimental results are presented in Table 4. Without using the rebalancing strategy, the DSC metric dropped substantially compared to the utilization of our gradient-based rebalancing strategy. In contrast to the rebalancing strategy based on class ratios, the gradient-based rebalancing strategy induces to performance gain of 6.05% and 1.63% DSC on the pancreas and prostate segmentation task respectively.

## 5    Conclusions

In this paper, a novel pipeline is presented to settle the unsupervised cross-site adaptation problem. For eliminating the domain gap between the source and target datasets, we first implement the global domain alignment via the feature norm regularization and the domain-aware adversarial learning. Then, the uncertainty minimization is adopted to achieve class-wise domain alignment. More importantly, a gradient-based rebalancing strategy is devised for preventing the learning bias in the uncertainty minimization process. Experiments on pancreas and prostate segmentation datasets collected from different sites, indicate that our method outperforms state-of-the-art unsupervised cross-site adaptation methods.

## References

1. Bateson, M., Kervadec, H., Dolz, J., Lombaert, H., Ben Ayed, I.: Source-relaxed domain adaptation for image segmentation. In: Martel, A.L., et al. (eds.) MICCAI 2020. LNCS, vol. 12261, pp. 490–499. Springer, Cham (2020). https://doi.org/10.1007/978-3-030-59710-8_48
2. Chen, H., Wang, X., Huang, Y., Wu, X., Yu, Y., Wang, L.: Harnessing 2D networks and 3D features for automated pancreas segmentation from volumetric CT images. In: Shen, D., et al. (eds.) MICCAI 2019. LNCS, vol. 11769, pp. 339–347. Springer, Cham (2019). https://doi.org/10.1007/978-3-030-32226-7_38

3. Chen, M., Xue, H., Cai, D.: Domain adaptation for semantic segmentation with maximum squares loss. In: Proceedings of the IEEE/CVF International Conference on Computer Vision, pp. 2090–2099 (2019)
4. Chiou, E., Giganti, F., Punwani, S., Kokkinos, I., Panagiotaki, E.: Harnessing uncertainty in domain adaptation for MRI prostate lesion segmentation. In: Martel, A.L., et al. (eds.) MICCAI 2020. LNCS, vol. 12261, pp. 510–520. Springer, Cham (2020). https://doi.org/10.1007/978-3-030-59710-8_50
5. Chiou, E., Giganti, F., Punwani, S., Kokkinos, I., Panagiotaki, E.: Unsupervised domain adaptation with semantic consistency across heterogeneous modalities for MRI prostate lesion segmentation. In: Albarqouni, S., et al. (eds.) DART/FAIR-2021. LNCS, vol. 12968, pp. 90–100. Springer, Cham (2021). https://doi.org/10.1007/978-3-030-87722-4_9
6. Cui, W., et al.: Semi-supervised brain lesion segmentation with an adapted mean teacher model. In: Chung, A.C.S., Gee, J.C., Yushkevich, P.A., Bao, S. (eds.) IPMI 2019. LNCS, vol. 11492, pp. 554–565. Springer, Cham (2019). https://doi.org/10.1007/978-3-030-20351-1_43
7. Degel, M.A., Navab, N., Albarqouni, S.: Domain and geometry agnostic CNNs for left atrium segmentation in 3D ultrasound. In: Frangi, A.F., Schnabel, J.A., Davatzikos, C., Alberola-López, C., Fichtinger, G. (eds.) MICCAI 2018. LNCS, vol. 11073, pp. 630–637. Springer, Cham (2018). https://doi.org/10.1007/978-3-030-00937-3_72
8. Deng, J., Dong, W., Socher, R., Li, L.J., Li, K., Fei-Fei, L.: ImageNet: a large-scale hierarchical image database. In: 2009 IEEE Conference on Computer Vision and Pattern Recognition, pp. 248–255. IEEE (2009)
9. Dou, Q., et al.: PnP-AdaNet: plug-and-play adversarial domain adaptation network with a benchmark at cross-modality cardiac segmentation. arXiv preprint arXiv:1812.07907 (2018)
10. Ganin, Y., Lempitsky, V.: Unsupervised domain adaptation by backpropagation. arXiv preprint arXiv:1409.7495 (2014)
11. Goodfellow, I.J., et al.: Generative adversarial networks. arXiv preprint arXiv:1406.2661 (2014)
12. He, K., Zhang, X., Ren, S., Sun, J.: Deep residual learning for image recognition. In: Proceedings of the IEEE Conference on Computer Vision and Pattern Recognition, pp. 770–778 (2016)
13. Hoffman, J., et al.: CyCADA: cycle-consistent adversarial domain adaptation. arXiv preprint arXiv:1711.03213 (2017)
14. Hoffman, J., Wang, D., Yu, F., Darrell, T.: FCNs in the wild: pixel-level adversarial and constraint-based adaptation. arXiv preprint arXiv:1612.02649 (2016)
15. Hu, M., et al.: Fully test-time adaptation for image segmentation. In: de Bruijne, M., et al. (eds.) MICCAI 2021. LNCS, vol. 12903, pp. 251–260. Springer, Cham (2021). https://doi.org/10.1007/978-3-030-87199-4_24
16. Landman, B., Xu, Z., Igelsias, J., Styner, M., Langerak, T., Klein, A.: MICCAI multi-atlas labeling beyond the cranial vault-workshop and challenge (2015)
17. Lemaître, G., Martí, R., Freixenet, J., Vilanova, J.C., Walker, P.M., Meriaudeau, F.: Computer-aided detection and diagnosis for prostate cancer based on mono and multi-parametric MRI: a review. Comput. Biol. Med. 60, 8–31 (2015)
18. Li, K., Wang, S., Yu, L., Heng, P.A.: Dual-teacher++: exploiting intra-domain and inter-domain knowledge with reliable transfer for cardiac segmentation. IEEE Trans. Med. Imaging 40, 2771–2782(2020)

19. Mao, X., Li, Q., Xie, H., Lau, R.Y., Wang, Z., Paul Smolley, S.: Least squares generative adversarial networks. In: Proceedings of the IEEE International Conference on Computer Vision, pp. 2794–2802 (2017)
20. Milletari, F., Navab, N., Ahmadi, S.A.: V-Net: fully convolutional neural networks for volumetric medical image segmentation. In: 2016 Fourth International Conference on 3D Vision (3DV), pp. 565–571. IEEE (2016)
21. Bloch, N., et al.: NCI-ISBI 2013 challenge: automated segmentation of prostate structures (2013). http://doi.org/10.7937/K9/TCIA.2015.zF0vlOPv
22. Ouyang, C., Kamnitsas, K., Biffi, C., Duan, J., Rueckert, D.: Data efficient unsupervised domain adaptation for cross-modality image segmentation. In: Shen, D., et al. (eds.) MICCAI 2019. LNCS, vol. 11765, pp. 669–677. Springer, Cham (2019). https://doi.org/10.1007/978-3-030-32245-8_74
23. Roth, H.R., et al.: DeepOrgan: multi-level deep convolutional networks for automated pancreas segmentation. In: Navab, N., Hornegger, J., Wells, W.M., Frangi, A.F. (eds.) MICCAI 2015. LNCS, vol. 9349, pp. 556–564. Springer, Cham (2015). https://doi.org/10.1007/978-3-319-24553-9_68
24. Tang, Y., Tang, Y., Sandfort, V., Xiao, J., Summers, R.M.: TUNA-net: task-oriented unsupervised adversarial network for disease recognition in cross-domain chest X-rays. In: Shen, D., et al. (eds.) MICCAI 2019. LNCS, vol. 11769, pp. 431–440. Springer, Cham (2019). https://doi.org/10.1007/978-3-030-32226-7_48
25. Tarvainen, A., Valpola, H.: Mean teachers are better role models: weight-averaged consistency targets improve semi-supervised deep learning results. arXiv preprint arXiv:1703.01780 (2017)
26. Tsai, Y.H., Hung, W.C., Schulter, S., Sohn, K., Yang, M.H., Chandraker, M.: Learning to adapt structured output space for semantic segmentation. In: Proceedings of the IEEE Conference on Computer Vision and Pattern Recognition, pp. 7472–7481 (2018)
27. Vu, T.H., Jain, H., Bucher, M., Cord, M., Pérez, P.: ADVENT: adversarial entropy minimization for domain adaptation in semantic segmentation. In: Proceedings of the IEEE Conference on Computer Vision and Pattern Recognition, pp. 2517–2526 (2019)
28. Wu, X., Zhou, Q., Yang, Z., Zhao, C., Latecki, L.J., et al.: Entropy minimization vs. diversity maximization for domain adaptation. arXiv preprint arXiv:2002.01690 (2020)
29. Xu, R., Li, G., Yang, J., Lin, L.: Larger norm more transferable: an adaptive feature norm approach for unsupervised domain adaptation. In: Proceedings of the IEEE International Conference on Computer Vision, pp. 1426–1435 (2019)
30. Yang, C., Guo, X., Zhu, M., Ibragimov, B., Yuan, Y.: Mutual-prototype adaptation for cross-domain polyp segmentation. IEEE J. Biomed. Health Inform. 25(10), 3886–3897 (2021)
31. Yang, Y., Soatto, S.: FDA: Fourier domain adaptation for semantic segmentation. In: Proceedings of the IEEE/CVF Conference on Computer Vision and Pattern Recognition, pp. 4085–4095 (2020)
32. Zakazov, I., Shirokikh, B., Chernyavskiy, A., Belyaev, M.: Anatomy of domain shift impact on U-Net layers in MRI segmentation. In: de Bruijne, M., et al. (eds.) MICCAI 2021. LNCS, vol. 12903, pp. 211–220. Springer, Cham (2021). https://doi.org/10.1007/978-3-030-87199-4_20
33. Zeng, G., et al.: Semantic consistent unsupervised domain adaptation for cross-modality medical image segmentation. In: de Bruijne, M., et al. (eds.) MICCAI 2021. LNCS, vol. 12903, pp. 201–210. Springer, Cham (2021). https://doi.org/10.1007/978-3-030-87199-4_19

34. Zeng, G., et al.: Entropy guided unsupervised domain adaptation for cross-center hip cartilage segmentation from MRI. In: Martel, A.L., et al. (eds.) MICCAI 2020. LNCS, vol. 12261, pp. 447–456. Springer, Cham (2020). https://doi.org/10.1007/978-3-030-59710-8_44

35. Zou, Y., Yu, Z., Vijaya Kumar, B.V.K., Wang, J.: Unsupervised domain adaptation for semantic segmentation via class-balanced self-training. In: Ferrari, V., Hebert, M., Sminchisescu, C., Weiss, Y. (eds.) ECCV 2018. LNCS, vol. 11207, pp. 297–313. Springer, Cham (2018). https://doi.org/10.1007/978-3-030-01219-9_18

# DeepEnReg: Joint Enhancement and Affine Registration for Low-contrast Medical Images

Xiaolin Wang[1,2], Ziyang Li[1,2], Zi Li[1,2], Yun Peng[3], Di Hu[4], Huanyu Luo[3], Huanjie Li[5], Zhongxuan Luo[1,2], and Xin Fan[2,6(✉)]

[1] School of Software Technology, Dalian University of Technology, Dalian, China
[2] DUT-RU Co-Research Center of Advanced ICT for Active Life, Dalian, China
xin.fan@dlut.edu.cn
[3] National Center for Children's Health, Capital Medical University, Beijing, China
[4] Beijing Children's Hospital, Beijing, China
[5] School of Biomedical Engineering, Dalian University of Technology, Dalian, China
[6] DUT-RU International School of Information Science and Engineering, Dalian University of Technology, Dalian, China

**Abstract.** Affine registration aims to find the low-dimensional parametric transformation that best aligns one data to another. However, existing registration methods, either classic energy optimization or deep learning are mainly designed for adult brain images and have limited performance on infant brain images with widely varied intensity distributions and low-contrast issues. To achieve fast and robust registration on low-contrast infant brain images, we propose an unsupervised deep registration framework DeepEnReg with a deep enhancement module and a deep affine registration module. Our affine registration module leverages a multi-resolution loss to guarantee consistency on sparsely sampled infant brain images. Our DeepEnReg achieves reasonable and reliable performance on the affine registration tasks of infant brain images and synthetic data and significantly reduces irregular registration results compared to other mainstream methods. Our proposed method significantly improves the computation efficiency over the mainstream medical image processing tools (from 13 to 0.570 s for a 3D image pair on affine registration) and outperforms state-of-the-art approaches.

**Keywords:** Affine registration · Enhancement · Low-contrast medical images · Infant brain image registration · Unsupervised learning

This work was partially supported by the National Key R&D Program of China (2020YFB1313503), the National Natural Science Foundation of China (Nos. 61922019), LiaoNing Revitalization Talents Program (XLYC1807088), and the Fundamental Research Funds for the Central Universities.
X. Wang—Student.

S. Yu et al. (Eds.): PRCV 2022, LNCS 13535, pp. 152–163, 2022.
https://doi.org/10.1007/978-3-031-18910-4_13

# 1   Introduction

Registration is a fundamental task in biomedical image analysis to establish spatial correspondences among different images [13,17]. In medical image registration problems, infant brain image registration is one of the difficulties. In addition to the difficulty in establishing the complex sulci and gyrus structure correspondence, the appearance of magnetic resonance images changes significantly over the same period, and the image contrast is overly low in certain age groups are unique difficulties of infant brain image registration [1,5,9]. One of the most challenging issues is image quality degradation including low-contrast and intensity non-uniformity, and it is necessary to develop a robust registration algorithm to deal with low-contrast and non-uniform infant brain images.

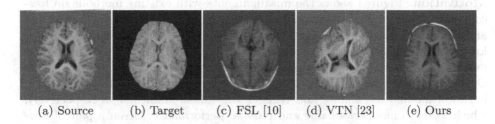

(a) Source         (b) Target         (c) FSL [10]         (d) VTN [23]         (e) Ours

**Fig. 1.** Given a low-contrast source image (a) and a target image (b), both the optimization-based method (c) and learning-based method (d) struggle to provide satisfying solutions. Our DeepEnReg (e) performs accurate registration for such scenarios.

As a critical processing step in image analysis, affine registration aims to obtain aligned images through global transformation (*e.g.*, rotations, translations, scaling, and shears), which is the main focus of this paper. To improve the registration performance on infant brain images, current mainstream methods [1,20] mainly rely on tissue segmentation maps, which are time-consuming and labor-intensive. Without segmentation maps, classic methods [6,10,11] involve an iterative optimization of registration energy over a space of transformation. The representative conventional affine algorithm in analysis tools FSL [10] and NiftyReg [18] is widely used for medical images, which employs a fast global optimization method using boundary-based registration. However, these methods have a strong constraint on images that must be of sufficient quality to extract surfaces/boundaries that separate tissue types. Recent learning-based strategies [2,3,12,14,15,21,22] leverage dataset of images to solve registration. They employ deep networks to output transformation parameters *e.g.*, affine or dense displacement field. Since the registration step is achieved via a single feed-forward pass, learning-based affine methods [3,23] are substantially faster than classic iterative methods. However, prior registration methods, either derived from energy optimization or deep learning, mostly acquiesce to an ideal situation that the images have high-quality acquisition, and frequently fail when encountering low-contrast and non-uniform infant brain images.

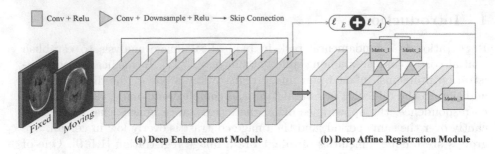

Conv + Relu   Conv + Downsample + Relu ⟶ Skip Connection

(a) Deep Enhancement Module          (b) Deep Affine Registration Module

**Fig. 2.** The proposed DeepEnReg scheme. The overall architecture is trained with self-supervised enhancement losses $\ell_E$ and unsupervised affine registration losses $\ell_A$.

**Motivation.** Figure 1 shows the misalignments with existing methods on low-contrast infant brain images. Traditional registration methods are misaligned and time-consuming, and existing deep learning affine networks lack design for low-contrast images. To overcome the aforementioned problems, we propose a multi-resolution unsupervised deep registration framework (DeepEnReg). Our DeepEnReg combines the deep enhancement module and the deep affine registration module to enhance and register the infant brain images respectively, which leads to more reasonable and reliable performance. Given a pair of low-contrast and non-uniform images, the deep enhancement module performs a pixel-wise enhancement on infant images. Then, the enhanced images are fed into the deep affine registration module with a multi-resolution regularization term to promote accuracy. Finally, the low-contrast source image is warped with the affine transformation to align with the target image. In summary, our main contributions are: (1) We introduce a deep enhancement module to help the affine registration module learn transformation from low-contrast images in an unsupervised manner. (2) The deep enhancement module is plug-and-play to effectively help deep learning and traditional methods in pixel-wise registration. (3) Our proposed method outperforms the state-of-the-art approaches qualitatively and quantitatively on clinical infant brain images and synthetic data with less time consumption.

## 2   The Proposed Method

Our architecture consists of two key parts: i) the deep enhancement network that estimates the optimal intensity enhancement results by enhancing the given input images, and ii) the deep affine registration module which obtains the best-fitting transformation matrix to align the source image and the target image. And we apply a multi-resolution strategy in the affine registration module.

### 2.1   Deep Enhancement Module

Considering low-contrast and widely varied intensity distribution issues in input scans, we refer to the recent unsupervised enhancement framework for natural images [7,16]. And the architecture of the deep enhancement module is elaborated as follows.

As shown in Fig. 2(a), we apply 3D convolution in our enhancement network which employs seven convolutional layers with kernels of size $3 \times 3$ and stride 1. Each layer except the last one is followed by the ReLU activation function and the last layer is followed by the Tanh activation function. The inputs of our enhancement module are low-contrast infant brain image slices and it outputs the enhanced brain image slices which are processed into a brain image. To ensure the effectiveness of the enhancement network, we introduce two losses to guide the training process. One of the losses is a spatial consistency loss, which preserves the local information of the adjacent regions between the enhanced image and the source image, thus ensuring the spatial consistency of the enhanced image. Besides, an intensity control loss function is also applied to control the difference between the average intensity value of the local region and the enhanced one.

## 2.2  Deep Affine Registration Module

As shown in Fig. 2(b), the affine registration network aims to align the source image $S_e \in \mathbb{R}_e$ and target image $T_e \in \mathbb{R}_e$ with an affine transform $f(x)$. Following the existing literature [4,23], our network progressively down-samples the input by doing stride convolution and a fully-connected layer is applied to produce 12 numeric parameters, which represent a transform matrix A and a displacement vector b. And in the actual implementation of the affine registration network structure, we adopt a multi-resolution strategy in the downsampling process. In detail, we perform fully connected convolutions on features of three different resolutions to obtain three affine registration matrices. The flow field produced by this network is defined as $f(x) = Ax + b$. To train our model in an unsupervised manner, we measure the similarity between the moving images warped by the last affine transform $S_e \circ \phi$ and the fixed image $T_e$. Furthermore, regularization losses are introduced on three transformation matrices to prevent the flow fields from over-fitting.

We employ a plain convolutional neural network of 5 down-sampling 3D convolutional layers with a kernel size of $3 \times 3 \times 3$ and stride 2 for the affine network. The fixed image and the moving image are concatenated as a 2-channel 3D image which is fed into the network and outputs the affine transformation matrix.

## 2.3  Loss Functions

**Deep Enhancement Module.** The loss function $\ell_E$ of the enhancement network consists of two components which is defined as:

$$\ell_E = \ell_{spa} + \ell_{con}. \tag{1}$$

And one is the spatial consistency loss $\ell_{spa}$ that preserves the difference of adjacent regions between the input image and the enhanced image to encourage spatial coherence. The $\ell_{spa}$ is as:

$$\ell_{spa} = \frac{1}{N} \sum_{i=1}^{N} \sum_{j \in \Omega(i)} (|(E_i - E_j)| - |(I_i - I_j)|)^2, \tag{2}$$

where $N$ is the number of adjacent regions, and $\Omega(i)$ represents the four adjacent regions centered at region $i$. $E$ and $I$ respectively denote the average intensity value of the local region in the enhanced image and input image. The other is the intensity control loss $\ell_{con}$ to control the intensity variation of low intensity and high intensity regions. The intensity control loss measures the distance between the average intensity of the local region and the expected intensity interval $O$. The $\ell_{con}$ is as:

$$\ell_{con} = \frac{1}{M} \sum_{i=1}^{M} |E_i - O|, \tag{3}$$

where $M$ represents the number of non-overlapping local regions and $O$ is set to be 0.6.

**Deep Affine Module.** The affine registration network is optimized by three losses, defined as:

$$\ell_A = \ell_{cc} + \lambda_{det}\ell_{det} + \frac{1}{2}\ell_{multi}. \tag{4}$$

The correlation coefficient loss $\ell_{cc}$ measures the degree of linear correlation between the warped source image $S \circ \phi$ and the target image $T$, and attains 0 if the two are a linear function of each other. And $\ell_{cc}$ is defined as:

$$\ell_{cc} = 1 - \frac{cov(S \circ \phi, T)}{\sqrt{cov(S \circ \phi, S \circ \phi)cov(T,T)}}. \tag{5}$$

The determinant loss penalizes the reflection in the affine alignment which is defined as:

$$\ell_{det} = (-1 + det(A + I))^2. \tag{6}$$

And we introduce a multi-resolution loss $\ell_{multi}$ to constrain the transformation matrices obtained under $\frac{1}{8}$ and $\frac{1}{16}$ resolution features respectively. The $\ell_{multi}$ is:

$$\ell_{multi} = \lambda_{det}\ell_{det}^{1/8} + \lambda_{det}\ell_{det}^{1/16}. \tag{7}$$

## 2.4   Implementation Details

Since it is difficult to obtain the ground truth of medical images, we train Deep-EnReg for 3D infant brain MRI registration in an unsupervised manner. Each 3D MRI scan $\mathbb{R}_i$ is fed into our enhancement module as slices and the enhanced slices are obtained. Then we reconstruct the enhanced slices into an enhanced 3D infant brain image $\mathbb{R}_e$. Next, we input the enhanced image pairs to the affine module and apply the obtained transform field to the original infant brain image $\mathbb{R}_i$.

And the hyper-parameter setting in the affine network is $\lambda_{det} = 0.1$. Our DeepEnReg is implemented with PyTorch on 3.20 GHz Intel(R) i7-8700 CPU with 32 GB RAM and an Nvidia TITAN XP GPU. Our network is trained in 100 epochs with a batch size of 1. We use the ADAM optimizer and fix the learning rate $1 \times 10^{-4}$.

## 3    Experiments

In this section, we introduce the data acquisition and preparation process. In addition, we conduct comprehensive and elaborate analyses and comparisons to evaluate our proposed DeepEnReg.

### 3.1    Data Preparation and Evaluation Metrics

We perform image-to-image registration on our infant brain MR dataset, including 14 T1 weighted MR volumes of $0.45 \times 0.45 \times 6$ mm isotropic resolution. Our infant brain images are acquired on a Philips Achieva 3T scanner (Philips Medical Systems). For T1 weighted images, the resolution of each slice is $432 \times 432$ mm$^2$. And 20 sagittal slices are obtained by using the spin echo (SE): Repetition Time = 534 ms, Echo Time = 12 ms, inversion time = 860 ms, Flip Angle = 70°. Data are collected longitudinally from one and a half years old to 2 years old.

Considering the large disparity among different data, all scans are preprocessed with skull stripping and normalization. The skull stripping is performed with FSL. Then the data is resampled to a size of $432 \times 432 \times 32$. We get 182 infant brain image pairs and randomly split these image pairs into two parts: 150 image pairs for training and the rest as a testing dataset. Moreover, we conduct experiments on synthetic data. To be specific, we split the 14 images into 10 training data and 4 testing data. For each training data, we randomly generate 6 reasonable transformation matrices and obtain 60 deformed images. Then, training data pairs are constructed by randomly combining training data and deformed training data and selecting 400 pairs from them. The training dataset contains pairs of brain images of the same individual and different individuals. For each test data, we randomly generate 5 transformation matrices, and a total of 20 pairs of test data are obtained.

We evaluate the performance of the proposed registration method with the following metrics:

**Registration Success Rate (RSR).** RSR is defined as the percentage of accurate registration results. It is insufficient to use only numerical metrics to measure the performance of registration. Therefore, we introduce the metric of registration success rate to measure the effectiveness and robustness of our proposed method. We pay more attention to the head position and image quality of the registered images, and classify the results with incorrect head position and incomplete anatomical structure information as false results, while other results are classified as correct results.

**Running Time.** It is the average time taken for each pair of images to be registered. A lower time means a more efficient registration.

**Local Normalized Cross-correlation Coefficient (LNCC).** LNCC is a measure of similarity of two series. We use LNCC to evaluate differences in appearance. In our setting, higher LNCC indicates that the warped image is more similar to the target image.

**End Point Error (EPE).** EPE is an indispensable error measurement that calculates the magnitude of the distance between the predicted transformation matrix and the true transformation matrix at the mean value of all elements. A lower EPE value indicates that the results are more close to the GT.

**Modality Independent Neighbourhood Descriptor (MIND)** [8]. MIND is proposed on the assumption that the small image patches of an image should be similar even in different image modalities. A higher MIND value indicates that the warped image is more consistent with the target image.

LNCC and MIND metrics measure the similarity between the target image and the source image to a certain extent. However, in practical clinical applications, the RSR and EPE of registration results and the time spent are more important indicators.

## 3.2 Comparison Results and Ablation Analysis

To quantitatively analyze the improvement of our method, two conventional affine algorithms FSL [10], NiftyReg [19], an unsupervised deep learning affine algorithm VTN [23], and a supervised-DeepEnReg are chosen as comparison methods. For the unsupervised algorithm, we conduct comparison experiments on in-house and synthetic datasets respectively. In addition, we compare the performance of our unsupervised DeepEnReg with that of the supervised approach on the synthetic dataset.

To verify the effectiveness of our joint enhancement and affine registration framework, we make some ablation experiments. To be specific, we first verify the necessity of the enhancement module via the performance of affine registration with and without the enhancement module respectively. Then while keeping the enhancement module, we verified the excellence of our alignment module. Finally, the strength of our multi-resolution strategy applied in the deep affine registration module is verified by the ablation analysis of the loss functions.

**Table 1.** Quantitative comparisons on in-house dataset of optimization-based and learning-based representative methods in terms of accuracy and efficiency. The best result is in red whereas the second best one is in blue.

| Method | RSR ↑ | Runtime (s) ↓ | LNCC ↑ | MIND ↑ |
|---|---|---|---|---|
| FSL [10] | **0.720** | 199.635 | 0.149 ± 0.053 | 0.963 ± 0.014 |
| NiftyReg [19] | 1 | 13 | 0.164 ± 0.031 | **0.967 ± 0.009** |
| VTN [23] | 0 | 0.563 | 0.087 ± 0.016 | 0.946 ± 0.008 |
| DeepEnReg | 1 | **0.570** | **0.157 ± 0.038** | 0.967 ± 0.008 |

**Comparison Results.** First, we count the registration success rate of our proposed method and other methods to demonstrate the effectiveness of the method. At the same time, we also calculate the computation time of each method to measure the efficiency. And we evaluate the LNCC and MIND between target images and images output from our DeepEnReg and comparison methods.

**Table 2.** Quantitative comparisons of optimization-based and learning-based representative methods on synthetic data. The best result is in red whereas the second best one is in blue.

| Method | EPE ↓ | Runtime (s) ↓ |
|---|---|---|
| FSL [10] | 0.243 ± 0.060 | 198.812 |
| NiftyReg | 0.204 ± 0.075 | 8.389 |
| VTN [23] | 0.283 ± 0.053 | 0.187 |
| DeepEnReg | **0.186 ± 0.034** | 0.265 |
| Supervised-DeepEnReg | 0.184 ± 0.035 | 0.343 |

As shown in Table 1, our method shows satisfying registration performance on in-house dataset with an obvious higher RSR value and much less running time. Our method achieves the highest RSR score as the conventional method

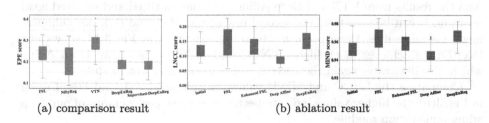

(a) comparison result          (b) ablation result

**Fig. 3.** The boxplots illustrate the affine registration performance on different evaluation metrics. Lower values mean better performance in (a). Higher values mean better performance in (b).

NiftyReg, which indicates that the warped results obtained by our method can achieve a comparable accuracy to that of the conventional method. With the guaranteed RSR, the LNCC and MIND values of our method are in a close race with NiftyReg. It demonstrates that our alignment results are very similar to the target images. And we improve the running time of NiftyReg from 13 s to 0.570 s, which is also a qualitative breakthrough.

**Table 3.** Ablation study of loss functions of the registration module on synthetic data.

| Loss Functions | EPE ↓ | Runtime (s) ↓ |
|---|---|---|
| DeepEnReg w/o $\ell_{multi}$ | 0.208 ± 0.047 | 0.182 |
| DeepEnReg | 0.186 ± 0.034 | 0.265 |

Table 2 shows that our proposed method achieves the lowest EPE value on synthetic data which indicates that the transformation matrix obtained by our method is the closest to the GT. And the DeepEnReg ranks second in running time, maintaining affine registration accuracy while being efficient. It can also be seen from Table 2 that the EPE value of our DeepEnReg is very close to the supervised method. And it indicates that our method using a large amount of training data without auxiliary labels can approach the affine alignment performance of the supervised method with only a few labels available and learn the correct transformation matrix. And Fig. 3(a) shows that our DeepEnReg yields minimal variation in results, indicating that our method is very stable and effective.

**Visual Comparisons and Ablation Analysis.** As shown in Figs. 4 and 3(b), our deep enhancement module effectively improves the problem of low-contrast image affine alignment and the superiority of our deep affine registration module when enhancement is applied to low-contrast images. We present two representative irregular registration results in Fig. 4. As shown in the first row of Fig. 4(A) and (B), the warped images from FSL have incomplete anatomical structures. And the results from VTN and Deep Affine both have a tilted and inverted head position. It can be seen from the second row of Fig. 4(A) and (B), our enhancement module solves these problems to some extent. And Fig. 3(b) shows our DeepEnReg achieves much higher LNCC and MIND values than Deep Affine which also illustrates again the necessity of our enhancement module.

Comparing the LNCC and MIND values of Enhanced FSL and DeepEnReg in Fig. 3(b), the higher values indicate better alignment performance of our deep affine registration module.

And Table 3 highlights the strength of our multi-resolution strategy and explains why our alignment model works. As mentioned above, the affine registration network is optimized by three loss functions. We test the alignment

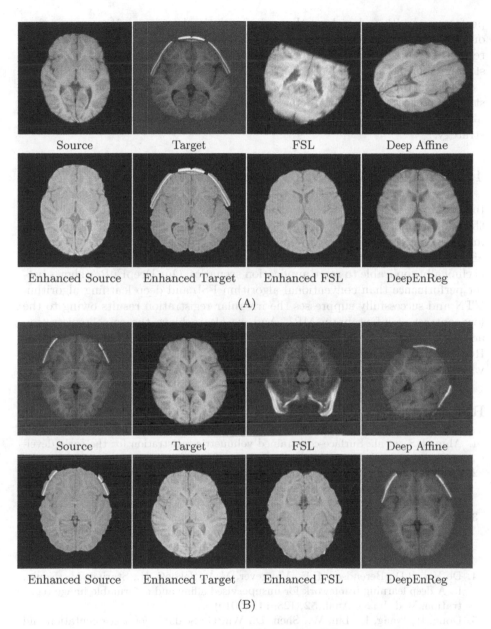

**Fig. 4.** Sample results of registering different images. (A) and (B) are respectively the visualization results of affine on two image pairs. From left to right, the first row represents the source image, target image, FSL affine on the source image (FSL), and our method only with the affine network on the source image (Deep Affine). The second row represents source image output from our enhancement network (Enhanced Source), target image output from our enhancement network (Enhanced Target), FSL affine on the enhanced source (Enhanced FSL), and our method on source image (DeepEnReg).

performance with and without the multi-resolution loss $\ell_{multi}$. It turns out that our DeepEnReg improves from 0.208 to 0.186 on EPE than without the multi-resolution loss. And it again shows that with the help of the multi-resolution strategy, our method can learn the transformation matrix much closer to GT.

The experiments indicate the advantages of our proposed method and demonstrate the effectiveness of the joint enhancement module and registration module of our DeepEnReg. And it also shows the strength of our multi-resolution strategy.

## 4  Conclusion and Future Work

In this paper, we propose a deep registration framework DeepEnReg and utilize the multi-resolution strategy for low-contrast infant brain images. We employ the image enhancement network to enhance medical images and affine network to affine registration. Our DeepEnReg is trained in an unsupervised manner which is clinically applicable to more application scenarios. Our DeepEnReg shows better performance than conventional algorithm FSL and deep learning algorithm VTN and successfully suppresses the irregular registration results owing to the low-contrast of infant brain MRI. And we also achieve the same registration accuracy as NiftyReg in less time which is a significant superiority of DeepEnReg. Further, we will improve our DeepEnReg into an end-to-end model and validate the performance on different types of medical data in the future.

## References

1. Ahmad, S., et al.: Surface-constrained volumetric registration for the early developing brain. Med. Image Anal. **58**, 101540 (2019)
2. Balakrishnan, G., Zhao, A., Sabuncu, M.R., Guttag, J., Dalca, A.V.: VoxelMorph: a learning framework for deformable medical image registration. IEEE Trans. Med. Imag. **38**(8), 1788–1800 (2019)
3. Chen, X., Meng, Y., Zhao, Y., Williams, R., Vallabhaneni, S.R., Zheng, Y.: Learning unsupervised parameter-specific affine transformation for medical images registration. In: de Bruijne, M., et al. (eds.) MICCAI 2021. LNCS, vol. 12904, pp. 24–34. Springer, Cham (2021). https://doi.org/10.1007/978-3-030-87202-1_3
4. De Vos, B.D., Berendsen, F.F., Viergever, M.A., Sokooti, H., Staring, M., Išgum, I.: A deep learning framework for unsupervised affine and deformable image registration. Med. Image Anal. **52**, 128–143 (2019)
5. Dong, P., Wang, L., Lin, W., Shen, D., Wu, G.: Scalable joint segmentation and registration framework for infant brain images. Neurocomputing **229**, 54–62 (2017)
6. Greve, D.N., Fischl, B.: Accurate and robust brain image alignment using boundary-based registration. Neuroimage **48**(1), 63–72 (2009)
7. Guo, C., et al.: Zero-reference deep curve estimation for low-light image enhancement. In: Proceedings of the IEEE/CVF Conference on Computer Vision and Pattern Recognition, pp. 1780–1789 (2020)
8. Heinrich, M.P., et al.: Mind: Modality independent neighbourhood descriptor for multi-modal deformable registration. Med. Image Anal. **16**(7), 1423–1435 (2012)

9. Hu, S., Wei, L., Gao, Y., Guo, Y., Wu, G., Shen, D.: Learning-based deformable image registration for infant MR images in the first year of life. Med. Phys. **44**(1), 158–170 (2017)

10. Jenkinson, M., Beckmann, C.F., Behrens, T.E.J., Woolrich, M.W., Smith, S.M.: FSL. NeuroImage **62**(2), 782–790 (2012)

11. Jenkinson, M., Smith, S.: A global optimisation method for robust affine registration of brain images. Med. Image Anal. **5**(2), 143–156 (2001)

12. Li, Z., Li, Z., Liu, R., Luo, Z., Fan, X.: Automated learning for deformable medical image registration by jointly optimizing network architectures and objective functions. arXiv preprint arXiv:2203.06810 (2022)

13. Li, Z., Li, Z., Liu, R., Luo, Z., Fan, X.: Coupling deep deformable registration with contextual refinement for semi-supervised medical image segmentation. In: 2022 IEEE 19th International Symposium on Biomedical Imaging (ISBI), pp. 1–5. IEEE (2022)

14. Liu, R., Li, Z., Fan, X., Zhao, C., Huang, H., Luo, Z.: Learning deformable image registration from optimization: perspective, modules, bilevel training and beyond. IEEE Trans. Pattern Anal. Mach. Intell. (2021). https://doi.org/10.1109/TPAMI.2021.3115825

15. Liu, R., Li, Z., Zhang, Y., Fan, X., Luo, Z.: Bi-level probabilistic feature learning for deformable image registration. In: Proceedings of the Twenty-Ninth International Conference on International Joint Conferences on Artificial Intelligence, pp. 723–730 (2021)

16. Liu, R., Ma, L., Zhang, J., Fan, X., Luo, Z.: Retinex-inspired unrolling with cooperative prior architecture search for low-light image enhancement. In: Proceedings of the IEEE/CVF Conference on Computer Vision and Pattern Recognition, pp. 10561–10570 (2021)

17. Maintz, J.B.A., Viergever, M.A.: A survey of medical image registration. Med. Image Anal. **2**(1), 1–36 (1998)

18. Modat, M., Cash, D.M., Daga, P., Winston, G.P., Duncan, J.S., Ourselin, S.: Global image registration using a symmetric block-matching approach. J. Med. Imag. **1**(2), 1–6 (2014)

19. Sun, W., Niessen, W.J., Klein, S.: Free-form deformation using lower-order B-spline for nonrigid image registration. In: Golland, P., Hata, N., Barillot, C., Hornegger, J., Howe, R. (eds.) MICCAI 2014. LNCS, vol. 8673, pp. 194–201. Springer, Cham (2014). https://doi.org/10.1007/978-3-319-10404-1_25

20. Wei, L., et al.: Learning-based deformable registration for infant MRI by integrating random forest with auto-context model. Med. Phys. **44**(12), 6289–6303 (2017)

21. Zhang, Y., Liu, R., Li, Z., Liu, Z., Fan, X., Luo, Z.: Coupling principled refinement with bi-directional deep estimation for robust deformable 3D medical image registration. In: 2020 IEEE 17th International Symposium on Biomedical Imaging (ISBI), pp. 86–90. IEEE (2020)

22. Zhao, A., Balakrishnan, G., Durand, F., Guttag, J.V., Dalca, A.V.: Data augmentation using learned transformations for one-shot medical image segmentation. In: Proceedings of the IEEE/CVF Conference on Computer Vision and Pattern Recognition, pp. 8543–8553 (2019)

23. Zhao, S., Lau, T., Luo, J., Eric, I., Chang, C., Xu, Y.: Unsupervised 3D end-to-end medical image registration with volume tweening network. IEEE J. Biomed. Health Inform. **24**(5), 1394–1404 (2019)

# Fluorescence Microscopy Images Segmentation Based on Prototypical Networks with a Few Annotations

Yuanhao Guo[1,2] , Yaoru Luo[1,2] , Wenjing Li[1,2] , and Ge Yang[1,2]([✉])

[1] Computational Biology and Machine Intelligence Lab, Institute of Automation, Chinese Academy of Sciences, Beijing 100190, China
{yuanhao.guo,luoyaoru2019,wenjing.li,ge.yang}@ia.ac.cn
[2] School of Artificial Intelligence, University of Chinese Academy of Sciences, Beijing 100049, China

**Abstract.** The objects in fluorescence microscopy images (FMIs) are rather densely populated, and often have complex structures as well as large color variations. These issues result in time-consuming manual annotations for training a segmentation model. Few-shot segmentation (FSS) models reduce the requirements of annotations by using prototypical networks to generalize the object regions given only a few annotation masks. These methods, however, often fail to generalize to FMIs due to the domain shift from the images of source class to those of target class. To tackle these challenges, we adapt the prototypical networks from the few-shot learning scheme as our base model architecture to learn a compact feature representation of the object, with only a few annotated masks. Then, to solve the domain shift problem, we propose a resampling strategy to regularize the model training. Specifically, we construct the training set using not only the images form the source class, but also the support set from the target class by resampling the latter for regularizing the training. To distinguish our FMIs segmentation method from the conventional FSS models, we define it as a **t**raining **r**egularization strategy based on the **p**rototypical **n**etworks (TRPN). Experimental results on three public datasets, *i.e.*the ER, MITO and NUC, have confirmed the advantages of our method, which provides robust and accurate segmentation performance on FMIs only with a few annotation masks. Source code and data of this work are made publicly available at: https://github.com/cbmi-group/TRPN-model.

**Keywords:** Fluorescence microscopy images segmentation · A few annotations · Prototypical feature learning · Training regularization strategy

This work was supported in part by research grants from Natural Science Foundation of China (No. 32101216, No. 91954201, No. 31971289), the Chinese Academy of Sciences (No. 292019000056), University of Chinese Academy of Sciences (No. 115200M001), and the Beijing Municipal Science & Technology Commission (No. 5202022).

S. Yu et al. (Eds.): PRCV 2022, LNCS 13535, pp. 164–177, 2022.
https://doi.org/10.1007/978-3-031-18910-4_14

# 1    Introduction

Accurate segmentation of fluorescence microscopy images (FMIs) is essential to quantitative analysis of biological samples [1]. For example, an overall structural representation of the endoplasmic reticulum (ER) can be obtained via image segmentation and can clearly present its network connectivity, which is playing an important role in regulating cellular physiology [2]. Recent development of deep learning methods enables robust segmentation of FMIs [3], which, however, requires a large quantity of human-assisted annotations [4]. This is extraordinarily difficult in segmenting complex structures. Take the ER images shown in Fig. 1A for an example, it may take hours for an annotator to manually segment even a small image patch (*e.g.* 256 × 256 pixels). To solve this problem, the few-shot learning [5,6] (FSL) models are developed and adapted in the task of image segmentation. The few-shot segmentation (FSS) models mimic the condition, in which the models learn to segment object regions in a query image given only a few annotated support images.

The architectures of the FSS models usually take the form of two-branch prototypical networks [7–10]. Given a few densely annotated support images from a source class, the prototype-learning branch of the network learns a prototypical feature (a compact feature representation) of the annotated object. The segmentation branch compares the acquired prototypical feature with a query image, obtaining a similarity map which indicates the correlation between the support and query images. By combing this similarity map with the feature representation of the query image, the FSS models are equipped with the capability to *segment the query images from an unseen target class guided by only a few annotated support images, without employing any finetuning.* This works in a similar way as the meta-learning [11] and transfer learning [12].

When adapting the general-purpose FSS models [13] to segment the FMIs, we face the following obstacles. First, the FSS models often use the middle-level features to learn the prototypes, which cannot handle the intricate structures of the objects densely populated in FMIs, such as the complex network structures of ER and mitochondria (MITO) in Fig. 1[1]. Second, in the setup of FSS, the source class is isolated to the target class. The FSS models may perform well on natural images, because the target class bear a certain semantic resemblance with the source class. For example, both buses and airplanes have wheels and windows. However, the FSS models is prone to be overfitting in segmenting FMIs. For example, when using the ER as source class and the MITO as target class, the domain shift problem arises due to the structure difference between them. Similar challenges are also found in medical image segmentation [14].

In this study, we make the following contributions to tackle the above challenges. We first adapt the prototypical feature learning networks [13] as the base model architecture to segment the FMIs with only a few annotation masks. Second, we train the networks in a similar way of FSS models which construct support-query image pairs from the source class and guide the networks to learn

---

[1] The MITO can present diverse shapes, like ribbon, pole, reticulation, *etc.*.

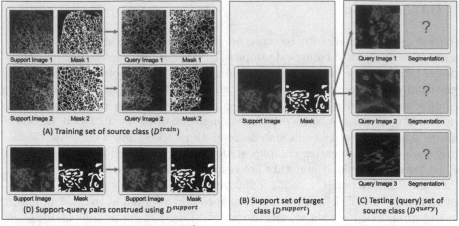

(A) Training set of source class ($D^{train}$)

(D) Support-query pairs construed using $D^{support}$

(B) Support set of target class ($D^{support}$)

(C) Testing (query) set of source class ($D^{query}$)

(E) Training set used in the proposed TRPN ($D^{train,*}$)

**Fig. 1. Construction of training and testing sets for the proposed TRPN.** We use a one-shot case to illustrate our method. (A) The training set consists of the images and their masks from the source class (ER). (B) The support set consists of one image and its mask from the target class (MITO), which is used to guide the segmentation for the referenced object of the target class. (C) The testing (query) set consists of the images from the target class that need to be segmented and evaluated. (D) The support set in (B) is constructed as the form of support-query pair. (E) The training set of the proposed TRPN is constructed using the images from (A) and (D).

a prototypical feature representation of the object. Differently, we propose a regularization training strategy by resampling the support set from the target class. In this way, we ensure the support image from the target class to appear in every training step to regularize the model training. To distinguish our method from the conventional FSS models, we define it as a training regularization strategy based on the prototypical networks (TRPN). At test time, we use the unique support image and its mask to segment all the remaining images from the target class. In Fig. 1, we use a one-shot case to illustrate our definition. By integrating the above contributions, our method has obtained the best performance on three public datasets, the ER, MITO [15] and NUC (nucleus) [3], compared to the competing methods.

## 2    Related Works

In this section, we briefly summarize the recent developments of the FSL models in several typical applications.

**Few-shot Classification.** Since the invention of the MAML [16], meta-learning has been widely used to deal with the deep neural networks based few-shot classification task. This type of models uses a meta-learner to generalize many few-shot

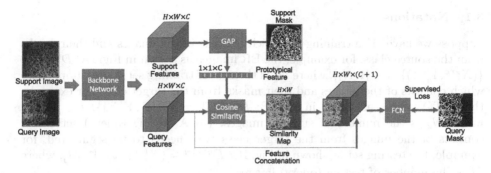

**Fig. 2. Model architecture of TRPN.** By using a global average pooling (GAP), the prototype-learning branch (upper branch) learns the prototypical feature of the object annotated by the support mask for the support image. The segmentation branch (lower branch) learns to segment the query image based on the acquired prototypical feature. Differently from its original version [13], we use the U-Net [28] as the backbone network and use feature concatenation to combine the extracted features with the similarity map of the query image. A two-layer fully-connected network (FCN) is used to complete the segmentation of the query image. At training time, the query mask of the query image is given to guide the trainings.

tasks, and then finetunes a base-learner on unseen tasks given only a few training examples. The TAML method improves the few-shot classification to be unbiased towards new tasks by introducing the entropy-based meta-learner [17]. The MTL model solves the problem that a relatively deeper neural network tend to overfit under the few-shot setup [18]. To further improve the performance of few-shot classification, an attention-based task-specific feature extraction module is proposed to guide the model to learn representative features for each task [6].

**Few-shot Segmentation.** Recent developed deep learning-based FSS models focus on improving the prototypical feature representation via feature refinement [10,19], dense comparison [20–22] and combining local information based on graph model [20] or attention model [23–25]. Some methods enhance the prototypical feature at inference time [9]. In [26], a base-learner is proposed to segment the base classes, which solves the problem that previous class-agnostic methods are biased to the source classes. Differently, our method mainly solves the domain shift problem in FMIs by a training regularization strategy and similar methods have been proven its efficacy in image classification task [27].

## 3 Methodology

In this section, we first formulate the mathematical notations of TRPN. We then describe the base model architecture for TRPN. Finally, we introduce our training strategy.

## 3.1   Notations

Suppose we have (1) a training set which consists of the images and their masks from the source class, for example, the ER images as shown in Fig. 1A: $D^{train} = \{(X_i^{src}, Y_i^{src})\}$, $i \in [1, N_1]$, where $N_1$ is the size of training set; (2) A support set which consists of the images and their masks from the target class, for example, the MITO images as shown in Fig. 1B: $D^{support} = \{(X_i^{tar}, Y_i^{tar})\}$, $i \in [1, N_2]$, where $N_2$ is the number of support images; (3) A testing (query) set which consists of the images from the target class that needs to be segmented, for example, the testing set as shown in Fig. 1C: $D^{query} = (X_j^{tar})$, $i \in [1, M]$, where $M$ is the number of testing (query) images [2].

In this work, we borrow the terminology from the few-shot learning domain. We use one-shot to represent that we have one support image and its mask to guide the segmentation of the query images, i.e. $N_2 = 1$. And we use few-shot to indicate that we have a few support images and their masks to guide the segmentation of the query images, e.g. $N_2 = 5$. Considering that our FMIs only contain one class of subject in one image, so we use a binary mask to represent the annotation, i.e. the values of 0 and 1 in the annotated mask represent the background and the object, respectively.

We aim to segment any query images from $D^{query}$ guided by the support set $D^{support}$, which can be denoted as the one-shot case $(X^{tar}, Y^{tar}) \rightarrow X_j^{tar}$. To this end, the segmentation model needs to be trained in a similar manner that the training images are also organized as support-query pairs $(X_i^{src}, Y_i^{src}) \rightarrow (X_j^{src}, Y_j^{src})$. Details will be elaborated in following sections.

## 3.2   Model Architecture

Fig. 2 shows the model architecture of the proposed TRPN, which is adapted from the prototypical feature learning network [13], a two-branch network. Our model consists of (1) a shared backbone network for feature extraction (2) a prototype-learning branch for learning the prototypical feature from the support image guided by its mask (3) and a segmentation branch for segmenting the query image.

In previous study [15], we have verified that accurate segmentation of FMIs requires leverage multi-scale features in the network. To this end, we use a standard encoder-decoder model, the U-Net [28] denoted as $F^b$, as the backbone network of TRPN. It should be noted that other models like U-Net++ [29] and HRNet [30] also apply. Given a support-query pair $(X_i^{src}, Y_i^{src}) \rightarrow (X_j^{src}, Y_j^{src})$, $F^b$, $F^b$ extracts features for both support and query images, and we use the features of the last convolutional layer of the U-Net, which integrates multi-level features.

$$f_i = F^b(X_i;\ W^b);\ f_j = F^b(X_j;\ W^b), \tag{1}$$

---

[2] Here, we use *testing* and *query* to indicate the identical definition that represents the image to be segmented.

where $W^b$ denotes the model weights of $F^b$; $f_i \in R^{H \times W \times C}$ and $f_j \in R^{H \times W \times C}$ are the extracted features for the support image $X_i$ and query image $X_j$, respectively. We omit the superscript $src$ and $tar$ for generalization.

The prototype-learning branch uses global average pooling (GAP) to obtain a compact feature representation for the object to be segmented.

$$proto_i = \frac{\sum_{p \in \mathcal{P}} f_i(p) \odot Y_i(p)}{\sum_{p \in \mathcal{P}} Y_i(p)} \in R^{1 \times 1 \times C}, \tag{2}$$

where $p$ denotes pixel location and $\mathcal{P}$ is the image domain. The prototypical feature $proto_i$ is obtained by masking the features in the object regions.

The segmentation branch first uses $proto_i$ to obtain a similarity map for the query image, implemented by a cosine distance:

$$sim_{ij}(p) = \frac{f_j(p) \cdot (proto_i)^T}{||f_j(p)|| \cdot ||proto_i||} \tag{3}$$

Then, we concatenate the acquired similarity map with the original features of the query image from the feature dimension $f_j = [f_j; \ sim_{ij}] \in R^{H \times W \times (C+1)}$. In other words, we enhance the feature representation of the query image by fusing its similarity score to the learned prototype. Next, a two-layer fully convolutional network (FCN) denoted as $F^{fcn}$ is used to complete the segmentation for the query image $\hat{Y}_j = F^{fcn}(f_j; W^{fcn})$, where $W^{fcn}$ is the model weights of the FCN.

At training time, we randomly construct the support-query pairs using the images of the training set. Considering leverage the data balance of the foreground and background, we use the IOU loss to supervise the training of the whole model:

$$\mathcal{L}_{IOU} = \frac{1}{N_1} \sum_{j=1}^{N_1} \left( 1 - \frac{\sum_{p \in \mathcal{P}} Y_j \hat{Y}_j}{\sum_{p \in \mathcal{P}} (Y_j + \hat{Y}_j - Y_j \hat{Y}_j) + \eta} \right), \tag{4}$$

where $\eta$ is a smoothing coefficient for numerical stability of the loss function. Here we omit the pixel location $p$ for simplicity.

## 3.3   Regularization Training Based on the Resampling Strategy

In the few-shot learning scheme, the prototypical networks are trained for once with the training set ($D^{train}$) consisting of source class. And later the networks are used to segment all the query images from the testing set ($D^{query}$) consisting of target class, guided by the support set ($D^{support}$) without any finetuning of the networks. This training setup may cause severe domain shift problem due to the structural difference of the objects from the source to the target class in FMIs. Accordingly, overfitting problem of standard FSS models will occur to segment the FMIs.

To solve the above problem, we propose a training regularization strategy. In this method, we first construct the training set using the images from the source class, for example, the ER images, in the form of support-query image pairs, as shown in Fig. 1A. Then, we extend the training set using the support set from the target class like the MITO images as shown in Fig. 1B. In this one-shot case, we use the unique support image as both the support and query image for the training set. We denote the extended training set as $D^{train,\star} = D^{train} \cap D^{support}$. Lastly, in each training step, we construct the mini-batch by randomly sampling a subset from $D^{train}$ and resampling the $D^{support}$ according to a probability $p$ which is empirically chosen to be 0.25. For example, in a mini-batch of size 8, we use 6 support-query image pairs from the source class, and replicate the support set from the target class for 2 times.

In fact, our resampling strategy acts as a regularizer to guide the model to better generalize the target class. Our TRPN requires to re-train the whole model for each novel target class. This differs from standard FSS models, which are trained only for once using the source class and then tested for all the other novel classes. Our method dramatically improves the robustness and stability in segmenting the FMIs and the results will be shown in the following sections. We stress that the proposed regularization training strategy does not violate the criterion that the training and test images are not overlapped, because we only use the support image of the target class to train our model and use all the remaining query images for evaluation. Similar fine-tuning strategy is also proposed in few-shot classification task [27].

## 4 Experiments

### 4.1 Datasets and Configurations

We use three datasets to evaluate the performance of the proposed method, i.e. MITO [15], ER [15] and NUC [3], which include 111, 134 and 340 training/validation images, and 72, 38 and 32 test images, respectively. Based on the definition in Sect. 3, we first formulate two evaluation setups. (1) MITO Test: MITO as target class and ER as source class; (2) ER Test: ER as target class and MITO as source class. We then devise a different evaluation setup for the NUC dataset later. We use IOU (intersection-over-union), F1 (F1 score), AUC (area under ROC curve) and ACC (accuracy) to measure the performance of all methods. All experiments are implemented using PyTorch [31] and performed on 2 NVIDIA 2080Ti GPU cards. From the webpage of our source codes, we list the specific training configurations for different methods.

We devise the following baseline methods to compare with our method. (1) Fully-Supervised: The U-Net trained in a fully-supervised manner with the whole training set from target class, which obtains the upper bound performance. (2) Finetune: The U-Net pretrained from the source class and then finetuned with $D^{support}$. (3) SG-One-UNet: We use the SG-One [13], one of the typical prototypical networks, as a baseline method of the FSS model. We replace its backbone network with the U-Net [28], because the original version of the SG-One does not

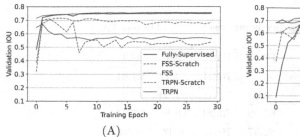
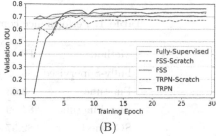

(A)    (B)

**Fig. 3. Efficacy of the proposed training strategy.** (A) and (B) are validation results on ER and MITO, respectively.

even convergence on our datasets. (4) RANet-TRPN: We adapt an attention-based FSS network, the RANet [32], as the base model architecture of our TRPN to evaluate its effect with an advanced model architecture.

## 4.2    Ablative Studies

In this experiment, we first use both ER Test and MITO Test to verify the efficacy of the proposed regularization training strategy. As a comparison, we only use the source class (Fig. 1A) to train our TRPN, which degenerates the model into a standard FSS model. We devise two training setups: train from scratch (FSS-Scratch, TRPN-Scratch) and finetune from a pre-trained backbone network (FSS, TRPN). In Fig. 3, we show the evaluation results during training. We have the following observations. (1) The FSS model overfits quickly on the ER dataset caused by the domain shift problem, and the TRPN performs better due to the resampling strategy. (2) By using a pre-trained backbone network, the performance of both FSS and TRPN are improved. (3) The performance of TRPN and Fully-Supervised are close on ER dataset, but remain a certain gap on the MITO dataset.

We then use the ER Test to verify the efficacy of the feature concatenation in the network architecture of TRPN. We use the original feature multiplication in [13] as a comparison. We finally obtain the IOU on ER Test as 74.94% and 73.28% of TRPN and the competing method, respectively. So, for the remaining experiments, we use feature concatenation in our method.

## 4.3    Performance Comparison

In Table 1, we compare the performance of all methods on MITO Test. Bracket denotes the performance gap from our TRPN to the upper bound. We can see that: (1) The domain shift problem from the train class to the target class results in a relatively low performance of the SG-One-UNet. Its performance is even worse than the simple Finetune method, because the SG-One-UNet is not trained with any images from the target class. (2) Our TRPN method outperforms both

**Table 1.** Performance comparison on MITO test (%)

| Method | F1 | IOU | AUC | ACC |
|---|---|---|---|---|
| Fully-Supervised | 86.52 | 76.24 | 99.42 | 97.61 |
| Finetune | 83.63 | 71.87 | 99.09 | 97.04 |
| Five-Finetune | 84.99 | 73.90 | 99.16 | 97.31 |
| SG-One-UNet | 82.57 | 70.31 | 99.00 | 86.80 |
| RANet-TRPN | 84.76 | 73.56 | 99.10 | 97.15 |
| TRPN | 84.80 | 73.62 | 99.25 | 97.24 |
| | (-1.72) | (-2.62) | (-0.17) | (-0.37) |
| Five-TRPN | **85.51** | **74.90** | **99.35** | **97.40** |
| | (-1.01) | (-1.34) | (-0.07) | (-0.21) |

**Table 2.** Performance comparison on ER test (%)

| Method | F1 | IOU | AUC | ACC |
|---|---|---|---|---|
| Fully-Supervised | 85.86 | 75.23 | 96.87 | 91.41 |
| Finetune | 84.20 | 72.72 | 95.98 | 90.23 |
| SG-One-UNet | 71.95 | 56.19 | 82.50 | 84.42 |
| RANet-TRPN | 83.92 | 72.30 | 94.28 | 86.89 |
| TRPN | **85.67** | **74.94** | **96.11** | **91.26** |
| | (-0.19) | (-0.29) | (-0.76) | (-0.15) |

**Table 3.** Performance comparison on NUC test (%)

| Method | F1 | IOU | AUC | ACC |
|---|---|---|---|---|
| Fully-Supervised | 87.91 | 78.42 | 99.72 | 98.71 |
| Finetune | 83.23 | 71.28 | 99.26 | 98.16 |
| Five-Finetune | 85.87 | 75.24 | 99.25 | 98.49 |
| SG-One-UNet | 83.50 | 72.87 | 99.08 | 98.20 |
| RANet-TRPN | 85.59 | 73.80 | 99.47 | 98.43 |
| TRPN | 86.07 | 74.67 | 99.63 | 98.51 |
| | (-1.84) | (-3.75) | (-0.09) | (-0.20) |
| Five-TRPN | **86.29** | **75.88** | **99.64** | **98.52** |
| | (-1.62) | (-2.54) | (-0.08) | (-0.19) |

the simple Finetune method and the SG-One-UNet model by a large margin, which shows the effects of our model adaptation and the training strategy. (3) However, a performance gap is found between our method and the upper bound performance. To further improve the performance of our TRPN, we first use a more advanced base model architecture, the RANet-TRPN model; We then try to use more support images (*e.g.* five) to train our TRPN, *i.e.* Five-TRPN. From the results, we can see that using more support images can obtain more performance improvement than using a more complex model for MITO Test.

In Table 2, we show the performance comparison on ER Test. We can see that the SG-One performs much worse than other methods, because it is only trained with the images from the source class (MITO). The complex structure of ER can not be handled by only using the MITO images for training. To be compared, the TRPN shows the best performance on ER Test, which performs even similarly as the Fully-Supervised method. Although only one support set is provided, the annotations in the support image is quite dense which may offer sufficient structure information of the ER (see Fig. 1A). This also explains that the simple Finetune method can obtain a relatively good performance on ER Test. In this experiment, the RANet-TRPN performs worse than TRPN. This overfitting problem may be caused by the complex model architecture with a few training data.

For NUC Test, we separately use ER and MITO as the source class to train our TRPN. The IOU obtained by TRPN are 71.20% and 72.43% respectively. These results are much lower than the upper bound performance (78.42%). This is, again, caused by the severe structural difference from NUC to ER and MITO. So, we use an extra NUC dataset [33] as the source class to construct the training set. In Table 3. We show the performance comparison on NUC Test. In this experiment, the SG-One-UNet can obtain slightly better performance than the simple Finetune strategy due to the similarity between the source and target class. The best results are obtained from TRPN (74.67%) and Five-TRPN (75.88%), respectively. Comparing the results of Five-TRPN and Five-Finetue, we can see that using more support images to train our model may reach a limited performance improvement.

In Fig. 4, we visualize some segmentation effects on the three datasets obtained from different methods.

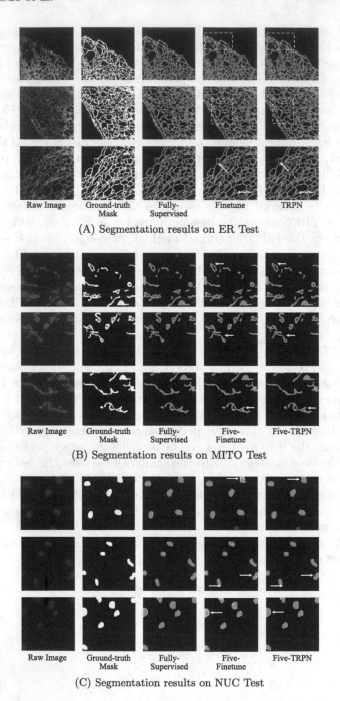

(A) Segmentation results on ER Test

(B) Segmentation results on MITO Test

(C) Segmentation results on NUC Test

**Fig. 4. Segmentation results comparison of different methods.** White boxes and arrows indicate the regions that the proposed TRPN method performs better. Red: True Positive; Green: False Negative; Blue: False Positive.

# 5  Conclusions and Discussions

In this work, we define the task of FMIs segmentation with only a few annotations and propose a feasible solution, the TRPN method. For the base model architecture of TRPN, we use the prototypical-feature learning model with sufficient adaptations. To deal with the domain shift problem in FMIs, we propose a training regularization strategy to leverage the model training. The experimental results have led us to draw several important conclusions. First, pre-training the backbone network can stabilize the training of TRPN. Second, resampling the support image from target class to train TRPN can dramatically improve its performance. Lastly, the source and target classes require certain structural similarity to ensure the successful TRPN. Compared to the existing FSS models, our method can handle the segmentation of totally novel class of FMIs given a few annotations, with the support of available datasets. Our method, in its current form, has several limitations. First, it needs to be re-trained when adapting to a new test class; Second, the performance gap between TRPN and the baselines decreases when employing more supported images. It should be noted that TRPN is less risky to be overfitting and obtains significant performance improvement in the one-shot case. To further improve our method, we may use the meta-transfer learning module to train a deeper model and verify the performance of our training regularization strategy in other prototypical networks.

# References

1. Moen, E., Bannon, D., Kudo, T., et al.: Deep learning for cellular image analysis. Nat. Methods **16**(12), 1233–1246 (2019)
2. Nixon-Abell, j., Obara, C.J., Weigel, A.V., et al.: Increased spatiotemporal resolution reveals highly dynamic dense tubular matrices in the peripheral ER. Science **354**(6311), aaf3928 (2016)
3. Caicedo, J.C., Goodman, A., Karhohs, K.W., et al.: Nucleus segmentation across imaging experiments: the 2018 Data Science Bowl. Nat. Methods **16**(12), 1247–1253 (2019)
4. Greenwald, N.F., Miller, G., Moen, E., et al.: Whole-cell segmentation of tissue images with human-level performance using large-scale data annotation and deep learning. Nat. Biotechnol. **40**(4), 555–565 (2022)
5. Wang, Y., Yao, Q., Kwok, J.T., Ni, L.M.: Generalizing from a few examples: a survey on few-shot learning. ACM Comput. Surv. **53**(3), 1–34 (2020)
6. Cheng, G., Li, R., Lang, C., Han, J.: Task-wise attention guided part complementary learning for few-shot image classification. Sci. China Inf. Sci. **64**(2), 1–14 (2021). https://doi.org/10.1007/s11432-020-3156-7
7. Snell, J., Swersky, K., Zemel, R.: Prototypical networks for few-shot learning. In: Advances in Neural Information Processing Systems, vol. 30 (2017)
8. Dong , N., Xing, E.P.: Few-shot semantic segmentation with prototype learnings. In: British Machine Vision Conference, vol. 3 (2018)
9. Nguyen, K., Todorovic, S.: Feature weighting and boosting for few-shot segmentation. In: IEEE International Conference on Computer Vision, pp. 622–631 (2019)

10. Tian, Z., Zhao, H., Shu, M., et al.: Prior guided feature enrichment network for few-shot segmentation. IEEE Trans. Pattern. Anal. Mach. Intell. (2020)
11. Hospedales, T., Antoniou, A., Micaelli, P., Storkey, A.: Meta-learning in neural networks: a survey. arXiv preprint arXiv:2004.05439 (2020)
12. Weiss, K., Khoshgoftaar, T.M., Wang, D.D.: A survey of transfer learning. J. Big Data **3**(1), 1–40 (2016). https://doi.org/10.1186/s40537-016-0043-6
13. Zhang, X., Wei, Y., Yang, Y., Huang, T.S.: SG-One: similarity guidance network for one-shot semantic segmentation. IEEE Trans. Cybern. **50**(9), 3855–3865 (2020)
14. Ouyang, C., Biffi, C., Chen, C., et al.: Self-supervised learning for few-shot medical image segmentation. IEEE Trans. Med. Imaging **41**(7), 1837–1848 (2022)
15. Guo, Y., Huang, J., Zhou, Y., Luo, Y., Li, W., Yang, G.: Segmentation of intracellular structures in fluorescence microscopy images by fusing low-level features. In: Chinese Conference on Pattern Recognition and Computer Vision, vol. 13021, pp. 386–397. Springer, Cham (2021). https://doi.org/10.1007/978-3-030-88010-1_32
16. Finn, C., Abbeel, P., Levine, S.: Model-agnostic meta-learning for fast adaptation of deep networks. In: International Conference on Machine Learning, pp. 1126–1135. PMLR (2017)
17. Jamal, M.A., Qi, G.J.: Task agnostic meta-learning for few-shot learning. In: IEEE Conference on Computer Vision and Pattern Recognition, pp. 11719–11727 (2019)
18. Sun, Q., Liu, Y., Chua, T., Schiele, B.: Meta-transfer learning for few-shot learning. In: IEEE Conference on Computer Vision and Pattern Recognition, pp. 403–412 (2019)
19. Siam, M., Oreshkin, B.N., Jagersand, M.: AMP: adaptive masked proxies for few-shot segmentation. In: IEEE International Conference on Computer Vision, pp. 5249–5258 (2019)
20. Zhang, C., Lin, G., Liu, F., et al.: Pyramid graph networks with connection attentions for region-based one-shot semantic segmentation. In: IEEE International Conference on Computer Vision, pp. 9587–9595 (2019)
21. Liu, W., Zhang, C., Lin, G., Liu, F.: CRNet: cross-reference networks for few-shot segmentation. In: IEEE Conference on Computer Vision and Pattern Recognition, pp. 4165–4173 (2020)
22. Zhang, B., Xiao, J., Qin, T.: Self-guided and cross-guided learning for few-shot segmentation. In: IEEE Conference on Computer Vision and Pattern Recognition, pp. 8312–8321 (2021)
23. Liu, Y., Zhang, X., Zhang, S., He, X.: Part-Aware prototype network for few-shot semantic segmentation. In: Europe Conference on Computer Vision, vol. 12354, pp. 142–158. Springer, Cham (2020). https://doi.org/10.1007/978-3-030-58545-7_9
24. Yang, B., Liu, C., Li, B., Jiao, J., Ye, Q.: Prototype mixture models for few-shot semantic segmentation. In: Europe Conference on Computer Vision, vol. 12353, pp. 763–778. Springer, Cham (2020). https://doi.org/10.1007/978-3-030-58598-3_45
25. Yang, Y., Meng, F., Li, H., Wu, Q., Xu, X., Chen, S.: A new local transformation module for few-shot segmentation. In: International Conference on Multimedia Modeling, vol. 11962, pp. 76–87. Springer, Cham (2020). https://doi.org/10.1007/978-3-030-37734-2_7
26. Lang, C., Cheng, G., Tu, B., Han, J.: Learning what not to segment: a new perspective on few-shot segmentation. In: IEEE Conference on Computer Vision and Pattern Recognition, pp. 8057–8067 (2022)
27. Shen, Z., Liu, Z., Qin, J., et al.: Partial is better than all: revisiting fine-tuning strategy for few-shot learning. In: AAAI Conference on Artificial Intelligence, vol. 35, pp. 9594–9602 (2021)

28. Ronneberger, O., Fischer, P., Brox, T.: U-Net: convolutional networks for biomedical image segmentation. In: International Conference on Medical Image Computing and Computer-Assisted Intervention, vol. 9351, pp. 234–241. Springer, Cham (2015). https://doi.org/10.1007/978-3-319-24574-4_28
29. Zhou, Z., Rahman Siddiquee, M.M., Tajbakhsh, N., Liang, J.: UNet++: a nested U-Net architecture for medical image segmentation. In: Deep Learning in Medical Image Analysis and Multimodal Learning for Clinical Decision Support, vol. 11045, pp. 3–11. Springer, Cham (2018). https://doi.org/10.1007/978-3-030-00889-5_1
30. Wang, J., Sun, K., Cheng, T., et al.: Deep high-resolution representation learning for visual recognition. IEEE Trans. Pattern. Anal. Mach. Intell. **43**(10), 3349–3364 (2020)
31. Paszke, A., Gross, S., Massa, F., et al.: Pytorch: an imperative style, high-performance deep learning library. In: Advances in Neural Information Processing Systems, vol. 32 (2019)
32. Wang, Z., Xu, J., Liu, L., et al.: RANet: ranking attention network for fast video object segmentation. In: IEEE International Conference on Computer Vision, pp. 3978–3987 (2019)
33. Arslan, S., Ersahin, T., Cetin-Atalay, R., Gunduz-Demir, C.: Attributed relational graphs for cell nucleus segmentation in fluorescence microscopy images. IEEE Trans. Med. Imaging **32**(6), 1121–1131 (2013)

# SuperVessel: Segmenting High-Resolution Vessel from Low-Resolution Retinal Image

Yan Hu[1]([✉]), Zhongxi Qiu[1], Dan Zeng[1], Li Jiang[2], Chen Lin[2], and Jiang Liu[1,3]

[1] Research Institute of Trustworthy Autonomous Systems and Department of Computer Science and Technology, Southern University of Science and Technology, Shenzhen 518055, China
huy3@sustech.edu.cn

[2] Department of Ophthalmology, Shenzhen People's Hospital (The Second Clinical Medical College, Jinan University; The First Affiliated Hospital, Southern University of Science and Technology), Shenzhen, China

[3] Guangdong Provincial Key Laboratory of Brain-inspired Intelligent Computation, Department of Computer Science and Engineering, Southern University of Science and Technology, Shenzhen 518055, China

**Abstract.** Vascular segmentation extracts blood vessels from images and serves as the basis for diagnosing various diseases, like ophthalmic diseases. Ophthalmologists often require high-resolution segmentation results for analysis, which leads to super-computational load by most existing methods. If based on low-resolution input, they easily ignore tiny vessels or cause discontinuity of segmented vessels. To solve these problems, the paper proposes an algorithm named SuperVessel, which gives out high-resolution and accurate vessel segmentation using low-resolution images as input. We first take super-resolution as our auxiliary branch to provide potential high-resolution detail features, which can be deleted in the test phase. Secondly, we propose two modules to enhance the features of the interested segmentation region, including an upsampling with feature decomposition (UFD) module and a feature interaction module (FIM) with a constraining loss to focus on the interested features. Extensive experiments on three publicly available datasets demonstrate that our proposed SuperVessel can segment more tiny vessels with higher segmentation accuracy IoU over 6%, compared with other state-of-the-art algorithms. Besides, the stability of Super-Vessel is also stronger than other algorithms. The code will be released at https://github.com/Qsingle/Megvision.

**Keywords:** Vessel segmentation · Super-resolution · Multi-task learning · Retinal image

## 1 Introduction

Retinal images are widely adopted as effective tools for the diagnosis and therapy of various diseases. The visual exploration of retinal blood vessels assists

S. Yu et al. (Eds.): PRCV 2022, LNCS 13535, pp. 178–190, 2022.
https://doi.org/10.1007/978-3-031-18910-4_15

ophthalmologists in diagnosing variety of abnormalities of eyes, such as diabetic retinopathy, glaucoma, age-related macular degeneration. Researchers also proved the changes of retinal vessels could be an early screening method for some brain diseases [11], cardiovascular diseases [5], or systematic diseases [16]. Retinal vessel segmentation is one fundamental step for retinal image analysis. Identifying the vessel structures based on high-resolution images can give doctors great convenience of precise disease diagnosis. It brings a great burden and consumes plenty of time for doctors to segment vessels manually since it requires specific medical training and technical expertise.

In recent years, researchers have proposed many automatic vessel segmentation algorithms based on deep-learning construction to lighten the burdens on doctors. They learn from the raw image data without adopting handcrafted features. Ronneberger et al. [14] proposed U-shape Net (U-Net) framework for biomedical image segmentation, which has become a popular neural network architecture for its promising results in biomedical image segmentation. Many variations have been proposed based on U-Net for different vessel segmentation tasks. For example, Fu et al. [3] adopted the CRF to gather the multi-stage feature maps for improving the vessel detection performance. Some researchers proposed to stack multiple U-net shape architectures [8], input image patches into U-net architecture [17], introduce multi-scale input layer to the conventional U-net [15], or cascade a backbone residual dense network and a fine-tune tail network [6]. For computation loads, the existing algorithms often output low-resolution vessel segmentation results or direct upsampling results leading to a discontinuity in the results, which cannot satisfy the requirement of ophthalmologists. They often require high-resolution continuous vessels for analyzing diseases like branch retinal vein occlusion (BRVO), high-resolution (HR) images can provide more details as tiny vessels.

Recently, Wang et al. [18] proposed a patch-free 3D brain tumor segmentation driven by super-resolution technique. An HR 3D patch is necessary to guide segmentation and super-resolution during training, which may increase the computation complexity. In natural image segmentation, researchers proposed some auxiliary segmentation tasks [7,19], which adopt the feature loss between segmentation and super-resolution branches to indicate the task fusion. However, only constrained by image feature similarity cannot provide effective features for the vessel segmentation task, as vessel proportion in an entire image is relatively small.

Therefore, to solve the above problems, we propose to output high-resolution vessel segmentation only based on low-resolution images, which supplies doctors with clear vessels for accurate diagnosis. Then we try to improve the vessel segment accuracy by focusing on our interested vessel regions with effective feature interaction. The contributions are as follows: 1) We propose a novel dual-stream learning algorithm that combines segmentation and super-resolution to produce the high-resolution vessel segmentation based on a low-resolution input. 2) We emphasize the interested features in two aspects, including an upsampling with a feature decomposition (UFD) module and a feature interaction module

(FIM) with a new constraint loss. They extract the spatial correlation between the decomposed features and super-resolution features. 3) The efficacy of our proposed SuperVessel is shown on three publicly available datasets compared with other state-of-the-art algorithms.

## 2    Methodology

The pipeline of our proposed SuperVessel is illustrated in Fig. 1. Given a retinal image $X$ of size $H \times W$, we first downsample the image by $n\times$ to simulate a low-resolution image, which is adopted as the input of the whole framework. To reconstruct more appealing vessels, we propose two modules with a new loss function: An upsampling with feature decomposition (UFD) module separates vessel and background features into different channels. The proposed feature interaction module (FIM) emphasizes the vessel features by optimizing the feature interaction between the UFD module and the super-resolution branch. In the testing phase (as shown in the light green box), only the vessel segmentation branch is adopted to segment vessels to output high-resolution vessel segmentation results without extra computational load.

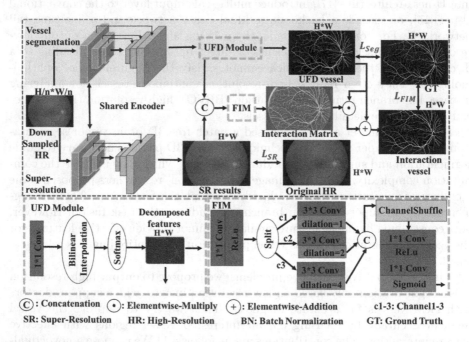

**Fig. 1.** The pipeline of the proposed SuperVessel framework. For the test phase, only the vessel segmentation branch is adopted, as shown in the light green box. (Color figure online)

## 2.1   SuperVessel Framework

Decoded features only upsampled by bilinear interpolation cannot bring any additional information, since the input is a low-resolution image. Thus, we adopt super-resolution as an auxiliary network for vessel segmentation to provide more details in our SuperVessel framework, and the super-resolution network can be removed during the test phase. Ground truth for vessel segmentation is the labeled segmentation mask of the original high resolution, and that for super-resolution is the original high-resolution image. For the two branches, the same encoder-decoder structures [14] are adopted as the backbones. The encoder $E$ is shared, and two parallel decoders $D_{Seg}$ and $D_{SR}$ realize vessel segmentation and super-resolution, respectively, as shown in Fig. 1. Therefore, the whole structure of the SuperVessel could be formulated as:

$$O_{Seg} = \text{UFD}(D_{Seg}(E(X))) \tag{1}$$

$$O_{FIM} = \text{FIM}(C(O_{Seg}, O_{SR})) \tag{2}$$

$$O_{SR} = D_{SR}(E(X)) \tag{3}$$

where $O_{Seg}, O_{FIM},$ and $O_{SR}$ are the output of vessel segmentation branch, the FIM module, and super-resolution branch, respectively. $X$ is the input image, $E(X)$ is encoded features of image $X$, D is the corresponding decoder, C is the concatenation operation.

The loss function of our framework is defined as: $\mathcal{L} = \mathcal{L}_{Seg} + \mathcal{L}_{SR} + \mathcal{L}_{FIM}$, where $\mathcal{L}_{Seg} = -\frac{1}{n}\sum_{i=0}^{n} GT_i \log O_{Seg_i}$ for the loss between UFD vessel and GT, $\mathcal{L}_{SR}(SR, HR) = \alpha * (SR - HR)^2 + (1 - \alpha) * (1 - \text{SSIM}(SR, HR))$ for the loss of super-resolution branch, $\mathcal{L}_{FIM}$ for the loss between interaction vessel and GT, $n$ is the number of the classes, $GT$ is the label, $GT_i$ is the ground truth of the class $i$, and $O_{Seg}{}^i$ is the probability of the class $i$ in the segmentation results. $SR$ is the predicted super-resolution image, $HR$ is the original high-resolution image as the ground truth.

## 2.2   Vessel Feature Enhancement

To enhance the interested vessel features, we propose two modules, upsampling with feature decomposition (UFD) module and feature interaction module (FIM) with a loss $\mathcal{L}_{FIM}$. The former module splits the vessel features from the background, and the latter emphasizes the vessel features by capturing the spatial relation between segmentation and super-resolution branches.

**Upsampling with Feature Decomposition (UFD) Module:** Previous algorithms constrain all features of the entire image by a loss function to the same degree. However, the background is not our interested target, and we hope the framework can focus on our interested vessels. Thus in our SuperVessel, we propose the upsampling with feature decomposition (UFD) module to split the background and vessel features, and the details are shown in the light green dotted frame of Fig. 1. The construction is simple but effective, only $1 \times 1$ Conv is adopted before bilinear interpolation [13] to output decomposed features in different channels. Then the features with two channels are input into our interaction module to obtain a vessel interaction matrix.

**Feature Interaction Module (FIM):** Most algorithms often fuse multiply tasks by various losses or similarities of entire images, which cannot focus on our interested vessel region, nor capture the spatial relation between separated segmentation features and super-resolution features. As the structure information, like vessels, should correspond to the two branches, we propose a feature interaction module (FIM) to capture the spatial relation between features and mainly focus on our interested vessels. The detailed construction is shown in the yellow dotted frame of Fig. 1. The decomposed background, vessel features from segmentation, and super-resolution features are concatenated together into the FIM. $1 \times 1$ Conv with ReLU as the activation is adopted to map the input features into tensors with dimension $d$. The tensors are split into three groups based on channel, and dimension of each group is $d/3$. Then three $3 \times 3$ Conv with different dilation rates $dilation = 1, 2, 4$ to capture different scale information from three groups. In this way, features with different scales can be obtained. Then we concatenate these features to be one tensor. One $1 \times 1$ Conv can be used to integrate information from different scales effectively, thus the spatial relevance can be obtained. To further emphasize the interaction between each group, we adopt ChannelShuffle [22] to exchange the information of concatenated features, which are output from three different dilated rates. Finally, $1 \times 1$ Conv with ReLU followed by one $1 \times 1$ Conv with the Sigmoid is adopted as the activation function to generate the weight matrix of spatial interaction.

The product of mask and high-resolution image is often adopted to produce the region of interest, which takes the whole image as an entire. This often brings some false similarity expressions, especially when some vessels labeled in the mask cannot clearly show up in the corresponding high-resolution image (such as blurry or hard to see). To solve such a problem, we propose to use the prediction of segmentation adding the product of the interaction matrix and prediction of segmentation, and take the segmentation mask of high-resolution as the ground truth. In this way, the framework focuses on the shared region of vessel structures. Thus the loss of FIM $\mathcal{L}_{FIM}$ is expressed as:

$$\mathcal{L}_{FIM} = -\frac{1}{n} \sum_{i=0}^{n} GT_i \log \left( O_{\text{Seg}} \odot O_{\text{FIM}} + O_{\text{Seg}} \right)_i \tag{4}$$

where $n$ is the number of the classes, $GT_i$ is the ground truth of the class $i$, $O_{\text{Seg}}$ is the output of the segmentation, $O_{\text{FIM}}$ is the output of the FIM, and $\left( O_{\text{Seg}} \odot O_{\text{FIM}} + O_{\text{Seg}} \right)_i$ is the probability of the class $i$.

## 3  Experiments

The vessel segment branch of our SuperVessel is adopted to conduct the following experiments. In the section, we first introduce the datasets, evaluation metrics, and experiment parameters. Then the ablation study is listed. Finally, the performance of our SuperVessel is evaluated compared with other state-of-the-art methods.

**Datasets:** We evaluated our SuperVessel with three modals of retinal images from three publicly available datasets, including Color fundus (**HRF**) [1], OCTA (**OCTA-6M**) [9], and ultra-widefield retinal images (**PRIME-FP20**) [2]:

**HRF:** The dataset contains 45 color fundus images from healthy person and patients with diabetic retinopathy or glaucoma. The image size is $3504 \times 2336$. 30 images are used for training, and the rest 15 images for test.

**OCTA-6M:** The dataset contains 300 subjects' images, from the OCTA-500 [9]. OCTA (Optical Coherence Tomography Angiography) is a novel non-invasive imaging modality that visualizes human retinal vascular details. The field of view is $6\,\text{mm} \times 6\,\text{mm}$, with resolution $400 \times 400$ pixels. We use the first 240 subjects to train the model, and the other 60 subjects for test.

**PRIME-FP20:** The dataset provides 15 high-resolution ultra-widefield (UWF) fundus photography (FP) images using Optos 200Tx camera. All images have the same resolution $4000 \times 4000$ pixels. The first 10 images are used for training, and the rest for test.

**Evaluation Metrics:** The evaluation metrics include Precision (P), Sensitivity (SE), Intersection over Union (IoU), Dice, Accuracy (ACC), and Area under the ROC curve (AUC).

**Implementation Details:** All the experiments are run on one NVIDIA RTX 2080TI GPU. We used SGD as the optimizer with the momentum of 0.9 and the weight decay of 0.0001. We used the poly learning rate adjust schedule strategy [10] to set the learning rate during training, where $lr = ((1 - \frac{iter}{max\_iter})^{power}) * init\_lr$, and we set $init\_lr = 0.01, power = 0.9$. In addition, the training epoch is set as 128. Due to the memory limit, we cannot use the original size of the HRF and PRIME-FP datasets to train the model, we use $1752 \times 1162$ and $1408 \times 1296$ as the target size of the high-resolution image for these two datasets respectively.

### 3.1  Ablation Study

An ablation study is conducted on the HRF dataset to investigate the effectiveness of designed modules in our SuperVessel, which takes U-net as the backbone. We also counted the computational parameters and FLOPs of our SuperVessel in both training and test phases. The parameters of SuperVessel for training and test are 29.73M and 28.95M, respectively. Its FLOPs for training and test are 5.86G and 4.72G, respectively. The parameters and FLOPs of SuperVessel for the test are the same as those of U-net. Thus our SuperVessel does not increase the computation load.

As shown in Table 1, we proposed three modules, including ASR (auxiliary super-resolution task), UFD, and FIM. Only adding ASR, meaning purely adding a super-resolution branch to the vessel segmentation, IoU and Dice

**Table 1.** Ablation study of SuperVessel (*mean* ± std).

| ASR | UFD | FIM | SE | IoU | Dice | ACC | AUC |
|---|---|---|---|---|---|---|---|
| × | × | × | 68.56 ± 1.96 | 56.73 ± 0.94 | 72.39 ± 0.76 | 95.87 ± 0.04 | 83.05 ± 0.96 |
| ✓ | × | × | 68.40 ± 2.38 | 56.13 ± 1.01 | 71.89 ± 0.83 | 95.78 ± 0.10 | 82.89 ± 1.08 |
| ✓ | ✓ | × | 68.31 ± 2.13 | 59.41 ± 0.97 | 74.53 ± 0.77 | 96.32 ± 0.05 | 83.08 ± 1.05 |
| ✓ | ✓ | ✓ | **72.29 ± 1.30** | **62.26 ± 0.38** | **76.74 ± 0.29** | **96.54 ± 0.03** | **85.06 ± 0.66** |

decrease a little, so simply combining the two tasks does not effectively improve the segmentation results. After UFD is inserted into the network, the IoU and Dice further increase by about 3% than the baseline, which illustrates that separating vessel features from the background can make the network focus on the vessel features. Finally, the network with FIM improves the IoU and Dice by about 6% and 4%, which means that the interaction between the two branches can further emphasize the vessel features. Our feature enhancement can effectively improve the segmentation accuracy for our SuperVessel. Therefore, the SuperVessel improves the vessel segmentation accuracy without increasing the computation load.

## 3.2   Comparison Results

Seven state-of-the-art methods are selected for comparison, four vessel segmentation networks including U-net [14], SA-UNet [4], CS-Net [12], SCS-Net [20]; three super-resolution-combined segmentation multi-task networks including DSRL [19], CogSeg [21] and PFSeg [18]. The proposed SuperVessel is compared with the above methods based on the three vessel segmentation datasets.

**Table 2.** Results on the HRF dataset (mean ± std).

| Model | SE | IoU | Dice | ACC | AUC |
|---|---|---|---|---|---|
| U-net | 68.56 ± 1.96 | 56.73 ± 0.94 | 72.39 ± 0.76 | 95.87 ± 0.04 | 83.05 ± 0.96 |
| SA-UNet | 68.19 ± 2.89 | 55.26 ± 1.02 | 71.18 ± 0.84 | 95.64 ± 0.07 | 82.70 ± 1.33 |
| CS-Net | 67.43 ± 2.45 | 55.09 ± 0.92 | 71.04 ± 0.76 | 95.66 ± 0.08 | 82.32 ± 1.13 |
| SCS-Net | 66.31 ± 1.76 | 54.63 ± 0.30 | 70.66 ± 0.25 | 95.65 ± 0.13 | 81.80 ± 0.73 |
| DSRL | - | - | - | - | - |
| CogSeg | 70.95 ± 1.72 | 59.68 ± 0.76 | 74.75 ± 0.6 | 96.22 ± 0.04 | 84.31 ± 0.81 |
| PFSeg | - | - | - | - | - |
| **SuperVessel** | **72.29 ± 1.30** | **62.26 ± 0.38** | **76.74 ± 0.29** | **96.54 ± 0.03** | **85.06 ± 0.66** |

**Comparison Results on HRF Datasets:** The sizes of input images for all the algorithms are the same $876 \times 584$, to simulate low-resolution input images. The sizes of output images for U-net, SA-UNet, CS-Net and SCS-Net are the same

as their input, and those for DSRL, CogSeg, PFSeg and our SuperVessel are
$1752 \times 1162$. From Table 2, our SuperVessel surpasses all the other state-of-the-
art networks, with an IoU of more than 2%. The std numbers of our SuperVessel
are the lowest, meaning that the segmentation stability of SuperVessel is superior
to other algorithms. DSRL and PFSeg cannot segment the HRF dataset, as the
gradient explosion happens during training. We will discuss this in the discussion
section. Thus, the superiority of our SuperVessel in the accuracy and stability
can be proved on the HRF dataset.

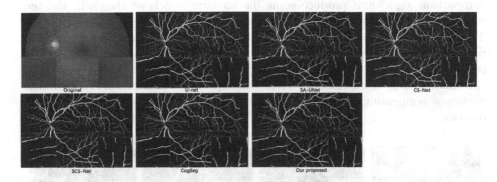

**Fig. 2.** The experiment examples on the HRF datasets. Green means the ground truth,
red is segmentation result, yellow means the corrected segmentation results. **(Please
zoom in for a better view.)** (Color figure online)

The experiment examples on HRF dataset are shown in Fig. 2. All the other
algorithms wrongly segment the edge of the disc as vessels, but our SuperVessel
gives out the exact classification. Then we selected two blocks with tiny vessels
to further analyze the results, the blue rectangle contains tiny vessels around
the macular, and the red rectangle contains the vessels' end. The SuperVessel
can segment more tiny vessels than other algorithms, especially, at the end of
all vessels. Thus, the proposed feature enhancement can effectively improve the
tiny vessel segmentation.

**Table 3.** Comparison results based on OCTA dataset.

| Model | SE | IoU | Dice | ACC | AUC |
|---|---|---|---|---|---|
| U-net | $64.06 \pm 0.41$ | $52.36 \pm 0.18$ | $68.73 \pm 0.15$ | $94.53 \pm 0.01$ | $80.97 \pm 0.18$ |
| SA-UNet | $59.65 \pm 0.41$ | $48.94 \pm 0.25$ | $65.72 \pm 0.23$ | $94.16 \pm 0.02$ | $78.86 \pm 0.20$ |
| CS-Net | $61.58 \pm 0.84$ | $50.32 \pm 0.25$ | $66.95 \pm 0.22$ | $94.29 \pm 0.03$ | $79.79 \pm 0.36$ |
| SCS-Net | $63.44 \pm 0.27$ | $51.17 \pm 0.04$ | $67.70 \pm 0.04$ | $94.32 \pm 0.02$ | $80.62 \pm 0.12$ |
| DSRL | - | - | - | - | - |
| CogSeg | $66.33 \pm 0.27$ | $56.46 \pm 0.48$ | $72.17 \pm 0.39$ | $95.2 \pm 0.08$ | $82.42 \pm 0.16$ |
| PFSeg | $\mathbf{74.92 \pm 2.68}$ | $56.35 \pm 2.55$ | $72.05 \pm 2.07$ | $94.55 \pm 0.39$ | $86.02 \pm 1.3$ |
| **SuperVessel** | $73.80 \pm 0.31$ | $\mathbf{64.56 \pm 0.10}$ | $\mathbf{78.46 \pm 0.07}$ | $\mathbf{96.20 \pm 0.02}$ | $\mathbf{86.30 \pm 0.13}$ |

**Comparison Results on OCTA Dataset:** The sizes of low-resolution input images for all the algorithms are the same $200 \times 200$. The sizes of output images for U-net, SA-UNet, CS-Net and SCS-Net are the same as their input, and those for DSRL, CogSeg, PFSeg and our SuperVessel are $400 \times 400$. From Table 3, our SuperVessel surpasses all the other state-of-the-art networks, with an IoU of more than 8%. The std numbers of our SuperVessel are lower than most other algorithms, meaning that the SuperVessel works stably. We will also discuss that DSRL cannot segment the OCTA dataset in the discussion section.

The experiment examples on the OCTA dataset are shown in Fig. 3. Most comparison algorithms produce some discontinue vessels as shown in the red rectangles, as the vessels around the macular are very tiny and indistinguishable. There are two tiny vessels away from the large vessels in the blue rectangles. Our SuperVessel can detect the tiny vessels, but other algorithms cannot correctly segment them, since our SuperVessel highlights the structure features based on the enhancement of the features. Thus, the superiority of our SuperVessel in the accuracy, segmenting of tiny vessels, and stability can be proved on the OCTA dataset.

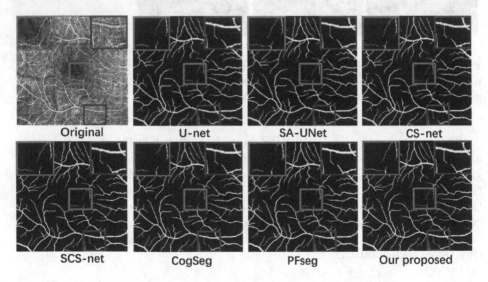

**Fig. 3.** The experiment examples on the OCTA datasets. Green means the ground truth, red is segmentation result, yellow means the corrected segmentation results. **(Please zoom in for a better view.)** (Color figure online)

**Comparison Results on PRIME-FP20 Dataset:** The sizes of input images for all the algorithms are the same $704 \times 648$, to simulate low-resolution input images. The sizes of output images for U-net, SA-UNet, CS-Net and SCS-Net are the same as their input, and those for DSRL, CogSeg, PFSeg and our SuperVessel are $1408 \times 1296$. From Table 4, our SuperVessel surpasses all the other state-of-the-art networks, with IoU of more than 11%, which is significant. The std

**Table 4.** Comparison results on PRIME-FP20 dataset

| Model | SE | IoU | Dice | ACC | AUC |
|---|---|---|---|---|---|
| U-net | 26.43 ± 1.34 | 22.77 ± 0.89 | 37.08 ± 1.18 | 97.77 ± 0.01 | 62.62 ± 0.70 |
| SA-UNet | 13.50 ± 5.90 | 12.43 ± 5.33 | 21.77 ± 8.94 | 97.66 ± 0.08 | 56.47 ± 2.82 |
| CS-Net | 19.37 ± 6.90 | 17.06 ± 5.31 | 28.86 ± 7.91 | 97.70 ± 0.04 | 59.26 ± 3.24 |
| SCS-Net | 18.91 ± 4.68 | 17.08 ± 3.72 | 29.04 ± 5.40 | 97.73 ± 0.04 | 59.05 ± 2.19 |
| DSRL | - | - | - | - | - |
| CogSeg | 11.14 ± 7.79 | 10.50 ± 7.25 | 18.36 ± 12.31 | 97.69 ± 0.13 | 55.52 ± 3.82 |
| PFSeg | - | - | - | - | - |
| **SuperVessel** | **38.47** ± 1.7 | **33.52** ± 1.12 | **50.21** ± 1.25 | **98.11** ± 0.03 | **68.67** ± 0.84 |

parameters of our SuperVessel are lower than most of the other algorithms, meaning that the SuperVessel works stably. For the situation of DSRL and PFSeg, we will also discuss this in the discussion section. The experiment examples on the dataset are shown in Fig. 4. As the view field of these images is about 200°, the vessels in these images are extremely tiny compared with the other two datasets. In the red rectangles, the segmented vessels by our SuperVessel are more continuous than those by other algorithms. In the blue rectangles containing more tiny vessels, the SuperVessel detects more vessels than other algorithms, as the spatial features such as vessels are emphasized by our feature enhancement. Therefore, our SuperVessel is superior to other state-of-the-art algorithms in the segmentation accuracy and stability with tiny vessels based on the three publicly available datasets.

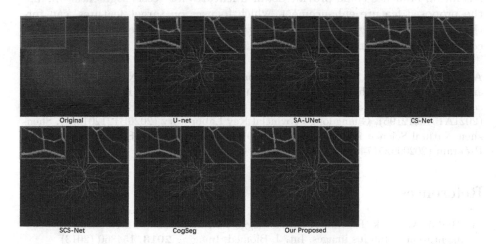

**Fig. 4.** The experiment examples on the PRIME-FP20 dataset. Green means the ground truth, red is segmentation result, yellow means the corrected segmentation results. **(Please zoom in for a better view.)** (Color figure online)

# 4    Discussion and Conclusions

In the study, we proposed the SuperVessel to provide high-resolution vessel segmentation results for analysis based on low-resolution input, and experiments prove its effectiveness. But previous super-resolution-combined segmentation multi-task networks such as DSRL and PFSeg cannot train on most of the vessel segmentation datasets, we observed that these methods often cause the model to collapse during training. We conjectured that the similarity loss between two tasks is not suitable when the targets of one task are the subset of another task. Since the similarity maybe make one of the tasks lose its constraint direction, the collapsing of models maybe happen, such as the two algorithms collapsed in the vessel segmentation task. Experiments on three datasets show that our proposed method can resolve this problem by finding the spatial relation between two tasks for vessel segmentation.

Although the SuperVessel can work well on most of the vessel segmentation datasets, there are still some improvements. For some extremely tiny blood vessels, especially for ultra-field fundus images in the PRIME-FP20 dataset, the model can only segment a little more vessels than other algorithms. The main reason is that the original image is very large but we cannot deal with so much redundant information. Limited by our computation devices we cannot train our SuperVessel to output the vessel of original image size for some extremely large-image-size datasets.

In conclusion, we proposed the SuperVessel for vessel segmentation, which outputs high-resolution vessel segmentation results based on low-resolution input images. Experiments on three publicly available datasets prove that super-resolution branches could provide detailed features for vessel segmentation, and the proposed feature enhancement, which focuses on target features, can further improve the segmentation accuracy with more tiny vessels and stronger continuity of the segmented vessels.

**Acknowledgement.** This work was supported in part by The National Natural Science Foundation of China (8210072776), Guangdong Provincial Department of Education (2020ZDZX3043), Guangdong Basic and Applied Basic Research Foundation (2021A1515012195), Guangdong Provincial Key Laboratory (2020B121201001), Shenzhen Natural Science Fund (JCYJ20200109140820699) and the Stable Support Plan Program (20200925174052004).

# References

1. Budai, A., Bock, R., Maier, A., Hornegger, J., Michelson, G.: Robust vessel segmentation in fundus images. Int. J. Biomed. Imaging **2013**, 154860 (2013)
2. Ding, L., Kuriyan, A.E., Ramchandran, R.S., Wykoff, C.C., Sharma, G.: Weakly-supervised vessel detection in ultra-widefield fundus photography via iterative multi-modal registration and learning. IEEE Trans. Med. Imaging **40**(10), 2748–2758 (2020)

3. Fu, H., Xu, Y., Lin, S., Kee Wong, D.W., Liu, J.: DeepVessel: retinal vessel segmentation via deep learning and conditional random field. In: Ourselin, S., Joskowicz, L., Sabuncu, M.R., Unal, G., Wells, W. (eds.) MICCAI 2016. LNCS, vol. 9901, pp. 132–139. Springer, Cham (2016). https://doi.org/10.1007/978-3-319-46723-8_16

4. Guo, C., Szemenyei, M., Yi, Y., Wang, W., Chen, B., Fan, C.: SA-UNet: spatial attention U-Net for retinal vessel segmentation. In: 2020 25th International Conference on Pattern Recognition (ICPR), pp. 1236–1242. IEEE (2021)

5. Ikram, M.K., Ong, Y.T., Cheung, C.Y., Wong, T.Y.: Retinal vascular caliber measurements: clinical significance, current knowledge and future perspectives. Ophthalmologica **229**(3), 125–136 (2013)

6. Karaali, A., Dahyot, R., Sexton, D.J.: DR-VNet: retinal vessel segmentation via dense residual UNet. arXiv preprint arXiv:2111.04739 (2021)

7. Lei, S., Shi, Z., Wu, X., Pan, B., Xu, X., Hao, H.: Simultaneous super-resolution and segmentation for remote sensing images. In: 2019 IEEE International Geoscience and Remote Sensing Symposium, IGARSS 2019, Yokohama, Japan, 28 July–2 August 2019, pp. 3121–3124. IEEE (2019)

8. Li, L., Verma, M., Nakashima, Y., Nagahara, H., Kawasaki, R.: IterNet: retinal image segmentation utilizing structural redundancy in vessel networks. In: IEEE Winter Conference on Applications of Computer Vision, WACV 2020, Snowmass Village, CO, USA, 1–5 March 2020, pp. 3645–3654. IEEE (2020)

9. Li, M., et al.: Image projection network: 3D to 2D image segmentation in octa images. IEEE Trans. Med. Imaging **39**(11), 3343–3354 (2020)

10. Liu, W., Rabinovich, A., Berg, A.C.: ParseNet: looking wider to see better. arXiv preprint arXiv:1506.04579 (2015)

11. London, A., Benhar, I., Schwartz, M.: The retina as a window to the brain-from eye research to CNS disorders. Nat. Rev. Neurol. **9**(1), 44–53 (2013)

12. Mou, L., et al.: CS-Net: channel and spatial attention network for curvilinear structure segmentation. In: Shen, D., et al. (eds.) MICCAI 2019. LNCS, vol. 11764, pp. 721–730. Springer, Cham (2019). https://doi.org/10.1007/978-3-030-32239-7_80

13. Press, W.H., Teukolsky, S.A., Vetterling, W.T., Flannery, B.P.: Numerical Recipes. The Art of Scientific Computing, 3rd edn. Cambridge University Press, Cambridge (2007)

14. Ronneberger, O., Fischer, P., Brox, T.: U-Net: convolutional networks for biomedical image segmentation. In: Navab, N., Hornegger, J., Wells, W.M., Frangi, A.F. (eds.) MICCAI 2015. LNCS, vol. 9351, pp. 234–241. Springer, Cham (2015). https://doi.org/10.1007/978-3-319-24574-4_28

15. Su, R., Zhang, D., Liu, J., Cheng, C.: MSU-Net: multi-scale U-Net for 2D medical image segmentation. Front. Genet. **12**, 140 (2021)

16. Sun, C., Wang, J.J., Mackey, D.A., Wong, T.Y.: Retinal vascular caliber: systemic, environmental, and genetic associations. Surv. Ophthalmol. **54**(1), 74–95 (2009)

17. Wang, B., Qiu, S., He, H.: Dual encoding U-Net for retinal vessel segmentation. In: Shen, D., et al. (eds.) MICCAI 2019. LNCS, vol. 11764, pp. 84–92. Springer, Cham (2019). https://doi.org/10.1007/978-3-030-32239-7_10

18. Wang, H., et al.: Patch-free 3D medical image segmentation driven by super-resolution technique and self-supervised guidance. In: de Bruijne, M., et al. (eds.) MICCAI 2021. LNCS, vol. 12901, pp. 131–141. Springer, Cham (2021). https://doi.org/10.1007/978-3-030-87193-2_13

19. Wang, L., Li, D., Zhu, Y., Tian, L., Shan, Y.: Dual super-resolution learning for semantic segmentation. In: Proceedings of the IEEE/CVF Conference on Computer Vision and Pattern Recognition (CVPR), June 2020

20. Wu, H., Wang, W., Zhong, J., Lei, B., Wen, Z., Qin, J.: SCS-Net: a scale and context sensitive network for retinal vessel segmentation. Med. Image Anal. **70**, 102025 (2021)
21. Zhang, Q., Yang, G., Zhang, G.: Collaborative network for super-resolution and semantic segmentation of remote sensing images. IEEE Trans. Geosci. Remote Sens. **60**, 1–12 (2022)
22. Zhang, X., Zhou, X., Lin, M., Sun, J.: ShuffleNet: an extremely efficient convolutional neural network for mobile devices. In: Proceedings of the IEEE Conference on Computer Vision and Pattern Recognition, pp. 6848–6856 (2018)

# Cascade Multiscale Swin-Conv Network for Fast MRI Reconstruction

Shengcheng Ye[1], Xinyu Xie[2], Dongping Xiong[1], Lijun Ouyang[1],
and Xiaozhi Zhang[2(✉)]

[1] School of Computing/Software, University of South China, Hengyang 421001, China
[2] School of Electrical Engineering, University of South China, Hengyang 421001, China
zxz_usc@163.com

**Abstract.** Compressed sensing magnetic resonance imaging (CS-MRI) is an important and effective tool for the fast MR imaging, which enables superior performance in restoring the anatomy of patients from the undersampled k-space data. Deep learning methods have been successful in solving this inverse problem and are competent to generate high quality reconstructions. While state-of-the-art deep learning methods for MRI reconstructions are based on convolutional neural networks (CNNs), which only consider the local features independently and lack long-range dependencies presented in images. In this work, inspired by the impressive performances of Transformers on high level vision tasks, we propose a Cascade multiscale Swin-Conv (CMSC) network, a novel Swin Transformer based method for the fast MRI reconstruction. The whole network consists of the shallow feature extraction, deep feature extraction and image reconstruction module. Specifically, the shallow feature extraction module is a Multiscale Cascade Convolution Block (MCCB), and the deep feature extraction module is a U-shaped network composed of several Cascade Multiscale Swin-Conv Blocks (CMSCB), each of which has several Cascade Swin Transformer Layers (STL) and an MCCB to highly model both the local and long-range information with multiscale features. Our framework provides three appealing benefits: (i) A new U-shaped deep feature extraction module combined with Swin Transformers and CNNs is introduced to hierarchically capture the local and global information. (ii) A novel CMSCB is designed for developing multiscale features via computing self-attention in a window with increasing size. (iii) Our MCCB is the first attempt for fusing multiscale information and deeply extracting local features with multiple residual convolutional layers. Experimental results demonstrate that our model achieves superior performances compared with other state-of-the-art deep learning-based reconstruction methods.

**Keywords:** MRI reconstruction · Swin transformer · Multiscale cascade convolution

## 1 Introduction

Magnetic resonance imaging (MRI) is a powerful and non-invasive medical imaging technique, which provides strong capabilities in obtaining rich anatomical and physiological information. However, acquiring a high spatial resolution image in MRI takes up

© The Author(s), under exclusive license to Springer Nature Switzerland AG 2022
S. Yu et al. (Eds.): PRCV 2022, LNCS 13535, pp. 191–203, 2022.
https://doi.org/10.1007/978-3-031-18910-4_16

to tens of minutes long, which causes problems with patient discomfort and leads to high exam costs. To shorten the long acquisition time of MRI, three traditional methods have been developed over the past decades and become the mainstream methods, namely, the physics based fast scanning sequences [1], parallel imaging [2], and compressed sensing (CS) techniques [3, 4]. These techniques along with their combinations have either reduced reconstruction time or shortened the acquisition time. Although those numerical methods have been proposed to optimize the free parameters in MRI, traditional reconstruction methods still have problems of the high computing complexity and aliasing artifacts [5].

With the rapid development of image processing techniques, deep learning (DL) methods have attracted unprecedented attention and shown great potential in various tasks [6–9]. Inspired by such success, deep learning methods have been applied to the field of MR imaging reconstruction, which is being increasingly to complement or replace the traditional algorithms. Compared with traditional algorithms, such as CS techniques, DL avoids complicated optimization parameter tuning and performs fast online reconstruction with the aid of offline training using enormous amounts of data [10]. CNN is the classic deep learning network which enable enhanced latent feature extraction through their highly hierarchical structure. Wang et al. first takes advantage of CNNs by extracting latent correlations between the undersampled and fully sampled $k$-space data for MRI reconstruction [11]. Yang et al. proposed an improved network by re-applying the alternating direction method of multipliers (ADMM) with CNN [12]. The ADMM achieved similar reconstruction results as classic CS-MRI reconstruction methods but dramatically reduced reconstruction time. The MRI reconstruction method based on CNNs also includes [13–19]. Yang et al. introduced Deep De-Aliasing Generative Adversarial Networks (DAGANs), in which a U-Net architecture was used to construct the generator [20]. It not only provides superior reconstruction results, but also retains more the perceptual details. Similarly, the GAN-based reconstruction methods also include [21, 22]. Moreover, Residual networks used in studies can effectively restore the high frequency details of MR images with long and short skip connections [23–27]. For a period, CNNs had a dominant position in the field of image tasks. However, it lacks the long-range dependency. In addition, the overly deep network depth and unfitted convolutional kernel size can cause Network training crashes.

Transformer derived from the Natural Language Processing (NLP) has gained much popularity in the Computer Vision (CV) task. It can exploit the global information by modeling the long-range dependency. It also takes advantage of sequence-to-sequence model design, even deeper mapping and adaptive self-attention setting with expanding receptive fields [28–31]. Benefiting from these superior abilities, Transformers have recently achieved state-of-the-art performances on different CV tasks [32–36]. Feng et al. adopted the model for reconstruction and super-resolution tasks by incorporating the model with task-specific cross-attention modules [37]. Although visual Transformers have advantages in CV tasks, the transplant from NLP to CV tasks leads to challenges. On the one hand, the quantity of pixels in images tends to be much higher than words in sentences, which causes high computational burdens [33]. On the other hand, visual elements in CV tasks tend to vary substantially in scale unlike language elements in NLP tasks. To address the above drawbacks, a hierarchical Shift Windows (Swin)

Transformer is developed in [38]. Swin Transformer substituted the traditional Multi-head Self-Attention (MSA) with the Windows or Shifted Windows based Multi-head Self-Attention (W-MSA/SW-MSA). Based on the Swin Transformer module, Cao et al. proposed a U-shaped network Swin-Unet for image segmentation tasks [39]. Liang et al. proposed a Swin Transformer-based image restoration model SwinIR, which achieves state-of-the-art performances on three representative image restoration tasks [40]. Huang et al. first applied Swin Transformer based network SwinMR for Fast MRI and discussed how powerful transformers are in Fast MRI Reconstruction task [41, 42]. Based on SwinIR, SwinMR is the first attempt at accelerated MRI reconstruction. These methods derived from Swin Transformer show great potential to be improved.

Motivated by the above success of Swin Transformers, we investigated how to further improve the performance in MRI reconstruction tasks by designing a powerful transformer model. We propose a Swin Transformer-based model to reconstruct the under-sampled MR images in this work. The Cascade multiscale Swin-Conv block (CMSCB) and Multiscale Cascade Convolution Block (MCCB) are incorporated to further improve the ability of extracting features. Specifically, the CMSC is composed of the shallow feature extraction, deep feature extraction and image reconstruction module. We performed comprehensive experiments and the CMSC achieved better results compared with other deep learning based models.

Concretely, our main contributions are:

- A new U-shaped deep feature extraction module combined with Swin Transformer and CNN as the deep feature extraction module is designed to capture the hierarchical local and global context feature representations from various scales of receptive field.
- A novel CMSCB is proposed to compute MSA in windows with increasing size to learn multiscale feature representations, which could capture more sufficient long-range dependencies.
- MCCB selectively fuses the multiscale long-range information and deeply extracts the local features using multiple residual convolutional layers. Multiple residual connections significantly stabilize model training, which enables a deeper network.

## 2 Method

### 2.1 CMSC Network Architecture

As shown in Fig. 1, CMSC consists of three modules: shallow feature extraction, deep feature extraction, and image reconstruction modules.

**Shallow Feature Extraction Module.** The shallow feature extraction module is designed to map the input image to a higher dimensional feature space for the following deep feature extraction module. We designed an MCCB (which will be illustrated in Sect. 2.3) to fully extract shallow features of the input image. Given the undersampled MR images $X_u \in \mathbb{R}^{H_0 \times W_0 \times C_u}$ ($H_0$, $W_0$ and $C_u$ are the image height, width, and channel numbers, respectively), the shallow feature extract operator $F_S$ can be formulated as

$$X_0 = F_S(X_u), \tag{1}$$

where $X_0 \in \mathbb{R}^{H_0 \times W_0 \times C_0}$ is the output shallow features representations with higher dimension $C_0$.

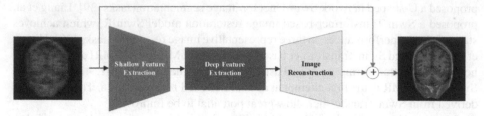

**Fig. 1.** The overview architecture of CMSC net.

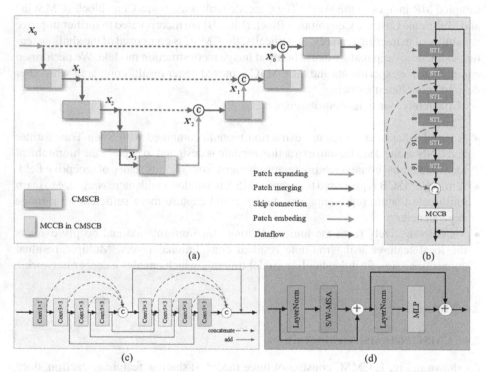

**Fig. 2.** The sub-network of CMSC. (a) U-shaped Deep Feature Extraction Module. (b) Cascade Multiscale Swin-Conv Block (CMSCB). (c) Multiscale Cascade Convolution Block (MCCB). (d) Swin Transformer Layer (STL).

**Deep Feature Extraction Module.** The overview of the deep feature extraction module and its data flow are illustrated in Fig. 2 (a). The deep features are extracted from the shallow features, which can be represented by

$$X_0' = F_D(X_0), \tag{2}$$

where $F_D$ is the deep feature extractor, and it is a U-shaped network composed of CMSCBs (which will be illustrated in Sect. 2.2). To completely save pixel features information as well as transform the input into sequence embeddings for the following CMSCB, the feature map $X_0$ is split into tokens with patch size of $1 \times 1$ by using a patch embedding operation, then it passes through several CMSCBs and patch merging layers to generate $L$ hierarchical long-range feature representations $X_i$. This process can be expressed by

$$X_{i+1} = F_{Merg_i}\big(F_{CMSCB_i}(X_i)\big), i = 0, 1, \ldots, L-1, \tag{3}$$

where $F_{Merg_i}$ is the $i$-th patch merging operation, $F_{CMSCB_i}$ denotes the $i$-th CMSCB and $X_i \in \mathbb{R}^{H_i \times W_i \times C_i}$ represents the $i$-th feature map while $X_{i+1} \in \mathbb{R}^{\frac{H_i}{2} \times \frac{W_i}{2} \times 2C_i}$ represents the $i+1$-th feature map. $F_{CMSCB_i}$ can adequately extract the long-range dependence of image context and capture the local features respectively under various scales receptive fields in each layer. After that, the fully extracted feature map $X_{L-1}$ is upsampled layer by layer from $X_{L-1}'$ to $X_0'$ and they are concatenated with downsampled features $X_i$ via skip connections. These steps can be formulated as

$$X_{L-i-1}' = F_{Expand_i}\Big(F_{CMSCB_i}'\big(Concat\big(X_{L-i}', X_{L-i}\big)A_{L-i}\big)\Big), i = 1, 2, \ldots, L-1, \tag{4}$$

where $F_{CMSCB_i}'$ is the $i$-th CMSCB in the upsampling layer, $Concat$ performs concatenation of features along dimensions and $F_{Expand_i}$ is the $i$-th patch expanding operation. $A_{L-i} \in \mathbb{R}^{2C_i \times C_i}$ conducts linear mapping to shrink the dimension from $2C_i$ to $C_i$ for the next $F_{CMSCB_i}'$.

**Image Reconstruction.** This model applies a single $3 \times 3$ convolution layer as the reconstruction module $F_R$ to map the high dimensional representations $X_0'$ to MR image space $X_R \in \mathbb{R}^{H_0 \times W_0 \times C_u}$ as

$$X_R = F_R(X_0'). \tag{5}$$

Besides, the residual connection between the input undersampled image $X_u$ and reconstructed image $X_R$ is used to stabilize training and aggregate more undersampled image information. The whole process can be expressed as

$$\widehat{X} = F_R(F_D(F_S(X_u))) + X_u, \tag{6}$$

where $\widehat{X}$ is the generated restored image via our method.

**Loss Function.** For this reconstruction task, we optimize the parameters of networks by minimizing the Normalized Mean Squared Error (NMSE) loss

$$L_{NMSE} = \sqrt{\frac{\|\widehat{X} - X\|_2^2}{\|X\|_2^2}}. \tag{7}$$

## 2.2 Cascade Multisacle Swin-Conv Block

As shown in Fig. 2 (b), the proposed Cascade Multiscale Swin-Conv Block $F_{CMSCB}$ is composed of a cascade of $Q$ Swin Transformer Layers (STL, as shown in Fig. 2 (d)) followed by a Multiscale Cascade Convolution Block $F_{MCCB}$ at the end. STL alternatively calculates window based multi-head self-attention (W-MSA) and shifted window based multi-head self-attention (SW-MSA). Given the $i$-th downsampling input $X_i$, the entire dataflow of the structure $F_{CMSCB_i}$ can be expressed by

$$X_{i,0} = X_i, \tag{8}$$

$$X_{i,j+1} = F_{STL_{i,j}}(X_{i,j}), j = 0, 1, \ldots, Q - 1, \tag{9}$$

$$X_{i,Q} = Concat(X_{i,Q-1}, X_{i,Q-3}, \ldots, X_{i,2}), \tag{10}$$

$$X_m = F_{MCCB}(X_{i,Q}) + X_{i,0}, \tag{11}$$

where $F_{STL_{i,j}}$ denotes the $j$-th STL in the $i$-th downsampling layer. In particular, the size of non-overlaping window within which MSA is computed doubles every two STLs starting from 4. Taking Fig. 2 (b) as an example, we set the window size in each STL layer to 4, 4, 8, 8, 16 and 16, respectively. This design aims to obtain multiscale feature maps that contain both local information and long-range dependency, which ensures the receptive field larger than that computed within a fixed size window. For $F_{MCCB}$, it fuses the concatenated multiscale information selectively as well as enhances the translational equivariance of our network by using spatially invariant convolution filters.

## 2.3 Multiscale Cascade Convolution Block

Inspired by the dense net [27] and residual net [23], we propose a novel convolution-based block (Fig. 2 (c)) named Multiscale Cascade Convolution Block. At first, the network channel number is reduced to a quarter by a $1 \times 1$ convolution operation. By doing this, the computation cost for the following layer will be saved. Then the followed 3 consecutive $3 \times 3$ convolution layers are applied to fully extract local information. Finally, the output feature maps from each layer are concatenated together to recover to the original channel number. These three steps as a stage are applied twice and several skip connections are employed between these two stages. These skip connections can significantly deepen the number of layers so as to alleviate the problem of gradient vanishing or gradient explosion during backpropagation.

# 3    Experiments and Results

## 3.1    Datasets

The proposed methods were experimented on the MICCAI 2013 grand challenge dataset [43]. We randomly sampled 15216 and 9854 slices of T1-weighted MRI brain images for training and validation, and 50 testing sets were chosen independently. All image data were resized to $256 \times 256$. For masks, we used three different types of udersampling patterns for training and testing, i.e., 1D Gaussian (G1D), 2D Gaussian (G2D) and 2D Poisson disc (P2D). 30% retained raw $k$-space data were applied to simulate $3.3\times$ accelerations.

## 3.2 Implementation Details

The proposed network was implemented based on Pytorch 1.1.0. The embed dimension (feature dimension in Swin Transformer) were set to 96. Basically, we applied 4 layers and 6 STLs in each CMSCB individually. We trained our model on Nvidia RTX 3090 with 24 GB memory using Adam optimizer; the learning rate was set to 1e−4 and the parameters $\beta_1$ and $\beta_2$ were set to 0.5 and 0.999 respectively. The learning rate decayed by half every 5 epochs; The total epochs were set to 40.

## 3.3 Comparison Results with Other Methods

Table 1 tabulates the comparison results of our method as well as some other representative methods, including ZF (zero-filling), Deep-ADMM [12], Cascade [13], DAGAN [20], Unet [14], Unet-Refine (with global residual) and SwinMR (nPI) [41] using G1D 30%, G2D 30%, and P2D 30% undersampling masks. In general, our method has outperformed other deep learning methods with a higher Peak signal-to-noise ratio (PSNR) and lower NMSE. The results show a greater advantage in reconstructing the image from ZF image, especially when the PSNR of ZF is higher. We can improve PSNR by 2.83 in G1D 30% mask compared with SwinMR (nPI) whose PSNR result is 45.89 dB.

Figure 3 shows a horizontal line profile across a randomly selected case comparison result using different reconstruction methods. The variation of image intensity of our method is closer to the Ground Truth (GT) and is smoother than comparison methods.

Figure 4 shows the visual quantity results and differences between ZF and reconstructed images. According to the results from (b) and (e), our model obtained better de-aliasing results compared to other methods. From the zoom in ROI G1D 30% (b), we can observe that the reconstructed texture information is more obvious than in other methods, and the image noise is fully reduced. Figure 4 (c) and (f) also demonstrate that our method gains the minimum difference between the restored image and GT image. For P2D 30% mask in Fig. 4 (f), we can hardly observe the visual differences between the reconstructed images and the GT.

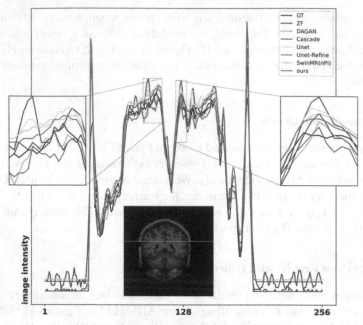

**Fig. 3.** Comparison of horizontal line profile.

**Table 1.** Quantitative results (PSNR and NMSE) of the comparison methods using different undersampling masks.

| MICCAI 2013 | G1D30% | | G2D30% | | P2D30% | |
|---|---|---|---|---|---|---|
| Method | NMSE | PSNR | NMSE | PSNR | NMSE | PSNR |
| ZF | $0.16 \pm 0.03$ | $35.30 \pm 5.22$ | $0.14 \pm 0.03$ | $36.51 \pm 5.01$ | $0.10 \pm 0.02$ | $39.17 \pm 4.85$ |
| ADMM [12] | $0.11 \pm 0.02$ | $37.77 \pm 4.82$ | $0.09 \pm 0.02$ | $39.64 \pm 4.64$ | $0.07 \pm 0.02$ | $41.65 \pm 3.39$ |
| Cascade [13] | $0.10 \pm 0.02$ | $39.39 \pm 4.38$ | $0.07 \pm 0.04$ | $42.75 \pm 4.27$ | $0.05 \pm 0.03$ | $46.38 \pm 4.29$ |
| DAGAN [20] | $0.08 \pm 0.03$ | $41.16 \pm 4.07$ | $0.06 \pm 0.02$ | $43.45 \pm 4.58$ | $0.05 \pm 0.02$ | $45.99 \pm 4.39$ |
| Unet [14] | $0.07 \pm 0.02$ | $42.01 \pm 4.81$ | $0.07 \pm 0.03$ | $42.51 \pm 4.77$ | $0.05 \pm 0.01$ | $45.47 \pm 4.44$ |

(continued)

**Table 1.** (*continued*)

| MICCAI 2013 | G1D30% | | G2D30% | | P2D30% | |
|---|---|---|---|---|---|---|
| Method | NMSE | PSNR | NMSE | PSNR | NMSE | PSNR |
| Unet | 0.06 ± 0.01 | 43.43 ± 5.05 | 0.05 ± 0.02 | 45.79 ± 5.20 | 0.03 ± 0.01 | 49.27 ± 5.37 |
| Refine SwinMR (nPI) [41] | 0.05 ± 0.01 | 45.89 ± 5.10 | 0.05 ± 0.01 | 46.07 ± 5.66 | 0.03 ± 0.01 | 49.59 ± 5.98 |
| **Ours** | **0.03 ± 0.01** | **48.72 ± 4.89** | **0.03 ± 0.01** | **50.93 ± 5.88** | **0.02 ± 0.01** | **54.53 ± 6.53** |

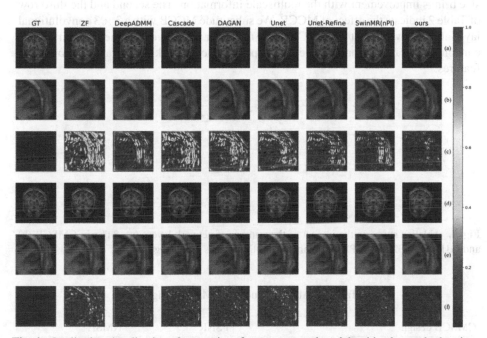

**Fig. 4.** Qualitative visualization of comparison for our proposed models with other methods using G1D 30% (top 3 rows a, b, c) and P2D 30% (bottom 3 rows d, e, f) random undersampling. (a), (d) displays the reconstructed image from different methods. (b), (d) zoomed in ROI from the red box in (a), (d) respectively. (c), (f) shows the difference in heating image between the reconstructed image and the GT of the same ROI. Color bars for the difference image are shown on the right. (Color figure online)

## 3.4 Ablation Study

We conducted ablation studies with the G1D30% mask to search for the hyper-parameters of the proposed model. Specifically, the number of network layers, STLs in RSTB, the window size and the effect of MCCB will be discussed below.

Figure 5 (a) illustrates that the PSNR increases as the number of network layers increases from 2 to 4. When the number of network layers equals 2, the PSNR result produces a large gap compared to 4 layers due to insufficient hierarchical features. Figure 5 (b) shows that when the number of STL $\geq$ 4, our model performance tends to be saturated and stable. In this case, global information modeling is fully exploited by a cascade of STLs with the same scales of receptive field in each layer. Figure 5 (c) displays the results of G1D30%, G2D30% and P2D30% mask. Our trained models reach a convergence stage in a few dozens of training iterations.

Table 2 demonstrates the effectiveness of the incremental window size and the use of MCCB in CMSCB. The first row and the third row of Table 2 shows the impact of fixed and incremental window size in CMSCB where self-attention is calculated. The fixed window size was set to 8. From the table, we can observe that the incremental window size brings improvement with the multiscale information. The second and the third row of Table 2 indicate the effect of MCCB. We substitude MCCB with a $3 \times 3$ convolutional layer and discovered that the MCCB performs better with fewer parameters than a $3 \times 3$ convolutional layer. It mainly owes to deepening the network for extracting more local features.

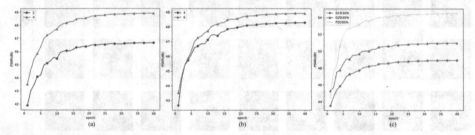

**Fig. 5.** Ablation study on the impact of the number of network layers (a), STLs in CMSCB (b) and G1D 30%, G2D30%, P2D30% undersampling masks (c) during training.

**Table 2.** Ablation study on CMSCB design.

| CMSCB design | PSNR | NMSE |
|---|---|---|
| CMSCB without incremental window size | 48.47 ± 4.85 | 0.034 ± 0.01 |
| CMSCB without MCCB | 48.49 ± 4.83 | 0.034 ± 0.01 |
| CMSCB | 48.72 ± 4.89 | 0.033 ± 0.01 |

## 4 Conclusion

In this work, we propose a Cascade Multiscale Swin-Conv (CMSC) network for accelerated MRI reconstructions, which is helpful to learn the local and global information in MR images. In particular, the proposed U-shaped deep feature extraction network can capture the hierarchical local and global information at the same time. STLs in the CMSCB capture the multiscale global information. The MCCB in CMSCB fuse the global information and deeply extract the local features. Furthermore, we conducted ablation studies on the variant of CMSCBs and the results indicated that the multiscale information and the use of the MCCB bring improvements. The comparison experiments demonstrated our model outperforms state-of-the-art methods on MICCAI 2013 grand challenge dataset. In the future, we will extend the model to other vision tasks.

**Acknowledgment.** This work was supported by the National Natural Science Foundations of China under Grant 62071213, Scientific research project of Hunan Provincial Department of Education under Grant 18C0413, 20C1632, 200SJY031.

# References

1. Fessler, J.A., Sutton, B.P.: Nonuniform fast Fourier transforms using min-max interpolation. IEEE Trans. Signal Process **51**, 560–574 (2013)
2. Lv, J., Wang, C., Yang, G.: PIC-GAN: a parallel imaging coupled generative adversarial network for accelerated multi-channel MRI reconstruction. Diagnostics **11**(1), 61 (2021)
3. Chen, Z., Huang, C., Lin, S.: A new sparse representation framework for compressed sensing MRI. Knowl. Based Syst. **188**, 104969 (2020)
4. Haldar, J.P., Hernando, D., Liang, Z.P.: Compressed-sensing MRI with random encoding. IEEE Trans. Med. Imaging **30**(4), 893–903 (2010)
5. Lee, D., Yoo, J., Tak, S., Ye, J.C.: Deep residual learning for accelerated MRI using magnitude and phase networks. IEEE Trans. Biomed. Eng. **65**(9), 1985–1995 (2018)
6. Isensee, F., Jaeger, P.F., Kohl, S.A., et al.: nnU-Net: a self-configuring method for deep learning-based biomedical image segmentation. Nat. Methods **18**(2), 203–211 (2021)
7. Li, H., Wu, X.J., Kittler, J.: RFN-Nest: an end-to-end residual fusion network for infrared and visible images. Inf. Fus. **73**, 72–86 (2021)
8. Tzinis, E., Wang, Z., Smaragdis, P.: Sudo RM-RF: efficient networks for universal audio source separation. In: 2020 IEEE 30th International Workshop on Machine Learning for Signal Processing (MLSP), pp. 1–6 (2020)
9. Krizhevsky, A., Sutskever, I., Hinton, G.: ImageNet classification with deep convolutional neural networks. Adv. Neural Inf. Process. Syst. **25**(2), 1097–1105 (2012)
10. Liang, D., Cheng, J., Ke, Z., et al.: Deep magnetic resonance image reconstruction: inverse problems meet neural networks. IEEE Signal Process. Mag. **37**(1), 141–151 (2020)
11. Wang, S., Su, Z., Ying, L., et al.: Accelerating magnetic resonance imaging via deep learning. In: 2016 IEEE 13th International Symposium on Biomedical Imaging, pp. 514–517 (2016)
12. Yang, Y., Sun, J., Li, H., et al.: Deep ADMM-Net for compressive sensing MRI. In: Proceedings of the 30th International Conference on Neural Information Processing Systems, pp. 10–18 (2016)
13. Schlemper, J., Caballero, J., Hajnal, J.V., et al.: A deep cascade of convolutional neural networks for dynamic MR image reconstruction. IEEE Trans. Med. Imaging **37**(2), 491–503 (2017)
14. Hyun, C.M., Kim, H.P., Lee, S.M., et al.: Deep learning for undersampled MRI reconstruction. Phys. Med. Biol. **63**(13), 135007 (2018)
15. Wu, Y., Ma, Y., Liu, J., et al.: Self-attention convolutional neural network for improved MR image reconstruction. Inf. Sci. **490**, 317–328 (2019)

16. Liang, D., Cheng, J., Ke, Z., et al.: Deep MRI reconstruction: Unrolled optimization algorithms meet neural networks. arXiv preprint arXiv:1907.11711 (2019)
17. Zhou, T., Fu, H., Chen, G., et al.: Hi-Net: hybrid-fusion network for multi-modal mr image synthesis. IEEE Trans. Med. Imaging **39**(9), 2772–2781 (2020)
18. Wu, Y., Ma, Y., Capaldi, D.P., et al.: Incorporating prior knowledge via volumetric deep residual network to optimize the reconstruction of sparsely sampled MRI. Magn. Reson. Imaging **66**, 93–103 (2020)
19. Wang, P., Chen, E.Z., Chen, T., et al.: Pyramid convolutional RNN for MRI reconstruction. arXiv preprint arXiv:1912.00543 (2019)
20. Yang, G., Yu, S., Dong, H., et al.: DAGAN: deep de-aliasing generative adversarial networks for fast compressed sensing MRI reconstruction. IEEE Trans. Med. Imaging **37**(6), 1310–1321 (2018)
21. Quan, T.M., Nguyen-Duc, T., Jeong, W.K.: Compressed sensing MRI reconstruction using a generative adversarial network with a cyclic loss. IEEE Trans. Med. Imaging **37**(6), 1488–1497 (2018)
22. Mardani, M., Gong, E., Cheng, J.Y., et al.: Deep generative adversarial neural networks for compressive sensing MRI. IEEE Trans. Med. Imaging **38**(1), 167–179 (2019)
23. He, K., Zhang, X., Ren, S., et al.: Deep residual learning for image recognition. In: Proceedings of the IEEE Conference on Computer Vision and Pattern Recognition, pp. 770–778 (2016)
24. Zeng, W., Peng, J., Wang, S., et al.: A comparative study of CNN-based super-resolution methods in MRI reconstruction and its beyond. Signal Process. Image Commun. **81**, 115701 (2020)
25. Li, X., Cao, T., Tong, X., et al.: Deep residual network for highly accelerated fMRI reconstruction using variable density spiral trajectory. Neurocomputing **398**, 338–346 (2020)
26. Bao, L., Ye, F., Cai, C., et al.: Undersampled MR image reconstruction using an enhanced recursive residual network. J. Magn. Reson. **305**, 232–246 (2019)
27. Huang, G., Liu, Z., Laurens, V., et al.: Densely connected convolutional networks. In: Proceedings of the IEEE Conference on Computer Vision and Pattern Recognition, pp. 4700–4708 (2016)
28. Parmar, N., Vaswani, A., Uszkoreit, J., et al.: Image transformer. In: International Conference on Machine Learning, pp. 4055–4064 (2018)
29. Matsoukas, C., Haslum, J.F., Söderberg, M., et al.: Is it time to replace CNNs with transformers for medical images? arXiv preprint arXiv:2108.09038 (2021)
30. Dosovitskiy, A., Beyer, L., Kolesnikov, A., et al.: An image is worth 16x16 words: transformers for image recognition at scale. arXiv preprint arXiv:2010.11929 (2020)
31. Ho, J., Kalchbrenner, N., Weissenborn, D., et al.: Axial attention in multidimensional transformers. arXiv preprint arXiv:1912.12180 (2019)
32. Strudel, R., Garcia, R., Laptev, I., et al.: Segmenter: transformer for semantic segmentation. In: Proceedings of the IEEE/CVF International Conference on Computer Vision, pp. 7262–7272 (2021)
33. Shamshad, F., Khan, S., Zamir, S.W., et al.: Transformers in medical imaging: a survey. arXiv preprint arXiv:2201.09873 (2022)
34. Arnab, A., Dehghani, M., Heigold, G., et al.: ViViT: a video vision transformer. In: Proceedings of the IEEE/CVF International Conference on Computer Vision, pp. 6836–6846 (2021)
35. Hatamizadeh, A., Yang, D., Roth, H., et al.: UNETR: transformers for 3D medical image segmentation. In: Proceedings of the IEEE/CVF Winter Conference on Applications of Computer Vision, pp. 574–584 (2021)
36. Chen, C.F.R., Fan, Q., Panda, R.: CrossViT: cross-attention multi-scale vision transformer for image classification. In: Proceedings of the IEEE/CVF International Conference on Computer Vision, pp. 357–366 (2021)

37. Feng, C.M., Yan, Y., Chen, G., et al.: Accelerated multi-modal mr imaging with transformers. arXiv preprint arXiv:2106.14248 (2021)
38. Liu, Z., Lin, Y., Cao, Y., et al.: Swin transformer: hierarchical vision transformer using shifted windows. In: Proceedings of the IEEE/CVF International Conference on Computer Vision, pp. 10012–10022 (2021)
39. Cao, H., Wang, Y., Chen, J., et al.: Swin-Unet: Unet-like pure transformer for medical image segmentation. arXiv preprint arXiv:2105.05537 (2021)
40. Liang, J., Cao, J., Sun, G., et al.: SwinIR: image restoration using swin transformer. In: Proceedings of the IEEE/CVF International Conference on Computer Vision, pp. 1833–1844 (2021)
41. Huang, J., Fang, Y., Wu, Y., et al.: Swin transformer for fast MRI. Neurocomputing **493**, 281–304 (2022)
42. Huang, J., Fang, Y., Wu, Y., et al.: Fast MRI reconstruction: how powerful transformers are? arXiv preprint arXiv:2201.09400 (2022)
43. MASI Lab. https://my.vanderbilt.edu/masi/workshops/. Accessed 14 Apr 2022

# DEST: Deep Enhanced Swin Transformer Toward Better Scoring for NAFLD

Renao Yan[1](ID), Qiming He[1], Yiqing Liu[1], Jizhou Gou[2], Qiehe Sun[1],
Guangde Zhou[2], Yonghong He[1], and Tian Guan[1](✉)

[1] Tsinghua Shenzhen International Graduate School, Shenzhen, China
guantian@sz.tsinghua.edu.cn
[2] The Third People's Hospital of Shenzhen, Shenzhen, China
guangdez@sina.com

**Abstract.** Nonalcoholic fatty liver disease (NAFLD) has become one
of the most common liver diseases. Image analysis of liver biopsy is
the gold standard for early diagnosis of NAFLD. Deep learning offers
an effective tool to evaluate NAFLD with histological feature scoring
on ballooning, inflammation, steatosis, and fibrosis. However, current
methods using convolutional neural networks (CNNs) may not extract
multi-scale and contextual information of histological images effectively.
For better performance, we introduce a Swin-Transformer-based model
using deep self-supervision with the residual module. To the best of our
knowledge, it is the first time Swin Transformer has been used in liver
pathology. The whole slide images (WSIs) were cropped into patches at
two scales and analyzed for four features. Experiments conducted on the
public dataset Biopsy4Grading and the in-house dataset Steatosis-Biopsy
indicate that our method achieves superior classification performance to
previous CNN-based methods in this field.

**Keywords:** Nonalcoholic fatty liver disease · Liver biopsy ·
Pathology · Swin transformer · Deep learning

## 1 Introduction

Nonalcoholic fatty liver disease (NAFLD) and its progressive form, nonalcoholic
steatohepatitis (NASH), have become common liver diseases [1,16,18]. Epidemi-
ological surveys have shown that the prevalence of NAFLD in Europe and the
United States is more than 20% [2,21]. Although noninvasive tests are preferred
when possible, liver biopsy remains the gold standard for the diagnosis of NAFLD
[8,13]. Between 10% and 20% of simple fatty livers can progress to NASH [5].
A widely used pathologist score is the 'Kleiner score', which demonstrated that
ballooning, inflammation, steatosis, and fibrosis are the main four pathological
features that correlate with the diagnosis of NASH [9]. Too many pathological images and cumbersome indicators lead to a heavy burden of diagnosis, so
computer-aided diagnosis is particularly important [14].

---

R. Yan and Q. He—Contribute equally to this work.

© The Author(s), under exclusive license to Springer Nature Switzerland AG 2022
S. Yu et al. (Eds.): PRCV 2022, LNCS 13535, pp. 204–214, 2022.
https://doi.org/10.1007/978-3-031-18910-4_17

In recent years, deep learning has performed well in classifying pathological images. Yu, et al. automated feature classification and fibrosis scoring by using AlexNet, with balanced AUROC values of up to 0.85–0.95 [19]. Qu, et al. used ResNet to score NAS and fibrosis stage on pathological images with different stains and magnifications [12]. Heinemann, et al. automate NAS and fibrosis stage with two different scale stained images by using Inception-V3 CNNs, each specialized for one of four features [7]. Yin, et al. proposed selective attention regularization to focus on clinically interpretable features, which helped deep learning methods like SCNet to perform better on NAS-related classification [17]. They all use CNN to extract pathological contextual and multi-scale information. To identify the macro-patterns and characterize fibrosis stages more efficiently, Wojciechowska, et al. utilized a GNN-based model to facilitate analysis of fibrosis with ResNet18 [15]. Meanwhile, on account of superiority in natural language processing, Alexey, et al. designed a subtle Transformer architecture to address vision classification tissues [4]. Ze, et al. use window-based multi-head self-attention, which reduces computational complexity to allow higher-resolution input [11]. The shifted-window method with the reverse cyclic shift is proved to be efficient and makes ST perform much better than the overwhelming majority of CNN frameworks.

In this paper, we introduce a transformer-based model named Deep Enhanced Swin Transformer (DEST) using deeper skip connection (DeeperSC) with weighted embedding branches (WEB) to classify the four pathological features of NASH. The model is trained and validated on a public dataset and tested on a private dataset. Data augmentation for pathological images is used to better generalization ability on test data. Results indicated that the model trained in the animal liver images from the public dataset has a good performance on human liver biopsy from the private dataset. Furthermore, the model showed good consistency in predicting the steatosis classification in different stained biopsy slides. Our contributions are:

- To the best of our knowledge, it is the first time Swin Transformer has been used for liver pathology. With more efficient extraction of pathological image context and multi-scale features, the proposed DEST achieves superior classification performance compared to CNN-based methods in this field.
- DeeperSC and WEB are introduced to better avoid vanishing gradient and semantic ambiguity, which enhanced feature extraction.
- A pathologist's rigorously reviewed human liver biopsy dataset was developed. Both Masson and HE stained slides are available, which can help address the current challenging NAFLD scoring problems.

## 2   Method

In this paper, we propose a model DEST with DeeperSC and WEB introduced for liver biopsy scoring. For the training phase, the Masson stained tiles are propagated forward through all stages. The low-level pathology features from

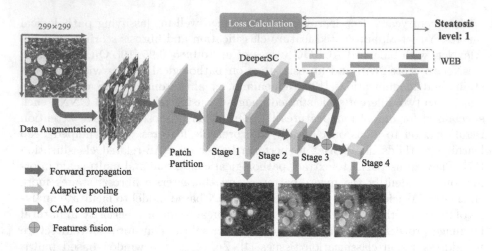

**Fig. 1.** The overview of the proposed Deep Enhanced Swin Transformer.

Stage 1 pass through DeeperSC to fuse with the high-level features from Stage 3. With macro and micro information extracted, the fusion results are then fed to Stage 4. The features output by Stage 2–4 contain semantics from cellular to sub-tissue scale. The classification costs are calculated by three branches of WEB and their weights, according to their contributions. For the inference phase, the whole process does not employ WEB, and scores are predicted by a trained fully connected layer after Stage 4. The overall framework is shown in Fig. 1.

### 2.1 Transformer-Based Liver Biopsy Images Scoring

The backbone of DEST is the tiny version of Swin Transformer. The settings of all stages are consistent with those in [11]. The scoring model DEST can be regarded as a function $f_\theta$ with weights $\theta$ that maps input tiles $t_i$ to probabilities for discrete scores. Assume $o_i^k$ denotes the $i$th output of the $k$th stage and given a scoring task, a list of pathological feature vectors $O = \{o_i^K : i = 1, 2, \cdots, n\}$ is obtained by computing a batch of $n$ tiles from a $K$-stage model. We then obtain the predicted score $s_i^K$ of each tile according to the highest-discrete-score probability: $s_i^K = argmax\left(o_i^K\right)$. With this prediction, the output of the network $\widehat{y_i} = f_\theta(t_i) = s_i^K$ can be compared to the true score $y_i$ through the cross-entropy loss $\mathcal{L}_{cls}$:

$$\mathcal{L}_{cls} = \frac{1}{N} \sum_{i=1}^{N} y_i \log \widehat{y_i} \tag{1}$$

### 2.2 DeeperSC and WEB

Pathological images, especially those obtained by puncture, have a huge variance in structures and textures compared to natural images, so directly applying ST to liver biopsy scoring is challenging. According to CNN-based deep learning theory [6], deeper stages of ST may imply vanishing gradient and semantic ambiguity. DeeperSC and WEB are introduced to enhance the capability of deeper stages of ST.

DeeperSC consists of feature encoding and fusion. The feature map $m_1$ output by the first stage undergoes batch normalization, $1 \times 1$ convolution, and adaptive pooling to obtain encoded feature maps $m_1^*$ with the shape matching $m_3$. DeeperSC causes $m_1^*$ to sparsely encode low-level features (e.g., textures and shapes of lymphocytes and fat droplets), making the significant low-level information more discriminative. In contrast, the feature map $m_3$ is output using the low-resolution tiles to obtain high-level vision representation related to scoring (e.g., characterization of immune cell dot foci and bridging). The feature map input to Stage 4 is obtained by pixel-wise summation operation of $m_1^*$ and $m_3$ and carries high-level and encoded low-level features. It encourages Stage 4 to learn more salient semantics, enhancing the global feature extraction of ST.

WEB contains three branches with feature compression and loss calculation. $m_1$ is not suitable to predict scores as its signal-to-noise ratio is too low. However, $m_2$ and $m_3$ contain some high-level features which contribute to the final prediction. This paper introduces three branches from Stage 2 to 4 for label comparisons. For feature compression, the prediction score $s_i^k$ is obtained by the feature maps through fully connected layers. For loss calculation, the weights of the three branches are set to 0.1, 0.1, and 0.8, respectively. The loss of DEST can be computed as

$$\mathcal{L} = \alpha * \mathcal{L}_{cls\ WEB2} + \beta * \mathcal{L}_{cls-WEB3} + \gamma * \mathcal{L}_{cls-WEB4},  \qquad (2)$$

where $\mathcal{L}_{cls-WEB2}$, $\mathcal{L}_{cls-WEB3}$, and $\mathcal{L}_{cls-WEB4}$ are the branching classification losses, and $\alpha$, $\beta$, and $\gamma$ are the corresponding weights.

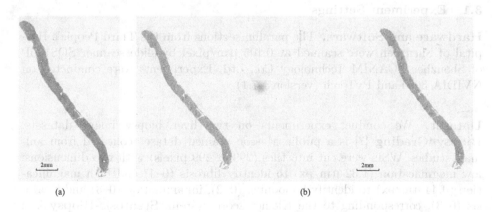

(a)                                        (b)

**Fig. 2.** Examples of Masson and H&E stained sections in Steatosis-Biopsy.

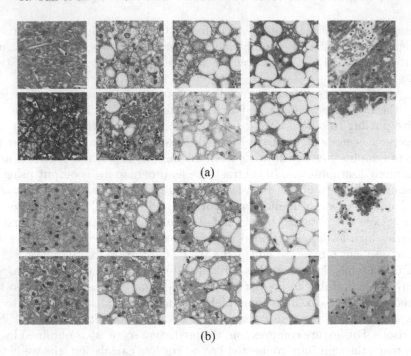

(a)

(b)

**Fig. 3.** (a) and (b) Examples of Masson and H&E tiles in Steatosis-Biopsy. Column 1–5 are cases of steatosis-score 0–3 and class ignore. These tiles show huge in-domain differences and out-of-domain differences from those in Biopsy4Grading, which is challenging for model trained on Biopsy4Grading.

## 3    Experiments

### 3.1    Experiment Settings

**Hardware and Software.** The paraffin sections from the Third People's Hospital of Shenzhen were scanned at 0.105 μm/pixel by slide scanner SQS120P of Shenzhen SCANIM Technology Co., Ltd. Experiments were conducted on NVIDIA 3090 and PyTorch (version 1.7.1).

**Dataset.** We conduct experiments on two liver biopsy image datasets. **Biopsy4Grading** [7] is a public Masson stained dataset collected from animals studies. WSIs were cut into tiles (299 × 299 pixels) with two dimensions: low magnification (1.32 μm/px) to identify fibrosis (0–4) and high magnification (0.44 μm/px) to identify ballooning (0–2), inflammation (0–3) and steatosis (0–3), corresponding to the Kleiner score system. **Steatosis-Biopsy** is a private liver biopsy image dataset of 14 cases of NAFLD (see Fig. 2, 3). The sections were stained Masson or H&E and cropped into 10132 and 10577 tiles (299 × 299 pixels), respectively. All tiles were manually labeled with 5 steatosis classes (including 'ignore') by experienced pathologists. **Biopsy4Grading** was randomly partitioned into a training set (~90%) and a validation set (~10%). **Steatosis-Biopsy** was used as a test set especially for steatosis scoring to show the generalization ability of the proposed model.

**Evaluation Metrics.** For fibrosis and NAS-related components quantification, we choose sensitivity, specificity, and weighted F1 score for evaluation.

**Data Augmentation.** Pathology images exhibit large intra-class variance, so complex data augmentation methods are a must to achieve accurate classification [10]. On top of Dropout used in ST, we use Auto-Augment [3] and random erasing [20] to reach data-efficient training.

**Training Details.** The model is trained using the AdamW optimizer with betas = (0.9, 0.999), weight decay = 5e−2 to minimize categorical cross-entropy loss on validation data. The initial learning rate is set to 1e−4. If the validation loss did not decrease for two epochs, the learning rate was reduced by multiplying with a factor of 0.8 to a minimum rate of 1e−7. We train the model with 50 epochs and the batch size is set to 64.

**Table 1.** Validation performance comparisons on the public dataset Biopsy4Grading for classification of fibrosis, ballooning, inflammation, and steatosis.

| Methods | Tasks | Metrics (%) | | |
|---------|-------|-------------|---|---|
| | | Sensitivity | Specificity | F1 |
| Fabian et al. [7] | Fibrosis | | | |
| | Ballooning | 79.36±2.27 | 94.60±0.60 | 80.16±1.63 |
| | Inflammation | 85.83±1.35 | 93.94±0.78 | 87.61±0.90 |
| | Steatosis | 94.20±1.50 | 98.73±0.38 | 93.78±1.16 |
| Yin et al. [17] | Fibrosis | | | |
| | Ballooning | 80.42±2.17 | **94.92±0.99** | 81.03±0.99 |
| | Inflammation | 86.46±2.93 | **94.13±1.15** | 88.01±1.84 |
| | Steatosis | 94.68±1.12 | **98.78±0.29** | 94.42±0.81 |
| ResNet34 | Fibrosis | 90.03±1.03 | 98.09±0.50 | 90.59±1.20 |
| | Ballooning | 95.94±0.73 | 87.21±3.32 | 96.46±0.57 |
| | Inflammation | 86.85±0.99 | 92.72±2.42 | 88.09±1.19 |
| | Steatosis | 92.83±0.86 | 97.54±0.28 | 92.87±0.87 |
| Ours | Fibrosis | **92.26±0.23** | **98.46±0.10** | **92.61±0.29** |
| | Ballooning | **96.43±0.18** | 87.98±1,47 | **96.74±0.12** |
| | Inflammation | **88.50±0.47** | 92.64±0.78 | **88.94±0.51** |
| | Steatosis | **95.21±0.31** | 98.34±0.10 | **95.33±0.28** |

## 3.2  Analysis

**Transformer-Based DEST Outperforms CNN in NAFLD Scoring.** We compared the results on Biopsy4Grading between DEST and previous methods. Since other methods did not score on fibrosis, we trained ResNet34 with the same configuration as DEST. Table 1 shows results that compared with CNNs, DEST shows a better overall performance, especially on sensitivity and F1 score.

For ResNet34, the best among CNNs, DEST shows improvement in all metrics. Generally, scoring NAFLD relies on the different perceptive fields, which requires models to be sensitive to multi-scale and contextual information. ST uses hierarchical feature refinement to efficiently represent high-level features. Therefore, transformer-based networks would be a strong competitor to CNNs in pathology image analysis.

**Transformer-Based DEST Better Highlights Discriminative Regions.** To better compare ST with CNN, we computed class activation maps (CAMs) of DEST and ResNet34. Figure 5 indicates DEST learned pathological relevant features better. On one hand, DEST is sensitive to local features, while ResNet only focuses on the most salient ones. On the other hand, DEST better fuses global and contextual semantics. For example, DEST targeted the tiny ballooning cell, while ResNet only captured the bigger one. And ResNet incorrectly added more attention to endothelial cells, which were surrounded by many fat drops than DEST (Fig. 4).

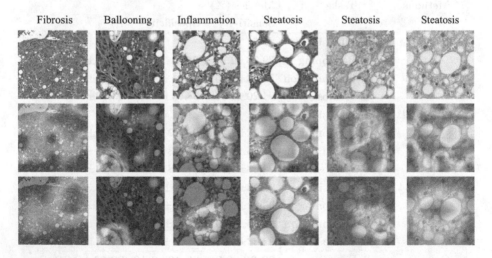

**Fig. 4.** Examples of CAMs. Row 1–3: original tiles, examples of DEST and ResNet34. Column 1–4 are from Biopsy4Grading. Column 5–6 are Masson and H&E tiles from Steatosis-Biopsy.

**Table 2.** Test performance of different configurations of modules.

| F1 (%) | Ablation on | None: Swin-T + Data Augmentation | | | |
|---|---|---|---|---|---|
| | DeeperSC | ✗ | ✓ | ✗ | ✓ |
| | WEB | ✗ | ✗ | ✓ | ✓ |
| Biopsy4-Grading | Fibrosis | 91.98±1.00 | **92.72±0.50** | 92.69±0.59 | 92.61±0.29 |
| | Ballooning | 96.62±0.60 | 96.67±0.40 | 96.69±0.3 | **90.74±0.12** |
| | Inflammation | 88.14±0.63 | 88.41±0.46 | 88.72±0.51 | **88.94±0.51** |
| | Steatosis | 94.01±0.93 | **95.48±0.46** | 95.18±0.32 | 95.33±0.28 |
| Steatosis-Biopsy | Steatosis (Masson) | 80.34±2.60 | 84.99±0.56 | 85.12±0.56 | **85.74±0.51** |
| | Steatosis (H&E) | 82.60±1.52 | 86.51±1.09 | 86.24±0.28 | **86.85±0.41** |

**DeeperSC and WEB Enhance Deeper Stages of ST.** To verify the performance of DeeperSC and WEB, we trained models on public datasets and tested them on both datasets. As shown in Table 2, DEST is the best of all, even surpassing ST by up to 5.40% and 4.25% in the private dataset. ST-DeeperSC ranks first in fibrosis and steatosis in the public dataset, and ST-WEB is higher than ST in all metrics.

DeeperSC. On the public dataset, ST-DeeperSC achieves more improvement to ST on fibrosis and steatosis than on ballooning and inflammation. This is because DeeperSC fuses the lowest and second-highest level features to extract higher-level features, which are gainful for the NASH features containing low and high level semantics, but introduce noise to ones only related to low-level information. Fibrosis scoring requires localization of fibers around central hepatocytes and confluent region of the lobule (cellular level) and bridging and pseudobullets (tissue level). Steatosis grading requires the identification of lipid droplets (cellular level) and predicts the proportion (tissue level). In contrast, scores of ballooning are judged by capturing edema or ballooning (cellular level); scoring inflammation only requires cells cluster features. Therefore, DeeperSC has a greater enhancement of the former two metrics.

WEB. On the public dataset, the improvement of ST-WEB to ST for ballooning is only 0.07%, while the improvement for the other three is above 0.5%. ST-WEB serve to integrate features from cellular to tissue scale and compensate for the loss of low-level information. It introduces feature maps from Stages 2 and 3 instead of Stage 1, so it has the least boost for ballooning and a larger boost for the other three NASH features.

These two modules were introduced with different focuses to enhance deeper stages. DEST combines these two, resulting in a 0.80% improvement in inflammation and a 0.12% improvement in ballooning to ST. There are also checks and balances between the two modules, with low-level noise and regularizing effects produced. Therefore, DEST showed poorer performance on scoring fibrosis and steatosis. On the private dataset, we see impressive performance of two modules, with an extra average improvement of 1.95% in steatosis scoring compared to the difference with ST on the public dataset. The reason may be that these two modules introduce extra model perturbation and Masson and H&E tiles in the private dataset have a large variance from public ones. The low-level noise and branching loss encourage the model to learn more contextual and multi-scale information.

**Data Augmentation Increases Generalization Performance.** We trained ST with and without data augmentation on the public dataset and test them on the more challenging private dataset. As shown in Fig. 5, ST has a slightly higher F1 score of 0.9436 on the validation dataset but its performance drops down drastically on the test dataset, especially on tiles with stains different from the training dataset. ST with data augmentation gets F1 scores over 0.8 on Masson and H&E stained tiles. This means Auto-Augment adaptively implements dataset-related data augmentation but not non-specific one. And random erasing encourages ST to learn more invariant features and improve performance.

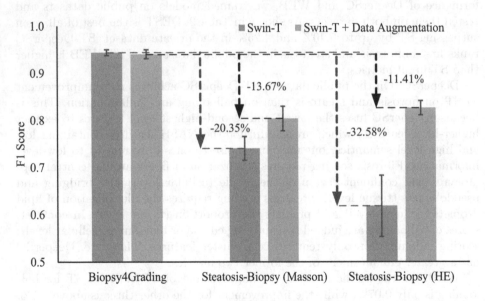

**Fig. 5.** Data augmentation leads to higher generalization performance.

## 4    Conclusion

In this paper, we demonstrate that DEST model better scores NAFLD features on both public and private datasets. Experiments conducted show DEST extract contextual and multi-scale features more effectively than CNNs. And DeeperSC and WEB proposed mitigates vanishing gradient and semantic ambiguity, enhancing the deeper stage of ST. Additionally, modules with pathology specificity can improve transformer architecture on challenging computational pathology. Future work is to develop a transformer-based WSI-level scoring model.

**Acknowledgements.** This work was approved by the Ethics Committees of Third People's Hospital of Shenzhen (No. 2021-028), and supported by Special project of Clinical toxicology, Chinese Society of Toxicology under Grant CST2020CT102.

# References

1. Arjmand, A., Tsipouras, M.G., Tzallas, A.T., Forlano, R., Manousou, P., Giannakeas, N.: Quantification of liver fibrosis – a comparative study. Appl. Sci. **10**(2), 447 (2020)
2. Chalasani, N., et al.: The diagnosis and management of non-alcoholic fatty liver disease: practice guideline by the American Association for the study of liver diseases, American College of Gastroenterology, and the American Gastroenterological Association. Hepatology **55**(6), 2005–2023 (2012)
3. Cubuk, E.D., Zoph, B., Mane, D., Vasudevan, V., Le, Q.V.: Autoaugment: learning augmentation policies from data. arXiv preprint arXiv:1805.09501 (2018)
4. Dosovitskiy, A., et al.: An image is worth $16 \times 16$ words: transformers for image recognition at scale. arXiv preprint arXiv:2010.11929 (2020)
5. Ekstedt, M., Nasr, P., Kechagias, S.: Natural history of NAFLD/NASH. Curr. Hepatol. Rep. **16**(4), 391–397 (2017)
6. He, K., Zhang, X., Ren, S., Sun, J.: Deep residual learning for image recognition. In: 2016 IEEE Conference on Computer Vision and Pattern Recognition (CVPR), pp. 770–778 (2016). https://doi.org/10.1109/CVPR.2016.90
7. Heinemann, F., Birk, G., Stierstorfer, B.: Deep learning enables pathologist-like scoring of Nash models. Sci. Rep. **9**(1), 1–10 (2019)
8. Jain, D., Torres, R., Celli, R., Koelmel, J., Charkoftaki, G., Vasiliou, V.: Evolution of the liver biopsy and its future. Transl. Gastroenterol. Hepatol. **6** (2020). https://tgh.amegroups.com/article/view/5958
9. Kleiner, D.E., et al.: Design and validation of a histological scoring system for nonalcoholic fatty liver disease. Hepatology **41**(6), 1313–1321 (2005)
10. Koohbanani, N.A., Unnikrishnan, B., Khurram, S.A., Krishnaswamy, P., Rajpoot, N.: Self-path: self-supervision for classification of pathology images with limited annotations. IEEE Trans. Med. Imaging **40**(10), 2845–2856 (2021)
11. Liu, Z., et al.: Swin transformer: hierarchical vision transformer using shifted windows. In: Proceedings of the IEEE/CVF International Conference on Computer Vision, pp. 10012–10022 (2021)
12. Qu, H., et al.: Training of computational algorithms to predict NAFLD activity score and fibrosis stage from liver histopathology slides. Comput. Methods Programs Biomed. **207**, 106153 (2021)
13. Soon, G., Wee, A.: Updates in the quantitative assessment of liver fibrosis for nonalcoholic fatty liver disease: Histological perspective. Clin. Mol. Hepatol. **27**(1), 44 (2021)
14. Su, T.H., Wu, C.H., Kao, J.H.: Artificial intelligence in precision medicine in hepatology. J. Gastroenterol. Hepatol. **36**(3), 569–580 (2021)
15. Wojciechowska, M., Malacrino, S., Garcia Martin, N., Fehri, H., Rittscher, J.: Early detection of liver fibrosis using graph convolutional networks. In: de Bruijne, M., et al. (eds.) MICCAI 2021. LNCS, vol. 12908, pp. 217–226. Springer, Cham (2021). https://doi.org/10.1007/978-3-030-87237-3_21
16. Wong, R.J., et al.: Nonalcoholic steatohepatitis is the second leading etiology of liver disease among adults awaiting liver transplantation in the United States. Gastroenterology **148**(3), 547–555 (2015)

17. Yin, C., Liu, S., Shao, R., Yuen, P.C.: Focusing on clinically interpretable features: selective attention regularization for liver biopsy image classification. In: de Bruijne, M., et al. (eds.) MICCAI 2021. LNCS, vol. 12905, pp. 153–162. Springer, Cham (2021). https://doi.org/10.1007/978-3-030-87240-3_15
18. Younossi, Z., et al.: Global perspectives on nonalcoholic fatty liver disease and nonalcoholic steatohepatitis. Hepatology **69**(6), 2672–2682 (2019)
19. Yu, Y., et al.: Deep learning enables automated scoring of liver fibrosis stages. Sci. Rep. **8**(1), 1–10 (2018)
20. Zhong, Z., Zheng, L., Kang, G., Li, S., Yang, Y.: Random erasing data augmentation. In: Proceedings of the AAAI Conference on Artificial Intelligence, vol. 34, pp. 13001–13008 (2020)
21. Zhu, J.Z., Dai, Y.N., Wang, Y.M., Zhou, Q.Y., Yu, C.H., Li, Y.M.: Prevalence of nonalcoholic fatty liver disease and economy. Dig. Dis. Sci. **60**(11), 3194–3202 (2015)

# CTCNet: A Bi-directional Cascaded Segmentation Network Combining Transformers with CNNs for Skin Lesions

Jing Wang[1], Bicao Li[1,2]([✉]), Xuwei Guo[3], Jie Huang[1], Mengxing Song[1], and Miaomiao Wei[1]

[1] School of Electronic and Information Engineering, Zhongyuan University of Technology, Zhengzhou 450007, China
lbc@zut.edu.cn
[2] School of Computer and Artificial Intelligence, Zhengzhou University, Zhengzhou 450001, China
[3] The 1st Affiliated Hospital of Henan University of Science and Technology, Luoyang 471000, China

**Abstract.** Dermoscopic images segmentation is a key step in skin cancer diagnosis and analysis. Convolutional Neural Networks (CNNs) has achieved great success in various medical image segmentation tasks. However, continuous downsampling operation brings network redundancy and loss of local details, and also shows great limitations in modeling of long-range relationships. Inversely, Transformer shows great potential in modeling global contexts. In this paper, we propose a novel segmentation network combining Transformers and CNNs (CTCNet) for Skin Lesions to improve the efficiency of the network in modeling the global context, while maintaining the control of the underlying details. Besides, a novel fusion technique - Two-stream Cascaded Feature Aggregation (TCFA) module, is constructed to integrate multi-level features from two branches efficiently. Moreover, we design a Multi-Scale Expansion-Aware (MSEA) module based on the convolution of feature perception and expansion, which can extract high-level features containing more abundant context information and further enhance the perception ability of network. CTCNet combines Transformers and CNNs in a parallel style, where both global dependency and low-level spatial details can be efficiently captured. Extensive experiments demonstrate that CTCNet achieves the better performance compared with state-of-the-art approaches.

**Keywords:** Skin lesion segmentation · Transformers · CNNs · Two-stream cascaded feature aggregation module · Multi-scale expansion-aware module

## 1 Introduction

Skin cancer is currently one of the most common types of cancer, which cause an increasing number of deaths each year. Dermoscopy is a non-invasive imaging method widely used in clinical dermatology, which is able to assist physician for the diagnosis and treatment in the initial stages of skin cancer and increase the chances of successful cure.

Dermoscopic skin lesions segmentation is of significance for the automated screening and detection of skin cancer. However, automatic segmentation of skin lesions remains a challenging task due to the subtle changes in the appearance of the skin lesions, and the ambiguity of the lesion boundaries. Several convolutional neural network (CNN) methods have been proposed for the automated segmentation of the skin lesions [1–5]. Most of these approaches have certain similarities. On the one hand, a considerable portion of networks are evolved from encoder-decoder structure, or some novel modules are designed for global context information extraction. At the same time, the attention mechanism that makes networks to pay attention interesting areas adaptively is also widely used. The SLSDeep is a typical encoder-decoder network to segment skin lesions precisely [6]. In their model, the encoder consists of extended residual layers, while the decoder employs a pyramid pooling module. A multi-scale strategy is adopted in FCA-Net to resize the input images to three different scales of the original size. Also, the factorized channel attention (FCA) module is introduced into the encoder, which can improve the low-contrast and boundary blur problems of skin lesions effectively [7]. To obtain good interpretability, Ran et al. proposed a novel network integrating space, channel and scale attention mechanisms [8]. In CPFNet, two new pyramid modules are designed to integrate both global and multi-scale contextual information respectively [9].

In summary, sensing the global information can effectively improve the generalization ability of model. However, existing works usually obtain global information by generating very large receptive domains, which is lacking efficiency in capturing global contextual information.

Transformer has attracted many researchers' attentions recently. The first purely visual transformer (ViT) based on self-attention has achieved competitive results in ImageNet dataset [10]. Meanwhile, the encoder was replaced with transformers in traditional encoder-decoder-based networks, achieving advanced results in natural image segmentation tasks [11]. The Transformer specializes in global context modeling, but it shows limitations in capturing fine-grained details, especially for medical images. To integrate the benefits of both, some hybrid models were introduced combining CNN with Transformer. For example, TransUnet [12] first utilizes CNN to extract low-level features and then model the global context through transformers, with good results in the CT multi-organ segmentation task. Transfuse [13] combines Transformers and CNN in a parallel manner, where both global dependency and low-level spatial details can be captured efficiently.

Inspired by the success of the above transformer model, in this paper, we present a novel framework which explores the potential of transformers in the context of medical image segmentation. Ours main contributions are trifold:

1. A novel segmentation network is proposed combining Transformers and CNNs for Skin Lesions to improve the efficiency of our network in modeling the global context, while maintaining the control of the underlying details.
2. A TCFA module is designed to aggregate the features from Transformers and CNNs efficiently in a parallel cascade manner. Besides, we construct a MSEA module

to acquire high-level features to preserve abundant context information and further enhance the scale perception ability of network by aggregating multi-level features selectively, which can solve the scale variation problem in skin lesions dataset.

3. Compared with state-of-the-art methods, the experimental results of our proposed method conducted on two skin lesions datasets demonstrate that the effectiveness of the proposed method for skin lesion segmentation.

## 2 Proposed Method

### 2.1 CTCNet

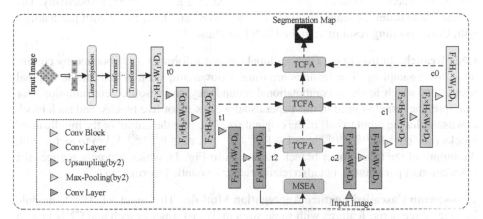

**Fig. 1.** The overall framework of the proposed CTCNet.

As shown in Fig. 1, CTCNet is composed of two parallel branches: 1) CNN branches. From local information encoding to global features; 2) Transformer branch. Encoding starts from the global features, and finally gradually recovers the local details. To exploit and fuse the rich context information in high-level features gradually, the features at the same resolution extracted from both branches are fed into multiple TCFA modules with a cascaded fashion. Additionally, a MSEA module is introduced at the bottom level of the network and employed as one of input features of the first-level TCFA module. The MSEA module extracts advanced features containing richer context information. Specifically, three parallel dilated convolutions [14] with sharing weights are leveraged to capture different scale context information, and two cascaded Scale-Aware Modules (SAM) [13] based on spatial attention mechanism are applied to integrate multi-scale information and compensate for lost details. In addition, a global average pooling (GAP) branch is introduced to integrate global context prior information.

TCFA module is utilized to integrate two parallel branches and recover the advanced features generated by MSEA module in the fusion process, which can take full advantage of CNN and Transformer. Global information can be captured without establishing a very deep network, while retaining more shallow information.

## 2.2  Fusion Technique

**Transformer Branch.** Inspired by SETR [11] and VIT [10], the Transformer branch (as shown in Fig. 2(a).) is designed as a typical u-shape structure. Specifically, the input image $x \in R^{H \times W \times 3}$ is first divided into $N = H/S \times W/S$ patches, where S is set to 16 in this paper. The patch is flattened and then fed into a linear embedding layer to obtain the embedding sequence $D \in R^{N \times D0}$. The resulting embeddings D is inputted into the Transformer encoder. The transformer encoder includes the L-layer multi-head self-attention (MSA) and the multi-layer perceptron (MLP). The output of the last transformer layer was layer-normalized to obtain the coding sequence $Z_L \in R^{N \times D0}$. AS for the decoder part, inspired by [32], $Z_L$ is first reshaped to $t0 \in R^{H/16 \times W/16 \times D0}$ and then fed to two consecutive up-sampling and convolution layers to recover spatial resolution, where we obtain $t1 \in R^{H/8 \times W/8 \times D1}$ and $t2 \in R^{H/4 \times W/4 \times D2}$, respectively. The features with different scales t0, t1, and t2 are saved and then fused with the features with Corresponding resolution in the CNN branches.

**CNN Branch.** In traditional CNNs, global context information is obtained by continuous down-sampling. The features are usually downsampled to a fifth of the original resolution, which leads to computational redundancy and resource consumption. For example, the resnet34 used in this paper usually consists of five blocks, and each block downsamples the input to half of the original size. We take the output of the middle three blocks (i.e., $c0 \in R^{H/16 \times W/16 \times C0}$, $c1 \in R^{H/8 \times W/8 \times C1}$, $c2 \in R^{H/4 \times W/4 \times C2}$) to merge with the output of the transformer branch (as shown in Fig. 1), which not only reduces the calculation of parameters, but also retains richer semantic information.

**Two-stream Cascaded Feature Aggregation Module.** The input of TCFA module includes three parts: features with same sizes in Transformer branch and CNN branch $(f_t, f_c)$, and the output of the previous level module $(f_{i-1})$. Firstly, the three input features are mapped to the same channel by standard $3 \times 3$ convolution, while the output of the previous level $(f_{i-1})$ is mapped to the same resolution as the output features of two parallel branch by upsampling operations. Then, in order to extract global contextual information from different levels of feature maps, four parallel separable convolutional [15] with different expansion rates of 1, 4, 8 and 16 are used. Finally, a standard convolution is exploited to obtain the final results. To simplify the formula, we omit the convolution operation, then the module can be summarized as:

$$F_i = C( \sum_{j}^{j=1,4,8,16} D_{sconv}^j (C(P(F_{i-1}), F_t, F_c))) \tag{1}$$

where, $F_i$ represents the feature maps of output of the TCFA module at stage i. P denotes upsampling operation, C represents concatenation operation, and $D_{sconv}^j$ represents four parallel separable convolutions with different expansion rates. By introducing multiple TCFA modules between two parallel branches, global semantic information flows from different stages can be fused gradually.

**Multi-scale Expansion-Aware Module.** Multi-scale context information can improve the performance of semantic segmentation tasks. a Multi-Scale Expansion-Aware

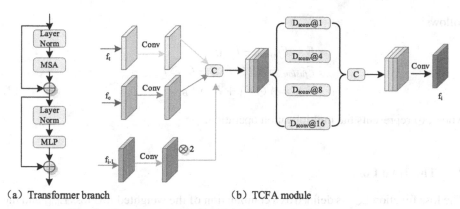

(a) Transformer branch                    (b) TCFA module

**Fig. 2.** Transformer branch and the framework of TCFA module.

(MSEA) module is constructed, as shown in Fig. 3. In the MSEA module, three parallel dilated convolutions with different dilation rates 1, 2, and 4 are employed to acquire multi-scale information. After this, two scale-aware modules are introduced, which can select and integrates the appropriate multi-scale information dynamically through self-learning. Meanwhile, a global average pooling block is introduced to integrate the global context prior information.

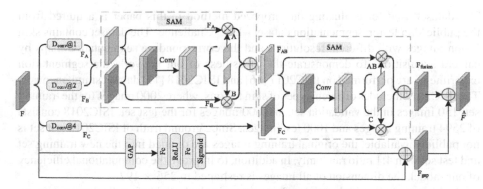

**Fig. 3.** The framework of MSEA module.

Specifically, the input is firstly fed into parallel dilated convolutions and obtain multi-scale features $F_A$, $F_B$, $F_C$. These features will be fed into two cascaded SAM modules, where multi-scale information will be further integrated and fused. Taking the first SAM module as example, $F_A$, $F_B$ are fed to convolution block and activation function to generate the feature maps A, B, then A and B are multiplied with original features to obtain $F_A$ and $F_B$, with the summation of both $F_{AB}$. We employ two cascade SAM modules to obtain the final fusion feature $F_{fusion}$ of $F_A$, $F_B$, $F_C$. Finally, the global pooling branch $F_{GAP}$ is added with $F_{fusion}$ to obtain the output of the MSEA module. The global average pooling branch adopts the residual structure, which consists of global average pooling, two consecutive FC layers and activation function. The formula is expressed as follows:

$$\hat{F} = F_{fusion} + F_{GAP}$$
$$F_{fusion} = AB \odot F_{AB} + C \odot F_C$$
$$F_{AB} = A \odot F_A + B \odot F_B \tag{2}$$

where, $\odot$ represents the multiplication operation.

## 2.3 The Total Loss

The loss function $L_{seg}$ is defined as a combination of the weighted IoU loss $L_{IoU}$ and the weighted binary cross entropy loss $L_{bce}$ with the following formula:

$$L_{seg} = L_{IoU}^W + \lambda L_{BCE}^W \tag{3}$$

where $\lambda$ is the weights and set to 1 in our experiments.

# 3   Experiments

## 3.1 Dataset and Evaluation Metrics

The dataset used for evaluating our proposed method in this paper is acquired from the public skin lesion segmentation dataset - ISIC Challenge. The dataset contains skin lesion images with different resolutions and the corresponding segmentation maps by camera acquisition. To demonstrate the robustness of our network, the segmentation experiments are performed on ISIC2017 [16] and ISIC2018 [17] dataset simultaneously. The ISIC2017 includes different types of skin lesions, where 2000 images for the training set, 150 images in the validation set, and 600 images for the test set. ISIC2018 consists of 2594 training images and 1000 test images. Since ground truth of ISIC2018 test set is not publicly available, the original training images are divided into the new training set and test set with 4:1 ratio randomly. In addition, to improve the computational efficiency of our model, the dimension of all images is reshaped to 256 × 192.

In this paper, two widely-used evaluation metrics in the field of medical segmentation, Dice similarity coefficient (Dice) and Intersection Over Union (IOU), are applied to evaluate our model. The formula is expressed as follows.

$$Dice = \frac{2 \times TP}{2 \times TP + FN + FP}$$
$$IOU = \frac{TP}{TP + FN + FP} \tag{4}$$

where TP, FP and FN represent the number of true positive pixels, false positive pixels, false negative pixels, respectively.

## 3.2 Implementation Details

Our proposed CTCNet is implemented in the PyTorch framework and trained with a NVIDIA-GTX1080GPU of 12G memory. In ISIC2017 segmentation experiments, Adam optimizer is leveraged with a learning rate of $7e^{-5}$ and a batchsize of 16. The epoch is set to 30. Besides, in ISIC2018 segmentation experiments, our model is trained untill 100 epochs with a learning rate of $1e^{-3}$.

## 3.3 Comparison Experiments

We demonstrate the efficiency of our proposed segmentation model and conduct a comparison with 6 state-of-the-art methods on ISIC2017 and ISIC2018 dataset respectively, including Unet [18], Att-Unet [19], Cdnn [20], CPFNet [9], DCL [21], Transfuse [13], ResUNet [22], MedT [23], TransUnet [12], Unext [24]. In addition, for a more intuitive comparison, the final predictions are also visualized in Fig. 3.

**Quantitative Evaluation.** Table 1 and Table 2 show the quantitative results of our network and other 6 state-of-the-art methods in the two datasets respectively. As shown in two tables, the Dice coefficient is notably improved by 2.82% compared with Unet and reaches 86.78% on the isic2017 dataset, while a better result for IOU with 1.5% improvement is achieved on isic2018 dataset compared with Unext. Furthermore, compared with the advanced method Transfuse, our CTCNet also obtain comparative accuracy on both datasets.

**Visual Comparison.** To illustrate the segmentation results of our method intuitively, Fig. 4 displays the visual results of our network and other advanced methods in the 2017 dataset. The from left to right columns denote the original image, the results of Unet, CPFNet, Transfuse, our proposed method, and ground truth. In the third and fourth rows, some fuzzy edges and false detection areas are appeared in the segmentation results of Unet and CPFNet, while the edge details of lesions segmented by our proposed algorithm are closer to the ground truth. Obviously, this algorithm has a significant improvement in skin lesions segmentation compared with previous algorithms.

**Table 1.** Quantitative evaluation of CTCNet with 6 state-of-the-art methods on ISIC2017 dataset.

| Model | Dice | IOU |
|---|---|---|
| Unet [18] | 0.8396 | 0.7533 |
| Att-Unet [19] | 0.8367 | 0.7506 |
| Cdnn [20] | 0.8490 | 0.7650 |
| CPFNet [9] | 0.8546 | 0.7705 |
| DCL [21] | 0.8570 | 0.7770 |
| Transfuse [13] | *0.8612* | *0.7814* |
| Ours | **0.8678** | **0.7876** |

**Table 2.** Quantitative evaluation of CTCNet with 6 state-of-the-art methods on ISIC2018 dataset.

| Model | Dice | IOU |
|---|---|---|
| Unet [18] | 0.8403 | 0.7455 |
| ResUNet [22] | 0.8560 | 0.7562 |
| MedT [23] | 0.8735 | 0.7954 |
| TransUnet [12] | 0.8891 | 0.8051 |
| Unext [24] | 0.8927 | 0.8095 |
| Transfuse [13] | **0.9029** | **0.8254** |
| Ours | *0.9022* | *0.8245* |

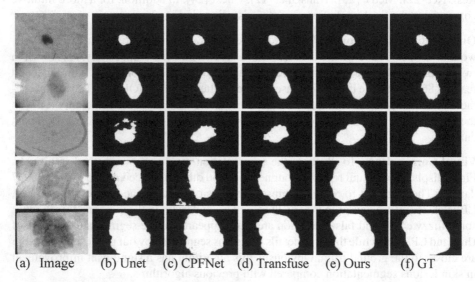

(a)  Image     (b) Unet    (c) CPFNet   (d) Transfuse    (e) Ours        (f) GT

**Fig. 4.** Visual comparison of our CTCNet and several state-of-the-art methods.

## 3.4  Ablation Study

In this section, we perform numerous ablation studies to verify the validity of the proposed module. Three groups of ablation experiments are carried out: the overall ablation experiment and the ablation experiment of two core components. To be more convincing, we take our ablation studies in the 2017 segmentation dataset with public test set labels. The test results of first group are illustrated in Table 3, and the output of CNN and Transformer branch in parallel is taken as baseline. Specifically, segmentation results of combining baseline with TCFA module are given in the second row, along with the results of adding TCFA and MSEA modules provided in the third row. As can be seen from Table 3, the Dice reach 0.8568 and 0.8604 respectively by adding the MSEA module and the TCFA module alone in baseline network, which is superior to original network, while the improvement of 1.32% in dice and 1.74% in IOU is achieved by adding two modules simultaneously, which is better than transfuse under the same device conditions. This ablation studies demonstrates the effectiveness of our proposed modules.

**Table 3.** Ablation study of the proposed method on ISIC2017 test set.

| Index | Baseline | TCFA | MSEA | Dice | IOU |
|-------|----------|------|------|------|-----|
| E.1 | ✓ | | | 0.8546 | 0.7702 |
| E.2 | ✓ | ✓ | | 0.8568 | 0.7719 |
| E.3 | ✓ | | ✓ | 0.8604 | 0.7775 |
| E.4 | ✓ | ✓ | ✓ | **0.8678** | **0.7876** |

**Validation of TCFA Module.** To demonstrate the effectiveness of the proposed TCFA module, we introduce it into the baseline network. As shown in Table 4, the ablation experiments of TCFA module mainly contains two main directions--feature fusion and receptive field, with MSEA module has been added. The first and second columns in table 4 show the results of the TCFA module with concatenation operation or residual structures respectively, while the third to fifth columns shows the results of TCFA module with separable convolutions of different dilation rates, where wide, wide1, wide2 represent separable convolutions of dilation rates are 1, 2, 4;1, 2, 4, 8;1, 4, 8, 16 respectively. For example, the wide_w/Concat in first column represents the TCFA module performing a concatenation operation in separable convolutions of dilation rates are 1, 2, 4 with the raw input features. The metrics in the last column have a significant improvement compared to the previous operation. The five experiments in the table can be represented by the formulas as follows:

$$F = C(P(F_{i-1}), F_t, F_c)))$$

$$F_i^{E.1} = C(\sum_{j}^{j=1,2,4} D_{sconv}^j(F), F),$$

$$F_i^{E.2} = C(\sum_{j}^{j=1,2,4} D_{sconv}^j(F)) \oplus F,$$

$$F_i^{E.3} = C(\sum_{j}^{j=1,2,4} D_{sconv}^j(F)),$$

$$F_i^{E.4} = C(\sum_{j}^{j=1,2,4,8} D_{sconv}^j(F)),$$

$$F_i^{E.5} = C(\sum_{j}^{j=1,4,8,16} D_{sconv}^j(F)) \tag{5}$$

where C represents the concatenation operation, $D_{sconv}^{j}$ denotes the separable convolution with dilation rate of j, and P is the upsampling operation. F represents the output feature integrating two branches and the previous level feature. $F_i$ is the output feature of the current level module, E denotes the current experimental serial number.

**Table 4.** Ablation study of TCFA module on ISIC2017 test set. Wide, wide1, wide2 represent separable convolutions of different dilation rates (as shown in formula 5).

| Index | MSEA | TCFA | Dice | IOU |
|-------|------|------|------|-----|
| E.1 | √ | +wide_w/concat | 0.8600 | 0.7769 |
| E.2 | √ | +wide_w/addition | 0.8617 | 0.7801 |
| E.3 | √ | +wide | 0.8668 | 0.7854 |
| E.4 | √ | +Wide1 | 0.8635 | 0.7826 |
| E.5 | √ | +Wide2 | **0.8678** | **0.7876** |

**Effectiveness of MSEA Module.** Table 5 shows the ablation experiments for MSEA module while TCFA has been added. Experiment 1, 2, 3 represent the test results of the segmentation model without MSEA module, removing FC branches and with the complete MSEA module respectively. The results are tabulated in Table 3, with an improvement of 1% compared to the baseline. Obviously, the results demonstrate the validity of the parts in our module.

**Table 5.** Ablation study of MSEA module on ISIC2017 test set. E1, E2, E3 represent the test results of the segmentation model without MSEA module, removing FC branches and with the complete MSEA module respectively.

| Index | TCFA | MSEA | Dice | IOU |
|-------|------|------|------|-----|
| E.1 | √ | W/o_MSEA | 0.8568 | 0.7719 |
| E.2 | √ | +SAMs | 0.8595 | 0.7768 |
| E.3 | √ | +FC branch | **0.8678** | **0.7876** |

# 4   Conclusion

In this paper, we propose a novel strategy to combine the transformer and CNN for skin image segmentation, termed as CTCNet. Its architecture takes advantage of the transformer's capacity in modeling global relationships while retaining more details. In CTCNet, we design a new feature fusion module (TCFA module) to integrate the global semantic information flow from different stages gradually. In addition, to deal with the complexity and diversity of the textures of skin lesions, a MSEA module is constructed to capture powerful features that can improve the ability of networks to solve scale changes. We validate the effectiveness of each component of our network in the ablation studies comprehensively. Extensive experimental results demonstrate that CTCNet achieves better performance on the skin lesions segmentation task. In the future, we plan to ameliorate the efficiency of our network and are devoted to other medically-related tasks.

**Acknowledgement.** This research was supported by the National Natural Science Foundation of China (No. 61901537), Research funds for overseas students in Henan Province, China Post-doctoral Science Foundation (No. 2020M672274), Science and technology guiding project of China National Textile and Apparel Council (No. 2019059), Postdoctoral Research Sponsorship in Henan Province (No. 19030018), Program of Young backbone teachers in Zhongyuan University of Technology (No. 2019XQG04), Training Program of Young Master's Supervisor in Zhongyuan University of Technology (No. SD202207).

# References

1. Wu, H., Pan, J., Li, Z., Wen, Z., Qin, J.: Automated skin lesion segmentation via an adaptive dual attention module. IEEE Trans. Med. Imaging **40**(1), 357–370 (2021)
2. Xw, A., et al.: Knowledge-aware deep framework for collaborative skin lesion segmentation and melanoma recognition. Pattern Recogn. **120**, 108075 (2021)
3. Xiao, J., et al.: A prior-mask-guided few-shot learning for skin lesion segmentation. Computing **120**, 108075 (2021)
4. Cerri, S., Puonti, O., Meier, D.S., Wuerfel, J., Leemput, K.V.: A contrast-adaptive method for simultaneous whole-brain and lesion segmentation in multiple sclerosis. Neuroimage **225**, 117471 (2021)
5. Li, W., Raj, A., Tjahjadi, T., Zhuang, Z.: Digital hair removal by deep learning for skin lesion segmentation. Pattern Recogn. **117**, 107994 (2021)
6. Sarker, M.M.K., et al.: SLSDeep: skin lesion segmentation based on dilated residual and pyramid pooling networks. In: Frangi, A.F., Schnabel, J.A., Davatzikos, C., Alberola-López, C., Fichtinger, G. (eds.) MICCAI 2018. LNCS, vol. 11071, pp. 21–29. Springer, Cham (2018). https://doi.org/10.1007/978-3-030-00934-2_3
7. Singh, V.K., et al.: FCA-Net: adversarial learning for skin lesion segmentation based on multi-scale features and factorized channel attention. IEEE Access **7**, 130552–130565 (2019)
8. Ran, G., Guotai, W., Tao, S., et al.: CA-Net: comprehensive attention convolutional neural networks for explainable medical image segmentation. IEEE Trans. Med. Imaging **40**(2), 699–711 (2021)
9. Feng, S., Zhao, H., Shi, F., et al.: CPFNet: context pyramid fusion network for medical image segmentation. IEEE Trans. Med. Imaging **39**(10), 3008–3018 (2020)
10. Dosovitskiy, A., Beyer, L., et al.: An image is worth 16 × 16 words: transformers for image recognition at scale. arXiv preprint arXiv:2010.11929 (2020)
11. Zheng, S., Lu, J., et al.: Rethinking semantic segmentation from a sequence-to sequence perspective with transformers. arXiv preprint arXiv:2012.15840 (2020)
12. Chen, J., Lu, Y., et al.: TransUNet: transformers make strong encoders for medical image segmentation. arXiv preprint arXiv:2102.04306 (2021)

13. Zhang, Y., Liu, H., Hu, Q.: TransFuse: fusing transformers and CNNs for medical image segmentation. In: de Bruijne, M., et al. (eds.) MICCAI 2021. LNCS, vol. 12901, pp. 14–24. Springer, Cham (2021). https://doi.org/10.1007/978-3-030-87193-2_2

14. Chen, L.C., Papandreou, G., Kokkinos, I., et al.: DeepLab: semantic image segmentation with deep convolutional nets, atrous convolution, and fully connected CRFs. IEEE Trans. Pattern Anal. Mach. Intell. **40**(4), 834–848 (2018)

15. Chollet, F.: Xception: deep learning with depthwise separable convolutions In: Proceedings of IEEE Conference on Computer Vision and Pattern Recognition (CVPR), pp. 1251–1258 (2017)

16. Codella, N.C., et al.: Skin lesion analysis toward melanoma detection: a challenge at the 2017 international symposium on biomedical imaging (ISBI), hosted by the international skin imaging collaboration (ISIC). arXiv preprint arXiv:1710.05006 (2017)

17. Codella, N.C., et al.: Skin lesion analysis toward melanoma detection: a challenge at the 2017 international symposium on biomedical imaging (ISBI), hosted by the international skin imaging collaboration (ISIC). arXiv preprint arXiv:1902.03368 (2018)

18. Ronneberger, O., Fischer, P., Brox, T.: U-Net: convolutional networks for biomedical image segmentation. In: Navab, N., Hornegger, J., Wells, W., Frangi, A. (eds.) MICCAI 2015. LNCS, vol. 9351, pp. 234–241. Springer, Cham (2015). https://doi.org/10.1007/978-3-319-24574-4_28

19. Oktay O, Schlemper J, Folgoc LL, et al.: Attention U-Net: learning where to look for the pancreas. arXiv Print, arXiv:1804.03999 (2018)

20. Yuan, Y., Lo, Y.C.: Improving dermoscopic image segmentation with enhanced convolutional-deconvolutional networks. IEEE J. Biomed. Health Inform. **23**, 519–526 (2017)

21. Bi, L., Kim, J., et al.: Step-wise integration of deep class-specific learning for dermoscopic image segmentation. Pattern Recogn. **85**, 78–89 (2019)

22. Jha, D., et al.: Resunet++: an advanced architecture for medical image segmentation. In: 2019 IEEE International Symposium on Multimedia (2019)

23. Valanarasu, J.M.J., Oza, P., Hacihaliloglu, I., Patel, V.M.: Medical transformer: Gated axial-attention for medical image segmentation. In: de Bruijne, M., et al. (eds.) MICCAI 2021. LNCS, vol. 12901, pp. 36–46. Springer, Cham (2021). https://doi.org/10.1007/978-3-030-87193-2_4

24. Valanarasu J, Patel V M.: UNeXt: MLP-based rapid medical image segmentation network (2022)

# MR Image Denoising Based on Improved Multipath Matching Pursuit Algorithm

Chenxi Li[1], Yitong Luo[2], Jing Yang[1], and Hong Fan[1(✉)]

[1] School of Computer Science, Shaanxi Normal University, Xi'an 710062, China
{lichenxi, fanhong}@snnu.edu.cn
[2] School of Computer Science and Technology, Beijing Institute of Technology,
Beijing 100081, China

**Abstract.** Magnetic resonance images are accompanied by random Rician noise due to the influence of uncertain factors in the process of imaging, storage, which brings a lot of inconvenience to the subsequent processing of the image and clinical diagnosis. This paper proposes an improved multipath matching pursuit algorithm based on learning Gabor pattern dictionary atom for image reconstruction and denoising. Firstly, Gabor wavelet transform based on neurophysiological constraints is used to generate dictionary atoms that match the local features of the image; Then this paper introduces adaptive differential evolution algorithm optimization to the process of solving multiple candidate atoms matching the local image features in each iteration of the multipath matching pursuit. It combines the advantages of adaptive differential evolution and multipath matching pursuit algorithm, not only avoids the genetic falling into the local optimal defect, but also obtains the best matching parameters with higher accuracy, and effectively reduces the computational complexity of the multipath matching pursuit. In the reconstruction experiment of the simulated MR images, compared with state-of-the-art denoising algorithms, our algorithm not only shows better denoising performance, but also retains more detailed information, and the running time is reduced nearly 50% than multipath matching pursuit; which fully shows the clinical application value.

**Keywords:** Gabor pattern · Multipath matching pursuit algorithm · Adaptive differential evolution algorithm · Dictionary atom · MR image denoising

## 1 Introduction

Magnetic resonance imaging (MRI) is a technology that uses static magnetic field and radiofrequency magnetic field to imaging human tissues. However, due to the influence of electronic components, there is always random noise in MR images, which brings a lot of inconvenience to the subsequent image processing. Therefore, MR images denoising has always been a challenging problem, many denoising methods have been applied to the processing of MR images [1]. These methods are based on different theoretical foundations, such as: statistical estimator, spatial domain filter, stochastic analysis, partial differential equation, transform domain method, hybrid domain method, low-rank clustering method, approximate theoretical method, ordinal statistics, and so on.

Spare representation (SR) can achieve a simple representation of complex images in a given overcomplete dictionary with a linear combination of atoms that are as few as possible but best fit the characteristics of the image to be decomposed. It models the image as $Y \approx DX$, where $Y$ is a complex signal, $D$ is an overcomplete dictionary, each column in $D$ is called as an atom, and $X$ is a coefficient matrix obtained by sparse decomposition algorithm. The noise is often accompanied by random characteristics, is difficult to be represented by fixed structure atoms. Therefore, using sparse coefficient matrix $X$ and overcomplete dictionary $D$ can denoise and reconstruct clean image.

Matching pursuit (MP) is the classic sparse decomposition algorithm [2, 3]. Its core principle is to adaptively decompose the signal $f$ into a set of linear combinations of basis functions $g_\gamma$ ($\|g_\gamma\| = 1$)for best matching the signal structure on the overcomplete dictionary $D$ in the Hilbert space. If decomposition is performed $m$ times, $f$ would be decomposed into:

$$f = \sum_{n=0}^{m-1} \langle R^n f, g_{\gamma n} \rangle g_{\gamma n} + R^m f \tag{1}$$

MP is suitable for many types of signals, especially suitable for extracting signal features with better time-frequency local characteristics. But it cannot be widely used due to the low reconstruction accuracy.

In recent years, there have been many improved sparse decomposition algorithms with good performance [4–6]. Among them, inspired by the combinatorial tree search problem, the multipath matching pursuit (MMP) algorithm transforms the optimal path search problem into a tree search problem, finds multiple candidate atoms in the search process, and selects the only one with the smallest residual as the final candidate support set when the iteration is completed, which greatly improves the accuracy of the final result [7]. The specific process is as follows:

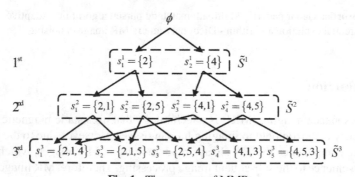

**Fig. 1.** The process of MMP

Under the guarantee based on the restricted isometric property (RIP), MMP has good reconstruction performance in both noisy and noise-free environments. However, the algorithm needs to screen the overcomplete atom dictionary one by one in each iteration process to find multiple optimal atoms that can match the signal structure, which results in a huge amount of computation.

The intelligent optimization algorithm is a kind of algorithm with strong universality, global optimization performance and suitable for parallel processing. It is widely used in the sparse decomposition process, which can reduce the computation of searching the best matching atom [8–10]. The differential evolution (DE) algorithm was proved to be the fastest evolution algorithm in the first IEEE evolutionary optimization competition [11].

SR based K-singular value decomposition (K-SVD) algorithm has been widely used and extended [12], for a short while, this algorithm was considered as state-of-the-art. However, over the years it has been surpassed by other methods, such as NLM (based on spatial domain) [13], BM3D (based on hybrid domain) [14] and DnCNN (based on deep-learning) [15].

Can we redesign the algorithm based on SR and apply it to MR image denoising, so that the denoising performance is close to or even better than state-of-the-art denoising algorithms? When the SR based algorithm is applied to MR image denoising, there are two core problems that need to be solved: the computational complexity and accuracy cannot be achieved simultaneously, and the selection of dictionary atoms. Around the two problems, the main contributions are as follows:

1. The Gabor wavelet transform based on neurophysiological constraints is used to generate overcomplete dictionary atoms;
2. DE is introduced to the process of image sparse decomposition by MMP, automatically adjusting the scaling factor and crossover probability, avoiding the algorithm falling into the local optimum and reducing the running time of MMP.

## 2 Proposed Method

### 2.1 Dictionary Atom Selection

The selection of dictionary atoms directly affects the accuracy and speed of MMP. The neurophysiological constrained Gabor wavelet has good local representation characteristics, direction and scale selectivity, and is sensitive to image edge information. So it is often used to match image features and generate dictionary atoms [16, 17]. According to [18–20], the Gabor wavelet transform based on neurophysiological constraints can finally be defined as (2):

$$G(u,v,x,y) = \sqrt{2\pi} \frac{f^u}{\kappa} \cdot \left\{ \exp\left[i \cdot 2\pi f^u \left(x\cos\theta_v + y\sin\theta_v\right)^2\right] - \exp\left(-\frac{\kappa^2}{2}\right) \right\}$$
$$\exp\left\{ \frac{\pi^2 \left(f^u\right)^2}{2\lambda^2 \kappa^2} \left( \lambda^2 \left(x\cos\theta_v + y\sin\theta_v\right)^2 + \left(-x\sin\theta_v + y\cos\theta_v\right)^2 \right) \right\}$$

(2)

Among them, $u$ and $v$ represent the atom size and rotation direction; the atom rotation operation can be defined as $\theta_v = \pi(v-1)/v_{\max}$, $f^u$ represents the spacing ratio between Gabor cores; $\kappa$ reflects the half-amplitude spatial frequency bandwidth, defined as $\kappa = \sqrt{2\ln 2}\left((2^{\phi}+1)/(2^{\phi}-1)\right)$; according to [18], select $\phi = 1.5$, $\kappa = 2.4654$; $\lambda$ represents the aspect ratio of the elliptic Gaussian function, select $\lambda = 2$. Figure 1 shows the magnitude, real and imaginary components of the Gabor wavelet transform based on neurophysiological constraints with $\phi = 1.5$, 5 scales ($u = 5$) and 8 directions ($v = 8$) (Fig. 2).

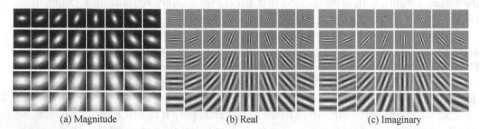

(a) Magnitude            (b) Real            (c) Imaginary

**Fig. 2.** Gabor wavelet transform based on biological constraints with 5 scales and 8 directions

### 2.1.1 The Influence of Different Dictionary Atom Numbers

The number of atoms is a factor that affects the quality of image reconstruction [3]. Figure 3 shows the reconstruction results, using 1000, 2500, 5000 and 6000 atoms for the standard test images and simulated brain MR images. Table 1 shows the evaluation values of peak signal to noise ratio (PSNR) [21] and structural similarity (SSIM) [22] for the reconstruction images with different numbers of atoms.

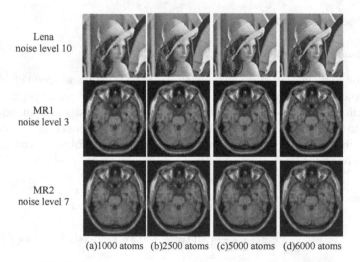

(a)1000 atoms   (b)2500 atoms   (c)5000 atoms   (d)6000 atoms

**Fig. 3.** Reconstruction results of different atom numbers

**Table 1.** The PSNR and SSIM values of different numbers of atoms

|  | Lena | | MR1 | | MR2 | |
|---|---|---|---|---|---|---|
|  | PSNR | SSIM | PSNR | SSIM | PSNR | SSIM |
| 1000 | 31.7382 | 0.7533 | 37.5032 | 0.7925 | 32.7609 | 0.7193 |
| 2500 | 33.7479 | 0.8610 | 39.7363 | 0.8335 | 33.0000 | 0.7304 |
| 5000 | **37.1470** | **0.9366** | **40.0412** | **0.8398** | **33.0167** | **0.7378** |
| 6000 | 36.6980 | 0.9272 | 39.9819 | 0.8394 | 33.0154 | 0.7377 |

It can be seen from Fig. 3 that some features in the image are not matched when using 1000 atoms for reconstruction, and the visual effect is blurred; When the number of the atoms is 2500, the noise has been suppressed, and it has obtained a good reconstruction result; Moreover, the visual effect with 5000 atoms and 6000 atoms has been further improved. Combining the data in Table 1: we can see that, as the number of atoms increases, the reconstruction effect gets better and better. But when it reaches a certain number, PSNR and SSIM start to decrease instead. The reason is that as the algorithm runs, there is less and less effective information in the residual image. When using too many atoms, the noise is also matched. Through this experiment, using 5000 atoms can obtain a better reconstruction result under different noise levels.

### 2.1.2 The Influence of Different Dictionary Atom Scales

The scale of atoms is another important factor affecting the quality of image reconstruction [23]. Atom $g_{\gamma-(x,y,u,v)}$ needs to determine its parameter range (upper and lower bounds), where $(x, y)$ represents the position, $u$ represents the scale parameter, and $v$ represents the deflection angle. [24] gives the upper and lower bounds of the four parameters $[x, y, u, v]$ as $[hx, hy, 2^j, 180]$ and $[0, 0, 0, 0]$, where $hx$, $hy$ represents the height and width of the image, and $j$ represents the index of the scale factor, through the experiment: $1 \leq 2^j < 40$.

Figure 4 shows the reconstruction results of the standard test images with different scales. Figure 4 (a) is the original image, and Fig. 4 (b–f) is the reconstruction result of the scale $2^1, 2^2, 2^3, 2^4, 2^5$ respectively.

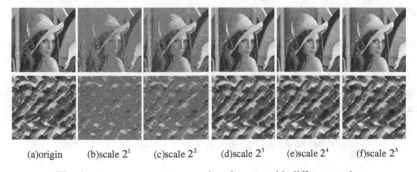

    (a)origin    (b)scale $2^1$    (c)scale $2^2$    (d)scale $2^3$    (e)scale $2^4$    (f)scale $2^5$

**Fig. 4.** The reconstruction results of atoms with different scales

It can be seen from Fig. 4 that the small-scale atoms represent the contour information of the image, only using the small-scale atoms can't reconstruct the image well; The middle-scale atoms are mainly concentrated in the content area of the image; and the large-scale atom is mainly responsible for matching a larger untextured area block in the image. Through this experiment: we can see that different scales play different roles in matching image features. If you want to reconstruct images with better quality, more combination of middle-scale and large-scale atoms is needed.

## 2.2   Improved Multipath Matching Pursuit Algorithm

The MMP algorithm needs to select several candidate atoms in each iteration, so the running time is long. Therefore, this paper introduces the adaptive differential evolution (ADE) algorithm to optimize MMP, which improves the solving speed.

In this paper, the 4-dimensional parameter of Gabor atom $\gamma$ is used as the parameter to be optimized in ADE (chromosome in ADE). The inner product of the residual signal and the atom is used as the fitness function, and the parameter encoding method is real number encoding, so that it can ensure higher accuracy in the process of atom optimization and avoid hexadecimal conversion, reducing the running time. In order to accelerate the decomposition speed of MMP improved by ADE, the following three key issues must be solved:

1. The parameter range of Gabor atoms. It is known from the above experiments that the combination of atoms of various scales can improve the reconstruction accuracy of the image. In this paper, the upper bound of the four parameters $[x, y, u, v]$ given in [24] is $[hx, hy, 2^j, 180]$ modified to $[hx, hy, bsloop, \min(hx, hy)]$, and the definition of $bsloop$ is shown in Eq. (3):

$$bsloop = \left(NN * \log_2^{\min(hx,hy)} - NN\right) * \left(1 - \frac{loop}{Nterm} * 0.5\right) \tag{3}$$

where $hx$ and $hy$ represent the height and width of the image respectively; $Nterm$ is the total number of iterations, $loop$ is the number of current iterations, and $NN$ is a constant. Through the experiment, taking the real constant 5 is to ensure $bsloop \in \left[1/2 * \left(5\log_2^{\min(hx,hy)} - 5\right), 5\log_2^{\min(hx,hy)} - 5\right)$, so that it can obtain more middle-scale and large-scale atoms within the value range.

2. The generation of the initial population. In this paper, the population is randomly initialized according to the range of atom parameters, the population size $P$ is 21 [25].

3. The determination of scaling factor and crossover probability. According to [26], the scaling factor (F) is designed as follows:

$$F = F_0 * 2^\lambda, \lambda = \exp\left(1 - \frac{G_m}{G_m + 1 - G}\right) \tag{4}$$

$F_0$ represents the initial scaling factor, $G_m$ represents the total evolution times, and $G$ represents the current evolution times.

According to [25], the crossover probability (CR) is designed as follows:

$$CR = \begin{cases} p_{c\_max} - \dfrac{(p_{c\_max} - p_{c\_min})(f' - \overline{f})}{f_{max} - \overline{f}}, & f' \geq \overline{f} \\ p_{c\_max}, & f' < \overline{f} \end{cases} \tag{5}$$

$f_{max}$ and $\overline{f}$ represents the maximum and average fitness value, $f'$ represents the larger fitness value of the two crossover individuals, $p_{c\_max}$ and $p_{c\_min}$ represents the maximum and minimum crossover probability. According to [27], take $p_{c\_max} = 0.9, p_{c\_min} = 0.6$ and $F_0 = 0.5$ to reasonably adjust the scaling factor and crossover probability in the evolution process, so that the algorithm can jump out of the local optimum.

The specific processing flow of the proposed algorithm is shown in Algorithm 1:

---

**Algorithm 1 Improved Multipath Matching Pursuit Algorithm**

---

**Input:** noisy image $y$, the number of path $L$, maximum number of iteration

**Output:** reconstruction clean image (denoised image) $\hat{x}$

Initialization: the number of iteration $k = 0$, the initial residual     , the candidate set $S^0 = \{\phi\}$ ;

1.  When $k < Nterm$ , the number of iteration: $k = k+1$ , the candidate index: $u = 0$ , the candidate support set: $S^k = \phi$ ; the initial population(generated according to the upper and lower limits of the atom parameters) $W$ ;

2.  When   |   | , use ADE to accelerate the search for $L$ optimal atoms $g_r = \{g_{r_1}, \ldots, g_{r_L}\}$ , and use these $L$ atoms to match the residual signals respectively, calculate $proj = < r_i^{k-1}, g_r >$ ;

3.  When $1 \leq j \leq L$ , establish a temporary path, $S_{temp} = S_i^{k-1} \cup \{g_{r_j}\}$ ;
    Check whether there is a shared path, if $S_{temp} \notin S^k$ , update the candidate index $u = u+1$ , update the path $S_u^k = S_{temp}$ , update the set of path $S^k = S^k \cup \{S_u^k\}$ , and then estimate and update the residuals, $\hat{x}_u^k = S_u^k y$ , $r_u^k = y - S_u^k \hat{x}_u^k$ ;Otherwise, return to step 3 until     , end step 3, return to step 2, and form the $k$ -th candidate path set $S^k = \{s_1^k, s_2^k, \ldots, s_u^k\}$ ;

4.  If $k \geq \Gamma$ , the candidate index set is pruned: According to the size of the corresponding reconstruction residual, the candidate support set in the candidate set $S^k$ is screened twice, and the     candidate support sets with the largest residuals are removed, and they are not allowed to procee the subsequent path expansion;

5.  When the given requirements are met, finding the candidate support set with the smallest residual to recovery signal.

---

## 2.3  The Time Complexity Analysis

For Gabor wavelet transform with fixed size, the time complexity is $O(w^2 NM)$, $w \times w$ is the window size of the biologically restricted Gabor filter function, $N$ and $M$ represent the height and width of the image. Therefore, for a biologically restricted Gabor wavelet transform of $U$-size and $V$-direction, the total time complexity is $O(w^2 UVNM)$.

In the sparse decomposition process of the image, MMP selects $L$ atoms in each iteration. According to [28], its time complexity should be $O\left((T^2L^2 + TL)d/2 + T^2L^2n\right)$, the image block size is $\sqrt{d} \times \sqrt{d}$, $n$ is the number of dictionary atoms, $T$ is the sparsity of the sparse matrix. Therefore, the total time complexity for image reconstruction using $U \times V$ Gabor transform and MMP is $O\left((T^2L^2 + T + 2T^2L^2n/d)UVNM\right)$.

For the proposed algorithm in this paper, the main factors affecting the algorithm are the number of redundant dictionary atoms and the population size. If the number of redundant dictionary atoms is $n$, the population size is $P$, then the time complexity of the proposed algorithm is $O\left(nPw^2UVNM\right)$.

## 3    Experiments

During the imaging process of MR images, the real and imaginary component of the signal usually have the same variance and zero mean Gaussian White Noise, and the noise brought by the real and imaginary component is independent of each other. It is generally believed that this noise has a Rician characteristic distribution, its probability density function is shown in (6):

$$f(z) = \frac{z}{\sigma^2} \exp\left[-\frac{1}{2\sigma^2}\left(z^2 + A^2\right)\right]I_0\left(\frac{Az}{\sigma^2}\right), z \geq 0 \tag{6}$$

$I_0$ represents the modified zero-order Bessel function of the first kind, and $A$ represents the peak value of the signal magnitude. When $A \rightarrow 0$, the Rician distribution is converted to the Rayleigh distribution.

For the experimental dataset, the images from the Mcgcill University MR Simulated Brain Image Database were selected. The brain MR images are T1-weighted, the 45th, 90th and 115th slices are selected, the noise levels are 1%, 5% and 9%, and the size is 217∗181. Figure 5 (b–h) shows the reconstruction results of NLM, KSVD, BM3D, DnCNN, MP, MMP and our algorithm under different noise levels. Among them, the search window radius of the NLM is 2, the field window radius is 5, and the smoothing parameter of the Gaussian function is 10; MP, MMP and our algorithm all use 5000 atoms for reconstruction. In order to compare the effects of reconstruction, two objective indicators commonly used for testing images were selected: PSNR and SSIM. The experimental platform is Windows10, the hardware is Inter (R) Core (TM) i5-6600M 3.30 GHz CPU, 8G RAM, and all algorithms are running in MATLAB R2020b environment.

Combine the data in Table 2 and 3, it can be found that under the same noise level, our algorithm has higher PSNR and SSIM values than the comparison algorithm, showing a better denoising performance. The subsequent processing of MR images and clinical diagnosis based on MR images have high requirements for the details. It can be seen from Fig. 5 that NLM and DnCNN blur the details of the MR image to a certain extent while denoising. Our algorithm not only has good denoising effect, but also better preserves the details of MR images. In terms of the running time, for NLM, the values of the search window radius and the neighborhood window radius affect the running time; For KSVD, the computational complexity of sparse decomposition, the iteration number, and error threshold affect the running time; For MP and MMP, in order to ensure the reconstruction accuracy, it is necessary to calculate the inner product of each atom and

**Table 2.** The PSNR values of denoising results of simulated brain MR images with different noise levels

|        | Noise level 1 | | | Noise level 5 | | | Noise level 9 | | |
|--------|---------|---------|----------|---------|---------|----------|---------|---------|----------|
|        | Slice45 | Slice90 | Slice115 | Slice45 | Slice90 | Slice115 | Slice45 | Slice90 | Slice115 |
| NLM    | 38.4831 | 39.5233 | 40.0376  | 28.9215 | 28.0658 | 28.9975  | 27.4003 | 27.0042 | 27.7918  |
| KSVD   | 41.0504 | 41.2084 | 41.9460  | 28.8095 | 28.1468 | 29.0501  | 27.4570 | 27.0845 | 27.9031  |
| BM3D   | 44.3907 | 43.9476 | 44.4151  | 28.9816 | 28.3217 | 29.1679  | 27.7353 | 27.3491 | 28.1536  |
| DnCNN  | 41.6528 | 41.7659 | 42.3846  | 29.0110 | 28.1310 | 29.0619  | 31.2234 | 30.6536 | 29.4043  |
| MP     | 39.9304 | 40.0041 | 40.8688  | 35.6002 | 34.8671 | 33.7138  | 31.1729 | 30.5768 | 29.3727  |
| MMP    | 43.6372 | 43.5168 | 43.1887  | 35.7044 | 34.8707 | 33.7311  | 31.1999 | 30.6661 | 29.4405  |
| OURS   | **44.7109** | **44.5166** | **44.7702** | **35.7340** | **34.9081** | **33.7362** | **31.2657** | **30.7070** | **29.5193** |

**Table 3.** The SSIM values of denoising results of simulated brain MR images with different noise levels

|        | Noise level 1 | | | Noise level 5 | | | Noise level 9 | | |
|--------|---------|---------|----------|---------|---------|----------|---------|---------|----------|
|        | Slice45 | Slice90 | Slice115 | Slice45 | Slice90 | Slice115 | Slice45 | Slice90 | Slice115 |
| NLM    | 0.9185 | 0.8993 | 0.8738 | 0.7720 | 0.7402 | 0.6581 | 0.7114 | 0.6865 | 0.5966 |
| KSVD   | 0.9025 | 0.9140 | 0.8880 | 0.7621 | 0.7389 | 0.6639 | 0.7089 | 0.6412 | 0.5692 |
| BM3D   | 0.9467 | 0.9160 | 0.8917 | 0.7871 | 0.6775 | 0.6120 | 0.5915 | 0.5544 | 0.4947 |
| DnCNN  | 0.9374 | 0.9111 | 0.8837 | 0.7883 | 0.7451 | 0.6678 | 0.7169 | 0.6843 | 0.5982 |
| MP     | 0.9175 | 0.9015 | 0.8836 | 0.7754 | 0.7352 | 0.6586 | 0.7006 | 0.6677 | 0.5881 |
| MMP    | 0.9589 | 0.9124 | 0.8915 | 0.8358 | 0.7371 | 0.6614 | 0.7561 | 0.6647 | 0.5849 |
| OURS   | **0.9635** | **0.9385** | **0.9093** | **0.8364** | **0.7956** | **0.7141** | **0.7564** | **0.7242** | **0.6412** |

the residual signal to obtain the best matching atom, and the running time is proportional to the number of atoms. Moreover, MMP needs to select multiple candidate atoms in each iteration, with the increase of the number of iterations, the number of candidate support sets will also increase, so the running time is longer than that of MP. It can be seen from Table 4 that after the introduction of ADE, the decomposition speed of MMP is accelerated. Both the matching of a single atom and the total running time are reduced by nearly 50% compared with MMP. More important, the quality of image reconstruction has also been improved. This experiment shows the effectiveness of the proposed algorithm.

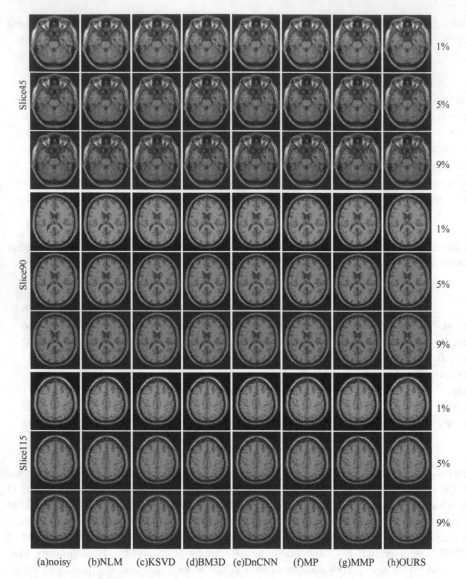

(a)noisy    (b)NLM    (c)KSVD    (d)BM3D    (e)DnCNN    (f)MP    (g)MMP    (h)OURS

**Fig. 5.** Denoising results of simulated brain MR images with different noise levels

**Table 4.** Running time (seconds), NLM and BM3D are the total running time; For KSVD, the left value is the time required for each iteration, and the right value is the algorithm running time; For MP, MMP and OURS, the left value in the algorithm of this paper are the time required to match a single atom, the value on the right is the running time of the algorithm

|          | NLM     | KSVD            | BM3D   | DnCNN  | MP              | MMP             | OURS            |
|----------|---------|-----------------|--------|--------|-----------------|-----------------|-----------------|
| Slice45  | 19.0625 | 3.0861/135.6581 | 0.6787 | 0.5282 | 0.1467/783.6968 | 0.2425/1850.0283 | 0.1406/925.1645 |
| Slice90  | 19.6568 | 5.8496/313.4582 | 0.7705 | 0.4696 | 0.1101/604.5600 | 0.2614/1861.1526 | 0.1268/787.0325 |
| Slice115 | 20.2586 | 5.4958/266.4625 | 0.7310 | 0.8523 | 0.1228/624.3360 | 0.2174/1817.5445 | 0.1338/797.8443 |

# 4  Conclusion

In this paper, an improved multipath matching pursuit algorithm based on learning Gabor pattern dictionary atom is proposed. Firstly, use the Gabor wavelet transform based on neurophysiological constraints to generate overcomplete dictionary atoms; Furthermore, ADE is effectively combined with MMP, taking advantage of the strong global search ability, fast convergence speed, adaptive adjustment of scaling factor and crossover probability of ADE to avoid falling into local optimization and to improving the decomposition speed and reconstruction accuracy. The secondary screening of the candidate sets can remove several candidate support sets with large residuals, and the pruning can prevent the excessive number of candidate support sets, so as to further reduce the running time. The Experimental results show that the running time is nearly 50% shorter than that of MMP. Compared with the state-of-the-art denoising algorithm, the effectiveness and robustness of this algorithm are verified, which fully verified that this algorithm not only obtains better denoising effect, but also reduces the time complexity of MMP.

**Acknowledgments.** This work was supported by the National Natural Science Foundation of China (Grant No. 11471004), the National Natural Science Foundation of Shaanxi Province (Grant No. 2022ZJ-39), the Open Project of the Key Laboratory of Forensic Genetics, Ministry of Public Security (Grant No. 2021FGKFKT07).

# References

1. Mishro, P.K., Agrawal, S., Panda, R., et al.: A survey on state-of-the-art denoising techniques for brain magnetic resonance images. IEEE Rev. Biomed. Eng. **15**, 184–199 (2022)
2. Mallat, St.G., Zhang, Z.: Matching pursuits with time-frequency dictionaries. IEEE Trans. Signal Process. **41**(12), 3397–3415 (1993)
3. Bergeaud, F., Mallat, S.: Matching pursuit of images. In: Proceedings of the Proceedings. International Conference on Image Processing, Washington, DC, USA, pp. 53–56. IEEE (1995)
4. Zhao, J., Xia, B.: An improved orthogonal matching pursuit based on randomly enhanced adaptive subspace pursuit. In: Proceedings of the 2017 Asia-Pacific Signal and Information Processing Association Annual Summit and Conference (APSIPA ASC), Kuala Lumpur, Malaysia, pp. 437–441. IEEE (2017)

5. Liu, W., Chen, X.: Research on identification algorithm based on optimal orthogonal matching pursuit. In: Proceedings of the 2021 4th International Conference on Electron Device and Mechanical Engineering (ICEDME), Guangzhou, China, pp. 185–188. IEEE (2021)
6. Zhang, Z., Xu, Y., Yang, J., et al.: A survey of sparse representation: algorithms and applications. IEEE Access 3, 490–530 (2015)
7. Kwon, S., Wang, J., Shim, B.: Multipath matching pursuit. IEEE Trans. Inf. Theory 60(5), 2986–3001 (2014)
8. Xiao-dong, X.U., Ying-jie, L.E.I., Shao-hua, Y.U.E., Ying, H.E.: Research of PSO-based intuitionistic fuzzy kernel matching pursuit algorithm. Acta Electronica Sinica 43(07), 1308–1314 (2015)
9. Li, J., Yan, H., Tang, J., Zhang, X., Li, G., Zhu, H.: Magnetotelluric noise suppression based on matching pursuit and genetic algorithm. Chin. J. Geophys. 61(07), 3086–3101 (2018)
10. Fan, H., Meng, Q.-F., Zhang, Y.: Matching pursuit via genetic algorithm based on hybrid coding. J. Xi'an Jiaotong Univ. 39(3), 295–299 (2005)
11. Storn, R., Price, K.: Differential evolution – a simple and efficient heuristic for global optimization over continuous spaces. J. Global Optim. 11(4), 341–359 (1997)
12. Elad, M., Aharon, M.: Image denoising via sparse and redundant representations over learned dictionaries. IEEE Trans. Image Process. 15(12), 3736–3745 (2006)
13. Buades, A., Coll, B., Morel, J.M.: A non-local algorithm for image denoising. In: Proceedings of IEEE Computer Society Conference on Computer Vision and Pattern Recognition, CVPR 2005, pp. 60–65. IEEE (2005)
14. Dabov, K., Foi, A., Egiazarian, K.: Image denoising by sparse 3D transform-domain collaborative filtering. IEEE Trans. Image Process. 16(8), 2080–2095 (2007)
15. Zhang, K., Zuo, W., Chen, Y.: Beyond a Gaussian denoiser: residual learning of deep CNN for image denoising. IEEE Trans. Image Process. 26(7), 3142–3155 (2016)
16. Cl, A., Yh, B., Wei, H.C., et al.: Learning features from covariance matrix of Gabor wavelet for face recognition under adverse conditions. Pattern Recogn. 119, 108085–108097 (2021)
17. Liu, J., Zhao, S., Xie, Y., et al.: Learning local Gabor pattern-based discriminative dictionary of froth images for flotation process working condition monitoring. IEEE Trans. Industr. Inf. 17(7), 4437–4448 (2020)
18. Jone, T.S.: Image representation using 2D Gabor wavelets. IEEE Trans. Pattern Anal. Mach. Intell. 18(10), 959–971 (1996)
19. Liu, J., Zhou, J., et al.: Toward flotation process operation-state identification via statistical modeling of biologically inspired gabor filtering responses. IEEE Trans. Cybern. 50, 4242–4255 (2019)
20. Jones, J.P., Palmer, L.A.: An evaluation of the two-dimensional Gabor filter model of simple receptive fields in cat striate cortex. J. Neurophysiol. 58(6), 1233–1258 (1987)
21. Huynh-Thu, Q., Ghanbari, M.: Scope of validity of PSNR in image/video quality assessment. Electron. Lett. 44(13), 800–801 (2008)
22. Wang, Z., Bovik, A.C., Sheikh, H.R., et al.: Image quality assessment: from error visibility to structural similarity. IEEE Trans. Image Process. 13(4), 600–612 (2004)
23. Qiang, G., Duan, C., Fang, X., et al.: A study on matching pursuit based on genetic algorithm. In: Proceedings of the 2011 Third International Conference on Measuring Technology and Mechatronics Automation (2011)
24. Ventura, R., Vandergheynst, P., Pierre, V.: Matching pursuit through genetic algorithms. Technical report: 86783, Signal Processing Laboratories LTS2, Lausanne, Switzerland (2001)
25. Wang, X.-P., Cao, L.-M.: Genetic Algorithms: Theory, Applications, and Software Implementation. Xi'an Jiaotong University Press, Xi'an (2002)
26. Georgioudakis, M., Plevris, V.: A comparative study of differential evolution variants in constrained structural optimization. Front. Built Environ. 6, 1–14 (2020)

27. Da Silva, A.R.F.: Atomic decomposition with evolutionary pursuit. Digit. Signal Process. **13**(2), 317–337 (2003)
28. Tropp, J.A., Gilbert, A.C.: Signal recovery from random measurements via orthogonal matching pursuit. IEEE Trans. Inf. Theory **53**(12), 4655–4666 (2007)

# Statistical Characteristics of 3-D PET Imaging: A Comparison Between Conventional and Total-Body PET Scanners

Yuejie Lin[1], En-tao Liu[2], and Tian Mou[1,2(✉)]

[1] School of Biomedical Engineering, Health Science Center, Shenzhen University, Shenzhen, China
linyuejie2021@email.szu.edu.cn, tian.mou@szu.edu.cn
[2] WeiLun PET Center, Department of Nuclear Medicine, Guangdong Provincial People's Hospital, Guangdong Academy of Medical Sciences, Guangzhou, China
liuentao@gdph.org.cn

**Abstract.** The performance of an operational PET scanner is affected by many factors, thus the detailed evaluation of imaging characteristics could contribute to ensuring the image quality. The routine quality assurance (QA) measurement of PET scanners can be used to provide an operational understanding of scanning properties. This study aims to compare the results obtained by the procedure for qualifying PET/CT scanners for clinical trials adopted by Guangdong Provincial People's Hospital on both conventional (Biograph 16HR, Siemens) and total-body (uEXPLORER) PET/CT scanners. Uniform phantoms filled with 18F-FDG used in static mode and Ge-68 PET cylinders & transmission rod source used in dynamic mode have both been analyzed. This comparison study focuses on statistical characteristics and spatial correlation within the region of interest. We evaluate axial and transaxial patterns in mean, variance, and covariance. In general, voxel values of dynamic images are more skewed than static images, indicating that the Normal-based image post-processing algorithms might not be applicable for dynamic PET scans. Since variance characteristics are dominated by effective counts– these are lower in the axial extremes of the scanner bed, there is always a U-shaped of variance over axial locations in conventional PET scanners, while the static mode of the uEXPLORER scanner does not have. The spatial correlation between adjacent slices shows a potential connection with scanning settings. Therefore, there is a certain difference in imaging characteristics between conventional and whole-body PET scanners. In addition, information from routine phantom scanning would enrich the knowledge of image processing and give a novel method of comparative studies. Investigation of this approach is currently underway and will be reported in future work.

**Keywords:** PET/CT · Image processing · Whole-body PET · Quality assurance · Imaging characteristic

© The Author(s), under exclusive license to Springer Nature Switzerland AG 2022
S. Yu et al. (Eds.): PRCV 2022, LNCS 13535, pp. 240–250, 2022.
https://doi.org/10.1007/978-3-031-18910-4_20

# 1   Introduction

With the increasing demands of multi-center clinical PET study, the assessment of image quality between different scanners [5] or scanning settings, such as radiopharmaceuticals [3,8], reconstruction methods [6] and dynamic/static scanning modes [2], needs to be investigated to enhance image consistency and comparability. Traditional total-body PET/CT scans are done by scanning multiple times and reconstructing in segments. One disadvantage of multiple scans is that the radioactivity of the tracer decreases as the scanning time increases, which will lead to the difference in the reconstructed value of segments. The total-body PET scanner, uEXPLORER, breaks this limitation by allowing a single scan to include the whole body area. Therefore, the empirical understanding of imaging characteristics, such as mean, variance, and spatial correlation pattern, of operational scanning data should be necessary for comparing image qualities of different scanners.

Most of the existing multi-center studies have focused on comparative studies of tracers, reconstruction methods, and scanners. And the indicators for evaluating the imaging performance are mostly lesion detection effect [4,9], image features variation [10,11] and standard uptake value (SUV) comparison [7,12]. *Shiri et al.* carried out multi-scanner studies including phantom and patient to investigate the impact of different reconstruction settings on image features using the coefficient of variation (COV) as a metric, where they believe that the variability and robustness of PET/CT image radiomics in advanced reconstruction settings is feature-dependent, and different settings have different effects on different features [13]. *Lantos et al.* conducted a study comparing the detection ability and imaging characteristics of two reconstruction algorithms, ordered subset expectation maximization (OSEM) and block sequential regularized expectation maximization (BSREM). The results showed that there were some differences in SUVmax, contrast recovery, and organ homogeneity in small lesions. Besides, the author believes that the BSREM algorithm is better than the OSEM algorithm after properly setting the parameters [9]. *Shimada et al.* analyzed the phantom images obtained by different scanners and concluded that scanning duration could have a significant impact on the image noise, which the variability in SUVmax and SUVpeak depended on [12].

In this paper, we consider the statistical characteristics of images as evaluation criteria to analyze the differences between scanners. Details of the data and specific evaluation methods for the data will be presented in the Methodology section. The presentation and analysis of the results will be presented in detail in the Results section.

# 2   Methodology

In this study, we use the voxel-level data of phantom scanning in different modes and scanners to analyze the difference in statistical characteristics and spatial correlation. Uniform phantom scans are collected from Guangdong Provincial

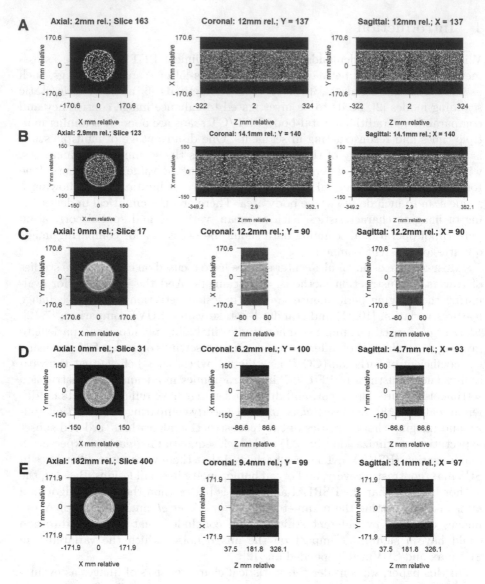

**Fig. 1.** Uniform phantom images of each scanner. A: Dynamic Biograph 16HR brain scan, B: Dynamic uEXPLORER brain scan, C: Static Biograph 16HR brain scan, D: Static uEXPLORER brain scan, E: Static uEXPLORER whole-body scan.

People's Hospital including conventional scanner Biograph 16HR and total-body scanner uEXPLORER. Biograph 16HR from Siemens is one of the traditional PET/CT scanners. The crystal size of Biograph 16HR is $4 \times 4 \times 20 \, mm^3$ and the axial field of view (AFOV) is 162 mm [1]. The uEXPLORER is the first 194-cm-long total-body PET/CT scanner built by United Imaging with

$2.85 \times 2.85 \times 18.1\,\mathrm{mm}^3$ crystal size and 194 cm AFOV [14]. There are two scanning modes for data from both scanners: dynamic and static brain scan and data from uEXPLORER have one more set of the static whole-body scan. The tracer options are Ge-68 PET Cylinders & Transmission rod source for dynamic scanning and uniform phantoms filled with 18F-FDG for static scanning. More details of mode settings are shown in Table 1, where the scan mode abbreviation is indicated in parentheses in the Scanner column. Besides, the example images of each scanner are displayed in Fig. 1. Voxel-level data in a cylindrical volume, within a white outline, are used in the analysis.

**Table 1.** More details about scan data

| Scanner | Scan mode | Reconstruction method | Radiopharmaceutical |
|---|---|---|---|
| Biograph 16HR (DBS) | Dynamic brain scan | OSEM 2D 6i16s | 68 Germanium |
| Biograph 16HR (SBS) | Static brain scan | DIFT | 18 Fluorine |
| uEXPLORER (DBS) | Dynamic brain scan | 3D iterative TOF PSF | 68 Germanium |
| uEXPLORER (SBS) | Static brain scan | 3D iterative TOF PSF | 18 Fluorine |
| uEXPLORER (SWB) | Static whole body scan | 3D iterative TOF PSF | 18 Fluorine |
| Scanner | Pixel spacing (mm) | Slice thickness (mm) | Total dose (MBq) |
| Biograph 16HR (DBS) | 1.33 | 2 | 93.43 |
| Biograph 16HR (SBS) | 2.03 | 5 | 70.30 |
| uEXPLORER (DBS) | 1.17 | 2.89 | 28.70 |
| uEXPLORER (SBS) | 1.56 | 2.89 | 70.3 |
| uEXPLORER (SWB) | 3.13 | 2.89 | 70.3 |

For analysis needs, the mean and variance of each slice will be calculated as the statistical characteristics of image data. Conventional analysis of the routine PET phantom data has focused on systematic deviations between the actual activity value and its regional mean of scanned data. But it is worth considering a more detailed evaluation of imaging characteristics. This work is more concerned with components of random variation, including axial patterns in variance and covariance. The full understanding of statistical characteristics from the phantom scanning would practically help the examination of performance between different scanners.

Here, the original set of voxel-level PET activity values will be normalized, which is to adjust mean of data to one, and let $\{z_{ijk}, i = 1, 2, \ldots, N; j = 1, 2, \ldots, N; k = 1, 2, \ldots, K\}$ represents the normalized values. Then we could use the equation below to calculate the mean and variance by slices.

$$\mu_k = \frac{\sum_{i=1}^{N} \sum_{j=1}^{N} z_{ijk}}{N \times N} \tag{1}$$

$$\phi_k = \frac{\sum_{i=1}^{N} \sum_{j=1}^{N} (\mu_k - z_{ijk})^2}{N \times N} \tag{2}$$

where $N$ represents the number of pixels in each row or column of the PET images, which should be the same in the scan, and $k$ represents which slice the voxels are on. Mean and variance will be expressed as $\mu$ and $\phi$ below. The residuals will calculate like Pearson residuals.

$$r_{ijk} = \frac{z_{ijk} - \mu_k}{\sqrt{\phi_k}} \tag{3}$$

The auto-correlation function (ACF) of images is calculated using the residuals through the Wiener-Khinchin theorem, to inspect the spatial neighborhood information that remains in it.

$$R(l) = \frac{Re\{\mathcal{F}^{-1}\{\mathcal{F}(r) \times Conj[\mathcal{F}(r)]\}\}}{N \times N \times K} \tag{4}$$

where $\mathcal{F}(\cdot)$ and $\mathcal{F}^{-1}(\cdot)$ represent the 3D Fourier transform and its inverse. $R(l)$ and $l$ represent the ACF results and the order of lags. $Re(\cdot)$ represents the real part of the result and $Conj(\cdot)$ represents the conjugate calculation. $N \times N$ and $K$ stand for the number of voxels on each slice and the number of slices. Furthermore, the ACF results are standardized based on the maximum point.

## 3   Results

As shown in Fig. 1, phantom images have different patterns across scanning modes and scanners. In the comparison of static and dynamic images from Biograph 16HR, radial artifacts are prominent in static scanning images. We consider this is caused by the differences in reconstruction methods. With the iteration calculation by the OSEM algorithm, the image quality has greatly improved compared to the image reconstructed by the DIFT algorithm–a traditional filtered back-projection (FBP) reconstruction algorithm in Fourier space. In addition, the brightness of dynamic scan images is much lower than the static. This may be because of the less scanning time of dynamic scanning per bed position than static images. The longer the scanning time at the same location, the more photons can be received, so that the brightness and quality of the images would be increased.

Figure 2 and 3 show the distributions of voxel values across transaxial slices. The x-axis is the axial location. For dynamic scans, all time frames are summarized for each slice. We compare histograms (Fig. 2) and boxplots (Fig. 3) of dynamic (A & B) and the static (C, D & E) images, where dynamic data show a Gamma-like skewness and static data are closer to Gaussian distribution.

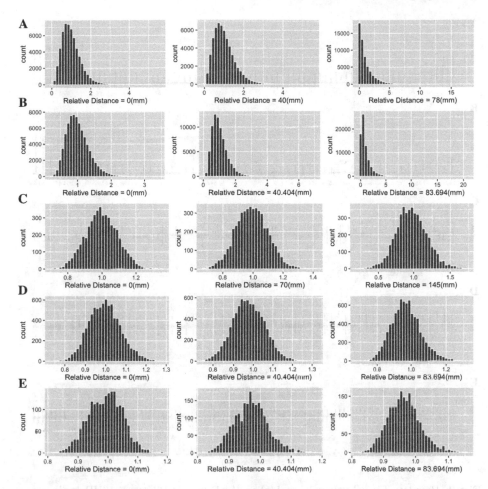

**Fig. 2.** Histograms of voxel values from middle to edge bed positions (from left to right column). A: Dynamic Biograph 16HR brain scan, B: Dynamic uEXPLORER brain scan, C: Static Biograph 16HR brain scan, D: Static uEXPLORER brain scan, E: Static uEXPLORER whole-body scan.

In Fig. 3, both dynamic and static scans from Biograph 16HR exhibit U-shaped variations across slices, that is lower variation in the middle and higher till the edge. However, the static data from uEXPLORER maintains relatively stable.

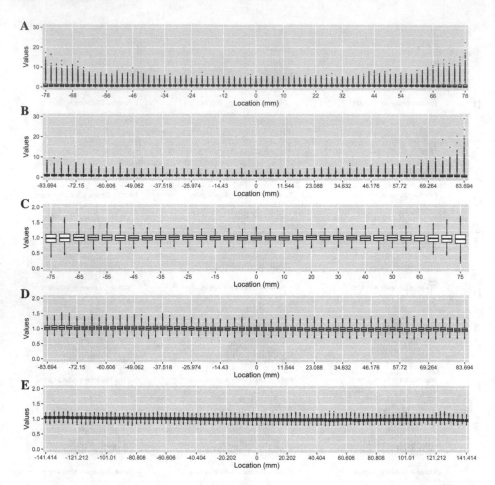

**Fig. 3.** Boxplot of voxel values in each slice. A: Dynamic Biograph 16HR brain scan, B: Dynamic uEXPLORER brain scan, C: Static Biograph 16HR brain scan, D: Static uEXPLORER brain scan, E: Static uEXPLORER whole-body scan.

In Fig. 4, the mean ($\mu$) and variance ($\phi$) of the dynamic scan is calculated for each slice across all time frames. For the static data, it is simply calculated for each slice. The values of voxels have been normalized by cases, which guarantees the mean of all voxels should be around 1 in each case. Note that the middle slice of the scan or each time frame is considered as 0 location.

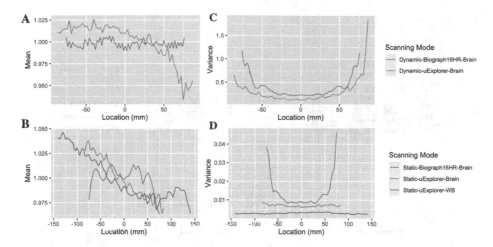

**Fig. 4.** Axial mean ($\mu_k$) and variance ($\phi_k$) in the PET measurement.

From $\mu$ of each slice in all the scanners in Fig. 4AB, we consider there are patterns for different scanners, where all the $\mu$ of uEXPLORER show a decreasing trend with slice moving backward. However, the $\mu$ of the Biograph 16HR swings around 1. Moreover, $\phi$ in all dynamic cases and static cases from Biograph 16HR show a U-shaped pattern which verifies the result in Fig. 3. Figure 4C and D show the $\phi$ of scanner Biograph 16HR are always greater than $\phi$ of scanner uEXPLORER, which is the same as Fig. 3 displayed. This may be caused by the different detectors and reconstruction methods in the scanner which are more sensitive and accurate in scanner uEXPLORER. With more sensitive detectors, the counting of photons will be higher and make the values more constant during reconstruction, where a more advanced reconstruction algorithm should also help but in different procedures of A. In addition, we discover a pattern of $\phi$ that a higher total dose of the radionuclide leads to lower $\phi$ in cases of the scanner uEXPLORER. This pattern shows the higher total dose can stable the value of voxels, which is by increasing the number of photons received. However, the scanner Biograph 16HR shows the opposite, the total dose of the dynamic scan of scanner Biograph 16HR is much higher than the static scan, but a higher dose leads to a bigger $\phi$. Since the $\phi$ of dynamic scans stay much higher than the static in all cases, we believe the possible reason for this is the scan time difference between dynamic and static scans, where the difference in reconstruction methods and radiopharmaceuticals may also influence on.

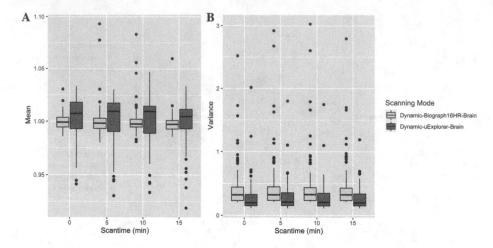

**Fig. 5.** The distribution of $\mu$ and $\phi$ in each time frame.

Figure 5 shows a little variation of $\mu$ and $\phi$ in each time frame which demonstrates the stability of the statistical characteristic of each time frame in a single multi-frame scan. In addition, images from scanner Biograph 16HR have twenty slices more than from scanner uEXPLORER in a single time frame. Under the same premise of slice thickness, this can bring a larger imaging area, but it will introduce noise in the extended part which is due to the reduction of photons received at the edge of the detector. Moreover, in Fig. 5B, The variance of each time frame both remain relatively constant in a multi-frame scan, and the variation of Biograph16HR stays higher than uEXPLORER in every time frame, which may be attributed to the fact that the number of slices in a single time frame of Biograph16HR is larger than that of uEXPLORER. We also performed an additional test of the significance of difference and p-values shown in Table 2, which confirmed that the difference between the two in variation is significant.

**Table 2.** P-values of t-test in $\mu$ and $\phi$ of dynamic scan

| P-values | Scan time | | | |
|---|---|---|---|---|
| | 0 min | 5 min | 10 min | 15 min |
| $\mathbf{P}_\mu$ | 0.61 | 0.68 | 0.94 | 0.97 |
| $\mathbf{P}_\phi$ | $6.0 \times 10^{-3}$ | $3.3 \times 10^{-4}$ | $4.1 \times 10^{-4}$ | $4.1 \times 10^{-4}$ |

Considering the specificity of the uEXPLORER whole body scan, in Fig. 6, we regard it as a separate category to display the ACF results. In Fig. 6A, compared to scanner Biograph16HR, the ACF of uEXPLORER maintains a more concentrated distribution across scans of different modes and a more consistent trend in transaxial ACF. Besides, uEXPLORER-WB shows a different trend

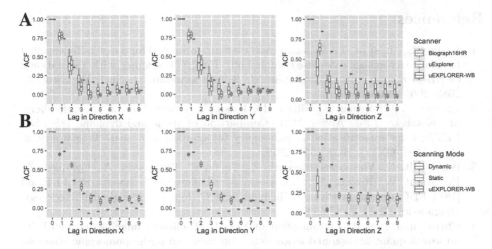

**Fig. 6.** The ACF comparison between scanners and scanning mode.

from the other two scanners. The ACF of Biograph16HR and uEXPLORER both drop rapidly in the first few lags and remain stable thereafter, while the ACF of uEXPLORER-WB gradually decreases with no sign of becoming constant. Figure 6B shows the ACF of dynamic scans is more consistent and much lower than that of static scans, which also shows the difference in trend variation in the comparison of uEXPLORER-WB and others. By combining the results in Fig. 6 with details in Table 1, we believe that the transaxial ACF and the axial ACF are related to pixel spacing and slice thickness, respectively. However, due to the small amount of data, we did not perform correlation analysis and further verification.

## 4 Conclusions

Uniform phantom scan from the clinical routine QA process provides an opportunity to analyze the statistical basis of reconstructed data, especially for comparative studies across multi-center trials. The analysis of conventional and whole-body PET scans demonstrates appreciable temporal and axial variation in the reliability of reconstructed images. Both scanners show their patterns in the regional mean, variance, and spatial covariance characteristics in their respective multi-frame scans. The ACF results reveal the potential connection of spatial relation with the thickness of slices and with pixel spacing. With the development of multi-center research, it is necessary to conduct a postprocessing technology with a complete statistical understanding of reconstructed images to improve the comparability of PET clinical indexes across different scanners or settings. A more detailed investigation of this phenomenon in the context of operational PET scanners is certainly warranted.

# References

1. Brambilla, M., et al.: Performance characteristics obtained for a new 3-dimensional lutetium oxyorthosilicate-based whole-body PET/CT scanner with the national electrical manufacturers association NU 2–2001 standard. J. Nucl. Med. **46**(12), 2083–2091 (2005)
2. Braune, A., Hofheinz, F., Bluth, T., Kiss, T., Wittenstein, J., Scharffenberg, M., Kotzerke, J., de Abreu, M.G.: Comparison of static and dynamic 18F-FDG PET/CT for quantification of pulmonary inflammation in acute lung injury. J. Nucl. Med. **60**(11), 1629–1634 (2019)
3. Burchardt, E., Warenczak-Florczak, Z., Cegła, P., Piotrowski, A., Cybulski, Z., Burchardt, W., Roszak, A., Cholewiński, W.: Differences between [18F] FLT and [18F] FDG uptake in PET/CT imaging in CC depend on vaginal bacteriology. Diagnostics **12**(1), 70 (2021)
4. Christian, P., et al.: Optimization of 89Zr-PET clinical imaging for multi-site improved quantification and lesion detection using an anthropomorphic phantom (2018)
5. Dondi, F., Pasinetti, N., Gatta, R., Albano, D., Giubbini, R., Bertagna, F.: Comparison between two different scanners for the evaluation of the role of 18F-FDG PET/CT semiquantitative parameters and radiomics features in the prediction of final diagnosis of thyroid incidentalomas. J. Clin. Med. **11**(3), 615 (2022)
6. Girard, A., et al.: Impact of point-spread function reconstruction on dynamic and static 18F-DOPA PET/CT quantitative parameters in glioma. Quant. Imaging Med. Surg. **12**(2), 1397 (2022)
7. Hanafi, M.H., Noor, N.M., Hassan, M.H.: Inconsistency of lesion quantitative assessment in 2D SUV and 3D SUV quantification techniques for [18F]-FDG PET/CT: a phantom study. Mal. J. Med. Health Sci. **17**(2), 289–293 (2021)
8. Hoffmann, M.A., et al.: Comparison of [18F] PSMA-1007 with [68Ga] Ga-PSMA-11 PET/CT in restaging of prostate cancer patients with PSA relapse. Cancers **14**(6), 1479 (2022)
9. Lantos, J., Mittra, E.S., Levin, C.S., Iagaru, A.: Standard OSEM vs. regularized PET image reconstruction: qualitative and quantitative comparison using phantom data and various clinical radiopharmaceuticals. Am. J. Nucl. Med. Mol. Imaging **8**(2), 110 (2018)
10. Matheoud, R., et al.: Comparative analysis of iterative reconstruction algorithms with resolution recovery and time of flight modeling for 18F-FDG cardiac PET: a multi-center phantom study. J. Nucl. Cardiol. **24**(3), 1036–1045 (2017)
11. Pfaehler, E., et al.: Experimental multicenter and multivendor evaluation of pet radiomic features performance using 3D printed phantom inserts. J. Nucl. Med. **61**(3), 469–476 (2020). https://doi.org/10.2967/jnumed.119.229724
12. Shimada, N., et al.: A multi-center phantom study towards harmonization of FDG-PET: variability in maximum and peak SUV in relation to image noise (2020)
13. Shiri, I., Rahmim, A., Ghaffarian, P., Geramifar, P., Abdollahi, H., Bitarafan-Rajabi, A.: The impact of image reconstruction settings on 18F-FDG PET radiomic features: multi-scanner phantom and patient studies. Eur. Radiol. **27**(11), 4498–4509 (2017)
14. Zhang, X., et al.: Total-body dynamic reconstruction and parametric imaging on the uexplorer. J. Nucl. Med. **61**(2), 285–291 (2020)

# Unsupervised Medical Image Registration Based on Multi-scale Cascade Network

Yuying Ge, Xiao Ma, Qiang Chen, and Zexuan Ji[✉]

School of Computer Science and Engineering, Nanjing University of Science and Technology, Nanjing 210094, China
`jizexuan@njust.edu.cn`

**Abstract.** As a core technique of medical image analysis task, image registration is the process of finding the non-linear spatial correspondence among the input images. Comparing with supervised learning methods, unsupervised learning methods can ease the burden of manual annotation by exploiting unlabeled data without supervision. For high-resolution medical images, existing methods would maintain the consistency of the global structure and have limited matching accuracy in local details. Moreover, the intensity distribution of the warped image tends to the fixed image, which is quite different from the moving image. To solve the above problems, in this paper, we propose a multi-scale cascade network based on unsupervised end-to-end network registration method. We cascade the registration subnetworks with multi-scale strategy, which can extract local features more comprehensively and realize the registration from coarse to fine. The cascading procedure can further maintain the consistency of both global structure and local details for high-resolution medical images. The cyclic consistency loss is introduced to ensure the content consistency between the moving image and the warped image, and the structural consistency loss is used to ensure the structural consistency between the fixed image and the warped image. Experiments on three datasets demonstrate that our algorithm achieves state-of-the-art performance in medical image registration. The source code would be available online.

**Keywords:** Medical image registration · Cascade network · Multi-resolution registration

## 1 Introduction

Deformable image registration [1–4] is the main research direction in the field of medical image registration. In medical image registration, due to the development of the patient's condition and other factors, different images would have structural changes. Global alignment occurs in the registration process, while

---

**Supplementary Information** The online version contains supplementary material available at https://doi.org/10.1007/978-3-031-18910-4_21.

the degree of alignment in some details is ignored [5,6]. Therefore, non-rigid registration [7,8] is particularly important. Non-rigid medical registration mainly solves the problem of non-rigid deformation between fixed image and moving image.

In the existing methods, the non-rigid registration method has gradually become perfect, but there are still many shortcomings. Zhao et al. [9] proposed an unsupervised end-to-end cascade registration method for large displacement, which deals with the accuracy of large displacement registration through a joint training cascade network. Vos et al. [10] trained the next network after preserving the weight of the previous hierarchical network in sequence. Neither of these two training methods allows intermediate cascade to register a pair of images step by step. In the process of training, intermediate networks are not cooperative, and the information obtained after previous network training is not shared to the next layer network. Therefore, even if a deeper network is added, the performance of registration can hardly be improved. Zhao et al. [11] improved their previous method, in which each of their cascades commonly takes the current warped image and the fixed image as inputs and the similarity is only measured on the final warped image, enabling all cascades to learn progressive alignments cooperatively. However, if only the image with a fixed resolution is registered in cascade for several times, the feature information extracted from the network is limited, and the registration of details cannot be well taken into account and satisfactory results cannot be achieved.

To solve the above challenges, we propose an unsupervised registration method based on multi-scale cascade network. In the registration task, the large displacement deformation field is decomposed into small displacement deformation fields by using the cascade recursive network. The registration network adopts a UNet-like structure by adding jump connections between feature maps of different scales to reduce information loss in the process of downsampling. Therefore, the network can take into account both global and local information learning and improve the registration accuracy. Meanwhile, the multi-resolution strategy is adopted to register with low resolution at the beginning, and then improve the resolution at each layer. So the network can extract local features more comprehensively and realize the registration from coarse to fine. Moreover, we find that the intensity distribution of the warped image is inconsistent with the original moving image in many unsupervised learning-based registration models. If there is a lesion in the moving image, and the warped image would change the texture information of the lesion due to the influence of the fixed image, which will lead to a great misleading for the clinical diagnosis. Therefore, the cyclic consistency loss is introduced to ensure the content consistency between the moving image and the warped image. Furthermore, the structural consistency loss is used to ensure the structural consistency between the fixed image and the warped image. Experimental results show that our method has significant advantages in registration performance compared with several state-of-the-art methods.

# 2   Methods

## 2.1   Overview of Proposed Method

As shown in Fig. 1, we first feed the moving image and fixed image into the affine network. The affine registration network predicts a set of affine parameters, and then generates a flow field to warp the moving image. Then the moving image is input into the flow field, and the image is warped by Spatial Transformer Networks (STN) [12], which allows the neural network to learn how to perform spatial transformations on the input image to enhance the geometric invariance of the model. The STN warps the input image by sampling the grid through linear interpolation to calculate the grayscale of the corresponding points. Note that the warped image obtained by the affine registration network is first converted to low resolution through interpolation as output. In this work, we use a resolution of 128×128 in the first-layer affine registration network. We keep the resolution of fixed image consistent with that of warped image of the previous layer through interpolation. Then, the i-th warped image and the i-th fixed image(i represents the scale id of the cascading network) are fed into the registration network RegNet as input. A flow field is generated by the registration network, and then the warped image of the previous layer is fed into the flow field. A new warped image is generated with STN, and then the warped image is interpolated to twice that of the previous layer. The i-th fixed image is interpolated to obtain the same resolution as the i-th warped image, and then input into RegNet together. After cascaded five-layer network, the image resolution is finally restored to the original resolution and warped image after registration is generated. The process of unsupervised end-to-end learning is guided by the structural similarity between the i-th warped image and the i-th fixed image as well as the content similarity between the i-th warped image and the (i − 1)-th warped image.

## 2.2   Registration Neural Network

In the whole registration process, two backbone networks are involved, i.e. AffineNet and RegNet. One AffineNet is the affine registration network at the first layer, which is used to perform affine transformation on the moving image, so as to achieve initial alignment registration with the fixed image. AffineNet uses the same network structure as Affine Subnetwork in VTN [9]. The moving image and fixed image are splice and input into the network, and down-sampling is carried out through 2D convolution layer. Finally, six parameters are output through the full connection layer, representing a 2×2 affine transformation matrix and a 2-dimensional displacement vector b respectively. The flow field generated by affine registration network can be expressed as follows:

$$f(x) = A(x) + b \tag{1}$$

The moving image is transformed through the output affine transformation parameters, and then the transformed image is used as the input of the subsequent network.

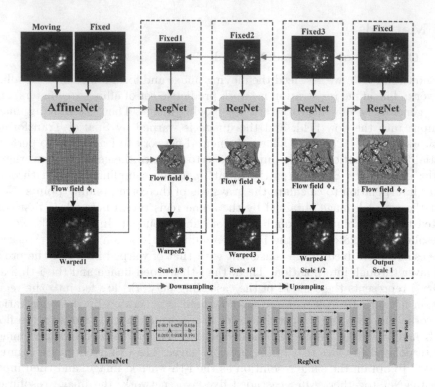

**Fig. 1.** An overview of the proposed registration methods.

RegNet is a deformable registration network. The warped image generated by the previous layer network and the fixed image adjusted by a specific resolution are spliced together as the input of the deformable registration network for each RegNet. In order to facilitate the whole registration process and reduce the computational burden, we use the same deformable registration network for each scale. RegNet is similar with Registration Subnetwork in VTN [9]. The feature convolution layer will concatenate to the corresponding upsampling layer, which can realize the effective use of feature maps for each layer and enhance the information representation of feature maps. RegNet outputs a dense flow field and a feature map with the same size as the input.

## 2.3 Loss Function

At present, the non-rigid registration method based on unsupervised end-to-end learning has become the mainstream research direction. If the deformation field produced by the traditional registration method is used as the monitoring information to train the network, it is easy to cause the over-fitting problem. To train our model in an unsupervised manner, we introduce loss functions to guide registration.

We used the correlation coefficient as a similarity measure. Suppose F is represented as fixed image, M is moving image, and $\phi$ is flow field, the similarity between M and F is expressed as

$$L_{sim}(F, M) = 1 - \frac{Cov[F, M]}{\sqrt{Cov[F, F]\, Cov[M, M]}} \tag{2}$$

where Cov is the covariance, which can be expressed as

$$Cov[F, M] = \frac{1}{|\Omega|} \sum_{x \in \Omega} F(x) M(x) - \frac{1}{|\Omega|^2} \sum_{x \in \Omega} F(x) \sum_{y \in \Omega} M(y) \tag{3}$$

where $\Omega$ denotes the cuboid (or grid) on which the input images are defined.

In the training process, by maximizing the similarity measure of images, discontinuous deformation field is often generated in the network, so we add a spatial smoothness constraint to the predicted deformation field.

$$L_{smooth}(\phi) = \sum_{p \in \Omega} ||\nabla \phi(p)||^2 \tag{4}$$

In addition, since the image needs to be similar with fixed image in structure and be similar with moving image in content after registration, structural similarity and cycle consistency loss are used to guide registration. The formula for structural similarity is based on three attributes between images F and M, i.e. brightness, contrast, and structure. Mean value is used to estimate brightness, standard deviation can estimate contrast, and covariance is utilized to estimate structural similarity. An N*N window is taken, and the window is continuously sliding for calculation. Finally, the average value is taken as the global structural similarity.

Cycle consistency means that for moving image and fixed image, warped image is generated after the moving image is registered to the fixed image, and then the warped image is registered back to the moving image. To ensure the consistency of moving image and warped image in content distribution, cycle consistency and bidirectional registration have similar ideas but different effects. In the cycle consistent registration, fixed image does not change, and the input task is only the moving image registration to fixed image. In bidirectional registration, the moving image is registered to the fixed image and the fixed image is registered to the moving image. The cycle consistency loss can be defined as

$$\begin{aligned} L_{cycle}(F, M) = E_{x \sim p_{data}(x)}\left[||F(M(x)) - x||_1\right] \\ + E_{y \sim p_{data}(y)}\left[||M(F(y)) - y||_1\right] \end{aligned} \tag{5}$$

where E represents expectation, $p_{data}$ represents distribution of real data, $|| \cdot ||_1$ denotes the l1-norm.

We use structural similarity loss [13] to ensure structural consistency between warped image and fixed image. Structural similarity loss is similar to the human visual system (HVS), which is sensitive to local structural changes. Structural similarity loss can be defined as

$$L_{ssim}(F, M) = 1 - \frac{(2\mu_F\mu_M + c_1)(2\sigma_{FM} + c_2)}{(\mu_F^2 + \mu_M^2 + c_1)(\sigma_F^2 + \sigma_M^2 + c_2)} \tag{6}$$

where $\mu$ represents the mean of the image, $\sigma$ represents the variance of the image.

Consequently, the total loss function of the proposed model can be summarized as follows

$$L_{total}(F, M, \phi) = L_{sim}(F, M) + \lambda L_{smooth}(\phi) + L_{ssim}(F, M) + L_{cycle}(F, M) \tag{7}$$

## 3   Result

### 3.1   Experimental Design

We trained and evaluated our method on three data sets, i.e. ADNI [14], RIRE [15], and UWF [16]. The ADNI dataset is a combination of brain MRI and PET information collected from people of different ages in order to study the causes of Alzheimer's disease which contains 200 pairs of MRI-PET images. RIRE is designed to compare retrospective CT-MR and PET-MR registration techniques used by a number of groups which contains 109 pairs of CT-MR images. UWF is an ultra-wide-angle image of the retinal region, which contains 399 pairs of UWFA images on the early and late phases from 280 diabetics and 119 normal subjects. For each dataset, we cropped the paired images to $1024 \times 1024$. We compared the proposed method with traditional registration methods, including SIFT [17] and Voxel [18], RSC [11], LapIRN [19], ProsReg-Net [20], MICDIR [21]. All experiments were conducted on NVIDIA Tesla T4 GPU.

### 3.2   Qualitative Results

Figure 2 shows the registration results for all the comparison methods on three data sets. In each subfigure, the bottom image is the enlarge view of the area with red box in the top image. In the first row, only our method is depressed on the structure circled by red box, which is consistent with the structure of fixed image in this part. In addition, our performance is also excellent for the registration of local vascular details. It can be observed from the third row that in terms of the registration effect of the shape of the brain, our size and shape are the closest to the moving image, which is consistent with the original intention due to the effect of circular consistency loss. The fifth row shows the CT-MRI registration. It can be seen from the red box that our method also achieves satisfactory results, indicating that our method is not only suitable for single-mode registration, but also for multi-mode registration. The qualitative results proves the superiority of our registration method.

| Fixed | Moving | Sift | Voxel | RSC | LapIRN | ProsRegNet | MICDIR | Our |

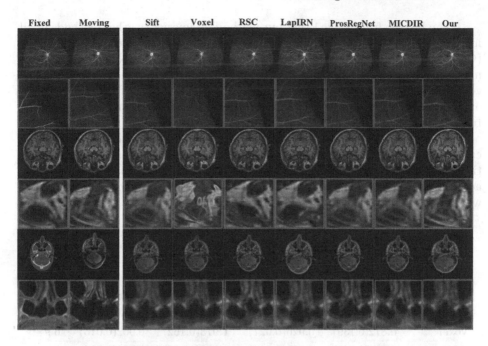

**Fig. 2.** Qualitative comparison results on three datasets. The first row are the result of registration on UWF, the third row are the result of registration on ADNI, and the fifth row are the result of registration on RIRE. The second, fourth, and sixth rows are the enlarge view of the area with red box in the corresponding top image. (Color figure online)

## 3.3    Quantitative Results

We evaluated our method using five evaluation indicators on three data sets, including DSC, SSIM, MI, CC, Time. DSC measures the degree of overlap between ROI in the image after registration and ROI in the fixed image, and its value range is [0,1]. The closer it is to 1, the higher the overlap degree will be. SSIM can measure the structural similarity between the registered image and fixed image. MI can measure the probability distribution of the intensity of fixed image and moving image, which has great reference value for evaluating the effectiveness of the cyclic consistency loss in our method. CC measures the correlation degree between the image after registration and the fixed image, and its value range is [−1,1]. The closer the value is to 1, the higher the correlation degree of the two images will be. Time will test the efficiency of our method.

It can be seen from Table 1 that our method is superior to other methods in all indicators of ADNI data set. For the UWF data set, our correlation coefficient (CC) is lower than that of LapIRN. This is because LapIRN, on the basis of multi-resolution, also ensures good differential properties, which makes it show good performance in the face of complex vascular structure. Table 3 shows that our DSC is slightly lower than ProsRegNet and higher than the other methods. In terms of SSIM and MI indicators, our performance on the three data sets is optimal, which also depends on the characteristics of our method. Moreover, it can be seen from the three tables that our method has a very short registration time, indicating that our method is also very efficient. In general, our method has achieved excellent results in all indicators, which also proves that our method is worthy of affirmation (Table 2).

**Table 1.** Quantitative results on ADNI datasets for all the comparison methods.

| Methods | DSC | SSIM | MI | CC | Time |
|---|---|---|---|---|---|
| Affine | 0.841(0.171) | 0.854(0.112) | 1.929(0.239) | 0.878(0.058) | 7 s |
| Sift | 0.843(0.140) | 0.873(0.103) | 1.955(0.173) | 0.883(0.045) | 9 s |
| Voxel | 0.872(0.139) | 0.926(0.027) | 1.973(0.162) | 0.902(0.015) | 6 s |
| RSC | 0.896(0.142) | 0.928(0.012) | 1.972(0.154) | 0.913(0.036) | 6 s |
| LapIRN | 0.892(0.036) | 0.925(0.021) | 1.980(0.101) | 0.914(0.017) | 5 s |
| ProsRegNet | 0.913(0.024) | 0.923(0.019) | 1.981(0.126) | 0.912(0.021) | 4 s |
| MICDIR | 0.902(0.016) | 0.917(0.014) | 1.976(0.118) | 0.911(0.032) | 4 s |
| **Ours** | **0.915(0.016)** | **0.932(0.037)** | **1.983(0.132)** | **0.915(0.041)** | **3 s** |

**Table 2.** Quantitative results on UWF datasets for all the comparison methods.

| Methods | DSC | SSIM | MI | CC | Time |
|---|---|---|---|---|---|
| Affine | 0.686(0.034) | 0.816(0.101) | 1.523(0.162) | 0.842(0.012) | 8 s |
| Sift | 0.701(0.182) | 0.818(0.092) | 1.463(0.149) | 0.867(0.031) | 11 s |
| Voxel | 0.719(0.016) | 0.821(0.124) | 1.529(0.151) | 0.870(0.016) | 5 s |
| RSC | 0.725(0.130) | 0.821(0.083) | 1.547(0.120) | 0.872(0.024) | 6 s |
| LapIRN | 0.720(0.111) | 0.822(0.026) | 1.542(0.150) | **0.876(0.029)** | **4 s** |
| ProsRegNet | 0.721(0.250) | 0.822(0.104) | 1.545(0.169) | 0.873(0.054) | 5 s |
| MICDIR | 0.724(0.179) | 0.821(0.121) | 1.546(0.103) | 0.872(0.102) | 6 s |
| **Ours** | **0.726(0.211)** | **0.823(0.119)** | **1.548(0.138)** | 0.874(0.014) | 5 s |

**Table 3.** Quantitative results on the RIRE datasets for all the comparison methods.

| Methods | Dice | SSIM | MI | CC | Time |
|---|---|---|---|---|---|
| Affine | 0.810(0.021) | 0.826(0.201) | 1.837(0.042) | 0.819(0.032) | 9 s |
| Sift | 0.811(0.103) | 0.819(0.038) | 1.840(0.126) | 0.821(0.047) | 10 s |
| Voxel | 0.818(0.097) | 0.837(0.156) | 1.843(0.114) | 0.820(0.015) | 7 s |
| RSC | 0.819(0.251) | 0.840(0.172) | 1.843(0.260) | 0.822(0.019) | 8 s |
| LapIRN | 0.817(0.027) | 0.843(0.112) | 1.847(0.089) | 0.821(0.025) | 8 s |
| ProsRegNet | **0.822(0.204)** | 0.842(0.108) | 1.845(0.163) | 0.820(0.016) | 5 s |
| MICDIR | 0.817(0.102) | 0.843(0.152) | 1.844(0.125) | 0.821(0.030) | 5 s |
| **Ours** | 0.820(0.034) | **0.845(0.140)** | **1.850(0.145)** | **0.823(0.020)** | 4 s |

## 4    Conclusion

This paper proposes a medical image registration method based on multi-resolution cascaded network. Different from the previous method that simply cascaded the network, our method uses different resolutions at each level of cascaded network, so that the network can learn more comprehensive information. The proposed model can realize the gradual alignment from coarse to fine, and give better consideration to the global and local details registration. At the same time, structural consistency and cyclic consistency loss are added to ensure the structural consistency between the image and fixed image and the content consistency between the image and moving image after registration. Experiments show that our method achieves excellent performance. In addition, our network is very flexible and can change the layers and resolution size of the cascade network according to different datasets.

**Acknowledgement.** This work was supported by the National Natural Science Foundation of China under Grant NO. 62072241.

## References

1. Sotiras, A., Davatzikos, C., Paragios, N.: Deformable medical image registration: a survey. IEEE Trans. Med. Imaging **32**(7), 1153–1190 (2013)
2. Mok, T.C.W., Chung, A.C.S.: Conditional deformable image registration with convolutional neural network. In: de Bruijne, M., et al. (eds.) MICCAI 2021. LNCS, vol. 12904, pp. 35–45. Springer, Cham (2021). https://doi.org/10.1007/978-3-030-87202-1_4
3. Dalca, A.V., Balakrishnan, G., Guttag, J., Sabuncu, M.R.: Unsupervised learning for fast probabilistic diffeomorphic registration. In: Frangi, A.F., Schnabel, J.A., Davatzikos, C., Alberola-López, C., Fichtinger, G. (eds.) MICCAI 2018. LNCS, vol. 11070, pp. 729–738. Springer, Cham (2018). https://doi.org/10.1007/978-3-030-00928-1_82

4. Rohé, M.-M., Datar, M., Heimann, T., Sermesant, M., Pennec, X.: SVF-Net: learning deformable image registration using shape matching. In: Descoteaux, M., Maier-Hein, L., Franz, A., Jannin, P., Collins, D.L., Duchesne, S. (eds.) MICCAI 2017. LNCS, vol. 10433, pp. 266–274. Springer, Cham (2017). https://doi.org/10.1007/978-3-319-66182-7_31

5. Wang, M., Li, P.: A review of deformation models in medical image registration. J. Med. Biol. Eng. **39**(1), 1–17 (2019)

6. Yang, X., Kwitt, R., Niethammer, M.: Fast predictive image registration. In: Carneiro, G., et al. (eds.) LABELS/DLMIA -2016. LNCS, vol. 10008, pp. 48–57. Springer, Cham (2016). https://doi.org/10.1007/978-3-319-46976-8_6

7. Krebs, J., et al.: Robust non-rigid registration through agent-based action learning. In: Descoteaux, M., Maier-Hein, L., Franz, A., Jannin, P., Collins, D.L., Duchesne, S. (eds.) MICCAI 2017. LNCS, vol. 10433, pp. 344–352. Springer, Cham (2017). https://doi.org/10.1007/978-3-319-66182-7_40

8. Hua, R., Pozo, J.M., Taylor, Z.A., Frangi, A.F.: Multiresolution eXtended Free-Form Deformations (XFFD) for non-rigid registration with discontinuous transforms. Med. Image Anal. **36**, 113–122 (2017)

9. Zhao, S., Lau, T., Luo, J., Eric, I., Chang, C., Xu, Y.: Unsupervised 3D end-to-end medical image registration with volume tweening network. IEEE J. Biomed. Health Inform. **24**(5), 1394–1404 (2019)

10. De Vos, B.D., et al.: A deep learning framework for unsupervised affine and deformable image registration. Med. Image Anal. **52**, 128–143 (2019)

11. Zhao, S., Dong, Y., Chang, E.I., Xu, Y.: Recursive cascaded networks for unsupervised medical image registration. In: 2019 IEEE/CVF International Conference on Computer Vision, pp. 10600–10610. IEEE (2019)

12. Jaderberg, M., Simonyan, K., Zisserman, A.: Spatial transformer networks. In: Advances in Neural Information Processing Systems 28 (2015)

13. Wang, Z., Bovik, A.C., Sheikh, H.R., Simoncelli, E.P.: Image quality assessment: from error visibility to structural similarity. IEEE Trans. Image Process. **13**(4), 600–612 (2004)

14. Petersen, R.C., Aisen, P.S., Beckett, L.A., et al.: Alzheimer's disease neuroimaging initiative (ADNI): clinical characterization. Neurology **74**(3), 201–209 (2010)

15. West, J., Fitzpatrick, J.M., Wang, M.Y., et al.: Comparison and evaluation of retrospective intermodality brain image registration techniques. J. Comput. Assist. Tomogr. **21**(4), 554–568 (1997)

16. Wang, X., et al.: Automated grading of diabetic retinopathy with ultra-widefield fluorescein angiography and deep learning. J. Diabetes Res. (2021). https://doi.org/10.1155/2021/2611250

17. Yi, Z., Zhiguo, C., Yang, X.: Multi-spectral remote image registration based on SIFT. Electron. Lett. **44**(2), 107–108 (2008)

18. Balakrishnan, G., Zhao, A., Sabuncu, M.R., et al.: VoxelMorph: a learning framework for deformable medical image registration. IEEE Trans. Med. Imaging **38**(8), 1788–1800 (2019)

19. Mok, T.C.W., Chung, A.C.S.: Large deformation diffeomorphic image registration with Laplacian pyramid networks. In: Martel, A.L., et al. (eds.) MICCAI 2020. LNCS, vol. 12263, pp. 211–221. Springer, Cham (2020). https://doi.org/10.1007/978-3-030-59716-0_21

20. Shao, W., et al.: ProsRegNet: a deep learning framework for registration of MRI and histopathology images of the prostate. Med. Image Anal. **68**, 101919 (2021)
21. Chatterjee, S., Bajaj, H., Siddiquee, I.H., et al.: MICDIR: multi-scale inverse-consistent deformable image registration using UNetMSS with self-constructing graph latent. arXiv preprint arXiv:2203, 04317 (2022)

# A Novel Local-Global Spatial Attention Network for Cortical Cataract Classification in AS-OCT

Zunjie Xiao[1], Xiaoqing Zhang[1], Qingyang Sun[1], Zhuofei Wei[1], Gelei Xu[1], Yuan Jin[3], Risa Higashita[1,2], and Jiang Liu[1,4(✉)]

[1] Research Institute of Trustworthy Autonomous Systems and Department of Computer Science and Engineering, Southern University of Science and Technology, Shenzhen 518055, China
liuj@sustech.edu.cn
[2] TOMEY Corporation, Nagoya 4510051, Japan
k-chen@tomey.co.jp
[3] Zhongshan Ophthalmic Center, Sun Yat-sen University, Guangzhou 510060, China
[4] Guangdong Provincial Key Laboratory of Brain-inspired Intelligent Computation, Southern University of Science and Technology, Shenzhen 518055, China

**Abstract.** Cataracts are the leading causes of reversible blindness and visual impairment. Cortical cataract (CC) is one of the most common cataract types. Early intervention is a useful way to improve the vision of CC patients. Anterior segment optical coherence tomography (AS-OCT) is a new ophthalmic image type that can capture the cortex region clearly. To our best knowledge, no previous work has paid attention to AS-OCT image-based CC classification. Thus, this paper presents an effective local-global spatial fusion network (LGSF-Net) to automatically recognize the severity levels of CC. In the LGSF-Net, we construct a novel local-global spatial fusion (LGSF) attention block by incorporating the clinical prior knowledge of CC. The extensive experiments conduct on the CASIA2 AS-OCT dataset of CC, and the results show that our LGSF-Net achieves better performance than state-of-the-art attention-based convolutional neural networks (CNNs). Moreover, we also demonstrate the generalization of our method on the public ChestXRay2017 dataset through comparisons to existing methods.

**Keywords:** Cortical cataract classification · AS-OCT · Local-global

## 1 Introduction

Cataracts are one of the most common ocular diseases of blindness and visual impairment in the world. According to the World Health Organization (WHO), by 2025, the number of blind patients caused by cataracts would reach 40 million worldwide [2]. According to the opacity location in the lens area, cataracts are generally grouped into three types: posterior subcapsular cataract (PSC), cortical cataract (CC), and nuclear cataract (NC). CC is the most common cataract

S. Yu et al. (Eds.): PRCV 2022, LNCS 13535, pp. 262–273, 2022.
https://doi.org/10.1007/978-3-031-18910-4_22

type, which forms spoke-like lines that lead into the centre of the cortical region in the lens. Under the standard of opacities classification system III (LOCS III) [19], the severity levels of CC can be divided into three stages according to clinical treatment [1]: normal, mild, and severe. Normal means healthy; Mild CC patients have asymptomatic opacity in the cortex, which can be relieved by early drug intervention; Severe CC patients have symptomatic opacity in the cortex, which requires surgery to cure.

Over the past years, researchers have developed computer-aided diagnosis (CAD) techniques for CC based on retro-illumination images [7,18,30]. For instance, Li et al. [17] proposed an automatic CC classification system in retro-illumination images. Following that, [7] proposed an enhanced texture feature for CC classification and achieved 84.8% accuracy. Anterior segment optical coherence tomography (AS-OCT) image is a new ophthalmic image type, which has been widely applied to ocular disease diagnosis, e.g., NC [26,31,32], glaucoma [6,20]. Compared with retro-illumination images, AS-OCT can capture both posterior and anterior cortex regions. However, no existing works have used AS-OCT images for automatic CC recognition.

To this end, we firstly proposed a local-global spatial fusion network (LGSF-Net) for automatic CC classification based on AS-OCT images. In the LGSF-net, we construct a local-global spatial fusion (LGSF) block by infusing the prior knowledge of CC, which fuses spatial feature representation information of anterior cortex-, posterior cortex-, and whole cortex- regions with three independent spatial attention blocks concurrently. To validate the effectiveness of our LGSF-Net, we conduct comprehensive experiments on the CASIA2 AS-OCT dataset of CC. The results show that our method achieves better performance than state-of-the-art attention-based convolutional neural networks (CNNs). For example, LGSF-ResNet34 obtains **92.48%** of accuracy and outperforms SRM with **3.43%** of accuracy. A public ChestXRay2017 dataset is used to demonstrate the generalization of LGSF-Net. Overall, the main contributions of this paper are summarized as follows:

- To the best of our understanding, this paper first proposes a novel CNN model named LGSF-Net for automatic AS-OCT-based CC classification.
- In the LGSF-Net, we construct a novel local-global spatial fusion attention (LGSF) block by incorporating the clinical prior knowledge, which is capable of highlighting more informative spatial feature representations and suppressing less important ones.
- We conduct experiments on the CASIA2 AS-OCT dataset and a public ChestXRay2017 dataset. The results show that our LGSF-Net performs better than strong baselines, demonstrating the effectiveness of our method.

## 2   Related Work

### 2.1   Automatic Cataract Classification

In the past years, CAD techniques have been widely applied to automatic cataract screening and classification based on different ophthalmic image types, such as slit-lamp images, fundus images, and AS-OCT images [15,16]. Xu et al. [28] developed the similarity weighted linear reconstruction (SWLR) method to predict the NC severity levels by using slit-lamp images. Zhou et al. [34] used fundus images for cataract screening with a deep neural network and achieved good classification results. Li et al. [17] detected CC based on retro-illumination images with a combination of canny edge detection and Laplacian filter. Gao et al. [7] further improved CC detection by extracting the texture features. Zhang et al. [31] proposed a novel CNN model named GraNet to classify the severity levels of NC based on AS-OCT images but obtained poor classification performance. Following the [31], [26,32,33] developed attention-based CNNs to classify AS-OCT image-based NC severity levels by considering the clinical prior knowledge of cataracts.

## 2.2  Attention Mechanism

Attention mechanisms have proved that they are capable of empowering the feature representations of CNNs on various learning tasks [22], e.g., medical image analysis. In general, attention mechanisms can be mainly grouped into three basic categories: channel attention, spatial attention, and the combination of channel attention and spatial attention.

Squeeze-and-Excitation network SENet [11] firstly proposed the channel attention mechanism, which aimed at recalibrating the relative weights of channels from convolutional layers. Inspired by SENet, various channel attention mechanism variants have been proposed to make CNNs pay more attention to informative channels and ignore useless ones. Efficient channel attention network (ECANet) [23] introduced a cross-channel interaction method for channel attention design. Lee et al. [14] constructed a style-based recalibration module (SRM) by adjusting the relative importance of styles in CNNs with a channel-independent style integration method. The spatial attention mechanism is another attention mechanism that can be considered an adaptive spatial location selection procedure. [27] pioneered the use of spatial attention mechanism, which first proposed two attention mechanisms (soft attention and hard attention) to select important spatial locations adaptively. Following [27], Non-Local [24] introduced the self-attention mechanism in computer vision for establishing the global relationship to recalibrate the relative weights in the spatial domain. However, self-attention also introduced much computation complexity at the same time. Therefore, GENet [10] proposed a lightweight spatial attention mechanism to efficiently establish a global relationship. Otherwise, Bottleneck attention module (BAM) [21] and convolutional block attention module (CBAM) [25] adopt a combination of both two attention mechanisms to further enhance the feature representation of CNNs.

## 3  Method

Figure 1(a) presents the general flowchart of the proposed Local-global spatial fusion network (LGSF-Net) for automatic CC classification based on AS-OCT

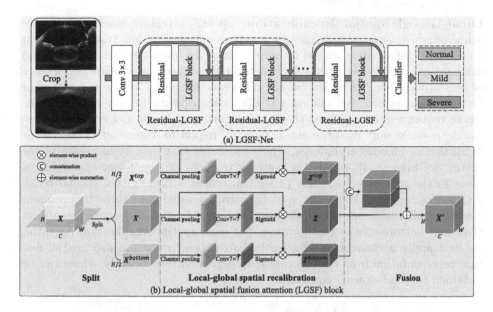

**Fig. 1.** In (a), a framework of the Local-global spatial fusion network (LGSF-Net) is used to generate the severity levels of CC based on AS-OCT images. In the LGSF-Net, we construct a local-global spatial fusion attention (LGSF) block (b) by injecting the clinical prior knowledge of CC, and then combine it with a residual block to the Residual-LGSF module. The proposed LGSF-Net is built on a stack of Residual-LGSF modules, and a classifier is used to generate the three severity levels of CC: normal, mild, and severe.

images. We adopt ShuffleSeg Network [3] to crop the whole cortex region from the original AS-OCT image and resize it into $224 \times 224$ as the inputs of LGSF-Net. In the LGSF-Net, we design an effective local-global spatial fusion attention (LGSF) block, as shown in Fig. 1(b)) to adaptively recalibrate the relative importance of spatial feature representation information in a local-global manner. Finally, a classifier automatically predicts the three severity levels of CC: normal, mild, and severe.

### 3.1 Local-Global Spatial Fusion Attention (LGSF) Block

Given an input $X \in \mathbb{R}^{H \times W \times C}$, our LGSF block can generate a augmented feature representations $X' \in \mathbb{R}^{H \times W \times C}$ in a local-global manner. The detailed structure of our LGSF block is presented in Fig. 1(b), which consists of three operators, split, local-global spatial recalibration, and fusion.

**Split:** For the input feature map $X$, we split it along with the height dimension and obtain the top half region $X^{top} \in \mathbb{R}^{H/2 \times W \times C}$ and bottom half region $X^{bottom} \in \mathbb{R}^{H/2 \times W \times C}$, respectively.

**Local-Global Spatial Recalibration:** Spatial attention mechanisms have achieved surpassing performance in various computer vision tasks, aiming at focusing on informative spatial locations. However, published spatial attention mechanisms usually adopt a global method to adjust the relative importance of spatial locations, which ignores the difference in spatial locations in different feature map regions. For clinical CC diagnosis, opacity usually occurs in the whole cortex region, including the anterior cortex and posterior cortex regions. Previous works only used the anterior cortex region to diagnose CC due to the limitation of imaging techniques, which indicates that opacity locations in the cortex are uneven. To enable the network to focus on significant opacity locations in the cortex regions, this paper constructs a Local-global spatial recalibration operator to follow the split operator, consisting of three independent spatial recalibration operators: whole-spatial recalibration, top-spatial recalibration, and bottom-spatial recalibration. For each spatial recalibration operator, we first apply a channel pooling method to extract *max* and *avg* spatial feature representation from each feature map region correspondingly, which can be obtained by the following equations:

$$\mu(i,j) = \frac{1}{C} \sum_{c=1}^{C} X_c(i,j) \quad (1 \le i \le H, 1 \le j \le W), \tag{1}$$

$$\mu^{top}(i,j) = \frac{1}{C} \sum_{c=1}^{C} X_c^{top}(i,j) \quad (1 \le i \le H/2, 1 \le j \le W), \tag{2}$$

$$\mu^{bottom}(i,j) = \frac{1}{C} \sum_{c=1}^{C} X_c^{bottom}(i,j) \quad (1 \le i \le H/2, 1 \le j \le W), \tag{3}$$

$$M(i,j) = max(\{x_c | x_c \in X(i,j)\} \quad (1 \le i \le H, 1 \le j \le W)), \tag{4}$$

$$M^{top}(i,j) = max(\{x_c | x_c \in X^{top}(i,j)\}) \quad (1 \le i \le H/2, 1 \le j \le W), \tag{5}$$

$$M^{bottom}(i,j) = max(\{x_c | x_c \in X^{bottom}(i,j)\}) \quad (1 \le i \le H/2, 1 \le j \le W), \tag{6}$$

where $(\cdot)(i,j)$ denotes the feature in spatial position $(i,j)$ and $(\cdot)_c$ denotes the feature map in $c$-th channel, e.g., $X_c(i,j)$ represent the $c$-th channel value of $X$ in position $(i,j)$; $\mu \in \mathbb{R}^{H/2 \times W}$, $\mu_{top} \in \mathbb{R}^{H/2 \times W}$ and $\mu_{bottom} \in \mathbb{R}^{H/2 \times W}$ denote the *avg* representations through channel average pool, similarly, $M \in \mathbb{R}^{H \times W}$, $M_{top} \in \mathbb{R}^{H/2 \times W}$ and $M_{bottom} \in \mathbb{R}^{H/2 \times W}$ denote the *max* features through channel maximum pooling. Then we apply a convolution layer to integrate representation features into the spatial weights map. The overall process can be summarized as:

$$Z = \sigma(f^{7 \times 7}([\mu; M])) \otimes X = F_s \otimes X, \tag{7}$$

$$Z^{top} = \sigma(f^{7 \times 7}([\mu^{top}; M^{top}])) \otimes X^{top} = F_s^{top} \otimes X^{top}, \tag{8}$$

$$Z^{bottom} = \sigma(f^{7 \times 7}([\mu^{bottom}; M^{bottom}])) \otimes X^{bottom} = F_s^{bottom} \otimes X^{bottom}, \tag{9}$$

where $\sigma$ denotes the *sigmoid* function, $f^{7 \times 7}$ denotes the convolution operator with $7 \times 7$ kernel size and $\otimes$ denotes element-wise production; $[]$ denotes concatenation over channels. $F_s$, $F_s^{top}$ and $F_s^{bottom}$ denote the spatial weights maps; $z$, $z^{top}$ and $z^{bottom}$ denote the spatial recalibrated features of the whole-, top- and bottom-, respectively.

**Fusion:** For the recalibrated features $Z$, $Z^{top}$ and $Z^{bottom}$ given by local-global spatial recalibration, we fuse them as follows:

$$X' = Concat(Z_{top}, Z_{bottom}) + Z, \tag{10}$$

where $Concat$ denotes concatenation over height dimension, which is a reverse of split operation; $X'$ denotes the final output of our LGSF block.

## 3.2   Network Architecture

ResNet [9] is a widely-used backbone network for various attention methods, such as SE [11], GCA [26], ECA [23], and CBAM [25]. These attention methods can be used as strong baselines to demonstrate the effectiveness of our LGSF block. As shown in Fig. 1(a), we combine the Residual block with the LGSF block to construct a Residual-LGSF module.

Given an input $X$, the output of the Residual-LGSF module can be formulated as:

$$S = LGSF(Residual(X)) + X. \tag{11}$$

As a comparison, the formulation of the basic Residual block is:

$$S = Residual(X) + X. \tag{12}$$

*LGSF* denotes the LGSF block and *Residual* denotes the Residual block in ResNet.

LGSF-Net is comprised of a convolutional layer, multiple Residual-LGSF modules, a global average pooling layer, a fully-connected layer (FC), and a classifier. This paper adopts softmax as the classifier and cross-entropy (CE) as the loss function, respectively.

# 4   Experiment and Result

## 4.1   Dataset

**CASIA2 AS-OCT Dataset:** We collected a clinical AS-OCT image dataset using the CASIA2 ophthalmology device (Tomey Corporation, Japan), namely CASIA2 AS-OCT dataset. The dataset comprises 279 right eyes and 263 left eyes from 303 participants. We collected 16 AS-OCT images from each eye and deleted low-quality images with the cooperation of ophthalmologists due to the effects of poorly opened eyelids. Overall, available images for 1,151 normal, 2,109 mild CC, and 1,672 severe CC. We use a deep segmentation network [3] to crop

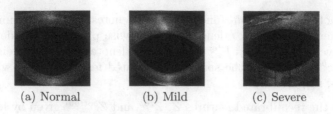

(a) Normal          (b) Mild          (c) Severe

**Fig. 2.** AS-OCT images for three severity levels of cortical cataract.

the cortex region from the anterior segment structure based on AS-OCT images. Due to lacking a standard cataract classification system in AS-OCT images, we map labels of AS-OCT images from slit-lamp images. Three experienced ophthalmologists labeled slit-lamp images based on LOCS III, confirming label quality. Figure 2 lists examples of each CC severity level on AS-OCT images.

We divide the CASIA2 AS-OCT dataset into three disjoint sub-datasets at the participant level: training, validation, and testing, which confirms AS-OCT images of each participant fall into the same sub-datasets. The image number of normal, mild, and severe in training dataset is 676, 1529, 1511; the image number of normal, mild, and severe in validation dataset is 242, 252, 83; and the image number of normal, mild, and severe in testing dataset is 233, 328, 78, respectively.

**ChestXRay2017 Dataset:** It is collected by Guangzhou Women and Children's Medical Center, Guangzhou, and contains a training dataset and a testing dataset [12]. The training dataset included 3,883 pneumonia images and 1,349 normal images, and the test set included 390 pneumonia images (242 bacterial and 148 viral) and 234 normal images.

### 4.2 Evaluation Metrics

We use five commonly-used evaluation metrics: accuracy ($Acc$), recall ($Rec$), precision ($Pre$), F1 score ($F1$) and kappa coefficient ($Kappa$) value to evaluate the performance of the model. The calculation formulas are as follows:

$$Acc = \frac{TP + TN}{TP + FP + TN + FN}, \tag{13}$$

$$Rec = \frac{TP}{TP + FN}, \tag{14}$$

$$Pre = \frac{TP}{TP + FP}, \tag{15}$$

$$F1 = 2 \times \frac{Rec \times Pre}{Rec + Pre}, \tag{16}$$

where TP, FP, TN, and FN denote True Positive, False Positive, True Negative, and False Negative, respectively.

$$Kappa = \frac{p_0 - p_e}{1 - p_0}, \tag{17}$$

where $p_0$ denotes the relative observed agreement among raters, and $p_e$ denotes the hypothetical probability of chance agreement.

## 4.3  Experiment Setting

On CASIA2 AS-OCT and ChestXRay2017 dataset, our LGSF-Net and other comparable models are trained on an NVIDIA TITAN V (11 GB RAM) GPU with a batch size 16 for 150 epochs. All the input images are resized to $224 \times 224$ pixels and implemented standard data augmentation methods like the random flipping method and the random cropping method for training images. The initial learning rate (lr) is 0.0035 and reduced by a factor of 10 every 50 epochs, and the optimizer is stochastic gradient descent (SGD) with a momentum of 0.9 and a weight decay of 1e−4.

**Table 1.** Performance comparisons of our LGSF-Net and advanced attention-based methods on the CIASIA2 AS-OCT dataset. (The best results are labeled in **bold**.)

| Method | Backbone | Acc/% | Pre/% | Rec/% | F1/% | Kappa/% |
|---|---|---|---|---|---|---|
| ResNet18 [9] | | 84.19 | 81.43 | 82.36 | 81.59 | 73.57 |
| SE [11] | | 87.32 | 80.72 | 81.94 | 81.29 | 78.65 |
| CBAM [25] | | 88.11 | 83.18 | **83.30** | 83.23 | 79.79 |
| GCA [26] | ResNet18 | 85.91 | 80.27 | 80.65 | 80.27 | 76.09 |
| SRM [14] | | 86.39 | 80.65 | 84.02 | 82.01 | 77.39 |
| ECA [23] | | 84.51 | 77.98 | 79.05 | 78.48 | 73.88 |
| BAM [21] | | 82.79 | 77.23 | 82.12 | 78.43 | 71.96 |
| LGSF(ours) | | **89.83** | **91.71** | 81.89 | **85.32** | **82.07** |
| ResNet34 [9] | | 86.39 | 84.31 | 77.78 | 80.21 | 76.09 |
| SE [11] | | 84.98 | 79.44 | 76.87 | 81.29 | 78.65 |
| CBAM [25] | | 83.18 | 88.70 | 83.43 | 85.51 | 82.13 |
| GCA [26] | ResNet34 | 81.22 | 74.40 | 78.14 | 75.15 | 69.57 |
| SRM [14] | | 89.05 | 84.01 | 84.12 | 84.03 | 81.37 |
| ECA [23] | | 85.76 | 79.48 | 78.81 | 79.11 | 75.73 |
| BAM [21] | | 88.42 | 83.26 | 84.81 | 83.85 | 80.45 |
| LGSF(ours) | | **92.48** | **93.71** | **86.81** | **89.49** | **86.96** |

## 4.4  Comparison with State-of-the-Art Methods on CASIA2 AS-OCT Dataset

Table 1 shows the classification results of our LGSF block with other stat-of-the-art attention blocks based on ResNet18 and ResNet34. Our LGSF block continuously improves the CC classification performance over other attention methods on CASIA2 AS-OCT dataset. For instance, LGSF-ResNet18 outperforms CBAM-ResNet18 by **1.72%** accuracy and **2.28%** of kappa value. Under the ResNet34 backbone, our LGSF block achieves **92.48%** of accuracy, **91.71%** of precision, 86.81% of sensitive, **89.49%** of F1, and **86.96%** of kappa value. Compared with SRM and GCA, LGSF-ReNet34 achieves **3.26%**, **2.21%**, **5.59%** gains of accuracy, F1 and kappa, demonstrating the superiority of our method. Especially, SE, GCA and CBAM hurt the performance on ResNet34 backbone, which demonstrates the generalization of our LGSF block.

## 4.5   Ablation Study

In this section, we adopt the local spatial attention block and global spatial attention block to test the effectiveness of the proposed Local-global spatial fusion attention (LGSF) block. In the global spatial attention block, we only use the whole-spatial recalibration; and in the local spatial attention block, we use top-spatial recalibration and bottom-spatial recalibration. Table 2 shows the classification results of three different spatial attention blocks: local, global, and fusion (LGSF). Compared with local or global spatial attention block, our LGSF block obtains the best performance, demonstrating that LGSF block can efficiently integrate local and global information into attention maps. Besides, the local spatial attention block performs better than the global spatial attention block, which indicates that the local spatial attention block has a more powerful representation ability.

**Table 2.** Comparison of different spatial attention blocks. (The best results are labeled in **bold**.)

| Spatial attention | Backbone | Acc/% | Pre/% | Rec/% | F1/% | Kappa/% |
|---|---|---|---|---|---|---|
| Global | | 85.29 | 79.43 | 81.47 | 80.19 | 75.33 |
| Local | ResNet18 | 85.91 | 79.81 | 78.38 | 79.01 | 75.82 |
| Global+local (LGSF) | | **89.83** | **91.71** | **81.89** | **85.32** | **82.07** |
| Global | | 88.11 | 83.18 | 83.30 | 83.23 | 79.79 |
| Local | ResNet34 | 88.89 | 85.87 | 84.50 | 85.12 | 80.95 |
| Global+local (LGSF) | | **92.48** | **93.71** | **86.81** | **89.49** | **86.96** |

## 4.6   Validation on the ChestXRay2017 Dataset

Table 3 lists the classification results of our LGSF-ResNet34 and published methods on ChestXRay2017 dataset. In general, our LGSF-ResNet34 achieves the best performance among all methods. It obtains **97.54%** of accuracy and outperforms SA-ResNet34 by **0.9%** of accuracy and **1.58%** of recall. The results further verify the generation ability of our method.

**Table 3.** Comparisons of our LGSF-Net and published methods on the ChestXRay2017 dataset. (The best results are labeled in **bold**.)

| Method | Acc/% | Rec/% | Pre/% | F1/% |
|---|---|---|---|---|
| VGG16 [4] | 86.26 | 85.22 | 87.73 | 86.46 |
| VGG19 [4] | 85.94 | 90.43 | 80.39 | 85.11 |
| Inception v3 [4] | 94.59 | 95.35 | 93.75 | 94.54 |
| ResNet50 [4] | 96.61 | 94.92 | **98.49** | 96.67 |
| Liang et al. [13] | 90.50 | 96.70 | 89.10 | 92.70 |
| ResNet34 [5] | 95.51 | 94.44 | 96.02 | 95.14 |
| SE-ResNet34 [5] | 96.31 | 95.77 | 96.35 | 96.04 |
| SA-ResNet34 [5] | 96.64 | 96.20 | 96.61 | 96.40 |
| CBAM-ResNet34 [5] | 96.80 | 96.33 | 96.82 | 96.56 |
| SPA [8] | 96.80 | 96.41 | 96.74 | 96.57 |
| Shuffle attention [29] | 96.64 | 95.86 | 96.99 | 96.37 |
| LGSF-ResNet34 (ours) | **97.54** | **97.78** | 95.98 | **96.83** |

## 5   Conclusion

This paper proposes a simple yet effective local-global spatial fusion network termed LGSF-Net to automatically recognize the severity levels of cortical cataracts on AS-OCT images. In the LGSF-Net, we design a local-global spatial fusion attention (LGSF) block to highlight the feature representation difference in spatial locations by infusing the clinical prior knowledge of CC with a local-global manner. The results on the CASIA2 AS-OCT dataset and a public ChestXRay2017 dataset show that LGSF-Net significantly improves the general CC classification through comparisons to advanced attention-based CNN. In the future, we will collect the AS-OCT images of CC to further validate the effectiveness of our LGSF-Net.

**Acknowledgement.** This work was supported part by Guangdong Provincial Department of Education (2020ZDZX3043, SJJG202002), and Guangdong Provincial Key Laboratory (2020B121201001).

## References

1. Benčić, G., Zorić-Geber, M., Šarić, D., Čorak, M., Mandić, Z.: Clinical importance of the lens opacities classification system III (LOCS III) in phacoemulsification. Coll. Antropol. **29**(1), 91–94 (2005)
2. Bourne, R.R., et al.: Magnitude, temporal trends, and projections of the global prevalence of blindness and distance and near vision impairment: a systematic review and meta-analysis. Lancet Glob. Health **5**(9), e888–e897 (2017)

3. Cao, G., et al.: An efficient lens structures segmentation method on AS-OCT images. In: 2020 42nd Annual International Conference of the IEEE Engineering in Medicine and Biology Society (EMBC), pp. 1646–1649. IEEE (2020)

4. El Asnaoui, K., Chawki, Y., Idri, A.: Automated methods for detection and classification pneumonia based on X-Ray images using deep learning. In: Maleh, Y., Baddi, Y., Alazab, M., Tawalbeh, L., Romdhani, I. (eds.) Artificial Intelligence and Blockchain for Future Cybersecurity Applications. SBD, vol. 90, pp. 257–284. Springer, Cham (2021). https://doi.org/10.1007/978-3-030-74575-2_14

5. Feng, Y., Yang, X., Qiu, D., Zhang, H., Wei, D., Liu, J.: PCXRNet: pneumonia diagnosis from chest X-Ray images using condense attention block and multiconvolution attention block. IEEE J. Biomed. Health Inform. **26**(4), 1484–1495 (2022)

6. Fu, H., et al.: Segmentation and quantification for angle-closure glaucoma assessment in anterior segment OCT. IEEE Trans. Med. Imaging **36**(9), 1930–1938 (2017)

7. Gao, X., Li, H., Lim, J.H., Wong, T.Y.: Computer-aided cataract detection using enhanced texture features on retro-illumination lens images. In: 2011 18th IEEE International Conference on Image Processing, pp. 1565–1568. IEEE (2011)

8. Guo, J., et al.: SPANet: spatial pyramid attention network for enhanced image recognition. In: 2020 IEEE International Conference on Multimedia and Expo (ICME), pp. 1–6. IEEE (2020)

9. He, K., Zhang, X., Ren, S., Sun, J.: Deep residual learning for image recognition. In: Proceedings of the IEEE Conference on Computer Vision and Pattern Recognition, pp. 770–778 (2016)

10. Hu, J., Shen, L., Albanie, S., Sun, G., Vedaldi, A.: Gather-excite: exploiting feature context in convolutional neural networks. In: Advances in Neural Information Processing Systems 31 (2018)

11. Hu, J., Shen, L., Sun, G.: Squeeze-and-excitation networks. In: Proceedings of the IEEE Conference on Computer Vision and Pattern Recognition, pp. 7132–7141 (2018)

12. Kermany, D.S., et al.: Identifying medical diagnoses and treatable diseases by image-based deep learning. Cell **172**(5), 1122–1131 (2018)

13. Khalil, M., Ayad, H., Adib, A.: MR-brain image classification system based on SWT-LBP and ensemble of SVMs. Int. J. Med. Eng. Inform. **13**(2), 129–142 (2021)

14. Lee, H., Kim, H.E., Nam, H.: SRM: a style-based recalibration module for convolutional neural networks. In: Proceedings of the IEEE/CVF International Conference on Computer Vision, pp. 1854–1862 (2019)

15. Li, H., et al.: Structure-consistent restoration network for cataract fundus image enhancement. arXiv preprint arXiv:2206.04684 (2022)

16. Li, H., et al.: An annotation-free restoration network for cataractous fundus images. IEEE Trans. Med. Imaging **41**, 1699–1710 (2022)

17. Li, H., Ko, L., Lim, J.H., Liu, J., Wong, D.W.K., Wong, T.Y.: Image based diagnosis of cortical cataract. In: 2008 30th Annual International Conference of the IEEE Engineering in Medicine and Biology Society, pp. 3904–3907. IEEE (2008)

18. Liu, J., et al.: Integrating research, clinical practice and translation: the Singapore experience. In: 2013 35th Annual International Conference of the IEEE Engineering in Medicine and Biology Society (EMBC), pp. 7148–7151. IEEE (2013)

19. Makhotkina, N.Y., Berendschot, T.T., van den Biggelaar, F.J., Weik, A.R., Nuijts, R.M.: Comparability of subjective and objective measurements of nuclear density in cataract patients. Acta Ophthalmol. **96**(4), 356–363 (2018)

20. Maslin, J.S., Barkana, Y., Dorairaj, S.K.: Anterior segment imaging in glaucoma: an updated review. Indian J. Ophthalmol. **63**(8), 630 (2015)

21. Park, J., Woo, S., Lee, J.Y., Kweon, I.S.: BAM: bottleneck attention module. arXiv preprint arXiv:1807.06514 (2018)
22. Qin, Z., Zhang, P., Wu, F., Li, X.: FcanNet: frequency channel attention networks. arXiv preprint arXiv:2012.11879 (2020)
23. Wang, Q., Wu, B., Zhu, P., Li, P., Zuo, W., Hu, Q.: ECA-Net: efficient channel attention for deep convolutional neural networks. In: The IEEE Conference on Computer Vision and Pattern Recognition (CVPR) (2020)
24. Wang, X., Girshick, R., Gupta, A., He, K.: Non-local neural networks. In: Proceedings of the IEEE Conference on Computer Vision and Pattern Recognition, pp. 7794–7803 (2018)
25. Woo, S., Park, J., Lee, J.-Y., Kweon, I.S.: CBAM: convolutional block attention module. In: Ferrari, V., Hebert, M., Sminchisescu, C., Weiss, Y. (eds.) ECCV 2018. LNCS, vol. 11211, pp. 3–19. Springer, Cham (2018). https://doi.org/10.1007/978-3-030-01234-2_1
26. Xiao, Z., et al.: Gated channel attention network for cataract classification on AS-OCT image. In: Mantoro, T., Lee, M., Ayu, M.A., Wong, K.W., Hidayanto, A.N. (eds.) ICONIP 2021. LNCS, vol. 13110, pp. 357–368. Springer, Cham (2021). https://doi.org/10.1007/978-3-030-92238-2_30
27. Xu, K., et al.: Show, attend and tell: neural image caption generation with visual attention. In: International Conference on Machine Learning, pp. 2048–2057. PMLR (2015)
28. Xu, Y., Duan, L., Wong, D.W.K., Wong, T.Y., Liu, J.: Semantic reconstruction-based nuclear cataract grading from slit-lamp lens images. In: Ourselin, S., Joskowicz, L., Sabuncu, M.R., Unal, G., Wells, W. (eds.) MICCAI 2016. LNCS, vol. 9902, pp. 458–466. Springer, Cham (2016). https://doi.org/10.1007/978-3-319-46726-9_53
29. Zhang, Q.L., Yang, Y.B.: SA-Net: shuffle attention for deep convolutional neural networks. In: 2021 IEEE International Conference on Acoustics, Speech and Signal Processing (ICASSP), ICASSP 2021, pp. 2235–2239. IEEE (2021)
30. Zhang, X., Hu, Y., Xiao, Z., Fang, J., Higashita, R., Liu, J.: Machine learning for cataract classification/grading on ophthalmic imaging modalities: a survey. Mach. Intell. Res. (2022). https://doi.org/10.1007/s11633-022-1329-0
31. Zhang, X., et al.: A novel deep learning method for nuclear cataract classification based on anterior segment optical coherence tomography images. In: 2020 IEEE International Conference on Systems, Man, and Cybernetics (SMC), pp. 662–668. IEEE (2020)
32. Zhang, X., et al.: Mixed pyramid attention network for nuclear cataract classification based on anterior segment OCT images. Health Inf. Sci. Syst. 10(1), 1–12 (2022)
33. Zhang, X., et al.: Nuclear cataract classification based on multi-region fusion attention network model. J. Image Graph. 27, 948–960 (2022). https://doi.org/10.11834/jig.210735
34. Zhou, Y., Li, G., Li, H.: Automatic cataract classification using deep neural network with discrete state transition. IEEE Trans. Med. Imaging 39(2), 436–446 (2019)

# PRGAN: A Progressive Refined GAN for Lesion Localization and Segmentation on High-Resolution Retinal Fundus Photography

Ao Chen, Xiao Ma, Qiang Chen, and Zexuan Ji[✉]

School of Computer Science and Engineering, Nanjing University of Science
and Technology, Nanjing 210094, China
jizexuan@njust.edu.cn

**Abstract.** Retinal-related diseases are the leading cause of vision loss and even blindness. The automatic methods for retinal disease segmentation based on medical images are essential for timely treatment. Fully supervised deep learning models have been successfully applied to medical image segmentation, which, however, particularly relies on a large number of pixel-level labels. To reduce the model's dependence on pixel-level labels, in this paper, we propose a progressive refined generative adversarial network (PRGAN) model by translating the abnormal retinal images to healthy images. The diseased area can be revealed by differentiating the synthetic healthy and real diseased images, thereby realizing the segmentation of lesions. The proposed framework is a weakly supervised approach with image-level annotations. A progressive generator is proposed with multi-scale strategy to generate images with more detail for large-scale color fundus images by refining the synthesis scale by scale. A visual consistency module is introduced to preserve color information in source domain images. Moreover, the domain classification loss is utilized to improve the convergence of the model. Our model achieves superior classification and segmentation performance on the IDRiD, DDR and Ichallenge-AMD datasets. With clear localization for lesion areas, the competitive results reveal great potentials for the proposed weakly supervised model.

**Keywords:** Retinal fundus photography · Generative adversarial networks · Lesion segmentation · Weakly supervised model

## 1 Introduction

Retinal-related diseases are the main causes of vision loss and blindness. The analysis of retinal fundus images can enable the diagnosis of a large number of

**Supplementary Information** The online version contains supplementary material available at https://doi.org/10.1007/978-3-031-18910-4_23.

ophthalmological-related blinding diseases, such as diabetic retinopathy [1], age-related macular degeneration [2], pathological myopia [3,4], etc. However, the diagnosis and analysis of retinopathy requires a large number of qualified ophthalmologists. Therefore, a highly accurate and efficient method for localization and segmentation of retinopathy is essential for timely treatment.

Detecting and accurately segmenting lesion regions in fundus images is a challenging task. In recent years, deep learning has achieved excellent results for retinal image analysis. Generative Adversarial Network (GAN) is an important branch of deep learning, and its excellent image simulation ability solves the limitation of data in retinal image analysis. Zheng et al. [5] achieved data augmentation through conditional GAN and proposed an integrated convolutional neural network (MU-net) to detect the retinal lesions. Siddiquee et al. [6] proposed a fixed-point GAN for disease detection and localization that imposes the limitations of the same domain and cross domain image conversion. Zhang et al. [7] jointly optimized CycleGAN and CNN classifiers to detect retinal diseases and localize lesion areas with limited training data. However, these methods are limited by the generation ability of GAN, especially for the retinal fundus images with high-resolution and large-size [8].

To address the above issues, we propose a weakly supervised approach for lesion localization and segmentation for high-resolution retinal fundus images, named progressive refine GAN (PRGAN), in which the backbone is based on StarGAN v2. StarGAN v2 [15] uses a single discriminator and generator, leveraging domain-specific style vectors from a style encoder or mapping network, to generate distinct images in each domain. In this paper, the fundus image with the lesion area is regarded as the "normal" domain, while the fundus image without the lesion area is regarded as the "abnormal" domain. The diseased area can be revealed by differentiating between the synthetic healthy and real diseased images, thereby realizing the segmentation of lesions. The main contributions of this work can be summarized as follows:

(1) A progressive generator is proposed with a multi-scale strategy to generate images with more detail for high-resolution color fundus photography by refining the synthesis scale by scale, which can further ensure the detail fidelity and content consistency of the generated images.
(2) A visual consistency module is introduced to preserve color information in source domain images. Moreover, the domain classification loss is utilized to improve the convergence of the model.
(3) The experimental results on three color fundus photography datasets demonstrate the stability and superior performances of the proposed model comparing with state-of-the-art weakly supervised models, and can produce similar or superior accuracy comparing with fully supervised approaches.

## 2   Methods

Figure 1 presents the architecture of our proposed model, which consists of the proposed generator, a discriminator, a style encoder, a visual consistency module,

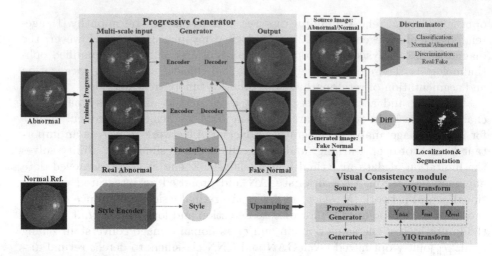

**Fig. 1.** The architecture of PRGAN.

and a localization and segmentation module. Adversarial loss, style reconstruction loss, cycle consistency loss and the proposed domain classification loss are combined to train PRGAN.

**Progressive Generator:** The resolution of medical images is usually large, and it is difficult for conventional generators to generate realistic and large-scale images, which also limits the segmentation performance. In order to ensure the detail fidelity and content consistency of the generated images for high-resolution color fundus photography, we design a progressive multi-scale generator $G$, as shown in Fig. 2(a). The small-scale encoder-decoder module is first trained to capture the global features in the fundus image. The resolution of the input image is then gradually increased (by a factor of 2 each time), while increasing the downsampling and upsampling blocks in the encoder-decoder. With the increasing of image scales, the generator learns more detailed local features. Therefore, the generator can gradually maintain the detail fidelity and content consistency scale by scale, instead of learning all scales simultaneously. Such a coarse-to-fine training procedure can further accelerate the training speed of the model. To guarantee that the progressive generator can generate the largest scale images, the outputs are upsampled to the largest resolution during training at each scale.

As shown in Fig. 2(a), our generator contains three sets of encoder-decoder modules, each of which consists of several residual blocks [10,11]. As the training progresses, low-level features will be gradually integrated into the high-level scale by smoothly fading in. The "fade in" scheme is similar with the work proposed by Karras et al. [9]. In StarGANv2 [15], the encoder of generator is constructed with ResBlk as shown in Fig. 2(b), and the decoder uses AdaINResBlk. In this paper, we use a similar encoder module. For the decoder part, we use Generator ModResBlk as shown in Fig. 2(c). Adaptive instance normalization (AdaIN) [12]

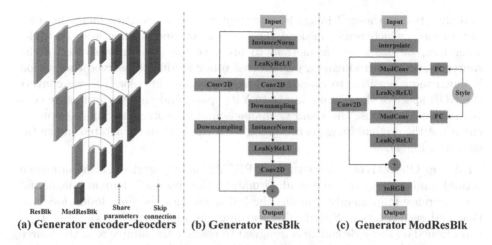

**(a) Generator encoder-deocders** | **(b) Generator ResBlk** | **(c) Generator ModResBlk**

**Fig. 2.** (a) The generator encoder-decoders. Each encoder-decoder is connected by skip connection and two adjacent scales are trained in "fade in" manner. (b) The generator ResBlk and (c) the generator ModResBlk.

is usually used for the normalization layer to control the influence of the source vector on the generated images [13]. AdaIN normalizes the mean and variance of each feature map separately, which may destroy the information found in the magnitude of features relative to each other. In order to avoid this problem, we improve the decoder part and use Modulated Convolutions to replace AdaIN, namely Generator ModResBlk.

**Style Encoder:** Given a "normal" domain fundus image $X_{ref}$ as a reference, our style encoder $S$ can extract the style encoding of $X_{ref}$ $s = S(X_{ref}, y)$, where $S(.)$ denotes the output of the style encoder and $y$ denotes the normal domain. For different reference images in normal domain, $S$ can generate corresponding style codes $s$, and then is sent to each decoder to guide the generator to synthesize output images that reflect the style of the reference image $X_{ref}$. Relevance can be found in Fig. 1 and Fig. 2(c), which show the relationship between style encoding $s$ and generator decoders.

**Discriminator:** Our discriminator has two roles. One is to play the role of the discriminator and complete the identification task of the generator's generated results, that is, to assist the generator in generating as realistic target domain images as possible, which is consistent with the role of the conventional discriminator. The second is to play the role of an auxiliary classifier to complete the classification task of the input image. To achieve this task, we impose a domain classification loss when training $D$ and $G$. Therefore, this strategy would further improve the convergence of the model.

**Visual Consistency Module:** Our proposed "de-disease" framework essentially guides image synthesis through style transfer, and it is experimentally verified that color information is largely independent of other style aspects. We find that the synthesized image is consistent with the reference image in color distribution, which would mislead the localization and segmentation module. Therefore, we use a simple method to preserve the color information of the source image by introducing a visual consistency module. Observed that vision is much more sensitive to changes in brightness than in color [14], we convert the RGB space of the original image to YIQ space, and only perform style conversion on Y, because the I and Q channels mainly store color information, so the IQ of the original image is combined with the Y of the generated image (as shown in Fig. 1).

**Training Objectives:** The purpose of PRGAN is to map the healthy unknown retinal fundus image (normal or abnormal) to the "normal" domain image, and the difference map mainly contains the lesion area for the final lesion localization and segmentation. Specifically, learning the mapping $G : X_{y_{src}} \rightarrow Y_{y_{trg}}$ conditioned on the style code $s$ is designed to convert the sample $\mathbf{x}$ in the source domain $y_{src}$ (normal or abnormal) to the sample $\mathbf{y}$ in the target domain $y_{trg}$ (normal). The objective function, like StarGANv2, includes adversarial loss $L_{adv}$, style reconstruction loss $L_{sty}$ and cycle consistency loss $L_{cyc}$. The adversarial loss can make the synthesized image indistinguishable from the real image. The style reconstruction loss is utilized to guarantee that the converted image can also be encoded with a consistent style code. The cycle consistency loss ensures that the translated image correctly preserves the key features of the source image. Please refer to Ref. [15] for more details.

For a given input image $\mathbf{x}$, we need to convert $\mathbf{x}$ to a normal image and simultaneously maintain the category attribute of $\mathbf{x}$. To achieve this purpose, when training both $D$ and $G$, we impose a domain classification loss. The proposed domain classification loss has two parts: one is to optimize $D$ using real images, and the other is to optimize $G$ using generated fake images. The former is defined as

$$L_{domain}^{real} = E_{\mathbf{x},y_{src}}[-logD_{domain}(y_{src}|\mathbf{x})] \tag{1}$$

where $D_{domain}(y_{src}|\mathbf{x})$ denotes the probability that the source image $\mathbf{x}$ is classified as category $y_{src}$ by the auxiliary classifier of discriminator. The latter is expressed as

$$L_{domain}^{fake} = \sum_{y\in\{y_{src},y_{trg}\}} E_{\mathbf{x},y}[-logD_{domain}(y|G(\mathbf{x},y))] \tag{2}$$

During training $G$, the model minimizes the domain classification loss to synthesis images that can be differentiated as the domain $y \in \{y_{src}, y_{trg}\}$ by $D$.

Finally, we can formulate our full objective functions for the discriminator and generator:

$$L_G = L_{adv} + \lambda_{sty}L_{sty} + \lambda_{cyc}L_{cyc} + \lambda_{domain}L_{domain}^{fake} \tag{3}$$

$$L_D = -L_{adv} + \lambda_{domain}L_{domain}^{real} \tag{4}$$

where $\lambda_{domain}, \lambda_{sty}, \lambda_{cyc}$ are hyperparameters, which are used to adjust the weight of domain classification loss, style reconstruction loss, and cycle consistency loss, respectively.

# 3    Experiments and Result

**Datasets and Implementation Details:** Three public datasets were utilized to train and validate the proposed model, i.e. IDRiD [16], DDR [23] and Ichallenge-AMD [17]. IDRiD consists of 516 retinal fundus images categorized into three categories, i.e. Diabetic Retinopathy (DR), Diabetic Macular Edema (DME) and normal images. DDR dataset consists 13,673 fundus images from 147 hospitals, covering 23 provinces in China. For segmentation task, 757 fundus images are provided with pixel-level annotation. The partition of training set, validation set and testing set is provided on DDR already, with 383 images for training, 149 images for validation and the rest 225 images for testing. Ichallenge-AMD contains 1200 images, labels for AMD and non-AMD patients, and masks for various lesions. 400 images with labels for AMD/non-AMD and masks of lesion regions were used in our work.

For the training of the proposed model, only images with image-level annotations were used. At the inference stage, we concentrated on translating any images (normal or abnormal) into the normal domain. Then the difference map could be calculated by subtracting the transformed normal image from the input image. We trained our model for 30K iterations. Adam optimizer with $\beta_1 = 0.5$ and $\beta_2 = 0.999$ was used and the batch size was set as $b = 6$ for all the experiments. During the training of the model procedure, we gradually decreased the learning rate (initially $10^{-6}$) for small scale layers of the progressive generator in order to avoid the sudden impact of the newly added large-scale layer on the small-scale layer. We added larger scale layers every 10K epochs and linearly decayed the learning rate to 0 over the next 20K epochs. The hyperparameters of objective functions were $\lambda_{domain} = 0.5$, $\lambda_{sty} = 1$, $\lambda_{cyc} = 1$, respectively.

**Comparison on Ichallenge-AMD Dataset:** In the first experiment, we evaluated our model on the Ichallenge-AMD dataset. We used 400 images with labels for AMD/non-AMD and masks of lesion regions, which were divided into training sets, validation sets and test sets according to the ratio of 6:2:2.

For image-level classification, we compared PRGAN with ResNet-50 [18], Inception-v3 [19], Fixed-Point GAN [6] and Join-CycleGAN-CNN [7]. We trained a ResNet-50 classifier and a Inception-v3 on the Ichallenge-AMD dataset, respectively. Table 1 shows the results of some comparison methods. The classification performance of various models is greatly hindered due to the difficulty of sizing lesions and the limitation of shape variation in the dataset. Comparatively, we can see that our method achieves the best results on each evaluation index. Especially on the F1 score, our method outperforms all other methods by at least 4.97%.

For pixel-level segmentation, we compared our method with three classical semantic segmentation methods (FCN [20], U-Net [21], DeeplabV3+ [22]) two fully supervised models dedicated to fundus image segmentation (namely SAA [24] and RTNet [25]), and three GAN-based models (StarGANV2 [15], Fixed-Point GAN [6], Join-CycleGAN-CNN [7]). Figure 3 shows the visualized segmentation results. For the classical semantic segmentation methods, we

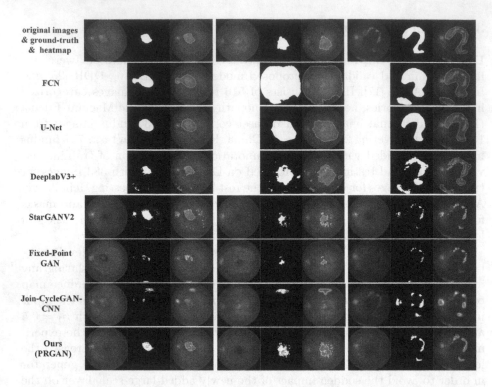

**Fig. 3.** Visualized comparison results on Ichallenge-AMD dataset with three examples. For each example, the 1st row shows the original image, ground truth of lesion segmentation, and heatmaps from left to right. The 2nd to 4th rows show the segmentation results and heatmaps of the classic segmentation algorithms. The 5th to 8th rows are the generated images, segmentation results, and heatmaps of the GAN-based methods.

**Table 1.** Quantitative comparison results on Ichallenge-AMD dataset for classification.

| Methods | Acc | Precision | Recall | F1 score |
|---|---|---|---|---|
| ResNet-50 [18] | 0.711 | 0.391 | 0.463 | 0.424 |
| Inception-v3 [19] | 0.795 | 0.502 | 0.553 | 0.530 |
| Fixed-Point GAN [6] | 0.832 | 0.765 | 0.794 | 0.779 |
| Join-CycleGAN-CNN [7] | 0.852 | 0.783 | 0.786 | 0.784 |
| Ours (PRGAN) | **0.895** | **0.805** | **0.841** | **0.823** |

can obtain the binary segmentation results and the heatmaps. For GAN-based weakly supervised methods, we also show the generated images. It is very clear to see that more small and large lesions are recognized in our models. From the case shown we can know that PRGAN works well both on generating healthy image and lesions segmentation. The quantitative results for pixel-level segmen-

**Table 2.** Quantitative comparison results on Ichallenge-AMD dataset for segmentation. The numbers with triangle superscript and bullet superscript indicate the highest values in fully superviesed model and weakly supervised model, respectively.

| Type | Methods | Accuracy | Precision | Sensitivity | Specificity |
|------|---------|----------|-----------|-------------|-------------|
| Fully supervised models | FCN [20] | 0.842 | 0.661 | 0.954 | 0.774 |
| | U-Net [21] | 0.955 | 0.702 | 0.986 | 0.832 |
| | DeeplabV3+ [22] | 0.962 | 0.835 | 0.983 | 0.895 |
| | SAA [24] | 0.971▽ | 0.842 | 0.992 | 0.901 |
| | RTNet [25] | 0.969 | 0.851▽ | 0.993▽ | 0.904▽ |
| Weakly supervised models | StarGANV2 [15] | 0.917 | 0.651 | 0.915 | 0.810 |
| | Fixed-Point GAN [6] | 0.925 | 0.695 | 0.937 | 0.826 |
| | Join-CycleGAN-CNN [7] | 0.947 | 0.731 | 0.952 | 0.821 |
| | Ours (PRGAN) | 0.958• | 0.795• | 0.992• | 0.906• |

**Table 3.** Quantitative comparison results on DDR dataset for classification.

| Methods | Acc | Precision | Recall | F1 score |
|---------|-----|-----------|--------|----------|
| ResNet-50 [18] | 0.544 | 0.365 | 0.463 | 0.408 |
| Inception-v3 [19] | 0.621 | 0.458 | 0.497 | 0.477 |
| Fixed-Point GAN [6] | 0.742 | 0.653 | 0.684 | 0.668 |
| Join-CycleGAN-CNN [7] | 0.886 | 0.727 | 0.711 | 0.719 |
| Ours (PRGAN) | **0.891** | **0.746** | **0.715** | **0.730** |

tation are displayed in Table 2. It is worth mentioning that our method achieves higher results than the fully supervised methods on Specificity (about 0.906). On other metrics, our method is comparable to fully supervised methods and far outperforms GAN methods, which further demonstrates the effectiveness of our method.

**Comparison on DDR Dataset:** We also verified the effectiveness of the proposed method on DDR dataset. The baselines utilized are the same as ones used on Ichallenge-AMD dataset.

For image-level classification, The results shown in Table 3 illustrate that PRGAN also ranks first in four individual evaluations. We can conclude that our method can accurately predict the image category (healthy or diseased) while segmenting lesions.

For pixel-level segmentation, Table 4 displays four metrics of quantificationally evaluation and Fig. 4 shows the visualized segmentation results on DDR dataset. It is obvious that our method is not doing the best job in pixel-level segmentation both on Ichallenge-AMD and DDR dataset, which may be explained by the fact that our model is a weakly supervised approach. Nevertheless, our method is comparable or even slightly better than some classical fully supervised segmentation methods and significantly outperforms other GAN-based weakly supervised models.

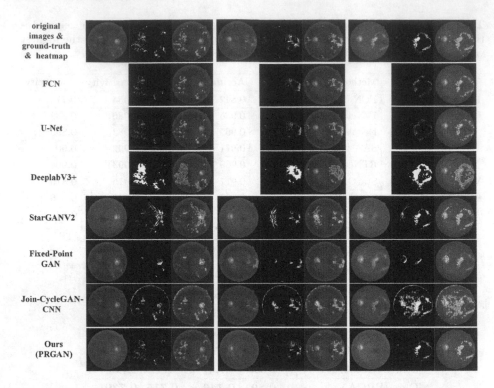

original
images &
ground-truth
& heatmap

FCN

U-Net

DeeplabV3+

StarGANV2

Fixed-Point
GAN

Join-CycleGAN-
CNN

Ours
(PRGAN)

**Fig. 4.** Visualized comparison results on DDR dataset with three examples. For each example, the 1st row shows the original image, ground truth of lesion segmentation, and heatmaps from left to right. The 2nd to 4th rows show the segmentation results and heatmaps of the classic segmentation algorithms. The 5th to 8th rows are the generated images, segmentation results, and heatmaps of the GAN-based methods.

**Ablation Study:** We conducted an ablation study to evaluate the role of each module in our proposed framework: multi-scale progressive generator (decoder uses ModResBlk instead of AdaINResBlk together), visual consistency module, and domain classification loss. To ensure the generalization ability of our model, Ichallenge-AMD dataset and 20% of IDRiD dataset are used for training, 40% of IDRiD dataset are used for validating and the remaining 40% are used for testing the model. Figure 5 shows the visualized ablation study results. Without the progressive encoder-decoders, the results generated by the model lose some details and produce artifacts (red boxes in Fig. 5(b)). Without the visual consistency module, the model can convert abnormal images to more normal images (more details are preserved). However, color and brightness have also been modified (Fig. 5(c)). In addition, without the domain classification loss, some lesions remain in the generated results (blue boxes in Fig. 5(d)). Comparatively, the integral model can obtain better lesion localization and segmentation performance (Fig. 5(e)). This is further confirmed by the qualitative analysis results of different model components (Fig. 5(f) and (g)), which show that the perfor-

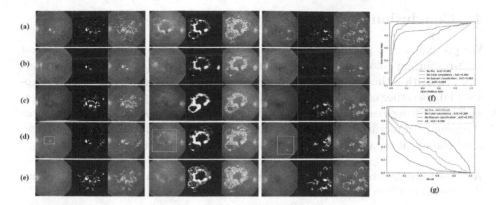

**Fig. 5.** The visualized ablation study results on IDRiD dataset. For each case, from left to right: (a) the original image, ground truth of lesion segmentation, heatmaps, (b) the result obtained by the model with a conventional generator, (c) the result without the visual consistency module, (d) the result without the domain classification loss, (e) the result of PRGAN. (f) ROC curves for classification and (g) PR curves for segmentation. (Color figure online)

**Table 4.** Quantitative comparison results on DDR dataset for segmentation. The numbers with triangle superscript and bullet superscript indicate the hightest values in fully superviesed model and weakly supervised model, respectively.

| Type | Methods | Accuracy | Precision | Sensitivity | Specificity |
|---|---|---|---|---|---|
| Fully supervised models | FCN [20] | 0.648 | 0.652 | 0.572 | 0.672 |
| | U-Net [21] | 0.640 | 0.654 | 0.559 | 0.686 |
| | DeeplabV3+ [22] | 0.673 | 0.662 | 0.583 | 0.689 |
| | SAA [24] | 0.719 | 0.685 | 0.614▽ | 0.741▽ |
| | RTNet [25] | 0.741▽ | 0.689▽ | 0.607 | 0.736 |
| Weakly supervised models | StarGANV2 [15] | 0.626 | 0.584 | 0.537 | 0.571 |
| | Fixed-Point GAN [6] | 0.643 | 0.614 | 0.548 | 0.596 |
| | Join-CycleGAN-CNN [7] | 0.652 | 0.628 | 0.573 | 0.603 |
| | Ours (PRGAN) | 0.725• | 0.661• | 0.609• | 0.693• |

mance of image-level classification drops significantly without the image-level progressive generator ('No-Pro' curve in Fig. 5(f)) or the domain classification loss ('No-Domain classification' curve in Fig. 5(f)). The integral model ('All' curve in Fig. 5(g)) outperforms other semi-finished models on pixel-level segmentation. In terms of the area under the curve (AUC), our method with all modules achieves state-of-the-art performance in both image-level classification and pixel-level segmentation.

## 4   Conclusion

We present a new paradigm for lesion localization and segmentation based on high-resolution color fundus photography in this research. It is a weakly supervised algorithm that obtains reliable lesion segmentation results by using image-level labels rather of pixel-level annotations. Furthermore, the progressive generator integrating visual consistency module and domain classification loss assures the generated pictures' detail fidelity and content consistency, improving image-level classification accuracy and pixel-level segmentation accuracy.

**Acknowledgements.** This work was supported by the National Natural Science Foundation of China under Grant NO. 62072241.

## References

1. Qummar, S., Khan, F.G., Shah, S., et al.: A deep learning ensemble approach for diabetic retinopathy detection. IEEE Access **7**, 150530–150539 (2019)
2. Peng, Y., Dharssi, S., Chen, Q., et al.: DeepSeeNet: a deep learning model for automated classification of patient-based age-related macular degeneration severity from color fundus photographs. Ophthalmology **126**(4), 565–575 (2019)
3. Rauf, N., Gilani, S.O., Waris, A.: Automatic detection of pathological myopia using machine learning. Sci. Rep. **11**(1), 1–9 (2021)
4. dell'Omo, R., et al.: Lamellar macular holes in the eyes with pathological myopia. Graefes Arch. Clin. Exp. Ophthalmol. **256**(7), 1281–1290 (2018). https://doi.org/10.1007/s00417-018-3995-8
5. Zheng, R., Liu, L., Zhang, S., et al.: Detection of exudates in fundus photographs with imbalanced learning using conditional generative adversarial network. Biomed. Opt. Express **9**(10), 4863–4878 (2018)
6. Siddiquee, M.M.R., Zhou, Z., Tajbakhsh, N., et al.: Learning fixed points in generative adversarial networks: from image-to-image translation to disease detection and localization. In: Proceedings of the IEEE/CVF International Conference on Computer Vision, pp. 191–200 (2019)
7. Zhang, Z., Ji, Z., Chen, Q., et al.: Joint optimization of CycleGAN and CNN classifier for detection and localization of retinal pathologies on color fundus photographs. IEEE J. Biomed. Health Inform. **26**(1), 115–126 (2021)
8. Chen, Q., Sun, X., Zhang, N., et al.: Mini lesions detection on diabetic retinopathy images via large scale CNN features. In: 2019 IEEE 31st International Conference on Tools with Artificial Intelligence (ICTAI), pp. 348–352. IEEE (2019)
9. Karras, T., Aila, T., Laine, S., et al.: Progressive growing of GANs for improved quality, stability, and variation. arXiv preprint arXiv:1710.10196 (2017)
10. Park, T., Liu, M.Y., Wang, T.C., et al.: Semantic image synthesis with spatially-adaptive normalization. In: Proceedings of the IEEE/CVF Conference on Computer Vision and Pattern Recognition, pp. 2337–2346 (2019)
11. Shaham, T.R., Dekel, T., Michaeli, T.: SinGAN: learning a generative model from a single natural image. In: Proceedings of the IEEE/CVF International Conference on Computer Vision, pp. 4570–4580 (2019)
12. Huang, X., Belongie, S.: Arbitrary style transfer in real-time with adaptive instance normalization. In: Proceedings of the IEEE International Conference on Computer Vision, pp. 1501–1510 (2017)

13. Karras, T., Laine, S., Aila, T.: A style-based generator architecture for generative adversarial networks. In: Proceedings of the IEEE/CVF Conference on Computer Vision and Pattern Recognition, pp. 4401–4410 (2019)
14. Wandell, B.A.: Foundations of Vision. Sinauer Associates (1995)
15. Choi, Y., Uh, Y., Yoo, J., et al.: StarGAN v2: diverse image synthesis for multiple domains. In: Proceedings of the IEEE/CVF Conference on Computer Vision and Pattern Recognition, pp. 8188–8197 (2020)
16. Porwal, P., Pachade, S., Kamble, R., et al.: Indian diabetic retinopathy image dataset (IDRiD): a database for diabetic retinopathy screening research. Data **3**(3), 25 (2018)
17. Fu, H., Li, F., Orlando, J.I., et al.: Adam: automatic detection challenge on age-related macular degeneration. IEEE Dataport (2020). https://dx.doi.org/10.21227/dt4f-rt59
18. He, K., Zhang, X., Ren, S., et al.: Deep residual learning for image recognition. In: Proceedings of the IEEE Conference on Computer Vision and Pattern Recognition, pp. 770–778 (2016)
19. Szegedy, C., Vanhoucke, V., Ioffe, S., et al.: Rethinking the inception architecture for computer vision. In: Proceedings of the IEEE Conference on Computer Vision and Pattern Recognition, pp. 2818–2826 (2016)
20. Long, J., Shelhamer, E., Darrell, T.: Fully convolutional networks for semantic segmentation. In: Proceedings of the IEEE Conference on Computer Vision and Pattern Recognition, pp. 3431–3440 (2015)
21. Ronneberger, O., Fischer, P., Brox, T.: U-Net: convolutional networks for biomedical image segmentation. In: Navab, N., Hornegger, J., Wells, W.M., Frangi, A.F. (eds.) MICCAI 2015. LNCS, vol. 9351, pp. 234–241. Springer, Cham (2015). https://doi.org/10.1007/978-3-319-24574-4_28
22. Chen, L.-C., Zhu, Y., Papandreou, G., Schroff, F., Adam, H.: Encoder-decoder with atrous separable convolution for semantic image segmentation. In: Ferrari, V., Hebert, M., Sminchisescu, C., Weiss, Y. (eds.) ECCV 2018. LNCS, vol. 11211, pp. 833–851. Springer, Cham (2018). https://doi.org/10.1007/978-3-030-01234-2_49
23. Li, T., Gao, Y., Wang, K., et al.: Diagnostic assessment of deep learning algorithms for diabetic retinopathy screening. Inf. Sci. **501**, 511–522 (2019)
24. Bo, W., Li, T., Liu, X., et al.: SAA: scale-aware attention block for multi-lesion segmentation of fundus images. In: 2022 IEEE 19th International Symposium on Biomedical Imaging (ISBI), pp. 1–5. IEEE (2022)
25. Huang, S., Li, J., Xiao, Y., et al.: RTNet: relation transformer network for diabetic retinopathy multi-lesion segmentation. IEEE Trans. Med. Imaging **41**(6), 1596–1607 (2022)

# Multiscale Autoencoder with Structural-Functional Attention Network for Alzheimer's Disease Prediction

Yongcheng Zong, Changhong Jing, and Qiankun Zuo[✉]

Shenzhen Institutes of Advanced Technology, Chinese Academy of Sciences,
Shenzhen 518000, China
{yc.zong,ch.jing,qk.zuo}@siat.ac.cn

**Abstract.** The application of machine learning algorithms to the diagnosis and analysis of Alzheimer's disease (AD) from multimodal neuroimaging data is a current research hotspot. It remains a formidable challenge to learn brain region information and discover disease mechanisms from various magnetic resonance images (MRI). In this paper, we propose a simple but highly efficient end-to-end model, a multiscale autoencoder with structural-functional attention network (MASAN) to extract disease-related representations using T1-weighted Imaging (T1WI) and functional MRI (fMRI). Based on the attention mechanism, our model effectively learns the fused features of brain structure and function and finally is trained for the classification of Alzheimer's disease. Compared with the fully convolutional network, the proposed method has further improvement in both accuracy and precision, leading by 3% to 5%. By visualizing the extracted embedding, the empirical results show that there are higher weights on putative AD-related brain regions (such as the hippocampus, amygdala, etc.), and these regions are much more informative in anatomical studies. Conversely, the cerebellum, parietal lobe, thalamus, brain stem, and ventral diencephalon have little predictive contribution.

**Keywords:** Channel and spatial attention mechanism · Multimodal fusion · Patch-level module · Alzheimer's disease

## 1 Introduction

Alzheimer's disease (AD) is a very serious and irreversible neurodegenerative disease among old people [1]. The diagnosis of Alzheimer's disease is a difficult task for neurologists, and traditional test scales such as memory tests cannot accurately determine the disease type [2]. With the help of machine learning algorithms emerging in recent years, computer-aided diagnosis has been widely used in the field of medical image analysis and achieved great success [3,4]. One of the major challenges in developing brain image-based AD diagnostic methods

S. Yu et al. (Eds.): PRCV 2022, LNCS 13535, pp. 286–297, 2022.
https://doi.org/10.1007/978-3-031-18910-4_24

is the difficulty in visually seeing AD-induced changes in the brain due to the very complex structure of brain tissue.

Magnetic resonance imaging is a non-invasive, repeatable, and high spatial resolution technique that is widely used in the diagnosis and research of various brain diseases [5]. Among them, fMRI imaging based on the BOLD effect, which uses the blood oxygen level-dependent signal as a neurophysiological indicator, is widely used in the identification of neurodegenerative diseases [6], especially in the classification of MCI and AD stages. The T1-weighted magnetic resonance imaging (T1WI) is used to extract brain tissue morphological features among the whole brain to capture volume change information in different brain regions. Since different modal images carry different disease-related information, researchers explore methods using T1WI or fMRI for disease diagnosis. For example, the work in [7] developed an MRI-based model and achieve good performance in AD diagnosis; Xiao et al. [8] utilized fMRI data to fully explore functional features and gain high detection accuracy. As multimodal images can provide complementary information about the disease, recent studies [9–11] with multimodal data have shown better performance compared with methods using unimodal data. Therefore, we make use of the T1WI and fMRI in our model to conduct multimodal feature fusion for disease diagnosis.

In recent years, deep learning has achieved great success in medical image analysis [12–17], especially the famous convolution neural network (CNN) [18–23]. It automatically learns the best features from data distribution because of its strong ability in local feature extraction. It was shown by Ju et al. [24] that the autoencoder model achieved better performance in diagnosis compared to methods such as support vector machines, logistic regression, linear discriminant analysis, etc. Most CNN-based segmentation models have an encoder-decoder structure, such as the fully convolutional network (FCN) [25]. The FCN first extracts feature through a series of convolutional layers and restore the size of the original image using the convolutional layers as decoders. This end-to-end mechanism enables the network to generate full-scale segmentation outputs. Meanwhile, the Generative adversarial network (GAN) [26] has become the most popular deep generation model in the fields of medical image recognition [27] since it can generate realistic data without explicitly modeling the data distribution. GAN can bee seen as variational-inference [28–31] based generative model and has also been widely applied in the Alzheimer's disease diagnosis, such as image generation [32,33], image recognition [34,35], image segmentation [36], image super-resolution [37], and brain network analysis [38–40]. The GANs can extract latent representations from brain imaging for AD recognition and prediction. However, different fusion strategies for the processing of the global and local features can affect the identification of key brain regions in AD [40], and influence the model's classification performance.

This paper proposes an end-to-end multiscale autoencoder-based Alzheimer's disease prediction network, which consists of three modules, a feature extraction network, a feature fusion network, and a classifier. In the feature extraction stage, the T1WI data is processed in patches and then input to the corresponding autoencoder modules, the two patch-level modules (sPM, fPM) for T1WI and fMRI, respectively. We improve Alzheimer's disease detection performance by leveraging learned multimodal complementary features and intramodal correlation information. The multimodal fusion network of our proposed self-attention mechanism plays a key role, where channel attention aims at dimensionality reduction and spatial attention aims at identifying the most important information. The mechanism effectively fuses the multimodal data, thereby improving the classification performance. Experiments on the Alzheimer's Disease Neuroimaging Initiative (ADNI) database show that compared with the H-FCN without the autoencoder structure, our method has achieved better results in AD classification.

The main innovations of this paper are as follows:

(1) Our model successfully learns the heterogeneity of different individual brain networks. The automatic alignment and brain atlas registration of general preprocessing software cannot adapt to the different brain structures of a large group of people. The preprocessed data is often based on the average value between regions, which loses a lot of potential information on the voxels.
(2) The multiscale autoencoder of the feature extraction network in our model can gain significant features by extracting features from different levels of sub-networks, which contribute to better classification prediction performance. We directly use 3D T1WI data and provide a visual representation of embedding, so the results have better interpretability.
(3) The self-attention mechanism integrates the data features of the two modalities in practice. Based on the visual display of the weights under different binary classification tasks, we obtain areas of structural changes that are consistent with the clinical practice, which is beneficial for disease diagnosis.

## 2    Method

Figure 1 shows the overall framework of the model proposed in this paper. The model consists of three main modules, namely, the multiscale autoencoder, the multimodal feature fusion with attention mechanism, and the final classification MLP network. In the feature extraction stage, the T1WI data is processed in patches and input to the corresponding autoencoder modules, that is, patch-level modules (sPM, fPM) for T1WI and fMRI, respectively. The network parameters of each module are independent of each other, so each module shares the same values of weights. Based on the learned features and fused features, it is finally used for the classification of AD subjects.

### 2.1    Feature Extraction Network: Autoencoder

Inspired by the successful application of Transformer [41] in CV, this paper also processes T1WI raw data into patches in the beginning. Different from [42] to

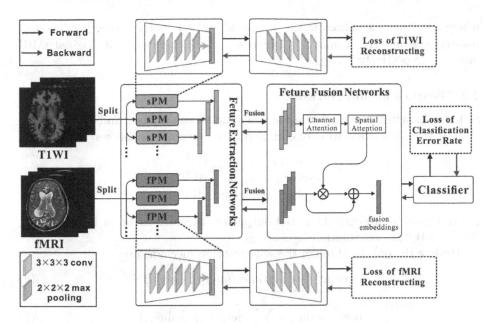

**Fig. 1.** The architecture of the proposed model.

divide the brain according to putative brain anatomy, we directly divide the brain image into $4 \times 4 \times 4$ non-overlapping sub-regions in three dimensions, and each patch is processed by a separate sub-network to extract the region features of the corresponding part. By using convolution downsampling operations three times, the sPM reduces the original dimension of the image to the size of $2 \times 2 \times 2$ in the first stage. Based on the analysis, the intermediate embedding results can be easily visualized.

The loss function of this stage is the reconstruction loss between the original and generated T1WI. To extract sparse features [43], a sparse penalty term for encoding is added to the loss function:

$$\Omega(h) = \lambda \sum_i |h_i| \tag{1}$$

where h is the encoding parameter.

The structure of the fPM and sPM design is similar. For fMRI data, the extra dimension of the time is added to the input. At last, we get features of each region of the brain. These features are then fused by the self-attention mechanism we propose.

Guided by image reconstruction loss [44], we first pre-train the feature extraction network of our model.

$$\begin{cases} L_s = \frac{1}{N} \sum_i^N \left\| \widehat{As}_i - As_i \right\|_2^2 + \Omega(h) \\ L_f = \frac{1}{N} \sum_i^N \left\| \widehat{Af}_i - Af_i \right\|_2^2 + \Omega(h) \end{cases} \tag{2}$$

where $\widehat{As_i}$ i and $\widehat{As_i}$ represent the generated and original T1 structure imaging, respectively and $\widehat{Af_i}$ i and $\widehat{Af_i}$ i represent the generated and original fMRI imaging, respectively.

## 2.2  Feature Fusion Network

Self-attention fusion is carried out in two dimensions of spaces and channels, and the self-attention calculation of each region is processed as follows:

$$\begin{cases} \text{key }_i = \text{region }_i \cdot W^{(k)} \\ \text{value }_i = \text{region }_i \cdot W^{(v)} \\ \text{query }_i = \text{region }_i \cdot W^{(q)} \end{cases} \tag{3}$$

where region$_i$ represents the initial output of $i$th patch of brain imaging, $W^k$, $W^v$, and $W^q$ are convolution layers.

Update the output through the self-attention mechanism:

$$\text{weight }_{ij} = softmax(\text{query }_i \cdot \text{key }_j) \tag{4}$$

$$\text{new\_region }_i = \sum_j^r \left(\text{weight }_{ij} \cdot \text{value }_j\right) \tag{5}$$

To effectively utilize both T1-weighted structural features and fMRI functional features, we must fuse these two different modalities [45]. In addition, any redundancy and information that is not important to either mode must be reduced. We design a multimodal module with an attention mechanism to improve the compatibility of two different modalities and then distinguish fusion features by a classifier for subsequent classification tasks.

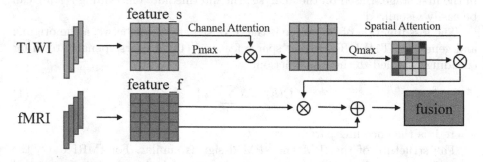

**Fig. 2.** The proposed feature fusion mechanism. Pmax represents the global max-pooling operation and Qmax denotes the global max pooling along the space axis. The T1 features are passed through Channel Attention and Spatial Attention to locate what and where is significant.

Learned from [46], we improve the original channel attention and spatial attention method. The fusion process of extracted features can be expressed by the following formula:

$$\begin{cases} \boldsymbol{f}_{T1}^c = \text{Attention}^c \left( \boldsymbol{f}_{T1} \right) \in \mathbb{R}^{H \times W \times C} \\ \boldsymbol{f}_{T1}^S = \text{Attention}^s \left( \boldsymbol{f}_{T1}^c \right) \in \mathbb{R}^{H \times W \times C} \\ \boldsymbol{f}_{fusion} = \boldsymbol{f}_{fMRI} \otimes \boldsymbol{f}_{T1}^S \oplus \boldsymbol{f}_{fMRI} \end{cases} \quad (6)$$

where $\oplus$ denotes element-wise addition, and $\oplus$ denotes element-wise multiplication. By combining T1 weighted features, the fusion feature will contain extra complementary information. We use a T1-guided attention module at each level of the feature fusion network to obtain the aggregation features. The specific mechanism of the feature fusion process is illustrated in Fig. 2.

## 2.3 Classifier Network

Considering that the full connection network has good classification capabilities and generalization, we choose the MLP network with easy implementation and high efficiency to calculate the classification regression loss with the labels of subjects.

We use cross-entropy as the loss function of the classifier. To be more specific, the loss function to this end is the combination of the loss for weakly-supervised discriminative localization and the loss for multi-task regression [47]

$$L_{reg} = -\frac{1}{N} \sum_{n=1}^{N} \sum_{c=1}^{C} \mathbf{1} \left( y_n = c \right) \log \left( y_n \right) \quad (7)$$

where $\mathbf{1}(\cdot)$ is a binary indicator and $y_n$ is the ground truth.

The total loss function is as follows:

$$L = \alpha L_s + \beta L_f + L_{reg} \quad (8)$$

where $\alpha$, $\beta$ are the super parameters, and both are set to 0.5.

## 3 Experiments

### 3.1 Dataset

The experiments are performed on the public Alzheimer's Disease Neuroimaging Initiative (ADNI) dataset [48]. We use the ADNI3 dataset and download 206 pairs of T1WI and fMRI imaging datasets in total. T1WI is a 3D MR image with a voxel resolution of $240 \times 256 \times 176$. fMRI is a 4D MR image, the original format is $704 \times 704 \times 976$ time slices, after conversion and removal of boundary padding, the input resolution is converted to $976 \times 60 \times 64 \times 44$. The dataset contains 72 AD, 34 EMCI, 36 LMCI, and 64 NC samples, respectively. 70% of the data is used as the training set, and the remaining 30% is used to test the classification performance. Since the same weight is assigned to the structural and functional brain networks, there is no validation set to adjust the hyperparameters of the model.

## 3.2    Experimental Settings

The model is trained on the TensorFlow1 platform. The data is directly fed into the network for training without general preprocessing methods such as skull stripping or registration. The NVIDIA TITAN RTX2080 GPU device is used to train the model for 24 h with about 800 epochs. The learning rate is set to 0.001 initially and the network parameters are updated by Adam optimizer [49]. Each layer of the network adopts group normalization and ReLU activation function in the feature extraction network. The classifier adopts a fully connected layer, and finally performs classification prediction through a softmax layer. The $\alpha$ and $\beta$ in our experiments is empirically set to 0.5 and 0.5, respectively.

The sPM network parameters are listed in the following Table 1, where GN denotes Group Normalization, and AddId denotes a residual structural connection. Like the encoder, the decoder has a symmetrical structure. The difference is that the downsampling of convolution with stride 2 in the encoder process is replaced by the upsampling of trilinear interpolation in the decoder. Other structures remain unchanged and are not listed in detail. It is worth noting that we also add concatenations between the encoder and decoders.

**Table 1.** The settings of the sPM network parameters.

| Name | Ops | Output size |
|------|-----|-------------|
| Input, T1WI | | $1 \times 240 \times 256 \times 176$ |
| InitConv | Conv | $32 \times 240 \times 256 \times 176$ |
| EncoderDown1 | Conv stride2 | $64 \times 120 \times 128 \times 88$ |
| EncoderBlock1 | [GN, ReLU, Conv]$\times 2$, AddId | $64 \times 120 \times 128 \times 88$ |
| EncoderDown1 | Conv stride2 | $128 \times 64 \times 64 \times 44$ |
| EncoderBlock1 | [GN, ReLU, Conv]$\times 2$, AddId | $128 \times 64 \times 64 \times 44$ |
| EncoderDown1 | Conv stride2 | $128 \times 30 \times 32 \times 22$ |
| EncoderBlock1 | [GN, ReLU, Conv]$\times 2$, AddId | $64 \times 30 \times 32 \times 22$ |

## 3.3    Results

**Performance Comparison.** The experiment performance is evaluated according to three metrics: classification accuracy, precision, and recall. We choose H-FCN as the baseline comparison, and CNN is used to hierarchically identify patch-level and region-level identification locations in whole-brain T1WI automatically since CNN can obtain good performance in brain tumor identification [50]. The accuracy and the recall rate are calculated by treating AD as the positive class (AD vs. NC and MCI).

**Table 2.** The prediction performance in three metrics. The training/testing sets ratio is 7:3. Values are reported as mean ± std deviation.

| Method | Accuracy | Precision | Recall |
|--------|----------|-----------|--------|
| H-FCN | 64.23 ± 5.33 | 68.35 ± 2.54 | **82.55 ± 4.73** |
| Ours | **67.55 ± 4.26** | **73.61 ± 3.16** | 79.82 ± 4.49 |

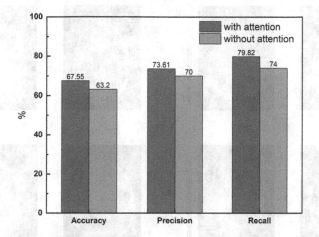

**Fig. 3.** The comparison of attention mechanism(with/without). The left blue bins denote the performance of our model, and the right origin bins denote the other method by simply element-wise addition. (Color figure online)

Based on the well-trained model, we have conducted 10 experiments in total in the test dataset. The best and largest results are labeled in bold in each row. It can be seen from Table 2 that the variance difference between the two methods is not large, reflecting the stability of the two methods is basically the same. In general, except for recall, which lags behind H-FCN, all other performance metrics lead by 2–3% points. The proposed model behaves in poor performance in the recall metric evaluation.

**Ablation Study.** The input of the experiment includes brain image data of two modalities. To verify the effect of our fusion mechanism on classification accuracy, we designed a set of ablation experiments. The following chart in Fig. 3 demonstrates the results by comparing with another simple strategy of element-wise addition on two features. All methods are trained using the same AD and NC subjects and also are tested on the same testing data. We can conclude that the proposed fusion mechanism does work by improving the classification performance in all three evaluation metrics.

**Feature Visualization.** Figure 4 shows the visual results of the same subject's brain sections and the corresponding extracted embedding. Some edge portion of the embedding visualization has a higher value which should be omitted (since original imaging data has not been pre-processed to eliminate the scalp regions). The weight values in the area of the cerebral cortex are distributed randomly overall, and there is a highlighted part (yellow) in the hippocampus area associated with the disease.

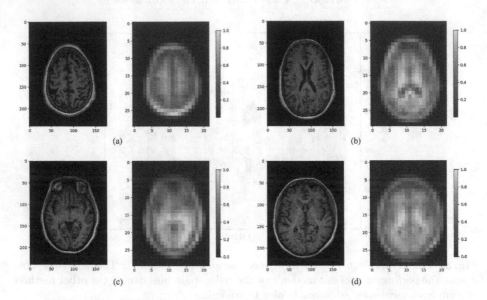

**Fig. 4.** Embedding visualization. The left is a T1WI slice of one subject, and the right is the weight values of the fusion embedding.

By visualizing the extracted features, we find that the hypothesized AD-related brain regions (such as the hippocampus, amygdala, etc.) have higher weights, and these regions contain more information. In contrast, the cerebellum, parietal lobe, thalamus, brain stem, and ventral interbrain control little predictive effect.

## 4    Conclusion

In this paper, we propose an end-to-end framework for Alzheimer's disease diagnosis based on a multiscale autoencoder. Specifically, a CNN-based encoder is used to extract features in the brain image representation space, and then attention-based fusion modality features are utilized for AD detection and brain region identification. The results on the ADNI dataset show that our method can effectively improve the classification performance, and the regions with high thresholds reveal abnormal brain regions in AD patients. In the future, we will explore the intrinsic mechanisms of multimodal fusion and extend this work to multi-task classification.

**Acknowledgment.** This work was supported by the Shenzhen Key Basic Research Projects under Grant JCYJ20200109115641762.

# References

1. Minati, L., Edginton, T., Bruzzone, M.G., et al.: Reviews: current concepts in Alzheimer's disease: a multidisciplinary review. Am. J. Alzheimer's Dis. Other Dement. **24**(2), 95–121 (2009)
2. Mahesh, G., Shazia, T.: Biomarker controversies and diagnostic difficulties in Alzheimer's disease. Am. J. Phytomed. Clin. Ther. **2**(4), 463–8 (2014)
3. Wang, S., Shen, Y., Zeng, D., et al.: Bone age assessment using convolutional neural networks. In: International Conference on Artificial Intelligence and Big Data (ICAIBD), pp. 175–178 (2018)
4. Hu, S., Yuan, J., Wang, S.: Cross-modality synthesis from MRI to pet using adversarial U-Net with different normalization. In: International Conference on Medical Imaging Physics and Engineering (ICMIPE), pp. 1–5 (2019)
5. Wang, S., Wang, X., Shen, Y., et al.: An ensemble-based densely-connected deep learning system for assessment of skeletal maturity. IEEE Trans. Syst. Man Cybern. Syst. **52**(1), 426–437 (2020)
6. Balachandar, R., Bharath, S., John, J.P., et al.: Resting-state functional connectivity changes associated with visuospatial cognitive deficits in patients with mild Alzheimer disease. Dement. Geriatr. Cogn. Disord. **43**229–236 (2017)
7. Yu, W., Lei, B., Shen, Y., et al.: Morphological feature visualization of Alzheimer's disease via multidirectional perception GAN. IEEE Trans. Neural Netw. Learn. Syst. (2021)
8. Xiao, L., Wang, J., Kassani, P.H., et al.: Multi-hypergraph learning-based brain functional connectivity analysis in fMRI data. IEEE Trans. Med. Imaging **39**(5), 1746–1758 (2019)
9. Yu, S., et al.: Multi-scale enhanced graph convolutional network for early mild cognitive impairment detection. In: Martel, A.L., et al. (eds.) MICCAI 2020. LNCS, vol. 12267, pp. 228–237. Springer, Cham (2020). https://doi.org/10.1007/978-3-030-59728-3_23
10. Huang, J., Zhou, L., Wang, L., et al.: Attention-diffusion-bilinear neural network for brain network analysis. IEEE Trans. Med. Imaging **39**(7), 2541–2552 (2020)
11. Zhang, L., Wang, L., Gao, J., et al.: Deep fusion of brain structure-function in mild cognitive impairment. Med. Image Anal. **72**, 102082 (2021)
12. Wang, S., Shen, Y., Shi, C., et al.: Skeletal maturity recognition using a fully automated system with convolutional neural networks. IEEE Access **6**, 29979–29993 (2018)
13. Wang, S., Hu, Y., Shen, Y., et al.: Classification of diffusion tensor metrics for the diagnosis of a myelopathic cord using machine learning. Int. J. Neural Syst. **28**(02), 1750036 (2018)
14. Lei, B., Yu, S., Zhao, X., et al.: Diagnosis of early Alzheimer's disease based on dynamic high order networks. Brain Imaging Behav. **15**(1), 276–287 (2021)
15. Lei, B., Liang, E., Yang, M., et al.: Predicting clinical scores for Alzheimer's disease based on joint and deep learning. Expert Syst. Appl. **187**, 115966 (2022)
16. Shen, Y., Huang, X., Kwak, K.S., et al.: Subcarrier-pairing-based resource optimization for OFDM wireless powered relay transmissions with time switching scheme. IEEE Trans. Signal Process. **65**(5), 1130–1145 (2016)

17. Wang, S., Yu, W., Xiao, C., et al.: Visualization method for evaluating brain addiction traits, apparatus, and medium. U.S. Patent Application No. 17/549,258 (2022)
18. Wang, S., Wang, H., Shen, Y., et al.: Automatic recognition of mild cognitive impairment and Alzheimer's disease using ensemble based 3D densely connected convolutional networks. In: 17th IEEE International Conference on Machine Learning and Applications (ICMLA), pp. 517–523 (2018)
19. Wang, H., Shen, Y., Wang, S., et al.: Ensemble of 3D densely connected convolutional network for diagnosis of mild cognitive impairment and Alzheimer's disease. Neurocomputing 333, 145–156 (2019)
20. Wang, S., Wang, H., Cheung, A.C., Shen, Y., Gan, M.: Ensemble of 3D densely connected convolutional network for diagnosis of mild cognitive impairment and Alzheimer's disease. In: Wani, M.A., Kantardzic, M., Sayed-Mouchaweh, M. (eds.) Deep Learning Applications. AISC, vol. 1098, pp. 53–73. Springer, Singapore (2020). https://doi.org/10.1007/978-981-15-1816-4_4
21. Wang, S.Q., Li, X., Cui, J.L., et al.: Prediction of myelopathic level in cervical spondylotic myelopathy using diffusion tensor imaging. J. Magn. Reson. Imaging 41(6), 1682–1688 (2015)
22. Hu, S., Yu, W., Chen, Z., et al.: Medical image reconstruction using generative adversarial network for Alzheimer disease assessment with class-imbalance problem. In: 2020 IEEE 6th International Conference on Computer and Communications (ICCC), pp. 1323–1327 (2020)
23. You, S., Shen, Y., Wu, G., et al.: Brain MR images super-resolution with the consistent features. In: 2022 14th International Conference on Machine Learning and Computing (ICMLC), pp. 501–506 (2022)
24. Ju, R., Hu, C., Li, Q.: Early diagnosis of Alzheimer's disease based on resting-state brain networks and deep learning. IEEE/ACM Trans. Comput. Biol. Bioinform. 16(1), 244–257 (2017)
25. Long, J., Shelhamer, E., Darrell, T.: Fully convolutional networks for semantic segmentation. IEEE Trans. Pattern Anal. Mach. Intell. 39(4), 640–651 (2015)
26. Bellegarda, J.R., Pagallo, G.: Neural typographical error modeling via generative adversarial networks. In: Advances in Neural Information Processing Systems, 3, pp. 2672–2680 (2014)
27. Wang, S.Q., Wang, X., Hu, Y., et al.: Diabetic retinopathy diagnosis using multichannel generative adversarial network with semisupervision. IEEE Trans. Autom. Sci. Eng. 18(2), 574–585 (2020)
28. Mo, L.F., Wang, S.Q.: A variational approach to nonlinear two-point boundary value problems. Nonlinear Anal. Theory Methods Appl. 71(12), e834–e838 (2009)
29. Wang, S.Q.: A variational approach to nonlinear two-point boundary value problems. Comput. Math. Appl. 58(11–12), 2452–2455 (2009)
30. Wang, S.Q. He, J.H.: Variational iteration method for a nonlinear reaction-diffusion process. Int. J. Chem. React. Eng. 6(1) (2008)
31. Wang, S.Q., He, J.H.: Variational iteration method for solving integro-differential equations. Phys. Lett. A 367(3), 188–191 (2007)
32. Hu, S., Shen, Y., Wang, S., Lei, B.: Brain MR to PET synthesis via bidirectional generative adversarial network. In: Martel, A.L., et al. (eds.) MICCAI 2020. LNCS, vol. 12262, pp. 698–707. Springer, Cham (2020). https://doi.org/10.1007/978-3-030-59713-9_67
33. Hu, S., Lei, B., Wang, S., et al.: Bidirectional mapping generative adversarial networks for brain MR to PET synthesis. IEEE Trans. Med. Imaging 41(1), 145–157 (2021)

34. Wang, S., Shen, Y., Zhang, W.: Enhanced generative adversarial network and target sample recognition method. U.S. Patent Application No. 16/999,118 (2020)
35. Yu, W., Lei, B., Ng, M.K. et al.: Tensorizing GAN with high-order pooling for Alzheimer's disease assessment. IEEE Trans. Neural Netw. Learn. Syst. (2021)
36. Wang, S., Chen, Z., You, S., et al.: Brain stroke lesion segmentation using consistent perception generative adversarial network. Neural Comput. Appl., 1–13, 8657–8669 (2022)
37. You, S., Lei, B., Wang, S., et al.: Fine perceptive GANs for brain MR image super-resolution in wavelet domain. IEEE Trans. Neural Netw. Learn. Syst. (2022)
38. Pan, J., Lei, B., Wang, S., et al.: DecGAN: decoupling generative adversarial network detecting abnormal neural circuits for Alzheimer's disease. arXiv preprint arXiv:2110.05712 (2021)
39. Zuo, Q., Lei, B., Wang, S., et al.: A prior guided adversarial representation learning and hypergraph perceptual network for predicting abnormal connections of Alzheimer's disease. arXiv preprint arXiv:2110.09302 (2021)
40. Pan, J., Lei, B., Shen, Y., Liu, Y., Feng, Z., Wang, S.: Characterization multimodal connectivity of brain network by hypergraph GAN for Alzheimer's disease analysis. In: Ma, H., et al. (eds.) PRCV 2021. LNCS, vol. 13021, pp. 467–478. Springer, Cham (2021). https://doi.org/10.1007/978-3-030-88010-1_39
41. Dosovitskiy, A., Beyer, L., Kolesnikov, A., et al.: An image is worth 16x16 words: transformers for image recognition at scale. arXiv preprint arXiv:2010.11929 (2020)
42. Zhao, Y.-X., Zhang, Y.-M., Song, M., Liu, C.-L.: Region ensemble network for MCI conversion prediction with a relation regularized loss. In: de Bruijne, M., et al. (eds.) MICCAI 2021. LNCS, vol. 12905, pp. 185–194. Springer, Cham (2021). https://doi.org/10.1007/978-3-030-87240-3_18
43. Shafay, M., Hassan, T., Damiani, E., et al.: Temporal fusion based mutli-scale semantic segmentation for detecting concealed baggage threats. In: IEEE International Conference on Systems, Man, and Cybernetics (SMC), pp. 232–237 (2021)
44. D'Souza, N.S., et al.: A matrix autoencoder framework to align the functional and structural connectivity manifolds as guided by behavioral phenotypes. In: de Bruijne, M., et al. (eds.) MICCAI 2021. LNCS, vol. 12907, pp. 625–636. Springer, Cham (2021). https://doi.org/10.1007/978-3-030-87234-2_59
45. Zuo, Q., Lei, B., Shen, Y., Liu, Y., Feng, Z., Wang, S.: multimodal representations learning and adversarial hypergraph fusion for early Alzheimer's disease prediction. In: Ma, H., et al. (eds.) PRCV 2021. LNCS, vol. 13021, pp. 479–490. Springer, Cham (2021). https://doi.org/10.1007/978-3-030-88010-1_40
46. Feng, C. M., Fu, H., Zhou, T., et al.: Multi-modal aggregation network for Fast MR imaging. arXiv preprint arXiv:2110.08080 (2021)
47. Lian, C., Liu, M., Wang, L., Shen, D.: End-to-end dementia status prediction from brain MRI using multi-task weakly-supervised attention network. In: Shen, D., et al. (eds.) MICCAI 2019. LNCS, vol. 11767, pp. 158–167. Springer, Cham (2019). https://doi.org/10.1007/978-3-030-32251-9_18
48. Jack Jr., C.R., Bernstein, M.A., Fox, N.C., et al.: The Alzheimer's disease neuroimaging initiative (ADNI): MRI methods. J. Magn. Reson. Imaging Off. J. Int. Soc. Magn.Reson. Med. **27**(4), 685–691 (2008)
49. Kingma, D.P., Ba, J.: Adam: a method for stochastic optimization. arXiv preprint arXiv:1412.6980 (2014)
50. Ronneberger, O., Fischer, P., Brox, T.: U-Net: convolutional networks for biomedical image segmentation. In: Navab, N., Hornegger, J., Wells, W.M., Frangi, A.F. (eds.) MICCAI 2015. LNCS, vol. 9351, pp. 234–241. Springer, Cham (2015). https://doi.org/10.1007/978-3-319-24574-4_28

# Robust Liver Segmentation Using Boundary Preserving Dual Attention Network

Yifan Yang, Xibin Jia$^{(\boxtimes)}$, and Luo Wang

Beijing University of Technology, Beijing, China
jiaxibin@bjut.edu.cn

**Abstract.** Accurate liver segmentation is essential for the diagnosis and treatment planning of liver diseases. Recently, deep-learning-based segmentation methods have achieved state-of-the-art performance in the medical image domain. However, due to low soft tissue contrast between the liver and its surrounding organs, most existing segmentation methods are difficult to capture the boundary information of the liver well. Considering boundary information is necessary for liver edge localization in liver segmentation, we propose a novel deep-learning-based segmentation network, called Boundary Preserving Dual Attention network (BPDA). In the proposed BPDA, the boundary is being concerned with the dual attention module which consists of the spatial attention module and the semantic attention module at each layer of U-Net with the feature maps of current and its neighboring layer as inputs. The spatial attention module enhances the perception of target boundaries by focusing on salient intensity changes. Meanwhile, the semantic attention module highlights the contribution of different filters in semantic feature extraction by weighting important channels. Moreover, to overcome the phenomena that the segmentation of left lobe performance bad especially in new datasets from different sources in practical use, we analyze the attribution of the liver, we devise a data augmentation strategy to expand the data of the left lobe of the liver under the guidance of professional radiologists. The comparative experiments have done on the self-build clinic liver dataset, which includes 156 clinic case images with Iterative Decomposition of Water and Fat with Echo Asymmetry and Least-squares Estimation Magnetic Resonance Imaging(IDEAL-IQ MRI). Experiments show that our proposed method outperforms other state-of-the-art segmentation methods.

**Keywords:** Liver segmentation · Attention mechanism · Boundary preserving · Guided augmentation

## 1 Introduction

Liver segmentation is important for facilitating quantitative pathology assessment, treatment planning and monitoring disease progression [1]. In clinical

S. Yu et al. (Eds.): PRCV 2022, LNCS 13535, pp. 298–310, 2022.
https://doi.org/10.1007/978-3-031-18910-4_25

surgery, radiological images which provide the high specificity resulting from optimal lesion-to-liver contrast and no radiation exposure is important for diagnosis of liver diseases [2]. Therefore, liver segmentation based on radiological images has important research value in the diagnosis of liver diseases. Recently, many significant advances have been made in liver segmentation. Most of existing liver segmentation methods are based on traditional image processing and level sets [3,4]. In the era of deep learning, there are plenty of methods applying convolutional neural networks to solve the liver segmentation problem and achieve good results [5,6].

Although these methods provide solutions for liver segmentation task, there are still some drawbacks. On the one hand, due to the ambiguity of structural boundaries, uncertainty of segmentation regions without domain knowledge [7], it is difficult to obtain accurate segmentation results. On the other hand, due to the tiny and variable shape of the left lobe of the liver, it is difficult for network to learn its discriminative features, which leads to a decrease in segmentation accuracy. Besides, the severity of the lesion also affects the accuracy of liver segmentation. The grayscale difference between the liver and the liver background of patients with severe fatty liver is small, which brings challenges to the network to capture the liver boundary information.

To solve the above mentioned problems, we propose a novel deep-learning-based method for liver segmentation with combining two kinds of attention modules, named Boundary Preserving Dual Attention network (BPDA). In our method, the spatial attention module and the semantic attention module are built to enhance the input feature maps in parallel from pixel and channel dimensions, respectively. We employ these two modules to emphasize fusion features that contain significant boundary information. We also propose a guided data augmentation strategy for the left lobe of the liver under the guidance of professional radiologists. With targeted cropping of the left lobe of the liver occurrence region, we expand the training data. Experimental results show the guided data augmentation strategy indeed improve the robustness and generalization performance of our BPDA. Our main contributions can be summarized as follows:

1. We propose a novel Boundary Preserving Dual Attention network for liver segmentation. In our proposed network, the dual attention module, which consists of the spatial attention module and the semantic attention module, makes full use of both spatial and semantic information related to boundaries at each level of the U-Net. As a result, the boundary information between the liver and its surroundings is enhanced.
2. Under the guidance of professional radiologists, a novel data augmentation strategy is designed to expand the data of the left lobe of the liver, which improves the generalization ability and segmentation accuracy of our BPDA.
3. A well-labeled dataset of livers is built from clinical cases. Comprehensive experiments have been done on the built dataset. The experiments demonstrate that our method achieves the state-of-the-art results.

## 2 Related Work

### 2.1 Medical Image Segmentation

Recently, deep convolutional neural networks (DCNNs) have achieved great success in the medical images domain. U-Net [8] is one of the most widely used segmentation networks for medical images, which consists of symmetric contracting and expanding paths, and the most important design in U-Net is the skip connection, which fuses the low-level features with rich detail information and the high-level features with rich semantic information. U-Net improves the accuracy of feature localization and boundary recovery. Inspired by U-Net, many variants of it have emerged in medical image segmentation. Attention U-Net [9] introduces the idea of soft attention into U-Net to suppress irrelevant regions in the input image while highlighting salient features in specific local regions; UNet++ [10] redesigns the skip connection to aggregate features with different semantic scales on the decoder to produce a highly flexible feature fusion scheme. In order to further improve the performance of the segmentation network, TransUNet [11] combines Transformer [12] and U-Net to complete the segmentation task, which can not only use the global self-attention mechanism for feature extraction, but also use skip-connection to recover local spatial information. MSN-Net [13] redesigns a novel skip connection and combines high-level and low-level features as well as multi-scale semantic information to obtain more representative features. This method performs well on liver segmentation tasks. However, these methods face great challenges when object boundaries are not clear in medical images. Our boundary preserving dual attention network enhances the extraction of boundary information and achieves better segmentation results.

### 2.2 Attention Mechanism

The attention mechanism is first proposed in natural language processing, and is later introduced to the computer vision with great success. Recently, there have been several attempts [14, 15] incorporating attention mechanism to improve the performance of CNNs in large-scale computer vision tasks. Hu et al. [16] introduces a attention module to exploit the inter-channel relationship, which called squeeze-and-excitation module, they use global average-pooled features to compute channel-wise attention. DANet [17] models the semantic interdependencies in both spatial and channel dimensions to integrate local features and global dependencies adaptively. CCNet [18] demonstrates that long-range dependency can capture useful contextual information and designs the recurrent criss cross attention module. This module obtains more effective target features by calculating the relationships between the pixels of the target feature and all other pixels in the feature map.

However, these methods ignore the boundary information when using attention mechanism and low-level feature map with rich boundary information is not fully utilized. We apply attention mechanism to capture important boundary information from both semantic and spatial perspectives, achieving more efficient performance of networks.

# 3    Method

## 3.1    Overview

In this section, we give the details of our proposed network (BPDA) for medical image segmentation. We first present a general framework of our method in Fig. 1. Then the dual attention module, which consists of the spatial attention module and the semantic attention module, is designed. The spatial attention module enhances the awareness of target boundaries by focusing on salient intensity changes. The semantic attention module highlights the contribution of different kernels in semantic extraction by weighting important channels. Finally, to better capture the discriminative feature of the left lobe of the liver, we propose a guided augmentation strategy for it to improve the liver segmentation and generalization performance of our BPDA.

In our network, we choose U-Net with residual blocks [19] as the backbone network. We deploy a dual attention module at each resolution level of the U-Net. A low-level feature map with significant boundary information and a high-level feature map with significant semantic information are used as the inputs of this module. The module then weights the input features to highlight boundary-related information from spatial and semantic perspectives, respectively. After that, the features with enhanced boundary information are passed to the decoding side of the current layer via skip connection.

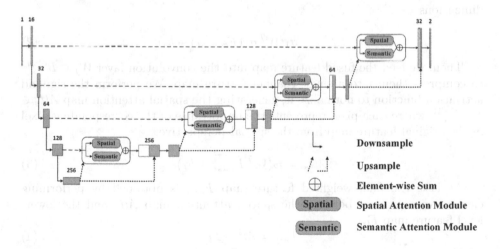

Fig. 1. Our proposed network

## 3.2    Spatial Attention Module

Boundary is the edge of an object, appearing in areas of varying intensity values in an image. However, due to human variations in the shapes of the liver and the similar intensity between the liver and nearby organs including the heart, pancreas, spleen, and kidneys, boundaries of the liver is difficult to locate. In order to discriminate pixels with boundary properties and enhance their feature representation, we design the spatial attention module to improve the feature representation of key regions in fused features containing important boundary information. Since the boundary of different channels in the feature map have position consistency, we use spatial attention module to weight spatial information of different channels of the feature map. As a result, important information such as liver boundaries and locations is significantly enhanced. Next, we elaborate the detailed process of this module.

As shown in Fig. 2, first, given the low-level feature map $F_l \in R^{C \times H \times W}$ from the encoding path, and the high-level feature map $F_h \in R^{C \times H \times W}$ from the decoding path, we feed them into two different convolution kernels $W_l \in R^{C \times C}$ and $W_h \in R^{C \times C}$, respectively, resulting in two feature maps $F_l^{'} \in R^{C \times H \times W}$ and $F_h^{'} \in R^{C \times H \times W}$. Then, we concat the two feature maps along the channel dimension to obtain the feature map $F_{concat} \in R^{2C \times H \times W}$.

$$F_{concat} = concat(W_l^T F_l + b_l, W_h^T F_h + b_h) \tag{1}$$

After that the feature map $F_{concat}$ is activated using ReLu function and then fed into the convolution layer $W_c \in R^{2C \times C}$, the BatchNorm layer and the ReLu nonlinear activation layer in turn to obtain the fused feature map $F_{fuse}^s \in R^{C \times H \times W}$. At this point, the low-level feature map and the high-level feature map are integrated while keeping the spatial information and reducing dimensions.

$$F_{fuse}^s = \sigma_1(W_c^T \sigma_1(F_{concat}) + b_c) \tag{2}$$

Then, we feed the fused feature map into the convolution layer $W_f \in R^{C \times C}$ to compress them into a single-channel feature map. We perform the sigmoid activation function to normalize it, generating the spatial attention map $Att_s \in R^{1 \times H \times W}$ where each pixel represents the importance of the corresponding pixel in the original feature map from the spatial perspective.

$$Att_s = \sigma_2(W_f^T F_{fuse}^s + b_f) \tag{3}$$

At last, the final weighted feature map $F_{att}^s$, is obtained by performing element-wise product between the spatial attention map $Att_s$ and the lower-level feature map $F_l$.

$$F_{att}^s = Att_s \cdot F_l \tag{4}$$

In the above equations, $b_l$, $b_h$, $b_c$, $b_f$ are bias terms corresponding to different convolutional layers, $\sigma_1$ and $\sigma_2$ are denoted as the ReLu activation function and the sigmoid activation function, respectively.

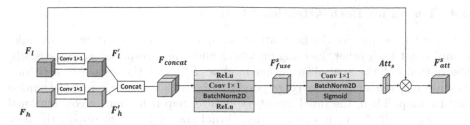

**Fig. 2.** Spatial attention module

## 3.3  Semantic Attention Module

The feature maps generated by different convolution kernels can reflect different attributions of semantic. Therefore, when revealing boundary semantics, enhancing importance of channels related to boundary semantics can improve segmentation accuracy. Inspired by this, we propose our semantic attention module that takes into account the differences between different kernels to better reflect boundary semantic information.

The structure of the semantic attention module is shown in Fig. 3. Different from the spatial attention module, in order to better ensure the consistency of semantic category information, the fusion method uses element-wise sum operation to generate the fused feature map $F_{fuse}^c \in R^{C \times H \times W}$.

$$F_{fusc}^c = W_l^T F_l + W_h^T F_h + b \tag{5}$$

In the above equation, $b = b_l + b_h$. Then the feature map use global average pooling to downsample each channel of it to obtain a vector, which represents the weight of each channel. After the sigmoid function is activated on this vector, the semantic attention map $Att_c \in R^{C \times 1 \times 1}$ is obtained.

$$Att_c = \sigma_2(GAP(\sigma_1(F_{fuse}^c))) \tag{6}$$

Finally we perform element-wise product between $Att_c$ and $F_l$.

$$F_{att}^c = Att_c \cdot F_l \tag{7}$$

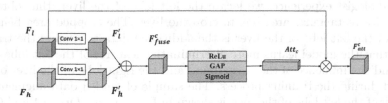

**Fig. 3.** Semantic attention module

### 3.4  Fusion for Both Attention Modules

We fuse the outputs of the both attention module. The two attention modules complement each other, focusing on where and what, respectively. Specifically, the outputs of the spatial attention module $F_{att}^s$ and the semantic attention module $F_{att}^c$ are summed by corresponding pixels to generate a fused attention feature map. Then, the fused attention feature map is fed into a convolutional layer $W_{att} \in R^{C \times C}$ with a convolution kernel size of $1 \times 1$ to obtain the final attention feature map $F_{final}$, the final attention map concatenates with high-level feature map $F_h$ to accomplish the skip-connection of U-Net.

$$F_{final} = W_{att}^T(sum(F_{att}^s, F_{att}^c)) + b_{att} \tag{8}$$

### 3.5  Guided Augmentation for the Left Lobe of the Liver

In segmental anatomy of the liver, the middle hepatic vein divides the liver into the right and left lobes [20]. In liver segmentation task, the left lobe of the liver is difficult to be segmented due to its small and variable characteristics in shape. Therefore, we propose a guided data augmentation strategy for the left lobe of the liver to improve segmentation performance. The detailed operations are as follows.

**Left Lobe Slice Selection.** Since the training data is 2D image, it is necessary to determine the range of 2D slice appearing in the left lobe of the the liver in the original 3D case data. Under the guidance of professional radiologists, we determined the range of slices the left lobe of the liver appearing in each case of training set, which is denoted as $slice_i^k$, where $i$ represents the $i$-th case, $k$ represents the $k$-th slice appearing in the left lobe of the liver. Second, since the range of slices appearing in the left lobe of the liver varies from case to case, we determine the intersection of it in each case as the final range, which is denoted as $S = [s_b, s_e]$, where $s_b$ represents the start slice and $s_e$ represents the end slice.

**Left Lobe Location and Enhancement.** Then, we locate the left lobe of the liver in the slices within the above range $S$. Due to the differences in the size and relative position of the left lobe of the liver in different cases and slices, with radiologist experience, we locate the left lobe of the liver, thus obtaining a fixed-size rectangular area box to crop the liver. The cropped area being the region of the left lobe of the liver is the additional data to expand the training set, so that the model learns more discriminative features of the left lobe of the liver, and the influence of the background and the right lobe of the liver on it is reduced during the training process. The sample of guided data augmentation strategy of the left lobe of the liver is shown in Fig. 4, where Origin 1 and Origin 2 are samples of training set while Aug 1 and Aug 2 are samples obtained by our proposed guided augmentation.

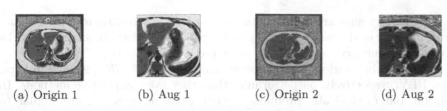

(a) Origin 1          (b) Aug 1          (c) Origin 2          (d) Aug 2

**Fig. 4.** Data augmentation of the left lobe of the liver

## 4    Experiments

### 4.1    Datasets and Evaluation Metrics

In this study, we collected a liver MRI dataset from Beijing Friendship Hospital, and IDEAL IQ (Iterative Decomposition of Water and Fat with Echo Asymmetry and Least Squares Estimation Quantification), which enables quantitative analysis of fat content, is selected for the experiment. There are 156 cases in this dataset, including 101 cases in the training set, 25 cases in the validation set, and 30 cases in the testing set. Another 50 cases with different sources from the training data are used for external qualitative experimental validation. The data are labeled with only two categories: the liver and the background. All experimental data and their corresponding labels are sliced into two-dimensional data and fed into the network for training and testing, In the end, we have 2185 training images, 553 validation images and 642 test images.

To evaluate the proposed method, we employ Dice, Sensitivity (Sens), Positive Predicted Value (PPV) [21] and Hausdorff Distance(HD) [22] as the evaluation metrics.

### 4.2    Implementation Details

Our system is implemented using Pytorch. The backbone of our method adds the residual block [19] to the U-Net to enhance information transfer and avoid network overfitting. The training uses an adaptive learning rate decay strategy, where the initial learning rate is multiplied by 0.1 if the Dice metric on the validation set does not decrease within 6 training rounds. We train our method using the Adam optimizer [23] with the batch size of 32, the initial learning rate of 0.001 and the weight decay of 0.0001.

### 4.3    Quantitative Results

**Comparison with Some Competitive Methods.** We conduct experiments on liver datasets to compare our method with several competitive segmentation methods, including U-Net, ResU-Net, SE+ResU-Net, Attention ResU-Net and DANet. As shown in Table 1, SE+ResU-Net [24] and DANet [17] achieve slightly better performance than U-Net, demonstrating that attention mechanism is helpful for the liver segmentation. Notably, our method (BPDA) achieves the best performance among all methods and is highly consistent with Ground Truth in terms of the target boundaries, corroborating that our method has the capability to enhance the awareness of boundary information.

In view of the metrics, our method achieves 94.82%, 94.75%, 94.90% in Dice, Sens, PPV, respectively, outperforming the other five competitive methods. In addition, our method also produces segmentation maps which are similar to ground truth regarding boundaries. This boundary similarity is obtained by Hausdorff Distance. From Table 1, it is clear that our method does well in capturing boundary information compared to other methods and achieves the best Hausdorff Distance of 18.55 mm. With the help of guided augmentation in the left lobe of the liver, the segmentation accuracy of our method is further improved, reaching 94.97%, 95.26%, 18.54 mm, respectively in Dice, PPV and Hausdorff Distance. In Table 1, Our Method w/ Guided Aug is our method with the guided augmentation.

**Table 1.** Segmentation results on testing set.

| Method | Dice(%) | Sens(%) | PPV(%) | HD(mm) |
|---|---|---|---|---|
| U-Net | 93.75 | 94.09 | 93.42 | 23.15 |
| ResU-Net | 94.32 | 93.44 | 94.70 | 21.37 |
| SE+ResU-Net | 94.57 | 94.46 | 94.69 | 23.82 |
| DANet | 94.44 | 94.67 | 94.22 | 23.82 |
| Attention ResU-Net | 94.54 | 94.49 | 94.59 | 21.34 |
| Our method | 94.82 | **94.75** | 94.90 | 18.55 |
| Our method w/Guided Aug | **94.97** | 94.70 | **95.26** | **18.54** |

To further verify the robustness and generalization performance of our method, we also conduct experiments on external qualitative validation dataset with 50 cases, 1250 images. Table 2 shows the quantitative comparison results, our proposed method is still superior to other competitive methods in liver segmentation, which reaches 94.18%, 95.85%, 92.59%, 20.61 mm in Dice, Sens, PPV and Hausdorff Distance. Due to the presence of data from patients with severe fatty liver in the external validation dataset, this convincing result shows that our method indeed has better robustness and generalization performance and is insensitive to the grayscale difference between the liver and the liver background, therefore our method has better segmentation performance for livers with different degrees of lesions. Besides, we also conduct the effectiveness of our proposed guided data augmentation for the left lobe of the liver. The results show that after using it, the segmentation accuracy and generalization ability of our method is further improved, reaching the best value at 94.52% in Dice and 93.30% in PPV.

**Table 2.** Segmentation results on external qualitative validation set.

| Method | Dice(%) | Sens(%) | PPV(%) | HD(mm) |
|---|---|---|---|---|
| U-Net | 93.27 | 95.32 | 91.33 | 27.16 |
| ResU-Net | 93.90 | 95.41 | 92.47 | 24.73 |
| SE+ResU-Net | 93.93 | 95.63 | 92.30 | 24.37 |
| DANet | 93.57 | 95.76 | 91.50 | 24.41 |
| Attention ResU-Net | 93.59 | 95.27 | 91.99 | 26.46 |
| Our method | 94.18 | **95.85** | 92.59 | 20.61 |
| Our method w/Guided Aug | **94.52** | 95.79 | **93.30** | **19.71** |

**Ablation Studies.** We further validate the importance of each module in dual attention by conducting ablation experiments. In Table 3, "spatial" indicates that our method only uses the spatial attention module, while "semantic" represents that only the semantic attention module is employed. As shown, the results support our intuition that dual attention with both modules turned on (denoted as full) outperforms the other two approaches.

**Table 3.** Result comparisons under different experiment settings of the dual attention.

| Method | Dice(%) | Sens(%) | PPV(%) | HD(mm) |
|---|---|---|---|---|
| U-Net(baseline) | 93.75 | 94.09 | 93.42 | 23.15 |
| Our method(spatial) | 94.64 | 94.61 | 94.69 | 20.84 |
| Our method(semantic) | 94.73 | 94.43 | 94.87 | 21.32 |
| Our method(full) | **94.82** | **94.75** | **94.90** | **18.55** |

## 4.4   Visualization Results

To demonstrate the performance of our proposed method to preserve boundary information of the target region during liver segmentation, we visualize our segmentation results in Fig. 5. As shown in Fig. 5, even the images have ambiguous structure boundary of target region, our method still outperforms other competitive methods.

To demonstrate the effectiveness of our proposed guided augmentation strategy in accurately segmenting the left lobe of the liver, we show the segmentation results with and without this strategy in Fig. 6. As shown in Fig. 6, the segmentation accuracy of our BPDA is further improved by this strategy, especially in the left lobe of the liver, which indicates that our guided augmentation strategy is indeed effective. In Fig. 6, Our Method w/o Augmentation refers to our method without guided augmentation.

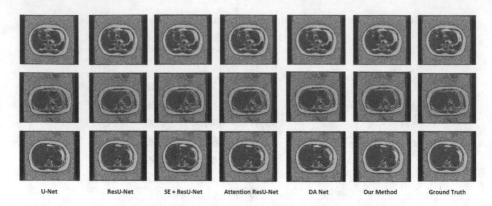

Fig. 5. Visualization of comparison experiment results on testing set.

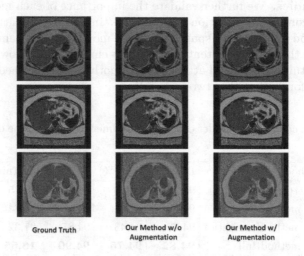

Fig. 6. Visualization of comparison experiment results on external qualitative validation set.

To qualitatively analyze the effectiveness of our BPDA in segmentation, we
used Grad-Cam [25] to visualize the heat map of the region of interest of our
method and compare it with other approaches. The comparison results are shown
in Fig. 7. We can clearly see that in the heat map, our method covers the liver
region and the liver boundary better than the other methods. This indicates that
our method is able to learn liver features more comprehensively, thus improving
the accuracy of segmentation.

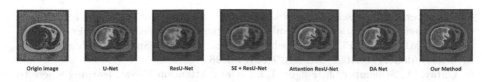

Origin image U-Net ResU-Net SE + ResU-Net Attention ResU-Net DA Net Our Method

**Fig. 7.** Grad-CAM visualization results.

## 5 Conclusion

In this paper, we propose the Boundary Preserving Dual Attention network for liver segmentation, which calculates the fused attention map at each layer of U-Net through the dual attention module to highlight boundary information and suppress irrelevant region. Specifically, the dual attention module is composed of the spatial attention module and the semantic attention module in parallel, calculating the attention map from both spatial and semantic aspects to enhance boundary-related information. Besides, we propose a guided augmentation strategy for the left lobe of the liver to improve the segmentation accuracy and generalization ability of our proposed method. We conduct comparative experiments to verify effectiveness of our method and results show that our method outperforms several state-of-the-art segmentation methods.

**Acknowledgement.** This work is partly supported by National Natural Science Foundation of China(No. 62171298, 61871276, 82071876). The adopted dataset is provided by Beijing Friendship Hospital. It is specially acknowledged with Dr. Cao Di and Prof. Yang Zhenghan with medical problem guiding and data annotation.

## References

1. Ahn, J.C., Connell, A., Simonetto, D.A., et al.: Application of artificial intelligence for the diagnosis and treatment of liver diseases. Hepatology **73**(6), 2546–2563 (2021)
2. Sung, Y.S., Park, B., Park, H.J., et al.: Radiomics and deep learning in liver diseases. J. Gastroenterol. Hepatol. **36**(3), 561–568 (2021)
3. Shu, X., Yang, Y., Wu, B.: Adaptive segmentation model for liver CT images based on neural network and level set method. Neurocomputing **453**, 438–452 (2021)
4. Zhou, L., Wang, L., Li, W., et al.: Multi-stage liver segmentation in CT scans using Gaussian pseudo variance level set. IEEE Access **9**, 101414–101423 (2021)
5. Aghamohammadi, A., Ranjbarzadeh, R., Naiemi, F., et al.: TPCNN: two-path convolutional neural network for tumor and liver segmentation in CT images using a novel encoding approach. Expert Syst. Appl. **183**, 115406 (2021)
6. Ahmad, M., Qadri, S.F., Qadri, S., et al.: A lightweight convolutional neural network model for liver segmentation in medical diagnosis. Comput. Intell. Neurosci. **2022** (2022)
7. Han, Y., Li, X., Wang, B., et al.: Boundary loss-based 2.5 D fully convolutional neural networks approach for segmentation: a case study of the liver and tumor on computed tomography. Algorithms **14**(5), 144 (2021)

8. Ronneberger, O., Fischer, P., Brox, T.: U-Net: convolutional networks for biomedical image segmentation. In: Navab, N., Hornegger, J., Wells, W.M., Frangi, A.F. (eds.) MICCAI 2015. LNCS, vol. 9351, pp. 234–241. Springer, Cham (2015). https://doi.org/10.1007/978-3-319-24574-4_28

9. Oktay, O., Schlemper, J., Folgoc, L.L., et al.: Attention U-Net: learning where to look for the pancreas. arXiv preprint arXiv:1804.03999 (2018)

10. Zhou, Z., Siddiquee, M.M.R., Tajbakhsh, N., et al.: UNet++: redesigning skip connections to exploit multiscale features in image segmentation. IEEE Trans. Med. Imaging **39**(6), 1856–1867 (2019)

11. Chen, J., Lu, Y., Yu, Q., et al.: TransUNet: transformers make strong encoders for medical image segmentation. arXiv preprint arXiv:2102.04306 (2021)

12. Vaswani, A., Shazeer, N., Parmar, N., et al.: Attention is all you need. Adv. Neural Inf. Process. Syst. **30** (2017)

13. Fan, T., Wang, G., Wang, X., et al.: MSN-Net: a multi-scale context nested U-Net for liver segmentation. SIViP **15**(6), 1089–1097 (2021)

14. Wang, X., Girshick, R., Gupta, A., et al.: Non-local neural networks. In: Proceedings of the IEEE Conference on Computer Vision and Pattern Recognition, pp. 7794–7803 (2018)

15. Cao, Y., Xu, J., Lin, S., et al.: GCNet: non-local networks meet squeeze-excitation networks and beyond. In: Proceedings of the IEEE/CVF International Conference on Computer Vision Workshops (2019)

16. Hu, J., Shen, L., Sun, G.: Squeeze-and-excitation networks. In: Proceedings of the IEEE Conference on Computer Vision and Pattern Recognition, pp. 7132–7141 (2018)

17. Fu, J., Liu, J., Tian, H., et al.: Dual attention network for scene segmentation. In: Proceedings of the IEEE/CVF Conference on Computer Vision and Pattern Recognition, pp. 3146–3154 (2019)

18. Huang, Z., Wang, X., Huang, L., et al.: CCNet: criss-cross attention for semantic segmentation. In: Proceedings of the IEEE/CVF International Conference on Computer Vision, pp. 603–612 (2019)

19. He, K., Zhang, X., Ren, S., et al.: Deep residual learning for image recognition. In: Proceedings of the IEEE Conference on Computer Vision and Pattern Recognition, pp. 770–778 (2016)

20. Abdel-Misih, S.R.Z., Bloomston, M.: Liver anatomy. Surg. Clin. **90**(4), 643–653 (2010)

21. Jia, X., Qian, C., Yang, Z., et al.: Boundary-aware dual attention guided liver segment segmentation model. KSII Trans. Internet Inf. Syst. (TIIS) **16**(1), 16–37 (2022)

22. Karimi, D., Salcudean, S.E.: Reducing the Hausdorff distance in medical image segmentation with convolutional neural networks. IEEE Trans. Med. Imaging **39**(2), 499–513 (2019)

23. Kingma, D.P., Ba, J.: Adam: A method for stochastic optimization. arXiv preprint arXiv:1412.6980, 2014

24. Zhang, Y., et al.: Multi-phase liver tumor segmentation with spatial aggregation and uncertain region inpainting. In: de Bruijne, M., et al. (eds.) MICCAI 2021. LNCS, vol. 12901, pp. 68–77. Springer, Cham (2021). https://doi.org/10.1007/978-3-030-87193-2_7

25. Selvaraju, R.R., Cogswell, M., Das, A., et al.: Grad-CAM: visual explanations from deep networks via gradient-based localization. In: Proceedings of the IEEE International Conference on Computer Vision, pp. 618–626 (2017)

# msFormer: Adaptive Multi-Modality 3D Transformer for Medical Image Segmentation

Jiaxin Tan[1], Chuangbo Jiang[2], Laquan Li[1,2], Haoyuan Li[1], Weisheng Li[1], and Shenhai Zheng[1(✉)]

[1] College of Computer Science and Technology, Chongqing University of Posts and Telecommunications, Chongqing 400065, China
zhengsh@cqupt.edu.cn
[2] School of Science, Chongqing University of Posts and Telecommunications, Chongqing 400065, China

**Abstract.** Over the past years, Convolutional Neural Networks (CNNs) have dominated the field of medical image segmentation. But they have difficulty representing long-range dependencies. Recently, the Transformer has been applied to medical image segmentation. Transformer-based architectures that utilize the self-attention (core of the Transformer) mechanism can encode long-range dependencies on images with highly expressive learning capabilities. In this paper, we introduce an adaptive multi-modality 3D medical image segmentation network based on Transformer (called msFormer), which is also a powerful 3D fusion network, and extend the application of Transformer to multi-modality medical image segmentation. This fusion network is modeled in the U-shaped structure to exploit complementary features of different modalities at multiple scales, which increases the cubical representations. We conducted a comprehensive experimental analysis on the Prostate and BraTS2021 datasets. The results show that our method achieves an average DSC of 0.905 and 0.851 on these two datasets, respectively, outperforming existing state-of-the-art methods and providing significant improvements.

**Keywords:** Transformer · Multi-modal · Medical image segmentation

## 1 Introduction

Medical imaging is widely used in medical diagnosis and interventional treatment [1,2]. In turn, medical image segmentation plays an important role in these applications. Typically, medical image segmentation is performed based on single-modality images, such as CT, PET and MRI. However, single-modality images can not fully reflect the true pathology. As shown in the first column in Fig. 1(a) and (b), in most cases, organs or lesion areas are visible in both different modalities. However, the other columns show that we can only localize

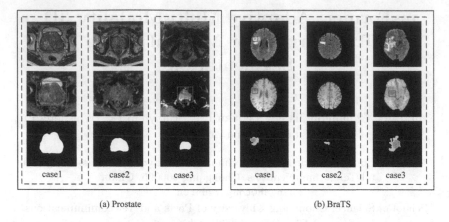

(a) Prostate                          (b) BraTS

**Fig. 1.** (a) T2-weighted images (the first row), ADC scattering coefficients images (the second row), and the ground truth of prostate (the third row). (b) FLAIR images (the first row), native T1 scan (the second row), and the ground truth of the brain tumor (the third row). Therefore, multi-modality scans can complement each other to obtain a better segmentation performance.

the organ or lesion region in one modality. Therefore, combining different modal images for segmentation is more effective in segmenting the real pathology.

Many methods have been devoted to multi-modality image segmentation. Several researchers conducted multi-modality segmentation studies with traditional methods, such as thresholding [3], random walk [4], and graph-cut [5]. However, with the continuous advancement of computational power and technology, an increasing number of researchers are focusing on the application of Convolutional Neural Networks (CNNs) in multi-modality medical image segmentation. Zhao et al. [6] proposed a multi-branch segmentation model based on fully convolutional networks. Fu et al. [7] applied a spatial transformation to the feature fusion process and quantified the importance of different modal feature maps. A multi-modality segmentation strategy combining shared downsampling of multi-scale features was proposed in [8]. However, CNNs excessively focus on local features of images and ignore the global representation, thus making it difficult to achieve optimal segmentation results.

Currently, with the continuous research on Transformer [9], it has been widely used in medical image segmentation [10]. TransUNet [11] was the pioneering work to introduce the Transformer into medical image segmentation, and the overall architecture is similar to U-Net [12]. Hatamizadeh [13] proposed a 3D medical image segmentation method (UNETR) based on Transformer and CNNs. While most works combine the properties of CNNs and Transformer to constitute a new segmentation approach, Swin-UNet [14] provided a novel segmentation method based entirely on Transformer. All these studies effectively indicate the feasibility of the Transformer model in medical image segmentation. However, these works have either considered a single modality or have simply concatenated multiple modalities in a single stream, and most of the existing vision Transformer models are based on 2D images and fail to handle 3D medical images perfectly.

In this paper, we propose a powerful 3D medical image segmentation network (msFormer) that extends the application of Transformer to multi-modality medical image segmentation. This proposed network is modeled as a U-shaped structure where complementary cubic features of different modalities are exploited at multiple scales between different modalities. The Prostate and BraTS datasets were evaluated and we observed an average DSC of 0.905 on Prostate and 0.851 on BraTS. The results show that msFormer significantly enhances the overall segmentation results.

## 2 Method

### 2.1 Overview

The overall structure of our proposed method is shown in Fig. 2, which comprises three branches: the encoding, fusion, and decoding parts.

### 2.2 Encoding

**3D-Embedding.** As the first part of the network encoding phase, the main role of the embedding layer is to divide the input image into patches, which is

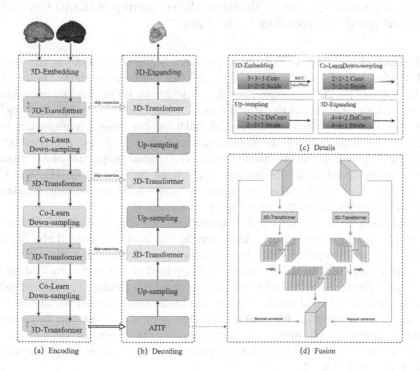

**Fig. 2.** (a) is the encoding phase of the network. (b) is the decoding phase. (c) is the details in msFormer. (d) is the fusion module (AITF).

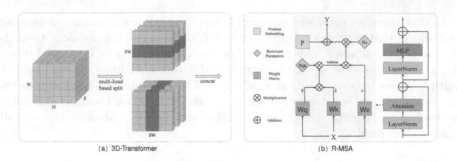

(a) 3D-Transformer                  (b) R-MSA

**Fig. 3.** Detail of the 3D-Transformer and R-MSA.

similar to Vision Transformer (VIT) [15], but with the difference that we embed the 3D image instead of 2D ones. In this module, we convert the input 3D image $x \in R^{H \times W \times S}$ into a high-dimensional tensor $x \in R^{H' \times W' \times S' \times C}$, where $H' \times W' \times S'$ represents the number of patch tokens and C represents the length of the sequence. As shown in Fig. 2(c), we extract features by using sequential 3D convolution in the 3D-Embedding module, which allows for a more detailed pixel-level encoding of patches and facilitates accurate segmentation tasks. And after the convolution, GELU [16] and layer normalization (LayerNorm) [17] are applied, and in real experiments, the size of the convolution in the 3D-Embedding is adjusted specifically according to the input.

**3D-Transformer.** Multi-head self-attention mechanism (MSA) is the core of the Transformer, which calculates the similarity between patches. The MSA in VIT is designed for 2D images and is not applicable to 3D medical images. And it computes the global similarity, which brings a huge computational effort, while many methods have demonstrated that with proper design, computing local similarity not only reduces the computational effort but also achieves better results [18,19]. In order to effectively utilize the spatial properties of 3D medical images, we designed a 3D Restricted Multi-head Self-Attention (R-MSA), as shown in Fig. 3(b). It calculates the similarity between 3D patches and constrains the model to converge by the restricted parameters $R$.

In addition to R-MSA, in 3D-Transformer, we also use local windows to reduce the computational effort. As shown in Fig. 3(a), we divided the 3D self-attention calculation process into two different parts by utilizing the multi-head mechanism (whether the third dimension is divided or not is determined by the size of the input image). Half of the *heads* are used to calculate the self-attention of the horizontal 3D local window, while the remaining are used to calculate the vertical 3D local window. We concatenate the results of these two branches to get the complete 3D self-attention calculation results finally.

Supposing that the 3D-Transformer input for the $l^{th}$ layer is $x_t^l$. The $qkv_{3D}$ is calculated as in Eq. (1):

$$qkv_{3D} : q = w_q x_t^l, k = w_k x_t^l, v = w_v x_t^l \tag{1}$$

where $q$, $k$, and $v$ represent the *query*, *key*, and *value* matrices, respectively. This is the same calculation as in the Transformer. The specific calculation of R-MSA is $x_t^l = concat\left(x_{th}^l, x_{tv}^l\right)$, where $x_{th}^l$ and $x_{tv}^l$ are the vertical and horizontal attention, as shown in Eq. (2) and Eq. (3). As opposed to the attention calculation in the original Transformer, we add a restriction parameter $R$ to constrain this attention so that the model does not have unnecessary outliers. Also changing the computational position of the position encoding makes the model better represent the real features of the image.

$$x_{th}^l = R_v \left(softmax\left(R_{qk}\left(q_h k_h^T \Big/ \sqrt{d}\right)\right)v_h\right) + p_h \tag{2}$$

$$x_{tv}^l = R_v \left(softmax\left(R_{qk}\left(q_v k_v^T \Big/ \sqrt{d}\right)\right)v_v\right) + p_v \tag{3}$$

where $p_h$ and $p_v$ are position encoding in both directions, $R_{qk}$ and $R_v$ are restricted parameters. In the 3D-Transformer module, the last part after self-attention $MLP$ is given as in Eq. (4). It aims to increase the nonlinear expression of the model.

$$MLP : x_t^l = mlp(LayerNorm(Drop(x_t^l))) \tag{4}$$

**Co-learn Down-sampling.** The advantage of the Transformer is able to focus on global pixel-level feature relationships. However, it is still significant to preserve the perception of local relationships for the fine segmentation task. CNNs are enabled to perceive local pixel relationships in an image. Therefore, we designed the Co-Learn Down-sampling module (CDS) to compensate for the perception of local features in our model and can reduce the feature map scale and the computational effort. In order to enable different modality features to co-guide the model, the information interaction between two modalities is strengthened by sharing parameters, and some misleading features are eliminated, thus realizing the multi-modality co-segmentation.

## 2.3   Adaptive Interleaved Transformer Feature Fusion

After the encoding part, feature maps generated in different modalities have certain variations, and the significance cannot be accurately expressed using ordinary addition operations. To deal with this problem, we designed an AITF module, as shown in Fig. 2(d), act as the core component of msFormer in the multi-modality features fusion process. The AITF module maps the feature maps of different modalities by a shared-weight 3D-Transformer module. Different modal feature maps have a certain similarity on the same channel, so we interleave the mapped feature maps for concatenation. During this process, the degree of contribution of different modal features to the segmentation results is automatically inferred by two learnable weight parameters. Finally, we restore the fused feature maps to the same scale as the input as the complete fused features.

## 2.4  Decoding

As shown in Fig. 2(b), the decoding part is similar to the encoding. The AITF module outputs the fused features and they are gradually restored to the same scale as the input by the Up-sampling module. In this stage, features from the encoding part are combined with decoding features through skip-connection, so we also designed the 3D-Transformer module to map the features again to obtain finer results. Finally, the output of the 3D-Expanding module will be used as the segmentation result with the same scale as the input.

In addition, our model outputs feature maps of different scales for depth supervision. Specifically, besides the final output, two additional feature maps with different scales (or over two, which can be adjusted according to the actual experimental procedure) are obtained in the decoding stage. For all the outputs, Cross-Entropy Loss and the Soft-Dice Loss will be calculated, and we do a simple summation of these two losses, as shown in Eq. (5). Therefore, in this paper, the final training loss function is the sum of all the losses at three scales, as shown in Eq. (6).

$$L_{all}\left(s, h, w\right) = w_{ce} \times L_{ce} - log\left(-L_{dice}\right) \times w_{dice} \tag{5}$$

$$L_{multi} = \sum_{i \in k} \lambda_i \times L_{all}\left(\frac{s}{i}, \frac{h}{i}, \frac{w}{i}\right), k = \{1, 2, 4\} \tag{6}$$

## 3  Experiments

To compare the strength and weakness of our model with existing models, we conducted experiments on the Prostate [20] and BraTS2021 [21–25] datasets.

### 3.1  Dataset

Prostate dataset is a subset of Medical Segmentation Decathlon (MSD)[1] which contains image data of 10 different body parts. It contains 48 MRI studies provided by Radboud University reported in a previous segmentation study, of which 32 cases are annotated (the training set occupies 85% and the test set 15%). The voxel size of T2-weighted scans is 0.65×0.65×3.59 mm, and the apparent diffusion coefficient (ADC) image is 2×2×4 mm. The image shape is 320×320×20.

BraTS2021 dataset is from the Brain Tumor Segmentation Challenge (BraTS)[2]. It delivers multi-modality MRI scans of 2000 patients, of which 1251 cases are annotated (the training set occupies 80% and the test set is 20%). Annotations are completed manually by experienced neuroradiologists. The voxel size of all sequences is 1×1×1 mm, and the image shape is 240×240×155. The labels include regions of GD-enhancing tumor (ET), the peritumoral edematous/invaded tissue (ED), and the necrotic tumor core (NCR).

---

[1]  http://medicaldecathlon.com/.
[2]  http://braintumorsegmentation.org/.

**Table 1.** The network configuration of our model on Prostate and BraTS datasets.

|  | Prostate | BraTS |
|---|---|---|
| Crop size | $128 \times 128 \times 16$ | $128 \times 128 \times 64$ |
| Batch size | 2 | 2 |
| Embed_dim | 192 | 96 |
| No. heads | [6, 12, 24, 12] | [6, 12, 24, 12] |
| No. Transformer | [2, 4, 7, 2] | [2, 4, 7, 2] |

## 3.2  Implementation Details

All experiments we conducted were based on Python 3.6, PyTorch 1.8.1, and Ubuntu 16.04. All training processes were performed using a single 12 GB NVIDIA 2080Ti GPU.

**Learning Rate and Optimizer.** The initial learning rate $init\_lr$ was set to 0.01, and it decayed during training with the decay strategy shown in Eq. (7). The optimizer used SGD with momentum weight decay was set to 0.99 and 3e-5. The number of training epochs was 400 and the iteration of each epoch was 250.

$$lr = init\_lr \times (1 - \frac{curr\_epoch}{training\_epochs})^{0.9} \tag{7}$$

**Data Processing.** We performed pre-processing and data enhancement operations on the images. In the data pre-processing, we resampled all the data uniformly to the same target spacing to prevent the discrepant information of the data itself from affecting the experiment. Meanwhile, we performed a series of enhancement operations on the data: image rotation and scaling operations according to the same settings, as well as adding Gaussian noise, Gaussian blurring operations, adjusting brightness and contrast, and performing low-resolution simulation, gamma enhancement, and mirroring.

**Network Settings.** In addition to the basic experimental environment configuration, in Table 1, we report some important configurations in msFormer on Prostate and BraTS. The *Crop_size* of the input network, *batch_size*, *Embed_dim*, the number of *heads* of MSA, and the number of Transformers per layer (No. Transformer).

## 3.3  Results on Prostate and BraTS

Metrics evaluation of Dice Similarity Coefficient (DSC), Jaccard similarity coefficient (Jaccard), Relative Volume Difference (RVD), and 95% Hausdorff distance (HD95) are shown in Table 2 and Table 3 which compared our msFormer with existing methods.

**Prostate.** We trained the overall prediction on the Prostate dataset for the whole organ region. As shown in Table 2, our msFormer were able to achieve an average DSC of 0.905 on this dataset. As a comparison, the MSAM [7], WNet [26], MAML [27], TCSM [6], and MFNet [28] methods had lower DSC than our proposed method by 3.8% to 11.9%. In addition, the HD95 of our method (2.431) was the best performance which are shown in bold.

**BraTS.** MRI scans have 4 sequences: native T1-weighted images, post-contrast T1-weighted images (T1GD), T2-weighted images, and T2 fluid-attenuated inversion recovery images (T2-Flair). We selected both native T1 and T2-Flair sequences to test our model.

Instead of predicting the three mutually exclusive subregions corresponding to the segmentation labels, we predicted three overlapping regions, the enhancing tumor (ET, original region), tumor core or TC (ET + NCR), and whole tumor or WT (ED + TC). As shown in Table 3 our msFormer average DSC in these regions was 0.851. However, the DSC of the comparison method was 1.3% to 6.6% lower than our proposed method. In addition, the HD95 of our method (2.736) was the best performance.

### 3.4 Ablation Study

In this section, we illustrate the relevance of the AITF. Compared results are listed in Table 4. To investigate the effect of the AITF module on the segmentation model, we added the AITF module to the UNETR and nnFormer models. Experiments show that the addition of the AITF module improves the model accuracy by 2.1% and 2.3% on the Prostate dataset, and by 3.1% and 4.9% on the BraTS dataset.

### 3.5 Visualization

In Fig. 4 and Fig. 5, we show the segmentation results of the test method in some hard samples of both datasets. Both Ground Truth and test results are superimposed on the original images. It is worth stating that Ground Truth is consistent

**Table 2.** Experiments on Prostate. The best results are bolded.

| Model | DSC | HD95 | Jaccard | RVD |
|---|---|---|---|---|
| MFNet [28] | 0.786±0.07 | 6.443±2.94 | 0.653±0.09 | 0.302±0.19 |
| TCSM [6] | 0.811±0.09 | 6.652±1.47 | 0.689±0.12 | 0.226±0.19 |
| MAML [27] | 0.816±0.08 | 3.786±1.83 | 0.713±0.09 | 0.243±0.18 |
| WNet [26] | 0.847±0.06 | 6.495±1.71 | 0.741±0.09 | 0.182±0.12 |
| MSAM [7] | 0.867±0.03 | 3.543±1.44 | 0.779±0.05 | 0.131±0.07 |
| Ours | **0.905±0.02** | **2.431±0.82** | **0.827±0.04** | **0.104±0.04** |

for both modalities, so the difference between the observed segmentation results and Ground Truth is also consistent for visualized images of different modalities.

On the Prostate dataset (Fig. 4), we superimpose the segmentation results on the T2-weighted image to focus more clearly on the segmentation details (the ADC image is more blurred and less favorable for observation). It is clear that our proposed method segments well in both relatively large (first row) and small (second row) regions. On the BraTS dataset (Fig. 5), the segmentation results are superimposed on the different modalities (T1 in the first row and Flair in the second row), and it can be seen that our method can predict the different regions of the tumor well, even in the case of irregular tumors, without a large degree of missegmentation, and only fails to predict accurately when there are few voids in Ground Truth, while the other methods showed more significant missegmentation. This shows that our proposed method has a more effective segmentation capability and is more stable.

**Table 3.** Experiments on BraTS. The best results are bolded.

| Model | Region | DSC | HD95 | Jaccard | RVD |
|---|---|---|---|---|---|
| MFNet [28] | ET | 0.549±0.03 | 9.358±1.69 | 0.301±0.09 | 0.647±0.13 |
| | TC | 0.869±0.07 | 3.892±0.84 | 0.774±0.10 | 0.122±0.03 |
| | WT | 0.939±0.03 | 2.482±0.53 | 0.887±0.04 | 0.068±0.02 |
| | AVG | 0.785±0.04 | 5.244±1.02 | 0.654±0.08 | 0.279±0.06 |
| TCSM [6] | ET | 0.621±0.04 | 6.124±0.69 | 0.451±0.04 | 0.303±0.08 |
| | TC | 0.889±0.05 | 3.393±0.87 | 0.805±0.08 | 0.133±0.07 |
| | WT | 0.942±0.02 | 3.041±1.08 | 0.892±0.04 | 0.082±0.03 |
| | AVG | 0.817±0.04 | 4.186±0.88 | 0.716±0.05 | 0.173±0.06 |
| MAML [27] | ET | 0.647±0.09 | 4.556±1.05 | 0.785±0.09 | 0.229±0.10 |
| | TC | 0.882±0.05 | 3.101±0.96 | 0.807±0.09 | 0.206±0.08 |
| | WT | 0.934±0.02 | 1.867±0.35 | 0.894±0.03 | 0.162±0.04 |
| | AVG | 0.821±0.05 | 3.175±0.79 | 0.729±0.07 | 0.199±0.07 |
| WNet [26] | ET | 0.658±0.07 | 4.443±0.99 | 0.511±0.08 | 0.325±0.06 |
| | TC | 0.884±0.06 | 3.016±0.64 | 0.815±0.10 | 0.203±0.07 |
| | WT | 0.945±0.02 | 2.016±0.21 | 0.910±0.03 | 0.121±0.02 |
| | AVG | 0.829±0.05 | 3.158±0.62 | 0.746±0.07 | 0.216±0.05 |
| MSAM [7] | ET | 0.661±0.08 | 4.063±0.92 | 0.499±0.09 | 0.362±0.07 |
| | TC | 0.901±0.06 | 2.569±0.79 | 0.825±0.10 | 0.155±0.06 |
| | WT | 0.952±0.02 | 2.084±0.49 | 0.910±0.04 | 0.103±0.03 |
| | AVG | 0.838±0.06 | 2.905±0.73 | 0.745±0.07 | 0.207±0.05 |
| Ours | ET | 0.692±0.05 | 3.909±0.66 | 0.532±0.06 | 0.225±0.05 |
| | TC | 0.904±0.04 | 2.511±0.62 | 0.827±0.07 | 0.126±0.05 |
| | WT | 0.956±0.02 | 1.789±0.27 | 0.917±0.03 | 0.056±0.02 |
| | AVG | **0.851±0.04** | **2.736±0.52** | **0.759±0.05** | **0.136±0.04** |

**Table 4.** Investigation of AITF. The bolded data in parentheses indicate the increased average DSC of the model after the addition of the AITF module

| Datasets | Region | UNETR [13] + AITF | nnFormer [29] + AITF |
|----------|--------|-------------------|----------------------|
| BraTS | ET | 0.565(**+0.042**) | 0.650(**+0.099**) |
| | TC | 0.897(**+0.029**) | 0.919(**+0.036**) |
| | WT | 0.947(**+0.019**) | 0.955(**+0.011**) |
| | AVG | 0.803(**+0.031**) | 0.841(**+0.049**) |
| Prostate | AVG | 0.847(**+0.021**) | 0.879(**+0.023**) |

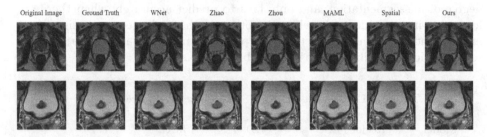

**Fig. 4.** Segmentation results of some hard samples on Prostate (superimposed on the T2-weighted image). The first column is the original image, the second column is the ground truth, and the remaining columns are the segmentation results of the comparison method and our proposed method.

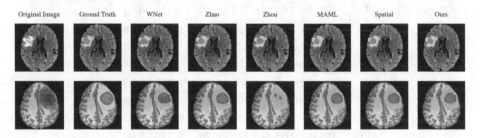

**Fig. 5.** Segmentation results of some hard samples on BraTS. The first column is the original image, the second column is the ground truth, and the remaining columns are the segmentation results of the comparison method and our proposed method.

## 4    Conclusions

This paper investigates a new Transformer-based 3D fusion network (msFormer) for the segmentation of multi-modality medical images. This proposed network has an overall U-shaped structure and consists of a 3D-Embedding block, 3D-Transformer blocks for different modalities, a shared collaborative learning down-sampling (CDS) block, and an adaptive interleaved Transformer feature fusion (AITF) module, an upsampling module, and a 3D-Expanding module. The network effectively utilizes the complementary features of different modalities and effectively eliminates the misleading information between modalities. Extensive experiments have confirmed its effectiveness. In the future, we hope that msFormer can be applied to semi-supervised medical image segmentation, and we also hope to provide more help for developing medical-related tasks, such as disease detection and classification.

**Acknowledgment.** This work was supported in part by the National Natural Science Foundation of China (Grant Nos. 61901074 and 61902046) and the Science and Technology Research Program of Chongqing Municipal Education Commission (Grant Nos. KJQN201900636 and KJQN201900631) and China Postdoctoral Science Foundation (Grant No. 2021M693771) and Chongqing postgraduates innovation project (CYS21310).

# References

1. Hastreiter, P., Bischoff, B., Fahlbusch, R., Doerfler, A., et al.: Data fusion and 3D visualization for optimized representation of neurovascular relationships in the posterior fossa. Acta Neurochirurgica **164**(8), 1–11 (2022)
2. Pereira, H.R., Barzegar, M., Hamadelseed, O., Esteve, A.V., et al.: 3D surgical planning of pediatric tumors: a review. Int. J. Comput. Assist. Radiol. Surg. **17**, 1–12 (2022). https://doi.org/10.1007/s11548-022-02557-8
3. Moussallem, M., Valette, P.-J., Traverse-Glehen, A., Houzard, C., et al.: New strategy for automatic tumor segmentation by adaptive thresholding on PET/CT images. J. Appl. Clin. Med. Phys. **13**(5), 236–251 (2012)
4. Liu, Z., Song, Y., Maere, C., Liu, Q., et al.: A method for PET-CT lung cancer segmentation based on improved random walk. In: 24th International Conference on Pattern Recognition (ICPR), PP. 1187–1192 (2018)
5. Song, Q., Bai, J., Han, D., Bhatia, S., et al.: Optimal co-segmentation of tumor in PET-CT images with context information. IEEE Trans. Med. Imaging **32**(9), 1685–1697 (2013)
6. Zhao, X., Li, L., Lu, W., Tan, S.: Tumor co-segmentation in PET/CT using multimodality fully convolutional neural network. Phys. Med. Biol. **64**(1), 015011 (2018)
7. Kumar, A., Fulham, M., Feng, D., Kim, J.: Co-learning feature fusion maps from PET-CT images of lung cancer. IEEE Trans. Med. Imaging **39**(1), 204–217 (2019)
8. Xue, Z., Li, P., Zhang, L., Lu, X., et al.: Multi-modal co-learning for liver lesion segmentation on PET-CT images. IEEE Trans. Med. Imaging **40**(12), 3531–3542 (2021)
9. Vaswani, A., Shazeer, N., Parmar, N., Uszkoreit J., et al.: Attention is all you need. In: Advances in Neural Information Processing Systems, vol. 30 (2017)
10. Shamshad, F., Khan, S., Zamir S.W., et al.: Transformers in medical imaging: a survey. arXiv preprint arXiv:2201.09873 (2022)
11. Chen, J., Lu, Y., Yu, Q., Luo X., et al.: TransuNet: transformers make strong encoders for medical image segmentation. arXiv preprint arXiv:2102.04306 (2021)
12. Ronneberger, O., Fischer, P., Brox, T.: U-Net: convolutional networks for biomedical image segmentation. In: Navab, N., Hornegger, J., Wells, W.M., Frangi, A.F. (eds.) MICCAI 2015. LNCS, vol. 9351, pp. 234–241. Springer, Cham (2015). https://doi.org/10.1007/978-3-319-24574-4_28

13. Hatamizadeh, A., Tang, Y., Nath, V., Yang, D., et al.: UNETR: transformers for 3D medical image segmentation. In: Proceedings of the IEEE/CVF Winter Conference on Applications of Computer Vision, pp. 574–584 (2022)

14. Cao, H., Wang, Y., Chen, J., Jiang, D.,et al.: Swin-unet: unet-like pure transformer for medical image segmentation. arXiv preprint arXiv:2105.05537 (2021)

15. Dosovitskiy, A., Beyer, L., Kolesnikov, A., Weissenborn, D., et al.: An image is worth $16 \times 16$ words: transformers for image recognition at scale. arXiv preprint arXiv:2010.11929 (2020)

16. Hendrycks, D., Gimpel, K.: Gaussian error linear units (gelus). arXiv preprint arXiv:1606.08415 (2016)

17. Ba, J.L., Kiros, J.R., Hinton, G.E.: Layer normalization. arXiv preprint arXiv:1607.06450 (2016)

18. Dong, X., Bao, J., Chen, D., Zhang, W., et al.: Cswin transformer: a general vision transformer backbone with cross-shaped windows. arXiv preprint arXiv:2107.00652 (2021)

19. Liu, Z., Lin, Y., Cao, Y., Hu, H., et al.: Swin transformer: hierarchical vision transformer using shifted windows. In: Proceedings of the IEEE/CVF International Conference on Computer Vision (2021)

20. Simpson, A.L., Antonelli, M., Bakas, S., Bilello, M., et al.: A large annotated medical image dataset for the development and evaluation of segmentation algorithms. arXiv preprint arXiv:1902.09063 (2019)

21. Menze, B.H., Jakab, A., Bauer, S., Kalpathy-Cramer, J., et al.: The multimodal brain tumor image segmentation benchmark (BRATS). IEEE Trans. Med. Imaging **34**(10), 1993–2024 (2014)

22. Bakas, S., Akbari, H., Sotiras, A., Bilello, M., et al.: Segmentation labels and radiomic features for the pre-operative scans of the TCGA-LGG collection. The cancer imaging archive 286, (2017)

23. Bakas, S., Akbari, H., Sotiras, A., Bilello, M., et al.: Segmentation labels and radiomic features for the pre-operative scans of the TCGA-GBM collection. Nat. Sci. Data **4**, 170117 (2017)

24. Bakas, S., Akbari, H., Sotiras, A., Bilello, M., et al.: Advancing the cancer genome atlas glioma MRI collections with expert segmentation labels and radiomic features. Sci. Data **4**(1), 1–13 (2017)

25. Baid, U., Ghodasara, S., Mohan, S., Bilello, M., et al.: The RSNA-ASNR-MICCAI BraTS 2021 benchmark on brain tumor segmentation and radiogenomic classification. arXiv preprint arXiv:2107.02314 (2021)

26. Xu, L., Tetteh, G., Lipkova, J., Zhao, Y., et al.: Automated whole-body bone lesion detection for multiple myeloma on 68GA-Pentixafor PET/CT imaging using deep learning methods. Contrast Media Mol. Imaging **2018**, 2391925 (2018)

27. Zhang, Y., et al.: Modality-aware mutual learning for multi-modal medical image segmentation. In: de Bruijne, M., et al. (eds.) MICCAI 2021. LNCS, vol. 12901, pp. 589–599. Springer, Cham (2021). https://doi.org/10.1007/978-3-030-87193-2_56

28. Zhou, T., Ruan, S., Guo, Y., Canu, S.: A multi-modality fusion network based on attention mechanism for brain tumor segmentation. In: 2020 IEEE 17th international symposium on biomedical imaging (ISBI), pp. 377–380 (2020)

29. Zhou, H.-Y., Guo, J., Zhang, Y., Yu, L., et al.: nnFormer: interleaved transformer for volumetric segmentation. arXiv preprint arXiv:2109.03201 (2021)

# Semi-supervised Medical Image Segmentation with Semantic Distance Distribution Consistency Learning

Linhu Liu, Jiang Tian, Zhongchao Shi$^{(\boxtimes)}$, and Jianping Fan

Lenovo Research, Beijing, China
{liulh7,tianjiang1,shizc2,jfan1}@lenovo.com

**Abstract.** Semi-supervised medical image segmentation has attracted much attention due to the alleviation of expensive annotations. Recently, many existing semi-supervised methods incorporate unlabeled data via the consistency learning. However, those consistency learning methods usually utilize the mean teacher structure, resulting in the different feature distribution on the intermediate representations. As for semi-supervised medical image segmentation, the different feature distribution limits the efficiency of consistency. In this paper, we propose Semantic Distance Distribution (SDD) Consistency Learning method, which has the ability to maintain the same feature distribution on the intermediate representations. On the one hand, to model invariance on feature distribution, we consider the shared encoder instead of averaging model weights. On the other hand, we introduce a SDD Map for consistency learning on the intermediate representations, where SDD Map is closely related to the feature distribution. SDD Map is characterized with the set of distances between the feature on each voxel and the mean value of all features in intra-cluster. Extensive experiments on two popular medical datasets have demonstrated our proposed method achieves state-of-the-art results.

**Keywords:** Medical image segmentation · Semi-supervised learning · Consistency learning · Semantic distance distribution

## 1 Introduction

Medical image segmentation is a fundamental step for medical image analysis and it is also a key component in delineating anatomical structure in medical images. The study of medical image segmentation usually requires large amounts of well-annotated data to train a deep neural network [10,13,14,17,20]. However, obtaining such high-quality data is extremely expensive and time-consuming in medical imaging domain. For example, about 79 s are taken to draw the accurate

**Supplementary Information** The online version contains supplementary material available at https://doi.org/10.1007/978-3-031-18910-4_27.

pixel-level annotations of an object [1]. NIH Pancreas[1] contains 231 slices on average for an object, raising the annotation time to about five hours per object. Therefore, the research of combining limited labeled samples with large amounts of unlabeled samples for medical image segmentation, denoted as semi-supervised medical image segmentation, is great meaningful.

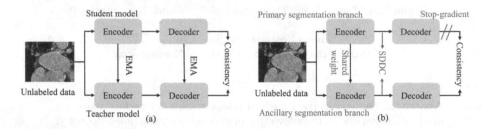

**Fig. 1.** Illustration of previous mean teacher based framework (a) and our proposed framework (b) for semi-supervised medical segmentation. EMA denotes exponential moving average. SDDC presents the SDD consistency.

Recently, many successful semi-supervised learning methods perform the medical segmentation by consistency learning [2,8,12,18], which enforces an invariance of the model's predictions on the unlabeled images via small perturbations or transformations. However, those existing consistency learning based methods usually use a mean teacher (MT) framework [15] to exert consistency of model's predictions between unlabeled data with/without perturbations (see Fig. 1(a)). In the framework, there have a teacher model and a student model, where the student model learns from the teacher model via a consistency loss. Each model has an encoder and a decoder. At each training step, the weights of the student model are updated with gradient descent, while the weights of teacher model are updated with an exponential moving average (EMA) of the student weights. Due to the EMA, the teacher model constructs average intermediate representations via the encoder, then the representations are inputted to decoder for segmentation.

Compared with the semi-supervised classification, semi-supervised segmentation pays more attention to the spatial structure which heavily depends on the details of the feature distribution, especially in medical domain. Therefore, feature distribution plays an important role in semi-supervised medical image segmentation. In MT, since the weights of teacher model are updated with an EMA of the student weights, the distribution of intermediate representations between student model and teacher model is different, especially on the object boundary distribution, resulting in the limited work efficiency.

To maintain the same feature distribution on the intermediate representations, we propose Semantic Distance Distribution (SDD) Consistency Learning

---

[1]  https://wiki.cancerimagingarchive.net/display/Public/Pancreas-CT/.

method. On the one hand, we consider the shared encoder instead of averaging model weights. The shared encoder can naturally introduce inductive biases for modeling invariance on the unlabeled data, leading the intermediate representations almost to have the same feature distribution. On the other hand, some works [4,11] have proved that intermediate representations maintain the cluster assumption, where the classes must be separable by low density regions, for the semantic segmentation. We introduce a SDD Map for consistency learning on the intermediate representations, and obtain regions of clusters with significant feature representations. Each cluster can be viewed as semantic representation, our purpose is to perform consistency constraint on the semantic level.

The proposed SDD Map is characterized with the set of distances between the feature on each voxel and the mean value of all features in intra-cluster. The SDD Map is closely related to the feature distribution and small changes in voxel of input-level will change SDD Map values of neighbouring multiple points. Therefore, imposing the consistency on such SDD Map could force the encoder more robust and better exploit the spatial structure information from the unlabeled data to improve the performance.

Concretely, we consider joint training of two branches, namely primary segmentation branch and ancillary segmentation branch (see Fig. 1(b)). Each branch shares the encoder's weights and a stop-gradient operation is utilized. A SDD consistency is performed on the encoder's output. Additionally, we also consider the original unsupervised consistency loss on the two branches' predictions. With extensive experiments, we demonstrate the effectiveness of our approach on left atrium (LA) and NIH Pancreas dataset.

Our contributions are summarized as follows.

- A novel SDD Consistency Learning approach is developed for semi-supervised medical image segmentation, which obtains training information from the unlabeled images by applying the consistency on the organ's semantic distance distribution in hidden feature space.
- A SDD Map is proposed to model the distance distribution by computing the distances between the feature of organ's voxel and the mean value of organ's features without any prior and additional parameters.
- Our method achieves the state-of-the-art segmentation performance on two public medical datasets with only a small number of labeled images.

## 2   Method

Our goal is to train a network for medical image segmentation in a semi-supervised manner by using SDD Consistency Learning. The overall pipeline of our proposed method is shown in Fig. 2. We will first introduce the overall framework design, followed by the SDD Map. We finally detail the proposed SDD Consistency Learning.

## 2.1  Overall Framework Design

Throughout the paper, we denote by $D_l = \{(x_1^l, y_1), ..., (x_n^l, y_n)\}$ the $n$ labeled images and $D_u = \{x_1^u, ..., x_m^u\}$ the $m$ unlabeled images, where $x_n^l$ and $x_m^u$ are the input volumes with spatial dimensions $H \times W \times D$ and $y_n \in \{0, 1\}^{H \times W \times D}$ is the ground truth annotation.

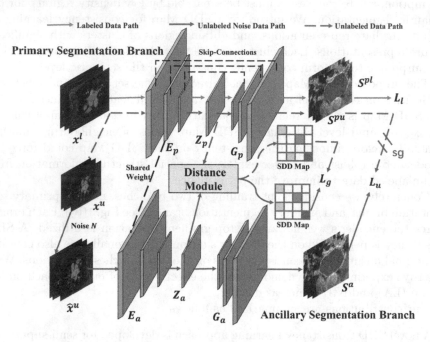

**Fig. 2.** Overview of the proposed method. The distance module is used to obtain the SDD Map for consistency learning. The original unsupervised consistency loss $L_u$ is also included in our pipeline. sg means stop-gradient.

As shown in Fig. 2, the architecture is composed of two branches, namely primary segmentation branch and ancillary segmentation branch. They have weight-shared encoder (e.g., $E_p$ or $E_a$) and individual decoder (e.g., $G_p$ or $G_a$). Given an input image $x^l \in D_l$, the primary segmentation branch $F_p = E_p \cdot G_p$ generates a confidence score map $S^{pl} \in [0, 1]^{H \times W \times D}$ in a traditional supervised manner. Given an input image $x^u \in D_u$, a noise $N$ is first injected into the input $x^u$ to obtain $\hat{x}_u$, then $x^u$ and $\hat{x}_u$ are respectively injected to the primary segmentation branch and ancillary segmentation branch for consistency learning. Specifically, each branch first generates the feature map $Z$ via the encoder $E$, a distance module is then utilized to obtain SDD Map, which models the organ's distance distribution for consistency learning. Finally, the feature map $Z$ via the decoder $G$ obtains prediction $S$ (e.g., $S^{pu}$ and $S^a$) for original unsupervised consistency learning. In practice, stop-gradient is used to prevent collapsing when the consistency is imposed for unsupervised learning and the ancillary segmentation branch does not have skip-connections.

## 2.2  SDD Map

The proposed SDD Map models the distance distribution of organ by computing the set of distances between the feature on organ's voxel and the mean value of organ's features. Based on the two branches design, the resulting representations of organ, as generic features via the weight-shared encoder, are more robust, comprehensive and discriminative. Therefore, we can select target organ's region more accurate on the hidden feature space. In order to utilize the training information from the unlabeled data as much as possible, we also consider the background distance distribution. Specifically, such SDD Map can be easily obtained in three steps via the distance module without any additional parameters. First, we select the regions of the target foreground or the background via a Sigmoid function on the feature map $Z$.

$$R = \Gamma(Sigmoid(Z) > H),  \tag{1}$$

where $H$ is a threshold to select the high activation voxels that generally represent the organ's region, and $\Gamma()$ is the indicator function. We denote the region of organ and background by the set of voxels having the same value in $R$. Second, an average operation is used to compute each region's mean feature in feature map $Z$. Finally, we perform the cosine similarity function to measure the distances between the feature of each voxel and its corresponding region's mean feature.

$$M = Cos(f(v), \frac{1}{|S_v|} \sum_{q \in S_v} f(q)),  \tag{2}$$

where $f(v)$ denotes the feature on voxel $v$, $S_v$ is the set of voxels that are in the same region as voxel $v$, $|S_v|$ stands for the size of the $S_v$. $Cos(\cdot)$ is the cosine similarity function and $M$ is the SDD Map.

## 2.3  SDD Consistency Learning

To extract training information from the unlabeled set $D_u$, we rely on enforcing a consistency between the SDD Map of two branches. Additionally, the original unsupervised consistency loss is a widely adopted objective for many semi-supervised tasks. It adds a strong congruent constraint on predictions. Therefore, the goal of the proposed SDD Consistency Learning is to minimize the following combined loss

$$L = L_l + \omega_u L_u + \omega_g L_g,  \tag{3}$$

where $L_l$ denotes the supervised loss to evaluate the quality of segmentation on the labeled data, while $L_u$ represents the original unsupervised consistency loss for measuring the consistency between the prediction of two branches on the unlabeled data under a perturbation of the input level. $L_g$ is the SDD consistency loss for estimating the distance distribution between the unlabeled data and the noised one. $\omega_u$ and $\omega_g$ are balance parameters. Following [6], to avoid using the initial noisy outputs of the encoders, $\omega_u$ and $\omega_g$ ramp up starting from zero along a Gaussian curve up to a fixed weight $\alpha_1$ and $\alpha_2$, respectively.

**Supervised Loss.** For a labeled example $x_i^l$ and its voxel-level label $y_i$, the primary segmentation branch is trained using a supervised manner.

$$L_l = \gamma_1 \frac{1}{n} \sum_{i=1}^{n} CE(y_i, S_i^{pl})) + \gamma_2 \frac{1}{n} \sum_{i=1}^{n} D(y_i, S_i^{pl})), \tag{4}$$

where $CE(\cdot)$ denotes cross-entropy loss and $D(\cdot)$ denotes dice loss [10]. $\gamma_1$ and $\gamma_2$ are weighting coefficients balancing two loss terms. $S_i^{pl}$ is the primary segmentation branch's prediction for one labeled example.

**Unsupervised Consistency Loss.** Given a unlabeled data $x_i^u$, unsupervised consistency loss $L_u$ enforces a consistency between the prediction of the primary segmentation branch and the ancillary segmentation branch.

$$L_u = \frac{1}{m} \sum_{i=1}^{m} d(sg(S_i^{pu}), S_i^a), \tag{5}$$

where $d(\cdot)$ is the mean squared error (MSE). $S_i^{pu}$ is the primary segmentation branch's prediction for one unlabeled example and $S_i^a$ denotes ancillary segmentation branch's prediction for the unlabeled example with a noise $N$. sg means stop-gradient.

**SDD Consistency Loss.** To utilize the unlabeled medical example's training information, the objective is to minimize the distance between SDD Map of the two branches as

$$L_g = \frac{1}{m} \sum_{i=1}^{m} d(M_p, M_a), \tag{6}$$

where $d(\cdot)$ is the MSE, $M_p$ and $M_a$ represent the corresponding SDD Map of the two branches.

## 3   Experiments

Similar to [9], we validate our method on two common medical datasets. (1) **LA**[2] contains 100 3D gadolinium-enhanced MR imaging scans (GE-MRIs) and LA segmentation masks. The dataset has an isotropic resolution of $0.625 \times 0.625 \times 0.625 \, mm^3$. Following [7,9,18], we split them into 80 scans for training and 20 scans for validation, and apply the same pre-processing. (2) **NIH Pancreas**[3] contains 82 abdominal CT volumes. Following [9], we split them into 62 images for training and 20 images for testing. For fair comparison, we apply the same pre-processing methods as in [9]. More details are in the Data Pre-processing section of supplementary material.

---

[2]   https://atriaseg2018.cardiacatlas.org/.
[3]   https://wiki.cancerimagingarchive.net/display/Public/Pancreas-CT/.

**Table 1.** Ablation study results on LA using 10% labeled data.

| Dataset | Method | # Scans used | | Metrics | | | |
|---------|--------|--------------|--------------|--------------|-----------------|----------------|---------------|
| | | Labeled | Unlabeled | Dice (%) | Jaccard (%) | ASD (voxel) | 95 HD (voxel) |
| LA | $L_l$ | 10% (8) | 0% (0) | 79.99 | 68.12 | 5.48 | 21.11 |
| | $L_l + L_u$ | 10% (8) | 90% (72) | 86.57 | 76.77 | 2.89 | 10.95 |
| | $L_l + L_u + L_g$ | 10% (8) | 90% (72) | **88.77** | **79.97** | **2.25** | **8.02** |

## 3.1 Experimental Setup

All experiments are implemented on the Pytorch platform. In practice, we employ the V-net [10] as backbone of the primary segmentation branch and the ancillary segmentation branch for fair comparison. We train our model from scratch with random initialization. The model is optimized using the SGD optimizer with a batch size of 8, consisting of 4 annotated images and 4 unannotated ones and a momentum of 0.9. The learning rate is set to 0.05 initially and decayed by 0.8 after every 1000 iterations. For LA dataset, we randomly crop $112 \times 112 \times 80$ cubes as the network input, while $96 \times 96 \times 96$ cubes on NIH Pancreas. In all experiments, we set $\gamma_1 = \gamma_2 = 0.5$ in Eq. 4. In Eq. 3, we empirically set the fixed weight $\alpha_1$ and $\alpha_2$ as 8 and 4, respectively. In order to select the target organ's region on feature map, we set the threshold $H$ as 0.8 in Eq. 1. $N$ is the Gaussian noise $N \sim G(-0.2, 0.2)$. During inference, only the primary segmentation branch is used for segmentation.

**Evaluation Metrics.** Similar to [7,9], we also use four standard evaluation metrics to quantitatively evaluate our method, including Dice, Jaccard, the average surface distance (ASD), and the 95% Hausdorff Distance (95HD). Dice and

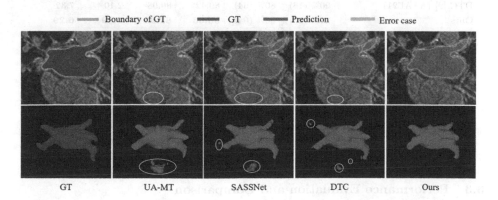

**Fig. 3.** Some qualitative comparisons on the LA, when models are trained with 10% labeled data. The first row shows 2D slices randomly selected from MR data and the second row demonstrates the corresponding 3D example.

Jaccard evaluate volumetric overlap, while ASD and 95HD compute geometric distance. Following the work in [7], we also consider two different data partition settings, where one takes 10% of the training data and another uses 20% of the training data as labeled data for model training.

## 3.2 Ablation Study

As mentioned in the Sect. 2, the proposed SDD Consistency Learning contains three loss items, $L_l$, $L_u$ and $L_g$. Therefore, we study the effect of enabling and disabling them on LA under 10% settings. Taking the $L_l$ as our baseline, which uses the limited labeled data for supervised learning. From Table 1, we see that: (1) When we add the loss $L_u$, denoted as $L_l + L_u$, the Dice performance is improved about $+6.58\%$ on LA, due to the information extracted from unlabeled data. (2) Further adopting the loss $L_g$ boosts the Dice improvement to $+8.78\%$. (3) The combination of two components gives the performance improvement on all metrics. These results indicate the advantage of the proposed SDD Consistency Learning. More additional experiments are in the supplementary material.

**Table 2.** Comparison of our model and state-of-the-art methods on the LA under two different data partition settings. Note that we do not use any post-processing.

| Method | # Scans used | | Metrics | | | |
|---|---|---|---|---|---|---|
| | Labeled | Unlabeled | Dice (%) | Jaccard (%) | ASD (voxel) | 95 HD (voxel) |
| V-net | 100% (80) | 0% (0) | 91.14 | 83.82 | 1.52 | 5.75 |
| V-net | 20% (16) | 0% (0) | 86.03 | 76.06 | 3.51 | 14.26 |
| DAP [19] (MICCAI'19) | 20% (16) | 80% (64) | 87.89 | 78.72 | 2.74 | 9.29 |
| UA-MT [18] (MICCAI'19) | 20% (16) | 80% (64) | 88.88 | 80.21 | 2.26 | 7.32 |
| SASSNet [7] (MICCAI'20) | 20% (16) | 80% (64) | 89.27 | 80.82 | 3.13 | 8.83 |
| DUWM [16] (MICCAI'20) | 20% (16) | 80% (64) | 89.65 | 81.35 | 2.03 | 7.04 |
| LG-ER-MT [5] (MICCAI'20) | 20% (16) | 80% (64) | 89.62 | 81.31 | 2.06 | 7.16 |
| DTC [9] (AAAI'21) | 20% (16) | 80% (64) | 89.42 | 80.98 | 2.10 | 7.32 |
| Ours | 20% (16) | 80% (64) | **90.63** | **82.95** | **1.89** | **6.29** |
| V-net | 10% (8) | 0% (0) | 79.99 | 68.12 | 5.48 | 21.11 |
| DAP [19] (MICCAI'19) | 10% (8) | 90% (72) | 81.89 | 71.23 | 3.80 | 15.81 |
| UA-MT [18] (MICCAI'19) | 10% (8) | 90% (72) | 84.25 | 73.48 | 3.36 | 13.84 |
| SASSNet [7] (MICCAI'20) | 10% (8) | 90% (72) | 86.81 | 76.92 | 3.94 | 12.54 |
| DUWM [16] (MICCAI'20) | 10% (8) | 90% (72) | 85.91 | 75.75 | 3.31 | 12.67 |
| LG-ER-MT [5] (MICCAI'20) | 10% (8) | 90% (72) | 85.54 | 75.12 | 3.77 | 13.29 |
| DTC [9] (AAAI'21) | 10% (8) | 90% (72) | 86.57 | 76.55 | 3.74 | 14.47 |
| Ours | 10% (8) | 90% (72) | **88.77** | **79.97** | **2.25** | **8.02** |

## 3.3 Performance Evaluation and Comparison

**Experiments on LA.** We first evaluate the performance of SDD Consistency Learning on the LA dataset. The quantitative comparison results are summarized in Table 2, we observe that: (1) SDD Consistency Learning outperforms all the other semi-supervised methods on all evaluation metrics under two settings. (2) Our SDD Consistency Learning trained on the 20% setting can achieve comparable Dice (90.63%) and Jaccard (82.95%) to that of 100% fully-supervised approach (91.14% and 83.82%), respectively. Figure 3 further shows some qualitative comparison examples, they show our SDD Consistency Learning pays more attention to inner regions of target objects and less to outliers than other methods. These qualitative and quantitative results verify the effectiveness of SDD Consistency Learning.

**Table 3.** The segmentation performance on NIH Pancreas. The results of two settings are reproduced through the released codes. Note that we do not use any post-processing.

| Method | # Scans used | | Metrics | | | |
|---|---|---|---|---|---|---|
| | Labeled | Unlabeled | Dice (%) | Jaccard (%) | ASD (voxel) | 95 HD (voxel) |
| V-net | 100% (62) | 0% (0) | 81.78 | 69.65 | 1.34 | 5.13 |
| V-net | 20% (12) | 0% (0) | 70.63 | 56.72 | 6.29 | 22.54 |
| MT [15] (NeurIPS'17) | 20% (12) | 80% (50) | 75.85 | 61.98 | 3.40 | 12.59 |
| UA-MT [18] (MICCAI'19) | 20% (12) | 80% (50) | 77.26 | 63.82 | 3.06 | 11.90 |
| SASSNet [7] (MICCAI'20) | 20% (12) | 80% (50) | 77.66 | 64.08 | 3.05 | 10.93 |
| CCT [11] (CVPR'20) | 20% (12) | 80% (50) | 76.58 | 62.76 | 3.69 | 12.92 |
| DTC [9] (AAAI'21) | 20% (12) | 80% (50) | 78.27 | 64.75 | 2.25 | 8.36 |
| Ours | 20% (12) | 80% (50) | **81.50** | **69.14** | **1.41** | **5.70** |
| V-net | 10% (6) | 0% (0) | 52.66 | 37.82 | 8.27 | 27.60 |
| MT [15] (NeurIPS'17) | 10% (6) | 90% (56) | 67.70 | 52.38 | 6.68 | 21.76 |
| UA-MT [18] (MICCAI'19) | 10% (6) | 90% (56) | 68.01 | 52.89 | 6.14 | 19.95 |
| SASSNet [7] (MICCAI'20) | 10% (6) | 90% (56) | 70.10 | 54.96 | 5.60 | 18.71 |
| CCT [11] (CVPR'20) | 10% (6) | 90% (56) | 68.17 | 53.79 | 3.93 | 16.85 |
| DTC [9] (AAAI'21) | 10% (6) | 90% (56) | 68.34 | 53.37 | 4.53 | 14.33 |
| Ours | 10% (6) | 90% (56) | **74.60** | **60.65** | **2.41** | **12.63** |

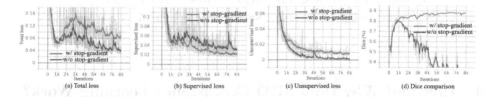

**Fig. 4.** Analysis with and without stop-gradient on LA under 10% setting. w/ denotes the with and w/o represents the without.

**Experiments on NIH Pancreas.** We also conduct experiments on NIH Pancreas to further verify the ability of the proposed SDD Consistency Learning. The experiment in [9] only reports the performance with 20% labeled data, we use the official codes to reproduce all the results of 10% setting. As listed in Table 3, SDD Consistency Learning outperforms others with an impressive margin under two settings, especially under the 10% setting. For example, SDD Consistency Learning improves the V-net using the 10% labeled data by 21.94% Dice while outperforms DTC by 6.26% Dice. Note that our method using 20% labeled data obtains comparable results, e.g. 81.50% vs 81.78% Dice, with the V-net using the 100% labeled data. Some qualitative comparisons are in the Visualization section of supplementary material.

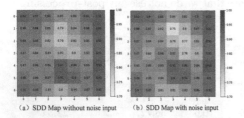

(a) SDD Map without noise input    (b) SDD Map with noise input

**Fig. 5.** Visualization example of SDD Map with or without noise on LA unlabeled data under 10% setting. The example is randomly selected from the slices of SDD Map.

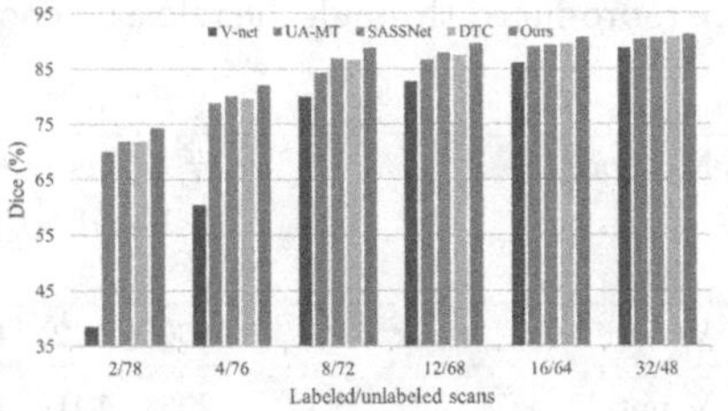

**Fig. 6.** Comparisons on the LA under different labeled/unlabeled scans.

**Table 4.** Comparison with or without the skip-connection of ancillary segmentation branch on LA under 10% setting.

| Method | # Scans used | | Metrics | | | |
|---|---|---|---|---|---|---|
| | Labeled | Unlabeled | Dice (%) | Jaccard (%) | ASD (voxel) | 95HD (voxel) |
| V-net | 10% (8) | 0% (0) | 79.99 | 68.12 | 5.48 | 21.11 |
| w/ skip | 10% (8) | 90% (72) | 87.60 | 78.29 | 2.30 | 8.42 |
| w/o skip | 10% (8) | 90% (72) | **88.77** | **79.97** | **2.25** | **8.02** |

## 4    How and Why Does SDD Consistency Learning Work?

In this section, we attempt to give some insights about how and why our method works. We first evaluate the network architecture, which has two key components. We then visualize the SDD Map and conduct experimental analysis with our SDD Consistency Learning over a very small amount of labeled data. Finally, we give additional discussion.

**Is Stop-gradient Essential?** Our network shares the encoders weights, but SimSiam [3] has proved that the operation exists the collapsing solutions in contrastive learning. Therefore, SimSiam uses stop-gradient to prevent collapsing, but we have an question in this work: is stop-gradient essential in semi-supervised manner? To answer this question, a comparison on "with vs. without stop-gradient" is presented in Fig. 4. Without stop-gradient, unsupervised loss reaches the minimum possible loss of 0 in Fig. 4(c), but the Dice performance is very worse in Fig. 4(d). In Fig. 4(b), supervised loss decreases slowly. Obviously, stop-gradient also plays an essential role in our architecture. Since the weight of unsupervised loss uses Gaussian curve to ramp up, the total loss appears inflection point at about $1k$ iterations (see Fig. 4(a)). Note that unsupervised loss's weight is larger than supervised loss's, blue curve thus decreases quickly than the orange curve in Fig. 4(a).

**Why Does not The Ancillary Segmentation Branch Have Skip-connections?** The reason is that: (1) It enlarges the differences between two branch decoders' features and also can be regarded as "negative" perturbations in feature level. Due to the consistency constraint on decoders' predictions, such differences or perturbations can force the encoder more robust on the organ. (2) Ancillary segmentation branch is not used during inference. The quantitative comparison on "with vs. without skip-connections" is listed in Table 4.

**SDD Map Visualization.** As shown in Fig. 5(a), it is observed that each value is greater than 0.75. Such situation verifies that all the voxels are very similar to its corresponding region's mean feature, since cosine similarity function is used to measure the distance. We further visualize the corresponding SDD Map of ancillary segmentation branch (see Fig. 5(b)), where it inputs the unlabeled data with noise. We can see Fig. 5(a) and Fig. 5(b) are very similar. These qualitative results demonstrate the effectiveness of the proposed method.

**Does SDD Consistency Learning Still Effectiveness over Very Limited Labeled Data?** From Fig. 6, it is observed that our method consistently performs better than other methods under different labeled/unlabeled scans, even if the amount of labeled data is very small, such as 2 labeled data.

**Discussion.** One may wonder what would happen if we directly use the feature map rather than the proposed the SDD Map for consistency learning. We have conducted such an experiment and the Dice performance reduced to 88.58% (−0.19%) on LA under 10% setting. Compared with the individual voxel-wise feature map where local changes only affect local points, small changes in voxel will change SDD Map values of neighbouring multiple points. To maintain the consistency between SDD Map of two branches, the encoder has to learn a holistic overview of the input volume. In this way, encoder's representation ability is further improved. In this work, we focus on single-class segmentation to simplify the presentation. As for multi-class case, a straightforward manner is regarding the different organs as one-class. Since it is not the optimal strategy when extending our method from single organ to multi-organ segmentation, we expect to explore better framework in our future work.

## 5  Conclusions

A SDD Consistency Learning method is developed in this paper to achieve semi-supervised medical image segmentation. Our proposed method is capable of gradually enforcing the consistency of the organ's distance distribution over the unlabeled images under a small perturbation. Comprehensive experimental results on two popular medical datasets have demonstrated that our proposed method can achieve the state-of-the-art segmentation performance, such improvement benefits from both the network design and the distance distribution modeling.

## References

1. Bearman, A., Russakovsky, O., Ferrari, V., Fei-Fei, L.: What's the point: semantic segmentation with point supervision. In: Leibe, B., Matas, J., Sebe, N., Welling, M. (eds.) ECCV 2016. LNCS, vol. 9911, pp. 549–565. Springer, Cham (2016). https://doi.org/10.1007/978-3-319-46478-7_34
2. Bortsova, G., Dubost, F., Hogeweg, L., Katramados, I., de Bruijne, M.: Semi-supervised medical image segmentation via learning consistency under transformations. In: Shen, D., et al. (eds.) MICCAI 2019. LNCS, vol. 11769, pp. 810–818. Springer, Cham (2019). https://doi.org/10.1007/978-3-030-32226-7_90
3. Chen, X., He, K.: Exploring simple siamese representation learning. In: Conference on Computer Vision and Pattern Recognition (2021)
4. French, G., Laine, S., Aila, T., Mackiewicz, M., Finlayson, G.: Semi-supervised semantic segmentation needs strong, varied perturbations. In: British Machine Vision Conference (2020)
5. Hang, W., et al.: Local and global structure-aware entropy regularized mean teacher model for 3D left atrium segmentation. In: MICCAI 2020. LNCS, vol. 12261, pp. 562–571. Springer, Cham (2020). https://doi.org/10.1007/978-3-030-59710-8_55
6. Laine, S., Aila, T.: Temporal ensembling for semi-supervised learning. In: International Conference on Learning Representations (2017)
7. Li, S., Zhang, C., He, X.: Shape-aware semi-supervised 3D semantic segmentation for medical images. In: Martel, A.L., et al. (eds.) MICCAI 2020. LNCS, vol. 12261, pp. 552–561. Springer, Cham (2020). https://doi.org/10.1007/978-3-030-59710-8_54
8. Li, X., Yu, L., Chen, H., Fu, C.W., Heng, P.A.: Semi-supervised skin lesion segmentation via transformation consistent self-ensembling model. In: British Machine Vision Conference (2018)
9. Luo, X., Chen, J., Song, T., Chen, Y., Wang, G., Zhang, S.: Semi-supervised medical image segmentation through dual-task consistency. In: AAAI Conference on Artificial Intelligence (2021)

10. Milletari, F., Navab, N., Ahmadi, S.A.: V-Net: fully convolutional neural networks for volumetric medical image segmentation. In: International Conference on 3D Vision, pp. 565–571 (2016)
11. Ouali, Y., Hudelot, C., Tami, M.: Semi-supervised semantic segmentation with cross-consistency training. In: Conference on Computer Vision and Pattern Recognition, pp. 12674–12684 (2020)
12. Perone, C.S., Cohen-Adad, J.: Deep semi-supervised segmentation with weight-averaged consistency targets. In: Deep Learning in Medical Image Analysis and Multimodal Learning for Clinical Decision Support, pp. 12–19 (2018)
13. Ronneberger, O., Fischer, P., Brox, T.: U-Net: convolutional networks for biomedical image segmentation. In: Navab, N., Hornegger, J., Wells, W.M., Frangi, A.F. (eds.) MICCAI 2015. LNCS, vol. 9351, pp. 234–241. Springer, Cham (2015). https://doi.org/10.1007/978-3-319-24574-4_28
14. Shen, H., Wang, R., Zhang, J., McKenna, S.J.: Boundary-aware fully convolutional network for brain tumor segmentation. In: Descoteaux, M., et al. (eds.) MICCAI 2017. LNCS, vol. 10434, pp. 433–441. Springer, Cham (2017). https://doi.org/10.1007/978-3-319-66185-8_49
15. Tarvainen, A., Valpola, H.: Mean teachers are better role models: weight-averaged consistency targets improve semi-supervised deep learning results. In: Neural Information Processing Systems, pp. 1195–1204 (2017)
16. Wang, Y., et al.: Double-uncertainty weighted method for semi-supervised learning. In: Martel, A.L., et al. (eds.) MICCAI 2020. LNCS, vol. 12261, pp. 542–551. Springer, Cham (2020). https://doi.org/10.1007/978-3-030-59710-8_53
17. Xiong, Z., Fedorov, V.V., Fu, X., Cheng, E., Macleod, R., Zhao, J.: Fully automatic left atrium segmentation from late gadolinium enhanced magnetic resonance imaging using a dual fully convolutional neural network. IEEE Trans. Med. Imaging 38(2), 515–524 (2019)
18. Yu, L., Wang, S., Li, X., Fu, C.-W., Heng, P.-A.: Uncertainty-aware self-ensembling model for semi-supervised 3D left atrium segmentation. In: Shen, D., et al. (eds.) MICCAI 2019. LNCS, vol. 11765, pp. 605–613. Springer, Cham (2019). https://doi.org/10.1007/978-3-030-32245-8_67
19. Zheng, H., et al.: Semi-supervised segmentation of liver using adversarial learning with deep atlas prior. In: Shen, D., et al. (eds.) MICCAI 2019. LNCS, vol. 11769, pp. 148–156. Springer, Cham (2019). https://doi.org/10.1007/978-3-030-32226-7_17
20. Zhou, Z., Siddiquee, M.M.R., Tajbakhsh, N., Liang, J.: Unet++: redesigning skip connections to exploit multiscale features in image segmentation. IEEE Trans. Med. Imaging 39(6), 1856–1867 (2019)

# MultiGAN: Multi-domain Image Translation from OCT to OCTA

Bing Pan, Zexuan Ji[✉], and Qiang Chen

School of Computer Science and Engineering, Nanjing University of Science and Technology, Nanjing 210094, China
{panbing,jizexuan,chen2qiang}@njust.edu.cn

**Abstract.** Optical coherence tomography (OCT) and optical coherence tomography angiography (OCTA) are important imaging techniques for assessing and managing retinal diseases. OCTA can display more blood vessel information than OCT, which, however, requires software and hardware modifications on OCT devices. A large number of OCT data does not have corresponding OCTA data, which greatly limits doctors' diagnosis. Considering the inconvenience of acquiring OCTA images and inevitable mechanical artifacts, we introduce image-to-image translation to generate OCTA from OCT. In this paper, we propose a novel method, MultiGAN, which uses one input image to get three target domain outputs without relying on domain code. We utilize the resnet block in skip connections to preserve details. A domain dependent loss is proposed to impose the restrictions among OCTA projection maps. The dataset containing paired OCT and OCTA images from 500 eyes diagnosed with various retinal diseases is used to evaluate the performance of the proposed network. The results based on cross validation experiments demonstrate the stability and superior performances of the proposed model comparing with state-of-the-art models.

**Keywords:** Multi-domain · Image-to-image translation · OCT-to-OCTA generation · Unsupervised methods

## 1 Introduction

Image-to-image translation aims to transform the image representation of an object into another image representation of the object [1]. That is, to find a function that can map the source domain to the target domain, which can be applied to many practical problems, such as image style transfer, attribute transfer, image resolution improvement and so on [2,3]. The existing methods have good results in one-to-one image translation, but they also have their disadvantages. They need to build multiple generators to build multiple mapping relationships, and are not suitable for multi-domain image translation tasks. Multi-domain image translation has also been widely developed [4,5].

Many diseases can be reflected on fundus image. In recent years, optical coherence tomography (OCT) [6] has been paid more and more attention in

S. Yu et al. (Eds.): PRCV 2022, LNCS 13535, pp. 336–347, 2022.
https://doi.org/10.1007/978-3-031-18910-4_28

the evaluation and diagnosis of retinal diseases due to its characteristics of high imaging speed, high resolution and non-invasive. Optical coherence tomography angiography (OCTA) [7] is a new imaging mode based on OCT technology. It displays the three-dimensional structure of retinal blood vessels, which makes up for the lack of blood flow information provided by OCT. OCTA can display the superficial and deep capillary plexus of the retinal vascular system [8,9].

Although it is theoretically possible to obtain OCTA using the same OCT hardware, in practice obtaining OCTA images requires some hardware and software modifications to existing OCT machines [10,11]. Some OCTA scanning methods are easy to introduce background noise, which reduces the image quality of OCTA [12]. In addition, due to the time difference between the development of OCT and OCTA models, a large number of OCT image in many hospitals lack corresponding OCTA images, and some hospitals even lack OCTA equipment. Therefore, it is of great significance to study the relationship between OCT and corresponding OCTA images, so as to conveniently obtain OCTA images from OCT images.

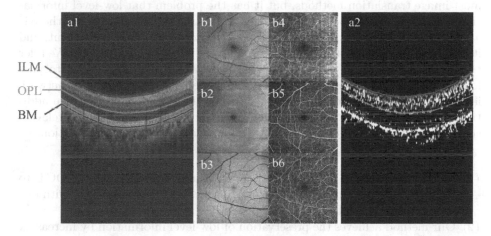

**Fig. 1.** Visualizations of OCT and OCTA images. (a1) OCT B-scan. (a2) Enhanced OCTA B-scan. (b1–b3) OCT projection images. (b4–b6) OCTA projection images.

OCT and OCTA directly obtain three-dimensional volume data of the retina, but the volume data cannot visually display detailed information. At present, the mainstream observation method is to observe three projection images of the retina, as shown in Fig. 1, a1 and a2 use B-scan to segment three retinal layers, which are internal limiting membrane (ILM), outer plexiform layer (OPL), and Bruch's membrane (BM) [13]. In Fig. 1, a2 is the result of intensity multiplied by six based on OCTA B-scan. The projection map is realized based on the result of layer segmentation. In the Fig. 1, b1 and b4 belong to FULL domain, which includes all information from ILM layer to BM layer. This domain contains global information. b2 and b5 belong to ILM-OPL domain and represent information between ILM and OPL layers. It can show the vessels in the inner retina with high reflection. b3 and b6 belong to OPL-BM domain and is the part between OPL and BM [9,14]. It displays the vessel shadows in the outer retina with low reflection. Both ILM-OPL and OPL-BM are products of layer segmentation. If the OCTA image is directly generated using OCT B-scan image and then the projection map is obtained by layer segmentation, the effect of layer segmentation has a great influence on the blood flow information in the OCTA projection map. In order to avoid the influence of layer segmentation, we use OCT FULL domain projection map to generate three OCTA projection maps.

CycleGAN [15] and pix2pix [16] need to train multiple models to achieve multiple target domains, while Stargan-v2 [17] realizes the generation of multiple target domains from one model by controlling the generator for many times by using Style encoder. SingleGAN [18] use domain code to generate images of three target domains simultaneously from one input image. In multi-domain translation, many models rely on domain code, but our method achieves the release of domain code [18] on the basis of using one input image to generate images of three target domains simultaneously. Encoder-decoder [19] is used in most image translation methods, but it has the problem that low-level information cannot be shared to decoder. As mentioned in the pix2pix method, there is a great deal of low-level information shared between the input and output, and it would be desirable to shuttle this information directly across the net. We refer to the skip connections [20] in U-Net [21] on the basis of SingleGAN to pass low-channel information to decoder. At the same time, the number of network layers is increased and resnet blocks [22] are used on skip connections. In addition, due to the correlation between OCTA projection images, we use correlation constraints to help the generator get better images for vascular information.

Overall, our contributions are as follows:

(1) We propose multiGAN, a multi-domain image translation from OCT to OCTA. Three target domain images are generated simultaneously with one input image without using domain code.
(2) Our method achieves the preservation of low-level information by increasing the number of network layers and using resnet block in skip connections.
(3) Due to the correlation between target domains, the full layer information of OCTA should include the deep and shallow layers of OCTA. We propose domain dependent loss to constrain the generated images.

## 2    Method

### 2.1    Network Structure

We use the one-to-many generator and discriminator architecture in SingleGAN. Figure 2 illustrates an overview of our framework, which consists of two modules described below.

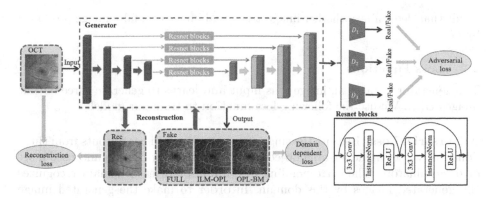

**Fig. 2.** The overview of the proposed method. Generator is composed of an encoder-decoder architecture and resnet blocks on the skip connection. The objective function includes: adversarial loss, reconstruction loss, domain dependent loss.

**Generator.** Many domain generation solutions have used encoder-decoder networks on generator, such as CycleGAN, StarGAN-v2, and SingleGAN. In these networks, input image is sampled progressively downsample through a series of layers, until a bottleneck layer [23], and then upsample. These networks contain two stride-2 convolution layers for downsampling, six resnet blocks and two stride-2 transposed convolution layers for upsampling. That is, the encoder compresses the information into a fixed length vector, which often results in the loss of information. For image translation problems, especially medical image translation problems, it is necessary to retain more details of the input image, such as vascular information. There is a lot of low-level information shared between the input and output that we want to be accessible to decoder [24].

To solve the problem of detail retention in medical images, we refer to the skip connections in U-Net on the basis of SingleGAN to pass low-channel information to decoder. In transferring information, we refer to the bottleneck and rather than directly linking the $i$ layer information to the $n-i$ layer information, where n is the total number of layers. Instead of using too many resnet blocks at the same time, we use two blocks to reduce the computation. The use of bottleneck can reduce the number of parameters and computation, and make data training and feature extraction more efficient and intuitive. In order to better capture the features of the deep layer, we also increased the downsample and upsample layers to three layers.

Furthermore, we do not use domain code $z$ in SingleGAN. By fixing the generator's domain information, our network generates these three domains at the time to reduce the amount of computation, which can greatly reduce the network burden.

**Discriminators.** We use three discriminators with the same structure to distinguish between images in different domains. Each discriminator gets a binary result that determines whether image $x$ is a real image or a false image produced by $G$.

## 2.2  Loss Functions

The generator G takes an image x as input and learns to generate three output images G(x). We use the following loss function to train our model.

**Adversarial Loss.** Because the single generator we used has outputs from three domains, we set up adversarial objectives for each target domain and used a set of discriminators. The corresponding discriminator to each domain recognizes the generated images by this domain. In order to make the generated image indistinguishable from the real image, we use an adversarial loss. The $\mathcal{L}_{adv}$ is redefined as

$$\mathcal{L}_{adv}(G, D_{\{B,C,D\}}) = \sum_{i \in \{B,C,D\}} (\mathbb{E}_{x_i}[\log(D_i(x_i))] + \mathbb{E}_{x_A}[\log(1 - D_i(G(x_A)))]), \tag{1}$$

where A is the FULL domain in OCT, B is the FULL domain in OCTA, C is the ILM-OPL domain in OCTA and D is the OPL-BM domain in OCTA. Among them, A is the source domain and B, C, D are target domains. In this paper, $D_i(\cdot)$ tries to distinguish between real and generated images [25].

**Reconstruction Loss.** Paired OCT and OCTA data often do not exist in actual hospitals because it requires two tests in a short period of time. In order to achieve translation between domains without paired input-output examples, we apply a Reconstruction loss to the generator, which is defined as

$$\mathcal{L}_{rec}(G) = \mathbb{E}_{x_A}[\|x_A - G(G(x_A))\|], \tag{2}$$

where $G(x_A)$ generates three target domain images and put these images back into the generator to get $G(G(x_A)) = \hat{x_A}$. The reconstruction loss is to make $\hat{x_A}$ close to $x_A$. Instead of the L1 norm in SingleGAN, we choose to use structural similarity (SSIM) [26] as a reconstruction loss to represent more texture details [27].

**Domain Dependent Loss.** The three generated images have domain dependent features. In other words, the full layer information of OCTA should include the deep and shallow layers of OCTA. Due to the special relationship between target domains, we introduce a new loss function called domain dependent loss, which is defined as

$$\mathcal{L}_{dom}(G) = \mathbb{E}_{x_A}[\|2G(x_A)_B - (G(x_A)_C + G(x_A)_D)\|], \tag{3}$$

where $G(x_A)_B$, $G(x_A)_C$ and $G(x_A)_D$ are the full layer, shallow layer and deep layer generation results of OCTA respectively. This allows better retention of vascular information, especially of small vessels, and improves vascular continuity.

**Full Objective.** Finally, the full objective function can be written as

$$\min_{G} \max_{D} \mathcal{L}_{adv} + \lambda_{rec}\mathcal{L}_{rec} + \lambda_{dom}\mathcal{L}_{dom}, \tag{4}$$

where $\lambda_{rec}$ and $\lambda_{dom}$ hyper-parameters that control the relative importance of reconstruction and domain dependent compared to the adversarial objective, respectively. We use $\lambda_{rec} = 10$ and $\lambda_{dom} = 5$ in all of our experiments.

## 3  Experiments

**OCTA-500.** OCTA-500 [9] contains two subsets, OCTA_6M and OCTA_3M, which is divided according to the FOV type. We use projection images portion of OCTA_6M dataset containing 300 subjects with an imaging range of 6 mm × 6 mm × 2 mm centered on the fovea. The dataset can be categorized into NORMAL, OTHERS and various retinal diseases, including age-related macular degeneration (AMD), diabetic retinopathy (DR), choroidal neovascularization (CNV), central serous chorioretinopathy (CSC) and retinal vein occlusion (RVO). We randomly select one-fifth of the data as the test set and use all remaining images for training data.

**Performances.** Figure 3 illustrates the performance of our approach in several diseases, containing the input FULL domain OCT projection images, three generated OCTA projection images and their corresponding ground truth respectively. In the diseased images, there are anomalies near the fovea of OCT, which may affect the results of image generation. However, our method can effectively extract vascular information in a variety of diseases without being affected by lesions, which indicates that our method is robust.

**Baselines and Metrics.** As our baseline models, we adopt CycleGAN, StarGANv2, HISD [28] and SingleGAN. CycleGAN belongs to two domain generation method, and the rest are multi-domain generation methods. All models of baselines are trained using the implementations provided by their authors.

The evaluation metrics include SSIM, feature similarity (FSIM) and Single Image Fréchet Inception Distance (SIFID) [29]. All the metrics are evaluated between the generated image and the ground truth (GT), averaged over all test in each domain.

SSIM can compute the perceptual distance between the generated image and its ground truth. The higher the SSIM is, the greater the similarity of the luminance, contrast and structure of two images will be. FSIM considers that all pixels in an image do not have the same importance, and it uses feature similarity for quality evaluation. The higher the FSIM value, the higher the consistency of human sensory images The SIFID captures the difference between the internal distributions of two images. A lower SIFID score indicates that the styles of two images are more similar [26].

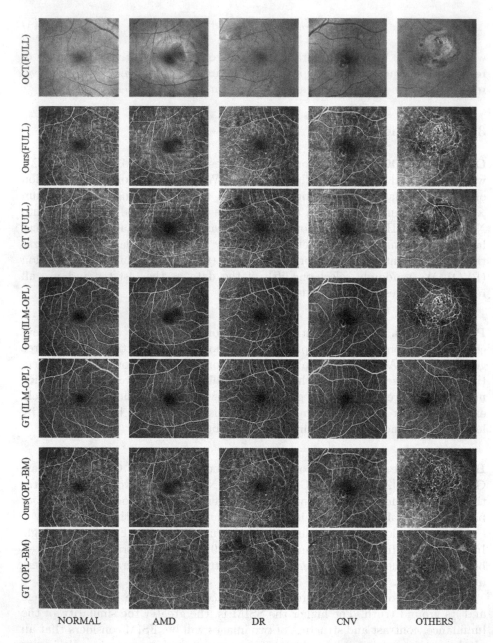

**Fig. 3.** Performances of our approach in several diseases. The first line is the input image. The other six lines are three domain of GT OCTA and generated OCTA projection images for each category.

**Comparison Results.** In this section, we will evaluate the performance of different models. The FULL domain of OCT generates three domain images for OCTA as shown in Fig. 4.

It is not difficult to see that the effect of several models is generally preferred when the target domain is ILM-OPL, and vascular information is obvious. In addition to our method, other methods have defects in the formation of fovea, too large or too small fovea will affect the formation of small vessels. The performance of these models, especially the Stargan-v2 and HISD models, is degraded in the generation of FULL target domain. At the same time, we can observe that our proposed method can present the best results in all three target domains. The vascular information is continuous and clear, and it is worth mentioning that the information of the small vessels near the fovea is also preserved. The contribution should contain no more than four levels of headings.

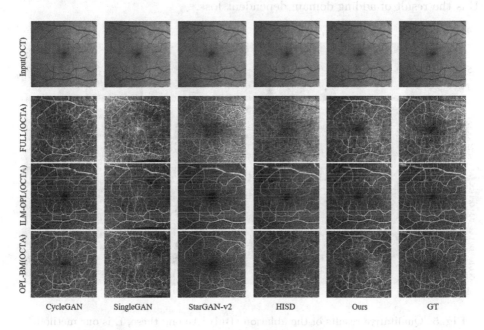

**Fig. 4.** OCTA projection images generation compared to baselines.

The quantitative evaluation results are shown in Table 1. Our approach achieves better performance than baselines in all the tasks. Our method achieves minimum SIFID and maximum SSIM and FSIM. However, other methods have poor indicators in SIFID, and the corresponding image cannot obtain the reserved details. The quantitative data prove that our model is stable and reliable.

**Table 1.** Quantitative results of the comparison experiment.

| Method | SSIM | | | FSIM | | | SIFID | | |
|---|---|---|---|---|---|---|---|---|---|
| | FULL | ILM-OPL | OPL-BM | FULL | ILM-OPL | OPL-BM | FULL | ILM-OPL | OPL-BM |
| CycleGAN | 0.0547 | 0.0206 | 0.0229 | 0.7239 | 0.6955 | 0.7174 | 0.4185 | 0.3800 | 0.2268 |
| SingleGAN | 0.0981 | 0.1332 | 0.0865 | 0.7198 | 0.7212 | 0.7143 | 0.2708 | 0.1838 | 0.1345 |
| StarGAN-v2 | 0.1074 | 0.0999 | 0.0760 | 0.7471 | 0.7238 | 0.7309 | 0.5779 | 0.5899 | 0.8961 |
| HISD | 0.0498 | 0.0352 | 0.0304 | 0.7360 | 0.6586 | 0.7101 | 0.6301 | 0.4741 | 0.2694 |
| Ours | **0.1420** | **0.2063** | **0.1458** | **0.7615** | **0.7473** | **0.7538** | **0.1963** | **0.1655** | **0.1286** |

**Ablation Study.** We conduct ablation study to validate the effect of each module of our proposed approach, as shown in Fig. 5. A is the result of increasing the number of network layers, B, C and D are the results of adding one layer, two layers and three layers of skip connections with resnet blocks, respectively. E is the result of adding domain dependent loss.

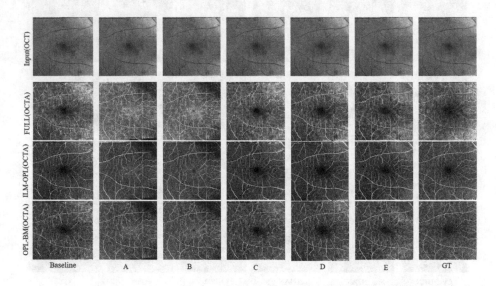

**Fig. 5.** Qualitative results of the ablation study. Among these, E is our method.

The baseline is the reconstruction loss using SingleGAN of the SSIM (baseline in Fig. 5). Compared with the SingleGAN result in Fig. 4, it can be seen that using SSIM can better express the structural similarity, which is more in line with the intuitive feeling of human eyes, and the generation of fovea is also significantly improved. Baseline deepens the number of network layers from the baseline while reducing the number of resnet blocks. This justifies the need to increase the number of network layers. But it is clear that decoder only retains deep information, leaving the fovea and its surrounding small blood vessels unlearned. B, C and D respectively add one layer, two layers and three layers of skip connections with resnet blocks.

Table 2. Quantitative results of the ablation study.

| Method | MSE | | | FSIM | | |
|---|---|---|---|---|---|---|
| | FULL | ILM-OPL | OPL-BM | FULL | ILM-OPL | OPL-BM |
| Baseline | 0.0617 | 0.0781 | 0.0879 | 0.7263 | 0.6698 | 0.7052 |
| A | 0.0857 | 0.0714 | 0.0806 | 0.7482 | 0.7515 | 0.7395 |
| B | 0.0872 | 0.0709 | 0.0817 | 0.7529 | **0.7605** | 0.7466 |
| C | 0.0583 | 0.0714 | 0.0858 | 0.7200 | 0.6763 | 0.7016 |
| D | 0.0534 | 0.0524 | 0.0730 | 0.7490 | 0.7554 | 0.7353 |
| E | **0.0497** | **0.0470** | **0.0687** | **0.7615** | 0.7473 | **0.7538** |

From the quantitative analysis in Table 2, we can see that it is very effective to use resnet block to retain shallow data on skip connections and pass it to decoder. The fovea is becoming more and more suitable in size. This proves that our method is valid. On this basis, we can see that the generation result of ILM-OPL domain is far better than that of FULL domain and OPL-BM domain, and the information of these three domains is correlated. In order to make better use of the results of ILM-OPL domain, we added domain dependent loss (E in Fig. 5). As can be seen from the results listed in Table 2, the overall evaluation of our method (E in Fig. 5) is excellent. It is optimal on MSE, that is, the difference between the generated image and the real image is the smallest. Although shallow information was added in methods C and D, FSIM results decreased, which was because the network learned the fovea and paid attention to small vessels around the fovea, but the continuity and retention of other vessels were missing. Our approach effectively solves this problem. It can be seen that our method better preserves the information of small vessels, and both large and small vessels are more continuous than the baseline.

## 4    Conclusion

In this paper, we propose a detail-preserving architecture based on SingleGAN, which generates detailed images by using resnet blocks on skip connections. In order to solve the problem of lack of OCTA projection images and avoid the use of layer segmentation, we add domain dependent loss to this architecture, which perfectly solves the requirement of generating three OCTA projection images from OCT FULL domain projection images. This perfectly solves the need for OCT FULL domain projection images to generate three kinds of OCTA projection images. In addition, due to the lack of corresponding OCTA image in a large number of OCT images in hospitals, the use of unpaired data in our method has important significance and application prospects. Extensive qualitative and quantitative experiments prove the effectiveness of our method. Our method is most similar to GT, especially in the continuity of great vessels, the formation of fovea and the formation of small vessels near the fovea.

# References

1. Pang, Y., Lin, J., Qin, T., Chen, Z.: Image-to-image translation: methods and applications. IEEE Trans. Multimed. **24**, 3859–3881 (2021)
2. Kazemi, H., Soleymani, S., Taherkhani, F., Iranmanesh, S., Nasrabadi, N.: Unsupervised image-to-image translation using domain-specific variational information bound. In: Advances in Neural Information Processing Systems, vol. 31 (2018)
3. Li, R., Cao, W., Jiao, Q., Wu, S., Wong, H.S.: Simplified unsupervised image translation for semantic segmentation adaptation. Pattern Recogn. **105**, 107343 (2020)
4. Cao, J., Huang, H., Li, Y., He, R., Sun, Z.: Informative sample mining network for multi-domain image-to-image translation. In: Vedaldi, A., Bischof, H., Brox, T., Frahm, J.-M. (eds.) ECCV 2020. LNCS, vol. 12364, pp. 404–419. Springer, Cham (2020). https://doi.org/10.1007/978-3-030-58529-7_24
5. Huang, X., Liu, M.-Y., Belongie, S., Kautz, J.: Multimodal unsupervised image-to-image translation. In: Ferrari, V., Hebert, M., Sminchisescu, C., Weiss, Y. (eds.) ECCV 2018. LNCS, vol. 11207, pp. 179–196. Springer, Cham (2018). https://doi.org/10.1007/978-3-030-01219-9_11
6. Yang, H.L., et al.: Weakly supervised lesion localization for age-related macular degeneration detection using optical coherence tomography images. PLoS ONE **14**(4), e0215076 (2019)
7. Chalam, K., Sambhav, K.: Optical coherence tomography angiography in retinal diseases. J. Ophthalmic Vis. Res. **11**(1), 84 (2016)
8. Laıns, I., et al.: Retinal applications of swept source optical coherence tomography (OCT) and optical coherence tomography angiography (OCTA). Prog. Retin. Eye Res. **84**, 100951 (2021)
9. Li, M., et al.: IPN-V2 and OCTA-500: methodology and dataset for retinal image segmentation. arXiv preprint arXiv:2012.07261 (2020)
10. Lee, C.S., et al.: Generating retinal flow maps from structural optical coherence tomography with artificial intelligence. Sci. Rep. **9**(1), 1–11 (2019)
11. Zhang, Z., Ji, Z., Chen, Q., Yuan, S., Fan, W.: Texture-guided U-Net for OCT-to-OCTA generation. In: Ma, H., et al. (eds.) PRCV 2021. LNCS, vol. 13022, pp. 42–52. Springer, Cham (2021). https://doi.org/10.1007/978-3-030-88013-2_4
12. Kadomoto, S., Uji, A., Muraoka, Y., Akagi, T., Tsujikawa, A.: Enhanced visualization of retinal microvasculature in optical coherence tomography angiography imaging via deep learning. J. Clin. Med. **9**(5), 1322 (2020)
13. Li, X.X., et al.: A quantitative comparison of five optical coherence tomography angiography systems in clinical performance. Int. J. Ophthalmol. **11**(11), 1784 (2018)
14. Chen, Q., Niu, S., Yuan, S., Fan, W., Liu, Q.: High-low reflectivity enhancement based retinal vessel projection for SD-OCT images. Med. Phys. **43**(10), 5464–5474 (2016)
15. Zhu, J.Y., Park, T., Isola, P., Efros, A.A.: Unpaired image-to-image translation using cycle-consistent adversarial networks. In: Proceedings of the IEEE International Conference on Computer Vision, pp. 2223–2232 (2017)
16. Isola, P., Zhu, J.Y., Zhou, T., Efros, A.A.: Image-to-image translation with conditional adversarial networks. In: Proceedings of the IEEE Conference on Computer Vision and Pattern Recognition, pp. 1125–1134 (2017)
17. Choi, Y., Uh, Y., Yoo, J., Ha, J.W.: StarGAN v2: diverse image synthesis for multiple domains. In: Proceedings of the IEEE/CVF Conference on Computer Vision and Pattern Recognition, pp. 8188–8197 (2020)

18. Yu, X., Cai, X., Ying, Z., Li, T., Li, G.: SingleGAN: image-to-image translation by a single-generator network using multiple generative adversarial learning. In: Jawahar, C.V., Li, H., Mori, G., Schindler, K. (eds.) ACCV 2018. LNCS, vol. 11365, pp. 341–356. Springer, Cham (2019). https://doi.org/10.1007/978-3-030-20873-8_22
19. Badrinarayanan, V., Kendall, A., Cipolla, R.: SegNet: a deep convolutional encoder-decoder architecture for image segmentation. IEEE Trans. Pattern Anal. Mach. Intell. **39**(12), 2481–2495 (2017)
20. Drozdzal, M., Vorontsov, E., Chartrand, G., Kadoury, S., Pal, C.: The importance of skip connections in biomedical image segmentation. In: Carneiro, G., et al. (eds.) LABELS/DLMIA -2016. LNCS, vol. 10008, pp. 179–187. Springer, Cham (2016). https://doi.org/10.1007/978-3-319-46976-8_19
21. Ronneberger, O., Fischer, P., Brox, T.: U-Net: convolutional networks for biomedical image segmentation. CoRR abs/1505.04597. arXiv preprint arXiv:1505.04597 (2015)
22. Wen, L., Li, X., Gao, L.: A transfer convolutional neural network for fault diagnosis based on ResNet-50. Neural Comput. Appl. **32**(10), 6111–6124 (2020). https://doi.org/10.1007/s00521-019-04097-w
23. Park, J., Woo, S., Lee, J.Y., Kweon, I.S.: BAM: bottleneck attention module. arXiv preprint arXiv:1807.06514 (2018)
24. Garg, A., Gowda, D., Kumar, A., Kim, K., Kumar, M., Kim, C.: Improved multi-stage training of online attention-based encoder-decoder models. In: 2019 IEEE Automatic Speech Recognition and Understanding Workshop (ASRU), pp. 70–77. IEEE (2019)
25. Wolterink, J.M., Leiner, T., Viergever, M.A., Išgum, I.: Generative adversarial networks for noise reduction in low-dose CT. IEEE Trans. Med. Imaging **36**(12), 2536–2545 (2017)
26. Sara, U., Akter, M., Uddin, M.S.: Image quality assessment through FSIM, SSIM, MSE and PSNR-a comparative study. J. Comput. Commun. **7**(3), 8–18 (2019)
27. Choi, Y., Choi, M., Kim, M., Ha, J.W., Kim, S., Choo, J.: StarGAN: unified generative adversarial networks for multi-domain image-to-image translation. In: Proceedings of the IEEE Conference on Computer Vision and Pattern Recognition, pp. 8789–8797 (2018)
28. Li, X., et al.: Image-to-image translation via hierarchical style disentanglement. In: Proceedings of the IEEE/CVF Conference on Computer Vision and Pattern Recognition, pp. 8639–8648 (2021)
29. Bates, R., Chocholek, M., Fox, C., Howe, J., Jones, N.: SIFID Scottish inshore fisheries integrated data system: WP 3 final report: development of a novel, automated mechanism for the collection of scallop stock data (2020)

# TransPND: A Transformer Based Pulmonary Nodule Diagnosis Method on CT Image

Rui Wang, Yangsong Zhang$^{(\boxtimes)}$, and Jiangtao Yang

Southwest University of Science and Technology, Mianyang 621000, China
zhangyangsong@vip.163.com

**Abstract.** Detection of Benign and malignant pulmonary nodules is a significant help for early lung cancer diagnosis. Owing to the superior performance of the transformer based deep learning methods in different computer vision tasks, this study attempts to introduce it into the CT image classification task of pulmonary nodules. However, the problems of rare samples and harrowing local feature extraction in this field still need to solve. To this end, we introduce a CT image-based transformer for pulmonary nodule diagnosis (TransPND). Specifically, firstly, we introduce a 2D Panning Sliding Window (2DPSW) for data enhancement, making it more focused on local features. Secondly, unlike the encoder of the traditional transformer, we divide the encoder part of TransPND into two parts: Self Attention Encoder (SA) and Directive Class Attention Encoder (DCA). SA is similar to the traditional self-attention mechanism, except that we introduce Local Diagonal Masking (LDM) to select the attention location and focus on the correlation between tokens rather than itself score. Meanwhile, based on SA, we improve it and propose DCA to guide attention to focus more on local features and reduce computational effort. Finally, to solve the model overfitting problem caused by the increasing depth, we choose the Weight Learning Diagonal Matrix (WLDM) to gate each residual connection in both the SA and DCA stages. We conducted extensive experiments on the LIDC-IDRI dataset. The experimental results show that our model achieves an accuracy of 93.33% compared to other studies using this dataset for lung nodule classification. To the best of our knowledge, TransPND is the first research on the classification of lung nodule CT images based on pure transformer architecture.

**Keywords:** ViT · 2D Panning Sliding Window · Directive Class Attention · Weight Learning Diagonal Matrix · Pulmonary nodule diagnosis

## 1 Introduction

Lung cancer is a malignant tumor originating from the bronchial mucosa epithelium or alveolar epithelium, and it has become one of the cancers with the highest

S. Yu et al. (Eds.): PRCV 2022, LNCS 13535, pp. 348–360, 2022.
https://doi.org/10.1007/978-3-031-18910-4_29

incidence and the fastest death rate in the world [1], among which lung cancer in men is located at the top of all malignant tumors [2]. Depending on the different types of cancer cells, primary lung cancer can be divided into Small Cell Lung Cancer and Non-Small Cell Lung Cancer [3]. Moreover, Small Cell Lung Cancer accounts for about 0.15 of the total incidence of lung cancer and is the most malignant type of lung cancer. However, its cause has not been fully elucidated, and only a few factors increase the risk of lung cancer [4]. So, early diagnosis is essential. As a non-invasive diagnosis, Low Radiation Dose Spiral CT is a medical examination specifically designed to screen for lung cancer. It can detect small nodular lesions at the millimeter level. These lesions can be divided into three types, as shown in Fig. 1, (a) is a pure ground-glass nodule (GGN), (b) is a mixed density nodule (partially solid nodule), and (c) is a solid nodule. This study focuses more on using benign\malignant classification of lung nodules to assist in the diagnosis of early lung cancer. Most existing medical image classification methods are established on CNNs [5–9], which we can classify into several categories based on deep convolution, multi-task convolution, and semi-supervised learning. For instance, Nibali et al. evaluated the effectiveness of in-depth CNN in expert pulmonary nodule classification tasks with ResNet and curriculum learning strategy [10]. Zhai et al. proposed multi-task convolution to learn the characteristics of three-dimensional (3-D) pulmonary nodules from a two-dimensional (2-D) view [11]. Xie et al. used labeled and unlabeled data for semi-supervised Learning, which was combined with the confrontation model for classification [12]. However, the transformer developed prosperously in Natural Language Processing (NLP) has gradually become the dominant model, achieving the most advanced performance in various computer vision tasks. One of the most distinguished contributions in the field of image classification is ViT [13], where Dosovitskiy et al. firstly divided the image into equal blocks and used the correlation between them for position embedding, and the results even outperformed various CNN architectures, such as ResNet [14].

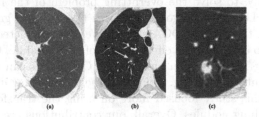

(a)                    (b)                    (c)

**Fig. 1.** Schematic diagram of Pulmonary nodules in the LIDC-LDRI dataset.

However, it does not resolve higher-order dependencies and lacks locally induced bias in structure compared with CNN. Thus, ViT requires a large amount of training data to obtain acceptable visual performance. For example, ViT can show its advantages after pre-train with JFT-300M [15]. Obviously, this is a fatal problem in the field of medical images. A large amount of image information, small local features, and inadequate training data hinder its development in this field. Some researchers have used transfer learning to solve these problems. Such as [16], they trained generic and non-medical datasets to analyze the impact of transfer learning on the classification accuracy of malignant tumors. Nevertheless, such datasets do not allow the network to thoroughly learn the features of medical images such as lung nodules and affect classification effectiveness. Simultaneously, others have focused on feature extraction. PiT, proposed by Xu et al., investigated the effectiveness of pooling layers in the architecture of converters concerning CNN [17]. Although it improved ViT performance, it was based on a hybrid architecture of CNN and Transformer. Furthermore, numerous research describes the reduction of reliance on large datasets by improving ViT. For example, the Swin Transformer proposed by Liu et al. used local attention for non-overlapping windows, with window-to-window merging to produce hierarchical representations, leading to higher efficiency [18].

Therefore, we introduce a novel pure transformer architecture model by reforming deep ViT, which efficiently uses lung nodule CT images for classification tasks. TransPND is built on 2DPSW and an architecture consisting of SA Encoder and DCA Encoder. Firstly, 2DPSW inputs more spatial information into the network by translating the sliding window into 2D space, entirely using the relationship between adjacent pixels, thus generating more compact local feature tokens. Afterward, tokens are input into a multi-layer transformer encoder combined with SA and DCA for feature extraction. Firstly, they are input into the SA stage, which is similar to the self-attention of the traditional transformer. The only difference is that SA introduces Local Diagonal Masking (LDM) to select attention locations. The essential effect is to ignore attention to the diagonal while highlighting correlations between other tokens. Then, we introduce DCA, a modification of SA. Unlike traditional ViT, where the class token and patch embedding were fed into the network simultaneously, at this stage, we propose to embed class tokens in the last two layers of the network to guide attention to focus more on local features and reduce the computational effort. Finally, to solve the overfitting problem of the increasing depth, we choose Weight Learning Diagonal Matrices (WLDM) to gate each residual connection in both the SA and DCA stages. We also conducted extensive ablation experiments to elucidate the effectiveness of each module. Our experiments show that applying TransPND on lung nodule CT images can achieve excellent performance without pre-training. Moreover, the results show its great potential in this field, and this study focused more on using the transformer to classify benign\malignant lung nodules. Overall, our contributions are as follows:

- We introduce a Transformer (TransPND) to efficiently use lung nodule CT images to extract local features in deep dimensions.
- We propose a new local feature extraction method, which embeds more spatial information labels by translating sliding windows in 2D space. This approach has significant advantages over the purely sliced image patch.

- Unlike the traditional deep transformer, we use the Weight Learning Matrix (WLDM) and Local Diagonal Masking (LDM) for the residual connection and attention computation process to improve classification accuracy.
- To the best of our knowledge, TransPND is the first study on lung nodule CT image classification performance using a pure Vit architecture without a pre-training basis and achieving 93.33% accuracy on the LIDC-IDRI dataset.

## 2  Related Work

### 2.1  Classification of Lung Nodules Based on CNN

Over the past decade, CNN has been the dominant model for lung nodule CT image classification [5–7]. Some studies want to improve the model's performance by increasing the depth of convolution [9,19]. Similar to [8], the method proposed in that paper was based on multi-model network architecture and applied Ensemble Learning. Sun et al., as one of the studies that did not use CNN, used Deep Belief Network (DBN) and Stacked Denoising Autoencoder (SDAE) to compare with CNN in the LIDC-IDRI dataset [20]. With extensive experiments, they showed that deep structured algorithms could automatically generate image features of relevant types, however, in this study, in terms of AUC, CNN outperformed.

In addition, inspired by the attention mechanism, Kai et al. firstly used the Residual Attention Network (RAN) and Squeeze-and-Excitation Network(SEN) to extract spatial and contextual features and invoked the novel Multi-Scale Attention Network (MSAN) to capture significant features of nodules [21]. This operation demonstrated the effectiveness of the attention mechanism in image classification.

### 2.2  Visual Transformer (ViT)

Recently, the frameworks based on ViT have consistently achieved state-of-the-art performance in various image classifications. According to previous experience, increasing the depth of the model allows the network to learn more complex representations, such as ResNet increased from 18 to 152 layers. In recent years, there has been a growing body of literature on deep ViT. For example, Brown et al. introduced multiple transformer blocks in GPT-3 to deepen the model [22]. Considering the performance, Mehta et al. used group-linear transformation and an expansion-reduction strategy to effectively vary the width and depth of the DeLightT block, making up for the disadvantage of the deep transformer by reducing the number of parameters in the network [23]. In contrast, we use Weight Learning Diagonal Matrices (WLDM) to gate the residual connections to prevent over-fitting problems due to depth.

In addition, much current research has recognized the critical role of self-attention operation in reducing its computational complexity. For instance, [24] used window attention and hole attention to save memory and improve long-range sequence modeling ability. In addition, Tay et al. used a fully-connected neural network to generate a self-attention matrix and proposed a synthetic attention mechanism [25]. However, neither of them considers that when Q and K are calculated, each position will interact with all parts in the sequence and calculate the attention, causing the superposition of similarity between itself, making the correlation more focused on itself than others. For this, we use Local Diagonal Masking (LDM), so that correlations concentrated on the diagonal are ignored, and locations with higher correlations are selected.

## 3    Method

### 3.1    Overall Architecture

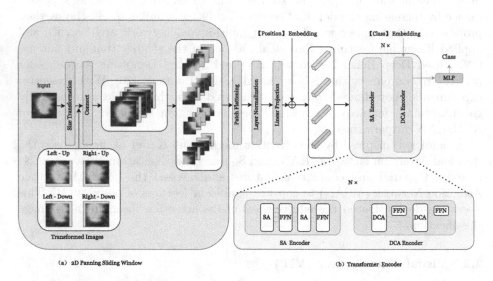

(a)  2D Panning Sliding Window                               (b)  Transformer Encoder

**Fig. 2.** Overview of the TransPND architecture. TransPND mainly consists of 2DPSW and a Transformer Encoder part that combines a SA encoder and a DCA encoder. It is worth mentioning that both LDM and WLDM are introduced in SA and DCA stages. FFN represents the Feed-Foward Network.

In this section, we detail the overall architecture of the proposed TransPND, as shown in Fig. 2. Our TransPND has two modules: a 2D Panning Sliding Window (2DPSW) that processes the input image into the feature vector (see (a)) and a Transformer Encoder composed of SA Encoder and DCA Encoder (see (b)). Next, we describe the individual components of TransPND in detail.

### 3.2    2D Panning Sliding Window (2DPSW)

Firstly, we input a $32 \times 32$ CT image $X$ and slide a 2D spatial window with half the size of $X$ in the diagonal direction (Left-Up, Right-Up, Left-Down,

Right-Down). In addition, we experiment with random sliding, standard sliding windows (Top, Bottom, Left, Right), and combinations of standard sliding and diagonal sliding methods. The results showed that the diagonal direction alone was more competitive. Therefore, we judged that 2DPSW focuses more on the spatial relationships between adjacent pixels than random cropping. Secondly, we crop the translated image whose size is the same as $X$ and then perform the concatenation. Thirdly, the layers need to be expanded and flattened after dividing the image from two planes into four sets of patches ($16 \times 16$), then we normalized and linearly projected to obtain $X_t$. Finally, $X_t$ is sent into the Transformer Encoder to learn long-range feature correlations further.

### 3.3  Weight Learning Diagonal Matrix (WLDM)

We declare that this module will be introduced into both SA and DCA. When we increase the depth of ViT, the following considerations are its computational power and stability. In order to solve the problem of vanishing gradients caused by deeper network layers, ReZero [26] chose to gate each residual connection with a single zero initialization parameter. The equations are as follows:

$$X'_t = X_t + \alpha_t SA(X_t)$$
$$X_c = X'_t + \alpha'_t FFN(X'_t) \tag{1}$$

where $\alpha_t, \alpha'_t$ represents the learnable scalar. But this is not the case when we apply it to TransPND. To this end, as shown in Fig. 3, we use a weight diagonal matrix instead of scalar. In addition, we continue to use normalization. The equations are as follows:

$$X'_t = X_t + D(\lambda_1, ..., \lambda_n) \times SA(LN(X_t))$$
$$X_c = X'_t + D(\lambda'_1, ..., \lambda'_n) \times FFN(LN(X'_t)) \tag{2}$$

where $\lambda_i, \lambda'_i$ are all denoted as learnable weights and initialized to small values. LN denotes Layer Normalization.

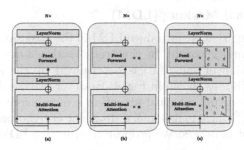

**Fig. 3.** Normalization strategies for multiple transformers. Where (a) is standard ViT. (b) ReZreo added a learnable scalar initialized to 0 while removing the layer normalization. (c) We propose to use a diagonal matrix with learnable weights.

## 3.4   Directive Class Attention (DCA)

In conventional ViT, the class token and patch embedding were sent into the network together. However, the main purpose of the class token is to obtain information related to the classifier. So, we propose DCA, which is an SA-like architecture. We embed class tokens in the last two layers of the network to focus exclusively on the essential features. This can guide the attention computation and reduce the computational effort. We will demonstrate its feasibility experimentally in the following.

We design a network with h heads and p patches, denoting $d_m$ as the embedding size, the biases $b_q, b_k, b_v, b_o \in R^{d_m}$ and $W^Q, W^K, W^V, W^O \in R^{d_m \times d_m}$. DCA receives $X_c$ from SA, so we represent the DCA attention with the following equation:

$$Q = \begin{cases} W^Q[x_{class}] + b_q \in R^{h \times 1 \times d_m/h} & if\ DCA\ exist \\ W^Q[x_{class}, X_c] + b_q \in R^{h \times p \times d_m/h} & others \end{cases} \tag{3}$$

$$K = W^K[x_{class}, X_c] + b_k \in R^{h \times p \times d_m/h} \tag{4}$$

$$V = W^V[x_{class}, X_c] + b_v \in R^{h \times p \times d_m/h} \tag{5}$$

$$Attention(Q, K, V) = Softmax(\frac{QK^T}{\sqrt{d_m/h}})V \tag{6}$$

where Q, K and V are three matrices and $x_{class}$ is a class token, the multi-attended results as follows:

$$Out_{DCA} = Concat(A_1, A_2, ..., A_n)W^O + b_o \tag{7}$$

$$A_i = Attention(QW_i^Q, KW_i^K, VW_i^V) \tag{8}$$

Meanwhile, the original self-attention calculates $QK^T \in R^{h \times p \times p}$, while in DCA, $QK^T \in R^{h \times 1 \times p}$. In other words, the initially quadratic complexity in the number of patches becomes linear in DCA layers.

## 3.5   Local Diagonal Masking (LDM)

It is worth mentioning that we introduce LDM in the attention calculation phase of SA and DCA simultaneously. In the traditional self-attention mechanism, the weight distribution of value (V) is determined by the similarity between query (Q) and key (K), as shown in Fig. 4. However, we use $R_{i,j}^{N \times N}$ to denote a linear matrix of obstructed diagonal attention scores before softmax, and $-\infty$ represents masking, which makes more diagonal correlations be ignored and highlights the weight of others. We propose interpreting LDM as:

$$R_{i,j}^{N \times N}(x) = \begin{cases} R_{i,j}(x), & i \neq j \\ -\infty, & i = j \end{cases} \tag{9}$$

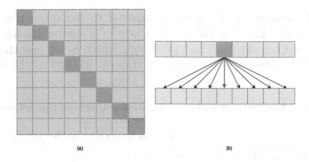

**Fig. 4.** Standard self-attention matrix and similarity computation.

# 4   Experiments

## 4.1   Datasets and Evaluation Metrics

The data used in this study is the LIDC-IDRI dataset [27] published by the National Cancer Institute of the National Institutes of Health. In total, 1,018 study instances of 1,010 patients are included. For each instance, a two-stage diagnostic annotation was performed by four experienced thoracic radiologists. We follow the same data preprocessing procedure explained in [28] and exclude nodules with indistinct IDs in this dataset. Meanwhile, similar to [29], we also exclude nodules with a fuzzy classification of rating 3. Eventually, 848 nodules are obtained, of which 442 are benign and 406 are malignant. The performance metrics are classification accuracy, precision, and AUC, calculated according to 10x cross-validation.

## 4.2   Experimental Design Details

Our model is written based on PyTorch. The number of training vit layers is 24, the hidden dimension is 192, and the head is 4. Furthermore, in our method, 50 epochs were trained with Adam optimizer [30] and learning rate set to 0.001, batch size to 128, and warm-up to 10. Simultaneously, we need to improve model performance through data augmentation because of limited data. First, we extract three 2D views for each nodule's three planes and then apply them to four rotation angles (0°, 90°, 180°, 270°). Moreover, we utilize other techniques, such as the Mixup [31], which improves the network's generalization ability by enhancing the linear representation between training samples.

## 4.3   Experimental Results

As shown in Table 1, we compare TransPND with other studies using the LIDC-IDRI dataset. Experiments show that TransPND achieves 93.33% accuracy, while in terms of AUC, it achieves 96.04%, significantly more than other CNN-centric models. At the same time, it is worth noting that we did not use transfer learning, which is more advantageous compared to the other results. In addition, in our experiment, even though we discover a moment with an accuracy of 93.73%, we checked its AUC and precision, which is far less than the stable moment of 93.33%. Hence, the experiment chooses 93.33% as the final result.

**Table 1.** Comparison with existing methods across the ten folds.

| | Year | Accuracy(%) | AUC($10^{-2}$) |
|---|---|---|---|
| Multi-scale CNN [6] | 2015 | 86.84 | – |
| Vanilla 3D CNN [32] | 2016 | 87.40 | 94.70 |
| Multi-crop CNN [29] | 2017 | 87.14 | 93.00 |
| DeepLung [9] | 2018 | 90.44 | – |
| Liu et al. [33] | 2018 | 89.50 | 93.18 |
| Local-Global [19] | 2019 | 88.46 | 95.62 |
| Liu et al. [8] | 2020 | 90.60 | 93.90 |
| NASLung [34] | 2021 | 90.07 | – |
| **TransPND (ours)** | | **93.33** | **96.04** |

### 4.4   Ablation Studies

In this section, we set different ablation groups. In order to ensure the individual variability of an experiment, the only parameter to be adjusted for each group is the variable to be evaluated, and the rest of the parameters are set to the optimal situations.

For the 2DPSW and LDM, we evaluate their presence or absence. Table 2 shows the validity of the ablation experiments (i.e., TransPND-NO-2DPSW vs. TransPND-NO-LDM). The former shows the importance of the 2DPSW for extracting spatial information. The accuracy rate increases by 1.96% (93.33%-91.37%), and the precision increases by 3.28% (90.98%–87.70%). The latter indicates that, after the diagonal shading, attention is more focused on other markers than itself. The accuracy rate is increased by 2.74% (93.33%–90.59%), and the precision is increased by 3.89% (90.98%–87.09%).

**Table 2.** Classification validity of 2DPSW, LDM on the LIDC-IDRI dataset.

| Methods | Accuracy(%) | Precision(%) |
|---|---|---|
| TransPND | 93.33 | 90.98 |
| TransPND-NO-2DPSW | 91.37 | 87.70 |
| TransPND-NO-LDM | 90.59 | 87.09 |

**Table 3.** Evaluate depth convergence of WLDM against the LIDC-IDRI dataset for accuracy.

| Depth | 10 | 14 | 18 | 22 | 24 | 36 |
|---|---|---|---|---|---|---|
| TransPND-NO-WLDM | 91.17 | 91.23 | 91.23 | 90.98 | 90.96 | 90.80 |
| Rezero | 92.28 | 92.37 | 92.37 | 92.37 | 92.39 | 92.27 |
| TransPND | 93.12 | 93.33 | 93.33 | 93.33 | 93.33 | 93.20 |

At the same time, we evaluated the effects of WLDM. In Table 3, the modified method can converge more layers without premature saturation, and the results improve the classification accuracy compared to Rezero. In addition, for the position embedding of the class token, we conduct experiments by setting different values of Class Depth and obtain Fig. 5 with blue. The results show that class tokens in the deep layer will improve classification accuracy (Class-Depth is defined as the reciprocal layer of the network). We suggest that it is better to embed it in the last two layers of the network (see Table 4).

**Table 4.** Evaluate the effectiveness of class patch embedding locations and network depth on classification accuracy.

| Depth | ClassToken | | | Model | | |
|---|---|---|---|---|---|---|
| | Accuracy(%) | AUC(%) | Precision(%) | Accuracy(%) | AUC(%) | Precision(%) |
| 2 | **93.33** | **96.04** | **90.98** | – | – | – |
| 4 | 93.33 | 95.26 | 89.68 | 92.04 | 94.33 | 86.59 |
| 6 | 93.33 | 96.04 | 89.68 | **93.73** | 94.73 | 86.61 |
| 8 | 93.33 | 95.18 | 88.09 | 92.94 | 95.24 | 90.24 |
| 10 | 92.94 | 95.61 | 88.88 | 93.12 | 94.45 | 90.83 |
| 14 | 92.94 | 95.26 | 88.88 | 93.33 | 94.86 | 90.90 |
| 18 | 92.94 | 95.26 | 90.98 | 93.33 | 96.06 | 90.40 |
| 22 | 92.94 | 95.26 | 90.98 | 93.33 | 96.04 | 90.90 |
| 24 | 92.55 | 94.83 | 90.16 | **93.33** | **96.04** | **90.98** |
| 36 | 92.53 | 94.80 | 90.10 | 93.20 | 95.58 | 90.56 |

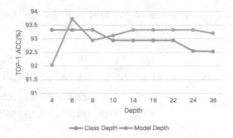

**Fig. 5.** Visualization for evaluating the impact of class patch embedding location and model depth on classification accuracy. (Color figure online)

Last but not least, we verify the advantage of depth on TransPND with guaranteed network convergence. Where convergence is possible, we expand the network depth as shown in Table 4. Although the model achieves 93.73% of the Accuracy when it reaches the sixth level, the AUC and Precision are far from the optimal consequence, of which AUC difference 1.31% (96.04%–94.73%), precision difference 4.37% (90.98%–86.61%). Meanwhile, the experimental results show that as the depth of the model increases, the model tends to be stable, and the classification accuracy is higher (see Fig. 5 with orange).

## 5    Conclusion

In this study, we apply the architecture based entirely on the transformer to CT images of lung nodules, addressing the problem of benign\malignant classification for the first time. In order to solve the difficulties of small local features and lack of data, we propose a new transformer architecture. The architecture skillfully uses 2DPSW for local feature extraction. At the same time, the LDM and WLDM are used in the multi-layer transformer's residual connection and attention calculation stage. In addition, we propose a mechanism named DCA to make the network pay more attention to local features and reduce the calculation. The experimental results show that TransPND significantly improves the final accuracy of classification, indicating that the ViT is a favorable trend for lung nodule classification, which opens a new window for applying pure attention mechanisms to other small datasets in the field of medical images.

## References

1. Siegel, R.L., Miller, K.D., Fuchs, H.E., Jemal, A.: Cancer statistics, 2022. CA: A Cancer J. Clin. **72** (2022)
2. Xia, C., et al.: Cancer statistics in china and united states, 2022: profiles, trends, and determinants. Chin. Med. J. **135**, 584–590 (2022)
3. Tang, H., Liu, W., Huang, K.: Tereotactic ablative radiotherapy for inoperable t1–2n0m0 small-cell lung cancer. Thoracic Cancer **13**, 1100–1101 (2022)

4. Kane, G.C., Barta, J.A., Shusted, C.S., Evans, N.R.: Now is the time to make screening for lung cancer reportable. Ann. Internal Med. (2022)
5. Kumar, D., Wong, A., Clausi, D.A.: Lung nodule classification using deep features in CT images. In: 2015 12th Conference on Computer and Robot Vision, pp. 133–138 (2015)
6. Shen, W., Zhou, M., Yang, F., Yang, C., Tian, J.: Multi-scale convolutional neural networks for lung nodule classification. In: Ourselin, S., Alexander, D.C., Westin, C.-F., Cardoso, M.J. (eds.) IPMI 2015. LNCS, vol. 9123, pp. 588–599. Springer, Cham (2015). https://doi.org/10.1007/978-3-319-19992-4_46
7. Shen, S., Han, S.X., Aberle, D.R., Bui, A.A.T., Hsu, W.: An interpretable deep hierarchical semantic convolutional neural network for lung nodule malignancy classification. Expert Syst. Appl. **128**, 84–95 (2019)
8. Liu, H., et al.: Multi-model ensemble learning architecture based on 3D CNN for lung nodule malignancy suspiciousness classification. J. Digital Imaging 1–15 (2020). https://doi.org/10.1007/s10278-020-00372-8
9. Zhu, W., Liu, C., Fan, W., Xie, X.: DeepLung: deep 3D dual path nets for automated pulmonary nodule detection and classification. In: 2018 IEEE Winter Conference on Applications of Computer Vision (WACV), pp. 673–681 (2018)
10. Nibali, A., He, Z., Wollersheim, D.: Pulmonary nodule classification with deep residual networks. Int. J. Comput. Assist. Radiol. Surg. **12**, 1799–1808 (2017)
11. Zhai, P., Tao, Y., Chen, H., Cai, T., Li, J.: Multi-task learning for lung nodule classification on chest CT. IEEE Access **8**, 180317–180327 (2020)
12. Xie, Y., Zhang, J., Xia, Y.: Semi-supervised adversarial model for benign-malignant lung nodule classification on chest CT. Med. Image Anal. **57**, 237–248 (2019)
13. Dosovitskiy, A., et al.: An image is worth 16 × 16 words: transformers for image recognition at scale. arXiv preprint arXiv:2010.11929 (2020)
14. He, K., Zhang, X., Ren, S., Sun, J.: Deep residual learning for image recognition. In: 2016 IEEE Conference on Computer Vision and Pattern Recognition (CVPR), pp. 770–778 (2016)
15. Sun, C., Shrivastava, A., Singh, S., Gupta, A.K.: Revisiting unreasonable effectiveness of data in deep learning era. In: 2017 IEEE International Conference on Computer Vision (ICCV), pp. 843–852 (2017)
16. Ali, I., Muzammil, M., ul Haq, I., Khaliq, A.A., Abdullah, S.: Efficient lung nodule classification using transferable texture convolutional neural network. IEEE Access **8**, 175859–175870 (2020)
17. Heo, B., Yun, S., Han, D., Chun, S., Choe, J., Oh, S.J.: Rethinking spatial dimensions of vision transformers. In: 2021 IEEE/CVF International Conference on Computer Vision (ICCV), pp. 11916–11925 (2021)
18. Liu, Z., et al.: Swin transformer: hierarchical vision transformer using shifted windows. In: 2021 IEEE/CVF International Conference on Computer Vision (ICCV), pp. 9992–10002 (2021)
19. Al-Shabi, M., Lan, B.L., Chan, W.Y., Ng, K.H., Tan, M.: Lung nodule classification using deep local-global networks. Int. J. Comput. Assist. Radiol. Surg. **14**, 1815–1819 (2019)
20. Sun, W., Zheng, B., Qian, W.: Automatic feature learning using multichannel ROI based on deep structured algorithms for computerized lung cancer diagnosis. Comput. Biol. Med. **89**, 530–539 (2017)
21. Xia, K.J., Chi, J., Gao, Y., Jiang, Y., Wu, C.: Adaptive aggregated attention network for pulmonary nodule classification. Appl. Sci. **11**, 610 (2021)
22. Brown, T., et al.: Language models are few-shot learners. Adv. Neural. Inf. Process. Syst. **33**, 1877–1901 (2020)

23. Mehta, S., Ghazvininejad, M., Iyer, S., Zettlemoyer, L., Hajishirzi, H.: Delight: Very deep and light-weight transformer. arXiv preprint arXiv:2008.00623 (2020)

24. Child, R., Gray, S., Radford, A., Sutskever, I.: Generating long sequences with sparse transformers. arXiv preprint arXiv:1904.10509 (2019)

25. Tay, Y., Bahri, D., Metzler, D., Juan, D.C., Zhao, Z., Zheng, C.: Synthesizer: rethinking self-attention in transformer models. In: ICML (2021)

26. Bachlechner, T.C., Majumder, B.P., Mao, H.H., Cottrell, G., McAuley, J.: Rezero is all you need: Fast convergence at large depth. In: UAI (2021)

27. Armato III, S.G., et al.: The lung image database consortium (LIDC) and image database resource initiative (IDRI): a completed reference database of lung nodules on CT scans. Med. Phys. **38**(2), 915–931 (2011)

28. Al-Shabi, M., Lee, H.K., Tan, M.: Gated-dilated networks for lung nodule classification in CT scans. IEEE Access **7**, 178827–178838 (2019)

29. Shen, W., et al.: Multi-crop convolutional neural networks for lung nodule malignancy suspiciousness classification. Pattern Recognit. **61**, 663–673 (2017)

30. Kingma, D.P., Ba, J.: Adam: a method for stochastic optimization. arXiv preprint arXiv:1412.6980 (2014)

31. Zhang, H., Cisse, M., Dauphin, Y.N., Lopez-Paz, D.: mixup: beyond empirical risk minimization. arXiv preprint arXiv:1710.09412 (2017)

32. Yan, X., et al.: Classification of lung nodule malignancy risk on computed tomography images using convolutional neural network: a comparison between 2D and 3D strategies. In: ACCV Workshops (2016)

33. Liu, Y., Hao, P., Zhang, P., Xu, X., Wu, J., Chen, W.: Dense convolutional binary-tree networks for lung nodule classification. IEEE Access **6**, 49080–49088 (2018)

34. Jiang, H., Shen, F., Gao, F., Han, W.: Learning efficient, explainable and discriminative representations for pulmonary nodules classification. Pattern Recognit. **113**, 107825 (2021)

# Adversarial Learning Based Structural Brain-Network Generative Model for Analyzing Mild Cognitive Impairment

Heng Kong[1,2], Junren Pan[2], Yanyan Shen[2], and Shuqiang Wang[2(✉)]

[1] Southern University of Science and Technology, Shenzhen 518000, China
12132527@mail.sustech.edu.cn
[2] Shenzhen Institutes of Advanced Technology, Chinese Academy of Sciences,
Shenzhen 518000, China
{jr.pan,yy.shen,sq.wang}@siat.ac.cn

**Abstract.** Mild cognitive impairment (MCI) is a precursor of Alzheimer's disease (AD), and the detection of MCI is of great clinical significance. Analyzing the structural brain networks of patients is vital for the recognition of MCI. However, the current studies on structural brain networks are totally dependent on specific toolboxes, which is time-consuming and subjective. Few tools can obtain the structural brain networks from brain diffusion tensor images. In this work, an adversarial learning-based structural brain-network generative model (SBGM) is proposed to directly learn the structural connections from brain diffusion tensor images. By analyzing the differences in structural brain networks across subjects, we found that the structural brain networks of subjects showed a consistent trend from elderly normal controls (NC) to early mild cognitive impairment (EMCI) to late mild cognitive impairment (LMCI): structural connectivity progressed in a progressively weaker direction as the condition worsened. In addition, our proposed model tri-classifies EMCI, LMCI, and NC subjects, achieving a classification accuracy of 83.33% on the Alzheimer's Disease Neuroimaging Initiative (ADNI) database.

**Keywords:** Structural feature extraction · Graph convolution · Structural brain networks · Separable convolutional block

## 1 Introduction

Alzheimer's disease (AD) is an irreversible neurodegenerative disease with a high prevalence in the elderly population, which is characterized by a severe clinical decline in memory and cognitive functions [1]. The pathogenic mechanisms of AD are not fully understood [2], and there is a lack of effective therapeutic drugs [3,4]. Mild cognitive impairment (MCI), a prodromal stage of AD [5–7], has attracted widespread interest in the study of patients with MCI because interventions at this stage can reduce the rate of conversion to AD. In order to

© The Author(s), under exclusive license to Springer Nature Switzerland AG 2022
S. Yu et al. (Eds.): PRCV 2022, LNCS 13535, pp. 361–375, 2022.
https://doi.org/10.1007/978-3-031-18910-4_30

detect AD patients as early as possible, medical image computational methods are used to help diagnose this type of brain disease with the help of computer vision [8,9]. As a critical method in the artificial intelligence field, deep learning has been widely applied in medical image computing [10,11]. Because of its excellent performance, many complex patterns of medical imaging can be identified, and it enables the auxiliary diagnosis of disease [12,13]. Medical images of AD have their complicated pattern and biomarkers, and a deep learning-based approach can handle them through its specific techniques. For example, convolution neural networks (CNN) is a universal imaging computing method. It can automatically learn the parameters of the convolution kernel and extract features that are highly correlated with the target [14,15]. Notably, 3D CNN has better processing performance for 3D brain image data such as DTI. However, the patterns of high-dimensional medical images are difficult to analyze and identify. Brain networks as a pattern of networks integrated by connections can better and more easily represent downscaled brain information. They can be derived from anatomical or physiological images, yielding structural and functional networks [16,17], respectively. Structural connectivity of brain networks describes the anatomical connections that connect a set of neuronal elements. Diffusion tensor imaging (DTI) shows changes in the number of fiber bundle connections, fiber bundle length, and anisotropy values, which can provide valid structural information for MCI detection [18].

The data of medical images have problems such as a small sample size and uneven distribution of categories. These problems are prone to overfitting and other problems when applying traditional deep learning methods. The generative adversarial network (GAN) method is more suitable for the medical image field due to the use of the idea of adversarial learning. GAN can be seen as variational-inference [19] based generative model. Recently, more and more researchers have used the GAN method to study Alzheimer's disease. Especially in the field of brain medical images, many classic GAN methods [20,21] have emerged. Yu et al. [22] proposed a GAN method that applied tensor decomposition to model training, effectively improving the model's generation effect. Hu et al. [23] proposed a bidirectional mapping mechanism applied to the training of the GAN network, and the generated image is more in line with the real effect. Hu et al. [24] proposed a cross-modal adversarial generation method applied to the generation of brain medical images, effectively improving the model's classification effect. You et al. [25] proposed the FP-GAN model to improve brain medical images' texture generation effectively. Yu et al. [26] proposed the MP-GAN method to successfully extract rich features from different types of MRI images and effectively improve the generation effect of the model. Zuo [27], Pan [28] and others introduced graph convolution and hypergraph operation [29] into the generative adversarial network and analyzed the pathological mechanism of Alzheimer's disease in the field of whole-brain topology. All of the above methods have promoted the in-depth exploration of the pathogenesis of Alzheimer's disease to some extent in some fields. Nevertheless, these methods still have much room for optimization. This paper proposed a GAN-based method, and the specific contributions are as follows:

This paper proposed an SBGM framework. This method integrates classification and reconstruction knowledge to realize the direct generation of structural brain networks from DTI. The structural networks generated by the model contain structural connection information and feature information between brain regions. The model proposed in this paper is able to classify three types of subjects: NC, EMCI, and LMCI. More importantly, this model provides a generative approach from DTI to structural brain networks. The experimental results on the ADNI database also prove that our proposed model has high classification accuracy. Moreover, the structural brain networks generated by the model have a consistent pattern of change with the structural brain networks obtained from the software template calculations: we found a gradual weakening of structural brain network connectivity in subjects from NC to EMCI to LMCI.

## 2    Methods

The framework diagram of SBGM is given in Fig. 1. Our proposed model consists of three main modules: generator, discriminator, and classifier. The generator consists of two sub-modules, SFENet (Structural Feature Extraction Network) and Structure Profile. SFENet is used to extract structural features of brain regions from 3-dimensional DTI as node features of the structural brain network, and Structure Profile maps structural features of brain regions into a matrix of structural connections between brain regions. The discriminator consists of two fully connected layers to distinguish whether the structural connection matrix comes from the generator or the AAL template. The classifier consists of a graph convolutional network (GCN) and a fully connected layer for the tri-classification of EMCI, LMCI, and NC subjects. The AAL template [30–35] is a commonly used template for brain region delineation. In this paper, we use it to process the DTI to obtain empirical knowledge of the brain structural connectivity matrix. The meanings of other symbols in the model are as follows: $G$ denotes the topology of the structural brain network, $\hat{A}$ denotes the brain structural connectivity matrix generated by Structure Profile, $P$ denotes the structural features of brain regions extracted by SFENet, $A$ denotes the structural connectivity matrix obtained from the AAL template, $L_D$ denotes discriminator loss, $L_G$ denotes generator loss, and $L_C$ denotes classification loss.

### 2.1    Generator

***Structural Brain Network.*** The generator's main function is to generate the structural network of the brain, which contains the structural connectivity matrix $\hat{A}$ between brain regions and the structural feature [36] matrix $P$. The structural network of brain is a weighted graph, which can be represented as $G(V, E, \hat{A}, P)$, where $V = \{v_1, v_2, ..., v_N\}$ denotes the $N$ brain regions and $E$

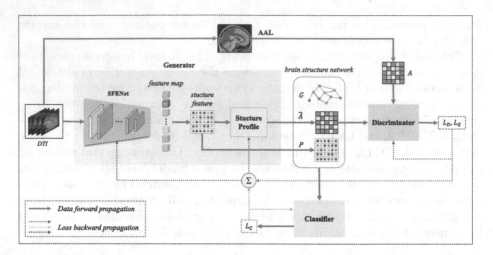

**Fig. 1.** Overall framework of the proposed SBGM.

denotes the edges connecting different brain regions [37]. The structural connectivity matrix $\hat{A}$ represents the relative connection strength between brain regions, $\hat{A}$ is a symmetric matrix, and all elements are continuous values between $[0, 1]$. If $\hat{A}_{ij} = \hat{A}_{ji} = 0$, indicates that there is no direct structural connection between brain region $v_i$ and $v_j$, then the corresponding edge $E(v_i, v_j)$ does not exist in the structural network of the brain. Generally, the structural connections between most brain regions are weak, so $\hat{A}$ is a sparse matrix. $P$ is the structural feature matrix of brain regions, and each row represents the feature vector $p_i$ of brain region $v_i$. In this study, to make the generated brain structural connectivity matrix have the same dimensionality as the structural connectivity matrix from the AAL template, we take $N = 90$ based on empirical knowledge.

***SFENet.*** CNN can automatically learn the parameters of the convolution kernel and extract features that are highly relevant to the task [38, 39], so we use CNN to extract structural features of brain regions from DTI. According to the definition and division of brain regions in neuroscience and medicine, a brain region is a complex irregular chunk in the volume of the brain. In order to fully extract the features of these brain regions, we need to extend the convolution kernel of CNN to 3 dimensions. However, extending the convolution kernel to 3 dimensions increases the parameter size linearly and increases the training difficulty.

To reduce the training difficulty of the model, we designed a lightweight 3D CNN model-SFENet, as shown in Fig. 2. SFENet performs feature extraction for DTI by combining one standard convolutional (Conv) layer and eight depthwise separable convolutional blocks, with each block containing a depthwise convolutional (DW Conv) layer and a pointwise convolutional (PW Conv) layer. The standard convolution layer sets one convolution kernels ($3 \times 3 \times 3 \times 8$) for each input channel to extract the lower-level structural feature information of DTI. The depthwise convolution layer has one convolution kernel ($3 \times 3 \times 3 \times 1$) for

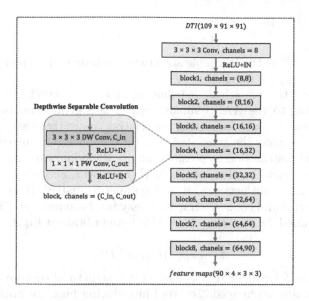

**Fig. 2.** Framework of SFENet.

each input channel, and the number of convolution kernels is the same as the number of channels $C_{in}$ of the input feature map. Depthwise convolution only uses the information of a single input channel, does not take full advantage of the information between channels, and cannot change the number of output channels $C_{out}$. To compensate for the shortcomings of depthwise convolution, we add a pointwise convolution layer afterward to weight the information of all channels and adjust the number of channels of the output feature map. After each convolution, we use a linear collation function (ReLU) as the activation function to alleviate the gradient disappearance problem and perform an instance normalization (IN) operation on the output feature map to prevent "gradient explosion". The DTI we use is a single channel 3-dimensional image of size $(109 \times 91 \times 91)$, and the desired output is 90 feature maps of size $(4 \times 3 \times 3)$. We spread each feature map as a structural feature vector of the corresponding brain region, and we can obtain the structural feature matrix $P \in R^{90 \times 36}$ of the brain region.

**Structure Profile.** It is still an open field of research on how to obtain the structural connectivity matrix $\hat{A}$ from the structural feature matrix $P$ of brain regions. A common approach is calculating the correlation, covariance, and mutual information between the structural feature vectors of brain regions [40]. One of the simplest methods is to make $\hat{A} = PP^T$ and then normalize $\hat{A}$. However, this approach relies excessively on structural features of brain regions and does not make full use of classification knowledge and structural network reconstruction knowledge. In the work of this paper, we use a more sophisticated parameterization method: we obtain the brain structural connectivity matrix $\hat{A}$ by learning a structural contour matrix $M$. The specific method is shown in Eq. 1.

$$\hat{A} = exp(-|PMP^T|) \tag{1}$$

where $M \in R^{36 \times 36}$ is the learnable structural contour matrix and $exp(-|\cdot|)$ is the nonlinear mapping function.

We compute the empirical distribution $A$ of the structural connectivity matrix according to the AAL template, which is a symmetric matrix and all elements lie between $[0, 1]$, indicating the relative connectivity strength between brain regions. To make the generated structural connectivity matrix $\hat{A}$ as close to the empirical distribution as possible, we use the nonlinear mapping function $exp(-|\cdot|)$ to restrict the elements to $[0, 1]$. Moreover, according to the definition of structural brain network, $\hat{A}$ is a symmetric matrix. If we follow Eq. 1, the resulting structural connection matrix may not be symmetric. Therefore, we further constrained $M$ such that $M = MM^T$ and obtained Eq. 2.

$$\hat{A} = exp(-|PMM^T P^T|) \tag{2}$$

Although the formula of $\hat{A}$ has changed, the structural contour matrix $M$ to be learned remains unchanged. To avoid introducing bias, we initialize $M$ as a identity matrix in the training phase.

## 2.2 Discriminator

If a structural connection matrix $\hat{A} \sim P_{\hat{A}}$ generated by the generator and a structural connection matrix $A \sim P_A$ from the AAL template, then the role of the discriminator is to determine whether the input samples come from the distribution $P_{\hat{A}}$ or empirical distribution $P_A$ and to distinguish them maximally. The goal of the generator, on the other hand, is to maximize the learning of the empirical distribution $P_A$ and eventually reach $\hat{A} \sim P_A$, but this is only the ideal case. Combining the generator and discriminator to get a GAN for simultaneous training and introducing W-divergence (W-div) to measure the distance between the two distributions can solve the problems such as training difficulties and training instability. The loss functions of the discriminator and generator are shown in Eq. 3 and Eq. 4, respectively.

$$L_D = E_{\tilde{x} \sim P_{\hat{A}}} D(\tilde{x}) - E_{x \sim P_A} D(x) + E_{(\tilde{x}, x) \sim (P_{\hat{A}}, P_A)} k||\nabla T||^p \tag{3}$$

$$L_G = -E_{\tilde{x} \sim P_{\hat{A}}} D(\tilde{x}) \tag{4}$$

where $\tilde{x}, x$ denotes the sample input to discriminator D, $(\tilde{x}, x) \sim (P_{\hat{A}}, P_A)$ denotes the joint distribution of $P_{\hat{A}}$ and $P_A$, $\nabla T$ is the distance between the 2 distributions, $k, p$ is the hyperparameter.

$$k||\nabla T||^p = \frac{k}{2}[\sum (\frac{\partial D(\tilde{x})}{\partial \tilde{x}})^2]^{\frac{p}{2}} + \frac{k}{2}[\sum (\frac{\partial D(x)}{\partial x})^2]^{\frac{p}{2}} \tag{5}$$

We use two fully connected layers as the discriminator, with 8100 neurons in the input layer, ten neurons in the hidden layer, and one neuron in the output layer. The hidden layer uses $LeakeyReLU$ as the activation function while the output layer doesn't, and the output value is a scalar.

## 2.3 Classifier

As shown in Fig. 3, the classifier consists of a GCN layer and a fully connected layer, where the GCN [41] layer is used to fuse the structural features of each node's neighboring nodes, and the fully connected layer performs whole graph level classification based on the fused feature matrix. The classifier is used to classify EMCI, LMCI, and NC, but more importantly, to learn the structural brain network using the classification knowledge. Using Laplace transform on the structural connectivity matrix not only requires a higher computational cost but also may have an unknown effect on the results. Therefore, we did not use Laplace transform for the structural connection matrix when using GCN to fuse the feature information of different nodes in the structural brain network. The convolution process is shown in Eq. 6.

$$H = ReLU((\hat{A} + I)PW) \tag{6}$$

where $H$ denotes the structural feature matrix after convolution, $ReLU$ is the activation function of the convolution layer, $W \in R^{F_{in} \times F_{out}}$ is the weight matrix, $F_{in} = 36, F_{out} = 18$. Considering the structural characteristics of each node itself, we add an identity matrix $I$ to $\hat{A}$.

The number of input neurons of the fully connected layer is 3240, the number of output neurons is 3, and the activation function of the output layer is $ReLU$. We use the output results of the classifier and the class labels to calculate the cross-entropy loss as the loss of the classifier, as shown in Eq. 7.

$$L_C = -\frac{1}{N} \sum_{i=1}^{N} p(y_i|x_i) log[q(\hat{y}_i|x_i)] \tag{7}$$

where $N$ is the number of input samples, $p(y_i|x_i)$ denotes the actual distribution of sample labels, and $q(\hat{y}_i|x_i)$ denotes the distribution of labels at the output of the classifier.

## 2.4 Trainning Strategy

We train the generator, discriminator, and classifier simultaneously, fixing the other two modules while training one of them. The discriminator is first trained by feeding the generated structural connection matrix $\hat{A}$ and the structural connection matrix $A$ from the AAL template into the discriminator and learning the parameters of the discriminator based on the discriminator loss $L_D$. The distance between distributions using the W-div metric does not cause the problem that the generator gradient disappears because the accuracy of the discriminator is too high, so we repeat the training of the discriminator five times during the iteration, which can speed up the convergence of the model. After training the

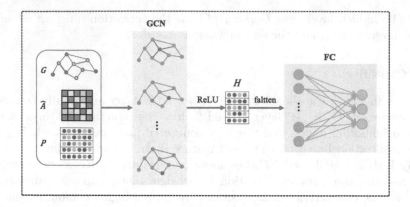

**Fig. 3.** Framework of classifier.

discriminator five times, we train the classifier one time and update the classifier's parameters according to the classification loss $L_C$. Finally, we train the generator one time. In order to integrate the classification knowledge into the generation of the structural brain network, we calculate the weighted sum of the generator loss $L_G$ and the classification loss $L_C$ as the total loss of the generator, as shown in Eq. 8, and then update the parameters of the generator using the $L_{G\_total}$.

$$L_{G\_total} = L_G + \beta L_C \tag{8}$$

where $\beta$ is the weight coefficient, which is a hyperparameter that determines the relative importance of the classification loss $L_C$ in training the generator. In the early stage of model training, the pattern of the structural brain network generated by the generator is relatively simple, and the classification loss $L_C$ calculated using such a structure network is almost constant, which not only cannot guide the learning process of the classifier and generator but may even cause gradient cancellation. To prevent this from happening, we used linearly increasing weight coefficient $\beta$, and dynamically adjusted $\beta$ values according to the training process, as shown in Eq. 9.

$$\beta = \frac{\beta_{max} - \beta_{min}}{Epoches} \times epoch \tag{9}$$

where $\beta_{max}$ is the maximum value of the weight coefficient, $\beta_{min}$ is the minimum value of the weight coefficient, $Epoches$ is the maximum number of iterations, and $epoch$ is the current number of iterations.

# 3    Experiments

## 3.1    Dataset

The primary purpose of this paper is to investigate the differences in the structural brain network between EMCI, LMCI, and NC subjects, so we used only DTI as the dataset. DTI of 298 subjects were selected from the ADNI database for this study, including 87 NC subjects (42 males and 45 females, mean age 74.1 years, standard deviation 7.4), 135 EMCI patients (69 males and 66 females, mean age 75.8, standard deviation 6.4), 76 LMCI patients (35 males and 41 females, mean age 75.9 years, standard deviation 7.5).

For the DTI, we performed cranial stripping, resolution resampling, eddy current correction, and fiber tracking preprocessing operations using the PANDA toolbox. The voxel of the resampled 3-dimensional DTI was $109 \times 91 \times 91$. Then we divided the whole brain into 90 brain regions using the AAL template and counted the number of DTI-derived fibers between brain regions to calculate the structural connectivity matrix $A$. Because the number of fiber tracts varies widely between brain regions, we normalized $A$ to $[0, 1]$ as the empirical distribution of the discriminator's input.

## 3.2    Experimental Settings

For each subject, we obtained their DTI and structural connectivity matrix $A$ and added labels as input data for the model. We divided 298 subjects into a training set containing 250 subjects and a testing set containing 48 subjects (16 each for EMCI, LMCI, and NC subjects). We used batch training to train the model with $batch\_size = 14$.

We detail the structure and parameters of the generator, discriminator, and classifier, as well as the training strategy of the model in Sect. 2. We train the three modules separately, thus defining 3 Adam optimizers with a learning rate of 0.005 for the generator, 0.001 for the discriminator, and 0.001 for the classifier. The hyperparameters in the discriminator loss $L_D$ are set to $k = 2, p = 6$, the joint loss $L_{G\_total}$ of the generator is taken to be $\beta_{max} = 3$ and $\beta_{min} = 0.1$, and the maximum number of iteration of the model is $Epoches = 300$.

## 3.3    Results

*Training Process.* To demonstrate the effectiveness of the training strategy, we present in Fig. 4 the training loss function curves using linearly increasing weight coefficient $\beta$ versus using fixed weight $\beta = 2$. As can be seen from the figure, the training process of the generator is more stable using a linearly increasing weight coefficient, and the loss function of the classifier is no longer a horizontal line at the early stage of training.

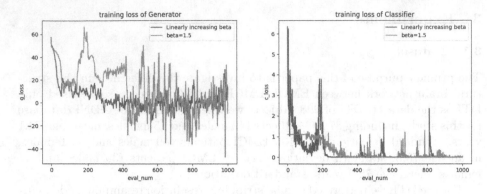

**Fig. 4.** Generator loss and discriminator loss curves for 2 training strategies.

***Classification Performance.*** In the current study, we were more interested in patients in the MCI phase, so the subjects selected for the study were mainly NC, EMCI, and LMCI subjects, and these subjects were tri-classified. Currently, there is a paucity of research work using these three subjects for tri-classification. Therefore, in this section, we mainly show the test results of our two training strategies, including accuracy, precision, recall, and f1-score, as shown in Table 1.

**Table 1.** Average detection performance of different training strategies. (%)

|                    | Accuracy  | Precision | Recall    | F1-score  |
| ------------------ | --------- | --------- | --------- | --------- |
| $\beta = 0.01$     | 61.04     | 56.83     | 58.53     | 56.31     |
| $\beta = 1.5$      | 72.50     | 68.87     | 64.25     | 65.08     |
| $\beta = 3$        | 67.77     | 62.50     | 61.33     | 60.83     |
| $\beta$-dynamic    | **83.33** | **88.58** | **74.28** | **76.75** |

It can be seen from Table 1 that better classification results can be achieved using linearly increasing weight coefficient, with a classification accuracy of 83.3%.

***Structural Brain Network Generation.*** Generating a structural brain network from DTI based on classification and reconstruction knowledge was our main goal in this study, and we tested the performance of the generator on 48 test samples. Our generator reconstructs the structural connectivity matrix of the brain well compared to the structural connectivity matrix from the AAL template. However, there are some differences in connectivity between local brain regions. This is because we introduced disease-related classification knowledge, and the generated structural connectivity matrix may better reflect patients' real brain structural connectivity. We hope to identify some brain regions that are highly correlated with MCI by analyzing the connectivity differences between these local brain regions.

***Brain Structural Network Connectivity Analysis.*** To analyze whether the structural connectivity matrix $\hat{A}$ generated by our proposed model was significantly changed compared to empirical distribution $A$, we tested $\hat{A}$ against $A$ using a paired-samples T-test at the significance level of 0.05. Dividing the testing set into three groups, EMCI, LMCI, and NC, with 16 individuals in each group, we used the generator to generate their structural connectivity matrix $\hat{A}$ and T-test it against the structural connectivity matrix $A$ from the AAL template, using a spin diagram to indicate those connections that have significant changes. As shown in Fig. 5, it can be found that the structural connectivity matrix $\hat{A}$ generated by our model has altered connectivity between many brain regions compared to empirical distribution $A$.

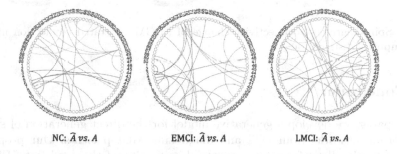

NC: $\hat{A}$ vs. $A$            EMCI: $\hat{A}$ vs. $A$            LMCI: $\hat{A}$ vs. $A$

**Fig. 5.** Changes in structural brain connectivity at different stages

To further analyze the differences in the distribution of the brain structural connectivity matrix generated by our proposed model between different types of subjects, we compare the changes in brain connectivity in NC versus EMCI, NC versus LMCI, and EMCI versus LMCI patients, respectively, in Fig. 6. This change in connectivity between brain regions was more pronounced in LMCI patients compared with NC subjects. Similarly, between EMCI patients and LMCI patients, there was a significant decrease in connectivity between brain regions in LMCI patients. These changes and trends reveal a stepwise progression toward AD pathology in NC subjects: a gradual decrease in connectivity of the structural brain network.

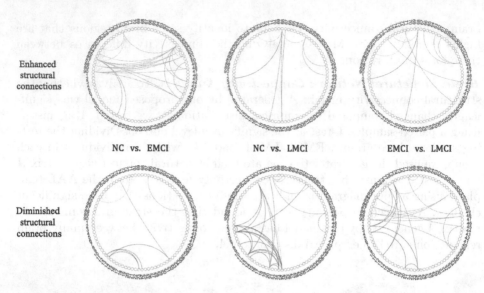

**Fig. 6.** Spin diagram of connectivity change of SBGM generated connection matrix with empirical distribution A.

## 4 Conclusion

In this paper, we develop a generative model for the direct generation of structural brain networks from DTI and diagnosing MCI patients. Our proposed model not only allows for more accurate classification of three subjects, EMCI, LMCI, and NC. More importantly, it provides a method to generate structural brain networks directly from DTI, which is free from the limitations of many existing software templates and toolboxes, providing a prerequisite for us to study the changes in the structural brain networks of MCI patients. Experimental results on the ADNI dataset demonstrate that our proposed model achieves an accuracy of 83.4% for the classification of three subjects, EMCI, LMCI, and NC. Moreover, we found that the brain structural connectivity of subjects gradually decreased from NC to EMCI to LMCI, which is consistent with some research findings in the field of neuroscience. In future research, we will focus on which brain regions with greater changes in structural connectivity of patients with AD as their disease worsens and extend our research work to the fusion of multimodal information.

**Acknowledgment.** This work was supported by the National Natural Science Foundations of China under Grants 62172403 and 61872351, the Distinguished Young Scholars Fund of Guangdong under Grant 2021B1515020019, the Excellent Young Scholars of Shenzhen under Grant RCYX20200714114641211 and Shenzhen Key Basic Research Projects under Grant JCYJ20200109115641762.

# References

1. DeTure, M.A., Dickson, D.W.: The neuropathological diagnosis of Alzheimer's disease. Mol. Neurodegener. **14**(1), 1–18 (2019)
2. Habib, N., McCabe, C., Medina, S., et al.: Disease-associated astrocytes in Alzheimer's disease and aging. Nat. Neurosci. **23**(6), 701–706 (2020)
3. Citron, M.: Alzheimer's disease: strategies for disease modification. Nat. Rev. Drug Discov. **9**(5), 387–398 (2010)
4. Mattson, M.P.: Pathways towards and away from Alzheimer's disease. Nature **430**(7000), 631–639 (2004)
5. Gauthier, S., Reisberg, B., Zaudig, M., et al.: Mild cognitive impairment. The Lancet **367**(9518), 1262–1270 (2006)
6. Petersen, R.C., Roberts, R.O., Knopman, D.S., et al.: Mild cognitive impairment: ten years later. Arch. Neurol. **66**(12), 1447–1455 (2009)
7. Petersen, R.C., Doody, R., Kurz, A., et al.: Current concepts in mild cognitive impairment. Arch. Neurol. **58**(12), 1985–1992 (2001)
8. Wang, H., Shen, Y., Wang, S., et al.: Ensemble of 3D densely connected convolutional network for diagnosis of mild cognitive impairment and Alzheimer's disease. Neurocomputing **333**, 145–156 (2019)
9. Lei, B., Yu, S., Zhao, X., et al.: Diagnosis of early Alzheimer's disease based on dynamic high order networks. Brain Imaging Behav. **15**(1), 276–287 (2021). https://doi.org/10.1007/s11682-019-00255-9
10. Wang, S., Wang, X., Shen, Y., et al.: An ensemble-based densely-connected deep learning system for assessment of skeletal maturity. IEEE Trans. Syst. Man Cybern. Syst. **52**(1), 426–437 (2020)
11. Wang, S., Shen, Y., Zeng, D., et al.: Bone age assessment using convolutional neural networks. In: 2018 International Conference on Artificial Intelligence and Big Data (ICAIBD), pp. 175–178. IEEE (2018)
12. Yu, S., et al.: Multi-scale enhanced graph convolutional network for early mild cognitive impairment detection. In: Martel, A.L., et al. (eds.) MICCAI 2020. LNCS, vol. 12267, pp. 228–237. Springer, Cham (2020). https://doi.org/10.1007/978-3-030-59728-3_23
13. Wang, S., Wang, X., Hu, Y., et al.: Diabetic retinopathy diagnosis using multichannel generative adversarial network with semisupervision. IEEE Trans. Autom. Sci. Eng. **18**(2), 574–585 (2020)
14. Wen, J., Thibeau-Sutre, E., Diaz-Melo, M., et al.: Convolutional neural networks for classification of Alzheimer's disease: overview and reproducible evaluation. Med. Image Anal. **63**, 101694 (2020)
15. Rashid, A.H., Gupta, A., Gupta, J., et al.: Biceph-Net: a robust and lightweight framework for the diagnosis of Alzheimer's disease using 2D-MRI scans and deep similarity learning. IEEE J. Biomed. Health Inform. (2022)
16. Filippi, M., Basaia, S., Canu, E., et al.: Changes in functional and structural brain connectome along the Alzheimer's disease continuum. Mol. Psychiatry **25**(1), 230–239 (2020)
17. Lei, B., Cheng, N., Frangi, A.F., et al.: Self-calibrated brain network estimation and joint non-convex multi-task learning for identification of early Alzheimer's disease. Med. Image Anal. **61**, 101652 (2020)
18. De, A., Chowdhury, A.S.: DTI based Alzheimer's disease classification with rank modulated fusion of CNNs and random forest. Expert Syst. Appl. **169**, 114338 (2021)

19. Mo, L.F., Wang, S.Q.: A variational approach to nonlinear two-point boundary value problems. Nonlinear Anal. Theory Methods Appl. **71**(12), e834–e838 (2009)

20. Hu, S., Yu, W., Chen, Z., et al.: Medical image reconstruction using generative adversarial network for Alzheimer disease assessment with class-imbalance problem. In: 2020 IEEE 6th International Conference on Computer and Communications (ICCC), pp. 1323–1327. IEEE (2020)

21. Hu, S., Yuan, J., Wang, S.: Cross-modality synthesis from MRI to PET using adversarial U-net with different normalization. In: 2019 International Conference on Medical Imaging Physics and Engineering (ICMIPE), pp. 1–5. IEEE (2019)

22. Yu, W., Lei, B., Ng, M.K., et al.: Tensorizing GAN with high-order pooling for Alzheimer's disease assessment. IEEE Trans. Neural Netw. Learn. Syst. **33**(9), 4945–4959 (2022)

23. Hu, S., Shen, Y., Wang, S., Lei, B.: Brain MR to PET synthesis via bidirectional generative adversarial network. In: Martel, A.L., et al. (eds.) MICCAI 2020. LNCS, vol. 12262, pp. 698–707. Springer, Cham (2020). https://doi.org/10.1007/978-3-030-59713-9_67

24. Hu, S., Lei, B., Wang, S., et al.: Bidirectional mapping generative adversarial networks for brain MR to PET synthesis. IEEE Trans. Med. Imaging **41**(1), 145–157 (2021)

25. You, S., Lei, B., Wang, S., et al.: Fine perceptive GANs for brain MR image super-resolution in wavelet domain. IEEE Trans. Neural Netw. Learn. Syst. (2022)

26. Yu, W., Lei, B., Wang, S., et al.: Morphological feature visualization of Alzheimer's disease via multidirectional perception GAN. IEEE Trans. Neural Netw. Learn. Syst. (2022)

27. Zuo, Q., Lei, B., Shen, Y., Liu, Y., Feng, Z., Wang, S.: Multimodal representations learning and adversarial hypergraph fusion for early Alzheimer's disease prediction. In: Ma, H., et al. (eds.) PRCV 2021. LNCS, vol. 13021, pp. 479–490. Springer, Cham (2021). https://doi.org/10.1007/978-3-030-88010-1_40

28. Pan, J., Lei, B., Shen, Y., Liu, Y., Feng, Z., Wang, S.: Characterization multimodal connectivity of brain network by hypergraph GAN for Alzheimer's disease analysis. In: Ma, H., et al. (eds.) PRCV 2021. LNCS, vol. 13021, pp. 467–478. Springer, Cham (2021). https://doi.org/10.1007/978-3-030-88010-1_39

29. Pan, J., Lei, B., Wang, S., et al.: DecGAN: decoupling generative adversarial network detecting abnormal neural circuits for Alzheimer's disease. arXiv preprint arXiv:2110.05712 (2021)

30. Rolls, E.T., Huang, C.C., Lin, C.P., et al.: Automated anatomical labelling atlas 3. Neuroimage **206**, 116189 (2020)

31. Zalesky, A., Fornito, A., Harding, I.H., et al.: Whole-brain anatomical networks: does the choice of nodes matter? Neuroimage **50**(3), 970–983 (2010)

32. Rolls, E.T., Joliot, M., Tzourio-Mazoyer, N.: Implementation of a new parcellation of the orbitofrontal cortex in the automated anatomical labeling atlas. Neuroimage **122**, 1–5 (2015)

33. Tzourio-Mazoyer, N., Landeau, B., Papathanassiou, D., et al.: Automated anatomical labeling of activations in SPM using a macroscopic anatomical parcellation of the MNI MRI single-subject brain. Neuroimage **15**(1), 273–289 (2002)

34. Evans, A.C., Janke, A.L., Collins, D.L., et al.: Brain templates and atlases. Neuroimage **62**(2), 911–922 (2012)

35. Sun, K., Liu, Z., Chen, G., et al.: A two-center radiomic analysis for differentiating major depressive disorder using multi-modality MRI data under different parcellation methods. J. Affect. Disord. **300**, 1–9 (2022)

36. Ashburner, J., Csernansk, J.G., Davatzikos, C., et al.: Computer-assisted imaging to assess brain structure in healthy and diseased brains. The Lancet Neurol. **2**(2), 79–88 (2003)

37. Zimeo Morais, G.A., Balardin, J.B., Sato, J.R.: fNIRS Optodes' Location Decider (fOLD): a toolbox for probe arrangement guided by brain regions-of-interest. Sci. Rep. **8**(1), 1–11 (2018)

38. Gómez, J.C.V., Incalla, A.P.Z., Perca, J.C.C., et al.: Diferentes configuraciones para MobileNet en la detección de tumores cerebrales: different configurations for MobileNet in the detection of brain tumors. In: 2021 IEEE 1st International Conference on Advanced Learning Technologies on Education & Research (ICALTER), pp. 1–4. IEEE (2021)

39. Sun, Y., Zhang, J., Han, C.: A flower recognition system based on MobileNet for smart agriculture. In: 2021 IEEE 3rd International Conference on Frontiers Technology of Information and Computer (ICFTIC), pp. 712–717. IEEE (2021)

40. Zhang, L., Wang, L., Gao, J., et al.: Deep fusion of brain structure-function in mild cognitive impairment. Med. Image Anal. **72**, 102082 (2021)

41. Li, C., Mo, L., Yan, R.: Rotating machinery fault diagnosis based on spatial-temporal GCN. In: 2021 International Conference on Sensing, Measurement & Data Analytics in the Era of Artificial Intelligence (ICSMD), pp. 1–6. IEEE (2021)

# A 2.5D Coarse-to-Fine Framework for 3D Cardiac CT View Planning

Xiaohan Yuan[1] and Yinsu Zhu[2(✉)]

[1] School of Automation, Southeast University, Nanjing, China
[2] Department of Radiology, The First Affiliated Hospital of Nanjing
Medical University, Nanjing, China
zhuyinsu@njmu.edu.cn

**Abstract.** Usually, the directly acquired CT images are from the axial views with respect to the major axes of the body, which do not effectively represent the structure of the heart. If CT imaging is first reformatted into the typical cardiac imaging planes, it will lay the foundation for the subsequent analysis. In this paper, we propose an automatic CT view planning method to acquire standard views of the heart from 3D CT volume, obtaining the equation of the plane by detecting landmarks that can determine this view. To face the challenge of memory cost brought by 3D CT input, we convert the 3D problem into a 2.5D problem, taking into account the spatial context information at the same time. We design a coarse-to-fine framework for the automatic detection of anatomical landmarks. The coarse network is used to estimate the probability distribution of the landmark location in each set of orthogonal planes, and the fine network is further used to regress the offset distance of the current result from the ground-truth. We construct the first known dataset of reformatted cardiac CT with landmark annotations, and the proposed method is evaluated on our dataset, validating its accuracy in the tasks of landmark detection and view planning.

**Keywords:** Cardiac CT · Automatic imaging view planning · Medical landmark detection

## 1 Introduction

According to the World Health Organization (WHO), cardiovascular disease (CVD) is the number one killer of deaths worldwide [1], and the analysis of cardiac images can support the diagnosis and treatment of heart disease. The raw CT images are obtained directly with respect to the main axes of the body (axial, sagittal, and coronal), while the heart itself has its own position and orientation, so it is necessary to re-plan the views suitable for observation. This procedure of converting the images produced by the original reconstruction process into a different orientation than the way they were originally produced is called view planning [12], and it has been applied to several anatomical sites such as the brain [6] and the heart [7]. The importance and challenges of automatic and rapid planning of standard views of the heart in clinical practice cannot be ignored.

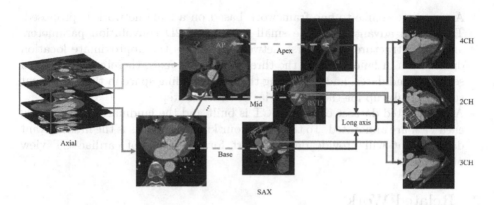

**Fig. 1.** The process of manually acquiring some anatomical landmarks to construct standard views of the heart.

Standard cardiac scans include images acquired at different angulated planes of the heart, such as short-axis (SAX), long-axis 2-chamber (2CH, vertical long-axis), and 4-chamber (4CH, horizontal long axis), and 3-chamber (3CH) views. As shown in Fig. 1, to generate these standard cardiac views, the physician manually obtains some anatomical landmarks through the following steps, which usually take roughly 3 min. The midpoint of the mitral valve (MV) and the apex (AP) of the heart is first selected from the original axial planes to obtain the long axis of the heart. A sequence of SAX views is obtained from a plane perpendicular to the long axis, from MV planning to AP. On the SAX basal slice, the midpoint of the aortic valve (AV) is selected, and combined with the long-axis to form a 3CH view. On the SAX intermediate slice, the RV lateral point (RVL) and the long-axis constitute a 4CH view. Two RV insertion points (RVI1, and RVI2) are also taken, and the 2CH view is defined as a plane parallel to the line connecting the two RV insertion points and passing through the long axis.

The objects of existing cardiac view planning methods are often MR images, and the approaches are divided into segmentation-based and landmark-based. The former needs to segment the cardiac chambers first, to complete the location of the long axis of the ventricle, but this will make the task more arduous because the difficulty of segmenting and labeling is much greater than that of landmarks. The method based on landmark detection is intended to determine the location of the view by detecting the anatomical landmarks that determine the plane, including the case where the input is 2D or 3D. Unlike MR images, raw cardiac CT images are high-resolution 3D volumes. Although the existing 3D methods can often obtain accurate results due to the effective use of spatial information, they are accompanied by high computational costs. To address this challenge, in this paper, we propose a view planning approach for CT images based on deep learning, which converts the 3D problem into a 2.5D problem while taking into account spatial context information. Specifically, we make the following contributions:

- A two-stage coarse-to-fine framework based on a 2.5D network is proposed. Taking full advantage of the small amount of 2D convolution parameters and light structure, our coarse network estimates the approximate location distribution of landmarks in the three coordinate axes, thereby generating a series of candidates, and extracting their surrounding space in the refinement stage to make up for the deficiencies of the first step.
- A reformatted dataset of cardiac CT is built and the landmarks determining each view are annotated. To the best of our knowledge, this is the first relevant dataset that will provide data support for the study of cardiac CT view planning.

## 2    Related Work

Automatic view planning is very important to obtain an image perspective that is convenient for subsequent analysis, much work has been devoted to this aspect, mainly in MRI images. Lelieveldt et al. [9] proposed an automated SA scan planning technique for cardiac MR images by matching the thorax model to scout images to estimate the position and orientation of the LV long axis. Jackson et al. [7] planned the acquisition of images aligned with the cardiac axes which are determined from a stack of localizer images. Lu et al. [11] first located and segmented the ventricle, and then obtained the landmarks to calculate the views. Similarly, after anatomy recognition using a model-based segmentation approach, Frick et al. [5] aligned landmarks with the reference frame to yield automatically defined scan geometry orientations. These methods are all carried out based on segmentation. Le et al. [8] proposed a method based on a 3D neural network, which first calculates a bounding box that tightly crops the heart and then detects the landmarks to generate the long and short-axis views. Alansary et al. [2] employed a multi-scale reinforcement learning (RL) agent framework to find standardized view planes in 3D image acquisitions. Blansit et al. [3] used deep learning-based localization of landmarks to prescribe imaging planes. Wei et al. [18] proposed a novel annotated-free system to mine the spatial relationship between the source and target views by training a deep network to regress the heatmaps defined by the intersection lines. However, these methods are based on 2D inputs and do not conform to the CT case.

For deep learning-based landmark detection methods in medical images, they can be divided into two categories according to their inputs: one is image-based and the other is patch-based. Image-based methods tend to be end-to-end, but are dominated by 2D inputs [17]. Patch-based methods include classification-based [19,21], regression-based [10,20], and a combination of the two [14,15].

As far as we know, few publications address the reformatting challenges of cardiac CT images. As the first full-automatic CT image reformatting method,

Nuñez-Garcia et al. [16] obtained surface meshes through deep learning-based segmentation and then detected shape features to find the transformation that locates the ventricle on its standard, mathematically defined short-axis position. However, the main disadvantage is that this method requires prior segmentation and relies on the quality of the segmentation masks.

# 3  Methodology

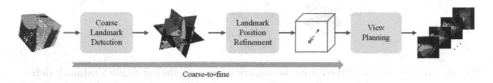

**Fig. 2.** Overview of the proposed method for automatic CT view planning.

The pipeline of the proposed automatic CT view planning method is shown in Fig. 2. The view plane is determined by specific anatomical key points, so it is necessary to accurately detect the location of these landmarks. The input is a CT volume, and after coarse-to-fine landmark detection, the output is a set of planned long- and short-axis views based on specific landmarks.

## 3.1  Coarse Landmark Detection

Due to the relatively large CT volume of the heart, using 3D methods requires more computational resources. To avoid the challenges of computational memory caused by direct input of the overall volume and the lack of resolution caused by downsampling to cater to memory consumption, we convert the 3D landmark detection problem into a 2.5D problem. Unlike previous methods, CT volume is not directly input to the network, but the high-resolution 2D image.

We first extract three sets of orthogonal planes along the X, Y, and Z axes of the anatomical coordinate system for the 3D CT volume: sagittal plane, coronal plane, and axial plane. Each set of planes consists of a series of 2D images along that coordinate axis. Our method separately estimates the location of surface points in the image sequence for each axis, localizing anatomical structures in 3D medical images by combining the three coordinate locations. The process is shown in Fig. 3.

Many current methods model the problem of landmark localization as a binary classification problem [4,19,22]. For each landmark, 2D images are marked as positive or negative depending on whether they contain it. Due to a large number of slices in each axis of the heart volume but only one correct landmark position, this processing will cause a serious imbalance of positive and negative samples, which will affect the training effect. Inspired by the method

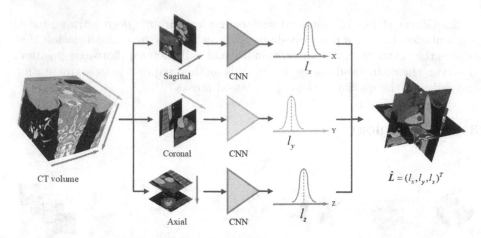

**Fig. 3.** The framework of the coarse landmark detection, taking single landmark detection as an example. After extracting three sets of orthogonal planes along the X, Y, and Z axes of the 3D CT volume, respectively estimate the probability distribution of the landmark location in each set of planes, and then combine the results to obtain the 3D landmark position.

of using regression heatmap for keypoint detection, we model the localization problem as a regression problem, that is, instead of judging whether a 2D image contains landmarks, we estimate the probability of landmarks appearing in the specified 2D image.

Since the cardiac CT is approximately cubic, we first normalize the 3D image to $N \times N \times N$, where $N$ is the size number, and then extract three sets of 2D image sequences based on this. For a series of 2D images on the coordinate axis $A_i, i \in \{1, 2, 3\}$ is $\mathbb{S}_i = \{\mathbf{S}_1, ..., \mathbf{S}_N\}$, where $\mathbf{S}_i \in \mathbb{R}^{N \times N}$. The ground-truth coordinate of the landmark point $\mathbf{L}_j, j \in \{1, ..., M\}$ on the axis $A_i$ is $l_{i,j} \in \{0, ..., N-1\}$, where $M$ is the number of landmarks. A Gaussian function is used to simulate its probability distribution $\mathbf{p}_{i,j}$. The value at $l_{i,j}$ is 1, and the closer the distance is, the closer the probability is to 1:

$$\mathbf{p}_{i,j} = [p_{i,j,0}, ..., p_{i,j,k}, ..., p_{i,j,N-1}] \in \mathbb{R}^N, p_{i,j,k} = exp(-\frac{(k - l_{i,j})^2}{2\sigma_1^2}), \quad (1)$$

where $i$, $j$ and $k$ are the indices of axis, landmark and coordinate, respectively, $k \in \{0, ..., N-1\}$, $\sigma_1$ is the standard deviation and $p_k$ will be the ground-truth of the probability at coordinate $k$.

We design a CNN-based neural network to regress the probability distribution of landmarks on each axis separately. The input to the network is a 2D slice on one axis, and the output is a 1D vector $\hat{\mathbf{P}}_{i,k} = \left(\widehat{p_{i,0,k}}, ..., \widehat{p_{i,j,k}}, ..., \widehat{p_{i,M-1,k}}\right)^T$. After predicting all the slices of the entire axis, take the value with the highest probability as the final result:

$$\hat{l_{i,j}} = \operatorname{argmax}_k \hat{\mathbf{P}}_{i,j} = \operatorname{argmax}_k \left[\widehat{p_{i,j,0}}, ..., \widehat{p_{i,j,k}}, ..., \widehat{p_{i,j,N-1}}\right] \quad (2)$$

where $l_{i,j}^{\hat{}}$ is the predicted coordinate value of landmark $L_j$ on axis $A_i$. The position of the coordinates in 3D space is combined on the three axis predictions $\hat{\mathbf{L}}_j = (l_{0,j}^{\hat{}}, l_{1,j}^{\hat{}}, l_{2,j}^{\hat{}})^T$.

## 3.2   Landmark Position Refinement

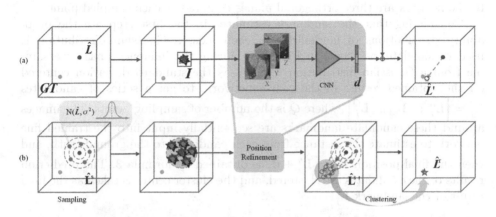

**Fig. 4.** The framework of the fine landmark detection, taking single landmark detection as an example. (a) The input of the fine network is the surrounding images of the coarse landmark detection result, and the output is the offset distance from the current landmark to the ground-truth. (b) Take the result of coarse landmark detection as the center to sample candidates, perform position refinement on each candidate, and cluster the obtained positions as the final result.

Since estimating landmark locations from 2D images does not utilize spatial context information, we try to further refine the results and introduce the output of coarse landmark detection into the refinement network as an initial condition. After getting the rough landmark positions from the first network, we design a regression network to estimate the offset distance from the current landmark to the ground-truth:

$$\mathbf{L}_j = \hat{\mathbf{L}}_j + \mathbf{d_j} \qquad (3)$$

where $\mathbf{d_j} = (d_{0,j}, d_{1,j}, d_{2,j})^T$ is the displacement vector of the distance between the current position and the ground-truth landmark position, as the output of the fine network.

As shown in Fig. 4(a), we hope to infer the relative position of the current point to the ground-truth point from the local spatial information of the current position. But directly taking the 3D volume around the current landmark as input is expensive, so we approximate it by taking three orthogonal planes centered at $\hat{\mathbf{L}}_j$ along the X, Y, and Z axes and concatenating them together as the input $\mathbf{I}_j \in \mathbb{R}^{3 \times S \times S}$ to the network to approximate the effect of 3D volume input. It is also to convert the 3D problem into a 2.5D problem and replace

3D convolution with 2D convolution, but at the same time consider the spatial context information.

To train the network, we structure the training data as follows. First, a series of rough landmark locations obtained from the coarse network is simulated by sampling from a Gaussian distribution centered at the location of the ground-truth landmark with $\sigma_2$ as the standard deviation. The locations of ground-truth will then be diffed with them, and the results are used as supervision. The inputs to the network are three orthogonal planes centered at each sampled point.

Considering that the landmark estimates in the first step are the probability distributions of landmarks on each axis, a Gaussian distribution is used to simulate, as shown in Fig. 4(b). During the inference phase, we sample from a Gaussian distribution with $\sigma_3$ as the standard deviation centered on the obtained results of the coarse network, to get a series of candidates $\hat{\mathbb{L}}_j^s = \left[ \hat{\mathbf{L}}_j^0, ..., \hat{\mathbf{L}}_j^q, ..., \hat{\mathbf{L}}_j^Q \right]$, where $Q$ is the number of sampling points. The images around these candidate landmarks are sequentially input into the trained fine network to estimate the distance from each candidate to the ground-truth, and then the final position $\hat{\mathbf{L}}_j^{'q} = \hat{\mathbf{L}}_j^q + \hat{\mathbf{d}}_j$ is obtained by formula 3. The prediction results of the candidates are clustered, and the cluster center is taken as the final result of the landmark $\hat{\mathbf{L}}_j^r$.

# 4   Experiments and Results

## 4.1   Data and Annotations

We collected more than 200 cardiac CTs from ***** for the study, each volume data from the upper abdomen to the aortic arch, covering the entire cardiac structure. We asked professional radiologists to plan the views (SAX, 2CH, 3CH, 4CH) of the acquired cardiac CT according to the standard defined by the American Heart Association (AHA) [13], and to annotate the landmarks that can determine each view plane(MV, AP, AV, RVL, RVI1, RVI2), as shown in Fig. 1. These landmarks have certain anatomical significance. The experiments were trained on 150 cases and tested on 75 cases.

## 4.2   Experimental Design

All CT volumes are resized to $N \times N \times N$ voxels ($N = 256$). The structure of both networks is similar to UNet's Encoder structure, followed by 3 fully connected layers. The input of the rough network is a 2D image with the size of $N \times N$, the last layer of the network is a sigmoid layer, and the output is a one-dimensional vector of length $K (K = 6)$ representing the probability. For each landmark, the input to the fine network is a $3 \times S \times S$ ($S = 96$) tensor and the output is the distances in three directions. Both networks use MSE loss for supervision. We trained with a 2080Ti GPU with batch sizes of 32 and 256, respectively, using the Adam optimizer with an initial learning rate set to 1e−4. In the experiment, take $\sigma 1 = \sigma 2 = \sigma 3 = 10$. Use the Euler distance between points to evaluate the performance of landmark detection, and use the angle between two plane normals to evaluate the performance of view planning.

## 4.3   Results

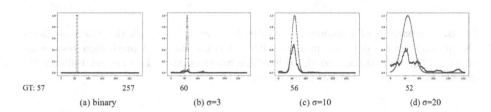

GT: 57                    257         60                   56                  52

(a) binary              (b) σ=3              (c) σ=10             (d) σ=20

**Fig. 5.** Analysis of coordinate representation, taking the z-axis results of AP as an example. Red represents the ground-truth distribution, and blue represents the predicted results. (Color figure online)

**Analysis of Coordinate Representation.** For the framework of coarse landmark detection, we verify the effect of different modeling approaches to the problem of detecting the location of landmarks from a set of 2D images along each axis. As shown in Fig. 5, when it is regarded as a binary classification problem, that is, whether each image contains landmarks is defined as positive or negative, in the process of training, due to the lack of supervision information provided, the positive and negative samples are seriously uneven, and its predicted results tend to be 0. By regressing the probability of each landmark, each position on the axis provides supervision information, the network can converge faster, and predicting each pixel position can improve the accuracy of landmarks. In this regard, we compare the effect of using different standard deviations to generate Gaussian distribution on the results, and it can be seen that the effect is optimal when $\sigma = 10$.

**Table 1.** Comparison of results from landmark detection. Shown are the mean and standard deviation of the distance (mm) between points.

| Method | MV | AP | AV | RVL | RVI1 | RVI2 |
|---|---|---|---|---|---|---|
| C | 6.61 (3.70) | 9.32 (8.38) | 8.12 (4.01) | 11.96 (7.06) | 11.66 (7.42) | 8.92 (4.73) |
| C2F | 6.10 (3.39) | 11.6 (6.51) | 6.36 (3.14) | 9.41 (6.77) | 10.58 (6.44) | 9.28 (5.64) |
| C2F (iter) | 5.42 (2.72) | 9.62 (8.09) | 5.65 (2.88) | 9.24 (5.58) | 9.79 (6.29) | 8.21 (4.25) |
| C2F (cluster) | **4.93 (2.45)** | **8.51 (7.87)** | **5.60 (2.72)** | **8.89 (5.13)** | **9.32 (5.85)** | **7.80 (3.77)** |

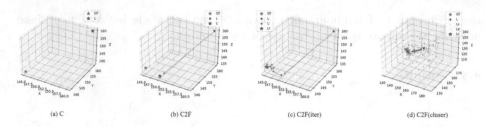

      (a) C                      (b) C2F                  (c) C2F(iter)              (d) C2F(cluser)

**Fig. 6.** Comparison of visualization results for several landmark detection methods. The ground-truth points are marked with red stars, the final prediction results are marked with green stars, and the others are intermediates. The arrows indicate the optimization direction. (Color figure online)

**Landmark Detection Results.** Table 1 compares the results of different methods for landmark detection, including coarse localization only (C), one-step fine localization after coarse localization (C2F), multiple iterations of fine localization after coarse localization (C2F (iter)), and fine localization performed by sampling candidates after coarse localization (C2F (cluster)), and their visualization results are shown in Fig. 6. It can be seen that using only the coarse network to estimate landmarks (Fig. 6(a)) is inaccurate but provides suitable initial values for the subsequent refinement. After adding the refinement network, the positions are all close to the ground-truth. However, the results of continuous iterative optimization (Fig. 6(c), $L'$ is the intermediate result after iterative refinement) is better than one-step optimization (Fig. 6(b), $L'$ is the one-step refinement result), constantly approaching the ground-truth. However, with the continuous search, the results are easy to oscillate around the true value, and if a large error occurs in one of the iterations, it will affect the overall detection. After a large number of sampling, the candidates are generated and then clustered (Fig. 6(d), $Ls$ is the sampled input candidate point, $Ls'$ is the refined result of $Ls$), which has a higher fault tolerance rate and reduces the impact of poor individual predictions.

**Table 2.** Comparison of the results of automatic view planning. Shown are the mean and standard deviation of the angle (°) between the normals.

| Methods | Normal deviation | | | | Running time |
|---------|------|------|------|------|--------------|
|         | SAX  | 2CH  | 3CH  | 4CH  |              |
| SSM  | 7.75 (2.70) | 13.8 (14.65) | 11.8 (12.74) | 14.64 (13.50) | 20.56 |
| Ours | **7.02 (8.70)** | **8.97 (10.81)** | **9.81 (8.15)** | **7.06 (8.47)** | **4.13** |

**View Planning Results.** Based on obtaining the landmark results, the plane position determined by these landmarks can be planned, and several examples are shown in Fig. 7. It can be seen from the visualization results that our method

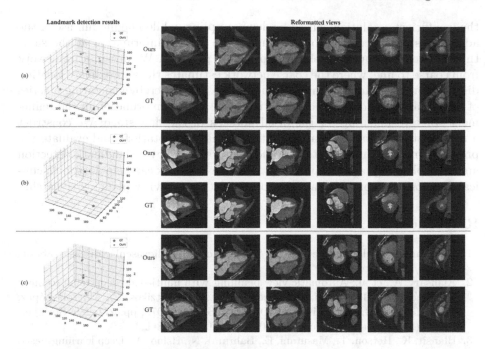

**Fig. 7.** Comparison between the results of ground-truth and our method for landmark detection and automatic planning. The reformatted views are obtained from the localized landmarks, from left to right are the 2CH, 3CH, 4CH, and base, middle, and top images of the SAX view.

can accurately detect the location of landmarks, thereby obtaining views that are almost consistent with the ground-truth views. We compare the proposed method with a statistical shape model-based method (SSM) [19], as shown in Table 2. The SSM needs to build the atlas of the heart in advance to construct the parametric model, which requires a lot of manual annotation. In the inference process, the CT volume is segmented first, and then the model parameters are regressed based on the segmentation. Because the 3D model obtained by the parameters has a consistent topology, the vertex index corresponding to the landmark can be directly read, complete the landmark positioning, and then perform view planning. But the biggest challenge of this method is that it requires segmentation information, and the quality of segmentation will affect the results of downstream tasks. There will also be a significant increase in runtime due to iterative operations. Our method performs better in both quantitative results and running time.

## 5    Conclusion

In this paper, we propose an automatic cardiac CT view planning method by detecting landmarks that can determine the view planes. To avoid the computational memory challenge caused by the direct input of the 3D volume and the insufficient resolution caused by downsampling, while making full use of the advantages of 2D convolution, leveraging the spatial information at the same time, we convert the 3D problem into a 2.5D problem. We design a framework from coarse to fine, where the coarse network estimates the approximate location distribution of landmarks on three coordinate axes, thereby generating a series of coordinate candidates, and extracting local spatial information in the refinement stage to make up for the disadvantages of the first stage. We construct a reformatted cardiac CT dataset with landmark annotations and evaluate the proposed method on our dataset, validating its accuracy in landmark detection and view planning tasks, respectively. We hope our work can help doctors in clinical diagnosis and provide data support for future CT view planning research.

# References

1. Who cardiovascular diseases. https://www.who.int/cardiovascular_diseases/about_cvd/en/. Accessed 29 July 2020
2. Alansary, A., et al.: Automatic view planning with multi-scale deep reinforcement learning agents. In: Frangi, A.F., Schnabel, J.A., Davatzikos, C., Alberola-López, C., Fichtinger, G. (eds.) MICCAI 2018. LNCS, vol. 11070, pp. 277–285. Springer, Cham (2018). https://doi.org/10.1007/978-3-030-00928-1_32
3. Blansit, K., Retson, T., Masutani, E., Bahrami, N., Hsiao, A.: Deep learning-based prescription of cardiac MRI planes. Radiol. Artif. Intell. **1**(6), e180069 (2019)
4. De Vos, B.D., Wolterink, J.M., de Jong, P.A., Leiner, T., Viergever, M.A., Išgum, I.: Convnet-based localization of anatomical structures in 3-D medical images. IEEE Trans. Med. Imaging **36**(7), 1470–1481 (2017)
5. Frick, M., et al.: Fully automatic geometry planning for cardiac MR imaging and reproducibility of functional cardiac parameters. J. Magn. Reson. Imaging **34**(2), 457–467 (2011)
6. Itti, L., Chang, L., Ernst, T.: Automatic scan prescription for brain MRI. Magn. Reson. Med. Off. J. Int. Soc. Magn. Reson. Med. **45**(3), 486–494 (2001)
7. Jackson, C.E., Robson, M.D., Francis, J.M., Noble, J.A.: Computerised planning of the acquisition of cardiac MR images. Comput. Med. Imaging Graph. **28**(7), 411–418 (2004)
8. Le, M., Lieman-Sifry, J., Lau, F., Sall, S., Hsiao, A., Golden, D.: Computationally efficient cardiac views projection using 3D convolutional neural networks. In: Cardoso, M.J., et al. (eds.) DLMIA/ML-CDS -2017. LNCS, vol. 10553, pp. 109–116. Springer, Cham (2017). https://doi.org/10.1007/978-3-319-67558-9_13
9. Lelieveldt, B.P., van der Geest, R.J., Lamb, H.J., Kayser, H.W., Reiber, J.H.: Automated observer-independent acquisition of cardiac short-axis MR images: a pilot study. Radiology **221**(2), 537–542 (2001)
10. Li, Y., et al.: Fast multiple landmark localisation using a patch-based iterative network. In: Frangi, A.F., Schnabel, J.A., Davatzikos, C., Alberola-López, C., Fichtinger, G. (eds.) MICCAI 2018. LNCS, vol. 11070, pp. 563–571. Springer, Cham (2018). https://doi.org/10.1007/978-3-030-00928-1_64
11. Lu, X., et al.: Automatic view planning for cardiac MRI acquisition. In: Fichtinger, G., Martel, A., Peters, T. (eds.) MICCAI 2011. LNCS, vol. 6893, pp. 479–486. Springer, Heidelberg (2011). https://doi.org/10.1007/978-3-642-23626-6_59
12. McNitt-Gray, M.F.: AAPM/RSNA physics tutorial for residents: topics in CT: radiation dose in CT. Radiographics **22**(6), 1541–1553 (2002)

A 2.5D Coarse-to-Fine Framework for View Planning 387

13. American Heart Association Writing Group on Myocardial Segmentation and Registration for Cardiac Imaging, et al.: Standardized myocardial segmentation and nomenclature for tomographic imaging of the heart: a statement for healthcare professionals from the cardiac imaging committee of the council on clinical cardiology of the American Heart Association. Circulation **105**(4), 539–542 (2002)
14. Noothout, J.M., et al.: Deep learning-based regression and classification for automatic landmark localization in medical images. IEEE Trans. Med. Imaging **39**(12), 4011–4022 (2020)
15. Noothout, J.M., de Vos, B.D., Wolterink, J.M., Leiner, T., Išgum, I.: CNN-based landmark detection in cardiac CTA scans. arXiv preprint arXiv:1804.04963 (2018)
16. Nuñez-Garcia, M., Cedilnik, N., Jia, S., Sermesant, M., Cochet, H.: Automatic multiplanar CT reformatting from trans-axial into left ventricle short-axis view. In: Puyol Anton, E., et al. (eds.) STACOM 2020. LNCS, vol. 12592, pp. 14–22. Springer, Cham (2021). https://doi.org/10.1007/978-3-030-68107-4_2
17. Payer, C., Štern, D., Bischof, H., Urschler, M.: Regressing heatmaps for multiple landmark localization using CNNs. In: Ourselin, S., Joskowicz, L., Sabuncu, M.R., Unal, G., Wells, W. (eds.) MICCAI 2016. LNCS, vol. 9901, pp. 230–238. Springer, Cham (2016). https://doi.org/10.1007/978-3-319-46723-8_27
18. Wei, D., Ma, K., Zheng, Y.: Training automatic view planner for cardiac MR imaging via self-supervision by spatial relationship between views. In: de Bruijne, M., et al. (eds.) MICCAI 2021. LNCS, vol. 12906, pp. 526–536. Springer, Cham (2021). https://doi.org/10.1007/978-3-030-87231-1_51
19. Yang, D., Zhang, S., Yan, Z., Tan, C., Li, K., Metaxas, D.: Automated anatomical landmark detection ondistal femur surface using convolutional neural network. In: 2015 IEEE 12th International Symposium on Biomedical Imaging (ISBI), pp. 17–21. IEEE (2015)
20. Zhang, J., Liu, M., Shen, D.: Detecting anatomical landmarks from limited medical imaging data using two-stage task-oriented deep neural networks. IEEE Trans. Image Process. **26**(10), 4753–4764 (2017). https://doi.org/10.1109/TIP.2017.2721106
21. Zheng, Y., Liu, D., Georgescu, B., Nguyen, H., Comaniciu, D.: 3D deep learning for efficient and robust landmark detection in volumetric data. In: Navab, N., Hornegger, J., Wells, W.M., Frangi, A.F. (eds.) MICCAI 2015. LNCS, vol. 9349, pp. 565–572. Springer, Cham (2015). https://doi.org/10.1007/978-3-319-24553-9_69
22. Zhou, X., et al.: Automatic anatomy partitioning of the torso region on CT images by using a deep convolutional network with majority voting. In: Medical Imaging 2019: Computer-Aided Diagnosis, vol. 10950, pp. 256–261. SPIE (2019)

# Weakly Supervised Semantic Segmentation of Echocardiography Videos via Multi-level Features Selection

Erna Chen[1], Zemin Cai[1(✉)], and Jian-huang Lai[2]

[1] Department of Electronic Engineering, Shantou University, Shantou 515063, Guangdong, People's Republic of China
{20enchen,zmcai}@stu.edu.cn
[2] School of Data and Computer Science, Sun Yat-sen University, Guangzhou 510006, China
stsljh@mail.sysu.edu.cn

**Abstract.** Echocardiogram illustrates what the capacity it owns of detecting the global and regional functions of the heart. With obvious benefits of non-invasion, visuality and mobility, it has become an indispensable technology for clinical evaluation of cardiac function. However, the uncertainty in measurement of ultrasonic equipment and inter-reader variability are always inevitable. Regarding of this situation, researchers have proposed many methods for cardiac function assessment based on deep learning. In this paper, we propose UDeep, an encoder-decoder model for left ventricular segmentation of echocardiography, which pays attention to both multi-scale high-level semantic information and multi-scale low-level fine-grained information. Our model maintains sensitivity to semantic edges, so as to accurately segment the left ventricle. The encoder extracts multiple scales high-level semantic features through a computation efficient backbone named Separated Xception and the Atrous Spacial Pyramid Pooling module. A new decoder module consisting of several Upsampling Fusion Modules (UPFMs), at the same time, is applied to fuse features of different levels. To improve the generalization of our model to different echocardiography images, we propose Pseudo-Segmentation Penalty loss function. Our model accurately segments the left ventricle with a Dice Similarity Coefficient of 0.9290 on the test set of echocardiography videos dataset.

**Keywords:** Echocardiography · Left ventricle · Semantic segmentation · Encoder-decoder · Pseudo-Segmentation Penalty Loss Function

## 1 Introduction

The heart is the key organ to pump blood to the whole body indicating the critical role of it's normal function. Cardiac dysfunction can lead to cardiovascular

S. Yu et al. (Eds.): PRCV 2022, LNCS 13535, pp. 388–400, 2022.
https://doi.org/10.1007/978-3-031-18910-4_32

diseases (CVDs) such as cardiovascular death, heart failure, hypertrophic cardiomyopathy, coronary heart disease and aneurysm [1–3] which are the primary diseases that endanger human health. Accurate and non-invasive evaluation of global and regional left ventricular function is of vital importance for the determination of diagnosis of the heart. The most common clinically useful parameter is left ventricular ejection fraction (LVEF). LVEF is the fraction of chamber volume ejected of the left ventricular end-systole volume (ESV) in relation to the left ventricular end-diastolic volume (EDV).

Echocardiography is a preferred imaging analytical method to detect the CVDs. It provides clear, concrete and real time displays of the shape, spatial distribution and mechanical displacement information of cardiac structure. As a result, echocardiography can be used to accurately and quantitatively assess not only cardiovascular hemodynamic information but also global and regional mechanical functions of myocardium. In the field of echocardiography research, at present, several techniques have been validated. M-mode echocardiography measures myocardial contraction and radius enlargement with excellent time resolution. In particular, two-dimensional (2D) echocardiography is widely used and can accurately quantify the overall and regional ventricular functions.

Precise diagnosis of CVDs based on 2D echocardiography video depends on accurate segmentation of left ventricle.

In this paper, we propose UDeep, a weak-supervised deep learning model which is used for the left ventricle semantic segmentation of echocardiography videos. The output of UDeep provides the necessary basis for subsequent cardiac function analysis and diseases prediction, such as the ejection fraction (EF) and heart failure prediction. UDeep is an encoder-decoder model that learns from the ideas of DeepLabv3+ [4] and Unet [5]. DeepLabv3+ has been improved on the basis of DeepLabv3 to enhance its segmentation ability for multi-scale targets. Nevertheless, the excessive expansion rates of the Atrous Spacial Pyramid Pooling (ASPP) structure make it difficult to accurately extract features of the target at the edge of the image. Beside aforementioned defects, it lacks the ability to perceive multi-scale low-level features. To this end, we absorb the ideas of Unet, and propose a new decoder module which improves the ability of our model to perceive multiple scales low-level fine-grained features. At the same time, we modify the backbone named Xception to avoid excessive calculation and gradient explosion, and improve the performance of the model significantly.

The main contributions of this paper are listed as follows:

- We propose an efficient encoder-decoder model, which places emphasis on both semantic information of multi-scale high-level features through ASPP module and fine-grained information of multi-scale low-level features through several UPFM modules, to perform weakly supervised semantic segmentation of left ventricle of echocardiography videos.
- We further modify the backbone named Xception not only in simplifying the kernel size but also in replacing the activation function achieving dual purpose of reducing the computation complexity and improving the segmentation performance. Several minor modifications are also conducted in ASPP

module to achieve better segmentation effect, including the number of projection layers and the dilated rates of atrous convolutions.

- A Pseudo-Segmentation Penalty (PSP) loss function based on Euclidean distance is also proposed to impose varying degrees of penalties for pseudo-segmentation.
- Sufficient experiments on echocardiography videos dataset, EchoNet-Dynamic [6], demonstrates the superiority of our approach over other state-of-the-art methods.

The rest of this paper is organized as follows. Section 2 describes the related works on the task of image segmentation. Section 3 explains the proposed semantic segmentation model serving for echocardiography videos. The numerical implementation of our multi-level features selection model is given in Sect. 4. Section 5 gives experimental details of the proposed model and the corresponding results. We finally discuss the conclusion in Sect. 6.

## 2   Related Works

The proposal of Fully Convolutional Networks (FCNs) [7] opens up the precedent of deep learning in the field of image semantic segmentation. Compared with FCNs, SegNet [8] and DeconvNet [9] can handle objects of different scales, and achieve more sophisticated segmentation. Unet [5] makes the feature maps of each layer smaller through a shrinking network similar to VGG [10], and then outputs pixel-level labels of the whole image through upsampling and convolution. Many of the current semantic segmentation works such as SPPNet [11], DeepLab series [4,12,13] and PSPNet [14] are more willing to pay attention to pooling and multi-scale atrous convolution operations. Especially, DeepLabv3 [13] provides a parallel global pooling layer to further capture global contextual feature. PSPNet proposes a pyramid pooling module to extract contextual information of different scales. DeepLabv3+ [4] uses the core of DeepLabv3 as an encoder, and employs a simple decoder to improve the accuracy of segmentation boundaries.

Being unsatisfied with traditional CNN models, scholars turn to attention mechanism and transformer that firstly designed for NLP tasks [15–17]. EMANet [18] applies the expectation maximization (EM) algorithm to the attention mechanism, combined with the non-local network idea to iterate a set of compact bases through the EM algorithm. TransUNet [19] can be counted as a model which applies the transformer to replace the encoder module of Unet achieving comparatively desirable segmentation on a magnetic resonance (MR) dataset.

The analysis of cardiac function using echocardiograms is a complicated process and this has spawned many application of automatic analysis techniques based on deep learning in echocardiography. The work of Zhang et al. [20] segmented the left ventricle and myocardium, and all of these outputs were used to quantify the cavity volume and left ventricular mass, determining the ejection fraction (EF), and automatically determined the longitudinal strain through speckle tracking. EchoNet-Dynamic [6] performed weak-supervised semanticsegmentation of the left ventricle based on DeepLabv3 [13] model, predicting EF, and evaluates cardiomyopathy based on EF decline. PLANet [21] also proposed a pyramid local attention module, which further enhanced the feature extraction by extracting multi-scale information, showing good performance in the echocardiographic image segmentation.

Inspired by the above works, the purpose of UDeep is to achieve the capacity of obtaining multi-scale and multi-level features. The encoder module perceives global and regional features while the decoder module combines high-level semantic features and multi-scale low-level features full of fine-grained information together. In addition, the generalization ability of current common deep learning based segmentation model is fairly limited. Therefore, UDeep is mainly to serve for a more satisfactory implementation in semantic segmentation of echocardiography videos.

## 3   The Proposed Semantic Segmentation Method

In this section, we will introduce our backbone named Separated Xception based on the modifications of DeepLabv3+ to Xception. Our backbone further improves the performance with lower computation complexity. We regard roughly double bilinear upsampling in decoder module of DeepLabv3+ as a risky behavior. So we propose a new decoder to fuse high-level features generated by encoder module with multi-scale low-level features. We then present a pseudo-segmentation penalty (PSP) loss function based on Euclidean distance to post-process the semantic pseudo-segmentation results, thereby improving the performance of the model.

### 3.1   Separated Xception Couples with ASPP as Our Encoder

In order to both further improve the performance and reduce the complexity of our proposed model, we apply Separated Xception coupled with ASPP as our encoder. As demonstrated in Fig. 1, after the input image is extracted through the backbone with atrous convolution, the ASPP module is applied to probe deep convolutional features at multiple scales in order to extract multi-scale contextual information. Especially, we modify the $1 \times 1$ convolution of ASPP with 256 filters to sequential convolutions with filters of 1024 and 256. Then the Dilated rates of 3, 5, 7 are applied to supersede the original dilated rates of atrous convolutions. After ASPP operation, we then use a $1 \times 1$ convolution to consolidate information from multiple channels. The output of the encoder module is a feature map with 256 channels, which contains rich high-level semantic information to serve for the decoder module. In addition to the aforementioned modifications, we replace all ReLU activation with PReLU activation [22].

### 3.2   Upsampling Couples with $3 \times 3$ Convolutions as Our Decoder

It is worth noting that the directly bilinear upsampling operation by 4 is a very violent behavior. This weakness results in low accuracy of semantic segmentation, especially in boundaries. Hence we propose a new decoder to apply skip

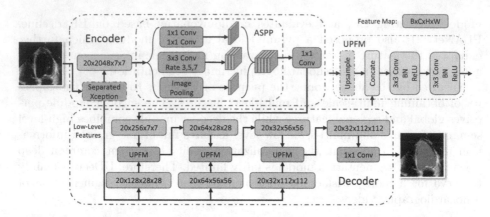

**Fig. 1.** The structure of UDeep. The encoder module encodes multi-scale features and global contextual information with focused semantic information extracted by backbone, the Separated Xception. Skip connection is applied between encoder and decoder modules. In decoder module, UPFM is applied to fuse different-scale feature maps. Multi-scale low-level features are extracted from Separated Xception including the outputs of Block1, Conv2, Conv1 modules (see Fig. 2 for details.). **ASPP**: Atrous Spacial Pyramid Pooling. **UPFM**: Upsampling Fusion Module. $\mathbf{B} \times \mathbf{C} \times \mathbf{H} \times \mathbf{W}$: batch × channel × height × width.

all ReLU activation with PReLU activation which avoids the gradient of 0 when ReLU is less than 0 almost without increasing the computational complexity, similar to [23]. Finally, to serve for the decoder module, we modify convolution strides of Conv1 and Conv2 to 1 and 2, respectively, as shown in Fig. 2 connection and fusion operations between feature maps of different levels. Several Upsampling Fusion Modules (UPFMs) composing of bilinear upsampling, concatenation and 3 × 3 fusion convolutions are applied to the decoder module to fuse multi-scale low- and high-level feature maps. This modification contributes to more accurate edge information recovery. Multiple scale low-level feature maps are generated by backbone and skip connection will be applied between them and the outputs of encoder module or UPFM. At the end, we apply a 1 × 1 classification convolution to generate pixel-level semantic segmentation result, as shown in Fig. 1.

### 3.3 Separated Xception

As demonstrated in [4], it makes more changes based on the modifications of what MSRA [24] has done to Xception. All of these changes make similar performance, and in the meantime, reduce computation complexity significantly. For the purpose of further reducing computation complexity and performing better, Firstly, we separate all 3 × 3 depthwise separable convolutions in Middle flow to 3 × 1 and 1 × 3 depthwise separable convolutions. Secondly, we replace

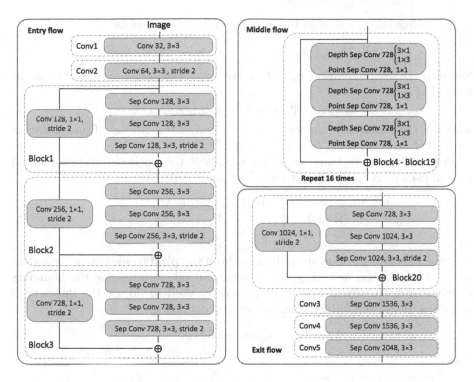

**Fig. 2.** The workflow of Separated Xception. **Depth Sep Conv**: depthwise separable convolution. **Point Sep Conv**: pointwise separable convolution.

### 3.4 Loss Function

The size and shape of the cardiac chambers are changed during the systole and diastole of the myocardium, combining with a certain similarity in shape throughout the cardiac cycle. Therefore, both the size difference and the shape similarity of the left ventricle are important in the left ventricle semantic segmentation task. The size difference of the left ventricle causes the model to be more effective in segmenting the left ventricle at the end systole, but less effective at the end diastole and vice versa. In conclusion, the generalization ability of previous models in different periods of the left ventricular motion cycle is unsatisfactory, resulting in left ventricular pseudo-segmentation. Inspired by the Dice Similarity Coefficient (DSC), a standard for evaluating binary classification effects, we propose a Pseudo-Segmentation Penalty (PSP) loss function based on Euclidean distance to impose varying degrees of penalties for pseudo-segmentation. As shown in Fig. 3(a), given the ground truth and segmentation output of the model, the ground truth has an intersection with the segmentation output (blue block in Fig. 3(a)). We regard the two cases of mismatches between the ground truth and output as pseudo-negative segmentation (brown block in Fig. 3(b)) and pseudo-positive segmentation (green block in Fig. 3(b)), respectively.

We define the pixels of an input image and their labels as

$$(X;Y) = \{(x_1, x_2, ..., x_i); (y_1, y_2, ..., y_i)\}, i \in N \tag{1}$$

Similarly, the segmentation output of the corresponding input image can be defined as

$$\hat{Y} = \{\hat{y_1}(x_1; \theta), \hat{y_2}(x_2; \theta), ..., \hat{y_i}(x_i; \theta)\}, i \in N \tag{2}$$

where $N$ represents the number of pixels of image. $\theta$ is the set of parameters of the model. In this paper, $N = 112 \times 112$.

Assuming that the boundary of the label is $B$, the Euclidean distance weight map of each pixel to its nearest boundary point is defined as,

$$W(x_i) = \begin{cases} -(e^{\beta d} - 1), & x_i \in M_{in} \\ 0, & x_i \in B \\ e^{\beta d} - 1, & x_i \in M_{out} \end{cases} \tag{3}$$

where $d$ indicates the Euclidean distance from the pixel to its nearest boundary point of labels. $M_{in}$ and $M_{out}$ denote regions inside and outside the boundary of labels, respectively. $\beta$ is a hyper-parameter used to adjust the intensity of penalties. Hence the full loss function can be defined as

$$\mathcal{L} = \mathcal{L}_{BCE} + \lambda \mathcal{L}_{PSP} \tag{4}$$

where

$$\mathcal{L}_{BCE} = -\frac{1}{N} \left[ \sum_{i=1}^{N} y_i \log \left( \hat{y}(x_i; \theta) \right) + (1 - y_i) \log \left( 1 - \hat{y}(x_i; \theta) \right) \right] \tag{5}$$

and

$$\mathcal{L}_{PSP} = \sum_{i=1}^{N} \hat{y}(x_i; \theta) \cdot B_{\hat{y}(x_i; \theta)} \cdot W(x_i) \tag{6}$$

We utilize $\mathcal{L}_{BCE}$ and $\mathcal{L}_{PSP}$ to denote the Binary Cross Entropy loss function and PSP loss function, respectively. In Eq. (4), $\lambda$ is a hyper-parameter. In Eq. (6), $B_{\hat{y}(x_i; \theta)}$ is a boolean 2-D matrix of dimension equal to segmentation output map that is true when pseudo segmentation happened. The symbol $\cdot$ is a dot product operation. We hope that when either pseudo-negative segmentation or pseudo-positive segmentation happened, each sample value for pseudo segmentation of $\mathcal{L}_{PSP}$ should be positive to achieve the purpose of penalty. Different signs (negative for $x_i \in M_{in}$, positive for $x_i \in M_{out}$) in Eq. (3) are applied to distinguish the Euclidean distance weight map corresponding to the sign of $\hat{y}(x_i; \theta)$.

## 4   Implementation

### 4.1   Echocardiography Video Datasets

In this paper, we performed the experiments on the public echocardiography dataset named EchoNet-Dynamic dataset. The EchoNet-Dynamic dataset made

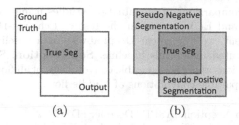

(a)                              (b)

**Fig. 3.** Pseudo segmentation. (a) The intersection between ground truth and segmentation output is the true segmentation. (b) Two cases of mismatches between ground truth and segmentation output are regarded as pseudo-negative segmentation (brown block) and pseudo-positive segmentation (green block) respectively. (Color figure online)

public by Ouyang et al., consisting of 10,030 apical four-chamber view echocardiography videos collected at Stanford University Hospital. The echocardiography videos are split to 7,465, 1,277, and 1,288 videos, respectively for training, validation, and test sets with pixel-level binary labels of left ventricular end systolic and end diastolic. Each echocardiogram video is $112 \times 112$ pixels in size.

## 4.2   Implementation Details

In this section, we will firstly introduce our implementation details. Then ablation experiments applied on the EchoNet-Dynamic dataset reveal the superiority of different parts of modification in our proposed model.

We use Separated Xception as our backbone to extract focused semantic information. For the purpose of uprating the performance of the proposed model, the Separated Xception is initialized by Xception model that is pretrained on ImageNet dataset [25], excepting the Middle flow which is initialized randomly. As to ASPP module, it is established by sequential $1 \times 1$ convolutions with filters of 1024 and 256, three $3 \times 3$ convolutions with different dilated rates of 3, 5, 7 and an image-level pooling operation [4]. Regarding of the decoder, we apply three Upsampling Fusion Modules (UPFMs) consisting of bilinear upsampling, concatenation and $3 \times 3$ fusion convolutions to fuse feature maps of different levels. In addition, a $1 \times 1$ convolution is applied to generate labels for each pixel. In addition, we replace all the ReLU activation with PReLU activation in Separated Xception and ASPP modules. We adopt Adam optimizer with initial learning rate $= 5e-3$, betas $= (0.9, 0.999)$, eps $= 1e-8$ to update parameters. As to the Euclidean distance weight map $W(x_i)$ (Eq. (3)) and loss function $\mathcal{L} = \mathcal{L}_{BCE} + \lambda \mathcal{L}_{PSP}$ (Eq. (4)), we define hyper-parameter $\beta = 5e-2$, and $\lambda = 1.05e-3 \times$ epoch.

**Ablation Studies:** We conduct the ablation studies to emphasize the meliority of different parts of application in our proposed model. In our ablation

**Table 1.** Statistical comparisons of our ablation studies using the average values of DSC at overall, ESV and EDV frames on the test of EchoNet-Dynamic dataset. In this ablation experiment, we implement DeepLabv3+ as a baseline method and our modifications are executed under this baseline. **SepXception**: Separated Xception. **AFs**: Separated operations apply to separable convolutions of all flows. **MF**: Separation operations apply to separable convolutions of Middle flow.

| Baseline | Sep Xception | | ASPP | Decoder | DSC | | |
|---|---|---|---|---|---|---|---|
| | AFs | MF | | | Overall | ESV | EDV |
| ✓ | | | | | 0.9138 | 0.8971 | 0.9246 |
| ✓ | ✓ | | | | 0.9180 | 0.9042 | 0.9266 |
| ✓ | | ✓ | | | 0.9238 | 0.9105 | 0.9323 |
| ✓ | | ✓ | ✓ | | 0.9257 | 0.9138 | 0.9331 |
| | | ✓ | ✓ | ✓ | **0.9290** | **0.9173** | **0.9364** |

experiments, we implement DeepLabv3+ [4] as a baseline method and our modifications are executed under this baseline.

We define $[k \times l, f]$ as a convolution operation with kernel $k \times l$ and $f$ filters. As described in Sect. 3.3, we separate all $3 \times 3$ depthwise separable convolutions to $3 \times 1$ and $1 \times 3$ depthwise separable convolutions in middle flow (MF) rather than in all flows (AFs). These two separated operations, comparing to Xception in baseline, namely, without modification, both contribute to relatively promotion of segmenting accuracy. A minor change to ASPP module likewise obtains a decent segmentation performance than previous ASPP module in [4].

By adding a new decoder composing of several UPFMs, our proposed model is completed which generates a more accurate segmentation performance. UPFMs are implemented including bilinear upsampling by different rates, concatenation and $3 \times 3$ fusion convolutions to fuse feature maps of different levels. At the end of decoder module, we apply a $[1 \times 1, 1]$ convolution to refine labels for each pixel. In this experiment, we define the rates of bilinear upsampling operations as 4, 2 and 2 coupled with fusion convolutions of $\{[3 \times 3, 192]\ [3 \times 3, 64]\}$, $\{[3 \times 3, 64]\ [3 \times 3, 32]\}$ and $\{[3 \times 3, 32]\ [3 \times 3, 32]\}$ severally. Table 1 gives the comparison results in the ablation studies, which state that when Separated operations are applied on MF of Xception, minor modification is achieved in ASPP, and a new decoder is utilized, the model achieves the best performance in all DSCs.

## 5 Experiments

Experiments are performed on the EchoNet-Dynamic dataset which has been mentioned in Sect. 4.1. In this section, we assess several deep learning baseline methods for natural segmentation (DeepLabv3+ [4], EMANet [18], TDNet [26]) and latest published medical segmentation methods (TransUNet [19], DCUNet

[27], EchoNet-Dynamic [6]) and our proposed UDeep on the test set of EchoNet-Dynamic dataset to state the superiority of UDeep. Then we will make a comparison of segmentation accuracy between EchoNet-Dynamic and UDeep on the test set of EchoNet-Dynamic dataset.

We firstly report performance of these baseline methods and our method named UDeep on the test set of EchoNet-Dynamic dataset in Table 2. Table 2 figures out the superiority of UDeep on the test set of EchoNet-Dynamic dataset. As illustrated in Table 2, through DSC, an indicator for segmentation evaluation, EchoNet-Dynamic performed 0.9068 (95%CI 0.9055–0.9086) for the ESV frames and was 0.9278 (95%CI 0.9261–0.9294) for the EDV frames on the test set which result in 0.9200 (95%CI 0.9187–0.9213) for overall labeled echocardiograms. Our proposed method segments the ESV and EDV frames reaching to 0.9173 (95%CI 0.9154–0.9192) and 0.9364 (95%CI 0.9350–0.9378) through the DSC, respectively. And these results in 0.9290 for overall labeled echocardiograms. By comparison, we may notice that no matter in the overall labeled frames, EDV frames or ESV frames, our model performs better than EchoNet-Dynamic and other baseline methods. The analysis of computational consumption and parameter requirements of above models is introduced in Table 3. The number of floating point operations (Flops) is calculated for an input with size of $3 \times 112 \times 112$. Owing to our simplification and modification to the baseline network, our model performed a more ideal segmentation effect with a small increase in computational consumption and parameter requirements.

Statistics of performance of our proposed method measured by DSC in Overall labeled frames, ESV and EDV frames are shown in Fig. 4(a). Qualitative effect of employing the proposed method and comparison with EchoNet-Dynamic are shown in Fig. 4(b). In Fig. 4(b), the first row illustrates the examples of echocardiographic frames and pixel-level ground truth of left ventricular EDV and ESV frames (blue regions). The second and third rows show the predictions of UDeep (red regions) and EchoNet-Dynamic (green regions) of left ventricle. The last two rows are the visual cross-contrast experiments between ground truth and predictions of UDeep and EchoNet-Dynamic. These two rows illustrate the pseudo semantic segmentation, in another word, incorrect prediction outputs between the ground truth and the prediction of UDeep and prediction of EchoNet-Dynamic, respectively.

As shown in Fig. 4, our proposed model UDeep performs better than EchoNet-Dynamic. The shape of our model's segmentation result of left ventricle is more relevant to the shape of ground truth. At the same time, benefiting not only from our new decoder which pays more attention to multiple scales low-level features but also PSP loss function, the segmentation boundary tends to be smooth rather than jagged. Similarly, the generalization capacity of our model is particularly suitable to different echocardiography images.

**Table 2.** Comparisons between baseline methods and our proposed UDeep on the test set of EchoNet-Dynamic dataset.

| Method | Year | Backbone | DSC Overall | ESV | EDV |
|--------|------|----------|---------|-----|-----|
| DeepLabv3+ [4] | 2018 | Xception-71 | 0.9138 | 0.8971 | 0.9246 |
| DeepLabv3+ [4] | 2018 | ResNet-101 | 0.9154 | 0.9039 | 0.9228 |
| TDNet [26] | 2020 | TD$^2$-PSP50 | 0.9162 | 0.9070 | 0.9217 |
| EMANet [18] | 2019 | ResNet-101 | 0.9168 | 0.9089 | 0.9234 |
| EchoNet-Dynamic [6] | 2019 | ResNet-50 | 0.9200 | 0.9068 | 0.9278 |
| TransUNet [19] | 2021 | ResNet-50+ViT-B/16 | 0.9205 | 0.9060 | 0.9295 |
| DCUNet [27] | 2020 | – | 0.9207 | 0.9036 | 0.9316 |
| Ours | 2022 | Separated Xception-71 | **0.9290** | **0.9173** | **0.9364** |

**Table 3.** Comparisons on computational consumption and parameter requirements between baseline methods and our proposed UDeep.

| Method | Backbone | Flops (**G**) | Params (**M**) |
|--------|----------|------------|-------------|
| DeepLabv3+ [4] | Xception-71 | **79.25** | 54.71 |
| DeepLabv3+ [4] | ResNet-101 | 85.02 | 61.39 |
| TDNet [26] | TD$^2$-PSP50 | 90.42 | 59.36 |
| EMANet [18] | ResNet-101 | 220.57 | 53.77 |
| EchoNet-Dynamic [6] | ResNet-50 | 156.81 | 39.63 |
| TransUNet [19] | ResNet-50+ViT-B/16 | 123.44 | 93.19 |
| DCUNet [27] | – | 109.90 | **10.26** |
| Ours | Separated Xception-71 | 85.68 | 55.83 |

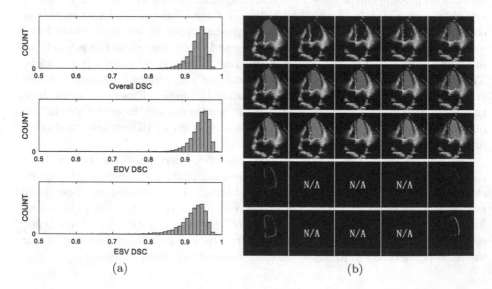

(a)                                        (b)

**Fig. 4.** (a) DSC shows the statistical information of performance of UDeep applied to overall labeled frames, each EDV and ESV frames. (b) Visual comparison between UDeep and EchoNet-Dynamic. (Color figure online)

# 6    Conclusion

We have presented an efficient encoder-decoder model named UDeep to segment the left ventricle on the echocardiography videos through multi-level features selection. The characteristic of UDeep is to lay more emphasis on the selection and fusion of multi-level features. This model further improves the performance in the task of left ventricular semantic segmentation, which serves for more downstream tasks such as prediction of EF and cardiovascular disease analysis. An efficient-higher and parameter-lesser backbone, which we called Separated Xception, is adopted to extract focused semantic information serving for ASPP in encoder module to obtain multi-scale high-level features. This backbone contributes multi-scale low-level features for decoder module likewise. Skip connections are also applied between encoder and decoder modules. UPFM in decoder module is used to fuse multi-scale high- and low-level features with different sizes of feature maps. Moreover, a PSP loss function is introduced to solve the problem of pseudo semantic segmentation. The proposed UDeep model further improve the precision of semantic segmentation of left ventricle, comparing with the state-of-the-art methods.

# References

1. Bui, A.L., Horwich, T.B., Fonarow, G.C.: Epidemiology and risk profile of heart failure. Nat. Rev. Cardiol. **8**(1), 30–41 (2011)
2. McMurray, J.J., Stewart, S.: Epidemiology, aetiology, and prognosis of heart failure. Heart **83**(5), 596–602 (2000)
3. Ziaeian, B., Fonarow, G.C.: Epidemiology and aetiology of heart failure. Nat. Rev. Cardiol. **13**(6), 368–378 (2016)
4. Chen, L.-C., Zhu, Y., Papandreou, G., Schroff, F., Adam, H.: Encoder-decoder with atrous separable convolution for semantic image segmentation. In: Ferrari, V., Hebert, M., Sminchisescu, C., Weiss, Y. (eds.) ECCV 2018. LNCS, vol. 11211, pp. 833–851. Springer, Cham (2018). https://doi.org/10.1007/978-3-030-01234-2_49
5. Ronneberger, O., Fischer, P., Brox, T.: U-Net: convolutional networks for biomedical image segmentation. In: Navab, N., Hornegger, J., Wells, W.M., Frangi, A.F. (eds.) MICCAI 2015. LNCS, vol. 9351, pp. 234–241. Springer, Cham (2015). https://doi.org/10.1007/978-3-319-24574-4_28
6. Ouyang, D., et al.: Video-based AI for beat-to-beat assessment of cardiac function. Nature **580**(7802), 252–256 (2020)
7. Long, J., Shelhamer, E., Darrell, T.: Fully convolutional networks for semantic segmentation. IEEE Trans. Pattern Anal. Mach. Intell. **39**(4), 640–651 (2015)
8. Badrinarayanan, V., Kendall, A., Cipolla, R.: SegNet: a deep convolutional encoder-decoder architecture for image segmentation. IEEE Trans. Pattern Anal. Mach. Intell. **39**(12), 2481–2495 (2017)
9. Noh, H., Hong, S., Han, B.: Learning deconvolution network for semantic segmentation. In: Proceedings of the IEEE International Conference on Computer Vision, pp. 1520–1528 (2015)
10. Simonyan, K., Zisserman, A.: Very deep convolutional networks for large-scale image recognition. In: Bengio, Y., LeCun, Y. (eds.) 3rd International Conference on Learning Representations, ICLR 2015, San Diego, CA, USA, 7–9 May 2015, Conference Track Proceedings (2015)

11. He, K., Zhang, X., Ren, S., Sun, J.: Spatial pyramid pooling in deep convolutional networks for visual recognition. IEEE Trans. Pattern Anal. Mach. Intell. **37**(9), 1904–1916 (2015)

12. Chen, L.C., Papandreou, G., Kokkinos, I., Murphy, K., Yuille, A.L.: DeepLab: semantic image segmentation with deep convolutional nets, atrous convolution, and fully connected CRFs. IEEE Trans. Pattern Anal. Mach. Intell. **40**(4), 834–848 (2017)

13. Chen, L., Papandreou, G., Schroff, F., Adam, H.: Rethinking atrous convolution for semantic image segmentation. CoRR abs/1706.05587 (2017)

14. Zhao, H., Shi, J., Qi, X., Wang, X., Jia, J.: Pyramid scene parsing network. In: Proceedings of the IEEE Conference on Computer Vision and Pattern Recognition, pp. 2881–2890 (2017)

15. Cho, K., et al.: Learning phrase representations using RNN encoder-decoder for statistical machine translation. Comput. Sci. (2014)

16. Sutskever, I., Vinyals, O., Le, Q.V.: Sequence to sequence learning with neural networks. In: Advances in Neural Information Processing Systems, pp. 3104–3112 (2014)

17. Vaswani, A., et al.: Attention is all you need. In: Advances in Neural Information Processing Systems, vol. 30 (2017)

18. Li, X., Zhong, Z., Wu, J., Yang, Y., Lin, Z., Liu, H.: Expectation-maximization attention networks for semantic segmentation. In: Proceedings of the IEEE/CVF International Conference on Computer Vision, pp. 9167–9176 (2019)

19. Chen, J., et al.: TransUNet: transformers make strong encoders for medical image segmentation. CoRR abs/2102.04306 (2021)

20. Zhang, J., et al.: Fully automated echocardiogram interpretation in clinical practice: feasibility and diagnostic accuracy. Circulation **138**(16), 1623–1635 (2018)

21. Liu, F., Wang, K., Liu, D., Yang, X., Tian, J.: Deep pyramid local attention neural network for cardiac structure segmentation in two-dimensional echocardiography. Med. Image Anal. **67**, 101873 (2021)

22. He, K., Zhang, X., Ren, S., Sun, J.: Delving deep into rectifiers: surpassing human-level performance on ImageNet classification. In: Proceedings of the IEEE International Conference on Computer Vision, pp. 1026–1034 (2015)

23. Paszke, A., Chaurasia, A., Kim, S., Culurciello, E.: ENet: a deep neural network architecture for real-time semantic segmentation. CoRR abs/1606.02147 (2016)

24. Qi, H., et al.: Deformable convolutional networks-COCO detection and segmentation challenge 2017 entry. In: ICCV COCO Challenge Workshop, vol. 15, pp. 764–773 (2017)

25. Russakovsky, O., et al.: ImageNet large scale visual recognition challenge. Int. J. Comput. Vis. **115**(3), 211–252 (2015). https://doi.org/10.1007/s11263-015-0816-y

26. Hu, P., Caba, F., Wang, O., Lin, Z., Sclaroff, S., Perazzi, F.: Temporally distributed networks for fast video semantic segmentation. In: 2020 IEEE/CVF Conference on Computer Vision and Pattern Recognition, CVPR 2020, Seattle, WA, USA, 13–19 June 2020, pp. 8815–8824. Computer Vision Foundation/IEEE (2020)

27. Lou, A., Guan, S., Loew, M.H.: DC-UNet: rethinking the u-Net architecture with dual channel efficient CNN for medical images segmentation. CoRR abs/2006.00414 (2020)

# Dformer: Dual-Path Transformers for Geometric and Appearance Features Reasoning in Diabetic Retinopathy Grading

Xiaoqiang Jin , Hongwei Li , and Ruirui Li$^{(\boxtimes)}$

Beijing University of Chemical Technology, Beijing 100029, China
liruirui@mail.buct.edu.cn

**Abstract.** In fundus screening, the accuracy of automatic grading of Diabetic Retinopathy (DR) is crucial for the early detection and intervention of DR. Existing methods are inaccurate in the judgment of DR grading, especially the grade of mild Non-proliferative DR (NPDR). There are two reasons for this. On the one hand, the microaneurysm, which is the main judgment basis, is very small. Their false detection and missed detection rates are very high. On the other hand, the existing Convolutional Neural Network (CNN) structure lacks the ability of global reasoning and comprehensive analysis. To address these issues, this paper proposes a transformer-based dual-path reasoning network that can infer from geometric and appearance features based on the preliminary clues discovered by the detection network. We also design exchange connections between the two paths to better integrate the learned weights. The proposed method can better identify early mild NPDR, thereby improving the accuracy of the overall DR grading. It was experimentally verified on the public DDR dataset and Messidor dataset, and the accuracy of early mild NPDR grading increased by 18.16%, and the overall DR grading accuracy increased by 1.93%. Ablation experiments and visualization analysis show that the proposed method can focus on lesions in images and effectively infer the correct DR level based on them.

**Keywords:** Diabetic retinopathy · Automatic grading · Transformer · Dual-path reasoning · Exchange connections · Microaneurysm detection · Geometric and appearance features

## 1 Introduction

Diabetic retinopathy is a complication of diabetes that can cause vision loss and blindness. Manual screening for diabetic retinopathy relies on a large number of experienced ophthalmologists, which is often time-consuming and expensive. Therefore, the development of automated grading algorithms for retinopathy screening is extremely important for early diagnosis and intervention. According to the diagnosis criteria of the American

**Supplementary Information** The online version contains supplementary material available at https://doi.org/10.1007/978-3-031-18910-4_33.

Academy of Ophthalmology (AAO) [1], the severity of DR can be divided into five grades: No DR, Mild NPDR, Moderate NPDR, Severe NPDR, and Proliferative DR. The specific diagnostic criteria are shown in Table 1. As can be seen, the severity of DR generally depends on the symptoms associated with lesions, such as microaneurysms, hemorrhages, cotton wool spots, and hard exudates. How to accurately extract information about these symptoms in fundus images and effectively represent and reason about them is the key and challenge for accurate DR grading.

**Table 1.** Severity levels of DR.

| DR level | Visual observations using fundoscopy | Severity level |
|---|---|---|
| 0 | No observable abnormalities | No DR |
| 1 | Observable microaneurysms | Mild NPDR |
| 2 | Observable microaneurysms OR retinal dots and hemorrhages OR hard exudates OR cotton wool spots | Moderate NPDR |
| 3 | Observable beading in 2 or more quadrants OR intra-retinal microvascular abnormality (IRMA) in 5 or more quadrants OR intra-retinal hemorrhages (more than 20) in each of the 4 quadrants | Severe NPDR |
| 4 | Observable Neo-vascularization OR pre-retinal hemorrhages | Proliferative DR |

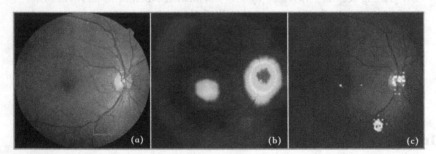

**Fig. 1.** Heatmap of regions of interest for the network. (a) a fundus image of Mild NPDR; (b) regions learnt by ResNet50 classification network; (c) regions gotten by DPformer.

Deep learning has achieved overwhelming success in the field of computer vision. Unlike traditional machine learning methods, convolutional neural networks (CNNs) can automatically extract features from images. Researchers such as Sankar et al. [2], Alban et al. [3], and Pratt et al. [4] have attempted to optimize automatic DR classification using specially designed CNNs and have achieved remarkable progress. However, due to the large variances in lesions, it is difficult for the network to pay attention to lesions such as microaneurysms (Fig. 1b), resulting in inaccurate DR grading. Li et al. [5] adopted an attention mechanism to optimize the extraction and representation of small lesion features. The visualization of attention opened the black box of neural networks. It has been discovered that CNNs do not always judge DR grades based on the correct lesions, raising concerns about the credibility of their output. Several studies thus tried to integrate lesion information to improve the accuracy and reliability of DR grading. For example, Zhou et al. [6] simultaneously optimize the two tasks of lesion segmentation and DR classification. CLPI [7] trains lesion detection and DR grading tasks in a multi-task fashion and fuses the features of the lesion region by re-weighting.

It was observed that a large factor contributing to inaccurate DR grading was inaccurate judgment of mild NPDR grading (Fig. 2a). This is because the microaneurysms, which are the main basis for judging mild NPDR, are small in size (Fig. 2b) and are not easily found. Mainstream detection networks, such as Faster RCNN [8] and CenterNet [9], have high false and missed detection rates for microaneurysms, which can easily lead to errors in subsequent calculations. In addition, the latest CNN-based DR grading method [7] also lacks correlation analysis among features when determining the DR grading.

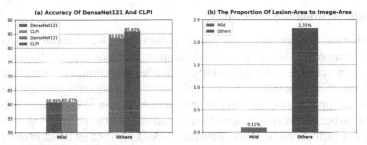

**Fig. 2.** A comparison between Mild NPDR and the others. (a) accuracy; (b) lesion size. It is found that the classification accuracy of Mild NPDR is much lower, and lesions for Mild NPDR are much smaller.

Unlike CNNs that extend the receptive field by sharing parameters, a transformer is good at learning correlation among features [10, 11]. Recently, transformer has been used to optimize DR grading [12]. However, their approach uses a transformer to learn the characteristics of the whole image indiscriminately. This approach cannot guarantee that the features of microaneurysm are effectively and reasonably used for subsequent diagnosis. Therefore, it is necessary to design better tokens and better transformer-based structures to optimize the perception of microaneurysms and reasoning based on them.

Inspired by the work in image caption [13], we design a novel DR grading framework. It contains two stages. Firstly, it detects potential microaneurysms and looks for patches around the detected positions. In the second stage, it treats the geometric and appearance features as tokens and designs a dual-path transformer network for better reasoning. We named it DPformer, in which one path is for geometric features and the other is for appearance features. We also design two exchange connections between the transformers to better aggregate the features. To evaluate the proposed method, we conduct experiments on two public datasets, DDR [14] and Messidor-1 [15]. The results show that the proposed method can better distinguish between mild and normal fundus images. Compared with CLPI [7], the grade accuracy of mild NPDR increased by 18.16%, and the overall DR grade accuracy increased by 1.93%. For clarity, our contributions can be summarized as follows:

(1) We propose a new DR grading framework, which consists of a detection network and a reasoning network. The framework takes the detected lesion cues as the content of reasoning. To the best of our knowledge, this is the first study to perform DR grading by establishing relationships among lesions in fundus images;
(2) A dual-path reasoning network based on the transformer is proposed, which can obtain reliable DR classification results by jointly inferring on the geometric and appearance features.
(3) We design exchange connections between the two transformers to better aggregate features and improve the accuracy of DR classification. We conduct extensive experiments and analyses on two publicly available datasets.

## 2 Related Work

### 2.1 Diabetic Retinopathy Assessment

Deep learning has become more and more popular in the task of automatic assessment of diabetic retinopathy. Existing DR classification methods can be divided into two categories: direct classification and classification after detection. The first category only requires image-level annotations, but it is difficult to learn effective lesion features. This is because the lesions are highly variable and the distribution of lesion data is extremely unbalanced. To better perceive the lesion features at different scales, M. Antony et al. [16] used images of various resolutions to train the CNNs. On the other hand, in order to solve the problem of insufficient DR samples, Lin et al. [17] proposed a data augmentation method, which uses the gradient class activation map [18] to find potential lesion areas and use them to synthesize more DR samples. Li et al. [5] added an attention mechanism to make the network pay more attention to the lesion area, but their work failed to focus on small lesions. More recently, Li et al. [6] adopted a self-supervised framework with a large amount of unlabeled data to better learn fundus image features, but this unsupervised method is currently far less accurate than supervised methods.

The second approach draws on the diagnosis criteria in the AAO [1] guideline. They first extract the lesions and then perform the classification based on them. For example, Antal and Hajdu et al. [19] grade DR according to the distribution of microaneurysms. Through multi-tasking, Lin et al. [20], Yang et al. [21], and CLPI [7] explicitly direct the network focus on the lesions by increasing the weights of the correspondent features. Unfortunately, due to the structural limitations of CNNs, it is difficult for such methods to reason on lesions as mentioned in the guideline. It urgently needs to introduce a new reasoning module. Graph Neural Networks (GNNs) can perform non-local reasoning, but their usage is a bit complicated. As a more general structure, the transformer naturally has the ability of feature relationship modeling and reasoning. Recently, LAT [12] tried to use the transformer to learn the correlation among pixels, so as to better improve the perceptual ability to the lesion area. However, this method does not apply the transformer to the lesion-aware reasoning. The DPformer proposed in this paper, to the best of our knowledge, is the first work that applies transformers to lesion-aware reasoning.

## 2.2 Transformer in Medical Images

The transformer has been widely applied in speech recognition, machine translation, and image processing since it was proposed by Vaswani et al. [22]. More recently, transformer structures have been used in medical image processing. Song et al. [23] optimized the relationship between Optical Coherence Tomography (OCT) features and Visual Field (VF) features for glaucoma diagnosis using a transformer. Sun et al. [12] employed a transformer to establish pixel correlation and grade DR by learning the relationship between lesion features and image features via cross-attention. The above methods use transformer structures to better learn image features. In addition, transformer structures are also used to establish the relationship between different objectives, such as the application of medical report generation [24] and image caption [13].

# 3   Dual-Path Transformers for Accurate DR Grading

## DR Grading Framework

The overall framework consists of two networks: a detection network and a reasoning network. The detection network adopts the FCOS [25] detector since it can better detect potential lesions. We compared various detection networks and found that it has the highest recall for lesion detection.

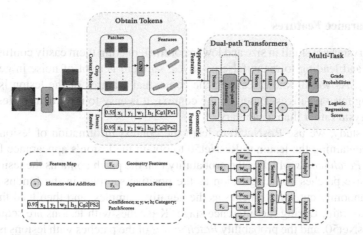

**Fig. 3.** Pipeline for the proposed method. The detector is used to obtain the lesions' geometric features, the CNN is used to obtain the lesions' appearance features, and a dual-path transformer is used to establish the association between lesions and integrate the lesions' features.

In order to better establish the correlation and reasoning between lesions in fundus images, we propose a dual-path transformer network named DPformer. One of the paths is for geometric features, and the other path is for appearance features. We carefully design novel tokens that are input to the transformer. Specifically, the geometric feature encodes the location and size information of the lesion, and the appearance feature is the ResNet50 feature of the patch near the lesion location. DPformer is a multi-task network that performs classification and regression tasks on features and locations, respectively, and finally obtains accurate classification results.

## 3.1 Geometric Features

The fundus image is fed into the detection network to get the confidence and coordinates of potential lesions. The detection results are sorted in order of confidence from high to low, and the fundus image lesion description set $G = \{g_1, g_2, \ldots, g_k\}$ is obtained, where $g_i$ is expressed as a one-dimensional row vector, i.e., (1).

$$g_i = \left[ Confidence, x_1, y_1, w/W, h/H, Category, PatchScores \right] \quad (1)$$

in which *Confidence* represents the lesions' confidence; $(x1, y1)$ represents the coordinates of the lesion's upper left corner; $w, h$ represents the lesion's width and height; $W, H$ represent the width and height of the fundus image; *Category* represents the lesion's category; and *PatchScores* represents the probability that the lesion patch contains a lesion. It is worth noting that the use of *PatchScores* can reduce the noise caused by false positives. Each $g_i$ is regarded as a word and embedded in a higher dimension for representation. The geometric features are given as $F_G$ after vector embedding, each element is a row vector with a length of K. To learn the relative position relationship of the elements in $F_G$, a learnable position embedding is added.

## 3.2 Appearance Features

Microaneurysms are small in size and low in contrast, making them easily confused with capillaries and leading to many false positives, so there is a lot of noise in geometric features $F_G$. As we all know, learning the contextual features of the lesion is crucial for reducing false positives. Based on the context, it is easy to infer that the lesion is a microaneurysm rather than a capillary.

In this study, we use ResNet50 to learn the context information of lesions. Input the patch containing the lesion to ResNet50 to obtain the lesion's appearance features, and output *PatchScores* which is the probability that the patch contains the lesion. Crop the k * k size patches containing lesion as the positive samples in the fundus images, and then randomly cut some patches as the negative samples, and then feed them into ResNet50 to train. During the inference stage, K patches with lesions are sequentially fed into ResNet50, and the probability *PatchScores* of the patches with lesions is output. Simultaneously, the features after the global average pooling layer are kept as the features set $A = \{A_1, A_2, \ldots, A_k\}$, the dimension of $A_i$ is $1 * 1 * 2048$. As mentioned above, each $A_i$ is regarded as a word and, embedded in a higher dimension for representation, a learnable position embedding is added. The appearance features are given as $F_A$ after vector embedding, each element is a row vector.

### 3.3  Dual-Path Transformers

The basic transformer encoder consists of multi-head self-attention blocks and MLP blocks alternately, applying LayerNorm before each block and residual connections after each block. The input of the self-attention module includes queries, keys and values, which are expressed as matrices $Q$, $K$, and $V$, respectively. The feature dimension after projection is $d_k$. The output can be expressed as i.e., (2).

$$V^{out} = softmax\left(QK^t/\sqrt{d_k}\right)V \tag{2}$$

As shown in Fig. 3, this study proposes dual-path transformer structures as encoders, which use the geometric features $F_G$ and appearance features $F_A$ of lesions to establish the global correlation between lesions, then weight their attention scores to reasoning the DR grading results.

The dual-path transformer branch input $F_A$ and $F_G$, both of length K, and each element is a row vector. Obtain $Q_A$, $K_A$, $V_A$, $Q_G$, $K_G$, $V_G$ as shown in (3), (4).

$$Q_A = W_{AQ}F_A, \quad K_A = W_{AK}F_A, \quad V_A = W_{AV}F_A \tag{3}$$

$$Q_G = W_{GQ}F_G, \quad K_G = W_{GK}F_G, \quad V_G = W_{GV}F_G \tag{4}$$

Then, the weight of the corresponding position can be obtained through the dot product and Softmax, as shown in (5) and (6), where $d$ is the feature dimension after projection.

$$\omega_A = softmax\left(Q_AK_A^t/\sqrt{d}\right) \tag{5}$$

$$\omega_G = softmax\left(Q_GK_G^t/\sqrt{d}\right) \tag{6}$$

In order to make dual-path features interact with each other, we obtain the new weight $\omega_A'$ and $\omega_G'$ by balancing $w_A$ and $w_G$, as shown in (7) and (8), where $\lambda_A$, $\lambda_G$ are the hyperparameter.

$$\omega_A' = \lambda_A w_A + (1 - \lambda_A)w_G \tag{7}$$

$$\omega_G' = (1 - \lambda_G)w_A + \lambda_G w_G \tag{8}$$

Then we output the weighted value $V_A^{out}$ and $V_G^{out}$, as shown in (9).

$$V_A^{out} = \omega_A'V_A, \quad V_G^{out} = \omega_G'V_G \tag{9}$$

Input $V_A^{out}$ and $V_G^{out}$ to the classification head and regression head respectively for training, where the classification head and regression head are linear layers.

### 3.4 Loss Function

Since DR grading is an ordered classification problem, we treat the branches of the input geometric features as logistic regression tasks and the branches of the input appearance features as classification tasks, and the multi-task joint way can achieve better performance. Weighted cross entropy loss $L_{cls}$ is used for the classification branch, and smooth L1 loss $L_{reg}$ is used for the regression branch. The total loss is computed as (10), where $\gamma$ is hyperparameter.

$$\mathcal{L} = L_{cls} + \gamma L_{reg} \tag{10}$$

## 4  Experiments

### 4.1  Dataset

**DDR Dataset [14].** The dataset contained 13,673 fundus images from 147 hospitals in 23 provinces of China, which can be used for lesion segmentation, lesion detection, and DR grading. Hard exudate (EX), hemorrhages (HE), microaneurysms (MA), and hard exudate (SE) pixel level annotations were provided for 757 fundus images. Ophthalmologists grade images according to the International Classification of Diabetic Retinopathy to assess the severity of DR. At the same time, images with more than 70% blur and no obvious lesions were considered ungradable. In other words, these images in DDR are divided into six categories: No DR, Mild NPDR, Moderate NPDR, Severe NPDR, Proliferative DR, and Ungradable.

**Messidor-1 Dataset [15].** It includes 1200 fundus images from three French hospitals. However, their grading scale only has four grades, which is slightly different from the five-level international protocol. Therefore, as in the previous method [5, 12], we achieved referral classification and normal classification. For referral classifications, Grade 0 and Grade 1 are marked as non-referrable, while Grade 2 and Grade 3 are considered referrable. For normal classification, only Grade 0 is designated as normal, the other grades are considered abnormal. Following the protocol in the previous method [12], we use 10-fold cross validation for the entire dataset.

### 4.2  Implementation Details

**Data Preparation.** Due to the small size of lesions in fundus images, we cut fundus images into patches of 640 * 640 and send them to the detector. Random horizontal flip, random vertical flip, and random rotation are used to reduce overfitting of detectors. The center of the detection results is taken as the center of the patches, and patches of 128 * 128 are inputted to ResNet50 to extract the contextual features of the lesion. Random horizontal flip, random vertical flip, and contrast enhancement are used to reduce the overfitting of the network. Then input $F_A$ and $F_G$ in dual-path transformer without any data enhancement.

**Parameter Settings.** FCOS is selected to detect lesions. Due to the small size of microaneurysms, P2, P3, P4, and P5 of FPN are selected to predict the location and category of lesions. The pre-training model of ImageNet is loaded into the backbone network. Dual-path transformer branches are configured with different heads and depths as described above, as seen in subsequent ablation experiments.

**Experimental Environment.** The whole framework was built on PyTorch with the Nvidia Tesla V100. During the training, the batch size is set to 512, and the initial learning rate is set to 0.0001. In addition, during the whole training, if loss is kept constant for 5 consecutive epochs, the learning rate is reduced, and the weight attenuation is set to 0.001. We train this network for 300 epochs using the SGD optimizer with a momentum set of 0.9.

### 4.3 Evaluation Metrics

In order to evaluate the performance of the proposed method, the DDR dataset [14] employs metrics including Accuracy and Kappa. The Messidor-1 dataset [15] uses the same metric of AUC as [12]. In addition, in order to verify the advancement of our method more comprehensively, AUC, F1-Score, and other metrics are used for comprehensive comparison between normal fundus images and mild NPDR fundus images.

### 4.4 Results

**Comparisons with State-of-the-Art Methods.** Table 2 compares the classification performances of different methods on the DDR dataset, which include VGG16 [26], ResNet18 [27], GoogLeNet [28], SE-BN-Inception [29] and CLPI [7]. In addition to Accuracy and Kappa, we also compared the accuracy of each category. Among them, the overall accuracy of CLPI [7] is the highest at 82.96%, that has greatly improved the accuracy of Mild, Server, and PDR compared with others. However, the improvement of the performance in Mild is limited. As mentioned above, this is because microaneurysms are smaller than other lesions, so the performance improvement of Mild with only microaneurysms in the image is limited by feature weighting.

In contrast, our proposed method's overall accuracy is 1.93% higher than CLPI [7], and Mild's accuracy is 18.16% higher than CLPI [7]. At the same time, the accuracy of other categories are basically the same as that of CLPI [7]. This is because we can better perceive the microaneurysms in the fundus image by using the detector. At the same time, we can infer the grading results by establishing a global relationship between the lesions in the fundus image from the geometric features and the contextual appearance features of the lesions, which is not sensitive to the size of the lesions.

In addition, we also compare it to other advanced DR grading methods in the Messidor-1 dataset [15]. We used the detector trained by the DDR dataset to find lesions in fundus images and retrain the dual-path transformer because the Messidor-1 dataset [15] does not provide bounding-box-level annotations. As shown in Table 3, in the absence of bounding-box-level annotations and the limited number of images in the Messidor-1 dataset [15], the AUC of our normal classification and referral classification still exceeds the most advanced method LAT [12].

**Table 2.** Performance comparison of different methods on DDR datasets.

| Method | NoDR | Mild | Moderate | Severe | PDR | Ungraded | Kappa | Accuracy |
|---|---|---|---|---|---|---|---|---|
| VGG16 | **0.9689** | 0.0873 | 0.7173 | 0.5532 | 0.7692 | **0.8826** | 0.7280 | 0.8182 |
| ResNet18 | 0.9505 | 0.0714 | 0.7564 | 0.3404 | 0.7747 | 0.8304 | 0.7220 | 0.8141 |
| GoogLeNet | 0.9585 | 0.0714 | 0.7542 | 0.4468 | 0.7473 | 0.8261 | 0.7286 | 0.8185 |
| DenseNet121 | 0.8252 | 0.3016 | 0.6637 | 0.5320 | 0.7527 | **0.8826** | 0.6158 | 0.7431 |
| SE-Inception | 0.9401 | 0.0714 | **0.8190** | 0.3617 | 0.6978 | 0.8696 | 0.7438 | 0.8284 |
| CLPI | 0.9361 | 0.3025 | 0.7239 | **0.7110** | **0.8035** | 0.8441 | 0.7534 | 0.8296 |
| **Ours** | 0.9449 | **0.4841** | 0.7911 | 0.7021 | 0.7802 | 0.8348 | **0.7766** | **0.8489** |

**Table 3.** Performance comparison with the state-of-the-art methods on the Messidor-1 dataset.

| Method | Referral AUC | Normal AUC |
|---|---|---|
| VNXK [30] | 0.887 | 0.870 |
| CKML [30] | 0.891 | 0.862 |
| Comp.CAD [31] | 0.910 | 0.876 |
| Expert A [31] | 0.940 | 0.922 |
| Expert B [31] | 0.920 | 0.865 |
| Zoom-in-Net [32] | 0.957 | 0.921 |
| AFN [20] | 0.968 | – |
| Semi+Adv [6] | 0.976 | 0.943 |
| CANet [5] | 0.963 | – |
| CLPI [7] | 0.985 | 0.959 |
| LAT [12] | 0.987 | 0.963 |
| **Ours** | **0.989** | **0.969** |

**Grading Results of Normal Fundus Images and Mild NPDR Fundus Images.**
Because mild NPDR fundus images are often confused with normal fundus images, in order to further illustrate our recognition ability of mild NPDR fundus images, we separately compared the classification performance of different methods for normal fundus images and mild NPDR fundus images. ResNet [27], ViT [10] and Swin-Transformer [11] all load the ImageNet pre-training model for training. As shown in Fig. 4, the receiving operating characteristic (ROC) curve and the precision and recall (PR) curve show that the performance of our method is superior to that of other methods. Meanwhile, in order to conduct a more comprehensive comparison between different methods, we made a quantitative comparison of area-under-the-curve (AUC), Accuracy, and F1-Score, as shown in Table 4.

ResNet50 struggles to recognize mild NPDR fundus images when the input image size is 224 * 224. When the input image size is 512 * 512, the performance of ResNet50 is significantly improved. For Swin-T [11] and ViT [10], we believe that the amount of data may limit its performance. In contrast, our method can achieve better performance only by using geometric features or appearance features. The joint training of the two types of features has achieved the best results, with an AUC of 0.9495 far exceeding the 0.697 obtained by ResNet50, and the F1-Score increased from 0.24 obtained by ResNet50 to 0.7843, indicating that this method can distinguish mild NPDR fundus images from normal fundus images well.

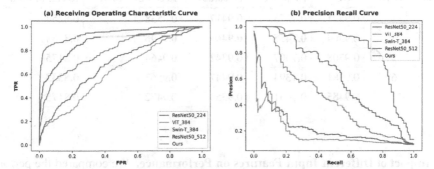

**Fig. 4.** Performance of different methods in normal fundus images and mild NPDR fundus images. (a) receiving operating characteristic (ROC) curve, (b) precision and recall (PR) curve.

**Table 4.** Performance comparison of different methods in mild NPDR fundus images and normal fundus images.

| Method | Input size | AUC | Accuracy | F1-Score | Recall of NoDR | Recall of mild |
|--------|-----------|-----|----------|----------|----------------|----------------|
| ResNet50 | 224 | 0.6971 | 0.8923 | 0.2404 | **0.9733** | 0.1842 |
| ResNet50 | 512 | 0.8702 | 0.9241 | 0.5654 | 0.9611 | 0.5423 |
| ViT | 384 | 0.6286 | 0.7817 | 0.1887 | 0.8324 | 0.2778 |
| Swin-T | 384 | 0.8067 | 0.9028 | 0.4463 | 0.9505 | 0.4286 |
| Ours($F_G$) | – | 0.9076 | 0.7407 | 0.3902 | 0.7261 | **0.8810** |
| Ours($F_A$) | – | 0.9216 | 0.8969 | 0.6080 | 0.9018 | 0.8492 |
| Ours($F_A$&$F_G$) | – | **0.9421** | **0.9417** | **0.7273** | 0.9538 | 0.8254 |

### 4.5 Ablation Experiments

In order to highlight the classification performance of mild NPDR fundus images, ablation experiments are carried out on the classification of mild fundus images and normal fundus images.

**The Effect of the Number of Head and Depth on the Performance.** We compared the impact of the depth of the transformer block and the number of self-attention heads on results in a dual-path transformer, as shown in Table 5. Experimental results show that using only a single transformer block and a single attention head outperforms other methods, and further deepening the network or increasing the attention header has little effect on the classification results.

**Table 5.** The effect of dual-path transformer head and depth on performance.

| Depth | Head | AUC | F1-Score | Accuracy | Recall of NoDR | Recall of mild |
|-------|------|--------|----------|----------|----------------|----------------|
| 1 | 1 | 0.9421 | 0.7273 | 0.9417 | 0.9538 | 0.8254 |
| 1 | 3 | 0.9364 | **0.7455** | **0.9469** | **0.9596** | 0.8254 |
| 3 | 3 | 0.9308 | 0.7007 | 0.9342 | 0.9464 | 0.8175 |
| 3 | 6 | 0.9381 | 0.7394 | 0.9447 | 0.9563 | **0.8333** |
| 12 | 12 | **0.9485** | 0.7031 | 0.9350 | 0.9472 | 0.8175 |

**The Impact of Different Input Features on Performance.** We compared the performance of inputting appearance features $F_A$ or geometric features $F_G$ separately with that of inputting both types of features simultaneously, as shown in Table 4. We find that classification performance far exceeded the ResNet50 classification results when the input $F_A$ or $F_G$, and the best results are obtained by inputting the two features simultaneously and interacting with each other.

**The Effects of Weighted Attention Hyperparameters on Performance.** We also compared the effects of different weights of attention on the results. As shown in (5) and (6), $\lambda_A$ represents the proportion of attention score when input $F_A$, and $\lambda_G$ represents the proportion of attention score when input $F_G$. As shown in Table 6, the best classification result is obtained when $\lambda_A = 0.5$ and $\lambda_G = 0.5$.

**Table 6.** Effects of different weights of attention scores on results.

| $\lambda_A$ | $\lambda_G$ | AUC | F1-Score | Recall of NoDR | Recall of mild |
|-------------|-------------|--------|----------|----------------|----------------|
| 0.3 | 0.3 | 0.9394 | 0.7128 | 0.9505 | 0.8175 |
| 0.5 | 0.5 | **0.9433** | **0.7331** | **0.9571** | 0.8175 |
| 0.3 | 0.7 | 0.9421 | 0.7273 | 0.9538 | 0.8254 |
| 0.7 | 0.3 | 0.9330 | 0.7148 | 0.9497 | 0.8254 |
| 0.7 | 0.7 | 0.9332 | 0.7123 | 0.9488 | 0.8254 |
| 1.0 | 1.0 | 0.9216 | 0.6080 | 0.9018 | **0.8492** |

**The Effect of the Number of Input Lesions on the Results.** As mentioned above, we sort detection results according to the confidence and input the appearance features $F_A$ and geometric features $F_G$ of the top K lesions for classification. We compare the influence of K on the results, as shown in Table 7. The experiment proves that K is insensitive to the classification results.

Table 7. The effects of lesion number K on the results.

| K | AUC | F1-Score | Recall of NoDR | Recall of mild |
|---|---|---|---|---|
| 16 | 0.9214 | 0.4417 | **0.9992** | 0.2857 |
| 25 | 0.9318 | 0.7059 | 0.9497 | 0.8095 |
| 49 | **0.9421** | **0.7273** | 0.9538 | **0.8254** |
| 100 | 0.9373 | 0.6823 | 0.9414 | 0.8095 |

**The Effect of Different Detectors on Classification Performance.** As shown in Table 8, we compare the performance of using different detection networks to classify normal fundus images and mild NPDR fundus images. Experimental results show that our method does not depend on specific detectors. This could be because we use geometric and appearance features to infer the relationship between all lesions from a global perspective, which reduces the need for detection precision.

Table 8. The effect of different detectors on classification performance.

| Method | mAP(IoU = 0.25) | AR50 | AUC | F1-Score |
|---|---|---|---|---|
| Faster RCNN | 0.3140 | 0.6953 | 0.9375 | 0.7175 |
| CenterNet | 0.3160 | 0.7074 | 0.9403 | 0.7190 |
| FCOS | 0.2960 | 0.7711 | **0.9421** | **0.7273** |

### 4.6 Qualitative Results

We visualize the classification results of both ResNet50 and our method, as shown in Fig. 5. As mentioned above, the only difference between a mild NPDR fundus image and a normal fundus image is whether there are microaneurysms in the image. For example, Fig. 5 (a) shows a mild fundus image with microaneurysms in the positions of the green circles. The classical classification network is used for DR grading, due to the continuous pooling operation, the network cannot pay attention to the microaneurysms, resulting in classification errors, as shown in Fig. 5 (b). Besides, because size of microaneurysms is small and the contrast of microaneurysms is low, there are a large number of false

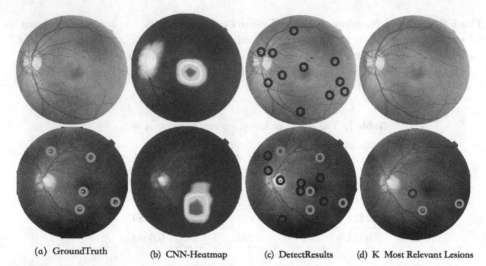

(a) GroundTruth        (b) CNN-Heatmap        (c) DetectResults        (d) K Most Relevant Lesions

**Fig. 5.** Visual classification basis. (a) mild NPDR fundus image with microaneurysms, green circles indicating the location of microaneurysms (b) Basis for Resnet50 (c) Lesion detection results (d) Basis of our method, green circles indicating true lesion, blue circles indicating false positive. In first line, K = 1, in second line, K = 3.

detections, which can be seen from the comparison between Fig. 5 (a) and Fig. 5 (c). Inputting the detection results with a large number of false detections to the dual-path transformer, we can still achieve good classification performance by making global reasoning on the possible lesions in the fundus image. We can ignore a large number of false detections in the fundus image and pay attention to the true lesion area. As shown in Fig. 5 (d), it is the position of the green circle where the lesions are located that affects the classification results.

## 5   Conclusion and Discussion

This paper proposes a transformer-based dual-path reasoning network that can infer from geometric and appearance features based on the preliminary clues discovered by the detection network. We also design exchange connections between the two paths to better integrate the learned weights. The proposed method can better identify early mild NPDR fudus images, thereby improving the accuracy of the overall DR grading. Although we propose a dual-path reasoning network to improve DR grading performance while focusing on true lesions, our method requires box-level lesion annotations to train the detector to discover lesion cues, which severely limits the method's applicability, which is the problem we'll address next.

## References

1. Wilkinson, C., et al.: Proposed international clinical diabetic retinopathy and diabetic macular edema disease severity scales. Ophthalmology **110**(9), 1677–1682 (2003)

2. Sankar, M., Batri, K., Parvathi, R.: Earliest diabetic retinopathy classification using deep convolution neural networks.pdf. Int. J. Adv. Eng. Technol **10**, M9 (2016)
3. Alban, M., Gilligan, T.: Automated detection of diabetic retinopathy using fluorescein angiography photographs. Report of Standford Education (2016)
4. Pratt, H., et al.: Convolutional neural networks for diabetic retinopathy. Procedia Comput. Sci. **90**, 200–205 (2016)
5. Li, X., et al.: CANet: cross-disease attention network for joint diabetic retinopathy and diabetic macular edema grading. IEEE Trans. Med. Imaging **39**(5), 1483–1493 (2019)
6. Zhou, Y., et al.: Collaborative learning of semi-supervised segmentation and classification for medical images. In: Proceedings of the IEEE/CVF Conference on Computer Vision and Pattern Recognition (2019)
7. Yang, Y., et al.: Robust collaborative learning of patch-level and image-level annotations for diabetic retinopathy grading from fundus image. IEEE Trans. Cybern. (2021)
8. Ren, S., et al.: Faster R-CNN: towards real-time object detection with region proposal networks. In: Advances in Neural Information Processing Systems 28 (2015)
9. Zhou, X., Wang, D., Krähenbühl, P.: Objects as points. arXiv preprint arXiv:1904.07850 (2019)
10. Dosovitskiy, A., et al.: An image is worth $16 \times 16$ words: transformers for image recognition at scale. arXiv preprint arXiv:2010.11929 (2020)
11. Liu, Z., et al.: Swin transformer: Hierarchical vision transformer using shifted windows. In: Proceedings of the IEEE/CVF International Conference on Computer Vision (2021)
12. Sun, R., et al.: Lesion-aware transformers for diabetic retinopathy grading. In: Proceedings of the IEEE/CVF Conference on Computer Vision and Pattern Recognition (2021)
13. Luo, Y., et al.: Dual-level collaborative transformer for image captioning. arXiv preprint arXiv:2101.06462 (2021)
14. Li, T., et al.: Diagnostic assessment of deep learning algorithms for diabetic retinopathy screening. Inf. Sci. **501**, 511–522 (2019)
15. Decencière, E., et al.: Feedback on a publicly distributed image database: the Messidor database. Image Anal. Stereol. **33**(3), 231–234 (2014)
16. Antony, M., Brggemann, S.: Kaggle diabetic retinopathy detection: team o_O solution. Technical report (2015)
17. Lin, C., et al.: ELLG: explainable lesion learning and generation for diabetic retinopathy detection. In: International Joint Conferences on Artificial Intelligence Workshop on Disease Computational Modeling. International Joint Conferences on Artificial Intelligence Organization (2020)
18. Chattopadhay, A., et al.: Grad-CAM++: generalized gradient-based visual explanations for deep convolutional networks. In: 2018 IEEE Winter Conference on Applications of Computer Vision (WACV). IEEE (2018)
19. Antal, B., Hajdu, A.: An ensemble-based system for microaneurysm detection and diabetic retinopathy grading. IEEE Trans. Biomed. Eng. **59**(6), 1720–1726 (2012)
20. Lin, Z. et al.: A framework for identifying diabetic retinopathy based on anti-noise detection and attention-based fusion. In: Frangi, A., Schnabel, J., Davatzikos, C., Alberola-López, C., Fichtinger, G. (eds.) MICCAI 2018. LNCS, vol. 11071, pp. 74–82. Springer, Cham (2018). https://doi.org/10.1007/978-3-030-00934-2_9
21. Yang, Y., Li, T., Li, W., Wu, H., Fan, W., Zhang, W.: Lesion detection and grading of diabetic retinopathy via two-stages deep convolutional neural networks. In: Descoteaux, M., Maier-Hein, L., Franz, A., Jannin, P., Collins, D., Duchesne, S. (eds.) MICCAI 2017. LNCS, vol. 10435, pp. 533–540. Springer, Cham (2017). https://doi.org/10.1007/978-3-319-66179-7_61
22. Vaswani, A., et al.: Attention is all you need. In: Advances in Neural Information Processing Systems 30 (2017)

23. Song, D., et al.: Deep relation transformer for diagnosing glaucoma with optical coherence tomography and visual field function. IEEE Trans. Med. Imaging **40**(9), 2392–2402 (2021)
24. Wu, L., et al.: Generative caption for diabetic retinopathy images. In: 2017 International Conference on Security, Pattern Analysis, and Cybernetics (SPAC). IEEE (2017)
25. Tian, Z., et al.: FCOS: fully convolutional one-stage object detection. In: Proceedings of the IEEE/CVF International Conference on Computer Vision (2019)
26. Simonyan, K., Zisserman, A.: Very deep convolutional networks for large-scale image recognition. arXiv preprint arXiv:1409.1556 (2014)
27. He, K., et al.: Deep residual learning for image recognition. In: Proceedings of the IEEE Conference on Computer Vision and Pattern Recognition (2016)
28. Szegedy, C., et al.: Going deeper with convolutions. In: Proceedings of the IEEE Conference on Computer Vision and Pattern Recognition (2015)
29. Hu, J., Shen, L., Sun, G.: Squeeze-and-excitation networks. In: Proceedings of the IEEE Conference on Computer Vision and Pattern Recognition (2018)
30. Vo, H.H., Verma, A.: New deep neural nets for fine-grained diabetic retinopathy recognition on hybrid color space. In: 2016 IEEE International Symposium on Multimedia (ISM). IEEE (2016)
31. Sánchez, C.I., et al.: Evaluation of a computer-aided diagnosis system for diabetic retinopathy screening on public data. Invest. Ophthalmol. Vis. Sci. **52**(7), 4866–4871 (2011)
32. Wang, Z., Yin, Y., Shi, J., Fang, W., Li, H., Wang, X.: Zoom-in-net: deep mining lesions for diabetic retinopathy detection. In: Descoteaux, M., Maier-Hein, L., Franz, A., Jannin, P., Collins, D., Duchesne, S. (eds.) MICCAI 2017. LNCS, vol. 10435, pp. 267–275. Springer, Cham (2017). https://doi.org/10.1007/978-3-319-66179-7_31

# Deep Supervoxel Mapping Learning for Dense Correspondence of Cone-Beam Computed Tomography

Kaichen Nie[1], Yuru Pei[1(✉)], Diya Sun[2], and Tianmin Xu[3]

[1] Key Laboratory of Machine Perception (MOE), Department of Machine Intelligence, School of Artificial Intelligence, Peking University, Beijing, China
peiyuru@cis.pku.edu.cn
[2] Peking University People's Hospital, Institute for Artificial Intelligence, Peking University, Beijing, China
[3] School of Stomatology, Peking University, Beijing, China

**Abstract.** Deep registration models have shown prominent online inference efficiency and competitive accuracies compared with traditional iterative optimization-based techniques. Most existing techniques rely on cascaded convolutional layers to parameterize the nonlinear mapping from volumetric images to dense displacement or velocity fields, introducing memory burden in model training, especially for high-resolution volumetric images. Moreover, the metric space alignment tends to fall into local minima when confronted with pose and shape perturbations, claiming prior affine transformation or sparse correspondence annotation. We propose an unsupervised deep supervoxel-wise correspondence network (SVNet) for dense correspondence of cone-beam computed tomography. In particular, we formulate the dense volumetric registration as solving the sparse supervoxel-wise permutation matrix. We design an unsupervised learning scheme for supervoxel descriptor learning and seek the optimal matching, relax the prior transformation or correspondence annotation. The proposed SVNet is optimized in an unsupervised manner by regularized appearance and geometric alignments regarding a supervoxel permutation matrix, aside from the metric space alignment of the volumetric images. Extensive experimental results showcase the effectiveness of the proposed approach in the supervoxel mapping with performance gains over compared deep registration models, avoiding memory-expensive training and computations.

**Keywords:** Supervoxel mapping · Correspondence · Cone-beam computed tomography

## 1  Introduction

Cone-beam computed tomography images (CBCT) have been widely applied in clinical orthodontics to provide quantitative assessments of patient-specific

S. Yu et al. (Eds.): PRCV 2022, LNCS 13535, pp. 417–427, 2022.
https://doi.org/10.1007/978-3-031-18910-4_34

craniofacial anatomies for clinical diagnosis and research on structural developments, which heavily rely upon the dense volumetric correspondence. With the advent of data-driven and deep learning-based techniques, the computationally expensive online optimization in the traditional registration is relaxed. The 3D U-Net-like encoder-decoder framework has shown prominent performances in estimating dense voxel-wise displacement and velocity fields [2,3]. The concatenated convolutional layers are feasible to parameterize the mapping from the volumetric image pair to the dense registration fields, significantly reducing the computational costs. However, representing the deformable registration as the voxel-wise displacement fields has two major disadvantages.

First, the memory burden to learn the displacement field decoder regarding the high-resolution volumetric image can not be neglected. Thus, many deep learning-based registration methods have resorted to down-sampling or decomposition of volumetric images into patches [17,22] for training. Though, these operations come with the price of losing fine-grained anatomical details or the spatial dependency of long-range contexts. The down-sampled 3D sift-based voxel subset has been used to estimate the rigid transformation of CBCTs via the manifold alignment [14], though the rigid model is limited to handle the structure deformations. Second, the metric space alignment-based volumetric image registration necessitates the prior affine or rigid registration, as well as the landmark and mask annotation, to handle the high-frequency pose and shape perturbations [5,6,16]. However, the prior annotation is tedious and prone to labeling errors. Supervoxel decomposition provides a compact volumetric representation by clustering the homogeneous neighboring voxels, greatly reducing the complexity of the high-dimensional volumetric images. The supervoxels have been deployed on scanned data registration [23], the multi-atlas segmentation [18], brain tumor segmentation [9,13], Glioblastoma Multiforme segmentation [7], and correspondence [8,15]. The supervised random forest has been used to build the classifier to find the supervoxel-wise correspondence for atlas-based segmentation [8]. The clustering forest enabled the supervoxel-wise affinity estimation [15]. Whereas, the prior descriptor extraction or post-processing regularization was required for dense correspondence.

We propose an unsupervised deep supervoxel mapping network (SVNet) for dense correspondence of CBCTs. More specifically, the volumetric image is decomposed into supervoxel clouds and the dense registration is explained by the relatively sparse supervoxel permutation matrix. We tackle both challenges mentioned above by 1) representing the volumetric image as supervoxel clouds and estimating the sparse supervoxel correspondence instead of directly computing dense registration fields. 2) We introduce an unsupervised supervoxel descriptor learning module for discriminative supervoxel descriptors to seek matching, relaxing the need for ground truth dense correspondence and sparse landmark annotations. Aside from the metric space alignment of the volumetric image, we design a novel criterion of supervoxel-level regularized appearance and geometric alignment for learning. The SVNet produces sparse supervoxel-wise correspondence and up-sampled dense registration fields of clinically obtained CBCTs, relieving the image down-sampling or decomposition in the patch-based registration. The main contributions are:

- We first introduce the deep supervoxel mapping framework for dense volumetric registration, relieving the memory burden in learning the dense registration fields.
- We optimize the discriminative supervoxel descriptor under an unsupervised learning manner, extending the metric space alignment of the volumetric image with the regularized supervoxel-level appearance and geometric alignment. Our approach relaxes the need for the supervision of correspondence and prior landmark annotation.
- Extensive experimental results showcase the effectiveness of the proposed approach in predicting the dense correspondence of clinically obtained CBCTs.

## 2  Method

Figure 1 shows the pipeline of the proposed SVNet. Given a pair of CBCTs $X, Y \in \mathbb{R}^n$ with $n$ voxels, we aim to find the correspondence between the supervoxels of $X$ and $Y$.

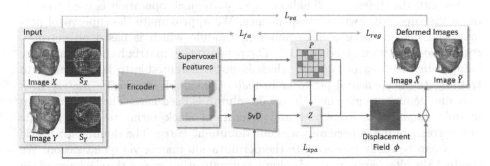

**Fig. 1.** The pipeline of the proposed SVNet. Given a pair of volumetric image $(X, Y)$ and the supervoxel cloud $S_X$ and $S_Y$, we exploit a graph CNN-based supervoxel descriptor refinement encoder and a Sinkhorn algorithm to compute the supervoxel permutation matrix $P$, which can be up-scaled to voxel-wise dense registration field $\phi$ via landmark interpolation. We obtain the displacements $Z$ of supervoxel centroids via supervoxel clouds deformer (SvD). We optimize the SVNet via a regularized supervoxel-wise alignment and voxel-wise alignment in an unsupervised manner.

We seek the permutation matrix $P \in \mathbb{R}^{n_X \times n_Y}$ of the supervoxel clouds $(S_x, S_y)$. $S_x = \{s_i^X | i = 1, \ldots, n_X\}$ and $S_Y = \{s_i^Y | i = 1, \ldots, n_Y\}$ denote the supervoxel cloud obtained by the SLIC [1]-based supervoxel decomposition. The entry $p_{ij}$ indicates the probability of supervoxel $s_i^X$ being assigned to supervoxel $s_j^Y$. The supervoxel cloud provides a compact representation of the volumetric images with $n_X, n_Y \ll n$, and supervoxel boundaries are consistent with the contours of craniofacial structures. We utilize a deep convolution network-based descriptor learning to embed and refine the supervoxel descriptors. The Sinkhorn layer [10] is utilized to compute the supervoxel permutation matrix $P$ from the supervoxel affinity matrix $A \in \mathbb{R}^{n_X \times n_Y}$. We present an unsupervised learning scheme to optimize the SVNet by exploiting the regularized supervoxel appearance and geometric alignments.

## 2.1   Supervoxel Correspondence

**Supervoxel Feature Learning.** The supervoxel clouds of the reference and the target images are fed to the graph CNN [20]-based module which consists of EdgeConv layers [20] and an MLP to account for volumetric contexts for feature refinements. EdgeConv layers can gather neighborhood information for feature embedding. The resultant supervoxel features are used to estimate the permutation matrix regarding the supervoxel cloud. Specifically, we first estimate the supervoxel-wise affinity matrix. Given latent supervoxel descriptor $F_X, F_Y$ obtained by the supervoxel feature refinement module, we compute the affinity matrix $A$, s.t. $A_{ij} = \frac{1}{\|f_i^X - f_j^Y\|_2})$. where $f_i^X$ and $f_j^Y$ denote the $d$-dimensional feature vectors of supervoxel $s_i^X \in S_X$ and supervoxel $s_j^Y \in S_Y$ obtained by feature refinement module.

Second, the differential Sinkhorn layer with slack operation is used to estimate the supervoxel-wise correspondence. We approximate the supervoxel permutation matrix using a Slack-Sinkhorn module which is based on entropy-regularized Sinkhorn algorithm [10]. The permutation matrix has only one entry being 1 in each row or column, which is not differentiable to be optimized in training the deep neural network. Instead, the doubly stochastic matrix with only one dominant entry in each row or column is used here. The Slack-Sinkorn module employs an extra row and column of slack terms to allow for the non-corresponding supervoxels without dominant entry. The doubly stochastic matrix can be easily converted to the permutation matrix via quantization. We conduct the alternating row and column normalization except the slack terms via the softmax operations with five iterations, yielding the doubly stochastic matrix $\hat{P} \in \mathbb{R}^{n_X \times n_Y}$. The permutation matrix $P_{ij} = 1$ when $\hat{P}_{ij} = \max_{1 \leq i' \leq n} \hat{P}_{i'j}$, and 0 otherwise.

**Supervoxel Alignment.** The supervoxel alignment loss $L_{sva}$ is composed of the supervoxel feature alignment loss $L_{fa}$ and the spatial alignment loss $L_{spa}$, and $L_{sva} = L_{fa} + \alpha L_{spa}$. When given the permutation matrix, the permuted supervoxel features of the reference volume are expected to be consistent with the target, and vice versa.

$$L_{fa} = \|P^T F_0^X - F_0^Y\|_F^2 + \|F_0^X - P F_0^Y\|_F^2. \tag{1}$$

$F_0$ denotes the input 653-dimensional supervoxel features, consisting of 3D coordinates of supervoxel centroids, the 200-dimensional HU histogram, and the 450-dimensional contextual features of supervoxels as [25].

Aside from the feature alignment, we address the spatial alignment of transformed supervoxel clouds. Let $Q_X \in \mathbb{R}^{n_X \times 3}$ denote coordinates of the supervoxel centroids of the volume $X$. The transformed supervoxel cloud $P^T Q_X + Z_X$ bears the same topology as that of the volume Y, and are expected to coincide with the supervoxel cloud $Q_Y \in \mathbb{R}^{n_Y \times 3}$. $Z_Y \in \mathbb{R}^{n_X \times 3}$ denote the supervoxel-wise displacement fields. The spatial alignment loss

$$L_{spa} = \|P^T Q_X + Z_X - Q_Y\|_F^2 + \|P Q_Y + Z_Y - Q_X\|_F^2. \tag{2}$$

We utilize the MLP-based supervoxel cloud deformation (SvD) module to infer the supervoxel-wise displacement vectors of the permutated supervoxel clouds $\hat{Q}_X = P^T Q_X$ and $\hat{Q}_Y = P Q_Y$. The SvD performs the bidirectional deformation and takes the concatenation of the global feature vector obtained by the encoder and the permutated supervoxel centroids $\hat{Q}$ as the input and outputs displacement vector $Z_X \in \mathbb{R}^{n_Y \times 3}$ and $Z_Y \in \mathbb{R}^{n_X \times 3}$. The $L_{spa}$ measures the distance between the supervoxel clouds of the same topology with the Frobenius metric instead of the Chamfer distance.

**Regularization.** The regularization is imposed on the supervoxel permutation matrix to enforce the spatial consistent correspondence between supervoxel clouds.

$$L_{reg} = \beta( \sum_{(i,j)\in \mathcal{E}_X} \|d_{i'j'}^Y - d_{ij}^X\|_F^2 + \sum_{(i,j)\in \mathcal{E}_Y} \|d_{i'j'}^X - d_{ij}^Y\|_F^2) + \|PP^T - I\|_F^2. \tag{3}$$

$\mathcal{E}_X$ and $\mathcal{E}_Y$ denote the nearest neighbors set of supervoxels. For each pair of neighboring supervoxels $(s_i^X, s_j^X)$ on volume $X$, the Euclidean distance of the supervoxel centroid $d_{ij}^X = \|q_i^X - q_j^X\|_2$ is expected to be consistent with its counterpart $d_{i'j'}^Y = \|q_{i'}^Y - q_{j'}^Y\|_2$. $q_{i'}^Y$ and $q_{j'}^Y$ denote the centroid of the correspondent supervoxel $s_{i'}^Y$ and $s_{j'}^Y$ on volume $Y$, s.t. $i' = \arg\max_{1 \leq k \leq n_Y} P_{ik}$ and $j' = \arg\max_{1 \leq k \leq n_Y} P_{jk}$. We regularize the permutation matrix $P$ using the edge length consistency for each pair of supervoxels. In the third term of $L_{reg}$, we enforce the orthogonal constraint on the permutation matrix.

## 2.2 Dense Registration Field

Given the displacement vector $Z_X$ of the permutated supervoxel cloud $\hat{Q}_X$, the displacement vector $\tilde{Z}_X$ of the supervoxel cloud $Q_X$ is recovered as $\tilde{Z}_X = P Z_X$. We further recover the dense registration field from the $\tilde{Z}$ by Nadaraya-Watson method [11,21]. We use a Gaussian heat kernel to interpolate the neighboring supervoxel centroids to estimate the value on the regular grid of the displacement field. As to the displacement field $\phi_X$ at position $x$, we consider the neighboring supervoxel centroids in $\mathcal{N}(x)$.

$$\phi(x) = \frac{\sum\limits_{q' \in \mathcal{N}(x)} G(x, q') \tilde{Z}(q')}{\sum\limits_{q' \in \mathcal{N}(x)} G(x, q')}, \tag{4}$$

where $G(u, v) = \exp(-\mu \|u - v\|_2)$ with the heat kernel parameter $\mu$. The operation is differentiable, enabling the loss back-propagation in the optimization. The dense voxel-wise registration loss is defined as follows:

$$L_{va} = \|X - Y \circ \phi_Y\|_F^2 + \|Y - X \circ \phi_X\|_F^2. \tag{5}$$

The final loss function $L$ is composed of supervoxel alignment loss $L_{sva}$, the regularization loss $L_{reg}$ on the supervoxel permutation matrix, and the voxel-wise registration loss $L_{va}$.

$$L = \gamma_1 L_{sva} + \gamma_2 L_{reg} + \gamma_3 L_{va}, \tag{6}$$

where the hyper-parameters $\gamma_1$, $\gamma_2$ and $\gamma_3$ are used to balance the supervoxel-level and the voxel-level alignments, as well as the regularization on the supervoxel permutation matrix.

The proposed SVNet realizes supervoxel-wise correspondence. The SVNet is similar to the B-spline-based registration, in that the registration field is computed by the linear interpolation of sparse supervoxel centroids. The supervoxel decomposition respects the anatomical shapes in locating supervoxels. However, the regular control grids do not consider the shape of anatomies. It is nonsense to compute the correspondence of the regular control grid in the B-spline-based registration.

## 3    Experiments

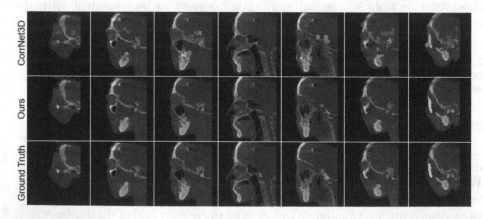

**Fig. 2.** Craniofacial bony structure segmentation obtained by the attribute transfer and dense correspondence of the proposed SVNet and the CorrNet3D [24]. (Red-maxilla, green-mandible, yellow-zygoma, cyan-frontal, magenta-sphenoid, beige-occipital, and brown-temporal) (Color figure online)

**Dataset and Metric.** We train and evaluate the proposed SVNet on a CBCT dataset obtained in clinical orthodontics. The dataset consists of 407 craniofacial CBCTs with a resolution of $128 \times 128 \times 128$, being randomly split into 370, 20, and 17 for training, validation, and testing, respectively. The isotropic voxel size is 1.56 mm $\times$ 1.56 mm $\times$ 1.56 mm. The SLIC algorithm [1] is used for supervoxel decomposition, where approx. 2000 supervoxels of soft and hard tissues are retained. The proposed SVNet is quantitatively evaluated using the Dice similarity coefficient (DSC) in the atlas-based segmentation of bony structures.

**Implemental Details.** The hyper-parameters in the loss function $L$ is set as: $\gamma_1 = 0.2$, $\gamma_2 = 1$ and $\gamma_3 = 200$. The hyper-parameter $\alpha$ in the supervoxel alignment loss $L_{sva}$ is set to 0.5. The hyper-parameter $\beta$ in the regularization loss $L_{reg}$ is set to 10. The parameter $\mu$ in the NW-regression method is set to 25. We implement the proposed SVNet using the PyTorch toolbox with the ADAM-based optimizer. The learning rate is set to 2e−5. We permute the data randomly in each epoch and the mini-batch is composed of the supervoxel clouds of a volume pair. The training of the SVNet takes 10 h with 477 epochs on a machine with a NVIDIA GTX 3090 GPU.

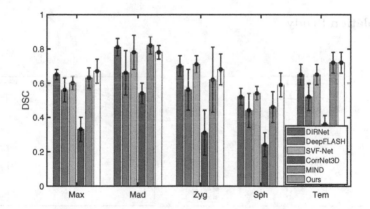

**Fig. 3.** The DSC of five craniofacial structures by the deep registration methods, including the DIRNet [17], the DeepFLASH [19], the SVF-Net [16], the MIND [4], the CorrNet3D [24], and our method.

## 3.1 Quantitative Assessment

The proposed SVNet has been evaluated on the dense correspondence of clinically obtained CBCTs. Figure 2 shows the craniofacial bony structure segmentation obtained by the attribute transfer and dense correspondence of the proposed SVNet and the CorrNet3D [24] compared with the ground truth. The segmentation obtained by the proposed approach is consistent with the ground truth on all reported structures. We compare the proposed approach with state-of-the-art deep registration methods, including the DIRNet [17], the DeepFLASH [19], the SVF-Net [16]. We compare with the functional map [12]-based correspondence using the handcrafted features of the MIND [4]. Figure 3 reports the DSC of five craniofacial structures, including the maxilla, the mandible, the zygoma, the sphenoid, and the temporal, by the deep registration methods. The proposed supervoxel-based SVNet achieves the comparable accuracies with existing registration techniques, with the DSC of 0.67 vs. 0.65 of the DIRNet, 0.56 of the DeepFlash, 0.60 of the SVF-Net and 0.33 of the CorrNet3D on maxilla. In the point cloud alignment method of the CorreNet3D, we use the coordinates of supervoxel centroids as the input. As shown in Fig. 2, the CorreNet3D failed in the supervoxel correspondence in that the 3D coordinates themselves could not account for variations of the hard and soft anatomies in the computation of the supervoxel correspondence. The proposed approach achieves comparable correspondence accuracies with the deep registration methods as shown in Fig. 3. Figure 4(b) shows the DSC of the proposed SVNet with an increasing number $K$ of nearest neighbors. The DSC regarding all structures reach more than 0.8 when $K = 4$. The proposed SVNet learns the discriminative supervoxel descriptor and computes the supervoxel matching, relieving the prior affine or rigid transformation in the deep registration methods.

## 3.2  Ablation Study

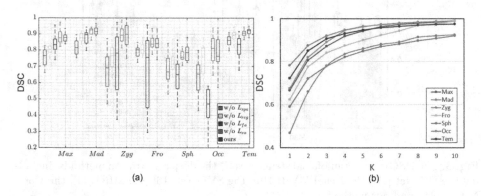

**Fig. 4.** (a) The DSC of the proposed SVNet and its variants without $L_{spa}$, $L_{reg}$, $L_{va}$ and $L_{fa}$ respectively. (b) The DSC of the proposed SVNet with an increasing number of nearest neighbors.

We conduct the ablation study on the spatial alignment loss, feature alignment loss, the registration loss, and the regularization of the supervoxel permutation matrix as shown in Fig. 4(a). We measure the DSC of the proposed SVNet and its variants without $L_{spa}$, $L_{reg}$, $L_{va}$, and $L_{fa}$ on five craniofacial bony structures, where the nearest neighbor number is set to 3. We illustrate the supervoxel correspondence in two viewpoints in Fig. 5, where pseudo colors indicate the corresponding supervoxels.

We observe the performance gap and the mapping ambiguity when removing the spatial alignment loss. For instance, the DSC decreases by 0.1 regarding the symmetric structures of the mandible. The feature alignment is feasible to discriminate supervoxels belonging to different anatomical structures, and contributes to the performance improvement regarding the dense correspondence. For instance, the DSC increases by 0.06 when given $L_{fa}$ regarding the mandible. The regularization facilitates the topology-preserving correspondence, where the counterparts of the neighboring supervoxels of the reference volume tend to be close in the target volume. We observe that the regularization term is feasible to remove mapping errors and enables the smooth correspondence between the reference and the target volumes.

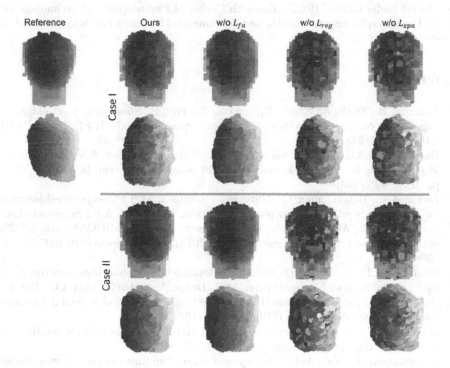

**Fig. 5.** The supervoxel correspondence of two cases obtained by the SVNet and its variants without $L_{spa}$, $L_{reg}$, and $L_{fa}$ respectively. We illustrate the supervoxel correspondence in two viewpoints, where pseudo colors indicate the corresponding supervoxels.

## 4   Conclusion

We have presented the SVNet for supervoxel correspondence and dense registration of volumetric CBCTs. We refrain from the CNN-based inference of dense displacements and velocity fields in existing deep registration models, and provides a lightweight registration models by estimating the sparse supervoxel permutation matrices. We design an unsupervised learning scheme by exploiting the regularized supervoxel-level and voxel-level image alignments, relaxing the need for prior transformation or correspondence annotation. Extensive experimental results demonstrate the efficacy of the SVNet in supervoxel correspondence on clinical CBCTs.

**Acknowledgments.** This work was supported in part by National Natural Science Foundation of China under Grant 61876008 and 82071172, Beijing Natural Science Foundation under Grant 7192227, Research Center of Engineering and Technology for Digital Dentistry, Ministry of Health, and Fundamental Research Funds for the Central Universities.

## References

1. Achanta, R., Shaji, A., Smith, K., Lucchi, A., Fua, P., Süsstrunk, S., et al.: SLIC superpixels compared to state-of-the-art superpixel methods. IEEE Trans. PAMI **34**(11), 2274–2282 (2012)
2. Balakrishnan, G., Zhao, A., Sabuncu, M.R., Guttag, J., Dalca, A.V.: An unsupervised learning model for deformable medical image registration. In: IEEE CVPR, pp. 9252–9260 (2018)
3. Dalca, A.V., Balakrishnan, G., Guttag, J., Sabuncu, M.R.: Unsupervised learning for fast probabilistic diffeomorphic registration. In: Frangi, A.F., Schnabel, J.A., Davatzikos, C., Alberola-López, C., Fichtinger, G. (eds.) MICCAI 2018. LNCS, vol. 11070, pp. 729–738. Springer, Cham (2018). https://doi.org/10.1007/978-3-030-00928-1_82
4. Heinrich, M.P., et al.: MIND: modality independent neighbourhood descriptor for multi-modal deformable registration. Med. Image Anal. **16**(7), 1423–1435 (2012)
5. Hu, Y., et al.: Label-driven weakly-supervised learning for multimodal deformable image registration. In: IEEE ISBI, pp. 1070–1074 (2018)
6. Hu, Y., et al.: Weakly-supervised convolutional neural networks for multimodal image registration. Med. Image Anal. **49**, 1–13 (2018)
7. Kadkhodaei, M., et al.: Automatic segmentation of multimodal brain tumor images based on classification of super-voxels. In: 2016 38th Annual International Conference of the IEEE Engineering in Medicine and Biology Society (EMBC), pp. 5945–5948 (2016)
8. Kanavati, F., et al.: Supervoxel classification forests for estimating pairwise image correspondences. In: Zhou, L., Wang, L., Wang, Q., Shi, Y. (eds.) MLMI 2015. LNCS, vol. 9352, pp. 94–101. Springer, Cham (2015). https://doi.org/10.1007/978-3-319-24888-2_12
9. Zhao, L., Sarikaya, D., Corso, J.J.: Automatic brain tumor segmentation with MRF on supervoxels. In: NCI MICCAI BraTS (2013)

10. Mena, G.E., Belanger, D., Linderman, S.W., Snoek, J.: Learning latent permutations with Gumbel-Sinkhorn networks. ArXiv abs/1802.08665 (2018)
11. Nadaraya, E.A.: On estimating regression. Theory Probab. Appl. **9**(1), 141–142 (1964)
12. Ovsjanikov, M., Ben-Chen, M., Solomon, J., Butscher, A., Guibas, L.: Functional maps: a flexible representation of maps between shapes. ACM Trans. Graph. **31**(4), 30 (2012)
13. Pei, L., Reza, S.M.S., Iftekharuddin, K.: Improved brain tumor growth prediction and segmentation in longitudinal brain MRI. In: 2015 IEEE International Conference on Bioinformatics and Biomedicine (BIBM), pp. 421–424 (2015)
14. Pei, Y., Ma, G., Chen, G., Zhang, X., Xu, T., Zha, H.: Superimposition of cone-beam computed tomography images by joint embedding. IEEE Trans. Biomed. Eng. **64**(6), 1218–1227 (2017)
15. Pei, Y., et al.: Spatially consistent supervoxel correspondences of cone-beam computed tomography images. IEEE Trans. Med. Imaging **37**, 2310–2321 (2018)
16. Rohé, M.-M., Datar, M., Heimann, T., Sermesant, M., Pennec, X.: SVF-Net: learning deformable image registration using shape matching. In: Descoteaux, M., Maier-Hein, L., Franz, A., Jannin, P., Collins, D.L., Duchesne, S. (eds.) MICCAI 2017. LNCS, vol. 10433, pp. 266–274. Springer, Cham (2017). https://doi.org/10.1007/978-3-319-66182-7_31
17. Vos, B.D., Berendsen, F., Viergever, M., Staring, M., Isgum, I.: End-to-end unsupervised deformable image registration with a convolutional neural network. ArXiv abs/1704.06065 (2017)
18. Wang, H., Yushkevich, P.A.: Multi-atlas segmentation without registration: a supervoxel-based approach. In: Mori, K., Sakuma, I., Sato, Y., Barillot, C., Navab, N. (eds.) MICCAI 2013. LNCS, vol. 8151, pp. 535–542. Springer, Heidelberg (2013). https://doi.org/10.1007/978-3-642-40760-4_67
19. Wang, J., Zhang, M.: DeepFLASH: an efficient network for learning-based medical image registration. In: IEEE CVPR, pp. 4443–4451 (2020)
20. Wang, Y., Sun, Y., Liu, Z., Sarma, S.E., Bronstein, M.M., Solomon, J.M.: Dynamic graph CNN for learning on point clouds. ACM Trans. Graph. (TOG) **38**, 1–12 (2019)
21. Watson, G.S.: Smooth regression analysis. Sankhyā Indian J. Stat. Ser. A **26**(4), 359–372 (1964)
22. Yang, X., Kwitt, R., Niethammer, M.: Quicksilver: fast predictive image registration–a deep learning approach. Neuroimage **158**, 378–396 (2017)
23. Yang, Y., Chen, W., Wang, M., Zhong, D., Du, S.: Color point cloud registration based on supervoxel correspondence. IEEE Access **8**, 7362–7372 (2020)
24. Zeng, Y., Qian, Y., Zhu, Z., Hou, J., Yuan, H., He, Y.: CorrNet3D: unsupervised end-to-end learning of dense correspondence for 3D point clouds. In: Proceedings of the IEEE/CVF Conference on Computer Vision and Pattern Recognition, pp. 6052–6061 (2021)
25. Zhang, Y., Pei, Y., Guo, Y., Ma, G., Xu, T., Zha, H.: Consistent correspondence of cone-beam CT images using volume functional maps. In: Frangi, A.F., Schnabel, J.A., Davatzikos, C., Alberola-López, C., Fichtinger, G. (eds.) MICCAI 2018. LNCS, vol. 11070, pp. 801–809. Springer, Cham (2018). https://doi.org/10.1007/978-3-030-00928-1_90

# Manifold-Driven and Feature Replay Lifelong Representation Learning on Person ReID

Tianjun Huang and Jianguo Zhang[✉]

Department of Computer Science and Engineering, Southern University of Science and Technology, Shenzhen 518055, China
{huangtj,zhangjg}@sustech.edu.cn

**Abstract.** Lifelong learning, which attempts to alleviate catastrophic forgetting in machine learning models, is gaining increasing attention for deep neural networks. Recent lifelong learning methods which continuously append new classes in the classification layer of deep neural network suffer from the model capacity issue. Representation learning is a feasible solution for this problem. However, representation learning in lifelong learning has not been cautiously evaluated, especially for unseen classes. In this work, we concentrate on evaluating the performance of lifelong representation learning on unseen classes, and propose an effective lifelong representation learning method to match image pairs, without the need of increasing the model capacity. Specifically, we preserve the knowledge of previous tasks in the manifolds learned from multiple network layer outputs. The obtained distributions of these manifolds are further used to generate pseudo feature maps which are replayed in a combination with knowledge distillation strategy to improve the performance. We conduct the experiments on three widely used Person ReID datasets to evaluate the performance of lifelong representation learning on unseen classes. The result shows that our proposed method achieves the state-of-the-art performance compared to other related lifelong learning methods.

**Keywords:** Lifelong learning · Feature replay · Person re-identifications

## 1 Introduction

Lifelong learning is closely related with the *"stability-plasticity"* dilemma, which is a common problem in biological system [4]. *Plasticity* refers to the ability of learning new knowledge, and *stability* represents the memory of past knowledge. Deep neural network models have been shown to have catastrophic forgetting issue on the memory of previously learned knowledge [9].

One intuitive solution for solving catastrophic forgetting is to keep a subset of raw data in previous tasks. Samples in those subsets are integrated into the

© The Author(s), under exclusive license to Springer Nature Switzerland AG 2022
S. Yu et al. (Eds.): PRCV 2022, LNCS 13535, pp. 428–440, 2022.
https://doi.org/10.1007/978-3-031-18910-4_35

training process of a new task to impel the network to remember previous knowledge [16]. However, most often, the data in previous tasks are not accessible due to *data privacy* (e.g., medical images of patients) and humans have the ability to remember previous knowledge regardless of the occurrence of previous data when learning new knowledge.

Most recent lifelong learning methods use the strategy that incrementally augments new classes on the classification layer of the network to integrate new task and previous tasks [14]. These methods suffer from the *model capacity* (i.e., the size of the model) problem as the number of classes increases. Representation learning is a feasible solution to avoid the expanding of *model capacity*. However, current lifelong representation learning methods [16,19] always assume that the classification labels in training set and testing set are the same, and then generate prototypes for training classes to estimate labels in testing set. Lifelong representation learning on unseen classes, such as in popular Person Re-identification and Image Retrieval scenarios, is not well explored.

In this paper, we propose an effective method to enhance the lifelong representation learning ability of a single deep neural network on unseen classes when given a sequence of tasks. Samples of previous tasks are *not required* so as to avoid *data storage* and *privacy* issues. Meanwhile, the structure of the network stays the same when testing on each task, which solves the problem of *model capacity*. Specifically, we leverage Variational Autoencoders (VAEs) to capture the distributions of manifolds for multiple output feature maps in the network. We find that minimizing the discrepancy of code distributions of feature maps can maintain compacted knowledge in previous tasks and leave more space for the network to learn new knowledge. In addition, the distributions are able to generate pseudo feature maps which mitigate the issue of *data privacy* compared to those that generate pseudo samples of previous tasks. The combination of distribution constraint and pseudo feature maps further improves the performance of our method on lifelong representation learning.

Three widely used Person Re-identification (ReID) datasets are sequentially evaluated in the experiments to simulate lifelong representation learning on unseen classes. ReID is an important research area for both academia and industry due to its applications on surveillance and security. The number of people occurred in camera views may continually increase and is hard to forecast. Most existing lifelong learning methods for conventional classification tasks, such as in CIFAR100 and MNIST, are hard to be applied in this scenario, since they need to solve the problem of continually labelling unseen person in real time and the constraint of *model capacity*. In testing, where person IDs are different from that of the training, each query image is compared to gallery images based on their representations to generate the results of match-ranking. Existing ReID methods mainly focus on achieving good performance on each individual ReID dataset [6]. However, the catastrophic forgetting problem is ignored when sequentially learning a sequence of tasks. We explore the existence of catastrophic forgetting in ReID area and demonstrate that our proposed method outperforms other related lifelong learning methods on unseen classes.

The contributions of our work are summarised as follows:

- We propose an effective lifelong learning method on representation learning and evaluate its performance on unseen classes. Our proposed method leverages the distributions of manifolds captured by VAEs to compact knowledge of previous tasks for easing the catastrophic forgetting problem in lifelong representation learning and enhancing the flexibility of deep neural network to learn new knowledge.
- Pseudo feature maps of previous tasks can be easily generated by our VAEs. The result demonstrates that these replayed feature maps are able to further improve our lifelong representation learning performance. One resulting advantage is that pseudo feature maps would naturally preserve the *data privacy* stronger than the use of pseudo input samples.
- Extensive experiments are conducted on three widely used ReID datasets. Results clearly demonstrate that our method is capable of resolving catastrophic forgetting problem in the ReID scenario, achieving the best performance compared to other lifelong methods on representation learning.

## 2 Related Work

### 2.1 Lifelong Learning

Recent lifelong learning methods are often categorized into three families: *replay-based* methods, *parameter isolation-based* methods and *regularization-based* methods [9]. *Replay-based* methods often add a subset of samples from previous tasks into the training process of the new task so as to replay the old knowledge [16]. The selection and storage of previous samples are the main problem of these methods and they are not able to deal with the scenario when samples of previous tasks are not accessible due to *data privacy*. Other approaches in this family are to generate pseudo samples for previous tasks by using generative models [17]. However, these pseudo samples still have *data privacy* issue. *Parameter isolation-based* methods normally gradually expand the network structure. Each task is corresponding to a part of the network parameters [2]. This family is restricted by the *model capacity* since the model size increases with the number of tasks. *Regularization-based* methods usually introduce an extra regularization term in the loss function for consolidating the information learned in previous tasks [5,8,12]. Elastic weight consolidation (EWC) [8] is a typical approach in the regularization family. The diagonal of Fisher information matrix is utilized to assign different levels of importance to the network parameters. When learning a new task, changes of important parameters will get high penalty.

Since different lifelong learning families have their own advantages, [14] starts to combine them together to obtain the state-of-the-art performance. They used conditional GAN to generate pseudo feature maps, plus a regularization loss between previous and current feature maps. Different from their approach, our proposed method integrates the discrepancy of distributions of manifolds and feature map replay into the lifelong learning structure by utilizing unified VAE structures. The obtained distributions maintain low-dimensional compacted knowledge compared to general feature map regularization.

A common issue in recent lifelong learning methods is the growing requirement of *model capacity*, since the classification layer is expanding as the number of tasks increases [14]. Representation learning can avoid the issue of the increase of *model capacity*. However, current lifelong representation learning methods [16,19] on conventional datasets (e.g., MNIST, CIFAR100 and ImageNet) often assume that training set and testing set have the same class labels and utilize nearest-class-mean as the classification method. The performance of lifelong representation learning on unseen classes is rarely considered, such as in Image Retrieval and ReID.

## 2.2   Person Re-Identification

Most existing ReID approaches mainly focus on transfer learning problem, that is, achieving the best performance on each individual ReID dataset [13]. Catastrophic forgetting is ignored in this area. To the best of our knowledge, recently, very few work start to solve the lifelong representation learning problem on ReID for unseen classes. [18] just simply applied Learning without Forgetting algorithm [12] on two ReID datasets. An flexible knowledge distillation approach which is also based on [12] was proposed by [20], but the mixing testing set from different datasets in their experiment is hard to illustrate the catastrophic forgetting issue on ReID and recently related lifelong learning methods were not evaluated. The most similar work to us is [5]. By constricting the distribution discrepancy and replaying features, our proposed method can better alleviate the problem of forgetting than [5], especially when the number of tasks increases.

## 3   Methodology

The overview of our method can be seen in Fig. 1. It shows the framework of two tasks lifelong learning. After learning the first task, feature generators $\{G_1, G_2, ...\}$ are trained for the feature maps of multiple layer outputs in the network. When the second task appears, its output feature maps will go through the corresponding pre-trained feature generators to calculate the distributions of manifolds. These distributions are constrained during the second task learning so as to maintain the previous knowledge. Meanwhile, pseudo feature maps $\{S_1, S_2, ...\}$ of different layers can be produced by the feature generators. We fuse the pseudo feature maps of the first task into the training of the second task by utilizing distillation loss to replay the previous knowledge. The representation learned before the classification layer is extracted for image matching.

### 3.1   Manifolds Learning with VAE

Regularizing all the model parameters is an intuitive way for alleviating catastrophic forgetting in previously learned tasks. It may be seen as an excessive

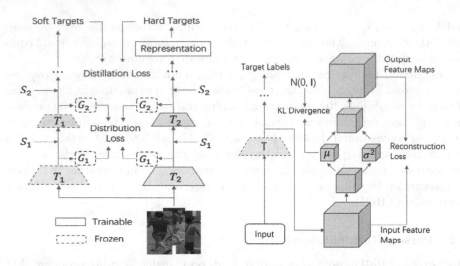

**Fig. 1.** Left: overview of our framework of two tasks lifelong learning. $T_1$ and $T_2$ represent the previous task and new task, respectively. $\{G_1, G_2, ...\}$ are the feature generators learned from multiple layer outputs in $T_1$. $\{S_1, S_2, ...\}$ are the pseudo features generated by $\{G_1, G_2, ...\}$. The training images are all from the new task $T_2$. Right: the structure of our Variational Autoencoders, two convolution layers for encoding and two transposed convolution layers for decoding.

restraint in terms of learning new knowledge due to the complexity of deep neural network models. Our motivation is that, only effective knowledge in the previous tasks should be constrained so that the network can be more flexible to learn the knowledge in new tasks. Specifically, we use Variational Autoencoders (VAEs) [7] to learn distributions of manifolds to compact knowledge in previous tasks.

Let $X$ denotes the input data and $\mathbf{z}$ is the corresponding latent variables on a low-dimensional manifold, the calculation of the posterior distribution $P(\mathbf{z}|X)$ is always intractable. Therefore, VAE creates an approximation distribution $Q(\mathbf{z}|X)$ to simulate $P(\mathbf{z}|X)$. Kullback-Leibler (KL) divergence is often used to measure the similarity between the two distributions [3]:

$$KL[Q(\mathbf{z}|X)||P(\mathbf{z}|X)] = E_{\mathbf{z}\sim Q}[logQ(\mathbf{z}|X) - logP(\mathbf{z}|X)] \tag{1}$$

By rewriting Eq. (1), we can obtain:

$$logP(X) - KL[Q(\mathbf{z}|X)||P(\mathbf{z}|X)] = E_{\mathbf{z}\sim Q}[logP(X|\mathbf{z})] \\ - KL[Q(\mathbf{z}|X)||P(\mathbf{z})] \tag{2}$$

The right hand side of Eq. (2) is called Variational Lower Bound or Evidence Lower Bound (ELBO). Since KL divergence is not less than zero, maximizing $logP(X)$ is equivalent to maximizing the lower bound. Assuming $Q(\mathbf{z}|X) = \mathcal{N}(\mathbf{z}|\mu, \Sigma)$ and $P(\mathbf{z}) = \mathcal{N}(0, I)$, where $\Sigma$ is a diagonal matrix and $I$ is the identity matrix, the $KL[Q(\mathbf{z}|X)||P(\mathbf{z})]$ can be computed as follows:

$$KL[Q(\mathbf{z}|X)||P(\mathbf{z})] = \frac{1}{2} \sum_{k=1}^{K} (\sigma_k^2 + \mu_k^2 - K - log\sigma_k^2) \tag{3}$$

where $K$ is the number of dimensions of $\mathbf{z}$ and $\sigma_k^2$ is the value on the diagonal of matrix $\Sigma$. Reconstruction error between the input data and reconstructed data is used to compute $E_{\mathbf{z}\sim Q}[logP(X|\mathbf{z})]$. Thus, we can train the VAE model by maximizing the lower bound. In our work, after the training of current task is completed, VAEs are trained on multiple layer outputs in the deep neural network to capture compressed knowledge of different levels. Our VAE structure has four layers and there is no fully connected layers, as it can be seen in Fig. 1. Assuming the convolution filter has size 3 by 3 and the number of output channels is $D$, the number of parameters for training a VAE for this layer output is equal to $(D \times 3 \times 3 \times D + 3 \times 0.5 \times D \times 3 \times 3 \times 0.25 \times D)$.

## 3.2 Distribution Discrepancy

When a new task appears, layer outputs of the new task go through the corresponding VAEs of previous tasks to produce the distributions of latent variables. The manifold consistency of VAEs is achieved by minimizing the discrepancy of distributions to preserve knowledge in previous tasks. Let $T$ denotes the total number of tasks and $N$ is the size of input data in the new task, we use Wasserstein distance to measure the discrepancy between the latent distributions $\hat{\mu}$ and $\hat{\sigma}$ in the new task and distributions $\mu$ and $\sigma$ in previous tasks:

$$Loss_t^n = \sum_{v=1}^{V} \sum_{k=1}^{K} ((\mu_k{}^v - \mu_k^v)^2 + (\hat{\sigma}_k{}^v - \sigma_k^v)^2) \tag{4}$$

$$Loss_D = \frac{1}{N(T-1)} \sum_{n=1}^{N} \sum_{t=1}^{T-1} Loss_t^n \tag{5}$$

where $v$ is the index for multiple VAEs and $K$ is the number of dimensions of multivariate Gaussian. The knowledge compacted in the low-dimensional distributions leaves the model more space to learn knowledge from new tasks. Another advantage is that the learned distribution can generate pseudo feature maps to assist memory replay. We will discuss it in the next section.

## 3.3 Feature Map Replay

Since VAEs are generative models, it is convenient to produce pseudo feature maps by utilizing the learned distributions of manifolds. Compared to sample replay methods such as [17], feature replay is a more appropriate solution for the issue of *data privacy*, and recent work [14] shows that the feature replay can achieve even better performance. Based on the learned VAEs, we can sample latent codes from the distribution $\mathcal{N}(0, I)$ and then pass these codes through decoders in VAEs to generate pseudo feature maps on different levels. These pseudo feature maps are then fused into the training process with real samples of a new task.

Knowledge Distillation loss is applied on the pseudo feature maps to preserve the knowledge of the network on previous tasks and soften the predictions produced by the pseudo feature maps. Specifically, let $\mathbf{p}_l = \{p_l^{(1)}, ..., p_l^{(C)}\}$ denotes the output of a pseudo feature map on the old task network and $\mathbf{p}_l' = \{p_l'^{(1)}, ..., p_l'^{(C)}\}$ is the output on the new task network but with the classifier of the old task, and $L$ is the number of pseudo feature maps, the Distillation loss is then defined as:

$$Loss_K = -\frac{1}{L}\sum_{l=1}^{L}\sum_{c=1}^{C} p_l^{(c)} log p_l'^{(c)} \tag{6}$$

where $C$ is the number of labels and $p_l^{(c)}$, $p_l'^{(c)}$ are computed as follows:

$$p_l^{(c)} = \frac{exp(p_l^{(c)}/M)}{\sum_j exp(p_l^{(j)}/M)}, \quad p_l'^{(c)} = \frac{exp(p_l'^{(c)}/M)}{\sum_j exp(p_l'^{(j)}/M)} \tag{7}$$

where $M$ is the temperature value.

For the classifier of the new task with its data of input size $N$, we use the cross-entropy loss:

$$Loss_E = -\frac{1}{N}\sum_{n=1}^{N}\sum_{c=1}^{C} y_n^c log(p_n^c) \tag{8}$$

The final optimization function is then the sum of the three losses:

$$L = Loss_E + Loss_K + \alpha Loss_D \tag{9}$$

where $\alpha$ controls the impact of the distribution discrepancy.

The feature representation before the final classification layer of the network is extracted to match image pairs in unseen testing set. Cosine distance is calculated to measure the similarity between two representations and rank the matching result.

## 4   Experiments

### 4.1   Datasets

We conduct the experiments on three widely used public ReID datasets: Market-1501, DukeMTMC and CUHK03. We use the original separations of training and testing sets for Market-1501 and DukeMTMC datasets. The new protocol proposed in [21] is used to separate CUHK03 dataset. For all the three datasets, we select the first image from each identity in the training set to construct the validation set. *It should be noted that person IDs in testing sets of the three datasets are unseen in their training sets.*

## 4.2    Implementation Details

The sequential order of learning the three datasets is Market-1501, DukeMTMC-reID and CUHK03, which is randomly decided for avoiding bias. The base model used in this work is ResNet-50 that is often used as the baseline in ReID [22]. Except the last two fully connected layers, parameters learned in the previous network will be transferred into the new task as the initialization. For the first task, we use ResNet-50 pre-trained on ImageNet dataset as the initialization. Images are resized to $256 * 128$ as the input. For the optimization, we use SGD with momentum of 0.9. The learning rate starts with 0.05 for the parameters transferred from previous model. For the re-initialized fully connected layers in the new task, the learning rate is set to 0.05. Learning rates are divided by 10 after 20 epochs during the total 60 epochs training. Parameter settings for training ResNet-50 networks on three datasets are the same.

We build our VAEs on the outputs of four layers (each layer contains several bottlenecks) of ResNet-50 network implemented by Pytorch. The learning rate of VAEs starts from 0.0001 and is divided by 10 after 25 epochs during the total 60 epochs training. Parameter settings for training VAEs on corresponding datasets are the same. The hyper-parameter $\alpha$ is found by using grid search. For feature replay, each VAE generates the same number of pseudo feature maps with the data size of a new task. Temperature $M$ is set to 5, consistent across all related experiments. The training time of our model (including VAEs) with feature replay is about seven hours using a single NVIDIA TITAN V GPU with 12G memory.

## 4.3    Results and Comparisons

Most lifelong learning methods use average accuracy and average forgetting to evaluate the performance of proposed methods. The learned model may prefer remembering previous tasks whose classification accuracies are relatively higher than others, while disregarding the performance on the current task. This strategy may go against with the aim of lifelong learning in practice. Therefore, we keep in step with [5], that is, *the performance on current task should be guaranteed first.* Our following experiments are based on this setting.

Two measurements are commonly used in ReID for evaluating the performance of a representation learning algorithm on unseen classes: mean Average Precision (mAP) and Rank-1. The former is a popular criterion in information retrieval. Rank-1 calculates the probability when the image with highest ranking is the correct match. Market-1501, DukeMTMC-reID and CUHK03 are corresponding to Task1, Task2 and Task3 in the experiments, respectively.

**Table 1.** Performance of lifelong representation learning on two continual tasks. Fine-tuning is the baseline approach which means the network is sequentially fine-tuned on each task. For lifelong learning setup, the network trained on Task 2 is tested on both Task 1 and Task 2 to evaluate the degree of forgetting by calculating the mean values of Rank-1 and mAP.

| Method | Task 1 | | Task 2 | | Mean | |
|---|---|---|---|---|---|---|
| | Rank-1 | mAP | Rank-1 | mAP | Rank-1 | mAP |
| Fine-tuning | 0.439 | 0.182 | 0.792 | 0.632 | 0.616 | 0.399 |
| LwF [12] | 0.508 | 0.242 | 0.780 | 0.610 | 0.644 | 0.426 |
| EWC [8] | 0.564 | 0.282 | 0.781 | 0.602 | 0.673 | 0.442 |
| Encoder Lifelong [15] | 0.534 | 0.264 | 0.782 | 0.606 | 0.658 | 0.435 |
| MAS [1] | 0.599 | 0.319 | 0.781 | 0.602 | 0.690 | 0.461 |
| $L_2$-$SP$ [11] | 0.533 | 0.249 | 0.785 | 0.608 | 0.659 | 0.429 |
| DELTA (without ATT) [10] | 0.604 | 0.313 | 0.782 | 0.610 | 0.693 | 0.462 |
| E-EWC [19] | 0.695 | 0.424 | 0.585 | 0.395 | 0.640 | 0.410 |
| GFR [14] | 0.602 | 0.314 | 0.776 | 0.604 | 0.689 | 0.459 |
| Auto-Weighted EC [5] | 0.627 | 0.341 | 0.778 | 0.607 | 0.703 | 0.474 |
| **VAE-D (Ours)** | 0.612 | 0.322 | 0.781 | 0.609 | 0.697 | 0.466 |
| **VAE-D-R (Ours)** | 0.635 | 0.340 | 0.781 | 0.609 | **0.708** | **0.475** |

**Table 2.** Performance of lifelong representation learning on three continual tasks. Fine-tuning is the baseline approach which means the network is sequentially fine-tuned on each task. The network trained on Task 3 is tested on Task 1, Task 2 and Task 3, respectively, to evaluate the degree of forgetting by calculating the mean values of Rank-1 and mAP.

| Method | Task 1 | | Task 2 | | Task 3 | | Mean | |
|---|---|---|---|---|---|---|---|---|
| | Rank-1 | mAP | Rank-1 | mAP | Rank-1 | mAP | Rank-1 | mAP |
| Fine-tuning | 0.444 | 0.210 | 0.438 | 0.252 | 0.504 | 0.466 | 0.462 | 0.309 |
| LwF [12] | 0.488 | 0.245 | 0.468 | 0.278 | 0.503 | 0.463 | 0.486 | 0.329 |
| EWC [8] | 0.578 | 0.324 | 0.433 | 0.247 | 0.494 | 0.461 | 0.502 | 0.344 |
| Encoder Lifelong [15] | 0.516 | 0.267 | 0.485 | 0.291 | 0.502 | 0.463 | 0.501 | 0.340 |
| MAS [1] | 0.574 | 0.313 | 0.456 | 0.273 | 0.494 | 0.458 | 0.508 | 0.348 |
| $L_2$-$SP$ [11] | 0.576 | 0.310 | 0.428 | 0.252 | 0.494 | 0.461 | 0.499 | 0.341 |
| DELTA (without ATT) [10] | 0.573 | 0.310 | 0.437 | 0.248 | 0.495 | 0.463 | 0.502 | 0.340 |
| E-EWC [19] | 0.644 | 0.392 | 0.430 | 0.241 | 0.361 | 0.325 | 0.478 | 0.319 |
| GFR [14] | 0.578 | 0.317 | 0.452 | 0.259 | 0.492 | 0.463 | 0.507 | 0.346 |
| Auto-Weighted EC [5] | 0.590 | 0.323 | 0.478 | 0.280 | 0.503 | 0.465 | 0.524 | 0.356 |
| **VAE-D (Ours)** | 0.563 | 0.296 | 0.486 | 0.288 | 0.497 | 0.463 | 0.515 | 0.349 |
| **VAE-D-R (Ours)** | 0.630 | 0.359 | 0.547 | 0.340 | 0.507 | 0.465 | **0.561** | **0.388** |

**Methods Comparison.** Table 1 and Table 2 show the comparison results of our proposed method with related lifelong learning approaches on two tasks and three tasks lifelong representation learning, respectively. To make a fair comparison, we only consider the methods that do not need samples or pseudo samples from previous tasks.

We replace the conditional GAN in the GFR [14] method with our VAEs to generate pseudo feature maps from multiple layer outputs. Meanwhile, previously learned VAEs are stored to directly generate pseudo feature maps when learning a new task rather than preserving a single conditional GAN in the GFR.

E-EWC represents the embedding method proposed in [19] without semantic drift compensation. Since the person IDs in testing set are unseen in training set, the semantic drift compensation [19] whose aim is to generate class prototypes is not feasible in this case. VAE-D represents our proposed method which uses the VAE distribution discrepancy. VAE-D-R means the combination of VAE distribution discrepancy and feature replay.

The results show that, even without the feature replay, VAE-D is able to outperform most of the methods except [5] which further investigates different levels of importance on the low-dimensional manifolds. By combining pseudo feature maps generated from VAEs with the minimization of distribution discrepancy, our VAE-D-R achieves the best performance on all the experiments. Especially when the number of tasks increases, VAE-D-R demonstrates a significant improvement compared with other methods (see Table 2). It may due to the reason that training with pseudo features maps is helpful to jointly learn the knowledge from all the tasks.

**Ablation Study.** For brevity, we report the performance of lifelong representation learning on three continual tasks for all the ablation studies.

**Distribution Discrepancy and Feature Replay.** To explore the impact of feature replay, we conduct the lifelong representation learning experiments by only using the pseudo feature maps generated from multiple VAEs. It can be seen in Table 3 that the feature replay is able to alleviate the forgetting in fine-tuning, but its performance is worse than distribution discrepancy. We suppose the main reason is that feature replay focuses on the classification result on the training set, while distribution regularization constrains the intermediate features which may be more important for representation learning on unseen classes. In addition, the quality of these pseudo feature maps may also affect the performance of feature replay.

**Table 3.** Mean Rank-1 and mAP values of distribution discrepancy and feature replay for three tasks lifelong representation learning. Feature replay only uses pseudo feature maps generated from the same VAEs with distribution discrepancy.

| Method | Rank-1 | mAP |
|---|---|---|
| Fine-tuning | 0.462 | 0.309 |
| Feature Replay | 0.477 | 0.323 |
| VAE-D | **0.515** | **0.349** |

**Distribution Discrepancy on Different Levels.** The distribution discrepancy proposed in our method is composed of four discrepancy items from VAEs trained on four different levels of feature maps in the network. The four levels (from low to high) are corresponding to the four layers in Resnet-50 implemented by Pytorch. Each layer consists of several bottlenecks. The left graph in Fig. 2 demonstrates the performance for minimizing distribution discrepancy of each individual layer output and their combination. Minimizing distribution discrepancy on higher level representation results in better performance. This is probably caused by the reason that high level feature maps are more close to the final representation, so that they can affect more pre-layer parameters in the network to maintain the old knowledge. The combination of minimizing distribution discrepancy from low level to high level generates the best performance, which implies the existence of complementary information among different levels.

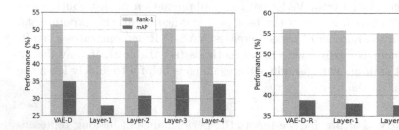

**Fig. 2.** Left: mean Rank-1 and mAP values for minimizing distribution discrepancy of different levels. The horizontal coordinates from Layer-1 to Layer-4 represents the feature maps from low level to high levels. Right: mean Rank-1 and mAP values for feature replay of different levels. This result is built on VAE-D.

**Feature Replay on Different Levels.** The right graph in Fig. 2 investigates the impact of adding feature replay of each layer on the VAE-D structure. Since parameters of last two fully connected layers in previous tasks are not transferred into the new task, the VAE built on the fourth layer is only used for distribution regularization and does not generate pseudo feature maps. On the contrary, with the result of distribution discrepancy on different levels, pseudo feature maps generated by low level VAE obtains better performance than high level pseudo feature maps. We suppose the reason is that pseudo feature maps affect the post-layer parameters in the network. Therefore, low level pseudo feature maps have the advantage of adjusting more parameters in the network to achieve a good trade-off of memories between new task and previous tasks. Same with the ablation studies in regularization, the combination of feature replay from all layers achieves the best performance due to the potential complementary information among different levels.

## 5    Conclusions

In this work, we evaluate the performance of lifelong representation learning on unseen classes and present a novel method that combines distribution discrepancy and feature replay learned from multiple VAEs. The classification layer of the network is not incrementally expanded in our proposed method so that the model capacity can remain the same after training. Experiments on three widely used ReID datasets show that the proposed method is able to achieve a better trade-off between stability and plasticity when continually learn tasks on representation learning, compared to other related lifelong learning methods. The results of ablation studies indicate that the combination of different levels can obtain the best performance due to the potential complementary information among different levels. The main limitation of the current work is the storage of previously learned VAEs, we could reduce the number of VAEs based on the ablation study and provide an online upgrading mechanism in the future work.

**Acknowledgement.** This work is supported by National Key Research and Development Program of China (2021YFF1200804), and National Key Research and Development Program of China (2021YFF1200800).

# References

1. Aljundi, R., Babiloni, F., Elhoseiny, M., Rohrbach, M., Tuytelaars, T.: Memory aware synapses: learning what (not) to forget. In: Ferrari, V., Hebert, M., Sminchisescu, C., Weiss, Y. (eds.) ECCV 2018. LNCS, vol. 11207, pp. 144–161. Springer, Cham (2018). https://doi.org/10.1007/978-3-030-01219-9_9
2. Aljundi, R., Chakravarty, P., Tuytelaars, T.: Expert gate: Lifelong learning with a network of experts. In: CVPR (2017)
3. Doersch, C.: Tutorial on variational autoencoders. In: arXiv:1606.05908 (2016)
4. Grossberg, S.T.: Studies of Mind and Brain: Neural Principles of Learning, Perception. Cognition, and Motor Control. Springer, Development (1982)
5. Huang, T., Qu, W., Zhang, J.: Continual representation learning via auto-weighted latent embeddings on person reid. In: PRCV (2021)
6. Jin, X., Lan, C., Zeng, W., Chen, Z., Zhang, L.: Style normalization and restitution for generalizable person re-identification. In: CVPR (2020)
7. Kingma, D.P., Welling, M.: Auto-encoding variational bayes. In: ICLR (2014)
8. Kirkpatrick, J., et al.: Overcoming catastrophic forgetting in neural networks. In: Proceedings of National Academy of Sciences (2017)
9. Lange, M.D., Aljundi, R., Masana, M., Parisot, S., Jia, X., Leonardis, A., Slabaugh, G., Tuytelaars, T.: Continual learning: A comparative study on how to defy forgetting in classification tasks. arXiv:1909.08383 (2019)
10. Li, X., Xiong, H., Wang, H., Rao, Y., Liu, L., Chen, Z., Huan, J.: Delta: deep learning transfer using feature map with attention for convolutional networks. In: ICLR (2019)
11. Li, X., Grandvalet, Y., Davoine, F.: Explicit inductive bias for transfer learning with convolutional networks. In: ICML (2018)
12. Li, Z., Hoiem, D.: Learning without forgetting. In: Leibe, B., Matas, J., Sebe, N., Welling, M. (eds.) ECCV 2016. LNCS, vol. 9908, pp. 614–629. Springer, Cham (2016). https://doi.org/10.1007/978-3-319-46493-0_37
13. Liu, J., Zha, Z.J., Chen, D., Hong, R., Wang, M.: Adaptive transfer network for cross-domain person re-identificaiton. In: CVPR (2019)
14. Liu, X., et al.: Generative feature replay for class-incremental learning. In: CVPR Workshop (2020)
15. Rannen, A., Aljundi, R., Blaschko, M.B., Tuytelaars, T.: Encoder based lifelong learning. In: ICCV (2017)

16. Rebuffi, S.A., Kolesnikov, A., Sperl, G., Lampert, C.H.: icarl: Incremental classifier and representation learning. In: CVPR (2017)
17. Shin, H., Lee, J.K., Kim, J., Kim, J.: Continual learning with deep generative replay. In: NIPS (2017)
18. Sugianto, N., Tjondronegoro, D., Sorwar, G., Chakraborty, P., Yuwono, E.I.: Continuous learning without forgetting for person re-identification. In: International Conference on Advanced Video and Signal Based Surveillance (AVSS) (2019)
19. Yu, L., Twardowski, B., Liu, X., Herranz, L., Wang, K., Cheng, Y., Jui, S., van de Weijer, J.: Semantic drift compensation for class-incremental learning. In: CVPR (2020)
20. Zhao, B., Tang, S., Chen, D., Bilen, H., Zhao, R.: Continual representation learning for biometric identification. In: WACV (2021)
21. Zhong, Z., Zheng, L., Cao, D., Li, S.: Re-ranking person re-identification with k-reciprocal encoding. In: CVPR (2017)
22. Zhong, Z., Zheng, L., Zheng, Z., Li, S., Yang, Y.: Camera style adaptation for person re-identification. In: CVPR (2018)

# Multi-source Information-Shared Domain Adaptation for EEG Emotion Recognition

Ming Gong[1], Wei Zhong[2(✉)], Jiayu Hu[3], Long Ye[2], and Qin Zhang[2]

[1] Key Laboratory of Media Audio and Video, Communication University of China,
Beijing 100024, China
gongming@cuc.edu.cn

[2] State Key Laboratory of Media Convergence and Communication,
Communication University of China, Beijing 100024, China
{wzhong,yelong,zhangqin}@cuc.edu.cn

[3] College of Letters and Science,University of California at Los Angeles,
Los Angeles 90095, USA
jiayuhu12@g.ucla.edu

**Abstract.** EEG-based affective computing aims to provide an objective method to evaluate people's emotional states in human-computer interactions, but it suffers the dilemma of individual differences in EEG signals. The existing approaches usually extract domain-specific features, which ignore the commonness of subjects or treat all subjects as one source for transfer. This paper proposes a novel multi-source information-shared domain adaptation framework for cross-subject EEG emotion recognition. In the proposed framework, we assume that all EEG data share the same low-level features, the shared representations and private components are captured by the shared extractor and private extractors, respectively. Besides the maximum mean discrepancy and diff losses, we also propose the was-loss to align the private domains for the purpose of extracting tight shared domain and thus enhancing the domain adaptation ability of the network. Finally, we build the domain-specific classifiers and shared classifier in parallel and dynamically integrate their predictions by the similarity of marginal distributions among domains. The experimental results on the SEED and SEED-IV datasets demonstrate that our framework outperforms the state-of-the-art domain adaptation methods with accuracies of 88.1% and 73.8% on average.

**Keywords:** EEG emotion recognition · Domain adaptation · Transfer learning

## 1 Introduction

In recent years, EEG-based emotion recognition has aroused the interest of researchers by its advantages in real-time with a high time resolution [1] and stable patterns over time [2]. The field of affective Brain-Computer Interface (aBCI) refers to detect people's emotional state through EEG signals [3], which

S. Yu et al. (Eds.): PRCV 2022, LNCS 13535, pp. 441–453, 2022.
https://doi.org/10.1007/978-3-031-18910-4_36

could contribute to detecting mental disorders [4] and objective evaluation of depression [5]. Due to the reason of head size, body states and experimental environment, the structural and functional variability of brain can be different cross subjects, and thus there are significant individual differences between their EEG signals [6]. The traditional machine-learning algorithms train an EEG-based recognition network with data from some subjects. However, the trained network can not generalize well to the new subject because of the domain shift problem [7]. To resolve this problem, the conventional operation is to collect the labeled data of new subject and finetune the network parameters for calibration. But it always provides an unfriendly experience for users and is less convenient.

With the development of deep-learning technologies, the researchers attempt to use the transfer learning methods to deal with the problem caused by nonstationary nature and inter-subject structural variability of EEG signals [8] in practical aBCI applications. The transfer learning can build the bridge between the source domain and unlabeled target domain through finding the similarity between them [9]. The existing transfer learning methods can be mainly classified into two categories, domain adaption (DA) and domain generalization (DG). The DG methods appeal to extract the domain-invariant feature, however, without the access to target domain data, it is hard to train a network generalized well to new subject [10,11]. In contrast, the DA methods use target domain information in the training phase to solve the domain shift problem, mainly by the ways of feature transformation, instance-based and model pretraining [9]. When applying the DA methods to the task of cross-subject EEG emotion recognition, the existing works either regard all source domains as the same or train source-specific learners directly, ignoring the relationship between individuality and commonality in different domains. Therefore, it is necessary to consider the individual difference and group commonality together among the multi-source domains, further improving the recognition performance.

In this paper, we propose a multi-source information-shared domain adaptation network for cross-subject EEG emotion recognition. In the proposed network, we firstly extract the domain-specific and domain-shared features to represent the individuality and commonality of EEG signals from different domains, respectively. And then in the training phase, besides using the maximum mean discrepancy (MMD) to make the marginal distribution between source and target domains closer, as well as the diff-loss to improve the astringency of network, another loss is also proposed to narrow the distance between target private domains, which enhances the mapping capability of private extractors by considering the information of other private domains. Furthermore, instead of artificially adjusting the weights of classifiers by experience, we integrate the outputs of classifiers by distribution distance between the source domains, realizing the adjustment of network optimization dynamically. The experimental results on SEED and SEED-IV datasets show that the performance of the proposed network outperforms the state-of-the-art domain adaptation methods. The contributions of this paper can be summarized as follows:

- We propose an efficient EEG emotional recognition network by integrating individual differences and group commonality of multi-source domains.
- The was-loss is proposed to make the marginal distribution of domain-specific features closer among target private domains. Conjuncted with the diff-loss, the domain adaptation ability of network can be enhanced.
- We propose a dynamic weighting strategy based on the MMD distribution distance between source private domains and shared domain to adjust the optimization of network.

## 2  Related Work

With the rapid developments of deep learning, the transfer learning has become the mainstream method in the field of EEG-based emotion recognition. There are two main branches in transfer learning to reduce inter-subject variability, DA and DG. The goal of DG is to learn a model from several source domains that generalizes to the unseen target domains through data manipulation, representation learning and learning strategy [12]. The scatter component analysis (SCA) [13] extended the kernel fisher discriminant by amplifying the information from the same category and domain, while dampening from different category and domain. Ma et al. [14] proposed a domain residual network (DResNet) by improving DG-DANN with ResNet. Since the DG methods do not utilize target domain information in training phase, they hardly achieve high recognition accuracy like DA methods.

In contrast, the DA methods use target domain information to transfer knowledge by minimizing the domain shifts between the source and target domains. Zheng et al. [15] applied transfer component analysis (TCA) and transductive parameter transfer (TPT) to the cross-subject EEG emotion recognition on the SEED dataset. Li et al. [16] provided another method of domain-adversarial neural networks (DANN) with adversarial training of feature extractor and domain classifier. Luo et al. [17] proposed the Wasserstein GAN domain adaptation network (WGANDA) by using the gradient penalty to alleviate domain shift problem. Zhao et al. [18] developed a plug-and-play Domain Adaptation (PPDA) network, which tried to disentangle the emotion information by considering the domain-specific and domain-invariant information simultaneously. Hao et al. [19] took the source data with different marginal distributions into account and proposed a multi-source EEG-based emotion recognition network (MEERNet). Meanwhile, they [20] used the disc-loss to improve domain adaptation ability and proposed a multi-source marginal distribution adaptation (MS-MDA) network for cross-subject and cross-session EEG Emotion recognition. It can be seen from above analysis, most of the DA methods either regard all source domains as the same or train source-specific learners directly, which may make the network learn unreasonable transfer knowledge, resulting in negative transfer. In this paper, we consider not only the domain-specific individuality and domain-shared commonality among different domains but also the relationship between them, further improving the recognition performance.

# 3 Methods

In this section, we propose a multi-source information-shared domain adaptation network for cross-subject EEG emotion recognition, which is defined as MISDA.

## 3.1 Framework

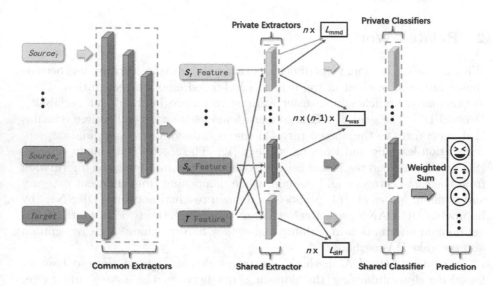

**Fig. 1.** The overall framework of our proposed MISDA network.

The overall framework of our proposed MISDA network is shown in Fig. 1, which consists of five components including common extractors, private extractors, shared extractor, private classifiers and shared classifier. To get a reliable network trained on the multiple source domain data to predict emotion state from newly collected data, we extract different domain-specific features and domain-invariant features for emotion recognition.

Assume that $\mathbf{X}_S$ is the source data matrices and $\mathbf{Y}_S$ is their labels, and $\mathbf{X}_T$ is the target unlabeled data matrices,

$$\mathbf{X}_S = \{\mathbf{X}_S^i\}_{i=1}^n, \ \mathbf{Y}_S = \{\mathbf{Y}_S^i\}_{i=1}^n, \tag{1}$$

where $n$ represent the numbers of subjects in source datasets. The common extractor $E_C$ maps the source data matrices $\mathbf{X_S}$ and target data matrices $\mathbf{X_T}$ to the low-level feature space,

$$\mathbf{X}_S' = \{\mathbf{X}_S'^i\}_{i=1}^n = \{E_C(\mathbf{X}_S^i)\}_{i=1}^n, \ \mathbf{X}_T' = E_C(\mathbf{X}_T). \tag{2}$$

Then for low-level features of each source domain, we build a private extractor to get its source domain-specific features. And for those of target domain, the domain-specific features are extracted by $n$ private extractors,

$$\mathbf{F}_{SP}^i = E_P^i(\mathbf{X}_S'^i), \ \mathbf{F}_{TP}^i = E_P^i(\mathbf{X}_T'), \ i = 1, 2, \ldots, n. \tag{3}$$

In the parallel pipeline, the shared extractor extracts shared deep features from all domains,

$$\mathbf{F}_{SS} = \{E_S(\mathbf{X}_S'^i)\}_{i=1}^n, \ \mathbf{F}_{TS} = E_S(\mathbf{X}_T'). \tag{4}$$

Subsequently, the private classifier $C_P^i$ and shared classifier $C_S$ take $(\mathbf{F}_{SP}^i, \mathbf{F}_{TP}^i)$ and $(\mathbf{F}_{SS}, \mathbf{F}_{TS})$ as inputs and output emotional prediction $(\hat{\mathbf{Y}}_{SP}^i, \hat{\mathbf{Y}}_{TP}^i)$ and $(\hat{\mathbf{Y}}_{SS}, \hat{\mathbf{Y}}_{TS})$, respectively,

$$\hat{\mathbf{Y}}_{SP}^i = C_P^i(\mathbf{F}_{SP}^i), \ \hat{\mathbf{Y}}_{TP}^i = C_P^i(\mathbf{F}_{TP}^i), \ i = 1, 2, \ldots, n,$$
$$\hat{\mathbf{Y}}_{SS} = C_S(\mathbf{F}_{SS}), \ \hat{\mathbf{Y}}_{TS} = C_S(\mathbf{F}_{TS}). \tag{5}$$

Finally, $\hat{\mathbf{Y}}_S$ is the weighted sum by $\hat{\mathbf{Y}}_{SP}^i$ and $\hat{\mathbf{Y}}_{SS}$, $\hat{\mathbf{Y}}_T$ by $\hat{\mathbf{Y}}_{TP}^i$ and $\hat{\mathbf{Y}}_{TS}$, respectively. We use $\hat{\mathbf{Y}}_S$ the to calculate the classification loss, and $\hat{\mathbf{Y}}_T$ to predict emotion category.

## 3.2   Modules

In this subsection, we describe the following modules included in the proposed framework in detail.

**Common Extractor.** Despite considering the individual differences on EEG signals, there still exist some common low-level features resulted by human brain activities and signal characteristics. And thus, we assume that the EEG signals from different subjects share the same shallow features. Similar to the pipelines of MEER-Net [19] and MS-MDA [20], a common extractor is used to map all domain data into a common latent space, extracting the low-level features.

**Private Extractors and Shared Extractor.** Considering the difference among domains, we set up a fully connected layer for each source domain to map the data from common feature space to latent domain-specific feature space, capturing the individual domain information. Here we choose MMD [21,22] to measure the marginal distribution distance between the source and target domains in the reproducing kernel Hilbert space $\mathcal{H}$,

$$MMD(\mathbf{F}_{SP}, \mathbf{F}_{TP}) = \frac{1}{n} \sum_{i=1}^n |(\psi(\mathbf{F}_{SP}^i) - \psi(\mathbf{F}_{TP}^i))|_{\mathcal{H}}, \tag{6}$$

where $\psi$ denotes the mapping function.

In order to make the marginal distributions of domain-specific features closer among target private domains, another metric named $L_{was}$ is also introduced, which is inspired by the Wasserstein loss [23],

$$L_{was} = \sum_{i=1}^{n} \sum_{j=1, j \neq i}^{n} \left| \overline{\mathbf{F}_{TP}^i} - \overline{\mathbf{F}_{TP}^j} \right|, \tag{7}$$

where $\overline{\mathbf{F}_{TP}^i}$ and $\overline{\mathbf{F}_{TP}^j}$ denote the mean vector across feature dimensions from the domain-specific features extracted by the $i$-th and $j$-th private extractors, respectively. The $L_{was}$ aligns the target private features inside and provides a closer private domain, which contributes to extracting the shared domain.

The shared extractor maps the low-level feature space to the shared one. Inspired by the DG disentanglement [9], we continue to extract shared information from the low-level features. To balance the learning ability between private and shared extractors, the shared extractor is built with the same structure as the private one. Moreover, the difference loss $L_{diff}$ is applied to encourage the shared and private extractors to extract different information of low-level features as

$$L_{diff} = \left| \overline{\mathbf{F}_{TP}^i} - \overline{\mathbf{F}_{TS}} \right|, \quad i = 1, 2, \ldots, n. \tag{8}$$

It is worth mentioning that, since all source domains are linearly independent, the shared domain can be identified by the conjunction of $L_{diff}$ and $L_{was}$ in each iteration. And thus the shared extractor could extract the closer domain-invariant features from different domains, which enhances the domain adaptation ability of the network.

**Private Classifiers and Shared Classifier.** Following the private extractors, the private classifiers use the domain-specific features to predict emotion states. The Softmax activate function is adopted after the fully connected layer corresponding to each source domain. Similarly, the shared classifier also has the same structure as the private ones in order to balance the classification ability between them. In the training process, we choose cross-entropy to measure the classification loss of private and shared classifiers as,

$$L_{cl_P} = -\mathbf{Y}_S^i \log \hat{\mathbf{Y}}_{SP}^i, \quad L_{cl_S} = -\mathbf{Y}_S^i \log \hat{\mathbf{Y}}_{SS}. \tag{9}$$

where $Y_S^i$ is the emotion label of $i$-th source domain.

**Weight Sum.** For the sake of dynamically adjusting the optimization process and balancing the weight of private and shared networks, we also propose a weight sum strategy according to the similarity between the private and shared domains. In the training process, we integrate the private and shared classifiers by calculating the MMD distance between the source private and shared domains

$$w_S = softmax(\left| (\psi(\mathbf{F}_{SP}^i) - \psi(\mathbf{F}_{SS})) \right|_{\mathcal{H}}). \tag{10}$$

Then the classification loss is calculated by,

$$L_{cl} = L_{cl_P} + w_S * L_{cl_S}. \tag{11}$$

The higher $w_S$ indicates that the distribution of shared domain is more similar to those of private ones, and thus more trust can be given to the shared classifier.

With $L_{mmd}$, $L_{was}$, $L_{diff}$ and $L_{cl}$ given above, the final loss can be represented as,

$$L = L_{cl} + \alpha L_{mmd} + \beta L_{wass} + \gamma L_{diff}. \tag{12}$$

where $\alpha$, $\beta$ and $\gamma$ are the hyper-parameters.

In the prediction phase, the proposed MISDA network predicts the final results by integrating the predictions of private and shared domains,

$$\hat{Y}_T = \frac{1}{n} \sum_{i=1}^{n} (C_P^i(\mathbf{F}_{TP}^i) + w_T^i * C_S(\mathbf{F}_{TS})), \tag{13}$$

where $w_T^i$ is calculated by the MMD distance between the $i$-th target private and shared domains.

In summary, the work flow of the proposed MISDA framework is given as follows.

---

**Algorithm 1:** The work flow of the proposed MISDA framework

**Input:** Source domain dataset $\mathbf{X}_S = \{\mathbf{X}_S^i\}_{i=1}^n$ and the labels $\mathbf{Y}_S = \{\mathbf{Y}_S^i\}_{i=1}^n$, target domain dataset $\mathbf{X}_T$

**Output:** Predicted target domain emotional state $\hat{\mathbf{Y}}_T$

1  Random initialize $E_P^{1 \sim n}$, $C_P^{1 \sim n}$, $E_C$, $E_S$ and $C_S$
2  **Training phase:**
3      **for** Epochs **do**
4          sources = 1: n
5          **for** sources **do**
6              $E_C(\mathbf{X}_S) \to \mathbf{X}_S'$, $E_C(\mathbf{X}_T) \to \mathbf{X}_T'$
7              $E_P(\mathbf{X}_S') \to \mathbf{F}_{SP}$, $E_P(\mathbf{X}_T') \to \mathbf{F}_{TP}$
8              $(\mathbf{F}_{SP}^{1 \sim n}, \mathbf{F}_{TP}^{1 \sim n}) \to (6)$, $(\mathbf{F}_{TP}^i, \mathbf{F}_{TP}^j)^{1 \sim n} \to (7)$
9              **Parallel:**
10                 $E_S(\mathbf{X}_S') \to \mathbf{F}_{SS}$, $E_S(\mathbf{X}_T') \to \mathbf{F}_{TS}$
11                 $(\mathbf{F}_{TP}^{1 \sim n}, \mathbf{F}_{TS}) \to (8)$, $(\mathbf{F}_{SP}^{1 \sim n}, \mathbf{F}_{SS}) \to (10)$
12                 $C_P^{1 \sim n}(\mathbf{F}_{SP}^{1 \sim n})$, $C_S(\mathbf{F}_{SS}) \to (9)(11)$
13                 Update network by minimizing the total loss $\to (12)$
14          **end**
15      **end**
16  **Test phase:**
17      $E_P^{1 \sim n}(E_C(\mathbf{X}_T)) \to \mathbf{F}_{TP}^{1 \sim n}$, $E_S(E_C(\mathbf{X}_T)) \to \mathbf{F}_{TS}$
18      Predict target labels $(\mathbf{F}_{TP}^{1 \sim n}, \mathbf{F}_{TS}) \to (13)$
19  **Return:** $\hat{\mathbf{Y}}_T$

# 4    Experiments

## 4.1    Dataset and Preprocessing

We evaluate the proposed network on SEED [3,24] and SEED-IV [25], which are commonly-used public datasets for emotion recognition based on EEG. For the datasets of SEED and SEED-IV, 15 Chinese participants were required to watch 15 film clips to elicit their emotion. The raw data are recorded at a sampling rate of 1000 Hz with an international 10–20 system using the ESI NeuroScan System by a 62-channel electrode cap. The preprocessed data is downsampled 200 Hz and filtered with a bandpass filter of 0–75 Hz to eliminate the interference of environment. The differential entropy (DE) features are then extracted with a non-overlapping one-second Hanning window from five frequency bands, $\delta$: 1–3 Hz, $\theta$: 4–7 Hz, $\alpha$: 8–13 Hz, $\beta$: 14–30 Hz, $\gamma$: 31–50 Hz [3]. The number of samples for each subject is 3394, and each sample has the feature dimensions of 310 (62 channels multiplied by five frequency bands). The SEED dataset includes three emotion categories, which are positive, neutral and negative. While the emotion categories in the dataset of SEED-IV are neutral, sad, fear and happy.

## 4.2    Implementation Details

To examine the effectiveness of handling the cross-subject emotion recognition problem and fairly compare with other research results, we evaluate the proposed network with Leave-One-Subject-Out strategy. Specifically in each epoch, we select one subject as the target one with unlabeled data and the other fourteen subjects as the source subjects.

The common extractor is a 3-layer multilayer perceptron with nodes 310-256-128-64 to extract the low-level features. We choose one linear layer for each private extractor to reduce the feature dimensions from 64 to 32 followed by a 1-D BatchNorm layer. Each private classifier is a single fully-connected network with a hidden dimension from 32 to the number of emotion categories. The shared extractor and shared classifier have the same structure as the private extractors and private classifiers, respectively. The LeakyRelu activation function is used in all hidden layers. In addition, we also normalize all the data by the electrode-wise method used in [20] to get better performance.

For the hyper-parameters in (12), considering the trade-off among the constituent losses, we set $\alpha = \frac{2}{1+e^{-10 \times i/iteration}} - 1$ and $\beta = \gamma = \frac{\alpha}{100}$. The different values of learning rate and batch size are compared on the SEED dataset in Fig. 2. It can be seen from Fig. 2 that with the learning rate being 0.01 and batch size 32, our model achieves the highest accuracy. Furthermore, the adam optimizer is applied as the optimizing function and the epoch is set to be 200. The whole framework is implemented by PyTorch.

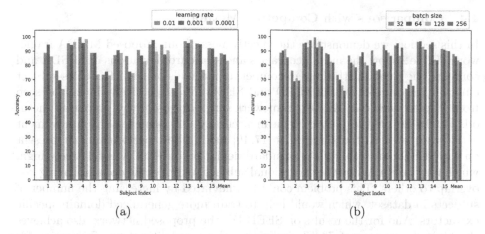

**Fig. 2.** The hyper-parameter selections on SEED, (a) learning rate and (b) batch size.

**Table 1.** Ablation study running on SEED and SEED-IV

| Variants | SEED | | SEED-IV | |
|---|---|---|---|---|
| | Mean | Std. | Mean | Std. |
| **MISDA** | **88.1%** | **9.5%** | **73.8%** | **11.9%** |
| w/o $L_{mmd}$ | 82.5% | 8.4% | 66.3% | 12.5% |
| w/o $L_{was}$ | 85.3% | 10.5% | 70.6% | 12.6% |
| w/o $L_{diff}$ | 84.5% | 10.9% | 70.8% | 10.7% |
| w/o $L_{was}$ and $L_{diff}$ | 83.6% | 10.3% | 68.6% | 11.4% |
| w/o $L_{mmd}$, $L_{was}$ and $L_{diff}$ | 76.1% | 9.7% | 67.5% | 12.8% |

w/o $L_*$ means the framework trained without the loss $L_*$.

### 4.3 Ablation Study

To demonstrate the effect of each module in MISDA, we give the performance of ablated framework on the datasets of SEED and SEED-IV as shown in Table 1.

Here the recognition performance is measured by the metrics of mean accuracy (Mean) and standard deviation (Std.). It can be seen from Table 1 that, three loss functions all contribute to improve the recognition performance, and achieve mean accuracies of 88.1% and 73.8% with standard deviations of 9.5% and 11.9% on the SEED and SEED-IV, respectively. In addition, the result without $L_{mmd}$ has a more significant drop compared with those removing one of other two losses, showing the importance of narrowing the distance between source and target domains. Furthermore it should be noticed that, depriving $L_{was}$ and $L_{diff}$ simultaneously would decrease the performance much more than removing either of them. This indicates by conjuncting $L_{was}$ to provide the closer private domain, the $L_{diff}$ loss could locate the shared domain more compactly, which contributes to strengthen the domain adaptation ability of network.

## 4.4    Comparisons with Competing Methods

In this section, we demonstrate the effectiveness of our proposed MISDA framework. Table 2 show the mean accuracies and standard deviations of MISDA and compare the results with those of competing methods on the EEG cross-subject emotion recognition task of SEED and SEED-IV, respectively. It can be seen from Table 2 that our MISDA framework outperforms other competing methods [14,16–20] in the metric of mean accuracy and achieves an improvement of 1% compared to the algorithms [17,19] having best performance at present on the SEED dataset. But the standard deviation of MISDA is relatively high, which may be caused by the exceptional subject with specific domain having less overlap to others. This problem could be alleviated by increasing the number of subjects in dataset, which would help to train more generalized domain-specific extractors. And for the results on SEED-IV, the proposed network also achieves the highest accuracy of 73.8%, indicating the generality of our framework for domain adaptation on EEG emotion recognition.

**Table 2.** Performance comparisons with competing methods on SEED and SEED-IV

| Methods | SEED | | SEED-IV | |
|---|---|---|---|---|
| | Mean | Std. | Mean | Std. |
| DResNET [14] | 85.3% | 8.0% | – | – |
| DANN [16] | 79.2% | 13.1% | - | – |
| DDC [16] | – | – | 54.3% | 4.2% |
| DAN [16] | 83.8% | 8.6% | 69.8% | 4.2% |
| WGANDA [17] | 87.1% | 7.1% | – | – |
| PPDA [18] | 86.7% | 7.1% | – | – |
| MEER-NET [19] | 87.1% | 2.0% | 71.0% | 12.1% |
| MS-MDA [20] | 81.6% | 9.1% | 59.3% | 5.5% |
| **MISDA (Ours)** | **88.1%** | **9.5%** | **73.8%** | **11.9%** |

Further in order to show the recognition ability of MISDA framework among different emotion categories, Fig. 3 shows the confusion matrix of predictions made on the SEED and SEED-IV datasets. It can be seen from Fig. 3(a) that on the SEED dataset, our network achieves the recognition accuracies of 83.8%, 90.4% and 87.8% respectively on the emotion categories of negative, neutral and positive, showing strong discriminative capability across emotion. The results on the SEED-IV dataset as shown in Fig. 3(b) indicate that, our model can obtain decent accuracies for the emotion categories of neutral, sad and happy. While for the category of fear, the proposed MISDA confuses it with sad because these two emotions are relatively similar on EEG signals.

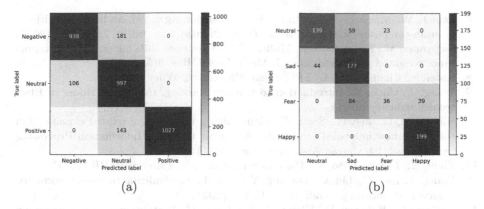

**Fig. 3.** The confusion matrices of predictions on (a) SEED and (b) SEED-IV, the value of square represents the number of samples.

## 5    Conclusion

In this paper, we propose the MISDA network for cross-subject EEG emotion recognition, which not only divides the EEG representations into private components specific to the subject and shared features universal to all subjects, but also cares the relationship between individual difference and group commonality. In order to narrow the distance among different private domains, the was-loss is also proposed in conjunction with diff-loss, enhancing the domain adaptation ability of the network. Furthermore, we also propose the dynamic weighting strategy to balance the shared and private information, so as to adjust the optimization of network. The performance of our network has been evaluated by conducting Leave-One-Subject-Out cross-validation on the datasets of SEED and SEED-IV, which outperforms competing methods by the mean accuracies of 88.1% and 73.8%, respectively. Our future work will concentrate on reducing the variance by improving the stability of network.

## References

1. Yang, H., Rong, P., Sun, G.: Subject-independent emotion recognition based on entropy of EEG signals. In: the 33rd Chinese Control and Decision Conference, pp. 1513–1518. IEEE (2021)
2. Zheng, W.L., Zhu, J.Y.: Identifying stable patterns over time for emotion recognition from eeg. IEEE Trans. Affect. Comput. **10**, 417–429 (2017)
3. Zheng, W.L., Lu, B.L.: Investigating critical frequency bands and channels for EEG-based emotion recognition with deep neural networks. IEEE Trans. Auton. Ment. Dev. **7**(3), 162–175 (2015)
4. Pfurtscheller, G., Müller-Putz, G.R., Scherer, R., Neuper, C.: Rehabilitation with brain-computer interface systems. Computer **41**(10), 58–65 (2008)
5. Putnam, K.M., McSweeney, L.B.: Depressive symptoms and baseline prefrontal EEG alpha activity: a study utilizing ecological momentary assessment. Biol. Psychol. **77**(2), 237–240 (2008)

6. Samek, W., Meinecke, F.C., Müller, K.R.: Transferring subspaces between subjects in brain-computer interfacing. IEEE Trans. Biomed. Eng. **60**(8), 2289–2298 (2013)
7. Sugiyama, M., Krauledat, M., Müller, K.R.: Covariate shift adaptation by importance weighted cross validation. J. Mach. Learn. Res. **8**(5) (2007)
8. Sanei, S., Chambers, J.A.: EEG Signal Processing. Wiley (2013)
9. Wang, J., Chen, Y.: Introduction to transfer learning. Publishing House of Electronics Industry (2021)
10. Blanchard, G., Lee, G., Scott, C.: Generalizing from several related classification tasks to a new unlabeled sample. In: Advances in Neural Information Processing Systems. vol. 24. Curran Associates, Inc. (2011)
11. Zhou, K., Liu, Z., Qiao, Y.: Domain generalization: a survey. CoRR (2021)
12. Wang, J., Lan, C., Liu, C., Ouyang, Y., Qin, T.: Generalizing to unseen domains: a survey on domain generalization. CoRR (2021)
13. Ghifary, M., Balduzzi, D., Kleijn, W.B., Zhang, M.: Scatter component analysis: a unified framework for domain adaptation and domain generalization. IEEE Trans. Pattern Anal. Mach. Intell. **39**(7), 1414–1430 (2016)
14. Ma, B.-Q., Li, H., Zheng, W.-L., Lu, B.-L.: Reducing the subject variability of EEG signals with adversarial domain generalization. In: Gedeon, T., Wong, K.W., Lee, M. (eds.) ICONIP 2019. LNCS, vol. 11953, pp. 30–42. Springer, Cham (2019). https://doi.org/10.1007/978-3-030-36708-4_3
15. Zheng, W.L., Lu, B.L.: Personalizing EEG-based affective models with transfer learning. In: Proceedings of the International Joint Conference on Artificial Intelligence, pp. 2732–2738 (2016)
16. Li, H., Jin, Y.-M., Zheng, W.-L., Lu, B.-L.: Cross-subject emotion recognition using deep adaptation networks. In: Cheng, L., Leung, A.C.S., Ozawa, S. (eds.) ICONIP 2018. LNCS, vol. 11305, pp. 403–413. Springer, Cham (2018). https://doi.org/10.1007/978-3-030-04221-9_36
17. Luo, Y., Zhang, S.-Y., Zheng, W.-L., Lu, B.-L.: WGAN domain adaptation for EEG-based emotion recognition. In: Cheng, L., Leung, A.C.S., Ozawa, S. (eds.) ICONIP 2018. LNCS, vol. 11305, pp. 275–286. Springer, Cham (2018). https://doi.org/10.1007/978-3-030-04221-9_25
18. Zhao, L.M., Yan, X., Lu, B.L.: Plug-and-play domain adaptation for cross-subject EEG-based emotion recognition. In: Proceedings of the 35th AAAI Conference on Artificial Intelligence, pp. 863–870 (2021)
19. Chen, H., Li, Z., Jin, M., Li, J.: MEERNet: multi-source EEG-based emotion recognition network for generalization across subjects and sessions. In: Annual International Conference of IEEE Engineering in Medicine & Biology Society. pp. 6094–6097 (2021)
20. Chen, H., Jin, M., Li, Z., Fan, C., Li, J., He, H.: MS-MDA: multisource marginal distribution adaptation for cross-subject and cross-session EEG emotion recognition. Frontiers in Neuroscience 15 (2021)
21. Borgwardt, K.M., Gretton, A., Rasch, M.J.: Integrating structured biological data by kernel maximum mean discrepancy. Bioinformatics **22**(14), e49–e57 (2006)
22. Pan, S.J., Tsang, I.W., Kwok, J.T., Yang, Q.: Domain adaptation via transfer component analysis. IEEE Trans. Neural Networks **22**(2), 199–210 (2011)
23. Arjovsky, M., Chintala, S., Bottou, L.: Wasserstein generative adversarial networks. In: International Conference on Machine Learning. pp. 214–223 (2017)

24. Liu, W., Qiu, J.L., Zheng, W.L., Lu, B.L.: Comparing recognition performance and robustness of multimodal deep learning models for multimodal emotion recognition. IEEE Trans. Cognitive Dev. Syst. (2021)
25. Zheng, W.L., Liu, W., Lu, Y., Lu, B.L., Cichocki, A.: Emotionmeter: a multimodal framework for recognizing human emotions. IEEE Trans. Cybern. **49**(3), 1110–1122 (2019)

# Spatial-Channel Mixed Attention Based Network for Remote Heart Rate Estimation

Bixiao Ling, Pengfei Zhang, Jianjun Qian[✉], and Jian Yang

PCA Lab, Key Lab of Intelligent Perception and Systems for High-Dimensional Information of Ministry of Education, and Jiangsu Key Lab of Image and Video Understanding for Social Security, School of Computer Science and Engineering, Nanjing University of Science and Technology, Nanjing, China
{lingbixiao,zhangpengfei,csjqian,csjyang}@njust.edu.cn

**Abstract.** Recently, remote heart rate (HR) estimation has attracted increasing attention. Some previous methods employ the Spatial-Temporal Map (STMap) of facial sequences to estimate HR. However, STMap ignores that each facial regions play a different role in HR estimation task. Moreover, how to focus on key facial regions to improve the performance of HR estimation is also a challenging problem. To overcome this issue, this paper proposes a novel Spatial-Channel Mixed Attention Module (SCAM) to select the facial regions with high correlation for HR estimation adaptively. To our best knowledge, we are the first to design an attention module for STMap in the HR estimation task. Furthermore, the whole HR estimation framework SCANet is proposed, including feature extraction, signal generation, and HR regression. The experiments performed on three benchmark datasets show that the proposed method achieves better performance over state-of-the-art methods.

**Keywords:** Remote heart rate estimation · Spatial-temporal map · Spatial-channel mixed attention

## 1 Introduction

Heart rate (HR) is an important physiological indicator of human health status. Traditionally, HR signals are measured based on electrocardiography (ECG) and photoplethysmography (PPG), both of which require direct contact with human skin, which limits the application to scenarios such as traumatized patients and daily patient monitoring. Due to this limitation, remote and non-contact HR measurement techniques based on remote photoplethysmography (rPPG) have attracted increasing interest in recent years [6,29]. The principle of this technique is that the skin color will periodically change with the periodic blood volume changes induced by the heartbeat. People can measure HR by capturing this skin color variations. It has been proved that the measurement of HR can be

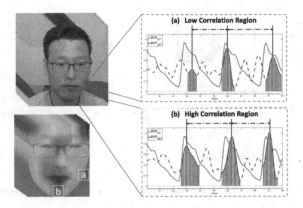

**Fig. 1.** Illustration of BVP signal estimated from different face regions. Due to motion, illumination, and uneven distribution of microvessel density in the face, different regions have inconsistent correlations with HR. The heatmap is generated by our method. $\mathbf{BVP}_{GT}$: the Ground-truth Blood Volume Pulse. $\mathbf{BVP}_{EST}$: the Estimated BVP signal generated by [3].

realised by extracting subtle color variations of facial skin from a distance of several meters using cameras [30].

Early rPPG-based HR measurement methods usually used CHROM [3] and POS [31] to extract the blood volumn pulse (BVP) signal or decomposed the raw temporal signal using PCA or ICA [1,16,22,23]. However, the traditional methods are relatively simple and cannot obtain critical physiological information, and there is still much room for improving the accuracy of HR measurement. With the great success of deep learning in various tasks of computer vision in recent years [7,25], rPPG-based HR measurement methods have also started to turn to deep learning methods [2,14,18,21,33].

Considering the low peak signal-to-noise ratio (PSNR) of the BVP signal in face video, dense sampling of the face image can introduce more noise to the HR signal. Some researches [14,17,18] first compute a preliminary feature representation Spatial-Temporal Map (STMap) [17] by spatial region segmentation and time series stitching of the face video. Because STMap can avoid the disadvantages of the above methods by suppressing extraneous noise while preserving color statistical information.

However, the human faces are not ideal Lambertian objects. As shown in Fig. 1, the rPPG signals estimated from various regions often lack consistency due to motion, illumination, and uneven distribution of microvessel density in the face. Only some regions called ROI are highly correlated with HR. How to select ROI is very important for HR estimation.

Several studies have analyzed the influence of different facial regions on the quality of rPPG signals in recent years [9,10,12]. Furthermore, there are also works [2,15,20,33] to improve the accuracy of HR estimation proposed from the perspective of spatial dimension. DeepPhys [2] and rPPGNet [33] select ROI based on the skin segmentation implemented by attention mechanism. Niu *et al.* [20] introduced CBAM [32] into the HR estimation model for changing

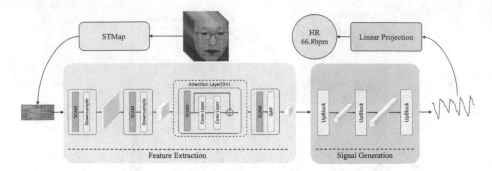

**Fig. 2.** The overview of our HR estimation approach with spatial-channel mixed attention network(SCANet).

the weights of feature. Nevertheless, these attentions are designed for traditional vision models and may not be suitable for HR estimation tasks.

To address these problems, we propose a Spatial-Channel Mixed Attention Network (SCANet) for HR estimation. Our framework consists of three parts: feature extraction, signal generation and HR estimation. Specifically, we design a novel spatial-channel mixed attention module (SCAM) in feature extraction. This module can weight the ROI and focus on the higher correlation region with the target HR to solve the problem of inconsistent correlation in each ROI.

In summary, our contributions can be summarized as follows:

- We propose a novel spatial-channel mixed attention module (SCAM) to highlight facial regions with strong HR signals and select the highly correlated regions with HR adaptively.
- Based on SCAM, the proposed HR estimation framework SCANet achieves state-of-the-art performance on three public datasets. It is worth mentioning that our method reduces the mean absolute error from 4.93 bpm to 4.64 bpm on the VIPL-HR dataset.

## 2    Spatial-Channel Mixed Attention Network

### 2.1    Spatial-Temporal Map

To learn the mapping from the input feature to the target signals, STMap extracted from ROI have recently been adopted as a refined form of input for deep learning frameworks to exclude major irrelevant elements such as face-shape attributes [14,17,19,20]. Following the method [20], we generate STMap with a size of $S \times T \times C$. $S$ represents the number of face regions, $T$ stands for the time sequence of T-frame images, and $C$ denotes the number of color channels.

### 2.2    Spatial-Channel Mixed Attention Module

Due to physiological variables such as uneven distribution of micro-vessel density in facial skin tissues, as well as external elements such as illumination variation,

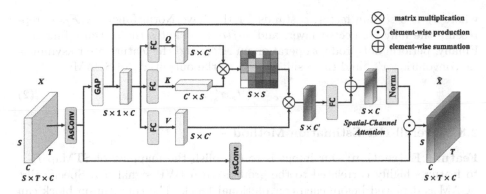

**Fig. 3.** The spatial-channel mixed attention module (SCAM), which aims to weight the ROI and focus on the higher correlation region with HR. **AsConv**: Asymmetric convolution, the default kernel size is 1×3.

occlusion, head movement, the BVP and noise distributions of each ROI are different. Since each row of the STMap represents the original temporal signal for one ROI on the face in the HR estimation task, existing methods, such as [20,33], adjust the weight of each row of the STMap by alternately performing spatial-temporal attention and channel attention to solve the above problem. However, such a manner also changes the weight of each column of the STMap which represents the raw spatial information for one frame. As indicated in [10,19], the BVP signals from different ROI should be nearly synchronized, which means that the contribution of each frame can be regarded as equal in the time dimension. Thus, using temporal attention may be unreasonable and will affect the waveform and period of the predicted BVP signal $S_{pre}$. In another aspect, it is difficult to adjust ROI weights by using attention in the channel dimension alone.

To solve these problems, we propose a spatial-channel mixed attention module inspired by ViT [5]. By calculating the correlation between each spatial-channel feature and others, SCAM can adjust the feature representation ability between signals in different regions, thereby filtering out feature information that can highly reflect HR. As shown in Fig 3, for the input $\mathbf{x}_{stc} \in \mathbb{R}^{S \times T \times C}$ of the module, the global average pooling layer is first used to aggregate the temporal dimension information and obtain the features $\mathbf{x}_{sc} \in \mathbb{R}^{S \times 1 \times C}$. Furthermore, $\mathbf{x}_{sc}$ is projected into the corresponding $q_{sc}$, $k_{sc}$ and $v_{sc}$ matrix through three different fully connected layers. Through the matrix operation of $q_{sc}$ and $k_{sc}^T$, the correlation matrix of each face region can be calculated. This matrix is then normalized using the softmax function and computed with $v_{sc}$ to obtain an attention weighted representation of different spatial regions. In addition, SCAM retains the original feature $\mathbf{x}_{sc}$ through residual connections. Through the above calculation, the attention matrix $Att_{sc}$ of different ROI and channels can be obtained. The specific calculation expression is as follows:

$$Att_{sc} = \phi(\mathcal{F}_{fc}(softmax(\frac{q_{sc}k_{sc}^T}{\sqrt{d_k}})v_{sc} + x_{sc}), \tag{1}$$

where $d_k$ is a scaling factor, $\phi$ stands for the LayerNorm function, $\mathcal{F}_{fc}(\cdot)$ represents the fully connected layer, and $softmax$ denotes the softmax function. Finally, perform dot product operation on $Att_{sc}$ and the feature after asymmetric convolution $x'_{sc}$, and the result is used as the output $\hat{x}_{sc}$ of SCAM:

$$\hat{x}_{sc} = Att_{sc}x'_{sc}. \tag{2}$$

## 2.3   Overall HR Estimation Method

**Feature Extraction:** Our intent is to establish the mapping of STMap $I_{stm}$ to features highly correlated to the ground-truth BVP signal $S_{gt}$. Specifically, SCAM is deployed before each convolutional block. The convolution block can be a downsampling layer or a residual convolution block borrowed from ResNet [7]. Given the input STMap $I_{stm}$, we can get the raw signal $S_{raw}$:

$$S_{raw} = P(B_n(B_{n-1}(...B_1(I_{stm})...))), \tag{3}$$

where $B_n$ denotes the $n$-th joint SCAM and convolutional block, $P(\cdot)$ stands for the average pooling function.

**Signal Generation and HR Regression:** These two steps simply include three upsample blocks to generate the predicted BVP signal $S_{pre}$ and a fully connected layer to regress the output $HR_{out}$:

$$HR_{out} = \mathcal{F}_{fc}(S_{pre}) = \mathcal{F}_{fc}(DeConv(S_{raw})), \tag{4}$$

where $\mathcal{F}_{fc}(\cdot)$ indicates the fully connected layer and $DeConv(\cdot)$ represents deconvolution operation.

**Loss Function:** Here, four constraint term are employed to improve the robustness of the generated signal.Specifically, We use a negative Pearson correlation loss [33] since it is proved to be an effective function to define the similarity between the ground-truth BVP signal $S_{gt}$ and the predicted BVP signal $S_{pre}$:

$$\mathcal{L}_p = 1 - \frac{Cov(S_{pre}, S_{gt})}{\sqrt{Cov(S_{pre}, S_{pre})}\sqrt{Cov(S_{gt}, S_{gt})}}, \tag{5}$$

where $Cov(x,y)$ is the covariance of x and y. Meanwhile, $L_1$ Loss is also used for evaluating the quality of predicted BVP signal $S_{pre}$:

$$\mathcal{L}_{sig} = \frac{1}{T}\sum_{t=1}^{T}|S_{pre}^{(t)} - S_{gt}^{(t)}|, \tag{6}$$

where $T$ is the length of time contained in the signal. To better calculate the estimated HR $HR_{est}$ from the predicted BVP signal $S_{pre}$, the SNR loss is applied which is a frequency domain loss to define the cross-entropy between the predicted BVP signal $S_{pre}$ and the ground-truth HR value $HR_{gt}$:

$$\mathcal{L}_{snr} = CE(PSD(S_{pre}), HR_{gt}), \tag{7}$$

**Table 1.** HR estimation results by our method and several state-of-the-art methods on the VIPL-HR database. Best: **bold**.

| Method | Std (bpm) ↓ | MAE (bpm) ↓ | RMSE (bpm) ↓ | r ↑ |
|---|---|---|---|---|
| DeepPhy [2] | 13.6 | 11.0 | 13.8 | 0.11 |
| Niu2019 [20] | 7.99 | 5.40 | 7.99 | 0.66 |
| RhythmNet [18] | 8.11 | 5.30 | 8.14 | 0.76 |
| CVD [19] | 7.92 | 5.02 | 7.97 | 0.79 |
| Dual-GAN [14] | 7.63 | 4.93 | 7.68 | 0.81 |
| SCANet(Ours) | **7.17** | **4.64** | **7.22** | **0.82** |

**Table 2.** HR estimation results by our method and several state-of-the-art methods on the MAHNOB-HCI database. Best: **bold**.

| Method | Std (bpm) ↓ | MAE (bpm) ↓ | RMSE (bpm) ↓ | r ↑ |
|---|---|---|---|---|
| HR-CNN [27] | – | 7.25 | 9.24 | 0.51 |
| STVEN+rPPGNet [33] | 5.57 | 4.03 | 5.93 | 0.88 |
| RhythmNet [18] | 3.98 | – | 4.00 | 0.87 |
| Meta-rPPG [11] | 4.90 | 3.01 | – | 0.85 |
| Deep-HR [24] | 3.47 | – | **3.41** | 0.92 |
| SCANet(Ours) | **3.40** | **2.90** | 3.42 | **0.93** |

where $CE(x,y)$ denotes the cross-entropy loss of the input $x$ and groud-truth $y$, $PSD(s)$ denotes the power spectral density of the input signal $s$. Naturally, for the final HR regression task, we also calculate the $L_1$ distance between the estimated HR $HR_{est}$ and the ground-truth HR value $HR_{gt}$ for supervision. The final loss for HR estimation is:

$$\mathcal{L} = \lambda_{hr}||HR_{est} - HR_{gt}||_1 + \lambda_p \mathcal{L}_p + \lambda_{sig}\mathcal{L}_{sig} + \lambda_{snr}\mathcal{L}_{snr}, \tag{8}$$

where $\lambda_{hr}, \lambda_p, \lambda_{sig}$ and $\lambda_{snr}$ are corresponding balancing parameters.

## 3 Experiment

### 3.1 Databases and Experiment Settings

**VIPL-HR** [17] is a large-scale database for HR estimation, which contains 2378 visible light videos. 107 subjects participated in the construction of the dataset, and the RGB videos are recorded by 3 different devices based on 9 facial scenarios. Each video records the subject's physiological information, such as HR, at a frame rate of 25 to 30 fps.

**MAHNOB-HCI.** [26] contains 527 facial videos of with 61 fps frame rate and 780×580 resolution from 27 subjects. Following [18], we downsample the videos from 61 fps to 30.5 fps for efficiency. By referring to the previous work [13,33],

**Table 3.** HR estimation results by our method and several state-of-the-art methods on the PURE database. Best: **bold**.

| Method | MAE (bpm) ↓ | RMSE (bpm) ↓ | r↑ |
|---|---|---|---|
| 2SR [4] | 2.44 | 3.06 | 0.98 |
| CHROM [3] | 2.07 | 9.92 | 0.99 |
| HR-CNN [27] | 1.84 | 2.37 | 0.98 |
| Dual-GAN [14] | **0.82** | 1.31 | 0.99 |
| SCANet(Ours) | 0.83 | **1.06** | **0.996** |

**Table 4.** Ablation study of effectiveness of SCAM for HR estimation on VIPL-HR. Best: **bold**.

| Attention | Std (bpm) ↓ | MAE (bpm) ↓ | RMSE (bpm) ↓ | r ↑ |
|---|---|---|---|---|
| – | 8.42 | 5.46 | 8.43 | 0.75 |
| CBAM [32] | 7.74 | 4.95 | 7.71 | 0.79 |
| SE [8] | 7.80 | 4.91 | 7.84 | 0.79 |
| SCAM(Ours) | **7.17** | **4.64** | **7.22** | **0.82** |

we use the EXG2 channel[1] signal to generate the corresponding HR value which is measured by an ECG sensor. Meanwhile, we clean-up and calculate the HR based on the ECG sensor information by *qrs_detector* function from the MNE package[2]. Following [2,33], we also use only a 30-second (frames 306 to 2135) clip of each video in our experiments.

**PURE** [28] is a widely used public database including 60 RGB videos from 10 subjects in 6 different head motion scenarios. Each video was recorded by an eco274CVGE camera with 30 fps frame rate and 640×480 resolution. Meanwhile, the BVP signals were captured using CMS50E and reduced to 30 fps to align with the videos.

**Training Details:** For all datasets, a uniform preprocessing method was applied. We set the number of face region divisions being $S = 25$, the sliding window of $T = 300$ frames, and the interval of the sliding window being 0.5s. The estimated HR is obtained according to its frame rate:

$$HR_{est} = \frac{HR_{out} \times fps}{T/60}, \tag{9}$$

where, $fps$ denotes the frame rate and 60 represents 60 s per minute. Random horizontal flip and random crop are applied to the STMap and corresponding signal before feeding input into the network. Meanwhile, the data augmentation method uses the strategy proposed in [20] as well as the random mask strategy to simulate the situation when the face is missing detected. Our method is

---

[1] The position of ECG sensor is upper left corner of chest and under clavicle bone.
[2] https://github.com/mne-tools/mne-python.

**Table 5.** Ablation study of loss function for HR estimation on VIPL-HR. Best: **bold**.

| $\mathcal{L}_{hr}$ | $\mathcal{L}_p$ | $\mathcal{L}_{sig}$ | $\mathcal{L}_{snr}$ | Std (bpm) ↓ | MAE (bpm) ↓ | RMSE (bpm) ↓ | $r$ ↑ |
|---|---|---|---|---|---|---|---|
| ✓ |   | ✓ | ✓ | 7.28 | 4.67 | 7.26 | 0.81 |
| ✓ | ✓ |   | ✓ | 7.35 | 4.71 | 7.37 | 0.80 |
| ✓ | ✓ | ✓ |   | 7.19 | 4.66 | 7.24 | 0.81 |
| ✓ | ✓ | ✓ | ✓ | **7.17** | **4.64** | **7.22** | **0.82** |

**Table 6.** Ablation study of muti-head for HR estimation on VIPL-HR. Best: **bold**.

| Head | Std (bpm) ↓ | MAE (bpm) ↓ | RMSE (bpm) ↓ | $r$ ↑ |
|---|---|---|---|---|
| 8 | 7.59 | 4.82 | 7.45 | 0.80 |
| 4 | 7.53 | 4.83 | 7.41 | 0.80 |
| 2 | 7.56 | 4.76 | 7.44 | 0.80 |
| 1 | **7.17** | **4.64** | **7.22** | **0.82** |

implemented in the PyTorch[3] and trained on NVIDIA TITAN RTX. We train all model for 50 epochs via the Adam optimizer with the initial learning rate of 0.001. The all balance parameter for loss functions defaults to 1. Especially, the batch size of VIPL-HR and MAHNOB-HCI databases being 128, and PURE being 32. The ground truth signal in VIPL-HR and PURE are BVP, but in MAHNOB-HCI is ECG.

**Performance Metrics:** To validate the performance of HR estimation approaches, a number of different evaluation metrics are appiled [13,18]. We choose four widely used metrics among them: the standard deviation (Std) of the HR error, the mean absolute HR error (MAE), the root mean squared HR error (RMSE), and Pearson's correlation coefficients $r$ [13].

## 3.2   Comparison with State-of-the-arts

We evaluate the effectiveness of the proposed method on three public datasets VIPL-HR [17], MAHNOB-HCI [26], and PURE [28]. For the sake of fairness, experiments follow [18,19] and use a 5-fold subject-exclusive cross-validation protocol on VIPL-HR. In addition, the train/test split is same as [17]. Our method is compared with five baseline methods on VIPL-HR, in which the results of other methods are directly from [14,18]. As shown in Table 1, our method achieves superior results over most of the significant metrics. Similarly, a three-fold subject-independent cross-validation protocol is adopt following [18,33] for the MAHNOB-HCI database. We compared our method with five baseline methods on this database. All experimental results are shown in Table 2, the proposed method again outperforms all the baseline methods. For PURE dataset, experiments follow [27] and use the same protocol to compare with four baseline

---

[3] https://pytorch.org/.

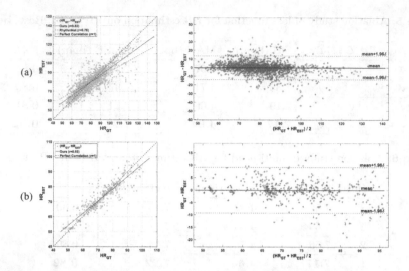

**Fig. 4.** The scatter plots and the Bland-Altman plot of HR$_{GT}$, HR$_{EST}$ on the VIPL-HR (a) and MAHNOB-HCI (b) database. HR$_{GT}$: the Ground-truth HR. HR$_{EST}$: the Estimated HR by our method. The green dashed line in (a) is borrowed from the original paper [18]. (Color figure online)

methods, for which their performance are directly borrowed from [14]. Table 3 shows that our method can achieve the same result as the best. According to the above results, our method is very effective for HR estimation, which achieves state-of-the-art performance and can generalize to other database.

### 3.3 Ablation Study

**Impact of SCAM:** As illustrated in the Table 4, the SCAM play vital roles in SCANet. We designed some experiments according to the attention previously used for the HR estimation task. Obviously, SCAM can help our method to reduce the MAE and RMSE by 0.82 and 1.21, respectively. This also support our view that SCAM is able to select ROI with higher correlation with HR information.

**Impact of Loss Function:** Further, the effectiveness of the loss function for training model is evaluated. We listed the prediction results by taking one loss function away for training as shown in Table 5. Here, we actually focus on evaluating three loss functions since the importance of the L1 loss $\mathcal{L}_{hr}$ of HR is obviously. From Table 5, we can see clearly that the absence of each loss function will cause the performance of the model to degrade. It is interesting to find that $\mathcal{L}_{sig}$ has the most impact on the model from the second row. However, many previous work on generating BVP signal overlook this loss constraint term.

**Impact of Muti-Head:** Comparing with multi-head attention in ViT [5], we design experiments with different numbers of heads. Table 6 shows that the best

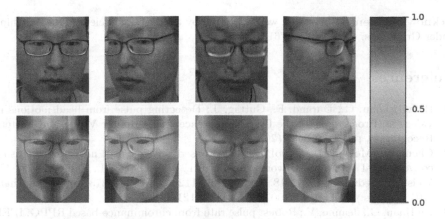

**Fig. 5.** Visualization of the discriminating face regions that the SCAM focused on.

result is achieved when head is set to 1. But it is not normal results as in common vision tasks. The results show that traditional attention models are not well for HR estimation task. HR feature is projected to multiple subspaces, which may destroy the information unity of STMap and interfere with the physiological information representation. Therefore, we discard the multi-head operation in our model.

### 3.4 Visualization and Analysis

We draw scatter plots and the Bland-Altman plot of $HR_{est}$ and $HR_{gt}$ on the VIPL-HR and MAHNOB-HCI database to clearly illustrate the improvement of the data correlation of our method in HR estimation task. As show in Fig. 4, this diagram indicates that most of the estimated HR are highly correlated with the ground-truth ones. Compare with RhythmNet which also gives the scatter, our method demonstrates a superior linear correlation of data on the VIPL-HR.

Furthermore, the attention map is visualized from the first SCAM acting on the input STMap. From the highlighted regions in the top of Fig. 5, we can draw a conclusion that SCAM focuses on the more continuous and larger skin regions facing the frontal view. Whether from the perspective of physiological principles or compared with previous work [9,12], these results are consistent with our prior knowledge.

## 4    Conclusion

This paper proposes an end-to-end spatial-channel mixed attention network (SCANet) based on the spatial-temporal map for HR estimation. The Spatial-Channel Mixed Attention Module can adaptively select effective ROI with richer physiological information. Extensive experiments demonstrate the superiority of our approach against the competed methods.

**Acknowledgments.** This work was supported by the National Science Fund of China under Grant Nos. 61876083,62176124.

# References

1. Balakrishnan, G., Durand, F., Guttag, J.: Detecting pulse from head motions in video. In: Proceedings of the IEEE Conference on Computer Vision and Pattern Recognition, pp. 3430–3437 (2013)
2. Chen, W., McDuff, D.: DeepPhys: video-based physiological measurement using convolutional attention networks. In: Ferrari, V., Hebert, M., Sminchisescu, C., Weiss, Y. (eds.) ECCV 2018. LNCS, vol. 11206, pp. 356–373. Springer, Cham (2018). https://doi.org/10.1007/978-3-030-01216-8_22
3. De Haan, G., Jeanne, V.: Robust pulse rate from chrominance-based RPPG. IEEE Trans. Biomed. Eng. **60**(10), 2878–2886 (2013)
4. De Haan, G., Van Leest, A.: Improved motion robustness of remote-PPG by using the blood volume pulse signature. Physiol. Meas. **35**(9), 1913 (2014)
5. Dosovitskiy, A., et al.: An image is worth $16 \times 16$ words: transformers for image recognition at scale. arXiv preprint arXiv:2010.11929 (2020)
6. Garbey, M., Sun, N., Merla, A., Pavlidis, I.: Contact-free measurement of cardiac pulse based on the analysis of thermal imagery. IEEE Trans. Biomed. Eng. **54**(8), 1418–1426 (2007)
7. He, K., Zhang, X., Ren, S., Sun, J.: Deep residual learning for image recognition. In: Proceedings of the IEEE Conference on Computer Vision and Pattern Recognition, pp. 770–778 (2016)
8. Hu, J., Shen, L., Sun, G.: Squeeze-and-excitation networks. In: Proceedings of the IEEE Conference on Computer Vision and Pattern Recognition, pp. 7132–7141 (2018)
9. Kwon, S., Kim, J., Lee, D., Park, K.: Roi analysis for remote photoplethysmography on facial video. In: 2015 37th Annual International Conference of the IEEE Engineering in Medicine and Biology Society, pp. 4938–4941. IEEE (2015)
10. Lam, A., Kuno, Y.: Robust heart rate measurement from video using select random patches. In: Proceedings of the IEEE Conference on Computer Vision and Pattern Recognition, pp. 3640–3648 (2015)
11. Lee, E., Chen, E., Lee, C.-Y.: Meta-rPPG: remote heart rate estimation using a transductive meta-learner. In: Vedaldi, A., Bischof, H., Brox, T., Frahm, J.-M. (eds.) ECCV 2020. LNCS, vol. 12372, pp. 392–409. Springer, Cham (2020). https://doi.org/10.1007/978-3-030-58583-9_24
12. Lempe, G., Zaunseder, S., Wirthgen, T., Zipser, S., Malberg, H.: Roi selection for remote photoplethysmography. In: Bildverarbeitung für die Medizin 2013, pp. 99–103. Springer, Heidelberg (2013)
13. Li, X., Chen, J., Zhao, G., Pietikainen, M.: Remote heart rate measurement from face videos under realistic situations. In: Proceedings of the IEEE Conference on Computer Vision and Pattern Recognition, pp. 4264–4271 (2014)
14. Lu, H., Han, H., Zhou, S.K.: Dual-gan: Joint bvp and noise modeling for remote physiological measurement. In: Proceedings of the IEEE/CVF Conference on Computer Vision and Pattern Recognition, pp. 12404–12413 (2021)
15. McDuff, D.: Deep super resolution for recovering physiological information from videos. In: Proceedings of the IEEE Conference on Computer Vision and Pattern Recognition Workshops, pp. 1367–1374 (2018)

16. McDuff, D., Gontarek, S., Picard, R.W.: Improvements in remote cardiopulmonary measurement using a five band digital camera. IEEE Trans. Biomed. Eng. **61**(10), 2593–2601 (2014)
17. Niu, X., Han, H., Shan, S., Chen, X.: VIPL-HR: a multi-modal database for pulse estimation from less-constrained face video. In: Jawahar, C.V., Li, H., Mori, G., Schindler, K. (eds.) ACCV 2018. LNCS, vol. 11365, pp. 562–576. Springer, Cham (2019). https://doi.org/10.1007/978-3-030-20873-8_36
18. Niu, X., Shan, S., Han, H., Chen, X.: Rhythmnet: end-to-end heart rate estimation from face via spatial-temporal representation. TIP **29**, 2409–2423 (2019)
19. Niu, X., Yu, Z., Han, H., Li, X., Shan, S., Zhao, G.: Video-based remote physiological measurement via cross-verified feature disentangling. In: Vedaldi, A., Bischof, H., Brox, T., Frahm, J.-M. (eds.) ECCV 2020. LNCS, vol. 12347, pp. 295–310. Springer, Cham (2020). https://doi.org/10.1007/978-3-030-58536-5_18
20. Niu, X., Zhao, X., Han, H., Das, A., Dantcheva, A., Shan, S., Chen, X.: Robust remote heart rate estimation from face utilizing spatial-temporal attention. In: 2019 14th IEEE International Conference on Automatic Face & Gesture Recognition, pp. 1–8. IEEE (2019)
21. Perepelkina, O., Artemyev, M., Churikova, M., Grinenko, M.: Hearttrack: Convolutional neural network for remote video-based heart rate monitoring. In: Proceedings of the IEEE/CVF Conference on Computer Vision and Pattern Recognition Workshops, pp. 288–289 (2020)
22. Poh, M.Z., McDuff, D.J., Picard, R.W.: Advancements in noncontact, multiparameter physiological measurements using a webcam. IEEE Trans. Biomed. Eng. **58**(1), 7–11 (2010)
23. Poh, M.Z., McDuff, D.J., Picard, R.W.: Non-contact, automated cardiac pulse measurements using video imaging and blind source separation. Opt. Express **18**(10), 10762–10774 (2010)
24. Sabokrou, M., Pourreza, M., Li, X., Fathy, M., Zhao, G.: Deep-hr: Fast heart rate estimation from face video under realistic conditions. arXiv preprint arXiv:2002.04821 (2020)
25. Simonyan, K., Zisserman, A.: Very deep convolutional networks for large-scale image recognition. arXiv preprint arXiv:1409.1556 (2014)
26. Soleymani, M., Lichtenauer, J., Pun, T., Pantic, M.: A multimodal database for affect recognition and implicit tagging. IEEE Trans. Affect. Comput. **3**(1), 42–55 (2011)
27. Špetlík, R., Franc, V., Matas, J.: Visual heart rate estimation with convolutional neural network. In: Proceedings of the british machine vision conference, Newcastle, UK, pp. 3–6 (2018)
28. Stricker, R., Müller, S., Gross, H.M.: Non-contact video-based pulse rate measurement on a mobile service robot. In: The 23rd IEEE International Symposium on Robot and Human Interactive Communication, pp. 1056–1062. IEEE (2014)
29. Ulyanov, S.S., Tuchin, V.V.: Pulse-wave monitoring by means of focused laser beams scattered by skin surface and membranes. In: Static and Dynamic Light Scattering in Medicine and Biology, vol. 1884, pp. 160–167. International Society for Optics and Photonics (1993)
30. Verkruysse, W., Svaasand, L.O., Nelson, J.S.: Remote plethysmographic imaging using ambient light. Opt. Express **16**(26), 21434–21445 (2008)
31. Wang, W., den Brinker, A.C., Stuijk, S., de Haan, G.: Algorithmic principles of remote ppg. IEEE Trans. Biomed. Eng. **64**(7), 1479–1491 (2016)

32. Woo, S., Park, J., Lee, J.-Y., Kweon, I.S.: CBAM: convolutional block attention module. In: Ferrari, V., Hebert, M., Sminchisescu, C., Weiss, Y. (eds.) ECCV 2018. LNCS, vol. 11211, pp. 3–19. Springer, Cham (2018). https://doi.org/10.1007/978-3-030-01234-2_1

33. Yu, Z., Peng, W., Li, X., Hong, X., Zhao, G.: Remote heart rate measurement from highly compressed facial videos: an end-to-end deep learning solution with video enhancement. In: Proceedings of the IEEE/CVF International Conference on Computer Vision, pp. 151–160 (2019)

# Weighted Graph Based Feature Representation for Finger-Vein Recognition

Ziyun Ye, Zihao Zhao, Mengna Wen, and Jinfeng Yang[✉]

Institute of Applied Artificial Intelligence of the Guangdong-Hong Kong-Macao Greater Bay Area, Shenzhen Polytechnic, Shenzhen 518055, China
jfyang@szpt.edu.cn

**Abstract.** Graph-based method is highly favorable for finger-vein recognition. The existing graph construct strategies are inflexible and unable to describe the vein networks effectively. In this paper, we propose a new weighted graph construction method for finger-vein network feature representation. First, a node-set generated by image division is reshaped according local vein-network skeleton. Then, the edges connecting adjacent nodes are weighted by considering both the content variations of blocks and the similarities between adjacent blocks. Therefore, the generated graphs using these nodes and weighted edges are capable in carrying both the global random patterns and the local variations contained in finger-vein networks. Experiments are implemented to show that the proposed method achieves better results than other existing methods.

**Keywords:** Finger-vein recognition · Weighted graph structure · Feature extraction

## 1 Introductionn

Finger-vein for human identification has been a hot topic in biometric recognition. Finger vein pattern has exhibited excellent advantages, for instance uniqueness, active liveness, anti-counterfeit and user friendliness, making it very suitable for many critical security applications. The morphology of vascular network shows strong randomness [1], and is the physiological basis for uniqueness and discrimination of finger vein. Since finger-vein stay in the subcutaneous tissue, its acquisition strategies cannot capture reliable finger-vein network. Thus, effectively representation of the vein network randomness is crucial for finger-vein recognition [2–4].

The randomness of finger vein network can be roughly described from two aspects: the randomness of vein topology and local image content variation. Hence, feature representation considering these two aspects are crucial, and

Supported by the National Natural Science Foundation of China under Grant 62076166.

S. Yu et al. (Eds.): PRCV 2022, LNCS 13535, pp. 467–478, 2022.
https://doi.org/10.1007/978-3-031-18910-4_38

graph-based method can satisfy these requirements. For a graph, its nodes can represent different image parts, and its edges can describe different connections between these image parts, such as spatial structure, relational structure, etc.

Graph theory have been widely used in machine learning, pattern recognition and many other fields. Its related researches include: graph based object recognition [5–7]; face and finger-vein recognition based on local graph coding [8–12]; weighted graph model based finger-vein feature description [13]; clinical analysis or verification of retina and coronary artery network based on biometric graph [14–16], etc.

Methods mentioned above are not suitable for finger-vein feature representation. Local graph structure (LGS) is more concerned with local content variation other than image global structure. The coding results of LGS indicate gray variation between central pixel and its neighborhood. The biometric graph represents the topology of vessel network, but can not describe the differences of local image. Further biometric graph makes graph matching more complex. Generally, graph aims to describe determined structural relationships, while finger-vein network structure is different from different samples. Therefore, this paper further explores graph construction strategies, aiming to effectively represent the randomness of finger-vein networks.

This paper proposes a weighted graph based feature representation method. Firstly, a node-set generated by image division is reshaped according local structure of vein network; Then the edges are formed to connect adjacent nodes and weights of edges are valued considering both the content variations of blocks and the similarities between adjacent blocks. The weighted graph describes the global structural randomness through edge-set generation and edge-weight evaluation; as well as describes the local randomness through blocks re-division and local content variation measurement. Compared with [13], our proposed method can describe the finger-vein randomness pattern better.

The main contributions of our work are highlight below: a. A new weighted graph based feature representation method is proposed, which can better represent the random variation of vein networks as well as the local variation of image contents. b. Based on several different finger vein image datasets, the proposed method can achieve a better classification performance.

## 2    Graph Construction Method

$G(V, E, M)$ is a weighted graph, $V$, $E$ and $M$ respectively denotes the node set, edge set and weight set. $V = \{v_1, v_2, \cdots, v_n\}$, $E = [e_{ij}]_{n \times n}$, $W = [w_{ij}]_{n \times n}$, $i \neq j$. The elements in $W$ are real non-negative numbers. When $w_{ij}=w_{ji}$, the weight function is symmetric and undirected; otherwise it is asymmetric.

### 2.1    Node Construction

Anatomy research shows that the network developing is a random process, so it is important to combine the random pattern of vein network with the generation of the node-set $V$. This proposes two node generation methods: block division based on border redefine, block re-division by block center adjustion.

**Block Division Based on Border Redefine (BDBR).** If image is divided evenly, there exists local bad division of vein network, as shown in Fig. 1(b). BDBR redefines blocks' boundary based on the partial vein skeleton contained in blocks, so that the local division tends to be reasonable. Thus the generated node-set somewhat contains the randomness information from network structure.

Taking Fig. 1(b) as an example, the image is divided evenly, with block-size $h \times h$. The vein skeleton curves in node $v_i$ are tracked and noted as $\{l_1, \cdots, l_i, \cdots, l_n\}$,

$$S_i = \frac{h^2}{4} - \sum_{n_1}^{n_2} l_i, \tag{1}$$

$$r_i = \frac{S_i}{h^2}, \tag{2}$$

$$t_i = \frac{|x_1 - x_2|}{|y_1 - y_2|}, \tag{3}$$

where $n_1$ and $n_2$ are the intersection points of curve $l_i$ and block boundary, the coordinates are labeled as $(x_1, y_1)$, $(x_2, y_2)$, $S_i$ is a area surrounded by curve $l_i$ and block boundary. According to the Eq. (2), a small $r_i$ denotes that curve $l_i$ is divided badly. Then according to the result of the Eq. (3), it choose a appropriate adjacent block and redefine the block's border to include the curve $l_i$. As shown in Fig. 1(b), where the green box is the new block boundary. The shape variation of block re-division result also reflects the random pattern of the vein network.

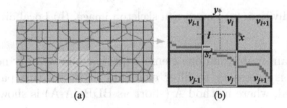

(a)                    (b)

**Fig. 1.** Block division. (a) Finger-vein skeleton image. (b) Local division result.

**Block Division by Block Center Adjustion (BDBCA).** For the finger vein skeleton, the location of minutiae and vein skeleton around them exhibit great individual discrimination, as shown in Fig. 2(a). However, these local skeletons are often divided into several blocks and can not be discussed as a whole part. Therefore, a block-re-divide operation is implemented by using those minutiae to relocate block-center and redefine block-size. The location, size and content of blocks reflect the random pattern of the vein network.

Firstly, the image is divided uniformly with block size $h \times h$ and the number of division nodes $m \times n$. Curve tracing is utilized to the vein skeletons in node $v_i$, denoted as $P = \{p_1, p_2, \cdots, p_N\}$. Suppose $p_i$ is a point of the vein skeleton, and the $3 \times 3$ neighborhood pixels around $p_i$ are denoted as $\{p_{i,0}, p_{i,1}, \cdots, p_{i,7}\}$. Skeleton minutiae are determined according to Eqs. (4), (5), and the block center is adjusted according to Eq. (6),

$$N_{trans}(p_i) = \sum_{j=0}^{7} |p_{i,j+1} - p_{i,j}|, \tag{4}$$

$$Z_i = \{p_i | N_{trans}(p_i) \geq 6\}, \tag{5}$$

$$c_i' = \begin{cases} Z_i & Z_i \neq \emptyset \\ p_{\lceil \frac{N}{2} \rceil} & Z_i = \emptyset \end{cases}, \tag{6}$$

where $N_{trans}(p_i)$ represents the number of pixel value changes from $p_{i,0}$ to $p_{i,7}$ with $p_{i,0} = p_{i,8}$. $N_{trans}(p_i) \geq 6$ means $p_i$ is an intersection. From Eq. (6), take the intersection or centroid as new block center $c_i'$. Redefine the size of node $v_i$ to $2D \times 2D$ where $D$ is the maximum distance from $c_i'$ to block's original boundary. Re-division results are is shown in Fig. 2(b).

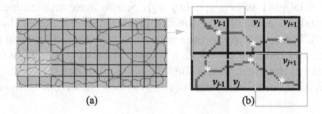

**Fig. 2.** Block division. (a) Finger-vein skeleton image. (b) Local division result.

$Z_i$ may contain more than one element $\{z_k\}$, while we only need one center per node, so it is necessary to filter elements in $Z_i$. In this paper, two filter methods are used, where method A (short as BDBCA-A) is shown in Eq. (7),

$$c_i' = \arg\min_{z_k}(\|z_k - O_i\|), \tag{7}$$

where $O_i$ is geometric center of $i$th pre-divided block. And method B (note as BDBCA-B) first adjusts the center of $v_i$ according to Eq. (7). $Z_i = Z_i - \{c_i'\} \neq 0$, denote the $3 \times 3$ neighborhood nodes of $v_i$ as $Q = \{v_j | v_j \in N_8(v_i)\}$. The centers $c_j$ in $Q$ are adjusted by Eqs. (8), (9).

$$c_j' = \arg\min_{z_k}(\|z_k - c_j\|), \text{if } c_j = O_j, Z_i \neq \emptyset, \tag{8}$$

$$Z_i = Z_i - \{c_j'\}, \tag{9}$$

As for these two filters, BDBCA-A focuses on local network structure around minutiae, while BDBCA-B focuses on both minutiae and local network nearby.

## 2.2  Edge Set Generation and Edge Weight Calculation

Edge connection widely used include: fully connected, regionally connected, K-nearest neighbor connected, and Delaunay triangulation. Triangulation is a classic and robust way, as shown in Fig. 3(a). Based on triangulation edge-set, here plan to add edges between two-hop neighbor nodes when these nodes are not blank, as shown in Fig. 3(b). Due to the random structure of vein network, the edge-set constructed by this way shows individual differences.

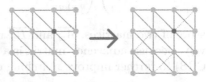

**Fig. 3.** Generation of edge-set. (a) Delaunay triangulation. (b) Connection between partial 2-hop nodes.

Weight function is shown in Eq. (10), where $S(v_i, v_j)$ measuring the similarity of block feature between $v_i$, $v_j$, and $I(v_i)$ represents local image content feature. To describe local image content variation, $I(v_i)$ is defined as Eqs. (12)–(14),

$$W_{ij} = I(v_i) \times S(v_i, v_j)|_{e_{ij} \subset E}, \tag{10}$$

$$S(v_i, v_j) = \exp(\frac{-\sum_{l=1}^{L}(f_i(l) - f_j(l))^2}{2\sigma^2}), \tag{11}$$

$$I(v_i) = 1, \tag{12}$$

$$I(v_i) = \text{AAD}(B_i), \tag{13}$$

$$I(v_i) = \sum_{l=1}^{L} f_i(l), \tag{14}$$

where $f_i$, $f_j$ respectively represent block feature corresponding to $v_i$, $v_j$, $L$ is feature length and $\sigma$ is a fixed value. AAD is the average absolute deviation operator, $B_i$ is the enhancement result of block corresponding to the $i$th node, and if $I(v_i) = 1$ means that image content variation is not considered.

## 2.3   Recognition Matching

Recognition based on graph $G(V, E, W)$ is complex and time consuming, thus we use adjacency matrix for matching simplification. The adjacency matrix of weighted is defined as follow:

$$\mathbf{A}_w(i,j) = \begin{cases} W_{ij} & \text{if } e_{ij} \in E \\ 0 & \text{otherwise} \end{cases}, \tag{15}$$

$$M_s = \frac{\sum\limits_{p=1}^{n} \sum\limits_{q=1}^{n} \left(A_w(p,q) - \overline{A_w}\right)\left(B_w(p,q) - \overline{B_w}\right)}{\sqrt{\left(\sum\limits_{p=1}^{n} \sum\limits_{q=1}^{n} \left(A_w(p,q) - \overline{A_w}\right)^2\right)\left(\sum\limits_{p=1}^{n} \sum\limits_{q=1}^{n} \left(B_w(p,q) - \overline{B_w}\right)^2\right)}}, \tag{16}$$

where $M_s$ is similarity score of two matrices, $\overline{A_w}$ and $\overline{B_w}$ represent mean values of $A_w$ and $B_w$, respectively. Because adjacency matrix is a sparse matrix, we use compress row storage (CRS) to further improve matching efficiency, as shown in Fig. 4.

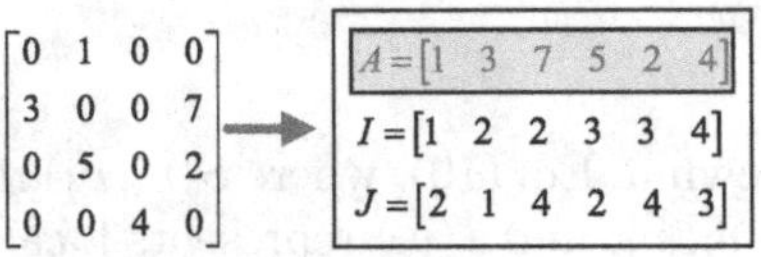

$$\begin{bmatrix} 0 & 1 & 0 & 0 \\ 3 & 0 & 0 & 7 \\ 0 & 5 & 0 & 2 \\ 0 & 0 & 4 & 0 \end{bmatrix} \longrightarrow \begin{array}{l} A = \begin{bmatrix} 1 & 3 & 7 & 5 & 2 & 4 \end{bmatrix} \\ I = \begin{bmatrix} 1 & 2 & 2 & 3 & 3 & 4 \end{bmatrix} \\ J = \begin{bmatrix} 2 & 1 & 4 & 2 & 4 & 3 \end{bmatrix} \end{array}$$

**Fig. 4.** CRS expression of the sparse matrix.

## 2.4   Image Preprocess and Feature Extraction

The image preprocess include: image enhancement [17], binary segmentation, and finger-vein skeleton extraction, some results are shown in Fig. 5.

(a)          (b)          (c)          (d)

**Fig. 5.** The results during skeleton extraction. (a) Original image; (b) The enhanced result; (c) Binary segmentation; (d) the skeleton of (c).

After preprocess and image division, we extract block feature by using steerable filter to compute the oriented energy [18]. Steerable filter is defined as follows,

$$h^\theta (x,y) = \sum_{j=1}^{N} k_j (\theta) f^{\theta_j} (x,y), \tag{17}$$

where $f(x,y)$ is a set of basic function, $N$ is the number of $f(x,y)$, $k(\theta)$ is interpolation function, $\theta$ is the orientation of Steerable filter, $\theta_j$ is the orientation of $f^{\theta_j}(x,y)$.

The oriented energy $E(\theta)$ is defined as a squared convolution between steerable filter and block $I_i$ at angle $\theta$,

$$E(\theta) = \left( \sum_{j=1}^{N} \sum_{x=1}^{X} \sum_{y=1}^{Y} \left( k_j (\theta) f^{\theta_j} (x,y) I_i (x,y) \right) \right)^2, \tag{18}$$

where $X$ and $Y$ are the sizes of $h_\theta$ and $I_i$. As shown in Eq. (18), we can find that the oriented energy $E$ is a function of angle $\theta$.

In order to describe local vein skeleton of $I_i$, we compute $E(\theta)$ at different $\theta$ as Eq. (19). The example of an image block and its oriented energy are shown in Fig. 6.

$$f_i = \{E(1), E(2), \cdots, E(\theta), \cdots, E(360)\}, \tag{19}$$

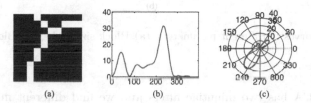

(a)                      (b)                      (c)

**Fig. 6.** Oriented energy. (a) A block of Fig. 5(d); (b) Oriented energy of (a); (c) Polar plot of (b).

## 3    Experiments and Analysis of Results

To evaluate the proposed weighted graph-based finger-vein network description method, two databases are used in our experiments. The HMD is a homemade finger trimodal image database which totally contains 5000 finger-vein images from 500 individual fingers, and the SDUMLA is an sub-set of the public Homologous Multimodal Traits Database [19] developed by Shangdong University, which contain 600 images from 100 individual fingers.

## 3.1   Impact of Node Construction Methods on Recognition

In BDBR method, a pre-design threshold $R$ is used to compare with $r_i$ to find out whether the local skeleton has been divided reasonably. From Eq. (2), we can see $r_i$ is determined by the pr-division block-size $h$. So different threshold $R$ and block-size $h$ have different effects on recognition performance, and experimental results are shown in Fig. 7. It illustrates that the value of the threshold $R$ is taken differently with different block-size $h$. The block-size $h$ is negatively correlated with the threshold $R$, within a certain range. When $h$ takes a certain value, the recognition rate is slightly improved for different values of $R$. Because finger-vein is a sparse network, and bad division only exists in a few blocks, so re-division results only affect the sub-structure of graph, such as weights of some edges. Therefore, recognition improvement is limited.

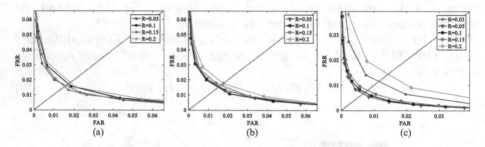

**Fig. 7.** ROC curves of different parameters. (a) Block size = 11; (b) Block size = 13; (c) Block size = 15.

The BDBCA has two minutiae filters and we find different minutiae filter have different impact on the graph constructed. The following experiments are conducted to compare recognition performance of these two method.

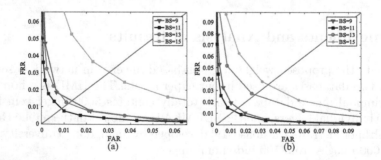

**Fig. 8.** ROC curves of different filter methods in different block-size. (a) BDBCA-A; (b) BDBCA-B.

From Fig. 8, we find that the recognition results vary considerably for different $h$. BDBCA redefines all nodes containing vein skeleton, which changes node features as well as local image content. Thus, the BDBCA method changes global structure of graph, and its performance is reflected in ROC curves. Comparing the recognition result of these two filters, BDBCA-A works better. This indicates that blank nodes also have a positive effect on network description and the large variance in block-size of BDBCA-B could reduce the recognition accuracy.

### 3.2   Performance of Edge Set Generation Method

Compare with the Delaunay triangulation used in [13], the edge set constructed here shows individual discrimination by considering the random pattern of vein network. In this part, we design several experiments to compare the performance of these two edge generation methods. In the experiments, the graph node-sets are generated by BDBR, BDBCA-A and BDBCA-B, respectively.

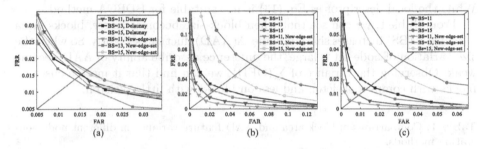

**Fig. 9.** Recognition performance comparisons between different edge-set generation methods. (a) BDBR; (b) BDBCA-A; (c) BDBCA-B.

Figure 9 shows that our method achieves better recognition accuracy, so the edge-set constructed in this paper has shown better individual discrimination. Experimental results demonstrate that the edge-set differences can expand inter-class gap of samples, promote the random pattern description ability of graph.

### 3.3   Impact of Weight Function on Recognition

Weights of graph edges should be valued considering the randomness of vein network structure as well as the variation of local image content. From Eq. (10), we can see that the weight of an edge $e_{ij}$ is determined by local descriptor $W(v_i)$ and different $W(v_i)$ are defined in Eqs. (12)–(14). In this part, we conduct experiments to compare the performance of these three $W(v_i)$ in terms of recognition performance and some statistic feature.

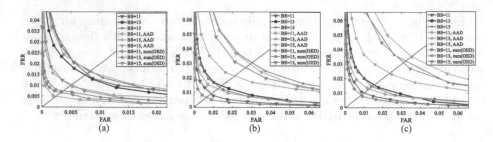

**Fig. 10.** ROC curves of different weight function. (a) BDBR; (b) BDBCA-A; (c) BDBCA-B.

From Fig. 10, we can see that weight functions using Eqs. (13)–(14) both achieve better performance in BDBR. For these three node-set generation methods, using the local descriptor as Eq. (14), they all have a certain promotion. While the local descriptor as Eq. (13) is not suitable for BDBCA method.

From Table 1, we can see that when block-size becomes larger, blocks' area variance $\triangle$(BS) increases sharply, while $\triangle$(AAD) fluctuates slightly. So when the size variation of node-set is large, the difference describe ability of AAD become weak. Observing the variance of $\sum$(OED), we can find that it more focuses on blocks with complex skeleton and less on blocks with little skeleton.

**Table 1.** Comparisons of block area and AAD feature variance in different node generation methods.

| Method | BDBR | | | BDBCA-A | | | BDBCA-B | | |
|---|---|---|---|---|---|---|---|---|---|
| Block size | $\triangle$(BS) | $\triangle$(AAD) | $\triangle(\sum$OED) | $\triangle$(BS) | $\triangle$(AAD) | $\triangle(\sum$OED) | $\triangle$(BS) | $\triangle$(AAD) | $\triangle(\sum$OED) |
| 11 | 18.01 | 19.82 | 237.34 | 113.44 | 15.65 | 1405.61 | 125.94 | 15.61 | 1596.63 |
| 13 | 26.72 | 19.61 | 404.16 | 165.40 | 14.96 | 2078.34 | 199.73 | 14.92 | 2425.41 |
| 15 | 39.03 | 19.16 | 632.76 | 208.64 | 14.27 | 2894.61 | 298.70 | 14.17 | 3735.90 |

## 3.4   Comparison Experiments

In order to further evaluate the performance of the proposed method, we compare our method with the state-of-the-art methods proposed in [13, 20–22]. [20] proposes an end-to-end CNN based finger-vein recognition method, referred to E2E-CNNfv. SCW-LGS is a finger-vein feature coding method by using local graph structure [21]. [22] classify weighted graphs by using Cheby-Mgpool GCNs instead of similarity measurement of adjcency matrixes. We compare these methods in terms of the recognition accuracy and efficiency.

From Fig. 11, we can see that the proposed method achieve the best recognition performance in HMD, and only slightly inferior to the Cheby-MgPool GCN method in SDUMLA. Because there exist significant pose variation and acquisition exposure in SDUMLA, and these problems affect the vein network skeleton

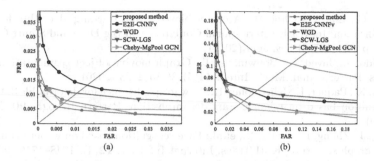

**Fig. 11.** Recognition performance comparisons of two database. (a) HMD; (b) SDUMLA.

extraction especially the skeleton minutiae. But from Table 2, we can see that the time cost of the proposed method is much less than Cheby-Mgpool GCNs method.

**Table 2.** The test time cost of single image (/s).

| Method | Ours | E2E-CNNFv [20] | WGD [13] | SCW-LGS [21] | CMGCNs [22] |
|--------|------|----------------|----------|--------------|-------------|
| MHD | 0.0265 | 0.0012 | 0.0362 | 0.0153 | 0.3472 |
| SDUMLA | 0.0166 | 0.0012 | 0.0281 | 0.0146 | 0.3942 |

## 4  Conclusions

In this paper, a new weighted graph based feature representation method had been proposed for finger-vein network. This method described the random pattern of finger-vein network by exploring the randomness existed in node-set, edge-set and edge-weight function. Based on two databases we conducted a series of experiments to evaluation different factors of graph construction on recognition rates and proved the effectiveness of the method.

## References

1. Yang, J., Shi, Y.: Finger-vein ROI localization and vein ridge enhancement. Pattern Recogn. Lett. **33**(12), 1569–1579 (2012)
2. Yang, J., Shi, Y., Jia, G.: Finger-vein image matching based on adaptive curve transformation. Pattern Recogn. **66**, 34–43 (2017)
3. Yang, J., Shi, Y.: Finger-vein network enhancement and segmentation. Pattern Anal. Appl. **17**(4), 783–797 (2014)
4. Li, S., Zhang B.: An adaptive discriminant and sparsity feature descriptor for finger vein recognition. In: IEEE International Conference on Acoustics, Speech, & Signal Processing, pp. 2140–2144. IEEE, Toronto Canada (2021)

5. Choi, G., Lim, C., Choi, H.: A center-biased graph learning algorithm for image classification. In: IEEE International Conference on Big Data and Smart Computing, pp. 324–327. IEEE, Jeju (2017)
6. Giraldo, J., Javed, S., Bouwmans, T.: Graph moving object segmentation. IEEE Trans. Pattern Anal. Mach. Intell. **44**(5), 2485–2503 (2020)
7. Madi, K., Paquet, E., Kheddouci, H.: New graph distance for deformable 3D objects recognition based on triangle-stars decomposition. Pattern Recogn. **90**, 297–307 (2019)
8. Yang, J., Zhang, L., Wang, Y., et al.: Face recognition based on weber symmetrical local graph structure. KSII Trans. Internet Inf. Syst. **12**(4), 1748–1759 (2018)
9. Kumar, D., Garain, J., Kisku, D.R., Sing, J.K., Gupta, P.: Ensemble face recognition system using dense local graph structure. In: Huang, D.-S., Gromiha, M.M., Han, K., Hussain, A. (eds.) ICIC 2018. LNCS (LNAI), vol. 10956, pp. 846–852. Springer, Cham (2018). https://doi.org/10.1007/978-3-319-95957-3_91
10. Li, S., Zhang, H., Yang, J.: Novel local coding algorithm for finger multimodal feature description and recognition. Sensors **19**(9), 2213 (2019)
11. Dong, S., Yang, J., Chen, Y., et al.: Finger vein recognition based on multi-orientation weighted symmetric local graph structure. Ksii Trans. Internet Inf. Syst. **9**(10), 4126–4142 (2015)
12. Zhao, Z., Ye, Z., Yang, J., Zhang, H.: Finger crystal feature recognition based on graph convolutional network. In: Feng, J., Zhang, J., Liu, M., Fang, Y. (eds.) CCBR 2021. LNCS, vol. 12878, pp. 203–212. Springer, Cham (2021). https://doi.org/10.1007/978-3-030-86608-2_23
13. Ye, Z., Yang, J.: A finger-vein recognition method based on weighted graph model. J. Shandong Univ. (Eng. Sci.) **48**(03), 103–109 (2018)
14. Lajevardi, S., Arakala, A., Davis, S., et al.: Retina verification system based on biometric graph matching. IEEE Trans. Image Process **22**(9), 3625–3635 (2013)
15. Arakala, A., Davis, S., Hao, H., et al.: Value of graph topology in vascular biometrics. IET Biometrics **6**(2), 117–125 (2017)
16. Zhao, J., Ai, D., Huang, Y., et al.: Quantitation of vascular morphology by directed graph construction. IEEE Access **7**, 21609–21622 (2019)
17. Yang, J., Wei, J., Shi, Y.: Accurate ROI localization and hierarchical hyper-sphere model for finger-vein recognition. Neurocomputing **328**, 171–181 (2019)
18. Simoncelli, E., Farid, H.: Steerable wedge filters for local orientation analysis. IEEE Trans. Image Process. **5**(9), 1377–1382 (1996)
19. Yin, Y., Liu, L., Sun, X.: SDUMLA-HMT: a multimodal biometric database. In: Sun, Z., Lai, J., Chen, X., Tan, T. (eds.) CCBR 2011. LNCS, vol. 7098, pp. 260–268. Springer, Heidelberg (2011). https://doi.org/10.1007/978-3-642-25449-9_33
20. Wen, M., Zhang, H., Yang, J.: End-to-end finger trimodal features fusion and recognition model based on CNN. In: Feng, J., Zhang, J., Liu, M., Fang, Y. (eds.) CCBR 2021. LNCS, vol. 12878, pp. 39–48. Springer, Cham (2021). https://doi.org/10.1007/978-3-030-86608-2_5
21. Li, S., Zhang, H., Jia, G., Yang, J.: Finger vein recognition based on weighted graph structural feature encoding. In: Zhou, J., Wang, Y., Sun, Z., Jia, Z., Feng, J., Shan, S., Ubul, K., Guo, Z. (eds.) CCBR 2018. LNCS, vol. 10996, pp. 29–37. Springer, Cham (2018). https://doi.org/10.1007/978-3-319-97909-0_4
22. Li, R., Su, Z., Zhang, H.: Application of improved GCNs in feature representation of finger-vein. J. Signal Process. **36**(4), 550–561 (2020)

# Self-supervised Face Anti-spoofing via Anti-contrastive Learning

Jiajiong Cao[1], Yufan Liu[2,3(✉)], Jingting Ding[1], and Liang Li[1]

[1] Ant Financial Service Group, Hangzhou, China
[2] National Laboratory of Pattern Recognition, Institution of Automation, Chinese Academy of Sciences, Beijing, China
yufan.liu@ia.ac.cn
[3] School of Artificial Intelligence, University of Chinese Academy of Sciences, Beijing, China

**Abstract.** Face Anti-Spoofing (FAS) protects face recognition systems from Presentation Attacks (PA). Though supervised FAS methods have achieved great progress recent years, popular deep learning based methods require a large amount of labeled data. On the other hand, Self-Supervised Learning (SSL) methods have achieved competing performance on various tasks including ImageNet classification and COCO object detection. Unfortunately, existing SSL frameworks are designed for content-aware tasks, which may fail on other tasks such as FAS. To deal with this problem, we propose a new SSL framework called Anti-Contrastive Learning Face Anti-Spoofing (ACL-FAS). ACL-FAS contains two key components, namely, one PAtch-wise vIew GEnerator (PAIGE) and one Disentangled Anti-contrastiVe lEarning (DAVE) framework. With the help of two components, ACL-FAS shows its superiority on four different FAS datasets compared with more than 10 supervised methods and 5 SSL methods.

**Keywords:** Face anti-spoofing · Self-supervised learning · Contrastive learning

## 1 Introduction

Face recognition provides an alternative identity verification approach for traditional pass word based methods. Though it has brought much convenience, it faces new safety issues such as face Presentation Attacks (PA). To detect different types of presentation attacks, Face Anti-Spoofing (FAS) is proposed. Researchers have made much progress on FAS by introducing FAS techniques with hand-crafted features or deep learning based features. To further improve the generalization of FAS methods, auxiliary supervisions including depth map and reflection map are adopted to train the FAS models. Although previous methods have achieved satisfying performance, all of them rely on a large amount of labeled data.

S. Yu et al. (Eds.): PRCV 2022, LNCS 13535, pp. 479–491, 2022.
https://doi.org/10.1007/978-3-031-18910-4_39

Recently, Self-Supervised Learning (SSL) has attracted much attention. A typical SSL pipeline usually contains a pre-training stage and a finetuning stage. Existing methods pre-train the model using contrastive learning or masked input reconstruction techniques. The pre-train stage can be accomplished without labeled data. Then the model is fixed (or partially fixed) and finetuned on the target task with labeled data, such as image classification and detection. Since SSL methods are able to make advantage of large amounts of unlabeled data, pre-trained models finetuned with limited labeled data can achieve satisfactory performance. However, existing SSL methods are designed for content-aware tasks including image classification tasks like ImageNet and image detection tasks like COCO. They heavily rely on content-invariant transformations such as different types of augmentations. These techniques may fail on FAS, since FAS is not a pure content-aware task, but also related to other factors such as illuminations and reflections.

To address the above issues and apply SSL techniques to FAS, we propose a novel self-supervised face anti-spoofing framework called Anti-Contrastive Learning Face Anti-Spoofing (ACL-FAS). ACL-FAS contains two key components, namely, one PAtch-wise vIew GEnerator (PAIGE) and one Disentangled Anti-contrastiVe lEarning (DAVE) framework. The former aims to provide both content-aware and content-neglected views with different augmentation techniques, while the latter extracts content-aware and content-neglected features from the views, and further introduces contrastive and anti-contrastive learning losses via disentanglement learning techniques to obtain high quality features for FAS. Different from previous SSL methods focusing on content-aware features, ACL-FAS learns both content-aware and content-neglected features from corresponding views. Consequently, the learned features are more suitable for FAS. To verify the effectiveness of the proposed method, we compare ACL-FAS with more than 10 supervised FAS methods and 5 popular SSL methods on four FAS datasets. The experimental results show the superior of ACL-FAS, especially under the self-supervised scheme.

The main contributions of this work are summarized as follows:

- This work analyzes that current SSL methods fail to obtain satisfactory performance on FAS. Extensive experimental results support this conclusion.
- A novel SSL framework called Anti-Contrastive Learning Face Anti-Spoofing (ACL-FAS) is proposed to learn more suitable features for FAS. It contains two novel components including one PAtch-wise vIew GEnerator (PAIGE) and one Disentangled Anti-contrastiVe lEarning (DAVE) framework.
- Extensive experiments on four datasets under both supervised and self-supervised schemes are conducted. The experimental results show the effectiveness over 10 supervised FAS methods and 5 popular self-supervised methods. The ACER is reduced by more than 50% under the self-supervised scheme.

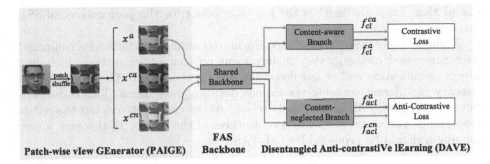

**Fig. 1.** Pipeline of the proposed Anti-Contrastive Learning Face Anti-Spoofing (ACL-FAS).

## 2    Related Work

### 2.1    Face Anti-spoofing

Face Anti-Spoofing (FAS) has been a vital component of face recognition system [2,8,23]. For recent years, thanks to the development of deep learning [13,18,19,22], great progress has been made in this area. Early works usually utilize hand-crafted features including HoG [7], LBP [10] and SIFT [20] and train classifiers such as SVM-based on these features. Thanks to the development of deep learning [15,33], deep neural networks have dominated FAS. [9] treats FAS as a binary classification problem and trains an end-to-end CNN to solve it. In order to avoid overfitting, recent works have turned to find structural supervision, such as depth map [16], reflection map [31] and supervision map generated by meta network [21]. Another important topic of FAS is domain generalization, where the model is trained on one domain while evaluated on another different one. To alleviate the performance drop across different domains, disentanglement techniques [30] and carefully designed convolutional operations [28] are proposed. However, previous works mainly focus on supervised learning, which are data-driven and require a large amount of labeled data.

### 2.2    Self-supervised Learning

Self-Supervised Learning (SSL) aims to learn features without labels that can be well applied to down-stream tasks. Contrastive learning is one of the main streams of SSL. Contrastive learning methods usually maximize the variance of negative pairs while minimizing the variance of positive pairs. For instance, SimCLR [3] introduces a linear projector to improve the feature quality, while BYOL [11] utilizes a momentum encoder as a teacher network to constrain the learning process. BYOL achieves SOTA performance without negative pairs. Recently, SimSiam [5] simplifies previous works and performs contrastive learning without negative pairs, large batch size as well as momentum encoder. It claims that "stop gradient" is the key component for the performance of SSL methods.

Though recent SSL methods have achieved similar performance compared with supervised methods, they mainly focus on content-aware tasks including object classification and object detection. SSL methods learn the semantic consistency of different contents via various data augmentations. This framework fails on FAS since FAS is not closely related to the content (face) but the reflections, moor waves and other low level features of the image. To this end, a new paradigm should be proposed for SSL-FAS.

# 3   Approach

The pipeline of proposed Anti-Contrastive Learning Face Anti-Spoofing (ACL-FAS) is shown in Fig. 1. It consists of two key components, including PAtch-wise vIew GEnerator (PAIGE) and Disentangled Anti-contrastiVe lEarning (DAVE). First, three views are generated by PAIGE. After that, three samples pass through a shared backbone to obtain three feature maps. Based on the patch-wise manner of PAIGE, a novel region-based similarity loss is computed for each sample pair. Then, the feature maps are fed into DAVE, which contains two paths. One path extracts content-aware features and performs contrastive learning for anchor sample and light-augmented sample, while the other path extracts content-neglected features and performs anti-contrastive learning for anchor sample and strong-augmented sample. For evaluation on FAS, both content-aware features and content-neglected features are concatenated to form the final feature for training linear binary classification. Details of PAIGE and DAVE are introduced respectively in the following sections.

## 3.1   Patch-Wise View Generator

For an input image $x$, it passes through PAtch-wise vIew GEnerator (PAIGE) and three views including anchor view $x^a$, content-aware view $x^{ca}$ and content-neglected view $x^{cn}$ are generated, as shown in Eq. 1.

$$\{x^a, x^{ca}, x^{cn}\} = PAIGE(x). \tag{1}$$

In particular, $x$ is first augmented with simple operations including random crop and horizontal flip. Then, it is further split into several $16 \times 16$ patches and the locations of the patches are random shuffled to destruct the structure of the face. Finally, the patch-wise sample is defined as the anchor view $x^a$. $x^a$ is further augmented to generate content-aware view $x^{ca}$ and content-neglected view $x^{cn}$. We adopt different augmentation operations and strengths to obtain $x^{ca}$ and $x^{cn}$. Then, three feature maps, $fm^a$, $fm^{ca}$ and $fm^{cn}$, are extracted via the shared backbone as shown in Eq. 2,

$$\{fm^a, fm^{ca}, fm^{cn}\} = F(\{x^a, x^{ca}, x^{cn}\}), \tag{2}$$

where $F(\cdot)$ indicates the forward function of the shared backbone, which can be formed with several residual blocks.

**Region-Based Similarity Loss (RSL):** RSL is proposed to learn general representations based on the region similarities of the same sample and across different samples. The formulation of RSL is shown in Eq. 3,

$$
Loss_{RSL} = \frac{1}{2N} \times ( \sum_{(l_1,l_2)\in L_1} < fm_a^{i-l_1}, fm_a^{j-l_2} > \\
- \sum_{(l_3,l_4)\in L_2} < fm_a^{i-l_3}, fm_a^{i-l_4} >), \tag{3}
$$

where $< x, y >$ indicates the cosine similarity of two features, $fm_a^{i-l_1}$ is the feature map of $i$-th anchor view $x_a^i$ at location $l_1$ and $L_1$ is the cross-sample location set while $L_2$ is the inner-sample location set. Both location sets have N elements and each location corresponds to one $16 \times 16$ region of the anchor view. Note that RSL only works on anchor views in order to reduce the influence of strong augmentations.

## 3.2 Disentangled Anti-contrastive Learning

The proposed Disentangled Anti-contrastiVe lEarning (DAVE) first splits the features from the shared backbone into two branches, one for content-aware contrastive learning and the other for content-neglected anti-contrastive learning. For example, as shown in Eq. 4, feature map obtained from the shared backbone of the anchor view $x^a$ is split from the channel dimension into two parts, namely, the content-aware feature map $fm_{cl}^a$ and the content-neglected feature map $fm_{acl}^a$. The operation on $x^{ca}$ and $x^{cn}$ is the same.

$$
\{fm_{cl}^a, fm_{acl}^a\} = split(fm^a) \tag{4}
$$

Then, the content-aware feature map and the content-neglected feature map are fed into the content-aware branch and content-neglected branch, respectively. For instance, as shown in Eq. 5, the refined content-aware feature map, $rfm_{cl}^a$, and the refined content-neglected feature map, $rfm_{acl}^a$, are obtained for $x^a$ after passing through two branches of DAVE. The operation on $x^{ca}$ and $x^{cn}$ is the same.

$$
rfm_{cl}^a = DAVE_{cl}(fm_{cl}^a), \\
rfm_{acl}^a = DAVE_{acl}(fm_{acl}^a), \tag{5}
$$

where $DAVE_{cl}(\cdot)$ is the forward function of the content-aware branch while $DAVE_{acl}(\cdot)$ is the forward function of the content-neglected branch.

Finally, two loss functions including contrastive loss and anti-contrastive loss are computed. As illustrated in Eq. 6, contrastive loss is computed on the anchor view $x^a$ and the corresponding content-aware view $x^{ca}$, while anti-contrastive loss is computed on the anchor view $x^a$ and the corresponding content-neglected view $x^{cn}$.

$$Loss_{CL} = ||rfm_{cl}^a - rfm_{cl}^{ca}||_2^2,$$
$$Loss_{ACL} = ||rfm_{acl}^a - rfm_{acl}^{cn}||_2^2. \tag{6}$$

Final objective can be formulated as the weighted sum of $Loss_{CL}$ and $Loss_{ACL}$ in Eq. 7.

$$Obj = Loss_{CL} + \lambda \times Loss_{ACL} \tag{7}$$

## 4   Experiments

### 4.1   Settings

**Dataset:** two datasets including SiW [16] and Oulu NPU [1] are adopted for intra-dataset testing while CASIA-MFSD [32] and Replay-Attack [6] are used for cross-dataset evaluation.

**Competing Methods:** more than 10 SOTA supervised FAS methods including DeSpoofing [14], Auxliary [16], FAS-TD [24], Disentagle [30], STDN [17], STASN [26], CDCN [28], BCN [27] and DCN [29] are compared under the supervised scheme while 6 self-supervised methods, including SimCLR [3], MoCo [4], BYOL [11], SimSiam [5], MAE [12] and MaskedFeat [25] are compared under the self-supervised scheme.

**Training and Evaluation Configs:** for the supervised scheme, the proposed method is trained with the proposed loss functions along with a binary classification loss, while for the self-supervised scheme, the proposed method is trained purely with the self-supervised loss. After training, we strictly follow the linear probe config in SimCLR [3] to evaluate the performance of all the self-supervised methods.

### 4.2   Ablation Analysis

In this section, the effectiveness of two key components, namely PAIGE and DAVE are verified under the self-supervised scheme. Note that without PAIGE and DAVE, the framework degrades to SimCLR. Therefore, SimCLR is used as the baseline. Additionally, no extra supervisions including depth map or reflection map are used for training. And we report the detailed results on Oulu-NPU in Table 1. One SOTA supervised method namely CDCN is also reported for better comparison.

As illustrated in Table 1, the baseline (SimCLR) performs much worse compared with the supervised method. It is because traditional self-supervised methods are designed for content-aware tasks instead of FAS. On the other hand, with the help of PAIGE and DAVE, the proposed method achieves much better performance, even compatible with that of supervised method. Further, compared with PAIGE, DAVE with anti-contrastive loss provides more performance gain. It indicates that most of the performance gain comes from the anti-contrastive learning framework while the traditional pure contrastive learning methods may not be suitable for self-supervised FAS.

**Table 1.** Ablation results on Oulu NPU. ACL-FAS is the proposed method (baseline+PAIGE+DAVE). CDCN is a SOTA supervised method, whose results are reported for better comparison.

| Method | Protocol | APCER | BPCER | ACER | Method | Protocol | APCER | BPCER | ACER |
|---|---|---|---|---|---|---|---|---|---|
| baseline | 1 | 6.5 | 22.9 | 14.7 | baseline | 2 | 8.5 | 23.7 | 16.1 |
| baseline+PAIGE | | 6.9 | 20.2 | 13.6 | baseline+PAIGE | | 10.2 | 21.8 | 16.0 |
| ACL-FAS | | **5.2** | **2.6** | **3.9** | ACL-FAS | | **5.3** | **3.3** | **4.3** |
| CDCN | | 0.4 | 1.7 | 1.0 | CDCN | | 1.5 | 1.4 | 1.5 |
| baseline | 3 | 8.7±5.4 | 27.1±7.8 | 17.9±6.6 | baseline | 4 | 11.2±8.4 | 35.4±15.6 | 23.3±12.0 |
| baseline+PAIGE | | 17.6±9.6 | 19.0±10.2 | 18.3±9.9 | baseline+PAIGE | | 20.5±10.7 | 26.6±14.2 | 23.6±12.5 |
| ACL-FAS | | **5.7±3.5** | **7.2±5.6** | **6.5±4.6** | ACL-FAS | | **6.9±6.0** | **10.5±7.1** | **8.7±6.6** |
| CDCN | | 2.4±1.3 | 2.2±2.0 | 2.3±1.4 | CDCN | | 4.6±4.6 | 9.2±8.0 | 6.9±2.9 |

## 4.3  Supervised Comparisons

In this section, the proposed method is compared with more than 10 SOTA supervised methods under both inner-dataset and cross-dataset settings. Since many SOTA methods take advantage of auxiliary supervisions including depth map, reflection map and rPPG signal, we introduce extra depth estimation supervision into the output feature map of the shared branch. Consequently, the supervised objective function is shown in Eq. 8 (the objective loss function for self-supervised scheme is as in Eq. 7).

$$Obj_{supervised} = Loss_{CL} + \lambda \times Loss_{ACL} + DE(\{fm^a, fm^{ca}, fm^{cn}\}), \qquad (8)$$

where, $DE(\cdot)$ is the depth estimation loss for all of the three views.

**Table 2.** Comparison with supervised methods on Oulu NPU.

| Method | Protocol | APCER | BPCER | ACER | Method | Protocol | APCER | BPCER | ACER |
|---|---|---|---|---|---|---|---|---|---|
| DeSpoofing | 1 | 1.2 | 1.7 | 1.5 | Disentangle | 2 | 2.7 | 2.7 | 2.4 |
| FAS-TD | | 2.5 | 0.0 | 1.3 | STASN | | 4.2 | 0.3 | 2.2 |
| Disentangle | | 1.7 | 0.8 | 1.3 | FAS-TD | | 1.7 | 2.0 | 1.9 |
| STDN | | 0.8 | 1.3 | 1.1 | STDN | | 2.3 | 1.6 | 1.9 |
| CDCN | | 0.4 | 1.7 | 1.0 | BCN | | 2.6 | 0.8 | 1.7 |
| BCN | | 0.0 | 1.6 | 0.8 | CDCN | | 1.5 | 1.4 | **1.5** |
| DCN | | 1.3 | 0.0 | **0.6** | DCN | | 2.2 | 2.2 | 2.2 |
| Ours | | 1.4 | 0.0 | 0.7 | Ours | | 1.8 | 1.4 | 1.6 |
| Auxliary | 3 | 2.7±1.3 | 3.1±1.7 | 2.9±1.5 | STASN | 4 | 6.7±10.6 | 8.3±8.4 | 7.5±4.7 |
| STDN | | 1.6±1.6 | 4.0±5.4 | 2.8±3.3 | CDCN | | 4.6±4.6 | 9.2±8.0 | 6.9±2.9 |
| STASN | | 4.7±3.9 | 0.9±1.2 | 2.8±1.6 | DeSpoofing | | 1.2±6.3 | 6.1±5.1 | 5.6±5.7 |
| BCN | | 2.8±2.4 | 2.3±2.8 | 2.5±1.1 | BCN | | 2.9±4.0 | 7.5±6.9 | 5.2±3.7 |
| CDCN | | 2.4±1.3 | 2.2±2.0 | 2.3±1.4 | Disentangle | | 5.4±2.9 | 3.3±6.0 | 4.4±3.0 |
| Disentangle | | 2.8±2.2 | 1.7±2.6 | 2.2±2.2 | STDN | | 2.3±3.6 | 5.2±5.4 | 3.8±4.2 |
| DCN | | 2.3±2.7 | 1.4±2.6 | 1.9±1.6 | DCN | | 6.7±6.8 | 0.0±0.0 | **3.3±3.4** |
| Ours | | 2.4±2.5 | 1.3±2.6 | **1.9±1.5** | Ours | | 7.6±8.0 | 0.0±0.0 | 3.8±4.0 |

We report inner-dataset results on Oulu NPU in Table 2. The proposed method achieved the best performance under protocol 3 and the second best under protocol 1, 2 and 4. Though the proposed method is designed for self-supervised FAS, the performance under supervised scheme indicates that it is also generalized for supervised FAS. Therefore, the proposed PAIGE and DAVE block can be used as a component for existing supervised FAS frameworks.

To further verify the cross-dataset generalization of the proposed method, we conduct cross-dataset experiments and report the results in Table 3. Our method outperforms most of the competing SOTA methods. It indicates that the proposed anti-contrastive learning framework and corresponding components can be well generalized from one dataset to another. It is important for real world applications, since the training data for FAS is usually different from that of the test scenarios.

**Table 3.** Cross-testing comparison with supervised methods on CASIA-MFSD and Replay-Attack.

| Method | Train | Test | Train | Test | Method | Train | Test | Train | Test |
|---|---|---|---|---|---|---|---|---|---|
| | CASIA MSFD | Replay Attack | Replay Attack | CASIA MSFD | | CASIA MSFD | Replay Attack | Replay Attack | CASIA MSFD |
| Motion-Mag | 50.1% | | 47.0% | | BASN | 23.6% | | 29.9% | |
| Spectral cubes | 34.4% | | 50.0% | | Disentangle | 22.4% | | 30.3% | |
| LowPower | 30.1% | | 35.6% | | BCN | 16.6% | | 36.4% | |
| CNN | 48.5% | | 45.5% | | CDCN | 15.5% | | 32.6% | |
| STASN | 31.5% | | 30.9% | | DCN | **15.3%** | | 29.4% | |
| Auxliary | 27.6% | | **28.4%** | | Ours | 16.4% | | 29.8% | |

### 4.4 Self-supervised Comparisons

In this section, we conduct experiments under the self-supervised scheme on 4 different datasets for both inner-dataset and cross-dataset settings. Note that the objective loss function for the self-supervised scheme is as in Eq. 7, where depth is not used as the supervision signal. In the mean time, competing methods do not use depth as supervision neither.

The self-supervised results on Oulu NPU and SiW are reported in Table 4 and Table 5, respectively. The proposed method achieves the best for both datasets and the ACER is reduced by more than 50%. In particular, for competing methods, contrastive learning based methods including SimCLR, MoCo, BYOL and SimSiam usually perform worse than the MAE based methods including MAE and MaskedFeat. It is because contrastive learning based methods introduce much noise when sampling negative pairs especially for binary classification tasks such as FAS. On the contrary, the proposed method adopts augmentations with different strengths are types to generate samples instead of pair-wise sampling. Consequently, the proposed method works under a more generalized condition. For MAE based methods, MaskedFeat continuously outperforms MAE. It is because using HoG instead of original RGB image as supervision is more suitable for FAS. HoG is a commonly used feature for FAS before the popularity of deep learning.

The self-supervised cross-dataset results are reported in Table 6. The proposed method and competing methods are first pre-trained on the training

**Table 4.** Comparison with self-supervised methods on Oulu NPU.

| Method | Protocol | APCER | BPCER | ACER | Method | Protocol | APCER | BPCER | ACER |
|---|---|---|---|---|---|---|---|---|---|
| SimCLR | 1 | 6.5 | 22.9 | 14.7 | SimCLR | 2 | 8.5 | 23.7 | 16.1 |
| MoCo | | 6.9 | 20.2 | 13.6 | MoCo | | 10.2 | 21.8 | 16.0 |
| BYOL | | 12.7 | 14.1 | 13.4 | BYOL | | 14.2 | 17.9 | 16.6 |
| SimSiam | | 10.3 | 12.8 | 11.6 | SimSiam | | 13.7 | 16.8 | 15.3 |
| MAE | | 14.2 | 6.0 | 10.1 | MAE | | 16.8 | 8.4 | 13.6 |
| MaskedFeat | | 11.5 | 4.7 | 8.1 | MaskFeat | | 12.7 | 5.3 | 9.0 |
| Ours | | **5.2** | **2.6** | **3.9** | Ours | | **5.3** | **3.3** | **4.3** |
| SimCLR | 3 | 8.7±5.4 | 27.1±7.8 | 17.9±6.6 | SimCLR | 4 | 11.2±8.4 | 35.4±15.6 | 23.3±12.0 |
| MoCo | | 17.6±9.6 | 19.0±10.2 | 18.3±9.9 | MoCo | | 20.5±10.7 | 26.6±14.2 | 23.6±12.5 |
| BYOL | | 15.9±8.3 | 17.7±10.2 | 16.6±9.3 | BYOL | | 20.1±11.3 | 23.5±13.6 | 21.8±12.5 |
| SimSiam | | 9.3±6.4 | 25.7±12.8 | 17.5±9.6 | SimSiam | | 12.7±7.9 | 31.9±17.5 | 22.3±13.7 |
| MAE | | 19.6±8.3 | 10.2±5.7 | 14.9±7.0 | MAE | | 25.8±13.0 | 12.4±8.4 | 19.6±10.7 |
| MaskedFeat | | 17.1±6.8 | 9.7±5.6 | 13.4±6.2 | MaskedFeat | | 23.3±12.9 | 13.1±7.0 | 18.2±10.0 |
| Ours | | **5.7±3.5** | **7.2±5.6** | **6.5±4.6** | Ours | | **6.9±6.0** | **10.5±7.1** | **8.7±6.6** |

**Table 5.** Comparison with self-supervised methods on SiW.

| Method | Protocol | APCER | BPCER | ACER | Method | Protocol | APCER | BPCER | ACER |
|---|---|---|---|---|---|---|---|---|---|
| SimCLR | 1 | 11.2 | 12.4 | 11.8 | SimCLR | 2 | 10.3±8.7 | 10.5±8.7 | 10.4±8.7 |
| MoCo | | 6.7 | 16.5 | 11.6 | MoCo | | 5.9±5.6 | 15.4±12.6 | 10.2±9.1 |
| BYOL | | 10.5 | 10.5 | 10.5 | BYOL | | 9.3±8.1 | 10.1±8.9 | 9.7±8.5 |
| SimSiam | | 7.4 | 14.7 | 11.1 | SimSiam | | 8.1±6.3 | 13.7±8.6 | 10.9±7.5 |
| MAE | | 9.3 | 9.9 | 9.6 | MAE | | 9.2±7.1 | 9.0±6.5 | 9.1±7.3 |
| MaskedFeat | | 6.6 | 9.1 | 7.9 | MaskedFeat | | 6.5±3.5 | 8.1±3.9 | 7.3±3.7 |
| Ours | | **3.8** | **2.8** | **3.3** | Ours | | **2.1±1.9** | **2.3±2.2** | **2.2±2.1** |
| SimCLR | 3 | 18.3±9.5 | 25.5±14.9 | 21.9±12.2 | MAE | 3 | 17.6±9.2 | 22.8±12.4 | 20.2±10.8 |
| MoCo | | 21.7±10.9 | 20.3±9.6 | 21.0±10.3 | MaskedFeat | | 18.5±8.6 | 16.7±7.0 | 17.6±7.8 |
| BYOL | | 19.4±12.3 | 18.9±11.5 | 19.2+11.9 | Ours | | **9.0±3.9** | **9.6±4.1** | **9.3±4.0** |
| SimSiam | | 20.5±10.7 | 21.9±12.6 | 21.2±11.7 | | | | | |

dataset. Then, they are trained under the linear probe setting on the training set. Finally, they are evaluated on the test dataset. To this end, the self-supervised cross-dataset evaluation is much more challenging than the supervised one. As illustrated in Table 6, SOTA self-supervised methods suffer from severe performance drop compared with supervised methods. For example, SimCLR shows around 15% performance drop compared with a simple CNN supervised baseline. On the contrary, with the help of PAIGE and DAVE, the proposed method outperforms the best SOTA methods (MaskedFeat) by around 20%. It verifies the effectiveness and generalization of the proposed method under the cross-dataset setting.

**Table 6.** Cross-testing comparison with self-supervised methods on CASIA-MFSD and Replay-Attack.

| Method | Train CASIA MSFD | Test Replay Attack | Train Replay Attack | Test CASIA MSFD | Method | Train CASIA MSFD | Test Replay Attack | Train Replay Attack | Test CASIA MSFD |
|--------|------|------|------|------|--------|------|------|------|------|
| SimCLR | 62.7% | | 56.8% | | MAE | 55.3% | | 54.9% | |
| MoCo | 61.4% | | 54.3% | | MaskedFeat | 54.1% | | 53.3% | |
| BYOL | 59.7% | | 55.6% | | Ours | **35.3%** | | **30.6%** | |
| SimSiam | 63.8% | | 56.2% | | | | | | |

**Evaluation with Limited Labeled Samples.** In this section, experiments with limited training data are conducted. Specifically, only a portion of the training set is used to train the self-supervised models, while the evaluation is performed on the whole testing set. The detailed results on SiW are reported in Table 7. According to the results, the proposed method shows continuous superiority over existing SSL methods. For instance, ACER is reduced by 30% to 50% under different settings. It indicates that the proposed method can be well applied to applications with limited available training data.

**Table 7.** Evaluation on SiW with limited training data. The ACER results on protocol 1 are reported

| Method | SimCLR | MoCo | BYOL | SimSiam | MAE | MaskedFeat | Ours |
|--------|--------|------|------|---------|-----|-----------|------|
| 1% training set | 35.5 | 34.7 | 32.1 | 34.5 | 31.8 | 30.7 | **24.8** |
| 5% training set | 24.3 | 24.5 | 23.7 | 24.4 | 21.7 | 21.5 | **15.3** |
| 10% training set | 17.9 | 18.2 | 16.4 | 17.1 | 15.6 | 13.5 | **9.6** |
| 20% training set | 14.3 | 13.9 | 13.7 | 14.1 | 12.5 | 10.7 | **5.1** |
| 50% training set | 12.7 | 12.4 | 11.3 | 12.5 | 10.3 | 8.9 | **4.6** |

## 5    Conclusion

We propose a novel self-supervised FAS pipeline to deal with the conflict between the existing SSL methods and FAS task. The proposed SSL framework is called Anti-Contrastive Learning Face Anti-Spoofing (ACL-FAS). ACL-FAS contains two key components, namely, one PAtch-wise vIew GEnerator (PAIGE) and one Disentangled Anti-contrastiVe lEarning (DAVE) framework. With the help of two components, ACL-FAS shows its superiority on four different FAS datasets compared with more than 10 supervised methods and 5 SSL methods.

**Acknowledgements.** This work was supported by the National Natural Science Foundation of China (No. 62192785, Grant No.61902401, No. 61972071), the Beijing Natural Science Foundation No. M22005.

# References

1. Boulkenafet, Z., Komulainen, J., Li, L., Feng, X., Hadid, A.: Oulu-npu: a mobile face presentation attack database with real-world variations. In: 2017 12th IEEE International Conference on Automatic Face & Gesture Recognition (FG 2017), pp. 612–618. IEEE (2017)
2. Cao, J., Li, Y., Zhang, Z.: Partially shared multi-task convolutional neural network with local constraint for face attribute learning. In: Proceedings of the IEEE Conference on Computer Vision and Pattern Recognition, pp. 4290–4299 (2018)
3. Chen, T., Kornblith, S., Norouzi, M., Hinton, G.: A simple framework for contrastive learning of visual representations. In: International Conference on Machine Learning, pp. 1597–1607. PMLR (2020)
4. Chen, X., Fan, H., Girshick, R., He, K.: Improved baselines with momentum contrastive learning. arXiv preprint arXiv:2003.04297 (2020)
5. Chen, X., He, K.: Exploring simple siamese representation learning. In: Proceedings of the IEEE/CVF Conference on Computer Vision and Pattern Recognition, pp. 15750–15758 (2021)
6. Chingovska, I., Anjos, A., Marcel, S.: On the effectiveness of local binary patterns in face anti-spoofing. In: 2012 BIOSIG-Proceedings of the International Conference of Biometrics Special Interest Group (BIOSIG), pp. 1–7. IEEE (2012)
7. Dalal, N., Triggs, B.: Histograms of oriented gradients for human detection. In: 2005 IEEE Computer Society Conference on Computer Vision and Pattern Recognition (CVPR 2005), vol. 1, pp. 886–893. IEEE (2005)
8. Deng, J., Guo, J., Xue, N., Zafeiriou, S.: Arcface: additive angular margin loss for deep face recognition. In: Proceedings of the IEEE/CVF Conference on Computer Vision and Pattern Recognition, pp. 4690–4699 (2019)
9. Feng, L., Po, L.M., Li, Y., Xu, X., Yuan, F., Cheung, T.C.H., Cheung, K.W.: Integration of image quality and motion cues for face anti-spoofing: a neural network approach. J. Vis. Commun. Image Represent. **38**, 451–460 (2016)
10. de Freitas Pereira, T., Anjos, A., De Martino, J.M., Marcel, S.: *LBP–TOP* based countermeasure against face spoofing attacks. In: Park, J.-I., Kim, J. (eds.) ACCV 2012. LNCS, vol. 7728, pp. 121–132. Springer, Heidelberg (2013). https://doi.org/10.1007/978-3-642-37410-4_11
11. Grill, J.B., Strub, F., Altché, F., Tallec, C., Richemond, P., Buchatskaya, E., Doersch, C., Avila Pires, B., Guo, Z., Gheshlaghi Azar, M., et al.: Bootstrap your own latent-a new approach to self-supervised learning. Adv. Neural. Inf. Process. Syst. **33**, 21271–21284 (2020)
12. He, K., Chen, X., Xie, S., Li, Y., Dollár, P., Girshick, R.: Masked autoencoders are scalable vision learners. arXiv preprint arXiv:2111.06377 (2021)
13. He, K., Zhang, X., Ren, S., Sun, J.: Deep residual learning for image recognition. In: Proceedings of the IEEE Conference on Computer Vision and Pattern Recognition, pp. 770–778 (2016)
14. Jourabloo, A., Liu, Y., Liu, X.: Face de-spoofing: anti-spoofing via noise modeling. In: Ferrari, V., Hebert, M., Sminchisescu, C., Weiss, Y. (eds.) ECCV 2018. LNCS, vol. 11217, pp. 297–315. Springer, Cham (2018). https://doi.org/10.1007/978-3-030-01261-8_18
15. Krizhevsky, A., Sutskever, I., Hinton, G.E.: Imagenet classification with deep convolutional neural networks. In: Advances in Neural Information Processing Systems, pp. 1097–1105 (2012)

16. Liu, Y., Jourabloo, A., Liu, X.: Learning deep models for face anti-spoofing: binary or auxiliary supervision. In: Proceedings of the IEEE Conference on Computer Vision and Pattern Recognition, pp. 389–398 (2018)
17. Liu, Y., Stehouwer, J., Liu, X.: On disentangling spoof trace for generic face anti-spoofing. In: Vedaldi, A., Bischof, H., Brox, T., Frahm, J.-M. (eds.) ECCV 2020. LNCS, vol. 12363, pp. 406–422. Springer, Cham (2020). https://doi.org/10.1007/978-3-030-58523-5_24
18. Liu, Y., Cao, J., Li, B., Hu, W., Maybank, S.: Learning to explore distillability and sparsability: a joint framework for model compression. IEEE Trans. Pattern Anal. Mach. Intell. (2022)
19. Liu, Y., et al.: Knowledge distillation via instance relationship graph. In: Proceedings of the IEEE/CVF Conference on Computer Vision and Pattern Recognition. pp. 7096–7104 (2019)
20. Patel, K., Han, H., Jain, A.K.: Secure face unlock: spoof detection on smartphones. IEEE Trans. Inf. Forensics Secur. 11(10), 2268–2283 (2016)
21. Qin, Y., Yu, Z., Yan, L., Wang, Z., Zhao, C., Lei, Z.: Meta-teacher for face anti-spoofing. IEEE Trans. Pattern Anal. Mach. Intell. (2021)
22. Szegedy, C., et al.: Going deeper with convolutions. In: Proceedings of the IEEE Conference on Computer Vision and Pattern Recognition, pp. 1–9 (2015)
23. Wang, H., et al.: Cosface: large margin cosine loss for deep face recognition. In: Proceedings of the IEEE Conference on Computer Vision and Pattern Recognition, pp. 5265–5274 (2018)
24. Wang, Z., et al.: Exploiting temporal and depth information for multi-frame face anti-spoofing. arXiv preprint arXiv:1811.05118 (2018)
25. Wei, C., Fan, H., Xie, S., Wu, C.Y., Yuille, A., Feichtenhofer, C.: Masked feature prediction for self-supervised visual pre-training. arXiv preprint arXiv:2112.09133 (2021)
26. Yang, X., et al.: Face anti-spoofing: model matters, so does data. In: Proceedings of the IEEE/CVF Conference on Computer Vision and Pattern Recognition. pp. 3507–3516 (2019)
27. Yu, Z., Li, X., Niu, X., Shi, J., Zhao, G.: Face anti-spoofing with human material perception. In: Vedaldi, A., Bischof, H., Brox, T., Frahm, J.-M. (eds.) ECCV 2020. LNCS, vol. 12352, pp. 557–575. Springer, Cham (2020). https://doi.org/10.1007/978-3-030-58571-6_33
28. Yu, Z., et al.: Searching central difference convolutional networks for face anti-spoofing. In: Proceedings of the IEEE/CVF Conference on Computer Vision and Pattern Recognition, pp. 5295–5305 (2020)
29. Zhang, K.Y., et al.: Structure destruction and content combination for face anti-spoofing. In: 2021 IEEE International Joint Conference on Biometrics (IJCB), pp. 1–6. IEEE (2021)
30. Zhang, K.-Y., et al.: Face anti-spoofing via disentangled representation learning. In: Vedaldi, A., Bischof, H., Brox, T., Frahm, J.-M. (eds.) ECCV 2020. LNCS, vol. 12364, pp. 641–657. Springer, Cham (2020). https://doi.org/10.1007/978-3-030-58529-7_38
31. Zhang, X., Ng, R., Chen, Q.: Single image reflection separation with perceptual losses. In: Proceedings of the IEEE Conference on Computer Vision and Pattern Recognition, pp. 4786–4794 (2018)

32. Zhang, Z., Yan, J., Liu, S., Lei, Z., Yi, D., Li, S.Z.: A face antispoofing database with diverse attacks. In: 2012 5th IAPR International Conference on Biometrics (ICB), pp. 26–31. IEEE (2012)
33. Zhou, B., Lapedriza, A., Xiao, J., Torralba, A., Oliva, A.: Learning deep features for scene recognition using places database. In: Advances in Neural Information Processing Systems, pp. 487–495 (2014)

# Counterfactual Image Enhancement
# for Explanation of Face Swap Deepfakes

Bo Peng[1,2], Siwei Lyu[3], Wei Wang[1], and Jing Dong[1(✉)]

[1] Center for Research on Intelligent Perception and Computing (CRIPAC),
Institute of Automation, Chinese Academy of Sciences, Beijing 100190, China
{bo.peng,wwang,jdong}@nlpr.ia.ac.cn
[2] Guangdong Key Laboratory of Intelligent Information Processing and Shenzhen
Key Laboratory of Media Security, Shenzhen 518060, China
[3] University at Buffalo, State University of New York,
Buffalo, NY 14260, USA
siweilyu@buffalo.edu

**Abstract.** Highly realistic AI generated face swap facial imagery known
as deepfakes can easily deceive human eyes and have drawn much attention. Deepfake detection models have obtained high accuracies and are
still improving, but the explanation of their decisions receives little attention in current research. Explanations are important for the credibility of
detection results, which is essential in serious applications like the court
of law. The explanation is a hard problem, apart from the deep detection
models are black boxes, the particular reason is that high-quality fakes
often have no human-eye-sensitive artifacts. We call the artifacts that
can be detected by models but are not human-eye-sensitive as subtle
artifacts. In this work, we attempt to explain model detected face swap
images to humans by proposing two simple automatic explanation methods. They enhance the original suspect image to generate its more real
and more fake counterfactual versions. By visually contrasting the original suspect image with the counterfactual images, it may become easier
for humans to notice some subtle artifacts. The two methods operate on
pixel and color spaces respectively, they do not require extra training
process and can be directly applied to any trained deepfake detection
models. We also carefully design new subjective evaluation experiments
to verify the effectiveness of proposed enhancement methods. Experiment
results show that the color space enhancement method is more preferred
by the tested subjects for explaining high-quality fake images, compared
to the other pixel space method and a baseline attribution-based explanation method. The enhancement methods can be used as a toolset that
helps human investigators to better notice artifacts in detected face swap
images and to add weights on proofs.

This work is supported by the National Key Research and Development Program of
China under Grant No. 2021YFC3320103 and the National Natural Science Foundation
of China (NSFC) under Grants 61902400, U19B2038, 61972395 and a grant from Young
Elite Scientists Sponsorship Program by CAST (YESS).

**Keywords:** Deepfake · Face swap · Explainable AI · Counterfactual explanation · Subjective study

# 1   Introduction

Deepfakes generally refer to synthesized or manipulated images, audios, or videos of a victim's likeness generated using deep learning models. The most widely known form of deepfake is the face swap videos created by a reddit user in 2017, which were fake celebrity pornography and then went virus on Internet. The model used to generate this type of deepfake is based on one shared encoder and two independent decoders for source and target faces. The model is very simple and easy to run, and later has multiple open source implementations that achieve better effects and wider attentions. Many concerns have been raised on the security and privacy risks of deepfakes, and there has been reports on misuses of deepfakes making serious harms and losses.

The media forensics community is taking actions on detecting deepfakes and has made some encouraging progress. Some methods are designed to detect specific artifacts leaved in the creation process, e.g. lack of eye-blinking [12] and lack of pulse signal [4]. However, these artifact-based methods are less general and require specific designs. Another branch of detection method relies on learning from large-scale datasets. Powerful deep-learning models [11,21] are actively studied for better detection accuracy on large deepfake datasets [5,8,13]. The learning-based methods are more popular according to recent competitions [5,18], as they are more general and easier to develop. With the fast development of deep learning methods and large-scale datasets, we foresee even more accurate and reliable detection models to emerge.

Although deepfake detection has improved greatly in terms of accuracy, the explanation of detection results is still a big problem, especially for the learning-based black-box detection models. Explanation is very important for the credibility of detection results, which is essential in serious application scenarios like the court of law. It is also important for understanding the similarities and differences between model and human perceptions of deepfakes. As detection models continuously becoming more accurate and widely deployed, the explanation problem will become more and more important.

In this work, we focus on the explanation of model detected face swap fake images to humans. And we only focus on explaining detected fakes instead of also explaining reals, since it is obviously more of a concern in actual applications. Also guided by application concerns, we put more stress on explaining the high-quality fakes, as obvious low-quality fakes are already easy to be spotted by human eyes. We note that the explanation of model detected high-quality fakes is a very hard problem. The particular reason that makes this explanation problem harder than those in semantic image recognition is that, deepfake detection models can often learn subtle artifacts that human eyes are not sensitive to. How to make these subtle artifacts more noticeable to human eyes is the key problem for the intuitive explanation of deepfakes.

Current works on explaining deepfakes [14,20] mainly use off-the-shelf attribution-based explanation methods, e.g. Grad-CAM [22], to localize important image regions with heat-maps. Like other attribution-based literature [6,7] and fake region localization methods [11,16], they only explain "where" the model thinks is fake, which is very frequently and without surprise the facial area in the face swap detection, but they cannot explain "why" it is fake. Even though they can draw the viewers' attention to some highlighted suspect regions, it may still be hard for human viewers to notice any artifacts, since human eyes are not sensitive to subtle artifacts. Hence, it is necessary to not only localize the suspect regions, but also enhance the image in certain aspects to make the subtle artifacts more noticeable.

To this end, we go deeper to attempt explaining the "why" problem. We propose two image enhancement methods that modify the original suspect image to generate its counterfactual versions that are more fake and more real, as perceived by the detection model. By comparing the original suspect image with the counterfactual images as references, human viewers are more likely to notice subtle artifacts and understand why the image is fake. Counterfactuals are imagined hypothetical realities that contradicts the observed facts that are useful for interpreting machine learning models [15]. Here, we call the more fake counterfactual as the explain-fake, and the other one as the explain-real. See Fig. 1 for examples. Human viewers may be able to discover some factors in the explain-fake image that make it appear more fake than the original image, and discover some factors in the explain-real image that make it appear more real than the original. We

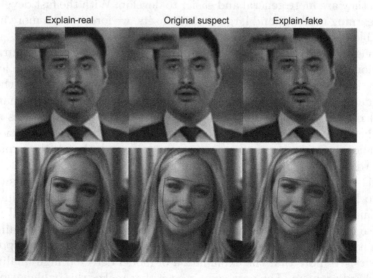

**Fig. 1.** Illustration of the proposed counterfactual enhancement results in the pixel space (top) and the color space (bottom). The proposed methods help human viewers better notice subtle artifacts by letting them compare the original image with the counterfactual images. For example, the jig-saw alike eyebrows in the first row and the color (contrast) mismatch in the second row. Best viewed in color and zoomed for details.(Color figure online)

note this comparing process is like using a pH scale chart to determine whether an aqueous solution is acidic or alkaline.

The first method enhances the original image directly in the pixel space. This method is inspired and adapted from the adversarial explanation work [23] of Woods et al.. The image pixels in the facial area are optimized to make the model prediction closer to the fake and the real end respectively. Although this method has more flexibility to reveal any kinds of artifacts, it is subject to pitfalls of generating unnatural adversarial examples that humans cannot understand. Hence, we propose to improve the interpretability in the second method by constraining the optimization space to only 6 color parameters of the facial area. Its motivation is that face swaps have splicing steps that may introduce the color-mismatch artifact between the insider facial area and its outer surroundings. This method only explains the color-mismatch artifact, but it is more interpretable.

To validate the effectiveness of the proposed methods, we devise new experimentation methods with user studies. Results show that the proposed enhancement methods can help human viewers to identify more deepfake samples, and they are useful in revealing subtle artifacts that human viewers previously missed. We also compare to the previous explanation method Guided Grad-CAM [22] and show the advantages of the proposed method.

In summary, this paper has the following contributions:

1. We tackle the problem of explaining face swap deepfakes to humans from a new perspective of counterfactual image enhancement to make subtle artifacts more noticeable.
2. We propose two methods to enhance the suspect image in the pixel space and the color space respectively, and we make our code publicly available for the convenience of future research[1].
3. We devise new experimentation methods to evaluate the effectiveness of deepfake explanation methods, and the experiment results show the proposed color space enhancement method achieves the best performance.

## 2 Proposed Methods

We propose two deepfake enhancement methods, which operate in the pixel space and the color space, respectively. The two methods use the same methodology that optimize a parameter space to push the suspect image further into the fake class or the real class. Finally, by contrasting with the generated explanation images, a human viewer may be more capable of identifying potential deepfake artifacts in the original suspect image.

### 2.1 Pixel Space Enhancement

As shown in Fig. 2, we propose a pixel space enhancement method by optimizing per-pixel perturbations. To constrain the perturbations to be in the interested

---

[1] Code available at https://github.com/NiCE-X/Deepfake_explain.

facial region, we first extract a facial mask using the convex hull of facial land-marks.

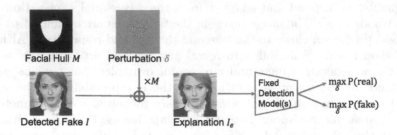

**Fig. 2.** Illustration of the proposed pixel space enhancement method.

Then the formation of the explanation image is as follows:

$$I_e = I + \delta \cdot M \qquad (1)$$

where $I_e, I, M$ are respectively the explanation image, the input image, and the facial mask, and $\delta$ is the perturbation image that has the same spatial size and number of channels as the input image. To obtain the pixel space explanation images, we optimize the perturbation $\delta$ to make the model classify it as more real or more fake. The optimization objective is as follows:

$$\hat{\delta} = \arg\max_{\delta} P(f(I_e), l) \qquad (2)$$

where $f$ represents a fixed deepfake detection model (or ensemble of models), and $P(\cdot, l)$ represents the probability of model classification to the target label $l$, which can either be real or fake. The probability $P$ is obtained as the Sigmoid of model output logit, in the range of $[0, 1]$. We use gradient decent to optimize the perturbation to generate both explain-real and explain-fake images, which are denoted as $I_e^{real}$ and $I_e^{fake}$ respectively. The maximization of the probability $P$ is converted to the minimization of the Binary Cross Entropy (BCE) loss in the optimization.

A challenge for the pixel space enhancement method is that adversarial examples can easily be generated to fool the classifier model, while human eyes cannot observe any meaningful pixel modifications. To alleviate this problem, we adopt the optimization algorithm from [23], that produces relatively large perturbations to generate visually prominent pixel modifications. We also propose to initialize the input image $I$ for multiple times by adding random noises and then optimize facial pixels to obtain multiple explanation images and finally average them. This trick can help suppress unstable adversarial perturbations and strengthen those stable artifacts, which is empirically found to obtain better enhancement results. The optimization process is detailed in Algorithm 1. In our experiments, the number of random initializations is set to $K = 3$, the number of optimization steps in set to $n = 10$, and the extent of perturbation is set to $\epsilon = 0.1$ for image values scaled in the range of [0,1]. Here, the parameter $\epsilon$ controls the magnitude of pixel perturbation, which is set as 10% of the range of image grey scale to produce relatively large perturbations. As with [23], the step size $\eta$ gradually decreases during optimization, as shown in Algorithm 1.

---

**Algorithm 1:** The Pixel Space Enhance Algorithm

---

    **input** : Suspect image $I$, facial mask $M$, fixed deepfake detection model(s) $f$,
            number of steps $n$, perturbation extent $\epsilon$, number of random
            initializations $K$.
    **output:** Explain-real image $I_e^{real}$, explain-fake image $I_e^{fake}$.

1   **for** *Target label* $l \in$ [real, fake] **do**
2     **for** $k = 1 : K$ **do**
3        Add random noise to $I$;
4        Initialize perturbation $\delta = 0$;
5        **for** $i = 1 : n$ **do**
6           Calculate $I_e^{(i)}$ using Eq. 1;
7           Calculate BCE loss $E^{(i)} = \mathrm{BCE}(f(I_e^{(i)}, l))$;
8           Calculate derivative $d_\delta = \partial E^{(i)} / \partial \delta^{(i-1)}$;
9           Update step size $\eta = 2\epsilon \cdot (n - i - 1)/n^2$;
10          Update perturbation $\delta^{(i)} = \delta^{(i-1)} - \eta \cdot d_\delta / \|d_\delta\|$;
11        **end**
12        $I_e^{(k)} \leftarrow I_e^{(i)}$;
13     **end**
14     $I_e^l = \sum_{k=1}^{K} I_e^{(k)}/K$;
15 **end**

---

## 2.2 Color Space Enhancement

As shown in Fig. 3, we propose a color space enhancement method by optimizing the color parameters. Since deepfake generation usually incorporates splicing the generated facial area, there may be color (or contrast) mismatch between the spliced facial area and its surrounding area. We propose to enhance the original image to generate the more natural and more unnatural images in terms of color matchiness to make this kind of artifact more noticeable.

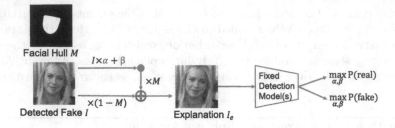

**Fig. 3.** Illustration of the proposed color space enhancement method.

---

**Algorithm 2:** The Color Space Enhance Algorithm

---

**input** : Suspect image $I$, facial mask $M$, fixed deepfake detection model(s) $f$,
step size $\eta$, tolerance $\epsilon$.
**output:** Explain-real image $I_e^{real}$, explain-fake image $I_e^{fake}$.

1 **for** *Target label* $l \in [\text{real}, \text{fake}]$ **do**
2 | Initialize $\alpha = 1$, $\beta = 0$ for all RGB channels;
3 | Initialize $i = 0$;
4 | **repeat**
5 | | $i = i + 1$;
6 | | Calculate $I_e^{(i)}$ using Eq. 3;
7 | | Calculate BCE loss $E^{(i)} = \text{BCE}(f(I_e^{(i)}, l))$;
8 | | Calculate derivative $d_\alpha = \partial E^{(i)} / \partial \alpha^{(i-1)}$;
9 | | Calculate derivative $d_\beta = \partial E^{(i)} / \partial \beta^{(i-1)}$;
10 | | Update $\alpha^{(i)} = \alpha^{(i-1)} - \eta \cdot d_\alpha / \|d_\alpha\|$;
11 | | Update $\beta^{(i)} = \beta^{(i-1)} - \eta \cdot d_\beta / \|d_\beta\|$;
12 | **until** $\|E^{(i)} - E^{(i-1)}\| < \epsilon$ *for 5 consecutive iterations*;
13 | $I_e^l \leftarrow I_e^{(i)}$;
14 **end**

---

More specifically, we first extract the facial mask using the convex hull of facial landmarks as in the pixel space method. Then the formation of the explanation image is as follows:

$$I_e = I \cdot (1 - M) + [(\alpha_r \cdot I_r + \beta_r), (\alpha_g \cdot I_g + \beta_g), (\alpha_b \cdot I_b + \beta_b)] \cdot M \quad (3)$$

where $I_r, I_g, I_b$ are respectively the RGB channels of the input image, and $\alpha, \beta$ are the contrast and bias parameters for adjusting each color channel. The border of the mask image is blurred to prevent introducing sharp blending edges. To obtain the explanation images in the color space, we optimize the color parameters $\alpha, \beta$ to make the model classify it as more real or fake. The optimization objective is as follows:

$$\hat{\alpha}, \hat{\beta} = \arg\max_{\alpha, \beta} P(f(I_e), l) \quad (4)$$

The parameters to be optimized here is the 6-dimensional color parameters. As in the pixel-space enhancement, we use gradient decent for optimization, and the maximization of the probability P is converted to the minimization of the BCE loss. The optimization process is detailed in Algorithm 2. In our experiment, the step size is set as $\eta = 10^{-3}$, and the tolerance for terminating the optimization is set as $\epsilon = 10^{-2}$.

## 3    Experiments

Since the main purpose of explaining deepfakes is to make the detection results more intuitive to humans, we design a set of experiments to allow human subjects to evaluate the effectiveness of the explanations provided by the proposed methods.

### 3.1    Datasets, Model and Baseline

To increase the diversity in the evaluation data, we combine 10 existing face swap datasets to form our evaluation dataset. The 10 datasets are FaceSwap [3], FaceShifter [10], FSGAN [17], UnifiedEncoder [19], DeepFakeDetection (DFD) [1], DFDC-test [5], Celeb-DF [13], DeeperForensics [9], WildDeepfake [24] (WDF), and ForgeryNet-3DMM [8]. The first 5 datasets are included in the FaceForensics++ dataset [21] or generated from its real images using the corresponding methods. FaceSwap and ForgeryNet-3DMM (named as "MM Replacement" in the original paper) are generated by two 3D face warping methods, and the rest are mainly by deep generation models. These datasets represent the general state of the art of current face swap deepfakes used in research papers or encountered in the wild.

Since we focus on explaining the detection of DeepFake examples, a pool of frames are first drawn from only the fake videos of each dataset, then 30 samples with detection scores above 0.6 using the chosen detection models (details below) are randomly selected from each dataset as the to-be-explained suspect images. The detection score represents the likelihood of being a fake that is predicted by the detection model. More specifically, we equally sample 10 images from three ranges of the detection scores, i.e. $[0.6,0.8),[0.8,0.92),[0.92,1]$, to represent different levels of detection confidence. As such, the total number of deepfake images to be explained and presented to human viewers is 300, i.e., $30\times10$.

We use the detection model corresponding to the top performer [2] of the Facebook DeepFake Detection Challenge. It is an ensemble model of seven EfficientNet-B7 models trained with heavy data augmentations. Because of the constraint of computational resources, we use five out of the seven pre-trained models to ensemble in our experiments. This method can be deemed as the SOTA face swap detection model.

As a comparison baseline to our methods, we use the Guided Grad-CAM (g-gradCAM) approach [22], which combines class-discriminative attribution heatmaps with back-propagated gradients to provide pixel-level granularity explanation results. The g-gradCAM result represents the importance of image pixels to the classifier output, and we convert it to a transparency map to be overlayed on the original image.

## 3.2  Query Settings

We recruited 10 subjects to independently examine the 300 deepfake images and their enhancement images and then answer several evaluation questions. Each of them was paid with 400 CNY as rewards (approximately 60 USD) and formally consented with the subjective evaluations. The 10 subjects compose of 6 females and 4 males with ages ranging from 20 to 31, and they are all college students or graduates. Of the 10 subjects, 7 reported familiar with portrait editing or deepfakes, and the remaining 3 reported unfamiliar with these topics. Before the experiments, they were given information on the backgrounds about typical deepfake artifacts, the aim of this test, how to interpret each explanation result, and the query procedure. They were also told that the testing images are classified as fake by a deepfake detection model, and they were requested to answer questions based only on their own observations of the images.

The 300 groups of images from different datasets are randomly mixed. Each group is composed of 4 images that are the original deepfake image (original), its enhanced explanation images by the g-gradCAM method (method A), our pixel space method (method B) and color space method (method C). All images are face crops resized to 380×380 in pixels. Examples of explanation images can be found in Fig. 7. The 4 images in each group were presented to each viewer sequentially, where they were pre-saved in a folder and the viewer used their computer screens for viewing and were free to control the time duration. Six questions were asked to the subjects for each group of images, which were in the form of a spread sheet to be filled by each subject. The specific questions are as follows:

1. q0: Observe the original suspect image and rate the noticeability level of artifacts in the image. Answers are selected from "very obvious" (indicated by the number 2), "relatively obvious" (indicated by 1) and "not obvious/not sure" (indicated by 0).
2. qA: Observe the enhanced images by method A, especially the explain-fake panel, does it highlight any artifacts of the original image? Answers are selected from "yes" (indicated by 1) and "no/not sure" (indicated by 0).
3. qB: Observe the enhanced images by method B, use the explain-fake and explain-real as references, do you notice any artifacts in the original image? Answers are selected from "yes" (indicated by 1) and "no/not sure" (indicated by 0).
4. qC0: Observe the enhanced images by method C, does the explain-real image seem more natural in color and contrast than the original image? Answers are selected from "more natural" (indicated by 1), "less natural" (indicated by −1) and "no difference/not sure" (indicated by 0).

5. qC1: Observe the enhanced images by method C, does it reveal the original image has color mismatch artifact? Answers are selected from "yes" (indicated by 1) and "no/not sure" (indicated by 0).
6. q1: Finally, which method do you think is most useful for revealing artifacts that explain this image is fake? Answers are selected from "A", "B", "C", and "none".

According to the 10 tested subjects, the mean time consumed to complete one group of queries is 1.55 min, with a 0.11 min standard deviation across different subjects. We also post-process the obtained query answers to eliminate obvious faults, such as choosing "no difference/not sure" for qC0 while choosing "yes" for qC1. Note that it is possible for a subject to rate the explain-real image of method C more natural while still think it does not reveal any color mismatch in the original image, because he or she may regard the original color matchiness natural enough.

### 3.3   Analysis of Query Results

**Distributions of Image Quality**
We first analyze the joint distribution of model prediction scores and Mean Opinion Scores (MOS) of the artifact noticeability level in original images, which is shown in Fig. 4a. The model prediction scores are directly obtained by inputting the original images into the detection model. The artifact MOS of an original image is obtained by averaging the 10 subject evaluations of artifact noticeability, as mentioned in q0, "very obvious", "relatively obvious" and "not obvious/not sure" are respectively represented by 2, 1 and 0. More formally,

$$\text{MOS} = \sum_{i=1}^{N_s} q0_i/N_s, \quad q0_i \in \{0, 1, 2\} \tag{5}$$

Here, $N_s = 10$ is the number of subjects, and $q0_i$ represents Subject i's answer to q0. From the marginal distribution of artifact MOS shown in Fig. 4a, we can see that the sampled dataset has diverse visual qualities. As shown in Fig. 4a, there is no correlation between model detection scores and human evaluated artifact scores (the correlation coefficient is 0.028). This implies that the artifacts perceived by the detection model and by the tested subjects are largely different. On the one hand, the detection model may have learnt some very subtle artifacts that cannot be very intuitively perceived by human eyes. On the other hand, obvious fake images as perceived by humans are not necessarily confident to be detected by the model, since learning-based models predict new samples based on their knowledge from the training set distribution, which may not include some kinds of obvious fakes.

For each of the 10 deepfake datasets, the distributions of per-answer artifact noticeability level that are evaluated by all the tested subjects are shown in Fig. 4b, and the mean artifact noticeability scores of each dataset are also shown. From this figure, we can see the difference in human observed quality of each face

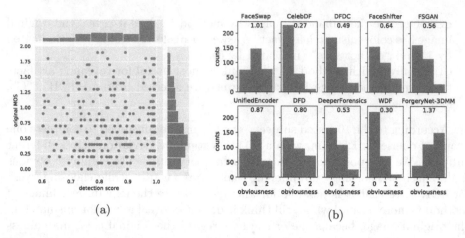

(a)    (b)

**Fig. 4.** Analysis of dataset. (a) The joint distribution of model detection scores and Mean Opinion Scores (MOS) of original suspect images. (b) The distribution of artifact noticeability level for each subset. The noticeability (obviousness) indicators 2, 1, 0 represents "very obvious", "relatively obvious" and "not obvious/not sure", respectively. The scores at the top of each subfigure are mean noticeability scores of each subset.

swap dataset. Notably, the Celeb-DF and WildDeepfake (WDF) datasets have the lowest overall artifact levels, and the two 3D warping based swap datasets ForgeryNet-3DMM and FaceSwap have the highest artifact levels.

**Distributions of Query Results**

The distributions of all subjects' answers to the six queries (in Sect. 3.2) are shown in Fig. 5a, which is a per-answer summation. Method A, B, C are respectively the g-gradCAM, the proposed pixel space and color pace method. Analyzing these answers, we have the following observations:

- a) Many answers (48.4%) to q0 are "not sure", indicating the subjects cannot directly identify clear artifacts in the original image for nearly half of all cases.
- b) The ratios of each method successfully revealing artifacts are respectively 35.2%, 20.6%, and 27.5% (qA, qB and qC1). Note that the artifacts in an image may be revealed by multiple methods in the same case.
- c) The preference rate for method A, B, C are respectively 26.6%, 4.9% and 23.8% according to q1, and still many answers (44.8%) think none of these methods reveals any artifacts.
- d) For method C, i.e., the color-space enhancement method, 33.8% answers think the explain-real image is more natural in color than the original, 48.7% choose not sure or no difference, and 17.6% choose less natural.

According to the above statistics, the g-gradCAM method reveals the most artifacts and is most preferred by the 10 subjects for the whole dataset. However, since the dataset has diverse image qualities, in the following, we compare these methods along different qualities, and in more details. We will show that the high preference rate for the g-gradCAM method is mostly for the relatively low-quality fakes, and its high artifact reveal rate is mostly from the artifacts that the subjects can already notice by directly viewing the original image.

## Comparison of Enhancement Methods

In Fig. 5b, we compare the performance of each method along different image qualities. In this figure, the histogram shows the distribution of artifact MOS* of original images. Different from the MOS in Fig. 4a and Eq. 5, here we merge the "relatively obvious" (1) and "very obvious" (2) into the same "obvious" category (1), so that there are only two opinions here:

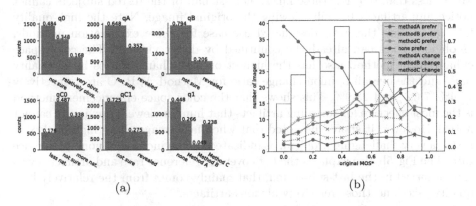

(a)                                (b)

**Fig. 5.** Analysis of query results. (a) The overall distributions of all subjects' answers to the 6 queries on all image samples. The number above each bar indicates the ratio of choosing that answer over the sum. (b) Comparison of each method's prefer ratio (pref) and opinion change ratio (ocr) along different image qualities. See the text for detailed explanations. Best viewed in digital color version.(Color figure online)

$$\text{MOS}* = \sum_{i=1}^{N_s} q0_i'/N_s, \quad q0_i' = \begin{cases} 0, & \text{if } q0_i = 0 \\ 1, & \text{if } q0_i \in \{1,2\} \end{cases} \tag{6}$$

The solid lines, i.e., the preference ratios, are the ratios of each method being preferred in answers to q1 for images in each quality bin. More formally, the preference ration for Method k in the m'th original MOS* bin, $\text{pref}_m^k$, is calculated as follows,

$$\text{pref}_m^k = \sum_{j}^{N_{im}} \sum_{i}^{N_s} \mathbb{1}(q1_i^j = k)/(N_s \cdot N_{im}), \quad k \in \{\text{A}, \text{B}, \text{C}, \text{none}\}. \tag{7}$$

Here, $N_s$ is the number of subjects, i.e., 10, $N_{im}$ is the number of images that have original artifact MOS* in this bin, $\mathbb{1}$ is the indicator function, and $q1_i^j$ represents Subject-i's answer to q1 for Image-j. The dashed lines, i.e., the opinion change ratios, are the ratios of the enhancement results successfully change the subject opinions on images they originally cannot notice artifacts (to can notice artifacts). More formally, the opinion change ratio of Method k in the m'th original MOS* bin, $\mathrm{ocr}_m^k$, is calculated as,

$$\mathrm{ocr}_m^k = \sum \mathbb{1}(q0 = 0, qk = 1)/\sum \mathbb{1}(q0 = 0), \quad qk \in \{qA, qB, qC1\}. \quad (8)$$

As can be seen from Fig. 5b, as the image quality increases (original MOS* moving from 1 to 0), the preference ratios for all methods decreases, and the g-gradCAM (Method A) decreases the most. The proposed color space enhancement method is the most preferred for high quality fake images with original MOS* less than 0.5. For these fakes, at least half of the tested subjects cannot notice any artifacts by only viewing the original image. Note the high-quality fake images are the most designated use case for these explanation methods, as obvious fakes can already be confirmed by direct viewing. The color space enhancement method also has the highest opinion change ratios in all quality bins, and the overall opinion change ratio for Method A, B, C are respectively 14.4%, 7.6%, and 23.9%. This shows that the color space enhancement method is the most effective for revealing artifacts that human viewers previously cannot notice. However, it should be noted that when fake images have high quality, it is still a very challenging problem, as indicated by the increasing none-preference rate. The Fig. 5b also explains the high overall preference rate and artifact reveal rate observed in the last subsection, that mainly comes from the relatively low-quality fakes and those relatively obvious artifacts.

**Explanation Toolset**

If we combine the three methods as a single toolset (i.e., at least one explanation method is effective (q1 ≠ "none")) to explain deepfakes, the artifact MOS* of the original and enhanced images are as shown in Fig. 6. Here the enhanced MOS* is calculated by regarding the noticeable artifacts both before (q0 > 0) and after seeing the enhancement results (q1 ≠ "none") as the positive opinion 1, and otherwise 0. As can be seen, the overall MOS* distribution is moved to the more obvious or revealed side. We can say that these enhancement methods

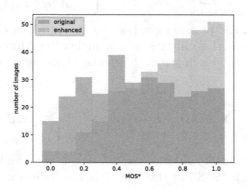

**Fig. 6.** Distributions of artifact MOS* before and after enhancement by using the three methods as toolset.

are useful to make subtle deepfake artifacts more noticeable to humans. Hence the credibility of detection results is improved.

### 3.4    Enhancement Examples

In Fig. 7, we show some enhanced images to give a qualitative overview of each method's results. These examples are mainly selected from the relatively high-quality fakes with one specific method being most preferred by the subjects. The model detection scores are also shown for the proposed methods in each example (which are not shown during subjective testing).

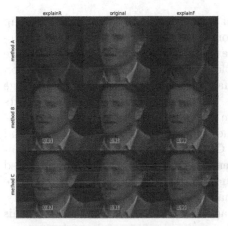 

(a) Original MOS* is 0.4, preference ratios for none, A, B, C are respectively 0.2, 0.2, 0.0, 0.6, enhanced MOS* is 0.9.

(b) Original MOS* is 0.2, preference ratios for none, A, B, C are respectively 0.4, 0.1, 0.0, 0.5, enhanced MOS* is 0.6.

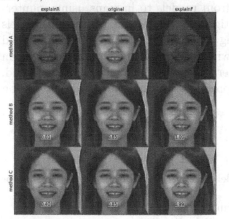

(c) Original MOS* is 0.4, preference ratios for none, A, B, C are respectively 0.4, 0.5, 0.0, 0.1, enhanced MOS* is 0.6.

(d) Original MOS* is 0.7, preference ratios for none, A, B, C are respectively 0.1, 0.3, 0.5, 0.1, enhanced MOS* is 0.9.

**Fig. 7.** Demonstration of enhancement examples. Best viewed in color and zoomed for details.

Take Fig. 7a for example, the model detection scores for the original, explain-real and explain-fake images of method B are 0.91, 0.01 and 0.99, respectively, and those for the explain-real and explain-fake of method C are 0.47 and 0.99. The original MOS* is 0.4, meaning only 4 tested subjects noticed artifacts by only viewing the original image (q0). While the enhanced MOS* is 0.9, meaning that with the help of the three methods as a toolset, finally 9 (out of 10) tested subjects noticed the artifacts. And the color space method is most preferred (q1) for this example.

## 4 Conclusions

In this paper, we focus on the problem of explaining model detected face swap deepfakes to human viewers, which is important for interpretable deepfake detection. To tackle this problem, we propose two enhancement methods that are based on optimizing image pixels and color parameters to make the detection model to classify as more real and more fake. By comparing the original image and enhanced images, a human viewer is more likely to notice subtle artifacts he or she previously missed and to believe the model detection results. We conducted comprehensive human subject study on a diverse deepfake dataset and compared to a popular baseline method - Guided GradCAM. Subjective evaluations show that the proposed color space enhancement method is more preferred by tested subjects for revealing artifacts in high-quality fakes, and it is also more effective in exposing fake images that human subjects previously cannot identify. When used together as a toolset, the enhancement methods investigated in this paper can considerably improve the human comprehension of deepfake images.

It should be noted that the explanation of deepfake is a very challenging problem, and this work is a small step towards this direction. For future research, the core idea of transferring knowledge from models to humans using counterfactual enhancement needs further investigation. As deepfake detection models constantly becoming stronger, developing methods that make model-captured artifacts more interpretable to humans will be more valuable. This work is an initial attempt in this direction, and other ways of enhancing may be explored. How to better constrain the method to prevent adversarial examples is also an important issue to be studied.

## References

1. DeepFakeDetection.     https://ai.googleblog.com/2019/09/contributing-data-to-deepfake-detection.html
2. DFDC top performer. https://github.com/selimsef/dfdc_deepfake_challenge
3. FaceSwap. https://github.com/MarekKowalski/FaceSwap
4. Ciftci, U.A., Demir, I., Yin, L.: FakeCatcher: detection of synthetic portrait videos using biological signals. IEEE Trans. Patt. Anal. Mach. Intell. (2020)
5. Dolhansky, B., et al: The DeepFake detection challenge dataset. arXiv preprint arXiv:2006.07397 (2020)

6. Fong, R., Patrick, M., Vedaldi, A.: Understanding deep networks via extremal perturbations and smooth masks. In: Proceedings of the IEEE/CVF International Conference on Computer Vision, pp. 2950–2958 (2019)
7. Fong, R.C., Vedaldi, A.: Interpretable explanations of black boxes by meaningful perturbation. In: Proceedings of the IEEE International Conference on Computer Vision, pp. 3429–3437 (2017)
8. He, Y., et al.: ForgeryNet: a versatile benchmark for comprehensive forgery analysis. In: Proceedings of the IEEE/CVF Conference on Computer Vision and Pattern Recognition, pp. 4360–4369
9. Jiang, L., Li, R., Wu, W., Qian, C., Loy, C.C.: DeeperForensics-1.0: a large-scale dataset for real-world face forgery detection. In: Proceedings of the IEEE/CVF Conference on Computer Vision and Pattern Recognition, pp. 2889–2898
10. Li, L., Bao, J., Yang, H., Chen, D., Wen, F.: FaceShifter: towards high fidelity and occlusion aware face swapping. arXiv preprint arXiv:1912.13457 (2019)
11. Li, L., et al.: Face X-ray for more general face forgery detection. In: Proceedings of the IEEE/CVF Conference on Computer Vision and Pattern Recognition, pp. 5001–5010
12. Li, Y., Chang, M.C., Lyu, S.: In Ictu oculi: exposing AI created fake videos by detecting eye blinking. In: 2018 IEEE International Workshop on Information Forensics and Security (WIFS), pp. 1–7. IEEE (2018)
13. Li, Y., Yang, X., Sun, P., Qi, H., Lyu, S.: Celeb-DF: a large-scale challenging dataset for DeepFake forensics. In: Proceedings of the IEEE/CVF Conference on Computer Vision and Pattern Recognition, pp. 3207–3216
14. Malolan, B., Parekh, A., Kazi, F.: Explainable deep-fake detection using visual interpretability methods. In: 2020 3rd International Conference on Information and Computer Technologies (ICICT), pp. 289–293. IEEE (2020)
15. Molnar, C.: Interpretable machine learning. Lulu. com (2020)
16. Nguyen, H.H., Fang, F., Yamagishi, J., Echizen, I.: Multi-task learning for detecting and segmenting manipulated facial images and videos. arXiv preprint arXiv:1906.06876 (2019)
17. Nirkin, Y., Keller, Y., Hassner, T.: FSGAN: subject agnostic face swapping and reenactment. In: Proceedings of the IEEE International Conference on Computer Vision, pp. 7184–7193
18. Peng, B., et al.: DFGC 2021: a DeepFake game competition. In: 2021 IEEE International Joint Conference on Biometrics (IJCB), pp. 1–8. https://doi.org/10.1109/IJCB52358.2021.9484387
19. Peng, B., Fan, H., Wang, W., Dong, J., Lyu, S.: A unified framework for high fidelity face swap and expression reenactment. IEEE Trans. Circ. Syst. Video Technol. **32**, 3673–3684 (2021)
20. Pino, S., Carman, M.J., Bestagini, P.: What's wrong with this video? Comparing explainers for deepfake detection. arXiv preprint arXiv:2105.05902 (2021)
21. Rossler, A., Cozzolino, D., Verdoliva, L., Riess, C., Thies, J., Nießner, M.: FaceForensics++: learning to detect manipulated facial images. In: Proceedings of the IEEE/CVF International Conference on Computer Vision, pp. 1–11
22. Selvaraju, R.R., Cogswell, M., Das, A., Vedantam, R., Parikh, D., Batra, D.: Grad-CAM: visual explanations from deep networks via gradient-based localization. In: Proceedings of the IEEE International Conference on Computer Vision, pp. 618–626

23. Woods, W., Chen, J., Teuscher, C.: Adversarial explanations for understanding image classification decisions and improved neural network robustness. Nat. Mach. Intell. **1**(11), 508–516 (2019)
24. Zi, B., Chang, M., Chen, J., Ma, X., Jiang, Y.G.: WildDeepfake: a challenging real-world dataset for DeepFake detection. In: Proceedings of the 28th ACM International Conference on Multimedia, pp. 2382–2390 (2020)

# Improving Pre-trained Masked Autoencoder via Locality Enhancement for Person Re-identification

Yanzuo Lu[1], Manlin Zhang[1], Yiqi Lin[1], Andy J. Ma[1,2,3(✉)], Xiaohua Xie[1,2,3], and Jianhuang Lai[1,2,3]

[1] School of Computer Science and Engineering, Sun Yat-sen University, Guangzhou, China
majh8@mail.sysu.edu.cn
[2] Guangdong Province Key Laboratory of Information Security Technology, Guangzhou, China
[3] Key Laboratory of Machine Intelligence and Advanced Computing, Ministry of Education, Guangzhou, China

**Abstract.** Person Re-identification (ReID) is a computer vision task of retrieving a person of interest across multiple non-overlapping cameras. Most of the existing methods are developed based on convolutional neural networks trained with supervision, which may suffer from the problem of missing subtle visual cues and global information caused by pooling operations and the weight-sharing mechanism. To this end, we propose a novel Transformer-based ReID method by pre-training with Masked Autoencoders and fine-tuning with locality enhancement. In our method, Masked Autoencoders are pre-trained in a self-supervised way by using large-scale unlabeled data such that subtle visual cues can be learned with the pixel-level reconstruction loss. With the Transformer backbone, global features are extracted as the classification token which integrates information from different patches by the self-attention mechanism. To take full advantage of local information, patch tokens are reshaped into a feature map for convolution to extract local features in the proposed locality enhancement module. Both global and local features are combined to obtain more robust representations of person images for inference. To the best of our knowledge, this is the first work to utilize generative self-supervised learning for representation learning in ReID. Experiments show that the proposed method achieves competitive performance in terms of parameter scale, computation overhead, and ReID performance compared with the state of the art. Code is available at https://github.com/YanzuoLu/MALE.

**Keywords:** Masked Autoencoders · Transformer · Self-supervised learning · Person re-identification

## 1 Introduction

Person re-identification (ReID) aims at retrieving and associating the same person from different cameras. In the last decade, Convolutional Neural Networks

S. Yu et al. (Eds.): PRCV 2022, LNCS 13535, pp. 509–521, 2022.
https://doi.org/10.1007/978-3-031-18910-4_41

(CNNs) have achieved great success for the ReID task [16,19,23,27]. However, recent research [17] shows that the CNN-based methods have several drawbacks compared to the transformer-based approach. On the one hand, the weight-sharing mechanism of convolutional kernels may be harmful to discovering global cues, such as the pedestrian silhouette and human pose. On the other hand, pooling operations in CNNs may result in losing subtle visual cues, which are crucial to help discriminate between different persons (e.g. whether someone is wearing a watch or carrying a bag). By contrast, transformer-based methods utilize the self-attention mechanism to automatically capture important information in the global scope by maintaining long-range dependencies spatially. However, due to strong representation capacity, transformers tend to overfit small datasets which impedes their direct applications on various downstream tasks including ReID.

To address this issue, several self-supervised learning methods [2,11,29] have been proposed to pre-train the Transformer on large-scale unlabeled datasets before fine-tuning. Recent self-supervised pre-training methods based on transformers can be divided into contrastive [3,7,25] and generative [1,14,26] self-supervised approaches depending on the different kinds of pretext tasks. The contrastive self-supervised approach learns feature representation by increasing (decreasing) the similarity between different views of the same image (different images), while the generative self-supervised approach predicts the original input based on the latent code of corrupted data. By using the Transformer-based contrastive self-supervised learning, TransReID-SSL [20] takes advantage of millions of unlabeled person images for pre-training the ReID model, in which the contrastive self-supervised method DINO [3] is applied to learn feature representations. Despite the success of the Transformer and self-supervised learning in many applications, the Transformer-based generative pre-training approach has not yet been explored for the ReID task.

In this paper, we propose to learn robust feature representation by using the generative self-supervised learning method Masked Autoencoders (MAE) [14], rather than contrastive, which reconstructs pixels from masked person images. Different from the contrastive self-supervised learning methods depending on data augmentation for pre-training, the generative pre-training approach is able to preserve subtle visual cues by optimizing for the pixel-level reconstruction loss. Moreover, the Transformer encoder in MAE outputs global features represented as the classification token which models dependencies between different patches by the self-attention mechanism.

To further take full advantage of local information in patch tokens, we propose a Locality Enhancement Module (LEM) to construct their reshaped feature maps, and then extract local features by applying convolution operations on them. In our method, the patch tokens are reshaped according to the resolution of the input image so that position information is preserved in the feature maps of the patch tokens encoding local features. Based on the reshaped feature maps, local features among patch tokens are aggregated via convolution operations, which can utilize the locality and translation invariance properties of CNNs. The proposed LEM is a plug-and-play module which can be integrated in any Transformer backbone network that generates a sequence of patch tokens. By combining the global features of the classification token with the local features extracted by the LEM, more robust features representations are obtained for improving the ReID performance.

In summary, we propose a new framework to pre-train the Transformer backbone with Masked Autoencoder and then fine-tune it with Locality Enhancement (**MALE**) for improving the person re-identification performance. The proposed method is illustrated in Fig. 1. The contributions of this work are in three folds:

- This is the first work to utilize the generative self-supervised learning method Masked Autoencoders for person ReID, such that feature representation with stronger generalization ability can be extracted for the downstream task.
- To fully exploit the local information in patch tokens, we propose a locality enhancement module (LEM) by using convolution on reshaped feature maps to extract local features for a more robust representation of person images.
- Experiment and ablation study results on publicly available benchmarks including Market-1501 [28] and MSMT17 [24] demonstrate the effectiveness of our method pre-trained on LUPerson [12].

## 2   Related Work

**Contrastive Self-supervised Learning.** In contrastive self-supervised learning methods, two different views of the same image are first obtained by performing random data augmentation, and then a loss function is used to make the positive/negative image pairs as close/far as possible in the feature space. MoCo [6,7,15] maintains a dynamic dictionary with a queue to store negative samples and encodes them using a momentum encoder, which maximizes consistency throughout the training process. SimCLR [4,5] explores in detail the impact of the combination of data augmentations on contrastive self-supervised methods and introduces a nonlinear projection head to improve the quality of the features. The difference between the above two methods is the construction of positive and negative pairs, while BYOL [13] makes a difference and removes negative pairs completely, utilizing the natural extraction capability of networks. DINO [3] combined with ViT [11] as a backbone also does not construct negative sample pairs but avoids collapse through centering and sharpening operations, replacing the asymmetric predictor in BYOL [13].

**Generative Self-supervised Learning.** Generative self-supervised methods usually follow the idea of autoencoders, corrupting the input signal and learning to reconstruct its original uncorrupted signal. BEiT [1] is motivated by BERT [10] in natural language processing, tokenizing the image to discrete visual tokens for prediction with discrete VAE proposed by [21]. Another approach is Masked Autoencoders (MAE) [14] that we adopt for the pre-training stage, which

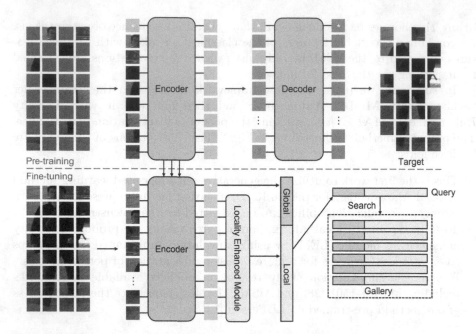

**Fig. 1. Overall Architecture.** In the pre-training stage, feature representations are learned by reconstructing masked person images to preserve subtle visual cues via the generative self-supervised learning method Masked Autoencoders (MAE). To fully utilize local information in the Transformer backbone, global features represented by the classification token and local features extracted by the proposed LEM module are combined in the fine-tuning stage to extract more robust feature representations.

designs an asymmetric encoder-decoder architecture to reconstruct original pixels instead of tokens. It achieves lightweight and effectiveness by giving partial observation and a high mask ratio to the encoder. More importantly, it is much simpler in implementation and does not depend on heavy data augmentation.

**Transformer-Based Person Re-identification.** TransReID [17] is the first to apply pure Transformer for ReID research, which proposes the Jigsaw Patch Module to shuffle and group patch tokens to learn local features and the Side Information Embedding to incorporate camera or viewpoint information. TransReID-SSL [20] goes further through a contrastive self-supervised learning method, i.e. aforementioned DINO [3], exploiting the large-scale unlabeled ReID dataset LUPerson [12] to learn discriminative features in the pre-training stage.

## 3    Approach

We first give an introduction to the transformer-based ReID (TransReID) [17] baseline (Sect. 3.1). To improve the representation robustness in person ReID, we propose to preserve subtle visual cues by reconstructing masked person images via Masked Autoencoders [14] pre-training on large-scale unlabeled data

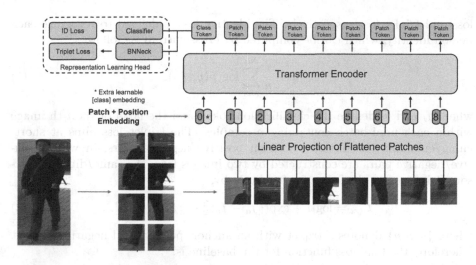

**Fig. 2. Transformer-based ReID Baseline.** In TransReID [17], only the classification token output by the Transformer encoder is sent to the classifier and the batch normalization neck to calculate identity loss and triplet loss respectively.

(Sect. 3.2). Then, the locality enhancement module (LEM) is presented to fully exploit local information from patch tokens for extracting local features combined with the global classification token to obtain the final representation (Sect. 3.3).

### 3.1 Preliminary: Transformer-Based ReID Baseline

The network architecture of our method is designed by following the TransReID [17] baseline, which consists of an encoder for feature extraction and a representation learning head, as shown in Fig. 2. Given a person image $\mathbf{x} \in \mathbb{R}^{H \times W \times C}$, we split it into $N$ image patches with the same size $(P, P)$, where $H, W, C$ denote height, width, number of channels for each image, and $N = HW/P^2$. The sequence of image patches $\mathbf{x}_p \in \mathbb{R}^{N \times (P^2 C)}$ is flattened and projected to $N$ patch embeddings of $D$ dimensions. Following the settings in ViT [11], 2D positional embeddings are added to the sequence of patch embeddings to keep spatial information for the Transformer encoder. It is worth noting that the person image size is not fixed across different models, so we need to perform 2D interpolation when the size of the pre-trained model and the fine-tuned model are different. Moreover, an extra learnable classification embedding $\mathbf{z}_0^0 = \mathbf{x}_{class}$ is prepended to the sequence to aggregate information from different image patches, and its corresponding output, i.e. the classification token $\mathbf{z}_L^0$, is the final representation of the image $x$.

The Transformer encoder consists of $L$ Transformer blocks as in [22], where the latent vector size throughout all layers is fixed. For the representation learning head, only the classification token $\mathbf{z}_L^0$ output by the Transformer encoder is sent to the classifier and the batch normalization neck to calculate the identity loss and triplet loss respectively. The identity loss is defined to recognize each person identity, which can be computed by cross-entropy as follows,

$$\mathcal{L}_{id} = -\frac{1}{n} \sum_{i=1}^{n} \log(p(y_i|f_i)), \tag{1}$$

where $f_i$ and $y_i$ denote the classification token and the label of the $i$-th image within each mini-batch containing $n$ samples. The triplet loss aims at shortening/enlarging the distance between positive/negative pairs, in which positive/negative pairs are constructed by two images from the same/different person. It is given in the form of soft-margin by,

$$\mathcal{L}_{tri} = \log[1 + \exp(\|f_a - f_p\|_2^2 - \|f_a - f_n\|_2^2)], \tag{2}$$

where $\{a, p, n\}$ denotes a triplet with an anchor, positive and negative sample. Therefore, the final loss function for the baseline is,

$$\mathcal{L}_{Baseline} = \mathcal{L}_{id} + \mathcal{L}_{tri}. \tag{3}$$

### 3.2 Masked Autoencoders Pre-training

Masked AutoEncoders (MAE) [14] proposes an asymmetric encoder-decoder architecture (See Fig. 1), in which the encoder maps visible image patches to latent representation, and the decoder reconstructs pixels for invisible image patches through these corrupted signals. The masking ratio is set to a relatively high value, e.g. 75%, in order to remove high redundancy in 2D image signals, preventing models from discovering shortcuts to easily perform the reconstruction. Both the encoder and decoder are ViT [11] models with positional embeddings. Differently, the lightweight decoder will be removed after pre-training and only the encoder will be used in the fine-tuning stage as a backbone.

The MAE pre-training approach can extract features sensitive to subtle visual cues of person images, which help discriminate different people for the downstream ReID task. This is because encoded features of the classification token and each visible-patch token with the mask token are learned to be able to reconstruct the masked image patches in pixel level. On the other hand, it is worth noting that we observe significant performance change when setting different aspect ratios in random crop augmentation, which means that the visible region for generative self-supervised methods is important. The aspect ratios need to be properly designed for the ReID task. In contrast, the contrastive self-supervised method DINO [3] utilized in TransReID-SSL [20] employs the multi-cropping operations to cover most areas of the person images. The MAE model does not rely on these complicated data augmentations of multi-cropping.

### 3.3 Fine-Tuning with Locality Enhancement Module

During the pre-training stage, the encoder is trained to provide patch tokens that embed rich local information for decoder reconstruction. In the fine-tuning stage,

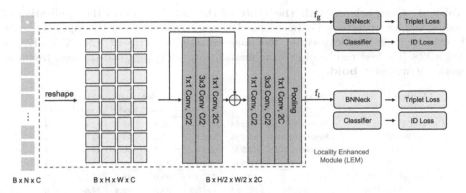

**Fig. 3. Locality Enhancement Module (LEM).** The sequence of patch tokens is unshuffled and reshaped into a feature map, in which the adjacency relation of the feature map is same as the input image. Then, we apply convolutional operations on the feature map to extract local features.

if the global classification token aggregating patch information in the encoder is used as the final representation, the extracted patch tokens containing rich subtle visual cues cannot be fully utilized, which causes the potential of the MAE pre-training undervalued. Thus, we propose the locality enhancement module (LEM) to fully exploit both the global and local features from the pre-trained encoder.

The Locality Enhancement Module (LEM) consists of three cascaded operations, i.e., reshaping, convolution, and pooling (Fig. 3). The sequence of patch tokens is unshuffled and reshaped into a feature map, in which the patch adjacency relation in the input image is preserved in the feature map of patch tokens. Then, convolution operations are designed to extract local features.

Local features generated by LEM are denoted as $\mathbf{f}_l$, and $\mathbf{f}_g$ represents the classification token output by the Transformer encoder. In the fine-tuning stage, local features and global features are processed separately and use different classifiers and batch normalization necks. The loss functions of local and global features are denoted as $\mathcal{L}_{id}^l, \mathcal{L}_{tri}^l$ and $\mathcal{L}_{id}^g, \mathcal{L}_{tri}^g$, respectively. The final loss function is,

$$\mathcal{L}_{MALE} = \alpha * (\mathcal{L}_{id}^l + \mathcal{L}_{tri}^l) + \beta * (\mathcal{L}_{id}^g + \mathcal{L}_{tri}^g). \tag{4}$$

where $\alpha, \beta$ are the trade-off hyper-parameters (which we simply set $\alpha = \beta = 0.5$ by default). During inference, local features and global features concatenated to improve the robustness of the final person representation.

## 4    Experiments

### 4.1    Implementation Details

**Datasets.** The large-scale unlabeled dataset LUPerson [12] is used for the pre-training stage. It contains about 4.18M person images and more than 200k identities. A subset of about 1.28M images are randomly selected (with similar size

**Table 1. Comparison with the state-of-the-art.** * indicates the application of sliding window operation, i.e. image patches are overlapping and the input sequence is extended. ↑384 indicates that the image scaling is increased from $256 \times 128$ to $384 \times 128$. The best results of existing methods are <u>underlined</u> and the best from our work are marked in **bold**.

| Method | Backbone | Params | GFLOPs | Market1501 | | MSMT17 | |
|---|---|---|---|---|---|---|---|
| | | | | Rank-1 | mAP | Rank-1 | mAP |
| BoT [19] | ResNet101-ibn | 44.6 M | 418.4 | 95.4 | 88.9 | 81.0 | 59.4 |
| AGW [27] | ResNet101-ibn | 44.7 M | 419.5 | 95.5 | 89.5 | 82.0 | 61.4 |
| SBS [16] | ResNet101-ibn | 44.7 M | 629.3 | 96.3 | 90.3 | 84.8 | 62.8 |
| MGN [23] | ResNet50-ibn | 70.9 M | 900.1 | 95.8 | 89.8 | 85.1 | 65.4 |
| TransReID [17] | ViT-B | 104.7 M | 787.1 | 95.0 | 88.2 | 83.3 | 64.9 |
| TransReID [17] | ViT-B↑384 | 104.8 M | 1191.6 | 95.0 | 88.8 | 84.6 | 66.6 |
| TransReID* [17] | ViT-B | 104.8 M | 1306.3 | 95.2 | 88.9 | 85.3 | 67.4 |
| TransReID* [17] | ViT-B↑384 | 104.9 M | 1962.5 | 95.2 | 89.5 | 86.2 | 69.4 |
| TransReID-SSL$^a$ [20] | ViT-B↑384 | 90.0 M | 1199.1 | <u>96.7</u> | <u>93.2</u> | <u>89.5</u> | **75.0** |
| Baseline | ViT-B | 86.5 M | 726.5 | 95.0 | 88.7 | 85.6 | 69.0 |
| Baseline | ViT-B↑384 | 86.6 M | 1101.5 | 95.3 | 88.6 | 86.4 | 70.0 |
| MALE | ViT-B | 96.6 M | 745.7 | 96.1 | 92.2 | 88.0 | 73.0 |
| MALE | ViT-B↑384 | 96.6 M | 1130.3 | **96.4** | **92.1** | **88.8** | 74.2 |

$^a$ Please note that TransReID-SSL compute the Catastrophic Forgetting Score (CFS) for the whole LUPerson dataset. Then, a subset of 50% data close to the down-stream ReID task is selected for pre-training. Differently, the implementation of our method randomly select 30% data for pre-training without additional computation on the whole dataset.

as ImageNet [9]) for pre-training the proposed MALE. Then, we evaluate our model on two benchmarks, i.e. Market-1501 [28] and MSMT17 [24]. The evaluation metrics are Rank-1 and mean Average Precision (mAP) accuracy.

**Pre-training.** The MAE [14] model is used for initialization. The default training settings are set as in [14], except that of data augmentation we modified the aspect ratio of random cropping from 1:1 to 2:1. In our experiments, this modification is able to improve the mAP accuracy on MSMT17 [24] by about 5.6%. For pre-training the proposed MALE on LUPerson [12], we use $2 \times$ NVIDIA A100 GPUs for 800 epochs by default.

**Fine-Tuning.** In the fine-tuning stage, all person images are resized to $256 \times 128$ (default) or $384 \times 128$. They are augmented with random horizontal flip, padding, random cropping, and random erasing, the same as TransReID [17]. The batch size is set to 64 with 8 images per identity, which means that we randomly sample 8 people per batch during training. The optimizer is AdamW [18] with $\beta_1, \beta_2$ set to 0.9 and 0.999, and the learning rate at the beginning of training is $8e-3$, in which a cosine decay schedule is applied along with training steps. Moreover, the layer-wise learning rate decay [8] is used with a default factor of 0.4. All fine-tuning experiments are trained using a single NVIDIA GeForce RTX 3090 GPU for 100 epochs, where the warmup epoch is set to 5.

**Table 2. Validate the effectiveness of LEM.** Trans. and Conv. refer to extra Transformer block and convolutional block respectively. * indicates a heavier convolutional block with more parameters and computation. Acc. is the average of Rank-1 and mAP accuracy.

| Method | Extra params | Extra GFLOPs | MSMT17 | | |
|--------|-------------|--------------|--------|-----|------|
| | | | Rank-1 | mAP | Acc. |
| Baseline | – | – | 85.64 | 68.97 | 77.31 |
| +Pooling | +0.9 M | +0.1 | 86.10 | 68.63 | 77.37 |
| +Trans.+Pooling | +7.9 M | +59.7 | 86.18 | 68.14 | 77.16 |
| +Conv.+Pooling(Ours) | +10.1 M | +19.2 | 88.02 | 72.96 | 80.49 |
| +Conv.+Pooling* | +77.2 M | +154.8 | 88.28 | 73.37 | 80.83 |

## 4.2 Comparison with the State-of-the-Art

Experimental results on the two benchmarks Market-1501 [28] and MSMT17 [24] are compared with the state-of-the-art methods in Table 1. It can be observed that our method outperforms the CNN-based methods on both benchmarks. Compared with TransReID [17], which is a transformer-based supervised learning method, our method achieves better performance with fewer parameters and computational cost. Moreover, the proposed MALE shows competitive results by randomly sampling 30% data from the LUPerson dataset for pre-training, while the state-of-the-art method TransReID-SSL [20] ranks the whole LUPerson dataset and select 50% data for representation learning. Different from the contrastive self-supervised learning method DINO [3] used in TransReID-SSL, our proposed method requires neither the carefully designed architecture like Jigsaw Patch Module (JPM) nor complicated data augmentations of multi-cropping.

## 4.3 Ablation Study

**The Effectiveness of LEM.** To validate the effectiveness of our proposed LEM, we conduct experiments on replacing the proposed module with global average pooling or the Transformer block. For the latter, we directly send all patch tokens into an additional block, in which the architecture is the same as the previous encoder, and the corresponding outputs after global average pooling are used as the local features. The results are shown in Table 2. We expect the additional module to capture the local information and aid the global classification token. Neither pooling nor extra Transformer block can hardly improve the baseline as they cannot exploit the 2D structure of the image. Moreover, replacing LEM with a more complex convolutional block only achieves comparable results with the proposed method, which validates that LEM can extract useful local features with smaller computation overhead.

**Table 3. Ablation of different aspect ratios.** The default setting is 1:1 in [14], while 2:1 is better for ReID in our method.

| Aspect ratio | Epochs | MSMT17 | | |
|---|---|---|---|---|
| | | Rank-1 | mAP | Acc. |
| 1:1 ([14]) | 200 | 74.47 | 52.36 | 63.42 |
| 1:1 ([14]) | 400 | 78.43 | 56.89 | 67.66 |
| 2:1 (Ours) | 200 | 79.93 | 58.92 | 69.43 |
| 2:1 (Ours) | 400 | 81.56 | 61.81 | 71.69 |

**Table 4. Comparison of different pre-training strategies.** PT is short for pre-training on LUPerson subset.

| MAE Init.[a] | PT Epochs | MSMT17 | | |
|---|---|---|---|---|
| | | Rank-1 | mAP | Acc. |
| ✓ | – | 80.73 | 60.18 | 70.46 |
| ✗ | 200 | 79.93 | 58.92 | 69.43 |
| ✗ | 400 | 81.56 | 61.81 | 71.69 |
| ✓ | 400 | 85.13 | 67.63 | 76.38 |
| ✓ | 800 | 85.64 | 68.97 | 77.31 |

[a] ✓ means initialization by the official MAE model in [14] while ✗ refers to random initialization.

**Random Crop Augmentation in MAE.** In the pre-training stage, we observe that the aspect ratio of random crop augmentation has a significant effect on the downstream ReID task (Table 3), which is not found in contrastive self-supervised learning methods. These results imply that contrastive self-supervised methods pay little attention to local details and generative pre-training methods can do a better job in this regard, thus subtle visual cues can be discovered for representation learning. On the other hand, it suggests that the visible region for generative self-supervised learning methods is crucial, which needs to be carefully designed according to different kinds of tasks.

**MAE Initialization Strategy.** We conducted experiments on varying the MAE Initialization strategy for comparison. As shown in Table 4, when the MAE model is initialized randomly and then pre-trained on the LUPerson subset after 400 epochs (line 3), the performance is better than the official MAE in [14] (line 1). By initializing with the official MAE and pre-training on the LUPerson subset, our method can further improve the performance, since the MAE model is adapted to the person ReID task.

### 4.4   Visualization

To illustrate that the proposed method is effective in enhancing the spatial relation for the person ReID, we further visualize the attention maps in Fig. 4. By comparing the higher response regions of the model with/without the additional LEM, we observe that more details and local cues are being captured after the enhancement, such as shoes, handbags, and backpacks, which can help the model discriminate between different people and improve the robustness of the final representations. For example, in the top-right group of images, our model can not only be attentive to the critical parts of the person but also notice the discriminating backpack.

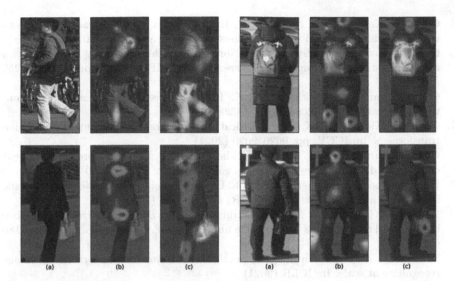

Fig. 4. **Visualization of attention maps.** (a) Input images, (b) Baseline, (c) MALE.

## 5   Conclusion

In this paper, we propose to learn robust feature representation by using the generative self-supervised learning method for pre-training on a large-scale unlabeled ReID dataset. In our method, global feature are extracted by aggregating information of different patches into the classification token in the Transformer backbone. To fully exploit local information in patch tokens, we propose the locality enhancement module (LEM) to obtain local features via convolution on reshaped feature maps of patch tokens. The combination of the global and local features improve the generalization ability of the feature representation for better performance in person Re-ID. Experimental results show that the proposed MALE achieves competitive results compared with state-of-the-art methods in terms of parameter scale, computation overhead, and ReID performance.

**Acknowledgments.** This work was supported partially by NSFC (No. 61906218), Guangdong Basic and Applied Basic Research Foundation (No. 2020A1515011497), and Science and Technology Program of Guangzhou (No. 202002030371).

## References

1. Bao, H., Dong, L., Wei, F.: BEiT: BERT pre-training of image transformers. In: ICLR (2022)
2. Carion, N., Massa, F., Synnaeve, G., Usunier, N., Kirillov, A., Zagoruyko, S.: End-to-end object detection with transformers. In: ECCV, pp. 213–229 (2020)
3. Caron, M., et al.: Emerging properties in self-supervised vision transformers. In: ICCV, pp. 9630–9640 (2021)

4. Chen, T., Kornblith, S., Norouzi, M., Hinton, G.: A simple framework for contrastive learning of visual representations. In: ICML, pp. 1597–1607 (2020)
5. Chen, T., Kornblith, S., Swersky, K., Norouzi, M., Hinton, G.: Big self-supervised models are strong semi-supervised learners. In: NeruIPS, vol. 33, pp. 22243–22255 (2020)
6. Chen, X., Fan, H., Girshick, R., He, K.: Improved baselines with momentum contrastive learning. arXiv:2003.04297 (2020)
7. Chen, X., Xie, S., He, K.: An empirical study of training self-supervised vision transformers. In: ICCV, pp. 9620–9629 (2021)
8. Clark, K., Luong, M.T., Le, Q.V., Manning, C.D.: Electra: pre-training text encoders as discriminators rather than generators. In: ICLR (2020)
9. Deng, J., Dong, W., Socher, R., Li, L.J., Li, K., Fei-Fei, L.: ImageNet: a large-scale hierarchical image database. In: CVPR, pp. 248–255 (2009)
10. Devlin, J., Chang, M.W., Lee, K., Toutanova, K.: BERT: pre-training of deep bidirectional transformers for language understanding. In: NAACL, pp. 4171–4186 (2019)
11. Dosovitskiy, A., et al.: An image is worth $16 \times 16$ words: transformers for image recognition at scale. In: ICLR (2021)
12. Fu, D., et al.: Unsupervised pre-training for person re-identification. In: CVPR, pp. 14750–14759 (2021)
13. Grill, J.B., et al.: Bootstrap your own latent a new approach to self-supervised learning. In: NeruIPS, vol. 33, pp. 21271–21284 (2020)
14. He, K., Chen, X., Xie, S., Li, Y., Dollár, P., Girshick, R.: Masked autoencoders are scalable vision learners. In: CVPR (2022)
15. He, K., Fan, H., Wu, Y., Xie, S., Girshick, R.: Momentum contrast for unsupervised visual representation learning. In: CVPR, pp. 9726–9735 (2020)
16. He, L., Liao, X., Liu, W., Liu, X., Cheng, P., Mei, T.: FastReID: a pytorch toolbox for general instance re-identification. arXiv:2006.02631 (2020)
17. He, S., Luo, H., Wang, P., Wang, F., Li, H., Jiang, W.: TransReID: transformer-based object re-identification. In: ICCV, pp. 15013–15022 (2021)
18. Loshchilov, I., Hutter, F.: Decoupled weight decay regularization. In: ICLR (2019)
19. Luo, H., Gu, Y., Liao, X., Lai, S., Jiang, W.: Bag of tricks and a strong baseline for deep person re-identification. In: CVPRW (2019)
20. Luo, H., et al.: Self-supervised pre-training for transformer-based person re-identification. arXiv:2111.12084 (2021)
21. Ramesh, A., et al.: Zero-shot text-to-image generation. In: ICML, pp. 8821–8831 (2021)
22. Vaswani, A., et al.: Attention is all you need. In: NeruIPS, vol. 30 (2017)
23. Wang, G., Yuan, Y., Chen, X., Li, J., Zhou, X.: Learning discriminative features with multiple granularities for person re-identification. In: ACM MM, pp. 274–282 (2018)
24. Wei, L., Zhang, S., Gao, W., Tian, Q.: Person transfer GAN to bridge domain gap for person re-identification. In: CVPR, pp. 79–88 (2018)
25. Xie, Z., et al.: Self-supervised learning with Swin transformers. arXiv:2105.04553 (2021)
26. Xie, Z., et al.: SimMIM: a simple framework for masked image modeling. In: CVPR (2021)
27. Ye, M., Shen, J., Lin, G., Xiang, T., Shao, L., Hoi, S.C.H.: Deep learning for person re-identification: a survey and outlook. TPAMI $\mathbf{44}$(6), 2872–2893 (2021)

28. Zheng, L., Shen, L., Tian, L., Wang, S., Wang, J., Tian, Q.: Scalable person re-identification: a benchmark. In: ICCV, pp. 1116–1124 (2015)
29. Zheng, S., et al.: Rethinking semantic segmentation from a sequence-to-sequence perspective with transformers. In: CVPR, pp. 6877–6886 (2021)

# Multi-modal Finger Feature Fusion Algorithms on Large-Scale Dataset

Chuhao Zhou[2], Yuanrong Xu[3], Fanglin Chen[2], and Guangming Lu[1,2](✉)

[1] Guangdong Provincial Key Laboratory of Novel Security Intelligence Technologies,
Guangzhou, China
[2] Harbin Institute of Technology, Shenzhen, China
{chenfanglin,luguangm}@hit.edu.cn
[3] Harbin Institute of Technology, Weihai, China

**Abstract.** Multimodal biometrics technologies have become dominant in the domain of biometric recognition since they exploit complementary information between modalities and usually have better recognition performance. Thg finger has abundant biometrical features, including fingerprint, finger vein, and finger knuckle, which make it one of the most important research fields in multimodal biometric recognition. Though plenty of multimodal finger recognition algorithms have been investigated in literatures, most of them are based on two of three modalities of the finger. Besides, there is no open, simultaneously-collected, and large-scale trimodal finger dataset together with convincing benchmarks for scholars to learn and verify their multimodal finger recognition algorithms. In this paper, we propose a novel large-scale trimodal finger dataset containing fingerprint, finger vein, and finger knuckle. Two benchmarks from a feature-level fusion strategy and a score-level fusion strategy are established. Finally, comprehensive ablation studies are used to analyze the contribution of each finger modality.

**Keywords:** Biometrics · Multimodal finger recognition · Fingerprint · Finger vein · Finger knuckle

## 1 Introduction

With the promotion of informatization and network algorithms, individual recognition has increasingly become an important issue. Due to high reliability and high precision, biometrics, including fingerprint, face, palm print, and

This work was supported in part by the NSFC fund 62176077, in part by the Guangdong Basic and Applied Basic Research Foundation under Grant 2019Bl515120055, in part by the Shenzhen Key Technical Project under Grant 2020N046, in part by the Shenzhen Fundamental Research Fund under Grant JCYJ20210324132210025, and in part by the Medical Biometrics Perception and Analysis Engineering Laboratory, Shenzhen, China. Guangdong Provincial Key Laboratory of Novel Security Intelligence Technologies (2022B1212010005).

S. Yu et al. (Eds.): PRCV 2022, LNCS 13535, pp. 522–536, 2022.
https://doi.org/10.1007/978-3-031-18910-4_42

iris, become one of the most important methods for person identification and verification. Moreover, combining multimodal biometrics to get more rich information and alleviate drawbacks of the single modality, can further improve the performance and security of a recognition system. For this reason, multimodal biometrics has become a prevalent research field.

The finger contains abundant biometric features, mainly including fingerprint, finger vein, and finger knuckle. Due to abundant information, high recognition accuracy, high user-friendliness, and portable acquisition devices, these features are widely utilized in the biometrics recognition system.

In the past decades, a variety of fingerprint, finger vein, and finger knuckle recognition approaches have been investigated and have shown adequate accuracy. However, existing recognition methods based on single modality suffer from many problems. First, among three modalities, fingerprint can provide sufficient information, but it can be easily forged, and its image quality can be greatly influenced by external factors [2,8]. Second, containing subcutaneous venous, finger vein shows powerful stability and anti-spoof capacity. However, few exploitable features and poor image quality will decrease the accuracy of the finger vein recognition system on large-scale datasets [3,19]. Third, finger knuckles are easy to acquire and have high recognition speed, however, with relatively simple texture and feature information, it is hard to reach a high recognition accuracy [12,18].

The aforementioned drawbacks of each modality promote research on multimodal finger recognition technologies. Among them, fusion strategies of two modalities have been studied extensively, and have shown their advantage in recognition accuracy [9,14,17]. However, current research on trimodal finger recognition suffers from several problems, which severely hinder the development of the trimodal finger recognition approach. First, there is no open, simultaneously-collected, and large-scale trimodal finger dataset that can be used to learn multimodal features and verify the recognition performance. Therefore, majority of literatures only focus on two modalities of finger and utilize homemade bimodal datasets in experiments. Besides, for the existing trimodal finger recognition algorithms, homemade small-scale trimodal datasets utilized in the experiments are not sufficient to demonstrate the advantage of trimodal features. Second, due to the absence of large-scale trimodal finger datasets, there have few convincing trimodal benchmarks for researchers to judge their recognition algorithms, thus few algorithms investigate the trimodal finger recognition in the large-scale application scenario.

To solve these issues, in this paper we build a simultaneously-collected large-scale trimodal dataset including 1,667 individuals' trimodal finger images. Each individual consists of fingerprint, finger vein, and finger knuckle modalities. Two fusion benchmarks respectively focus on feature-level and score-level fusion strategy are established. Finally, extensive ablation experiments on both benchmarks are carried out to show the contributions of different modalities.

The main contributions of this paper lie in the following aspects:

(1) Large-scale Trimodal Finger Dataset: We create a trimodal finger database namely MFD-HITSZ, which contains fingerprint, finger vein, and finger knuckle. These images are collected from 1,667 individuals simultaneously. The characteristics of large-scale and synchronism make it possible to run trimodal recognition algorithms over the dataset and evaluate the recognition performance of multimodal finger features.

(2) Two Benchmarks on both Feature-level and Score-level Fusion Strategies: Based on our large-scale trimodal finger dataset, we establish two fusion benchmarks. For feature-level fusion strategy, a multimodal Siamese network is implemented, the feature of each modality is extracted by different deep networks and fused by weighted concatenation. For score-level fusion strategy, three unimodal Siamese networks are trained to get embedding of each modality separately. Then a novel fusion strategy that fully considers matching score distributions of all modalities is proposed to obtain the fusion matching score.

(3) Comprehensive Ablation Analysis and Evaluation: We do abundant ablation experiments to show the contributions of different modalities. Note that our results of ablation experiments can be treated as benchmarks toward bimodal finger recognition algorithms as well.

## 2 Related Works

### 2.1 Multimodal Representation Learning Algorithms

Multimodal representation learning aims to learn feature representations of multimodal data that contain complementary information between modalities. It is widely used in many tasks, including classification, object detection, recognition, etc.

Generally, multimodal representation learning algorithms can be classified into two categories [10]. Those in the first category purpose to capture the correlations among multiple modalities through feature alignment. These algorithms learn representation for each modality separately and keep learned representations under some constraints. The typical algorithms are Canonical Correlation Analysis (CCA) [7] and its variants [1,6]. CCA utilizes covariance matrix to model correlation between two feature sets explicitly, and tries to find two linear projections that maximize the correlation between projected feature sets. The algorithms in the second category seek to directly learn a shared and compact representation from multiple modality-specific representations. Multimodal Deep Autoencoder [4,11,15] takes embeddings of audio and video as input and passes them to a shared representation layer. The fusion representation allows the model to capture the relation between two modalities and it will be optimized by minimizing the reconstruction error caused by each modality. Multimodal CNN [13] extracts embeddings of multiple modalities by a shared CNN, then fuses all embeddings by an elementwise maximum operation. It finally learns a joint representation by another CNN based on the fusion embedding. Besides, with the development of attention mechanisms, an increasing number of multi-modal representation fusion models have equipped attention in their frameworks to attain more expressive and discriminative joint representation. In the context of multimodal classification and recognition, the attention mechanism is mainly utilized to evaluate the relationship among different modalities. Based on the evaluation, complementary information can be selected and fused into a joint representation to ease semantic ambiguity [5]. For example, Xu et al. [16] obtain modality-specific features by a series of neural networks, then complementary information among them can be captured through outer product and a shared mapping module.

### 2.2 Multimodal Finger Recognition Algorithms

Multimodal finger recognition approaches have been investigated in many literatures. Yang et al. [17] extract features from fingerprint and finger vein through Gabor filter banks, and then learn aligned representations by canonical correlation analysis. To preserve more information lying in line patterns, S. Veluchamy et al. [14] utilize the repeated line tracking method to extract features from finger knuckle and finger vein. Then, a feature-level fusion using fractional firefly (FFF) optimization is used to get the fusion feature. Besides considering two modalities, Li et al. [9] combine fingerprint, finger vein, and finger knuckle. They initially calculate local discriminant codes for each modality, then map them to feature embeddings by convolution neural network. Concatenation is finally utilized to fuse all modality-specific embeddings.

## 3 MFD-HITSZ Dataset

### 3.1 Acquisition System

The acquisition system contains an acquisition device and a corresponding sampling program. The acquisition device consists of an A/D converter, control circuits, and three sampling modules, as shown in Fig. 1. Note that the height of infrared light sources is adjustable, which is designed to keep finger vein moderately penetrated. To obtain multimodal finger images simultaneously, a control program is implemented to execute each sampling module successively in a very short time. After initialization, all sample modules are started, when a user presses his finger on the fingerprint module, the inside pressure sensor will send a signal to the control program and let all modules capture images at the same time. Subsequently, the A/D converter transmits images to a computer, and the computer shows previews for people to decide whether to save them.

### 3.2 Statistics Information

In this paper, we build the MFD-HITSZ (Multimodal Finger Dataset HITSZ) dataset for multimodal finger recognition tasks. In detail, our MFD-HITSZ dataset contains 1,667 identities. Each identity provides 7–29 images, mostly 10 images. Besides, all modalities are collected simultaneously, and the quantity of each modality is identical. As a result, 20,524 images are captured for every modality and the whole dataset contains 61,572 images in total. Table 1 summarizes the brief information of our dataset. Figure 2 displays some samples from our dataset.

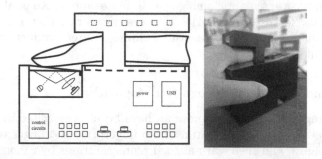

**Fig. 1.** Components of synchronous acquisition device and an illustration of the sampling process.

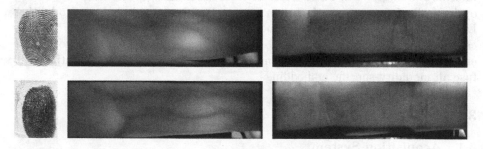

**Fig. 2.** Images samples from proposed MFD-HITSZ dataset. The first column shows the fingerprint images, the second row and the third column is the corresponding finger vein IR images and finger knuckle RGB images.

**Table 1.** Statistic information of MFD-HITSZ dataset.

| #Identities | #Images per identity | Images size | #Images |
|---|---|---|---|
| 2,000 | 7–29 | Fingerprint: 300 × 400 | 20,524 each modality; 61,572 in total |
| | | Finger vein: 750 × 225 | |
| | | Finger knuckle: 750 × 220 | |

# 4    Feature-Level Fusion Strategy

In this section, we establish a feature-level fusion strategy for the MFD-HITSZ dataset, serving as the first benchmark.

## 4.1    Feature Extraction and Fusion Framework

In this paper, we establish an end-to-end feature-level fusion framework, which integrates feature networks, an aggregation network, a matching module, and a concatenation weight learning module. The illustration of our model is shown in Fig. 3.

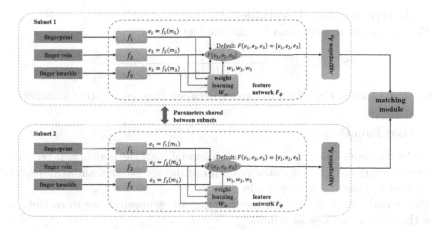

**Fig. 3.** Network architecture of feature-level fusion strategy. $f_1$, $f_2$, $f_3$ are three independent feature extractors. $W_\varphi$ is the weight learning module that is shared among three modalities. Aggregation network $A_\theta$ projects the weighted concatenated embeddings to the aggregative embedding. Components in two subnets share parameters.

The backbone of our model is overall a multimodal Siamese network that consists of two parameter-sharing branches. Each branch contains a feature network $F_\phi$, an aggregation network $A_\theta$, and a weight learning module $W_\varphi$, where $\phi$, $\theta$ and $\varphi$ are learnable parameters. Two branches converge at the matching module. To describe our model in one sentence: The feature network computes embedding for each modality, the weight learning module learns a concatenation weight for each embedding, the aggregation network fuses all weighted embeddings, and the matching module compares two aggregative embeddings to compute contrastive loss or similarity score.

The feature network $F_\phi$ contains three feature extractors whose output embeddings have unified dimension $d$:

$$e_i = f_i(m_i) \in R^d, \quad i = 1, 2, 3 \tag{1}$$

Once embeddings are produced, the **weighting learning module** $W_\varphi$, which is a series of fully connected layers, maps each embedding to a scalar as concatenation weight:

$$w_i = W_\varphi(e_i), \quad R^d \longmapsto R^1 \tag{2}$$

Based on learned weight, we concatenate all weighted embeddings to get fusion embedding:

$$fused\_emb = [w_1 e_1, w_2 e_2, w_3 e_3] \tag{3}$$

The fusion embedding is sent to the aggregation network $A_\theta$ to obtain the aggregative representation of each sample:

$$agg\_fea = A_\theta(fused\_emb), \quad R^{M \times d} \longrightarrow R^d \tag{4}$$

where $M$ is the number of modalities.

Finally, matching score can be obtained as follows:

$$SIM(A, B) = \frac{1}{1 + dist(agg\_fea_A, agg\_fea_B)} \tag{5}$$

where $dist()$ means Euclidean distances between two aggregative features.

### 4.2   Loss Function

Since the backbone of our model is a multimodal Siamese network, it requires us to generate genuine and impostor pairs for training. We will show more details about how to generate data pairs in Sect. 6.

Particularly, once data pairs for training are generated, we iteratively optimize the contrastive loss as follows:

$$L = \frac{1}{2B} \sum_{n=1}^{B} yd^2 + (1 - y)max(margin - d, 0)^2 \tag{6}$$

where $B$ refers to batch size, $y$ is the prediction made by the model whose value is set to 1 if two samples are from the same identity, otherwise, $y$ is set to 0. $d$ is Euclidean distance between two compared aggregative embeddings and $margin$ is a set threshold. The contrastive loss function minimizes intra-class distances while forces between-class distance to be larger than the $margin$.

## 5   Score-Level Fusion Strategy

In this section, we establish a score-level fusion strategy for the MFD-HITSZ dataset, serving as the second benchmark.

### 5.1   Network Architecture

In the score-level fusion strategy, we establish a model that contains three independent matching networks and a score fusion module. The illustration of the model is shown in Fig. 4.

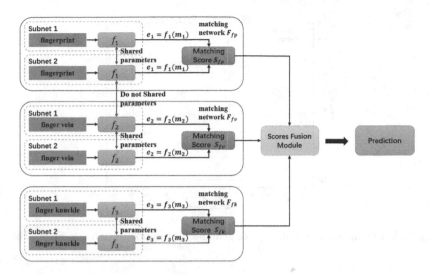

**Fig. 4.** Network architecture of score-level fusion strategy. $f_1, f_2, f_3$ are three independent feature extractors. In the training phase, three matching networks are trained separately. In the inference phase, modality-specific scores can be obtained through each matching network, then a score fusion strategy is conducted to attain the fusion score.

Each matching network can be treated as the unimodal version of the model in Sect. 4, thus we adopt some similar settings, specifically, there are three points. First, we utilize the same feature extractors to compute modality-specific embeddings, as shown in Eq. (1). Second, in the training phase, we use the same data pairs generation method and contrastive loss (shown in Eq. (6)) to train three matching networks separately. It is noticeable that feature extractors within a matching network share parameters while feature extractors between two matching networks do not. Third, in the inference phase, we utilize the same similarity score (shown in Eq. (5)) for each modality.

## 5.2  Score-Level Fusion Strategy

Once modality-specific matching scores are produced, we propose a score-level fusion strategy that simultaneously takes matching score distributions of all modalities into consideration. During the inference phase, we initially obtain matching scores for all genuine and impostor pairs in each modality, then score distributions can be generated. Figure 5, Fig. 6, and Fig. 7 show score distribution in fingerprint, finger vein, and finger knuckle respectively. Significantly, our similarity score always ranges from 0 to 1.

Therefore, we divide [0,1] region into 100 bins with interval 0.01. For all genuine or impostor pairs in each modality, we count the number of matching scores falling into each bin, then the frequency can be calculated as follows:

$$f_i = \frac{N_i}{N}, \quad i = 1, 2, ..100 \tag{7}$$

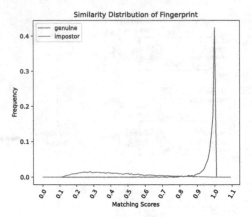

**Fig. 5.** Matching score distribution of genuine and impostor pairs on fingerprint.

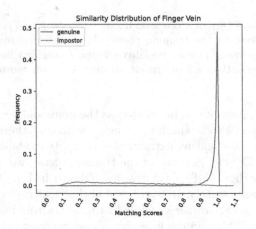

**Fig. 6.** Matching score distribution of genuine and impostor pairs on finger vein.

where $N$ refers to the number of all genuine or impostor pairs, $N_i$ is the number of matching scores falling into the $i$-th bin.

With the observation of score distribution for each modality, we can find that the score corresponding to the peak in the impostor distribution is much lower than it in the genuine distribution. Besides, there is an intersection between score distributions of genuine and impostor pairs, it is the intersection that samples, which are hard to discriminate, lie in.

The main idea of the score fusion strategy is that we only focus on samples that are hard to discriminate in all modalities. To achieve that, we set the upper bound and lower bound of matching scores and establish a hash table $P$ for each modality. The hash table $P$ maps a matching score to a probabilistic value. The value represents the probability that the corresponding pair of samples belong

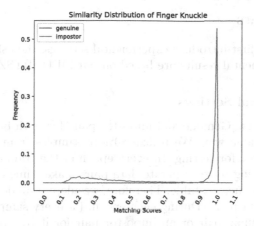

**Fig. 7.** Matching score distribution of genuine and impostor pairs on finger knuckle.

to genuine pairs. $P_m$ means the hash table for modality $m$, it can be established as follows:

$$P_m[s_m] = \frac{N_{i,m}^{genuine}}{N_{i,m}^{genuine} + N_{i,m}^{impostor}} \tag{8}$$

where $s_m$ means the matching score of a pair of samples for modality $m$, $i = round(s_m \times 100)$ means the corresponding bin index of $s_m$. $N_{i,m}^{genuine}$ and $N_{i,m}^{impostor}$ refers to the number of genuine pairs and impostor pairs falling into $i$-th bin for modality $m$.

Let $s_m^l$, $s_m^u$ represent the lower bound and upper bound of matching scores for modality $m$ respectively. Then, the fusion score can be calculated as follows:

$$S_{fusion} = \begin{cases} 0, & \exists s_m < s_m^l, \quad m = 1, 2, ...M \\ \sum_m^M P_m[s_m], & otherwise \\ 3, & \exists s_m > s_m^u, \quad m = 1, 2, ...M \end{cases} \tag{9}$$

where $M$ means the number of modalities.

The fusion score $S_{fusion}$ fully demonstrates our main idea. For a pair of samples, if any matching score is lower than the lower bound of its corresponding modality, we set $S_{fusion} = 0$. It means that it's almost impossible for the pair to be genuine. In the same way, we set $S_{fusion} = 3$ if any matching score is greater than the upper bound of its corresponding modality. It means that the pair belongs to genuine pairs with a high possibility. If all matching scores fall into the region between lower bound and upper bound, three probabilities that the pair belongs to genuine pairs can be obtained, then we assign the sum of the three probabilities to $S_{fusion}$.

The fusion score $S_{fusion} \in [0, 3]$ represents the possibility that a pair of samples belongs to genuine pairs, which can be treated as a novel similarity metric that focuses on samples whichs are hard to discriminate in all modalities.

## 6    Experiments

In this section, we first introduce experimental settings, then show experimental results, all experimental results are based on our MFD-HITSZ dataset.

### 6.1    Experimental Settings

**Pairs Generations.** Genuine and impostor pairs for both benchmarks can be generated in the same way. We utilize 80% of samples from each identity for training and the rest for testing. In every epoch of the training phase, traversing the whole training set to generate data pairs makes time consumption grow rapidly and become unacceptable. Therefore, we adopt a random sampling strategy to generate data pairs. During each epoch, for every sample in the training set, we form a genuine pair or an impostor pair for it by randomly sampling. It guarantees that the model can see each sample in both positive and negative scenarios after a few epochs and keeps the randomness of pairs generation to avoid the overfitting problem. During the testing phase, pre-sampled data pairs are utilized to keep testing set fixed.

Based on the aforementioned generation strategy, the number of generated data pairs is summarized in Table 2.

**Table 2.** Data pairs generation in both feature-level and score-level fusion strategy for the training phase and testing phase.

|  | Genuine pairs | Impostor pairs | Total |
|---|---|---|---|
| Training phase | 4,540 for each epoch | 4,540 for each epoch | 9080 for each epoch |
| Testing phase | 8,128 | 13,370 | 21,498 |

**Parameters Setup.** There are several predefined parameters in two fusion benchmarks. In the feature-level fusion benchmark, three feature extractors have the same structure whose output embeddings have unified 64-dim. Each feature extractor consists of a resnet-18 (without final fully-connected layers) and a fully-connected neural network with three hidden layers, including 512, 256, and 256 units, equipped with PReLU activation function. The weight learning module contains a fully-connected layer that maps the 64-dim input embedding to a scalar. In the score-level benchmark, lower bound and upper bound of matching scores need to be set for each modality. In this work, we set the lower bound $s^l_{fp} = 0.7, s^l_{fv} = 0.5, s^l_{fk} = 0.6$ and the upper bound $s^u_{fp} = 0.9, s^u_{fv} = 0.95, s^u_{fk} = 0.9$ respectively.

### 6.2    Experiment Results

In this section, experimental results are presented to show the performances of the proposed methods. The performance of every single modality is firstly calculated, followed by the performances of two fusion algorithms. Finally, ablation analysis is conducted on both fusion algorithms to demonstrate the contribution of each modality.

Table 3 and Fig. 8 shows the performance and ROC curves of the single modality respectively. Among all modalities, finger knuckle achieves the best performance with an EER of 1.158%, followed by fingerprint and finger vein with EER of 1.256% and 1.451%. Performances of the single modality serve as a baseline to be compared by two fusion algorithms, which can be treated as benchmarks for unimodal recognition algorithms on our dataset as well.

**Table 3.** EERs of single modality.

| Modality | EER (%) |
|---|---|
| Fingerprint (fp) | 1.256 |
| Finger vein (fv) | 1.451 |
| Finger knuckle (fk) | 1.158 |

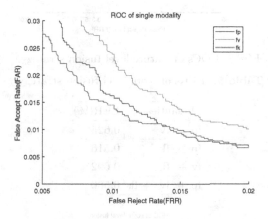

**Fig. 8.** ROCs of single modality.

The performance of feature-level fusion algorithm is shown in Table 4. It is shown in the table that, fusion of fingerprint and finger vein achieves the best performance with an EER of 0.955%, corresponding ROC curves are shown in Fig. 9. It is noticeable that the performance of feature-level fusion will decrease when finger knuckle is added in. The reason is that there is a relatively large modal gap between finger knuckle and the other two modalities, since line features are dominant in fingerprint and finger vein, but features lied in finger knuckle are mainly texture features. Elimination of modal gap between finger knuckle and the other two modalities can be regarded as a future trend for multimodal finger recognition.

**Table 4.** EERs of feature-level fusion strategy.

| Modalities | EER(%) |
|---|---|
| fp + fv | 0.955 |
| fp + fk | 1.350 |
| fv + fk | 1.381 |
| fp + fv + fk | 0.959 |

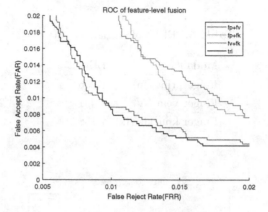

**Fig. 9.** ROCs of feature-level fusion strategy.

**Table 5.** EERs of score-level fusion strategy.

| Modalities | EER(%) |
|---|---|
| fp + fv | 0.625 |
| fp + fk | 0.516 |
| fv + fk | 0.692 |
| fp + fv + fk | 0.500 |

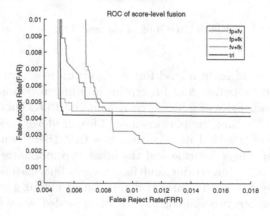

**Fig. 10.** ROCs of score-level fusion strategy.

In score-level fusion strategy, we first obtain modality-specific matching scores for all testing pairs, then fusion scores are generated to calculate EER and ROC curves which are shown in Table 5 and Fig. 10 respectively. From Table 5, trimodal fusion achieves the best performance with an EER of 0.500%. Besides, performances of any two or three modalities are better than their corresponding single modality, which demonstrates the effectiveness of score-level fusion strategy. Furthermore, we remove a modality alternately at each time, performance decreases the most when fingerprint has been removed. It shows that in our score-level fusion strategy, fingerprint plays a relatively more important role, followed by finger knuckle and finger vein. In score-level fusion strategy, we only focus on matching scores of samples that are hard to discriminate and do not care about correlations between features from different modalities, consequently, the inferior influence caused by the modal gap can be ignored. However, we still advocate that the feature-level fusion strategy has potential of acquiring better performance and the key point is to eliminate modal gap when learning shared feature representation among modalities.

## 7 Conclusion

In this paper, we propose a novel large-scale trimodal finger dataset namely MFD-HITSZ, including 2,000 individuals with simultaneously-collected fingerprint, finger vein, and finger knuckle images. It's capable to run and evaluate multimodal finger recognition algorithms. Besides, two benchmarks for both feature-level and score-level fusion strategies are established, providing researchers with convincing baselines to judge recognition algorithms. Furthermore, comprehensive ablation analysis is conducted to show different contributions of finger modalities whose results can also be treated as benchmarks toward bimodal finger recognition algorithms.

## References

1. Andrew, G., Arora, R., Bilmes, J., Livescu, K.: Deep canonical correlation analysis. In: International Conference on Machine Learning, pp. 1247–1255. PMLR (2013)
2. Babatunde, I.G.: Fingerprint matching using minutiae-singular points network. Int. J. Signal Process. Image Process. Patt. Recogn. **8**(2), 375–388 (2015)
3. Cappelli, R., Ferrara, M., Maltoni, D.: Fingerprint indexing based on minutia cylinder-code. IEEE Trans. Pattern Anal. Mach. Intell. **33**(5), 1051–1057 (2010)
4. Feng, F., Wang, X., Li, R.: Cross-modal retrieval with correspondence autoencoder. In: Proceedings of the 22nd ACM International Conference on Multimedia, pp. 7–16 (2014)
5. Guo, W., Wang, J., Wang, S.: Deep multimodal representation learning: a survey. IEEE Access **7**, 63373–63394 (2019)
6. Hardoon, D.R., Szedmak, S., Shawe-Taylor, J.: Canonical correlation analysis: an overview with application to learning methods. Neural Comput. **16**(12), 2639–2664 (2004)

7. Hotelling, H.: Relations between two sets of variates. In: Breakthroughs in Statistics, pp. 162–190. Springer (1992). https://doi.org/10.1007/978-1-4612-4380-9_14
8. Kumar, A., Wang, B.: Recovering and matching minutiae patterns from finger knuckle images. Pattern Recogn. Lett. **68**, 361–367 (2015)
9. Li, S., Zhang, B., Zhao, S., Yang, J.: Local discriminant coding based convolutional feature representation for multimodal finger recognition. Inf. Sci. **547**, 1170–1181 (2021)
10. Li, Y., Yang, M., Zhang, Z.: A survey of multi-view representation learning. IEEE Trans. Knowl. Data Eng. **31**(10), 1863–1883 (2018)
11. Ngiam, J., Khosla, A., Kim, M., Nam, J., Lee, H., Ng, A.Y.: Multimodal deep learning. In: ICML (2011)
12. Qin, H., El-Yacoubi, M.A.: Deep representation-based feature extraction and recovering for finger-vein verification. IEEE Trans. Inf. Forensics Secur. **12**(8), 1816–1829 (2017)
13. Su, H., Maji, S., Kalogerakis, E., Learned-Miller, E.: Multi-view convolutional neural networks for 3D shape recognition. In: Proceedings of the IEEE International Conference on Computer Vision, pp. 945–953 (2015)
14. Veluchamy, S., Karlmarx, L.: System for multimodal biometric recognition based on finger knuckle and finger vein using feature-level fusion and k-support vector machine classifier. IET Biometrics **6**(3), 232–242 (2017)
15. Wang, W., Arora, R., Livescu, K., Bilmes, J.: On deep multi-view representation learning. In: International Conference on Machine Learning, pp. 1083–1092. PMLR (2015)
16. Xu, J., Li, W., Liu, X., Zhang, D., Liu, J., Han, J.: Deep embedded complementary and interactive information for multi-view classification. In: Proceedings of the AAAI Conference on Artificial Intelligence, vol. 34, pp. 6494–6501 (2020)
17. Yang, J., Zhang, X.: Feature-level fusion of fingerprint and finger-vein for personal identification. Pattern Recogn. Lett. **33**(5), 623–628 (2012)
18. Yang, L., Yang, G., Yin, Y., Xi, X.: Finger vein recognition with anatomy structure analysis. IEEE Trans. Circuits Syst. Video Technol. **28**(8), 1892–1905 (2017)
19. Zhou, W., Hu, J., Wang, S.: Enhanced locality-sensitive hashing for fingerprint forensics over large multi-sensor databases. IEEE Trans. Big Data **7**(4), 759–769 (2017)

# MINIPI: A MultI-scale Neural Network Based Impulse Radio Ultra-Wideband Radar Indoor Personnel Identification Method

Lingyi Meng[1], Jinhui Zhang[2], Xikang Jiang[1], Wenyao Mu[1], Yili Wang[1],
Lei Li[1(✉)], and Lin Zhang[1]

[1] School of Artificial Intelligence, Beijing University of Posts
and Telecommunications, Beijing 100876, China
leili@bupt.edu.cn
[2] Equipment Support Room of Logistic Support Center,
Chinese PLA General Hospital, Beijing, China

**Abstract.** Impulse Radio Ultra-WideBand (IR-UWB) radar has great potential in personnel identification due to its characteristics of low power consumption and high time resolution. Several radar-based personnel identification methods collect gait data and use Convolutional Neural Network (CNN) for training and classification. However, gait data methods require each person to move in a specific way, which can be improved by using vital signs data instead including body shape and micro movement. In this paper, A MultI-scale Neural network based impulse radio ultra-wideband radar Indoor Personnel Identification method (MINIPI) is proposed, which can extract vital signs of radar signals and map them into identity information. The input of the network is a matrix reshaped from the maximum energy waveform in a radar signal slice and the corresponding vital signs. MINIPI uses a three-layer structure to extract features of three scales from the matrix. These features are concatenated, then input into an attention module and a fully connected layer to achieve identification. To evaluate the performance of MINIPI, we set up a dataset containing 10 persons indoors. The experiment result shows that the accuracy of MINIPI is 94.8% among these 10 persons, which is better than the gait data method using CNN by 3%. The indoor radar signal dataset and the source code are available at https://github.com/bupt-uwb/MINIPI.

**Keywords:** IR-UWB radar · Personnel Identification · Artificial Intelligence · Multi-scale Neural Network

---

L. Meng and J. Zhang—These authors contributed equally to this work and should be considered co-first authors.

This work was supported by the National Natural Science Foundation of China (Grant No. 62176024) and project A02B01C01-201916D2.

# 1    Introduction

Impulse Radio Ultra-WideBand (IR-UWB) radar has the characteristics of low power consumption and high time resolution [1]. When a person is in the detection area of radar, radar echoes will be modulated by the movement (including micro-movements of body parts). It is known as the micro-Doppler (MD) effect [2] and can characterize a person in realistic scenarios, making radar-based personnel identification possible. IR-UWB radar has its unique advantages in personnel identification. Compared with facial recognition [3], radar does not rely on light conditions and does not cause privacy problems. Compared with fingerprint collection [4], radar can provide a non-contact solution, and it even requires no interaction or cooperation with the target. Therefore, as a method of personnel identification, radar is very attractive and shows great application potential in the field of security and monitoring.

Nowadays, there are many types of researche on using radar for personnel identification. V. S. Papanastasiou et al. [5] use X-band monostatic Continuous Wave (CW) radar at 10 GHz to measure 22 persons walking at a fixed route and perform gait classification based on micro-Doppler. Kenshi Saho et al. [6] use Doppler radar to measure 10 persons sitting down or standing up at their own speed to achieve identification. Using a neural network to process radar signals has been proved to be effective. Zhaoyang Xia et al. [7] design a lightweight multi-branch convolutional neural network (CNN) with an Inception-Pool module and a Residual-Pool module to learn and classify gait Doppler features. B. Vandersmissen et al. [8] use deep CNN (DCNN) to obtain the MD features provided by frequency-modulated continuous-wave radar.

However, most radar-based identification methods are based on gait [9–11]. Gait data collection requires people to move in a specific way, which cannot be achieved in some cases. For example, when students check in at school, they will not have enough space to walk or run. Vital signs refer to the innate characteristics of a person, such as the heartbeat and breathing. It can explicitly reflect identity information and can be obtained in various scenarios.

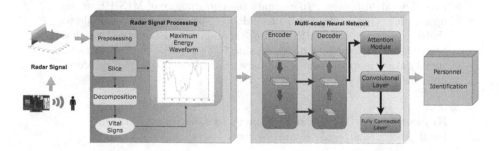

**Fig. 1.** Flowchart of the MINIPI.

In this paper, a multi-scale neural network based impulse radio ultra-wideband radar indoor personnel identification method is proposed. As shown in the Fig. 1, after preprocessing the original radar signal, the energy concentration area in the radar signal matrix is selected as the effective area. MINIPI slice the matrix with the length of 100 rows and the central interval between adjacent slices is 20 rows. Vital signs of all signal slices are extracted. The waveform with the maximum energy in the signal slice and its corresponding vital signs are reshaped into a 20×5 matrix and sent to the network. The network consists of the Encoder and the Decoder with three layers, which extract features of three scales from the input matrix and concatenate them to obtain new features. After the new feature at top layer passes through the attention module, convolutional layer and fully connected layer, the network obtains the result vector. In summary, the main contributions are listed as follows:

- We propose an indoor personnel identification network based on multiple scales, which can combine radar signals with corresponding vital signs to get identity information.
- We propose an IR-UWB radar personnel identification method using vital signs instead of gait, so it can be applied in more scenarios.
- We set up a radar vital signs dataset containing 10 persons, each with data of 4 min, altogether 40 min. Each person stands about 1 m in front of the radar. This dataset is available at https://github.com/bupt-uwb/MINIPI.

The rest of this paper is organized as follows. Section 2 describes radar signal processing. Section 3 describes methods of personnel identification. Section 4 and Sect. 5 describe the experimental setup, results and analysis. Section 6 concludes the paper.

## 2   Radar Signal Processing

In this Section, the radar signal model and its preprocessing, which is the basis of MINIPI, are introduced.

### 2.1   Radar Signal Model

IR-UWB radar transmits pulses in the form of sine waves with Gaussian envelope. The signal reflected from radar contains vital signs signals, clutters and noise. We assume that the environment in which the radar operates is static, then the vital signs signals are contained in the time-varying channel impulse response $h(t, \tau)$:

$$h(t, \tau) = \sum_i \alpha_i \sigma \left( \tau - \tau_i \right) + \alpha_b \sigma \left( \tau - \tau_b(t) \right) \tag{1}$$

where $t$ represents the cumulative time of the total pulse transmitted by the radar. $\tau$ represents the sampling time of each pulse transmitted by the radar, which is closely related to the distance from each position in space to the radar. When the radar signal reaches the human body and is reflected, there will be a delay. The delay related to the static part is represented by $\tau_i$ and the delay related to the moving part is represented by $\tau_b$.

The received radar signal is expressed as $r(t,\tau)$. $p(t)$ is a pulse in the form of a sine wave with Gaussian envelope transmitted from the radar transmitting end. Ignoring the influence of pulse distortion and noise, the received signal $R$ can be expressed as the convolution of the transmitted pulse and channel impulse response. The signal received at the pulse accumulation time $t$ can be expressed as:

$$r(t,\tau) = p(t) * h(t,\tau) = \sum_i \alpha_i p(\tau - \tau_i) + \alpha_b p(\tau - \tau_b(t)) \tag{2}$$

Sample the received radar signal at the discrete time of pulse accumulation time $t = mT_s (m = 1,, M)$ as:

$$r(mT_s, \tau) = \sum_i \alpha_i p(\tau - \tau_i) + \alpha_b p(\tau - \tau_b(mT_s)) \tag{3}$$

We sample $M$ pulse sequence signals and store them in a two-dimensional matrix with $M$ rows and $N$ columns. The matrix is expressed as:

$$r[m,n] = \sum_i \alpha_i p(n\sigma_\tau - \tau_i) + \alpha_b p(n\sigma_\tau - \tau_b(mT_s)) \tag{4}$$

where $m$ represents the cumulative time of receiving radar pulses, and $n$ represents the sampling point of each pulse received by the radar, which can be converted into the distance from each position in space to the radar.

## 2.2   Signal Preprocessing

In order to eliminate the impact that noise and clutters in the environment cause on vital signs signals, we need to preprocess the radar signal. First, we need to remove the static components in the data that cause interference. The simplest method is to average all pulse waveforms in the radar matrix and subtract the corresponding average value from each row. Then, we use Hamming window to construct a band-pass filter to obtain radar band-pass data in the frequency range of 6.5 GHz to 8 GHz.

Clutters still remain to be removed. We assume that the static clutters in the environment are similar in different radar echo signals. A method based on Principal Component Analysis (PCA) is used to suppress clutters. As a commonly used algorithm to reduce matrix dimensions, PCA can retain the most original matrix information while reducing the number of matrix dimensions. PCA essentially decomposes the radar signal into subspaces containing different pivot elements with different energy, so we can regard the radar signal matrix as the sum of pivot elements. The pivot elements containing clutter signals often occupy most of the energy in the whole radar matrix, and the energy proportion of vital signs signals in the matrix is often low. We usually regard the first pivot element, that is, the pivot element with the most energy, as the clutters in the whole environment and eliminate it.

# 3   Methodology

Height, width and thickness differ among different people, and when radar signals return after contacting the human body, these differences can be reflected in the mathematical features such as mean and variance. At the same time, the respiratory and heartbeat rates can be labels that distinguish persons. Therefore, the main idea of MINIPI is using the vital signs extracted from the radar signal matrix for personnel identification.

## 3.1   Vital Signs

Since the distance between the target and the radar will not change significantly when they are measured by the radar, the effective signals related to vital signs will be concentrated in a specific number of columns of the radar signal matrix. As shown in Fig. 2, the signal energy is concentrated around column 160. This is consistent with the fact that the target is standing about one meter in front of the radar in the actual measurement. Therefore, we calculate the mean value of each column of the radar signal matrix, take the number of columns where the maximum value is located as the center, and take a total of 100 columns around it as the effective signal.

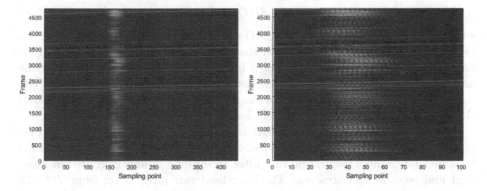

**Fig. 2.** Radar signal matrix after preprocessing and effective area.

The measured time of each participant is 4 min, and the radar signal matrix has a total of 4800 rows, which means every 20 rows in the matrix are 1 s. The radar signal matrix is sliced with the length of 100 rows, and the center interval between each adjacent slices is 10 rows. By slicing the radar data of 10 people in this way, we get about 4000 radar signal slices, which is used to extract vital signs.

Six mathematical features are selected to reflect body shape, all of which are calculated after taking the absolute value of the radar signal matrix. The proposed mathematical features are given in Table 1.

**Table 1.** Proposed mathematical features.

| | |
|---|---|
| Maximum energy | $\max(M(i,j))$ |
| Mean value | $\frac{\sum_{i,j} M(i,j)}{(i*j)}$ |
| Variance | $\frac{\sum_{i,j}(\mu - M(i,j))^2}{(i*j)}$ |
| Skewness | $E[(M-\mu)/\sigma]^3$ |
| Kurtosis | $\frac{E\left[(M-\mu)^4\right]}{\left(E\left[(M-\mu)^2\right]\right)^2}$ |
| Root Mean Square | $\sqrt{\sum_{i,j} M(i,j)^2/(i*j)}$ |

The human chest moves periodically and can be expressed as the sum of chest displacement caused by respiration and heartbeat [12–15]. This displacement can be reflected in the change of the distance between the human body and radar. We assume that the distance change caused by respiration and heartbeat is the superposition of sinusoidal functions, and the period of these functions depends on rates of respiration and heartbeat. In order to decompose the respiration and heartbeat rates from the preprocessed radar signal matrix, the variational mode decomposition (VMD) algorithm [11,13] is used.

VMD algorithm defines intrinsic mode functions (IMF) as:

$$\mu_k(t) = A_k(t) \cos\left(\varphi_k(t)\right) \tag{5}$$

where the phase of $\mu_k(t)$ is $\varphi_k(t)$. VMD can decompose the given signal into $K$ IMFs. Each IMF is a sub-signal with the same length as the original signal and has its own center frequency. Preset a large enough $K$ value in the algorithm and select the signal with the largest energy from the radar signal as the vital sign signal for decomposition, then we can get several sub-signals, which include the respiration and heartbeat information.

After obtaining a series of sub-signals, in order to obtain heartbeat and respiration rates from many central frequencies, it is necessary to construct a heartbeat rate filter and a respiration rate filter to exclude signals that are not heartbeat and respiratory waveforms. The heartbeat rate range is set from 50 to 120 per minute. The respiration rate range is set from 5 to 40 per minute.

For each radar signal slice, the column with the maximum mean value is selected as the maximum energy waveform. VMD is applied on the maximum energy waveform to extract heartbeat and respiration rates. The last eight elements of the maximum energy waveform are replaced by vital signs to obtain a $1\times100$ vector, which is used as the input of the neural network.

## 3.2 Multi-scale Neural Network

In the current use of neural network, Convolutional Neural Networks is more widely used and mature than Necurrent Neural Networks and the latest transformer. Therefore, we choose to use CNN for comparative experiment. Because the identification task has the characteristics of massive data and few categories (fewer than 100), We choose the U-Net [16] network as the baseline for the experiment. The advantage of the multi-scale information ensures that the original information will not be lost. When the signal duration increases, we can simply deepen the network depth to adapt without increasing the training burden. Due to the superiority of the attention mechanism in Transformer in recent years, we use the lightweight CNN global attention module proposed in [17] to modify the network. The overall network structure is shown in Fig. 3.

Multi-scale Neural Network is mainly composed of the Encoder and the Decoder, both of which have a three-layer structure. The input of the network is a 1×100 signal vector combined with vital signs. Since the radar signal is 20 rows per second, we reshape the vector into a 20×5 matrix to extract features better.

The top layer of the Encoder adjust the matrix channel to 16, and the middle and bottom layers extract features of different scales as:

$$E^{16}_{20\times5}, E^{32}_{10\times3}, E^{32}_{2\times5} = E(\text{Input}) \tag{6}$$

These features are all input into the Decoder. The middle layer of the Decoder will up sample the feature of bottom layer and concatenate it with the feature of the same layer in the Encoder. The concatenated feature is up sampled and sent to top layer as:

$$D^{16}_{20\times5} = D\left(D^{32}_{10\times3}, E^{32}_{10\times3}\right) \tag{7}$$

At the top layer, we perform a 3×3 convolution on the concatenated feature after inputting it into the attention module. Then we perform a 20×1 convolution to obtain the 1 channel feature of 1×5 scale, which will be sent to the fully connected layer. Then, we obtain a 1×8 vector, which is the result of personnel identification.

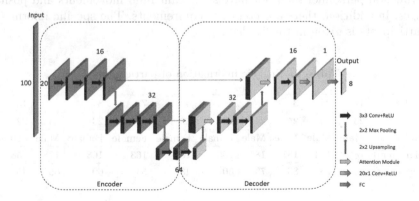

**Fig. 3.** Multi-scale neural network.

## 4    Experiment Setup

In this experiment, Xethru X4M03 radar is used for data collection. Figure 4 shows our experimental equipment and scene setup. The working frequency of IR-UWB radar is 6.0–8.5 GHz and can collect information 0.2–3 m ahead. The experiment was conducted in an indoor room. The radar was set 1.5 m above the ground, basically the same as the chest of the tested person. The frames are collected at a rate of 20 samples per second.

 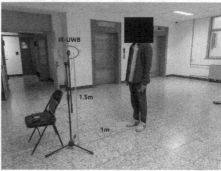

(a) The IR-UWB radar                    (b) Experimental scene

**Fig. 4.** Experimental equipment and scene.

The participants in the experiment were composed of 10 graduate students, all aged about 23 years old, with height ranging from 158 cm to 185 cm and weight ranging from 45 kg to 83 kg, including 5 females and 5 males. Each participant was asked to stand 1 m in front of the radar for 4 min. It is required that the experimental personnel shall not have significant limb movements and position changes. In addition, there are no other requirements. The specific information of participants is given in the Table 2.

**Table 2.** Specific information of participants.

| Number | 1 | 2 | 3 | 4 | 5 | 6 | 7 | 8 | 9 | 10 |
|---|---|---|---|---|---|---|---|---|---|---|
| Age | 23 | 23 | 24 | 24 | 23 | 22 | 23 | 23 | 23 | 22 |
| Gender | Male | Male | Male | Male | Female | Female | Female | Female | Male | Female |
| Height (cm) | 182 | 174 | 187 | 185 | 165 | 160 | 163 | 168 | 178 | 158 |
| Weight (kg) | 65 | 76 | 83 | 73 | 50 | 48 | 54 | 60 | 65 | 45 |

We collected data from each person for 4 min, all together 40 min. The data is processed using a notebook (Lenovo y7000p 2019).

# 5    Result and Analysis

After removing the contaminated data and invalid data, we obtained a dataset consisting of 4600 radar signal vectors combined with vital signs and corresponding identity tags. For comparison, we first input it into the random forest classifier. The accuracy of the prediction is represented by the confusion matrix. Each row of the confusion matrix represents the probability that the label of this row is predicted as various labels, and the value on the diagonal is the probability that the label is correctly predicted. When we divide the dataset into training set and test set with the ratio of 8:2, the confusion matrix is shown in Fig. 5(a). The average test accuracy is 81.2%. It can be seen that the identification accuracy of some specific targets is low.

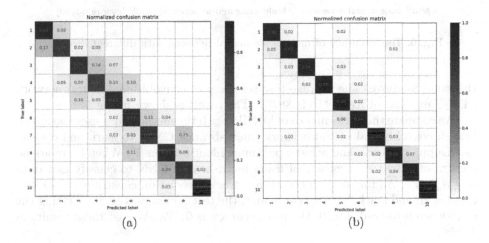

**Fig. 5.** Test accuracy of random forest classifier (a) and multi-scales neural network (b)

We input the dataset into our multi-scale neural network and also divide the dataset into training set and test set with the ratio of 8:2. The batch size is set as 16 and the number of epochs is 100. The confusion matrix is shown in Fig. 5(b)

From the confusion matrix, it can be seen that MINIPI can effectively identify 10 different targets. The identification accuracy of all targets on the test set is higher than 85%, and the average accuracy is 94.8%. In order to show the advantages of multi-scale features, we removed the middle layer of the network and carried out experiments in the same way. The result is shown in Fig. 6. It can be seen that the deepening of network layers helps to improve the identification accuracy.

For further analysis, we build two other neural network architectures and test their performance on this dataset. One is a convolutional neural network composed of three one-dimensional convolutional layers and a full connection layer. The other is ResNet18 [18]. The division of training set and test set is

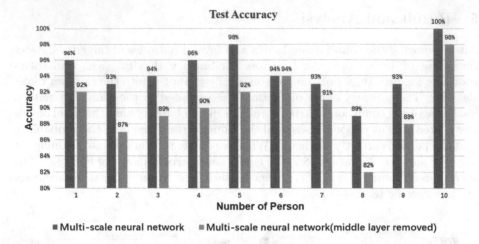

**Fig. 6.** Test accuracy of multi-scale neural network with different layers.

the same as above. The average test accuracy of convolutional neural network 84.5%, and that of ResNet18 is 88.3%. The result is shown in Fig. 7.

We compare the performance of MINIPI with the method that uses the multi-branch convolutional neural network (multi-branch CNN) to learn and classify gait Doppler features and achieve personnel identification [7]. When there are no constraints, the test accuracy of using multi-branch CNN to classify gait data sets is 74.4%. Adding motion constraint, track association constraint, track size constraint, and track linearity constraint, the test accuracy is 85.8%. Setting the confidence threshold $\mu$ 0.99, the test accuracy is 91.5%. We list these results in Table 3.

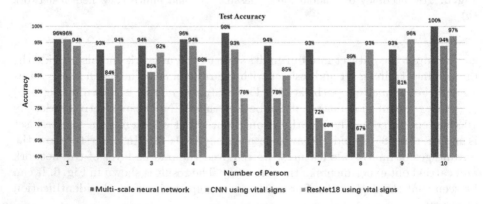

**Fig. 7.** Test accuracy of different neural network architectures.

It can be seen that MINIPI can perform indoor personnel identification accurately.

**Table 3.** Test accuracy of MINIPI and other methods.

| Method | Test accuracy |
|---|---|
| Multi-branch CNN [7] | 74.4% |
| Multi-branch CNN with four constraints [7] | 85.8% |
| Multi-branch CNN with four constraints, $\mu = 0.99$ [7] | 91.5% |
| **Random forest using vital signs** | **81.2%** |
| **CNN using vital signs** | **84.5%** |
| **ResNet18 using vital signs** | **88.3%** |
| **MINIPI** | **94.8%** |

## 6 Conclusion

To improve the wildly-used gait data based IR-UWB radar personnel identification method, we propose a multi-scale neural network based impulse radio ultra-wideband radar indoor personnel identification method. The radar signal matrix is sliced after preprocessing and the slices are used to extract vital signs. The maximum energy waveform in the slice and its corresponding vital signs are input into the multi-scale neural network. The network is mainly composed of the Encoder and the Decoder. Three layers are constructed to extract and concatenate features from the reshaped matrix. The feature at the top layer of the Decoder is sent into the attention module and the fully connected layer, then we get the identification results. A radar dataset containing 10 persons is set up. The average identification accuracy of MINIPI among these 10 persons is 94.8%. Results show that MINIPI performs accurately in indoor personnel identification.

## References

1. Li, H.-B., Takizawa, K., Kagawa, T., Kojima, F., Miura, R.: Improvement on localization accuracy of IR-UWB by adapting time bias inner transceiver. In: 2019 International Conference on Computing, Networking and Communications (ICNC), 2019, pp. 116–120 (2019). https://doi.org/10.1109/ICCNC.2019.8685621
2. Chen, V.: The Micro-Doppler Effect in Radar. Second Edition, Artech (2019)
3. Ranjan, R., et al.: A fast and accurate system for face detection, identification, and verification. IEEE Trans. Biometrics Behav. Identity Sci. IEEE Trans. Biometrics Behav. Identity Sci. 1(2), 82–96 (2019). https://doi.org/10.1109/TBIOM.2019.2908436

4. Tshomo, K., Tshering, K., Gyeltshen, D., Yeshi, J., Muramatsu, K.: Dual door lock system using radio-frequency identification and fingerprint recognition. In: 2019 IEEE 5th International Conference for Convergence in Technology (I2CT), 2019, pp. 1–5. https://doi.org/10.1109/I2CT45611.2019.9033636

5. Papanastasiou, V.S., Trommel, R.P., Harmanny, R.I.A., Yarovoy, A.: Deep Learning-based identification of human gait by radar micro-Doppler measurements. In: 2020 17th European Radar Conference (EuRAD), 2021, pp. 49–52 (2021). https://doi.org/10.1109/EuRAD48048.2021.00024

6. Saho, K., Shioiri, K., Inuzuka, K.: Accurate person identification based on combined sit-to-stand and stand-to-sit movements measured using doppler radars. IEEE Sensors J. **21**(4), 4563–4570 (2021). https://doi.org/10.1109/JSEN.2020.3032960

7. Z. Xia, G. Ding, H. Wang and F. Xu, Person Identification with Millimeter-Wave Radar in Realistic Smart Home Scenarios, in IEEE Geoscience and Remote Sensing Letters, vol. 19, pp. 1–5, 2022, Art no. 3509405, https://doi.org/10.1109/LGRS.2021.3117001

8. Vandersmissen, B., et al.: Indoor person identification using a low-power FMCW radar. IEEE Trans. Geosci. Remote Sens. **56**(7), 3941–3952 (2018). https://doi.org/10.1109/TGRS.2018.2816812

9. Connor, P., Ross, A.: Biometric recognition by gait: a survey of modalitiesand features. Comput. Vis. Image Underst. **167**, 1–27 (2018)

10. Ni, Z., Huang, B.: Human identification based on natural gait micro-Doppler signatures using deep transfer learning. IET Radar, Sonar Navigat. **14**(10), 1640–1646 (2020). https://doi.org/10.1049/iet-rsn.2020.0183

11. Ni, Z., Huang, B.: Open-set human identification based on gait radar micro-doppler signatures. IEEE Sens. J. **21**(6), 8226–8233 (2021). https://doi.org/10.1109/JSEN.2021.3052613

12. Duan, Z., Liang, J.: Non-contact detection of vital signs using a UWB radar sensor. IEEE Access **7**, 36888–36895 (2019). https://doi.org/10.1109/ACCESS.2018.2886825

13. Shen, H., et al.: Respiration and heartbeat rates measurement based on autocorrelation using IR-UWB radar. IEEE Trans. Circuits Syst. II Express Briefs **65**(10), 1470–1474 (2018). https://doi.org/10.1109/TCSII.2018.2860015

14. Yang, X., Ding, Y., Zhang, X., Zhang, L.: Spatial-temporal-circulated GLCM and physiological features for in-vehicle people sensing based on IR-UWB Radar. IEEE Trans. Instrumentation Measur. **71**, 1–13, 2022, Art no. 8502113, https://doi.org/10.1109/TIM.2022.3165808

15. Yang, X., Yin, W., Li, L., Zhang, L.: Dense people counting using IR-UWB radar with a hybrid feature extraction method. IEEE Geosci. Remote Sens. Lett. **16**(1), 30–34 (2019). https://doi.org/10.1109/LGRS.2018.2869287

16. Ronneberger O, Fischer P, Brox T. U-Net: Convolutional Networks for Biomedical Image Segmentation[J]. Springer International Publishing: Lecture Notes in Computer Science(), vol 9351. Springer, Cham. (2015). https://doi.org/10.1007/978-3-319-24574-4_28

17. Li, X., Jiang, Y., Li, M., Yin, S.: Lightweight attention convolutional neural network for retinal vessel image segmentation. IEEE Trans. Industr. Inf. **17**(3), 1958–1967 (2021). https://doi.org/10.1109/TII.2020.2993842

18. He, K., Zhang, X., Ren, S., Sun, J.: Deep residual learning for image recognition. In: IEEE Conference on Computer Vision and Pattern Recognition (CVPR) 2016, pp. 770–778 (2016). https://doi.org/10.1109/CVPR.2016.90

# PSU-Net: Paired Spatial U-Net for Hand Segmentation with Complex Backgrounds

Kaijun Zhou, Wenjing Qi$^{(\boxtimes)}$, Ziqiang Gui, and Qi Zeng

Hunan University of Technology and Business, Changsha 410000, China
pppyuyan@163.com

**Abstract.** Hand segmentation, as a key part of human-computer interaction, palmprint recognition and gesture recognition, is prone to interference from complex backgrounds subsequently resulting in poor segmentation accuracy. In this paper, a paired spatial U-Net (PSU-Net) hand image segmentation network is proposed. Firstly, we improve the traditional dilated pyramid pooling into the paired spatial pyramid pooling (PSPP) module. Through low-dimensional feature pairing, the PSPP can exploit the low-dimensional feature information, thus enhancing the network's ability to capture edge detail information. Then we design the global attention fusion module (GAF), which can efficiently combine low-dimensional spatial details and high-dimensional semantic information to solve blurred edges in complex backgrounds. Some experimental results on HOF, GTEA and Egohands databases show the proposed approach has quite good performance. The mIOU of PSU-Net can achieve 76.19% on HOF dataset, while the mIOU of DeeplabV3 is 74.45%.

**Keywords:** Hand image segmentation · Attention mechanism · Pyramid pooling structure

## 1 Introduction

Hand segmentation is vital to many computer vision applications, such as human-computer interaction, palmprint recognition and hand gesture recognition. But hand image in complex backgrounds is disturbed by many factors, which has posed a great challenge to hand region segmentation. In recent years, semantic segmentation is widely used in the fields of autonomous driving, video surveillance and robot perception, etc. It performs well in terms of segmentation accuracy. However, there are still problems such as large number of parameters and high volume of computation, inaccurate segmentation and edge details loss of complex background.

Meanwhile, current studies on hand segmentation are limited to traditional methods, with little involvement in deep learning semantic segmentation methods. Most of the traditional methods are based on skin color thresholding segmentation. Zhang [1] proposed a method based on suitable thresholding to separate hand images from the background, but it is only applicable to segmentation in simple backgrounds. Han [2] extracted hand regions by computing their distribution in Ycrcb color space, which can

© The Author(s), under exclusive license to Springer Nature Switzerland AG 2022
S. Yu et al. (Eds.): PRCV 2022, LNCS 13535, pp. 549–563, 2022.
https://doi.org/10.1007/978-3-031-18910-4_44

get more reasonable thresholds to complete the segmentation task compared with the previous method. Shuping Liu [3] combined the skin segmentation model with the gradient direction histogram, which effectively improved the hand segmentation accuracy. Hand segmentation based on skin color has been widely studied for decades due to its simplicity and intuitiveness [4]. Li [5] proposed a segmentation method based on saliency and skin color, which deeply integrates bottom-up saliency information and bottom-up skin color information to achieve segmentation. Many scholars have further researched and proposed to use the saliency information of images for compression, segmentation or classification.

Although the traditional method based on skin color can achieve fast and stable segmentation, and focus more on the theoretical basis of mining image information. But it is extremely vulnerable to similarity interference resulting in poor segmentation effect, cannot effectively extract the deep-level feature map. Its segmentation accuracy is far from meeting the application needs of people in daily life. And with the rapid development of deep learning, its segmentation performance has obvious advantages over traditional methods [6, 7].

In response to the problems of low accuracy of traditional skin color segmentation methods and poor segmentation of complex background images, we take high accuracy of semantic segmentation network as the research direction, and design a PSU-Net hand image segmentation model based on pyramid pooling and global attention mechanism.

The contributions of this paper are as follows:

Firstly, the mainstream semantic segmentation model U-net is improved and used in the field of biometric recognition for hand segmentation. We propose a PSU-Net based on the Paired Spatial Pyramid Pooling (PSPP), aiming to improve the efficiency of using feature maps and greatly enhance the accuracy of semantic segmentation.

Secondly, we combine the PAnet and Convolutional Block Attention Module (CBAM) and design the Global Attention Fusion module (GAF). The GAF can recover the lost high-dimensional edge information and produce a more accurate low-dimensional feature map, which communicates more smoothly with the high-dimensional information, thus increasing the speed of information fusion.

Finally, we have sufficient experiments to demonstrate the effectiveness of our model. Some experimental results on HOF, GTEA and Egohands databases show the proposed approach has quite good performance. The mIOU of PSU-Net reached 76.19% on the HOF dataset, while the mIOU of DeeplabV3 is 74.45%.

## 2  Related Work

### 2.1  Efficient Module Designs

Model design plays an important role in computer vision tasks. SqueezeNet [8] uses fire module and certain strategies to reduce model parameters. MobileNet V1 [9] uses depth-wise separable convolution to reduce FLOPs in the inference phase. ResNet [10] uses a residual construction layer to achieve excellent performance. MobileNet V2 [11] and ShuffleNet [12] use grouped convolution to reduce computational cost while maintaining comparable accuracy. These works are specifically designed for image classification tasks and their extensions to semantic segmentation applications should be carefully tuned.

## 2.2 Generic Semantic Segmentation

Jonathan [13] proposed a fully convolutional network, replacing the fully connected network with a convolutional network, combining deconvolution and classifier to form the basic structure of convolution-deconvolution-classifier. Badrinarayanan [14] proposed SegNet, which preserves the high-resolution feature maps at the deepest coded output and uses a decoder to decompose the low-resolution images. DeepLabv2 [15] proposed Atrous Spatial Pyramid Pooling (ASPP), and DeepLabv3 [16] enhanced the ASPP module on the basis of v2 by adding the final block of ResNet cascaded up and removing except the CRFs block. Hengshuang Zhao [17] proposed PSPNet, whose core contribution is Global Pyramid Pooling. It scales the feature map into several different sizes to give features better global and multi-scale information. Lin [18] illustrated the properties of the dilated pyramid pooling structure and introduced dilated convolution to extend the perceptual domain, thus to obtain image features with different scale information. However, due to the high resolution and complex network connectivity of most feature pyramid methods, significant computational costs are required.

Based on the above analysis, we propose a PSU-Net based on the PSPP module, which aims to improve the efficiency of feature map and greatly enhance the accuracy of semantic segmentation. Considering the low utilization of high-dimensional feature maps in the Pyramid module, we design the PSPP module by changing the Atrous Spatial Pyramid Pooling, which can effectively enhance the extraction of low-dimensional feature information.

## 2.3 Attention Mechanisms

When the network extracts image feature layers, adding channel attention mechanism and spatial attention mechanism between convolutional layers can enhance the ability of the network to extract images. The Recurrent Attention Model (RAM) [19] is an adaptive approach that continuously selects important regions from an image or video and processes them at high resolution, while using low resolution or discarding the less important ones. The essence of the Sequeeze and Excitation Net (SENet) [20] is to model the importance of each feature channel in order to enhance or suppress different channels for different tasks. The Convolutional Block Attention Module (CBAM) [21] is an adaptive feature refinement that inferred the attention of a picture sequentially along two independent dimensions, channel and space, given an intermediate feature map, and then multiplied the attention map by the input feature map.

Based on the above analysis, we combine the PAnet and CBAM to propose the GAF module. The GAF combines the attention obtained from the low-dimensional feature maps to complement the high-dimensional semantics, making the low-dimensional information more comprehensive. The GAF recovers the high-dimensional information lost at the edges and produces a low-dimensional feature map with a higher degree of accuracy. The module enables a more fluid exchange of low-dimensional feature maps with higher-dimensional information and can effectively increase the speed of fusion.

## 3   Proposed Method

The network structure of PSU-Net is shown in Fig. 1, which consists of an up-sampling module, a down-sampling module, a GAF module, a PSPP module, a batch normalization layer and a hopping connection. The encoder side consists of PSPP module, down-sampling and batch normalization layer, the decoder side consists of PSPP module, up-sampling and batch normalization layer, and the number of convolutional kernels is the same as the number of segmentation categories. The GAF module are added at the end of the last up-sampling. In the subsequent decoding and encoding process, the GAF is able to further enhance the dependency between feature maps, so as to more directly display the available features and to focus the attention of the network on features with high representativeness.

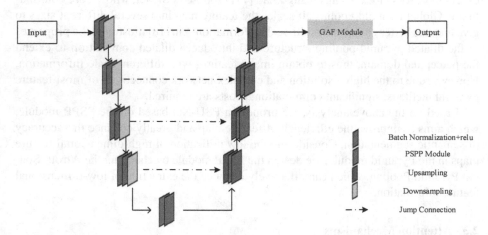

**Fig. 1.** Structure of the PSU-Net network

### 3.1   Paired Spatial Pyramid Pooling Module

DeepLab makes full use of the features of dilated convolution to obtain ASPP, which aims to obtain more semantic information in high-dimensional map. The above approach is good for obtaining high-dimensional information, but not for low-dimensional feature map. In general, in most Encoder-Decoder structures, the encoder mainly extracts the high-dimensional feature information from the input feature map but neglects low-dimensional features, which leads to a lack of multi-scale information and specific spatial details. To extract distinguishing information from shallow features, we introduce the PSPP module, which collects low-dimensional information from all phases of the backbone and fuses them by means of pairing.

The conventional ASPP module uses four parallel convolutional kernel operations for stitching. Unlike ASPP, the PSPP module combines low-dimensional feature maps in a paired way many times to the last stage, which is able to capture more low-dimensional scale information while preserving low-dimensional spatial information.. The specific

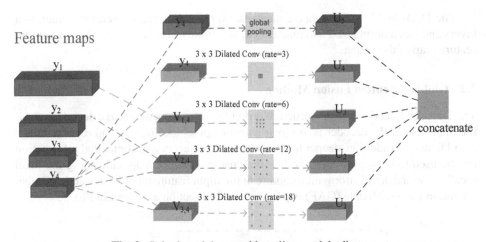

**Fig. 2.** Paired spatial pyramid pooling module diagram

structure of the PSPP module is shown in Fig. 2, y1, y2, y3 and y4 represent four feature maps with different dimensional information, {ys}s = 1, ..., 4 are higher-order representations of each stage, and then the first three feature maps are combined in a paired manner.

$$V_{1,4} = \text{Concat} \ (y_1, y_4) \tag{1}$$

$$V_{2,4} = \text{Concat} \ (y_2, y_4) \tag{2}$$

$$V_{3,4} = \text{Concat} \ (y_3, y_4) \tag{3}$$

Four $3 \times 3$ dilated convolutions with rates of (3, 6, 12, 18) and a global pooling are used on V1,4, V2,4, V3,4 and y4 respectively. Each dilated convolution is able to capture information at two scales, covering as large a span of scales as possible by using different dilated convolution rates. Therefore, due to the large receptive field of y3 and y4, a dilated convolution with a rate of 18 was applied on V3,4. At the same time, a low-rate dilated convolution of 6 and 12 was applied to V1,4 and V2,4, due to low level feature requires low-rate dilated convolution to maintain the spatial information.

$$U_1 = \text{Conv}_{\text{rates}=18}(V_{3,4}) \tag{4}$$

$$U_2 = \text{Conv}_{\text{rates}=12}(V_{2,4}) \tag{5}$$

$$U_3 = \text{Conv}_{\text{rates}=6}(V_{1,4}) \tag{6}$$

$$U_4 = \text{Conv}_{\text{rates}=3}(y_4) \tag{7}$$

$$U_5 = GAP(y_4) \tag{8}$$

The {Ui}i = 1, ..., 5 are then concatenated, passed through several convolutional layers and batch normalized and reactivated, and finally fused to obtain the final output feature map of the output.

### 3.2 Global Attention Fusion Module

The Decoder-Encoder network structure is divided into an encoder and a decoder, where the main role of the decoder is to repair category pixel localization and recover image detail feature. In addition, deeper feature with multi category and contextual information can be used to reassign weights to low-dimensional feature map, enhancing the pixel localization and detail information capture of the input feature map. To this end, a Global Attention Fusion Module (GAF) is proposed in this section as shown in Fig. 3.

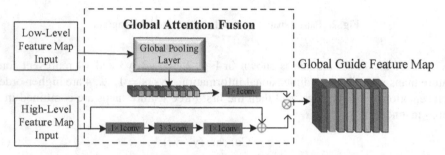

**Fig. 3.** Global attention fusion module

The principle of the GAF module proposed in this paper is as follows. The low-level feature map input is first globally pooled and subsequently plugged into a convolution kernel. Meanwhile, the high-level feature input is weighted and fused with the initial input after passing through three convolutions. Then, the outputs of the two ports are multiplied to obtain the low-dimensional attention feature map. This process produces global contextual features, which act as the attentional feature map and enable more accurate category pixel localization. A weighted feature map mapping is generated by applying element-by-element multiplication between the attention low-level features and the global attention mapping. And the output is connected to the context-embedded feature map to produce the final prediction.

### 3.3 Improved Loss Function

In the traditional U-Net, the cross-entropy loss function is calculated based on the output of Softmax as the loss function for the whole network. The distribution of weights corresponding to each pixel in the image is pre-calculated as shown in Eq. 9.

$$w(x) = w_c(x) + w_0 \cdot exp\left(-\frac{(d_1(x) + d_2(x))^2}{2\sigma^2}\right) \tag{9}$$

Equation 9 uses w(x) to compensate for the imbalance between different types of pixels in the dataset. The second part enhances the learning ability of the network for the target task by calculating the square of the sum of the distance from the current pixel to the nearest edge and the distance from the current pixel to the second nearest edge, with the network focusing more on edge learning for pixels that are in contact with each other. Equation 9 mainly addresses the sample imbalance problem and the low accuracy of edge segmentation in the segmentation task. Based on these two problems, the loss function is improved in this paper, taking into account the specific situation of hand image segmentation.

Cross entropy as a loss function can only indirectly estimate the effect of the existing model, and when the loss function reaches a minimum value, it does not guarantee that the model gets the best performance. As the Dice coefficient only cares about the gap between the segmentation result and the ground truth, using the opposite Dice coefficient can directly avoid the problem of uneven number of pixels in different categories without using weighting. Therefore, this paper uses the function opposite to the Dice coefficient as the loss function, which can directly avoid the problem of uneven number of pixels in different categories without weighting. The formula is shown in Eq. 10. The second improvement is to modify the weights of each pixel, where the gap between most image segments is significantly larger than the gap between cells. For smaller hand parts, there is a tendency for over-or under-cutting; or the hand edges are not segmented with high accuracy and the segmented hand size is slightly smaller than the real hand size. Determining the loss function as the inverse of the color block enables pixel imbalance to be avoided.

$$l = -\frac{2 \times \sum w_x Y_{\text{pre\_x}} Y_{\text{true}} + \varepsilon}{\sum_x w_x Y_{\text{pre\_x}} + \sum_x w_x Y_{\text{true\_x}} + \varepsilon} \tag{10}$$

where $Y_{pre\_x}$ denotes the prediction result for the xth pixel in the prediction result, $Y_{true\_x}$ denotes the category label for the xth pixel in the actual label, $w_x$ is the weight of the xth pixel, and $\varepsilon$ is used to prevent the numerator or denominator from being zero.

# 4  Experimental Results

In this paper, we validate our method on three datasets, the HOF [22], the GTEA [23], and the Egohands [24] respectively, in order to evaluate the effectiveness of our proposed backbone network and segmentation network. We first present the datasets used and the experimental deployment details, and then we validate the effectiveness and reliability of our model by comparing the accuracy and speed results of the experiments and with other algorithms on different benchmarks, as well as a series of ablation experiments.

## 4.1  Benchmarks and Evaluation Metrics

**HOF Dataset.** HOF-2018 is a segmentation dataset of common HandOverface scenes, where all images contain hands obscuring faces of different shapes, sizes and positions. People in the dataset come from different races, ages and genders. Each image has a pixel mask that is labelled as a hand or background entity. In this paper a proportion of the data is chosen for the experiments, split between 70% training, 10% validation and 20% testing.

**GTEA Dataset.** Our method is evaluated on a public GTEA recorded using a head-mounted wearable camera. This dataset contains 7 different cooking activities performed by 4 different subjects. Each action annotation contains an action and a set of objects (with start and end frames). There are 10 action categories and 525 instances (video segments) in the original label.

**Egohands Dataset.** This dataset is primarily an approach to understanding hands in different data-driven odd PC visuals, and contains 15,000 ground truth masks of the best quality. It contains both basic quality and pixel-level annotations. All images are taken from different egocentric perspectives, such as playing chess, stacking blocks, puzzles, etc., and contain images from 48 different situations.

**Evaluation Metrics.** We use the mean intersection-over-union (mIoU), a common model performance evaluation metric in the field of image segmentation, to characterize the segmentation performance of the model, mIoU can be expressed as Eq. 11. In addition, we also use F1 Score, The F1 score is based on Precision and Recall a comprehensive evaluation index, as expressed in Eq. 12. Precision represents the result evaluation that the hand image is correctly segmented, and Recall represents the result evaluation that the target sample in the hand image is correctly predicted.

$$\text{mIoU} = \frac{1}{k+1} \sum_{i=0}^{k} \text{IoU}_i \tag{11}$$

$$\text{F1} = 2 \times \frac{\text{Precision} \times \text{Recall}}{\text{Precision} + \text{Recall}} \tag{12}$$

### 4.2 Experimental Details

In order to evaluate the method proposed in this paper, a comprehensive experiment is conducted. This experiment will be completed on a high-performance laboratory computer with the main experimental configuration shown in Table 1, and all processes of the experiment are completed in this environment configuration. The validation of the PSU-Net is carried out on the pre-processed dataset, and all processes are implemented based on the Python language. The experiments are conducted on the common Tensorflow framework, and a poly learning rate strategy is used to tune the model learning rate and set the initial learning rate to 0.0002, the batchsize to 32 for both testing and training, and the training epoch to 500, while stochastic gradient descent with a weight decay of 0.00002 is used to optimize the network model. The proposed PSU-Net network model is trained for 200 iterations, and mIoU is used to judge the merit of the network model during the testing phase.

**Table 1.** Experimental software and hardware configuration

| Name | Value | Name | Value |
|------|-------|------|-------|
| CPU | Inter(R)Core(TM)i7-8700K | GPU | NVIDIA GeForce GTX2080Ti |
| Operating systems | Ubuntu 16.04 | Programming languages | Python3.6.5 |

### 4.3 Ablation Experiments

**PSPP Module Ablation Experiments.** In order to verify the effectiveness of the PSPP we proposed, the PSU-Net with only the PSPP module added was compared with the PSPNet, and the experimental results are shown in Table 2. From the experimental results, it can be seen that mIoU shows an increasing trend when no GAF is employed, which is able to prove that both branches are able to improve the accuracy of segmentation. The PSPP module can significantly improve the fusion efficiency of high and low dimensional feature maps by reducing the information gap between them through paired fusion, thus effectively improving the network performance.

**Table 2.** PSPP module ablation experiments

| Experimental method | Whether to use low-dimensional feature maps | mIoU(%) |
|---------------------|---------------------------------------------|---------|
| U-Net | × | 72.21 |
| PSPNet | × | 73.19 |
| PSU-Net(×GAF) | √ | 76.52 |
| PSU-Net | √ | **78.38** |

**Ablation Experiments of Attentional Mechanisms.** The fusion module has the function of weight assignment, which can allocate more weight to the necessary information, and if the GAF module is added, it can further improve the accuracy of the feature map in all aspects of information. This part of the experiment compares the PSU-Net with the GAF module removed to the one without, and the segmentation can be viewed as shown in Fig. 4, and the quantitative results of the GAF as shown in Table 2. We find that the model is able to complete the segmentation more accurately without a large degree of error, indicating that the GAF module can significantly improve the segmentation performance of the network, allowing the network to obtain more accurate boundary and detail information.

**Low-Dimensional Feature Maps and Different Ablations Rate of Dilated Convolution Block Experiments.** Since the hand occupies a relatively small portion of the experimental image and belongs to the small-scale target semantic information, this experiment is conducted to demonstrate the importance of low-dimensional feature maps

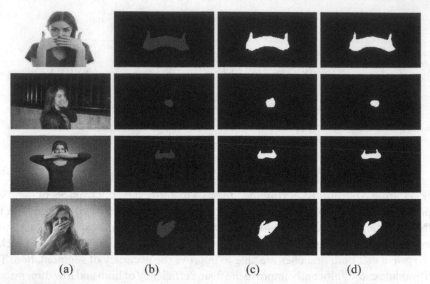

(a)          (b)          (c)          (d)

**Fig. 4.** Visualization results of the GAF on the HOF dataset. (a) Original plot. (b) Ground truth of the original plot. (c) The visualization result of PSU-Net (×GAF). (d) The result of PSU-Net moving out of the GAF.

in the extraction of small-scale target semantic feature information by excluding the feature maps of output 1 or removing both the feature maps of output 1 and output 2, and the experimental results are shown in Table 3. The experimental results show that the F1 score of the hand decreases more than the mIoU after removing the low-dimensional feature maps from the network.

In dilated convolution, different dilated rates result in different receptive field area sizes for the dilated convolution kernel. In order to test the effect of the size of the dilated rate in different dilated convolutions on the ability of the PSPP module to capture feature information, we set the dilated rate within the PSPP module to three different dilated rates, and different combinations of dilated rate also affect the performance of the PSPP module, so we took different combinations of dilated rate to complete this experiment, and from the experiments in the Table 3. The results show that the 6/12/18 rate shows better performance than the other two groups, so this combination is chosen as the rate for the proposed method.

### 4.4   Comparison Experiments

The HOF dataset is used to validate the model proposed in this paper and to compare it with other related segmentation methods as an indication of how advanced the model is. The visualization results of the experiments are shown in Fig. 5 and the quantitative analysis results are shown in Table 4. The original image is cropped to a size of 512 × 512 during the experimental training process, while the resolution of the original image is maintained during the testing phase.

**Table 3.** Different levels of feature maps and dilated rate ablation experiments

| Model name | Feature map hierarchy | mIoU (%) | F1(%) |
|---|---|---|---|
| PSU-Net | Output (3) | 74.59 | 85.20 |
| | Output (2, 3) | 75.89 | 84.72 |
| | Output (1, 2, 3) | 91.46 | 95.91 |
| | PSPP dilation rate | mIoU (%) | F1(%) |
| | PSPP (5/10/15) | 74.92 | 93.01 |
| | PSPP (6/12/18) | 75.81 | 94.12 |
| | PSPP (7/14/21) | 72.01 | 92.75 |

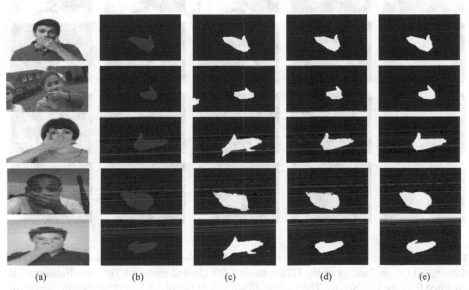

(a)          (b)          (c)          (d)          (e)

**Fig. 5.** Experimental results of different segmentation methods for the HOF dataset. (a) Original image of the HOF dataset. (b) Ground truth. (c) The visualization result obtained from the PSPNet. (d) The visualization result of DeeplabV3. (e) The visualization result of the PSU-Net.

In the experiments, in order to further analyze the feasibility of the method proposed in this paper, the FCN and SegNet are added to the quantitative analysis to further demonstrate that the PSU-Net we proposed has better results in segmentation performance. In the results shown in Table 4, it can be seen that on the HOF dataset, the mIOU of PSU-Net reached 76.19% and the F1 Score reached 96.29%, which is a significant improvement over PSPNet, DeeplabV3, U-Net, FCN and SegNet.

To further validate the segmentation performance of the PSU-Net, the comparison of the accuracy with other mainstream semantic segmentation networks is continued on the GTEA dataset. During the training process, the dataset is still divided according to the ratio of 7:2:1, and finally the test set is used to test the quantitative analysis results of the obtained network models. The visualization of each network on the GTEA dataset is shown in Fig. 6, and the quantitative analysis results are shown in Table 4. The mIOU of our proposed model on the GTEA dataset is able to achieve 72.89% and the F1 Score is 94.29%.

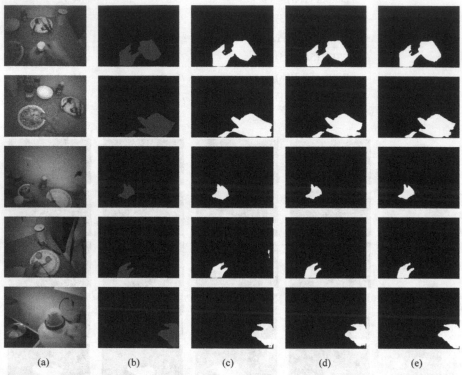

|  (a) | (b) | (c) | (d) | (e) |

**Fig. 6.** Comparison of experimental results of different segmentation methods for the GTEA dataset. (a) Original image of the GTEA dataset. (b) Ground truth. (c) The visualization result obtained from the PSPNet. (d) The visualization result of DeeplabV3. (e) The visualization result of the PSU-Net.

We also conducted experiments on the EgoHands, and the visualization results are shown in Fig. 7. Combining the five different scenes in the Egohands dataset, the PSU-Net is the network model with the best performance. Comparing the first complex scene, due to the presence of playing cards and interference under different illumination, PSPNet and DeepLabV3 mistakenly segmented the wrist part of the left hand in the figure as the hand, and the detail information is seriously lost, and the segmentation result is poor. In the rest of the scenes, the results achieved by PSU-Net are also better and can accomplish the task of hand segmentation well.

**Table 4.** Results of the quantitative analysis of the HOF and GETA

| Model | Results on HOF | | Results on GTEA | |
|---|---|---|---|---|
| | F1 (%) | mIoU(%) | F1 (%) | mIoU(%) |
| FCN | 65.81 | 58.05 | 59.68 | 51.79 |
| U-Net | 89.02 | 70.41 | 85.29 | 65.98 |
| PSPNet | 89.19 | 71.15 | 87.89 | 67.29 |
| DeeplabV3 | 94.59 | 74.45 | 90.87 | 68.89 |
| SegNet | 92.32 | 72.29 | 89.82 | 67.26 |
| **PSU-Net** | **96.29** | **76.19** | **94.29** | **72.89** |

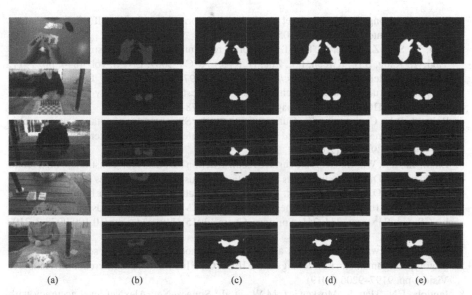

(a)          (b)          (c)          (d)          (e)

**Fig. 7.** Comparison of experimental results of different segmentation methods for the EgoHands dataset. (a) Original image of the EgoHands dataset. (b) Ground truth. (c) The visualization result obtained from the PSPNet. (d) The visualization result of DeeplabV3. (e) The visualization result of the PSU-Net.

## 5 Conclusions and Future Work

In order to solve the problems of large number of parameters in deep learning based on image segmentation models, and the small scale of individual hands and the difficulty of distinguishing edge detail information in complex backgrounds, we propose a hand image segmentation network based on PSU-Net. We design the paired spatial pyramid pooling (PSPP), the global attention fusion module (GAF) and an improved loss function, which can utilize the low-dimensional spatial detail information and high-dimensional semantic information more efficiently and improve the detail capture capability of the network, thus improve segmentation accuracy further. Some experimental results on

HOF, GTEA and Egohands databases show the proposed approach has quite good performance. The mIOU of PSU-Net reached 76.19% on the HOF dataset, while the mIOU of DeeplabV3 is 74.45%.

The proposed model can handle hand segmentation in complex backgrounds. In the future, we will develop lightweight networks and depth-wise convolutions networks to further enhance hand segmentation performance.

**Acknowledgements.** This research is funded by the National Natural Science Foundation of China under Grant 61976224 and 61976088. We would also like to thank University of Central Florida, GeorgiaTech, Indiana University for sharing the hand image databases.

# References

1. Zhang, D., Kong, W.K., You, J., et al.: Online palmprint identification. IEEE Tran. Pattern Anal. Mach. Intell. **25**(9), 1041–1050 (2003)
2. Han, Y., Sun, Z., Wang, F., Tan, T.: Palmprint recognition under unconstrained scenes. In: Yagi, Y., Kang, S.B., Kweon, I.S., Zha, H. (eds.) ACCV 2007. LNCS, vol. 4844, pp. 1–11. Springer, Heidelberg (2007). https://doi.org/10.1007/978-3-540-76390-1_1
3. Shuping, L., Yu, L., et al.: Hierarchical static hand gesture recognition by combining finger detection and HOG features. J. Image Graph. **20**(6), 781–788 (2015)
4. Rahmat, R.F., Chairunnisa, T., Gunawan, D., et al.: Skin color segmentation using multi-color space threshold. In: 2016 3rd International Conference on Computer and Information Sciences, pp. 391–396 (2016)
5. Li, S., Tang, J., Wu, G.: Geologic surface reconstruction based on fault constraints. In: Second Workshop on Digital Media and its Application in Museum and Heritages (2007)
6. Ronneberger, O., Fischer, P., Brox, T.: U-Net: convolutional networks for biomedical image segmentation. In: Navab, N., Hornegger, J., Wells, W.M., Frangi, A.F. (eds.) MICCAI 2015. LNCS, vol. 9351, pp. 234–241. Springer, Cham (2015). https://doi.org/10.1007/978-3-319-24574-4_28
7. Wang, K., Liew, J.H., Zou, Y., et al.: PANet: few-shot image semantic segmentation with prototype alignment. In: Proceedings of the IEEE/CVF International Conference on Computer Vision, pp. 9197–9206 (2019)
8. Iandola, F.N., Han, S., Moskewicz, M.W., et al.: SqueezeNet: AlexNet-level accuracy with 50x fewer parameters and <0.5 MB model size. arXiv preprint arXiv:1602.07360 (2016)
9. Howard, A.G., Zhu, M., Chen, B., et al.: MobileNets: efficient convolutional neural networks for mobile vision applications. arXiv preprint arXiv:1704.04861 (2017)
10. He, K., Zhang, X., Ren, S., et al.: Deep residual learning for image recognition. In: Proceedings of the IEEE Conference on Computer Vision and Pattern Recognition, pp. 770–778 (2016)
11. Sandler, M., Howard, A., Zhu, M., et al.: MobileNetV2: inverted residuals and linear bottlenecks. In: Proceedings of the IEEE Conference on Computer Vision and Pattern Recognition, pp. 4510–4520 (2018)
12. Zhang, X., Zhou, X., Lin, M., et al.: ShuffleNet: an extremely efficient convolutional neural network for mobile devices. In: Proceedings of the IEEE Conference on Computer Vision and Pattern Recognition, pp. 6848–6856 (2018)
13. Long, J., Shelhamer, E., Darrell, T.: Fully convolutional networks for semantic segmentation. In: Proceedings of the IEEE Conference on Computer Vision and Pattern Recognition (2015)
14. Badrinarayanan, V., Kendall, A., Cipolla, R.: SegNet: a deep convolutional encoder-decoder architecture for image segmentation. IEEE Trans. Pattern Anal. Mach. Intell. **39**, 2481–2495 (2017)

15. Chen, L.C., Papandreou, G., Kokkinos, I., Murphy, K., Yuille, A.L.: DeepLab: semantic image segmentation with deep convolutional nets, atrous convolution, and fully connected CRFs. IEEE Trans. Pattern Anal. Mach. Intell **40**(5), 834–848 (2017)
16. Chen, L.C, Papandreou, G., Schroff, F.: Rethinking atrous convolution for semantic image segmentation. arXiv preprint arXiv:1706.05587 (2017)
17. Zhao, H., Shi, J., Qi, X., et al.: Pyramid scene parsing network. In: Proceedings of the IEEE Conference on Computer Vision and Pattern Recognition (2017)
18. Lin, T.Y., Dollár, P., Girshick, R., et al.: Feature pyramid networks for object detection. In: Proceedings of the IEEE Conference on Computer Vision and Pattern Recognition (2017)
19. Mnih, V., Heess, N., Graves, A.: Recurrent models of visual attention. In: Advances in Neural Information Processing Systems 27 (2014)
20. Hu, J., Shen, L., Sun, G.: Squeeze-and-excitation networks. In: Proceedings of the IEEE Conference on Computer Vision and Pattern Recognition (2018)
21. Woo, S., Park, J., Lee, J.Y., et al.: CBAM: convolutional block attention module. In: Proceedings of the European Conference on Computer Vision, pp. 3–19 (2018)
22. Urooj, A., Borji, A.: Analysis of hand segmentation in the wild. In: Proceedings of the IEEE Conference on Computer Vision and Pattern Recognition, pp. 4710–4719 (2018)
23. Fathi, A., Ren, X., Rehg, J.M.: Learning to recognize objects in egocentric activities. In: Proceedings of the IEEE Conference on Computer Vision and Pattern Recognition, pp. 3281–3288 (2011)
24. Bambach, S., Lee, S., Crandall, D.J., et al.: Lending a hand: detecting hands and recognizing activities in complex egocentric interactions. In: Proceedings of the IEEE International Conference on Computer Vision, pp. 1949–1957 (2015)

# Pattern Classification and Clustering

# Human Knowledge-Guided and Task-Augmented Deep Learning for Glioma Grading

Yeqi Wang[1,2], Cheng Li[2], and Yusong Lin[3,4,5]([✉])

[1] School of Computer and Artificial Intelligence, Zhengzhou University,
Zhengzhou, Henan, China
[2] Paul C. Lauterbur Research Center for Biomedical Imaging, Shenzhen Institutes of
Advanced Technology, Chinese Academy of Sciences, Shenzhen, Guangdong, China
[3] School of Cyber Science and Engineering, Zhengzhou University, Zhengzhou,
Henan, China
yslin@ha.edu.cn
[4] Collaborative Innovation Center for Internet Healthcare Zhengzhou University,
Zhengzhou, Henan, China
[5] Hanwei IoT Institute, Zhengzhou University, Zhengzhou, Henan, China

**Abstract.** Traditional radiomics and deep learning have been widely employed for magnetic resonance imaging (MRI)-based glioma grading. Despite the reported promising grading performances, existing methods still have two limitations. One is that the strengths of radiomics and deep learning have not been integrated sufficiently. The other is that they cannot generalize well to different MR sequences. In this paper, we propose a human knowledge-guided and task-augmented deep learning network (HTNet) to address these issues. Particularly, radiomics hand-crafted signatures are constructed to describe brain lesions and then used to guide the training of deep learning models. Furthermore, an auxiliary MRI sequence classifier is added to the original classification task to learn versatile sequence properties and thus helps the model generalize to different MR sequences without extra training cost. Extensive experiments are conducted utilizing the public dataset BraTS2020, whose results show that the proposed method has competitive capabilities in glioma grading for different MR sequences.

**Keywords:** Human knowledge · Task-augmented deep learning ·
MRI · Glioma grading

## 1 Introduction

Gliomas are the most common type of primary neuroepithelial malignant tumors [8]. According to the degree of malignancy, the World Health Organization (WHO) classifies gliomas into low-grade gliomas (LGGs, grades I and II) and high-grade gliomas (HGGs, grades III and IV). The clinical manifestations

S. Yu et al. (Eds.): PRCV 2022, LNCS 13535, pp. 567–575, 2022.
https://doi.org/10.1007/978-3-031-18910-4_45

and prognostic effects of patients with different glioma grades vary significantly [7,11]. Therefore, accurate glioma grading is critical, which can help physicians develop personalized treatment plans.

Magnetic resonance imaging (MRI) has been widely utilized for glioma grading [14]. Because of its superior imaging contrast and resolution, MRI can help physicians localize the lesions preoperatively and evaluate the curative effects postoperatively. However, reading the acquired brain MR images manually requires rich domain knowledge and experience, which is time-consuming and error-prone. To assist physicians in achieving fast and accurate diagnoses, automatic MRI-based glioma auxiliary grading models are urgently needed.

Many computer-aided diagnosis (CAD) systems have been developed to achieve automatic glioma grading [1,5]. These methods can be broadly divided into radiomics-based methods and deep learning-based methods. Radiomics methods follow a general procedure of extracting quantitative handcrafted features from the lesion regions, then selecting the key features, and training a grading model [4]. The extracted handcrafted features are engineered to describe the size, shape, and texture attributes of the lesions. Representative works include Zhao et al. [13] and Vamvakas et al. [10], etc. Recently, deep learning, especially convolutional neural networks (CNNs), has presented unprecedented performance in medical imaging. CNN-based methods can extract high-dimensional features from the images automatically and accomplish the glioma grading task in an end-to-end manner. Exemplar works include Sultan et al. [9] and Yang et al. [12], etc. Both types of methods have obtained promising glioma grading results. However, there are still some issues that remain to be addressed. Although radiomics and deep learning show high potential on glioma grading, their strengths on medical image analysis have not been integrated and investigated sufficiently. Another issue is the sensitivity of the grading model to different MR sequence data. It is required to independently construct grading models on each different MR sequence, which is time-consuming and resource-consuming. As a result, the developed models can only be tested with the data acquired by the same MRI sequence as that of the training data, where the acquirement of MRI data may be limited by the clinical equipment or the patient physiology. To summarize, there is an urgent need for the development of patient-friendly and physician-friendly glioma grading models, combining the strengths of different methods and alleviating the reliance on specific MRI sequences.

In this paper, we propose a human knowledge-guided and task-augmented deep learning network (HTNet) for glioma grading. Firstly, we integrate the strengths of radiomics and deep learning methods. Specifically, we construct radiomic signatures with handcrafted quantitative features to guide the training of the deep learning model. With the minimization of a designed loss function, the human knowledge contained in the signatures help the model capture the latent representation of the brain lesion regions. Then, the flexibility of the deep learning model is enhanced by an elaborately designed task-augmented model optimization method. In detail, the glioma grading model is trained using MR images of multiple sequences, and an auxiliary classifier is added to differentiate the specific sequences of the inputs. This auxiliary classifier is expected to

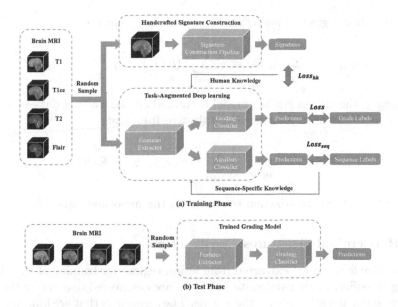

**Fig. 1.** Overall framework of HTNet

empower the grading model with MRI sequence-specific knowledge, and thus, the model can be tested with data of different sequences. Our major contributions can be summarized as follows:

1) A human knowledge loss function is designed to integrate the strengths of both radiomics and deep learning methods, to capture the latent representations.
2) By adding an auxiliary classifier during the model training, the grading model becomes flexible regarding the testing data, which can be acquired using different MRI sequences.
3) Extensive experiments have been conducted utilizing a public dataset, BraTS2020, and promising glioma grading performance has been achieved by the proposed method.

## 2    Methods

Given a patient sample $s = (x, y) \in \mathcal{X} \times \mathcal{Y}$, $x$ represents the MR image, and $y$ is the corresponding glioma grading label. A glioma grading model is trained to achieve the mapping from the MR image $x$ to the grading label $y$. Here, the hypothesis of the glioma grading model $h \in \mathcal{H}$ is a mapping function, where $\mathcal{H}$ is a hypothesis class. A loss function $\ell : h(\mathcal{X}) \times \mathcal{Y} \to \mathbf{R}_+$ is calculated, where $\ell(h(x), y)$ is the loss value of hypothesis $h$ for a sample $s = (x, y)$. Let $\mathcal{D}_{train} = \{s_i = (x_i, y_i)\}_{i=1}^N$ represent a set of training samples, the empirical loss of the glioma grading model on $\mathcal{D}_{train}$ can be defined as:

$$\mathcal{L}_{train}(h) = \frac{1}{N} \sum_{i=1}^{N} \ell(h(x_i), y_i). \qquad (1)$$

In summary, the glioma grading model is trained on the training dataset $\mathcal{D}_{train}$, which aims to optimize the following objective function:

$$h^*(x) = \underset{h \in \mathcal{H}}{\arg\min} \frac{1}{N} \sum_{i=1}^{N} \ell(h(x_i), y_i) + \mathcal{R}(h), \qquad (2)$$

where $\mathcal{R}(h)$ is the regularization to constrain the hypothesis space $h$.

## 2.1   Handcrafted Signatures Construction

Quantitative features are extracted from lesion regions for training of the glioma grading classifier. These handcrafted features are engineered to describe the size, shape, and texture attributes of the lesions. The signatures that are built on these features contain lesion-sensitive information. In this paper, these signatures are adopted as human knowledge to guide the training of the deep learning glioma grading model. A loss function is designed to achieve this target. Under the guidance of the human knowledge, the deep learning model can focus more on the brain lesion regions without requiring brain lesion segmentation maps. In this way, the model is able to capture the latent representations from lesion regions.

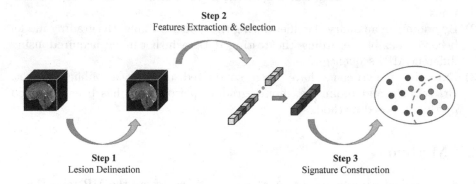

**Step 2**
Features Extraction & Selection

**Step 1**
Lesion Delineation

**Step 3**
Signature Construction

**Fig. 2.** Construction of the handcrafted signatures

Following the guideline [2], the construction of the handcrafted signatures can be simply divided into three steps: lesion region delineation, feature extraction and selection, and signature construction (Fig. 2). In the first step, brain lesions are delineated manually. Then, in the second step, handcrafted features are extracted from the delineated brain lesions, and key features are selected. A total of 1618 features are extracted. They are normalized to the same value range of $[0, 1]$. Then, the key features are selected by using a three-level cascaded feature selection algorithm (student t-test, lasso, and recursive feature elimination algorithm). In the third step, a logistic regression classifier is trained to construct the signatures with the selected key features. After obtaining the signatures, a Human Knowledge (HK) loss function is designed to transfer the implicit information from the constructed signatures to the deep learning model. Let $h_{hk}$ represent the mapping function from the MR images to the handcrafted signatures. The HK loss function is defined as:

$$\ell_{hk}\left(h\left(x\right), h_{hk}\left(x\right)\right) = h_{hk}\left(x\right) log \frac{h_{hk}\left(x\right)}{h\left(x\right)}. \tag{3}$$

By minimizing the HK loss, the distribution of $h$ is forced to gradually approach the distribution of $h_{hk}$, so that the human knowledge is transferred to deep learning models.

## 2.2 The Task-Augmented Deep Learning Glioma Grading Model

Due to the intrinsic imaging properties, each MRI sequence (T1ce, T1, T2, and FLAIR) shows different glioma grading features. However, the contrasts may not always be fully accessible. Furthermore, the grading models often need to be independently trained on each MR sequence data, which is troublesome and resource-consuming. To address this issue, we develop a task-augmented glioma grading model, which can achieve similar grading performance when data from different MRI sequences are inputted. An auxiliary classifier is added to the deep learning model that is trained with the proposed HK loss function. This auxiliary classifier aims to distinguish the specific MRI sequences of the input data. During model training, MR images of four sequences (T1, T1ce, T2, and FLAIR) are utilized. By minimizing the loss of the auxiliary classifier, the grading model can learn extra sequence-specific features, and the model becomes flexible regarding the input data type.

In addition to the hypothesis $h$ of existing deep learning models, an additional hypothesis function $h_{seq}$ for the auxiliary classifier is included in the proposed task-augmented model. The feature extractor is shared between the glioma grading task and the auxiliary MRI sequence classification task. For the auxiliary MRI sequence classification task, let $s = (x, y_{seq}) \in \mathcal{X} \times \mathcal{Y}_{seq}$ be the training sample, where $x$ represents a 3D brain MR image, $y_{seq}$ is the corresponding sequence label of the MRI image. The loss function of the auxiliary sequence classifier is defined as:

$$\ell_{seq}\left(h_{seq}\left(x\right), y_{seq}\right) = y_{seq} log h_{seq}\left(x\right). \tag{4}$$

## 2.3 Implementation Details

The total loss function of the HTNet proposed in this work is defined as:

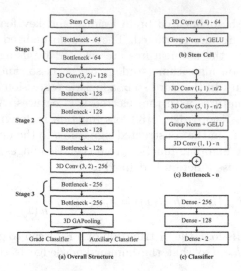

**Fig. 3.** Network structure of the proposed glioma grading model. Conv(k, s)-n means a convolution layer with a kernel size of k, a stride of s, and a channel number of n. Bottleneck-n represents a bottleneck module shown as (c) with a channel number of n.

$$\ell_{total} = \alpha \ell \left( h \left( x \right), y \right) + \beta \ell \left( h_{seq} \left( x \right), y_{seq} \right) + \gamma \ell_{hk} \left( h \left( x \right), h_{hk} \left( x \right) \right) \qquad (5)$$

where $\alpha$, $\beta$, and $\gamma$ are three constants to balance the contributions of the three terms.

The detailed network structure we developed is shown in Fig. 3. ResNet-style architectures are employed to handle the 3D brain MR images for glioma grading. Different from the original ResNet [3], non-overlapping convolutions (kernel size = stride) are used in the stem cell, and fewer activation and normalization layers are used in the bottleneck blocks. In addition, group normalization and GELU activation are used to replace the batch normalization and the ReLU activation in all modules.

The network is trained for 100 epochs using the AdamW optimizer. The initial learning rate is 1e-5, and a cosine decay schedule is utilized. The model is trained using a batch size of 32 for 100 epochs. To alleviate serious overfitting, the early-stopping mechanism is implemented with a patience of 20. Experiments are run on two NVIDIA TITAN V GPUs (12 GB memory). The open-source platform TensorFlow v2.5.1 is employed. The area under the receiver operating characteristic curve (AUC) is utilized as the main evaluation metric.

## 3   Experiments and Results

**Dataset.** The Brain Tumor Segmentation Challenge (BraTS [6]) 2020 dataset is adopted to evaluate the effectiveness of the proposed method. In total, MR images, as well as brain lesion segmentation maps, of 369 patients are provided, including LGG samples and HGG samples. Four MRI sequences (T1, T1ce, T2, and FLAIR) are included for each sample. The samples are divided into a training dataset and a testing dataset with a ratio of 4:1. The brain lesion regions in each MR image were delineated manually following the same annotation protocol and were then approved by experienced neuro-radiologists [6].

**Main Results.** Two comparison models are implemented, including a radiomics-based grading model and a 3D ResNet. Radiomics-based models for different MRI sequences were built with the process described in Sect. 2.2. The 3D ResNet models were developed with the ResNet-style structure, where three residual stage were adopted. Model training was performed by minimizing the loss function defined in Eq. 1. Results are listed in Table 1.

The proposed method obtain the similar grading performance in each single MR sequence data. For data from T2 and FLAIR sequences, our method achieve the better results than the two baseline methods. Overall, with the introduction of radiomics and auxiliary classifier, our proposed method can obtain the best glioma grading results averaged over the four MRI sequences. This suggests that our method can integrate the strengths of radiomics and deep learning, reducing the additional training costs for models on different data.

**Table 1.** Glioma grading performance of different methods

| Method | AVE_AUC | T1_ACU | T1ce_AUC | T2_AUC | FLAIR_AUC |
|---|---|---|---|---|---|
| Radiomics [2] | 0.8673 | 0.7907 | 0.9405 | 0.8710 | 0.8644 |
| 3D ResNet [3] | 0.8764 | 0.8534 | 0.9194 | 0.8694 | 0.8642 |
| Our Method | **0.8841** | 0.8293 | 0.9312 | 0.8827 | 0.8736 |

**Ablation Studies.** To evaluate the contributions of the human knowledge and sequence-specific knowledge to the performance enhancement of the proposed method, ablation studies were conducted. Results with different $\alpha$, $\beta$, and $\gamma$ are reported in Table 2, where $\alpha$, $\beta$, and $\gamma$ represent the weights of glioma grading loss, the sequence classification loss, and the human knowledge loss as defined in Eqs. 3 and 4. It can be summarized that grading models with the introduction of the human knowledge and the sequence-specific knowledge can outperform the baseline without the two types of knowledge ($\alpha = 0$, $\beta = 0$, and $\gamma = 0$), and our method with $\alpha = 0.5$, $\beta = 0.5$, and $\gamma = 0.1$ can obtain the best grading performance.

**Table 2.** Results of ablation studies. The **wo seq** means without sequence-specific knowledge, and the **wo hk** means without human knowledge.

| Method | $\alpha$ | $\beta$ | $\gamma$ | AVE_AUC |
|---|---|---|---|---|
| Our Method/wo seq&hk | 1 | 0 | 0 | 0.8652 |
| Our Method/wo seq | 1 | 0 | 0.1 | 0.8724 |
| Our Method/wo seq | 1 | 0 | 0.01 | 0.8670 |
| Our Method/wo hk | 0.5 | 0.5 | 0 | 0.8729 |
| Our Method/wo hk | 0.8 | 0.2 | 0 | 0.8748 |
| Our Method | 0.5 | 0.5 | 0.1 | **0.8841** |
| Our Method | 0.8 | 0.2 | 0.1 | 0.8800 |

# 4 Conclusion

In this paper, a human knowledge-guided and task-augmented deep learning glioma grading model is proposed. The introduction of the prior knowledge from constructed handcrafted signatures can help the deep learning grading model integrate the strength of radiomics. Meanwhile, to enhance the flexibility of the developed model, an auxiliary distinguishing classifier for MRI sequence is added to help the model learn the sequence-specific knowledge. With the introduction of the human knowledge and sequence-specific knowledge, our final model obtains promising glioma grading performance on input image data acquired with different MRI sequences, reducing the extra training costs of model on different MR sequence data. In this way, the proposed method possesses a potential to assist physicians in achieving fast and accurate diagnoses of gliomas.

**Acknowledgments.** This research was partly supported by Scientific and Technical Innovation 2030 - "New Generation Artificial Intelligence" Project (2020AA A0104100, 2020AAA0104105), the National Natural Science Foundation of China (61871371, 81772009), Guangdong Provincial Key Laboratory of Artificial Intelligence in Medical Image Analysis and Application (2022B1212010011), the Basic Research Program of Shenzhen (JCYJ20180507182400762), Shenzhen Science and Technology Program (RCYX20210706092104034), Youth Innovation Promotion Association Program of Chinese Academy of Sciences (2019351), Collaborative Innovation Major Project of Zhengzhou (20XTZX06013, 20XTZX05015), and the Key Technologies R&D Program of Henan Province (222102210281).

# References

1. Cho, H.H., Lee, S.H., Kim, J., Park, H.: Classification of the glioma grading using radiomics analysis. PeerJ **6**, e5982 (2018)
2. Gillies, R.J., Kinahan, P.E., Hricak, H.: Radiomics: images are more than pictures, they are data. Radiology **278**(2), 563–577 (2016)

3. He, K., Zhang, X., Ren, S., Sun, J.: Deep residual learning for image recognition. In: Proceedings of the IEEE Conference on Computer Vision and Pattern Recognition, pp. 770–778 (2016)
4. Lambin, P., et al.: Radiomics: the bridge between medical imaging and personalized medicine. Nat. Rev. Clin. Oncol. **14**(12), 749–762 (2017)
5. Matsui, Y., et al.: Prediction of lower-grade glioma molecular subtypes using deep learning. J. Neuro-oncol. **146**(2), 321–327 (2020)
6. Menze, B.H., et al.: The multimodal brain tumor image segmentation benchmark (brats). IEEE Trans. Med. Imaging **34**(10), 1993–2024 (2014)
7. Obara, T., et al.: Adult diffuse low-grade gliomas: 35-year experience at the Nancy France neurooncology unit. Front. Oncol. 1873 (2020)
8. Ostrom, Q.T., Patil, N., Cioffi, G., Waite, K., Kruchko, C., Barnholtz-Sloan, J.S.: Cbtrus statistical report: primary brain and other central nervous system tumors diagnosed in the united states in 2013–2017. Neuro-oncology **22**(Supplement_1), iv1–iv96 (2020)
9. Sultan, H.H., Salem, N.M., Al-Atabany, W.: Multi-classification of brain tumor images using deep neural network. IEEE Access **7**, 69215–69225 (2019)
10. Vamvakas, A., et al.: Imaging biomarker analysis of advanced multiparametric MRI for glioma grading. Phys. Med. **60**, 188–198 (2019)
11. Wu, W., et al.: Joint NCCTG and NABTC prognostic factors analysis for high-grade recurrent glioma. Neuro-oncology **12**(2), 164–172 (2010)
12. Yang, Y., et al.: Glioma grading on conventional MR images: a deep learning study with transfer learning. Front. Neurosci. 804 (2018)
13. Zhao, G., et al.: Ai-powered radiomics algorithm based on slice pooling for the glioma grading. IEEE Trans. Indust. Inf. (2021)
14. Zhuge, Y., et al.: Automated glioma grading on conventional MRI images using deep convolutional neural networks. Med. Phys. **47**(7), 3044–3053 (2020)

# Learning to Cluster Faces with Mixed Face Quality

Zhiwei Pan[1,2(✉)], Zhihua Guo[3], Huiting Yang[4], Congquan Yan[1],
and Pengju Yang[1]

[1] Hikvision Research Institute, Hangzhou, China
{panzhiwei5,yancongquan,yangpengju}@hikvision.com
[2] Zhejiang University, Hangzhou, China
[3] Xiamen University, Xiamen, China
31520191153352@stu.xmu.edu.cn
[4] Nanjing University of Aeronautics and Astronautics, Nanjing, China
yanghuiting@nuaa.edu.cn

**Abstract.** Face clustering is the task of grouping faces by their underlying identity, and is still a challenging task in practical use due to the common low-quality face images caused by pose, blur, occlusion, illumination etc. To address the issue, this paper proposes a face clustering algorithm, referred as FC-Q, that takes the quality score as extra input. Based on the main observation that two nodes similar in feature subspace but with different identity may have larger score difference, the algorithm first integrates this prior with the modified self-attention mechanism of Transformer to infer reliable linkage likelihood between similar node pairs. Then the algorithm combines the face quality information with the label propagation module to further suppress the abnormal pairings. The effectiveness of the algorithm is evaluated on two public face datasets in good and bad quality. Experimental results validate that our algorithm outperforms the state-of-the-arts under the general circumstance of clustering faces with mixed face quality.

**Keywords:** Face clustering · Face quality · Linkage estimation · Label propagation · Self-attention mechanism

## 1 Introduction

Face clustering is a fundamental task in face analysis and has been extensively studied in resent years [8,15,20,22,23]. Existing face clustering methods roughly fall into two categories, i.e., unsupervised methods and supervised methods. Unsupervised approaches, such as K-Means [10] and DBSCAN [6], rely on specific assumptions and lack the capability of resonating with high-dimensional structured data information. Supervised face clustering methods mainly aim to

This work was supported by the Postdoctoral Merit Funding Project of Zhejiang Province under Grant ZJ2020050.

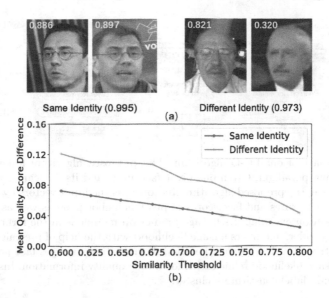

**Fig. 1.** (a) Demonstration of two node pairs with quality score shown on the images and similarity given in the parentheses. (b) Mean absolute value of quality score difference between every two pair nodes on IJB-C dataset [11] under the same and different identities with respect to similarity threshold. The node pairs with similarity higher than threshold are involved in this statistic. The face score is obtained by EQFace [9], the identity feature is extracted by pre-trained IResNet50 [4,5].

learn more distinguishing embedding subspace [3,14] or the complex cluster patterns [23]. These existing methods mainly based on the node distance in feature space, while ignore the negative effect caused by the face images in low quality. Face node with low quality is common and goes against the clustering due to its ambiguous identity. Figure 1(a) shows the example that the pair nodes with one in low quality can also have high similarity even they are under different identity. These low face quality nodes will obviously degrade the face clustering precision if not handled appropriately. It is essential for face clustering algorithms to have the ability to deal with this general application circumstance.

Fortunately, face quality score provides helpful auxiliary information for clustering. Figure 1(b) shows the mean absolute value of quality score difference between every two pair nodes under same and different identities with respect to similarity threshold. The node pairs in IJB-C dataset [11] with similarity higher than threshold are involved in this statistic. There always exists a gap between the score differences, which implies that two nodes similar in feature subspace but with different identity may have larger score difference. Based on this main observation, this paper proposes a face clustering algorithm, which is referred as FC-Q, intuitively takes the face quality as extra input to exploit unlabeled face data.

Face quality can be conveniently assessed beforehand by recent deep learning based methods. SER-FIQ [17] obtains the face quality by measuring the

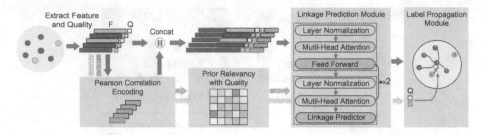

**Fig. 2.** Flowchart of our FC-Q algorithm. The proposed algorithm follows the link-based clustering paradigm, Given one pivot face node and its $K$ nearest neighbors in feature subspace, the proposed algorithm first obtains the input vectors by concatenating the identity features and face scores of pivot-neighbor pairs as well as the specific Pearson correlation encoding. Its linkage prediction module is in the form of modified Transformer encoder, and infers linkage likelihood with the help of pre-calculated prior relevancy matrix. Its label propagation module transitively merges face nodes according to the linkage likelihood refined with local face quality information. Instances with the same pseudo label constitute a cluster.

embedding variations generated from random sub-networks of the face recognition model. A deep tiny network [13] is also proposed to learn a face quality prediction function that is recognition-oriented. Meanwhile, face quality can be explicitly given along with the identity feature by face recognition network. Mag-Face [12] introduces an adaptive mechanism to learn a universal feature embedding with magnitude measuring the face quality. EQFace [9] outputs face quality and identity feature at the same time by adding a quality network branch to the baseline network of face recognition. Such methods make our work more efficient in gathering input data.

The proposed FC-Q algorithm incorporates the face quality into its two main modules, i.e., the linkage prediction module and the label propagation module. In the linkage prediction module, the algorithm adopts the framework of Transformer encoder [18]. It is specially modified to fit the general clustering circumstance. One relevancy prior is designed according to the quality score relationship among nodes in neighborhood. The prior helps the self-attention mechanism of Transformer encoder better infer the linkage likelihood between node pairs. In the label propagation module, the algorithm utilizes the face quality to recalibrate the abnormal linkage likelihood based on the local quality information. The linkage with one node having inconsistent quality score with its neighbors will be suspected of being unreliable, and its likelihood will be suppressed if the two pair nodes have a large gap with respect to their local quality information. Finally, our proposed algorithm transitively merges face nodes according to the refined linkage likelihood, and obtains the clusters.

To summarize, the main contributions of this work are as follows:

- A face clustering algorithm named FC-Q is proposed with the face quality as extra input. Compared with the state-of-the-arts, this algorithm deals with the more general circumstance that the face nodes are not all guaranteed in good quality.

- The proposed FC-Q algorithm modifies the Transformer encoder and designs the relevancy prior with face quality to infer more reliable linkage likelihood between similar pairs in feature subspace.
- The proposed FC-Q algorithm utilizes the local quality information of each node to further suppress the pairing with abnormal high linkage likelihood.
- The proposed FC-Q algorithm specifically conducts face clustering experiments on IJB-C dataset with low face quality and achieves 91.7% *pairwise* F-score on partial IJB-C, which provides a strong baseline for low-quality face clustering.

## 2 Methodology

In this section, we introduce the details of the proposed FC-Q algorithm, which includes the specific linkage prediction module and label propagation module. Figure 2 shows the flowchart.

### 2.1 Linkage Prediction with Prior Attention

Following the link-based clustering paradigm, the proposed algorithm selects every face node as a pivot, and estimates the linkage likelihood between the pivot and its $K$ nearest neighbors in feature subspace.

Given $i$th pivot face node $\mathbf{f}_0^i \in \mathbb{R}^{d_f}$ and its $K$ nearest neighbors $\mathbf{f}_j^i, j \in \{1, ..., K\}$, the input of the linkage prediction module consists of $K+1$ vectors with each has the form

$$\mathbf{g}_j = cat\left(\mathbf{f}_j^i, \mathbf{f}_0^i, q_j^i, q_0^i, \mathbf{p}_j\right) \in \mathbb{R}^{d_g}, \quad j \in \{0, ..., K\}, \tag{1}$$

where $q_0^i \in \mathbb{R}$ denotes the face quality score of pivot node, and $q_j^i, j \in \{1, ..., K\}$ denotes the face quality score of its neighbor. Operator $cat()$ denotes concatenation operation along the feature dimension, thus $d_g = 2d_f + 2 + K + 1$. Vector $\mathbf{p}_j \in \mathbb{R}^{K+1}$ represents Pearson correlation encoding of each involved face node. The element in $\mathbf{p}_j \in \mathbb{R}^{K+1}$, i.e., the Pearson correlation coefficient, is calculated as

$$\mathbf{p}_j^k = \frac{\operatorname{cov}\left(\mathbf{f}_j^i, \mathbf{f}_k^i\right)}{\sigma_{\mathbf{f}_j^i}\sigma_{\mathbf{f}_k^i}}, \quad k \in \{0, ..., K\}, \tag{2}$$

where cov and $\sigma$ denote the covariance and the standard deviation of $\mathbf{f}_j^i$ and $\mathbf{f}_k^i$ respectively. Concatenating pivot feature $\mathbf{f}_0^i$ in (1) aims to inform the linkage prediction module to learn the relationship between pivot-neighbor pair. Concatenating quality scores $q_j^i, q_0^i$ in (1) aims to let the linkage prediction module infer the link likelihood with more references. Concatenating Pearson correlation encoding $\mathbf{p}_j$ in (1) is under the consideration that the Pearson correlation coefficient can offer the linkage prediction module robust linear relations between pair nodes, which is highly sensitive to outliers [2].

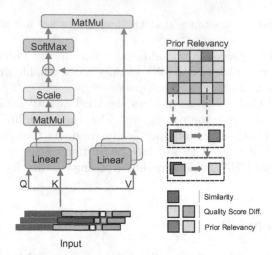

**Fig. 3.** Architecture of our modified self-attention mechanism. The input vectors are first projected into three super vectors named *key*, *query* and *value*. The *key* and *query* are forced to share the same projection. A prior relevancy matrix is added into the learned relevancy, and offers the negative relevancy information if the pair nodes have large quality score difference. The brighter the color, the larger the value.

With the input vectors generated, the linkage prediction module adopts the framework of modified Transformer encoder to estimate the linkage likelihood of pivot-neighbor pair. Compared with the GCN based framework [20], the Transformer encoder framework has the ability to learn relation weights based on its effective self-attention mechanism. As shown in Fig. 2, the linkage prediction module is composed of a stack of 3 identical layers. Each layer has three sub-layers. The first is a pre-layer normalization [21], the second is a modified multi-head self-attention mechanism, and the third is a simple fully connected feed-forward network. Note that the skip connections of the last two sub-layers are specifically removed to let the whole module focus more on inferring the difference between pivot and neighbor nodes. The last feed-forward sub-layer performs the binary node classification followed by softmax activation, which outputs the probability of whether the corresponding input belongs to the same class as the pivot.

Figure 3 further shows the architecture of our three modified self-attention mechanism sub-layers. Taking the first one as an example, every normalized vector $\mathbf{g}'_j$ in $i$th input $\mathbf{G}'_i \in \mathbb{R}^{(K+1) \times d_g}$ is first linearly projected into three super vectors named *key*, *query* and *value*, which can be expressed in matrix form as

$$
\begin{aligned}
\mathbf{K} &= \mathbf{G}'_i \mathbf{W}^S, \mathbf{K} \in \mathbb{R}^{(K+1) \times d_s}, \\
\mathbf{Q} &= \mathbf{G}'_i \mathbf{W}^S, \mathbf{Q} \in \mathbb{R}^{(K+1) \times d_s}, \\
\mathbf{V} &= \mathbf{G}'_i \mathbf{W}^V, \mathbf{V} \in \mathbb{R}^{(K+1) \times d_v},
\end{aligned}
\tag{3}
$$

where matrices $\mathbf{W}^S \in \mathbb{R}^{d_g \times d_s}$ and $\mathbf{W}^V \in \mathbb{R}^{d_g \times d_v}$ denote the learnable project matrices. The *key* and *query* are forced to share the same projection, thus the relevancy between the corresponding two samples will be symmetric. This setting is helpful for face clustering, which is shown in the following experiment section.

The relevancy between the samples are constructed as

$$\frac{1}{\sqrt{d_s}} \mathbf{Q} \mathbf{K}^T + \mathbf{A}, \qquad (4)$$

where matrix $\mathbf{A} \in \mathbb{R}^{(K+1) \times (K+1)}$ represents the prior relevancy, and its element in the $m$th row and $n$th col is of the form

$$\mathbf{A}_{m,n} = \text{sim}\left(\mathbf{f}_m^i, \mathbf{f}_n^i\right) \cdot \left(1 - \text{abs}(q_m^i - q_n^i)\right), \qquad (5)$$

where operator sim() calculates similarity between the identity features $\mathbf{f}_m^i$ and $\mathbf{f}_n^i$, and operator abs() denotes the absolute operation. Prior relevancy matrix $\mathbf{A}$ is also symmetric, and can offer the negative relevancy information between two samples if they have large quality score difference.

The output $\mathbf{Z} \in \mathbb{R}^{(K+1) \times d_v}$ in self-attention mechanism is the aggregation of *value* matrix $\mathbf{V}$ by attention weights, i.e.,

$$\mathbf{Z} = \text{softmax}\left(\frac{\mathbf{Q} \mathbf{K}^T + \mathbf{A}}{\sqrt{d_s}}\right) \mathbf{V}, \qquad (6)$$

where the attention weights are obtained by applying softmax normalization to (4).

The modified self-attention is further incorporated into the multi-head mechanism, where the self-attention is performed $H$ times in parallel. The outputs of each self-attention are concatenated and once again projected, resulting in the final output of multi-head self-attention sub-layer

$$\mathbf{Z}_M = \text{cat}\left(\mathbf{Z}_1, ..., \mathbf{Z}_H\right) \mathbf{W}_M, \qquad (7)$$

where matrix $\mathbf{W}_M \in \mathbb{R}^{H d_v \times d_g}$ denotes learnable project matrix.

During the training stage, the whole linkage prediction module is trained by cross-entropy loss

$$\mathcal{L} = -\sum_{k=0}^{K} \log(\hat{y}_{k_1}^i), \qquad (8)$$

where $\hat{y}_{k_1}^i$ denotes the output probability, i.e., linkage likelihood, of whether the $i$th pivot and its corresponding $k$th neighbor belong to the same class.

## 2.2 Label Propagation with Anomaly Suppression

As all the pivot nodes are involved in linkage prediction module, a set of pivot-neighbor pairs $\mathcal{E} = \{\mathbf{e}_j\}_{j=1,...,NK}$ will be obtained along with the corresponding linkage likelihood set $\mathcal{P} = \{p_j\}_{j=1,...,NK}$. The goal of the label propagation module is to assign pseudo label $y_i$ to every face image $\mathbf{x}_i$ with the help of quality score set.

**Algorithm 1.** Label propagation with anomaly suppression

---

**Input**: Pivot-neighbor pair set $\mathcal{E}$, linkage likelihood set $\mathcal{P}$, quality score set $\mathcal{Q}$.
**Parameter**: Initial likelihood threshold $\tau_p$, quality threshold $\tau_q$, maximum size $M$, maximum iteration number $T$.
**Output**: Pseudo labels.

1: Let $i = 0$.
2: **while** $i < T$ and $\mathcal{E} \neq \emptyset$ **do**
3:     **for** every pair $\mathbf{e}_j$ in $\mathcal{E}$ **do**
4:         Find connected neighbors of nodes $m$ and $n$ in $\mathbf{e}_j$.
5:         Calculate mean absolute value of quality score difference $\check{q}_m$ and $\check{q}_n$ using (9).
6:         **if** $\check{q}_m < \tau_q$ or $\check{q}_n < \tau_q$ **then**
7:             Suppress linkage likelihood using (10).
8:         **end if**
9:     **end for**
10:    Remove pairs from $\mathcal{E}$ with its likelihood below $\tau_p$.
11:    Find connected components.
12:    Annotate components with the node number below $M$ and remove its pairs from $\mathcal{E}$.
13:    Let $\tau_p = \tau_p + (1 - \tau_p) * 0.15$, and $i = i + 1$.
14: **end while**
15: Annotate orphan nodes.
16: **return** pseudo labels for all nodes

---

The label propagation module starts with the initial linkage threshold $\tau_p$, and performs in an iterative manner. In each iteration, the module first finds all the connected neighbors of every unlabeled node according to the current pair set $\mathcal{E}$. Then Given one pivot-neighbor pair $\mathbf{e}_j$ connecting nodes $m$ and $n$, the module calculates the mean absolute value of quality score difference between each node and its connected neighbors,

$$\check{q}_* = \frac{1}{|\mathcal{N}_*|} \sum_{k \in \mathcal{N}_*} \text{abs}\,(q_* - q_k)\,, \quad * = m, n, \tag{9}$$

where $\mathcal{N}_*$ denotes the set of neighbor index, and $|\mathcal{N}_*|$ denotes the number. If the value $\check{q}$ of either node is larger than a predefined threshold $\tau_q$, the pivot-neighbor pair will be considered unreliable and its linkage likelihood will be suppressed as

$$p_j = p_j \cdot (1 - \text{abs}\,(\bar{q}_m - \bar{q}_n))\,, \tag{10}$$

where $\bar{q}_m$ and $\bar{q}_n$ denote the mean value of quality scores of the very node and its connected neighbors. The gap in local face quality information between the two nodes determines the degree to which the corresponding linkage likelihood is suppressed.

With the linkage likelihood all updated, the label propagation module first removes the pivot-neighbor pairs from $\mathcal{E}$ whose linkage likelihood are below the threshold $\tau_p$. Then the module finds connected components based on the remaining pivot-neighbor pairs. If the node number of one component is below the predefined maximum size $M$, all nodes in the component are annotated with a new pseudo label, and the corresponding pivot-neighbor pairs are also removed from set $\mathcal{E}$. The threshold $\tau_p$ is increased at the end of every iteration.

The process mentioned above is iterated until the pair set $\mathcal{E}$ is empty. The neglected orphan nodes are also annotated with new pseudo labels individually. Finally, the face nodes with same pseudo label constitute a cluster. To summary, Algorithm 1 lists the whole procedure of this label propagation. The maximum computational complexity of one iteration is of order $\mathcal{O}(3NK)$, and decreases as the iteration progresses. It is observed that involving face quality can help improve the clustering precision along with a slight drop of recall.

# 3 Experiments

## 3.1 Experimental Settings

**Datasets.** We use the IJB-C dataset [11] of low face quality as well as the refined MS1M dataset [4,7] of good face quality for training and testing in *face clustering*. The IJB-C contains about 138K face images from 3.5K identities, and the MS1M contains about 5.8M face images from 85K identities. The IJB-C dataset is randomly partitioned into 10 splits with equal identity number, and each part has the same distribution of nodes per identity. As IJB-C dataset is small, 9 parts are used for training to alleviate overfitting and 1 part for testing. The MS1M dataset is partitioned in the same way with 1 part for training and the other 9 parts for testing.

We evaluate the performance of face clustering by three commonly used metrics, i.e., *Pairwise* [16], *BCubed* [1] and *NMI* [19]. *Pairwise* and *BCubed* both measure the precision and recall of clustering, with F-score being their harmonic mean. The former metric emphasizes more on large clusters. *NMI* measures the global closeness of the output pseudo labels and the ground-truth. All the metrics have a range of [0, 1] with 1 being the perfect. Four state-of-the-art algorithms, namely, L-GCN [20], GCN-DS [23], GCN-VE [22], and STAR-FC [15] are used for comparison.

Our framework is implemented in Pytorch. We first use the pre-trained IResNet50 [4,5] to extract the identity features of face nodes with dimension $d_f = 512$, and EQFace [9] to obtain the corresponding face quality scores. All the competing algorithms share the same input. We then set the neighbor number $K = 80$, the dimension of *key*, *query* and *value* $d_s = d_v = 2048$, and the number of multi-head attention $H = 2$. We also empirically set the initial linkage threshold $\tau_p = 0.9$, the quality threshold $\tau_q = 0.3$, and the maximum cluster size $M = 1000$. The maximum iteration number $T$ is set to 20 which is sufficient to obtain a satisfactory clustering. These parameter values remain the same in following experiments.

In addition, we train the model with 20 epochs from scratch, and optimize the loss with the SGD optimizer. The weight decay and the momentum are set to 0.0005 and 0.9, respectively. The initial learning rate is set to 0.01 and is empirically divided by 10 at 8, 12 and 18 epochs. All the experiments are performed on a single Tesla-P40 GPU, and one can use more for acceleration.

**Table 1.** Results on IJB-C dataset and MS1M dataset. "P" is short for "*Pairwise*", and "B" is short for "*BCubed*"

| | IJB-C | | | MS1M | | |
|---|---|---|---|---|---|---|
| | P F-score | B F-score | NMI | P F-score | B F-score | NMI |
| L-GCN | 0.876 | 0.818 | 0.925 | 0.959 | 0.975 | 0.994 |
| GCN-D | 0.686 | 0.710 | 0.871 | 0.899 | 0.906 | 0.980 |
| GCN-DS | 0.614 | 0.649 | 0.869 | 0.857 | 0.880 | 0.975 |
| GCN-V | 0.585 | 0.526 | 0.863 | 0.961 | 0.927 | 0.981 |
| GCN-VE | 0.535 | 0.474 | 0.844 | 0.975 | 0.963 | 0.991 |
| STAR-FC | 0.814 | 0.826 | 0.931 | **0.989** | 0.981 | 0.995 |
| FC-Q | **0.917** | **0.856** | **0.941** | 0.987 | **0.982** | **0.995** |

## 3.2 Experimental Results

Table 1 first shows the competing results on IJB-C dataset. The GCN-D only uses its detection module. The GCN-DS further incorporates the segmentation module but archives no performance improvement. This is because the algorithm fails in learning the complex cluster patterns as the identity similarities are not so reliable among low-quality faces. Algorithms GCN-V and GCN-VE present the same phenomenon, where the corresponding vertex confidence and edge connectivity estimation modules are heavily dependent on the identity similarity in feature subspace. The STAR-FC performs relatively better under the influence of its structure-preserved sub-graph sampling strategy. Overall, our FC-Q algorithm outperforms other algorithms on this dataset, and achieves 91.7% *pairwise* F-score under the employment of face quality scores. Table 1 also shows the competing results on MS1M dataset. It is observed that all the algorithms achieve performance improvements when the faces are in good quality. Overall, although the assistance role of face quality is diluted, our FC-Q algorithm still gets the satisfactory result. This indicates that our algorithm can be the first choice when implementing face clustering under general circumstance where the face quality is unknown or mixed.

## 3.3 Ablation Studies

In this subsection, we evaluate some design elements used in our algorithm. The following experiments are all conducted on IJB-C dataset. Table 2 presents the clustering results of our algorithm when individually removing the following four design elements, i.e., concatenating the quality scores, concatenating the Pearson correlation encoding, adding the prior relevancy matrix, and making *key* and *query* share the same projection. It is observed that all these four design elements contribute to the performance improvement, and the last element helps the most.

**Table 2.** Results on IJB-C when four design elements are removed successively. "P" is short for *"Pairwise"*, and "B" is short for *"BCubed"*.

|                                  | P F-score | B F-score | NMI   |
|----------------------------------|-----------|-----------|-------|
| FC-Q                             | **0.917** | **0.856** | **0.941** |
| Remove $q$ in (1)                | 0.902     | 0.848     | 0.938 |
| Remove **p** in (1)              | 0.895     | 0.799     | 0.921 |
| Remove **A** in (4)              | 0.886     | 0.840     | 0.935 |
| Remove *Sharing* $\mathbf{W}^S$ in (3) | 0.828 | 0.726     | 0.883 |

**Table 3.** Results of L-GCN and FC-Q algorithms with their label propagation modules swapped. "A+B" denotes using A for linkage prediction and B for label propagation.

|              | Pairwise |       |         | Bcubed |       |         |
|--------------|----------|-------|---------|--------|-------|---------|
|              | Pre      | Rec   | F-score | Pre    | Rec   | F-score |
| L-GCN+L-GCN  | 0.869    | 0.882 | 0.876   | 0.890  | 0.756 | 0.818   |
| L-GCN+FC-Q   | 0.935    | 0.870 | 0.901   | 0.942  | 0.730 | 0.823   |
| FC-Q+L-GCN   | 0.943    | 0.885 | 0.913   | 0.961  | 0.771 | 0.855   |
| FC-Q+FC-Q    | **0.952** | **0.885** | **0.917** | **0.964** | **0.770** | **0.856** |

We further swap the label propagation modules of L-GCN and FC-Q to validate the effectiveness of incorporating the face quality. We can see from Table 3 that equipping our proposed label propagation module evidently improves the clustering precision of L-GCN with a slight drop of recall. This is because our module can further suppress the abnormal pairing based on extra local quality information. The improvement is not so significant on FC-Q as its linkage prediction module has already incorporated the face quality to output more reliable linkage likelihood.

Figure 4 further shows the effectiveness of our modified self-attention mechanism. An attention map extracted from the last layer is list on the left, which involves one pivot example and its $K = 80$ nearest neighbors. The neighbors are sorted in descend order with respect to the similarity. The attention values are taken as logarithm to better demonstrate the numerical differences. The sequence above the attention map describes the identity consistency, where the black dot indicates the neighbor node at same sequence position having the different identity. Three pivot-neighbor pairs are also list on the right, with quality score shown on the image and similarity below the arrow. We can see that the first pivot-neighbor pair in red box and the second pivot-neighbor pair in rosy box have close similarity but opposite identity consistency. The self-attention mechanism successfully suppresses the attention values of the former neighbor node based on the large score difference prior. Note that although the third neighbor node in black box with different identity has small score difference, the self-attention mechanism can also suppress its attention value based on the relevancy aggregation among involved nodes.

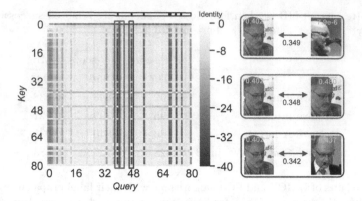

**Fig. 4.** Effect of self-attention mechanism. One attention map is list on the right and three pivot-neighbor pairs are list on the right.

## 4    Conclusion

This paper has introduced a face clustering algorithm, referred as FC-Q, to tackle with face nodes with mixed quality. The algorithm takes face quality score as extra input, which is incorporated into the linkage prediction module and label propagation module as a prior. The algorithm first modifies the Transformer encoder, and uses quality relevancy to infer more reliable linkage likelihood. Then the algorithm utilizes the local quality information to further suppress the abnormal pairing with high linkage likelihood. Experimental results validate that our algorithm gets the satisfactory clustering result under general circumstance where the face quality is unknown or mixed.

## References

1. Amigó, E., Gonzalo, J., Artiles, J., Verdejo, F.: A comparison of extrinsic clustering evaluation metrics based on formal constraints. Inf. Retriev. **12**(4), 461–486 (2009)
2. Benesty, J., Chen, J., Huang, Y., Cohen, I.: Pearson Correlation Coefficient, pp. 1–4. Springer, Vienna (2009)
3. Chen, D., Lv, J., Zhang, Y.: Unsupervised multi-manifold clustering by learning deep representation. In: The Thirty-First AAAI Conference on Artificial Intelligence (2017)
4. Deng, J., Guo, J., Xue, N., Zafeiriou, S.: Arcface: additive angular margin loss for deep face recognition. In: Proceedings of the IEEE Conference on Computer Vision and Pattern Recognition, pp. 4690–4699 (2019)
5. Duta, I.C., Liu, L., Zhu, F., Shao, L.: Improved residual networks for image and video recognition. arXiv preprint arXiv:2004.04989 (2020)
6. Ester, M., Kriegel, H.P., Sander, J., Xu, X.: A a density-based algorithm for discovering clusters in large spatial databases with noise. In: Proceedings of the Second International Conference on Knowledge Discovery and Data Mining, pp. 226–231 (1996)

7. Guo, Y., Zhang, L., Hu, Y., He, X., Gao, J.: Ms-celeb-1m: a dataset and benchmark for large-scale face recognition. In: European Conference on Computer Vision, pp. 87–102 (2016)

8. Li, P., Zhao, H., Liu, H.: Deep fair clustering for visual learning. In: Proceedings of the IEEE Conference on Computer Vision and Pattern Recognition, pp. 9070–9079 (2020)

9. Liu, R., Tan, W.: Eqface: a simple explicit quality network for face recognition. In: Proceedings of the IEEE Conference on Computer Vision and Pattern Recognition, pp. 1482–1490 (2021)

10. Lloyd, S.: Least squares quantization in PCM. IEEE Trans. Inf. Theory **28**(2), 129–137 (1982)

11. Maze, B., et al.: Iarpa janus benchmark - c: face dataset and protocol. In: 2018 International Conference on Biometrics, pp. 158–165 (2018)

12. Meng, Q., Zhao, S., Huang, Z., Zhou, F.: Magface: a universal representation for face recognition and quality assessment. In: Proceedings of the IEEE Conference on Computer Vision and Pattern Recognition, pp. 14225–14234 (2021)

13. Peng, B., Liu, M., Yang, H., Zhang, Z., Li, D.: Deep tiny network for recognition-oriented face image quality assessment. arXiv preprint arXiv:2004.04989 (2021)

14. Peng, X., Feng, J., Zhou, J.T., Lei, Y., Yan, S.: Deep subspace clustering. IEEE Trans. Neural Netw. **31**(12), 5509–5521 (2020)

15. Shen, S., et al.: Structure-aware face clustering on a large-scale graph with $10^7$ nodes. In: Proceedings of the IEEE Conference on Computer Vision and Pattern Recognition, pp. 9085–9094 (2021)

16. Shi, Y., Otto, C., Jain, A.K.: Face clustering: Representation and pairwise constraints. IEEE Trans. Inf. Forens. Secur. **13**(7), 1626–1640 (2018)

17. Terhorst, P., Kolf, J.N., Damer, N., Kirchbuchner, F., Kuijper, A.: Ser-fiq: unsupervised estimation of face image quality based on stochastic embedding robustness. In: Proceedings of the IEEE Conference on Computer Vision and Pattern Recognition, pp. 5651–5660 (2020)

18. Vaswani, A., et al.: Attention is all you need. In: International Conference on Neural Information Processing Systems, vol. 30, pp. 5998–6008 (2017)

19. Vinh, N.X., Epps, J., Bailey, J.: Information theoretic measures for clusterings comparison: variants, properties, normalization and correction for chance. J. Mach. Learn. Res. **11**(95), 2837–2854 (2010)

20. Wang, Z., Zheng, L., Li, Y., Wang, S.: Linkage based face clustering via graph convolution network. In: Proceedings of the IEEE Conference on Computer Vision and Pattern Recognition, pp. 1117–1125 (2019)

21. Xiong, R., et al.: On layer normalization in the transformer architecture. In: International Conference on Machine Learning, pp. 10524–10533 (2020)

22. Yang, L., Chen, D., Zhan, X., Zhao, R., Loy, C.C., Lin, D.: Learning to cluster faces via confidence and connectivity estimation. In: Proceedings of the IEEE Conference on Computer Vision and Pattern Recognition, pp. 13369–13378 (2020)

23. Yang, L., Zhan, X., Chen, D., Yan, J., Loy, C.C., Lin, D.: Learning to cluster faces on an affinity graph. In: Proceedings of the IEEE Conference on Computer Vision and Pattern Recognition, pp. 2298–2306 (2019)

# Capturing Prior Knowledge in Soft Labels for Classification with Limited or Imbalanced Data

Zhehao Zhong[1], Shen Zhao[2(✉)], and Ruixuan Wang[1,3(✉)]

[1] School of Computer Science and Engineering, Sun Yat-sen University, Guangzhou, China

[2] School of Intelligent Systems Engineering, Sun Yat-sen University, Shenzhen, China
zhaosh35@mail.sysu.edu.cn

[3] Key Laboratory of Machine Intelligence and Advanced Computing MOE, Guangzhou, China
wangruix5@mail.sysu.edu.cn

**Abstract.** Successful applications of deep learning often depend on large amount of training data. However, in practical image recognition tasks, available training data are often limited or imbalanced across classes, causing the over-fitting issue or the prediction bias issue during model training. In this paper, based on word embedding models from studies in natural language processing, the prior knowledge about the relationships between image classes is utilized to help train more generalizable classifiers under the condition of limited or class-imbalanced training data. Such inter-class relational knowledge is captured in the word embedding vectors for the textual names of image classes. Using these word embedding vectors as soft labels for corresponding image classes, the feature extractor part of a deep learning model can be guided to learn to extract visual features which contain both class-specific and class-shared information. Experiments on multiple image classification datasets confirm that the proposed learning framework helps improve model performance when training data is limited or class-imbalanced.

**Keywords:** Prototype learning · Image classification · Limited data · Imbalance data · Soft label

## 1 Introduction

Deep learning has shown its superior performance in various image recognition applications with the help of sufficient number of training data, such as for face recognition and intelligent diagnosis of specific diseases [1–3]. However, in practice, it may be difficult or even impossible to collect enough number of

This work is supported by NSFCs (No. 62071502, U1811461), the Guangdong Key Research and Development Program (No. 2020B1111190001), and the Meizhou Science and Technology Program (No. 2019A0102005).

S. Yu et al. (Eds.): PRCV 2022, LNCS 13535, pp. 588–600, 2022.
https://doi.org/10.1007/978-3-031-18910-4_47

training data for certain less frequent classes, e.g., images of rare diseases [4–6]. In this case, deep learning models would often suffer from limited or class-imbalanced training data (Fig. 1), due to over-fitting of the model when all classes of training data are limited or/and biased prediction toward frequent classes when training data are class-imbalanced.

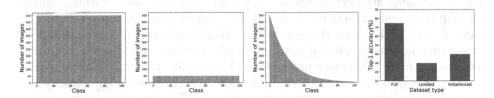

**Fig. 1.** Model performance (Left) often suffers from limited (Middle left) or imbalanced (Middle right) training data compared to sufficient training data (Right).

To alleviate the over-fitting issue, two main groups of approaches have been developed for training of deep learning models. The first group is based on trans-ferring knowledge from a relatively large auxiliary dataset which contains differ-ent classes but in content is often visually similar to the dataset of the current task. The auxiliary dataset is often used to train a feature extractor which is then fixed or fine-tuned for the current task, as in training of matching network [7], prototypical network [8] and relation network [9] for few-shot learning. However, in some scenarios like intelligent medical diagnosis, such large auxiliary dataset is generally not available because of difficulty in collecting large-scale data of many other diseases. Different from the first group of approaches, the second group does not reply on auxiliary datasets but employs various data augmen-tation techniques to increase the amount of the original training data. Besides the conventional data augmentations like random cropping, scaling, rotating, flipping and color jittering of each training image, advanced augmentation tech-niques including Cutout [10], Random erasing [11] and Grid mask [12] have been recently developed to further alleviate the over-fitting issue. These augmenta-tions operate directly on images and may not effectively introduce additional high-level semantic information compared with original data, thus still often lim-ited for improving generalizability of deep learning models. In addition, training tricks like label smoothing have also shown to be able to improve model gen-eralization. However, such tricks do not consider specific semantic relationships between classes.

Besides alleviating the over-fitting issue, class-imbalanced recognition tasks also need to reduce the prediction bias issue. Traditional class-balancing approaches include the class re-weighting [13] to increase the importance of training samples from less frequent classes in the loss function, and the re-sampling [14] of training samples to make training data balanced across classes. More recently developed approaches mainly focus on the loss design by consider-ing the instance-level prediction challenge [15] or class-level distribution [16]. Due to the essential data imbalance between small-sample (i.e., minority) and large-sample (i.e., majority) classes, these class-balancing approaches often achieve trade-off in accuracy between the majority and minority classes, particularly resulting in under-fitting of majority classes and/or over-fitting of minority classes [17].

In this paper, presuming that no auxiliary dataset is available, we propose a simple yet novel strategy to embed prior knowledge into deep learning models to help train more generalizable models with limited or imbalanced data. The prior knowledge is about the semantic relationships between classes, and such semantic relationships are implicitly captured by word embeddings from certain pre-trained natural language processing (NLP) model. The prior knowledge can also be leveraged for computer vision domain [18]. In this model, semantically related words have more similar feature vectors. By associating each (image) class with a specific embedding vector of the class-corresponding word(s), such semantic vector can be considered as the soft label for the class. The semantic relationship between any two classes can be implicitly represented by the proximity between the corresponding two soft labels. Guided by these semantically related soft labels, the feature extractor of a deep learning model can be trained to learn to extract visual features capturing inter-class relationships even with limited or class-imbalanced training data. Considering that knowledge distillation with soft labels has shown its effectiveness in transferring knowledge from one model to another in plenty of studies, it is expected that the soft labels from the NLP model can also help transfer the prior knowledge about class relationships into the deep learning model for image recognition tasks. Since soft labels do not affect designs of model architectures, the proposed strategy can be considered as a plug-in component and flexibly applied to any model backbones. The contributions of this study are summarized below.

- Prior knowledge about class relationships is introduced as soft labels to help train more generalizable models with limited or class-imbalanced training data.
- A learning framework is proposed to effectively train the feature extractor of deep learning models which can capture inter-class relationships with the help of soft labels using limited or class-imbalanced training data.
- Extensive empirical evaluations on multiple image classification tasks with limited data and imbalanced data confirmed the effectiveness and generalizability of the proposed approach.

## 2   Methodology

The main objective of training a deep learning model for image recognition is to make the model learn knowledge of classes from training images such that it can accurately recognize any new image. However, with limited or class-imbalanced training data, it becomes challenging for the model to well learn the knowledge of particularly small-sample classes. In this case, transferring or embedding prior knowledge of these classes to the model would help the model effectively grasp the knowledge of classes. Here, the word embedding vector of each (image) class is novelly considered as the soft label of the class, and thus inter-class relationship as part of class knowledge is naturally embedded into the training process of the deep learning model.

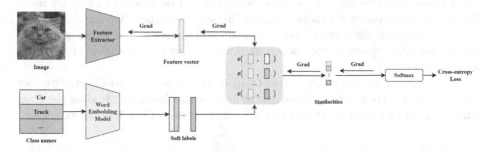

**Fig. 2.** Illustration of the proposed learning framework. Soft labels for all classes are generated based on a pre-trained and fixed word embedding model. Such soft labels capture semantic inter-class knowledge learned by the word embedding model with enormous amount of text data. The feature extractor is trained with the help of soft labels to learn to extract both class-shared and class-specific features even when training samples are limited or class-imbalanced.

## 2.1 Learning Framework

The proposed learning framework is illustrated in Fig. 2. The goal is to train the feature extractor $F$ for image recognition of $C$ classes. Suppose the soft label $\mathbf{w}_c \in \mathbb{R}^D$ of the $c$-th class ($c = 1, \ldots, C$) has been obtained based on a pre-trained word embedding model $W$ (see Sect. 2.2 for details). Given the training set $\mathcal{D} = \{(\mathbf{x}_i, \mathbf{y}_i), i = 1, \ldots, N\}$, where $\mathbf{x}_i$ is the $i$-th training image and $\mathbf{y}_i$ is the corresponding ground-truth one-hot label vector, denote by $\mathbf{f}_i = F(\mathbf{x}_i)$ the $D$-dimensional vector output of the feature extractor $F$ for input $\mathbf{x}_i$, and $\mathbf{z}_i \in \{\mathbf{w}_c, c = 1, \ldots, C\}$ the corresponding soft label of image $\mathbf{x}_i$. If the feature extractor $F$ is trained such that its output $\mathbf{f}_i$ is close to the corresponding soft label $\mathbf{z}_i$ for each image $\mathbf{x}_i$, the feature extractor would be expected to be able to extract visual features which contain inter-class relationships as in the soft label vectors. Thus, using the soft labels to guide the training of the feature extractor would help it learn the prior inter-class relational knowledge even under the condition of limited or class-imbalance training data. The guided training can be achieved by the minimization of the cosine distance loss $\mathcal{L}$ [19], which is actually a special form of the cross-entropy loss based on the cosine similarity between the feature extractor output $\mathbf{f}_i$ and each of the $C$ soft labels, i.e.,

$$\mathcal{L} = -\frac{1}{N} \sum_{i=1}^{N} \log \frac{e^{s(\mathbf{f}_i, \mathbf{z}_i)/\tau}}{\sum_{c=1}^{C} e^{s(\mathbf{f}_i, \mathbf{w}_c)/\tau}}. \tag{1}$$

Here $s(\mathbf{f}_i, \mathbf{w}_c)$ is the cosine similarity between vectors $\mathbf{f}_i$ and $\mathbf{w}_c$, and $\tau$ is the temperature hyper-parameter (set 1.0 in this study). Note that since the soft labels of all the $C$ classes participate in the calculation of the cosine distance loss for each image $\mathbf{x}_i$, the feature extractor would be trained to minimize the distance (i.e., maximize similarity) between each $\mathbf{f}_i$ and the corresponding soft label $\mathbf{z}_i$, and meanwhile to maximize the distance between $\mathbf{f}_i$ and the soft labels of all the other classes. In this way, the feature extractor can be trained to extract more discriminative features for those semantically similar classes (having similar soft labels), otherwise the corresponding similar soft labels would cause relatively larger loss. Consequently, the trained model would be more capable of discriminating between classes.

Once the feature extractor is well trained, it can be used to directly predict class of any new (test) image based on the nearest soft label, i.e., finding the class whose soft label vector is nearest to the vector output of the feature extractor.

## 2.2 Soft Label Generation

The generation of soft label for each class is mainly based on a pre-trained word embedding model. The word embedding model (e.g., Word2Vec [20] and GloVe [21]) is often trained in a self-supervised manner on a large-scale text dataset (like YFCC100M [22]), e.g., by predicting the masked word based on its context words or by predicting its context words based on the centered word in a sentence [20]. Once the self-supervised model is well trained, its feature encoder part (after removing the task-specific model head) can then be used as the word embedding model, i.e., the output of the feature encoder for each input word is the semantic representation of the input word in the embedded feature space. Since the word embedding model is trained based on millions or even billions of sentences, the embedded feature vector for each word captures the potential semantic relationships between the word and each other word. In particular, two words which are semantically closely related (e.g., 'boy' and 'man') are often closer to each other in the embedded feature space [20].

**Fig. 3.** Cosine similarity between soft labels of every paired classes. Left: each pixel represents the cosine similarity between the soft labels of the corresponding two image classes, with brighter pixels representing higher cosine similarities. Right: exemplar images of two classes with higher similarity (as indicated within the red box on the left) between corresponding soft labels. Both visually similar and class-specific features exist in the images. (Color figure online)

Based on the word embedding model, the soft label of each image class can be generated as follows. When one image class can be named by a single word (e.g., class of 'Cat'), then the output of the word embedding model for the word can be directly used as the soft label of the image class. On the other hand, when one image class is named by a sequence two or more words (e.g., class of 'Great white shark'), the weighted sum of the outputs of the word embedding model for the multiple words can be used as the soft label of the image class. In this study, simply the average of the outputs is adopted to represent the soft label for each multi-word class, although potentially more adaptive weight setting can be further investigated in future work. Figure 3 (Left) shows the cosine similarities between the soft labels of every two classes in the well-known CIFAR100 dataset. For those paired classes which have higher cosine similarities, similar visual features do often appear in the images of the classes, as demonstrated in Fig. 3 (Right). In this case, the soft label will guide the feature extractor to learn to extract such shared visual features during model training, meanwhile to extract class-specific features to discriminate between these semantically similar classes. Extraction of such more comprehensive (i.e., both class-shared and class-specific) features particularly from small-sample classes indicates that the feature extractor can be trained to extract representative features for each class, even with limited of imbalanced training samples.

### 2.3 Comparison with Relevant Methods

The soft labels can be considered as class centers in the semantic feature space. Different from the proposed generation of soft labels from a word embedding model in this study, several previous studies have proposed to directly learn one or multiple class centers for each class during the training of the classifier, where the class centers and model parameters are learned jointly. Examples include the center loss [23], the convolutional prototype learning (GCPL) [24] and the prototypical networks [8]. Since all these methods learn class centers solely based on training data, it is expected that the jointly learned classifier and the class centers would become over-fitting particularly when training data are limited or class-imbalanced. In comparison, the proposed soft label in this study is based on the word embedding model which is trained on large-scale text data, and therefore the semantic inter-class knowledge in the soft label may help train a more generalizable model with limited training samples.

## 3 Experiments

### 3.1 Experimental Setting

To evaluate the effectiveness and generalizability of the proposed method for image recognition under the condition of limited or class-imbalanced training samples, three public image datasets, i.e., CIFAR-10, CIFAR-100, and mini-ImageNet, were employed to create the limited (i.e., small-sample) and class-imbalanced training sets. For small-sample training sets, three versions were created from each original dataset, with 50, 100, and 200 images randomly sampled from each class of CIFAR-10 and CIFAR-100 respectively, and 10, 50, and 100 images per class randomly sampled from mini-ImageNet respectively. To create the class-imbalanced versions, the number of training samples were exponentially reduced across classes, while the test set was kept class-balanced. Denote by $\rho$ the imbalance ratio between sample sizes of the largest class and the smallest class. $\rho$ was set 10 and 100 respectively in relevant experiments.

In experiments, Resnet18 was used as the default model backbone, and two word embedding models GloVe [21] and Bert [25] were used to generate 300-dimensional and 768-dimensional soft labels respectively, with GloVe used by default in each experiment. During model training, conventional data augmentations were applied on each training set, including random cropping and horizontal flipping for each image. Stochastic gradient descend with momentum 0.9 and weight decay $10^{-4}$ was used to optimize each model for 200 epochs. The batch size is 128 for CIFAR-10 and CIFAR-100 and 64 for mini-ImageNet. The initial learning rate 0.1 was decayed by 0.1 respectively on epochs 120, 160, and 180. The linear warm-up learning rate schedule was also used for the first 5 epochs. During testing, the average and standard deviation of classification accuracy over five runs were reported. In addition, for the model trained with class-imbalanced data, the classification accuracy on larger-size classes (i.e., those 1/3 classes with larger training samples), smaller-size classes (i.e., those 1/3 classes with smaller training samples), and medium-size classes (i.e., the remaining 1/3 classes) were also reported respectively.

## 3.2   Effectiveness Evaluation with Limited Training Data

The proposed method was first evaluated with limited training samples. The baseline methods for comparison include the basic cross-entropy loss (CE), the center loss (CenterLoss) [23], the convolutional prototype learning (GCPL) [24], the prototypical network (ProtoNet) [8], and the label smoothing (LabelSmooth). The released source codes and suggested settings from the original studies were adopted for CenterLoss, GCPL and ProtoNet. Smooth factor of label smoothing was set 0.1.

As shown in Tables 1 and 2, compared to all the baseline methods (rows 1–5), the proposed method (last two rows) significantly improves model performance when the training samples are very limited, i.e., with 50 images per class on CIFAR-10 and CIFAR-100, and 10 images per class on mini-Imagenet. With relatively more training samples (i.e., respectively 100 and 200 images per class on CIFAR, and 50 and 100 images per class on mini-Imagenet), the proposed method still achieves satisfactory performance, often slightly better than the strongest baseline at each setting. Additional evaluations on different model backbones (e.g., ResNet50 and VGG16, Table 3) also confirm the effectiveness of the proposed method under the condition of limited training samples. Furthermore, when the proposed method is combined with existing methods like Cutout [10], Random erasing [11], and Grid mask [12], the classification performance is often significantly boosted compared to these individual methods, as demonstrated in Fig. 4 with varying number of training samples on the three datasets. These results support that the inter-class knowledge in the soft label can help train more generalizable models with limited training samples, and this method can be flexibly combined with (some of) existing strategies to further improve their effectiveness.

**Table 1.** Performance comparison on datasets with limited training data from CIFAR. '50/100/200': training samples per class. In brackets: standard deviations.

| Methods | CIFAR-10 | | | CIFAR-100 | | |
|---|---|---|---|---|---|---|
| | 50 | 100 | 200 | 50 | 100 | 200 |
| CE | 37.44 (0.74) | 48.68 (0.41) | 54.51 (0.45) | 31.76 (1.31) | 49.99 (0.94) | 63.41 (0.79) |
| CenterLoss | 35.44 (0.99) | 47.17 (1.45) | 59.04 (1.28) | 26.49 (0.40) | 50.53 (0.19) | 64.61 (1.16) |
| GCPL | 35.38 (1.18) | 48.65 (0.93) | 63.25 (0.52) | 27.10 (1.02) | 51.38 (0.40) | 64.34 (0.85) |
| ProtoNet | 36.47 (1.17) | 49.78 (0.87) | 61.73 (0.74) | 29.65 (1.48) | 49.90 (0.45) | 61.53 (0.70) |
| LabelSmooth | 35.99 (1.48) | 48.80 (0.85) | 63.07 (0.25) | 34.04 (1.21) | 52.13 (0.32) | 64.44 (0.92) |
| Ours (Bert) | **41.85** (0.34) | **52.41** (0.88) | **64.03** (0.50) | 39.22 (0.21) | 52.19 (0.35) | 64.17 (0.15) |
| Ours (GloVe) | 41.74 (0.57) | 51.23 (0.50) | 63.56 (0.56) | **39.51** (0.36) | **53.06** (0.36) | **64.84** (0.57) |

**Table 2.** Performance comparison on datasets with limited training data from mini-ImageNet. '10/50/100': training samples per class. In brackets: standard deviations.

| Methods | 10 | 50 | 100 |
|---|---|---|---|
| CE | 13.25 (0.16) | 39.68 (0.68) | 51.79 (0.11) |
| CenterLoss | 13.71 (0.26) | 40.96 (0.91) | 54.61 (0.50) |
| GCPL | 12.45 (0.95) | 42.03 (0.83) | 54.81 (0.73) |
| ProtoNet | 13.57 (0.89) | 41.03 (1.35) | 52.00 (0.73) |
| LabelSmooth | 13.80 (0.23) | 42.16 (0.34) | 53.98 (0.65) |
| Ours (Bert) | **18.31** (0.34) | 42.75 (0.18) | 54.24 (0.38) |
| Ours (GloVe) | 17.62 (0.50) | **43.37** (0.34) | **55.03** (0.61) |

**Table 3.** Performance comparison on different model backbones with limited (50 per class) training images

| Methods | Resnet50 | | Vgg16 | |
|---|---|---|---|---|
| | CIFAR-100 | Mini-ImageNet | CIFAR-100 | Mini-ImageNet |
| CE | 26.08 (0.69) | 40.56 (0.68) | 25.45 (1.48) | 29.54 (0.92) |
| CenterLoss | 24.17 (0.65) | 39.16 (1.34) | 21.83 (1.18) | 28.13 (1.48) |
| GCPL | 26.79 (1.21) | 39.23 (1.44) | 25.20 (1.20) | 29.62 (1.09) |
| ProtoNet | 31.95 (0.66) | 40.43 (1.01) | 28.30 (1.09) | 28.49 (1.26) |
| LabelSmooth | 29.56 (0.28) | 41.47 (0.27) | 29.79 (1.13) | 29.54 (0.28) |
| Our (Bert) | 32.13 (0.99) | 43.78 (0.69) | **38.20** (0.98) | **39.64** (0.59) |
| Our (GloVe) | **33.25** (0.53) | **44.01** (0.19) | 33.85 (0.51) | 39.06 (0.86) |

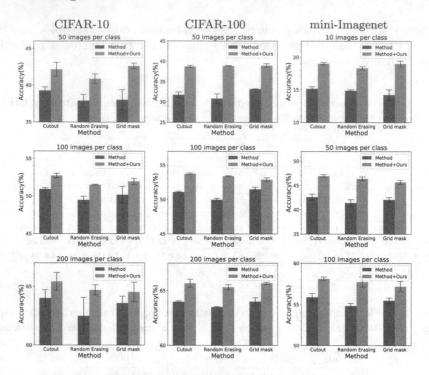

**Fig. 4.** Performance comparison based on limited training samples between each baseline and its combination with the proposed method. The baselines include Cutout, Random erasing, and Grid mask. Vertical lines for standard deviations.

**Table 4.** Performance comparison with class-imbalanced training set from CIFAR-10. Test set is class-balanced.

| Methods | $\rho = 100$ | | | | $\rho = 10$ | | | |
|---|---|---|---|---|---|---|---|---|
| | All | Larger | Medium | Smaller | All | Larger | Medium | Smaller |
| CE | 71.20 | 92.73 | 72.63 | 55.20 | 87.35 | 94.17 | **85.23** | 85.08 |
| Resample | 70.64 | 92.23 | 70.30 | 53.27 | 87.92 | 94.67 | 84.40 | 85.20 |
| Reweight | 70.39 | 90.50 | 69.90 | **55.67** | 87.61 | 94.20 | 84.50 | 85.50 |
| Ours | **72.13** | **93.27** | **73.33** | 55.38 | **88.21** | **95.00** | 84.93 | **85.58** |
| LDAM | 76.48 | 93.70 | 76.50 | 63.55 | 88.80 | 94.27 | 85.27 | 87.35 |
| LDAM+Ours | **77.30** | **93.93** | **76.73** | **65.25** | **89.17** | **95.13** | **85.93** | **87.55** |
| CB Focal | 74.10 | **93.37** | 74.80 | 59.12 | 88.88 | 93.33 | 85.37 | **88.17** |
| CB Focal+Ours | **74.63** | 93.19 | **75.53** | **60.06** | **89.19** | **93.70** | **86.53** | 87.05 |

## 3.3   Evaluation with Imbalanced Training Data

The proposed method also helps under the condition of class-imbalanced training data. As shown in Tables 4, 5 and 6, the proposed method (4-th row, 'Ours') overall outperforms the baselines (rows 1–3) under all settings ('All' columns, top-1 accuracy on all classes; note that test data are class-balanced). Interest-

**Table 5.** Performance comparison with class-imbalanced training set from CIFAR-100. Test set is class-balanced.

| Methods | $\rho = 100$ | | | | $\rho = 10$ | | | |
|---|---|---|---|---|---|---|---|---|
| | All | Larger | Medium | Smaller | All | Larger | Medium | Smaller |
| CE | 39.85 | 67.79 | 38.97 | 13.59 | 56.97 | 71.97 | 58.67 | 41.97 |
| Resample | 35.26 | 66.45 | 36.97 | 13.03 | 55.78 | 70.45 | 57.58 | 39.79 |
| Reweight | 39.56 | 67.58 | 38.79 | 13.85 | 56.19 | 68.85 | 58.09 | 42.05 |
| Ours | **41.81** | **69.36** | **41.33** | **15.53** | **60.35** | **73.48** | **61.24** | **46.74** |
| LDAM | 42.04 | **69.94** | 42.03 | **14.97** | 60.14 | 72.91 | 60.33 | **47.56** |
| LDAM+Ours | **42.49** | 69.85 | **43.58** | 14.88 | **60.29** | **73.45** | **60.82** | 46.91 |
| CB Focal | 39.85 | 67.79 | 38.97 | 13.59 | 57.85 | 70.06 | 58.52 | 45.35 |
| CB Focal+Ours | **42.87** | **70.94** | **42.06** | 16.41 | **62.05** | **75.33** | **62.06** | **49.15** |

**Table 6.** Performance comparison with class-imbalanced training set from mini-ImageNet. Test set is class-balanced.

| Methods | $\rho = 100$ | | | | $\rho = 10$ | | | |
|---|---|---|---|---|---|---|---|---|
| | All | Larger | Medium | Smaller | All | Larger | Medium | Smaller |
| CE | 50.92 | 79.88 | 50.70 | 23.03 | 70.04 | 83.06 | 69.61 | 57.82 |
| Resample | 46.25 | 77.18 | 45.15 | 20.12 | 68.99 | 82.70 | 69.03 | 55.65 |
| Reweight | 47.44 | 78.65 | 48.54 | 23.09 | 69.20 | 81.97 | 68.82 | 57.18 |
| Ours | **51.80** | **80.03** | **52.67** | **23.56** | **71.35** | **84.88** | **72.45** | **59.29** |
| LDAM | 52.20 | 79.36 | 52.12 | 25.91 | 70.50 | 81.15 | 70.42 | **58.94** |
| LDAM+Ours | **52.41** | **79.39** | **52.97** | **26.41** | **71.12** | **82.76** | **71.12** | 58.82 |
| CB Focal | 51.66 | **80.03** | 51.97 | 24.47 | 69.08 | 79.70 | 69.21 | 58.65 |
| CB Focal+Ours | **51.83** | 79.79 | 51.20 | **26.18** | **70.20** | **80.73** | **70.06** | **59.59** |

ingly, the proposed method improves the performance not only on those classes with smaller training samples ('Smaller' columns) under most settings, but also on those classes with larger-size ('Larger') and medium-size ('Medium') training samples. In addition, as with limited training data, the proposed method can also further improve the performance of existing methods by fusing them together (Tables 4, 5 and 6, last four rows). For example, models trained with the combination of CB Focal and the proposed method achieve the best classification performance on CIFAR-100 with different imbalance ratios. These results suggest that the proposed method can be applied to class-imbalanced image recognition either individually or in combination with existing strategies.

### 3.4   Ablation Study

To confirm the soft labels from a pre-trained word embedding model is essential to improve model performance with limited or class-imbalanced training set, an ablation study was performed by replacing the soft labels with randomly generated soft vectors. The element in each random vector was randomly sampled from uniform distribution. Figure 5 shows that, under the conditions of both limited and class-imbalanced training sets, the proposed soft labels often perform better than the randomly generated soft labels, while the latter is comparable to (i.e., either slightly better or worse than) the basic CE method under various settings. This supports that the implicit inter-class relationship in soft labels from the pre-trained word embedding model may help classifiers gain more semantic knowledge and generalizable performance.

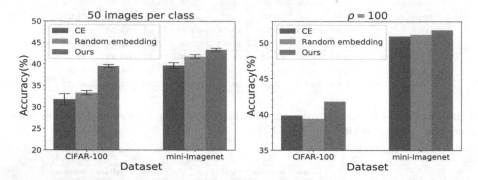

**Fig. 5.** Ablation study of soft labels. Left: classification performance of models with limited training set by the CE baseline, the randomly generated soft labels, and the proposed soft labels respectively. Right: performance of models with class-imbalanced training set.

## 4   Conclusions

In this study, soft labels containing inter-class relationships are proposed to guide the training of image recognition models under the condition of limited or class-imbalanced training samples. Extensive evaluations with three image classification datasets consistently support that the proposed learning framework is effective in improving the performance of classifiers, and its combination with existing strategies for small-sample or class-imbalanced learning can further improve the performance of these strategies. The proposed learning framework might also help train classifiers under more extreme conditions, such as those in zero-shot learning and open-set recognition. These extensions will be investigated in future work.

## References

1. Sun, Y., Liang, D., Wang, X.G., Tang, X.O.: DeepID3: face recognition with very deep neural networks. arXiv preprint arXiv:1502.00873 (2015)
2. Litjens, G., et al.: A survey on deep learning in medical image analysis. Med. Image Anal. **42**, 60–88 (2017)
3. Zhao, S., Wu, X., Chen, B., Li, S.: Automatic spondylolisthesis grading from MRIs across modalities using faster adversarial recognition network. Med. Image Anal. **58**, 101533 (2019)

4. Chen, K., et al.: Alleviating data imbalance issue with perturbed input during inference. In: de Bruijne, M., et al. (eds.) MICCAI 2021. LNCS, vol. 12905, pp. 407–417. Springer, Cham (2021). https://doi.org/10.1007/978-3-030-87240-3_39

5. Hu, Y., Zhong, Z., Wang, R., Liu, H., Tan, Z., Zheng, W.-S.: Data augmentation in logit space for medical image classification with limited training data. In: de Bruijne, M., et al. (eds.) MICCAI 2021. LNCS, vol. 12905, pp. 469–479. Springer, Cham (2021). https://doi.org/10.1007/978-3-030-87240-3_45

6. Zhuang, J., Cai, J., Wang, R., Zhang, J., Zheng, W.-S.: Deep kNN for medical image classification. In: Martel, A.L., et al. (eds.) MICCAI 2020. LNCS, vol. 12261, pp. 127–136. Springer, Cham (2020). https://doi.org/10.1007/978-3-030-59710-8_13

7. Vinyals, O., Blundell, C., Lillicrap, T., Wierstra, D.: Matching networks for one shot learning. In: Proceedings of Advances in Neural Information Processing Systems (NeurIPS), vol. 29, pp. 3630–3638 (2016)

8. Snell, J., Swersky, K., Zemel, R.: Prototypical networks for few-shot learning. In: Proceedings of Advances in Neural Information Processing Systems (NeurIPS), vol. 30, pp. 4077–4087 (2017)

9. Sung, F., Yang, Y., Zhang, L., Xiang, T., Torr, P.H.S., Hospedales, T.M.: Learning to compare: relation network for few-shot learning. In: Proceedings of the IEEE Conference on Computer Vision and Pattern Recognition (CVPR), pp. 1199–1208 (2018)

10. DeVries, T., Taylor, G.W.: Improved regularization of convolutional neural networks with cutout. arXiv preprint arXiv:1708.04552 (2017)

11. Zhong, Z., Zheng, L., Kang, G., Li, S., Yang, Y.: Random erasing data augmentation. In: Proceedings of the AAAI Conference on Artificial Intelligence (AAAI), vol. 34, no. 7, pp. 13001–13008 (2020)

12. Chen, P., Liu, S., Zhao, H., Jia, J.: Gridmask data augmentation. arXiv preprint arXiv:2001.04086 (2020)

13. Huang, C., Li, Y., Loy, C.C., Tang, X.: Learning deep representation for imbalanced classification. In: Proceedings of the IEEE Conference on Computer Vision and Pattern Recognition (CVPR), pp. 5375–5384 (2016)

14. Shen, L., Lin, Z., Huang, Q.: Relay backpropagation for effective learning of deep convolutional neural networks. In: Leibe, B., Matas, J., Sebe, N., Welling, M. (eds.) ECCV 2016. LNCS, vol. 9911, pp. 467–482. Springer, Cham (2016). https://doi.org/10.1007/978-3-319-46478-7_29

15. Cui, Y., Jia, M., Lin, T.Y., Song, Y., Belongie, S.: Class-balanced loss based on effective number of samples. In: Proceedings of the IEEE/CVF Conference on Computer Vision and Pattern Recognition (CVPR), pp. 9268–9277 (2019)

16. Cao, K., et al.: Learning imbalanced datasets with label-distribution-aware margin loss. In: Proceedings of Advances in Neural Information Processing Systems (NeurIPS), vol. 32, pp. 1565–1576 (2019)

17. Zhao, S., Chen, B., Chang, H., Chen, B., Li, S.: Reasoning discriminative dictionary-embedded network for fully automatic vertebrae tumor diagnosis. Med. Image Anal. **79**, 102456 (2022)

18. Zhao, S., Gao, Z., Zhang, H., Xie, Y., Luo, J., et al.: Robust segmentation of intima-media borders with different morphologies and dynamics during the cardiac cycle. IEEE J. Biomed. Health Inf. **22**, 1571–1582 (2017)

19. Van den Oord, A., Li, Y., Vinyals, O.: Representation learning with contrastive predictive coding. arXiv preprint arXiv: 1807.03748 (2018)

20. Mikolov, T., Chen, K., Corrado, G., Dean, J.: Efficient estimation of word representations in vector space. arXiv preprint arXiv:1301.3781 (2013)

21. Pennington, J., Socher, R., Manning, C.D.: Glove: global vectors for word representation. In: Proceedings of the 2014 Conference on Empirical Methods in Natural Language Processing (EMNLP), pp. 1532–1543 (2014)
22. Thomee, B., Shamma, D.A., Friedland, G., Elizalde, B., Ni, K., Poland, D., et al.: YFCC100M: the new data in multimedia research. Commun. ACM **59**(2), 64–73 (2016)
23. Wen, Y., Zhang, K., Li, Z., Qiao, Y.: A discriminative feature learning approach for deep face recognition. In: Leibe, B., Matas, J., Sebe, N., Welling, M. (eds.) ECCV 2016. LNCS, vol. 9911, pp. 499–515. Springer, Cham (2016). https://doi. org/10.1007/978-3-319-46478-7_31
24. Yang, H.M., Zhang, X.Y., Yin, F., Liu, C.L.: Robust classification with convolutional prototype learning. In: Proceedings of the IEEE Conference on Computer Vision and Pattern Recognition (CVPR), pp. 3474–3482 (2018)
25. Devlin, J., Chang, M.W., Lee, K., Toutanova, K.: Bert: pre-training of deep bidirectional transformers for language understanding. arXiv preprint arXiv:1810.04805 (2018)

# Coupled Learning for Kernel Representation and Graph Tensor in Multi-view Subspace Clustering

Man-Sheng Chen[1,2], Chang-Dong Wang[1,2(✉)], Dong Huang[3],
and Jian-Huang Lai[1,2]

[1] School of Computer Science and Engineering, Sun Yat-sen University,
Guangzhou 510006, China
chenmsh27@mail2.sysu.edu.cn, changdongwang@hotmail.com,
stsljh@mail.sysu.edu.cn
[2] Key Laboratory of Machine Intelligence and Advanced Computing,
Ministry of Education, Guangzhou, China
[3] College of Mathematics and Informatics, South China Agricultural University,
Guangzhou 510642, China

**Abstract.** An increasing amount of attention have been attracted in multi-view subspace clustering, whose impressive performance can be achieved by means of the self-expressive property, under the assumption of linear relations between multi-view data samples. However, most of them fail to recover the nonlinear relations between multi-view data for deeper study, and additionally they are incapable of discovering the comprehensiveness and higher-order correlations among multiple views. To deal with these challenges, we propose a novel model termed Coupled Learning for Kernel Representation and Graph Tensor (CLKT) in Multi-view Subspace Clustering, where both nonlinear relations and higher-order correlations among multiple affinity graphs are jointly learned in a unified framework. Optimal solutions of the proposed method can be obtained by an alternative minimizing optimization strategy. Extensive experiments on six real-world datasets indicate the superiority of CLKT compared with the state-of-the-art methods.

**Keywords:** Multi-view clustering · Kernel learning · Low-rank tensor representation

## 1 Introduction

Data are often collected from different fields or obtained from multiple feature extractors in many real-world applications, which is then named with the multi-view data. For instance, a webpage can be represented by multi-view features based on text, image and video. News can be reported by different languages. Multiple views or feature subsets comprehensively show different aspects of the data, motivating the development of multi-view learning. Multi-view learning

S. Yu et al. (Eds.): PRCV 2022, LNCS 13535, pp. 601–613, 2022.
https://doi.org/10.1007/978-3-031-18910-4_48

could combine all different features and make use of correlations between multiple views to obtain more deeper semantic information. In this paper, multi-view clustering is focused, where the ground-truth to guide the learning process is absent.

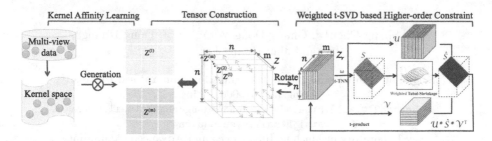

**Fig. 1.** Illustration of the CLKT model. Both nonlinear relations and higher-order correlations among multiple affinity graphs are jointly learned in a unified framework.

In the past few years, considerable efforts have been made in the development of multi-view clustering methods, which can be mainly classified into three categories: co-training style algorithms, multiple kernel learning based approaches, and subspace learning based methods. To be specific, the co-training style algorithms attempt to maximize the agreement on two different views of data by alternately training [8,9]. The work in [8] was proposed to seek for the clusters consistent across multiple views. Likewise, another strategy tried to co-regularize the clustering hypotheses such that multiple graphs could agree with each other [9]. Multiple kernel learning based approaches treat each kernel as a view, and linearly or non-linearly combine those kernels to improve their clustering performance [3,12,14]. The work in [3] aimed to learn nonlinear combinations of kernels via direct combination of multiple kernels. Tzortzis and Likas developed a general strategy to explore the weights of different kernels [14]. Under the assumption that multiple views are generated from a latent subspace, subspace learning based methods target at finding such a latent subspace shared by different views [4,18,20,22], which are in the majority. For instance, Gao et al. proposed to learn subspace representations of different views, and the common clustering results were obtained by adopting these subspace representations [4]. The work in [22] attempted to discover a underlying latent representation of multiple views, and then perform the data reconstruction on the learned latent representation rather than the original data space. Furthermore, Zhang et al. proposed a more generalized model to deal with general correlations between multi-view data samples [20]. The work in [23] studied a common similarity matrix from multiple views for kernel multi-view subspace clustering in one step. Recently, based on the emerging strategy of tensor singular value decomposition (t-SVD) based tensor nuclear norm, a few tensor based multi-view subspace clustering methods are proposed to discover the spatial structure and higher-order information of multi-view data [2,5,17,19], by which the clustering capability is well improved. In [19], Xie et al. put forward a compact t-SVD based subspace clustering model, where the rotated representation tensor was constrained by the tensor multi-rank to explore the higher-order cross-view correlations. The work in [5] studied the t-SVD based weighted tensor nuclear norm minimization to shrink different matrix singular values with the corresponding confidence. In [2], the low-rank representation tensor and affinity matrix were jointly learned while keeping the local structures. Unfortunately, despite the great success of these methods, most of them either assume linear relations among multi-view samples, failing to recover the nonlinear relations hidden in the data, or are incapable of discovering the higher-order correlations in different affinity graphs.

To deal with the aforementioned issues, in this paper, a novel Coupled Learning for Kernel Representation and Graph Tensor (CLKT) in Multi-view Subspace Clustering method is developed, in which both nonlinear relations and higher-order correlations among multiple affinity graphs are jointly learned in a unified framework. For clarity, the flowchart of CLKT is illustrated in Fig. 1. To be specific, nonlinear relations between multi-view data samples can be captured via mapping the multi-view features into a new kernel space. In order to comprehensively explore the higher-order correlations among different views, multiple affinity graphs are stacked into a tensor, and particularly the t-SVD based weighted tensor nuclear norm is employed to recover the underlying complementary and higher-order correlations from multiple views, considering the salient cues between different singular values of the matrix.

The main contributions of our work are summarized as follows:

- A novel framework is formulated to simultaneously learn both nonlinear relations and higher-order correlations among multiple affinity graphs.
- The prior information of singular values corresponding to multiple views is explicitly considered via the t-SVD based weighted tensor nuclear norm.
- An alternative minimizing optimization algorithm is developed to solve the proposed CLKT method. Extensive experiments on six datasets demonstrate the superiority of our method compared with the state-of-the-art multi-view clustering methods.

## 2  Preliminaries

Throughout this paper, the bold calligraphy letters (e.g., $\mathcal{B}$), bold upper case letters (e.g., $\mathbf{B}$) and bold lower case letters (e.g., $\mathbf{b}$) are respectively used for tensors, matrices and vectors. $\mathbf{B}^{(k)}$ is deployed to represent the $k$-th frontal slice of tensor $\mathcal{B}$, and $\overline{\mathcal{B}} = \text{fft}(\mathcal{B}, [\,], 3)$ denotes the fast Fourier transformation (FFT) along the third dimension. Similarly, $\mathcal{B}$ can be obtained from $\overline{\mathcal{B}}$ by the inverse FFT, i.e., $\mathcal{B} = \text{ifft}(\overline{\mathcal{B}}, [\,], 3)$.

**Definition 1 (t-SVD [6] ).** *For a tensor $\mathcal{B} \in \mathbb{R}^{n_1 \times n_2 \times n_3}$, its t-SVD can be factorized as,*

$$\mathcal{B} = \mathcal{U} * \mathcal{S} * \mathcal{V}^T, \tag{1}$$

where $\mathcal{U} \in \mathbb{R}^{n_1 * n_1 * n_3}$ and $\mathcal{V} \in \mathbb{R}^{n_2 * n_2 * n_3}$ are orthogonal tensors, and $\mathcal{S} \in \mathbb{R}^{n_1 * n_2 * n_3}$ is an f-diagonal tensor, whose frontal slices are all diagonal matrices.

Correspondingly, the t-SVD problem above can be solved by matrix SVD in the Fourier domain [7], i.e., $\overline{\mathbf{B}}^{(k)} = \overline{\mathbf{U}}^{(k)}\overline{\mathbf{S}}^{(k)}\overline{\mathbf{V}}^{(k)^T}, k = 1, \cdots, n_3$.

**Definition 2 (t-SVD based tensor nuclear norm [24] ).** *Given a tensor* $\mathcal{B} \in \mathbb{R}^{n_1 \times n_2 \times n_3}$, *its t-SVD based tensor nuclear norm (t-TNN) can be defined as,*

$$\|\mathcal{B}\|_{\circledast} = \sum_{k=1}^{n_3} \|\overline{\mathbf{B}}^{(k)}\|_* = \sum_{k=1}^{n_3} \sum_{i=1}^{min(n_1,n_2)} \sigma_i\left(\overline{\mathbf{B}}^{(k)}\right), \tag{2}$$

*where* $\sigma_i\left(\overline{\mathbf{B}}^{(k)}\right)$ *denotes the i-th largest singular value of* $\overline{\mathbf{B}}^{(k)}$. *It has been demonstrated that the t-TNN is not only valid, but also the tightest convex relaxation to* $l_1$ *norm of the tensor multi-rank [24].*

In addition, the weighted t-SVD based tensor nuclear norm can be further denoted as [5],

$$\|\mathcal{B}\|_{\omega,\circledast} = \sum_{k=1}^{n_3} \sum_{i=1}^{min(n_1,n_2)} \omega_i \sigma_i\left(\overline{\mathbf{B}}^{(k)}\right), \tag{3}$$

where $\omega_i$ is the weighted coefficient of $\sigma_i\left(\overline{\mathbf{B}}^{(k)}\right)$, and the prior knowledge of matrix singular values is explicitly considered.

## 3   The Proposed Methodology

In this section, we will first describe the proposed Coupled Learning for Kernel Representation and Graph Tensor (CLKT) in Multiview Subspace Clustering model, followed by the detailed optimization and algorithm summary.

### 3.1   Formulation

Assuming that each instance can be reconstructed as a linear combination of the other instances, the self-expressive subspace based multi-view clustering methods attempt to construct an informative affinity graph for better feeding into the later clustering algorithm (e.g. spectral clustering). Given a multi-view dataset $\mathbf{X} = \{\mathbf{X}^{(1)}, \ldots, \mathbf{X}^{(V)}\}$ consisting of $V$ views, where $\mathbf{X}^{(v)} \in \mathbb{R}^{d^v \times n}$ stands for the $v$-th view feature representation with dimensionality $d^v$, the objective function can be commonly formulated as [4]

$$\min_{\mathbf{Z}^{(v)}} \sum_{v=1}^{m} \|\mathbf{X}^{(v)} - \mathbf{X}^{(v)}\mathbf{Z}^{(v)}\|_F^2 + \alpha\Omega(\mathbf{Z}^{(v)}),$$

$$\text{s.t.} \quad \mathbf{Z}^{(v)} \geqslant 0, \mathbf{Z}^{(v)^T} = \mathbf{Z}^{(v)}, \tag{4}$$

where $\alpha > 0$ is a trade-off parameter. $\mathbf{Z}^{(v)} \in \mathbb{R}^{n \times n}$ is named with the learned affinity graph, and $\Omega(\mathbf{Z}^{(v)})$ denotes the certain regularization term on $\mathbf{Z}^{(v)}$. Especially, the existing works distinguish each other by employing different regularization terms or constraint sets [4,16]. Despite wide applications of self-expressive subspace methods, they mostly assume the linear relations among multi-view data samples, restricting the ability to deal with the nonlinear data.

To overcome this drawback, we extend the multi-view subspace clustering model to kernel spaces via a general kernelization framework. Let $\phi^{(v)}$ : $\mathbb{R}^{d^v} \rightarrow \mathcal{H}^{(v)}$ be a kernel that is able to map data samples from the $v$-th view to the corresponding reproducing kernel Hilbert space $\mathcal{H}^{(v)}$. Specifically, for $\mathbf{X}^{(v)} = \left[\mathbf{x}_1^{(v)}, \cdots, \mathbf{x}_n^{(v)}\right] \in \mathbb{R}^{d^v \times n}$ containing $n$ data samples, the transformation is $\phi(\mathbf{X}^{(v)}) = [\phi(\mathbf{x}_1^{(v)}), \ldots, \phi(\mathbf{x}_n^{(v)})]$. Moreover, the kernel similarity between data samples $\mathbf{x}_i^{(v)}$ and $\mathbf{x}_j^{(v)}$ can be defined as $\mathbf{K}_{i,j}^{(v)} = \mathcal{K}(\mathbf{x}_i^{(v)}, \mathbf{x}_j^{(v)}) = <\phi(\mathbf{x}_j^{(v)}), \phi(\mathbf{x}_j^{(v)}) >$ by a predefined kernel. In particular, there is no need to explicitly know what the transformation $\phi^{(v)}$ is, and all the similarities can be obtained by only employing the kernel function, which is well-known as the kernel trick. Since the kernel matrices are precomputed, the computations in the kernel space can be greatly simplified. In the new kernel space, we can reformulate the problem in Eq. (4) as

$$\min_{\mathbf{Z}^{(v)}} \sum_{v=1}^{m} \|\phi^{(v)}(\mathbf{X}^{(v)}) - \phi^{(v)}(\mathbf{X}^{(v)})\mathbf{Z}^{(v)}\|_F^2 + \alpha\|\mathbf{Z}^{(v)}\|_F^2,$$

$$\Leftrightarrow \min_{\mathbf{Z}^{(v)}} tr(\mathbf{K}^{(v)} - 2\mathbf{K}^{(v)}\mathbf{Z}^{(v)} + \mathbf{Z}^{(v)^T}\mathbf{K}^{(v)}\mathbf{Z}^{(v)}) + \alpha\|\mathbf{Z}^{(v)}\|_F^2, \quad (5)$$

$$\text{s.t.} \quad \mathbf{Z}^{(v)} \geqslant 0, \mathbf{Z}^{(v)^T} = \mathbf{Z}^{(v)},$$

where $\|\cdot\|_F^2$ is used in the regularizer about $\mathbf{Z}^{(v)}$ to avoid the trivial solution. The model in Eq. (5) recovers the linear relations between multi-view data samples in the new kernel spaces, corresponding to the nonlinear relations in the original data space.

Furthermore, to capture the higher-order correlations among different data samples in multiple views, the emerging tensor construction technique is utilized, in which the constructed tensor $\mathcal{Z} \in \mathbb{R}^{n \times n \times m}$ is composed of multiple affinity graphs, and thus the objective function of the proposed CLKT method can be reformulated as follows

$$\min_{\mathbf{Z}^{(v)}} \sum_{v=1}^{m} tr(\mathbf{K}^{(v)} - 2\mathbf{K}^{(v)}\mathbf{Z}^{(v)} + \mathbf{Z}^{(v)^T}\mathbf{K}^{(v)}\mathbf{Z}^{(v)}) + \alpha\|\mathbf{Z}^{(v)}\|_F^2 + \beta\|\mathcal{Z}\|_{\omega,\circledast}, \quad (6)$$

$$\text{s.t.} \quad \mathbf{Z}^{(v)} \geqslant 0, \mathbf{Z}^{(v)^T} = \mathbf{Z}^{(v)}, \mathcal{Z} = \Phi(\mathbf{Z}^{(1)}, \cdots, \mathbf{Z}^{(m)}).$$

where $\beta$ is a penalty parameter, and $\Phi(\cdot)$ constructs the tensor $\mathcal{Z}$ via merging multiple affinity graphs $\mathbf{Z}^{(v)}$ to a 3-mode tensor. In this paper, the weighted t-SVD based tensor nuclear norm is specifically employed to recover the higher-order correlations hidden among multi-view affinity graphs. By virtue of the weighted tensor nuclear norm minimization, the corresponding singular values are unequally regularized, and the soft-threshholding function can be deployed to shrink all different singular values with different weighting parameters.

Before the further detailed computation, rotation needs to be made on the constructed tensor $\mathcal{Z}$ so that we can better capture the low-rank property of inter-views and significantly reduce the computational complexity, and correspondingly its dimensionality changes from $n \times n \times m$ to $n \times m \times n$, whose transformation can be illustrated in Fig. 1 positioning in rotation. Observed from the model in Eq. (6), both nonlinear relations and higher-order correlations between multiple affinity graphs are jointly learned in a unified framework. After obtaining the learned affinity graphs $\mathbf{Z}^{(v)}$, the final consensus affinity matrix $\mathbf{S}$ can be computed by averaging all different $\mathbf{Z}^{(v)}$, i.e.,

$$\mathbf{S} = \frac{1}{m} \sum_{v=1}^{m} \mathbf{Z}^{(v)*}. \tag{7}$$

Subsequently, the consensus $\mathbf{S}$ is fed into the spectral clustering method to pursue the final clustering performance.

## 3.2 Optimization

To make $\mathcal{Z}$ separable in the optimization problem, the variable-splitting technique is adopted and one auxiliary tensor variable $\mathcal{A} \in \mathbb{R}^{n \times n \times m}$ is introduced to replace $\mathcal{Z}$, and the corresponding augmented Lagrangian function can be reformulated as the following optimization problem,

$$\min_{\mathbf{Z}^{(v)}, \mathcal{A}} \sum_{v=1}^{m} tr(\mathbf{K}^{(v)} - 2\mathbf{K}^{(v)}\mathbf{Z}^{(v)} + \mathbf{Z}^{(v)^T}\mathbf{K}^{(v)}\mathbf{Z}^{(v)}) + \alpha\|\mathbf{Z}^{(v)}\|_F^2 + \beta\|\mathcal{A}\|_{\omega,\circledast}$$
$$+ \frac{\mu}{2}\|\mathcal{Z} - \mathcal{A} + \frac{\mathcal{Y}}{\mu}\|_F^2, \tag{8}$$
$$\text{s.t.} \quad \mathbf{Z}^{(v)} \geqslant 0, \mathbf{Z}^{(v)^T} = \mathbf{Z}^{(v)},$$

where $\mathcal{Y} \in \mathbb{R}^{n \times n \times m}$ is the Lagrange multiplier, and $\mu > 0$ is the penalty factor. To solve the above problem, an alternative minimization strategy is adopted, by which the optimization problem in Eq. (8) can be divided into two sub-problems, and we can alternately optimize one variable while fixing the other one.

$\mathbf{Z}^{(v)}$-subproblem: With $\mathcal{A}$ fixed, $\mathbf{Z}^{(v)}$ can be updated by solving the following problem,

$$\min_{\mathbf{Z}^{(v)}} \sum_{v=1}^{m} tr(\mathbf{K}^{(v)} - 2\mathbf{K}^{(v)}\mathbf{Z}^{(v)} + \mathbf{Z}^{(v)^T}\mathbf{K}^{(v)}\mathbf{Z}^{(v)}) + \alpha\|\mathbf{Z}^{(v)}\|_F^2$$
$$+ \frac{\mu}{2}\|\mathbf{Z}^{(v)} - \mathbf{A}^{(v)} + \frac{\mathbf{Y}^{(v)}}{\mu}\|_F^2, \tag{9}$$
$$\text{s.t.} \quad \mathbf{Z}^{(v)} \geqslant 0, \mathbf{Z}^{(v)^T} = \mathbf{Z}^{(v)}.$$

---

**Algorithm 1.** Coupled Learning for Kernel Representation and Graph Tensor in Multi-view Subspace Clustering

---

**Input:** Multi-view dataset $\mathbf{X} = \left\{ \mathbf{X}^{(v)} \in \mathbb{R}^{d_v \times n} \right\}_{v=1}^{m}$, trade-off parameters $\alpha, \beta > 0$, weight vector $\omega > 0$, and cluster number $c$.

**Output:** Multiple affinity graphs $\mathbf{Z}^{(v)}$.

1: Initialize $\mathcal{Y} = 0, \mathcal{A} = \mathcal{I}$.
2: **while** not converged **do**
3:    **for** $\forall v = 1, \dots, m$ **do**
4:       Update $\mathbf{Z}^{(v)}$ by solving the problem in Eq. 11.
5:    **end for**
6:    Update $\mathcal{A}$ by solving the problem in Eq. 15.
7:    Update $\mathcal{Y}$ by $\mathcal{Y} = \mathcal{Y} + \mu(\mathcal{Z} - \mathcal{A})$.
8:    Update $\mu$ by $\mu = \rho\mu$.
9: **end while**

---

Accordingly, we can reformulate the above problem separately for each view,

$$\min_{\mathbf{Z}^{(v)}} tr(\mathbf{K}^{(v)} - 2\mathbf{K}^{(v)}\mathbf{Z}^{(v)} + \mathbf{Z}^{(v)^T}\mathbf{K}^{(v)}\mathbf{Z}^{(v)}) + \alpha\|\mathbf{Z}^{(v)}\|_F^2$$

$$+ \frac{\mu}{2}\|\mathbf{Z}^{(v)} - \mathbf{A}^{(v)} + \frac{\mathbf{Y}^{(v)}}{\mu}\|_F^2, \tag{10}$$

$$\text{s.t.} \quad \mathbf{Z}^{(v)} \geqslant 0, \mathbf{Z}^{(v)^T} = \mathbf{Z}^{(v)}.$$

The optimal solution $\mathbf{Z}^{(v)}$ can be obtained by differentiating Eq. (10) with respect to $\mathbf{Z}^{(v)}$ and setting it to zero [13],

$$\mathbf{Z}^{(v)} = (2\mathbf{K}^{(v)} + 2\alpha\mathbf{I} + \mu\mathbf{I})^{-1}(2\mathbf{K}^{(v)} + \mu\mathbf{A}^{(v)} - \mathbf{Y}^{(v)}). \tag{11}$$

Considering the constraints, i.e., $\mathbf{Z}^{(v)} \geqslant 0, \mathbf{Z}^{(v)^T} = \mathbf{Z}^{(v)}$, the symmetric non-negative affinity matrix $\mathbf{Z}^{(v)^*}$ can be computed by using $\mathbf{Z}^{(v)^*} = \frac{|\mathbf{Z}^{(v)}| + |\mathbf{Z}^{(v)^T}|}{2}$, where $|\cdot|$ is the absolute operator.

**$\mathcal{A}$-subproblem:** With $\mathbf{Z}^{(v)}$ fixed, $\mathcal{A}$ can be updated by solving the following problem,

$$\min_{\mathcal{A}} \frac{\beta}{\mu}\|\mathcal{A}\|_{\omega,\circledast} + \frac{1}{2}\|\mathcal{A} - (\mathcal{Z} + \frac{\mathcal{Y}}{\mu})\|_F^2. \tag{12}$$

In order to deal with the above weighted tensor nuclear norm minimization problem, we introduce the following theorem.

**Theorem 1.** *[5] Given $\mathcal{B} \in \mathbb{R}^{n_1 \times n_2 \times n_3}$, $l = min(n_1, n_2)$, we have $\mathcal{B} = \mathcal{U} * \mathcal{S} * \mathcal{V}^T$. For the model*

$$\arg\min_{\mathcal{X}} \frac{1}{2}\|\mathcal{X} - \mathcal{B}\|_F^2 + \tau\|\mathcal{X}\|_{\omega,\circledast}. \tag{13}$$

**Table 1.** Statistics of six real-world datasets.

| Datasets | Type | #Objects | View dimensions | #Classes |
|----------|----------|----------|-----------------------|----------|
| Yale | Image | 165 | 4096, 3304, 6750 | 15 |
| ORL | Image | 400 | 4096, 3304, 6750 | 40 |
| BBC4view | Document | 685 | 4659, 4633, 4665, 4684 | 5 |
| COIL-20 | Image | 1440 | 1024, 3304, 6750 | 20 |
| UCI | Image | 2000 | 240, 76, 6 | 10 |
| Notting-Hill | Image | 4660 | 6750, 3304, 2000 | 5 |

*And then, the optimal solution of the above model can be defined as*

$$\mathcal{X}^* = \Gamma_{\tau*\omega}(\mathcal{B}) = \mathcal{U} * ifft(\mathbf{P}_{\tau*\omega}(\overline{\mathcal{B}})) * \mathcal{V}^T, \tag{14}$$

*where $\overline{\mathcal{B}} = fft(\mathcal{B}, [\,], 3)$. $\mathbf{P}_{\tau*\omega}(\overline{\mathcal{B}})$ is a tensor, where $\mathbf{P}_{\tau*\omega}(\overline{\mathcal{B}}^{(i)})$ stands for the i-th frontal slice of $\mathbf{P}_{\tau*\omega}(\overline{\mathcal{B}})$, and $\mathbf{P}_{\tau*\omega}(\overline{\mathcal{B}}^{(i)}) = diag(\xi_1, \xi_2, \cdots, \xi_l)$ with $\xi_i = sign(\sigma_i(\overline{\mathcal{B}}^{(i)}))max(\sigma_i(\overline{\mathcal{B}}^{(i)}) - \tau * \omega_i, 0)..*

According to Theorem 1, the solution of Eq. (12) can be easily obtained,

$$\mathcal{A}^* = \Gamma_{\frac{\beta}{\mu}*\omega}[\mathcal{Z} + \frac{1}{\mu}\mathcal{Y}]. \tag{15}$$

$\mathcal{Y}$ and $\mu$-**subrpoblems:** The Lagrange multiplier $\mathcal{Y}$ and the penalty factor $\mu$ can be updated by:

$$\begin{aligned} \mathcal{Y} &= \mathcal{Y} + \mu(\mathcal{Z} - \mathcal{A}); \\ \mu &= \min(\rho\mu, \mu_{\max}), \end{aligned} \tag{16}$$

where $\rho > 1$ is used to boost the convergence speed [1]. For clarity, the procedure of solving the proposed model is summarized in Algorithm 1.

## 4   Experiments

In this section, extensive experiments are conducted on six real-world datasets to compare the proposed CLKT method with the state-of-the-art methods in terms of clustering performance. In the meantime, for a comprehensive study, parameter analysis and empirical convergence analysis are also conducted.

### 4.1   Experimental Settings

Six real-world datasets are utilized to evaluate the effectiveness of the proposed method: Yale, ORL, BBC4view, COIL-20, UCI and Notting-Hill. The statistics of these six datasets are summarized in Table 1.

CLKT is compared with the following baselines. $\mathbf{SC}_{best}$ [10] is a standard spectral clustering method designed for clustering each single view, and the best performance from multiple views is reported. **RMSC** [18] performs via the standard Markov chain. **LTMSC** [21] considers the unfolding tensor with low-rank constraint to capture the higher-order correlations. **MLAN** [11] simultaneously conducts clustering and local manifold learning in a framework by considering the adaptive neighborhood. **tSMC** [19] constructs the tensor by multiple subspace representations to capture the higher-order correlations among different views. **ETMC** [17] focuses on the Markov chain method to learn the essential tensor to discover the principle information from different views. **WTNM** [5] regularizes different singular values by different weighting coefficients. **GMC** [15] learns the similarity-induced graphs from different views and unified fusion graph in a mutual manner.

**Table 2.** Comparison results in terms of NMI (%) on six real-world datasets.

| Methods | Yale | ORL | BBC4view | COIL-20 | UCI | Notting-Hill |
|---|---|---|---|---|---|---|
| $SC_{best}$ | $65.73_{\pm 3.10}$ | $89.11_{\pm 1.38}$ | $54.27_{\pm 0.11}$ | $82.81_{\pm 1.29}$ | $58.74_{\pm 0.11}$ | $67.07_{\pm 0.04}$ |
| RMSC | $64.84_{\pm 1.24}$ | $88.41_{\pm 0.45}$ | $53.39_{\pm 0.58}$ | $83.16_{+0.29}$ | $82.25_{\pm 0.93}$ | $77.25_{\pm 0.00}$ |
| LTMSC | $76.00_{\pm 0.76}$ | $90.27_{\pm 1.04}$ | $79.62_{\pm 0.00}$ | $80.99_{\pm 1.63}$ | $76.89_{\pm 0.70}$ | $77.90_{\pm 0.00}$ |
| MLAN | $71.72_{\pm 0.00}$ | $83.84_{\pm 0.00}$ | $70.05_{\pm 0.00}$ | $85.58_{\pm 0.00}$ | $92.58_{\pm 0.00}$ | $11.49_{\pm 0.00}$ |
| tSMC | $91.90_{\pm 2.79}$ | $99.25_{\pm 0.39}$ | $97.75_{\pm 0.00}$ | $90.22_{\pm 0.34}$ | $98.91_{\pm 0.00}$ | $89.03_{\pm 0.03}$ |
| ETMC | $66.82_{\pm 1.59}$ | $85.79_{\pm 0.58}$ | $89.99_{\pm 1.91}$ | $92.77_{\pm 0.85}$ | $96.10_{\pm 0.78}$ | $91.10_{\pm 0.00}$ |
| GMC | $68.92_{\pm 0.00}$ | $85.71_{\pm 0.00}$ | $56.28_{\pm 0.00}$ | $94.07_{\pm 0.00}$ | $81.53_{\pm 0.00}$ | $9.23_{\pm 0.00}$ |
| WTNM | $96.41_{\pm 1.76}$ | $99.34_{\pm 0.44}$ | $98.37_{\pm 0.00}$ | $90.34_{\pm 0.06}$ | $99.04_{\pm 0.00}$ | $95.60_{\pm 0.00}$ |
| CLKT | $\mathbf{100.00}_{\pm 0.00}$ | $\mathbf{100.00}_{\pm 0.00}$ | $\mathbf{98.82}_{\pm 0.00}$ | $\mathbf{97.61}_{\pm 0.00}$ | $\mathbf{100.00}_{\pm 0.00}$ | $\mathbf{99.79}_{\pm 0.00}$ |

**Table 3.** Comparison results in terms of Fscore (%) on six real-world datasets.

| Methods | Yale | ORL | BBC4view | COIL-20 | UCI | Notting-Hill |
|---|---|---|---|---|---|---|
| $SC_{best}$ | $48.91_{\pm 3.79}$ | $71.20_{\pm 3.15}$ | $65.28_{\pm 0.09}$ | $71.21_{\pm 2.39}$ | $55.42_{\pm 0.09}$ | $77.23_{\pm 0.02}$ |
| RMSC | $47.39_{\pm 1.50}$ | $69.81_{\pm 1.09}$ | $59.09_{\pm 0.96}$ | $71.68_{\pm 0.33}$ | $80.06_{\pm 1.45}$ | $82.27_{\pm 0.00}$ |
| LTMSC | $61.87_{\pm 1.21}$ | $73.93_{\pm 2.44}$ | $87.38_{\pm 0.00}$ | $66.83_{\pm 2.56}$ | $74.89_{\pm 0.90}$ | $82.50_{\pm 0.00}$ |
| MLAN | $54.75_{\pm 0.00}$ | $50.97_{\pm 0.00}$ | $81.02_{\pm 0.00}$ | $74.05_{\pm 0.00}$ | $93.70_{\pm 0.00}$ | $37.62_{\pm 0.00}$ |
| tSMC | $85.76_{\pm 5.01}$ | $97.42_{\pm 1.33}$ | $99.05_{\pm 0.00}$ | $81.77_{\pm 0.96}$ | $99.20_{\pm 0.00}$ | $91.79_{\pm 0.03}$ |
| ETMC | $50.47_{\pm 2.04}$ | $64.03_{\pm 1.34}$ | $91.18_{\pm 3.22}$ | $85.15_{\pm 1.57}$ | $93.93_{\pm 1.30}$ | $92.40_{\pm 0.00}$ |
| GMC | $48.01_{\pm 0.00}$ | $35.99_{\pm 0.00}$ | $63.33_{\pm 0.00}$ | $79.43_{\pm 0.00}$ | $71.34_{\pm 0.00}$ | $36.94_{\pm 0.00}$ |
| WTNM | $93.69_{\pm 3.41}$ | $97.74_{\pm 1.52}$ | $99.33_{\pm 0.00}$ | $81.23_{\pm 0.07}$ | $99.30_{\pm 0.00}$ | $97.50_{\pm 0.00}$ |
| CLKT | $\mathbf{100.00}_{\pm 0.00}$ | $\mathbf{100.00}_{\pm 0.00}$ | $\mathbf{99.55}_{\pm 0.00}$ | $\mathbf{96.72}_{\pm 0.00}$ | $\mathbf{100.00}_{\pm 0.00}$ | $\mathbf{99.91}_{\pm 0.00}$ |

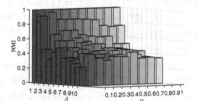
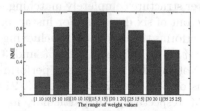

**Fig. 2.** The performance in terms of NMI when using different trade-off parameters $\alpha$, $\beta$ and the weighting factor $\omega$ on the Yale dataset.

Experiments are conducted twenty times for each method and the average performance as well as the standard deviation (std. dev.) are reported. For our method, the trade-off parameters $\alpha$ is tuned in the range of $[0.1, 1]$, $\beta$ is tuned in the range of $[1, 10]$ and the weight $\omega$ for shrinking different singular values of different views is tuned in the range of $(0, 20]$. Besides, the kernel matrix $\mathbf{K}$ in this paper is simply set as the linear kernel for different benchmark datasets, i.e., $\mathcal{K}(\mathbf{x}, \mathbf{y}) = \mathbf{x}^T \mathbf{y}$. For the baselines, the best parameters are tuned as suggested by the corresponding papers. Two widely used metrics are adopted to comprehensively evaluate the clustering performance, i.e., normalized mutual information (NMI) and Fscore. For the evaluation measures, higher values indicate better clustering performance.

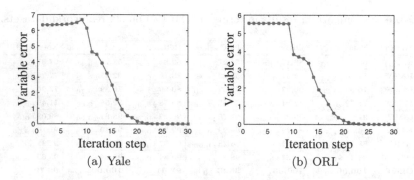

(a) Yale    (b) ORL

Fig. 3. Convergence versus iteration on Yale and ORL datasets.

## 4.2  Comparison Results

The detailed clustering results in terms of NMI and Fscore obtained by different clustering methods on six real-world datasets are respectively reported in Table 2 and Table 3. In each table, the best performance for distinct datasets is highlighted in terms of each measure in boldface.

According to these tables, the proposed CLKT method achieves the best clustering performance on all the benchmark datasets, especially obtaining the cluster structure completely matching with the ground-truth labels (i.e., all 1) on three out of six datasets. For instance, on the Yale dataset, CLKT significantly outperforms the baselines by achieving improvements of 37.27%, 35.16%, 24.0%, 28.28%, 8.1%, 33.18%, 31.08% and 3.59% respectively in terms of NMI. On the Notting-Hill dataset, the performance improvements over the baselines in terms of NMI are 32.72%, 22.54%, 21.89%, 88.3%, 10.76%, 8.69%, 90.56% and 4.19% respectively. In particular, it can be observed that methods with the tensor nuclear norm based on SVD, i.e., CLKT, WTNM, ETMC and tSMC, often obtain better clustering results than the other methods, confirming the effectiveness of the deployment of tensor nuclear norm in capturing the higher-order correlations between multi-view data. Despite of this, the proposed CLKT method significantly outperforms the other ones by simultaneously recovering the nonlinear relations and higher-order correlations among multiple learned affinity graphs. Besides, considering different confidences of multiple views, the proposed CLKT method unequally treats different singular values of multiple views during the exploration of higher-order correlations via tensor.

### 4.3 Parameter Analysis

Three free parameters needs to be tuned in the proposed CLKT method, including the trade-off parameters $\alpha$, $\beta$ and the weighting factor $\omega$. In this subsection, parameter analysis about these three parameters is conducted on the Yale dataset, which is illustrated in Fig. 2. From the figure, we can observe that the best performance can be found over the corresponding ranges of parameter values. Meanwhile, it can be concluded that the two trade-off parameters and weighting factor on the three views of the Yale dataset are significantly important for improving the clustering performance.

### 4.4 Convergence Analysis

In this subsection, the empirical convergence analysis is conducted on the Yale and ORL datasets to verify the convergence property of CLKT, and the convergence results are plotted in Fig. 3, where the corresponding variable error $\sum_{v=1}^{m} \| \mathcal{Z}_{(k+1)}^{(v)} - \mathcal{A}_{(k+1)}^{(v)} \|_\infty$ of each iteration step is recorded. In each subfigure, the horizontal axis stands for the iteration step while the vertical axis stands for the corresponding variable error. Obviously, we can observe that the value of the variable error would decrease within the first 20 iterations and then stays steady with more iterations. In other words, the convergence can be reached.

## 5    Conclusion

In this paper, a novel unified model termed Coupled Learning for Kernel Representation and Graph Tensor in Multi-view Subspace Clustering is developed. Different from the existing multi-view subspace clustering methods, both nonlinear relations and higher-order correlations among multiple affinity graphs are jointly studied in the unified model. Within this framework, multi-view observations are mapped into a new high-dimensional kernel space to recover the nonlinear relations in the original data space. Meanwhile, multiple learned affinity graphs are stacked in a low-rank tensor constrained by the t-SVD based weighted tensor nuclear norm to recover comprehensiveness and higher-order correlations among multiple views, and especially the prior information of singular values corresponding to multiple views is explicitly considered by assigning different contributions. Extensive experimental results on six datasets demonstrate the superiority of CLKT compared with the state-of-the-art clustering methods.

**Acknowledgements.** This work was supported by NSFC (61876193).

# References

1. Chen, Y., Wang, S., Zheng, F., Cen, Y.: Graph-regularized least squares regression for multi-view subspace clustering. Knowl. Based Syst. **194**, 105482 (2020)
2. Chen, Y., Xiao, X., Zhou, Y.: Multi-view subspace clustering via simultaneously learning the representation tensor and affinity matrix. Pattern Recognit. **106**, 107441 (2020)
3. Cortes, C., Mohri, M., Rostamizadeh, A.: Learning non-linear combinations of kernels. In: NIPS, pp. 396–404 (2009)
4. Gao, H., Nie, F., Li, X., Huang, H.: Multi-view subspace clustering. In: ICCV, pp. 4238–4246 (2015)
5. Gao, Q., Xia, W., Wan, Z., Xie, D., Zhang, P.: Tensor-SVD based graph learning for multi-view subspace clustering. In: AAAI, pp. 3930–3937 (2020)
6. Kilmer, M.E., Martin, C.D.: Factorization strategies for third-order tensors. Linear Algebra Appl. **435**(3), 641–658 (2011)
7. Kilmer, M.E., Braman, K.S., Hao, N., Hoover, R.C.: Third-order tensors as operators on matrices: a theoretical and computational framework with applications in imaging. SIAM J. Matrix Anal. Appl. **34**(1), 148–172 (2013)
8. Kumar, A., Daumé III, H.: A co-training approach for multi-view spectral clustering. In: ICML, pp. 393–400 (2011)
9. Kumar, A., Rai, P., Daumé III, H.: Co-regularized multi-view spectral clustering. In: NIPS, pp. 1413–1421 (2011)
10. Ng, A.Y., Jordan, M.I., Weiss, Y.: On spectral clustering: analysis and an algorithm. In: NIPS, pp. 849–856 (2002)
11. Nie, F., Cai, G., Li, J., Li, X.: Auto-weighted multi-view learning for image clustering and semi-supervised classification. IEEE Trans. Image Process. **27**(3), 1501–1511 (2018)
12. Ren, Z., Mukherjee, M., Bennis, M., Lloret, J.: Multikernel clustering via nonnegative matrix factorization tailored graph tensor over distributed networks. IEEE J. Sel. Areas Commun. **39**(7), 1946–1956 (2021)
13. Ren, Z., Sun, Q., Wei, D.: Multiple kernel clustering with kernel k-means coupled graph tensor learning. In: AAAI, pp. 9411–9418 (2021)
14. Tzortzis, G., Likas, A.: Kernel-based weighted multi-view clustering. In: ICDM, pp. 675–684 (2012)
15. Wang, H., Yang, Y., Liu, B.: GMC: graph-based multi-view clustering. IEEE Trans. Knowl. Data Eng. **32**(6), 1116–1129 (2020)
16. Wang, X., Guo, X., Lei, Z., Zhang, C., Li, S.Z.: Exclusivity-consistency regularized multi-view subspace clustering. In: CVPR, pp. 1–9 (2017)
17. Wu, J., Lin, Z., Zha, H.: Essential tensor learning for multi-view spectral clustering. IEEE Trans. Image Process. **28**(12), 5910–5922 (2019)
18. Xia, R., Pan, Y., Du, L., Yin, J.: Robust multi-view spectral clustering via low-rank and sparse decomposition. In: AAAI, pp. 2149–2155 (2014)
19. Xie, Y., Tao, D., Zhang, W., Liu, Y., Zhang, L., Qu, Y.: On unifying multi-view self-representations for clustering by tensor multi-rank minimization. Int. J. Comput. Vis. **126**(11), 1157–1179 (2018)
20. Zhang, C., Fu, H., Hu, Q., Cao, X., Xie, Y., Tao, D., Xu, D.: Generalized latent multi-view subspace clustering. IEEE Trans. Pattern Anal. Mach. Intell. **42**(1), 86–99 (2020)
21. Zhang, C., Fu, H., Liu, S., Liu, G., Cao, X.: Low-rank tensor constrained multiview subspace clustering. In: ICCV, pp. 1582–1590 (2015)

22. Zhang, C., Hu, Q., Fu, H., Zhu, P., Cao, X.: Latent multi-view subspace clustering. In: CVPR, pp. 4279–4287 (2017)
23. Zhang, G.Y., Zhou, Y.R., He, X.Y., Wang, C.D., Huang, D.: One-step kernel multi-view subspace clustering. Knowledge-Based Systems 189 (2020)
24. Zhang, Z., Ely, G., Aeron, S., Hao, N., Kilmer, M.E.: Novel methods for multilinear data completion and de-noising based on tensor-svd. In: CVPR, pp. 3842–3849 (2014)

# Combating Noisy Labels via Contrastive Learning with Challenging Pairs

Yipeng Chen[1], Xiaojuan Ban[1], and Ke Xu[2(✉)]

[1] School of Computer and Communication Engineering, University of Science and Technology Beijing, Beijing 100083, China
[2] Collaborative Innovation Center of Steel Technology, University of Science and Technology Beijing, Beijing 100083, China
xuke@ustb.edu.cn

**Abstract.** The predictive performance of deep neural networks (DNNs) depends on the quality of labels, yet imperfect labels are ubiquitous in real-world datasets. Several recent methods training DNNs robust to label noise have been proposed mainly focusing on two techniques: label filtering by a model after standard warm-up training to discriminate noisy labels and pseudo-labeling to optimize the model with the divided dataset. The performance of these methods depends on the quality of warm-up training, while noisy labels affect the training to some extent. In this paper, we propose to solve the problem by warming-up the models without any labels. Specifically, we optimize the models by a specified contrastive learning way combining with adversarial training. By getting rid of the noisy labels, the method creates more challenging pairs by computing adversarial noises in an unsupervised manner. Thus, we can obtain a high-quality feature extractor through the proposed contrastive learning method with challenging pairs (CLCP). Extensive experimental results on CIFAR-10 and CIFAR-100 demonstrate that the proposed approach is compatible with the existing methods and can significantly outperform the state-of-the-art counterparts.

**Keywords:** Noisy labels · Contrastive learning · Adversarial examples

## 1 Introduction

Deep neural networks (DNNs) have achieved remarkable advances in many machine learning tasks owing to the collection of large datasets with reliable annotated labels. However, obtaining quality annotations at scale is usually extremely expensive and time-consuming. Existing methods to solve the problem, such as semi-supervised learning and weakly supervised learning, seek to combine little well annotated data with a large number of unlabeled data [1,2] or data with inexpensive annotations [3,4]. These approaches are severely affected by noisy labels, either from the generated pseudo-labels or inherent noise in the dataset, leading to the poor performance without high-quality labels. Although pre-training on a large clean dataset may seem to be a possible solution to this problem, the availability of such data may be limited in some domain.

Thus, We seek to solve the problem without introducing additional data. Several recent studies haven demonstrated the efficiency on training with noisy labels by selecting the noisy labels firstly with a warm-up trained model, and then processing the divided data in a semi-supervised way [5–7]. Since the selection phase is conducted with the full dataset, the warm-up training is affected by the inherent noisy labels. Though DNNs have been proved to be robust to noisy labels due to the memorization effect in the early stage of training [8,9], it is still prone to memorizing noise degrading the model performance [7].Thus, it is of importance to seek suitable methods to prevent the model from over-fitting to noisy labels in the warm-up phase.

The recent success of self-supervised learning inspires us to adopt unsupervised pre-training to solve the problem. Self-supervised models without labels can even achieve almost the same performance with the supervised models trained by abundant quality labeled data [12,13,15]. Our method is based on the unsupervised contrastive learning [10–12,14], which has been shown efficient in large-scale computer vision tasks [10,17,18]. It is implemented by generating a pair of examples per instance, and feeding them through an encoder, which is trained with a constrastive loss. And the better design of positive pairs, which are defined as the pairs generated from the same instance, can help training better warm-up model [19]. Furthermore, previous studies [19,20] have shown that contrastive learning benefits from definitions of positive pairs that pose a greater challenge to the learning of the invariant instance representation.

Based on the above theories, we seek to adopt unsupervised contrastive learning to warm-up the model with challenging pairs (CLCP). Specifically, we search for the instance augmentation sets leading to the highest optimization cost for contrastive learning by applying adversarial examples [20,22,24]. Building on the success of recent contrastive learning [11,12] and adversarial training [20,23], we generate high-quality feature extractor by pre-training with specified adversarial examples on the raw dataset without introducing any external data.

To summary, the proposed approach for dealing with noisy labels benefits simultaneously from several effects. Initially, external well-annotated datasets are not required, and as a result, there will not be domain gap between different datasets. Furthermore, labels in the noisy dataset are not used and the warm-up training will not be corrupted by inherent noisy labels. Additionally, adversarial examples are applied to generate challenging pairs to further improve the warm-up training performance. Last but not least, the method can be combined with most of the existing state-of-the-art methods processing noisy labels. The main contribution of this work are as below:

- To optimize the warm-up training phase of noisy label processing, we propose to improve the unsupervised contrastive learning method by searching for challenging data pairs (CLCP). And the experimental results show that the introduction of adversarial examples brings the model better performance on dividing noisy labels.

- We show that the proposed method performs well in the beginning of the latter stage of noisy label processing. And the final experimental results on CIFAR-10 and CIFAR-100 outperform the state-of-the-art counterparts. Our experiments also show that the proposed method can be combined with most of the state-of-the-art methods and achieve good performance under different noise ratios.

## 2    Related Works

### 2.1    Self-supervised Learning

Self-supervised learning aims at learning representations that are meaningful in some general sense, without using externally provided labels. It is commonly implemented by designing and training with the pretext tasks. Some methods are based on reconstructing a corrupted version of the input [15,25], while some others seek to train a classifier based on other context predictions [26–28]. However, these methods are faced with an inherent problem when deploying the pre-trained feature extractor to a particular downstream task, which is not be well correlated with the self-supervised objective [29]. Recent studies on contrastive learning improve the performance in large-scale vision tasks to solve the problem [10–12,30].

Contrastive learning is implemented by generating a pair of examples per instance, and feeding them through an encoder, which is trained with a constrastive loss [10]. The design of positive pairs which are defined as pairs generated from the same instance, is always one of the research focuses. Most methods tend to apply transformation, such as rotation or scaling, to the data to generate positive pairs [10,15,17]. Previous studies [19,20] have proved that it is beneficial to generate positive pairs that pose a greater challenge to the learning of the invariant instance representation. Recently, Chih-Hui et al. [20] proposed to generate these challenging pairs by computing and applying adversarial noises.

### 2.2    Combating Noisy Labels

Two families of methods have been conducted to handle the issue of poor generalization performance attributed to noisy labels. On one hand, some approaches propose to construct a loss function that encourages the model to abstain from learning samples with noisy labels [33–35,41] or compute the noise transition matrix directly [31,32]. Although possessing low computational complexity, they have problems in training the clean samples and thus, achieve a sub-optimal point in training.

On the other hand, the other methods tend to detect the noisy labels by judging whether they are mislabeled to either relabel or discard them. Techniques for detecting noisy labels include utilizing multiple networks in a teacher-student architecture [37] or mutual teaching framework [38], and mixture models [5]. These are often based on the observation that samples with noisy labels converge slower than those with clean ones [9,39,40]. Recent studies have combined self-supervised learning with the mixture models to get rid of the noisy labels in warm-up phase [7]. While some approaches propose to apply two sets of augmentations to optimize the framework [6].

## 3 Proposed Method

The proposed method aims at improving the performance of unsupervised contrastive learning model, and thereby improves its abilities of discriminating noisy labels.

### 3.1 Preliminaries

Considering a $C$-class classification problem with a training set with $N$ labeled samples $\mathcal{D} = \{(x_1, y_1), \cdots, (x_n, y_n)\}$, where $x_i \in \mathbb{X}$ is the $i^{th}$ sample from the training set and $y_i \in \mathbb{Y}$ is a one-hot vector representing the label over $C$ classes associated with $x_i$. A supervised learning classifier seeks to learn a function $f : \mathbb{X} \to \mathbb{Y}$, which maps the input space to the label space. The training objective of the classifier is to find the optimal parameters $\theta$ that minimize an empirical risk defined by a loss function. Given a loss function $\mathcal{L}$ and the classifier $f(\cdot)$, the normal cross entropy loss of one sample for classification is defined as:

$$\mathcal{L}_{SL}(f(x_i), y) = -y^T \log(f(x_i)) \tag{1}$$

And the normal adversarial example $x_i^{adv}$ is computed as:

$$x_i^{adv} = x + \delta \quad \text{s.t.} \quad \|\delta\|_p < \epsilon \quad \text{and} \quad \arg\max_{\delta} \mathcal{L}_{SL}(f(x_i + \delta), y) \tag{2}$$

where $\delta$ is an adversarial perturbation of $L_p$ norm smaller than $\epsilon$.

While in unsupervised contrastive learning, the dataset is considered unlabeled, i.e. $\mathcal{U} = \{x_i\}$. Each example $x_i$ is mapped into an example pair $\{x_i^p, x_i^q\}$, where $p$ and $q$ are the transformation operations sampling from a set of transformations $\mathcal{A}$. Contrastive learning seeks to learn the representations of image $x_i$ by minimizing the contrastive cost:

$$\mathcal{L}_{CL}(f(x_i^{p_i}), f(x_i^{q_i})) = -\log \frac{\exp\left(f(x_i^{p_i})^T f(x_i^{q_i})/\tau\right)}{\sum_{k=1}^{B} \exp\left(f(x_i^{p_i})^T f(x_i^{q_i})/\tau\right)} \tag{3}$$

where $p_i$ and $q_i$ are sampled from the transformation set $\mathcal{A}$, $\tau$ is the sharpening temperature, and $B$ is the size of a mini-batch.

## 3.2   Challenging Pairs for Unsupervised Contrastive Learning

To generate the most challenging pairs for the above contrastive learning, we choose to apply the adversarial attacks [23,24] to maximize the contrastive cost. Following the route of previous work [20], we fix one of the two transformations i.e. $p$ or $q$, to compute the suitable adversarial perturbations for contrastive learning. Suppose that $p$ is fixed, the adversarial example $x_i^{adv_i}$ can be defined as:

$$x_i^{adv_i} = x_i^{p_i} + \delta \quad \text{s.t.} \quad \|\delta\|_p < \epsilon \quad \text{and} \quad \arg\max_\delta \mathcal{L}_{CL}\left(f\left(x_i^{p_i} + \delta\right), f\left(x_i^{p_i}\right)\right) \quad (4)$$

where $p_i$ is sampled from the transformation set $\mathcal{A}$, and $\delta$ is an adversarial perturbation of $L_p$ norm smaller than $\epsilon$. Then we conduct adversarial training with the generated challenging pairs $\left(x_i^{p_i}, x_i^{adv_i}\right)$ together with the original contrasive learning pairs $(x_i^{p_i}, x_i^{q_i})$ and the entire process is shown in Fig. 1. The adversarial training target is defined as:

$$\mathcal{L}_{AT}\left(f\left(x_i^{p_i}\right), f\left(x_i^{adv_i}\right)\right) = -\log \frac{\exp\left(f\left(x_i^{p_i}\right)^T f\left(x_i^{adv_i}\right)/\tau\right)}{\sum_{k=1}^B \exp\left(f\left(x_i^{p_i}\right)^T f\left(x_i^{adv_i}\right)/\tau\right)} \quad (5)$$

The final cost of contrastive learning with challenging pairs (CLCP) is consists of adversarial training loss term with these challenging pairs and the original contrastive loss:

$$\begin{aligned} \mathcal{L}_{CLCP}\left(f\left(x_i^{p_i}\right), f\left(x_i^{adv_i}\right), f\left(x_i^{q_i}\right)\right) &= \mathcal{L}_{CL}\left(f\left(x_i^{p_i}\right), f\left(x_i^{q_i}\right)\right) \\ &+ \omega\mathcal{L}_{AT}\left(f\left(x_i^{p_i}\right), f\left(x_i^{adv_i}\right)\right) \end{aligned} \quad (6)$$

where $\omega$ is the hyper-parameter balancing the original contrastive loss and adversarial loss.

## 3.3   Combating Noisy Labels with the Pre-trained Model

Inspired by the recent success of noisy label processing [5–7], we propose to apply a two-phase framework, which is similar to the architecture of DivideMix [5]. In the first stage, we warm-up a feature extractor by the method introduced in Sect. 3.2. By getting rid of the inherent noisy labels in the raw dataset, our method provides better feature extraction for the next stage. In the second stage, we deploy the model to divide the dataset into clean and noisy subsets, and then train the model in a semi-supervised learning style. We also prove that the pre-trained model can be well combined with the most state-of-the-art methods coping with noisy labels. Taking no account of labels, all methods adopting our pre-trained model achieve higher performance under even extreme noise level conditions. The experimental results are displayed in Sect. 4.

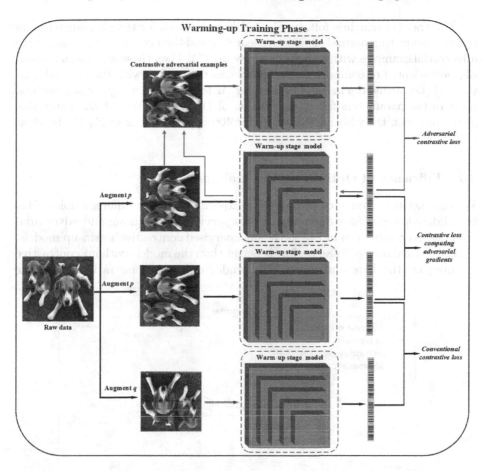

**Fig. 1.** Improving contrastive learning by creating challenging pairs in warm-up training. The black and red arrow denote the forward and backward propagation computing adversarial perturbations. The blue arrow represents the process of calculating the adversarial loss. And only the adversarial and conventional contrastive loss need backward propagation when optimizing the whole model. (Color figure online)

## 4    Experiments

The experiments are conducted on CIFAR-10 and CIFAR-100 dataset to demonstrate the efficiency of the proposed method (CLCP) on dealing with noisy labels. The synthetic noises are generated following the practice of common benchmarks [5,42,43]. We uses two types of label noise: symmetric and asymmetric. Following the common practice [42], symmetric noise is generated by randomly replacing the labels in a percentage of the training set with a random label sampled from a uniform distribution over all labels. And for asymmetric noise, it is designed to mimic the structure of real-world label errors, where classes that are generally similar in appearance are more likely to switch labels [43].

The training schedule follows Fig. 1. We first search for the challenging pairs by first conducting normal contrastive learning and then generate the contrastive adversarial examples with the gradients by Eq. (5). Then these adversarial examples are adopted to compute a adversarial contrastive loss with the original augmented (i.e. augment $p$ in Fig. 1) examples. As for the training hyper-parameters, most of the parameters follow the setting of DivideMix. We set the batch size as 64 and train the whole architecture for 400 epochs. The $\omega$ in Eq. (6) is set as 0.40.

## 4.1   Efficiency of Optimizing Pre-training

We conduct two groups of comparative experiment under different noise rates to validate the efficiency of deploying unsupervised pre-training and adversarial training. As can be seen in Fig. 2, the unsupervised contrastive warm-up models, i.e. the red and orange lines, performs better than the models without contrastive learning i.e. the blue and green lines, under different noise ratios. Since the

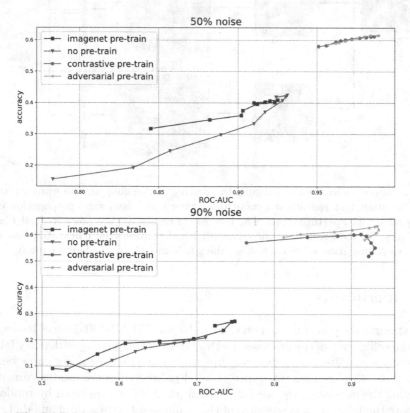

**Fig. 2.** The ROC-AUC and accuracy figure for different warm-up pre-training methods under various noise ratios on CIFAR-100. The points are sampled every five epochs during training (Color figure online)

unsupervised contrastive learning ignores the annotations, the pre-trained model performs much better than the models adopting supervised learning. And this can also explain the phenomenon of the larger gap between the two kinds of warming-up methods under higher noise ratio. On one hand, supervised learning suffers from more disturbance from labels as the noise rate increases, while on the other hand, unsupervised contrastive learning can avoid these perturbations. Thus, the gap between the kinds of methods increases as noise ratio grows.

Comparing to normal unsupervised contrastive learning [10], the proposed method performs better when noise ratio grows. Explanation for the phenomenon might be the adversarial training, which not only provides the better feature extracting ability, but also improves the robustness against perturbations.

## 4.2 Compatibility and Efficiency

We conduct experiments on CIFAR-10 and CIFAR-100 to demonstrate the compatibility of the proposed method with other state-of-the-art methods. ResNet-34 and ResNet-50 are pre-trained by unsupervised contrastive learning with challenging pairs (CLCP). We adopt two state-of-the-art methods: DivideMix [5] and ELR+ [41]. The experimental results on the two datasets are shown in Table 1 and Table 2 respectively.

**Table 1.** The test accuracy of different architectures with ResNet-34 on CIFAR-10 under different noise rates

| Method | 50% | 80% | 90% | asym-40% |
|---|---|---|---|---|
| ELR+ [41] | 94.2 | 92.6 | 76.3 | 92.2 |
| DivideMix [5] | 96.0 | 94.0 | 76.5 | 93.8 |
| ELR+ with CLCP | **96.2** | 93.5 | 88.6 | 93.9 |
| DivideMix with CLCP | 96.0 | **94.4** | **93.2** | **94.1** |

**Table 2.** The test accuracy of different architectures with ResNet-50 on CIFAR-100 under different noise rates

| Method | 20% | 50% | 80% | 90% | asym-40% |
|---|---|---|---|---|---|
| ELR+ [41] | 78.2 | 75.7 | 62.9 | 33.8 | 78.4 |
| DivideMix [5] | 77.7 | 74.8 | 61.8 | 31.0 | 73.3 |
| Augment-DivideMix [6] | 79.6 | 77.5 | 66.4 | 41.0 | **79.7** |
| C2D-DivideMix [7] | 80.9 | 79.5 | 71.5 | 64.1 | 77.8 |
| ELR+ with CLCP | 80.7 | 76.9 | 65.6 | 57.8 | 78.6 |
| DivideMix with CLCP | **81.0** | **80.1** | **72.3** | **66.2** | 77.7 |

As can be seen in Table 1 and Table 2, the proposed method surpasses the state-of-the-art counterparts under most of the noise rates. When the symmetric noise ratios are 50%, 80%, 90% together with the asymmetric noise, DivideMix with CLCP outperforms the other versions on CIFAR-10. And the increase become larger as the noise rate grows. The reason for this is the unsupervised contrastive learning ignoring the perturbation of noisy labels. Similar explanation also works on CIFAR-100 when there exists symmetric noise. As for the asymmetric noise, the proposed method has a 0.2% increase with ELR+, while get a improvement of 4.4% with DivideMix. The possible reason may be that DivideMix relies more on the warm-up phase than ELR+. And the asymmetric noise simulating the real-world is harder to process than symmetric noise, while the adoption of early stopping in ELR+ benefits the noisy label learning preventing the model from overfitting to the noise. In our opinion, the specified augmentation strategies counting for more situations may be closer to the real-world, thus are more beneficial to optimize DivideMix under the asymmetric noise. As a result of this, the specified augmentation [6] surpasses all other approaches under the asymmetric noise on CIFAR-100.

## 5    Conclusion

As noisy labels severely degrade the generalization performance of deep neural networks, learning from noisy labels is becoming an important task in modern deep learning applications. Existing methods failed to train a warm-up model whose target is to detect noisy labels. We proposed to solve the problem by getting rid of the labels and adopting unsupervised contrastive learning to obtain a high-quality feature extractor. In addition, we sought to improve the training by searching for challenging pairs by deploying adversarial attacks. The experimental results have shown that not only the performance of noisy label processing could be improved by the proposed method, but also the robustness increased as a result of the adversarial examples. The approach was well state-of-the-art methods. The proposed method outperformed most of the counterparts under different noise rates without introducing any external data.

## References

1. Kihyuk, S., et al.: FixMatch: simplifying Semi-Supervised Learning with Consistency and Confidence. In: Advances in Neural Information Processing Systems 2020, virtual (2020)
2. David, B., et al.: MixMatch: a holistic approach to semi-supervised learning. In: Advances in Neural Information Processing Systems 2019, pp. 5050–5060, Vancouver (2019)
3. Wen, L., et al.: WebVision Database: Visual Learning and Understanding from Web Data. CoRR abs/1708.02862 (2017)
4. Alina, K., et al.: The open images dataset V4: unified image classification, object detection, and visual relationship detection at scale. Int. J. Comput. Vision 128(7), 1956–1981 (2020)
5. Junnan, L., Richard, S., Steven, C.H.H.: DivideMix: learning with noisy labels as semi-supervised learning. In: 8th International Conference on Learning Representations, Addis Ababa (2020)

6. Kento, N., et al.: Augmentation strategies for learning with noisy labels. In: 2021 IEEE/CVF International Conference on Computer Vision, pp. 8022–8031, virtual (2021)
7. Evgenii, Z., et al.: Contrast to divide: self-supervised pre-training for learning with noisy labels. In: 2022 IEEE/CVF Winter Conference on Applications of Computer Vision, pp. 387–397, Waikoloa (2022)
8. Devansh, A., et al.: A closer look at memorization in deep networks. In: Proceedings of the 34th International Conference on Machine Learning, pp. 233–242, Sydney (2017)
9. Yingbin, B., et al.: Understanding and improving early stopping for learning with noisy labels. In: Advances in Neural Information Processing Systems 2021, pp. 24392–24403, virtual (2021)
10. Ting, C., et al.: A simple framework for contrastive learning of visual. In: Proceedings of the 37th International Conference on Machine Learning, pp. 1597–1607, virtual (2020)
11. Ting, C., et al.: Big self-supervised models are strong semi-supervised learners. In: Advances in Neural Information Processing Systems 2020, virtual (2020)
12. Xinlei, C., et al.: Improved Baselines with Momentum Contrastive Learning. CoRR abs/2003.04297 (2020)
13. Richard, Z., et al.: Split-brain autoencoders: unsupervised learning by cross-channel prediction. In: 2017 IEEE/CVF International Conference on Computer Vision, pp. 645–654, Honglulu (2017)
14. Kaiming, H., et al.: Momentum contrast for unsupervised visual representation learning. In: 2020 IEEE/CVF International Conference on Computer Vision, pp. 9726–9735, Seattle (2020)
15. Spyros, G., et al.: Unsupervised representation learning by predicting image rotations. In: 6th International Conference on Learning Representations, Vancouver (2018)
16. Prannay K. et al.: Supervised contrastive learning. In: Advances in Neural Information Processing Systems 2020, virtual (2020)
17. Olivier, J.H.: Data-efficient image recognition with contrastive predictive coding. In: Proceedings of the 37th International Conference on Machine Learning, pp. 4182–4192, virtual (2020)
18. Saining, X., et al.: PointContrast: unsupervised pre-training for 3D point cloud understanding. CoRR abs/2007.10985 (2020)
19. Nikunj, S., et al.: A theoretical analysis of contrastive unsupervised representation learning. In: Proceedings of the 36th International Conference on Machine Learning, pp. 5628–5637, Long Beach (2019)
20. Chih-Hui, H., Nino, V.: Contrastive learning with adversarial examples. In: Advances in Neural Information Processing Systems 2020, virtual (2020)
21. Anirban, C., et al.: Adversarial Attacks and Defences: A Survey. CoRR abs/1810.00069 (2018)
22. Cihang, X., Alan, L.Y.: Intriguing properties of adversarial training at scale. In: 8th International Conference on Learning Representations, Vancouver (2020)
23. Cihang, X., et al.: Adversarial examples improve image recognition. In: 2020 IEEE/CVF International Conference on Computer Vision, pp. 816–825, Seattle (2020)
24. Takeru, M., et al.: Virtual adversarial training: a regularization method for supervised and semi-supervised learning. IEEE Trans. Pattern Anal. Mach. Intell. **41**(8), 1979–1993 (2019)

25. Deepak, P., et al.: Context encoders: feature learning by inpainting. In: 2016 IEEE/CVF International Conference on Computer Vision, pp. 2536–2544, Las Vegas (2016)
26. Carl, D., Abhinav, G., Alexei, A.E.: Unsupervised visual representation learning by context prediction. In: 2015 IEEE International Conference on Computer Vision, pp. 1422–1430, Santiago (2015)
27. Spyros, G., Praveer, S., Nikos, K.: Unsupervised representation learning by predicting image rotations. In: 6th International Conference on Learning Representations, Vancouver (2018)
28. Alexander, K., Xiaohua, Z., Lucas, B.: Revisiting self-supervised visual representation learning. In: 2019 IEEE/CVF International Conference on Computer Vision, pp. 1920–1929, Long Beach (2019)
29. Ishan, M., Laurens van der M.: Self-supervised learning of pretext-invariant representations. In: 2020 IEEE/CVF International Conference on Computer Vision, pp. 6706–6716, Seattle (2020)
30. Yonglong, T., et al.: What makes for good views for contrastive learning? In: Advances in Neural Information Processing Systems 2020, virtual (2020)
31. Dan, H., et al.: Using trusted data to train deep networks on labels corrupted by severe noise. In: Advances in Neural Information Processing Systems 2018, pp. 10477–10486, Montréal (2018)
32. Filipe, R.C., Gustavo, C.: A survey on deep learning with noisy labels: how to train your model when you cannot trust on the annotations? In: 33rd SIBGRAPI Conference on Graphics, Patterns and Images, pp. 9–16, Recife/Porto de Galinhas (2020)
33. Lei, F., et al.: Can cross entropy loss be robust to label noise? In: Proceedings of the Twenty-Ninth International Joint Conference on Artificial Intelligence, pp. 2206–2212, Yokohama (2020)
34. Yang, L., Hongyi, G.: Peer loss functions: learning from noisy labels without knowing noise rates. In: Proceedings of the 37th International Conference on Machine Learning, pp. 6226–6236, virtual (2020)
35. Ehsan, A., et al.: Robust bi-tempered logistic loss based on bregman divergences. In: Advances in Neural Information Processing Systems 2019, pp. 14987–14996, Vancouver (2019)
36. Hongxin, W., et al.: Combating noisy labels by agreement: a joint training method with co-regularization. In: 2020 IEEE/CVF Conference on Computer Vision and Pattern Recognition, pp. 13723–13732, Seattle (2020)
37. Lu, J., et al.: MentorNet: learning data-driven curriculum for very deep neural networks on corrupted labels. In: Proceedings of the 35th International Conference on Machine Learning, pp. 2309–2318, Stockholmsmässanl (2018)
38. Bo, H., et al.: Co-teaching: robust training of deep neural networks with extremely noisy labels. In: Advances in Neural Information Processing Systems 2018, pp. 8527–8537, Montréal (2018)
39. Mingchen, L., Mahdi, S., Samet, O.: Gradient descent with early stopping is provably robust to label noise for overparameterized neural networks. In: The 23rd International Conference on Artificial Intelligence and Statistics, pp. 4313–4324 Online (Palermo, Sicily, Italy) (2020)
40. Xiaobo, X., et al.: Robust early-learning: hindering the memorization of noisy labels. In: 9th International Conference on Learning Representations, virtual (2021)
41. Sheng, L., et al.: Early-learning regularization prevents memorization of noisy labels. In: Advances in Neural Information Processing Systems 2020, virtual (2020)

42. Eric, A., et al.: Unsupervised label noise modeling and loss correction. In: Proceedings of the 36th International Conference on Machine Learning, pp. 312–321, Long Beach (2019)

43. Giorgio, P., et al.: Making deep neural networks robust to label noise: a loss correction approach approach. In: 2017 IEEE/CVF Conference on Computer Vision and Pattern Recognition, pp. 2233–2241, Honolulu (2017)

44. Kun Y., Jianxin W.: Probabilistic end-to-end noise correction for learning with noisy labels. In: 2019 IEEE/CVF Conference on Computer Vision and Pattern Recognition, pp. 7017–7025, Long Beach (2019)

45. Yongdong, K., et al.: Joint negative and positive learning for noisy labels. In: 2021 IEEE/CVF Conference on Computer Vision and Pattern Recognition, pp. 9442–9451, virtual (2021)

46. Lu, J., et al.: Beyond synthetic noise: deep learning on controlled noisy labels. In: Proceedings of the 37th International Conference on Machine Learning, pp. 4804–4815, virtual (2020)

# Semantic Center Guided Windows Attention Fusion Framework for Food Recognition

Yongxin Zhou, Jiale Chen, Xiong Zhang, Wenxiong Kang$^{(\boxtimes)}$, and Zeng Ming

South China University of Technology, Guangzhou, China
zhou_yongxin@outlook.com, {mschenjiale19,auzhangxiong}@mail.scut.edu.cn
{auwxkang,zengm}@scut.edu.cn

**Abstract.** Food recognition has attracted a great deal of attention in computer vision due to its potential applications for health and business. The challenge of food recognition is that food has no fixed spatial structure or common semantic patterns. In this paper, we propose a new semantic center guided window attention fusion framework (SCG-WAFM) for food recognition. The proposed Windows Attention Fusion Module (WAFM) utilizes the innate self-attention mechanism of Transformer to adaptively select the discriminative region without additional box annotation in training. The WAFM fuses the windows attention of Swin Transformer, crops the attention region from raw images and then scales up the region as the input of next network to iteratively learn discriminative features. In addition, the names of food categories contain important textual information, such as the major ingredients, cooking methods and so on, which are easily accessible and helpful for food recognition. Therefore, we propose Semantic Center loss Guidance(SCG) which utilizes the context-sensitive semantic embedding of food labels as category centers in feature space to guide the image features. We conduct extensive experiments on three popular food datasets and our proposed method achieves the state-of-the-art performance in Top-1 accuracy, demonstrating the effectiveness of our approach.

**Keywords:** Food recognition · Attention fusion · Context semantics · Transformer

## 1 Introduction

Food-related study has attracted more and more attention for its importance in people's lives and health. Understanding of food intake can help in personal diet management, nutritional analysis and so on, which is healthy for people. Automatical food recognition can enable a variety of business applications, such as mobile visual food diary [24], smart restaurants [1]. As the basic task in

**Supplementary Information** The online version contains supplementary material available at https://doi.org/10.1007/978-3-031-18910-4_50.

Cheesecake        Chocolate Cake        Carrot Cake

Spaghetti Bolognese    Spaghetti Carbonara

**Fig. 1.** Different foods with similar appearance

food applications, visual food recognition has made great progress with the rapid development of deep learning networks. Early food recognition approaches mostly extracted hand-crafted image features to classify. For example, Bossard et al. [2] exploited random forests to extract the discriminative features. In contrast, food recognition approaches based on convolutional neural networks [9,20] can capture discriminative features and have becoming prevalent solutions.

However, unlike the general recognition tasks, visual food recognition needs the fine-grained information to capture discriminative image representations for distinguishing sub-ordinate categories. Furthermore, foods do not have distinctive spatial configuration or fixed semantic pattern. As Fig. 1 shows, foods cooked in the same way have a similar appearance and foods vary greatly between different cooking methods, with few common semantic patterns and no similar structure. Therefore, the fine-grained recognition approaches based on fixed semantic pattern cannot well address visual food recognition.

In addition to visual information, food data is also rich in other modal information, such as ingredient [16,21], cooking recipes [26] and so on. Introducing such context information and external knowledge in training can mitigate the fine-grained recognition problem mentioned above and enhance the performance of food recognition. However, these approaches are always considered as laborious and hard to apply and promote in the general business scenarios for collecting the additional information.

In this work, we propose a semantic center guided windows attention fusion framework (SCG-WAFM). The proposed Windows Attention Fusion Module (WAFM) fuses the window multi-head self-attention of Swin Transformer [19] in different scales to adaptively locate the discriminative region. And then the region are scaled up and taken as the input of next fine-grained network to iteratively learn discriminative features. The WAFM address the issue of food without fixed spatial structure or common semantic patterns.

Furthermore, compared to other modal information, food names are more accessible and contain important textual information associated with food, such as principal ingredients, cooking methods and so on. Figure 1 shows similar food categories which are tough to distinguish only with image features and they differ in local details caused by different principal ingredients. However, the food names contain principal ingredients, such as carrot in "Carrot Cake", which we can use to generate context-sensitive embeddings to guide the network to focus on the corresponding local details. Therefore, we propose Semantic Center loss Guidance (SCG), which takes the semantic embeddings of food labels as the class centers in feature space and minimizes the distance between image features and semantic embeddings. The joint learning of semantic center loss and cross-entropy loss enables model to focus less on the non-essential ingredients of the food, improves the performance of food recognition and obtains more discriminative features.

Extensive experiments demonstrate that our proposed method achieves the state-of-the-art results in food recognition for Top-1 accuracy on three popular food images datasets (Food-101, VireoFood-172 and ChineseFoodNet datasets).

## 2   Related Work

### 2.1   Visual Food Recognition

Due to the rapid development of deep learning, visual food recognition has made great progress. Martinel et al. [20] proposed a slice convolution block in deep residual network to capture the common vertical structure from some food images. Qiu et al. [25] proposed PAR-Net to mine the significant regions of food images based on adversarial erasure method. Min et al. [23] proposed PRENet which adopts progressive training and self-attention to enhance local features.

In addition, introducing additional context information or external knowledge can also enhance the performance of food recognition, such as GPS, ingredient information, food recipes and so on. For example, Min et al. [21] designed an ingredient-guided cascaded multi-attention network (IG-CMAN), which utilized STN and LSTM to locate different scale image regions under both category-level and ingredient-level guidance. Jiang et al. [16] proposed a multi-scale multi-view feature aggregation (MSMVFA) scheme for food recognition, which incorporates both food images and ingredient information to aggregate different detail level features. However, these approaches using such additional information are not easy to apply and promote in the general food recognition as the collection is less cost-effective. Considering food names contains rich context information, Zhao et al. [30] proposed a semantic loss in their proposed framework by taking the distance of image features belong to different categories close to the distance of their corresponding class label semantic embeddings.

In this work, we propose a semantic center loss which guides transformer to learn the context-sensitive semantic embeddings of food labels by bringing the image feature close to the semantic embeddings.

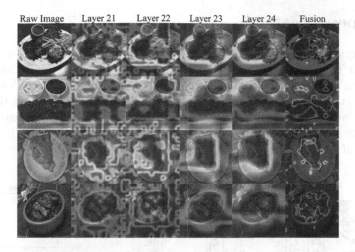

**Fig. 2.** Visualization results of self-attention weights from Swin Transformer. The first column is raw images, while from the second to fifth columns show the window attention maps of layers from 21 to 24 and the last column show the fusion attention map. Best viewed in color. (Color figure online)

## 2.2 Fine-Grained Image Recognition

There are two main directions for fine-grained classification recognition, end-to-end feature encoding and localization-classification sub-networks. Compared to the first way, the second one is able to obtain finer-grained information about key regions by the localization sub-networks to improve the classification performance. Some works of localization sub-networks [29] leveraged the extra annotations of bounding box in training, which are expensive and usually unavailable. The attention-based approach generates attention regions only with image-level annotations. For example, Fu et al. [8] proposed a recurrent attention convolutional network (RA-CNN), which is based on region attention sub-network to recursively learn discriminative regions.

ViT [7] has successfully applied transformer in computer vision, and makes transformer a hot research topic. ViT serializes images into patch tokens and utilizes self-attention mechanism to learn the correlation among patches. There are some works utilizing attentions of transformer in the fine-grained recognition. TransFG [10] integrates self-attention weights of ViT to focus on the target region by excluding non-target patches of the last transformer layer input. RAMS-Trans [13] measures the importance of the input patch tokens and recursively learn discriminative region attention in a multi-scale manner. However, the ViT-based approaches are limited by the fixed receptive field of the patch tokens to obtain finer-grained attention regions.

In this work, the proposed WAFM exploits the window attention weights of Swin Transformer [19] in different receptive fields, to adaptively extract more detailed target regions without the limit of fixed spatial structure or common semantic patterns.

## 3    Proposed Method

In this section, we elaborate on the SCG-WAFM framework. The framework takes Swin Transformer as backbone and the brief review of Swin Transformer can be seen in supplementary material. The WAFM fuses the windows multi-head self-attention weights of Swin Transformer to adaptively locate the target region. In addition, we propose semantic center loss to guide image features close to the semantic embeddings of food labels extracted by BERT. We take two stage of the framework in Fig. 3 as an example.

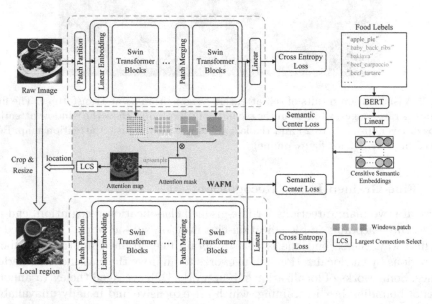

**Fig. 3.** The SCG-WAFM framework. The inputs of Swin Transformer are from full-size raw images to local region attention. The attention weights of Swin Transformer blocks are aggregated to attention mask matrix. In training, we joint cross-entropy loss and semantic center loss. Note that the patch partition, the swin transformer blocks and linear layers are parameter-sharing.

### 3.1    Windows Attention Fusion Module (WAFM)

Patch partition split an input RGB image ($H \times W$) in non-overlapping patches with a patch size of $4 \times 4$ and the feature dimension of each patch token is $4 \times 4 \times 3 = 48$. The linear embedding layer would project the feature to an arbitrary dimension. The framework of Swin Transformer can be seen in supplementary material.

Swin transformer blocks calculates self-attention of these patch tokens within windows. Each window takes the fixed number of patch tokens ($7 \times 7$ patch tokens per window). The total number of tokens is reduced by patch merging layers as the network gets deeper. Taking Swin-B model as example, the last two layers (layer 23, 24) take only one window to split the input feature map and calculate global self-attention which only focus on target region, the output resolutions is $\frac{H}{32} \times \frac{W}{32}$. Layers from 5 to 22 use 4 windows to split the input feature map which calculate local self-attention and their output resolution is $\frac{H}{16} \times \frac{W}{16}$, and similarly layers 1–2 and 3–4 use 64, 16 windows with the resolution of $\frac{H}{4} \times \frac{W}{4}$ and $\frac{H}{8} \times \frac{W}{8}$ respectively. As shown in Fig. 2, the local attention maps of the second, third column still focus on non-target objects and looks scattered over the whole image. Therefore, we propose to fuse the multi-head self-attention weights of each swin transformer block to mine the discriminative region attention, as shown in the attention map of Fig. 3. Based on the largest connection region of fusion attention map, we obtain the local region from the raw image. Finally, the local region is scaled up and inputs to the same network. The attention map generated by the WAFM based on the self-attention mechanism is able to adaptively select the most discriminative parts of food, excluding background and distractors.

The calculation of self-attention in window is the same as that of ViT, except that Swin Transformer adds the relative position bias $B \in \mathbb{R}^{M^2 \times M^2}$. We take out the window attention weights of each transformer layer as:

$$W_h^l = SoftMax(\frac{QK^T}{\sqrt{d}} + B) = [w_0, w_1, ..., w_{M^2-1}],$$

$$l \in [1, 2, ..., L], h \in [1, 2, ..., H], \tag{1}$$

$$w_p = [w_p^1, w_p^2, ..., w_p^k], \ p \in [0, 1, ..., M^2 - 1],$$

where $Q, K, V \in \mathbb{R}^{M^2 \times d}$ are Query, Key and Value matrix respectively. $d$ is the dimension of Key. $M^2$ is the patch number in a window. The relative position on each axis covers the range $[-M + 1, M - 1]$ and the values in $B$ is token from the parameterized variance matrix $\hat{B} \in \mathbb{R}^{(2M-1) \times (2M-1)}$. $l(L)$ denotes the index(total number) of swin transformer block. $h(H)$ denotes the index(total number) of windows in block. $p$ denotes the patch index in a window.

We integrate each patch's self-attention weights of k multi-head for each swin transformer block as

$$w_p = \frac{1}{k} \sum_{i=1}^{k} w_p^i, \tag{2}$$

We integrate and reshape all the windows of swin transformer block into the attention map and regularize the attention map as:

$$W^l = [W_0^l, ..., W_H^l],$$

$$G_l = \frac{W^l}{mean(W^l)}, \tag{3}$$

Then the fused attention map is computed as:

$$M = \prod_{l=1}^{L} G_l \tag{4}$$

We takes the mean value $\bar{M}$ over all the elements in $M$ as threshold to determine the target location. We propose a amplification factor $\gamma$ as a hyper-parameter to raise the threshold, which can improve the ability to further mine discriminative region. We extract the largest connected component of attention map $\hat{M}$ to locate and scale up the region attention in the raw image.

$$\hat{M}(x,y) = \begin{cases} 1 & if\ M(x,y) > \gamma\bar{M} \\ 0 & otherwise \end{cases} \tag{5}$$

where $\hat{M}(x,y)$ is the attention mask matrix and $(x,y)$ is the position.

### 3.2 Semantic Center Loss Guidance (SCG)

BERT [6] is a bidirectional transformers encoder that utilizes Masked Language Model (MLM) to pre-train model, alleviating the unidirectionality constraint, and BERT-based embeddings are context-sensitive. Food names contain important textual information on food, which can be considered as additional supervision information in training. We utilize BERT to extract context-sensitive semantic embeddings of the corresponding class label, as the class center in feature space to guide image feature.

The parameters of BERT are fixed in training and we consider the output of second last hidden layer as the semantic embedding $t$.

$$t = FC\left(\frac{1}{n}\sum_i^n e(y_i)\right) \tag{6}$$

where a sequence of tokens $\{y_1, y_2, ..., y_n\}$ from label $y$ denote the input of the transformer encoder BERT, $e(.)$ denotes the output of the second last hidden layer of BERT, $FC(.)$ denotes the trainable fully connected layer which makes the dimension of semantic embeddings same as the image features.

We consider that the semantic embeddings of labels extracted by BERT are in the same feature space as the image features extracted by Swin Transformer and they have a similar distribution since food labels are highly correlated with food images. In addition, BERT, pre-trained on large-scale text datasets, is able to extract the important information contained in the food labels. Therefore, we propose context-sensitive semantic center loss to align image feature $x_j$ to corresponding semantic embedding $t_j$ to learn key semantic information.

$$L_{sc} = \frac{1}{N}\sum_{j=1}^N \|x_j - t_j\|_2^2, \tag{7}$$

where $N$ denotes the batch size.

### 3.3 Implementation

We present our implementation details on loss function in training. Our loss function is formulated as multi-task loss consisting of classification loss and semantic center loss. We take the cross-entropy loss as classification loss.

$$L_{total} = \alpha(L_{cls1} + L_{cls2}) + \beta(L_{sc1} + L_{sc2}) \tag{8}$$

where $\alpha, \beta$ are the factors that balance the weight between classification loss and semantic center loss. $L_{cls1}$ denotes classification loss of first stage and $L_{cls2}$ denotes the guided loss which utilizes the WAFM to guide the model to mine the more discriminative regions. $L_{sc1(2)}$ denotes the context-sensitive semantic center loss of first(second) stage to guide the image feature close to the semantic embedding of the corresponding food label.

## 4 Experiments

### 4.1 Implementation Details

We load the model weights from the official Swin-B pre-trained on ImageNet-1k dataset. And we load the official pre-trained BERT [6] and MacBERT [5] to generate the semantic embeddings of English and Chinese labels, respectively. In training, the raw images are processed with random horizontal flips and color jitter, then randomly cropped and scaled to $224 \times 224$ as input. In inference, we resize the raw image to $224 \times 224$.

In all experiments, we train the model using the AdamW optimizer with the weight decay of 5e-2 and a mini-batch size of 24. We set 5 groups of learning rate, which are 2e-5, 1e-5, 5e-6, 1e-6 and 5e-7. The interval of learning rate change are 7, 8, 6 epochs for Food-101, VireoFood-172, ChineseFoodNet respectively.

We set the amplification factor $\gamma$ to 1.1 for the window attention fusion module and take two stage networks for the inference. The balance coefficient $\alpha, \beta$ are set to 0.6, 0.4 for the classification loss and the semantic center loss, respectively.

### 4.2 Experimental Results

Table 1 shows the overall results on the test sets. SCG denotes the semantic center loss guidance, which extracts the semantic embeddings of English labels, while SCG(Chinese) utilizes the Chinese labels. WAFM(wo train) indicates that WAFM is not involved in training and is just used in inference with $\gamma$ of 1. WAFM(first) denotes just using the prediction of the first stage in inference, while WAFM combines the predictions of two stages. The experiments demonstrate the power of SCG and WAFM for food recognition. Combining the two components yields better recognition performance. SCG-WAFM using the sum of two-stage predictions achieves 91.17%, 90.83%, 82.26% the Top-1 performance in Food-101, VireoFood-172 and ChineseFoodNet, with the improvements of 1.61%, 1.19% and 1.99% respectively, compared with the baseline. Then, we compare our proposed methods with recent state-of-the-art methods, including the basic classification networks and improved methods. As shown in Table 2,

**Table 1.** Experiment with different component

| Method | Food-101 | | VireoFood-172 | | ChineseFoodNet | |
|---|---|---|---|---|---|---|
| | Top-1 | Top-5 | Top-1 | Top-5 | Top-1 | Top-5 |
| Baseline | 89.56 | 98.26 | 89.64 | 98.36 | 80.27 | 96.34 |
| SCG | 90.06 | 98.35 | 89.71 | 98.44 | – | – |
| SCG (Chinese) | – | – | 90.04 | 98.41 | 81.0 | 96.70 |
| WAFM (wo train) | 90.11 | 98.31 | 90.53 | 98.54 | 81.04 | 96.58 |
| WAFM (first) | 89.92 | 98.36 | 89.87 | 98.3 | 80.55 | 96.50 |
| WAFM | 91.01 | 98.54 | 90.68 | 98.56 | 82.06 | 96.89 |
| SCG-WAFM (first) | 90.44 | 98.43 | 90.0 | 98.45 | 81.10 | 96.82 |
| SCG-WAFM | **91.17** | **98.66** | **90.83** | **98.71** | **82.26** | **97.07** |

**Table 2.** Performance comparison on Food-101 dataset

| Method | Top-1 | Top-5 | Method | Top-1 | Top-5 |
|---|---|---|---|---|---|
| AlexNet-CNN [2] | 56.40 | – | SGLANet (ISIA-500) [22] | 90.47 | 98.21 |
| DCNN-FOOD [9] | 70.41 | – | MSMVFA [16] | 90.59 | 98.25 |
| DeepFood [18] | 77.40 | 93.70 | PRENet [23] | 90.74 | 98.48 |
| Inception V3 [9] | 88.28 | 96.88 | PRENet (Food2K) [23] | 91.13 | 98.71 |
| ResNet-200 [11] | 88.38 | 97.85 | Gpipe [15] | 93.0 | – |
| DenseNet-161 [14] | 86.94 | 97.03 | EfficientNet-B7 [28] | 93.0 | – |
| WRN [20] | 88.72 | 97.92 | Swin Transformer [19] | 89.56 | 98.26 |
| WISeR [20] | 90.27 | 98.71 | SCG-WAFM | 91.17 | 98.66 |
| IG-CMAN [21] | 90.37 | 98.42 | Swin Transformer [19] | 92.65 | 98.98 |
| PAR-Net [25] | 89.30 | – | (ImageNet-22K) | | |
| SGLANet [22] | 89.69 | 98.01 | SCG-WAFM (ImageNet-22K) | **93.48** | **99.22** |

SCG-WAFM(ImageNet-22K) denotes the initial weights of model is from Swin-B pre-trained on ImageNet-22k. SCG-WAFM(ImageNet-22K) achieves the stat-of-the-art Top-1 performance, outperforms GPipe [15] which trains super-scale network and EfficientNet-B7 [28] which scales up network. As shown in Tables 3 and 4, SCG-WAFM, which loads the weights of Swin-B pre-trained on ImageNet-1k, also achieves the stat-of-the-art Top-1 results. The methods based on neural networks [16,21,23] need to use ingredient information to extract local details of food images layer by layer and fuse them with global features for recognition. In contrast, WAFM ia able to extract key region using the self-attention weight of Transformer without additional network structure, and SCG is able to further enhance the ability to focus on the main ingredients and reduce the interference of non-essential ingredients. SCG-WAFM combines the advantages of both methods and achieves state-of-the-art results in three datasets.

### 4.3 Ablation Studies

**Impact of Balance Factor $\alpha, \beta$ for SCG.** The hyperparameters $\alpha, \beta$ are multi-tasks factors to balance the weight between classification loss and semantic

**Table 3.** Performance comparison on VireoFood-172 dataset

| Method | Top-1 | Top-5 |
|---|---|---|
| AlexNet [17] | 64.91 | 85.32 |
| VGG-16 [27] | 80.41 | 94.59 |
| DenseNet-161 [14] | 86.93 | 97.17 |
| MTDCNN (VGG-16) [3] | 82.06 | 95.88 |
| MTDCNN (DenseNet-16) [3] | 87.21 | 97.29 |
| SENet-154 [12] | 88.71 | 97.74 |
| PAR-Net [25] | 89.60 | – |
| IG-CMAN [21] | 90.63 | 98.40 |
| MSMVFA [16] | 90.61 | 98.31 |
| SGLANet [22] | 89.88 | 97.83 |
| SGLANet (ISIA500) [22] | 90.78 | 98.16 |
| Swin Transformer [19] | 89.64 | 98.36 |
| SCG-WAFM | **90.83** | **98.71** |

**Table 4.** Performance comparison on ChineseFoodNet dataset

| Method | Top-1 | Top-5 |
|---|---|---|
| SqueezeNet [4] | 58.24 | 85.43 |
| VGG19-BN [4] | 79.22 | 95.99 |
| ResNet-152 [4] | 79.0 | 95.79 |
| DenseNet-201 [4] | 79.05 | 95.79 |
| DenseNet Fusion [4] | 80.47 | 96.26 |
| MultiCNN Fusion [4] | 81.55 | 96.76 |
| MSMVFA [16] (DenseNet-161) | 81.94 | 96.94 |
| Swin Transformer [19] | 80.27 | 96.34 |
| SCG-WAFM | **82.26** | **97.07** |

center loss. In order to analyze the effect of different combinations of $\alpha, \beta$, we set up 7 groups experiments. We experiment semantic center loss with English labels and Chinese labels in Food-101 and VireoFood-172 datasets, respectively. As we can seen from Tables 5 and 6, the experiments with factor $\alpha$ set to 0.6 and $\beta$ set to 0.4 work best in both food datasets.

**Impact of Food Labels Representation for SCG.** The official English labels provided by VireoFood-172 dataset are not accurate enough to describe Chinese food, for example, some of the foods use the same English name but their Chinese food names are different and more accurate. Thus, we translate the English labels into more accurate Chinese labels by ourselves, We set up 2 groups of parameters $\alpha, \beta$ to verify the validity of the accurate representation of food labels for semantic center loss (SCG). In Table 7, we can find that SCG using the Chinese labels boosts Top-1 accuracy more than the one using official English labels.

**Table 5.** Imapct of factor $\alpha, \beta$ with BERT on Food-101 dataset

| Approach | $\alpha$ | $\beta$ | Top-1 | Top-5 |
|---|---|---|---|---|
| Baseline | – | – | 89.56 | 98.26 |
| SCG | 1 | 1 | 89.76 | **98.37** |
| SCG | 0.4 | 0.6 | 89.8 | 98.28 |
| SCG | 0.5 | 0.5 | 89.84 | 98.27 |
| SCG | 0.6 | 0.4 | **90.06** | 98.35 |
| SCG | 0.7 | 0.3 | 89.97 | 98.34 |
| SCG | 0.8 | 0.2 | 89.96 | 98.31 |
| SCG | 0.9 | 0.1 | 89.94 | 98.33 |

**Table 6.** Impact of factor $\alpha, \beta$ with MacBERT on VireoFood-172 dataset

| Approach | $\alpha$ | $\beta$ | Top-1 | Top-5 |
|---|---|---|---|---|
| Baseline | – | – | 89.64 | 98.36 |
| SCG (Chinese) | 1 | 1 | 89.85 | 98.36 |
| SCG (Chinese) | 0.4 | 0.6 | 89.70 | 98.38 |
| SCG (Chinese) | 0.5 | 0.5 | 89.88 | 98.40 |
| SCG (Chinese) | 0.6 | 0.4 | **90.04** | 98.41 |
| SCG (Chinese) | 0.7 | 0.3 | 89.92 | **98.44** |
| SCG (Chinese) | 0.8 | 0.2 | 90.03 | 98.40 |
| SCG (Chinese) | 0.9 | 0.1 | 89.92 | 98.39 |

**Impact of Threshold $\gamma$ for WAFM.** The WAFM hyper-parameter $\gamma$ is the threshold to set up the size of discriminative target region. We set 5 groups of

**Table 7.** Impact of labels representation on VireoFood-172 dataset

| Approach | $\alpha$ | $\beta$ | Top-1 | Top-5 |
|---|---|---|---|---|
| Baseline | – | – | 89.64 | 98.36 |
| SCG (Chinese) | 0.6 | 0.4 | **90.04** | 98.41 |
| SCG (English) | 0.6 | 0.4 | 89.71 | 98.43 |
| SCG (Chinese) | 1 | 1 | 89.85 | 98.36 |
| SCG (English) | 1 | 1 | 89.79 | **98.44** |

experiments to investigate the effect of different value of $\gamma$ for food recognition performance. As shown in Table 8, we can get better accuracy with the sum predictions than the first prediction for the same parameters setting, indicating the complementary effect of the local region cropped by WAFM. And we can obtain the best Top-1 performance from the sum predictions of WAFM when the value of $\gamma$ is 1.1 and the Top-1 performance in general first increases and then decreases. When $\gamma$ is small, the WAFM will crop more regions resulting more non-critical region involved in the next stage, while when $\gamma$ is large, the input of next model will lose many critical region. Both of the above cases can lead to performance decreasing of food recognition, so it is important to choose the right threshold $\gamma$.

**Table 8.** Impact of $\gamma$ on Food-101 dataset

| Approach | $\gamma$ | First prediction | | Sum predictions | |
|---|---|---|---|---|---|
| | | Top-1 | Top-5 | Top-1 | Top-5 |
| Baseline | – | 89.56 | 98.26 | – | – |
| WAFM | 1 | 89.93 | 98.31 | 90.86 | 98.53 |
| WAFM | 1.1 | 89.92 | **98.36** | **91.01** | 98.54 |
| WAFM | 1.2 | 89.93 | 98.31 | 90.92 | 98.47 |
| WAFM | 1.3 | **89.97** | 98.28 | 90.76 | 98.48 |
| WAFM | 1.4 | 89.91 | 98.28 | 90.77 | **98.55** |

## 5    Conclusion

In this paper, we propose a new semantic center guided window attention fusion framework (SCG-WAFM) for food recognition. On the one hand, our proposed Semantic Center loss Guidance (SCG) utilizes the semantic embeddings of food labels as the class centers in feature space to guide the image representations. With the supervised learning utilizing joint semantic center loss and cross-entropy classification loss, the deeply learned features can greatly improve the performance of food recognition. On the other hand, our proposed Window

Attention Fusion Module (WAFM) is able to measure the importance of each pixel of the raw images and adaptively crop the discriminative region as the input of the next stage by fusing the inherent window attention weights of Swin Transformer. Through two stages of global-local complementary learning, WAFM can learn robust, discriminative features and highly enhance the performance of food recognition. SCG-WAFM combines the advantages of both proposed approaches and achieves the state-of-the-art results in Food101, VireoFood172 and ChineseFoodNet datasets.

# References

1. Aguilar, E., Remeseiro, B., Bolaños, M., Radeva, P.: Grab, pay, and eat: semantic food detection for smart restaurants. IEEE Trans. Multim. **20**(12), 3266–3275 (2018)
2. Bossard, L., Guillaumin, M., Van Gool, L.: Food-101 – mining discriminative components with random forests. In: Fleet, D., Pajdla, T., Schiele, B., Tuytelaars, T. (eds.) ECCV 2014. LNCS, vol. 8694, pp. 446–461. Springer, Cham (2014). https://doi.org/10.1007/978-3-319-10599-4_29
3. Chen, J., Ngo, C.W.: Deep-based ingredient recognition for cooking recipe retrieval. In: Proceedings of the 24th ACM International Conference on Multimedia, pp. 32–41 (2016)
4. Chen, X., Zhu, Y., Zhou, H., Diao, L., Wang, D.: Chinesefoodnet: A large-scale image dataset for Chinese food recognition. arXiv preprint arXiv:1705.02743 (2017)
5. Cui, Y., Che, W., Liu, T., Qin, B., Wang, S., Hu, G.: Revisiting pre-trained models for chinese natural language processing. arXiv preprint arXiv:2004.13922 (2020)
6. Devlin, J., Chang, M.W., Lee, K., Toutanova, K.: Bert: pre-training of deep bidirectional transformers for language understanding. In: NAACL (2019)
7. Dosovitskiy, A., et al.: An image is worth 16x16 words: transformers for image recognition at scale. arXiv preprint arXiv:2010.11929 (2021)
8. Fu, J., Zheng, H., Mei, T.: Look closer to see better: recurrent attention convolutional neural network for fine-grained image recognition. In: 2017 IEEE Conference on Computer Vision and Pattern Recognition (CVPR), pp. 4476–4484 (2017)
9. Hassannejad, H., Matrella, G., Ciampolini, P., De Munari, I., Mordonini, M., Cagnoni, S.: Food image recognition using very deep convolutional networks. In: Proceedings of the 2nd International Workshop on Multimedia Assisted Dietary Management, pp. 41–49 (2016)
10. He, J., et al.: Transfg: a transformer architecture for fine-grained recognition. arXiv preprint arXiv:2103.07976 (2021)
11. He, K., Zhang, X., Ren, S., Sun, J.: Deep residual learning for image recognition. In: 2016 IEEE Conference on Computer Vision and Pattern Recognition (CVPR), pp. 770–778 (2016)
12. Hu, J., Shen, L., Sun, G.: Squeeze-and-excitation networks. In: Proceedings of the IEEE Conference on Computer Vsion and Pattern Recognition, pp. 7132–7141 (2018)
13. Hu, Y., et al.: Rams-trans: recurrent attention multi-scale transformer for fine-grained image recognition. In: Proceedings of the 29th ACM International Conference on Multimedia, pp. 4239–4248 (2021)

14. Huang, G., Liu, Z., Weinberger, K.Q.: Densely connected convolutional networks. In: 2017 IEEE Conference on Computer Vision and Pattern Recognition (CVPR), pp. 2261–2269 (2017)

15. Huang, Y., et al.: Gpipe: efficient training of giant neural networks using pipeline parallelism. Adv. Neural Inf. Process. Syst. **32** (2019)

16. Jiang, S., Min, W., Liu, L., Luo, Z.: Multi-scale multi-view deep feature aggregation for food recognition. IEEE Trans. Image Process. **29**, 265–276 (2019)

17. Krizhevsky, A., Sutskever, I., Hinton, G.E.: Imagenet classification with deep convolutional neural networks. Commun. ACM **60**, 84–90 (2012)

18. Liu, C., Cao, Y., Luo, Y., Chen, G., Vokkarane, V., Ma, Y.: DeepFood: deep learning-based food image recognition for computer-aided dietary assessment. In: Chang, C.K., Chiari, L., Cao, Y., Jin, H., Mokhtari, M., Aloulou, H. (eds.) ICOST 2016. LNCS, vol. 9677, pp. 37–48. Springer, Cham (2016). https://doi.org/10.1007/978-3-319-39601-9_4

19. Liu, Z., et al.: Swin transformer: Hierarchical vision transformer using shifted windows. In: 2021 IEEE/CVF International Conference on Computer Vision (ICCV), pp. 9992–10002 (2021)

20. Martinel, N., Foresti, G.L., Micheloni, C.: Wide-slice residual networks for food recognition. In: 2018 IEEE Winter Conference on applications of computer vision (WACV), pp. 567–576. IEEE (2018)

21. Min, W., Liu, L., Luo, Z., Jiang, S.: Ingredient-guided cascaded multi-attention network for food recognition. In: Proceedings of the 27th ACM International Conference on Multimedia, pp. 1331–1339 (2019)

22. Min, W., et al.: ISIA food-500: a dataset for large-scale food recognition via stacked global-local attention network. In: Proceedings of the 28th ACM International Conference on Multimedia, pp. 393–401 (2020)

23. Min, W., et al.: Large scale visual food recognition. arXiv preprint arXiv:2103.16107 (2021)

24. Myers, A., et al.: Im2calories: towards an automated mobile vision food diary. In: 2015 IEEE International Conference on Computer Vision (ICCV), pp. 1233–1241 (2015)

25. Qiu, J., Lo, F.P.W., Sun, Y., Wang, S., Lo, B.P.L.: Mining discriminative food regions for accurate food recognition. In: British Machine Vision Association (BMVC) (2019)

26. Salvador, A., Hynes, N., Aytar, Y., Marín, J., Ofli, F., Weber, I., Torralba, A.: Learning cross-modal embeddings for cooking recipes and food images. In: 2017 IEEE Conference on Computer Vision and Pattern Recognition (CVPR), pp. 3068–3076 (2017)

27. Szegedy, C., et al.: Going deeper with convolutions. In: 2015 IEEE Conference on Computer Vision and Pattern Recognition (CVPR), pp. 1–9 (2015)

28. Tan, M., Le, Q.: Efficientnet: rethinking model scaling for convolutional neural networks. In: International Conference on Machine Learning, pp. 6105–6114. PMLR (2019)

29. Wei, X.S., Xie, C.W., Wu, J.: Mask-CNN: localizing parts and selecting descriptors for fine-grained image recognition. arXiv preprint arXiv:1605.06878 (2016)

30. Zhao, H., Yap, K.H., Kot, A.C.: Fusion learning using semantics and graph convolutional network for visual food recognition. In: 2021 IEEE Winter Conference on Applications of Computer Vision (WACV), pp. 1710–1719 (2021)

# Adversarial Bidirectional Feature Generation for Generalized Zero-Shot Learning Under Unreliable Semantics

Guowei Yin[1], Yijie Wang[1], Yi Zhang[1], and Sheng Huang[1,2(✉)]

[1] School of Big Data and Software Engineering, Chongqing University, Chongqing, China
{yinguowei,wyj,zhangyii,huangsheng}@cqu.edu.cn
[2] Ministry of Education Key Laboratory of Dependable Service Computing in Cyber Physical Society, Chongqing, China

**Abstract.** Although extensive methods have been proposed for Generalized Zero-shot Learning (GZSL), studies are still scarce for GZSL with unreliable data, which is a common issue in real circumstances. In this paper, we introduce a new problem of Generalized Zero-shot Learning with Unreliable Semantics (GZSL-US), based on which we study the GZSL under the partially ambiguous or even missing semantics. To address such a problem, we present a unified generative framework named Adversarial Bidirectional Feature Generation (ABFG), which introduces two extra operations, namely Bidirectional Matching (BM) and Adversary Injection (AI), to the basic generation process. The BM is to guarantee the consistency of the visual and semantic spaces by matching them with a learned metric, which alleviates the domain bias problem in GZSL. Meanwhile, AI is not only introduced for further exploiting the sampling space, but also for endowing the model with a strong resistance ability to semantic interference. The experimental results of Generative Adversarial Network (GAN)-based and Variational AutoEncoder (VAE)-based ABFG instances on four popular benchmarks not only prove the superior robustness of ABFG to the unreliable semantics but also demonstrate the encouraging GZSL performances in comparison with the state-of-the-arts.

**Keywords:** Generalized zero-shot learning · Generative model · Adversarial attack · Object recognition · Robustness analysis

## 1 Introduction

Transfer learning has been widely concerned by the machine learning community, since it adopts the knowledge-driven fashion for realizing the intelligence

---

**Supplementary Information** The online version contains supplementary material available at https://doi.org/10.1007/978-3-031-18910-4_51.

which is more like the ones of human beings. Zero-shot Learning (ZSL), as a typical transfer learning problem, aims to transfer the knowledge learned on source domain to target domain which denote as seen and unseen domains separately. As illustrated in Fig. 1, compared with other knowledge transfer tasks, *e.g.* Domain Adaptation, there is no class overlap between the source and target domains in ZSL. This is why ZSL is also known as a "Hard Knowledge Transfer" problem. In order to achieve such knowledge transfer, ZSL employs class-level intermediate semantic representation, such as attributes or word embedding, as the knowledge transfer vehicle between seen and unseen classes. Assisted by such semantic representations, plenty of impressive approaches [6,8,31,37,40] have been proposed for tackling ZSL task. Among these methods, the generative approach is currently the most potential one which enjoys the good generalization ability to unseen classes due to the fact that the generative approaches, *e.g.* Variational Auto-Encoder (VAE) based or Generative Adversarial Network (GAN) based methods, can well model the intrinsic distribution of data.

Despite of the outstanding performances of those generative methods, there are rare studies that investigate the robustness of proposed models to the contaminative or unreliable semantics. However such an issue is very common in the wild particularly for the semantics of the rare objects. For example, the dinosaur is deemed as a featherless animal in many early archaeological works while many recent works indicate that quite a lot of dinosaurs have the feathers which leads to the ambiguous semantic descriptions of the dinosaur. Recent studies [28] on Adversarial Attack indicates that the deep learning model is very frail to the small perturbation of input. These discoveries imply that the current deep learning-based ZSL approaches are very sensitive

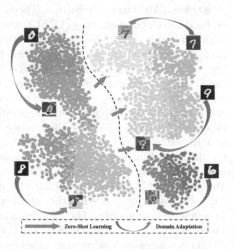

**Fig. 1.** The concept of "Hard Knowledge Transfer" problem (MNIST). Compared with Domain Adaptation which transfer knowledge among intra-class samples, the domains among which knowledge are transferred in Zero-shot Learning are exclusive.

to the semantic noise and the unreliable semantics will clearly lead to the unreliable knowledge transfer. Although the existing ZSL approaches are susceptible to interference due to the inherent characteristics of neural networks, the good news is that the disturbed samples elaborated by the aforementioned adversarial attack approaches have been proven effective to improve the performance and robustness of neural networks [13,35,36], which provides us a possible way to improve the robustness of ZSL.

In this paper, we intend to introduce the Generalized Zero-Shot Learning with Unreliable Semantics (GZSL-US) task formally and investigate it more systematically. We design two types of semantic noise attacks, namely semantic noise and semantic absence, for simulating the semantic unreliability in reality. In order to improve the robustness to these attacks in GZSL, we propose a novel generative framework named Adversarial Bidirectional Feature Generation (ABFG). It introduces the adversarial attack into the generative GZSL models for acquiring the adversarial samples which effectively simulates the different types of fatal data interference, and then trains the generative model with these adversarial samples to gain its robustness to the unreliable semantics. Moreover, an additional network is also introduced for bidirectionally aligning between semantic and visual spaces. Such a bidirectional generation part not only enriches the representational ability of visual feature that may indirectly benefit the model robustness, but also alleviate the domain shift problem between seen and unseen spaces. We validate ABFG on four popular ZSL datasets under our elaborately designed robustness evaluation metric. The experimental results not only show the strong robustness of our proposed framework to the unreliable semantics, but also indicate that ABFG can generally improve the GZSL performances of generative models.

In summary, the main contributions of our study are:

- We formally introduce a very meaningful in reality, but long-neglected issue in GZSL named Generalized Zero-Shot Learning with Unreliable Semantics which studies the GZSL under different types of semantic unreliability.
- To tackle GZSL-US, we develop a novel generative framework named Adversarial Bidirectional Feature Generation (ABFG), which employs adversarial attacks for improving the robustness of the generative models and the bidirectional generation for alleviating the domain shift. The experimental results show that the proposed ABFG not only improves the robustness of the model, but also improves the performance the model in GZSL tasks.
- We elaborately design an evaluation protocol for GZSL-US which includes the unreliable semantics generation strategy and the GZSL robustness evaluation metric. It is the first work that systematically and quantitatively analyzes the robustness of GZSL to the unreliable or noisy semantics.

## 2    Related Work

### 2.1    Zero-Shot Learning

Zero-shot Learning (ZSL) aims to predict the classes of unseen objects. In ZSL, the categories of training and testing data are not overlapped, so we need to produce intermediate representation, such as manually annotated attributes and word embeddings learned on text corpus, for transferring knowledge among these classes. Existing GZSL approaches mainly fall into two categories: embedding approaches [6,8,37] and generative approaches [12,22,31,40]. Embedding approaches address GZSL by learning an embedding space where the compatibility of visual features and semantic representations can be well measured. Such embedding space can be the semantic space [8], the visual space [37] or a common latent space [6]. Inspired by the recent remarkable success of Generative Adversarial Network (GAN) [20,21] and Variational AutoEncoder (VAE) [22], the generative approaches are advanced rapidly over recent years [12,15,22,31,40]. For example, Xian et al. [31] leveraged Wasserstein GAN (WGAN) [20] to synthesize visual features for unseen classes based on the attributes and then the GZSL task was considered as a normal classification issue for solution. Generally speaking, generative approaches often perform much better than embedding approaches particularly in the generalization ability to unseen classes.

## 2.2  Adversarial Attack

Szegedy *et al.* [28] discover that CNN is highly vulnerable to attack, which fueled the development of numerous techniques to attack deep visual models. According to the knowledge of attackers, there are generally two categories of threat models in the literature [4]. One is white-box settings where attackers acquire full access to the victim model, it enjoys great popularity among early work on attacking DNNs [5,9,16,28]. Different from the process of model training, they feature an optimization in input space to elevate training loss, such as Fast Gradient Sign Method (FGSM) [9], Basic Iterative Method (BIM) [16], and Projected Gradient Descent (PGD) [19].

However, white-box attacks hardly reflect the threat to models in practice since only query access is allowed in most realistic cases. Therefore, black-box attacks have attracted increasing attention recently. There are roughly two sorts of black-box attacks according to the mechanism they adopt. Query-based black-box attacks [3,10,25] can settle the susceptible direction of the victim model as per the response of the target model to given inputs [10], which usually require excessive queries before a successful trial. Transfer-based black-box attacks [7, 18,23,32,38] first launch attacks on off-the-shelf local models to which they have white-box access. Then the deceptive samples are directly transferred to fool the remote victim model. Therefore, transfer-based attackers can apply any white-box attack algorithm in this task, such as FGSM and BIM.

## 3  Methodology

### 3.1  Problem Definitions

In the context of zero-shot learning, there are two sets of classes $\mathcal{C}^s = \{c_i^s\}_{i=1}^{k_s}$ and $\mathcal{C}^u = \{c_i^u\}_{i=1}^{k_u}$, which represent seen and unseen classes respectively and satisfy $\mathcal{C}^s \cap \mathcal{C}^u = \emptyset$. For the exclusiveness of seen and unseen classes, the class-level semantic representations $\mathcal{V} = \{v_i\}_{i=1}^{k^s+k^u}$ are required for knowledge transfer.

**GZSL:** Let $\mathcal{S} = \{(x_i^s, y_i^s, v_i^s)\}_{i=1}^{N^s}$ be the labeled instance collection from $\mathcal{C}^s$ for training, where $N^s$ is the number of instance, $x_i^s \in \mathbb{R}^d$ is an image instance associated with its class label $y_i^s$ and its corresponding semantic representation $v^s$. In addition, the class label and corresponding semantic representation $\mathcal{U} = \{(y_i^u, v_i^u)\}_{i=1}^{k_u}$ from $C^u$ are also accessible in training stage. The goal of GZSL is devise a classifier $f : x \rightarrow y$ which is only trained on $\mathcal{S} \cup \mathcal{U}$ but capable to classify images from both seen $\mathcal{C}^s$ and unseen $\mathcal{C}^u$.

**GZSL-US:** In the existing GZSL approaches, all the used semantics are considered as the clean and completed ones as is the custom. However, the unseen classes are often the rarely observed objects who are difficult to semantically depicted in an accurate way. Consequently, the semantics of these categories may be ambiguous or even partially absence which are all referred to as the unreliable semantics by us. In such a manner, to study the GZSL under Unreliable Semantics (GZSL-US) is very meaningful task in real world scenarios. In the unreliable semantic representation setting, the semantic representation for unseen classes are partially missing $\mathcal{V}^m = \{v_i^m\}_{i=k^s+1}^{k^s+k^u}$ or noised $\mathcal{V}^n = \{v_i^n\}_{i=k^s+1}^{k^s+k^u}$ which increases the difficulty for knowledge transfer. We denote the derived unreliable $\mathcal{U}$ for training as $\mathcal{U}^{m|n}$. Same to the GZSL, GZSL-US aims to learn a classifier $f : x \rightarrow y$ which is trained on $\mathcal{S} \cup \mathcal{U}^{m|n}$ for recognizing the objects from both seen $\mathcal{C}^s$ and unseen $\mathcal{C}^u$.

## 3.2   Adversarial Bidirectional Feature Generation

In this section, we intend to introduce a concise but effective framework named Adversarial Bidirectional Feature Generation (ABFG) for generally endowing the generative GZSL approaches with the resistance ability to the unreliable semantics and further improving their GZSL performances. ABFG introduces the adversarial injection in model training step and an extra bidirectional generation module for achieving the aforementioned goals.

**Adversary Injection.** In the process of solving the zero-shot learning problem, the transfer of knowledge relies on additional descriptions of the dataset to complete the construction of the unknown data space. However, in the condition of unreliable semantics, the additional descriptions of unknown data is undependable, which means that when exploring the unknown data space, the additional description of the dataset will no longer be reliable.

Because of no reliable inference information supplied during the testing phase, the direct impact of which is that we may not be able to construct a true data representation during the testing phase. In the process of our consideration about the GZSL-US problem, a feasible method is to directly train the model during the training process to adapt to this learning process with lack of support information. In fact, this idea is feasible. On the one hand, we know that there is some redundancy in the existing category annotations. When the missing category descriptions are to some extent keep the key information retained, we can still make a relatively accurate distinction. On the other hand, when we add this kind of information-missing learning to

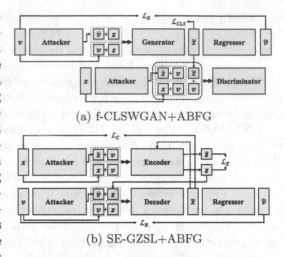

(a) f-CLSWGAN+ABFG

(b) SE-GZSL+ABFG

**Fig. 2.** The plus version of f-CLSWGAN and SE-GZSL with Adversarial Bidirectional Feature Generation framework assistance. In the training stage, only one space will be attacked and one combination of visual and semantic features are selected, which represents in same color (red or blue rectangle), for forward pass. The dot-starter arrow represents the selection of one combination. Better viewed in color. (Color figure online)

the training process, compared to pure category representation, we can make our model explore richer semantic representation (draw a picture, a single semantic representation only focuses on one point, and after interference, it also explores the surroundings of that point), to achieve a more detailed mapping between semantics and vision.

To incorporate the learning with support information absence into training, we introduce the Adversarial Attack into GZSL problem which can simulate the process effectively and give out the intuitive explanation of how each of them boost the robustness.

**Semantic:** Intuitively, the simplest way to simulate the unreliability of semantic representation is directly incorporate it into the training stage. Therefore, we conduct adversarial perturbation calculations in the semantic space for the training process to simulate the unreliable situations encountered in the test.

**Visual:** Compared with directly attacking the semantic space to simulate the testing process, another attack view is to start from the visual space to indirectly expand the model's ability to deal with semantic interference. The calculation of adversarial samples in the visual space can realize a more extensive exploration of the visual features of the same category, so as to realize the complete perception of the category.

**Bidirectional Generation.** The domain shift problem is an inevitable problem of GZSL, since the trained model is often more inclined to classify the unknown samples as seen classes in the inference stage. A lot of recent work has realized that if we perform a mapping of *visual* → *semantic* parallel with the *semantic* → *visual* generation, this problem can be mitigated well.

In our ABFG framework, the bidirectional matching are also conducted between semantic and visual spaces to realize the discrimination for unknown data. Specifically, as depicted in Fig. 2(a), we add a semantic regressor $R(·)$ which map the visual features generated by generator to the semantic space:

$$\hat{v} = R(G(z, v; \theta_G); \theta_R), \tag{1}$$

where the $\theta_G$ and $\theta_R$ refers to the parameters of generator and regressor.

### 3.3 Instances

In order to verify the efficacy of our proposed ABFG framework for solving the GZSL-US problem, we select f-CLSWGAN (cGAN-based) [31] and SE-GZSL (cVAE-based) [15] as representative for testing. Before giving the specific calculation process, we first explain the definitions and formula of selected attack algorithms.

**Adversaries.** While there are assorted attack algorithms, we choose FGSM proposed in the pioneer research [9] and PGD [19], for the effectiveness and simplicity of validation.

- **Fast Gradient Sign Method (FGSM)** The goal of FGSM is to fool the classification of the input by adding an unnoticeably small vector. The entries of the vector are computed by taking the sign of the gradient of the loss function associated with input feature. It is demonstrated that this method reliably misclassifies the model's input.
- **Projected Gradient Descent (PGD)** Recent work [19] on adversarial attack has shown that Projected Gradient Descent (PGD) is a universal adversary among first-order approaches. Given the visual feature and label pairs $(x, y)$ from training data, PGD computes adversarial perturbation $\delta$ by solving:

$$\delta = \underset{\|\delta\|_\infty \le \delta_{max}}{\arg\max} \ \mathcal{L}(N_\theta(x + \delta, y)), \tag{2}$$

where $N(·)$ is the network parameterized by $\theta$ and $\delta_{max}$ is the given upper bound of $\delta$.

**F-CLSWGAN with ABFG.** As depicted in Fig. 2(a), f-CLSWGAN is one of the GAN-based generative GZSL approaches which adopt conditional Wasserstein GAN as the basis for generation:

$$\mathcal{L}_{WGAN} = \mathbb{E}[D(x, v)] - \mathbb{E}[D(\tilde{x}, v)] - \lambda \mathbb{E}[(\| \nabla_{\tilde{x}} D(\hat{x}, v)\|_2 - 1)^2], \tag{3}$$

where $\tilde{x} = G(z, v)$, $\hat{x} = \alpha x + (1 - \alpha)\tilde{x}$ with $\alpha \sim U(0, 1)$, and $\lambda$ is the penalty coefficient.

In the core of f-CLSWGAN, there is an additional classifier attached to WGAN which encourages the generator to construct features that can be correctly classified by a discriminative classifier trained on the input data:

$$\mathcal{L}_{CLS} = -\mathbb{E}[P(y|\tilde{x}; \theta)], \tag{4}$$

where $\tilde{x} = G(z, v)$, $y$ is the class label of $\tilde{x}$, $P(y|\tilde{x}; \theta)$ denotes the probability of $\tilde{x}$ being predicted with its true class label $y$.

We also perform *visual → semantic* decoding, $R(\cdot)$, which can be deemed as the semantic representation generation step based on the generated features. The cosine similarity is adopted for measuring the similarity,

$$\mathcal{L}_R = \frac{1}{N} \sum_{i=1}^{N} \frac{c(y_i)^T \cdot \tilde{c}(y_i)}{\|c(y_i)\| \cdot \|\tilde{c}(y_i)\|}, \tag{5}$$

where $\tilde{c}(y_i) = R(\tilde{x}_i)$ is the decoded version of $c(y_i)$.

The full objective of f-CLSWGAN becomes:

$$\min_G \max_D \mathcal{L}_{WGAN} + \mathcal{L}_{CLS} + \mathcal{L}_R. \tag{6}$$

**SE-GZSL with ABFG.** For the VAE-based GZSL approaches, we select SE-GZSL as the test base which is depicted in Fig. 2(b). The basic conditional VAE consists of the conditional decoder(generator) $p_G(x|z, a)$, which are responsible for generating the exemplars that will subsequently be used to train the final classifier. Denoting the VAE encoder as $p_E(z|x)$, and the VAE loss function is given by:

$$\mathcal{L}_{VAE}(\theta_E, \theta_G) = -\mathbb{E}[\log p_G(x|z, a)] + KL(p_E(z|x)\|p(z)). \tag{7}$$

In the structure of SE-GZSL, except the core VAE process, there is an extra regressor. While the trained VAE performing the final unseen visual sample generation, the regressor plays the exactly same function as the bidirectional matching of our ABFG which learns to map the visual samples (real/generative) to its corresponding semantic vector:

$$\min_\theta \mathcal{L}_R = \mathcal{L}_{Sup} + \lambda_R \cdot \mathcal{L}_{Unsup}. \tag{8}$$

The $\mathcal{L}_{Sup}$ refers to the loss for real visual samples while $\mathcal{L}_{Unsup}$ means the loss for generated visual samples. The $\lambda_R$ is the compensation coefficient.

Since the addition of regressor, the generation cost for VAE becomes different to standard cVAE. The cost now consists of four parts rather than traditional two portions of KL divergence and reconstruction loss:

$$\min_{\theta_G, \theta_E} \mathcal{L}_{VAE} + \lambda_c \cdot \mathcal{L}_c + \lambda_{reg} \cdot \mathcal{L}_{Reg} + \lambda_Z \cdot \mathcal{L}_Z. \tag{9}$$

The $\mathcal{L}_c$ simply assumes that the regressor has optimal parameters and any reason for it not regressing to the correct value is because of the poor generation by the generator:

$$\mathcal{L}_c = -\mathbb{E}[\log p_R(a|\hat{x})], \tag{10}$$

which encourages the generator to create samples such that the regressed attribute vector by the regressor is correct. The $\mathcal{L}_{Reg}$ is added which acts as a regularizer that encourages the generator to generate a good class-specific sample:

$$\mathcal{L}_{Reg} = -\mathbb{E}[\log p_G(\hat{x}|z, a)]. \tag{11}$$

Additionally, SE-GZSL also enforce the independence of the unstructured component $z$ from the class-attribute $a$ which realized by ensuring that the sampling distribution and the one obtained from the generated exemplar follow the same distribution:

$$\mathcal{L}_Z = -KL[p_E(z|\hat{x})\|q(z)]. \tag{12}$$

**Classification.** While the semantic representation for unseen classes are genuine in GZSL setting, in GZSL-US they are assumed unreliable. We design two manually disturbance for unseen semantic representations: semantic noise (contamination) $v^n$ and semantic absence (missing) $v^m$, to simulate the unreliability.

For the setting of semantic absence, we randomly zero out the original semantic representation according to the given ratio that can effectively simulate the situation of information lost. Besides, we use semantic noise to simulate the information distortion. Similar to the semantic absence, we perform random Gaussian interference on the semantic representation according to a given ratio.

The test seen data coupled with the generated unseen samples are used for supervised multi-class classification training. Specifically, we adopt softmax classifier for simplicity and fair comparison with other generative approaches. The standard softmax classifier minimizes the negative log likelihood loss:

$$\min_\theta -\frac{1}{|T|} \sum_{(x,y)\in T} \log P(y|x; \theta), \tag{13}$$

where $\theta$ is the weight matrix of a fully connected layer which maps the image feature $x$ to $K$ unnormalized probabilities with $K$ being the number of classes.

# 4   Experiments

## 4.1   Datasets

**Datasets.** We conduct our experiments on four widely used datasets, including Caltech-UCSD-Birds 200-2011 (**CUB**) [29], SUN attributes (**SUN**) [26], Oxford

Flowers (**FLO**) [24], and Animals with Attributes 2 (**AWA2**) [30]. More details about dataset settings and implementation details can be found in Supplementary Material.

### 4.2 Criteria

**GZSL.** In the GZSL setting, after having computed the average per-class top-1 accuracy on seen and unseen classes, we compute the harmonic means of them:

$$H = \frac{2 * S * U}{S + U}. \tag{14}$$

**GZSL-US.** Under the discussion of the performance for GZSL-US, the semantic representation for unseen classes are disturbed before used to generate unseen samples which will further utilized to train the multi-class classifier. When it comes to the disturbance strength, we apply 6 level of disturbance: 0%, 10%, 20%, 30%, 40%, 50%. Then we compute the per-class top-1 accuracy under these 6 disturbance strength separately for seen and unseen test classes in which the computation are keep same with the standard GZSL:

$$H^{usr} = \frac{2 * S^{usr} * U^{usr}}{S^{usr} + U^{usr}}, \tag{15}$$

where the *usr* superscript denotes unreliable semantic representations.

**Table 1.** Comparisons with the state-of-the-art GZSL methods. U and S are the Top-1 accuracies tested on unseen classes and seen classes, respectively, in GZSL. H is the harmonic mean of U and S. The bold ones indicate the best results.

| Methods | | CUB | | | SUN | | | FLO | | | AWA2 | | |
|---|---|---|---|---|---|---|---|---|---|---|---|---|---|
| | | U | S | H | U | S | H | U | S | H | U | S | H |
| Embedding | DeViSE [8] | 23.8 | 53.0 | 32.8 | 16.9 | 27.4 | 20.9 | 9.9 | 44.2 | 16.2 | 17.1 | 74.7 | 27.8 |
| | SJE [1] | 23.5 | 52.9 | 33.6 | 14.7 | 30.5 | 19.8 | 13.9 | 47.6 | 21.5 | 8.0 | 73.9 | 14.4 |
| | SYNC [6] | 11.5 | 70.9 | 19.8 | 7.9 | 43.3 | 13.4 | 7.4 | 66.3 | 13.3 | 10.0 | 90.5 | 18.0 |
| | SAE [14] | 7.8 | 54.0 | 13.6 | 8.8 | 18.0 | 11.8 | – | – | – | 1.1 | 82.2 | 2.2 |
| | RelationNet [27] | 38.1 | 61.1 | 47.0 | – | – | – | – | – | – | 30.0 | 93.4 | 45.3 |
| | PSR-ZSL [2] | 24.6 | 54.3 | 33.9 | 20.8 | 37.2 | 26.7 | – | – | – | 20.7 | 73.8 | 32.3 |
| | PREN [33] | 35.2 | 55.8 | 43.1 | 35.4 | 27.2 | 30.8 | – | – | – | 32.4 | 88.6 | 47.4 |
| | VSE [39] | 39.5 | 68.9 | 50.2 | – | – | – | – | – | – | 45.6 | 88.7 | 60.2 |
| | PQZSL [17] | 43.2 | 51.4 | 46.9 | 35.1 | 35.3 | 35.2 | – | – | – | – | – | – |
| | DARK [11] | – | – | 41.6 | – | – | 32.8 | – | – | – | – | – | 38.3 |
| Generative | CVAE-ZSL [22] | – | – | 34.5 | – | – | 26.7 | – | – | – | – | – | 51.2 |
| | SE-GZSL [15] | 41.5 | 53.3 | 46.7 | 40.9 | 30.5 | 34.9 | – | – | – | 58.3 | 68.1 | 62.8 |
| | f-CLSWGAN [31] | 43.7 | 57.7 | 49.7 | 42.6 | 36.6 | 39.4 | **59.0** | 73.8 | 65.6 | – | – | – |
| | SR-GAN [34] | 31.3 | 60.9 | 41.3 | 22.1 | 38.3 | 27.4 | – | – | – | – | – | – |
| | GDAN [12] | 39.3 | 66.7 | 49.5 | 38.1 | 89.9 | **53.4** | – | – | – | 32.1 | 67.5 | 43.5 |
| f-CLSWGAN+ABFG | | **47.1** | 56.1 | **51.2** | **46.3** | 37.2 | 41.3 | 58.9 | 78.5 | **69.4** | 58.1 | 72.8 | **64.7** |
| SE-GZSL+ABFG | | 45.3 | 52.0 | 48.4 | 45.6 | 32.5 | 38.0 | 56.8 | 74.9 | 64.6 | **58.5** | 69.2 | 63.4 |

## 4.3 GZSL Results

Table 1 tabulates the GZSL performance of ABFG assisted models and representative approaches. The results indicate that the ABFG does great boost the performance for both GAN-based and VAE-based methods. There are 1.5%, 1.9% and 3.8% more gains for CUB, SUN and FLO dataset respectively of ABFG plus version f-CLSWGAN when compares to plain version of f-CLSWGAN. Similarly, when we compare SE-GZSL with SE-GZSL+ABFG, the performance are also elevated by 1.7%, 3.1% and 0.6% on CUB, SUN and AWA2 which further demonstrate the superiority of our proposed ABFG framework. Moreover, compared with SE-GZSL with ABFG which is VAE-based model, it can be observed that GAN-based f-CLSWGAN with ABFG achieves a higher level of GZSL performance for which reason the GAN-based methods are the main stream of generative approach of recent advancement. In summary, our ABFG shows its superiority and good generalization ability to unseen classes in comparison with the state-of-the-art approaches.

## 4.4 GZSL-US Results

**Table 2.** The results on CUB for Generalized Zero-shot Learning with Unreliable Semantic (GZSL-US) task.

| Type | Methods | Clean | Noise | | | | | Absence | | | | |
|---|---|---|---|---|---|---|---|---|---|---|---|---|
| | | | 10% | 20% | 30% | 40% | 50% | 10% | 20% | 30% | 40% | 50% |
| VAE-based | CVAE-ZSL | 34.5 | 5.2 | 5.5 | 4.0 | 4.5 | 4.1 | 12.3 | 10.3 | 5.7 | 4.9 | 5.7 |
| | SE-GZSL | 46.7 | 7.2 | 5.7 | 6.2 | 6.7 | 7.2 | 19.6 | 11.1 | 5.7 | 5.7 | 5.9 |
| | SE-GZSL+ABFG | 48.4 | 33.3 | 30.2 | 18.2 | 15.7 | 16.0 | 45.3 | 40.3 | 35.2 | 29.9 | 28.8 |
| GAN-based | SR-GAN | 41.3 | 7.3 | 5.2 | 5.4 | 6.0 | 3.3 | 20.8 | 11.0 | 13.2 | 8.8 | 7.2 |
| | GDAN | 49.5 | 11.6 | 8.7 | 8.3 | 6.5 | 5.3 | 30.1 | 18.8 | 18.6 | 5.6 | 5.5 |
| | f-CLSWGAN | 49.7 | 8.3 | 5.6 | 6.1 | 5.7 | 6.3 | 29.4 | 15.5 | 9.8 | 7.3 | 6.5 |
| | f-CLSWGAN+ABFG | 51.2 | 49.8 | 36.5 | 33.2 | 30.0 | 25.3 | 50.2 | 45.8 | 45.9 | 32.1 | 30.6 |

**Table 3.** The results on SUN for Generalized Zero-shot Learning with Unreliable Semantic (GZSL-US) task.

| Type | Methods | Clean | Noise | | | | | Absence | | | | |
|---|---|---|---|---|---|---|---|---|---|---|---|---|
| | | | 10% | 20% | 30% | 40% | 50% | 10% | 20% | 30% | 40% | 50% |
| VAE-based | CVAE-ZSL | 26.7 | 5.6 | 5.0 | 5.1 | 5.4 | 3.3 | 21.0 | 18.8 | 15.1 | 12.3 | 10.2 |
| | SE-GZSL | 34.9 | 13.3 | 9.3 | 9.0 | 5.4 | 6.8 | 27.5 | 23.2 | 20.9 | 18.0 | 15.1 |
| | SE-GZSL+ABFG | 38.0 | 29.2 | 25.5 | 20.7 | 19.3 | 16.0 | 31.2 | 31.5 | 26.6 | 24.0 | 21.2 |
| GAN-based | SR-GAN | 27.4 | 8.7 | 6.5 | 5.0 | 5.2 | 5.7 | 19.8 | 12.0 | 8.7 | 4.1 | 4.3 |
| | GDAN | 53.4 | 16.5 | 10.3 | 8.5 | 8.3 | 6.0 | 48.5 | 46.3 | 40.2 | 33.1 | 28.6 |
| | f-CLSWGAN | 39.4 | 17.1 | 11.4 | 8.3 | 6.3 | 6.3 | 36.5 | 33.2 | 30.7 | 29.2 | 27.3 |
| | f-CLSWGAN+ABFG | 41.3 | 35.8 | 32.3 | 31.2 | 28.5 | 20.8 | 39.6 | 39.1 | 39.3 | 36.1 | 35.4 |

**Setting.** To demonstrate the prevalence of the semantic unreliability, we first implement CVAE-ZSL and SR-GAN since the official code are not accessible while the code for f-CLSWGAN, GDAN are provided by the author. In the result Tables 2 and 3, there is a column "clean" which is excerpt from the original paper, for the data existed, or the result implemented by ourselves. Results on FLO and AWA2 are shown in Supplementary Material.

**The Phenomenon.** Both GAN-based and VAE-based approaches suffer dramatic accuracy loss when it comes to the semantic disturbance no matter which kind of disturbance it is. Specifically, the accuracy of CVAE-ZSL, SE-GZSL, SR-GAN, GDAN and f-CLSWGAN decreased to 5.2%, 7.2%, 7.3%, 11.6%, and 8.3% when the semantics are contaminated with Gaussian noise on CUB.

While both semantic disturbance caused devastating consequence on both GAN-based and VAE-based methods, the disturbance of semantic noise lead to greater destruction of performance. As the results on CUB of CVAE-ZSL shows, the gaps between noise and absence semantic representations with increasing disturbance ratio are 7.1%, 4.8%, 1.7%, 0.4%, 1.6%, which demonstrate the performance decreasing when the semantic representation are partially missing is much depressing than the semantic representations are contaminated. Similarly, the GAN-based models, such as SR-GAN and GDAN, are also show such characteristics in which the gaps are 13.5%, 5.8%, 7.8%, 2.8%, 3.9% and 18.5%, 10.1%, 10.3%, -0.9%, 0.2% on CUB dataset respectively. As the basis of our proposed ABFG framework, the SE-GZSL and f-CLSWGAN suffer the same way. More than that the performance gaps of all the mentioned models on SUN, FLO and AWA2 are also huge, for which we draw the conclusion of "the more confusion in data, other than data missing, the little valuable knowledge for transfer learning".

### 4.5    Adversary Discussion

In this part, we present the detail experimental results of our ABFG when we adopt different attack algorithms and attack views. To illustrate the role of attack view, Tables 4 and 5 tabulates the result for GZSL and Tables 6 and 7 tabulates the result for GZSL-US. We also present the results for f-CLSWGAN and SE-GZSL with various of attack algorithms in the Supplementary Material.

**Attack View.** We have carried out adversarial calculation in the semantic and visual space respectively, and discussed the role of adversarial samples from different types of sample spaces. Different from the attack in the visual space, the semantic attack directly simulates the seman-

**Table 4.** Attack view comparison for f-CLSWGAN.

| Model | CUB | SUN | FLO | AWA2 |
|---|---|---|---|---|
| FGSM+Visual | 49.5 | 39.8 | 68.2 | **63.7** |
| FGSM+Semantic | **50.7** | **40.5** | **69.1** | 63.5 |
| FGSM+Visual&Semantic | 44.2 | 33.5 | 65.7 | 59.3 |
| PGD+Visual | 51.0 | 41.1 | 68.7 | 64.2 |
| PGD+Semantic | **51.2** | **41.3** | **69.4** | **64.7** |
| PGD+Visual&Semantic | 48.1 | 37.0 | 66.2 | 60.1 |

tic interference during the training process which can derive the model with the ability to adapt to the semantic interference. Moreover, in addition to the better effect of semantic adversary than visual adversary, we found that the calculation of adversarial samples for semantic and visual space at the same time, which are utilized in the training process, will greatly reduce the performance of the model, as shown in Tables 4 and 5.

In addition, we also tested the performance on the AWA2 dataset for GZSL-US task with the same condition, as shown in Tables 6 and 7. Similarly, performing adversarial sample calculations for both spaces at the same time greatly reduces the performance of the model, and has

**Table 5.** Attack view comparison for SE-GZSL.

| Model | CUB | SUN | FLO | AWA2 |
|---|---|---|---|---|
| FGSM+Visual | 45.7 | 35.9 | 62.8 | 62.5 |
| FGSM+Semantic | **48.2** | **37.7** | **63.9** | **62.8** |
| FGSM+Visual&Semantic | 40.2 | 31.3 | 57.1 | 55.4 |
| PGD+Visual | 47.5 | 37.5 | 63.2 | 63.0 |
| PGD+Semantic | **48.4** | **38.0** | **64.6** | **63.4** |
| PGD+Visual&Semantic | 43.2 | 31.3 | 53.0 | 56.4 |

no direct relationship with the adversarial attack algorithm. Whether it is when the interference is weak or when the it is enhanced, the results obtained by simultaneous attacking are not as good as the results obtained by calculating the adversarial samples in only one space.

By comparing the improvement of f-CLSWGAN+PGD+Semantic relative to f-CLSWGAN on the GZSL-US task, and the improvement of SE-GZSL+PGD+Semantic relative to SE-GZSL, we can find that the improvement of GAN-based is more obvious. We call this phenomenon adversarial matching degree. This phenomenon exists not only when using PGD as an attacker, but also when using FGSM. A higher degree of matching indicates that our ABFG has a better effect and further proves the effectiveness of our proposed ABFG.

**Table 6.** Different attack view comparison on AWA2 for f-CLSWGAN.

| Methods | Noise | | | | | Absence | | | | |
|---|---|---|---|---|---|---|---|---|---|---|
| | 10% | 20% | 30% | 40% | 50% | 10% | 20% | 30% | 40% | 50% |
| PGD+Visual | 60.3 | 53.8 | 45.8 | 41.9 | 37.4 | 61.5 | 57.4 | 50.6 | 48.7 | 48.1 |
| PGD+Semantic | 61.2 | 57.2 | 45.8 | 41.0 | 38.6 | 61.6 | 58.8 | 53.8 | 49.6 | 47.3 |
| PGD+Visual&Semantic | 55.6 | 22.5 | 15.3 | 14.1 | 15.0 | 54.8 | 31.6 | 21.2 | 19.5 | 17.3 |
| FGSM+Visual | 60.7 | 53.4 | 46.4 | 38.6 | 32.8 | 60.8 | 56.2 | 50.1 | 45.1 | 43.0 |
| FGSM+Semantic | 60.9 | 55.7 | 45.7 | 39.4 | 38.8 | 62.1 | 57.8 | 51.3 | 47.4 | 45.8 |
| FGSM+Visual&Semantic | 51.0 | 33.1 | 30.5 | 29.7 | 31.3 | 48.8 | 37.2 | 35.8 | 30.3 | 26.9 |

**Table 7.** Different attack view comparison on AWA2 for SE-GZSL.

| Methods | Noise | | | | | Absence | | | | |
|---|---|---|---|---|---|---|---|---|---|---|
| | 10% | 20% | 30% | 40% | 50% | 10% | 20% | 30% | 40% | 50% |
| PGD+Visual | 56.9 | 43.2 | 36.2 | 33.7 | 28.4 | 58.3 | 55.8 | 50.9 | 46.7 | 44.6 |
| PGD+Semantic | 58.3 | 44.3 | 35.4 | 33.8 | 30.9 | 60.0 | 56.7 | 53.2 | 45.1 | 45.0 |
| PGD+Visual&Semantic | 49.2 | 20.3 | 13.0 | 11.5 | 11.2 | 48.9 | 31.3 | 24.6 | 15.7 | 15.1 |
| FGSM+Visual | 54.3 | 41.0 | 35.5 | 31.8 | 24.3 | 59.7 | 56.1 | 52.4 | 45.3 | 42.1 |
| FGSM+Semantic | 58.6 | 43.0 | 36.1 | 31.5 | 27.5 | 59.1 | 54.8 | 51.7 | 45.6 | 43.5 |
| FGSM+Visual &Semantic | 45.3 | 27.1 | 16.7 | 15.2 | 16.1 | 51.8 | 39.2 | 35.8 | 28.3 | 20.9 |

# 5 Conclusion

In this work, we propose the task of Generalized Zero-shot Learning with Unreliable Semantic (GZSL-US) which consider Generalized Zero-shot Learning (GZSL) with more realistic configuration and practical application. To address the GZSL-US problem, we propose a unified generative framework named Adversarial Bidirectional Feature Generation (ABFG) which introduce the adversarial samples and bidirectional matching into GZSL. The experimental results on four challenging datasets validate that ABFG assisted generative model indeed preserves strong robustness to various disturbance of semantic representation and achieves promising GZSL performance in comparison with the state-of-the-arts.

# References

1. Akata, Z., Reed, S., Walter, D., Lee, H., Schiele, B.: Evaluation of output embeddings for fine-grained image classification. In: Proceedings of the IEEE Conference on Computer Vision and Pattern Recognition, pp. 2927–2936 (2015)
2. Annadani, Y., Biswas, S.: Preserving semantic relations for zero-shot learning. In: Proceedings of the IEEE Conference on Computer Vision and Pattern Recognition, pp. 7603–7612 (2018)
3. Bhagoji, A.N., He, W., Li, B., Song, D.: Practical black-box attacks on deep neural networks using efficient query mechanisms. In: Ferrari, V., Hebert, M., Sminchisescu, C., Weiss, Y. (eds.) ECCV 2018. LNCS, vol. 11216, pp. 158–174. Springer, Cham (2018). https://doi.org/10.1007/978-3-030-01258-8_10
4. Biggio, B., Roli, F.: Wild patterns: ten years after the rise of adversarial machine learning. Pattern Recogn. **84**, 317–331 (2018)
5. Carlini, N., Wagner, D.: Towards evaluating the robustness of neural networks. In: 2017 IEEE Symposium on Security and Privacy (SP), pp. 39–57. IEEE (2017)
6. Changpinyo, S., Chao, W.L., Gong, B., Sha, F.: Synthesized classifiers for zero-shot learning. In: Proceedings of the IEEE Conference on Computer Vision and Pattern Recognition, pp. 5327–5336 (2016)
7. Dong, Y., Pang, T., Su, H., Zhu, J.: Evading defenses to transferable adversarial examples by translation-invariant attacks. In: Proceedings of the IEEE Conference on Computer Vision and Pattern Recognition, pp. 4312–4321 (2019)
8. Frome, A., et al.: Devise: a deep visual-semantic embedding model. In: Advances in Neural Information Processing Systems, pp. 2121–2129 (2013)
9. Goodfellow, I.J., Shlens, J., Szegedy, C.: Explaining and harnessing adversarial examples. arXiv preprint arXiv:1412.6572 (2014)
10. Guo, C., Gardner, J.R., You, Y., Wilson, A.G., Weinberger, K.Q.: Simple black-box adversarial attacks. arXiv preprint arXiv:1905.07121 (2019)
11. Guo, Y., et al.: Dual-view ranking with hardness assessment for zero-shot learning. In: Proceedings of the AAAI Conference on Artificial Intelligence, vol. 33, pp. 8360–8367 (2019)
12. Huang, H., Wang, C., Yu, P.S., Wang, C.D.: Generative dual adversarial network for generalized zero-shot learning. In: Proceedings of the IEEE Conference on Computer Vision and Pattern Recognition, pp. 801–810 (2019)
13. Inkawhich, N., Wen, W., Li, H.H., Chen, Y.: Feature space perturbations yield more transferable adversarial examples. In: Proceedings of the IEEE Conference on Computer Vision and Pattern Recognition, pp. 7066–7074 (2019)

14. Kodirov, E., Xiang, T., Gong, S.: Semantic autoencoder for zero-shot learning. In: Proceedings of the IEEE Conference on Computer Vision and Pattern Recognition, pp. 3174–3183 (2017)
15. Kumar Verma, V., Arora, G., Mishra, A., Rai, P.: Generalized zero-shot learning via synthesized examples. In: Proceedings of the IEEE Conference on Computer Vision and Pattern Recognition, pp. 4281–4289 (2018)
16. Kurakin, A., Goodfellow, I., Bengio, S.: Adversarial examples in the physical world. arXiv preprint arXiv:1607.02533 (2016)
17. Li, J., Lan, X., Liu, Y., Wang, L., Zheng, N.: Compressing unknown images with product quantizer for efficient zero-shot classification. In: Proceedings of the IEEE Conference on Computer Vision and Pattern Recognition, pp. 5463–5472 (2019)
18. Liu, Y., Chen, X., Liu, C., Song, D.: Delving into transferable adversarial examples and black-box attacks. arXiv preprint arXiv:1611.02770 (2016)
19. Madry, A., Makelov, A., Schmidt, L., Tsipras, D., Vladu, A.: Towards deep learning models resistant to adversarial attacks. arXiv preprint arXiv:1706.06083 (2017)
20. Martin Arjovsky, S., Bottou, L.: Wasserstein generative adversarial networks. In: Proceedings of the 34th International Conference on Machine Learning, Sydney (2017)
21. Mirza, M., Osindero, S.: Conditional generative adversarial nets. arXiv preprint arXiv:1411.1784 (2014)
22. Mishra, A., Krishna Reddy, S., Mittal, A., Murthy, H.A.: A generative model for zero shot learning using conditional variational autoencoders. In: Proceedings of the IEEE Conference on Computer Vision and Pattern Recognition Workshops, pp. 2188–2196 (2018)
23. Moosavi-Dezfooli, S.M., Fawzi, A., Fawzi, O., Frossard, P.: Universal adversarial perturbations. In: Proceedings of the IEEE Conference on Computer Vision and Pattern Recognition, pp. 1765–1773 (2017)
24. Nilsback, M.E., Zisserman, A.: Automated flower classification over a large number of classes. In: 2008 Sixth Indian Conference on Computer Vision, Graphics and Image Processing, pp. 722–729. IEEE (2008)
25. Papernot, N., McDaniel, P., Goodfellow, I., Jha, S., Celik, Z.B., Swami, A.: Practical black-box attacks against machine learning. In: Proceedings of the 2017 ACM on Asia Conference on Computer and Communications Security, pp. 506–519 (2017)
26. Patterson, G., Hays, J.: Sun attribute database: discovering, annotating, and recognizing scene attributes. In: 2012 IEEE Conference on Computer Vision and Pattern Recognition, pp. 2751–2758. IEEE (2012)
27. Sung, F., Yang, Y., Zhang, L., Xiang, T., Torr, P.H., Hospedales, T.M.: Learning to compare: relation network for few-shot learning. In: Proceedings of the IEEE Conference on Computer Vision and Pattern Recognition, pp. 1199–1208 (2018)
28. Szegedy, C., et al.: Intriguing properties of neural networks. arXiv preprint arXiv:1312.6199 (2013)
29. Wah, C., Branson, S., Welinder, P., Perona, P., Belongie, S.: The caltech-UCSD birds-200-2011 dataset (2011)
30. Xian, Y., Lampert, C.H., Schiele, B., Akata, Z.: Zero-shot learning-a comprehensive evaluation of the good, the bad and the ugly. IEEE Trans. Pattern Anal. Mach. Intell. **41**(9), 2251–2265 (2018)
31. Xian, Y., Lorenz, T., Schiele, B., Akata, Z.: Feature generating networks for zero-shot learning. In: Proceedings of the IEEE Conference on Computer Vision and Pattern Recognition, pp. 5542–5551 (2018)

32. Xie, C., et al.: Improving transferability of adversarial examples with input diversity. In: Proceedings of the IEEE Conference on Computer Vision and Pattern Recognition, pp. 2730–2739 (2019)
33. Ye, M., Guo, Y.: Progressive ensemble networks for zero-shot recognition. In: Proceedings of the IEEE Conference on Computer Vision and Pattern Recognition, pp. 11728–11736 (2019)
34. Ye, Z., Lyu, F., Li, L., Fu, Q., Ren, J., Hu, F.: Sr-gan: semantic rectifying generative adversarial network for zero-shot learning. In: 2019 IEEE International Conference on Multimedia and Expo (ICME), pp. 85–90. IEEE (2019)
35. Yin, D., Lopes, R.G., Shlens, J., Cubuk, E.D., Gilmer, J.: A fourier perspective on model robustness in computer vision. In: Advances in Neural Information Processing Systems, pp. 13276–13286 (2019)
36. Zeng, X., et al.: Adversarial attacks beyond the image space. In: Proceedings of the IEEE Conference on Computer Vision and Pattern Recognition, pp. 4302–4311 (2019)
37. Zhang, L., Xiang, T., Gong, S.: Learning a deep embedding model for zero-shot learning. In: Proceedings of the IEEE Conference on Computer Vision and Pattern Recognition, pp. 2021–2030 (2017)
38. Zhou, W., et al.: Transferable adversarial perturbations. In: Proceedings of the European Conference on Computer Vision (ECCV), pp. 452–467 (2018)
39. Zhu, P., Wang, H., Saligrama, V.: Generalized zero-shot recognition based on visually semantic embedding. In: Proceedings of the IEEE Conference on Computer Vision and Pattern Recognition, pp. 2995–3003 (2019)
40. Zhu, Y., Elhoseiny, M., Liu, B., Peng, X., Elgammal, A.: A generative adversarial approach for zero-shot learning from noisy texts. In: Proceedings of the IEEE Conference on Computer Vision and Pattern Recognition, pp. 1004–1013 (2018)

# Exploiting Robust Memory Features
# for Unsupervised Reidentification

Jiawei Lian[1,2], Da-Han Wang[1,2(✉)], Xia Du[1,2], Yun Wu[1,2], and Shunzhi Zhu[1,2]

[1] School of Computer and Information Engineering,
Xiamen University of Technology, Xiamen 361024, China
`wangdh@xmut.edu.cn`
[2] Fujian Key Labarotory of Pattern Recognition and Image Understanding,
600 Ligong Road, Xiamen 361024, People's Republic of China

**Abstract.** Unsupervised re-identification (ReID) is a task that does not use labels for classification and recognition. It is fundamentally challenging due to the need to retrieve target objects across different perspectives, and coupled with the absence of ID labels for supervision. However, the most severe aspect is that the appearance features of vehicles can be shifted under different viewpoints, which may cause an imbalance in inter-class and intra-class variation. In this work, we propose a fully unsupervised re-identification method applied to the person and vehicle domain. In particular, different from previous methods of cluster pseudo-labelling, we compress the feature dimensions used to generate the labels and improve the quality of the pseudo-label. Then, in the update memory feature module, we introduce the idea of partitioning to construct algorithms for dynamically finding inter-class and intra-class boundaries to improve the robustness of the model. To demonstrate the effectiveness of the proposed method, we conduct experiments on one vehicle dataset (VeRi-776) and one person datasets (MSMT17). Experimental results demonstrate that our method is effective in enhancing the performance of the ReID task, and the proposed method achieves the state-of-the-art performance. The code has been made available at https://github.com/ljwwwiop/unsupervised_reid.

**Keywords:** Re-identification · Intelligent transport systems · Unsupervised learning · Computer vision · Deep learning

## 1 Introduction

Re-identification (ReID) aims to match vehicle or person images in a camera network. With the development of convolutional neural networks, re-identification techniques have been used with great success in smart cities, and intelligent transport systems [16]. And there exists significant work using labels for supervised learning, and they effectively enhance the ability of models to extract features and improve the performance of models on datasets. However, constructing a label for a large-scale dataset is very expensive and will consume much time. In

© The Author(s), under exclusive license to Springer Nature Switzerland AG 2022
S. Yu et al. (Eds.): PRCV 2022, LNCS 13535, pp. 655–667, 2022.
https://doi.org/10.1007/978-3-031-18910-4_52

addition, manual miss-labeling can interfere with the supervised model's ability to extract features, and that noise is not easily resolved. As a result, there has been a growing interest in unsupervised methods in recent years, which significantly reduces labor costs as miss-labeling information is required.

Many methods for learning to discriminate features without labels have been proposed in the field of re-identification, which can be divided into two main categories: unsupervised domain adaptation learning (UDA) and fully unsupervised learning. Unsupervised domain adaptation (UDA) learning, which focuses on cross-domain methods by transferring feature information from labeled datasets (source domain) to unlabelled datasets (target domain) [2,10]. It is applied to person ReID [28] and vehicle ReID [19,27], and these methods have achieved significant performance. However, UDA-based methods cannot avoid the requirement for using labels in the source domain. Although the difference between two domains is measurable in terms of distribution, but UDA-based performance is not satisfactory when dealing with feature shifts and class distance problems.

**Fig. 1.** Examples of vehicles in VeRi-776 dataset. The same vehicle captured in different views of the camera, the representative features are highly varied.

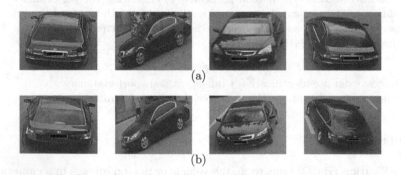

(a)

(b)

**Fig. 2.** Illustration of vehicles from VeRi-776. Two different vehicles with the same car model and color may look very similar from the same viewpoint.

Apart from the use of domain adaptation learning methods, fully unsupervised-based methods have also made significant contributions to unsupervised ReID [1,6,15,20,26]. However, the exploration of fully unsupervised-based methods is still inadequate compared to UDA-based methods. Fully unsupervised-based methods typically use cluster algorithms to generate pseudo-labels [6] or construct feature groups by the similarity of feature pairs [20]. It is worth noting that the quality of the pseudo-label and the hyperparameter settings affect the model differently. Next, the training model updates the features via a memory bank, which is crucial for unsupervised learning and can effectively influence the relationship between positive and negative samples. When the appearance features are shifted as the perspective changes, as in Fig. 1 and 2, it is crucial to reduce the intra-class distance and widen the inter-class distance, which makes the memory bank design more challenging.

In this paper, we propose a fully unsupervised approach applied to the field of person and vehicle re-identification. We improve the memory updates strategy by introducing mean distance response intra-class variation and not using the minimum distance inter-class as the sole basis for updates, enhancing the robustness of memory features. Correlation analysis (PCA) is used to compress feature dimensions and improve the quality of pseudo-label generation. We evaluate our method on the vehicle datasets and person datasets, as well as the ablation studies, which demonstrate that our method is competitive among existing ReID models.

## 2    Related Work

### 2.1    Supervised ReID

Supervised learning is the primary learning method used ReID tasks. In recent years, with the application of convolutional neural networks(CNN) in deep learning, many large-scale ReID datasets (person [25,29] and vehicles [16]) have been proposed, which has improved the performance of supervised ReID methods. Deep supervised ReID method can be summarized into three categories: discrimination-based features [17,21], metric-based learning [3,22] and spatial-based features [12,23]. The idea of discrimination-based feature methods lies in the fact that representative subtle features of different IDs can be effectively extracted for distinction. Such as, Wang et al. [21] propose a multi-branch network for extracting vehicle global features of different dimensions. Liu et al. [17] propose a network for learning global discriminative features across perspectives and correlating discriminative features with perspective information. These two supervised approaches bring significant improvements to ReID performance. However, when different objects have similarities (inter-class distance is smaller than intra-class), the performance of global features is not satisfactory. Therefore, to alleviate the similarity problem, metric-based learning methods are proposed. Wang et al. [22] propose a method for computing a multi-pair similarity measure, the results of which are used to generate different weights for sample pairs. Chu et al. [3] propose a learning viewpoint feature network and distinguishes between different viewpoint features and calculates the distance metric similarity separately. These two methods effectively alleviate the similarity problem and greatly enhance the performance of the model based on the global discriminative features.

Besides considering metric learning, there are some approaches have been introduced to the spatial perspective transformation problem. They guide the model to learn spatial information by additional manual labeling for annotation. Wang et al. [23] propose using vehicle keypoints (lights, wheels, etc.) to guide the model to construct spatial information. Khorramshahi et al. [12] introduce a two-stage network, one to train the spatial information decoder, and then combine the discriminative features with the spatial information to jointly discriminate. These two methods effectively reduce the noise problem caused by spatial transformation. Supervised learning methods greatly enhance the performance of ReID models. However, the performance of these supervised models is dependent on the manually prepared labels.

## 2.2 Unsupervised ReID

Compared to the methods of supervised learning-based of ReID, there is still not enough research on unsupervised ReID, as accurate extraction to discriminative features without label constraints is very difficult. Existing unsupervised ReID methods can be roughly categorised into two types: unsupervised domain adaptation (UDA) [7,8,28] and fully unsupervised learning [6,14,27]. The unsupervised domain adaptation ReID methods utilize transfer learning (source domain to unlabelled target domain) to enhance unsupervised performance. Such as, Song et al. [19] propose the theory of unsupervised domain adaptation learning in person ReID and constructs the UDA framework. Huang et al. [10] propose a dual-domain multi-task model to divide vehicle images into two domains for training by frequency estimation. The two methods have made significant contributions to the unsupervised domain, improving the discriminative power of unsupervised models. However, the source domain is label-dependent for training, and it is difficult for these methods to be applied when labels are missing. Therefore, it is necessary to propose an unsupervised method not relying on labels to overcome the necessity of source domains.

Different from the unsupervised domain adaptation (UDA) learning approach, fully unsupervised learning requires more complex model design in ReID. The pure unsupervised ReID framework generally consists of three modules: memory banking, pseudo-label generation and model training. Previous work improved significantly on the overall structure and the local modules. Wang et al. [20] propose a dictionary memory bank structure that stores all discriminative features and uses key values for multi-label classification. Lin et al. [15] propose a similarity-based approach that generates reliable pseudo-labels by computing global and local distances. Dai et al. [4] propose a cluster contrast learning-based approach to extract representative features by constructing a dynamic memory bank using momentum combined with minimum inter-cluster distance. These three methods have contributed significantly to the development of pure unsupervised ReID. However, the variation between different pseudo-labeled clusters is considered in their memory bank module, while the variation within the same pseudo-labeled clusters is ignored, so it is necessary to balance the inter-class and intra-class differences to improve the robustness of memory features.

## 2.3   Innovation of Our Method

In this paper, we propose a fully unsupervised-based approach for the person and vehicle ReID. To alleviate the problem of unbalanced inter-cluster and intra-cluster variation caused by pseudo-labeling, we propose a new update approach where the average intra-cluster variance is combined with the minimum inter-cluster distance, and this simultaneous update of inter-class and intra-class features significantly alleviates the imbalance of variation. Moreover, in the pseudo-label generation module, we try to improve the quality of pseudo-labels by compressing the feature dimension using linear analysis. Finally, we conduct experiments on different datasets and demonstrate that our proposed method is effective for enhancing the robustness of the model.

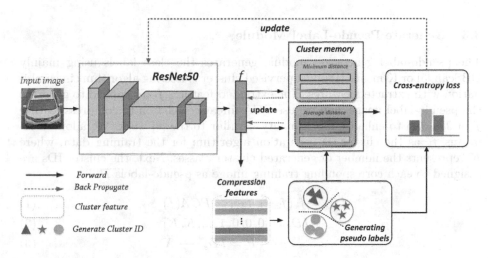

**Fig. 3.** The framework of our approach for Re-identification. The architecture has three modules: Backbone feature module, generation pseudo-labeling module and memory module.

## 3   Methodology

### 3.1   Methodology Overview

Our architecture consists of three modules: the backbone feature module, the cluster generation pseudo-labeling module, and cluster memory module. Figure 3 illustrates the details. The following content describes the model structure and methodology in detail.

Given an input image $X_i \in R^{H \times W \times C}$, $i \in N$, where $N$, $H$, $W$ and $C$ represent the number of training sets, the height, the width, and the channel number of the image, respectively. We extracted feature $f$ from the backbone network $\phi$ (ResNet50 [9]). The features $f$ then enter two branches, one for pseudo-label $p$ generation and the other for memory features combined with pseudo-label $p$ to generate cluster memory features $M_{inter}$ and $M_{intra}$, which then update the model $\phi$ parameters. Finally, pseudo-label $p$ and cluster memory features compute the cross-entropy loss, and the resulting loss gradient is backward propagated to the model.

### 3.2   Backbone Feature Module

In the backbone feature module, we utilize it to extract representative features from the input. The input image $X_i$ is passed through the backbone function $\phi$ to obtain the feature $f$: $\phi(X_i) \longrightarrow f$. The extracted feature $f$ is regularised by the $L2$-norm, so the scale of all features is fixed by 1.

### 3.3   Generate Pseudo-Label Module

The pseudo-label generation module generates the class labels using mainly DBScan [5] or K-means [18] unsupervised cluster clustering algorithms in combination with extracted features. The extracted features $f$ are applied to generate the pseudo-label image, and we use PCA linear correlation to compress feature $f$ of 256-dim to enhance label quality. Similar to the [6] work. We adopted K-means $f_k$ as the cluster-ID generation algorithm for the training data, where $K$ represents the number of generated cluster classes. Next, the cluster IDs are assigned to each corresponding training image as pseudo-labels $P$.

$$ID_s = f_k(f_{256}), f_{256} = PCA(f) \tag{1}$$
$$ID_s = [0, 0, 0, 1, ..., K, K] \tag{2}$$
$$P = ID_s \longrightarrow X \tag{3}$$

### 3.4   Memory Module

The cluster memory module is an essential part of improving the robustness of the features. To demonstrate the effectiveness of our proposed method, we try to keep the design as simple as possible and the same as the previous method, while our improved strategy is specified in Fig. 4. The mean distance of the same cluster-ID and the minimum boundary distance between different clusters are used to update the cluster features, and this strategy balances boths intra-class and inter-class distance variations.

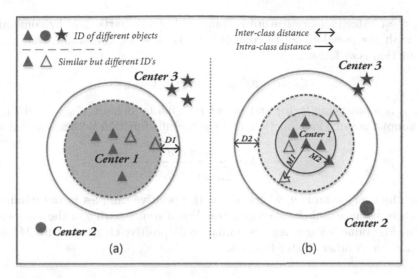

**Fig. 4.** Comparison of our proposed cluster memory update strategy with existing approaches. (a) Consider the minimum boundary distance D1 of the cluster, while ignoring the internal differences within the cluster. (b) The method proposed in our paper considers intra-class variation M1 and M2 apart from inter-class distance D2.

Memory initialisation settings: we average each cluster of $\phi(P)$ to generate the central cluster feature $[C_1, C_2, C_3, ..., C_{K-1}, C_K]$, thus obtaining a memory feature dictionary $M$ of length $K$. The clustering algorithms are improved with the model as it is continuously trained.

Memory Updating: we follow the extant working [4] protocol for querying in-memory features for the update using momentum comparison learning. Specifically, we query the extracted features $\phi(P)$ in the feature memory dictionary, and update the corresponding cluster feature vectors by selecting the sample with the smallest inter-cluster distance and the mean distance of the same cluster-ID sample. For a specific cluster with the same ID, its feature vector is updated via:

$$M_{inter} \longleftarrow \arg\min_{j}[M \cdot \phi(P_j)]_2, j \in K \qquad (4)$$

$$M_{intra} \longleftarrow Mean_j([M \cdot \phi(P_j)]_2), j \in K \qquad (5)$$

where $M_{inter}$ and $M_{intra}$ denote the minimum distance feature and the mean distance intra-cluster feature of the j-th cluster, and $[]_2$ represents the vector distance. We update the instance memory bank as follows:

$$\phi(P_j) \longleftarrow (M_{inter}^j, M_{intra}^j) \qquad (6)$$

Thus, the cluster memory feature is composed of two parts, and by combining them with the pseudo-label to compute the ID loss for constraint, the overall loss function is as follows:

$$\mathcal{L}_{total} = \mu \mathcal{L}_{inter} + (1 - \mu) \mathcal{L}_{intra} \tag{7}$$

where $\mu$ is a balancing factor and we set $\mu = 0.5$ by default. $\mathcal{L}_{inter}$ and $\mathcal{L}_{intra}$ both adopt the same loss function, and the specific function design is as follows:

$$\mathcal{L} = -\log \frac{exp(q \cdot M^+)}{\sum_{i=0}^{K} exp(q, M_i)} \tag{8}$$

For the query sample $q$, where $M_+$ is the positive samples in the minimum inter-class distance and the average intra-class distance with $q$ in the same cluster. The loss value is low when $q$ is similar to its positive cluster feature $M^+$ and dissimilar to all other cluster features.

## 4　Experiments

### 4.1　Dataset

We conducted extensive experiments on one public large-scale benchmarks for vehicle ReID (i.e., VeRi-776 [16]) and one dataset for person ReID (i.e., and MSMT17 [25]). The statistics of the two datasets are summarized in Table 1.

**Table 1.** Statistics of datasets used in the paper.

| Dataset | Object | ID | Image | Cam | View |
|---|---|---|---|---|---|
| MSMT17 [25] | Person | 1041 | 126,441 | 15 | –0 |
| VeRi-776 [16] | Vehicle | 776 | 51,003 | 20 | 8 |

Implementation Details: we used ResNet50 [9] as our backbone and used a pre-trained model [11] for the initial model parameters. For training, the input images were normalized to channel-wise zero-mean, with a standard variation of 1 and spatial resolution of vehicles and person is $224 \times 224$ and $256 \times 128$. Data augmentation was performed by resizing images to 105% width and height and random erasing [30], as well as random horizontal flipping with a probability of 0.5. Models were trained for 50 epochs, with a batch size of 256. A batch consists of 16 identities, each containing 16 samples. The parameters were optimized using the Adam [13] optimizer to train on the ReID model with weight decay $5 \times 10^{-4}$. The initial learning rate is set to $3.5 \times 10^{-4}$, and is reduced to 1/10 of its previous value every 20 epochs during total 50 epochs. For a fair comparison with other existing methods, the CMC rank-1 accuracy (r1), rank-5 accuracy (r5) and mAP are reported as the evaluation metrics. During the testing phase we follow the protocol of the previous method [4,6].

## 4.2   Ablation Studies

On the study of hyperparameters K in the K-means algorithm. Since K-means requires pre-set K clusters and the setting of different numbers of K affects the generation of pseudo-labels, it is essential to analyze the hyperparameter K to find reasonable pre-set values. From the Table 2, we can see that the best performance on the VeRi-776 dataset was achieved when K = 800. K values are difficult to set and usually require several iterations to find a suitable point Therefore, we set K values to 2000 for the other one pedestrian dataset(MSMT17).

**Table 2.** Comparison of the mAP, R1 and R5 obtained by setting different K values on the VeRi-776 dataset.

| Method | mAP | R1 | R5 |
|--------|-----|----|----|
| K = 600 | 67.6 | 89.6 | 96.2 |
| K = 800 | 69.0 | 90.5 | 96.2 |
| K = 1000 | 68.4 | 89.9 | 95.5 |

Regarding the effect of the loss function hyperparameter $\mu$. Experimental results can be seen in Table 3, $\mu$ is a balance factor between 0 and 1 and the model performs satisfactorily best when $\mu = 0.5$. When $\mu = 0$, then the loss function only considers intra-class variation. When $\mu = 1$, then only inter-class variation is considered.

**Table 3.** Comparison of mAP, R1 and R5 obtained by setting different balance factor $\mu$ on the VeRi-776 dataset.

| $\mu$ | mAP | R1 | R5 |
|-------|-----|----|----|
| $\mu = 0$ | 57.7 | 81.6 | 90.9 |
| $\mu = 0.25$ | 65.1 | 87.2 | 94.8 |
| $\mu = 0.5$ | 69.0 | 90.5 | 96.2 |
| $\mu = 0.75$ | 68.9 | 89.9 | 96.1 |
| $\mu = 1$ | 61.2 | 85.5 | 93.7 |

## 4.3   Comparison with State-of-the-Arts

The experimental results are shown in Tables 4 and 5. On the MSMT17 dataset, the results of our method are excellent, but the accuracy of R1 and R5 is low compared to ICE [1]. On the VeRi-776 vehicle dataset, our proposed method achieves 69.0%, 90.5%, and 96.2% for mAP, R1, and R5. Compared to CCL [4] and VACP [27], our method achieves a significant improvement and the results demonstrate the generalizability of our method to different domain data. Combining the performance of these two datasets, the overall performance well exceeds that of the unsupervised method, and our proposed fully unsupervised method is more satisfactory.

**Table 4.** Comparison on unsupervised person ReID with state-of-the-art methods, UDA is an unsupervised domain adaptation method.

| Method | MSMT17 | | | Where |
|---|---|---|---|---|
| | mAP | R1 | R5 | |
| UDA | | | | |
| MMT [7] | 24.0 | 50.1 | 63.5 | ICLR'20 |
| SPCL [8] | 26.8 | 53.7 | 65.0 | NeurIPS'20 |
| GCL [2] | 29.7 | 54.4 | 68.2 | CVPR'21 |
| GLT [28] | 26.5 | 56.6 | 67.5 | CVPR'21 |
| Fully Unsupervised | | | | |
| SPCL [8] | 19.1 | 42.3 | 55.6 | NeurIPS'20 |
| CycAS [24] | 26.7 | 50.1 | – | ECCV'20 |
| ICE [1] | 38.9 | 70.2 | 80.5 | ICCV'21 |
| CCL [4] | 33.3 | 63.3 | 73.7 | Arxiv'21 |
| Our proposed | 39.7 | 62.2 | 77.7 | |

**Table 5.** Comparison with state-of-the-art fully unsupervised method on the VeRi-776 vehicle dataset.

| Method | VeRi-776 | | | Where |
|---|---|---|---|---|
| | mAP | R1 | R5 | |
| BUC [14] | 21.2 | 54.7 | 70.4 | AAAI'19 |
| MMLP [20] | 24.2 | 71.8 | 75.9 | CVPR'20 |
| SPCL [8] | 38.9 | 80.4 | 86.8 | NeurIPS'20 |
| SSL [15] | 37.8 | 71.7 | 83.8 | CVPR'20 |
| MLFD [26] | 26.7 | 74.5 | 80.3 | IROS'21 |
| VACP-TO [27] | 30.4 | 76.2 | 81.2 | TITS'21 |
| CCL [4] | 42.5 | 87.7 | 91.4 | Arxiv'21 |
| Our proposed | 69.0 | 90.5 | 96.2 | |

# 5    Conclusion

In this work, we propose a fully unsupervised re-identification method applied to the vehicle and pedestrian domain. Specifically, we introduce linear correlation analysis to compress the features and improve the quality of the pseudo-label. In the memory module, we dynamically divide the intra-cluster and inter-cluster distances, and adopted the average distance and minimum distance to reflect the cluster feature variation to enhance the model's performance. Specially, the experimental results on one vehicle dataset and one person datasets demonstrate the effectiveness of our approach.

**Acknowledgements.** This work is supported by Industry-University Cooperation Project of Fujian Science and Technology Department (No. 2021H6035), and the Science and Technology Planning Project of Fujian Province (No. 2021J011191, 2020H0023, 2020Y9064), and the Joint Funds of 5th Round of Health and Education Research Program of Fu-jian Province (No. 2019-WJ-41).

# References

1. Chen, H., Lagadec, B., Bremond, F.: Ice: inter-instance contrastive encoding for unsupervised person re-identification. In: Proceedings of the IEEE/CVF International Conference on Computer Vision, pp. 14960–14969 (2021)
2. Chen, H., Wang, Y., Lagadec, B., Dantcheva, A., Bremond, F.: Joint generative and contrastive learning for unsupervised person re-identification. In: Proceedings of the IEEE/CVF Conference on Computer Vision and Pattern Recognition, pp. 2004–2013 (2021)
3. Chu, R., Sun, Y., Li, Y., Liu, Z., Wei, Y.: Vehicle re-identification with viewpoint-aware metric learning. In: 2019 IEEE/CVF International Conference on Computer Vision (ICCV) (2019)
4. Dai, Z., Wang, G., Zhu, S., Yuan, W., Tan, P.: Cluster contrast for unsupervised person re-identification. arxiv 2021. arXiv preprint arXiv:2103.11568 (2021)
5. Ester, M., Kriegel, H.-P., Sander, J., Xu, X., et al.: A density-based algorithm for discovering clusters in large spatial databases with noise. In: KDD, vol. 96, pp. 226–231 (1996)
6. Fan, H., Zheng, L., Yan, C., Yang, Y.: Unsupervised person re-identification: clustering and fine-tuning. ACM Trans. Multimedia Comput. Commun. Appl. (TOMM), **14**(4), 1–18 (2018)
7. Ge, Y., Chen, D., Li, H.: Mutual mean-teaching: pseudo label refinery for unsupervised domain adaptation on person re-identification. arXiv preprint arXiv:2001.01526 (2020)
8. Ge, Y., Zhu, F., Chen, D., Zhao, R., et al.: Self-paced contrastive learning with hybrid memory for domain adaptive object re-id. Adv. Neural. Inf. Process. Syst. **33**, 11309–11321 (2020)
9. He, K., Zhang, X., Ren, S., Sun, J.: Deep residual learning for image recognition. In: 2016 IEEE Conference on Computer Vision and Pattern Recognition (2016)
10. Huang, Y., et al.: Dual domain multi-task model for vehicle re-identification. IEEE Trans. Intell. Transp. Syst. **23**, 2991–2999 (2020)

11. Jia, D., Wei, D., Socher, R., Li, L.J., Kai, L., Li, F.F.: Imagenet: a large-scale hierarchical image database. In: Proceedings of IEEE Computer Vision Pattern Recognition, pp. 248–255 (2009)
12. Khorramshahi, P., Kumar, A., Peri, N., Rambhatla, S.S., Chen, J.-C., Chellappa, R.: A dual-path model with adaptive attention for vehicle re-identification. In: Proceedings of the IEEE/CVF International Conference on Computer Vision (ICCV), October 2019
13. Kingma, D., Ba, J.: Adam: a method for stochastic optimization. Comput. Sci. (2014)
14. Y. Lin, X. Dong, L. Zheng, Y. Yan, and Y. Yang. A bottom-up clustering approach to unsupervised person re-identification. In: Proceedings of the AAAI Conference on Artificial Intelligence, vol. 33, pp. 8738–8745 (2019)
15. Lin, Y., Xie, L., Wu, Y., Yan, C., Tian, Q.: Unsupervised person re-identification via softened similarity learning. In: Proceedings of the IEEE/CVF Conference on Computer Vision and Pattern Recognition, pp. 3390–3399 (2020)
16. Liu, X., Liu, W., Mei, T., Ma, H.: A deep learning-based approach to progressive vehicle re-identification for urban surveillance. In: Leibe, B., Matas, J., Sebe, N., Welling, M. (eds.) ECCV 2016. LNCS, vol. 9906, pp. 869–884. Springer, Cham (2016). https://doi.org/10.1007/978-3-319-46475-6_53
17. Liu, X., Liu, W., Zheng, J., Yan, C., Mei, T.: Beyond the parts: learning multi-view cross-part correlation for vehicle re-identification. In: MM 2020: The 28th ACM International Conference on Multimedia (2020)
18. MacQueen, J., et al.: Some methods for classification and analysis of multivariate observations. In: Proceedings of the fifth Berkeley Symposium on Mathematical Statistics and Probability, Oakland, CA, USA, vol. 1, pp. 281–297 (1967)
19. Song, L., et al.: Unsupervised domain adaptive re-identification: theory and practice. Pattern Recogn. **102**, 107173 (2020)
20. Wang, D., Zhang, S.: Unsupervised person re-identification via multi-label classification. In: Proceedings of the IEEE/CVF Conference on Computer Vision and Pattern Recognition, pp. 10981–10990 (2020)
21. Wang, H., Peng, J., Jiang, G., Xu, F., Fu, X.: Discriminative feature and dictionary learning with part-aware model for vehicle re-identification. Neurocomputing **438**, 55–62 (2021)
22. Wang, X., Han, X., Huang, W., Dong, D., Scott, M.R.: Multi-similarity loss with general pair weighting for deep metric learning. In: Proceedings of the IEEE Conference on Computer Vision and Pattern Recognition (2019)
23. Wang, Z., et al.: Orientation invariant feature embedding and spatial temporal regularization for vehicle re-identification. In: Proceedings of the IEEE International Conference on Computer Vision (ICCV), October 2017
24. Wang, Z., et al.: CycAs: self-supervised cycle association for learning re-identifiable descriptions. In: Vedaldi, A., Bischof, H., Brox, T., Frahm, J.-M. (eds.) ECCV 2020. LNCS, vol. 12356, pp. 72–88. Springer, Cham (2020). https://doi.org/10.1007/978-3-030-58621-8_5
25. Wei, L., Zhang, S., Gao, W., Tian, Q.: Person transfer GAN to bridge domain gap for person re-identification. In: Proceedings of the IEEE Conference on Computer Vision and Pattern Recognition, pp. 79–88 (2018)
26. Yu, J., Oh, H.: Unsupervised vehicle re-identification via self-supervised metric learning using feature dictionary. In: 2021 IEEE/RSJ International Conference on Intelligent Robots and Systems (IROS), pp. 3806–3813. IEEE (2021)
27. Zheng, A., Sun, X., Li, C., Tang, J.: Aware progressive clustering for unsupervised vehicle re-identification. IEEE Trans. Intell. Transp. Syst. **23**, 11422–11435 (2021)

28. Zheng, K., Liu, W., He, L., Mei, T., Luo, J., Zha, Z.-J.: Group-aware label transfer for domain adaptive person re-identification. In: Proceedings of the IEEE/CVF Conference on Computer Vision and Pattern Recognition, pp. 5310–5319 (2021)
29. Zheng, L., Shen, L., Lu, T., Wang, S., Qi, T.: Scalable person re-identification: a benchmark. In: 2015 IEEE International Conference on Computer Vision (ICCV) (2015)
30. Zhong, Z., Zheng, L., Kang, G., Li, S., Yang, Y.: Random erasing data augmentation. In: Proceedings of the AAAI Conference on Artificial Intelligence (2020)

# TIR: A Two-Stage Insect Recognition Method for Convolutional Neural Network

Yunqi Feng[iD], Yang Liu[✉][iD], Xianlin Zhang[iD], and Xueming Li[iD]

School of Digital Media and Design Arts, Beijing University of Posts
and Telecommunications, Beijing, China
yang.liu@bupt.edu.cn

**Abstract.** Recognition of insect images has been a challenge work due to variation in appearance within a category and similarity between classes. Although it can be regarded as a fine-grained vision classification (FGVC) problem, the nature of insect metamorphosis, that insects within the same class may have very different form at different growth stage, makes it diffierent from other FGVC problems. In this paper, we first refine the IP102 dataset and build IP102-YOLO, an adjusted insect dataset which is more suitable for recognition, and propose a Two-stage Insect Recognition method for convolutional neural network (CNN), namely TIR, to improve its performance. TIR extracts deep features from insect images, then divides them into K groups by appearance similarity, and trains K recognition heads for CNN, each for a group of deep features. Our experimental results indicate that: (1) our dataset (IP102-YOLO) has better recognition performance with the same algorithm; (2) TIR outperforms the state-of-the-art insect recognition methods; (3) some of the most commonly used backbone CNN models achieve higher accuracy by following our TIR protocol. We will make our new IP102-YOLO dataset and code publicly available at https://github.com/Fengqiqif77/TIR.

**Keywords:** Insect pest recognition · Fine-grained visual classification · Convolutional neural network

## 1 Introduction

Insects are the most diverse animal group on the earth. Their distribution is extremely wide, and they are closely linked to human life. Pests can cause huge losses to agriculture, the pathogens they transport can cause diseases and allergies in humans, animals and plants. Insect pest recognition plays an important role in agriculture, forestry and biological control. There are about a million named insect species around us, and even insect experts can only identify the species of insects they are familiar with based on their expertise [1], and it is

S. Yu et al. (Eds.): PRCV 2022, LNCS 13535, pp. 668–680, 2022.
https://doi.org/10.1007/978-3-031-18910-4_53

impossible for non-professionals to distinguish so many kinds of insects. Recognition of insect images by machine learning is effective and can greatly reduce the consumption of human capital.

Traditional methdos mainly relied on experts to manually extract image features and classified them with classifiers such as SVM [2–4], which is not only inefficient, but also time-consuming to design feature extractors for recognizing diverse insect pests. To address these issues, there has been an increasing amount of researches in recent years using CNNs for the task of insect image recognition.

As we know, large-scale dataset is very important to reduce overfitting and improve learning performance in deep learning. Most insect datasets contain limited species and samples, which are not ideal for training deep learning networks with a large number of parameters, so Wu et al. [2] proposed the large-scale insect dataset IP102. However, we notice that some of the data in this dataset do not match the actual situation, so we propose a new insect recognition dataset IP102-YOLO based on it (see Sect. 3 for details).

Recent works on IP102 are either based on integrating CNNs together [5] or solving it as a general FGVC problem [6,14,16]. However, there are few studies take into account the metamorphosis of insects, which allows the same insect to have very different shapes at different growth stages, but different species of insects are more similar in appearance, making it difficult for deep networks to extract discriminative features from insect images. Hence we propose a two-stage learning framework to address this problem (see Sect. 4 for details).

In this paper, (1) we build a large-scale insect dataset (IP102-YOLO) based on the IP102 dataset. (2) We propose TIR to address the problem of large intra-class differences and small inter-class differences in insect pest recognition. (3) We conduct experiments on IP102 and IP102-YOLO using CNNs, and the results show that the IP102-YOLO dataset is more suitable for insect recognition tasks. (4) The backbone in our method can be changed and can improve its insect recognition performance.

## 2 Related Work

### 2.1 Insect Pest Dataset

Although insects are common in our daily lives, creating a labelled pest dataset is not an easy task, it requires not only a lot of time and specialist equipment, but also entomological expertise. Most of the images in insect image recognition datasets were collected in a specific area, resulting in a small number of images and species [7,8,27,28]. For example, Liu et al. [9] collects a dataset only consists of 5136 images in 12 common species of crop pest. [8] present a dataset which contains 563 samples and 10 common insect pests of field crops. Yet on average it only has 56 samples per class, which is also hard to train a CNN.

Recently, Wu et al. [2] proposed a large-scale insect pest image dataset named IP102 with 75,222 images covering 102 common insect pest species and images belonging to the same category may capture different growth forms of the same type of insect, which makes it the most popular insect image classification dataset

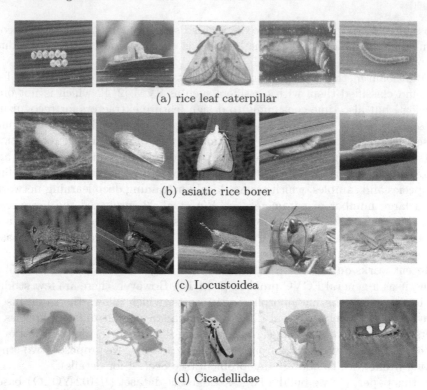

(a) rice leaf caterpillar

(b) asiatic rice borer

(c) Locustoidea

(d) Cicadellidae

**Fig. 1.** There are considerable variations in the appearance of insects at different stages of development. Each row shows images from the same category with large intra-class variations: pose variation, background variation and appearance variation.

(Fig. 1). The authors obtained images of insects through a search engine, worked with entomologists to filter the images to make sure an image contained only the same category of insects, and then annotated the images with the category label or bounding boxes. It contains two datasets, which can be used for object detection (IP102-OD) and image classification (IP102-IC), respectively.

## 2.2    Deep Learning in Insect Pest Recognition

With larger pest datasets emerged, insect recognition based on deep convolutional neural networks became mainstream. As we know, CNNs were created to solve a wide range of computer vision problems. AlexNet [10], proposed by Krizhevsky et al. in 2012, achieved good results in image classification tasks, after which much deeper and more efficient convolutional neural networks emerged, such as VggNet [11], GoogleNet [12] and ResNet [13]. Recently, almost all of the insect classification research in the field of computer vision based on deep learning networks. Zhou et al. [14] proposed a new network with fewer parameters and faster training than ResNet, achieving an accuracy of 53% on IP102.

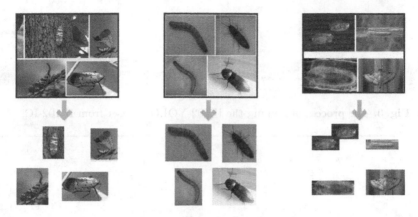

**Fig. 2.** There are some unreasonable images in the IP102 dataset. For example, the three images with black boxes in the first row, one image is stitched from multiple different insect images, which is not only bad for the CNN to learn discriminative features but also reduces the practicality of the research. We trained the YOLO network for object detection, then cropped unreasonable images into multiple images, and constructed a new dataset IP102-YOLO.

Liu et al. [6] [introduced a structure with an attention mechanism on the CNN, allowing the network to pay more attention to insects rather than the background environment. There are studies that integrate several basic CNNs together to improve classification results [15]. Xu et al. [17] used DenseNet [18] to deal with classification problems and achieved an accuracy of 61.06% on IP102. Luo et al. [16] proposed a multitasking framework capable of learning global features while learning local features, and its ResNet50-based network achieved 71.16% classification accuracy on IP102. As we know, CNNs relies on the image features information extracted from the convolutional layer for classification, and two images with similar content are likely to be classified in the same class by the CNN. Even though the aforementioned methods obtain promising results, they didn't take the intra-class similarity and inter-class difference in insect images into account.

## 2.3  Fine-Grained Visual Classification

In recent years, a number of deep learning methods have emerged for FGVC and it is widely used in fields such as species conservation, commodity manufacture and intelligent drive [19,29,30]. The purpose of FGVC is to classify images belonging to the same base class into more detailed subclasses, but due to the small inter-class differences and large intra-class differences between subclasses, fine-grained image classification is more difficult than the ordinary image classification task. To deal this problem, Xie et al. [20] divided the car dataset into different subsets according to the shooting direction by a manual method to reduce inter-class differences. Similarly, Ge et al. [21] pre-clustered visually similar images into subsets and use subset-specific CNNs. By dividing the dataset,

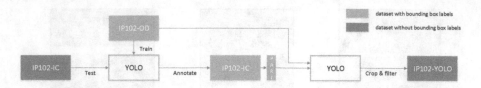

**Fig. 3.** The process of refining the IP102-YOLO dataset from IP102-IC.

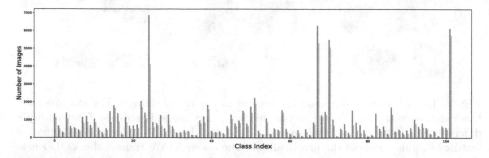

**Fig. 4.** Distribution of IP102-YOLO dataset (blue lines) and IP102 dataset (red lines). IP102-YOLO contains more data than IP102. (Color figure online)

they intelligently address the problem of large differences between classes and small differences within classes. However, Xie's experiment requires a lot of work-force to add super-class labels to the dataset, and the method proposed by Ge et al. requires training all parameters of $k + 3$ ($k$ is the number of subsets) classification networks, which is very time-consuming.

Many studies use fine-grained classification methods to classify insect images, but the classification results are not very good. As stated in [16], inset recognition is not an exact FGVC problem. Thus, in this paper, we mainly focus on the procedure with deep CNNs for insect pest categories and intend to explore how to build a scientific image classification system with CNNs to achieve better performance on IP102 dataset.

## 3    IP102-YOLO

IP102 [2] is currently one of the most popular large-scale insect image datasets. Although the creators of the dataset were thoughtful enough to remove images that contained multiple insects, there were still some unreasonable images in the dataset that made it difficult for the deep network to learn the characteristics of the insects.

As the Fig. 2 shows, some of the images in the IP102 dataset are unrealistic and are assembled from multiple images of the same species with different life cycles. It is unusual for a single image to contain multiple developmental forms of insects in real life. To deal this problem, we decide to segment this image to generate a new dataset.

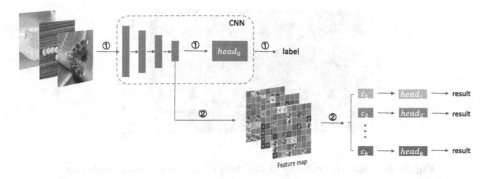

**Fig. 5.** Overview of TIR. It mainly consists of two steps for global features extracting and fine-grained features mining. At the ① step, we fine-tune all layers of CNN. In ②, the dataset is clustered into K subsets according to features of images, and each subset corresponds to a *head* for image classification.

We use a semi-supervised approach to make a new dataset IP102-YOLO. The YOLO [26] target detection model is trained based on the labeled IP102-OD dataset to obtain $model_1$, and then $model_1$ predicts the target detection pseudo-label of the IP102-IC dataset. We take the part of the pseudo-label data whose confidence is higher than 0.25 and Intersection over Union (IoU) is less than 0.45, and train a new object detection $model_2$ together with the IP102-OD data. Finally, apply $model_2$ on the unlabeled IP102-IC dataset to predict and cut the insect area, filter out images that are less than 50 pixels long or wide to prevent low-resolution images from affecting the classification task. We use the YOLOV5X model, set the input image size to 320, and train for 100 epochs (Fig. 3).

We obtain a new dataset of 97,494 images. The dataset is divided in a 6:1:3 split with the same proportions as the original dataset, with 58,540 images for training, 9,698 images for validation and 29,256 images for testing, and ensuring that there are enough samples of each category to participate in testing. As shown in Fig. 4, each category in IP102-YOLO contains more images than those in IP102, and the proportion of images in each category is basically the same.

## 4   TIR

In this section, we introduce the proposed method in detail. It consists of two main stages: First, we use image appearance similarity to divide the dataset into K subsets. Second, using separate CNNs to learn K subsets features and classify, respectively (Fig. 5).

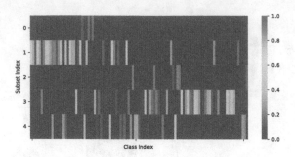

**Fig. 6.** Normalized heatmap of the data distribution after clustering.

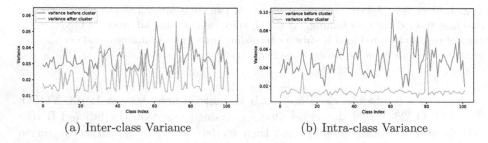

(a) Inter-class Variance                    (b) Intra-class Variance

**Fig. 7.** Comparison variance after cluster (blue lines) and variance before cluster (red lines). (Color figure online)

## 4.1 Pre-clustering

Inspired by [21], we train a CNN on the IP102-YOLO dataset by means of transfer learning and use it to extract global features of insect images.

We choose the features from the last module of CNN as the basis to generate subsets in terms of visual similar images. These were selected due to their are often used by researchers for image classification and clustering [21,31]. The growth stages of pests can generally be divided into four stages: eggs, larvae, pupa, and adults, we set the value $k$ of K-means to 5.

We denote the number of images in class $i$ as $N_i$. $f$ represents image features, $f_{i,j}$ is the feature of image $j$ in class $i$, and $\bar{f}_i$ is the mean of the features of class $i$. The intra-class variance is calculated by:

$$V_i^{intra} = \frac{1}{N_i} \sum_{j \in [0, N_i)} (f_{i,j} - \bar{f}_i)^2 \tag{1}$$

The inter-class variance of class $i$ is calculated by:

$$V_i^{inter} = \frac{1}{101} \sum_{t \in [0,102), t \neq i} (\bar{f}_i - \bar{f}_t)^2 \tag{2}$$

We draw a heatmap (Fig. 6) based on the distribution of each subset and category after clustering. The warmer the color of the block is, the more images

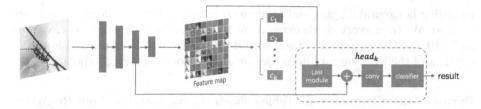

**Fig. 8.** The feature representation of the test image is from the backbone.

of this category are in the subset; conversely, the colder the color of the block is, the less images of this category are in the subset.

As can be seen from Fig. 7 that, clustering can significantly reduce the intra-class variance while keeping the inter-class variance basically unchanged.

### 4.2  Subset Feature Learning and Classification

As we mentioned earlier, images of the same pest can look very different due to the stage of growth, environment and posture of the pest. It is a major difficulty in insect image classification is that the metamorphosis of insects leads to large differences in the morphology of the same insect in different growth stages, so we added a clustering step before classification. After clustering, the images in each subset have high similarity in appearance, and we want to learn small differences between them.

However, it takes a lot of time to train k CNNs from scratch, so we construct K head structures for classification of K subsets respectively. We define head composition rules that apply to any backbone, it contains the last feature extraction base module of the pre-trained backbone CNN (LFM), a feature fusion module and a classifier composed of three linear layers. For example, the LFM corresponding to the backbone ResNet50 and Densenet are layer4 and dense-block4, and the deep feature information of the image can be quickly obtained through LFM. The purpose of the feature fusion module is to introduce the shallow information of the image and improve the classification effect.

When testing, we extract the global features of the test images using the pre-trained global CNN, then decide which subset the test image belongs to by the distance from the test image feature to the center feature of each subset, and then use the corresponding *head* to predict the category (see Fig. 8).

## 5   Experiment

### 5.1  Performance Comparison

**Experimental Parameters.** We use the standard metric accuracy and F1-score to evaluate the accuracy of the test model. For fair comparisons, we resize each input image to $224 \times 224$. Common training augmentation approaches including horizontal flipping and random cropping, as well as colour jittering are applied. We train every single experiment for 70 epochs with weight decay value as $5\times10^{-4}$. SGD optimizer is used with initial learning rate of unfixed layers to 0.001, and the learning rate decreases by a factor of 0.1 every 30 epoch.

**Performance Comparison.** Table 1 shows the comparisons of our ResNet50-based results with reported results, that for the backbone network ResNet50 the accuracy of TIR achieves 83.64% which is a considerable improvement over the previous state-of-the-art system [16]. This result shows that pre-clustering and training each subset separately can effectively reduce the influence of insect metamorphosis and background in images on the insect recognition task, and guide the backbone network to extract discriminative features more effectively.

Among them, Luo et al. [16] also believes that the IP102 dataset needs preprocessing. They proposed SGDL-Net, which is mainly composed of two modules, one module to crop the raw image by locating the subject, and the other module to classify the cropped image. We believe that the comparison of SGDL-Net with TIR based on IP102 dataset is unfair and should be compared with TIR based on IP102-YOLO. Furthermore, GAEnsemble uses an ensemble network and finally achieves a higher F1 score than the TIR method based on the IP102 dataset. Our method can also be added to [15] as part of an ensemble network to improve classification results.

**Table 1.** F1-score and test accuracy (%) by ours method and other state-of-art methods.

| Method | Backbone | Accuracy (%) | F1-score |
|---|---|---|---|
| ExquisiteNet [14] | ResNet50 | 52.32 | N/A |
| DMF-ResNet [6] | ResNet50 | 59.22 | 58.37 |
| GAEnsemble [15] | Ensemble | 67.13 | 65.76 |
| Nanni et al. [25] | DenseNet201 | 61.93 | 59.20 |
| Xu et al. [17] | DenseNet121 | 61.10 | N/A |
| SGDL-Net [16] | ResNet50 | 71.16 | 63.89 |
| TIR(IP102) | ResNet50 | 68.51 | 64.33 |
| TIR(IP102-YOLO) | ResNet50 | **83.64** | **82.96** |

**Comparison with IP102.** In this section, we evaluate the performance of state-of-the-art deep convolutional networks on the IP102 and IP102-YOLO dataset, including AlexNet [10], VggNet16 [11], ResNet50 [13] and DenseNet [18].

All the networks are pre-trained on the ImageNet [24] and then fine-tuned on IP102 and IP102-YOLO respectively. The results of DenseNet are taken from [17]. During training, we resize images to 224 × 224 and set the batch size to 64, use Stochastic Gradient Descent (SGD) optimizer and an initial learning

**Table 2.** Comparision of classification results on IP102 and IP102-YOLO. The '*' denotes results are taken from other papers.

| Dataset | Method | Accuracy (%) | F1-score |
|---|---|---|---|
| IP102 | AlexNet | 48.6 | 47.3 |
| | VGG16 | 52.3 | 50.9 |
| | ResNet50 | 55.1 | 53.5 |
| | DenseNet121* | 61.1 | N/A |
| IP102-YOLO | AlexNet | 62.8 | 57.6 |
| | VGG16 | 63.3 | 56.6 |
| | ResNet50 | 66.9 | 60.5 |
| | DenseNet121 | 70.4 | 64.3 |

rate of 0.01, decreasing by a factor of 0.1 every 40 epochs. The weight decay and momentum parameters are set to 0.0005 and 0.9.

Table 2 shows results of AlexNet, VGG16, ResNet50, and DenseNet on two datasets, and the classification performance of IP102-YOLO is better than that of IP102 on these CNNs, the accuracy rate is 11.575% higher on average. There are two main reasons for this: on the one hand, IP102-YOLO has 97,494 images, which is 22,272 more than the IP102 dataset, improving the generalization performance of CNN. On the other hand, the insects occupy a larger area of images in the IP102-YOLO dataset, which reduces the interference of the background and is beneficial to CNNs to extract useful features.

**Feature Fusion.** To pay attention to both global and fine grained features in image classification, we investigate three types of features for feature fusion. Features are obtained from layer1, layer2 and layer3 of ResNet50 and fused with the features of layer4. Through experiments, we found that selecting layer3 features for feature fusion can get the best classification results (Table 3).

**Table 3.** F1-score and test accuracy (%) for features fusion with different features.

| Features | Accuracy (%) | F1-score |
|---|---|---|
| layer1 | 81.79 | 80.76 |
| layer2 | 82.38 | 81.02 |
| layer3 | 83.64 | 82.96 |

## 5.2 Classification Results Based on Different Backbone

Additionally, we deploy our TIR protocol on some of the most popular CNN backbones, AlexNet, VGG16, ResNet50, DenseNet, on IP102-YOLO and compare performance with their original networks. We specify the rules for building

**Table 4.** F1-score and test accuracy (%) by ours method with different backbone. The "*" denotes using TIR.

| Method | Accuracy (%) | F1-score |
|---|---|---|
| AlexNet | 62.8 | 57.6 |
| AlexNet* | 79.9 | 79.0 |
| Vgg16 | 63.3 | 56.6 |
| Vgg16* | 66.9 | 61.1 |
| ResNet50 | 66.9 | 60.5 |
| ResNet50* | 83.6 | 83.0 |
| DenseNet121 | 70.4 | 64.3 |
| DenseNet121* | 85.4 | 84.7 |

the head module in TIR, which consists of the last feature extraction block of the backbone CNN, a feature fusion module and a classifier. The classifier consists of three linear layers. Table 4 proves that our method can improve the insect pest recognition performance of most CNNs, and users can replace the backbone according to their needs. We employ pre-clustering to increases inter-class variance and reduces intra-class variance, which further improved the overall performance.

## 6    Conclusion

In this paper, we build a large-scale dataset, named IP102-YOLO, for insect recognition. In addition, we propose a classification system to address the problem of insect pest recognition with large intra-class differences and small inter-class differences. Through an unsupervised approach, similar images in the insect dataset are grouped together, and then the CNN furthers learn features of the images in each cluster. We test this scheme on the IP102-YOLO dataset and achieve excellent image recognition results, in which the classification accuracy rate with ResNet50 as the backbone reached 83.6%. Furthermore, the backbone of this method can be replaced with any CNN, and we demonstrate that our method can improve its classification accuracy for insect images by using different CNNs as the backbone.

## References

1. Hiary, H.A.: Fast and accurate detection and dlassification of plant diseases. Int. J. Comput. Appl. **17**(1), 31–38 (2011)
2. Wu, X., Zhan, C., Lai, Y.K., Cheng, M.M.: Ip102: a large-scale benchmark dataset for insect pest recognition. In: 2019 IEEE/CVF Conference on Computer Vision and Pattern Recognition (CVPR), pp. 8787–8796 (2019)
3. Manoja, M.: Early detection of pest on leaves using support vector machine. Int. J. Electr. Electr. Res. **2**(4), 187–194 (2014)

4. Ams, A.: Pest identification in leaf images using SVM classifier. Int. J. Comput. Intell. Inform. **6**(1), 30–41 (2016)
5. Ayan, E., Erbay, H., Varn, F.: Crop pest classification with a genetic algorithm-based weighted ensemble of deep convolutional neural networks. Comput. Electr. Agric. **179**(4), 105809 (2020)
6. Liu, W., Wu, G., Ren, F.: Deep multi-branch fusion residual network for insect pest recognition. In: IEEE Transactions on Cognitive and Developmental Systems, pp. 1–1 (2020)
7. Ghosh, R.: Tea insect pests classification based on artificial neural networks. Int. J. Comput. Eng. Sci. **2**(6), 336 (2012)
8. Deng, L., Wang, Y., Han, Z., Yu, R.: Research on insect pest image detection and recognition based on bio-inspired methods. Biosys. Eng. **169**, 134–148 (2018)
9. Liu, Z., Gao, J., Yang, G., Zhang, H., He, Y.: Localization and classification of paddy field pests using a saliency map and deep convolutional neural network. Sci. Rep. **6**, 20410 (2016)
10. Krizhevsky, A., Sutskever, I., Hinton, G.: ImageNet classification with deep convolutional neural networks. In: Advances in Neural Information Processing Systems (2012)
11. Simonyan, K., Zisserman, A., Hinton, G.: Very deep convolutional networks for large-scale image recognition. Comput. Sci. (2014)
12. Szegedy, C., Wei, L., Jia, Y., Sermanet, P., Rabinovich, A.: Going deeper with convolutions. In: 2016 IEEE Conference on Computer Vision and Pattern Recognition (CVPR) (2016)
13. He, K., Zhang, X., Ren, S., Sun, J.: Deep residual learning for image recognition. In: Advances in Neural Information Processing Systems (2012)
14. Zhou, S. Y., Su, C. Y.: Efficient convolutional neural network for pest recognition - ExquisiteNet. In: 2020 IEEE Eurasia Conference on IOT, Communication and Engineering (ECICE) (2020)
15. Ayan, E., H Erbay, Varn, F.: Crop pest classification with a genetic algorithm-based weighted ensemble of deep convolutional neural networks. Comput. Elect. Agric. **179**(4), 105809 (2020)
16. Luo, Q., Wan, L., Tian, L., Li, Z.: Saliency guided discriminative learning for insect pest recognition. In: 2021 International Joint Conference on Neural Networks (IJCNN), pp. 1–8. (2021). https://doi.org/10.1109/IJCNN52387.2021.9533421
17. Xu, L., Wang, Y.: XCloud: design and implementation of AI cloud platform with RESTful API service (2019)
18. Huang, G., Liu, Z., Laurens, V., Weinberger, K.Q.: Densely connected convolutional networks. In: 2017 IEEE Conference on Computer Vision and Pattern Recognition (CVPR), pp. 2261–2269 (2017). https://doi.org/10.1109/CVPR.2017.243
19. Zhang, J., Xie, Y., Wu, Q., Xia, Y.: Medical image classification using synergic deep learning. Med. Image Anal. **54**, 10–19 (2019)
20. Yang, T., Wang, X., Lin, Y., Xie, S.: Hyper-class augmented and regularized deep learning for fine-grained image classification. In: 2015 IEEE Conference on Computer Vision and Pattern Recognition (CVPR), pp. 2245–2254 (2015). https://doi.org/10.1109/CVPR.2015.7298880
21. Ge, Z., Mccool, C., Sanderson, C., Corke, P.: Subset feature learning for fine-grained category classification. In: 2015 IEEE Conference on Computer Vision and Pattern Recognition Workshops (CVPRW), pp. 46–52 (2015). https://doi.org/10.1109/CVPRW.2015.7301271

22. Aggarwal, C.C.: On randomization, public information and the curse of dimensionality. In: 2007 IEEE 23rd International Conference on Data Engineering, pp. 136–145 (2007). https://doi.org/10.1109/ICDE.2007.367859
23. Tibshirani, R.: Estimating the number of clusters in a data set via the gap statistic. J. R. Stat. Soc. B **63**(2), 411–423 (2001)
24. He, K., Zhang, X., Ren, S., Sun, J.: Delving deep into rectifiers: surpassing human-level performance on imagenet classification. In: 2015 IEEE International Conference on Computer Vision (ICCV), pp. 1026–1034 (2015). https://doi.org/10.1109/ICCV.2015.123
25. Nanni, L., Maguolo, G., Pancino, F.: Insect pest image detection and recognition based on bio-inspired methods. Eco. Inform. **57**, 101089 (2020)
26. Redmon, J., Divvala, S., Girshick, R., Farhadi, A.: You only look once: unified, real-time object detection. In: 2016 IEEE Conference on Computer Vision and Pattern Recognition (CVPR), pp. 779–788 (2016). https://doi.org/10.1109/CVPR.2016.91
27. Xie, C., Wang, R., Jie, Z., Chen, P., Wei, D.: Multi-level learning features for automatic classification of field crop pests. Comput. Electron. Agric. **152**, 233–241 (2018)
28. Xie, C., Zhang, J., Li, R., Li, J., Hong, P.: Automatic classification for field crop insects via multiple-task sparse representation and multiple-kernel learning. Comput. Electr. Agric. **129**, 123–132 (2015)
29. Chang, D., Pang, K., Zheng, Y., Ma, Z., Song, Y.-Z., Guo, J.: Your "Flamingo" is my "Bird": fine-grained, or not. In: 2021 IEEE/CVF Conference on Computer Vision and Pattern Recognition (CVPR), pp. 11471–11480 (2021). https://doi.org/10.1109/CVPR46437.2021.01131
30. Zhang, J., Xie, Y., Wu, Q.: Medical image classification using synergic deep learning. Med. Image Anal. **54**, 10–19 (2019)
31. Donahue, J., Jia, Y., Vinyals, O., Hoffman, J., Darrell, T.: DeCAF: a deep convolutional activation feature for generic visual recognition. In: 2013 International Conference on Machine Learning. JMLR.org

# Discerning Coteaching: A Deep Framework for Automatic Identification of Noise Labels

Qiliang Wei[1], Peng Fu[1,2(✉)], Peng Zhang[1], and Tao Wang[1]

[1] School of Computer Science and Engineering, Nanjing University of Science and Technology, Nanjing, China
fupeng@njust.edu.cn
[2] Jiangsu Key Laboratory of Spectral Imaging and Intelligent Sense, Nanjing University of Science and Technology, Nanjing, China

**Abstract.** Training datasets for deep models inevitably contain noisy labels, such labels can seriously impair the performance of deep models. Empirically, all labels will be remembered after enough epochs, while pure labels will be remembered first and then noise labels. Inspired by this, we propose a new deep framework named *"Discerning Coteaching"* (DC). It can automatically identify noise and pure labels during training without additional prior knowledge. Specifically we train two networks at the same time, each network will contain an additional categorical cross entropy (CCE) loss. Then a threshold is dynamically selected based on the CCE, samples with a loss value greater than the threshold will be discarded directly, the rest will be sent to its peer network for updating. We validate the framework on Cifar10 and UCMD, and the results reveal that DC has a positive effect in dealing with noisy labels.

**Keywords:** Deep learning · Noise label · Coteaching · Sample selection

## 1 Introduction

Deep learning is an integral part of research in the field of computer vision, such as image classification [1,2], object detection [3,4], semantic segmentation [5] and so on. This significant success extremely relies on correctly labeled datasets, but a considerable part of the data set is not correctly labeled in many cases. These labels fail to classify the samples correctly are called the "noise label", on the contrary those correct labels are called "pure label". Noise labels can seriously affect the performance of deep models and hinder applications.

This work was in part supported by the National Natural Science Foundation of China under Grant no. 61801222, and in part supported by the Fundamental Research Funds for the Central Universities under Grant no. 30919011230, and in part supported by the Fundamental Research Funds for the Central Universities under Grant no. JSGP202204, and in part supported by the Natural Science Foundation of Shandong Province under Grant No. ZR2021MF039.

S. Yu et al. (Eds.): PRCV 2022, LNCS 13535, pp. 681–692, 2022.
https://doi.org/10.1007/978-3-031-18910-4_54

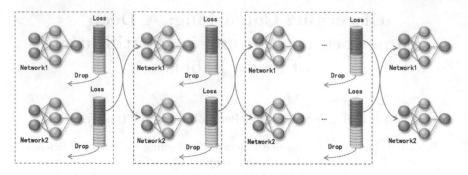

**Fig. 1.** The framework of Discerning Coteaching. We train two networks simultaneously, where each network computes two different loss functions. One of these two loss functions is used for sample selection and the other is used to update the network. It is worth noting that the two networks pick data for each other to update, and the unpicked data will be discarded.

Using samples with noise labels to train deep neural networks is a subject of widespread concern, and one of the most important methods named "Coteaching" [6,10], which trains two networks at the same time then select part of samples for update. However, this kinds of methods rely on the ratio of noise labels, which is always unavailable.

Another series of methods is dedicated to replacing the categorical cross entropy loss with "robust loss" [7–9,11], related researchers achieve better performance by improving the robustness of the model. Unfortunately, this approach suffers from overfitting in some cases.

After that, a class of methods that cannot be neglected of this field is based on the confusion matrix of the noise labels which records the probability that one label is misjudged as another [15–19]. Method of this kind utilize matrix as prior knowledge to assist or guide training. However, the confusion matrix is usually not available or hard to be estimated in practice.

The main idea of last category in this field is similar to semi-supervised learning, its revise noise labels with corrects. [20–24] Methods of this type need to separate noise labels and pure labels, besides an extra set of data with clean labels is needed.

In this paper, we propose a framework named "*Discerning Coteaching*" (DC), which can handle noise labels supernumerary pure set or prior knowledge. In addition, our framework also can separate pure labels and noise labels automatically. DC contains two networks, and each network computes two loss when every batch is fed to them. One loss value is for updating, the other is for sample selection. It is worth noting that these two networks select samples for each other not for themselves, we call this operation as "cross updating". Traditional deep learning tends to have only one network, when the network misjudges a noise label as pure label, this label will participate in network updates. Next time the network meets the label, this label will be judged as pure label again, so the

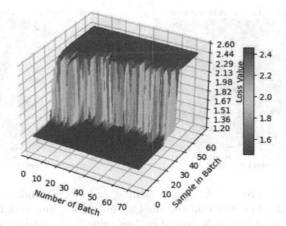

**Fig. 2.** The step in loss value of samples after sorting. Deep models tend to memorize correctly labeled samples first, such samples always have smaller loss values. Combined with the characteristics of CCE, the loss values of sample in the same batch will look like a step after sorting as shown in the figure.

single network structure is more susceptible to the influence of noisy labels. For dual network structure, a label will be used for updating only if both networks consider this label to be pure label at the same time. Since the two networks have different learning capabilities, our framework will improve the robustness and discrimination ability of the network against noisy labels. The schematic of Discerning Coteaching is shown in Fig. 1.

The main contributions of this paper can be summarised as the following three points:

- We propose a framework for dealing with noisy labels without using additional datasets or prior knowledge.
- We propose a method to automatically separate pure labels and noise labels.
- We analyze the impact of different loss functions on our framework and indicate the applicable scenarios.

## 2    Discerning Coteaching

### 2.1    Theory of Sample Selection

Our framework can recognizes the pure labels during training, the rest of labels are considered as noise labels, they will be dropped directly before updating.

Categorical cross entropy (CCE) loss described by formula (1) is the most widely used loss function in the training of neural networks loss. In formula (1), $L_i$ is the loss corresponding to the i-th sample, $k$ represents the number of types of samples, $\hat{y}_{ij}$ is element in $\hat{y}_i$ predicted by model for $i$th sample, which also represents the probability sample belongs to the $j$th category. Labels come from

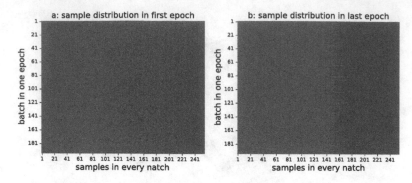

**Fig. 3.** Every pixel represent for a single sample, and a row stands for a batch in the training. Color of pixel express that the label is right or not, blue is right and red is the opposite, and the samples will be sorted by loss value from smallest to largest. These two figure are the first epoch (left) and last epoch (right) of Discerning Coteaching while dealing with Cifar10 with 40% symmetric noise labels. (Color figure online)

dataset is converted to one-hot encoding, $y_{ij}$ comes from $y_i = [y_{i1}, y_{i2}...y_{ik}]$ in which only one element is 1, and the rest are 0.

$$L_i = -\sum_k^{j=1} y_{ij} \ln \hat{y}_{ij} \tag{1}$$

It can be obtained by uncomplicated analysis that loss value of inaccurate predicted samples is obviously larger than those correct predicted, the specific performance in the experiment is that there is a visible step in loss value of samples after sorting, shown in Fig. 2.

An obvious property of deep models is that they always remember pure labels instead of noise labels early in training, we have proven this empirically. This property is based on an assumption that the most labels should be pure labels. Otherwise, the model will consider the label with the largest proportion as the correct label, which will cause noise labels to participate in the update of the model and invalidate the model.

According to the characteristics of the deep model and CCE mentioned above, it is not difficult to infer that the loss value of noise labels is larger than that of pure labels in the early stage of training. So we can separate noise labels and pure labels where the loss value has the largest gradient. It is worth pointing out that updating the model requires another loss function rather than CCE in order to prevent overfitting.

## 2.2   Dealing Noise Labels with Discerning Coteaching

Discerning Coteaching is described in algorithm 1. To pick pure labels from every batch, we compute an additional CCE before updating. This CCE loss function is only used for sample selection, it does not participate in updating. Models updated by CCE learn faster and be more susceptible to noise labels. Therefore, a more robust loss function is required when updating the network.

In the beginning of training, all samples will be used to update the network. Due to the nature of neural networks, only correctly labeled samples will be remembered. So the corresponding CCE value will be smaller than that of noise labels, and a step will emerge after sorting by CCE value. The samples with the smaller CCE value is considered labeled by pure labels and participates in subsequent updates. After seeing enough pure labels, the model can accurately separate pure labels and noise labels.

Figure 3 shows the sample distribution of first epoch and last epoch in Discerning Coteaching. From first few lines in $a$ of Fig. 3, we can easily find out that the pure samples and noise samples are uniform distribution, because all the samples have the same probability to be selected while forming a batch. Yet, potential to separate noise samples and pure samples start emerging after model learns from adequate samples. So in the lower part of $a$, the samples aggregate into two categories after sorted by loss value, however boundary of the two samples is still less obvious after first epoch. The $b$ of Fig. 3 are sample distribution in the last epoch, it is obvious that there are clear boundaries.

---

**Algorithm 1.** Discerning Coteaching Algorithm

**Require:** $w_f, w_g$: parameters of network $f$ and network $g$; $\eta$: learning rate; $T_{max}$:
   Maximum number of epochs; $T_{cross}$: Epoch when cross updating start;
**Ensure:** $w_f$ and $w_g$;
1:  **for** $T = 1, 2, ..., T_{max}$ **do**
2:     **Shuffle** training set $\mathcal{D}$;
3:     **for** $N = 1, 2, ..., N_{max}$ **do**
4:        **Fetch** mini-batch $\overline{\mathcal{D}}$ from $\mathcal{D}$;
5:        **Obtain** $e_f = sorted(CCE(f, \overline{\mathcal{D}}))$, $e_g = sorted(CCE(g, \overline{\mathcal{D}}))$;
6:        **Obtain** $G_f$, $G_q$ where $e_g$, $e_f$ have max gradient;
7:        **if** $T < T_{cross}$ **then**
8:           $\overline{\mathcal{D}}_f = \overline{\mathcal{D}}, \overline{\mathcal{D}}_g = \overline{\mathcal{D}}$;
9:        **else**
10:          $\overline{\mathcal{D}}_f = \overline{\mathcal{D}}$ correspond to $e_g [0 : G_g]$;
11:          $\overline{\mathcal{D}}_g = \overline{\mathcal{D}}$ correspond to $e_f [0 : G_f]$;
12:       **end if**
13:       **Update** $w_f = w_f - \eta \nabla \mathcal{L}(f, \overline{\mathcal{D}}_f)$;
14:       **Update** $w_g = w_g - \eta \nabla \mathcal{L}(g, \overline{\mathcal{D}}_g)$;
15:    **end for**
16: **end for**

---

In the algorithm we train two networks parameterized by $w_f$ and $w_g$ separately at the same time, $N_{max}$ is the number of mini-batches which is decided by the size of data set $\mathcal{D}$ and mini-batch, $\mathcal{L}$ is a robust loss. During the training, we feed nets with all the samples in the initial $T_{cross}$ epochs indiscriminately. After that only specifically samples could take part in training, remaining part would be drop directly. $e_f$ and $e_g$ are loss value calculated by CCE, instead of calculate average value of samples, we recorded its all. Specifically speaking every sample

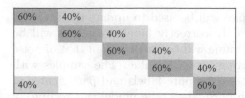 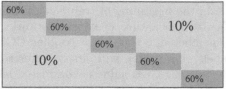

**Fig. 4.** Transition matrices of asymmetry (left) and symmetry (right) noise with 60% labels correct and we use five classes as an example.

in the same batch could find the corresponding loss in both $e_f$ and $e_g$, so they are lists with length equal to mini-batch. In the epoch later than $T_{cross}$ these two lists of loss are sorted from smallest to largest, then find where the gradient maximum $G_f$ and $G_g$ is, corresponding loss values are $e'_f$ and $e'_g$. Samples whose loss is smaller than $e'_f$ and $e'_g$ would be picked as $\overline{D}_f$ and $\overline{D}_g$. At last picked samples are feed to peer network to update their parameter.

## 3 Experiment

We verified our algorithm in the datasets named Cifar10 and UCMerced LandUse respectively, then compared the experimental result with GCE [7], SCE [8], NCE [9] and Coteaching [6].

### 3.1 Datasets Description

Cifar10 is collected by Alex Krizhevsky etc. [12], consists of 60 thousand color images, and all of them have been cropped into $32 \times 32$. This dataset contains 10 class, with 6 thousand images per class. Besides 50 thousand images are selected as training set and the rest of images are treated as test set, both training set and test set have the same number of every class.

University of California, Merced remote sensing image data set (UCMD), Yi Yang and Shawn Newsam [13] collected aerial orthoimageries from the United States Geological Survey (USGS), images from this data set contains 21 US regions, and they are devided into 21 land-use classes, every class contains 100 images. In addition images share have the same size ($256 \times 256$) and resolution (a pixel resolution of one foot). In this paper, we randomly select eighty percent of images as train set and the remaining twenty percent of images are treated as test set.

### 3.2 Experimental Setup

We choose PyTorch as frame to implement the mentioned methods, all the networks are the DenseNet-121 [14] which is pretrained by the researchers of PyTorch team and the number of epochs is set to 100 for all the experiments. In dealing with Cifar10, 256 images are contained in one batch, while 128 images could be found in the batch for UCMD because of insufficient sample size. To ensure that all the batch contains enough correctly labelled samples, so the batch size should be larger than other methods. We choose Adam with default parameters as optimizer for all the methods, and the initial learning rate is set as 0.0001, 0.0005 and 0.001 respectively, and $T_{cross}$ is selected from 10, 15 and 20 then we pick the result with highest accuracy.

For the noisy label, most of researchers choose to add two types of noise: symmetry and asymmetry [6–11]. Both of them will shift the correct label to another, symmetry noise means all the incorrect labels have the same probability to be selected, on the contrary asymmetry noise stand for all the instances in identical group have same incorrect labels. Figure 4 shows the transition matrices of two type of noise. The noise rate is range from 0.1 to 0.5 when the noise type is symmetry, and the upper limit of asymmetry noise decreases to 0.4 to make sure most labels are correct, otherwise the model would regard the noise labels as correct.

### 3.3 Experimental Result and Analysis

**Result on Cifar10.** First, we choose Cifar10 with artificial noise label as the dataset for training. Result of experts are shown in Table 1, Cot stands for Coteaching, DC stands for Discerning Coteaching. The font of highest accuracy is bold in the Table 1, from which we can see the methods we proposed outperforms other methods in most situation, expect SCE with 0.1 noise ratio in both type of noise and Coteaching with 40% asymmetrical noise.

**Table 1.** The best accuracy of different methods on Cifar10

| Noise ratio | Symmetry | | | | | Asymmetry | | | |
|---|---|---|---|---|---|---|---|---|---|
| | 0.1 | 0.2 | 0.3 | 0.4 | 0.5 | 0.1 | 0.2 | 0.3 | 0.4 |
| NCE | 87.18 | 85.74 | 84.94 | 83.53 | 80.76 | 87.21 | 85.65 | 83.01 | 66.41 |
| SCE | **87.82** | 86.50 | 85.16 | 83.48 | 81.23 | **87.73** | 85.83 | 83.28 | 64.38 |
| GCE | 87.09 | 85.29 | 83.46 | 81.14 | 78.68 | 86.88 | 83.90 | 80.32 | 75.68 |
| Cot | 85.72 | 84.79 | 83.55 | 81.87 | 79.33 | 85.51 | 84.45 | 82.88 | **76.88** |
| DC | 87.80 | **86.87** | **86.29** | **85.08** | **83.25** | 87.31 | **86.70** | **84.78** | 72.93 |

In addition, we also tested the effect of using different loss functions on the results when updating. The best accuracy is recorded by Table 2. From Table 1 and 2 we can find out that there is little difference between these methods except Coteaching while the noise ratio is 0.1 regardless which noise type is. When Discerning Coteaching updated by GCE, it achieves the best accuracy with 40% asymmetrical noise, but it does not perform well in other cases.

**Table 2.** The best accuracy of Discerning Coteaching utilizes different loss function on Cifar10

| Noise ratio | Symmetry | | | | | Asymmetry | | | |
|---|---|---|---|---|---|---|---|---|---|
| | 0.1 | 0.2 | 0.3 | 0.4 | 0.5 | 0.1 | 0.2 | 0.3 | 0.4 |
| $DC_{NCE}$ | 87.64 | 86.72 | 85.99 | 84.82 | 83.48 | 87.34 | 86.77 | 82.93 | 70.76 |
| $DC_{GCE}$ | 87.59 | 86.03 | 84.80 | 81.87 | 78.25 | 86.93 | 85.36 | 80.80 | 77.21 |

Table 3 reveals ability to separate noise and pure labels of our models, the first row of cell is the ratio of samples selected by model to the total number of samples, meanwhile the second row stands for the ratio of pure samples to the number of samples selected by model, in addition we regard the selected samples as pure samples in all experiments. From the second row we can find out easily that the label corrosion has been ameliorated obviously through our methods. Separation accuracy (second row of cell) also suffer from noise labels, falls as noise ratio rises, when the noise type is symmetry, separation accuracy seems to be more stable than the noise type is asymmetry, the same phenomenon can also be found in classification accuracy described in Table 1. There is a rapid decline in separation accuracy when noise ratio shift from 0.3 to 0.4 at asymmetry noise type, however only classification accuracy of DC and $DC_{NCE}$ contain same drops, $DC_{GCE}$ is on the contrary.

**Table 3.** How many labels are considered as pure labels by model, second row of same cell stands for how many labels are really pure labels after selected by model.

| Noise ratio | Symmetry | | | | | Asymmetry | | | |
|---|---|---|---|---|---|---|---|---|---|
| | 0.1 | 0.2 | 0.3 | 0.4 | 0.5 | 0.1 | 0.2 | 0.3 | 0.4 |
| DC | 87.16 | 68.18 | 77.57 | 59.29 | 50.36 | 88.38 | 77.97 | 72.43 | 60.76 |
| | 99.093 | 97.72 | 98.73 | 96.05 | 93.84 | 99.05 | 98.34 | 94.00 | 76.47 |
| $DC_{NCE}$ | 88.21 | 77.58 | 67.90 | 58.87 | 49.63 | 86.82 | 77.41 | 66.87 | 53.56 |
| | 99.19 | 98.74 | 97.74 | 96.30 | 94.37 | 99.46 | 98.50 | 91.30 | 74.75 |
| $DC_{GCE}$ | 90.24 | 80.28 | 71.43 | 63.60 | 60.17 | 90.53 | 83.36 | 86.65 | 90.92 |
| | 98.83 | 97.85 | 95.96 | 92.19 | 82.25 | 98.57 | 95.07 | 79.83 | 64.26 |

In more detail, $DC_{GCE}$ selects 90.92% of all samples while noise ratio is 0.4, and the ratio of truly labeled samples to selected is 64.28% which is not much different with initial noise ratio. So under this circumstance $DC_{GCE}$ almost degenerates into pure GCE, and GCE seems to be great for handling this situation, that is why $DC_{GCE}$ achieved the best accuracy.

Table 4. The best accuracy of different methods on UCMD

| Noise ratio | Symmetry | | | | | Asymmetry | | | |
|---|---|---|---|---|---|---|---|---|---|
| | 0.1 | 0.2 | 0.3 | 0.4 | 0.5 | 0.1 | 0.2 | 0.3 | 0.4 |
| NCE | 94.79 | 93.49 | 92.97 | 89.58 | 78.91 | 94.79 | 94.53 | 87.5 | 60.42 |
| SCE | 96.88 | 92.19 | 89.06 | 86.46 | 83.07 | 95.31 | 93.23 | 90.89 | 73.44 |
| GCE | 94.01 | 93.49 | 89.58 | 85.42 | 81.51 | 94.27 | 87.76 | 79.17 | 63.02 |
| Cot | 96.62 | 95.05 | 92.97 | 90.37 | 86.20 | 96.35 | 94.01 | 87.24 | 70.05 |
| DC | **97.40** | **96.62** | **95.05** | **94.53** | **86.46** | **97.14** | **96.09** | **93.23** | **78.39** |

**Result on UCMD.** In this section, we apply the proposed method to UCMD to demonstrate the effectiveness of the methods. The data set is processed in the same way as Cifar10, and methods are also named in the same way as Cifar10. Table 4 and Table 5 shows the highest accuracy of various methods on this dataset calculated with different parameters, besides the highest accuracies in Table 4 have been bolded. In addition, UCMD has less samples than Cifar10, which makes the validation set smaller, so some experiments have the same accuracy.

Table 5. The best accuracy of Discerning Coteaching utilizes different loss function on UCMD

| Noise ratio | Symmetry | | | | | Asymmetry | | | |
|---|---|---|---|---|---|---|---|---|---|
| | 0.1 | 0.2 | 0.3 | 0.4 | 0.5 | 0.1 | 0.2 | 0.3 | 0.4 |
| $DC_{NCE}$ | 97.66 | 97.40 | 95.83 | 92.45 | 89.06 | 97.14 | 95.57 | 90.63 | 75.26 |
| $DC_{GCE}$ | 98.18 | 96.62 | 94.27 | 94.01 | 82.55 | 96.62 | 95.57 | 92.97 | 81.25 |

Table 6 records the same thing as Table 3 of experiments in Cifar10. From Table 6, it is not difficult to find out methods proposed by us have the potential to split samples correct labeled from those with noise labels. In most instances, our methods can accurately estimated noise ratio with the error within 3% expect when the label noise ratio is particularly high. Moreover, the ratio of pure samples is significantly increased after selected by our model except for a few special cases such as $DC_{GCE}$ with half symmetrical noise labels. Corresponding to this is lower separation accuracy recorded in Table 3, the accuracy of $DC_{GCE}$ with half symmetrical noise labels is even worse than pure Coteaching.

When we focus on asymmetry noise, we can unearth that accuracy of all the methods contain a sharp decline along with noise ratio converting to 0.4 from 0.3, include our method. For this phenomenon, the same position of Table 6 gives an explanation, there also a sharp decline in separation accuracy recorded in the second row of cell. Consider factors above, it is not difficult to infer that when deal with datasets contain 40% asymmetry noise labels, the original

**Table 6.** How many labels are considered as pure labels by model, second row of same cell stands for how many labels are really pure labels after selected by model.

| Noise ratio | Symmetry | | | | | Asymmetry | | | |
|---|---|---|---|---|---|---|---|---|---|
| | 0.1 | 0.2 | 0.3 | 0.4 | 0.5 | 0.1 | 0.2 | 0.3 | 0.4 |
| DC | 90.99 | 78.49 | 70.49 | 62.98 | 58.29 | 91.65 | 80.71 | 73.20 | 81.43 |
| | 99.60 | 98.93 | 98.38 | 93.19 | 84.12 | 99.48 | 97.39 | 97.04 | 71.14 |
| $DC_{NCE}$ | 90.99 | 80.53 | 72.42 | 64.66 | 55.77 | 90.39 | 80.23 | 71.83 | 60.46 |
| | 99.34 | 99.10 | 97.93 | 95.26 | 89.22 | 99.34 | 97.38 | 92.80 | 75.35 |
| $DC_{GCE}$ | 91.71 | 82.75 | 71.58 | 63.10 | 51.61 | 90.33 | 80.71 | 72.96 | 67.67 |
| | 99.28 | 98.11 | 97.15 | 97.43 | 94.47 | 99.67 | 98.36 | 95.14 | 79.70 |

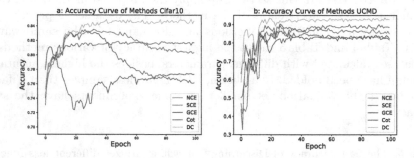

**Fig. 5.** The accuracy on the test set, figure a record the accuracy of experiment on cfar10 with 40% symmetry noise while b second row record the accuracy of experiment on UCMD with 40% symmetry noise.

model performed poorly so that our models cannot pick samples accurately, and ultimately leads to poor performance.

**Analysis on Discerning Coteaching.** Our experiments reveal that robust losses mentioned above can only alleviate overfitting in some cases. Figure 5 records the curve of the accuracy on the test set which changes with epoch, among which figure a reveals that overfitting still occurs even models equipped with robust loss, we can clearly see that accuracy curve of models with NCE, SCE and GCE all contain a obvious peak in the beginning of learning, varying degrees of decline also can be found after peaks. On the contrary, Coteaching seems to be more stable, accuracy of which only contain some tiny fluctuations after reaching the highest. The shortcomings of Coteaching are also obvious, both figures show that the highest accuracy of Coteaching is lower than others. From the accuracy curve, our methods combine the advantages of both Coteaching and robust loss, while improving the accuracy, the model output is still stable.

The accuracy curve of UCMD is recorded by b in Fig. 5, reassuringly all the methods are not affected by the overfitting compared to dealing with Cifar10, even though there were sharp fluctuations in the beginning. More specifically, accuracy of methods with robust loss are all slightly lower than Coteaching after stable, so in this situation Discerning Coteaching can separate samples with noise label and pure label exactly, and Table 2 confirms this. So as a result of training on a cleaner training set, our methods perform better.

## 4 Conclusion

In this paper, we propose a framework named Discerning Coteaching against noisy labels without using additional prior knowledge or dataset. Specifically, Discerning Coteaching can estimate the proportion of noise labels and further separate noisy samples from clean samples through distribution characteristics of CCE and learning properties of deep networks, and we have empirically proved that. Above all, our Discerning Coteaching can be used as a basis for subsequent research such as semi-supervised learning.

## References

1. Korot, E., Guan, Z., Ferraz, D., et al.: Code-free deep learning for multi-modality medical image classification. Nat. Mach. Intell. **3**(4), 288–298 (2021)
2. Lei, Z., Zeng, Y., Liu, P., et al.: Active deep learning for hyperspectral image classification with uncertainty learning. IEEE Geosci. Remote Sens. Lett. **19**, 1–5 (2021)
3. Wu, X., Sahoo, D., Hoi, S.C.H.: Recent advances in deep learning for object detection. Neurocomputing **396**, 39–64 (2020)
4. Wang, W., Lai, Q., Fu, H., et al.: Salient object detection in the deep learning era: an in-depth survey. IEEE Trans. Pattern Anal. Mach. Intell. **44**(6), 3239–3259 (2021)
5. Khan, M.Z., et al.: Deep neural architectures for medical image semantic segmentation. IEEE Access **9**, 83002–83024 (2021)
6. Han, B., et al.: Co-teaching: robust training of deep neural networks with extremely noisy labels. In: Advances in Neural Information Processing Systems, vol. 31 (2018)
7. Zhang, Z., Sabuncu, M.: Generalized cross entropy loss for training deep neural networks with noisy labels. In: Advances in Neural Information Processing Systems, vol. 31 (2018)
8. Wang, Y., et al.: Symmetric cross entropy for robust learning with noisy labels. In: Proceedings of the IEEE/CVF International Conference on Computer Vision (2019)
9. Ma, X., et al.: Normalized loss functions for deep learning with noisy labels. In: International Conference on Machine Learning. PMLR (2020)
10. Yu, X., et al.: How does disagreement help generalization against label corruption?. In: International Conference on Machine Learning. PMLR (2019)
11. Lyu, Y., Tsang, I.W.: Curriculum loss: robust learning and generalization against label corruption. arXiv preprint arXiv:1905.10045 (2019)
12. Krizhevsky, A., Hinton, G.: Learning multiple layers of features from tiny images, vol. 7 (2009)
13. Yang, Y., Newsam, S.: Bag-of-visual-words and spatial extensions for land-use classification. In: Proceedings of the 18th SIGSPATIAL International Conference on Advances in Geographic Information Systems (2010)

14. Huang, G., et al.: Densely connected convolutional networks. In: Proceedings of the IEEE Conference on Computer Vision and Pattern Recognition (2017)
15. Sukhbaatar, S., Fergus, R.: Learning from noisy labels with deep neural networks. arXiv preprint arXiv:1406.2080 **2**(3) (2014)
16. Dai, A.M., Le, Q.V.: Semi-supervised sequence learning. In: Advances in Neural Information Processing Systems, vol. 28 (2015)
17. Feurer, M., et al.: Efficient and robust automated machine learning. In: Advances in Neural Information Processing Systems, vol. 28 (2015)
18. Han, B., et al.: Masking: a new perspective of noisy supervision. arXiv preprint arXiv:1805.08193 (2018)
19. Hendrycks, D., Mazeika, M., Wilson, D., Gimpel, K.: Using trusted data to train deep networks on labels corrupted by severe noise. arXiv preprint arXiv:1802.05300 (2018)
20. Xiao, T., et al.: Learning from massive noisy labeled data for image classification. Proceedings of the IEEE Conference on Computer Vision and Pattern Recognition (2015)
21. Vahdat, A.: Toward robustness against label noise in training deep discriminative neural networks. In: Advances in Neural Information Processing Systems, vol. 30 (2017)
22. Sohn, K., et al.: Fixmatch: simplifying semi-supervised learning with consistency and confidence. In: Advances in Neural Information Processing Systems, vol. 30, pp. 596–608 (2020)
23. Lee, D.-H.: Pseudo-label: the simple and efficient semi-supervised learning method for deep neural networks. In: Workshop on Challenges in Representation Learning, ICML, vol. 3, no. 2 (2013)
24. Zhang, B., et al.: Flexmatch: boosting semi-supervised learning with curriculum pseudo labeling. In: Advances in Neural Information Processing Systems, vol. 34 (2021)

# VDSSA: Ventral & Dorsal Sequential Self-attention AutoEncoder for Cognitive-Consistency Disentanglement

Yi Yang[1] , Yong Su[1] , and Simin An[2]([✉])

[1] Tianjin Normal University, Tianjin 300387, China
suyong@tju.edu.cn
[2] Tianjin Normal University College of Management and Economics,
Tianjin 300387, China
ansm@tju.edu.cn

**Abstract.** Learning compact and interpretable disentangled representation is considered to be the key challenge in unsupervised learning. Although current methods which could capture the essence of the input from the perspective of Bayesian inference, have achieved some promising results, there still exists a gap between cognitive mechanisms and disentanglement techniques. To tackle this problem, inspired by the two-streams hypothesis in the visual cortex, we propose a *Ventral & Dorsal Sequential Self-attention AutoEncoder* (VDSSA), which introduces a self-attention based disentangled representation to capture both *cognitive-consistent* and semantic consistent factors in sequential data. In particular, cognitive-consistent factors include Global Shape Information (GSI) in the Ventral stream and Global Dynamic Information (GDI) in the Dorsal stream. We introduce a modified self-attention module to capture the GSI which denotes the cognitive-consistent factor in the spatial domain, allowing to overcome the limitation of receptive field in CNN. The GDI is encoded by Self-attention LSTM to obtain cognitive-consistent factors in the temporal domain. To the best of our knowledge, this is the first work to use cognitive-consistency in disentanglement model. The experiments on artificially generated cartoon video clips show that the proposed VDSSA could disentangle ventral and dorsal stream information from video sequences. Furthermore, the experimental results on the MNIST dataset show that the proposed method also has the ability to disentangle style and content factors from static data, and the encoded content features have better clustering characteristics.

**Keywords:** Ventral · Dorsal · Disentanglement representation and cognitive-consistency

**Supplementary Information** The online version contains supplementary material available at https://doi.org/10.1007/978-3-031-18910-4_55.

# 1    Introduction

In recent years, deep learning technology has gained remarkable success in many fields [1]. Among them, performance of supervised learning has already surpassed human ability in many important fields, such as imaging and voice recognition. Supervised learning which is a feed-forward, bottom-up approach, assumes that there always exists a teacher providing the correct label at each learning event. However, most human cognition is top-down, interpreting input data through feedback connections in the brain. Moreover, to achieve high recognition accuracy, supervised learning may ignore the essence of structure in data [2].

In contrast, unsupervised learning and self-supervised learning are more practical and cognitive-consistent in real-world scenarios [3]. To analyze the semantic information of unsupervised representation, disentanglement representation learning has attracted increasing attention in recent years. According to the topological theory and causal reasoning, in an ideal disentanglement model, semantic features and representation features should satisfy surjections. Intuitively, disentanglement can be defined as a separation in the representation of a certain object's attributes. Imagine a photo containing a specific object which is made up of a large number of pixels. These pixels are highly entangled, as changing the colour of the object would change a large number of pixels. Representation would be more disentangled when changing a subset of variables only influencing a subset of attributes. Furthermore, a disentangled representation is defined as a separable representation, in which each part represents an exclusive subset of attributes, and each subset is not related, but the set of all subsets together can represent a complete set.

Based on Bayesian inference [4] and information theory, many disentanglement methods have achieved promising results by trying to find a balance between independence and representation ability of features [5]. Although cognitive guidance has been proved to be very effective in many downstream tasks, such as attention mechanism, as far as we know, most disentanglement methods still only focus on semantic consistent disentanglement, few models conform to both cognitive consistency and semantic consistency. Typically, cognitive consistency is usually embodied in model structure, while semantic consistency is usually embodied in features.

In 1994, Haxby [6] has confirmed the two visual systems hypothesis which suggests processing of visual information into two distinct pathways in the brain, by measuring PET activity while subjects performed object identity and spatial location tasks. Inspired by the mechanism of two-streams hypothesis streams in the visual cortex, which states that the dorsal pathway and the ventral pathway encode the position information and shape information the object respectively. Many human cognitive inspired methods have been proposed to solve visual recognition and control tasks [7]. We generalize the ability of dorsal stream coding to temporal domain, which suggests the dorsal stream can capture dynamic information in the sequences. In this work, we propose a Ventral & Dorsal Sequential Self-attention Autoencoder (VDSSA), which top-down encodes global spatio-temporal features, and achieves feature disentanglement with cognitive consistency and semantic consistency at the same time.

Specifically, the proposed VDSSA can disentangle the global shape information (GSI) in the ventral stream and global dynamic information (GDI) in the dorsal stream. We introduce a modified self-attention module to overcome the local receptive field constraint of the convolution operator at frame level. Thus integrating self-attention LSTM, the cognitive consistency features of sequence can be disentangled from the global spatio-temporal information. The overview of the structure of VDSSA is given in Fig. 1, and we present the details of each technical component below. The contributions of this work are three folds:

- We propose a cognitive consistent sequential disentanglement model, besides information theory and statistics, it provides cognitive guidance for the theory of disentanglement.
- The modified self-attention module used in VDSSA can improve the global feature representation ability of the variational autoencoder.
- Experiments on two publicly available sequence and still image datasets demonstrate the effectiveness of the proposed approaches.

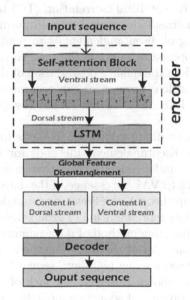

**Fig. 1.** Architecture of ventral & dorsal sequential transformer encoder

## 2    Related Work

In recent years, Disentanglement Representation Learning (DRL) has shown superior performance and attracted considerable research interest in the field of machine learning, due to the fact that it could capture independent explainable factors in data. The aiming of DRL is mostly about finding how independent factors are encoded in the feature representation. Recent works argue that the DRL has many advantages: when used in downstream tasks, it can improve prediction performance, reduce sample complexity and provide interpretability for the model, which is regarded as an effective method to overcome the "black box" in the deep network [8]. According to the topological theory and causal reasoning, there is a strong correspondence between the semantics independent factors and encoded features in the disentanglement model. In most methods, the unsupervised disentanglement model is mostly achieved by improving the Variational AutoEncoders (VAEs) which learn an inference model and a generative model jointly. These methods provide various regularization terms to constrain the encoder structure, allowing them to disentangle semantics independent factors automatically.

Higgins [9] represents the optimization problem in VAE as a Lagrange equation, where the Lagrange multiplier is set as a hyperparameter to balance the representation and independence of features. When $\beta = 1$, it is the standard VAE. A higher $\beta$ value means that the information representation ability of the eigenspace is reduced, but the disentanglement ability of the model is increased. By decomposing ELBO, Chen [10] demonstrates that the reason for the success of $\beta$VAE lies in the role of Total Correlation (TC) term. $\beta$VAE encourages lower TC values and penalizes index-code Mutual Information. They think that the most important thing of disentanglement is to punish the TC term. Similarly, the Factor VAE proposed by penalize the total correlation with adversarial training, which can alleviate the quality degradation of $\beta$VAE. Burgess [11] proposed AnnealedVAE, in which the encoder can accurately reconstruct the input signal while focusing on learning changing factors, by gradually increasing the bottleneck capacity.

In addition to the above disentanglement methods for static data, there are also some works on the disentanglement methods for sequential data. These methods could capture the independent factors that change with time by adding Recurrent Neural Network to VAE. In essence, if the data has a symmetric structure (represented by group theory), the linear disentanglement representation is equivalent to the irreducible representation of group elements. Although Higgins [9] may not give a clear modeling method of data symmetric structure, they provide reasonable suggestions. All of the above methods are based on statistical models, which focus on disentangling high-level semantic consistency features by statistical optimization methods. However, the lack of low-level cognitive consistency guidance in the process of sequence modelling may cause confusion or missing of spatial-temporal features, which are also the key bottleneck of the current sequential disentanglement models.

## 3   Proposed Scheme

*If a deep neural network model can imitate the human perception process, then the feature generative process must be consistent with the cognitive mechanism of human brain.* Take the visual system as an example, when the human brain is stimulated by visual signals, different visual neural pathways will receive specific types of signals, and then integrate the information received from these pathways. It is naturally to imitate the separation and fusion mechanism of human visual system by multi-stream or multi-channel deep neural network, the key point is to define the content in different channels. In order to understand the information contained in different pathways, some neuroscience researcherss [12] have given the basic models for processing and integrating information in the visual cortex when the brain is stimulated by visual signals. The human visual system consists of many different regions of the cerebral cortex, collectively known as the visual cortex. According to the division of cognitive function, the visual cortex contains the ventral stream for processing the shape information of objects and the dorsal stream for processing the location information. The parvocellular layer of the lateral geniculate nucleus of the thalamus is the information source of the ventral stream, each visual area provides a complete representation of visual space. The dorsal stream describes the way and direction of information flow in the visual cortex.

The mechanism of visual cortex processing visual signals can be described as follows:

$$F(x) \rightarrow F(z, s) \rightarrow F(z) \cup F(s) . \tag{1}$$

where $x,z$ and $s$ denote feature sequence, dorsal stream and ventral stream separately. In particular, for the video sequence, the model can be expressed in the following form:

$$F(x_{1:F}) \rightarrow F(z, s_{1:F}) \rightarrow F(z) \cup F(s_{1:F}) . \tag{2}$$

where $x_{1:F}$ denotes a discrete video feature with an input length of 1 to $F$. $z$ denotes the global dynamic component in sequence $x_{1:F}$ , corresponding to the information in dorsal stream. $s_{1:F}$ represents the appearance or shape information of the object at frame level, which belongs to the ventral stream information in the visual cortex.

Specifically, in this paper, we use the following conditional probability to model the pattern of information flow in the ventral and dorsal streams. In particular, we use the framework of generative model, which is consistent with human cognitive process:

$$p(z, s_{1:F}|x_{1:F}^{\text{global}}) = p(s_{1:F}|x_{1:F}^{\text{global}})p(z|x_{1:F}^{\text{global}}, s_{1:F}) \tag{3}$$

where $x_{1:F}^{\text{global}}$ represents the global features extracted from the input sequence. The global features mean that the model must have global representation capabilities both in the frame-level and temporal domain. Only in this way, dynamic information $z$ in the dorsal stream can be effectively retained and further to be disentangled.

However, most CNNs with local receptive field may limit the ability of global feature representation at frame level. In order to solve this problem, we use self-attention module to improve the global feature representation ability of CNN.

The input of self-attention block consists of queries $Q \in R^{d_k}$, keys $K \in R^{d_k}$ and values $V \in R^{d_v}$. $d_f = d_v + 2d_k$ is the number of output channels after the first convolution module. A softmax function is applied to the dot products of the query with all keys, and obtain the weights on the values.

$$Att(Q, K, V) = Softmax(\frac{QK^T}{d_k})V \tag{4}$$

The self-attention weights representing the correlation of features, which is close to the adjacency matrix of graph convolution neural network, can capture the long range correlation in high-dimensional space. In order to enhance the generalization ability of the model, we also use the multi-heads mechanism in self-attention block.

$$Multi(Q, K, V) = Concat(Att(Q_1, K_1, V_1)\dots Att(Q_h, K_h, V_h))W_0 \tag{5}$$

The global features at frame level can be obtained by concatenating convolutional features with a set of features produced via multi-heads self-attention $x_{1:F}^{ventral} = [Conv(x_{1:F}), Multi(x_{1:F})]$. $x_{1:F}^{ventral}$ enforces locality, to self-attentional features capable of modeling longer range dependencies.

After obtaining the global feature sequence at frame level, we need to capture the global dynamics from feature sequence. The Eq. 3 can be further rewritten as follows:

$$p(x_{1:F}^{global}, z_{1:F}, s) = \prod_{f=1}^{F} p(z_f|z_{1:f-1})p(x_f^{global}|z_f, s_f)p(s_f) . \tag{6}$$

where $p(z_f|z_{1:f-1})$ encodes the global motion information.

The dynamic information contained in the dorsal stream can be addressed by time gating mechanisms, such as RNN, LSTM and GRU. These approaches can well handle the length variations and the intra-sequence variations. While not every temporal stage are equally important for global dynamic cognition [13]. Therefore, determining the key stage is not only consistent with the principle of information compression in cognition, but also more conducive to the accurate transmission of key information. The proposed method adopts a self-attention LSTM to identify key stages by assigning different weights to the hidden variables at frame level.

For the long-time series, we use the self-attention LSTM to encode the global temporal features. Combining spatial domain and the temporal domain, the global feature can be expressed as:

$$x_{1:F}^{global} = x_{1:F}^{dorsal} = LSTM_{self-attention}(x_{1:F}^{ventral}) \tag{7}$$

Given the global feature $x_{1:F}^{global}$, we can use variational inference to learn an approximate posterior of latent variables.

$$p(z_f, s_{1:F}|x_{1:F}^{global}) = \frac{p(z_f, x_{1:F}^{global}, s_{1:F})}{p(x_{1:F}^{global})} \tag{8}$$

A distribution $q$ is introduced to approximate to the intractable true posterior. The variational lower bound can be written as:

$$\log p_\theta(x) \geq \mathcal{L}(\theta, \phi, x) = \mathrm{E}_{q_\phi(z, f|x)} \left[ -\log q_\phi(z, f|x) + \log p_\theta(x, f, z) \right] . \qquad (9)$$

Therefore, the posterior probabilities of ventral and dorsal information can be rewritten as follows:

$$q_\phi(z_{1:F}, s_{1:F} | x_{1:F}^{\text{global}}) = q_\phi(s_{1:F} | x_{1:F}^{\text{global}}) q_\phi(z_{1:F} | x_{1:F}^{\text{global}}, s_{1:F}) \qquad (10)$$

It is worth noting that, in Eq. 10, $q_\phi(z_{1:F} | x_{1:F}^{\text{global}}, s_{1:F})$ means that the perception of dynamic information needs the assistance of shape information. Intuitively, for example, in motion recognition tasks, if the shape information of human body is discarded, the dynamic information will become meaningless.

Through the above description, the proposed model is consistent with visual cognition and can model the information of the ventral and dorsal streams separately. In order to ensure the convergence of variational lower bound, we use the reparameterization trick (Eq. 11) to sample hidden variables and then generate realistic samples based on sampled hidden variables.

$$z = \mu + \epsilon \sigma \qquad (11)$$

where $\epsilon \sim N(0, 1)$, $\mu \in R^{hf}$ and $\sigma \in R^{hf}$ are the mean and standard deviation features generated by linear layer.

After cognitive consistent coding, in order to ensure the integrity of sequence information, it is necessary to integrate the information of ventral stream and dorsal stream, decode the coding features, and reconstruct the input sequence. The decoder consists of a full connection layer and four transposed convolution modules. The training objective of the proposed method is to minimize the following loss function:

$$L_{total} = L_{MSE} + L_{\mu,\sigma^2}^{dorsal} + L_{\mu,\sigma^2}^{ventral} \qquad (12)$$

where the $L_{MSE}$ is the sequence reconstruction loss (Eq. 12), $L_{\mu,\sigma^2}^{ventral}$ and $L_{\mu,\sigma^2}^{dorsal}$ represent Kullback-Leibler loss of the ventral and dorsal streams, respectively.

$$L_{MSE} = \frac{1}{n} \sum_{i=1}^{n} \left( X_i - X_i^{decoder} \right) \qquad (13)$$

$$L_{\mu,\sigma^2}^{ventral} = -\frac{1}{2} \sum_{i=1}^{f} \left( 1 - \mu_i^2 - \sigma_i^2 + \log \sigma_i^2 \right) \qquad (14)$$

$$L_{\mu,\sigma^2}^{dorsal} = -\frac{1}{2} \sum_{i=1}^{f} \left( 1 - \mu_i^2 - \sigma_i^2 + \log \sigma_i^2 \right) \qquad (15)$$

# 4    Experiment

In this section, we conduct extensive experiments on two public benchmark datasets.

## 4.1    Datasets and Settings

We test the proposed VDSSA on a dataset of video game "sprites", which comes from an open-source video game Liberated Pixel Cup2 [14]. This dataset is commonly used to test the disentanglement method [10]. In this dataset, the animated cartoon characters have four controllable appearance covariant factors (skin color, tops, pants and hairstyle) and 9 action categories (walking, casting spells and slashing, each with three viewing angles). For sprites dataset, we follow the protocol as in earlier work [15], and use 1000 of 1296 for training/validation and the rest of them for testing. Each sequences with 3 channels and 8 frames of dimension $64 \times 64$. Our experiments in this dataset show that the generated video can retain the static attributes well, and the dynamic factors can be transferred by exchanging with other dynamic factors.

The MNIST data set of hand-written digits has been extensively benchmarked. We used a standard splitting of the MNIST dataset into training, testing, and validation sets of sizes 55K, 10K and 5K images, respectively. Each image with 1 channel of dimension $28 \times 28$.

## 4.2    Implementation Details

We implement the VDSSA, Encoder and Decoder of our model as an end-to-end learnable neural networks. The Encoder of VDSSA consists of a spatial coding module with multi-head self attention and a sequential temporal coding module. The attention layers use multi-head attention with 4 heads and leaky ReLU slope of 0.1, then we applied four $4 \times 4$ convolutional layers with multi-head attention to increase the number of channels from 3 to 256, the pooling stride is 2. The dimensions of ventral and dorsal feature in reparameterization trick are 32 and 16. The Decoder consists of a full connection layer and four transposed convolution modules. In the first three transposed convolution modules, we first use a batch normalization operation normalizes each input channel across a mini-batch. Then we use a Leaky Relu activation function and dropout operations to enhance the nonlinear expression ability of network and avoid over fitting. The last transposed convolution module has only Tanh activation operation. We applied four $4 \times 4$ convolutional layers to reduce the number of channels from 256 to 3. We choose Adam [16] as our optimizer, and the momentum is set to 0.9. The learning rate is set to 0.0001. We trained on each dataset for 100 epochs, save the model checkpoints every epoch, and then evaluate on the validation set to find the best one for testing.

In MNIST dataset, the input channel is 1 and the input image size is $28 \times 28$, so the structure of the model has a slight change. For Encoder, we applied four $4 \times 4$ convolutional layers with multi-heads self-attention to increase the number of channels from 1 to 128, the pooling stride is 2. The LSTM layer is reset to a simple linear layer and the number of transposed convolution modules in Decoder is set to three with kernel size $5 \times 5$, $4 \times 4$ and $4 \times 4$ .

## 4.3 Sprites

In order to provide a qualitative evaluation on VDSSA model, we visualize some sampled reconstructions along with some real input sequences, the results are shown in Fig. 2. The top of each subgraph is the original input sequences, and the bottom is the reconstructions. It is not difficult to find that with the increase of the number of epochs, the reconstruction error decrease, and the reconstruction results are close to the original input.

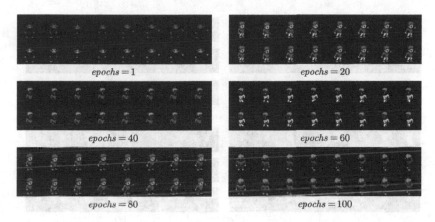

**Fig. 2.** Reconstructed results of sampled examples in sprites dataset. The top of each subgraph is the original input sequence, and the bottom is the reconstructed sequence.

In order to verify the effectiveness of the proposed model for ventral and dorsal stream modeling, we retain the ventral stream information $F\left(s_{1:F}^{1}\right)$ of the target sequence obtained by the encoder, and add the dorsal stream information $F\left(z_{1:F}^{2}\right)$ of other sequences, and then reconstruct it through the trained decoder $F\left(x_{1:F}\right) = F\left(z_{1:F}^{2}\right) \cup F\left(s_{1:F}^{1}\right)$. Figures 3 (a)–(c) are the synthesis results of side view. The first and second lines are two real input sequences respectively. We retain the static information captured by ventral stream in the first sequence, extract the dynamic information captured by dorsal stream in the second sequence, and the third is the synthesis dynamic sequence. This experiment contains two covariant factors, namely hair color and action. We can see that the synthesized sequence keeps the static factor (hair color) of the first sequence very well, and migrates the action of the second sequence to the first sequence. The results also show that the proposed method can effectively disentangle the dynamic and static factors by modeling the ventral and dorsal stream. Figure 3(d) tests the ability of the proposed VDSSA to model ventral and dorsal stream information from different perspectives. We can see that the perspective of the first sequence is retained as a static factor. As shown in Fig. 3e), similar results can be obtained from front view. We add more covariant factors in Fig. 3(f), which are hair color, action and coat color. It is not difficult to find that in the synthetic sequence, the static factors in the first sequence: hair color and coat color are retained, while the dynamic factors are completely removed.

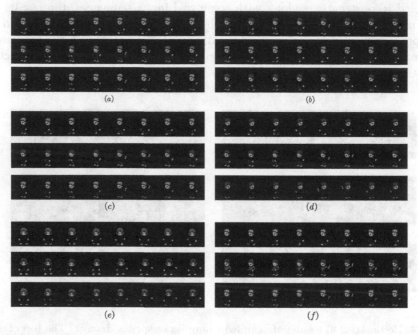

**Fig. 3.** Synthesize new samples by changing ventral & dorsal stream information from different sequences.

## 4.4 MNIST

The proposed VDSSA model can not only disentangle information of the ventral and dorsal streams, but also could disentangle the factors from static image. To this end, we exploit the most commonly used MNIST dataset to verify the disentanglment ability of the model to still images. The dimensions of ventral and dorsal feature in reparameterization trick are 6 and 6, respectively.

Instead of disentangling shape and dynamic factors from motion sequences, static images contain no dynamic components, so we turn to disentangle content and style factors in MNIST dataset. Intuitively, for example, Different people write the same content, each person's font has its own unique style. This style includes global style and local detail style. Traditional convolution operators can only extract local styles due to the limitation of the receptive field, and the global style composed of these local styles may be inconsistent with human perception. While the self-attention module we used can capture the image context information, and finally provide both global style information and local style.

In Fig. 4, we show the style transfer results of different numbers. The first two rows are the original input images, and the third row is the synthesized images. It is worth noting that the synthesized images with a red border in the third row, can be regarded as failure cases, which could not have clear semantics. Although these failure cases are not counterfactual, these ambiguous results may have an impact on downstream tasks, such as classification.

**Fig. 4.** The style transfer results of sampled examples in MNIST dataset.

In order to quantitatively evaluate the effectiveness of the proposed method in semi-supervised classification task, we have compared the performance of the proposed method with other existing variational Autoencoders [16]. We use the latent features from all trained encoders and fit a dense classification layer on them. The layer of differnt models is trained on only few number of labelled samples in the training set against cross-entropy. The three baseline methods we choose to compare are as follows:

**VAE** [16]. Theoretically, the variational autoencoder (VAE) is different from the standard deep autoencoder. But in practice, their difference lies only in the uncertainty brought about by the reparameterization trick.

$\beta$**-VAE** [9]. Beta Variational Autoencoder ($\beta$-VAE) is a generalization of the VAE that simply changes the ratio between reconstruction and divergence loss.

**VQ-VAE** [17]. The vector-quantized variational autoencoder (VQ-VAE) is a VAE that uses a uniform categorical distribution to generate latent features. Each output of the encoder is replaced by the categorical value of the distribution.

As shown in Table 1, we observed that the proposed method obtains substantially better performance in classification tasks than the other three approaches. In particular, compared with $\beta$-VAE wich is also a disentanglement method, the higher accuracy rate means that the proposed method can better disentangle the factors that are not related to the category in the data.

**Table 1.** Compared with the STOA method in different numbers of training samples (TS denotes the number of training samples).

| Scenario | $TS = 500$ | $TS = 700$ | $TS = 900$ | $TS = 1100$ |
|---|---|---|---|---|
| VAE | 59.76% | 61.68% | 64.29% | 65.71% |
| $\beta$-VAE | 61.32% | 64.43% | 65.32% | 66.32% |
| VQ-VAE | 69.38% | 72.27% | 77.84% | 78.62% |
| VDSSA (ours) | 75.24% | 78.55% | 81.43% | 81.56% |

# 5   Conclusion

In this paper, we propose a disentanglement method VDSSA, which is constructed according to the cognitive consistency of the two-streams hypothesis in the visual cortex. In the proposed method, the dynamic factor in the dorsal stream and the static factor in the ventral stream are obtained by disentangling the global Spatio-temporal features simultaneously. Extensive experimentation with both experimental and real datasets yielded quite encouraging results, suggesting that the self-attention-based disentanglement model could have the potential to capture more complete global information, so as to improve the disentanglement ability for the cognitive consistency factors. The proposed method can be extended to other complex downstream tasks, such as recognition tasks, and the robustness of the model can be improved by training synthetic samples.

# References

1. Lecun, Y., Bengio, Y., Hinton, G.: Deep learning. Nature **521**(7553), 436 (2015)
2. Szegedy, C., et al.: Going deeper with convolutions. In: IEEE Conference on Computer Vision and Pattern Recognition, CVPR, pp. 1–9 (2015)
3. Radford, A., Metz, L., Chintala, S.: Unsupervised representation learning with deep convolutional generative adversarial networks. In: Bengio, Y., LeCun, Y. (eds.) International Conference on Learning Representations, ICLR (2016)
4. Jordan, M.I., Ghahramani, Z., Jaakkola, T.S., Saul, L.K.: An introduction to variational methods for graphical models. Mach. Learn. **37**(2), 183–233 (1999)
5. Kingma, D.P,, Welling, M.: Auto-encoding variational bayes. In: Bengio, Y., LeCun, Y. (eds.) International Conference on Learning Representations, ICLR (2014)
6. Haxby, J.V., Horwitz,B., Ungerleider, L.G., Maisog, J.M., Pietrini, P., Grady, C.L.: The functional organization of human extrastriate cortex: a pet-RCBF study of selective attention to faces and locations. J. Neurosci. **5**(11), 6336–6353 (1994)
7. Collins, E., Freud, E., Kainerstorfer, J.M., Cao, J., Behrmann, M.: Temporal dynamics of shape processing differentiate contributions of dorsal and ventral visual pathways. J. Cogn. Neurosci. **31**(6), 821–836 (2019)
8. van Steenkiste, S., Locatello, F., Schmidhuber, J., Bachem, O.: Are disentangled representations helpful for abstract visual reasoning? In: Advances in Neural Information Processing Systems, pp. 14222–14235 (2019)

9.  Higgins, I., et al.: Towards a definition of disentangled representations, CoRR abs/1812.02230

10. Chen, T.Q., Li, X., Grosse, R.B.D., Duvenaud, D.K.: Isolating sources of disentanglement in variational autoencoders. In: Bengio, S., Wallach, H.M., Larochelle, H., Grauman, H., Bianchi, N.C., Garnet, R. (eds.) Advances in Neural Information Processing Systems, pp. 2615–2625 (2013)

11. Burgess, C.P., et al.: Understanding disentangling in $\beta$-VAE. CoRR abs/1804.03599 (2018)

12. Molnair, Z., Rockland, K.S.: Cortical columns. In: Neural Circuit and Cognitive Development, 2nd edn. pp. 103–126. Academic Press, Pittsburgh (2020)

13. Weng, J., Weng, C., Yuan, J.: Spatio-temporal Naive-Bayes nearest-neighbor (ST-NBNN) for skeleton-based action recognition. In: IEEE Conference on Computer Vision and Pattern Recognition, CVPR, pp. 445–454 (2017)

14. Mathieu, M., Zhao, J.J., Sprechmann, P., Ramesh, A., LeCun, Y.: Disentangling factors of variation in deep representation using adversarial training. In: Advances in Neural Information Processing Systems, pp. 5041–5049 (2015)

15. Li, Y., Mandt, S.: Disentangled sequential autoencoder. In: Dy, J.G., Krause, A. (eds.) International Conference on Machine Learning, pp. 5656–5665. ICML (2018)

16. Kingma, D.P., Ba, J., Adam: a method for stochastic optimization, In: International Conference on Learning Representations, ICLR (2015)

17. van den Oord, A., Vinyals, O., Kavukcuoglu, K.: Neural discrete representation learning. In: Advances in Neural Information Processing Systems, pp. 6306–6315 (2017)

# Bayesian Neural Networks with Covariate Shift Correction For Classification in γ-ray Astrophysics

Shengda Luo[1], Jing Luo[1], Yue Chen[2], Sangin Kim[3], David Hui[3], Jianguo Zhang[1(✉)], Alex Leung[2], and Roberto Bugiolacchi[4]

[1] Department of Computer Science and Engineering, Southern University of Science and Technology, Shenzhen, China
zhangjg@sustech.edu.cn
[2] Department of Physics, University of Hong Kong, Pokfulam Road, Hong Kong, Hong Kong
[3] Department of Astronomy and Space Science, Chungnam National University, Daejeon, Korea
[4] State Key Laboratory of Lunar and Planetary Sciences, Macau University of Science and Technology, Macao, China

**Abstract.** Machine learning techniques are successfully used for source classification on different wavelengths. In gamma-ray source classification, sources of more luminous are used to train machine learning models to classify fainter sources compiled in later surveys. This makes the distribution of unlabeled sources different from that of labeled sources. In addition, there are some unlabeled gamma-ray sources with insignificant features. Machine learning models are difficult to classify them. In this work, we propose a cascade framework for pulsars (PSRs)/active galactic nucleus (AGNs) classification. In the proposed framework, kernel mean matching is first used to make the distribution of training samples close to that of the samples in the test set. Then, samples with insignificant features are picked out from unlabeled data via Bayesian neural networks. Extensive experiments demonstrate that our method is effective for covariate shift correction and hard sample selection.

**Keywords:** Covariate shift · Epistemic uncertainty · Gamma-ray classification

## 1 Introduction

After Fermi Gamma-ray Space Telescope is launched, its observation ability creates conditions for the study of high-energy radiation bodies. Its Large Area Telescope (LAT) is a powerful tool for observing and studying high-energy celestial bodies due to its all-sky survey and monitoring functions. It makes the knowledge discovery in dataset become feasible. Machine learning is one of the most

---

J. Luo—Co-first Author

© The Author(s), under exclusive license to Springer Nature Switzerland AG 2022
S. Yu et al. (Eds.): PRCV 2022, LNCS 13535, pp. 706–719, 2022.
https://doi.org/10.1007/978-3-031-18910-4_56

important approaches for astronomic data analysis, and it is successfully applied in source classification in different wavelengths, such as gamma-ray and x-ray sources [9–11].

Pulsars are neutron stars that emit beams of radiation out of their magnetic poles. Astronomers can identify pulsars with the lighthouse-like beams of radiation which often contain gamma-ray. Due to the large number of gamma-ray sources, manual classification is too expensive. Recently, machine learning techniques are used to build prediction models for gamma-ray sources classification [13,17]. The assumption in these methods is that training and test feature vectors are independently and identically drawn from the same distribution. When the distributions on the training and the test sets do not match, we have sample selection bias or covariate shift. More specifically with sample selection bias, given feature vectors $X$ and labels $Y$, we have training samples $Z = \{(x_1, y_1), \ldots, (x_m, y_m)\} \subset X \times Y$ from a particular probability distribution $Pr(x, y)$, and test $Z' = \{(x'_1, y'_1), \ldots, (x'_m, y'_m)\} \subset X \times Y$ drawn from another distribution $Pr'(x, y)$.

In gamma-ray classification, the training sources can be biased towards brighter sources as these sources are detected easier. For variable stars, samples of more luminous or well-understood stars are mostly used to train machine learning models to classify fainter stars compiled in later surveys [19]. This lead to potential problems as the classification models perform the best with bright objects, not faint objects. Sample selection bias has been ignored in most work in astronomy with machine learning techniques. Especially in astronomy and astrophysics, the problem with bias arises fairly naturally, i.e., with the training data collected in a biased manner (strong sources are more easily found), inevitably the trained model is used to classify objects from a more general target population if sample selection bias is not considered. In the case of gamma-ray classification, samples of previously detected pulsars and active galactic nucleus (AGNs) do not reflect the general population in view of various possible observational biases. This issue of covariate shift was ignored in most of previous studies about gamma-ray classification.

In this paper, a novel cascade model is proposed to classify gamma-ray sources, where we attempt to bridge covariate shift correction and Bayesian neural networks. Bayesian neural networks allow us to simultaneously pick out fainter stars and to classify well-understood stars. The main contributions of this work are described as follows: 1) We present a cascade model which consists of three modules: feature selection, covariate shift correction, and Bayesian neural networks. Feature selection effectively reduces the dimensionality of the feature vectors, which is significantly to improve the interpretability of our model and the efficiency of subsequent covariate shift correction. Covariate shift correction can be used to reduce the sample bias between labeled sources and unknown sources. Bayesian neural networks are used to calculate the uncertainty scores for hard-sample detection. 2) Extensive experiments are carried out to demonstrate an advantage of the proposed model over the state-of-the-art methods. Experimental results show that, in our method, the distribution of training data are the same as that of test data. 3) Because there are many machine learning algorithms and training ways, the number of combinations is large. To make it easy for astronomers to use the novel method to predict their sources, a website is built with the state-of-the-art approaches and our method: https://anonymous.

We divide the remainder of this paper into four sections. In Sect. 2, a brief introduction of the related work is given. The details of our cascade model are presented in Sect. 3, and it is compared with the state-of-the-art methods in Sect. 4. The last section concludes our work.

## 2   Related Work

In 2010, the first Fermi Large Area Telescope catalog [1] (1FGL) is launched based on eleventh months data. Ackermann et al. attempt to apply classification tree and logistic regression to classify sources in 1FGL [3]. Due to the relatively small dataset, their approach only achieves an average accuracy of 80%. After the second Fermi Large Area Telescope catalog [16] (2FGL) is proposed in 2012, Mirabal et al. build their automatic models with random forest for gamma-ray classification [14]. They carry on feature selection based on previous knowledge. Mirabal et al. prove that the classification accuracy of the methods is slightly reduced when the feature called absolute galactic latitude (GLAT) is used. It is possibly because that using absolute galactic latitude as a feature could cause a tiny bias against AGNs close to the Galactic plane and the pulsar away from it. In [18], various algorithms are tried to classify the sources in the third Fermi Large Area Telescope catalog [2] (3FGL) that contains more sources than 2FGL and 1FGL. Saz Parkinson et al. carry on manual feature selection before training [18]. Feature selection operation can significantly improve the performance of gamma-ray classification, and they obtain the best overall accuracy of 96% for pulsars (PSRs) and AGNs classification by using the random forest technique. The manual feature selection in previous works relied on the knowledge of researchers. Luo et al. applied automatic feature selection algorithm in gamma-ray classification [13]. Their models achieve the best classification accuracy in both 3FGL and 4FGL. The authors also construct a cross-matched data set and shows that some features they used to build classification models with the identified sources have significant covariate shift issue. Such an issue can make the performance of the actual classification of the unidentified objects can possibly be lower. The reason for the covariate shift issue is that the distribution of the training set is different from that of the test set. Both the training set and the test set are derived from the identified gamma-ray sources, they are all based on the assumption that both the training set and the test set come from the same distribution in the feature space. This issue of covariate shift was ignored in most of the previous studies about gamma-ray classification.

## 3   Our Methods

In this work, a cascade framework with covariate shift correction is proposed. Our framework consists of following five stages:

(i) Data Pre-processing,
(ii) Feature Selection,
(iii) Covariate Shift Correction,
(iv) Sample Filtering, and
(v) Classification.

Algorithm 1 shown the details of the novel framework. In Algorithm 1, Stage 1 to 3 are performed on the training set, and Stage 4 and 5 is performed on the test set. The stages are described in following subsections.

---

**Algorithm 1.** The Proposed Cascade Framework

---

**Input:**

The set of training samples: $\mathbb{S} = \{(s_1, y_1), ..., (s_n, y_n)\}, s_i \in \mathbb{R}^d, y_i \in \mathbb{R}$

The set of test samples: $\mathbb{T} = \{(t_1, v_1), ..., (t_m, v_m)\}, t_i \in \mathbb{R}^d, v_i \in \mathbb{R}$

A threshold: $\delta$

**Output:**

The list of prediction results: $\hat{y} \in \mathbb{R}^n$

  **Stage 1: Data Preprocessing**

1: For $\mathbb{S}$ and $\mathbb{T}$, remove features with more than $\delta$ empty items

2: The empty items of the remaining features are filled with the mean of the corresponding features

  **Stage 2: Feature Selection**

3: recursive feature elimination (RFE) with random forest (RF) are trained with $\mathbb{S}$

4: Pick out important features with RFE with RF

  **Stage 3: Covariate Shift Correction**

5: For $\mathbb{S}$, correct sample bias with Kernel Mean Matching (see Algortithm 3)

  **Stage 4: Sample Filtering**

6: Build Bayesian neural networks with corrected $\mathbb{S}$, and uncertainty sources are calculated

7: Filter test samples with uncertainty sources, and $t \subseteq \mathbb{T}$ is obtained

  **Stage 5: Classification**

8: Train classifiers with corrected $\mathbb{S}$, and predict $t$ to obtain $\hat{y}$

---

## 3.1  Data Pre-processing and Feature Selection

As shown in Algorithm 1, training and test samples are clean in Stage 1. For $\mathbb{S}$ and $\mathbb{T}$, the number of empty items of feature vectors are counted. Features with more than $\delta$ empty items are removed. The empty items of the remaining features are filled with the average value of corresponding features. For example, the $i$-th features with $\mu, \mu < \delta$ empty items, the $\mu$ items are filled with the average values of $d - \mu$ non-empty items $\sum_{j=1}^{d-\mu} s_j^{(i)}$.

We attempt to reduce the number of input variables with feature selection when developing predictive models. It is desirable to reduce the number of input variables to both reduce the computational cost of modeling and, in some cases, to improve the performance of the machine learning model. Recursive feature

---

**Algorithm 2.** Recursive Feature Elimination in the Proposed Framework.

---

**Input:**

The set of training samples: $\mathbb{S} = \{(s_1, y_1), ..., (s_n, y_n)\}, s_i \in \mathbb{R}^d, y_i \in \mathbb{R}$

**Output:**

The set of selected features: $F$

1: Train the random forest model with $\mathbb{S}$

2: Evaluate the performance of the classifier (RF)

3: Initialize the importance scores of $d$ features, $D \in \mathbb{R}^d$ is the set of the scores

4: Record the performance and the features with their importance scores in $D$.

5: Update $D$ iteratively

**for** i = 1 ... $d - 2, d - 1$ **do**

   Eliminate the feature with the lowest importance score

   Re-train random projection model using $\mathbb{S}$ with remaining $d - i$ features

   Update $D$

**end for**

6: Obtain the set of selected features, $F$

---

elimination with random forest shown in Algorithm 2 are used to selected important features.

Recursive feature elimination is a backward selection method so it removes the least important features whose deletion will have the least effect on training errors to improve the machine learning model performance. As the selection of features is based on the best performance on the training set, Algorithm 2 is only applied on training data $\mathbb{S}$. In Algorithm 2, the unimportant features are eliminated iteratively. For example, in the $i$-th iteration, the remaining features will be fitted in combination with the classification method of recursive feature elimination, and then the performance of the fitting model is evaluated. The fitting model is used to generate the important scores of features, and the features with the lowest important scores are eliminated. The remaining features are used for the next iteration. The output of recursive feature elimination is the feature used to construct the fitting model with the best classification performance.

### 3.2 Covariate Shift Correction

The covariate shift issue is commonly existing in astronomical tasks such as gamma-ray classification. $p_{tr}(\cdot)$ and $p_{te}(\cdot)$ represent the probability distribution of training and test data, respectively. For a training sample $x$, covariate shift means $p_{tr}(x) \neq p_{te}(x)$. The usual assumption in supervised learning is that training and test feature vectors are independently and identically. However, covariate shift make this assumption no longer holds. Sample re-weighting is an important way to solve covariate shift. The important weights of training samples are obtained by estimating a density ratio $\beta(x) = \frac{p_{te}(x)}{p_{tr}(x)}$. Re-weighting makes the distribution of the training data more closely match that of the test data. In our cascade model, the Kernel Mean Matching [8] method is used for re-weighting. In KMM, samples are first mapped into a Reproducing Kernel Hilbert

Space (RKHS), and then compute the $\beta(x)$ without distribution estimation of $p_{tr}(\cdot)$ and $p_{te}(\cdot)$. Algorithm 3 shows the details of Kernel Mean Matching used in our model. The $\sigma$ is a hyper-parameter of the Gaussian kernel function.

---

**Algorithm 3.** Kernel Mean Matching in Our Framework.

---

**Input:**
The set of source samples: $\mathbb{S} = \{s_1, ..., s_n\}, s_i \in \mathbb{R}^d$;
The set of target samples: $\mathbb{T} = \{t_1, ..., t_m\}, t_i \in \mathbb{R}^d$;
**Output:**
The list of important weight: $\hat{\beta} \in \mathbb{R}^n$.

1: Calculate the matrix $E \in \mathbb{R}^{n \times n}$,
where $E^{(i,j)} = K(s_i, s_j) = exp(\frac{\|s_i - s_j\|^2}{2\sigma^2})$;
2: Calculate $\varepsilon \in \mathbb{R}^n$,
where $\varepsilon^i = \frac{n}{m} \sum_{j=1}^m K(s_i, t_j) = \frac{n}{m} \sum_{j=1}^m exp(\frac{\|s_i - t_j\|^2}{2\sigma^2})$;
3: Estimate important weights: $\hat{\beta} \approx \underset{\beta}{argmin} \frac{1}{2} \beta^T E\beta - \varepsilon^T \beta$,
subject to $\beta(x) \in [0, B], \forall i \in \{1, ..., n\}$, and $\left|\sum_{i=1}^n \beta_i - n\right| < \alpha$.

---

In Algorithm 3, the mean distance between weighted source sample distribution $\beta(x)p_{tr}(x)$ and target sample distribution $p_{te}(x)$ is minimized in the Reproducing Kernel Hilbert Space. The mean distance is calculated with the Maximum Mean Discrepancy. In the third step of Algorithm 3, parameter $B$ is a upper bound on the solution search space.

### 3.3 Bayesian Neural Networks

Different from the point estimation of weights in neural networks, the weights of Baye-sian neural networks $w$ are sampled from some predefined prior distribution i.e. $w \sim P(w)$. The prior distribution $P(w)$ provides some information about the target task. Thus, given training set $\mathbb{S} = (s, y)$, Bayesian neural networks model the joint distribution on targets $y$ and weights $w$ conditioned on inputs $s$ i.e. $P(y, w|s)$. The posterior distribution on weights then can be:

$$P(w|s, y) = \frac{P(y, w|s)}{P(y|s)} = \frac{P(y|s, w)P(w)}{\int P(y|s, w)P(w)dw}. \tag{1}$$

However, it is intractable to calculate the denominator in Eq. 1. Bayes by Backprop (BbB) [4] was proposed to learning a probability distribution on the weights of a Bayesian neural network. Via minimizing the Kullback-Leibler (KL) divergence between a distribution on the weights $Q_\theta(w)$ and the true posterior on the weights, BbB obtains a variational approximation to the true posterior on the weights. The detailed process of BbB can be formulated as:

$$\theta^* = \arg\min_{\theta} \mathrm{KL}\left[Q_\theta(w)\|P(w|s,y)\right]$$

$$= \arg\min_{\theta} \mathbb{E}_{Q_\theta(w)}\left[\log \frac{Q_\theta(w)}{P(w|s,y)}\right]$$

$$= \arg\min_{\theta} \mathbb{E}_{Q_\theta(w)}\left[\log Q_\theta(w) - \log P(y|s,w) - \log P(w)\right] \tag{2}$$

$$= \arg\min_{\theta} \mathrm{KL}\left[Q_\theta(w)\|P(w)\right] - \mathbb{E}_{Q_\theta(w)}\left[\log P(y|s,w)\right].$$

Therefore, the loss function for a Bayesian neural network is:

$$\mathcal{L} = \frac{n_b}{n}\mathrm{KL}\left[Q_\theta(w)\|P(w)\right] - \mathbb{E}_{Q_\theta(w)}\left[\log P(y|s,w)\right]$$

$$= \mathbb{E}_{Q_\theta(w)}\left[\frac{n_b}{n}\log Q_\theta(w) - \frac{n_b}{n}\log P(w) - \log P(y|s,w)\right], \tag{3}$$

where $n_b$ is the number of samples in a batch and $n$ is the number of samples in training set. Then, given test set $\mathbb{T} = (t, v)$, the posterior predictive distribution is:

$$P(v|t,s,y) = \int P(v|t,w)P(w|s,y)\mathrm{d}w$$

$$\approx \int P(v|t,w)Q_\theta(w)\mathrm{d}w \tag{4}$$

$$\approx \frac{1}{M}\sum_{m=1}^{M} P(v|t,w_m).$$

While Bayesian neural networks can quantify uncertainty effectively, its computational cost is relatively high. Gal [7] proved that samples from the posterior predictive distribution can be obtained via several stochastic forwards at inference time and proposed an alternative method, called Monte Carlo (MC) dropout, to estimate uncertainty. In MC dropout, dropout is applied on every layer except the last fully connected layer in a model at training and test time. The final prediction of MC dropout is the mean of all Monte Carlo predictive samples. The variance of all samples can be used to quantify uncertainty.

## 4   Experiments

In this experiment, we would like to verify that our method can solve the covariate shift correction and hard sample identification issues in gamma-ray classification. Gamma-ray sources are classified as pulsars (PSRs) and active galactic nucleus (AGNs). We first examine the effectiveness of Kernel Mean Matching of our framework for covariate Shift correction. Then, the corrected training data are used to build prediction models with various machine learning techniques. The performance of these trained models is evaluated in terms of classification accuracy. Finally, Bayesian neural networks of our framework are used to predict the unknown sources of 3FGL, and uncertainty scores of unknown sources are obtained.

## 4.1   Experimental Setting

3FGL and 4FGL are used in the experiments. 70% of the PSR and AGN sources in 3FGL are randomly selected to form the training set, and the remaining 30% sources are used as test samples. Since 4FGL was released later than 3FGL, there were more dedicated analyses in compiling 4FGL. Hence, 275 unidentified sources in the 3FGL catalog now have their natures revealed. These 275 sources are used to construct the 3FGL/4FGL cross-matched test set.

To make a fair comparison, we follow the previous paper [13,18] to process the original 3FGL data before feeding them into Algorithm 1. The data pre-processing stage of the proposed framework is used to process the missing data. As shown in Algorithm 1, $\delta$ is the manually defined threshold that is used in Stage 1. In the experiments, $\delta$ is equal to 95%.

In the experiments, all methods are evaluated with the classification accuracy that is calculated with true positive (TP), true negative (TN), false positive (FP) and false negative (FN):

$$Accuracy = (TP + TN) / (TP + TN + NP + NF). \tag{5}$$

## 4.2   Correction Quality

After Stage 1 and 2 of the proposed framework (see Algorithm 1), five features are selected with Algorithm 2: Signif Curve, Variability Index, Spectral Index, and Unc Flux1000, hr45. In addition to the set of selected features $F$, Algorithm 2 also generated a root mean squared error (RMSE) profile shown in Fig. 1. The

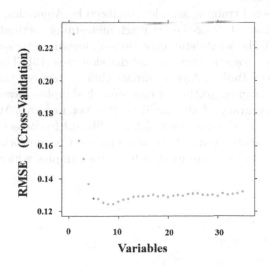

**Fig. 1.** For PSR/AGN classification, the root mean squared error (RMSE) profile of Algorithm 2 in the 3FGL catalog. Prediction models with the best trade-off between classification accuracy and model simplicity is trained with five features (the red point). (Color figure online)

classifier with the best trade-off between model prediction accuracy and model simplicity is trained with five features (the red point).

All training samples with five selected features are fed into Algorithm 3. In our framework, the distribution of training samples are corrected with Algorithm 3, and the results are shown in Fig. 2 and Fig. 3. The values of 'Unc Flux1000' are small and very similar. To clearly show the distributions, we used the max-min normalization to process 'Unc Flux1000'. The normalized values of 'Unc Flux1000' are not used to train classifiers. In these figures, black, red and green dots denote the training, testing and corrected samples respectively. With five features produced by Algorithm 2, we can obtain $C_5^2 = 10$ combinations. For each combination, samples with two features of the combination can be presented in two-dimensional Euclidean space, and are described in a 2-D coordinate system. For example, samples with two features (hr45 and Spectral Index) are shown in the in sub-figure(b) of Figure ??. In Fig. 2 or Fig. 3, the distributions of five combinations are shown. In the first column of these two figures, the distributions of original training samples (black), corrected training samples (green), and test samples (red) are shown in a 2-D coordinate system. The distributions of the test samples (red) are mostly obscured by the corrected training samples (green). In Column 2 and 3, the distribution of test samples and corrected training samples are shown alone. It's obvious that the distribution of the black dots is different from that of the red dots. This is due to the difference in the distribution of training samples (black) and test samples (red). The training samples are corrected with Algorithm 3, and corrected samples are obtained. The distribution of corrected samples is similar to that of testing samples. It means that Algorithm 3 of our framework can be used to alleviate the covariate shift issue.

With the corrected training samples produced by Algorithm 3, classifiers are built based on various state-of-the-art machine learning methods including random projection [21], boost logistic regression [6], logistic regression [12], support vector machine [20], logistic tree [5], and decision tree [15]. Their classification accuracy is shown in Table 1. After covariate shift correction, the distribution of training samples is similar to that of cross-match samples. However, in Table 1, the classification accuracy of all classifiers does not improve. We consider that this situation is due to the samples which are difficult to correctly predict in the 3FGL/4FGL cross-match dataset. In our proposed framework, Bayesian neural networks (see Sect. 3.3) are used to filter the samples which are difficult to correctly predict.

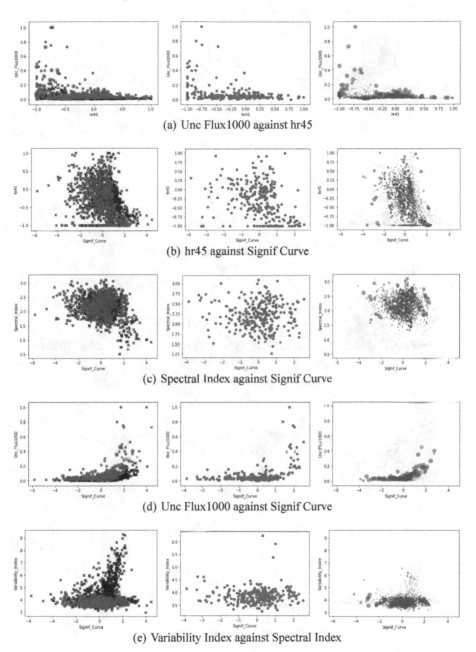

(a) Unc Flux1000 against hr45

(b) hr45 against Signif Curve

(c) Spectral Index against Signif Curve

(d) Unc Flux1000 against Signif Curve

(e) Variability Index against Spectral Index

**Fig. 2.** Correction Quality of Algorthm 3. With five selected features, $C_5^2 = 10$ combinations is obtained. Samples with two-features of a combination can be presented in a 2-D coordinate system. Corrected results of five combinations are shown in this figure. Black, red and green dots denote training, testing, and corrected samples. The distributions of three kind of samples are shown in Column 1. In Column 2 and 3, distributions of test samples and corrected training sample are shown alone. (Color figure online)

716    S. Luo et al.

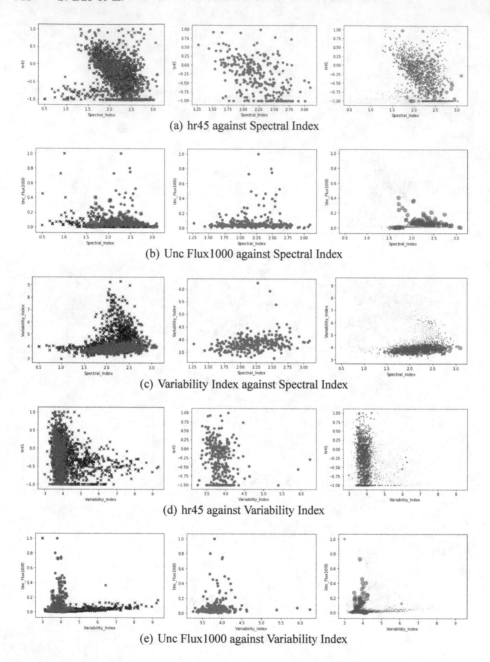

(a) hr45 against Spectral Index

(b) Unc Flux1000 against Spectral Index

(c) Variability Index against Spectral Index

(d) hr45 against Variability Index

(e) Unc Flux1000 against Variability Index

**Fig. 3.** Correction Quality of Algorthm 3. With five selected features, $C_5^2 = 10$ combinations is obtained. Samples with two-features of a combination can be presented in a 2-D coordinate system. Corrected results of five combinations are shown in this figure. Black, red and green dots denote training, testing, and corrected samples. The distributions of three kind of samples are shown in Column 1. In Column 2 and 3, distributions of test samples and corrected training sample are shown alone. (Color figure online)

**Table 1.** Classification accuracy of various machine learning models. 70% 3FGL sources are used to train models, and the remaining 30% sources are used as the test set. In 3FGL, 275 unknown sources are labeled in 4FGL. These 275 sources are used as the 3FGL/4FGL cross-match set. Results show that the accuracy of models is not improved after covariate shift correction.

| Classifiers | BEFORE shift coorection | | AFTER shift correction | |
|---|---|---|---|---|
| | Test set | Cross-match set | Test set | Cross-match set |
| Random Projection [21] | 98.6 % | 96.4 % | 97.7 % | 96.0 % |
| Boost LR [6] | 98.6 % | 95.6 % | 97.5 % | 95.6 % |
| Logistic Regression [12] | 97.4 % | 96.0 % | 98.0 % | 96.0 % |
| SVM [20] | 97.7 % | 95.6 % | 97.5 % | 95.6 % |
| Logistic Tree [5] | 98.0 % | 95.6 % | 97.5 % | 95.6 % |
| Decision Tree [15] | 97.4 % | 95.6 % | 92.8 % | 95.6 % |

## 4.3   Sample Filtering for the 3FGL/4FGL Cross-matched Test Set

In the cross-matched test set, there are some gamma-ray sources with insignificant features. Machine learning models are difficult to classify them. However, most machine learning models only classify sources as positive or negative, even if they are not sure which class the difficult samples belong to. Hence, in our framework, Bayesian neural networks are used to obtain the uncertainty scores. In the test set, samples with higher uncertainty scores are difficult samples. Difficult samples should be picked out rather than classified. With uncertainty scores, classification accuracy of various models is shown in Table 2. In Table 2, the classification accuracy is measured on the 3FGL/4FGL cross-matched test set.

The samples with higher uncertainty scores are removed from the 3FGL/4FGL cross-match dataset, and the remaining samples are used as the test set. For example, 95% of remaining samples denote that 5% of samples with the highest uncertainty scores are removed, and the 95% remaining samples are used as the test set. When the number of removed samples increases, the classification accuracy on the 3GL/4FGL cross-matched set increases. Finally, the accuracy on the cross-match set is similar to that on the test set (about 98.4%). Therefore, we consider that it is necessary to take the uncertainty of models into account when classifying unknown sources. The proposed cascade framework is effective for covariate shift correction and sample filtering.

**Table 2.** Classification accuracy with uncertainty scores of Bayes by backpropagation (BbB) and Monte Carlo (MC) dropout. Hard samples are picked out and standard samples are used as the test set. For example, 95% remaining samples denote that 5% samples with the highest uncertainty scores are removed, and 95% remaining samples are used as the test set. Classification accuracy of all methods is improved when the samples with higher uncertainty scores are removed.

| Classifiers | BbB | | | | MC dropout | | | |
|---|---|---|---|---|---|---|---|---|
| | Remaining samples | | | | Remaining samples | | | |
| | 95% | 90% | 80% | 70% | 95% | 90% | 80% | 70% |
| Random Projection | 97.7 % | 97.6 % | 98.6 % | 98.4 % | 96.2 % | 97.2 % | 98.2 % | 98.4 % |
| Boost LR | 98.0 % | 98.0 % | 98.6 % | 98.4 % | 96.7 % | 97.4 % | 98.2 % | 98.4 % |
| Logistic Regression | 97.7 % | 97.6 % | 98.6 % | 98.4 % | 96.2 % | 97.2 % | 98.2 % | 98.4 % |
| SVM | 97.7 % | 97.6 % | 98.6 % | 98.4 % | 95.4 % | 96.4 % | 98.2 % | 98.4 % |
| Logistic Tree | 97.7 % | 97.6 % | 98.6 % | 98.4 % | 94.6 % | 96.8 % | 98.2 % | 98.4 % |
| Decision Tree | 97.3 % | 97.2 % | 98.6 % | 98.4 % | 95.8 % | 97.2 % | 98.2 % | 98.4 % |

## 5   Conclusion

The covariate Shift issue and samples with insignificant features in gamma-ray sources affect the performance of machine learning models on PSR/AGN classification. To address these bottlenecks, a novel cascade framework is proposed. In this work, we attempt to bridge kernel mean matching and Bayesian neural networks in an easy way. Kernel mean matching is first used to make the distribution of training samples close to that of testing samples, in order to solve the covariate shift issue. Then, uncertainty scores are calculated with Bayesian neural networks. Samples with higher uncertainty scores are picked out, and the remaining samples are used as the test set for sources classification. Experimental results show that the proposed methods are effective for covariate shift correction and sample filtering.

**Acknowledgement.** This work is supported by National Key Research and Development Program of China (2021YFF1200804), and National Key Research and Development Program of China (2021YFF1200800). Roberto Bugiolacchi is supported by Macau Science and Technology Development Fund (No. 0079/2019/A2).

## References

1. Abdo, A.A., et al.: Fermi large area telescope first source catalog. Astrophys. J. Suppl. Ser. **188**(2), 405 (2010)
2. Acero, R., et al.: Fermi large area telescope third source catalog. Astrophys. J. Suppl. Ser. **218**(2), 23 (2015)
3. Ackermann, M., et al.: A statistical approach to recognizing source classes for unassociated sources in the first Fermi-LAT catalog. Astrophys. J. **753**(1), 83 (2012)

4. Blundell, C., Cornebise, J., Kavukcuoglu, K., Wierstra, D.: Weight uncertainty in neural network. In: International Conference on Machine Learning, pp. 1613–1622. PMLR (2015)
5. Clark, L.A., Pregibon, D.: Tree-based models. In: Statistical Models in S, pp. 377–419. Routledge, Abingdon (2017)
6. Friedman, J., Hastie, T., Tibshirani, R.: Additive logistic regression: a statistical view of boosting (with discussion and a rejoinder by the authors). Ann. Stat. **28**(2), 337–407 (2000)
7. Gal, Y., Ghahramani, Z.: Dropout as a Bayesian approximation: representing model uncertainty in deep learning. In: International Conference on Machine Learning, pp. 1050–1059. PMLR (2016)
8. Gretton, A., Smola, A., Huang, J., Schmittfull, M., Borgwardt, K., Schölkopf, B.: Covariate shift by kernel mean matching. Dataset Shift Mach. Learn. **3**(4), 5 (2009)
9. Hui, C., et al.: Searches for pulsar-like candidates from unidentified objects in the third catalog of hard Fermi-LAT sources with machine learning techniques. Mon. Not. R. Astron. Soc. **495**(1), 1093–1109 (2020)
10. Kang, S.J., Fan, J.H., Mao, W., Wu, Q., Feng, J., Yin, Y.: Evaluating the optical classification of fermi BCUs using machine learning. Astrophys. J. **872**(2), 189 (2019)
11. Kerby, S., et al.: X-ray spectra and multiwavelength machine learning classification for likely counterparts to fermi 3fgl unassociated sources. Astron. J. **161**(4), 154 (2021)
12. Kleinbaum, D.G., Dietz, K., Gail, M., Klein, M., Klein, M.: Logistic Regression. Springer, New York (2002). https://doi.org/10.1007/978-1-4419-1742-3
13. Luo, S., Leung, A.P., Hui, C., Li, K.: An investigation on the factors affecting machine learning classifications in gamma-ray astronomy. Mon. Not. R. Astron. Soc. **492**(4), 5377–5390 (2020)
14. Mirabal, N., Frías-Martinez, V., Hassan, T., Frias-Martinez, E.: Fermi's sibyl: Mining the gamma-ray sky for dark matter subhaloes. Monthly Notices R. Astron. Soc. Lett. **424**(1), L64–L68 (2012)
15. Myles, A.J., Feudale, R.N., Liu, Y., Woody, N.A., Brown, S.D.: An introduction to decision tree modeling. J. Chemom. Soc. **18**(6), 275–285 (2004)
16. Nolan, R.L., et al.: Fermi large area telescope second source catalog. Astrophys. J. Suppl. Ser. **199**(2), 31 (2012)
17. Parkinson, P.S., Xu, H., Yu, P., Salvetti, D., Marelli, M., Falcone, A.: Classification and ranking of Fermi LAT gamma-ray sources from the 3fgl catalog using machine learning techniques. Astrophys. J. **820**(1), 8 (2016)
18. Parkinson, P.S., Xu, H., Yu, P., Salvetti, D., Marelli, M., Falcone, A.: Classification and ranking of Fermi LAT gamma-ray sources from the 3fgl catalog using machine learning techniques. Astrophys. J. **820**(1), 8 (2016)
19. Richards, J.W., et al.: Active learning to overcome sample selection bias: application to photometric variable star classification. Astrophys. J. **744**(2), 192 (2011)
20. Schölkopf, B., Smola, A.J., Williamson, R.C., Bartlett, P.L.: New support vector algorithms. Neural Comput. **12**(5), 1207–1245 (2000)
21. Vempala, S.S.: The Random Projection Method, vol. 65. American Mathematical Society Providence (2005)

# Author Index

Printed in the United States
by Baker & Taylor Publisher Services